Contemporary
Literary Criticism

Guide to Gale Literary Criticism Series

When you need to review criticism of literary works, these are the Gale series to use:

If the author's death date is: **You should turn to:**

After Dec. 31, 1959
(or author is still living)

CONTEMPORARY LITERARY CRITICISM

for example: Jorge Luis Borges, Anthony Burgess,
William Faulkner, Mary Gordon,
Ernest Hemingway, Iris Murdoch

1900 through 1959

TWENTIETH-CENTURY LITERARY CRITICISM

for example: Willa Cather, F. Scott Fitzgerald,
Henry James, Mark Twain, Virginia Woolf

1800 through 1899

NINETEENTH-CENTURY LITERATURE CRITICISM

for example: Fedor Dostoevski, Nathaniel Hawthorne,
George Sand, William Wordsworth

1400 through 1799

LITERATURE CRITICISM FROM 1400 TO 1800
(excluding Shakespeare)

for example: Anne Bradstreet, Daniel Defoe,
Alexander Pope, François Rabelais,
Jonathan Swift, Phillis Wheatley

SHAKESPEAREAN CRITICISM

Shakespeare's plays and poetry

Antiquity through 1399

CLASSICAL AND MEDIEVAL LITERATURE CRITICISM

for example: Dante, Homer, Plato, Sophocles, Vergil,
the Beowulf Poet

Gale also publishes related criticism series:

CHILDREN'S LITERATURE REVIEW

This series covers authors of all eras who have written for the preschool through high school audience.

SHORT STORY CRITICISM

This series covers the major short fiction writers of all nationalities and periods of literary history.

ISSN 0091-3421

Volume 62

Contemporary Literary Criticism

Excerpts from Criticism of the
Works of Today's Novelists, Poets,
Playwrights, Short Story Writers, Scriptwriters,
and Other Creative Writers

Roger Matuz
EDITOR

Cathy Falk
Mary K. Gillis
Sean R. Pollock
David Segal
Bridget Travers
ASSOCIATE EDITORS

 Gale Research Inc. · DETROIT · NEW YORK · LONDON

STAFF

Roger Matuz, *Editor*

Cathy Falk, Mary K. Gillis, Sean R. Pollock, David Segal,
Bridget Travers, *Associate Editors*

Elizabeth P. Henry, Susan Peters, Susanne Skubik, Debra A. Wells, *Assistant Editors*

Jeanne A. Gough, *Production & Permissions Manager*
Linda M. Pugliese, *Production Supervisor*
Suzanne Powers, Maureen A. Puhl, Jennifer Van Sickle, *Editorial Associates*
Donna Craft, Lorna Mabunda, James G. Wittenbach, *Editorial Assistants*

Victoria B. Cariappa, *Research Manager*
H. Nelson Fields, Judy L. Gale, Maureen Richards, *Editorial Associates*
Jennifer Brostrom, Paula Cutcher, Alan Hedblad, Robin Lupa, Mary Beth McElmeel, *Editorial Assistants*

Sandra C. Davis, *Permissions Supervisor (Text)*
Josephine M. Keene, Denise Singleton, Kimberly F. Smilay, *Permissions Associates*
Maria L. Franklin, Michelle Lonoconus, Shalice Shah, Rebecca A. Stanko, *Permissions Assistants*

Patricia A. Seefelt, *Permissions Supervisor (Pictures)*
Margaret A. Chamberlain, *Permissions Associate*
Pamela A. Hayes, *Permissions Assistant*

Mary Beth Trimper, *Production Manager*
Shanna G. Philpott, *External Production Assistant*

Art Chartow, *Art Director*
C.J. Jonik, *Keyliner*

Laura Bryant, *Production Supervisor*
Louise Gagné, *Internal Production Associate*
Yolanda Y. Latham, *Internal Production Assistant*

Contents

Preface   vii

Acknowledgments   xi

Authors Forthcoming in *CLC*   xvii

v

Preface

Named "one of the twenty-five most distinguished reference titles published during the past twenty-five years" by *Reference Quarterly*, the *Contemporary Literary Criticism (CLC)* series has provided readers with critical commentary and general information on more that 2,000 authors now living or who died after December 31, 1959. Previous to the publication of the first volume of *CLC* in 1973, there was no ongoing digest monitoring scholarly and popular sources of critical opinion and explication of modern literature. *CLC*, therefore, has fulfilled an essential need, particularly since the complexity and variety of contemporary literature makes the function of criticism especially important to today's reader.

Scope of the Series

CLC presents significant passages from published criticism of works by creative writers. Since many of the authors covered by *CLC* inspire continual critical commentary, writers are often represented in more than one volume. There is, of course, no duplication of reprinted criticism.

Authors are selected for inclusion for a variety of reasons, among them the publication or dramatic production of a critically acclaimed new work, the reception of a major literary award, revival of interest in past writings, or the adaptation of a literary work to film or television.

The present volume of *CLC* includes Martin Amis and Thomas Pynchon, whose novels generate significant commentary and are especially popular among college students; Margaret Laurence, a major figure in Canadian literature; and John Berryman, an important post-World War II American poet whose works are represented in the recently published *Collected Poems*.

Perhaps most importantly, works that frequently appear on the syllabuses of high school and college literature courses are represented by individual entries in *CLC*. Lorraine Hansberry's *A Raisin in the Sun* and Sylvia Plath's *The Bell Jar* are examples of works of this stature appearing in *CLC*, Volume 62.

Attention is also given to several other groups of writers—authors of considerable public interest—about whose work criticism is often difficult to locate. These include mystery and science fiction writers, literary and social critics, foreign writers, and authors who represent particular ethnic groups within the United States.

Format of the Book

Altogether there are about 500 individual excerpts in each volume—with approximately seventeen excerpts per author—taken from hundreds of book review periodicals, general magazines, scholarly journals, monographs, and books. Entries include critical evaluations spanning from the beginning of an author's career to the most current commentary. Interviews, feature articles, and other published writings that offer insight into the author's works are also presented. Students, teachers, librarians, and researchers will find that the generous excerpts and supplementary material provided by *CLC* supply them with vital information needed to write a term paper, analyze a poem, or lead a book discussion group. In addition, complete bibliographical citations facilitate the location of the original source and provide all of the information necessary for a term paper footnote or bibliography.

A *CLC* author entry consists of the following elements:

- The **author heading** cites the form under which the author has most commonly published, followed by birth date, and death date when applicable. Uncertainty as to a birth or death date is indicated by a question mark.

- A **portrait** of the author is included when available.

- A brief **biographical and critical introduction** to the author and his or her work precedes the excerpted criticism. The first line of the introduction provides the author's full name, pseudonyms (if applicable), nationality, and a listing of genres in which the author has written. Since *CLC* is not intended to be a definitive biographical source, *cross-references* have been included to direct readers to these useful sources published by Gale Research: *Short Story Criticism* and *Children's Literature Review*, which provide excerpts of criticism on the works of short story writers and authors of books for young people, respectively; *Contemporary Authors*, which includes detailed biographical and bibliographical sketches of nearly 97,000 authors; *Something about the Author*, which contains heavily illustrated biographical sketches of writers and illustrators who create books for children and young adults; *Dictionary of Literary Biography*, which provides original evaluations and detailed biographies of authors important to literary history; and *Contemporary Authors Autobiography Series* and *Something about the Author Autobiography Series*, which offer autobiographical essays by prominent writers for adults and those of interest to young readers, respectively. Previous volumes of *CLC* in which the author has been featured are also listed in the introduction.

● A list of **principal works**, arranged chronologically and, if applicable, divided into genre categories, notes the most important works by the author.

● The **excerpted criticism** represents various kinds of critical writing, ranging in form from the brief review to the scholarly exegesis. Essays are selected by the editors to reflect the spectrum of opinion about a specific work or about an author's literary career in general. The excerpts are presented chronologically, adding a useful perspective to the entry. All titles by the author featured in the entry are printed in boldface type, which enables the reader to easily identify the works being discussed. Publication information (such as publisher names and book prices) and parenthetical numerical references (such as footnotes or page and line references to specific editions of a work) have been deleted at the editor's discretion to provide smoother reading of the text.

● A complete **bibliographical citation** designed to help the user find the original essay or book follows each excerpt.

● A **further reading** section appears at the end of entries on authors who have generated a significant amount of criticism other than the pieces reprinted in *CLC*. In some cases, it includes references to material for which the editors could not obtain reprint rights.

Other Features

● A list of **Authors Forthcoming in *CLC*** previews the authors to be researched for future volumes.

● An **Acknowledgments** section lists the copyright holders who have granted permission to reprint material in this volume of *CLC*. It does not, however, list every book or periodical reprinted or consulted during the preparation of the volume.

● A **Cumulative Author Index** lists all the authors who have appeared in *CLC, Twentieth-Century Literary Criticism, Nineteenth-Century Literature Criticism, Literature Criticism from 1400 to 1800, Classical and Medieval Literature Criticism,* and *Short Story Criticism*, with cross-references to these Gale series: *Children's Literature Review, Contemporary Authors, Contemporary Authors Autobiography Series, Contemporary Authors Bibliographical Series, Dictionary of Literary Biography, Something about the Author, Something about the Author Autobiography Series, Yesterday's Authors of Books for Children,* and *Authors & Artists for Young Adults*. Readers will welcome this cumulated author index as a useful tool for locating an author within the various series. The index, which lists birth and death dates when available, will be particularly valuable for those authors who are identified with a certain period but whose death date causes them to be placed in another, or for those authors whose careers span two periods. For example, Ernest Hemingway is found in *CLC,* yet a writer often associated with him, F. Scott Fitzgerald, is found in *Twentieth-Century Literary Criticism.*

● A **Cumulative Nationality Index** alphabetically lists all authors featured in *CLC* by nationality, followed by numbers corresponding to the volumes in which they appear.

● A **Title Index** alphabetically lists all titles reviewed in the current volume of *CLC*. Listings are followed by the author's name and the corresponding page numbers where the titles are discussed. English translations of foreign titles and variations of titles are cross-referenced to the title under which a work was originally published. Titles of novels, novellas, dramas, films, record albums, and poetry, short story, and essay collections are printed in italics, while all individual poems, short stories, essays, and songs are printed in roman type within quotation marks; when published separately (e.g., T.S. Eliot's poem *The Waste Land*), the title will also be printed in italics.

● In response to numerous suggestions from librarians, Gale has also produced a **special paperbound edition** of the *CLC* title index. This annual cumulation, which alphabetically lists all titles reviewed in the series, is available to all customers and will be published with the first volume of *CLC* issued in each calendar year. Additional copies of the index are available upon request. Librarians and patrons will welcome this separate index: it saves shelf space, is easy to use, and is disposable upon receipt of the following year's cumulation.

A Note to the Reader

When writing papers, students who quote directly from any volume in the Literary Criticism Series may use the following general forms to footnote reprinted criticism. The first example pertains to material drawn from periodicals, the second to material reprinted from books:

[1]Anne Tyler, "Manic Monologue," *The New Republic* 200 (April 17, 1989), 44-6; excerpted and reprinted in *Contemporary Literary Criticism,* Vol. 58, ed. Roger Matuz (Detroit: Gale Research, 1990), p. 325.

[2]Patrick Reilly, *The Literature of Guilt: From 'Gulliver' to Golding* (University of Iowa Press, 1988); excerpted and reprinted in *Contemporary Literary Criticism,* Vol. 58, ed. Roger Matuz (Detroit: Gale Research, 1990), pp. 206-12.

Suggestions Are Welcome

The editors welcome the comments and suggestions of readers to expand the coverage and enhance the usefulness of the series.

Acknowledgments

The editors wish to thank the copyright holders of the excerpted criticism included in this volume, the permissions managers of many book and magazine publishing companies for assisting us in securing reprint rights, and Anthony Bogucki for, assistance with copyright research. We are also grateful to the staffs of the Detroit Public Library, the Library of Congress, the University of Detroit Library, Wayne State University Purdy/Kresge Library Complex, and the University of Michigan Libraries for making their resources available to us. Following is a list of the copyright holders who have granted us permission to reprint material in this volume of *CLC*. Every effort has been made to trace copyright, but if omissions have been made, please let us know.

COPYRIGHTED EXCERPTS IN *CLC*, VOLUME 62, WERE REPRINTED FROM THE FOLLOWING PERIODICALS:

"Marge Piercy Makes War" by Dorothy Allison; v. XXXII, December 1, 1987 for "Yob Action" by Graham Fuller; v. XXXIII, October 4, 1988 for "We Fall to Pieces" by Rebecca Martin; v. XXXIV, April 25, 1989 for "Knight Life" by Bill Marx; v. XXXV, April 24, 1990 for "Murder He Wrote: Martin Amis's Killing Fields" by Graham Fuller. Copyright © News Group Publications, Inc., 1987, 1988, 1989, 1990. All reprinted by permission of *The Village Voice* and the author.—*VLS*, n. 39, October, 1985 for a review of "Watson's Apology" by William Grimes. Copyright © 1985 News Group Publications, Inc. Reprinted by permission of *The Village Voice* and the author.—*West Coast Review of Books*, v. 15, September–October, 1989. Copyright 1989 by Rapport Publishing Co., Inc. Reprinted by permission of the publisher.—*Western American Literature*, v. XVI, Fall, 1981; v. XXI, May, 1986. Copyright, 1981, 1986 by the Western Literature Association. Both reprinted by permission of the publisher.—*The Women's Review of Books*, v. I, August, 1984 for "Suburban Housewife Makes Good" by Susan Mernit; v. IV, July–August, 1987 for "Fiction at the Front" by Mary Biggs; v. V, July, 1988 for "Bodily Fluent" by Diane Wakoski. Copyright © 1984, 1987, 1988. All rights reserved. All reprinted by permission of the author.—*Women's Studies: An Interdisciplinary Journal*, v. 12, 1986. © Gordon and Breach Science Publishers. Reprinted by permission of the publisher.—*Yiddish*, v. 6, 1987. Reprinted by permission of the publisher.

COPYRIGHTED EXCERPTS IN *CLC*, VOLUME 62, WERE REPRINTED FROM THE FOLLOWING BOOKS:

Abramson, Doris E. From *Negro Playwrights in the American Theatre 1925–1959*. Columbia University Press. Copyright © 1967, 1969, Columbia University Press. Used by permission of the publisher.—Agosin, Marjorie. From *Pablo Neruda*. Translated by Lorraine Roses. Twayne, 1986. Copyright 1986 by Twayne Publishers. All rights reserved. Reprinted with the permission of Twayne Publishers, a division of G. K. Hall & Co., Boston.—Alexandrova, Vera. From *A History of Soviet Literature, 1917–1964*. Translated by Mirra Ginsburg. Doubleday & Company, Inc., 1963. Copyright © 1963 by Vera Alexandrova-Schawarz. All rights reserved. Used by permission of Doubleday, a division of Bantam, Doubleday, Dell Publishing Group, Inc.—Allen, Mary. From *The Necessary Blankness: Women in Major American Fiction of the Sixties*. University of Illinois Press, 1976. © 1976 by the Board of Trustees of the University of Illinois. Reprinted by permission of the publisher and the author.—Baraka, Amiri. From " 'A Raisin in the Sun's' Enduring Passion," in *A Raisin in the Sun; and The Sign in Sidney Brustein's Window*. By Lorraine Hansberry, edited by Robert Nemiroff. New American Library, 1987. Copyright © 1986 by Amiri Baraka. Reprinted by permission of Sterling Lord Literistic, Inc.—Bayley, John. From "John Berryman: A Question of Imperial Sway," in *The Salmagundi Reader*. Edited by Robert Boyers and Peggy Boyers. Indiana University Press, 1983. Copyright © 1983 by Robert Boyers and Peggy Boyers. All rights reserved. Reprinted by permission of the publisher.—Bigsby, C. W. E. From *Confrontation and Commitment: A Study of Contemporary American Drama, 1959–66*. University of Missouri Press, 1968. © 1967 and 1968 by C. W. E. Bigsby. Reprinted by permission of the author.—Bourjaily, Vance. From "Victoria Lucas and Elly Higginbottom," in *Ariel Ascending: Writings About Sylvia Plath*. Edited by Paul Alexander. Harper & Row, 1985. Reprinted by permission of Harper & Row, Publishers, Inc.—Bourjaily, Vance, and Harry T. Moore. From an interview in *Talks with Authors*. Edited by Charles F. Madden. Southern Illinois University Press. All rights reserved. Reprinted by permission of the author.—Bradbury, Malcolm. From *No, Not Bloomsbury*. Andre Deutsch, 1987. Copyright © 1987 by Malcom Bradbury. All rights reserved. Reprinted by permission of the author.—Cruse, Harold. From *The Crisis of the Negro Intellectual*. Morrow, 1967. Copyright © 1967 by Harold Cruse. All rights reserved. Reprinted by permission of William Morrow and Company, Inc.—Disch, Thomas M. From an introduction to *The Heat Death of the Universe and Other Stories*. By Pamela Zoline. McPherson & Company, 1988. Copyright © 1988 by Pamela Zoline. All rights reserved. Reprinted by permission of the publisher.—Evans, Robert O. From "The 'Nouveau Roman', Russian Dystopias, and Anthony Burgess," in *British Novelists Since 1900*. Edited by Jack I. Biles. AMS Press, 1987. Copyright © AMS Press, Inc., 1987. All rights reserved. Reprinted by permission of the publisher.—Goldberg, Anatol. From *Ilya Ehrenburg: Writing, Politics and the Art of Survival*. Weidenfeld and Nicolson, 1984. Copyright © Anatol Goldberg 1984. All rights reserved. Reprinted by permission of the publisher.—Hawthorn, Jeremy. From *Multiple Personality and the Disintegration of Literary Character: From Oliver Goldsmith to Sylvia Plath*. St. Martin's Press, 1983. © Jeremy Hawthorn 1983. All rights reserved. Used with permission of St. Martin's Press, Inc.—Huf, Linda. From *A Portrait of the Artist as a Young Woman: The Writer as Heroine in American Literature*. Frederick Ungar Publishing Co., 1983. Copyright © 1983 by Linda M. Huf. Reprinted by permission of the publisher.—Keyassar, Helene. From *The Curtain and the Veil: Strategies in Black Drama*. Franklin, 1981. © 1981 by Burt Franklin & Co., Inc. All rights reserved. Reprinted by permission of the publisher.—Kress, Susan. From "In and Out of Time: The Form of Marge Piercy's Novels," in *Future Females: A Critical Anthology*. Edited by Marleen S. Barr. Bowling Green State University Popular Press, 1981. Copyright © 1981 by Bowling Green State University Popular Press. Reprinted by permission of the publisher.—Morley, Patricia. From *Margaret Laurence*. Twayne, 1981. Copyright 1981–87 by Twayne Publishers, 1978 by the author. All rights reserved. Reprinted with the permission of the author, Patricia Morley.—Newman, Robert D. From *Understanding Thomas Pynchon*. University of South Carolina Press, 1986. Copyright © University of South Carolina 1986. Reprinted by permission of the publisher.—Orgel, Shelley. From "Fusion with the Victim: A Study of Sylvia Plath," in *Lives, Events, and Other Players: Directions in Psychobiography, Vol. IV*. Edited by Joseph Coltrera. Jason Aronson, 1981. Copyright © 1981 by Jason Aronson, Inc. All rights reserved. Reprinted by permission of the publisher.—Redmond, Eugene B. From an introduction to *Goodbye, Sweetwater: New & Selected Stories*. By Henry Dumas, edited by Eugene B. Redmond. Thunder's Mouth Press, 1988. Copyright © 1988 by Loretta Dumas and Eugene B. Redmond. All rights reserved. Reprinted by permission of the publisher.—Rose, Mark. From *Alien Encounters: Anatomy of Science Fiction*. Cambridge, Mass.: Harvard University Press, 1981. Copyright © 1981 by the President and

Fellows of Harvard College. Excerpted by permission of the publishers and the author.—Schmitt, Jack. From an introduction to *Art of Birds*. By Pablo Neruda, translated by Jack Schmitt. University of Texas Press, 1985. Copyright © 1985 by Herederos de Pablo Neruda. All rights reserved. Reprinted by permission of the publisher.—Stonehill, Brian. From *The Self-Conscious Novel: Artifice in Fiction from Joyce to Pynchon*. University of Pennsylvania Press, 1988. Copyright © 1988 by the University of Pennsylvania Press. All rights reserved. Reprinted by permission of the publisher.—Thomas, Clara. From *The Manawaka World of Margaret Laurence*. McClelland and Stewart, 1975. © McClelland and Stewart Limited 1975. All rights reserved. Used by permission of the Canadian Publishers, McClelland and Steward Limited, Toronto.—Wallace, Ronald. From *God Be with the Clown: Humor in American Poetry*. University of Missouri Press, 1984. Copyright © 1984 by The Curators of the University of Missouri. All rights reserved. Reprinted by permission of the publisher.

PHOTOGRAPHS APPEARING IN *CLC*, VOLUME 62, WERE RECEIVED FROM THE FOLLOWING SOURCES:

Photograph by Mark Gerson: **pp. 1, 21;** UPI/Bettmann Newsphotos: **pp. 41, 383;** Photographs by Adrienne F. Morgan. Courtesy of Vance Bourjaily: **p. 79;** Cyril Grossman/NYT Pictures: **p. 110;** © Lütfi Özkök: **pp. 122, 166;** © copyright Billett Potter, Oxford: **p. 183;** Photograph by Gin Brigg. Courtesy of Robert Nemiroff: **p. 209;** Photograph by Barney Hillerman. Courtesy of Tony Hillerman; **p. 249;** Photograph by Paul Orenstein: **p. 264;** The Granger Collection, New York: **p. 319;** © Jerry Bauer; **p. 339;** Photograph by Ira Wood. Courtesy of Marge Piercy: **p. 360;** © 1989 Harvey Ferdschneider. Courtesy of Stephanie Vaughn: **p. 456;** Photograph by John Fago. Courtesy of Pamela Zoline: **p. 460.**

Authors Forthcoming in *CLC*

To be Included in Volume 63

Christy Brown (Irish autobiographer and poet)—Crippled from birth by cerebral palsy, Brown is recognized for his celebrated autobiography *My Left Foot*, which was adapted into an Academy Award-winning film. Brown also wrote several novels, including *Down All the Days* and *A Shadow on Summer*, as well as numerous volumes of poetry.

Albert Camus (Algerian-born French novelist and essayist)—Awarded the Nobel Prize in 1957, Camus is renowned for writings that defend the dignity and decency of the individual and assert that one can transcend absurdity through purposeful actions. This entry will focus on his novels.

Tess Gallagher (American poet and short story writer)—Gallagher won acclaim for her direct yet subtle approach to family relations and the passage of time in two recent publications, *Amplitude: New and Selected Poems* and *The Lover of Horses and Other Stories*.

Shelby Hearon (American novelist and short story writer)—Described as a "female Larry McMurtry," Hearon sets much of her fiction in Texas or surrounding locales and presents strong and colorful female protagonists.

Joseph Heller (American novelist)—Heller is a popular contemporary satirist whose provocative blend of farce and tragedy is most often applied to the absurd machinations of large bureaucracies. His entry will focus on his most famous work, *Catch-22*, an irreverent portrayal of American armed forces during World War II.

Elia Kazan—(Turkish-born American filmmaker and novelist)—An award-winning director of such films as *A Streetcar Named Desire*, *On the Waterfront*, and *A Face in the Crowd*, Kazan also drew attention for several novels he wrote following his film career.

Boris Pasternak (Russian poet and novelist)—Awarded the 1958 Nobel Prize in Literature, which he was forced to decline under political pressure, Pasternak is best known for his novel *Dr. Zhivago*, an account of the Russian Revolution, but is equally respected for his complex, mystical poetry.

Upton Sinclair (American journalist and novelist)—A leading figure in the Muckraking movement, a term denoting the aggressive style of exposé journalism that flourished in the United States during the early 1900s, Sinclair aroused international furor with his best-selling novel *The Jungle*. Exposing exploitative, unsanitary, and hazardous conditions in American meat-packing plants, *The Jungle* is considered an exemplary work of social protest literature.

Gloria Steinem (American nonfiction writer and editor)—Among the most well-known leaders of the contemporary feminist movement, Steinem cofounded *Ms.* magazine and wrote essays that influenced the personal and political lives of many women. Her best-known works include the essay collection *Outrageous Acts and Everyday Rebellions* and her feminist biography of Marilyn Monroe.

Tom Stoppard (English dramatist)—A leading playwright in contemporary theater, Stoppard examines moral and philosophical themes within the context of comedy. Often described as "philosophical farces," his plays frequently draw upon Shakespeare's works to examine modern concerns, as in his his acclaimed work *Rosencrantz and Guildenstern Are Dead*, which will be the focus of Stoppard's entry.

Anna Akhmatova (Russian poet and translator)—Banned from publishing in the Soviet Union virtually her entire career, Akhmatova is nonetheless considered one of the premier Russian poets of the twentieth century. This entry will feature criticism on Akhmatova from the 1980s, when much of her previously unpublished or untranslated works appeared in various English-language collections.

E. M. Cioran (Rumanian-born philosopher and essayist)—Cioran is considered a formidable successor to the nihilistic tradition of thought espoused by Friedrich Nietzsche. In his philosophical essays, Cioran employs irony and elegant, aphoristic prose to explore such themes as alienation, absurdity, history, God, and death.

Jules Feiffer (American cartoonist, playwright, and novelist)—Feiffer brings to his plays and fiction the rueful scrutiny of middle-class idealism that characterizes his widely-syndicated cartoons. In his plays, Feiffer blends farce and satire with black humor to examine the psychological and social conditions of modern life. The entry will include criticism on his most recent play, *Elliot Loves.*

Ken Kesey (American novelist and short story writer)—Kesey is considered a transitional figure linking the Beat generation of the 1950s with the counterculture movement of the 1960s. This entry will focus on his experimental novel *One Flew over the Cuckoo's Nest,* an important work of contemporary American literature.

Hanif Kureishi (English playwright, screenwriter, and novelist)—Kureishi gained international recognition with the screenplays *My Beautiful Laundrette* and *Sammy and Rosie Get Laid,* which examine racial and class conflict in present-day London. His first novel, *The Buddha of Suburbia,* is a semiautobiographical account of a British Pakistani coming of age in the 1960s.

Philip Larkin (English poet and critic)—Among England's most popular and respected post-World War II poets, Larkin wrote witty, self-deprecating verse addressing such topics as love, loneliness, the passage of time, and contemporary life. The entry will focus on the posthumously published *Collected Poems,* which contains his best-known verse as well as many previously unpublished works.

Peter Matthiessen (American novelist, nonfiction writer, and short story writer)—Matthiessen is a naturalist who writes with compassion and conviction about vanishing cultures, oppressed peoples, and exotic wildlife and locales. His recent works include *On the River Styx and Other Stories* and *Killing Mr. Watson.*

Vladimir Nabokov (Russian-born American novelist, poet, and essayist)—Recognized as one of the greatest literary stylists of the twentieth century, Nabokov investigated the illusory nature of reality in his fiction. By emphasizing stylistic considerations over social and political issues, Nabokov championed the primacy of wit and imagination. The entry will focus on his notorious novel *Lolita,* which satirizes American culture and values.

Tom Robbins (American novelist and short story writer)—Robbins is acclaimed for his wildly playful, metafictional novels that advocate nonconformist behavior to overcome the absurdity of existence. This entry will include criticism on his latest novel, *Skinny Legs and All.*

Tobias Wolff (American short story writer and novelist)—A prize-winning author, Wolff has garnered praise for his stark portraits of ordinary lives. Although he depicts characters of diverse ages and backgrounds, Wolff is perhaps best known for his early stories about Vietnam veterans. This entry will provide an overview of Wolff's career, including his most recent work, *This Boy's Life.*

Martin Amis

1949-

(Born Martin Louis Amis) English novelist, critic, short story writer, editor, scriptwriter, and nonfiction writer.

Regarded as an outstanding novelist, Amis satirizes the scabrous excesses of youth and contemporary society with an irreverent and incisive wit similar to that of his father, author Kingsley Amis. Employing fast-paced prose infused with contemporary slang and profanity, Amis portrays characters who are obsessed with sex, drugs, violence, and materialistic pursuits. Like such satirists as Jonathan Swift and Angus Wilson, with whom he has been compared, Amis is widely regarded as a moralist whose novels admonish the vices of his age. Jerome Charyn commented: "Amis is so horrified by the world he sees in the process of formation that he feels compelled to warn us all about it."

Amis's first novel, *The Rachel Papers,* concerns a young man's passage from adolescence into adulthood. The protagonist, Charles Highway, an egocentric English youth on the eve of his twentieth birthday, relates his misadventures in graphic, humorous detail. Most critics found this work skillfully written but were impressed, as John Mellors noted, "more with promise and felicities en route than with achievement." Amis's second novel, *Dead Babies,* is a black comedy about a group of deviant youths who gather at a country home for a weekend of sex, drugs, verbal abuse, and physical violence. Rejecting the political idealism widespread among youth in the 1960s, Amis's characters revel in decadent behavior.

Amis's next novel, *Success,* centers on the relationship between two cohabiting foster brothers, one aristocratic and one working-class, and their comparative degrees of social, economic, and sexual success. The upper-class brother's fall and the proletarian brother's rise have prompted critics to interpret this novel as an allegorical commentary on the decline of traditional British social order. *Other People: A Mystery Story* is an ambiguous tale in which Amis relates the dual experiences of Mary Lamb, an amnesiac, and the wayward Amy Hide, who may represent Mary's former self. Naive and disoriented, Mary wanders innocently into London in search of her previous identity only to discover anew the complexities of contemporary society.

Money: A Suicide Note has been praised as Amis's best work. This ambitious and complicated novel explores such topics as greed, excess, self-destruction, cultural deprivation, sex, and love. Through satire Amis exposes the incessant debaucheries of John Self, a producer of commercials who is preparing to direct his first major American film. Using metaphor, allegory, caricature, and a cast of eccentric characters in an intricately designed plot, Amis delineates the surrealistic and squalid urban existence of his comic hero. Jonathan Yardley noted that Amis "has created a central character of consummate vulgarity and irresistible charm," adding that Self "emerges

as one of the indisputably memorable, not to mention haunting, characters of postwar fiction."

London Fields, set in 1999 against a backdrop of impending environmental, economic, and military disaster, is a satirical novel that enlarges upon themes examined in *Money.* This work focuses on Nicola Six, an amoral, self-destructive woman whom many critics identified as the personification of the death of love. Nicola seduces two men—a repugnant petty criminal and a simple-minded, affluent family man—with the hope that one will submit to her demands to kill her. She confesses her sordid adventures to Samson Young, a terminally ill American writer who has come to London with the intention of overcoming his writer's block and finishing his murder mystery novel before he dies or, as Amis insinuates, the planet expires. In a manner common to much postmodern fiction, Amis ambiguously suggests that the characters of *London Fields* may actually be creations of Samson Young. Using what some critics deemed overwrought symbolism, Amis links Earth's physical deterioration with humanity's spiritual and moral decay.

Amis's only volume of short fiction, *Einstein's Monsters,* comprises an essay on the consequences of living under the threat of nuclear annihilation and five parables concerning life before and after nuclear holocaust. While critics generally disputed Amis's contention that the sense of malaise prevalent in contemporary society results from nuclear weapons proliferation, they nevertheless noticed a broader, more generous emotional range in this collection. Amis has also written *The Moronic Inferno and Other Visits to America,* a compendium of essays that address literary and cultural issues in America. Included in this collection are profiles on Saul Bellow and Gloria Steinem and articles on AIDS and evangelical Christianity.

(See also *CLC,* Vols. 4, 9, 38; *Contemporary Authors,* Vols. 65-68; *Contemporary Authors New Revision Series,* Vols. 8, 27; and *Dictionary of Literary Biography,* Vol. 14.)

PRINCIPAL WORKS

NOVELS

The Rachel Papers 1973
Dead Babies 1975
Success 1978
Other People: A Mystery Story 1981
Money: A Suicide Note 1984
London Fields 1989

OTHER

The Moronic Inferno and Other Visits to America (essays) 1986
Einstein's Monsters (short stories) 1987

Richard Poirier

[The pieces collected in *The Moronic Inferno*] include mere snippets, like a note on the resurrection of *Vanity Fair,* or on William Burroughs ("most of Burroughs is trash"), or on Kurt Vonnegut. There are more extensive review-interviews of writers, such as Gore Vidal ("I cannot get through Vidal's fiction") and of film directors, such as Brian De Palma (his films "make no sense") or Steven Spielberg. There are news-story commentaries, on **"The Case of Claus von Bulow"** and on **"The Killings in Atlanta"**, where Amis discovers that the Peachtree Plaza Hotel is "a billion dollar masterpiece of American efficiency, luxury, and robotic good manners". And there are predictably disapproving reports on Jerry Falwell's evangelical Right and on Hugh Hefner and his Key Clubs, which have since been banished from the Playboy empire. The best items are the sensitive and well-researched **"Double Jeopardy: Making Sense of AIDS"** and **"Gloria Steinem and the Feminist Utopia"**. The book begins and ends with obsequies to Saul Bellow. "Saul Bellow", we are assured, "really is a great American writer."

The "really" is quite unnecessary since, so far as Amis's reading has taken him, all other American writers are more or less bushleagued. The book's title is from a phrase in Bellow's *Humboldt's Gift* (Bellow himself found it in Wyndham Lewis) and Amis's use of it, which is much broader than Bellow's, is a clue to his rather awkward, retrospective ambitions for this collection. The title encourages one to suppose that a reportorial assignment has somehow been transformed into a cultural one, without any intervening effort at rewriting or rethinking. And yet he admits that nearly all of the pieces "were written left handed", not by choice, that is, but at the request of various editors. No wonder he himself betrays some uncertainty about the results. First we're told that he had been asked on a couple of occasions "to write a book about America"; then, that in going over his selected journalism he discovered that "I had already written a book about America"; then that he is giving us merely "a collection of peripatetic journalism", and finally, having imposed on it so portentous a title, that the title does not in fact refer to America. "The moronic inferno is not", he says, "a peculiarly American condition. It is global and perhaps eternal. It is also, of course, primarily a metaphor, a metaphor for human infamy: mass, gross, ever-distracting human infamy."

Amis is a very OK writer, but he shouldn't expect his prose to carry that kind of baggage. He tends to chug and wheeze with incremental repetitions whenever it occurs to him that he ought to be solemn. . . .

The trouble is, Amis doesn't seem to have much fun on his visits. One inferable reason is that he has yet to master a requirement of good cultural reporting: that you must learn how to enjoy a lot of things you disapprove of, and that you have to find out why some other people seem to enjoy them instinctively. There are, inevitably, figures whose delight in themselves is contagious, like Steinem, Capote and Vidal, though even in these cases Amis has to be pulled into the party, and he manages so successfully to resist the charm, energy and audacity of Norman Mailer that he is left only with personal abuse:

> In the United States, provided you are Norman Mailer, it seems you can act like a maniac for forty years—and survive, prosper and multiply, and write the books. The work is what it is: sublime, ridiculous, always interesting. But the deeds—the human works—are a monotonous disgrace.

Why so heavy a hand? The fact that the "human works" conspicuously include nearly a dozen bright, healthy and happy offspring, all of them devoted to a father who remains friendly to their various mothers, is the kind of factor Amis is so determined to miss that he shouldn't have brought the matter up in the first place.

Bellow might have told him that it is always dangerous to try to be interesting when you are insufficiently engaged in a personal way with your subjects. In one of his better moments (*Salmagundi,* No 30, Summer 1975), Bellow allows that,

> if I were terribly moralistic I would scold everyone about this: that people do feel that there's something wrong, unappetising, unappealing in the ordinary—that they have to do something supererogatory, make themselves appeal; that the world is very boring, that they, themselves, are very boring and that they must discover some way not to be.

While Amis the journalist cannot afford to be boring or bored, he never wants to let himself go, to risk the self-exposures of an unguarded liking for something other than the monumental. Deeply hostile to artists who willingly put themselves forward in their work, like Philip Roth, Woody Allen and Mailer, he is a sort of neoclassicist manqué, distressed by a force of monstrosity, appetite and vulgarity which he calls "America". In Florida he boasts, "drop me down anywhere in America and I'll tell you where I am: in America"; while in the New York of Gloria Steinem he complains that "as soon as you leave New York you see how monstrously various, how humanly balkanised America really is". Nice thing about America, you can say anything you want about it, even if it's contradictory. "American novels are big all right", he tells us in the opening piece on Bellow, "but partly because America is big too", a bromide discarded long since by anyone who has bothered to ask himself why, in that case, *Middlemarch* and *Ulysses* are not small. On his visit to Palm Beach ("Never in my life have I seen such clogged, stifling luxury") he drives inland and discovers himself "immediately confronted by the booming chaos of middle America", a transition achieved less, I suspect, by driving than by typing. If wearing name tags has to be mentioned in the Ronald Reagan piece, what can be said about them? Obviously, that this is "something that Americans especially like doing", and if nothing else can be made out of the conviviality of the news-cameramen on the campaign plane, then why not propose that "their laughter, like so much American laughter, did not express high spirits but a willed raucousness". Enough, I say, of this willed raucousness! If, as he proposes in **"Mr Vidal: Unpatriotic Gore"**, "humorless people . . . include a great many Americans" who none the less obligingly laugh a good deal, then Amis's style seems to me better suited to them than to his compatriots, with their more cagey risibility. Anyway, Americans "tend to reduce argument to a babble of interested personalities". And so it goes. Hugh Hefner's alleged confusions of money and sex, consumerism and need, is "a very American mix", while euphemisms represent "a very American dishonesty". And when evocations of America are not put to work in place of a more personally engaged attentiveness, the function is just as glibly assigned to the easily maligned Sixties: "the usual rag-bag of Sixties sophistries" or "the Sixties, that golden age of high energy and low art", though, as it happens, it was a triumphant decade in American painting (which is mentioned not at all), in fiction (notably with Pynchon, who is referred to once) and in poetry, with Lowell, Bishop and Ashbery, to name only a few who are not mentioned anywhere in the book.

I'm not suggesting that a survey is the answer; rather that Amis's rhetoric and buzzwords exist in default of a willingness to find what he might have looked for. There is instead a kind of tightness and huffiness, issuing in such phrases as "our present permissiveness about turning tragedy into entertainment"—even though that seems to some of us what much literature tries to do—in the course of making a quite misleading point about so-called "non-fiction fiction". The trouble, so he opines, is that "what is missing . . . is moral imagination, moral artistry. The facts cannot be arranged to give them moral point." . . .

Except at points in the Steinem, the AIDS, and the Vidal pieces, it is mostly impossible to find in Amis's style those local, intimate, inquisitive reactions that might complicate the settled opinions of the communities for which he writes. He would like to suppose himself exempt from the criticisms he makes of Joan Didion, and for the reason that he assumes that what he calls "literature" is on his side, though I'm afraid he has a way to go. "Probably all writers", he remarks,

> are at some point briefly under the impression that they are in the forefront of disintegration and chaos, that they are among the first to live and work after things fell apart. The continuity such an impression ignores is a literary continuity. It routinely assimilates and domesticates more pressing burdens than Miss Didion's particular share of vivid, ephemeral horrors.

This is the familiar voice of a contemporary cultural conservatism trying to enlist a literature whose inner turmoils it fails and does not want to comprehend. There is, besides, a conspicuous inability in the book to elicit such literary continuities as might have allowed Amis some better sense of the American scene and the American writers he visits. It isn't necessarily that he needs to read more, though that wouldn't hurt in the case of authors he discusses, but that he needs to discover *how* to read the complicated inflections I mentioned at the beginning. This is true especially of Bellow's novels. Their distinction resides not in what Amis calls their "High Style . . . and exalted voice appropriate to the twentieth century", a formula not only at odds with the actual experience of reading Bellow but so gaseous as to be applicable to any ambitious writer of any time. Bellow is most alive precisely in his capacity to extemporize a style in which ordinary slang, coterie usages, the vulgarities, provincialities and waywardness of speech continually work against the pontifications of characters like Mr Sammler and Herzog, and in a manner contrived to redeem them. This is the sort of responsiveness, nuance, and play that Amis hasn't made his own, not yet anyway.

Richard Poirier, "Conservative Estimates," in The Times Literary Supplement, *No. 4346, July 18, 1986, p. 785.*

Sven Birkerts

The Moronic Inferno has as its points of entry and exit a review and a profile of Bellow, which is fitting in view of the fact that Bellow is one of the very few writers we have who has tried to sustain a panoramic, eagle's-eye view of our social landscape. The other 27 items break down pretty evenly between profiles of popular, middlebrow, or overrated American writers (Capote, Roth, Mailer, Vidal, Heller, Vonnegut, Burroughs, Updike, Didion, Theroux, and Talese) and chat-pieces on various prominent—and obvious—extrusions from the collective national psyche (von Bülow, De Palma, Presley, Reagan, Falwell, Steinem, Spielberg, and Hefner). In addition, there are bits of reportage on the Atlanta killings, Palm Beach, the evangelical right, *Vanity Fair,* and, yes, AIDS.

Looking at a culture from without has certain advantages. The observer (most of these pieces were written for the English journal of that name) can command some of the anthropologist's detachment, for one thing. He also has a tonal freedom denied to the native—he can sneer, mock, and condescend to his heart's content. Amis avails himself of all three options, most liberally of the last. Any American who has traveled abroad will recognize the friendly, bemused, confidential manner. And though Amis is clever enough to point his attitudes out even as he indulges them

("Oh God, we think"—he is referring to British critics on American novelists—"here comes another sweating, free-dreaming maniac with another thousand-pager; here comes another Big Mac"), the reader feels upon finishing that he has just passed an evening with somebody's "very nice, you'll like them" intellectual friends from Paris or London.

One of the subtle *dis*advantages of inspecting a culture from without is that it's very difficult for the outsider to tell a fresh insight from a commonplace. Unless, of course, that person is endowed with a decisively singular temperament, in which case every observation is of interest. Amis has not been thus endowed. His sensibility is precisely that of the literate John Doe. He is superficially cultivated—he is up to date—but not insightful; snide, but not dangerous; observant, but only of the cliché. What he notices about American fauna are precisely the things that our own journalists and supplement hacks long ago converted into received opinion. Palm Springs is a spiritual wasteland; Gore Vidal is a vain patrician pretender; Philip Roth is only concerned with Philip Roth. Ask me another! This stuff may be new to the readers of the *Observer,* but attentive culture-browsers will zip through it and go right back to *Vanity Fair* without so much as a transitional bump. (pp. 36-7)

My own hope, after my disappointment with the literary pieces, was that the rest of the collection might somehow make up the deficit. No such luck. Elvis, I learned, ended his days as an incontinent baby in diapers. Claus von Bülow is a shallow and avaricious—but not *stupid,* for God's sake—con. Hugh Hefner is, it seems, a vapid sybarite. Brian De Palma, about whom I knew nothing at all, turns out to be the very creature I would have imagined: a monomaniacal stringer-together of inchoate and violent imagery. Why he might be this kind of person is never questioned, nor is any understanding proffered about what the success of his spurting fantasies might say about the "deep and troubled . . . dreamlife" that so haunts Amis.

The two essays that rise above readable bitchiness are positioned shrewdly at the end of the book. **"Double Jeopardy: Making Sense of AIDS,"** while it delivers nothing new on a topic that shifts its contours daily, is a sane and remarkably empathic piece of reportage, combining information with sensitive ethical deliberation. Again, though, I have to lament an opportunity missed. Had this book been conceived as a real exploration of our moronic inferno, Amis might have gone on to pursue some of the more suggestive implications of his subject. He has a positive genius for brushing against what really matters—

> . . . one cannot avoid the conclusion that AIDS unites certain human themes—homosexuality, sexual disease, and death—about which society actively resists enlightenment. . . . We don't want to understand them. We would rather fear them . . .

—and then letting it go.

Saul Bellow is the one writer who escapes being spanieled at heels by the rebarbative Amis. This is because Bellow has done from within what Amis aspires to do from without. He has burrowed down past the obvious contradictions of the culture; he has reached that place where images and longings move like a miasma over the rock-scape of material conditions. And in **"Saul Bellow in Chicago,"**

it is the American who shows us how to think about America. A handful of quotations are enough to remind us what a book like Amis's could be. "For the first time in history," says Bellow, "the human species as a whole has gone into politics. . . . What is going on will not let us alone. Neither the facts nor the deformations." And: "You can say this for Chicago—there's no hypocrisy problem here. Everyone's *proud* of being a bastard." Maybe it's sensibility, maybe it's just that he's had seven decades to get the picture straight in his mind. Whatever the reason, Bellow's acerbic seriousness carries the day. Beside him, our young British friend looks like what Bellow in another context called "a contrast gainer." (pp. 37-8)

Sven Birkerts, "On Little Cat's Feet," in The New Republic, *Vol. 196, No. 4, January 26, 1987, pp. 36-8.*

Bruce Bawer

The Moronic Inferno and Other Visits to America is a collection of twenty-seven articles and reviews from the years 1977 to 1985, most of them originally printed in the English newspaper *The Observer,* all of them concerned with American culture or American writers. The topics include the Playboy mansion, AIDS, life in Palm Beach, the child killings in Atlanta, Truman Capote, Gore Vidal, Kurt Vonnegut, presidential candidate Ronald Reagan (1979), Gloria Steinem, Brian De Palma, and Steven Spielberg. None of these documents—the average length of which is about seven pages—could be described as deeply thoughtful or profound, or even (with one or two exceptions) substantial; at least one, a three-and-a-third-page "profile" of Diana Trilling, is so underdeveloped as to be virtually pointless: Amis doesn't arrive at the Trilling apartment until the top of the second page, and doesn't even get a word out of Mrs. Trilling until the middle of the third page. Several of the longer items in the book, meanwhile, are pastiches of two or more brief scraps. Amis's seventeen-page-long **"Norman Mailer: The Avenger and the Bitch,"** for instance, consists of a 1981 profile of Mailer, a 1982 report on Mailer and his "protégé" Jack Henry Abbott, a "postscript" review of Abbott's *In the Belly of the Beast,* and a 1985 review of Peter Manso's *Mailer: His Life and Times.* Amis has not added a single transitional sentence or paragraph to make a more coherent whole of these cobbled-together fragments; he just runs them in sequence, marking each break with three asterisks. So it goes throughout the book. Nor has he taken the trouble to improve upon the crude, newspapery prose that mars many of the pieces.

But then, one could hardly expect such efforts from Amis. After all, the unwritten code of the sassy young English literary man—a code which Amis obeys religiously—is not to try too hard. The literary man, according to this code, should be clever, not brilliant; energetic, not profound. Chatty and cheeky, impudent and self-indulgent, he should be ready to take on any topic, however serious, but must never behave as if anything could really touch him personally; he should, indeed, regard seriousness as a sort of intellectual version of a dinner jacket—a style he wears when the occasion calls for it, or when he finds himself possessed by a whim to make a somewhat more formal impression than usual. For the most part, however, the tone of his work should be decidedly brisk, sardonic, and offhand, as if he had dictated it hurriedly while on his way to something more important—a literary party, the West End theater, an Oxford banquet. Whereas many a young critic might attempt to establish an air of authority by developing a command of his material, by choosing his words with care, and by assuming a solemn tone, a sassy young English literary man more typically establishes his importance by making it clear that he is above such things—that he has better things to do than polish his prose or try to sound like Edward Gibbon or read everything his subject ever wrote. (pp. 20-1)

Once in a while, to be sure, Amis plays social critic. Indeed, in a manifest attempt to bolster his credibility as a professional observer of life in these United States, he wears his tenuous connections to the Republic on his sleeve—the sleeve of his book, that is: "Martin Amis, who lived in Princeton, New Jersey, as a ten-year-old, whose mother lived in America for years, and whose wife is American, feels 'fractionally American' himself." We are meant to understand from this, I suppose, that this is a man who knows his way around America. (And indubitably we are also meant to understand that, since Amis is at least "fractionally" one of us, it's acceptable for him to call America a "moronic inferno"—a phrase which, as he hastens to inform us, comes from Wyndham Lewis by way of Saul Bellow.) . . . At the end of his otherwise inconsequential introduction, he soberly pronounces that

> the moronic inferno [the meaning of which he never precisely explains] is not a peculiarly American condition. It is global and perhaps eternal. It is also, of course, primarily a metaphor, a metaphor for human infamy: mass, gross, ever-distracting human infamy. One of the many things I do not understand about Americans is this: what is it like to be a citizen of a superpower, to maintain democratically the means of planetary extinction? I wonder how this contributes to the dreamlife of America, a dreamlife that is so deep and troubled.

One should, of course, take this rhetoric with a grain or two of salt—after all, what we have here is really nothing more than a sassy young English literary man flirting with seriousness. But the fact that Amis chooses to characterize the United States as the prime emblem of "human infamy" *is* worth noting. Why does Amis perceive (or, at least, pretend to perceive) America in this way? Part of the reason, apparently, is that America is the world capital of serial murders (**"The Killings in Atlanta"**), of murder suspect as celebrity (**"The Case of Claus von Bülow"**), of serious writer as self-destructive buffoon (**"Norman Mailer," "Truman Capote: Knowing Everybody"**), of the vulgar rich (**"Elvis Presley: He Did It His Way," "Palm Beach: Don't You Love It?"**), of pre-Darwinian Protestantism (**"Here's Ronnie," "The New Evangelical Right," "Vidal vs. Falwell"**), and of impersonal sex (**"In Hefnerland," "Gay Talese: Sex-Affirmative"**); it is a "drive-in, shopping-mall land" of "condominiums, conurbations, the bleak toytowns formed by mobile homes." (How on earth, incidentally, can anyone from *England,* of all places, have the audacity to call American lower-class dwellings bleak?)

America is, in short, the seat of "excess"—a word that Amis returns to time and again. But the logic by means

of which he manages to reach this conclusion is ridiculously circular: he seeks out the most grotesque individuals and gruesome events in America to write about, and then decides (mostly, one suspects, because it provides him with a handy way of uniting these fugitive pieces thematically and of making them seem more important, more *representative* of something) that America itself is, on the evidence of these pieces, grotesque and gruesome. Singlemindedly, he equates one *outré* American phenomenon after another with the nation as a whole: "Like America, [Mailer] went too far in all directions. . . . " "Driving inland from Palm Beach, you are immediately confronted by the booming chaos of middle America." (There's a lot of booming in this book; also a lot of chaos.) As for Capote's life, "All the excess, solipsism, enmity, paranoia and ambition of American letters was crammed into those years. . . . " There is nothing Amis loves more than a sweeping generalization, especially one about the unavoidably drastic (and usually dire) effects of success upon a writer in America, and he makes such a generalization easier to draw by interviewing only writers like Mailer, Capote, Vonnegut, and Vidal, who have indeed allowed themselves to be "transformed" (as Amis puts it) to become media darlings. (Rest assured, there is no interview in *The Moronic Inferno* with Isaac Bashevis Singer.) As for the cases of the Atlanta child murders and of Claus von Bülow, what seems to interest Amis most about them is their luscious ambiguity—which he apparently considers an American characteristic. But why should one be surprised by any of this? As I say, considering that Amis has spent most of his time in America reporting on murders, hanging around Palm Beach and the Playboy mansion, and tagging along after the likes of Jerry Falwell, Norman Mailer, and Truman Capote, one would be astonished if America *didn't* strike him as bizarre, vulgar, crazy, and materialistic. (pp. 21-3)

Amis's own novels make it plain that his vision of America—and, indeed, of life itself—is close to Bellow's. His plotless, frenetic, Rabelaisian novels—*The Rachel Papers* (1973), *Dead Babies* (1975), *Success* (1978), *Other People: A Mystery Story* (1981), and *Money* (1985)—are for the most part darkly satiric tales about drug addicts, prostitutes, muggers, sensualists, and assorted grubby, amoral types; though Amis, to be sure, doesn't *like* such people, it is clear that for some reason he likes to think that the world is populated almost entirely by them. He certainly likes to think that America is populated by them (with a few million Falwellites, one supposes, thrown in for good measure). Yet to read a few of his pieces in *The Moronic Inferno* is to realize that when he complains about America's chaos, crudity, and cupidity—and this is true not only of him but of many English literary types—what is actually bugging him is our relative classlessness. Indeed, it is this very classlessness that, from Amis's upper-crust British point of view, makes America seem so anarchic and vulgar. The one constant throughout *The Moronic Inferno* is Amis's amused, supercilious attitude toward the lives and values and tastes of middle-class and lower-middle-class Americans, the cheapness of their homes, the modesty of their cultural attainments, the primitiveness of their *Weltanschauung,* and his amazement that these values and tastes are reflected on television, in fashion design, and in the speeches of presidential candidates. His unspoken complaint throughout the book is that America is the land of the rabble; one piece after another implicitly contrasts Martin Amis, a tiny package of English sophistication, with the huge and tacky people and houses and department stores and office buildings and billboards that constitute America. Perhaps the closest he comes to drawing this contrast explicitly is in the piece on Gloria Steinem, in which the Oxford graduate finds himself strolling around a building at Suffolk Community College on Long Island, "marvell[ing] at [the] variety" in shape and size of the American college students, and wondering: "Do all these people actually *have* a human potential?" (His answer, quite plainly: No, in Thunder!)

This supercilious point of view informs the entire book. (p. 23)

Size is a preoccupation throughout *The Moronic Inferno.* Amis keeps talking about the heights of his subjects. . . . And it is not just the size of *people* that interests Amis. American novels, he suggests, are big perhaps as "an inescapable response to America—twentieth-century America, racially mixed and mobile, twenty-four hour, endless, extreme, superabundantly various. American novels are big all right, but partly because America is big too." And Amis, as he himself cannot help telling us, is small. . . . One has the feeling that if America were not so big, Amis wouldn't think it was so bad. At any rate, it seems pretty clear that something is going on in *The Moronic Inferno* that has relatively little to do with America itself and a good deal to do with Amis.

For all its peculiarities and offenses, however, there is much to like—or at least much that one must (sometimes grudgingly) agree with—in this book. For one thing, in spite of his own sloppiness and superficiality, Amis appears sincerely to admire seriousness in other writers and to have minimal tolerance for the more self-indulgent creations (and personal antics) of Norman Mailer, William Burroughs, and the like. Generally, his taste is reliable: he rightly finds the essays of Gore Vidal and Joan Didion, for example, more accomplished than their novels. And he can be perceptive, even witty, about writers and their books. He recognizes that Vidal's primary characteristics are a "fundamental coldness" toward other human beings and a towering self-love. "Here is a man, you feel, who would walk a thousand miles for one of Gore's smiles." He observes that "never being satisfied is [Philip] Roth's great theme," and notes about Roth's Zuckerman trilogy that "There is not enough laughter or lyricism, there is not enough weather, there is not enough happening on the page. The Zuckerman novels look like life before art has properly finished with it. And Roth's corpus still gives the impression of a turbulent talent searching for a decorous way to explode." He can be relied on for a good quip: "As a filmmaker, Brian De Palma knows exactly what he wants. The only question is: why does he want it?" . . . Among the book's more disappointing items—considering Amis's gift for sarcasm and his preoccupation with sex—is the piece on "Hefnerland," which is dull and obvious and (uniquely in this book) overlong; Bob Greene has written more vividly and wittily about the Playboy mansion and William F. Buckley has more succinctly dispatched the Playboy Philosophy. On the other hand, the twelve-page article entitled **"Double Jeopardy: Making Sense of AIDS,"** originally published in *The Observer* in 1985, is perhaps Amis's most solid, sensible, and consistently intelligent piece, utterly free of the self-indulgent

touches that damage so many of the other things in the book.

Amis, then, understands many things about certain American subjects. Yet he doesn't really understand America itself—at least not as well as he thinks he does. After reading *The Moronic Inferno* one has the feeling that Amis has noticed everybody in America except the everyday people, the man and woman on the street; he doesn't seem to have the slightest idea what it is like to live a typical American life. In truth, he doesn't seem to *care* what it is like to live a typical American life. In *Money,* when he injected himself into the novel as a character, one was not all that surprised: one had already gathered the impression that here was a man who was bored contemplating other people—whether real or fictional—when he could be contemplating himself. In *The Moronic Inferno* Amis seems not so much to be observing America as to be observing himself in America; time and again one finds him writing not about Mr. Vidal, say, but about how Mr. Vidal reacted to Martin Amis. Nor does he have an ear for the American language. In *Money* he has American characters using British colloquialisms; in *The Moronic Inferno,* he reports Norman Mailer as saying, "I've written twice as many books as I should have done." He may have lived in New Jersey as a ten-year-old, may be married to an American, and for all I know may even drive a Chevy, but Martin Amis knows America in only the most superficial way—a way which makes for witty and even occasionally discerning articles and reviews, but which cannot make for a consistently penetrating book. (pp. 24-6)

> *Bruce Bawer, "Martin Amis on America," in* The New Criterion, *Vol. 5, No. 6, February, 1987, pp. 20-6.*

Richard T. Marin

[In *Einstein's Monsters*] Martin Amis has a cause to champion. He is *engagé.* Just as some people "get" religion, he has gotten Peace, or The Fear—not of God but the split atom. *Einstein's Monsters,* Amis announces in its 24-page introduction, titled **"Thinkability,"** is all about living with, and hating, the bomb.

Jonathan Schell's doomsday prognostications (in *The Fate of the Earth* and *The Abolition*) served as the catalyst for Amis's sudden awakening to the present danger. He thanks Schell both "for ideas and for imagery," while praising him reverentially: "He has moral accuracy. He is unerring."

As for the ideas, they are shopworn and uncharacteristically woolly: unilateral disarmament, "dismantling" nuclear weapons. The imagery is more provocative: it evokes life in a "Manhattan of missiles," which "squat on our spiritual lives." Ask what lies on "the other side of the firebreak" and Amis will tell you—"Necropolis." Take his ideas or leave them, Amis is still pushing words hard across the page. It's not easy to argue with someone who's talking so fast. But read on, and you discover that the five stories in this collection are not pitched to the high style promised in the introduction.

The first, **"Bujak and the Strong Force,"** tells of a hulking Polish émigré *cum* Samaritan who polices his neighborhood not so much with physical violence as the threat of it. That this bullet-headed tower of a man is actually a Minuteman/SS-20 in disguise is made just a little too clear by the narrator (one of the neighborhood's policed and protected), who calls Bujak "our deterrent." He is a weepy sort, this narrator, prone to saying things like, "I have nothing to fear, except the end of the world." After John Self's rollicking stream of consciousness [in *Money*], the diffuse, nondescript voices through which the stories in *Einstein's Monsters* trickle down come as something of an anticlimax. In the end, we are told, Bujak "laid down his arms," and the moral shouts through loud and clear. A little too loud, actually.

If these stories "arouse political feelings then that is all to the good," Amis says, after insisting that their primary purpose is to give "various kinds of complicated pleasure." Always a stern moralist, Amis has never before been a dour one. *Dead Babies,* his quintessential gross-out novel, was a graphic cry of revulsion at the sight of decency's decline and fall. Random copulation laced with deviant sexual practices, brain-frying drugs—these things disgusted Amis, but he could still laugh at them. In *Einstein's Monsters* he's so busy hanging crepe over the last days of Western Civilization he can't even muster a few *Strangelove*-style barbs, black though they might be.

Perhaps the problem lies in the species of writing undertaken. As Amis points out, most imaginative fiction to deal with this subject "belongs to the genres": fully one-quarter of science fiction novels are set after "W.W. III." To me, that adds up to several hundred-thousand pages of crushing tedium—and to Amis as well. Thus the problem he sets for himself: how to write about the holocaust differently, more skillfully?

The five stories in *Einstein's Monsters* are set sequentially, two pre- then three post-holocaust. The one closest to Amis's "thinkability" mindset is the second, called **"Insight at Flame Lake."** It recounts the diary of a mad teenager, a boy of 13 resembling "Franz Kafka or Ivan Lendl," whose thermonuclear obsession sends him first into schizophrenia then self-destruction. But as in **"Bujak,"** the symbolism squats flatly on the story's spiritual life. Neither the boy nor his uncle "Ned" comes off as real flesh-and-blood folk, but rather as didactic stand-ins, ideas in search of a character.

"The Time Disease" conjures a cyber-punk Hollywood future-world, where life imitates TV and sex is moribund. Now it's *"time"* (always in italics) that looms as the omnipresent oppressor. Nuclear winter persists and the heavens have gone dark. . . . But, a nit-picker might ask, how come all the TVs are working? After the blasts wiped out the electromagnetic field? It seems Amis chooses only those aspects of Schell's post-nuclear dystopia that suit his fictional purposes.

Time is also the lead player in **"The Immortals,"** a pompous lament by a man literally as old as the hills, who finds himself stuck on a dead earth with a few millennia to kill. "The first batch of ape people were just a big drag as far as I was concerned . . . " And so on. The tone is closer to Mel Brooks than Borges, whom Amis claims as the inspiration for **"The Immortals."** The gags miss the mark, though, leaving us a protracted bromide by the world's oldest and most boring raconteur.

Of all these stories, **"The Little Puppy That Could"** is the

most traditional piece of SF speculation—and the most lively. Set in a ragged village on the edge of chaos, a small contingent of our descendants live in mortal fear of a terrible creature called "the dog." They sacrifice "Queers" (their mal-evolved cousins) to the evil canine's voracious appetite until a lesser beast (the doglet of the title) intervenes. Lassie-like storyboard aside, there are several deft and welcome brushstrokes here. In this inverted community the women are "all rugged and ruddy and right; the men all drab, effaced, annulled." Genetic bedlam reigns and human beings are "mildly dismayed to find themselves travelling backward down their evolutionary flarepaths—or worse, sideways, into some uncharted humiliation of webs and pouches, of trotters and beaks."

At last, a whiff of the old (the young?) Martin Amis, cataloguing the nasty byways of perversity, as Balzac did cheeses in the market square; spinning an improbable but compelling yarn, and relaxing, enjoying it. To hell with polemics, "thinkability," and the moronic superinferno. The surest way to a reader's heart isn't through his conscience, but a good story. Or a good joke. (pp. 51-2)

Richard T. Marin, in a review of "Einstein's Monsters," in The American Spectator, *Vol. 20, No. 5, May, 1987, pp. 51-2.*

Adam Mars-Jones

Martin Amis in his new book of stories [*Einstein's Monsters*] seeks to enact that individual human rending which is the equivalent, in the only terms we seem able to understand, of the destruction done by nuclear weapons, by their very existence. Nuclear issues resist dramatization, but unless the attempt is made, nuclear war may become a physical reality without ever being an emotional, or even an intellectual reality. And if it happens, the only reality will be physical.

Amis provides a polemical introduction, on **"Thinkability"**, that is a powerful piece of rhetoric. He is at his best with one-liners. . . . At greater length, his rhetoric can be suspect. He is inconsistent, recognizing at one point that "we are slowly learning how to write about [nuclear weapons]", at another point lambasting those writers whose careers "straddled the evolutionary firebreak of 1945" for their silence, with the comment "they evidently did not find the subject suggested itself naturally", as if lack of interest could be the only obstacle.

Amis's rhetoric is sometimes unwontedly utopian, when for instance he says that "in our biosphere everything is to do with everything else. In that they are human, all human beings feel it—the balance, the delicacy. We have only one planet, and it is *round.*" It can't be quite that easy to disengage from human destructiveness. In any case the assertion that everything is to do with everything else sits particularly oddly with the fact that Amis considers nuclear weapons in isolation. He freely quotes writers on the subject but nowhere mentions the Campaign for Nuclear Disarmament, as if nuclear politics were self-evidently a matter for writers rather than activists. . . .

Amis is passionately eloquent in his introduction, without—as he acknowledges—providing any new answers, and his passion sometimes leads him to dangerous arguments. At one point, for instance, he asserts: "By threatening extinction, the ultimate anti-personnel device is in essence an anti-baby device. One is not referring here to the babies who will die but to the babies who will never be born, those that are queueing up in spectral relays until the end of time." Would he acknowledge the cogency of such an argument if it was advanced by someone who opposed both contraception and abortion, or is this that worrying development even within single-issue politics, the single-issue argument?

The nuclear dilemma has none of the traditional advantages of the single issue; it is an issue without edges. In the two of the stories in *Einstein's Monsters* that have a present-day setting, Amis's nuclear preoccupations seem to be imposed on the fiction. If everything has been undermined by the existence of nuclear weapons, how do you single out an area of collapse? In **"Bujak and the Strong Force"**, an American writer living in London tells how his Polish neighbour Bujak, in his sixties but still "hugely slabbed and seized with muscle and tendon", a self-appointed vigilante, reacts to the casual murder of his mother, daughter and granddaughter. The calamity is announced as "in some sense post-nuclear, einsteinian", but doesn't feel so. The extensive use of nuclear metaphor in the story—of *nuke* to mean "destroy utterly", of *fallout* as a strong word for "consequences", of *neutronium* to describe a powerful fist—feels appliqué rather than naturally emerging. If the story's dramatization of a post-atomic age needed no bolstering, there would be less call for the overkill.

Bujak for once takes no revenge. The narrator comments: "And now that Bujak has laid down his arms, I don't know why, but I am minutely stronger." This would be an effective turning-point, except that strength and weakness in the story are very much rhetorical constructs. The narrator is weak in the Woody Allen way, stridently, insistently weak, weak with all the resources at Martin Amis's disposal:

> What is it with objects? Why are they so aggressive? What's their beef with *me*? Objects and I, we can't go on like this. We must work out a compromise, a freeze, before one of us does something rash. I've got to meet with their people and hammer out a deal.

In a first-person story above all, control of language is the real strength, and this narrator is actually invulnerable.

Amis keeps up a steady verbal pressure. His narrators don't venture abroad without a suit, a shield, without a testudo of style to protect them. . . .

[Sometimes] it seems that the need to stamp each sentence with his literary personality defeats his ambitions as a literary artist. This is perhaps a peculiarly modern artistic dilemma. Fear of inauthenticity can lead to inauthenticity of a different sort, not an unsigned painting but a painting composed entirely of signatures. A reader of *Einstein's Monsters* is unlikely to forget at any point that he is reading Martin Amis, and when the stories are constructed according to a different assumption they necessarily misfire. The brilliant but suicidal narrator of **"Insight at Flame Lake"** turns out to have been twelve years old. The self-proclaimed "Immortal" of the last story, soon to be alone on an irradiated planet, suddenly wonders if he isn't a second-rate New Zealand schoolteacher after all. But the reader of *Einstein's Monsters* is likely to be too oversti-

mulated by Amis's hyperactive prose to be moved, or even convinced, by these revelations. The fireworks at these funerals distract from grief.

No such problems affect the collection's most successful story, and also its nearest approach to pure science fiction, **"The Time Disease"**. The characters in the story are terrified of "coming down with *time*", though it turns out that what they dread is not age but resurgent youth and vitality. What makes the story so funny and exciting is its enactment of a stupefied and stupefying society, where people say only, "It's a feature", or "It's a thing", to convey their response to extreme events. Amis makes this hampered speech, hardly an improvement on autism, both eloquent and unpredictable.

He has always been fascinated with the possibilities of debasement. Much of his writing has been the literary equivalent of tantric yoga, the path to enlightenment that works not by controlling the body and by austerity, but by systematic pollution and the cultivation of impure appetites. The typical Martin Amis sentence will force together high and low elements, pedantry and taboo slang, aesthetics and bestial cynicism.

Perhaps this is why, when he attempts the genre of innocence, in **"The Little Puppy That Could"**, the results are so uncomfortable. The story tells a version of the Andromeda myth, in a post-apocalyptic village where a mutated dog demands human sacrifices. The style wavers between cute and pseudo-cute, from deliberately ersatz sentiment to less obviously false naivety: "Why do people love children? Why do children love babies? Why do we all love animals? What do animals love, that way?" The effect is cloying, particularly as the celebration of natural virtue is accompanied by an unlikeable adult agenda.

The women of the village are strong, the men weak. The women are called Keithette, Clivonne, and Kevinia, while the men are feeble Tims, Tams and Toms. What surfaces in the story, not presumably by design, is a dread of power and desire in the female, unmanliness in the male, of identity in women and loss of it in men. And this time, unnatural strength and unnatural weakness are both rendered weak in literary terms, by being excluded from the point of view. The story ends with the recreation of a real man, "strong and warlike", to complement the heroine's submissive emotionalism.

There may be an irony intended, but if so it has failed to take, and that in a writer as scrupulous as Amis is itself significant. As so often in science fiction, it is the present that is being discussed, disguised as the future. It may be that Amis considers the breakdown of sex roles a consequence of deeper breakdowns (of the existence of nuclear weapons, for instance), but he can still seem to use sexual irregularity as a scapegoat, in a way that is highly conventional despite his career of iconoclasm. Here the hostile instincts too easily disavowed in the introduction return to mar, just for a few moments, this provocative and highly accomplished collection.

Adam Mars-Jones, "Fireworks at the Funeral," in The Times Literary Supplement, *No. 4387, May 1, 1987, p. 457.*

Francis King

The most interesting item in this always interesting collection [*Einstein's Monsters*] is not any one of its five stories but its introduction. In that introduction ["Thinkability"], Martin Amis brings a relentlessly grating logic to a problem which, by his own admission, no one knows how to solve. The crux of this problem is that (I paraphrase his words) nuclear weapons deter a nuclear holocaust by threatening a nuclear holocaust, but that if things go wrong then it is a nuclear holocaust that occurs. . . .

Amis—born in 1949, four days before the Russians tested their first atom bomb—confesses to clinical nausea when he thinks too deeply or too long about nuclear weapons. Literally, he grows sick of them. Even those who robustly maintain that they never give the issue a thought, cannot really, he claims, be uninterested—'The man with the cocked gun in his mouth may boast that he never thinks about the cocked gun. But he tastes it all the time.' A potent image.

Often in the stories Amis gives the impression not merely of constantly tasting the metal of that cocked gun but of greedily sucking on it, as though, irresistible but deadly, it were a delicious lollipop laced with cyanide. It is a strange and terrible fact of human nature that what we dread we also, in part at least, desire. All right, fine, take me, do what you want with me: the acceptance helps to minimise the horror. It is therefore with an almost voluptuous pleasure that Amis, like a hospital patient describing his sufferings to an increasingly disgusted visitor, lingers on all the consequences of the nuclear holocaust that he postulates in three of his five stories: for example, a dog-mutation, eight feet long and four feet high, which is both homovorous and the host to innumerable bacteria and viruses, or human survivors who, in one story, 'crackle with cancers . . . fizz with synergisms, under the furious and birdless sky' and in another must eschew sexual intercourse and cultivate boredom if they are not to succumb to the new disease of Time.

As in Amis's novels, so in these five stories, it is not always easy to discern precisely what is happening, so thick is the swirling impasto with which they are composed. The blurb tells one that, in "**Insight at Flame Lake**", 'a virulent new strain of schizophrenia overwhelms the 13-year-old boy who is one of its two narrators. But of this 'virulent new strain' I remained unaware throughout my reading, merely seeing the story as a brilliant description of how, on renouncing his drugs, a schizophrenic slips from the real world into a hallucinatory one, which then destroys him. Again, the blurb describes "**The Little Puppy that Could**" as a Kafkaesque love-story, but this post-Holocaust version of the story of the Frog Prince is surely far closer, in matter and manner, to Hans Andersen. . . .

Consisting of a mere 127 pages, this is a thin book. To say that the stories are also thin is not derogatory. Their thinness is that of an athlete, his body pared down so that its musculature is revealed in all its straining pathos; or of a wire, glittering and tensile, which can lift enormous weights or at a single tug garotte a man. What gives each paragraph its furious, famished energy is precisely what Amis describes himself as feeling when he contemplates a possible Holocaust: nausea. Sick to his stomach—the Americanism is his own—Amis cries out in desperation

for some kind of spiritual Dramamine or Kwells. But who can dispense it? 'What am I to do with thoughts like these? What is anyone to do with thoughts like these?' He cannot provide an answer and no one can provide one for him.

Francis King, "The Sin of the Fathers," in The Spectator, *Vol. 258, No. 8286, May 2, 1987, p. 31.*

John Lanchester

'I would certainly sacrifice any psychological or realistic truth for a phrase, for a paragraph that has a spin on it,' [Martin Amis told an interviewer]: 'that sounds whorish, but I think it's the higher consideration. Mere psychological truth in a novel doesn't seem to me all that valuable a commodity. I would sooner let the words prompt me, rather than anything I was representing.' *Einstein's Monsters* is a collection of five stories and an introductory essay, a collection which represents a spectacular retreat from—or advance beyond—the detached aestheticism of that loftily Nabokovian credo. The book announces an obsession with nuclear weapons; it also announces a new tonality in Amis's writing, a darkening and a loss of exuberance in his address to the world. Saul Bellow, an exemplary figure for Amis in more than one respect, is relevant to the transition we are witnessing here: 'Bellow has made his own experience resonate more memorably than any living writer. And yet he is also the first to come out on the other side of this process, enormously strengthened to contemplate the given world.'

The experience which resonates most memorably in Amis's five novels is described by Charles Highway, narrator of *The Rachel Papers:* 'One of the troubles with being overarticulate, with having a vocabulary more developed than your emotions, is that every turn in the conversation, every switch of posture, opens up an estate of verbal avenues with a myriad side-turnings and cul-de-sacs—and there are no signposts but your own sincerity and good taste, and I've never had much of either. All I know is that I can go down any one of them and be welcomed as a returning lord.' In creating themselves through language, Amis's protagonists—as well as being a laugh a line—have a fluidity of character that can be dangerous, and not only to themselves. The business of educating yourself out of this condition parallels the ethical self-training that all writers of fiction undergo. When, in *Money,* we meet the character Martin Amis, he seems, in his fully developed selfhood, a curiously stiff and priggish figure ('I get up at seven and write straight through till twelve. Twelve to one I read Russian poetry—in translation, alas. A quick lunch, then art history until three . . . ') compared to the unformed, uneducated John Self, the attractive monster of language and of appetite. A sentence of Northrop Frye's has a lot of bearing on *Money:* 'The culture of the past is not only the memory of mankind, but our own buried life, and study of it leads to a recognition scene, a discovery in which we see, not our past lives, but the total cultural form of our present life.' Amis has passed through that recognition scene, but Self has not: he is not free. This theme is another source of Amis's kinship with Bellow: 'Many times in Bellow's novels we are reminded that "being human" isn't the automatic condition of every human being. Like freedom or sanity, it is not a given but a gift, a talent, an accomplishment, an objective. In achieving it, some will need time or thought or help.' 'Human' is, in Amis's writing, a word which always has a special weight, a special glow.

In *Einstein's Monsters,* Amis writes about becoming human, but in a form new for him—the parable. **'The Little Puppy That Could'** (debts acknowledged to Nabokov and Kafka) is set in a post-apocalyptic world in which 'natural selection had given way to a kind of reverse discrimination or tokenism. Any bloody fool of an amphibious parrot or disgraceful three-winged stoat had as much chance of survival, of success, as the slickest, the niftiest, the most singleminded dreck-eating ratlet or invincibly carapaced predator.' A village is being terrorised by a giant, homovorous, dog; an adorable little puppy arrives, is adopted by the anomalously beautiful Andromeda and is given a home and a name (Jackajack). Eventually there is a catastrophic immolation, and a rebirth:

> She opened the door and said,
>
> 'Jackajack?'
>
> The boy stood there, against a swirl of stars, his body still marked by the claws and the flames. She reached up to touch the tears in his human eyes.
>
> 'John,' she said.
>
> His arms were strong and warlike as he turned and led her into the cool night. They stood together on the hilltop and gazed down at their new world.

The tone of this, and the explicit sentimentality it risks—perhaps more than risks—is something new in Amis's work. The story leaves a blurred, uneasy feeling in the reader's mind: a feeling you get used to in *Einstein's Monsters.* **'The Immortals'**, again set in a post-apocalyptic landscape, is narrated by a character who has lived for millions of years ('I think I must have been a dud god or something') and is now in New Zealand, watching the last human beings die. But there is a twist: it turns out that one of the symptoms of radiation sickness is the victim's illusion of immortality. 'Sometimes I have the weird idea that I am just a second-rate New Zealand schoolteacher who never went anywhere or did anything and is now painfully and noisily dying of radiation sickness along with everybody else.' On a first reading, the story is a Woody Allen sketch ('If I thought the Permian age was the pits it was only because I hadn't yet lived through the Triassic') with a darker-than-usual ending. With further readings, however, the story takes on a more sustainedly compassionate timbre and its focus seems to shift, so that its emotional centre is no longer the surprise ending but the pain and loss which are evoked almost parenthetically: 'A million times I have been bereaved, and then another million. What pain I have known, what megatons of pain.' This modulates into the truth: 'It's strange how palpable it is, this fake past, and how human: I feel I can reach out and touch it. There was a woman, and a child. One woman. One child . . . ' The stories in *Einstein's Monsters* are haunted, as is the introduction, by the imagined deaths of children. Often, this death (these deaths) is where the real imaginative weight of the story seems to be placed; the emotional balance is, as in **'The Immortals'**, slightly off-centre. In **'Insight at Flame Lake'**, the schizophrenic son of a recently-dead atomic scientist holidays with his uncle

and aunt and their newborn baby. The baby is at risk from the schizophrenic, who has thrown his medication into the lake (he has 'insight'—he knows he's sick); unborn children are at risk from the bomb (the scientists have a standing joke—'Dad: "Death to the babies." Andrei: "And to your babies." Dad: "And to your babies' babies" '); children at large are just plain at risk. The nephew kills himself, and the story ends with the voice of his uncle, in a passage whose strength comes from the restraint with which it hides real bitterness and despair behind a casual, throwaway manner:

> On the back of the half-gallon carton of homogenised, pasteurised, vitamin-D-fortified milk there are two mugshots of smiling children, gone missing (Have You Seen Them?). Date of birth, 7/7/79. Height, 3′6″. Hair, brown. Eyes, blue. Missing, and missed too, I'll bet—oh, most certainly. Done away with, probably, fucked and thrown over a wall somewhere, fucked and murdered, yeah, that's the most likely thing. I don't know what is wrong.

We get Amis's answer to the question 'what is wrong?' in the first story in the collection, **'Bujak and the Strong Force'**. It describes Bujak, a sixty-year-old strongman and philosopher whose mother, daughter and granddaughter are murdered. Bellow gets the source-acknowledgment, but the story also owes a debt to Capote, Mailer and the 'nonfiction novel' of murder, a form which Amis has criticised for its lack of 'moral imagination, moral artistry . . . When the reading experience is over, you are left, simply, with murder—and with the human messiness and futility which attend all death.' **'Bujak'** is an examination of murder which seeks to restore the moral artistry by seeking a cause for apparently random action—seeking it, and finding it too. 'All peculiarly modern ills, all fresh distortions and distempers, Bujak attributed to one thing: einsteinian knowledge, knowledge of the strong force. It was his central paradox that the greatest—the purest, the most magical—genius of our time should introduce the earth to such squalor, profanity and panic.' The murderers are 'vivid representatives of the 20th century—Einstein's monsters', just as the Author's Note has told us that 'we are Einstein's monsters, not fully human, not for now.'

It's **'Bujak'** which, while providing the strongest evidence of a new range and a new compassion in Amis's writing, also brings the difficulties with *Einstein's Monsters* into clearer focus. 'What is the hidden determinant that could explain it *all?*' asks the narrator. It's a dangerous question for a writer of fiction to be interested in. 'The truth is,' Amis wrote once, 'that in the vacuum of success Mailer had fallen prey to the novelist's fatal disease: ideas. His naïveté about "answers", "the big illumination", "the secret of everything", persists to this day.' Amis is alert to this naivety because he is also prone to it: there's a curious simplemindedness in the idea that there will be a 'hidden determinant' at all, let alone one as concrete as nuclear weapons. It's not that **'Thinkability'** is not brilliant, and it's not that the stories aren't compelling—it is, they are—it's just that the book's polemic is suggestive rather than convincing. **'Thinkability'** in fact undermines the stories by alerting us pre-emptively to their concerns: this effect is at its worst on the imagistic level. 'My impression is that the subject resists frontal assault. For myself, I feel it as a background, a background which then insistently foregrounds itself.' That isn't what the reader feels when he reads of 'the strong force, the energy locked in matter', of 'spin and charm, redshifts and blueshifts', of the lake which 'is like an explosion, in the last second before it explodes', of 'the leptons of the sun' which 'warily encircled the waiting earth and its strong force', of the puppy which 'seemed freer than air, whimsically lithe, subatomic, superluminary, all spin and charm, while the dog moved on rails like a bull, pure momentum and mass, and forever subject to their laws'. There are a lot of these images, and every single one of them is like a twenty-five-stone sunbathing nudist—very conspicuous, very inert. . . .

Einstein's Monsters is an uneven, unsettled book. Where *Money* seems, on each further reading, to be more and more of an achievement . . . *Einstein's Monsters* doesn't give a clear impression either of success or of failure. There is certainly a new emotional range in it, but at the same time, the attempt to focus on nuclear weapons as an all-embracing explanation of late 20th-century malaise does not convince. If the book lived by that idea, it would die by it too—but it doesn't, its real life is elsewhere. 'Clearly, a literary theme cannot be selected, cannot be willed; it must come along at its own pace.' That 'clearly' is partly a bluff: it seems to me that Amis, at some level of consciousness, chose the subject of nuclear weapons as a vehicle to demonstrate a new manner and new range of concerns; and that discrepancy between declared intention and real imaginative nexus is what causes the sense of provisionality and of strainedness in this book. Its real imaginative focus is hard to pinpoint, but it is something to do with the death of children—something to do with dead babies. In any case, however Amis got into this subject, it's too late now: he clearly hasn't finished with it, nor it with him. Middle Amis is upon us. (p. 11)

> John Lanchester, "As a Returning Lord," in London Review of Books, Vol. 9, No. 9, May 7, 1987, pp. 11-12.

Merle Rubin

Success is a kind of companion work to Amis's fifth book, *Money*. The themes—like the titles—are closely related: the frenetic pursuit of money, power, success, sex. As Amis takes us into the psyches of his desperate, empty-headed, manipulative characters, we well may wonder why he bothers to devote such a lot of attention to people he disapproves of so much. For, unlike the hydrogen bomb, the fast-lane fashionable set *can* be avoided!

But fashions do shape lives, and "life styles" substitute themselves for more substantive values. The characters in *Success* embody pervasive trends. And the great strength of this novel (like *Money*) is that it shows us what is wrong, not from the detached perspective of the critical outsider, but from the inside.

Two voices narrate the story, each talking at us with the compulsiveness of Coleridge's Ancient Mariner. One belongs to Terry Service, a hapless, lowborn, pathetically repulsive "yob" (his word). The other belongs to his "posh," upper-class foster brother, Gregory Riding, who is handsome, athletic, fashionable, disdainful, homosexual, and wildly in demand by men and women alike. Terry seems doomed to "service" and servility, while Gregory seems destined for "riding" high. Poor Terry has a meaningless

job he is terrified of losing, while Gregory deigns to take on a "fun" job in an art gallery. Terry can scarcely get a girl to look at him, while Gregory turns away girls in droves.

And so we are given the world according to Terry and the world according to Gregory. It's really the same world, but viewed from different angles, and expressed in different *styles*.

The seesaw shift about two-thirds of the way through the book, when success averts her shining face from Gregory to smile upon Terry, is essentially a shift in the way the characters see themselves. Between Gregory's preening self-love and Terry's bitter self-loathing there seems a world of difference.

But, as Amis skillfully illustrates, these two states of mind are a mere hair's breadth apart. Different though they are, Terry and Gregory are adrift in a world where no quality seems to exist in and of itself. Value is entirely arbitrary in the mind of the beholder. The situation recalls Shakespeare's *Troilus and Cressida:* "What is aught, but as 'tis valued?" and the reply, " . . . value dwells not in particular will." Gregory and Terry are caught up in the pursuit of things that have no intrinsic value and suffer accordingly. Devastating as Amis's satire is, its sting also exposes the sheer pathos—and the dreadful vertigo—of leading an empty life.

> Merle Rubin, "Martin Amis's Stinging Satire of Empty Lives in the Late '70's," in The Christian Science Monitor, September 4, 1987, p. B4.

Jay Parini

[Amis] wrote *The Rachel Papers*—an energetic but immature novel about a young man's obsessive quest for sexual fulfillment—soon after graduating from Oxford in the early 1970's. He soon became a fixture on the London literary scene, a satirist of the smart set in the tradition of Evelyn Waugh—with whom he shares a profound misanthropy, the sine qua non of all successful satirists. His third novel, *Success* (originally published in Britain in 1978 and now issued here for the first time), might easily have been called *Vile Bodies* had Waugh not got there before him.

Misanthropy becomes misogyny in *Success,* another novel on the theme of sexual obsession. The novel's two narrators, Gregory Riding and Terry Service, hate women almost as much as they hate themselves, though it remains unclear where Mr. Amis stands on all this. . . .

The novel is a double memoir, told in alternating and remarkably distinct voices. Gregory is an esthete, endlessly supercilious and charming, prone to view the world through rose-tinted pince-nez. "I work in an art gallery," he tells us. "Yes, the job *is* rather a grand one, as you'd expect. High salary, undemanding hours, opportunities for travel, lots of future." More to the point of *Success,* Gregory is sexually overactive. A bisexual, he would happily be a trisexual if a third sex suddenly materialized. People offer him their favors at every turn, much to the chagrin of unsuccessful Terry, his foster brother and reluctant flatmate.

Unlike Gregory, Terry is down on himself. "I look like educated lower-class middle-management, the sort of person you walk past in the street every day and never glance at or notice or recognize again," he informs us at the beginning. Even worse, from his viewpoint, he has not seduced a woman for six months, and it's driving him crazy. . . . One feels sorry for Terry, whose mother is dead and whose father butchered his little sister, thus forcing him upon the charity of the upper-class Ridings (Mr. Riding stumbles through the novel like a lost character from P. G. Wodehouse). But Terry's self-denigrations and complaints soon wear thin, and one quickly looks forward to Gregory's preening and strutting.

As Terry's prospects at work begin to improve through dealings with a seedy union organizer, and his relationship with Ursula, Gregory's psychotic sister, takes on a sinister aspect, one senses a shift in the wind. Eerily, Terry's rise seems to precipitate Gregory's fall, and Mr. Amis holds our attention quite skillfully as we wait, like a gallows crowd, for the floor to drop beneath Gregory's feet. Yet *Success* is, finally, a distasteful book, full of loathing that the author seems not fully to have understood or drawn through the crucible of art.

> Jay Parini, "Men Who Hate Women," in The New York Times Book Review, *September 6, 1987, p. 8.*

Graham Fuller

Success, Amis's third novel, bridges the postadolescent sexual angst of his first, *The Rachel Papers,* and the feverish junk-consumerism of his fifth, *Money.* First published in Britain in 1978, *Success* extends the "street sadness" introduced in his second novel, *Dead Babies,* to the ultimate degree of alienation. It's a parody of England's class war, with Gregory and Terry symbolizing the spiritual decay of the landed gentry and the greedy self-betterment of the "yobs," each appraising the other's position with eloquent disgust or shameless envy. Terry capitalizes on his status as a lackey serving his nouveau riche union organizer, Gregory squanders his nights in debauchery.

The title, of course, is ironic, and the structure embodies an elaborate practical joke. Building to a half-glimpsed shudder of schizophrenia "on the evening our lives sorted themselves out for good," *Success* takes the form of a year-long double diary, a pair of paranoid confessions, which traces a switch of fortunes. Plain, balding, sex-starved, but basically decent prole Terry (who's so fucked up but unfucked that on one page he savors the word "fuck" 48 times) graduates from maudlin self-pity to exploitative nastiness, while narcissist Gregory (the most malevolent portrait of a Sloane Ranger in English fiction), whose every twirled adjective reeks of sex and money, makes the reverse trip into humiliation and incipient madness. (pp. 66, 69)

Behind the comedy of Terry's whining and Gregory's lies, however, is a history of murder and incest. At the age of nine (prior to his adoption by Gregory's father), Terry witnessed the killing of his sister by his father, who'd already killed their mother. In their teens, Gregory fucked (and fucked up) *his* sister, Ursula, and—back in the present—he attempts to fuck Terry's new-found girlfriend,

Jan. It soon becomes apparent to Terry what he must do to get his revenge. Ursula and Jan are pawns, a thin, mindless, upper-class waif and a voluptuous, sardonic, working-class strumpet. In keeping with their creator's misogyny, they're discarded once they've served their purpose.

Perhaps Amis plays God too well. His Nabokovian wordplay is beautifully wrought, but the design is schematic, and such constant contriving seems a little soulless. Still, it also produces some delicious jolts to the memory—the November image of Gregory negotiating a pool of vomit, frozen in an alleyway, has, for example, a curiously poignant nostalgic value that wouldn't have been anticipated from seeing the fizzing, belching Terry leave it there six months before. (p. 69)

> Graham Fuller, "Yob Action," in The Village Voice, *Vol. XXXII, No. 48, December 1, 1987, pp. 66, 69.*

Melvyn Bragg

Martin Amis is our own nuke, nuked, new clear fall-out novelist. *London Fields* is set ten years hence as the world frazzles out. His quartet of main characters and their full supporting orchestra are swirled down the drain at the end of the century.

The basic plot, discovered by the writer, is a murder. Nicola Six, ex-actress to say the least, in her mid-thirties, decides against the second half of her life and plays the murderee. Keith Talent, poor working cheat, darts chump-champ, super-yob, is part of her drama; as is Guy Clinch, leisured rich, husband champ-chump, super fool; and Samson Young, the writer, Jewish American, living in the flat of an English writer with initials 'M. A.'. The location is Notting Hill Gate. The writing is hard-edged, funny, rifted with literary allusion—Nabokov puts in his usual appearance, and Larkin and Shakespeare of course, *et al.* But it is equally stuffed with gobbits from the *Sun* and *Star,* and flecked by aped television football commentary's peculiarly private lingo. The characters, too, come as much out of comics as Eng. Lit. There is a wonderfully monstrous child, Marmaduke (twinned, as you would expect from M. A., by a passively perfect child called Kim), who roars with the sound of a baby Dennis the Menace as much as any phenomenon from Dickens.

It is the mix of the well-bred in the traditional and the well-read in the flashiest contemporary which gives to Amis prose its rich bite. Sometimes it is too pummelling, occasionally straining. Alliterations and repetitions threaten to become cluttered and self-imitative, hammering at the prose like hail until you want to stop. But this is small beer. Taken all in all, *London Fields* is a rare achievement. In terms of old-fashioned accessibility, it is his best read since *The Rachel Papers.* The jokes work, the character/caricatures convince, the ambition is laudable, and the energy ferociously impressive. . . .

If you try to be a careful reader, then the novel will best be enjoyed as serialised treats. Sprinters will find good turf but the patient, even a plodder, will get more reward. This is a book for the tortoise written by someone who looks like a hare. The main thesis, which began, I suspect, pre-Gorbachev and had to be bent to fit an alternative scenario, is that a world on permanent pre-nuclear sufferance and further (perhaps a little later fortification) worn by the bombardment of pollution, is running out of its future. Nicola—'Miss World' someone wolf whistles at her down the street—wants to take the hemlock; but being an ornate artist wants much artifice. Her enlisting of a supporting cast, and her soft-porn character confused with role modelling, is the beginning of implausibilities which lever the book firmly away from realism. At its best, it floats three feet above the ground. Now and then there's a bump as the accuracy of the descriptive writing induces a state of suspended disbelief betrayed by the too contrived arrival of the plot. Nevertheless, the gains far outweigh the losses, and the tensions which are offered can work in the book's favour.

Melvyn Bragg, "Nuclear Reaction," in The Listener, *Vol. 122, No. 3132, September 21, 1989, p. 30.*

Martyn Harris

[*London Fields*] is set in 1999 London, a city even more squalidly gridlocked than today; alternately grilling and drenching under the greenhouse effect, where rain has come to sound "like industrial gas, escaping from the rooftops".

Political, economic and military crises are converging towards an apocalyptic millennium. Everyone is wasted by mysterious diseases. The narrator, Sam, is dying of something-like-Aids. His girlfriend Lizzyboo is eating herself sick. Nicola Six is plotting her own murder. Her would-be lover, Guy Clinch, is crippled by an erection of titanic tumescence. His baby, Marmaduke, is a sociopathic monster. Keith Talent, a typical Amis superyob. . . .

Amis was always great with the words, of course: the only English writer of his generation to kick his way out of the reticent, genteel language of the contemporary novel into a modern idiom which manages to be both coarse and eloquent, demotic and cerebral. He has a sharp ear for the cant phrases of everyday life like "heritage" and "prestigious" and the tics of pub talk with an "as such" and "innit" suffixed to every inanity. . . .

The question is, can Amis do anything else? Superheated rhetoric is okay, but novels need structure, and Amis's have a habit of collapsing into anticlimax where you find it was the mysterious psychopath who dunnit, for no reason whatever. Amis isn't interested in character, plot, motivation. "Motivation is pretty shagged out by now," says the Amis character in **Money**. "Go for a walk in the streets. How much motivation do you see?"

Well, quite a lot actually, and it is a remark which reveals a remoteness and lack of human curiosity in Amis, which can make his novels unsympathetic and snobbish. Keith Talent is simply brutish; Guy Clinch is simply a drip; Sam is simply a cipher for the authorial presence. Three quarters through **London Fields** I was bored with wondering which would kill Nicola Six and wishing somebody would just get on with it. In denying motive Amis denies his characters the capacity for change, which in turn rules out the manipulation of reader sympathy—the strongest lever in fiction.

Instead of character the book offers chronocentrism—the conceit that your own age is more special, more scary, more apocalyptic than any other. It might be—but it is a truth which must be glimpsed from the corner of the authorial eye, not harped on with the portentousness of the reborn eco freak and the whine of the nuke neurotic. The pursuit of the millennium is for lunatics, preachers and second-rate novels—of which this, sadly, is one.

Martyn Harris, "Pursuit of the Millennium," in New Statesman & Society, *Vol. 2, No. 68, September 22, 1989, p. 34.*

Francis King

The blurb of Martin Amis's [*London Fields*] describes it as 'many-layered.' But in the exact sense of the word, as distinct from the blurb-writer's sense, multi-layered is precisely what this novel is not. It has as many layers as a club-sandwich, which is three.

The middle of these layers concerns Nicola Six, 'tall, dark and thirty-four', who 'always knows what is going to happen next and who goes through life with two firm assurances: that no one will ever love her enough, and that those who do love her enough are not worth being loved by.' Beautiful, elegant, cool, devious, amoral, and with a taste for being sodomised (in describing this taste, Amis refers punningly to black holes) she is an amalgam of all the masturbatory fantasies of every male reader of the *Star* or the *Sun*. Like the protagonist of Muriel Spark's *The Driver's Seat*, Nicola is also a murderee, who, having opted for her murderer, then directs how and when the murder should take place.

The top layer of the sandwich is Keith Talent—'a bad guy . . . a very bad guy. You might even say that he was the worst guy'. . . .

The lower layer of the sandwich is Guy Clinch, of whom the author writes 'He wanted for nothing and lacked everything. He had a tremendous amount of money, excellent health, handsomeness, height, a capriciously original mind; and he was lifeless.' (p. 36)

What holds the three layers of the club sandwich together is Sam, a writer whom one of Keith's pub cronies describes in rhyming slang as 'a four wheel Sherman'. (Four wheel = four-wheel skid = yid. Sherman = Sherman tank = Yank). Sam, dying of some never clearly defined malady which one assumes to be radiation sickness, becomes the observer and confidant of the other three, whom he intends—here we are in the territory of Gide's *Les Faux-Monnayeurs*—to make the central characters of the fiction which he is incapable of imagining. What Sam does not realise is that his 'fiction' is really being controlled not by himself but by Nicola—who has planned for it a surprising dénouement.

As Sam moves painfully towards annihilation, so, it seems, does the earth. The threat of nuclear conflicts looms; and with it also looms the threat of a sun which, by some perversity of science, veers closer and closer to the horizon, causing freakish rain-storms—'the oceans are about to levitate, the sky to fall.' But the connection of this doomsday scenario with Nicola's setting up of her murder never became wholly clear to me at a single reading.

This 'multi-layered' novel has a plot less complex than that of *Pride and Prejudice;* geographically it hardly moves outside a small area defined by the three underground stations of Notting Hill Gate, Holland Park and Ladbroke Grove. How then does it stretch to 470 closely printed pages? The answer is: through reiteration. Amis uses reiteration not merely as a stylistic device—'She giggled uglily: ugly giggling', for example—but also uses it in the manner of a comedian who repeats a joke because it has happened to raise a laugh, and then goes on repeating it in the hope that it will continue to do so *ad infinitum.* (pp. 36-7)

What makes this book so much worth reading is the brilliance of its style. The hair of a Rastafarian is described as looking like an onion *bhagi;* some cumbersome panties as looking like bunion-pads. Here is Amis describing the pub in which his three characters so often meet each other:

> The place was ruined and innocuous in its northern light: a clutch of dudes and Rastas playing pool over the damp swipe of the baize, a pewtery sickliness of the whites (they looked like war footage), the twittering fruit-machines, the fuming pie-warmer.

There is no English novelist whose writing can match Amis's in this combination of fastidiousness and power.

The experience of reading this book is akin to listening to a conversationalist of genius dominate a dinner-table into the early hours. Enraptured, one hangs on every word. Marvellous stuff! Savage, racy, daring, poignant. The next morning one wakes up. One's head is throbbing, one feels vaguely nauseated. One asks oneself: 'Now what was all that about?'

Sadly, for all its energy, intelligence and stylistic virtuosity, *London Fields* is not in the class of *Money*—in my estimation one of the half-dozen finest English novels of the last decade. (p. 37)

> *Francis King, "A Thin Plot in a Fat Sandwich," in* The Spectator, *Vol. 263, No. 8411, September 23, 1989, pp. 36-7.*

Jonathan Yardley

[*London Fields*] is a slippery creature, one that defies easy categorization or description or, for that matter, judgment. Like *Money,* the best of its predecessors, it is astonishingly energetic, inventive and scabrous, not to mention richly contemptuous of virtually all that Margaret Thatcher hath wrought; beyond that, both books employ the technique, at once disingenuous and willfully deconstructionist, of introducing the author into his own tale. In these respects *London Fields* is a great success. But it is also a homily—"a murder story for the end of the millennium," Amis calls it—and as such is more notable for windy righteousness than for the merciless bite that is its author's salient characteristic.

Amis is at the age of 40 a force unto himself among those of his generation now writing fiction in English; there is, quite simply, no one else like him. Though his debt to Saul Bellow has been noted by others and happily acknowledged by Amis himself, the language he writes and the uses to which he puts it are his alone. While most of his

counterparts in Britain content themselves with painting cozy pictures on small canvases, and those in the United States gaze rapturously at the undulations of their own navels, Amis plunges like Dickens reincarnate into the life of the city, wallowing in its messiness and nastiness and desperation; by contrast with the muck and mire into which the reader is dragged by *Money* and *London Fields,* even [Tom Wolfe's] *The Bonfire of the Vanities* seems almost effete and fastidious.

Which is to say, to begin with, that *London Fields* is not a book for all tastes. Its humor, though less ebullient than that of *Money,* tends to obscenity and invective; its London bears no resemblance to the city beloved by Anglophilic tourists but is instead inhabited by "yokels and village idiots, turnip-swaggers, ditch people"; its prose soars to breathtaking literary heights and then, without warning, crashes in depths of pop-sloppy idiom; its plot lurches in various directions, some of them dead-end streets; its sermonizing is simplistic and intrusive and, at this moment in history, oddly anachronistic, yet it gnaws at certain unwelcome 20th-century truths.

London Fields is in sum a mad and maddening book, irate and deranged, and the reader can expect no compromises or comforts from it. In my judgment it borders on but never quite achieves brilliance, largely because of Amis's insistence on mounting the pulpit, but its shortcomings are more than outweighed by its heartbreaking ambition and the huge risks it takes in trying to do nothing less than tell the story of our times. . . .

A summary of *London Fields*? It would be easier to summarize [Thomas Pynchon's] *Vineland* if not *Gravity's Rainbow.* A beautiful and capricious woman, Nicola Six, "an ill wind, blowing no good," is blessed and cursed with the power to see into the immediate if not distant future; she knows that "some minutes after midnight, on her 35th birthday," she will be murdered; she is, as she sees herself, a "murderee." The murderer, she believes, will be a man named Keith Talent, a pub-crawling thug who has no talent at all except for drink, sex, darts and craven . . . brutality; but the murderer might also be Guy Clinch, "a good guy—or a nice one, anyway," who "wanted for nothing and lacked everything."

Their story is told by Samson Young: "A valued stylist, in my native America. My memoirs, my journalism, praised for their honesty, their truthfulness. I'm not one of those excitable types who get caught making things up. Who get caught improving on reality. I can embellish, I can take certain liberties. Yet to invent the bald facts of a life (for example) would be quite beyond my powers." Young has traded his New York residence for that of a successful London hack playwright and alter ego named Mark Asprey . . . and is now holed up there, writing the story of Nicola and Keith and Guy while, at the same time, befriending each of them.

Fiction and fact, reality and illusion; the webs they weave are the deconstructionist's delight, and Amis explores them with such pleasure and ingenuity that even the most ardent New Critic can only look on in wonder and admiration. In alternating chapters we are given the story of Nicola's impending doom and the story of how that story is told, and so persuasively does Amis intertwine the two that conventional objections must simply be shrugged aside even as we're wholly aware of the trick that's being played on us. Even the parallel Amis insists on drawing between Nicola's impending death and the planet's approaching millennium is, however irritating and overwrought, plausible within the context of a novel written by "a gaunt zero, zilched by death," in which everything is headed for destruction:

> We're all in it together now. As is the case with the world situation, something will have to give, and give soon. It will all get a lot woollier, messier, Everything is winding down, me, this, mother earth. More: the universe, though apparently roomy enough, is heading for heat death. I hope there are parallel universes. I hope alternatives exist. Who stitched us up with all these design flaws? Entropy, time's arrow—ravenous disorder. The designer universe: but it was meant to give out all along, like something you pick up at GoodFicks. So maybe the universe is a dog, a pup, a dud, slipped our way by the *Cheat*.

Yes, it sounds just like the piously apocalyptic twaddle merchandised in circles where retrograde '60s perspectives are still in fashion, and it doesn't do anything for *London Fields,* which insists that the age's "central question" is: "If, at any moment, nothing might matter, then who said that nothing didn't matter already?" That's chic absurdism and it's a pity that Amis has fallen for it; he's discovered The Bomb at exactly the moment when everyone else is trying to figure out how to get rid of it, with the result that he looks rather absurd, not to mention self-indulgent, himself.

No matter. The maunderings of *London Fields* are trivial by comparison with the intelligence and energy and sheer ferocity that otherwise characterize it. The doomed Nicola Six is a marvel to watch as she torments her two fancied executioners, playing them out on a string of sexual torment that becomes ever more excruciating as the novel progresses; the portrait of London, the polar opposite of the mythical London Fields where "the foliage is tropical and innocuous, the sky is crystalline and innocuous," is merciless and, in its accumulation of nasty detail, shattering; as for Keith Talent, he is quite simply a tour de force, a person utterly without redeeming qualities for whom one nonetheless feels a grudging but real sympathy.

> Jonathan Yardley, "Martin Amis: Waiting for the Millennium," in Book World—The Washington Post, *February 18, 1990, p. 3.*

Bette Pesetsky

With evangelical ardor, [Amis] sets his sixth novel, *London Fields,* in the grimmest of times. The approach of a global catastrophe he simply calls "the Crisis" provides the background for a bitter tragicomedy of life in a world going noisily to hell.

In Mr. Amis's last novel, *Money: A Suicide Note,* society was on its way to total corruption, a condition embodied in the greed of the character John Self, a truly horrific antihero. And *Einstein's Monsters,* a recent collection of short stories, brought forth exactly what its title predicted.

By insisting on such a relentlessly dark vision of life, Mr. Amis has certainly prepared us for what we are to encoun-

ter in *London Fields.* The title itself has a sinister twist, suggestive as it is of some rural paradise rather than the malignity of Mr. Amis's setting, the futuristic but all-too-familiar city of London in 1999. (p. 1)

What do people do in a world that feels "more and more nugatory"? Fortunately, this is no tale of generals barking menacing orders. The people in *London Fields* tend, by and large, to do exactly what they would probably always have done, crisis or no crisis. And this is where the book saves itself from the burden of its symbolism, setting a small-scale story of personal destruction against the backdrop of the larger doom.

London Fields is a virtuoso depiction of a wild and lustful society. In an age of attenuated fiction, this is a large book of comic and satirical invention. As he did in *Money,* Mr. Amis again employs the device of the intrusive and all-knowing author within the story. His stand-in here is an American writer, Samson Young. Sam, who is dying (perhaps of radiation poisoning), is preparing to write a murder mystery. . . .

London Fields offers Dickensian complications—but don't worry, they all unravel. For the basic plot is straightforward. The "murderee," the aforementioned Nicola Six (read that "Sex"), has been identified by Sam, an easy chore because Nicola has already dreamed, on several occasions, of her own death, which she knows will occur on her next birthday. The two possible murderers, also identified by Sam, are Keith Talent, a low-life criminal who is also a dart-throwing champion, and Guy Clinch, a wealthy and appallingly honorable gentleman. The question is, who will kill Nicola?

Mr. Amis's characters bear the burden of a satire that turns them into caricatures. But once this has been said, we can move on to the fact that Mr. Amis's language imbues these caricatures with a vitality and an erotic intensity seldom found in current fiction. *London Fields* is not a safe book, it is controlled and moved not by plot but by the density of its language. The author freely offends sensibilities. Indeed, it's difficult to think of anything he spares us when it comes to the concerns of the flesh. But his language is demonically alive.

Mr. Amis has a virtuoso's ear for street talk, and he gives his characters a rich bazaar of language. . . .

Keith Talent represents Mr. Amis's best creation in the book—a grotesque who is nevertheless both surprisingly vivid and desperate. It is a portrait done in verbal glitter. Yet Keith's dispassionate cruelty is almost mythlike. Born into poverty and emotionally without resources, he seeks escape by becoming a petty thief and professional cheat. He yearns for the best that life offers, at least in his terms—a dart-throwing championship and television-celebrity status.

As a criminal, Keith is a failure who is not clever enough to know when he is being cheated. So the taker gets taken. . . .

Keith's prodigious sexual appetite is multiracial, and followed by ample bragging. ("When it came to kissing and telling, Keith was a one-man oral tradition.") He is a man formed by television clichés and tabloid headlines. His natural home is a grim pub called the Black Cross, where misogyny and cruelty rule. His true passion is not women but darts, a game in which, with a mindless flow of energy, he succeeds. . . .

Keith as timeless hooligan mistreats both his wife, Kath, and their infant daughter, Kim. What will be his downfall? He will meet Nicola Six.

Guy Clinch is the other potential murderer. Unlike Keith, Guy is rich, handsome and wholesomely simple—in short, a man destined for vicissitudes. Mr. Amis seems unable to equate goodness with anything other than a gullibility bordering on imbecility.

Guy represents the aristocrat drained of vitality and isolated from the world by money and position. The author has administered an especially fiendish *coup de grâce* to poor Guy and his hapless American wife, Hope: meet Marmaduke, their 18-month-old monster child. . . .

Nicola Six is ready to meet her potential murderers. In fact, she is truly addicted to the idea. Just ask Sam, who from time to time invites Guy, Keith and Nicola to his apartment—or visits them on their own turf. Nicola is a problem, though; she makes us yield to a sneaking suspicion that a misogynist lingers here somewhere. She is not truly satisfying as character or caricature. She seems to be another of Mr. Amis's plastic women.

Beautiful Nicola is 34 years old and promiscuous by choice. In a world abloom with asthma, lesions and eczema, she is in the pink of health. Furthermore, Nicola is a repository of underwear philosophy and pornographic fiction—a sexual savant. . . .

As the novel proceeds, the Crisis approaches—and also the murder. Unfortunately, Mr. Amis endows the former with some painfully obvious symbolism, a series of painted arrows to guide the simple reader through the allegorical overkill. To Nicola Six falls the unenviable task of carrying the message: Nicola has always had an imaginary friend named Enola Gay, who in turn has a child called Little Boy. In case the reader's memory needs refreshing, Nicola obligingly lends Guy a book, which explains that Enola Gay was the name of the plane that carried the first atomic bomb (Little Boy). Nicola also refuses to wear a bikini (remember Bikini Atoll?): "Nicola Six disapproved of bikinis. She execrated bikinis."

As a tale of nuclear warning, *London Fields* is unconvincing. It succeeds, however, as a picaresque novel rich in its effects. . . .

Oh yes, the murder finally happens. But knowing who does it is somewhat beside the point, innit? (p. 42)

> Bette Pesetsky, "Lust Among the Ruins," in The New York Times Book Review, *March 4, 1990, pp. 1, 42.*

Graham Fuller

Named not after the eponymous district of East London but after the force fields where we lure and wreck one another, Martin Amis's [*London Fields*] is a mordant allegory of *fin de millénaire* entropy in the post-Thatcherite toilet that Britain has become by 1999. Having excoriated the 20th century's addictive vices in *Money* and sweated

about nuclear holocaust in *Einstein's Monsters,* Amis merges these themes in a slim, contrived plot modeled on Nabokov's *Despair* and narrated by a Bellovian American writer, Samson Young. Dying of an undisclosed disease, Sam has chanced upon beautiful Nicola Six, and is racing to novelize the infernal triangle she has created before time runs out—for her, for him, for the moribund planet itself.

It's a lingering chronicle of death foretold: Nicola knows she is destined to die on her 35th birthday, a few hours after Guy Fawkes night, and—a victim of men—she has decided to incinerate two guys in the process: her elected murderer Keith Talent, a streetunwise proletarian cheat; and her foil, Guy Clinch, a nice, titled, unhappily married dreamer. She bewitches Guy with the myth that she is a virgin dedicated to finding the lost son, Little Boy, of her friend Enola Gay. She patronizes Keith's dream of fame as a TV darts champion, encouraging him by performing sex videos in lewd underwear bought with Guy's money. After some 400 pages of playing these dupes against each other, Nicola girds herself up as the ultimate slut and heads across London like a cruise missile, a sex dart, to annihilate them. . . .

That Amis luxuriates in the concupiscent disenfranchisement of Nicola is unarguable, and yet it seems witless to dismiss *London Fields* without allowing for the irony with which, through Sam, he aloofly lacerates the sexism implanted in the story. His satirizing of it is intrinsic to the text, just as, for example, Dickens's satirizing of utilitarianism is intrinsic to the impacted language of *Hard Times.*

If Amis was overlooked by the Booker judges partly because he refuses to condemn a superyob hero who uses his numerous bimbette girlfriends like latrines, and who believes that Nicola is "Dreaming of it. Begging for it. Praying for it" (it's death she desires, not sex), nothing, of course, condemns slobbering Keith more than such pornfed assumptions about women. . . .

Keith himself is damned by class, a victim of cancerous cultural conditioning and forlorn dreams of betterment, the sleaziest excrescence of Thatcherite greed in fiction. In *London Fields,* as in *Success,* Amis balances the rise of a yob with the fall of an aristo, with a doomed female as the fulcrum; where lumpen opportunism prevails in the earlier book, in *London Fields* the scales tip marginally in favor of Guy's monied strength, but there are no winners here, none at all.

Nicola is, of course, also Old Nick, the clichéd she-devil who will nullify the men who objectify her. If men want women to be boy toys, Amis is saying, then the cockteasing necromancer Nicola is what they deserve. That she is a masturbatory figment of male imagination, not really a woman at all, is essential to Amis's sardonic analysis of the anesthetizing effects of pornography. . . .

The suggestion that women "devastate" men like their own personal nuclear bombs, most ruefully adumbrated in bikini-clad Nicola's commentary on the commemoration of the atom bomb test at Bikini atoll, may seem misogynistic in the extreme. Amis's men inflict pain, too. Like Sam, Nicola has failed in art and love. Her death wish is the result of "the death of love," romantic and humanistic, which Amis contemplates with unalloyed sadness. It's easier, perhaps, to marvel at Amis's show-off wordplay, his lofty mannerism, and his gleeful harnessing of English tabloid culture than to appreciate his mournful storm warnings:

> The diagnosis was in on love, the diagnosis was coming in; and love was as weak as a kitten, and pitifully confused, and not nearly strong enough to be brave or even understand. . . . Women would of course be expected to soldier on a little longer, with their biological imperative and so on, and the gentle feeling for children would naturally be the last thing to disappear, but women would never get very far with lovelessness and they too would weaken in the end. Nicola used to think (not often, and long ago) that even she might have been saved by love. Love was Plan B. But it never happened. . . . And if love was dead or gone then the self was just self, and had nothing to do all day but work on sex. Oh, and hate. And death.

The Enola Gay/Little Boy metaphor is strained: Amis decides late in the day that he has to spell out the symbolic significance of these names. It is also complicated by our perceptions of Amis himself. While "Martin Amis" doesn't appear in *London Fields* as he does in *Money,* the one man Nicola has loved is a successful absentee writer, Mark Asprey, whose initials are all too familiar. The Little Boy lost turns up hilariously as Marmaduke, a permanently exploding 50-megaton bomb of a baby born to Guy's wife, who is American like Amis's wife; Keith has meanwhile unaccountably fathered an angelic little girl, Kim, a symbol of threatened goodness. You begin to see signs that *London Fields* is a roman à clef wistful for the polarities of unobtainable whorishness and incorruptible innocence.

It's been suggested, with some truth, that Amis cannot write a wholly sympathetic female character, that whereas his male characters are lovable in their awfulness—Keith Talent, Charles Highway in *The Rachel Papers,* Keith Whitehead in *Dead Babies,* Terry Service in *Success,* John Self in *Money*—his women are usually ciphers, sluts or Sloanes or both. But if *Money*'s Selina Street is no more than a bankroll in the hay ("authentically corrupt, seriously vulgar"), then the same novel's Martina Twain (the female Martin A.) is a real, kind, flesh-and-blood woman—and, of course, ripe for Amis's humiliation. Then again, if Amis is hard on his women characters, you should see what he does to his men. Long before the end of *London Fields,* Guy's (and the heterosexual male reader's) repressed longing for Nicola is subverted into sadomasochistic anguish of the most gruesome kind.

Amis's most fully realized woman is Mary Lamb, the heroine of the excellent *Other People,* his first attempt to explore the magnetism of human force fields. True, she is another self-destructive nympho left for dead by a jealous lover, but when she is resurrected as an amnesiac at the start of the novel, you get the sense of someone who is far more than a collection of underwear and male yearnings. She sits, though, at the nexus of Amis Jr's trouble with girls; where Nicola Six is all sex, Mary Lamb (the name surely Blakean) is all innocence—a woman who wields her inalienable sex power unwittingly—and therefore equally unreal. *London Fields* is virtually a prequel to *Other People,* with Mary given a reprieve—Nicola lives!—but only temporarily. Amis remains in awe of women's sexual

power, and he takes unforgivably consistent delight in grimly expunging it.

If *London Fields* inevitably fails as an indictment of social malaise rooted in the man-made image of a promiscuous woman, it is because Amis himself is unable to resist Nicola's pornographic promise or the lascivious lexicon of sexism—which alone should offend many women readers. That doesn't mean Amis endorses sexism as a cultural given, any more than he endorses child abuse (a tangential theme of *London Fields*), or the misanthropy which leaves most of the characters in his books dead. He is a novelist wallowing in the spiritual bankruptcy of the late 20th century; his methods may make you feel increasingly queasy, but there is always a moral beneath the miasma.

> *Graham Fuller, "Murder He Wrote: Martin Amis's Killing Fields," in* The Village Voice, *Vol. XXXV, No. 17, April 24, 1990, p. 75.*

Luc Sante

The difference between a thin novel and a fat one is more than just a matter of length. From a big book—which can semi-arbitrarily be designated as anything over 400 pages—the reader feels entitled to more, quantitatively: not just more characters, more locations, more romances and death scenes and comic interludes, but more *stuff,* more digressions, arcana, crash courses in diverse subjects. The fat novel must be a miscellany of information, a multitiered box of trinkets and gewgaws. All this stuff should be judiciously arranged, however, in the hollows and contours of a real story, propulsive and engaging.

Martin Amis's *London Fields,* which measures 470 pages stripped, would seem to fill this bill with verve. There is its story: the triangle consisting of lowlife Keith Talent, high-born and -minded Guy Clinch, and belle dame sans merci Nicola Six, observed by fourth party and fifth wheel (and first-person narrator) Samson Young. It is propulsive, since we know from page one that the story will end in the murder of Nicola Six, although we don't know whose hand will direct it. It is engaging, since there is ample opportunity to browse among the dominant and recessive traits of Guy and Keith and Samson. (Nicola Six, per tradition, is fated to remain an impenetrable ice queen.)

There are its perquisites: a philosophy of underwear, a manual of darts, a comparative study of London dialects, several stabs at a taxonomy of the English underclass, various à clef japeries at the expense of current English literary personages, a veritable thesaurus of the kiss. . . . And there are its ambitions: it is intended to be a satirical portrait of present-day London life, an allegory of existence in the shadow of the Apocalypse, a sort of winged monument to the fallen of both the class war and the war between the sexes, and a large-scale metafictional braintwister. It's packed with jokes, too.

Somehow, though, all these features and intentions put together add up to a small, rather shrill book. Why should this be? Amis, who to date has written five other, variously satisfying novels—one of them (1984's *Money*) very good—as well as one collection of short stories and two collections of essays, is a gifted joker, an inspired verbal cartoonist with a particular flair for the grotesque, a connoisseur of comic misery. He is one of those prose stylists who can set up a subject and write the proverbial hell out of it. . . .

Amis wields a deadly pen and, one suspects, a deadly tongue, so that one would avoid being on the other side of a restaurant scrap. In the London press he is written about not only as a rising young author but as a ringleader, a social arbiter, an urban public wit of a sort not seen in years. Perhaps Amis felt that these skills and attributes were insufficient, that it was time to write a really important novel, a Big Book not just in size and density, but in stature. And while it could be said that his strongest suits—satire, caricature, apothegms, one-liners, asides—might not be the ideal ones for the task of major-novel construction, it could likewise be pointed out that major novels have been built using just such materials. (*Tristram Shandy* comes to mind.)

But **London Fields** doesn't seem to *want* to be a major novel. The reader can sense its core of gleeful malice throwing off the more self-consciously important of its grafted appurtenances the way a body rejects an ill-matched foreign organ. The book's subject is cheating, primarily. Keith Talent is a *cheat*—always italicized, this word—who pursues every variety of the short con. Guy Clinch is cheating on his wife, pursuing Nicola Six. Nicola is cheating on life by arranging for her own death at the hands of one or another of the besotted men around. Samson Young is cheating on the rules of his journalistic task of recording the entwined stories of the other three by (metafictionally) fiddling with their destinies.

Samson is an American, or at least he has come from New York via an apartment exchange ad in *The New York Review of Books,* swapping a crummy walk-up for the vast London flat of a grandiosely successful writer; at the same time, misty allusions are made to an English childhood, and he uses Brit slang terms more often and less self-consciously than American ones. He is dying of some vaguely defined ailment that might be AIDS but sounds more like the traditional movie disease, and his moribund condition is apparently the thing that turns him from a more-or-less journalist into a real Author, godlike and fateful.

Thus he selects the constituents of his triangle from out of the crowd and sets them to work on one another to give him the matter of his book. Meanwhile the news fragments come winging in, dimly: there is a Crisis (always capitalized), the Russians this, the mullahs that, the President's wife some other thing. This obscure tension is presumably supposed to mount. The plot hurtles along like an opera pastiche with cardboard sets, every convention emptied and reinflated, until it crashes to a close with a device, half Pirandello and half O. Henry, that rings so hollow and feels so antiquated that one wants to believe its hollowness and mustiness are deliberate.

There is real desperation in many of these choices. The toying with authorship and voice and point of view and destiny serves no purpose, except as packaging: some backdated flash for the squares, some makeshift complexity for the professors. The world-crisis tease is even less pertinent, merely there to simulate historical significance. (pp. 45-6)

Stripped of such trappings, the book begins to seem more

plausible, although it is still way too long. Much of the padding comes from Amis's unstoppable compulsion for shtick. . . . The trouble is that, having scored once with a given routine, Amis feels compelled to repeat the gambit again and again, without at all varying the tone or the nuance or the import. Perhaps it is only fitting, on the other hand, that compulsion should be so enmeshed in the novel's fabric, since virtually every character in it is a certifiable compulsive.

Reduced to essentials, then, the story (now about 250 pages or so in length) is a basic sexual triangle. Keith and Guy are cartoons, to be sure, but they are at least as complex and sympathetic as the more celebrated rabbits and coyotes. Keith is the king of his pub, the local darts phenomenon, a hustler who is always able to extract money from some small-time ploy or other . . . and then blow it all the next day at the turf accountant's. He is also a low-rent satyr with a long string of hapless, drunken, insane, or underage women scattered all over London. He's not a bad guy, really; he just can't help himself.

Amis clearly enjoyed writing about Keith and detailing his dank, malnourished world of pubs, petty crime, dirty jokes, hit-and-run sex, tabloids, canned lager, scotch eggs, council flats, caseworkers. . . .

Amis is less interested in the upper class, and Guy, being helplessly noble, is assigned an interestingly terrible family life, with an overbearing American wife and a literal monster of a child, who as an infant assaults and maims his nurses and requires muscular handlers with psycho-ward experience. In their differing ways, both men are obsessed with Nicola, whose job description sounds like something Amis cooked up to bait feminists: she is at once the story's nominal victim and the engineer of men's doom. Oddly enough, she is not altogether unsympathetic herself, principally because she can briefly appear human in the presence of the one man who has any power over her: the narrator, whose power derives from the fact that he is dying and thus is beyond sex. Nicola's vocation is sex, not that she cares much about it per se; what truly interests her is the intricate art of the tease. She is the embodiment of every male fear about women. She is beautiful, intelligent, self-sufficient, disinterested, and she treats men like bugs.

To call the premise thus skeletally outlined mechanical would be to belabor the obvious. It *is* a mechanism, the way a Tom and Jerry escapade is a mechanism, only in this case every pratfall is informed by rich sociological context. It is a panoramic cartoon that takes in a whole world of culture and custom and speech. (Amis, who has a prodigious ear, seems almost totally devoid of a visual sense.) At its best it is wildly entertaining, and the narrator/author's conniving voice engages the reader as a crony—the jokes become inside jokes between him and us. What keeps **London Fields** from being anything more than a cartoon, however, is the complete absence of a heart.

The deadly accurate pinpointing of human weaknesses has no counterweight in acknowledgment of human value. What makes the characters funny is their shortcomings, and what makes them sympathetic is also their shortcomings. The characters all operate from the basest possible motives at all times (except for Guy, but in this, too, he is merely embodying a class joke, as his nobility itself becomes a failing). In a quick read, all this entomological skewering would merely be malicious fun, but in such a long and dense novel it eventually reveals a quality of extreme emotional parsimony, of real, deep-dish cheapness. And this is a flaw that all the cosmetic layers of literary embellishment and current-events tomfoolery cannot ennoble or disguise. (p. 46)

Luc Sante, "Cheat's Tale," in The New Republic, *Vol. 202, No. 18, April 30, 1990, pp. 45-6.*

Donna Rifkind

If *Money* seemed on publication like an exercise in gross exaggeration, in comparison with *London Fields* it now appears as modest as a Barbara Pym novel. Set in 1999, on the brink of an apocalypse, the new novel enlarges upon many of *Money*'s themes. Once again we're in the heart of a crowded city (London), an inferno full of schemers and cheats, the most prominent of whom is a nasty bit of lowlife named Keith Talent. When not involved in petty crime, abusing his wife Kath in their squalid council flat, or sleeping with an international assortment of girlfriends, Keith wastes time at a pub called the Black Cross, dreaming of celebrity in the world of championship darts. Another figure often found slumming at the Black Cross is Guy Clinch, a wealthy, handsome, and very gullible representative of that endangered species known as the English upper class.

Keith and Guy are both entranced by the "potentially, magically, uncontrollably attractive" figure of Nicola Six, an enigmatic seductress who can predict the future. . . .

Lately, Nicola is preoccupied with the foreknowledge of her own murder, which is to take place after midnight on her next birthday—her thirty-fifth—on the dead-end street where she lives. She takes comfort in the fact that the planet itself is showing signs of imminent destruction: "she welcomed and applauded the death of just about anything. It was company. It meant you weren't quite alone. . . . The Death of the Planet. The Death of God. The death of love. It was company."

Just what, on the eve of the millennium, does the "Death of the Planet" entail? Amis never offers a straightforward description; he prefers to hover nervously on the edge, throwing out hints of imminent political, meteorological, physical, and moral destruction. A likely confrontation between the superpowers known as "the Crisis" is a source of vague general anxiety, as is the health of the American president's wife, who seems to be dying of cancer. An eclipse is predicted for November 5—Guy Fawkes Day—and the sun has lately been appearing suspiciously low on the horizon.

In addition, the ozone layer is in pieces; there are "gigawatt thunderstorms, multimegaton hurricanes and billion-acre bush fires"; the water is poisoned; food is irradiated beyond recognition; violence and vandalism flourish; and always, unavoidably, there is the threat of impending nuclear war: "It takes all kinds to make a world," warns the book's narrator, an American novelist named Samson Young; "It takes only one kind to unmake it." (p. 74)

Not surprisingly, all this approaching doom is causing a lot of physical wear and tear. Keith Talent suffers from a "bad chest, his curry-torn digestive system, the itchings and burnings of his sedimentary venereal complaints, his darts elbow, his wall-eyed hangovers." Guy Clinch, afflicted with perpetual nausea, can't bring himself to eat. And Sam Young, who is in and out of the narrative just as Martin Amis kept popping up in *Money*, is dying of a mysterious wasting disease. Amis couldn't make it any more clear: everyone, everything, the environment, the entire planet, is sick nearly to death. (pp. 74-5)

Against this rotting backdrop, a somewhat less significant drama is being played out—the drama of Nicola's eventual murder. She knows when and where it will take place, but she doesn't know who the murderer will be. Could it be the lovestruck, jealous Guy? Nicola has lured him into intimacy by pretending to need his help locating an imaginary childhood friend, a Cambodian girl who was sent back to Indochina just as a "superwar," "a new kind of conflict," was erupting in the area. Or will Nicola's killer be Keith, whom she entraps by offering him help with his darts career, and by supplying him with pornographic videos starring herself? Will it be Nicola's ex-lover, Mark Asprey, the insufferably successful British writer whose flat Sam Young is renting while Asprey pursues fresh triumphs in America?

Or perhaps, Amis suggests, the murderer will be Sam Young himself. As Sam explains at the beginning, he isn't actually inventing *London Fields;* he's only recording the action as he watches it unfold. The book, he says, is "not a whodunit. More a whydoit. . . . I think I am less a novelist than a queasy cleric, taking down the minutes of real life." Nicola gives Sam tips on what ought to happen next in the novel; he's writing *London Fields* with hopes of big money and a movie deal, but he depends on Nicola's ability—and her willingness—to tell him the future. As the novel progresses, he talks about his difficulties in planning the narrative, his anxiety that Nicola will refuse to cooperate, his writer's block. Will he decide to kill Nicola out of sheer artistic frustration?

A narrator who relies on one of his characters to write his story for him; atmospheric conditions that outdazzle the plot in dramatic effects: what exactly is going on here? Amis is using the popular tricks of metafiction to divert our attention away from his plot toward a series of Big Themes. Nicola and the others aren't characters so much as they are mediums through which the omniscient voice of Martin Amis can channel his opinions about the decay of civilization and its certain end in nuclear war. The narrator's voice, ostensibly Sam Young's, often adopts a preachy manner that no one could mistake for anything but Amis's own:

> We used to live and die without any sense of the planet getting older, of mother earth getting older, living and dying. We used to live outside history. But now we're all coterminous. We're inside history now all right, on its leading edge, with the wind ripping past our ears. Hard to love, when you're bracing yourself for impact. And maybe love can't bear it either, and flees all planets when they reach this condition, when they get to the end of their twentieth centuries.

While apocalyptic fantasies are certainly nothing new in modern literature, Amis's timing with this one could not possibly be worse. He can't of course be blamed for the vicissitudes of history, but, as we are reminded every day, it is nevertheless the case that the likelihood of a nuclear catastrophe is fainter now than it has been at any time in the last forty years. . . .

If you took away all the end-of-the-world melodrama in *London Fields,* you'd be left with little more than an outline.

The novel's murder plot—what there is of it—is nothing but a haphazard send-up of detective fiction, with liberal appropriations from Nabokov. . . . Amis doesn't even bother to make improvements on Nabokov, Raymond Chandler, James M. Cain, or any of his other predecessors. In fact, he seems barely interested in the murder story at all.

If the plot is insubstantial, the characters involved in it are practically nonexistent. Amis freely acknowledges that his characters are mere clichés; he observes that Nicola, who understands that men want to see "the female form shaped and framed, packaged and gift-wrapped, stylized, cartoonified," has obligingly stylized herself. But he tries to do the impossible with these cartoon figures: to make them live not as individual personalities but as allegorical figures. As a result, each is forced to pull too heavy a load of metaphorical weight. (pp. 75-6)

As it should by now be abundantly clear, Amis is much more interested in finding clever ways to subvert his own narrative than in supplying readers with a representation of reality. He is more than aware of the limitations of subversion and, in fact, is happy to go on at length about those limitations. As only a true believer in subversion could, he is willing to subvert himself. For one thing, it would be hard to overlook the possibility that Amis's ironic portrait of Marmaduke, Guy Clinch's horrifically hyperactive baby son, is a self-portrait. Is not this terrible infant, who is ceaselessly intent on gouging out his father's eyes and damaging his genitals, a comic mirror of Amis *fils,* the *enfant terrible* who is trying so hard to outdo his own father, the now conventional, middle-aged Kingsley Amis?

Other subversions follow as the novel drifts toward its conclusion. The dreaded eclipse passes without incident, the ominous weather improves, "the Crisis" shows signs of easing, the President's wife recovers, and there are signs that life on earth will continue. Subversively, Sam Young feels free to criticize the shortcomings of his own characters: "The people in here, they're like London, they're like the streets of London, a long way from any shape I've tried to equip them with, strictly non-symmetrical, exactly lopsided—far from many things, and far from art." This confession is immediately recognizable as the kind of coy apology that intelligent writers use to deflect potential

criticism. It is also by far the most genuine sentiment in the book.

In the end, all the noise about apocalypse in *London Fields* is merely an elaborate disguise for the author's failed enterprise, his book that strays so "far from art." Despite Amis's love of excess, the book has no exuberance, no sense of engagement. . . . (p. 76)

Amis's latest work challenges readers to acknowledge once again that, of all the bright young British novelists, he is the most ambitious of them all. Yet when an author's interest in himself comes across as the most prominent aspect of his work, it becomes difficult to take that work seriously. Amis's ambition has eclipsed his interest in the necessary aesthetic concerns that a big novel like this one must incorporate. No amount of pompous doomsaying about nuclear destruction can conceal the fact that Amis's new book is ill-conceived, sloppily executed, and rickety beyond repair. This would be true even if current events were not pointing to the fact that the only bomb being dropped around here is *London Fields.* (p. 77)

> *Donna Rifkind, "Apocalypse Now," in* The New Criterion, *Vol. 8, No. 9, May, 1990, pp. 73-7.*

FURTHER READING

Miller, Karl. "Twins." In his *Doubles: Studies in Literary History,* pp. 402-15. Oxford: Oxford University Press, 1985.
    Examines the dualistic nature of Amis's protagonists in the novels *Success, Other People,* and *Money.*

Morrison, Susan. "The Wit and the Fury of Martin Amis." *Rolling Stone,* No. 578 (17 May 1990): 95-102.
    Interview with Amis in which he discusses his work, literary influences and techniques, and reputation as a misogynist, among other topics.

Stout, Mira. "Down London's Mean Streets." *The New York Times Magazine* (4 February 1990): 32-6, 48.
    Profile of Amis's personal life and literary career, with an emphasis on his novel *London Fields.*

Wolcott, James. "Cool Hand Nuke." *Vanity Fair* 53, No. 3 (March 1990): 62, 68, 72.
    Largely favorable summary of Amis's career, with a focus on *London Fields.*

Beryl Bainbridge

1933-

(Born Beryl Margaret Bainbridge) English novelist, scriptwriter, short story writer, travel writer, and editor.

A popular and prolific author, Bainbridge often focuses upon lonely and solipsistic characters from England's lower and middle classes. The personal problems of her protagonists often result in physical or psychological violence, which usually occurs amid the mundane normality of everyday life. She is frequently compared to such British writers as Harold Pinter, Iris Murdoch, and Henry Green for her use of black comedy and emphasis on malevolent aspects of ordinary existence. Bainbridge has been variously categorized during her career as a writer of thrillers, psychological novels, gothic horror fiction, and absurdist or naturalistic works, yet many critics maintain that her work defies such compartmentalizations. Many concur that as a chronicler of modern life, Bainbridge has exerted a positive impact on contemporary British fiction, avoiding what John Barth has identified as the exhaustion of modern narrative modes through the imaginative vigor of her concise, disciplined style.

Born in Liverpool, England, Bainbridge was raised in a strained family environment that resulted from her mother's preoccupation with class distinctions and her father's temperamental disposition. At age fifteen she began acting, and then moved to London shortly after to work on stage, radio, and television. She gave up her acting career in 1972, the year her first major novel, *Harriet Said,* was published. Based on a story in an Australian newspaper about two girls who had committed matricide, the novel is narrated by an overweight thirteen-year-old who presents the act as unremarkable through her description of the competitive relationship that develops between herself and a charming but manipulative friend. Bainbridge's next novel, *The Dressmaker* (published in the United States as *The Secret Glass*), is set in Liverpool in 1944. In this work, a reticent, homely girl from an impoverished family dominated by her repressive Aunt Nellie meets and brings home a crude American soldier she hopes to marry. The soldier is more interested in sex than commitment, however, and Aunt Nellie murders him after discovering that he has inadvertently scratched a piece of family furniture while making advances toward the protagonist's younger aunt. Although some reviewers faulted Bainbridge's ending as sensational or unconvincing, *The Dressmaker* was praised for its grim humor, psychological plausibility, and realistic evocation of wartime England.

Bainbridge's next novel, *The Bottle Factory Outing,* is regarded as one of her most sustained works. Described by Dorothy Rabinowitz as an "absorbing social comedy," this work uses black humor to describe the situation of two women working in an Italian wine-bottling factory in England, who attempt to escape their unhappiness through romantic intrigues. When one woman is inadvertently killed, her friend seeks to avoid the disapproval of company management by placing the woman's body in an empty brandy cask and returning it to Italy, where she

hopes it will be discarded. *Sweet William,* which Bainbridge described as a "love story of sorts," is considered less bizarre and more overtly comic than her previous works. After breaking a wedding engagement because of parental disapproval, the protagonist becomes involved with a philandering playwright who victimizes her through his personal magnetism and charm.

Bainbridge has described her early novels as attempts to exorcise her feelings regarding her early home life. Her next novel, *A Quiet Life,* offers an autobiographical portrayal of an impoverished family of four, each of whom compete for psychological and emotional dominance. The novel's action is observed by Alan, a conformist adolescent who blocks out painful truths about his family. Alan is prompted by his father's manic fits of jealousy to reveal that his mother, rather than meeting a lover at night, leaves the house because "she can't stand being in the same room" with him. Following this disclosure, Alan's father dies of a heart attack as his family watches indifferently. Bainbridge claimed that her next novel, *Injury Time,* was intended to be "definitive on middle-aged love affairs, but ended up absurd." The book attracted positive critical notices in its satirical story of an unmarried middle-aged woman who convinces her married lover to throw a dinner party for his friends. Premonitions of disaster stalk Binny as she prepares for the party, which reaches its nadir as bank robbers fleeing from police take the party-goers as hostages.

Bainbridge attracted strong mixed reviews with *Young Adolf* which is based on an entry in the diary of Bridget Hitler, the wife of Adolf's half-brother, Alois. The novel proceeds from the assumption that Hitler visited his relatives in Liverpool, England while fleeing a military draft. Bainbridge focuses on Hitler's as yet unformed personal traits, including his ambition and sensitivity to criticism, suggesting through various humiliating episodes the victimizer he will later become. Although American reviewers expressed anxiety with Bainbridge's uncritical approach to her subject, a critic for *The Atlantic* asserted that in *Young Adolf* "she has succeeded in the seemingly impossible task of making Adolf interesting and human without giving him any sympathy whatsoever." In *Winter Garden* Bainbridge makes use of impressions she gathered while travelling in the Soviet Union as part of a cultural exchange tour. This book relates the story of a married man who confronts the confusion and bureaucracy of Russia after losing his luggage and mistress while on a tour of Russia with a group of artists.

Bainbridge's next published work is a revised and rewritten version of her first novel, *A Weekend with Claude*. In this work, an old photograph prompts the novel's eponymous protagonist to recall a weekend he spent with a group of cynical and eccentric individuals. Together, they attempt unsuccessfully to help their friend, Lily, trap her new lover into marriage by falsely claiming that he is the father of her unborn child. The book attracted scant critical attention following its initial publication in 1967, and while some reviewers of Bainbridge's 1981 revision faulted her characters as unconvincing, *A Weekend with Claude* was praised for its grim ambience. Tim Murray commented: "Bainbridge's eye for detail and atmosphere results in a compelling piece of fiction of the first order." *Another Part of the Wood* is also a substantially revised version of an early novel that suffered critical neglect. This book depicts a weekend holiday in which Joseph, a recently divorced father, takes his friends and young son to a country cabin. Absorbed in the solipsistic pursuit of power games while playing Monopoly, Joseph fails to notice that his son has taken a fatal dose of pills and is silently dying in the next room. As in many of Bainbridge's novel, disaster occurs amid the self-absorption and frivolity of ordinary life. *Filthy Lucre; or, The Tragedy of Andrew Ledwhistle and Richard Soleway,* a novel of revenge written in 1946 when Bainbridge was thirteen years old, makes use of the epic scope of works by Charles Dickens to chronicle the events of three generations in England and the United States. Lindsay Duguid commented: "What Bainbridge is really interested in is style, and it is here that she really lets herself go. The book bursts with dramatic touches and with the recklessly abundant vocabulary of early adolescence."

In *Watson's Apology,* Bainbridge fictionalizes a famous Victorian murder case in which a respected English headmaster, scholar, and ordained minister beat his wife to death after twenty-five years of marriage, a crime for which he served a fifteen-year prison sentence. Bainbridge includes letters, newspaper articles, and trial reports to suggest reasons for the homicide. Although some critics

asserted that Bainbridge remained unsympathetic to the character of the headmaster's wife, the novel received generally positive reviews. James Lasdun commented that the protagonist's "qualities are singled out by Bainbridge with impeccable judgment, the result being an individual with a complexity of mind that is rare in fiction." In *An Awfully Big Adventure,* Bainbridge draws on her experience in English theater following World War II to describe the disasters that befall the leading players of a repertory company in Liverpool after an aspiring sixteen-year-old actress becomes infatuated with the theater manager and attempts to make him jealous by seducing an aging character actor. Peter Parker remarked: "As well as being extremely funny, the book is also beautifully written, particularly in its luminous description of an impoverished, postwar Liverpool."

Bainbridge has also written numerous scripts for radio and television, including adaptations of her own work. She is also the author of *English Journey: or, The Road to Milton Keynes,* a journal of her assignment from the British Broadcasting Corporation to follow the path of J. B. Priestley on the fiftieth anniversary of his classic travelogue, *English Journey.* Noting similarities and differences along the route, Bainbridge expresses a nostalgia for the destroyed buildings that Priestley despised, providing comparisons to the poverty and unemployment that characterizes Northern England as described in both books. Most critics concurred with the opinion of Richard Eder: "Bainbridge's etherized travels do not make nearly as good a book as Priestley's; yet, in their way, and dismayingly, they convey as true a picture of the country and its times."

(See also *CLC,* Vols. 4, 5, 8, 10, 14, 18, 22; *Contemporary Authors,* Vols. 21-24, rev. ed.; and *Dictionary of Literary Biography,* Vol. 14.)

PRINCIPAL WORKS

NOVELS

A Weekend with Claude   1967; revised edition, 1981
Another Part of the Wood   1968; revised edition, 1979
Harriet Said   1972
The Dressmaker   1973; published in the United States as
    The Secret Glass, 1974
The Bottle Factory Outing   1974
Sweet William   1975
A Quiet Life   1976
Injury Time   1977
Young Adolf   1978
Winter Garden   1980
Watson's Apology   1984
*Filthy Lucre; or, The Tragedy of Andrew Ledwhistle and
    Richard Soleway*   1986
An Awfully Big Adventure   1989

TELEVISION SCRIPTS

Tiptoe through the Tulips   1976
Blue Skies from Now On   1977
The Warrior's Return   1977
It's a Lovely Day Tomorrow   1977
Words Fail Me   1979
Sweet William   1979

A Quiet Life 1980
The Journal of Bridget Hitler [with Phillip Seville]
    1980
Somewhere More Central 1981

OTHER

Clap Hands, Here Comes Charlie (radio script) 1981
English Journey: or, The Road to Milton Keynes (travel-
    ogue) 1984
Mum and Mr. Armitage: Selected Stories 1985

Marion Glastonbury

To begin her selection of favourite poems for a recent
radio programme, Beryl Bainbridge chose the coda of the
Four Quartets:

> The end of all our exploring
> Will be to arrive where we started
> And know the place for the first time.

These lines are borrowed, unacknowledged and in slightly
garbled form, by the sententious Claude of her latest title
[*A Weekend with Claude*]. (He's an antique dealer so perhaps the plagiarism is deliberate.) In the same spirit of cyclical recapitulation, her tenth novel in ten years turns out
to be a recasting of her earliest work [*A Weekend with
Claude*], originally published in 1967 and a sad disappointment.

A photograph discovered in the drawer of a desk . . . reminds Claude of a bygone visit from assorted friends. Fey,
beautiful, wayward Lily sought to inveigle naive Edward
into marriage by claiming disingenuously that he was the
father of her unborn child. To this end, she contrived a
gathering of rich mentors and threadbare devotees, con-
noisseurs of their own eccentricity, each of whom solilo-
quised about lost loves, missed opportunities and blighted
hopes, unfolding telescopic vistas of nostalgia several
times removed.

Much is made of the faded charm and zany hilarity of this
lonely crowd, and the pathos of being 'dreadfully impaled
upon my own . . . personality'. Yet there's little enough
in the characters to compensate for the stasis of the plot
and the monotony of the mood. In Claude's exquisite
household, raffish cynicism has settled wistfully down
with bland domesticity. So, when Julia detects traces of
woodworm in the furniture, we guess they have been
planted there for symbolic effect: the worm in the bud, the
flaw in the idyll. But what sense can be made of Victorian
Norman, proletarian sage and shop-floor stoic? No wonder his manifestos baffle his work-mates: 'Believing as I do
in Marxist ideology . . . politically, I do not recognise
class.' (Is it possible that Marx has been more travestied,
more misrepresented, in literature than in life?)

Shebah, the derelict actress, cavorting in her cups, singing
music hall songs and knocking over china cabinets, is supposed to be good for a laugh. She looks 'like a demented
nun', dramatises herself as a wandering Jew, and, when
struck by a pellet from an air-gun, is consoled with large
helpings of ham: 'It will give her something personal to
add to her list of Jewish persecutions.' Such Aryan ironies,

insistently repeated, raise doubts about what happens to
young writers when they swallow Eliot whole:

> Shadow of its own shadows, spectre in its own gloom,
> Leaving disordered papers in a dusty room.

(pp. 17-18)

Marion Glastonbury, "Disordered Papers," in
New Statesman, *Vol. 102, No. 2634, September 11, 1981, pp. 17-18.*

Anthony Thwaite

[Beryl Bainbridge's early novels] are being brought back
into print: not only that, but 'radically revised and rewritten.' *Another Part of the Wood,* first published in 1968,
had this treatment a couple of years ago, and now Beryl
Bainbridge's actual debut, *A Weekend With Claude,* has
been overhauled and resprayed.

As in *Another Part of the Wood, A Weekend with Claude*
has as its cast what I called an ill-assorted mob of solipsists, emotional cripples and bores. At the centre is the
Claude of the title, a reformed but hardly rehabilitated
drunk who runs an antique business. We meet him first
selling a desk to the sort of people Beryl Bainbridge likes
to bring in subordinately—a couple so straight that their
behavior seems twice as bizarre as the solipsists etc. who
are dominant. The comedy of this commerce is interleaved
between three flashbacks, each told by three weekend visitors to Claude. It's their group photograph which is found
pushed to the back of a drawer in the desk.

Lily is one of Miss Bainbridge's characteristic emotional
disasters; 'always in some sort of trouble,' says one of the
others, 'but she has amazing resilience.' It's hard to say
whether she's naïve or *faux-naïf,* but at any rate . . . ,
since she's pregnant, she must—somehow, but quickly—
acquire a husband. Will it be Edward, latest of a long line
of unsatisfactory boy friends? Down at Claude's, she
hopes to enlist Norman (known as Victorian Norman)
and Shebah to this end.

Victorian Norman is a solemnly pedantic Marxist, a sort
of Pooter of the Left, and almost as disaster-prone as Lily:
his earnest fumblings of Julia, Claude's mistress, are inevitably witnessed by Claude himself. Shebah is elderly, Jewish, paranoid and histrionic. She strenuously disapproves
of almost everything that goes on about her, and—
whether by accident or design—is shot in the ankle by
Claude.

This brief recital of persons and events may serve to show
that we are in familiar Bainbridge territory, a place of
fecklessness, deception and self-deception, and bloody
farce, all of it laced together with a style of mannered precision, mind-bending inconsequentiality, disarming whimsy, and almost total heartlessness. It's an acquired taste
which took a long time for me to acquire: in *A Weekend
With Claude,* it hasn't evolved into the brisk narrative inevitability she was later to find, and is apt to wander off
(particularly in the three monologues) into arabesques of
self-indulgent feyness. It's the slender thread of Claude
and the desk-buyers that is most persuasively true Bainbridge, and there's not enough of it.

Anthony Thwaite, "The Bainbridge Recipe for

Disaster," in The Observer, *September 20, 1981, p. 26.*

Tim Murray

[Bainbridge's recent novel, *A Weekend with Claude*], is a no-frills flight of the imagination. We land in the English countryside, at the home of an antique dealer who's had a few friends in for the weekend. The friends traipse into the picture weighted down with seemingly immeasurable suspicions, worries and conniving schemes. Their every word is a thrusting double-edged blade. Their predominant concern is sex. Their weekend luggage, so to speak, consists of life-sized valises of lost hopes and sputtering new dreams.

The entire tale is spun from a single photograph taken by Claude. In the picture are Edward and Lily. Lily believes she is pregnant by another man and plots an opportunity this weekend to give Edward reason to believe he is the father. Seated behind them in the snapshot is Shebah, an old woman dedicated to honest and worthy causes, of which she self-confessedly lists herself as the most honest and worthiest adherent. Next to Shebah sits a chap named Victorian Norman, a Communist theorist who prefers self-pity over success.

Bainbridge is superb in conveying the worth of these characters' lives. Their concerns and fears are neither contrived nor foolish. Bainbridge's eye for detail and atmosphere results in a compelling piece of fiction of the first order.

Tim Murray, in a review of "A Weekend with Claude," in Best Sellers, *Vol. 41, No. 12, March, 1982, p. 447.*

Judith Gies

Beryl Bainbridge, the English novelist whose strange, dislocated fiction has attracted something of a cult following, is interested in the aspect of suffering that "takes place," as Auden observed, "while someone else is eating or opening a window or just walking dully along."

Her characters suffer violence in a kind of vacuum—while the people around them walk along dully, preoccupied with their own psychic aches and pains. Often, the violence is physical. *Harriet Said* and *Secret Glass* end with macabre killings. In *The Bottle Factory Outing,* an abrasive young woman is throttled while revelers picnic a few yards away. (p. 10)

When her characters are not meeting violent ends, their psyches are being pummeled. Drawn largely from the English lower middle class, they exist in a stifling and dangerous atmosphere of claustrophobic domesticity, crippling gentility and pretension. Her protagonists (generally women) make fumbling, gallant attempts to get out from under their bell jars—usually through love.

But Bainbridge's characters never quite connect; they talk *through* each other, as Pinter's do. The disturbing edge this produces is intensified by the author's use of naturalism—with its careful attention to detail—and the grotesque details she chooses to use. Her vision is as glittering

and as narrow as a needle. Reading Bainbridge is like being given a geodetic map of a place that doesn't exist.

These qualities are apparent, if somewhat blunted, in *A Weekend With Claude,* the 10th Bainbridge novel to be published in this country. In an earlier incarnation, the book was published in England in the mid-60's to little or no critical notice. Now, her American publisher tells us, she has "radically revised and rewritten it, so that it is virtually a new book." Since the first version was never available in this country, and seems to have vanished entirely in England, I have no way of knowing what she's done with it. (It is interesting to note that this is the second novel Beryl Bainbridge has rewritten. *Another Part of the Wood,* published in England in 1968, was rewritten and appeared here in 1979).

In any case, the new *Weekend With Claude* is interesting—for the way it both conforms to and diverges from the rest of her work. In some respects, the territory is familiar. There are the usual ill-assorted characters looking for love and bungling it. They are thrown together in the usual confining situation. There is violence, but it is chiefly psychic, and more muted than usual. Like the suffering Auden speaks of, it takes place in "some untidy spot," namely the country home of a vaguely malign antique dealer named Claude, and Julia, a genteel earth mother who "shapes her vowels so beautifully."

As the novel opens, a conventional middle-class couple is buying a desk from Claude. In the back of a drawer the wife comes upon a letter and a photograph (the photograph is represented on the book jacket; it has the curious, proto-Punk quality that pervades Bainbridge's work). The picture was taken four years earlier, during the weekend of the title. It shows Claude's friend Lily and her two companions, Norman (called "Victorian Norman" because of his taste in clothes) and Shebah, an extraordinary, half-mad woman in her early 60's.

Edward is also in the picture. He is a young geologist who has been brought along in the hope that he can be tricked into believing he is the father of Lily's unborn child. The real father, it seems, is Billie, a somewhat shadowy churl who has recently disappeared. The weekend is a setup: Lily's friends have been instructed to put her in a good light, to convince Edward (who is unaware of her pregnancy) that he would like to marry her.

Most of the story is told in a series of flashbacks, punctuated every so often by the conversation between Claude and the antique hunters. Lily, Norman and Shebah are each given some 40 pages to provide their impressions of the weekend. There is a shooting (bloodless), a good deal of sexual fumbling, and intimations aplenty. Lily's friends do not do their job.

Lily, who combines the intellectual inertness and eternal hope of many Bainbridge women ("She has gone to bed with numerous strangers rather than offend"), tries to make the best of a bad job. "It's not really such a mean trick to play on anyone—well, not on Edward," she reflects, "because he's always smiling at children and patting them on the head." Norman, who spends most of the weekend pursuing Julia, is a fine comic creation. . . . Shebah, the most bizarre and affecting of the three, suffers from poverty, ill health and acute paranoia. "Knowing so much," she observes, "my bitterness can only be self-directed, there being nobody worthier to receive it."

They are a fine lot of eccentrics, but the Rashomon device has an oddly draining effect: the characters and their stories seem almost anemic, as if they had faded along with their photograph. Perhaps this is intentional. Certainly the novel has a ghostly, half-remembered quality that is seductive. But I miss the more robust style of *The Bottle Factory Outing* or even the near slapstick of *Injury Time.* Much of Miss Bainbridge's success is achieved through distancing. When she writes in the third person, we see her tragi-comic characters from the outside. Because we never totally understand the almost rudimentary thought processes that propel them, they linger in our memories. The first-person narratives in *A Weekend With Claude* interfere with the sense of dislocation that we look for in Bainbridge's work. For this reason, I prefer the running action between Claude and his customers; it has a raw comic immediacy.

And it is her skewed and deadly grasp of the immediate that makes Bainbridge's work unique. Formerly an actress, she has an uncanny ear for dialogue, a perfect sense of timing and a terse, elliptical narrative style that combine to create a dramatic, or cinematic, tension. This novel, rich as it is in grotesquerie, has the kind of dreamy, evocative quality we associate with the films of Eric Rohmer. But it lacks the jarring dazzle of her best work. (pp. 10, 25)

> *Judith Gies, "Looking for Love in Vain," in*
> The New York Times Book Review, *March 21, 1982, pp. 10, 25.*

Peter Campbell

They should be called the Kondratieff Laureates. Fifty years ago, when the economic cycle last hit bottom, J. B. Priestley made his *English Journey.* A few years later Orwell wrote *The Road to Wigan Pier,* and Edwin Muir *Scottish Journey.* Now, as the succeeding wave reaches the bottom of its downward swing, the BBC send out Bainbridge to follow Priestley [with *English Journey: or, The Road to Milton Keynes*]. . . . Why novelists? Perhaps because it is reckoned that they will give a human dimension to the changes documented in unemployment statistics and land-use maps. . . .

Priestley, peering through an atmosphere 'thickened with ashes and sulphuric fumes, like Pompeii on the eve of its destruction', gives bravura descriptions of industrial devastation. 'Between Manchester and Bolton,' he writes, 'the ugliness is so complete it is almost exhilarating.' Bainbridge, who has had a sentimental attachment to the mean streets that have fallen beneath the wrecker's ball, reserves her hardest words for Billingham: 'a mess of concrete flats and dingy housing, vulgar precincts and civic centres, not to mention the winged monstrosity of the Arts Forum Theatre'. Her villains are the people who tried to carry out the kind of changes Priestley might have approved of. She is almost as hard on what they have made as Priestley was on the buildings that have been knocked down. Thus Priestley, writing on small shops, says: 'one large clean shed, a decent warehouse, would be better than these pitiful establishments with their fly-blown windows and dark

reeking interiors'. Bainbridge complains about a Southampton shopping precinct: 'Traffic-free areas are a silly idea. The trick with shopping is to get the whole wretched business over with as quickly as possible—nobody in their right minds would want to sit down in the middle of it.' The shops, the housing, the hopes of the planners of the Fifties and the builders of the Sixties, are dismissed in asides of this kind.

Can England be saved? 'In a crowded dirty little country like ours,' Orwell wrote, 'one takes defilement almost for granted . . . slagheaps and chimneys seem a more normal, probable landscape than grass and trees, and even in the depths of the country when you drive your fork into the ground you half expect to lever up a broken bottle or a rusty can.' . . . Orwell was writing a tract, Priestley and Bainbridge are writing travel books. They are outraged by poverty, distressed by shabbiness and boredom, and appreciative of tolerance, variety and eccentricity. What they saw made them uncomfortable. It did not, however, lead them to uncomfortable conclusions. They are curiously incurious about facts, and even about explanations. Priestley took a *Blue Guide* and Stamp and Beaver's *Economic Survey* with him, but made little use of them. Bainbridge set off with the Sunday papers.

These novelists make comments which only need to have 'Beryl mused' or 'Jack protested' tacked on here and there to make the narrators products of their own imaginations. 'Whoever said that England can't produce enough food for her own consumption? All the way to Birmingham the land was heavy with apple orchards and fields of cabbages and sugar beet, barley and turnips . . . I swear it never stopped, the blooming and the growing and the grazing, until the big transporters began lumbering up the slope from Longbridge and we saw the sign welcoming us to Birmingham. ('Thought Beryl,' one might add, 'realising that she had no notion how many pigs it took to give London its breakfast, or whether the country could keep itself in Brussels sprouts come to that. Perhaps she would find out one day. There was certainly a lot of food about.') . . . That is what novelists are good at—showing how unsubstantiated conclusions come into people's heads and how protestations of ignorance can sound insincere.

The dyspeptic travel-writer has become more common now that abroad is so unromantic and home is so down-at-heel. The traveller who suffered from bandits and fevers could afford to be harsher on the natives than the one who has nothing more grisly to complain of than a British Rail breakfast. The least you can ask is that they be interested in the countryside they cover. Often Bainbridge gives the impression that she was not. Her objectivity is refreshing, her prose lively, the final result is rather chilling. For all her modesty of intention her view is Martian, and a Martian's view of one's own country proves unhelpful. Considering the decline of Liverpool, she writes:

> If I were an historian I could chart the reasons for all this chaos: decline of trade, loss of Empire, aeroplanes instead of ships, cars instead of railways, synthetics instead of cotton, the trade unions, the rise of the Japanese. I could blame the Conservatives for greed, the Liberals for lack of confidence, the socialists for naivety and jumping on the bandwagon of progress. But it hardly matters now. It's too late. Someone's murdered Liverpool and got away with it.

What is missing from this kind of rhetoric is the thought that we all murdered Liverpool, and are all responsible. . . .

Part of Bainbridge's problem with the present is the past:

> All my parents' bright days had ended before I was born. They faced backwards. In so doing they created within me so strong a nostalgia for time gone that I have never been able to appreciate the present or look to the future. The very things that Mr Priestley deplored, and which in part have been swept away, 'the huddle of undignified little towns, the drift of smoke, the narrow streets that led from one dreariness to another', were the very things I lamented. Show me another motorway, I thought, another shopping precinct, another acre of improved environment and I shall pack up and go home.

Bainbridge, uncomprehending of or depressed by new townscapes, gives few marks for the cars, television sets, bathrooms and freezers, public buildings and state services, which are what, for better or worse, we bought with the profits of the fat years. She finds the human damage equally depressing. Bing, 19 and looking 13, wearing tight jeans, cropped hair and big boots, had 'cold black buttons for eyes'. He was about to go to court, having attacked someone with a screwdriver.

> 'Don't you want to do something?' I asked. 'Something worthwhile.' I felt stupid the moment I'd said it. 'Wouldn't you like something to happen,' I amended. 'Something good, a nice home, someone who minds?' 'I'd like wheels,' he said. 'That's what I'd like' . . . I wished him good luck, that nearly came out as good riddance, and he crossed the road and from the back he was a little boy in seven-league boots, pathetically alone and possibly trying not to cry.

(p. 20)

Peter Campbell, "England's End," in London Review of Books, *Vol. 6, No. 10, June 7-20, 1984, pp. 20-2.*

Richard Eder

In 1933, J. B. Priestley set out by bus and car to reconnoiter the England of Depression years and report on its condition. The result was *English Journey,* a work fueled by a mix of indignation and exasperated love—fine-honed by Priestley's shrewd eye, speculative wit and a voracious, buttonholing curiosity about how coal is mined, a dry wall built and what the coal miner and dry waller think of their lives and times. It is one of the best travel books of the century. More than that, it is a portrait of a country whose ebbing tide exposed great scrofulous patches but retained a memory of its high-water days.

Fifty years later, the BBC commissioned novelist Beryl Bainbridge to retrace Priestley's journey [in her own *English Journey*]. She went from Southampton through Bristol and the Cotswolds, and up through the gritty industrial cities of Liverpool, Newcastle, Stockton and Birmingham; the first three devasted by stagnation and the last by prosperity.

What a passage of time and alteration between the two English journeys! Part of the change is marked by what the two writers found. Southampton and Liverpool were bustling ports then; now the one harbors yachts and moth-balled tankers; the other is virtually silent. There are similarities as well, though. The industrial north was dying in Priestley's day; it is dying still. Instead of men on the dole bunching on street corners, Bainbridge finds them in government offices, enmeshed in the high-mindedly punitive red tape of welfare programs. . . .

But more than the material, the style of the two books and their authors mark how much has gone and how little has taken its place. Priestley's book, twice as long as Bainbridge's, bristled with facts, encounters, opinions and the overwhelming energy provided by a sense of discovery. He took us firmly by the hand and gave us the news, usually bad.

Bainbridge travels palely and with reluctance. She is there and then she isn't, having retreated with a headache. She is not so much journeying as having herself pulled along by that myopic but formidable motor: the mobile television team with its producer, director, two cameramen and sound crew. What it captures is largely the dust it raises, and out of that dust, Bainbridge nervously emerges, wondering if the sound box strapped to her waist will suggest a prosthetic device, reflecting upon the differences between walking for one's self and walking for the camera.

She wanly interviews hotel porters and pub-sitters about the local economy. A retired steward on the Cunard Lines wafts into television range: "I was expected to talk to him about his life aboard the great liners," she writes, keeping her distance and consuming the chocolate cake he has baked. The cake is more real to her than the steward. In a touristy Cotswold village, she reports that "it was hoped I would talk to a vicar, but he was out."

Bainbridge is a most particular and quicksilver novelist, and this kind of scatty daze is irritating and puzzling. Perhaps it is her distrust of journalistic reality as against the reality of the imagination. Part of it may be a sardonic protest against television's invasive prison-visitor approach. How are you being treated?, the camera asks, while the world looks on and the subject triangulates his reply.

Still, Bainbridge signed on for this. What can she mean by her hazy recalcitrants, her insistence on looking at England as if it might not be there? She means a great deal, in fact.

Where is Southampton? she asks her driver as they go through feeder roads, past scattered housing developments and along dusty green spaces dotted with occasional shopping centers. This is it, he tells her. Priestley's decaying post-Victorian England of squalid row-houses and blackened factories has been replaced by a featureless blobbiness. There is, as the Gertrude Stein saying goes, no there there; and Bainbridge's fogginess is a commentary on fog. . . .

[As] she moves north out of Bristol and the Cotswolds, Bainbridge's memories assail her; she begins to emerge. Her portrait of her father, a failed commercial impresario with an eye for beauty, is as affecting as it is sardonic. He would visit cemeteries and lay his head on the gravestones, saying that "memories escaped if there were no walls to keep them trapped." Where will memories live in the redeveloped cities? Bainbridge asks. In Birmingham, with its urban maelstrom, she shouts at workmen having their lunch upon a tombstone being dug up to make room for a park.

Memory angers her, and anger rouses her and reassures us. Bainbridge's frivolousness is like that of mourners in the first shock of bereavement; it is more ghastly than grief, yet it is the surest sign of grief. Bainbridge's etherized travels do not make nearly as good a book as Priestley's; yet, in their way, and dismayingly, they convey as true a picture of a country and its times.

> *Richard Eder, "A Following in Priestley's Footsteps," in* Los Angeles Times Book Review, *September 9, 1984, p. 2.*

Benedict Nightingale

It must have sounded a bright, bold idea to the program planners. Why not mark the half-centenary of the publication of J. B. Priestley's *English Journey* by sending a camera crew along a route very similar to the one he classically traced back in 1933? Yes, and why not invite another north-country writer to do the interviews and the commentary? And so it was that the BBC came to screen a well-received series of documentaries earlier this year, and the novelist Beryl Bainbridge can now give us [*English Journey*], the diary she kept as she hurried from Southampton to Bristol to Manchester to Newcastle-on-Tyne to the new town of Milton Keynes, chatting to the local populace and wryly observing its social health.

Her native Liverpool is on roughly the same latitude as Priestley's native Bradford; but in most other respects she seems a curious successor to the late author. His *English Journey* was hearty, opinionated, magisterial, veering from robust enthusiasm to yeomanly outrage as he recorded instances of eccentricity, urban desolation or human waste. Her *English Journey* is by comparison nervous, flustered, a bit unsure of itself and its insights, and only very occasionally capable of a similarly forthright passion. Again, Priestley's plain-man, pipe-in-the-mouth socialism, always more a matter of good companionship than of theory and analysis, nevertheless seems considerably more sophisticated than the thinking of Miss Bainbridge, who tends to flinch and flounder whenever a political or economic idea threatens to waylay her. And this is a pity, because her journey takes her, as it took him during the Depression, to company towns and ports, factories and shipyards, at a time of national recession.

It is a not altogether different England that Miss Bainbridge breathlessly chronicles. The difference is apparent on the very first page, when she sees elderly Sikhs playing soccer on the outskirts of Southampton, and even more apparent when she gets to Bradford itself, where Asian-Englishmen in Nehru hats are parading their principled opposition to coeducation at a meeting in city hall.

The urban architecture has changed too, not altogether for the better. The smoky red-brick slums so eloquently deplored by Priestley have substantially disappeared, only to be replaced by cut-rate travesties of Alphaville, with pedestrian walkways, monotonous shopping malls and huge, anonymous concrete towers for the poor. As Miss Bainbridge sees it, the fools and knaves of contemporary En-

gland are the planners, who were asked to build a new Jerusalem and instead managed to put up Milton Keynes, a maze of expressways and traffic circles.

Yet this *English Journey* makes it clear that one thing has not changed since its prototype was published; or, rather, one thing did change, only to reappear and reassert itself. That, of course, is high unemployment, especially in the big northern industrial towns. It was Priestley's vivid portrayal of dying and dead communities, inhabited by men with the "strained, greyish, faintly decomposed look" of prisoners of war, that gave his book its power, its influence and importance in its day. He made his fellow countrymen see, smell, taste the "perpetual penniless bleak Sabbath" of afflicted areas like Jarrow.

And now Miss Bainbridge visits precisely the same town, to find a new shopping center, an art gallery in an old air-raid shelter—and the grandchildren of that same penniless generation once again on the dole.

If her account hasn't the same force, it's for several reasons. The dole is more generous these days, poverty less terrible. The human damage inflicted by unemployment is much more familiar to the public than in Priestley's time, thanks both to television and to print journalists distantly indebted to his pioneering reportage. Except for her account of Liverpool, Miss Bainbridge says nothing new about recession—and, one fears, isn't the right writer for the subject anyway. Her strength would seem to be recording the quirks and oddities of contemporary England—the thin boy she spots sniffing glue on the Bristol quayside, the topless woman fire-eater she meets in Southampton—. . . and not in conveying and mourning the nation's profounder woes.

> *Benedict Nightingale, "Priestley's Footsteps," in* The New York Times Book Review, *September 23, 1984, p. 24.*

Jonathan Raban

In 1933, when Priestley made his English journey, the number of people registered as being out of work was 2,498,100. That is the dominant fact of Priestley's book [*English Journey*]. It sets him traveling and it colors almost every perception that he has of England. (p. 46)

In 1983, when Beryl Bainbridge made her English journey, the number of people registered as being out of work was 3,104,700. (In the last year, that number has swollen by nearly a quarter of a million.) The figure is not to be found in Bainbridge's book [*English Journey*], nor is it by any means the book's dominant fact. She has borrowed Priestley's title and Priestley's itinerary, but there the resemblance stops.

Bainbridge is not on a mission; she is on commission.

> Last year, in celebration of Mr Priestley's classic book, *English Journey,* BBC Bristol sent a team of eight, which included me, to follow in his footsteps, recording on film the route he had taken and making a documentary series of what we saw and heard in the towns and villages of England during the summer of 1983.

Alas, how are the traveling writers fallen, from the proud

and solitary iconoclasm of Priestley in his Daimler to "a team of eight, which included me." Tied to a shooting script, wired for sound, continually watched by the gleaming mauve eye of an Arriflex, Beryl Bainbridge traveled in tune with her time, as a component, like a coil or a resistor, in a high-tech electronic system. She was not so much a person as a part of "the media"—a singular noun for which at least half the British population now harbors a well-founded dislike and mistrust. Any striking miner would identify the television industry as a fat rich man intent on exploiting and misrepresenting him.

Bainbridge is, of course, far too good a writer not to spot such ironies for herself. Her book, or notebook, has a fugitive quality. Written up in the odd moments when she could escape from the other seven people in her crew, it often reads like a prison diary as it annotates the cigarettes gone up in smoke, the drinks knocked back, the conversations forgotten, the expensive, repetitive tedium of filming. Whereas Priestley confidently booms, Beryl Bainbridge squeaks from inside the cage like an ailing budgerigar on tour in a circus.

Yet—because she is an accomplished novelist and because she is, thank God, one of the world's least likely television performers—her book manages to catch (often in an oblique and inadvertent way) a lot of the atmosphere of contemporary England. The "England" of her fiction is an infinitely unreliable place, chiefly inhabited by strays and fugitives, and Beryl Bainbridge's authorial manner has always been a touch elfin. So it is in her *English Journey*. She catches the spirit of 1983 best in the uncertainty of her own tone. The crispest enunciation of her attitude is set down in her preface:

> I have never been able to appreciate the present or look to the future. The very things that Mr Priestley deplored and which in part have been swept away, "the huddle of undignified little towns, the drift of smoke, the narrow streets that led from one dreariness to another," were the very things I lamented. Show me another motorway, I thought, another shopping precinct, another acre of improved environment and I shall pack up and go home.
>
> Some of the time I didn't know where home was. . . .

To account for "England in the 1980s" it would be hard to improve on these sentences. For what Beryl Bainbridge is looking for, in the company of Mrs. Thatcher, a large section of the British electorate, and the tourists who foregather round ruined villages in dried-up reservoirs, is an England she can recognize and put a name to as home. (pp. 47-8)

Whatever else was wrong with Priestley's England, it was recognizable. People had been taught to see it through the eyes of Dickens and Gustave Doré. The slums looked like authentic slums. The poor were dressed in what were obviously rags. The unemployed stood in the street, their pathos visible and affecting. . . .

It is not surprising that Priestley was able to write so well about it. Nor is it surprising that Beryl Bainbridge finds herself at a loss when she follows Priestley's route. For although the statistics have increased, the images have disappeared. She goes hopefully to Newcastle in search of the unemployed, and finds only a shopping precinct full of people spending money. Nothing to write about, or make a television film of, there. She goes to an "Action Centre" for the unemployed in Hanley:

> I talked to the dedicated young woman who runs the centre and asked her about the problems she deals with. She said the unemployment round here was higher than the national average and that the youth job employment scheme was a fiddle. It was exploitation, and besides, it could only deal with about one per cent of the population. Things weren't just bad, they were hopeless. People came in on Wednesday asking for money to buy tea and bread for the rest of the week. "But I expect they smoke," I said severely. "And I bet they've all got televisions and even videos."

With that culpably silly line, Bainbridge misses the most important fact around her. They *have* all got televisions, and even (rented by the week) videos. Therein lies the single most important distinction between Priestley's and Bainbridge's Englands.

For in 1933, most of English life took place out of doors. You even left your house to go to the lavatory. Out of a job, you stood in full view of the street. Because the slums were usually two stories high at the most, their streets and backyards became communal living spaces, open to the gaze of visiting writers and photographers. It would have been possible for Priestley to see unemployment at first hand without stepping from his Daimler.

It is not so now. Since the 1950s we have moved, or been moved, indoors and upstairs. Unemployment, like so many other features of our social life, has gone private. It happens on the twentieth floor, in a room full of plastic furniture, where a man in an ill-fitting but not ragged polyester shirt and jeans watches an old episode from *Dallas* on the video and (if Ms. Bainbridge's prim sense of how the working class should spend their money can take the strain) listens simultaneously to a cassette on his Sony Walkman. As an image, it's not a patch on the lines of washing (now dried in a machine, probably in a public launderette) or the men in scarves and flat caps loitering under the rusty girders of a railroad bridge filmed *contre jour*. It is an image that would make any televison cameraman yawn. Considered not as an image but as a plight, it is surely just as shocking, pitiable, and arousing as anything described by Priestley. To convey it requires the right of access not just to the outside of the man's house, to his squalid and depressing plot of civic green space, but to the inside of his head.

This, one might have thought, was a classic job for a writer, to go into regions prohibited to the televison camera and make the condition of unemployment legible—as it was legible in 1933. But Bainbridge is not that writer. She is the eighth member of her TV crew, looking for recognizable pictures that turn out to be in bafflingly short supply. Her best insights are fleetingly sad pictorial ones. On the top of a block of flats in Castlevale, outside Birmingham, she remarks, "I wouldn't fancy living in one of those top-floor flats. Not without wings." For a moment, as one is afforded a glimpse of angels dwelling at the tops of urban housing projects and drifting from high windows on their wings, one is reminded of just how good and odd a writer Bainbridge can be—and of how adrift she is in this England that she doesn't understand. It's true that she is attached to the Liverpool of her childhood, to bits and pieces of England remembered from her life as a young actress on tour during the 1960s, even to the England of her current London literary conventions—but these ties only serve to undermine Beryl Bainbridge's homelessness in the country at large.

Indeed, Bainbridge's incomprehension is her ticket of entry to the world she describes. Even by English standards, she comes across as curiously ill-traveled. Half the places she visits appear to be brand-new to her, and even now she seems to be under the innocent illusion that Skegness is in Scotland. Unlike Priestley, she is shy of advancing causes for what she sees, and even shyer of hazarding solutions to our unenviable problems. She is closer in spirit than she realizes to the manager of a crankshaft factory whom she meets in Lincoln:

> I asked him what he thought about the bomb. I kept thinking that here I was, almost at the end of my journey, and not once had we mentioned it. Ken looked taken aback for a moment, and then, looking sideways at the camera, he said, "It's not for the likes of me to say."

It's not for the likes of us to say. There is a line that deserves to go on England's tombstone.

Priestley in 1933 answered the optimistic national need for a sage; Bainbridge in 1984 caters to a peculiarly recent British taste for helpless irony. She claims no power over the world she charts. She finds it on the whole pretty alien. It would be nice if it were otherwise but it isn't, so she tries to make the best of it by taking a mild and mournful pleasure in its oddities. I very much fear that in this glancing, quirky, breathless little book, Beryl Bainbridge really does speak authentically for England. (pp. 48-9)

> *Jonathan Raban, "Hard Times," in* The New York Review of Books, *Vol. XXXI, No. 16, October 25, 1984, pp. 46-9.*

Valentina Yakovleva

In the last decades of the present century Great Britain has produced a whole galaxy of prominent women writers. Suffice it to name Doris Lessing, Muriel Spark, Pamela Hansford Johnson, Iris Murdoch, and among those dealing with more specifically feminine problems Margaret Drabble, Edna O'Brian, Susan Hill, and Rose Tremain.

Why then choose Beryl Bainbridge? No special reason except that she has been very much in the limelight lately and besides I happened to meet her once, which added a personal touch to my literary interest in her development as a writer. (p. 141)

I first read her work in 1975. On one of my regular visits to the Moscow Library of Foreign Literature I noticed on the stand of new acquisitions Beryl Bainbridge's novel *The Dressmaker,* first published in England in 1973. Not knowing the author at that time, I read the book out of curiosity and was soon rejoicing at the discovery of yet another doubtlessly gifted writer. The action of that rather short but skilfully structured novel is set in war-time England. The characters belong to what in England would

be most likely described as lower middle class. They are drawn with laconic precision and psychological insight.

Pretty and happy-go-lucky Valerie is the friend of Rita, a reticent, homely girl, cowed by the oppressive atmosphere of her cheerless home and particularly by her despotic old-maid aunt Nellie, the dressmaker. Valerie is going to marry one of the American soldiers posted in England. He is rich. He gives Valerie a good time and expensive presents, including a fridge. Valerie helps Rita to meet another American soldier who, however, turns out to be poor, illiterate and interested only in sex.

The general picture of the people's life during the Second World War serves only as a background for the individual drama of an unhappy family. The rationing of food and other goods, queues and bombings are only mentioned in passing but these and other aptly chosen details vividly convey the war-time atmosphere. So do some of the remarks made by the characters. Valerie's brother, a British soldier on leave, who is against her marriage, eagerly repeats the saying current at the time, "There's only three things wrong with them Yanks. They're overpaid, oversexed and over here." He also remarks bitterly that "Yanks had taken their time coming into the war" . . . Because of this background one begins to forget the narrow bounds of the story—narrow as compared with the enormous scope of the historical tragedy of the war; the story is perceived as an enlarged detail of a big canvas. There is a reason to mention the concluding episode of the novel: the dressmaker, annoyed by the appearance of a man (and an American soldier at that) in the life of her niece and at one particular moment enraged by the fact that he has carelessly scratched a sacred piece of furniture inherited by her from her mother, stabs him in the neck with her large scissors and kills him. However stern and grim the woman may be, her subsequent behaviour is hardly "in character", for after all, the author describes her as a God-fearing creature with a set pattern of moral standards. Meanwhile, she is not at all shocked by what she has done—quite calmly and soberly, she sets out to dispose of the dead body. (pp. 141-42)

After *The Dressmaker* I found *The Bottle Factory Outing* disappointing. The situation and the scene of action are different but the characters of the two English women working at the Italian run factory are painted in the same gloomy colours—miserable, lonely creatures ineptly trying to find some escape from their joyless existence. Situations in the novel are annoyingly contrived and the author's attempt at comedy (making the participants in the outing drive around in the car with the body of an inadvertently killed woman) is utterly unsuccessful. If this is humour, then what a strange, even perverted humour it is! And then comes the denouement—once again a search for a "professionally expedient" way of disposing of the body. This time it is put into an empty wine barrel, which is sent from the bottle factory in England to Italy with a batch of empties in the hope that on arrival it will simply be dumped into the sea since it is marked as being damaged. This reads almost like a parody by the author of her own writing. (pp. 142-43)

The more I read Bainbridge novels the more disappointed I grew in her attitude to the surrounding reality and in her choice of characters. She deliberately strives to remain "outside the story", an impartial observer. Yet the personality of the author cannot be hidden—the very striving after complete objectivity, the abstaining from judgements, from taking sides, from any commitment is in itself a "position", a revelation of the writer's world outlook and of her moral principles.

In my view, Miss Bainbridge is at her best in *A Quiet Life* and *Injury Time. A Quiet Life,* considering its spontaneity and freshness, might well have been her first novel. One feels that the writer had an ample store of personal experiences to rely on. *Injury Time,* which is considered by some Soviet critics as her nearest approach to satire, in my opinion does not rise to that status. Actually the book is written on two planes and dwells on two themes. The first part, written with sad humour, describes the life of an unattached woman who goes through all the humiliating experiences of being a married man's clandestine mistress. The author handles this situation with great sensitivity and insight and with many a sad and humorous detail. The further development of the plot, dealing with a hold-up and the embarrassing position in which the wayward husband-lover finds himself, is executed in the form of a grotesque. The two parts, however, possess an artistic unity, and the book as a whole is another proof of the author's talent.

At the end of 1979 I attended a meeting with Miss Bainbridge in Moscow. She came on a visit with another English writer, William Cooper, and was received as a guest of the Writers' Union of the USSR. (p. 143)

Someone asked Miss Bainbridge why she had given up her career as an actress and turned to literature. She said that perhaps the main reason was her desire to tell people about her far from easy childhood, and to sort out for herself in the process her attitude to the various events in her life, her own views and emotions. She spoke frankly and willingly, apparently enjoying the friendly contact with the audience. She said that at the age of about 14 she had first read Dostoevsky, who made a staggering impression on her and probably also strengthened her desire to become a writer. It was also under Dostoevsky's influence that she later used newspaper items as the basis for the plots of some of her novels, the first example being *Harriet Said* (. . . "loosely based on an actual murder case of the fifties in New Zealand . . . ").

As I read more of Miss Bainbridge's works, however, I could not help coming to the conclusion that the influence of the Russian classic on her work has never been profound: actually it can be seen only in rather imitative attempts at using purely formal "devices" or borrowing some incidental motifs and situations from Dostoevsky's writings or even resorting to the imitation of personal traits. For example, in *Another Part of the Wood* one of the characters, for no artistically logical reasons at all, is made to suffer from epileptic fits. This, apparently one of the most "Dostoevskian" of Miss Bainbridge's novels, produces a rather strange and unpleasant impression. The plot, the behaviour of the characters, the dramatic ending are all unnatural; they are reminiscent of a whimsical theatrical performance which has no point to it besides demonstrating the arbitrariness of the author's tastes. The story is cluttered with meaningless details in the description of the surroundings and the characters' appearance and mannerisms. One cannot help being surprised to learn that the novel was rewritten in 1979, having first been produced in 1965 and unfavourably received by the press (no

wonder!). I have not read the first version but the second makes one doubt the worth of the effort.

Miss Bainbridge, it seems, has developed something like a habit of rewriting her first-version books. Another example is *A Weekend With Claude* (1967-1981). Again I have read only the second version. It contains several rather freakish lonely characters who are engaged in settling their mundane affairs and at the same time uttering some rather trite philosophical maxims. Claude, for example, proclaims that "for every crime there is punishment" (a sample of Dostoevsky's influence?) or "Babies must be fed naturally, not handed the bottle every four hours" . . . , etc. The structure of the novel is not exactly original—it has been used in literature and cinema many times before: the events and emotional experiences are presented as viewed by several different people.

Among the so far one-version novels there is one entitled *Sweet William.* Beryl Bainbridge herself classifies *Sweet William* as a "love story of sorts". With the exception of one somewhat disgusting passage Miss Bainbridge is quite restrained in the depiction of love-making scenes in this "love story". One should note that in general, as far as the portrayal of sex life in the "permissive society" is concerned, Beryl Bainbridge may be said to be almost as chaste as a nun (compared, for instance, with Erica Jong).

The novel was filmed; it added to Miss Bainbridge's success, but it has little claim to be classed as a socially meaningful work of art. It abounds in deliberately contrived comical situations but the characters remain just the same pathetic human flotsam. (pp. 144-45)

Her book *Young Adolf* (1978-1979) did not come up for discussion at our meeting in Moscow as it had remained in Miss Bainbridge's suitcase, which happened to be mislaid by British Airways somewhere at Heathrow Airport, and failed to arrive at the same time as its author (the episode was later on worn threadbare by her in the novel *Winter Garden*). Subsequently, when the book arrived and I read it, my attitude towards Miss Bainbridge's writing rather changed for the worse. On the cover of a paperback edition a *Listener* critic is quoted, who has discovered in the book "an almost Chaplinesque glee", and an *Atlantic* critic says that "she has succeeded in the seemingly impossible task of making Adolf interesting and human without giving him any sympathy whatsoever". Whatever the enthusiastic critics say, the impossible remained unachieved. First of all, the very choice of the subject is too much of a concession to the fashionable, but by no means harmless, trend of "exonerating" Hitler—the trend that reached its peak a few years ago. Books of that kind seemed to crop up in the West like mushrooms. I am sure that writing on that subject could be justified only if the author's aim was to explain the social, political and economic reasons and the international situation which made the appearance of the monstrosity called Hitler possible, or if it was a devastating satire exposing and condemning the notorious "Führer" and his present-day dangerous young followers. But Miss Bainbridge is far from setting such an aim. How does the young Hitler look as portrayed by Miss Bainbridge? He is morbid and hysterical, his habits are strange and unpleasant, but all this is blamed on certain painful and demeaning experiences of his childhood and early youth. At the same time, as those around him stress more than once, he is clever and knowledgeable and has the markings of an orator and leader.

There is a saying that to understand means to forgive. Why should Miss Bainbridge try to understand and, consequently, to forgive Hitler? If the subject attracts her so much, one may ask, why not concentrate her attention on the none too sparse flocks of "young Adolfs" marching down the streets of London and other cities in the country of her birth? . . . [They] could certainly provide enough material for not only the blackest of "comedies", as Miss Bainbridge likes to classify her novels, but the blackest of tragedies. Maybe, this is an indiscriminate attempt at attracting public attention by resorting to the old device known as "Epater le bourgeois" as long as you hope to attract attention with your creation, the more weird and morbid it is, the better?

As for the Chaplinesque quality of that book, one can only marvel how any critic could suggest a comparison between Chaplin's mercilessly ridiculed "dictator" and the character produced by Miss Bainbridge. Chaplin uses mockery to brand Hitler as a dangerous freak of nature; there is no attempt on the artist's part "to understand and forgive."

In Chaplin's other films it is precisely the irreconcilable contradiction between the cruel, callous, corrupted world and the candid, trustful, kind man that produces the tragicomical effect. The spectators' hearts go out to the little man in compassion and sympathy. The readers' hearts seldom go out in compassion and sympathy to Miss Bainbridge's characters in her "everyday English life" novels because she does not strive for that. She accepts the world as it is, and there is a feeling that she expects her characters and her readers to do the same.

But to return to *Young Adolf.*

Besides arousing indignation in any reader who, even if he has not personally experienced, then has heard or read about the atrocities against humanity committed by Hitler, the book has another unforgivable defect—it is hopelessly, unbearably boring.

In another of her latest books, *Winter Garden,* the author's position is again bewildering to say the least. The book is not a travelogue, though the desire of the author to share her travelling impressions and the acquired half-knowledge of the "exotic country" called the Soviet Union, is evident enough. Since the author calls it a novel, it should have carried the usual publishers' note: "This novel is a work of fiction. Names, characters, places and incidents are either the product of the author's imagination or else are used fictitiously, and any resemblance to actual persons . . . " The rest of the usual warning is superfluous for there is no resemblance, however coincidental, to the real life of Soviet people which the writer tries to portray.

I would even say that characters, places and incidents are used in the book not simply "fictitiously" but maliciously. The four English people who go on a visit to the Soviet Union allegedly on the invitation of the Artists' Union, are no credit to their country. They do not seem to have any idea why they want to go there at all with the exception of the dull, stuffy Admiralty lawyer Mr. Ashburner, who joins the delegation because he hopes that it may provide a chance of greater intimacy with his wayward mistress, Nina St. Clair, the wife of a famous brain specialist.

In beautiful, sunny Georgia the English visitors, three of whom are supposed to be artists of sorts, never ask to be shown the works of Georgian painters (they probably do not know of their existence), they never go to a theatre, they are not interested in the works of sculptors or architects, they know nothing about the excellent modern Georgian films which have won prizes at several international film festivals. When they do ask to be taken to "the flicks", it is strangely enough in some half-built hall where they see a tedious old picture, and the only thing that provokes Mr. Ashburner's thought is his visit to a lavatory (a favourite subject with the author).

After a few opening pages the reader begins to receive generous doses of long worn-out derogatory outpourings about Soviet life: when you go to the Soviet Union you must take along bath plugs for they don't exist there, or if the plugs exist, then "the water gushing from the hot taps is a brackish brown". In another hotel, "The shower did not work and he was unable to open the window", in the washroom "the paste lathered like soap and the brush disintegrated in his mouth". (pp. 145-47)

Such things go on and on. To make her novel something of a thriller, the author invents quite a lot of "gothic" mysteries and adventures which are devoid of either meaning or suspense; or is it an attempt to pay tribute to what is now called post-modernism? In some places she loses both tact and taste. For example, Miss Bainbridge does not even hesitate to mock the famous Piskarev Cemetery in Leningrad, where the defenders of the city and victims of the Nazi blockade (1941-1944) lie buried. Why did the author feel obliged to do this? Are there no sacred things left in the present-day world? (pp. 147-48)

To write a book like *Winter Garden* about a trip to the Soviet Union one does not have to leave London at all. Just like a bride who, according to an old English (or is it American?) superstition, is advised to wear at her wedding "something old, something new, something borrowed and something blue," an author who seeks commercial success, is advised by a publishing firm editor to put into the novel "a bit of gory violence, perversion and lust, a sense of coming holocaust, and an anti-Soviet thrust." But does an author with an established reputation have to follow the rules of the book-market game? Alas, *Young Adolf* and *Winter Garden* show that some of them feel they have to conform . . .

An erosion of a literary talent is a sad thing to witness.

We in the Soviet Union are often reproached by Western critics for treating literature "too seriously", not as an entertainment but as a source of enlightenment and food for thought. No denying, such indeed is the case. This Russian-Soviet attitude to literature has a deeply rooted historical tradition. (p. 148)

Miss Bainbridge is what is called a successful writer. The fact that she is widely advertised by her publishers is easy to understand: "You've got to speak well of the things you mean to sell" (a Russian saying). But she also gets prizes and good reviews from some critics, and her books have a wide enough circulation. There may be two main explanations for this: one, her innate giftedness, and the other,

her deliberate stance as an indifferent, "impartial" observer of a world of alienated, muddled, hollow people of little use and human value to themselves or others. A position, which, as we have seen, is not as "impartial" as all that since it adds fuel to anti-Soviet propaganda and answers perfectly the "demand of the Establishment" prevailing in the Western world today. To comply with such a demand is the beginning of the end for any artist worth the name. (p. 149)

Valentina Yakovleva, "On Reading Beryl Bainbridge," in Soviet Literature, *No. 11, 1984, pp. 141-49.*

James Lasdun

Watson's Apology is an ambitious, original novel that manages to do full justice to its setting in the last century, without ever forgetting it is a [novelization of a famous Victorian murder case]. Letters, newspaper articles, Home Office papers and trial reports provided Beryl Bainbridge with the bare bones of her story, and many of these documents are included in the book. As for the flesh—as she herself puts it: "What has defeated historical inquiry has been the motives of the characters, their conversations and their feelings. These it has been the task of the novelist to supply."

In 1844 the Rev. J. S. Watson, headmaster of a school in Stockwell, began writing to Anne Armstrong, a woman he had met years earlier in Ireland. The burden of his cautious, polite letters was marriage, and although Anne Armstrong had no recollection of her suitor, her present circumstances were so dismal that any prospect of release from them was to be leapt at. The two married early the following year, and spent the next 25 gradually destroying each other with a deepening mixture of carelessness, misunderstanding, resentment, and bad luck. By 1871, Anne had disintegrated into a bitter, incontinent old woman, tormented by jealousy and scorn for her husband, who in turn was so disastrously thwarted in his career, his literary ambitions, and his marriage, that his reason had begun to stray. In October 1871, after a particularly quarrelsome period, he beat Anne to death with a pistol butt.

Beryl Bainbridge unearths no mysteries to account for the catastrophe. On the contrary, her achievement is to show how very ordinary and unmysterious were the forces at play upon Mr Watson and his wife. Both had their share of oddities and personal traumas to put up with, but what propelled them towards tragedy was an accumulation of the kinds of mutual disappointments that could afflict any marriage under similar circumstances—a promise of a holiday that takes Watson eight years to fulfil because of his consuming literary endeavours, irrational jealousy on Anne's part bred out of neglect, vindictiveness born from jealousy. . . . Marriage, in short, as a slow, protracted quarrel, where the original misdeed is long forgotten, but where blow and counterblow continue to be exchanged mercilessly.

Historical reality is a notoriously difficult proposition for a novelist to tackle, dead people being much more difficult to bring to life than purely imaginary ones. It takes some time for the Watsons to emerge into visibility from the sometimes fragmentary conversations and incidents with

which Bainbridge evokes them. Anne remains a perplexing character to the end; a solution—not always wholly satisfactory—to the enigmatic shreds of documentation from which Bainbridge has assembled her. In her husband, however, contradiction and inconsistency somehow acquire the texture of real life. His schoolmasterly pedantry, his impulsive charitableness, the disastrous combination of pity and selfishness he exhibits towards his wife, his abhorrence of violence in general and his own private act of violence, even his apparent lack of remorse—all these qualities are singled out by Bainbridge with impeccable judgment, the result being an individual with a complexity of mind that is rare in fiction. There is a poignant moment about half-way through the novel: presented, to his surprise and joy, with a silver salver for his service to the school, Watson is moved to extemporise on one of his beloved subjects:

> "The purpose of Tragedy was not to free one from
> pity or terror, nor to purge one by allowing the dis-
> charge of such feelings, but to bring one face to face
> with the awful truths of human existence."

On the next page, four years later, he is dismissed from his headmastership without reason, a blow that effectively sentences him to penury for the rest of his days. The intent of the juxtaposition is clear: Watson is to be regarded as a figure of tragic stature. An unlikely candidate perhaps, but it is with no feelings at all of having been manipulated that one acquiesces in Bainbridge's implicit judgment of her character, and that is a measure of the depth and fullness with which she has imagined him. (p. 44)

James Lasdun, "Pre-Modern, Post-Modernist," in Encounter, *Vol. LXIV, No. 2, February, 1985, pp. 42, 44-7.*

William Grimes

The apologetic Watson of Beryl Bainbridge's [novel *Watson's Apology*] was a schoolmaster, ordained minister, and prolific scholar who in 1871 inexplicably bludgeoned his wife to death with a pistol butt. Though he was condemned to hang, the sentence was commuted to life imprisonment. The 67-year-old murderer died in his cell nearly 15 years later. Beryl Bainbridge fleshes out these bare historical bones in a quasi-symbolist "docu-fiction" that integrates courtroom transcripts, letters, and newspaper articles into an elliptical study of love and the modern personality.

Watson's Apology begins with a short author's note assuring us that all documents are genuine: this is followed by a series of stilted love letters from John Selby Watson to Anne Armstrong, a woman he admired some 20 years earlier and now, mysteriously, wishes to marry. Armstrong, in straitened circumstances, agrees to meet with Watson, whose face she cannot recall, and a wedding quickly follows. Bainbridge chronicles, in harrowing fashion, the disintegration of their relationship.

Both Watson and Armstrong have deep-seated grievances against life: he was given away by his mother at birth; she came down in the world after her father lost every penny in a bank collapse. Pain and desperate need draw them together, but they manage only to compound each other's suffering. Minor criticisms and unspoken reproaches accumulate, ill will breeds, until even acts of kindness are sniffed at suspiciously. They are driven in upon themselves and neither can find a way back to the outside world; in time, their egos begin to unravel. . . .

The violent drama unfolds in an eerie stillness which derives from the laconic Bainbridge style, with its perfect pitch and unerring eye for the disturbing detail. The conversation is more Pinteresque than usual: Characters talk past one another, respond to unasked questions, pick up half-heard or misinterpreted phrases, and launch into seemingly irrelevant confessions. The spaces between words are as charged with meaning as the words themselves. In this rarefied atmosphere, metaphoric electrical pulses leap from pole to pole, eliminating time and distance. A woman, startled by the sound of sobbing, imagines that she is hearing her own child, many miles away. On a seashore outing, the murder is prefigured when a sudden breeze lifts Watson's hat, revealing a white scar on his temple. These images, bound together by a dream logic, communicate a sense of clammy dread.

Bainbridge gives a thoroughly contemporary and convincing account of a disastrous marriage. Both parties enter into matrimony with a clear idea of what they want, and only vague, conventional notions of what they might be expected to give. Both wish to love; neither knows how. Love becomes harmful to both the lover and the beloved, and therein, perhaps, lies Watson's apology. "He had not harmed her," he thinks after the murder, "merely rid her of the bad things that had kept them apart."

None of these subtleties is touched upon at the trial, which is presented entirely in courtroom transcripts. This section drags on far too long, with numerous witnesses (including several doctors attributing Watson's crime to "melancholia") going over the same ground in great detail. As if in recompense, however, Bainbridge concludes with a stunning coda describing Watson's final years in prison, when the outside world withers away and he lives in dreams. Even then, he finds no release. Watson suffers the torment of modern man: Bereft of faith, hope, or charity, he dwells in the purgatory of the will, forever demanding, forever frustrated. It is perhaps the most remarkable account of a mind in confinement since Richard II paced the stones of Pomfret Castle.

> *William Grimes, in a review of "Watson's Apology," in* VLS, *No. 39, October, 1985, p. 5.*

Marilyn Stasio

All the world loves a murderer. Victorian society, in particular, rationalized its morbid fascination with murderers by drawing uplifting moral lessons from their crimes. As early as 1827, Thomas De Quincey wrote on murder as a fine art arguing that the murderer's passion was a heroic transcendence of a milquetoast age. Henry James greatly admired "the dear old human and sociable murders" chronicled by his contemporary William Roughead, for the light they shed "on manners and conditions . . . the testimony to manners and morals." . . .

What, then, can be made of the 1871 case of John Selby Watson, an elderly schoolmaster in London who returned home from church one Sunday to thump his wife to death? To the crime chroniclers of his own age, this unprepossess-

ing murderer was largely a footnote. Poor dull Watson lacked the transcendent passions of the lusty wife-murderer Dr. Thomas Neill Cream: he had none of the subtlety of that sexy poisoner Madeleine Smith; and no scholar could make a case for his being a by-blow of the sociological barbarisms of industrial England. It also seems unlikely that Watson's career and subsequent fate will tweak the interest of the present-day public, which stands in awe only of serial and sex murderers. . . . (p. 7)

In *Watson's Apology,* Beryl Bainbridge has taken the historical facts of this mundane murder case and, by supplying "the motives of the characters, their conversations and their feelings," fashioned them into an enthralling novel about a pernicious marriage. It is an extraordinarily lively work of the imagination because the facts themselves remain so obdurately dull.

According to the court depositions and newspaper accounts included in the story, J. S. Watson was a solid specimen of middle-class respectability. A clergyman "of good character" as well as a classics scholar, he was for 22 years the headmaster of a grammar school, until his summary dismissal from that post cut off his career and income. He had few friends and no children of his marriage with Anne Armstrong, the daughter of a ruined Dublin banker. According to the same sources, Mrs. Watson was a holy terror who drove her husband batty with her black moods and fierce tempers.

In her previous novels, which include *Injury Time* and *The Bottle Factory Outing,* Miss Bainbridge trained her fine irony on people whose disorderly emotions turn them into ridiculous figures. Applying her probe to the wretched Watson, she draws an almost indecently intimate character study of a man who loses his equilibrium when he falls in love with a woman's glittering gypsy eyes. Confounded by his wife's passionate, theatrical ways (and despairing that "she was incapable of reading a book"), he evades her needs, crawling ever deeper into his uncommunicative privacies, leaving her to howl outside the door.

In the early stages of her dissection of this ill-fated match, Miss Bainbridge parcels out her brilliant insights evenly: "She had overestimated his faculty for understanding; he had always underestimated her capacity for feeling," Anne realizes during one of her less truculent moods. Up to a point, the author also finds a dreadful hilarity in the pathetic fumblings of both parties throughout their marriage. One hardly knows whether to laugh or cry when the obtuse Watson defends his habitual yawns during his wife's conversation as "a muscular spasm, a dependence of the platysma myoides, or what is known as the misorius Santorini."

But as these petty outbursts multiply and the domestic tensions intensify, it is Watson to whom Miss Bainbridge holds out her arms. "My marriage has destroyed me," he whimpers as he stumbles deeper into melancholia. "I am buried under trivialities."

As we have come to expect of this dazzling miniaturist, Miss Bainbridge is at her most penetrating when she dwells on the very minutiae that oppress Watson—a trip to the dentist, the family dog scratching at the door, a small matter of horseflies. They all add up to a character study of terrible sad beauty. One wishes only that she had listened more acutely to Anne Watson's complaint: "I have become invisible." For all her compassion for poor Watson's unarticulated miseries, she's a bit miserly with her sympathy for Anne, who had to howl like a vixen to make herself heard. In the end, Miss Bainbridge almost makes us forget who made the glitter go out of those gypsy eyes. (pp. 7, 9)

Marilyn Stasio, "He Hid, She Howled," in The New York Times Book Review, *October 20, 1985, pp. 7, 9.*

Michele Slung

The impulse which draws writers to recreate long-ago murders in their fiction is not difficult to understand: here is a bloody drama that has been played out, yet the curtain can always be rung up again and the actors put once more through their paces.

Not only, then, is the author omniscient in the usual manner but now holds sway over persons who actually witnessed, suffered or committed unspeakable acts. Says Beryl Bainbridge, in her brief prefatory note to *Watson's Apology* which explains that it is based on a true Victorian case, "What has defeated historical inquiry has been the motives of the characters, their conversations and their feelings. These it has been the task of the novelist to supply."

And so she does, in typical Bainbridge fashion—the meticulous accumulation of unsettling small events, the persistent sounding of off-key notes, the imaginative instinct for the place where banality and derangement intersect. Thus, what might be remarkable for another writer, that the crime—an elderly man kills his elderly wife—which inspired the book is so very ordinary, is for her its consummate feature.

Watson's Apology opens with six peculiar letters of courtship, sent by an obviously unworldly and awkward schoolmaster to an impoverished old maid. Though they were never introduced, John Selby Watson has continued to cherish the memory of Miss Anne Armstrong since once catching a glimpse of her many years before. Deciding at last to marry, he can think only of the entrancing figure dressed in some bright shade of pink or lilac and "that . . . same husky intonation of voice which he had picked out above all others in that crowded drawing-room in Marlborough Street."

Not exactly an unlikely match—each would otherwise remain single—it is, nonetheless, according to Bainbridge's psychological portraiture, doomed from the very start. The foreshadowing is hardly subtle, but the reader, like the two inept lovers, is both mesmerized and disoriented at the same time. Perhaps, even, it is the disorientation itself which casts the spell.

At their second meeting, Watson watches the face of his bride-to-be who is, of course, something quite different from his memory of her, and it seems to him "that when she looked at him directly the melancholy little room with its dusty curtains and dark linoleum was swept by flame." For her part, Anne forces herself "to look sympathetically at Watson, but it [is] a terrible effort." Still, within four

days, they join their lives together and for nearly 30 years more exist in a state of mutual torment.

Neither of them, for entirely different reasons, dwells altogether in the realm of reality. United by deep, thwarted yearnings to love and be loved, Watson and Anne struggle to communicate in a world where today's easily tossed-off jargon of self-realization, the language of Relationship, hasn't yet been invented. "She had overestimated his faculty for understanding; he had always underestimated her capacity for feeling."

When we hear this analysis, for example, it's hard to tell whether it is Bainbridge's authorial voice speaking, or Anne's own recognition. If it is the latter, though, what good does it do her? She, like her husband, is incapable of connecting self-awareness to action, and any efforts made by either in the direction seem like a sort of dementia.

This, added to the impossibility of the one seeing the other as he/she actually is created; a marital dance of death relentlessly choreographed by Bainbridge. Fascinated as ever by the hollow cavities where lie human pain, she steadily marks the ugly moments in which, for the luckless Watsons, frustration and bitterness take the place of any simple companionability.

The story of these two pathetic creatures is unfolded in Bainbridge's tantalizing style, which gives the reader the impression that something is happening just out of earshot, some detail which would make it all come right or at least render it less allusive and opaque. It's creepy, sad and suspenseful, all at once, the way she summons up the wraiths of "the strange murder at Stockwell," and the confusion between victim and villain is deliberate, given this 20th-century backward look. (pp. 14-15)

Bainbridge, by choosing such a commonplace but once celebrated crime, reveals the inevitable forgetfulness of a public which lusted for details, then turned its attention quickly elsewhere. Inside the gory, outward sensation, she reminds us, were fully dimensional people—by her reckoning, a querulous spinster *manqueé* and a pedantic hack who tried, haplessly, to love one another. (p. 15)

Michele Slung, "Strange Murder at Stockwell," in Book World—The Washington Post, *November 17, 1985, pp. 14-15.*

Peter Kemp

Only one of the stories collected in *Mum and Mr Armitage* is actually set during the Second World War (two others occur just after it, and the remaining nine are located in a contemporary world of tower blocks and Leisure Centres). Over all of them, though, the atmosphere of that period seems to linger. Surrounded by a hinterland of menace, characters soldier on in a chirpy, chin-up way. Bouts of chummy cheeriness are favoured—so are make-do enjoyments: even at a modern street carnival, trestle-tables offer a nostalgic array of hand-knitted tea cosies, fudge and rag-dolls.

Homely old-fashioned Englishness is the element in which Beryl Bainbridge's imagination thrives. It's no accident that the collection's flimsiest work—a lightweight piece called **"The Man Who Blew Away"**—is a cosmopolitan fantasy unballasted by those gritty everyday oddities her fiction usually delights in digging out. The other tale of the supernatural included here is firmly grounded in the realm of Minis and municipal tennis-courts. For all its uncanny flourishings, it's basically a spirited account of that *petit bourgeois* combativeness that Bainbridge never tires of scrutinizing.

Edgy egotism keeps breaking through matiness in these stories. Though communal activities—nights out, parties, dances—are stressed, individuals constantly fall out of step. Scuffles for position and dissatisfaction with partners regularly disrupt social occasions. Rancour and revelry get snarled up with particular ferocity in [**"Mum and Mr Armitage"**, the only story] specially written for this collection and a vintage specimen of Bainbridge fiction. Crammed with the period lumber she loves—a stuffed stoat is used to administer a *coup de grâce*—it trains a beady eye on the eventual discomfiting of two practical jokers who've long been leaving a trail of humiliation and palpitation in their guffawing wake. Come-uppances often come up in these stories. Another exercise in blackly comic retaliation shows a man, asked to take the part of a clairvoyant at a local fête, suddenly seeing how he can use this to exact a long-deferred revenge [in **"Through a Glass Brightly"**].

Like most of the pieces here, that story moves through nicely calculated permutations to an emphatic concluding twist that fastens everything into place. Another hallmark of the stories is a fondness for comic effects achieved by highlighting rather lowly topographical reference—as with "the two middle-aged men from Wigan—they were always referred to as 'the lads'—who habitually wore shorts in the hotel". Catching background figures in an artless-sounding but epitomizing thumb-nail sketch is a technique that Bainbridge relishes. . . .

Sprightly in tone, the stories are bleak-ish in content. A jaunty observer of human quirks and absurdities, Bainbridge also penetrates to deeper warpings and aberrations. One of the baleful, retarded pranksters in the title story has, it is remarked, eyes that are "frightening, not for what they had seen, but for what they hadn't." A later piece takes this notion further as a sinister bland narrator, given to unappetizing locutions like "I've never been enamoured of fruit", not only reveals himself to be a loveless monster but, without realizing it, makes clear that he has unknowingly hounded his wife into a mental breakdown and her lover to his death. Another oblique murderer—who specializes in ushering forlorn tenants of a rented room to suicide by his malign mixture of sympathy and suggestion—appears in the final work, **"Helpful O'Malley"**. At first playing on surface peculiarities, it seems, the stories then go on to delve deeper, often disinterring something particularly grisly in a final trenchant thrust. One of the narratives sets a cranky old woman's catch-phrase, "I don't like the sound of that", echoing comically through a spry account of her life, only to alter its timbre in the closing moments: as earth hits the lid of the woman's coffin her grand-daughter shiveringly reflects, "I didn't like the sound of it".

Terminal graveness of this kind opens up in a number of these lively stories. Solitaries snuff it in a bed-sitter filled with gas fumes; one man shoots himself with the revolver he's kept as a war-souvenir; another expires during a performance of *Peter Pan,* just as Tinkerbell is being resuscitated by the audience's applause. Usually, though, it's more mundane glumness that comes in for attention: long-harboured domestic grudges, reined-in resentments between friends, routine social callousness. "Life wasn't all roses" is the last line of one of these stories. With mocking nonchalance, its thornier aspects are pressed home in all of them.

Peter Kemp, "Beneath the Make-Do and the Mundane," in The Times Literary Supplement, *No. 4316, December 20, 1985, p. 1463.*

Neil Berry

[Beryl Bainbridge was raised] in the 1940s and '50s, the so-called Age of Austerity. And if her fiction typically seems soaked in the grey, ration-book atmosphere of the period, that does nothing to lessen its topicality in our new Age of Austerity, which is not discontinuous with the last one. Bainbridge's characters are a luckless, sometimes brutish lot. **"Bread and Butter Smith"**, a story in her recent collection of short fiction [*Mum and Mr. Armitage: Selected Stories*], set in post-War Liverpool and evocative of its grin-and-bear-it spirit, concerns a non-communicating couple who used to spend Christmas in a Liverpool hotel. The husband/narrator recalls how Smith, a fellow guest, would join them for Christmas dinner, always eating his regular four slices of bread and butter along with a few cuts of breast. Growing exasperated with the attention Smith pays to his wife, the husband fabricates for her a murky private life. The point, we gather, is that Smith is a prude who confines his romantic aspirations to sedate dances with respectable married ladies. With chilling imperceptiveness, the husband mentions that Smith killed himself and that his wife ended up in a mental hospital. Smith, apparently, had been an annual ray of light in her otherwise dim existence.

Smith's isn't the only suicide in these stories. The concluding tale, **"Helpful O'Malley"**, deals with a seedy rent-collector who inveigles lonely girl tenants into gassing themselves. But Beryl Bainbridge isn't always so gruesome, though her forte is black comedy sustained by unfaltering irony. The funniest moments in her fiction stem from the embarrassments incurred by extra-marital sex. In **"The Worst Policy"**, neurotic, self-conscious Sarah has contrived at last to meet her fancy man by borrowing a friend's house for the afternoon. As they begin to grapple with one another, the friend's son, for whom Sarah reserves a long-standing loathing, suddenly clambers in through the window.

The world of Beryl Bainbridge, full of shabbiness and struggle, offers little scope for personal happiness or for social harmony. In dingy, cluttered rooms her knobbly, demoralised, utterly unheroic characters blunder from one humiliation to the next. Inadequates to the last man and woman, they appear victims of a cripplingly limited culture. (p. 55)

Neil Berry, "Stepping Eastward," in Encounter, *Vol. LXVI, No. 5, May, 1986, pp. 55-8.*

Lorna Sage

[Bainbridge's novel *Filthy Lucre*] was the cause of much innocent amusement even before publication, when a story went round that the Booker judges had perused their proof copies with disappointment and dismay, not having realised that it was written in 1946 when Beryl Bainbridge was 13. Not a likely story—though not quite impossible, since its style is just about jaded enough to pass for a failed joke.

But then, as the preface points out, 'difficult' children in the 1940s scribbled away to themselves rather than being sent to psychiatric social workers. And (one might add) few of them were taught at school to write *like children,* to be fresh, direct, impressionable and so on. The novel is set in the mid-nineteenth century and written in a Dickensian grand style, spiced with Defoe and Stevenson, and is positively middle-aged in its outraged overview of the messes its characters make of their lives.

The plot starts with a City law firm, a misunderstanding about legacies, and a deathbed promise of vengeance. It then rushes headlong to the New World, and across three generations, before dishing out rewards and punishments in a playful, vindictive fashion which is credited to the Almighty ('God is not mocked') but which is disconcertingly prophetic of Ms Bainbridge in her prime. There are a great many 'characters' most of whom have something picturesquely wrong with them (not least their names). Dickens's influence is clear, too, in the author's spectacular lack of interest in the 'straight' romantic characters. Someone only has to be described as honest, or truthful, or (best of all) 'sunny-haired' to be marked for destruction.

There's no mistaking the bits where 13-year-old Beryl is really having fun ('shudder, reader'). Perhaps her most striking invention is Rupert Bigarstaff, misanthrope, animal-lover, charismatic healer—a murderer who does people in out of visionary principle, saying things like 'That was not violence, Gasper Liverwick, that was tidiness.' . . .

But I shouldn't make it sound quite so consistently and unnaturally black. Really, the effect is more like a tomboy on paper. Writing obviously seemed a manly business to Beryl. As she boasts in the preface, *her* very first stories were about an old sea-dog called Cherry-Blossom Bill, while her little friends tended to write about 'fairies living inside marigolds.' How lucky we are that no child-psychologist went to work on her penchant for grey whiskers and wooden legs.

Lorna Sage, "Not a Likely Story," in The Observer, *October 5, 1986, p. 25.*

Lindsay Duguid

Filthy Lucre, written in 1946 when the author was thirteen, comes quite late in Beryl Bainbridge's juvenile literary career. . . . It was written, Bainbridge tells us in her disarmingly detached introduction, as a distraction from the bickering of her mother and father, there being no television in those days. It is dedicated to the author of *Dismal England.*

Clearly a book that demanded to be written, *Filthy Lucre* displays few compositional uncertainties, few of those enemies of promise with which adult authors have to contend. The plot—a complicated saga, stretched over several generations, involving inheritance, impersonation, revenge, shipwreck, drunkenness and many deaths—has, one feels, hardly been a bother at all. What Bainbridge is really interested in is style, and it is here that she really lets herself go. The book bursts with dramatic touches and with the recklessly abundant vocabulary of early adolescence. . . .

The influence of Dickens is everywhere apparent—in the broad canvas, the large cast of characters (the Ledwhistle family tree which the author kindly provides contains sixteen members, some neatly characterized as "A spinster", "A drunkard", "A girl" and "No one important") and, above all, the frontal address to the reader: "Shudder reader for it is none other than . . . "; "God is not mocked"; and at one stage, "Read more slowly". But the exotic settings, which include a tropical island where oil is discovered and a Virginian plantation echoing to snatches of Negro spirituals, recall Defoe and Stevenson. The piling on of dramatic pressure and the technical virtuosity that Bainbridge shows in her use of flashbacks are alarmingly confident, and it is somewhat reassuring to find that she thinks a mongoose is a large bird.

The whole has an appealing naivety which her publishers have done their best to preserve. Now that Beryl Bainbridge has grown up, her best friend's husband has produced the book for her, artfully reproducing the family tree, correcting the spelling and even having her own detailed and striking illustrations redrawn.

Lindsay Duguid, "Shudder Reader," in The Times Literary Supplement, *No. 4359, October 17, 1986, p. 1168.*

Michiko Kakutani

The postwar England depicted by Beryl Bainbridge in such quick, pointed novels as *The Bottle Factory Outing* (1975), *Injury Time* (1978) and *A Quiet Life* (1977) is a drab, depressing place where lives are circumscribed and expectations diminished. Families tend to be the source of suffocation rather than sustenance, and romance, too, has a way of dwindling into comedy instead of blossoming into hope. In fact, most of the author's characters live blankly with a vague cloud of menace hovering over their heads.

A similar mood and landscape can be found in the stories of this collection, *Mum and Mr. Armitage.* The tennis courts where the ill-fated yuppies in **"Beggars Would Ride",** meet for their twice-weekly games are full of potholes and surrounded by grounds strewn with broken glass and beer cans. The garden belonging to Margaret and Richard in **"People for Lunch"** is so tiny that their outdoor luncheon must take place alongside some unsavory garbage bins. And the building that figures so prominently in **"Helpful O'Malley"** is one of those dark, clammy apartment houses in which coin-fed gas heaters supply insufficient warmth.

Obviously, such bleak settings are meant to mirror the emotional emptiness of the characters' lives. Nearly everyone in this collection suffers from alienation, loneliness or suppressed rage; not one has what could be considered a satisfying day-to-day existence or a sustaining relationship. Miss Emmet, an old lady from the Midlands, expects "to be left out of things"; and when she's finally invited along on an outing, disaster (in the form of a dangerous encounter with a dog) is nearly the result. A mousy young woman rents a small room on the second floor of a rooming house and, like her predecessors in that flat, commits suicide by shutting the windows and turning up the gas. . . .

For that matter, those folks with families or friends are hardly much better off in Ms. Bainbridge's view. In **"The Longstop,"** members of the Jones family speak to themselves in self-absorbed monologues that rarely intersect in anything resembling a real conversation; and in **"Perhaps You Should Talk to Someone,"** talks between mother and daughter devolve into "just words." "If you ask me," says the daughter,

> it's her that can't communicate. She's so screwed up about this trust thing that she's been rendered practically speechless except for muttering about tidiness and such like. She's like to tell me to work harder at school but she knows it's a losing battle.

In an effort, no doubt, to escape the confines of home life, some of Ms. Bainbridge's people turn to adultery or shadowy couplings, but more often than not, these liaisons also become cheerless affairs. The one between Margaret and Charles in **"People for Lunch"** seems to consist entirely of nasty, furtive meetings and acrimonious exchanges of guilt; and the one between Pinkerton and Agnes in **"The Man Who Blew Away"** begins with angry recriminations and ends with feigned affection. "Pinkerton said he wanted to buy Agnes a piece of jewelry," Ms. Bainbridge writes.

> They both knew that it was his farewell gift to her. She pretended that it was kind of him. When she returned to England he would telephone her once or twice to ask how she was, perhaps even take her out to lunch, and then the relationship would be over. Something had changed in him; he no longer needed her to berate him, and she was too old to change her ways.

Reading these stories, it's clear that Ms. Bainbridge has a dry, dark-humored wit as well as a sharp eye for incongruous details. She notices things like a woman's turban "printed all over with the heads of dogs" and the Christmas cards knocked off the mantlepiece by a fierce wind. But while her gift for irony has made for some maliciously comic novels, it tends, in the more compressed form of the short story, to result in implausible and overly tricked-up plots. Several of the stories in this collection rely on contrived deaths or descents into madness to underscore their characters' sad plights. Others pivot around heavy-handed reversals that fail to encompass the ambiguities and complexities of life.

"Beggars Would Ride" is a flimsy *Twilight Zone* episode, in which a clumsy estate agent discovers the mystical powers of an ancient talisman. **"Through a Glass Brightly"** uses a fortuneteller's crystal ball and a surprise ending, reminiscent of O. Henry, to relate the story of a cuckold's revenge. And **"The Longstop"** ends on a similarly ironic note when a man is bopped on the head with a cricket ball tossed by his hated father-in-law.

To make matters worse, these stories share a severely limited image bank. At least three of them (**"Mum and Mr. Armitage," "Through a Glass Brightly"** and **"The Man Who Blew Away"**) feature similar scenes depicting trees or flowers planted in ugly concrete tubs; and two of them (**"People for Lunch"** and **"The Worst Policy"**) use the same narrative setup, in which an obnoxious teen-age boy harasses an adulterous couple. In the end, such repetitions do a disservice to Ms. Bainbridge's usually agile talent. Indeed, they contribute to the feeling that these stories are nearly as attenuated as the world portrayed by the author.

> *Michiko Kakutani, "Cheerless Affairs," in*
> The New York Times, *July 11, 1987, p. 18.*

Elizabeth Ward

Bainbridge's many novels carry a curiously bitter aftertaste. Like ashes, they sting, but also put you in mind of death.

Like the novels, too, the stories gathered in *Mum and Mr. Armitage* define a highly particularized world. Bainbridge casts her net wide in search of subjects, settings and characters—from a postwar Christmas at Liverpool's Adelphi Hotel to a lunchtime game of tennis (interrupted by magic) in modern Hampstead or the strange spiritual odyssey of a contemporary English adulterer abroad—but all the stories distill an unmistakably English quality of rooted eccentricity. Possibly not since Joyce's *Dubliners* has there been so depressing a group-portrait of people trapped and stunted by their cultural circumstances.

Still, Monty Python rather than James Joyce is Beryl Bainbridge's true compatriot and her satirical gift, based on an unerring eye for the killer detail—"the stuffed stoat on the mantelpiece"; offspring who are constantly "gone hop-picking"—has the effect of relieving the stories' otherwise relentless melancholy. Thus the best of them juggle menace with hilarity in a surprisingly pleasurable, if slightly unsettling, balancing act.

The title story [**"Mum and Mr. Armitage"**] is the most sheerly Pythonesque. A group of ill-assorted holidaymakers of all ages is staying in a hotel in the Welsh border country sometime after World War II (a favorite Bainbridge period). Coquettish Mum and her "companion" Mr. Armitage are the life of the party for everybody but Miss Emmet, a "thin lady from the Midlands," the only one apparently aware of the subtle malice underlying Mum's frenzied antics. When Mum finally gets her shocking come-uppance at Miss Emmet's hands, it is only mildly ironic that in this instance Mum was not personally responsible for Miss Emmet's injury.

"Clap Hands, Here Comes Charlie" is a genteel little horror story which also lodges thrillingly in the mind. "Two weeks before Christmas, Angela Bisson gave Mrs. Henderson six tickets for the theatre. Mrs. Henderson was Angela Bisson's cleaning lady. 'I wanted to avoid giving you money,' Angela Bisson told her. ' . . . Somehow the whole process is so degrading.' " Mrs. Henderson, who "had never, when accepting money, felt degraded," nevertheless takes her family—scoffing husband, snooty son and daughter, obnoxious grandson—to a performance of *Peter Pan.* But then the gaudy pantomime being acted out on stage is counterpointed and mocked by the slow, unnoticed pantomime of Mr. Henderson's death by heart attack in the private darkness of the auditorium.

And what is one to make of **"Helpful O'Malley,"** a marvelously creepy tale of a tenant who, in the absence of the landlady, assiduously undertakes to rent out the difficult-to-let second floor room? Why had several recent occupants "moved on in the space of a few weeks"? Why were "none of those ever likely to come back"? It is chilling to speculate on O'Malley's interest in the free gas a broken meter supplies to that particular room. (pp. 3, 6)

Several of the stories, less flamboyant than these, focus on the furtive activities of suburban philanderers, a type which seems to fascinate Bainbridge. In **"People for Lunch,"** Margaret and Richard invite their toney friends Dora and Charles for a Sunday meal, which they are forced to hold al fresco, next to the rubbish bins, since their teenage son refuses to budge from the "telly" in the dining room. Before lunch is over, it is clear that relationships are more squalidly complicated than they appear. **"The Worst Policy"** dramatizes an amusing variation on the same scenario: a cheating wife contrives to entertain her lover in her best friend's bedroom, only to be caught in flagrante delicto by her friend's son, climbing in the bedroom window in pursuit of some underhanded activity of his own.

All dozen stories in **Mum and Mr. Armitage** are pretty funny; what limits them is that the laughter they prompt is so often uneasy. The humor which leavens these scenes of people getting, in various ways, their just deserts, is after all thoroughly dismissive. There are no second chances, no possibilities of redemption or life-altering revelation, such as Joyce or Flannery O'Connor or even Raymond Carver, all quite as keenly aware of life's little hampering threads, allow their characters. It is hard not to ask: even though the house is English, must it be so bleak? (p. 6)

> *Elizabeth Ward, "Beryl Bainbridge and Life's Little Ironies," in* Book World—The Washington Post, *July 26, 1987, pp. 3, 6.*

Anita Brookner

A self-denying ordinance seems to be operating in Beryl Bainbridge's new novel [**An Awfully Big Adventure**], which leaves out all of the plot and most of the characters. Signalled only by their names, these last seem fairly interchangeable; I had great difficulty in telling Grace from Dotty and Geoffrey from George. I was a little clearer on Meredith and Bunny, largely because they tend to be recognisable from other stories about provincial rep. Meredith is the one with the bow tie and the monocle, and Bunny is his friend, or even his 'friend', and together they run a theatre in Liverpool in the grim days after the second world war.

But perhaps I have misunderstood the story altogether: perhaps the main character—the only character—is Liverpool itself, ugly, dirty, damaged and deprived, and memorialised street by street and in loving detail by the author, who grew up there and was briefly, if I am not mistaken, in the theatre herself. The action of the story concerns a wave of anarchy in the fortunes of this not very illustrious company; the prime mover appears to be Stella, the 16-year-old heroine or poltergeist who brings about the downfall of all the leading players, ensnares the prodigious guest artist, and ruins every production with her gift of attracting attention and not knowing what to do with it.

Stories about women who are also witches seem to be issuing from Duckworth, in anorexic form, rather frequently these days. No doubt the idea of a woman possessing superior but also nefarious powers is one dear to the feminist heart, although if we are to take it seriously it would seem to proceed from a sense of frustration or inadequacy. The interesting thing about **An Awfully Big Adventure** is that the quirky and slightly perfunctory narrative hides another story which has its roots in the territory that produced that marvellous novel, **The Dressmaker.** The prodigious Stella, lethal to all those around her, is in fact a foundling. Her career is masterminded by Uncle Vernon and Lily, who are probably brother and sister, although this is never made clear, and who together run a fearful lodging house for commercial travellers, all of them afflicted with some form of disorder or deformity. Stella's mother was a bad lot who ran away after winning a competition for Miss Speaking Clock: obviously show business is in the blood. The child was abandoned in an empty house, in a cot surrounded by night lights. Stella's appeals to her vanished mother are not revealed until the final line of the novel and are all the more effective for that reason.

This then is the background. . . . It is all good quirky stuff and recognisably if bizarrely English. It is of course also the stuff of sadness, but sadness dressed up as grotesquerie, the two qualities which usually combine to give Beryl Bainbridge's novels a character far above the merely regional. They prove the curious fact that it is possible to feel nostalgia for something awful, and that the stuff of memory is so potent that it is simply not subject to alteration and continues to thrust its inconvenient head into all subsequent material.

There are signs here that glumness is winning. The residual story is fronted by the story about the luckless theatre company and its productions of *Dangerous Corner, Caesar and Cleopatra,* and *Peter Pan,* all sturdy English fare, with bleak comic effects thrown in. Bleak too is the absence of description, of particularity, which is denied to everyone and everything except the names of the streets, churches, and restaurants. A very strange novel indeed, gritty, sad, not quite realised. And a reminder that Beryl Bainbridge could, if she wanted, go all out for the darker effects, as she did in that strange and haunting novel, **Watson's Apology,** and thus restore integrity to a style which is beginning to look arbitrary and a little threadbare.

> *Anita Brookner, "Nostalgia for Something Awful," in* The Spectator, *Vol. 263, No. 8422, December 9, 1989, p. 37.*

Lindsay Duguid

An Awfully Big Adventure is a dark version of *The Good Companions;* the story of an orphan seeking a surrogate family in the raffish society of weekly rep. Its catarrhal young heroine, Stella, imaginative, illegitimate and with a talent for wringing the last drop of drama out of the smallest incident, progresses, thanks to a family connection, straight from elocution lessons with Mrs Ackerley to the post of assistant stage manager at the Liverpool Playhouse. Taught the practicalities by sad Bunny (stage manager) and salt-of-the-earth George (stage carpenter), before long she is running out for cigs and bets and bacon sandwiches for the cast and has fallen in love with the duffel coat and monocle of Meredith Potter (director). She also learns a lot about life. Not long after the production of *Dangerous Corner,* she is given a small part in *Caesar and Cleopatra,* but Stella does not become a star. Her most creative theatrical coup is at a matinée of *Peter Pan,* when she fails to re-illuminate the torch that represents Tinkerbell to the children who are clapping because they believe in fairies. . . .

Neither companionship nor true love—in this the book differs from J. B. Priestley's romance—are to be found among the backstage grime and casual behaviour; part of Stella's role as an innocent among adults is to show how far the world of make-believe extends behind the scenes. The personal lives of the members of the company are largely animated by self-delusion and unrequited love leading to histrionic displays: tears, rows and walkings out, an attempted suicide, even a broken leg. A great deal is made of loyalty and betrayal. The stagey speeches quoted from *Dangerous Corner* are only a shade more exaggerated than Meredith's telegram to his boyfriend: "Am in hell. Do ten years count for nothing. You must ring", or Dawn Allenby's farewell note which begins "Dear Swine". There is a grim layer of cruelty, too, beneath the bohemian glamour, but a combination of innocence and pragmatism makes Stella blind to it and she receives the various sticky sexual advances made to her with a similar lack of comprehension. In her reaction to losing her virginity—"I expect there's a knack to it. It's very intimate, isn't it?"—one can hear the mordant Liverpudlian glottal stop signifying low expectations. As might be expected, it is her passive presence rather than the spite and scheming of the players that causes the final tragedy.

Liverpool in this cautionary tale is a semiderelict city in the depths of its post-war gloom. Beryl Bainbridge, who was herself briefly employed by Liverpool Rep, is at home with its hills and squares and basements. She employs her matter-of-fact Gothic technique to depict the foggy Mersey, peeling paint and caved-in roofs, shop windows and telephone kiosks spots of light in the wet darkness. The actors live their lives from tea-room to hotel lounge to bar, and the theatre itself is always a haven. Outside the bombed churches, the black-clad Catholic priests are sinister bogeymen to Protestant Stella, while the city is inhabited by drunks, beggars and children with ringworm. Stella's home, the Aber House Hotel run by her Uncle Vernon, is full of disabled commercial travellers with terrible tales of their war experiences to tell.

Despite the grim setting and the characteristically bleak view of human nature, there is a mellowness about *An Awfully Big Adventure* which may come partly from the autobiographical element, but which is perhaps also due to its being set in the past. However sharp the details of poverty, of icy bathrooms and bugs and boils and kippers in digs, the retrospective picture has inevitably a blurred sepia halo. One laughs fondly as well as with relief. The themes and settings may be familiar ones in Bainbridge's work, but they have a new richness and complexity in this book. As well as memories and tradition (the actors constantly recall past triumphs and legendary disasters), it incorporates a significant text. The contradictions inherent in *Peter Pan,* its use as a Christmas play and the tension between its saccharine surface and what it tells of loss and death, are pointed out. The play has appeared in Bainbridge's fiction before, but here . . . it suggests an emotional subtext involving neglectful mothers and lost children which provides the key to one of the novel's several mysteries. The portrait of Stella as stubborn but infinitely malleable sounds a wistful note, as does the evocation of the yearning, genteel homosexuality of the period. Above all, there is much broad entertainment in the ripe backstage anecdotes, the theatrical characters and the jokes about Hoylake. Perhaps there is still some banked-up warmth in the props-room fire for this bitter season after all.

> *Lindsay Duguid, "The Lost Children of the Props-Room," in* The Times Literary Supplement, *No. 4254, December 15-21, 1989, p. 1385.*

Christina Koning

The title of Beryl Bainbridge's new novel [*An Awfully Big Adventure*] is from J. M. Barrie's *Peter Pan.* The awfully big adventure is, of course, death, and it is characteristic of Bainbridge's work that death is never far away, however much its grim exigencies may be obscured by euphemism or childish fantasy.

At one point in the novel, two of the characters, Stella and Meredith, are watching a rehearsal of Priestley's *Dangerous Corner.* Meredith asks Stella what she thinks it is about and her reply ("People loving people who love somebody else") nicely encapsulates the book's other main theme. Meredith, however, thinks the play is about death and our relation to it. Life, he says, is like a funeral procession, in which some of the mourners have temporarily fallen behind. . . .

If the novel's ultimate concern is with the latter of these two perceptions, its action is largely preoccupied with the former. Everyone in it is in love with somebody who loves somebody else, including Stella herself, the book's main protagonist.

Stella is 16, an ASM and "character juvenile" in a Liverpool repertory company in the 1950s. Abandoned by her mother as a child, she has been brought up by her aunt and uncle, who run a small hotel. Stella is old for her years, but cynicism does not preclude naivete, and much of the book's humour is derived from her misinterpretation of situations which are plain to everyone else.

The most serious of these misunderstandings is her infatuation with Meredith, the theatre manager. Her pathetic attempts to make him jealous result in an involvement with another member of the company, the ageing character actor, O'Hara, for whom the affair has disastrous consequences. Both relationships are sardonic illustrations of the adage that love is blind.

Blindness to the true state of affairs is a narrative device which works especially well in the context of the theatre, a world in which real and illusory passions have a tendency to become confused. The moment when Stella loses her innocence is not, therefore, when she loses her virginity to O'Hara—an almost perfunctory act—but one of much greater theatrical intensity, when she learns that Meredith is gay, and can never reciprocate her feelings for him.

This realisation is dramatised when Stella drops the torch with which she has been attempting to suggest the gradually fading presence of the dying Tinkerbell, during a performance of *Peter Pan.* It is of course, the moment she herself discovers, in more ways than one, that she can no longer believe in fairies. . . .

Bainbridge's evocation of period relies on the accretion of incidental detail rather than on the panoramic view. Postwar austerity is suggested in a few deft sentences: the difficulty of taking a hot bath in a run-down boarding house; the rarity value of Eccles cakes in a genteel tea-shop. The era's seedy glamour is conveyed, with similar economy, in the worldly gossip of a couple of ageing actresses; in the aroma of Capstan and eau de Cologne pervading a dressing-room.

> *Christina Koning, "Forgetting to Clap for Tinkerbell," in* Manchester Guardian Weekly, *December 24, 1989, p. 22.*

Peter Parker

Beryl Bainbridge's new novel [*An Awfully Big Adventure*] is set in the Liverpool of her youth amongst a down-at-heel repertory company. At one level, it is standard Bainbridge fare, an elegant and economical tragi-comedy, with a nice seasoning of the macabre and grotesque. Like many of Bainbridge's protagonists, 16-year-old Stella (a partial self-portrait of the writer as a young woman) stands at an odd angle to the world. Her Uncle Vernon, who has brought her up, is so alarmed by her character that he propels her towards a career in the theatre . . .

Stella is not really in control of her feelings, at one moment over-reacting wildly to some minor upset, at another remaining eerily impassive during experiences that others would regard as traumatic. She attends the funerals of strangers in order to give grief a dummy run; it is as if everything she does and feels is a rehearsal for real life. 'It wasn't my fault,' she says of the tragedy she precipitates in her quest for experience. 'I'll know how to behave next time. I'm learning.' Her unsentimental education in the complexities of adult relationships forms the core of the novel.

Bainbridge was herself an actress before turning to writing, and the dismal world of 1950s provincial rep is deftly recreated: squalid digs and faded tea-rooms, cameraderie and forced gaiety, *Dangerous Corner* and *Caesar and Cleopatra.* She captures perfectly the atmosphere not only of camp banter and theatrical bitchiness, but also of genuine

pathos, where no amount of greasepaint can mask despair. Appropriately in a novel about a profession in which looks count for much, Bainbridge is particularly good at describing physical details—a sleeveless dress exposing the slack flesh of an upper arm, or the actress 'whose features were a little too Frinton-on-Sea to suggest Cleopatra'; she also provides a memorably revolting description of a sexual encounter in a cinema. As well as being extremely funny, the book is also beautifully written, particularly in its luminous description of an impoverished, postwar Liverpool.

An Awfully Big Adventure not only takes its title from *Peter Pan* (Peter's brave salute to death at the end of Act III), but uses Barrie's dark masterpiece as a constant source of reference. . . . The wilful figure of 'The Boy Who Wouldn't Grow Up', first seen on the stage in 1904, has survived to haunt generations less innocent than the one that ended up in the trenches. Indeed, *Peter Pan* is intimately concerned with the death of innocence. . . .

Bainbridge is alert to the disturbing intimations of sexuality which tick through the play with rather more menace than the crocodile's clock, and the 'corruption' of minors forms an important strand of her story. Like Barrie's eponymous, other-worldly hero, Stella has apparently been abandoned by and is looking for her mother. She also, like Peter, inhabits a disconcerting limbo, neither wholly a child, nor yet an adult. Further echoes haunt the book: one character, hoping to impress, delivers a verdict upon the lead actor's performance as Hook which is lifted wholesale from Daphne du Maurier's account of the impression made by her father in the role in 1904. Similarly, Meredith's exposition of *Dangerous Corner* appropriates Barrie's notebook entry about death: 'One who died is only a little ahead of the procession all moving that way. When we round the corner we'll see him again. We have only lost him for a moment because we fell behind, stooping to tie a shoe-lace.' This image reverberates throughout the book, with increasing irony, until the very last page.

This may be an awfully short novel, but it packs in more than many books twice its length. Bainbridge's laconic narrative builds unobtrusively to a terrific ending, which itself depicts a small-scale massacre of the innocents—or, at any rate, of innocence (including the reader's own). *An Awfully Big Adventure* is a marvellous book, showing a novelist in absolute command of her material. Fizzing with energy and black humour, it may be prescribed as the perfect post-Christmas pick-me-up.

> *Peter Parker, "Straight on Till Mourning," in* The Listener, *Vol. 123, No. 3147, January 11, 1990, p. 25.*

John Berryman

1914-1972

(Born John Smith) American poet, biographer, novelist, critic, and editor.

Berryman is best known as the author of *The Dream Songs,* an unconventional, innovative poem sequence often compared to Walt Whitman's *Leaves of Grass* for its magnitude and uniquely American voice. Credited as an early practitioner of such postmodern techniques as unreliable narration, multiple viewpoints, and pastiche, Berryman created fragmentary verses that reflect his view of the chaotic nature of existence. Berryman is associated with both the "Middle Generation" of poets, those who came to maturity between the World Wars, as well as with such "Confessional" poets as Sylvia Plath and Robert Lowell, who wrote intense lyrics reflecting their volatile emotional states. Berryman's distinctive verse encompasses a broad range of subject matter, occasional use of strict, traditional forms, and a skillful mixture of pathos, farce, and sentimentality. Influenced by W. B. Yeats, Gerard Manley Hopkins, and W. H. Auden, Berryman's poetry has been described as nervous, humorous, and difficult. Edwin Morgan commented: "Berryman is a noted example of the poet who is hard to like and equally hard to forget. He drags his reader protesting almost continuously through a landscape of intense, jagged, contorted, often obscure, often touching subjectivity; no one conveys better the sheer *mess* of life, the failures and disappointments, betrayals and jealousies, lust and drunkenness, the endless nagging disjunction between ambition and reality." Much of the critical attention Berryman's work received in the 1980s focused on the literary and biographical sources of *The Dream Songs,* as well as its themes and motifs.

Berryman's experiences played a crucial role in determining the subject and form of his poetry. He was born John Smith in McAlester, Oklahoma, and was twelve years old when his father committed suicide. His mother quickly remarried, and his surname changed from Smith to Berryman. As an adolescent, Berryman attended a private school in Connecticut where he was bullied by fellow students and unsuccessfully attempted suicide. At Columbia University in New York, Berryman studied poetry under Mark Van Doren, whom he considered his mentor. He received an academic fellowship to Cambridge University in England, where he studied Shakespeare and met Auden, Dylan Thomas, and the elderly Yeats. Berryman taught at various universities throughout his adult life, including Harvard, Princeton, and, from 1958 until his death, at the University of Minnesota. He was renowned as a charismatic and formidably intelligent teacher. Berryman's public demeanor contrasted greatly with the insecure and sometimes morbid personality found in much of his work. Like his friend Dylan Thomas, Berryman was given to outrageous public behavior, including drunkenness and inappropriate sexual conduct. Berryman was married three times, and, during the final two decades of his life, he struggled to overcome an alcohol and pill addiction. In 1972, he took his own life. Many literary historians believe

that the death of his biological father heavily influenced both Berryman's poetry and his life.

Much of the poetry Berryman produced in the 1940s is imitative of the highly allusive, impersonal verse favored by critics and academics at the time. Berryman's first collection, simply titled *Poems,* is characterized by well-crafted verse often focusing on other works of art rather than human concerns. Although noting the poems were products of an obviously educated and sensitive mind, critics generally found the pieces in *Poems* too studied and rhetorical to be moving. Berryman's second volume, *The Dispossessed,* was also faulted for these reasons. While critics generally agree that Berryman had yet to master the distinctive voices he emulated, "The Nervous Songs" from *The Dispossessed* are considered exceptional. Utilizing a flexible, though regular form, and taking the poet himself for its subject, "The Nervous Songs" are often seen as forerunners of *The Dream Songs.*

In 1947, Berryman began an adulterous affair with the wife of a Princeton graduate student. The intense feelings of guilt, joy, and pain he felt throughout this period inspired a frenzied outpouring of verse, which, when it was published twenty years later, became *Berryman's Sonnets.* Republished in the posthumous *Collected Poems 1937-*

1971 as *Sonnets to Chris,* these verses chronicle the ongoing affair in broken and twisted syntax mixed with archaic phrases within the form of the Petrarchan sonnet. Berryman's name for his lover in the sonnets, "Lise," was changed to "Chris," the real name of the woman who had been his lover, in *Collected Poems 1937-1971.* "Lise" is considered an anagram after the Elizabethan fashion for "lies." Although it was published after *Homage to Mistress Bradstreet* and *The Dream Songs, Berryman's Sonnets* is the poet's first successful incorporation of the events of his life into his art. Critics find the volume oddly split, however, between homages to Lise, who functions as the poet's Muse as much as his lover, and highly rhetorical attempts to invoke her presence, resulting in clever, sometimes ingenious, linguistic effects that are nonetheless considered devoid of the passion and energy that infuses the others. Brad Leithauser located the problem in this way: "Maybe because they feel so deliberately worked—the outcome of so effortful a grapple with language—they fail to convey what no successful sequence of love sonnets lacks: an outward-flowing passion. As Berryman contends with Berryman (the emerging poet of the freewheeling *Dream Songs* tussling with the receding poet of the straitened *Dispossessed*), his beloved Lise/Chris get nudged aside."

Homage to Mistress Bradstreet, Berryman's next published volume, is often viewed as a sublimation of his adultery and consequent guilt and remorse. This long poem blends historical facts regarding Anne Bradstreet's life with creative embellishments, as Bradstreet, the first American poet, is summoned by the speaker, who falls in love with her. Although Berryman's personal obsessions, including adulterous longings, loss, creative difficulties, God, and the poet's relation to his society, are thematic elements in *Homage to Mistress Bradstreet,* Bradstreet herself speaks, gives birth, and eventually dies within the parameters of the poem. Some critics accused Berryman of creating an elaborate mirror for his personal concerns, yet the poem is generally considered a successful work of art in which structure and theme cohere on a number of metaphorical levels. Gary Q. Arpin remarked: "*Homage to Mistress Bradstreet* is in many ways Berryman's central work, the breakthrough that fulfills earlier promises of genius and makes new promises for the future."

The Dream Songs is Berryman's most celebrated accomplishment. First published in two parts as *77 Dream Songs* and *His Toy, His Dream, His Rest,* several hundred dream songs have been published, including those collected in a posthumous volume, *Henry's Fate and Other Poems: 1967-1972.* Each song is comprised of three six-line stanzas of irregular rhyme and meter. The persona, variously called Henry House, Henry Pussycat, and Mr. Bones, shares similar life circumstances, experiences, and friends with Berryman, and is usually considered interchangeable with him. *The Dream Songs* is an ambitious amalgam of obscure allusions, twisted and fragmented syntax, and minstrel-show language. The tone of these songs ranges from comedy to pathos, and the series of elegies for Theodore Roethke, Delmore Schwartz, Randall Jarrell, and Sylvia Plath are considered among the best in the dream song mode. Topical issues are also a concern in some of the songs, including the deaths of such prominent figures as President John F. Kennedy and Rev. Martin Luther King. Death, particularly the suicide of Berryman's father, is

considered to overshadow this extended poem sequence. Unlike Walt Whitman's *Song of Myself,* one of Berryman's models, *The Dream Songs* does not contain a philosophy but rather an extended character study of a multifaceted, troubled, American persona.

Love and Fame and *Delusions, Etc.* are the last collections of Berryman's work published under his own direction. The poems collected in these two volumes mark a return to the lyric form, and, most critics agree, comprise the product of Berryman's waning poetic skills. Extremely personal in subject matter, the majority of these poems are memoirs in verse regarding such unusual poetic matters as money and Berryman's grades in school. Although some critics appraise the lyrics in these two collections as deliberately over-stated and, hence, ironic and witty commentary on the excesses, pain, and brutality of youth, neither *Love and Fame* nor *Delusions, Etc.* is accorded the place of *The Dream Songs* or *Homage to Mistress Bradstreet* in Berryman's *oeuvre.* His "Eleven Addresses to the Lord," which conclude *Love and Fame,* are an exception to this judgment, and are considered among the most moving and subtle religious poems in contemporary American literature.

Berryman also published a critical biography, *Stephen Crane.* This work and his unfinished novel, issued posthumously as *Recovery,* are often read in relation with his own life experiences. *The Freedom of the Poet* which contains Berryman's critical essays and short stories, has been well received.

(See also *CLC,* Vols. 1, 2, 3, 4, 6, 8, 10, 13, 25; *Contemporary Authors,* Vols. 15-16, Vols. 33-36, rev. ed. [obituary]; *Contemporary Authors Permanent Series,* Vol. 1; *Contemporary Authors Bibliography Series,* Vol. 2; *Dictionary of Literary Biography,* Vol. 48; and *Concise Dictionary of Literary Biography 1941-1965.*)

PRINCIPAL WORKS

POETRY

Poems 1942
The Dispossessed 1948
Homage to Mistress Bradstreet 1956
77 Dream Songs 1964
Berryman's Sonnets 1967
His Toy, His Dream, His Rest 1968
The Dream Songs 1969
Love and Fame 1970
Delusions, Etc. 1972
Selected Poems 1938-1968 1972
Henry's Fate and Other Poems 1967-1972 1977
Collected Poems 1937-1971 1989

OTHER WORKS

Stephen Crane (criticism) 1950
Recovery (novel) 1973
The Freedom of the Poet (essays) 1976

Martin Dodsworth

Even though with the publication of *His Toy, His Dream, His Rest* in 1969 Berryman was supposed to have finished writing the poem for which he devised the six-line dreamsong stanza, he went on writing dream songs, as though he could not bear to be parted from his own creation. Readers sense this ambiguous attitude to completion and to "finish" in the awkward ellipses and unexpectedly public privacies of his poetry. *The Dream Songs* have that capacity to shock and embarrass the reader aimed at by surrealist poets but rarely achieved; but the shock and embarrassment do not here translate themselves into an index of value—they do not, for example, identify themselves as aspects of a revolutionary energy, promising to refashion society. They provoke anxiety.

Berryman understood this perfectly, and one of the later songs, collected by John Haffenden in the posthumous volume *Henry's Fate,* addresses itself to the matter in his characteristic fashion:

> There's madness in the book. And
>   sanenesses,
> he argued. Ha! It's all a matter of control (and so forth)
>   of the subject.
> The subject? Henry House & his
>   troubles, yes
> with his wife & mother & baby, yes
> we're now at the end, enough.

Here he goes out of his way to tell us that the "subject" of *The Dream Songs* is not John Berryman but "Henry House"—it is not a reassuring assurance, because there is something patently evasive in the idea of *controlling* the subject: if it is a question of madness, then surely it is Berryman himself that needs taking in hand. Indeed, he cannot even invoke an over-riding sanity in his art—just "sanenesses" that may or may not counterbalance the undesirable force of unreason. It is difficult not to feel that something is still being fought out in Berryman's poetry that in the works of poets he admired, like Yeats and Eliot, finds a kind of resolution or composure. The unpremeditated air of the dream songs and their successors may be the creation of art, but it directs us to think more readily in terms of the case-history than of the poem, whether viewed as Romantic organism or Mayakovskian machine. . . .

Berryman rarely had much sense of the whole into which his poem-parts were to fit. His continuing to write dream songs even though *The Dream Songs,* his "long poem", was completed is symptomatic of an uncertainty of direction. . . . The *Sonnets* were begun well before Berryman knew that the series was to end unhappily: he started it in the middle of the adulterous affair whose unhappy ending it records. The poet changed his mind many times about the structure of *The Dream Songs:* should the model be Homer or Dante, Don Quixote or Joseph Campbell's *Hero with a Thousand Faces*? The model chosen should obviously imply an idea of the intrinsic nature of the poem itself: as one replaced another in his thoughts, surely the poem's nature altered. *Love & Fame* began as a set of racy autobiographical poems, for the writing of which their author repented half way through, converting the latter part of the book to an unpremeditated palinode. . . . It is not essential to the vindication of Berryman's art that we should believe conception and achievement in every case, large and small, to be at one with each other. Some poems and some books are always going to be better than others in the complete works: most readers will probably settle for the proposition that *The Dream Songs* is uneven and does not cohere, but it does not follow that it is not Berryman's finest work nor that he is not a very good and important poet. . . .

In these degenerate days, of course, it has become very difficult to say what poetic coherence is or may be. [In his *John Berryman: A Critical Commentary,* John] Haffenden consigns *Love and Fame* to luck and *The Dream Songs* to paradox; he judges *Homage to Mistress Bradstreet* to be held together by personal concerns of the poet, notably his guilt about adultery. It is necessary to go carefully here, as we are given much new and interesting information, but it seems to me that Haffenden's immersion in the poet's biography results in a false emphasis on the poem's cathartic role for Berryman. What matters, surely, is the extent to which this aspect of the poem takes precedence over others. The poem is about a woman who is a poet, and about a poet whose imagining of her in the past is a kind of love; its focal moment is her admission that she wants this poet brooding on her from the future as her lover. Love and poetry are here inextricably tangled, and it is wrong to give one primacy over the other. The poem's last stanza significantly joins the two and its final injunction might as well be addressed to the Idea of poetry itself as to any loved woman: "Hover, utter, still, / a sourcing whom my lost candle like the firefly loves". Haffenden deploys his biographical knowledge, as he conjures up his coherence in *The Dream Songs,* in order to reduce the burden of anxiety with which Berryman charged his poems. Referring the poems back to their maker or imputing an internal logic to them takes pressure off the reader. . . .

Berryman needs a critical commentary. His idiosyncratic poetry needs the readers whom that commentary might secure; for Berryman is emphatically one of the great difficult modern poets, as John Bayley, in the only really interesting essay about him (in the American journal *Salmagundi*), has made plain: "a new verse and a new self in it" [see excerpt below]. The anxiety to which that verse gives rise is of the kind that comes from facing the wholly new.

Berryman's novelty does not, however, isolate him in the history of modern literature; it is just that a different and larger perspective is needed to supplement John Haffenden's if we are to understand that poet fully. He might have followed up Gary Q. Arpin's suggestion that Berryman's style owes something to that of Corbière, for example; it hints at an interesting line of descent for the poet from the French poetry of the nineteenth century via Eliot and Allen Tate, who was in some sense Berryman's literary mentor. Among the poet's unpublished papers there is an essay on Eliot and France—this may permit our seeing more than a casual reference in the single citation of Corbière in the *Sonnets.*

The similarities are many, especially stylistic. Like Corbière (who was known by the fisherman of Roscoff as an "Ankou": Death, "Mr Bones" himself), Berryman has a taste for conspicuously unliterary language, and a willingness to identify himself with the poor and underprivileged, and he creates a new form of writing which, like Corbière's, thrives on its own subversiveness:

> . . . *ça c'est naivement une*
>
> *impudente pose;*
>
> *C'est, ou ce n'est pas ça: rien ou*
>
> *quelque chose*

Corbière's two greatest poems both make their contribution to **The Dream Songs,** "Le Poète Contumace" by its characterization of the poet as already dead and buried, but liable to resurrect at the wrong moment—

> *N'apparais pas, mon vieux, triste et*
>
> *faux déterré . . .*
>
> *Fais le mort si tu peux . . .*

—and "La Rhapsode foraine" by the directness with which religion, the image of St Anne, embodiment of centuries of passionate idealism, is brought face to face with the diseased and mutilated inhabitants of the world over which she reigns. Just so does Berryman ("Noises from underground made gibbersome, / others collected & dug Henry up") confront God himself with human miseries:

> did once the Lord frown down
> Upon her ancient cradle thinking
>
> 'This one
>
> will do before she die
> for two and seventy years of
>
> chipped indignities
>
> at least' and with his thunder
> clapped a promise?

The Dream Songs are written in reaction to a poetry which, like that of Yeats and Eliot, of Mallarmé, Rilke or Valèry, sought an impossible ideal: the appearance of perfection in an imperfect world. The stillness of the Chinese jar, the fire and the rose becoming one, are not for Berryman, but his poetry is a scarifying commentary on the effort at transcendence that is Symbolism. Indeed he was not himself able to abandon the quest for an absolute, though his Songs tilt at conventional formulations of it ("God's Henry's enemy"); the coherence of **Love & Fame** is not a matter of "luck" because conversion, the discovery of the absolute, is a perpetual possibility for him. Berryman was trapped in a relative universe, one that he could not dismiss as *merely* relative, and it is the sense of the trap that essentially distinguishes his poetry from that of Corbière, whose own *épatement* of the bourgeoisie was a dandyish display of cool—liberty, not enslavement. Berryman was not only in himself anxious; his poetry is a channel by which anxiety is communicated to the world. He said of the Songs that they were not to be understood (in a relative world knowledge is not to be understood—at least, not as knowledge); they were "to terrify & comfort". Such comfort as they afford lies in their perceiving clearly the increasing area of uncertainty in human knowledge, in their being deconstructed texts *avant la lettre,* and perhaps in their revealing the fundamental state in a deconstructed world: loneliness.

> *Martin Dodsworth, "The Worries of Henry,"*
> *in The Times Literary Supplement, No. 4052,*
> *November 28, 1980, p. 1353.*

Roger Pooley

I start from the kind of praise that greeted the publication of **The Dream Songs.** Both Robert Lowell and Helen Vendler sketched Berryman's career to that date as a 'search for an inclusive style' (Lowell's phrase). Certainly Berryman managed to include in that work most of the virtues (and some of the vices) of his earlier writing. Only the act of historical imagination that is central to **Homage to Mistress Bradstreet** is lacking; and that is balanced by the kind of contemporary history that is involved in his urgent worried elegies for his own generation.

Inclusiveness is a particular characteristic of long poems written after Poe argued that long poems were no longer possible. *Song of Myself* (one of the models for **The Dream Songs**), *The Waste Land, The Cantos,* all of them face the problem of writing something in extended form by trying to write everything. If the signatures on things are not God's, they have to be the poet's. 'I am very ambitious' said Berryman when he compared his work to Whitman's and Eliot's. There is an important contrast with Whitman's achievement, however. In the work of containing everything in his writing Whitman also claims to be reconciling everything. Berryman and his Henry find that act of reconciliation impossible. **The Dream Songs** record a series of attempts to reconcile things. In the cautiously hopeful final Dream Song Berryman provides a gloss on that, in referring to the death of Ralph Hodgson. It is the last of a long series of elegies for dead poets. Hodgson was interviewed shortly before his death, and made the remark, 'I don't try to reconcile anything. This is a damn strange world'. Berryman liked the phrase so much that it appears twice in his published work, in the essay on Dreiser and in the second of the **"Eleven Addresses to the Lord",** the closing section of **Love and Fame.** His admiration thus stretched over twenty years, and perhaps illustrates as well as anything the felt need and the felt impossibility.

Christopher Ricks labelled this attempt at reconciliation 'theodicy'. That remains the single most illuminating critical comment on **The Dream Songs,** though it is plain that it leaves out much. The specifically theological questioning comes out in Berryman's characteristically allusive fashion, from the sycamore of Zaccheus in the first song to St Paul and the Church Fathers. But the theological comforts are few at this stage. While Berryman reflects often on the dark side of God, eroticism (Ricks's suggestion) and the Wordsworthian theodicy that suffering promotes personal development (Charles Thornbury's suggestion) produce most of the hope; to which add: 'Working & children & pals are the point of the thing' (**Dream Song 303**).

Berryman's inclusiveness is positive, energetic, erotic in the widest sense. But he is worried. The problems are those of theodicy (the theology and ethics of including the unaccountable suffering), of loss (the counterpart of eroticism), and of inspiration (as with all Romantic poets, the problems of the artist come centre-stage).

John Haffenden has a different emphasis: "Berryman's theodicy is based, I believe, on a text from St. Paul (Rom. 5:20) referred to in **Dream Song 20,** 'The Secret of the Wisdom' ":

> . . . We hear the more
> sin has increast, the more
> grace has been caused to abound.

'We hear' puts a certain distance between doctrine and experience anyway; but the doctrine, memorably reformulated by Berryman as 'the God of rescue', is most notable for its absence in the majority of the Dream Songs, and its distance in many of the poems in *Delusions Etc.* (the posthumous volume; the title uneasily recalls Freud's judgement on religion).

Grace *ought* to be central; one reason why it is not is that fear usurps most of the place reserved for sin in theodicy. Fear is a structural principle in *The Dream Songs,* generating much of its energy. But of Berryman's proposed theological solutions, two are heretical. One way is Origen's: that hell is empty. **Dream Song 56** celebrates it, **"The Facts & Issues"** in *Delusions Etc.* repeats it more agnostically, and there are other suggestions that hell cannot be any worse than the world as it is. Equally important is a kind of Pelagianism about work (numerous memoirs testify to Berryman the hard worker);

> He can advance no claim,
> save that he studied thy Word & grew afraid,
> work & fear be the basis for his terrible cry
> not to forget his name.
>
>   **(Dream Song 266)**

In his discussion of the controversy between Pelagius and Augustine, Peter Brown sees a 'cold streak' in the Pelagian reliance on works, thinking that the will can be stunned into good works by the example of Christ and the threat of punishment. Certainly it offers no lifeline to the self-disgusted alcoholic, and Berryman's adoption of the distinctly anti-Pelagian tenets of Alcoholics Anonymous as a framework for his novel *Recovery* recognizes it. It is a tendency towards Pelagianism rather than a constant part of his credo; but the combination with Origen gives disastrous substance to the reflection at the end of the sixth **"Address to the Lord"**:

> Now, brooding thro' a history of the early Church,
> I identify with everybody, even the heresiarchs

—disastrous because the combination of the two can make suicide a Christian act. If you carry on living you increase the amount of sin you commit; if you cannot work effectively any longer (literary judgements aside; if you *feel* you cannot) then how else will sin cease? And if hell is empty, or on this earth, then suicide does not carry the traditional sanction. The final section of **"Surveillance"**, written in 1971, puts it this way:

> The only really comforting reflection is not
> 'We will all rest in Abraham's bosom' & rot of that purport
> but: after my death there will be *no more sin.*

The logic carried on beyond the poetry to Berryman's suicide the following year, compounded with alcoholism and his obsession with the event, as committed by others including his own father. But it is odd to validate a reading of the poems with the biographical outcome, however closely the poet invites the connexion ('my strong disagreement with Eliot's line—the impersonality of poetry . . . it seems to me on the contrary that poetry comes out of personality'). What one can do is to parallel the theological/devotional problems with what happens to the language from the late Dream Songs to the final poems, and argue that the search for an inclusive reconciling style becomes the search for a vital Christian language. Paradoxically for such a complex and allusive writer, this is closely connected to Berryman's love/hate relationship

with plain simple statement. In some poems this plainness is seen as the distinctive feature of God's voice:

> After a Stoic, a Peripatetic, a Pythagorean,
> Justin Martyr studied the words of the Saviour,
> finding them short, precise, terrible, & full of refreshment.
> I am tickled to learn this.

Yet even here plainness is seen as emerging out of complexity, cutting through it, but needing its context.

Many of the stylistic devices in *The Dream Songs* depend for their effect on the reader recognizing that a plain statement has been avoided. Here is an example from **Dream Song 27**, where Henry promises pastoral comforts of a sort, Lycidas writing his own elegy to Milton, as it were:

> My friends,—he has been known to mourn,—I'll die;
> live you, in the most wild, kindly, green
> partly forgiving wood,
> sort of forever and all those human sings
> close not your better ears to, while good Spring
> returns with a dance and a sigh.

The agnostic hesitations are obvious enough: 'partly forgiving', 'sort of forever'. The inversions ('live you', 'close not') sound a little archaic, which fits the pastoral mood, though they might be attributed to the simple rarity of the imperative mood without the auxiliary 'do'. 'Sings' is a way of saying 'things' and 'songs' without saying either. The complete emotional effect is harder to describe. It might be described as precision, reticence, and unwillingness to say more than is truthfully felt; but that sounds uncomfortably like a description of Philip Larkin, and that is not the tone at all. Really these hesitations are like some features of the mask 'Henry' throughout *The Dream Songs,* an attempt to avoid sentimentality and plangency. (pp. 291-93)

By the end of *The Dream Songs* we have become aware of the success and failure of Berryman's directness within the idiom of the sequence as a whole. The key factor is restraint; when the emotional plangency of the plain self-pitying statement is surrounded by the black-face humour, or when it is transformed by witty allusiveness, or genuine sympathy for and questions about the fate of the dead poets, it works. It provides a core of seriousness and personality. But on its own, when Henry, in the penultimate song, is trying to dispose finally of his dead father's memory, it does not work. Like Sylvia Plath's "Daddy", which uses a similar strategy, it is too vehement to be convincing. The essence of plainness is restraint; the masters of plainness, like Ben Jonson, work by convincing us that the pyrotechnics of wit and emotion could have been invoked, but have been held back.

Another way of considering the matter would be to see plain statement as the natural idiom for concluding a certain sort of dramatic poem. The role of the black-face friend suggests comparisons with the comforters of Job ('the traditional Jewish jazz—namely, you suffer, therefore you are guilty') and the Fool in *King Lear* (which Berryman spent years editing). The Fool does his best to keep Lear sane, but he disappears from the climax of the play, much as the minstrel show fades from the end of *The Dream Songs.* The plain blunt speakers, Kent and Cordelia, are at last recognized for their worth. So far the parallel holds. But what of the note of repentance and self-knowledge in Lear's voice towards the end? Or Job's responding to God's voice with a simple statement of repentance, an admission that he has spoken of things he has not understood? To get from simplicity to repentance we have to read Berryman's final poems in *Delusions Etc.*

Joel Conarroe has said of the plain statements in that volume: 'These spontaneous laments of a man in distress make much of the surrounding verbiage sound cluttered, cranked out by a nervous, tinkering imagination'. That judgement would make them the opposite of those in *The Dream Songs.* But in context there is more to it than a spontaneity/complexity kind of opposition. "Vespers", for instance, is really all about trying to get out of the simple commands of Christ. So the tension between simple and complex syntax is an ethical one, between obedience and evasion. Compare:

> I have not done well.

with:

> Frantic I cast about abroad
> for avenues of out: Who really this this?
> Can *all* be lost, then? (But some do these things . . .
> I flinch from some horrible saints half the happy morn-
> ings—
> so that's blocked off.)

The technique is rather similar to some of Herbert's poems, like 'The Collar', though Berryman rarely comes to rest on the plain, assured, obedient statement as the earlier poet does. None the less, there is a new tone to those statements; 'I have not done well' would not be thinkable in *The Dream Songs,* not that sort of humility.

There is an example, quite out of character in some respects, of a very fine plain-style poem by Berryman, **"He Resigns"**: alarming that this should be a resting-place.

> Age, and the deaths, and the ghosts.
> Her having gone away
> in spirit from me. Hosts
> of regrets come & find me empty.
>
> I don't feel this will change.
> I don't want any thing
> or person, familiar or strange.
> I don't think I will sing
>
> any more just now;
> or ever. I must start
> to sit with a blind brow
> above an empty heart.

It is a dejection ode, a lament for the passing of inspiration. It is in a style that most of his poetry refuses, the restraint, the uncomplicated metre, the skills with run-on lines, phrasing and punctuation bent towards evenness rather than audacity. Apart from making the point that Berryman's plain style can produce a whole poem which steers clear of embarrassing self-indulgence, the poem also gives us a clue to Berryman's inclusiveness, which was our starting point. The picture in the first stanza is of a man still surrounded by the sources of his inspiration: his own increasing age, the recent deaths of many of his contemporaries, those literary heroes and reputations that haunt him, lost love and guilt. But he is unable to transform them by his singing because he no longer desires them. They find him empty.

Yet this new kind of plainness in *Delusions Etc.* is found

alongside a fascination with the grandeur of complexity, in particular the astronomical intricacies of pulsars and quasars, perhaps recalling the sense of power which is at least as important to a biblical theodicy like *Job* as is a God of love. There are times when God as the artist of all-inclusiveness and reconciliation takes over the burden from the human artist; but not for long:

> 'Behold, thou art taken in thy mischief,
> because thou art a bloody man' with horror
> loud down from Heaven did I not then hear,
> but sudden' was received,—appointed even
>
> poor scotographer, far here from Court,
> humming over goodnatured Handel's Te Deum.
> I waxed, upon surrender, strenuous
> ah almost able service to devise.

'Scotographer' means 'writer in the dark'.

The dead poets, notably Anne Bradstreet in the *Homage,* and Delmore Schwartz in *The Dream Songs,* had been potent sources of inspiration, anxiety, and anger. The artists celebrated in *Delusions Etc.,* Beethoven, Emily Dickinson, Trakl, Dylan Thomas, Frost, Gislebertus, and David (an eclectic mixture) produce some of the finest moments in the book. The poet's admiration is crucial to the way they work, but the self-comparisons are less intrusive, even when he is considering his own memories of his exact contemporary Dylan Thomas:

> Apart a dozen years, sober in Seattle
> 'After many a summer' he intoned
> putting out a fat hand. We shook hands,
>   How very shook to see him.

The tone is relaxed without being slack or uninventive. Part of the reason is that fragments of anecdote, phrases from the subject included, are pushed into the foreground with the same kind of technique as the plain phrases discussed above. And the anxiety about ranking, still present in the earlier *Love and Fame* poems, is not so urgent. Berryman's final lack of serenity has little to do with literary ambition.

The final poems, *Love and Fame* and *Delusions Etc.,* are not as substantial an achievement as *The Dream Songs;* rather, they deal with some of the problems raised by the idiom of that sequence. But that is not to relegate them to the status of footnotes to the masterpiece. They take some important steps forward in the areas of plain style and poetry and belief; and in doing so contain some of Berryman's most urgent and distinguished writing. (pp. 295-97)

Roger Pooley, "Berryman's Last Poems: Plain Style and Christian Style," in The Modern Language Review, *Vol. 76, No. 2, April, 1981, pp. 291-97.*

Alan Shapiro

The myth of the tragic artist, whose unhappiness is the inevitable price he pays for artistic power, was an article of faith for the poets of Berryman's generation. As Lowell wrote in his elegy for Berryman, "we had the same life/the generic one/our generation offered." Lowell himself, Theodore Roethke, Dylan Thomas, Delmore Schwartz and even at times Randall Jarrell all lived disordered lives; to varying degrees they regarded marital chaos, alcoholism and suicidal despair as occupational hazards and found in each other's suffering a terrible sanction for their own. Of course, the assumption that pathology and inspiration, art and suffering, are somehow related did not originate with them, but is as old as western civilization. Since the Romantic period especially, it has troubled and preoccupied every generation of poets. But to see the latest mutation of this idea we need only compare Wordsworth's version with Berryman's.

The poet, as Wordsworth defines him in the preface to the *Lyrical Ballads,* differs from other men only in degree, not kind, and this difference resides in what he calls "a greater promptness to think and feel without immediate external excitements, and a greater power of expressing such thoughts and feelings." The poet's mind is so primed, so heightened naturally, that it does not require, as less heightened minds do, "the application of gross and violent stimulants." This power, moreover, lies not in any special kind of experience (for his experiences are essentially the same as other men's), but rather in his intensity of recollection and his skill of expression. However, Wordsworth does believe that poets often live unhappy lives, for if by virtue of their heightened sensibility they derive more pleasure from ordinary experience, they also derive more pain. Although poets may be more tempted by the satisfaction of their appetites, and this may get them into trouble, Wordsworth never equates trouble with inspiration or artistic skill.

In Berryman's view, on the other hand, "this greater promptness to think and feel" is dependent on, even addicted to, "external excitements." His thinking is tightly circular and goes something like this: as a poet, I'm entitled to indulge in all temptations because they make me feel more alive and thereby stimulate my creative energies; but these indulgences also make me suffer because, being more sensitive than others, I feel extraordinarily guilty; yet suffering is a good not only because it gives me something to write about, but because it also justifies the painkiller of more self-indulgence. Thus, Berryman not only confuses excitement with inspiration, he confuses pleasure with pain, especially in *The Dream Songs,* where he continually draws connections between trauma (whether in the form of womanizing, drugs or emotional catastrophe) and poetry: "Hunger was constitutional" with Henry, "women, cigarettes, liquor, need need need/ until he went to pieces. / The pieces sat up & wrote"; "Feeling no pain, / Henry stabbed his arm and wrote a letter"; "They are shooting me full of sings." (pp. 114-16)

The Dream Songs, along with Lowell's *Life Studies,* have been praised for breaking from what is often called "the fifties poem," a poem of highly wrought aesthetic surfaces, disciplined, polished, learned and complex in tone and language, and obliquely related, if at all, to personal experience. As A. Alvarez describes it in *The Savage God,* this overly refined, overly sophisticated poetry could take "no account of the confusions and depressions of a life unredeemed by art." The direct autobiographical style of *The Dream Songs* represents an effort to "push . . . at the limits of what poetry can be made to bear," to invite into the domain of art "the tentative, flowing, continually improvised balance of life itself." Yet what emerges from a close reading of *The Dream Songs,* and from John Haffenden's 400-page biography of Berryman, is a portrait of an artist who held mere life in contempt, for whom life had no intrinsic worth except in so far as art could validate it. Since great art demanded, in Berryman's words, "gigantic, unspeakable but articulate disaster," Berryman arranged his circumstances so that he would be bound to suffer. As Haffenden puts it, he resolved "to adopt the mantle of the suffering life, to live intensively and to use his life as discipline . . . in arrogating to himself fundamental exercises in tragic art, he was in a way courting disaster in his personal life." Berryman himself described these aspirations in a poem written on his twenty-second birthday:

> What breaks about my head next year or next
> Let it be intolerable, let it be
> Agony's discipline, let it not be strange.

Such ideas are anything but strange in a twenty-two-year-old poet. When "agony's discipline" is only an imagined, not a real, experience, it is easy to romanticize. The strangeness is that Berryman would adhere so tenaciously to this adolescent program and continue throughout his life to rationalize his own pain and the pain he caused others by claiming they were indispensable conditions of his art. So in 1950 he confides to his journal, "My decision last week . . . was not to worry so but to take fucks when they turned up . . . perhaps that is not an abominable programme *if it lets me work whereas I otherwise wouldn't*" (italics his). . . . Older, though no wiser, in a 1962 interview, thinking of himself, he says of Mozart, "His whole life was at the mercy of his art. It is incredible. I'm thinking of that and I'm also thinking about the kind of hysterical states that modern artists go in very much for—an extreme case would be Van Gogh's cutting off his ear—periods of masochism and blasphemy—that kind of business . . ." Compulsive as he surely was, early and late Berryman was nonetheless a very "businesslike" manipulator of experience; even at his most destructive, he assumed, in Haffenden's words again, "the aspect of spectator of his own drama" and measured the value of each experience strictly in terms of the poetry it might produce.

Perhaps the most outrageous example of this specialized mentality (though the biography is full of them) is the infamous "Lise Affair." In the summer of 1947 Berryman became involved with the wife of a Princeton graduate student. It was during this affair that he started drinking heavily; not surprisingly, the excitement of the affair inspired a manic outpouring of sonnets—over a hundred in a two-month period. In the journal which he kept during this period he excused his infidelity by claiming, "my will has been at the service of my passion and my imagination." An Aeolian harp played by erotic impulse and inspiration alike, he used the same language to describe his passion for Lise that he often used to describe the poems he was writing. As Haffenden observes, he often commenced writing sonnets "helplessly," that many were "unexpected," that he couldn't "stop writing," that they "go on," and that he was surprised to find "I have eleven sonnets planned." At other times the language of obsession and hysteria ("All upside down, mad, guilty and frightening") alternated with the language of the cool, self-conscious artist, paring his fingernails as he falls apart: "Isn't my ideal of style at present: what will be lucid and elegant, but also surprising, frightening and various?" In [*Berryman's Sonnets*], this detachment takes the form of identifications with past adulterers and sonneteers—Bathsheba's David, Sidney, Petrarch, Balzac—identifications which cast an immortal literary glamor around his personal chaos. So when the affair ended, despite the damage it did to his marriage and despite how much Lise made him suffer, he could look back gratefully: "I owe her, besides times and days of unspeakable happiness: 1) the sonnets, though I abhor them just now, 2) a knowledge of women extraordinary and new, 3) a deterioration in my nervous state . . . which now looks to draw me out of much *more* pain than Lise made me herself and older difficulty." How quickly Berryman slid over the mention of "unspeakable happiness" in order to get to the poems and the pain! And more pain, of course, meant more poems. Why else have an affair? In her memoir, *Poets in Their Youth,* Eileen Simpson, Berryman's wife at the time, offers the same motive:

> As for John, was it Lise he wanted? Or the sonnets Lise inspired, as Yeats had been inspired by Maud Gonne? "If Miss Gonne had called Willie's bluff and gone to bed with him, she wouldn't have filled his days with misery. No misery, no poems. You can bet your life that what Yeats was after was the *poems,*" John used to say when asked what he made of their relationship. Was a new subject for poems what he too was after?

To suggest, as Berryman and Simpson do, that Yeats deliberately cultivated what he bitterly called, in "Pardon, Old Fathers," "a barren passion" for Maud Gonne, that he preferred misery to fulfillment for the sake of the poetry that misery would generate, is to simplify self-servingly Yeats' life and work. It is, furthermore, to forget that Yeats wrote only minor poetry during the unhappy period of his love for Maud Gonne, and that his greatest poetry came only after he had married Georgie Hyde-Lees and finally achieved a state of marital contentment and stability. . . . Berryman's correspondence then, "No misery, no poems," reduces the rich and complex figure of Yeats into a mirror within which Berryman could find a justifying precedent for all the wayward aspects of his personal life.

Similarly, throughout *The Dream Songs,* Berryman identifies himself with artists and cultural heroes in order to explain his suffering or justify his self-indulgence:

> Scarlatti spurts his wit across my brain,
> so too does *Figaro:* so much for art
> after the centuries yes
> who had for all their pains above all pain
> & who brought to their work a broken heart . . .
> —Dream Song 258
> (pp. 116-19)

Yet Berryman is also the master poet of the guilty conscience, tormented by an unrelenting and indefinable sense of sin:

> But never did Henry, as he thought he did,
> end anyone and hack her body up
> and hide the pieces, where they may be found.
> He knows: he went over everyone, & nobody's missing . . .
> Nobody is ever missing.
> —Dream Song 29

But such self-loathing is often merely self-exaltation in disguise. As an Artist in the Modern World, Henry is a kind of Everyman. His heightened sensibility compels him to respond so fully, so intensely, to the world that he comes to embody, in all aspects of his experience, the spirit of his age. This yoking together of public and private experience is, according to A. Alvarez, the crucial feature of the extremist poetry that Berryman and Lowell wrote, a poetry in which "the nihilism and destructiveness of the self . . . turns out to be an accurate reflection of the nihilism of our own violent societies." By identifying Henry with criminals (mass murderers, Nazis, corrupt politicians) to illustrate his violence and rage, or with Jews and blacks to illustrate the intensity of his suffering, Berryman gives Henry "a ruin-prone proud national mind" and thereby tries to turn his personal experience, good and bad, as victim and victimizer, into an internalized expression of his culture. . . . (p. 120)

Throughout this essay I treat Henry and Berryman as interchangeable, and some readers may object to this. After all, Berryman did dissociate himself from Henry in the introductory note to *The Dream Songs,* calling him "an imaginary character (not the poet, not me)." And insofar as Henry speaks in vaudevillian dialects, in rhyme and meter, and has experiences Berryman couldn't possibly have had (at one point he even dies and comes back to life), this is obviously true. On the other hand, if Henry is only an imaginary character (not the poet, not Berryman), how is it that he has the same friends and relatives, the same vices, the same obsessions—not to mention the same profession? And why did Berryman occasionally refer to himself as Henry in letters and conversation? The fact is Berryman wanted it both ways, for Henry is really his ventriloquist's dummy, through whom he could speak directly of himself and at the same time evade complete responsibility for what he says. It's precisely Henry's exaggerated mannerisms, his obviousness as a persona, that legitimizes, as it were, even the most intimate disclosures, the most puffed-up and egocentric attitudes. So in poems like **Dream Song 66,** Berryman can imply through Henry a causal link between his inner disarray and national disorder, or arrogate the suffering of blacks to dramatize his own unhappiness, and still deflect the charge of self-indulgence. But such poems *are* self-indulgent, however cagily Berryman throws his voice, and for this reason: the experiential authority that would justify the self-inflated claims is only asserted through a trick of style, not dramatized or discovered within the detailed tensions of private life.

But compare **Dream Song 66** with **Dream Song 191,** a poem in which Berryman does persuasively and movingly elicit general significance from his own experience. The poem is about old age and the death of friends, and the manner is unusually plain with little of the tricks and fripperies that dominate the Dream Song style. It is a manner appropriate to the quiet, yet deeply troubled, meditation on surviving those one loves, of living to an age when one's very consciousness becomes "a house of death":

> The autumn breeze was light & bright. A small bird
> flew in the back door and the beagle got it
> (half-beagle) on the second try.
> My wife kills flies & feeds them to the dog,
> five last night, plus one Rufus snapped herself.
> This is a house of death
>
> and one of Henry's oldest friends was killed,
> It came on a friend' radio, this week,
> whereat Henry wept.
> All those deaths keep Henry pale & ill

and unable to sail through the autumn world & weak,
a disadvantage of surviving.

The leaves fall, lives fall, every little while
you can count with stirring love on a new loss
& an emptier place.
The style is black jade at all seasons, the style
is burning leaves and a shelving of moss
over each planted face.

Despite the plainness, the poem is intricately structured: as Berryman moves toward the elegiac language of the closing lines, he unobtrusively changes from the blank verse of the first stanza, to the partial rhymes of the second, to the full rhymes of the third. Likewise, as the relatively trivial details of animal death give way in the second stanza to the death of "one of Henry's oldest friends," Berryman switches from the first-person pronoun to the third; though by means of this he distances the sorrow from himself, the distance itself intensifies rather than dilutes that sorrow, suggesting that his sense of loss is so acute that he can articulate it only by turning the part of himself that feels it into Henry. Yet Henry, too, disappears in the last stanza, generalized into the second person "you," just as his grief is generalized into a style of "black jade at all seasons," a style necessitated by "the disadvantages of surviving." There are traces of the Dream Song manner in the juxtaposition of "leaves" and "lives" and in the pun on "burning leaves," but the manner is subdued even at such moments, and remains throughout a sensitive response to the occasion it presents. The general meaning, moreover, rises through the particular biographical details, instead of being, as in so many of the Dream Songs, merely an effect of style, or an assertion.

But this is a rare exception. For the most part, the assumption that his experience is intrinsically significant or representative allows Berryman merely to indulge in all the petty, egotistical worriments of daily life: "Henry as a landlord made his eight friends laugh / but Henry laughed not: the little scraggly-bearded jerk / has not paid his rent for two months"; "Your first day in Dublin is your worst. / I just found my fly open: panic!" "Trunks & impedimenta. My manuscript won't go / in my huge Spanish briefcase, some into a bag." The same assumption also allows him to seem a harsh judge of himself, but it's only an apparent harshness, because his judgments invariably shade off into indictments of the world that ultimately made him what he is: "What the world to Henry / did will not bear thought." "Baseball, & the utter fucking bloody news, / converged on miserable Henry." (pp. 121-23)

No one would deny that we are products of culture or that our individual neuroses have social and political as well as psychological causes. But in Berryman's life and work this conflation of public and private experience, and the related assumption that the poet risks his life in order to confront the repressed truth about himself and his society, amounted to an evasion of responsibility: instead of drawing from his personal history the sympathy that would take him imaginatively into the experience of other sufferers, Berryman merely arrogated the credentials of other sufferers, in order to invest his own despair with special dignity and confer upon himself a kind of privileged immunity from social norms. Living the life he thought high art required, he believed he could redeem and ennoble everything he did, however base or brutal, by virtue of the poetry he wrote.

Yet Berryman is praised for being almost Christlike in his devotion to disaster. As Joel Conarroe puts it: "Artists like Berryman . . . who live perilously close to the abyss make it possible for us to journey over threatening terrain, to experience its terror and to return intact. . . . In courting certain kinds of disaster, Henry spares us the necessity of doing so ourselves, overpowering as the attractions sometimes are." In this view, Berryman surrenders to the impulses the rest of us repress so that we can feel the terror of the abyss without the danger, and thereby be spared from following his example. He drinks himself into a stupor, sleeps around and destroys his marriage, and so saves us from the same temptations. This shamanistic view of the poet is as naive as Berryman's self-serving belief that trauma in all its forms is an indisputable sign of artistic election. Even had he treated his addictions as addictions, not as a muse, I doubt that *The Dream Songs* could keep anyone seriously tempted by disaster from going mad, or drinking heavily, or cheating on his or her spouse. But those who are not seriously tempted by disaster—only trivially so—can read *The Dream Songs* and be titillated or, worse, feel justified in their prurient fantasies. Reading for them becomes a form of armchair debauchery whereby they can convince themselves that their temptations, however mild or ordinary, make them compellingly human, even poetic, without their suffering any of the consequences of "the poetic life."

In the conclusion to *Poets in Their Youth*, Eileen Simpson refuses to blame Berryman's suicide on his having been a poet. Though "the litany of suicides [among poets] is long . . . it was the poetry that had kept him alive . . . that he died a 'veteran of life' was thanks to his gift. . . . Only when there were no more [poems] did he feel . . . that 'It seems to be DARK all the time.'" This may seem at first like a sane corrective to the confessional cant that Berryman and his critics utter, but in effect it's no less horrifying. For it rests serenely on the assumption that a poet's exclusive source of value is his poetry, that his life is "at the mercy of his art." If, as Simpson claims, poetry kept Berryman alive, his idea of poetry ratified the kind of life he led, a life that could have ended only in suicide. His assumptions about the poet and his relation to the world may not have caused his appetite for self-destructive drama, but they did encourage it.

And the same ideas which exacted and excused the imperfections of the life also encouraged the imperfections of the work. Since poetry alone could validate his existence, he erected a conception of the poet that would enable him to write at will, and to mistake an aesthetics of suffering for an articulation of the underlying structures of suffering, the personal conflicts at its source. The tortured syntax, the punning and neologisms, the black-face dialect, the mingling of profane and sacred language coincident with the manic fluctuations of self-mockery and self-exaltation—these are merely the rhetorical effects of pain. Granted, the rhetoric is almost always impressive; moreover, there are poems in *The Dream Songs* that redeem the victimized buffoonery from mere mannerism, or that work by sheer force of verbal ingenuity, despite the highly mannered surface. That Berryman managed to write well at all is all the more remarkable given the extent and seriousness of his suffering. In assessing his work, however, we should not confuse, as he did, his suffering with his poetic gifts, dissolving the complex powers of aesthetic realization into a set of pat experiences. If ordeal were the most important ingredient of artistic achievement (especially the particular ordeals which Berryman was prone to), our de-tox centers and mental hospitals would be full of artists. No one but God perhaps can say whether Berryman would have written better had he lived and thought differently. But one thing is certain: however much his talent may have thrived on trauma, trauma in turn confined his talent to the narrow range of experience which he believed to be the most profound because the most extreme.

But the extreme in style as well as content is at best a marginal position. If poets are exemplars of consciousness, then our greatest poets should be those who exercise the widest range of faculties upon the widest range of life. Against this standard, Berryman can be regarded not as a representative man whose self-destruction was a badge of authenticity or of deep responsiveness to an irredeemably corrupt society, but rather as a brilliant eccentric. (pp. 123-25)

> *Alan Shapiro, " 'A Living to Fail': The Case of John Berryman," in TriQuarterly 58, No. 58, Fall, 1983, pp. 114-125.*

David K. Weiser

Published in 1967, about twenty years after their composition, *Berryman's Sonnets* were quickly recognized as more than a virtuoso performance. By reviving some long-dead conventions of the Renaissance love lyric, the poet expressed his own highly original personality. As William J. Martz pointed out, the hallmarks of that personality are "his energy, his humor and his exuberance." More recent critics have dealt with the sonnets as an anticipation of Berryman's concern for self-depiction, a task that was best fulfilled in his *Dream Songs.* Joel Conarroe, in the longest study so far, concludes that the sonnet sequence "is important in the development of Berryman's craft because for the first time . . . he drops the mask of neutral objectivity." Berryman's poetic speaker "emerges as a unique man who records his own sensibility in a voice that, at least in the strongest, truest sonnets, is recognizably his own."

But *Berryman's Sonnets* have intrinsic value, quite apart from the poet's later development. Like George Meredith's *Modern Love,* they illustrate the process of creative imitation, in which old forms are deliberately reshaped to express new attitudes. Berryman is far closer to the Renaissance model than was Meredith, who made no attempt to echo sixteenth-century style. Writing a century later, the American poet immersed himself in the past without excluding his present experience. His language can combine American slang with Elizabethan euphony in lines like "Snug, slim and supple-breasted girl for play," or "On a thousand greens the late slight rain is gleaming" and "Doomed cities loose and thirsty as a dune." Such intricate sound patterns attest to Berryman's familiarity with metrical techniques of the Renaissance. Joined with Elizabethan diction, in words like "toys," "roil," "lickerish," "rack", and "lusk," the iambic pentameter adds resonance to Berryman's Renaissance imitations.

Berryman's sonnets actually employ the theory of *inventio* that prevailed in the Renaissance. They are "imitations" in the sixteenth-century sense, deviating from their models much as the sonnets of Sidney and Shakespeare vary from those of Petrarch and Wyatt. By comparing Berryman's sonnets with their sources and analogues, we can discover how perfectly he assimilated old poetic forms but not their content. For all his technical prowess, the modern poet could not sustain belief in such postulates as right reason and natural law. A radical discrepancy thus separates his sonnets from their tradition.

The title *Berryman's Sonnets* boldly suggests a parallel with Shakespeare. Unlike the elusive Bard, this poet requires us to see his sonnets as a personal document; he defines himself through his uses of the past. When he echoes Shakespeare we are more impressed by deviations from the source than by fidelity to it. **Sonnet 40** is a case in point: "Marble nor monuments whereof then we spoke / We speak of more." The impersonal plural of "we spoke" and "we speak" implies a continuity of poetic voices from past to present. The speaker represents a consensus of poets, especially the moderns who are characterized by "our short songs." He contends at first that poetic immortality is an ideal for which "none hopes now." It is "a Renaissance fashion, not to be recalled." Moreover, an element of progress is implied: "We dinch 'eternal numbers' and go out. / We understand exactly what we are." Then the poet's individual voice enters the sonnet to complete it. He reverses the previous argument, making the *volta* coincide with his shift to a personal perspective:

> Do we? Argent I craft you as the star
> Of flower-shut evening: who stays on to doubt
> I sang true? ganger with trobador and scald!

The formative assertion of Shakespeare's sonnet 55 has now been vindicated. Yet Berryman never matches its confidence: "Not marble, nor the gilded monuments / Of princes, shall outlive this pow'rful rhyme." The appeal of his own sonnet lies in the unresolved conflict between the two opposing viewpoints, cynical and affirmative. In itself, his closing tercet is unconvincing because it ignores all that was said before. It reaffirms poetic immortality but unaccountably limits what Shakespeare had called "all posterity" to a small circle of poets. Similarly, the first eleven lines are unattractive in their cynicism. Their smug generalizations seem to cry out for refutation. The entire sonnet thus embodies the sustained tension characteristic of Berryman. Two contradictory sections actually complement each other, so that the complex whole most accurately reflects the poet's mind. Shakespeare's simpler and stronger expression of confidence in his art has been absorbed into a new complexity. Berryman, we find, has imitated a model only to represent himself. (pp. 388-90)

Again, in **sonnet 100** the phrase "mock the time" is a concealed quotation from *Macbeth.* Berryman puts it in a broader context of dissimulation:

> Burnt cork, my leer, my Groucho crouch and rush,
> No more my nature than Cyrano's: we
> Are 'hindered characters' and mock the time. . . .

Conarroe claims that "the poet is unable to make known his passion, and so puts on a comic mask." But mocking the time is derived from Macbeth's tragic acquiescence:

> Away, and mock the time with fairest show:
> False face must hide what the false heart doth know.

Both echoes of *Macbeth,* in **sonnets 105** and **100,** are meant to brand the speaker's adultery as tragic and unnatural. Since guilt feelings are placed within a wider range of associations, some of them comic, the resulting tone is richly complex. Just as Berryman could not duplicate Shakespeare's boast of immortality, so in acknowledging his pangs of conscience he creates a further conflict. The allusions are instrumental in helping the reader define that interplay of opposing emotions, so that familiar meanings are ironically modified by the modern context that absorbs them.

Another example of this process is **sonnet 20,** whose background is the Princeton University bicentennial. Playing on the colloquialism "two bands are raising hell," Berryman modulates to a weightier tone: "O hell is empty and Knowlton Street is well, / The little devils shriek." What he means will become clear when we recognize his borrowing from *The Tempest:* "Hell is empty, / And all the devils are here!" These words, spoken by Ferdinand during the shipwreck scene, are vital to Berryman; they enable him to transmute everyday reality. A public event, "the bicentennial of an affair with truth," seems unreal to the speaker who is obsessed with his own, much less truthful affair. The same clash is presented schematically in the sestet, where three lines parodying the ceremony are interwoven with parenthesized lines that relate the speaker's love-longing: "Two centuries here have been abused our youth: / (Your grey eyes pierce the miles to meet my eyes)." Ferdinand's exclamation is thus applied to the Princeton ceremony, registering the speaker's extreme dissociation from society. Shipwreck, being a conventional image of Petrarchan despair, forebodes even greater suffering than that caused here by the mistress' absence. At present, the speaker can endure and even enjoy his contradictory emotions: "an angelic tear / Falls somewhere, so (but I laugh) would mine." (pp. 390-91)

The form of *Berryman's Sonnets* is not Shakespearean, however, but Petrarchan; the inner lines of each quatrain make one rhyme and the outer lines another. Strictly following this pattern with a rhyme link between lines four and five, he allows himself only two rhyme sounds in the octet and three in the sestet. There are only five rhymes in these sonnets as against Shakespeare's seven. Moreover, in the chronological form of the sequence, with its specific dates and locations, we discern the direct influence of Petrarch rather than Shakespeare. The earlier poet had fused art and life in his sonnet-sequence instead of leaving their relation equivocal. Petrarch did not lend words for Berryman to echo but he supplied a structural model for individual sonnets and their arrangement. In addition, the familiar "conceits" derived from Petrarch and his imitators furnished a basis for Berryman's ironic variations.

Sonnet 75, for example, explicitly compares the two poets. Its first eight lines review main events in Petrarch's career, while the sestet contrasts his love for Laura with Berryman's passion for Lise: "He never touched her. Swirl our crimes and crimes." Although the historical facts are uncertain ("the old brume seldom clears"), Berryman is sure that his physicality compares unfavorably with Petrarch's ideal love. His mistress has nothing in common with Laura except her appearance, being "gold-haired (too)."

He ends the poem by addressing her directly: "Two guilty and crepe-yellow months / Lise! be our bright surviving actual scene." The specific contrast is between two months and twenty-one years. But the difference in duration is less revealing than that in the quality of love. The key word, I believe, is "guilty" since the many descriptions of sensual delight throughout these sonnets rarely conceal their brooding remorse.

Berryman is constantly aware of the unbridgeable gap between his own practice and the Renaissance ideal of love. His use of Petrarchan conceits, like the borrowings from Shakespeare, highlights basic differences by means of superficial likeness. **Sonnet 14** begins with one such conceit, "moths white as ghosts," but the speaker quickly puts this image at a distance by giving it another, less venerable source: "I am one of yours, / Doomed to a German song's stale metaphors." He then breaks down the compound image, dwelling on "ghost" in quatrain two: "I am your ghost. . . . on Denmark's moors / I loiter, and when you slide your eyes I swing." The allusion is to Lise's Danish ancestry as well as to the ghost in *Hamlet.* Moth and ghost are helplessly dependent, fitting the speaker's representation of himself. The Petrarchan conceit thus finds its place within an eclectic range of associations. In the sestet of this sonnet, love itself is epitomized in starkly colloquial language: "The billiard ball slammed in the kibitzer's mouth" and "this diamond meal to gag on." The impact of love receives a direct, objectified description, while the speaker's self-portrait is mockingly sentimental.

In **sonnet 52** we note a Petrarchan theme, one that is used by Sidney in *Astrophel and Stella.* However, detachment from these sources is obtained through translation into German: *"Da ist meiner Liebstens Haus."* Another parallel with Sidney, "the English Petrarke," is drawn explicitly in **sonnet 16.** Its rather convoluted opening explains that the poet had seen his lady three times before falling in love:

> Thrice, or I moved to sack, I saw you: how
> Without siege laid I can as simply tell
> As whether below the dreams of Astrophel.
> Lurks local truth some scholars would allow
> And others will deny in ours!

Undoubtedly, the first two lines employ the Petrarchan conceit of love as a conquering army. Berryman's deviation from this idea is complete; he wonders how he could have seen Lise without falling into the siege of love. However an earlier sonnet, the second, explains that the poet had tried to resist temptation: "I said / A month since, 'I will see that cloud-gold head, / Those eyes lighten, and go by': then your thunder rolled." For that matter, Sidney himself had repudiated the convention: "Not at first sight, nor with a dribb'd shot, / Love gave the wound which while I breathe will bleed." Perhaps it is this resemblance which reminds Berryman of Astrophel. He compares his own uncertainty to that of scholars about the biographical element, the "local truth," in Sidney's sonnet-sequence. Anticipating future commentators on his own sequence, he uses an ambiguous construction in which the contrast "some scholars would allow / And others will deny" refers both to Sidney and to Berryman. There is also a hint that future readers, presumably "new critics," will play down the biographical background to these poems. The speaker thus enjoys the irony of having an experience whose living reality will be denied. (pp. 392-94)

Despite his extensive debts to the past, it is typical of Berryman to mock the tradition that he writes in. Quite a few sonnets are openly self-critical. They ask whether *Berryman's Sonnets* are not merely an antiquarian exercise. Berryman's self-consciousness, his awareness of possible flaws in his method, implies that he is not subservient to conventions but in control of them. In **sonnet 23** he asserts that he loves but "would not cloy your ear . . . / With 'love' and 'love'." In fact, "love" appears frequently throughout the sequence despite these strictures against the word, "pompous and vague on the stump of his career." Loyal to the modern notion of authenticity, Berryman's speaker continues his verbal blacklist:

> Also I fox 'heart', striking a modern breast
> Hollow as a drum, and 'beauty' I taboo;
> I want a verse as a bubble breaks,
> As little false. . . .

The ideal of freshness within a Petrarchan framework may seem paradoxical. Yet the resultant tension is a main source of the sonnets' appeal. Even if "love" is a tasteless cliché, Berryman has no choice but to use it and its well-worn Renaissance antithesis, "lust." He denies the possible charge that "I *loved* you not, but blurred / *Lust* with strange images" (italics mine). We infer from this argument that the poet will require traditional words and connotations as long as he celebrates the idea of love. To redeem those words, he must employ them sparingly and ironically. We find that linguistic predicament at the end of **sonnet 23**: "I am in love with you— / Trapped in my rib-cage something throes and aches!" Modern poetics forbids calling that something the "heart" but the modern poet has not found an alternative. He turns to the past, despite its inadequacy, for a context against which he can define himself. In **sonnet 97** the stock phrases, *"I laid siege— you enchanted me,"* are italicized and labelled as "magic and warfare, faithful metaphors." The value of such phrases seems exhausted until Berryman invests them with a series of atavistic associations, imagining himself and his beloved as "the hunter and the witchwife." This hackneyed imagery of magic and war, presented hesistatingly at first, is finally justified by the keenly felt physical contact that generates it, the core of sexuality then as now: "Abrupt as a dogfight, the air full of / Tails and teeth."

The most thoroughly anti-Petrarchan sonnet is **103**, which begins by examining yet another catch-phrase: "A 'broken heart' . . . but *can* a heart break, now?" The succeeding lines echo Rosalind's well-known remarks in *As You Like It:* "The poor world is almost six thousand years old, and in all this time there was not any man died in his own person, videlicet, in a love cause." Berryman's version mocks poetic conventions rather than the mythological lovers debunked by Rosalind:

> Lovers have stood bareheaded in love's 'storm'
> Three thousand years, changed by their mistress' 'charm',
> Fitted their 'torment' to a passive bow,
> Suffered the 'darts' under a knitted brow,
> And has one heart *broken* for all this 'harm'?

Admittedly, self-criticism is an integral part of the Petrarchan mode. The earlier poets had often berated their vanity and its terms of expression. But Berryman's contrast of old conceits with "something definite," his aching arm, shows his radical departure from tradition. He prefers a unique, physically demonstrable ailment as the symbol of his suffering. The arm, "a piece of pain joined to me," does not entirely ruin him but it spoils his tennis: "after fifteen minutes of / Serving, I can't serve more." This precise account contradicts the vague improbability of a "broken heart." It resembles Petrarchan tradition only in that the pain is mysterious, perhaps supernatural: "no doctor can find a thing." The sonnet's final words, "still, it is something," remind us that a limited area of pain corresponds better to the lover's state than do the extravagant figures of his predecessors.

These qualifications of thought and style, however, do not alter the basic premise of *Berryman's Sonnets.* The poet's decision to revive an outmoded structure with all its conventions implies a firm belief in the continuity of literary culture. He seems to have adopted quite literally what T. S. Eliot calls "the historical sense . . . a perception not only of the pastness of the past, but of its presence." . . .

[An] echo of Eliot will be heard in **sonnet 101,** whose opening lines recall those of "Ash Wednesday" and create a subtle parody due to the difference between the ladies addressed:

> Because I'd seen you not believe your lover,
> Because you scouted cries come from no cliff,
> Because to supplications you were stiff. . . .

Eliot's influence (at its height in the late forties) clearly stimulated Berryman toward revitalizing the past. Rather than founding a latter-day School of Petrarch, he placed the old tradition squarely within the new. Such adaptation occurs in the questioning of old concepts, in the broadening contexts of quotations and allusions, in references to features of modern life (cars, planes and frozen daiquiris) and in the frequent mention of contemporary poets. Not only Eliot but Yeats, Thomas, Pound, Cummings and Stevens are also alluded to. Perhaps the most surprising contemporary reference is a quotation from Book II of W. C. Williams' *Paterson,* wedged into **sonnet 58:** "Since the corruption of the working classes / I am speaking of the Eighteenth Century." The subject here is the speaker's rejection of a conventional life, "sensible, coarse, and moral." This enables him to parody ordinary happiness and its clichés: "the water's fine, come in and drown." But by the sonnet's conclusion he admits his own complicity in the corruption that Williams had noticed: "The Reno brothels boom, suddenly we writhe." The borrowing from *Paterson* thus marks the speaker's exile from community mores and his use of poetry as a source of value. His references to contemporary poets only complete the literary continuum that begins with Pindar and Vergil and includes writers as disparate as Donne, Hölderin and Villon.

The speaker of *Berryman's Sonnets* identifies himself primarily as a poet rather than a lover. It follows that love itself is neither castigated nor praised as lavishly as in the Renaissance lyrics. It is a consistently sensual need that, for a time, is shared and gratified. In this context, the figure of Lise remains a real person with very real faults. Her name, on the analogy of Samuel Daniel's "Delia," could be read as an anagram yielding "lies" rather than the Renaissance poet's "ideal." Berryman's precise descriptions of love-making, his acceptance of it as a good, brings him closer in spirit to Ovid's *Ars Amoris* than to Shakespeare, let alone Petrarch or Dante. It is appropriate that Sigmund Freud is referred to as "the Master," echoing Dante's epithet for Aristotle. Nothing could better point out the contrast of world-views between Berryman and the poets whose forms he has borrowed. Like his master, he stresses the individual's urges against social norms that restrain them. This acceptance of irrational man weakens the basic tension inherent in the genre that Berryman imitates. For if the Renaissance poets felt anguish and shame for their supposed depravity, they could also transform love into a symbol of the divine. Since Berryman does not uphold the rational ideal, he has no basis for isolating in his mistress either the angelic or the animal elements that traditionally coexisted in human nature. There is, as we have seen, a persistent sense of guilt underlying the sequence. However, Berryman's guilt is no less irrational than his love.

A comparative reading of **sonnet 15** will best demonstrate how the modern poet's intellectual distance from the Renaissance influences the form and style of his work. This is the only sonnet out of one hundred and fifteen that acknowledges a specific source, carrying the subscription: "after Petrarch and Wyatt." It is based on Petrarch's sonnet 189, as well as Sir Thomas Wyatt's sixteenth-century translation. Assimilating the content of the two earlier poems, Berryman extends their vision. Many words and phrases from the Wyatt poem, itself an imitation rather than an exact rendering, are retained. However, no line is repeated verbatim. At some points Berryman is more faithful to Petrarch's original than Wyatt had been, while at others he deviates from both his predecessors. On the level of auditory coherence he outdoes them by using only two rhyme-sounds in the sestet rather than three. The rhyme scheme is cddccc, with the last two lines yielding the half-rhyme "art" and "port." This sestet is closer to Petrarch than is Wyatt's, which divides into a third quatrain and a couplet: cddcee. As a result, Berryman's *volta* or change of thought is located where Petrarch had made it, in line twelve rather than line thirteen. Elsewhere, his sonnet tends to correspond with Wyatt's on a line-by-line basis, just as Wyatt had corresponded to Petrarch. However, in lines three, four, ten and twelve he breaks the pattern of lineation by substituting run-ons for the earlier poems' end-stopped lines. (pp. 396-400)

The most illuminating change made by Berryman occurs at the sonnet's end. The Renaissance poets, however enamoured, viewed courtly love as an unfortunate lapse of reason. As Wyatt put it:

> Drowned is reason that should me comfort
> And I remain dispering of the port.

The English poet placed an even greater burden on reason than did the Italian, for Petrarch had combined reason with art:

> *Celansi duo mei dolci usati segni;*
> *Morta fra l'onde e la ragion et l'arte*
> *Tal ch'i'ncomincio a desperar del porto.*

For Berryman, however, the ideal of reason does not exist. The contest of reason and passion, which pervaded the love poetry of the Middle ages and the Renaissance, has been resolved in favor of the irrational. He is forced to make a major revision, therefore, when he describes the effects of love:

> Muffled in capes of waves my clear signs, torn,
> Hitherto most clear,—Loyalty and Art.
> And I begin now to despair of port.

The substitution of "Loyalty" for reason (*ragion*) reveals Berryman's departure from Renaissance thought. We are not told what sort of loyalty is meant, or to whom, but the term implies an emotional bond rather than a logically defined commitment. In this way, although Berryman intensifies the Petrarchan account of love as a perilous sea-voyage, he fundamentally alters its conclusion. As a psychological study of the lover's changing mood, his poem is the most effective of the three. As a juxtaposition of two radically opposed ideas, it is the least articulate.

A more typical example of Berryman's creative imitation, incorporating many Renaissance features but lacking a specific model, is **sonnet 25**. The poem is a striking expression of the turmoil that results when feelings of loyalty are pitted against stronger feelings of passion. It too employs the imagery of storm-tossed sailing to depict the speaker's state of mind. However, Berryman is now free to develop the image in his own way. He begins by setting forth his predicament:

> Sometimes the night echoes to prideless wailing
> Low as I hunch home late and fever-tired,
> Near you not, nearing the sharer I desired,
> Toward whom till now I sailed back. . . .

The wailing must be his own, occasioned by his return to his wife and separation from his love. The former is "the sharer I desired," but the memory of his earlier passion does not diminish his current obsession. The basic change in the poem, then, lies in his attitude toward his wife. When he loved her, his homecoming had been a "sailing." The same return now "yaws," or strays from course. It declines into the melodramatic shipwreck that the rest of the poem describes. The scene, from line five on, is vintage Hollywood:

> . . . The men are glaring, the mate has wired
> *Hopeless:* locked in, and humming, the Captain's nailing
> A false log to the lurching table.

This extended series of images for a single idea is a "Petrarchan conceit." The separate details, the men, the mate and captain, have no precise reference of their own. Together, they compose a single analogy to what the speaker feels. The figure of the captain, however, corresponds most closely with his own awareness of losing control. "Locked in, and humming," he is eccentric, isolated from others, and possibly mad.

As the sonnet ends, a subtle shift blends the captain's image with that of the poet-speaker: "Lies / And passion sing in the cabin on the voyage home." The voyage is both the speaker's reluctant homecoming and its symbolic equivalent, in which the "cabin" or control-room stands for the speaker's mind. Finally, the madness suggested by the captain's behavior is explicitly endorsed:

> . . . wind
> Madness like the tackle of a crane (outcries
> Ascend) around to heave him from the foam
> Irresponsible, since all the stars rain blind.

The last phrase, "since all the stars rain blind," is a description of the raging inner weather that the speaker endures. Madness is a consequence of his suffering, but also provides a means for accepting it. We can readily agree that a captain should not be blamed for the rainstorm that destroys his ship. But when we apply this image to its referent, we find it less than compelling. The speaker who abandoned one love for another has created the storm that ruins him. He is hardly "irresponsible." Berryman was indeed "nailing a false log" when he devised this metaphor, though surely not deliberately. His reference to madness constitutes an implicit plea for innocence. In addition, there is probably a pun intended in "rain," suggesting the misrule of blind fortune. This, too, should be seen as a desperate, guilt-ridden rationalization.

John Berryman did not write these sonnets, then, merely as a formal exercise but in order to explore, however inconclusively, a theme that would concern him throughout his career. Love was not for him the transcendent force that Renaissance poets had deified. But an illicit love affair brought out his awareness of an underlying conflict between inner impulses and outer norms. For Renaissance poets that clash had been internal, between a man's own powers of reason and passion. For Berryman, as with other American writers, it was another version of the conflict between the individual and society. He could not be reconciled to the seemingly arbitrary bonds that hindered his pleasure. Nor could he understand his mistress' refusal to give up her family. If we look ahead to the **Dream Song 4** we find the same problem represented with far greater discernment. Here "Henry" is attracted to a married woman whom he watches in a restaurant. He is dismayed by her lack of interest in him, as she sits and eats beside her husband. The situation is a paradigm for **Berryman's Sonnets,** except that the protagonist's desire is not requited. He comes to realize that the law is, after all, an inescapable reality:

> The restaurant buzzes. She might as well be in Mars.
> Where did it all go wrong? There ought to be a
> law against Henry.
> —Mr. Bones: there is.

(pp. 401-04)

David K. Weiser, "Berryman's Sonnets: 'In and Out of the Tradition'," in American Literature, *Vol. 55, No. 3, October, 1983, pp. 388-404.*

John Bayley

Berryman, like Lowell and perhaps more so, is the poet of the time whose size and whose new kind of stylistic being shrugs off any attempt at enclosure. But one thing about both is obviously true. *Life Studies, Notebook,* and **Dream Songs** show that verses, old-fashioned *numbers,* are still capable of being what Byron wanted—"a form that's large enough to swim in and talk on any subject that I please"—and not only the capable but the imperially inevitable form. Compare their talking verse—dense as lead one moment and light as feathers the next—with the brutal monotony of that dimension of talking prose which Hemingway evolved, and which Miller, Mailer, Burroughs and others have practised in their various ways. In the **Dream Songs** and **Love and Fame** Berryman makes

that kind of prose appear beside his verse not only doltish and limited but incapable even of straight talking.

Formalistically speaking, curiosity has no place in our reception of the Berryman experience. The medium makes the message all too clear. In spite of all the loose ends of talk, the name-dropping and the facts given, we have no urge to find out with whom, when, why, and what; and this is not a bit like Byron. "I perfect my metres," writes Berryman, "until no mosquito can get through." Let's hope he's right. In every context today we sup full of intimacies. The group therapy of our age is its total explicitness; privacy and reticence have lost all artistic function and status: and so a lack of curiosity is not abnormal in the reader or even unusual. But Berryman seals off curiosity with a degree of artistic justification against which there is no *ad hominem* appeal.

The implications of these two phenomena—a new verse and a new self in it—seem to me what discussion of Berryman has to be about. There is no point in prosing along with detailed technical discussion of his verse, for its idioms and techniques are all completely self-justifying and self-illuminating.

"Poetry," said Thoreau, "is a piece of very private history, which unostentatiously lets us into the secret of a man's life." The matter would only have been put thus by a North American, at once orphan and contemporary of romanticism. The triumph of Berryman's poetry is that in becoming itself it has learnt how to undermine the apparent relevance to the poetic art of that niggling adverb: by flinging it suddenly on its back he has revealed that utter and shameless ostentation can become the same thing as total form, and virtually the same thing as the impersonality which our knowledge and love of the traditions of poetry condition us to expect. To let us in unostentatiously usually means today to be *confiding.* Elizabeth Bishop makes her Fish her poem, but is at the same time both confiding and self-justifying, as is such a typical poem of Wallace Stevens's final period as "The Plant on The Table." So at the other extreme of length and technique is *Paterson.* These confidences produce the impression that the poet is (to turn Stevens's own words against him) "an obstruction, a man / Too exactly himself." Such confidences cease to be important when they are made by a poet as far back as Wordsworth, but in our own time they are very important because they collapse style, the only thing that enables us to guess at the authority of a modern poet. At the moment they are not "soluble in art" (the phrase from the prologue to **Berryman's Sonnets**) though they may dissolve in time—or the whole poem may.

One thing which that in other respects overrated European author Beckett shares with Berryman and Lowell is the masterly inability to confide. None of them are deadpan: indeed all seem very forthcoming, but what Berryman calls "imperial sway" (Pound was "not fated like his protegé Tom or drunky Jim / or hard-headed Willie for imperial sway") manifests in them as a kind of regal blankness: it is not for them to know or care whether or not their subjects are listening.

Berryman cannot be "exactly himself," for he is so present to us that the thought of the real live Berryman is inconceivable, and scarcely endurable. His poetry creates the poet by a process opposite to that in which a novelist creates a character. We get to know Macbeth, say, or Leopold Bloom, to the point where we enter into him and he becomes a part of us; like Eurydice in Rilke's poem he is *geben aus wie hundertfacher vorrat*—bestowed upon the world as a multitudinous product. Berryman, by contrast, creates himself as an entity so single that we cannot share with or be a part of him. Such an autobiography as his does not make him real in the fictional sense. Everything is there, but so is the poetry, "language / so twisted and posed in a form / that it not only expresses the matter in hand / but adds to the stock of available reality."

That is Blackmur, one of Berryman's heroes: his wisdom put into a lapidary stanza and three quarters, ending with the poet's comment: "I was never altogether the same man after *that.*" *That* is after all, though, a conventional formalistic and Mallarméan utterance, and the great apparent size of Berryman and Lowell is that they have achieved a peculiarly American breakthrough: the emancipation of poetry from its European bondage as *chose preservée* and its elevation into a form which can challenge and defeat the authority and easygoingness of prose at every point. As Valèry perceived when he coined the phrase, Europe can never get over its tradition that poetry occupies a special place, and that prose has grown all round it like some rank and indestructibly vital weed, isolating it in an unmistakable enclave. (pp. 499-501)

Coleridge's and Wordsworth's "I" is usually themselves, the "man speaking to men," in either verse or prose. Even in such a masterpiece as "Resolution and Independence" "I" is not metamorphosed by the medium, by the poetry. Hence, even there, the poetry is not doing its poetic job to the hilt. A prose Wordsworth is, or would be, perfectly acceptable, but a prose Whitman "I", or a prose "Henry" Berryman would be intolerable. To make a poetic "I" as free and even more free, as naturalistic and even more so, than a prose ego, and yet quite quite different: that is the secret of the American new poetry which appears to reach its apogee in Lowell and Berryman. By this they show not only that verse can still do more than prose, but that the more closely it is involved in the contingent, the more it can manifest itself as the aesthetically and formalistically absolute.

I must return to this point in a moment, but let us first dispose of Berryman's own comments about the "I" of the ***Dream Songs.***

> Many opinions and errors in the songs are to be referred not to the character Henry, still less to the author, but to the title of the work . . . . The poem, then, whatever its wide cast of characters, is essentially about an imaginary character, (not the poet, not me) named Henry, a white American in early middleage in blackface, who has suffered irreversible loss and talks about himself sometimes in the first person, sometimes in the third, sometimes even in the second; he has a friend, never named, who addresses him as Mr. Bones and variants thereof.

This of course is rubbish in one sense, but in another it is a perfectly salutary and justified reminder by the author that when he puts himself into a poem he formalises himself. To labour the point again: Mailer is always Mailer, but Berryman in verse is Berryman in verse. That does not mean that he is exaggerated or altered or dramatised: on the contrary, if he were so the poem would be quite differ-

ent and much more conventional. Berryman of course deeply admired and was much influenced by Yeats, who helped him to acquire the poet's imperial sway over himself and us, but he is not in the least concerned with Yeats's doctrine of the Masks, and with trying out contrasting dramatic representations of the self; such a cumbrous and courtly device of European poetry does not go with American directness and the new American expansiveness. Why bother to put on masks when you can make the total creature writing all the form that is needed?

Byron and Pushkin also emphasised the formal nature of their poetic device, often in facetious terms and in the poems themselves—making characters meet real friends and themselves, etc.—Berryman's gambit to emphasise a comparable formalism has a long history. None the less his comments are misleading in so far as they imply something like a dramatic relation between characters and ideas in the ***Dream Songs.*** The hero of Meredith's *Modern Love* would be as impossible in any other art context as Henry, but he is in a dramatic situation, and in that situation we can—indeed we are positively invited to—judge him, as we judge Evgeny Onegin. And to judge here is to become a part of. The heroes of such poems with dramatic insides to them are not taken as seriously as heroes in prose; they are unstable and frenetic, capable of all or nothing, because we do not get accustomed to them: they appear and vanish in each line and rhyme. None the less they are stable enough to be sat in judgment on, and Berryman's Henry is not. Ultimately, the formal triumph of Henry is that because he is not us and never could be, he has—like our own solitary egos—passed beyond judgment.

The paradox is complete, and completely satisfying. Clearly Berryman knew it. "These songs are not meant to be understood you understand / They are only meant to terrify and comfort." But though it is not dramatic the interior of the ***Dream Songs*** is grippingly exciting, deep, detailed and spacious. Moreover it is not in the least claustrophobic in the sense in which the world of Sylvia Plath involuntarily constricts and imprisons: on the contrary, like the world of early Auden it is boisterously exhilarating and liberating. It has no corpus of exposition, sententiousness, or pet theory, which is why it is far more like *Modern Love* or *Evgeny Onegin* than the *Cantos* or, say, *The Testament of Beauty.* It never expounds. Another thing in common with the Meredith and Pushkin is the nature of the pattern. Each "Number" is finished, as is each of the intricate stanzas of their long poems, but in reading the whole we go with curiosity unslaked and growing, as if reading a serial. The separate numbers of the ***Dream Songs*** published in magazines could not of course indicate this serial significance, which is not sequent, but taken as a whole reveals unity.

The Russian formalists have a term *pruzhina,* referring to the "sprung" interior of a successful poetic narration, the bits under tension which keep the parts apart and the dimensions open and inviting. Thus, in *Evgeny Onegin,* Tatiana is a heroine, a story-book heroine, and a parody of such a heroine; while Evgeny is, conversely, a "romantic" hero for her, a parody of such a hero, and a hero. The spring keeps each separable in the formal art of the poem, and the pair of them in isolation from each other. I am inclined to think that Berryman's quite consciously contrived *pruzhina* in the **Dream Songs** is a very simple and very radical one: to hold in opposed tension and full view the poet at his desk at the moment he was putting down the words, and the words themselves in their arrangement on the page as poetry. When one comes to think of it, it is surprising that no one has thought of exploiting this basic and intimate confrontation before. (The weary old stream of consciousness is something quite other, being composed like any other literature in the author's head, irrespective of where he was and what he was being at the time.) The extreme analogy of such a confrontation would be Shakespeare weaving into the words of "To be or not to be," or "Tomorrow and tomorrow and tomorrow" such instant reactions and reflections as "Shall I go for a piss now or hold it till I've done a few more lines"—or—"I wonder what size her clitoris is"—or—"We must be out of olive oil." Of course there is no effect of interpretation in Berryman; but the spring does hold apart, and constantly, a terrifying and comforting image of the poet as *there*—wrestling in his flesh and in his huddle of needs—while at the same time poetry is engraving itself permanently on the page. It is this that keeps our awed and round-eyed attention more than anything else: our simultaneous sense of the pain of being such a poet, and of the pleasure of being able to read his poetry.

It is also instrumental in our not judging. The poet is not asking us to pity his racked state, or to understand and sympathize with the wild bad obsessed exhibitionist behaviour it goes with. These things are simply there, as formal achievement. . . . (pp. 501-03)

How judge someone who while talking and tormenting himself is also writing a poem about the talk and torment? Except that we know, deeper down, that this effect *is* a formalistic device and that Berryman's control of it is total. And this knowledge makes us watch the taut spring vibrating with even rapter attention. There is a parallel with the formalism so brilliantly pulled off by Lowell in *Life Studies,* where the poetry seemed itself the act of alienation and cancellation, as if poet and subject had died the instant the words hit the paper. The formal device or emblem above the door framing the two collections might be, in Lowell's case, a speech cut off by the moment of death: in Berryman's, a Word condemned to scratch itself eternally, in its chair and at its desk.

Lowell forsook that frame, and in *Notebook* approaches the idiom of the **Dream Songs** (I waive any enquiry, surely bound to be inconclusive, into questions of mutual sympathetic influencing). But in achieving the note of continuing casualness, in contriving to stay alive as it were, *Notebook* remains individual pieces, fascinating in themselves, but lacking the tension that makes **Dream Songs** a clear and quivering serial. The comparison may be unfair, because *Notebook* may not be intended to be a narrative poem, but it shows how much and how successfully **Dream Songs** is one, and **Love and Fame.**

If I am right in thinking that Berryman's aim is to hold in opposed tension and full view the poet and his words, I may also be right in supposing that **Homage To Mistress Bradstreet** was inspired, in the form it took, by the same preoccupation. What seems to have been the donnée for Berryman there was the contrast between the woman as she presumably was, and the poems that she wrote. Berryman's ways of suggesting this are on the whole crude—I

do not see they could be anything else; but the idea obviously fascinates him. Why couldn't her poems be *her,* as he wills his to be him? . . . **Homage to Mistress Bradstreet** is far from being a masterpiece; it is a very provisional kind of poem. Its virtues grow on one, but so does a sense of the effort Berryman was making to push through a feat of recreation for which a clarified version of the style of Dylan Thomas was—hopefully—appropriate. Had Thomas, instead of lapsing into "Fern Hill," been able to write a long coherent poem on a real subject—the kind of subject touched on in "The Tombstone Told When She Died"—it might have been something like this. But Thomas never got so far. We know from **Love and Fame** that Berryman felt the impact of Thomas early—in Cambridge, England, before the war—found him better than anyone writing in America, and made great use of him, the kind of use a formidably developing poet can make of an arrested one. The superiority of **Mistress Bradstreet** over the poems that are unemancipated from Auden—**"World-Telegram"**, **"1 September 1939"**, **"Desire Is a World by Night"**, etc.—strikingly show how Auden was far too intellectually in shape to be successfully digested by Berryman as Thomas had been.

The feeling imagination, the verbal love, in fact, of **Mistress Bradstreet,** is most moving; and the image of her reading Quarles and Sylvester ("her favourite poets; unfortunately") is, I am convinced, a counter-projection of the image later willed on us by the grand, fully "voiced" Berryman of his own self at his own desk. Finding his own voice is for Berryman a consummation in which his own self and his poetry become one. Nor would it be fanciful to see this as the climax of a historical as well as of a personal process. Poetry, in its old European sense, *was* very largely a matter of getting out of your own perishable tatty self into a timeless metaphysical world of order and beauty. (pp. 504-05)

From Bradstreet to "Henry," who is no mask but a nickname in the formal spousals of poet to reader, is therefore a journey of almost symbolic dimensions, and one which only Lowell and Berryman could have successfully accomplished. Whatever their technical interest and merits, all their early poems were strangely clangorous and muffled, as if a new god were trying to climb out from inside the machinery: they needed the machinery to establish but not to *be* themselves. **Berryman's Sonnets** are brilliantly donnish in the way they cavort around the traditions and idioms of the genre, and it is indeed part of that idiom that there is no inside to them, no personal, non-dramatic reality.

> Keep your eyes open when you kiss: do: when
> You kiss. All silly time else, close them to;

In combination with such admirable and witty pastiche the gins and limes and so on of the **Sonnets** strike one as mere modern properties, and quite singularly not about what Berryman is. (p. 506)

Yeats had always affirmed the self: he took it for granted, he did not have to find it: and in "Sailing to Byzantium" he exaggerates almost to the verge of parody the traditional view that seems to start Berryman off in **Mistress Bradstreet:** that "once out of nature" and in the world of art the perishable and tatty self enters a new dimension of being, becomes a poet. What is fascinating about Berryman's enterprise is that starting from "the proportioned spiritless poems" he tries to reconstitute, so to speak, the perishable being who so improbably produced them. That seems to me the significant American poetic journey—to discover the living ego as it has to be ("I renounce not even ragged glances, small teeth, nothing")—and it is the exact reverse of Yeats's pilgrimage. In finding themselves Lowell and Berryman must indeed renounce nothing, not a hair of their heads, "forever or / so long as I happen." Such an achievement is a triumph quite new to poetry and confers on it a new and unsuspected authority. Thomas Wolfe said something like: "I believe we are lost in America but I believe we shall be found." Lowell and Berryman could have nothing to do with the lush fervour of the sentiment. None the less, in terms of poetry they embody such a faith and justify it.

This is indeed glorious but not necessarily satisfactory. Let us try to see what has been lost as well as gained. My contention would be that the two poets reverse completely one canon of the European aesthetic tradition, as represented by Yeats, and those other European Magi Rilke and Valéry, but in another way they are willy-nilly bound to it. Their spectacular breakthrough into contingency is only possible because of the other Magi article of belief that things have no existence except in the poet's mind. So that in the iron selfhood the two poets have created, the most apparently feeble, hasty, or obviously untrue comment, sloughed off from day to day, acquires an imperishable existence when it is unsubstantiated on the page. The poems in *Love and Fame,* where even the nick-name "Henry" has been dropped between us (as nick-names come to be dropped between old married couples) are apparently barroom comments on Berryman's past, nothing more, and the people, events, feuds and boastings in them are as commonplace as the lunch-hour. The lines are like a late Picasso drawing, the realised personality of genius implicit in every flick of the pencil. (pp. 507-08)

Temperamentally, one infers, Berryman could hardly be more different from either Yeats or Auden. He was "up against it" in a sense (I take it) unknown to their basically sane and self-centering personalities, but he adapts the mirror world of their invention to sound like what he wants to be. Success is shown by the failure of the alternatives taken by poets in a comparable situation (not of course of Berryman's stature, but that begs the question): the "confidences" of Anne Sexton and the "blown top" meaninglessness of Kenneth Fearing, for example. Berryman takes from Auden not only the mirror world but the wry unswerving knowledge of its use, which adds—as it does in Auden—a further dimension to the meaning of the poem. An instance would be **97** in the **Dream Songs,** which deliberately lapses delicately into gibberish and concludes:

> Front back and backside go bare!
> Cat's blackness, booze, blows, grunts, grand groans.
> Yo-bad yom i-oowaled bo v'ha'l lail awmer h're gawber!
> —Now, now, poor Bones.

This is not like Lear's fool, clowning to hide desolation and fear, though something like his voice can be heard at times in the **Dream Songs.** It is a humorous, rather than a witty, exploitation of the formal idiom; its camp "blackface" touch not unlike Auden's handling of Jewish Rosetta in *The Age of Anxiety.* Both poets know that they can

only move us by means of a sort of carnival exploitation of the mirror world: Caliban, with his virtuoso eloquence, and Rosetta with her day dreams, would be equally at home among the exuberance and desperation of the **Dream Songs.** "A man speaking to men" does not say, as Henry does "He stared at ruin. Ruin stared straight back." The humour of Groucho Marx, even if corny, also belongs to the mirror world.

And so does the straight talk. We can have no objection to sentiments like

> Working & children & pals are the point of the
> thing for the grand sea awaits us which will then
> us toss & endlessly us undo.

or

> We will die, & the evidence
> is: nothing after that.
> Honey, we don't rejoin.
> The thing meanwhile, I suppose, is to be courageous and
>   kind.

because they are less earnest than sparkles from the wheel, and have been so wholly cauterised by contrivance. We can have "a human relation," for what that's worth, with poets far less good than Berryman. We can enter into such and share their feelings in a way impossible with him, for all the openness and Olympianly inclusive naturalness of his method. It is strangely unsatisfactory that in his poetry the poet cannot put a foot wrong. He can go off the air (Auden can too) but that is a different thing. If any technological habit has unconsciously influenced this kind of poetry it may be the record player with its click on and off, its hairline acoustics and relentless sensitivity. Both Lowell's and Berryman's poems have the flat finality of something perfectly recorded, and just the right length for perfect transmission. I notice writing down quotations that they do not sound very good, even when I had admired them as part of the poem: for the proper rigorous effect every word of the poem must be there. (pp. 509-10)

[Can] it be that Berryman's preoccupation—for it appears to be that—with establishing the poet's existence in all its hopeless contingency ("I renounce not even ragged glances, small teeth, nothing,") is both an attempt at what earlier poets—and bad poets today—do without meaning to, and a recognition that only a formalisation of such directness is possible to him? We can see it in the cunning control of that . . . poem, "The Heroes," which slides casually into the subject *a propos* of Pound, a "feline" figure ("zeroing in on feelings, / hovering up to them, putting his tongue in their ear"); then goes on to distinguish this from the "imperial sway" exercised by Eliot, Joyce and Yeats; rises to the celebration of heroism . . . ; and in the last verse shows us where the first six came from.

> These gathering reflexions, against young women,
> against seven courses in my final term,
> I couldn't sculpt into my helpless verse yet.
> I wrote mostly about death.

The ideas are referred to a pre-poetic stage in the poet, when they were tumbling in the dark together with feelings about girls and resentment against classes. That self could not have written the poem, but it had the ideas, and is coincident with the self that is now sculpting the poetry effectively—perhaps more than coincident, because its topic was the inclusive and unsculpturable one of death. Imperial sway can only be exercised over the words that make up the self.

The last line does not nudge us; it simply looms up—a perspective on the dark contingency of the self that heroes don't have, for they can be sculptured into verse. The self that can't remains pervasively present, disembodied above the poem like a Cheshire Cat. There is no question of making or remaking that self in Yeatsian style, nor of making legendary figures out of the poet's *entourage,* as both Yeats and Lowell in their different ways have done. Professor Neff who gave Berryman a C out of malice at Columbia, in the next poem **"Crisis"** is paid the subtle compliment of a rapid, unimpartial write-off; there is no attempt to enshrine him in some immortal rogues' gallery, and Mark Van Doren in the poem is also and simply a real person, as in conversation. The poet's mother and father appear in an equally unspectacular way (contrast again with Lowell), figures briefly revealed by night, unless the night, or pre-dawn, time of most pieces, like the seeming traces of drink or drugs, is another convention for conveying the continuity and actuality of the self.

The self can appear in that dark past as in grand guignol, surrounded by ghosts indistinguishable from itself ("riots for Henry the unstructured dead") or it can be transposed into a hauntingly meticulous *doppelganger,* as in **Dream Song 242.**

> About that "me." After a lecture once
> came up a lady asking to see me. "Of course.
> When would you like to?"
> Well, *now,* she said.

After a precise, casual, brittle account of the quotidian campus scene—the poet with lunch date, the lady looking distraught—comes the payoff.

> So I rose from the desk & closed it and turning back
> found her in tears—apologising—"No,
> go right ahead", I assur-
> ed her, "here's a handkerchief. Cry". She did. I did.
> When she got control, I said "What's the matter—if you
>   want to talk?"
> "Nothing, Nothing's the matter." So.
> I am her.

Naturally: she could be nobody else. Only through Berryman can the poem move us, but it does move. The hopelessness, the stasis, is completely authentic. Not so, I think, those poems in **Love and Fame** about the others in the mental hospital, Jill and Eddie Jane and Tyson and Jo. For all their "understanding" **"The Hell Poem"** and **"I know"** have something insecure about them, as if threatened by the presence of other people. The poet was not threatened of course—we feel his openness, his interest—but the poem is caught between its equation with contingency and the fact that, as form, its contingency can only be "me."

The Berryman *pruzhina,* or spring, snaps as the real presence of these others pulls it too far apart. For the young Berryman, as he tells us in **"Two Organs,"** the longing was to write "big fat fresh original & characteristic poems."

> My longing, yes, was a woman's.
> She can't know can she *what kind* of a baby
> she's going with all the will in the world to produce?
> I suffered trouble over this.

"I couldn't sleep at night, I attribute my life-long insomnia / to my uterine struggles." Nothing is more graphic in Berryman than the sickness and struggle of finding oneself about to become a poet, lumbered with an unknown foetus that when it arrives will be oneself. We may note that this is the exact opposite, in this mirror world, of true childbirth, which produces *another person.* Still, the pains are real enough, and so is the comedy. Indeed the black comedy of Beckett again comes to mind, a theatre of one. "By virtue of the aesthetic form," generalises Marcuse, the "play" creates its own atmosphere of "seriousness" which is *not* that of the given reality, but rather its "negation." That kind of portentousness is here in a way, and the theory of the "living theatre" has certain affinities with Berryman's drive—if I am right about it—to coincide poet as man with poem as thing.

Berryman's fascination with becoming himself as a poet has—given his genius—an almost equal fascination for us, but it has a drawback too. We can contemplate it but not share it—it is not really a part of the universally identifiable human experience, the experience in Byron or in Gray's "Elegy," to which, as Dru Johnson observed, every bosom returns an echo. What we have instead is extreme singularity, the Berrymanness of Berryman, which we and the poet stare at together: that he absorbs us as much as he absorbs himself is no mean feat. We want indeed to know "of what heroic stuff was warlock Henry made"—the American hero whose tale can be only of himself and who is (unlike Wordsworth) bored by it.

> Life, friends, is boring. We must not say so.
> After all, the sky flashes, the great sea yearns,
> we ourselves flash and yearn,
> and moreover my mother told me as a boy
> (repeatedly) "Ever to confess you're bored
> means you have no Inner Resources.". . .

Delightful! Our bosoms return an echo to *that,* as to the celebration of the same mother in **Dream Song 100,** and her "two and seventy years of chipped indignities," but what principally gets to us is the performance of birth, the pleasure of finding the foetus so triumphantly expelled. *"Le chair est triste, hélas, et J'ai lu tous les livres"*—that sensation, too, for Mallarmé, existed to end up in a book, and so it is with the perpetual endgame of Berryman— "after all has been said, and all *has* been said. .."

We do miss a *developing* world. Having found himself on the page the poet has found hell, or God—it is much the same, for in either case there is nothing further there. Compare with the world of Hardy, say, who was not bored but went on throughout a long calvary continuing to *notice* things outside himself, able to bring the outside world into his poetry while leaving it in its natural place (Marianne Moore and Elizabeth Bishop have done the same). And among Hardy's preoccupations "the paralysed fear lest one's not one"—a poet that is—did not as far as we can see, figure. But it is the detriment and dynamic of Berryman's book. Hardy had things easier, for he did not in the least mind writing bad relaxed poems, and this itself helps to keep him in the outer world, the world of *true* contingency. His is the natural contrast to the place discovered and developed by our two in some ways equally Anglo-Saxon giants.

> I say the paralysed fear that one's not one
> is back with us forever. .

So it may be. The struggle to become a great poet, to exercise imperial sway, may indeed be increasingly and ruinously hard, obsessing the poet's whole outlook. But they have shown it can be done.

The novelists of our time have not succeeded in creating a new fictional form as they have created a new poetic one—and that seems to me to have real significance. The bonds that enclosed the novelist and compelled him into his form have up till lately been social as well as aesthetic ones. There was much that he could not say "in so many words," and which therefore had to be said by other means—a style had to be found for creating what society could not tolerate the open expression of: such a style as is created, for example, in the opening lines of *Tristram Shandy*. But in a wholly permissive age the formal bonds of poetry remain drawn taut because they depend on sculpting a voice, graving a shape and pattern. The bonds of fiction slacken into unrecognisability because the pressures of society itself, not of mere craft, which used to enforce them, have withdrawn. The novel form today has no inevitable response to make to its unchartered freedom; it can only concoct unnecessary ones, resurrected devices like those of Barth, Burroughs, Vonnegut and others, which do not impress us with self-evident authority but act as an encumbrance, get in the way. Like the novelist the poet can say anything now, but he must exercise imperial sway as he does so. If he can, poetry has the edge again, and Lowell and Berryman have honed it to a razor sharpness. Despairing art critics, we learn, have been asking not what art is possible today but *is* art possible. As regards poetry, we have our answer. It is still adding to the stock of available reality while expressing the matter in hand. (pp. 512-16)

> *John Bayley, "John Berryman: A Question of Imperial Sway," in* The Salmagundi Reader, *edited by Robert Boyers and Peggy Boyers, Indiana University Press, 1983, pp. 499-516.*

Ronald Wallace

T. S. Eliot remarks in "Tradition and the Individual Talent," "Some one said: 'The dead writers are remote from us because we *know* so much more than they did.' Precisely, and they are that which we know." Berryman knew well the dead (or dying) writers . . . , both rejecting them and incorporating them into his own work. He reserved places in his *Dream Songs* for Dickinson, Frost, Stevens, and Whitman, among others, a fact that would indicate to Harold Bloom a certain amount of anxiety. Although Berryman's (and most poets') anxieties usually involve matters more threatening than influences, Berryman's combination of the voices and techniques of earlier poets helps to define his own uniqueness. Although he is clearly ambivalent about most of his poetic forebears, he imagines "Miss Dickinson—fancy in Amherst bedding hér," and he devotes a trilogy of songs to Robert Frost, evincing a grudging respect for him: "His malice was a pimple down his good / big face . . . / he couldn't hear or see well"; but "Quickly, off stage with all but kindness, now," he was "an unusual man." Dickinson's and Frost's underlying tragic sense and their ambivalent attitudes toward the self, God, and religion appealed to Berryman and inform his own comic method.

Wallace Stevens and Walt Whitman have even more interest for Berryman. Stevens prods him into a rowdy quibble: "He lifted up, among the actuaries, / a grandee crow. Ah ha & he crowed good. / That funny money man." Berryman clearly appreciates Stevens's comic method. Adopting Stevens's oxymoronic humor ("grandee crow," "He mutter spiffy"), Berryman sees Stevens as both a funny money-man and a funny-money man, suggesting that while his poems are comic, they may also be counterfeit. What is missing for Berryman in Stevens, what is "not there in his flourishing art," is a capacity to "wound": "It is our kind / to wound, as well as utter / a fact of happy world." Berryman's ambivalence is clear in his final assessment of Stevens, who is "brilliant . . . / better than us; less wide." The comment suggests that Stevens is both less wide (has less breadth and range) than Berryman and less wide of the mark. Stevens's gaudy language and his method of exaggeration and deflation appealed to Berryman. Although he criticizes Stevens for a lack of heart, he couldn't dismiss him. The question mark in the title of **Dream Song #219, "So Long? Stevens"** (one of the few titles in *The Dream Songs*), suggests his ambivalence.

Berryman drew on Dickinson, Frost, and Stevens, but he felt the closest affinity with Walt Whitman. In his sensitive essay on "Song of Myself" in *The Freedom of the Poet,* Berryman confesses, "I like or love Whitman unreservedly." Berryman loved "Song of Myself" for its sense of "Welcome, self-wrestling, inquiry, and wonder . . . (not exulting as over an accomplished victory, but gradually revealing, puzzling, discovering)." The description is a good one of *The Dream Songs* as well; Berryman's own long poem is consciously modeled on Whitman's: "I think the model in *The Dream Songs* was the other greatest American poem—I am very ambitious—'Song of Myself.' " But if Berryman admired Whitman's poem unreservedly, he was not prepared to duplicate it. Like Stevens, he lacked Whitman's transcendental faith; like Dickinson and Frost, he had a sense of potential tragedy and loss that qualified Whitman's exaggerated optimism.

Thus *The Dream Songs* becomes a kind of parody of "Song of Myself," embuing Whitman's barbaric yawp with more sadness, doubt, worry, and fear than Whitman would have acknowledged. Whitman begins his poem in health and optimism: "I, now thirty-seven years old in perfect health begin, / Hoping to cease not till death." Berryman ends his poem in ill health and ambiguity: "I, Henry Pussy-cat, being in ill-health / & 900 years old, begin & cease, / to doubt." Likewise, while Whitman can boldly insist that the persona of "Song of Myself" is himself, Berryman must distance his persona by insisting that it is an imaginary character, not himself. Berryman quotes Whitman's statement in his essay on "Song of Myself"— "to put *a Person,* a human being (myself, in the latter half of the Nineteenth Century, in America) freely, fully and truly on record"—and then parodies that statement in a note on his own *Dream Songs,* which are "essentially about an imaginary character (not the poet, not me) named Henry, a white American in early middle age." Whitman claims to be writing about himself while clearly writing about a symbolic figure; Berryman, like Dickinson, claims to be writing about a fictional character while clearly writing about himself.

Thus Berryman's characteristic comic voice and method

reflect a combination of the backwoods and Yankee strains of American humor. . . . For Whitman, comedy is a mode of celebration, a means of absurdly affirming a transcendent faith in the self. For Dickinson and Frost, comedy is more often an evasive tactic, a way of seeing truth aslant. For Stevens, comedy is a means of achieving a balance, of keeping things and ideas moving, vital, and alive. For Berryman, comedy is a combination of these things, incorporating celebration and sadness, self-aggrandizement and self-deprecation, attack and evasion, into an essentially confessional mode. Berryman adds to the inherited voices a more personal note, a new self-consciousness about his own capabilities and inadequacies. For Berryman, comedy is a means of confession and a tactic for facing fear and dread without seeming lugubrious or self-pitying. Death is omnipresent; God is a bad joke; life is boring or painful; people's capacities fall woefully below their aspirations. By exaggerating his suffering comically, Berryman is able both to express it and to rebuke it.

Constance Rourke prophesied the coming of Berryman in her 1931 study of American humor when she described the "minstrel voice." According to Rourke, the two major strains of American humor, the Yankee and the backwoods voice, were merging into a third strain, best evidenced in the Negro minstrel show. Combining the Yankee's characteristic pose of ignorance and witty self-deprecation with the Kentuckian's characteristic pose of omnipotence and boastful self-aggrandizement, the minstrel voice added its own distinct note of melancholy. "Triumph was in his humor," suggests Rourke, "but not triumph over circumstances. Rather this was an unreasonable headlong triumph launching into the realm of the preposterous." Combining the language, banter, dance, ego, and flamboyance of Whitman and Stevens with the sadness, doubt, uncertainty, private pain, and humiliation of Dickinson and Frost, Berryman adopted the mode of the Negro minstrel show as a paradigm for his own life.

In general, the critics quickly perceived the spirit of *The Dream Songs.* Robert Lowell, in a review of the first *77 Dream Songs,* notes, "This great Pierrot's universe . . . is more tearful and funny than we can easily bear." William J. Martz concurs that Berryman "is preeminently a poet of suffering and laughter." Berryman himself knew the effect the songs would have on an audience. He warned a Harvard audience in 1966, "Prepare to weep, ladies and gentlemen. Saul Bellow and I almost kill ourselves laughing about *The Dream Songs* and various chapters in his novels, but other people feel bad. Are you all ready to feel bad?" (pp. 171-73)

In his otherwise excellent study of the epic poem in America, James E. Miller implies that we do not know the source of one of Berryman's epigraphs for *The Dream Songs,* "Go in brack man, de day's yo' own." We *do* know that source, and reference to the book from which Berryman got his information on minstrel shows is instructive. Berryman's epigraph is taken from Carl Wittke's history of the American minstrel show, *Tambo and Bones,* a book that helps clarify both character and structure in *The Dream Songs.*

Wittke traces the origins of the American minstrel show to Daddy "Jim Crow" Rice, who in 1828 corked his face black and imitated the comical strut of an old black crip-

ple on stage in Louisville. Rice's mimicry was an immediate hit and became known as "jumping Jim Crow." . . . Indeed, Rice's performance was so well received both in this country and abroad that it eventually developed into the loosely structured but elaborate minstrel shows of the 1830s and 1840s. Berryman pays tribute to Daddy Rice in his **Dream Song #2,** referring to Rice's "Big buttons" (gold coins, an extravagance that eventually led to his downfall) and to the "cornets" that were used in the advance parade announcing the show. It is appropriate that Berryman begins his own minstrelsy with Rice, the father of minstrelsy, and with the cornets of the advance parade. As Wittke notes, Rice's performance hovered somewhere "between tragedy and farce" and the audience "cried and laughed" as he jumped Jim Crow. Berryman expects the same response from his audience as he jumps and sings his *Dream Songs.*

From Rice's act, the minstrel show developed into a loosely structured variety show, combining humor, song and dance, and theatrical performance. As it came to be standardized by such troupes as the Christy Minstrels, the show divided into two parts, the first part consisting of humorous repartee between the black-faced white "end men" in a semicircle and the white "interlocutor" in the center. The end men, called Mr. Bones and Mr. Tambo after the instruments they played, were ignorant darky clowns who suffered greatly but were eternally resilient. They put on airs, made humorous mistakes, got comeuppances, and remained blissfully unaware of their own foolishness. Like Berryman's Mr. Bones, the minstrel end men drank too much, loved not wisely but too well, and had periodic literary aspirations and delusions of adequacy. According to Wittke, the end men were supposed to cultivate an eccentric vocabulary complete with faulty pronunciation, bad grammar, and bombastic ignorance, answering the interlocutor's serious questions with puns, spoonerisms, willful misunderstandings, and conundrums. When not talking, the end men's job was to keep the audience laughing by grimacing while the balladists performed, or by performing their own comic songs and grotesque dances in parody of the serious entertainers.

The interlocutor, responsible for running the show, was a humorless straight man who served as a foil to the end men, exposing both their foolishness and his own and sometimes being unwittingly undercut by their antics. The end men were humorous in their ignorance and ineptness and willfulness. The interlocutor was humorous in his pompousness and humorlessness and authority. But the interlocutor's main function was not self-exposure, as one can easily perceive in the recently reprinted *Minstrel Gags and End Men's Hand-Book.* His main function was to serve as a friend, confidant, and critic of Bones and Tambo. He kept the end men talking or shut them up when it was time for a ballad. He deflated their foolishness when they put on airs, and he cheered them up when they fell into humorous excesses of despair.

The relationship between end men and interlocutor was adapted by subsequent comic duos like Abbott and Costello, Martin and Lewis, Burns and Allen, and Crosby and Hope. Abbott, Martin, Burns, and Crosby played the role of interlocutor to Costello, Lewis, Allen, and Hope, who played the role of end man or clown. John Berryman also adapted the traditional conflict for his own purposes in

The Dream Songs. Berryman is not writing a minstrel show, and his characters don't always correspond to the traditional roles (Berryman's Mr. Bones never, for example, undercuts the interlocutor, and Berryman's interlocutor occasionally puts on blackface himself, something the traditional figure never did). But the parallels are instructive, clarifying the conflicting voices in the poem and reflecting the poem's tone and spirit. Generally, there are three voices in ***The Dream Songs:*** Henry, who is variously the feisty but lovable Henry Pussycat, the solid Henry House, the pompous Dr. Bones, and the lugubrious Mr. Bones; an unnamed voice who is variously the interlocutor, Tambo, critic, confidant, and friend; and the poet himself. The three voices are all elements of a single individual struggling to be whole and keep his balance.

Thus, when Henry/Mr. Bones puts on airs and gets too high on himself, the unnamed voice assumes the role of Mr. Interlocutor, soberly bringing Henry down. In **Dream Song #25**, for example, when Henry's literary pretensions get out of hand (a favorite pretension of the minstrel Mr. Bones as well, who is always writing his own biography or aspiring to be a great author), the interlocutor steps in to calm him: "Euphoria, / Mr Bones, euphoria." In **Dream Song #69** when Henry lusts after the body of Miss Boogry (Berryman must have chuckled at the dirty joke implicit in the number), the interlocutor similarly steadies him: "Mr Bones, *please.*" Conversely, when Henry/Mr. Bones gets too low, benumbed by fear and dread (another favorite topic of the traditional minstrel repartee), the interlocutor himself puts on blackface and tries to pull Henry up: "you is bad powers," he mocks in **Dream Song #50**. And in **Dream Song #76**: "You is from hunger, Mr Bones." Often, the interlocutor is merely moderator and straight man, as in **Dream Song #26**: "What happen then, Mr Bones?" he repeats in each stanza to keep Henry talking.

As Berryman clearly knew, the comic conflict that structures his ***Dream Songs*** extends further back in the comic tradition than the American minstrel stage. Berryman's characters, and their minstrel predecessors as well, are merely modern versions of the two archetypal comic characters we have seen before in Whitman, Dickinson, Stevens, and Frost—the *eiron* and the *alazon*. . . . Henry/Mr. Bones is the pretentious but scared *alazon* who, in his baby talk and babbling, seems to strive to become baby or brook. The unnamed voice or interlocutor is the *eiron,* or ironical man, who continually jostles Henry into remaining comic and human. Berryman, containing both *eiron* and *alazon,* is both at war with Henry and on his side, balancing his pathos and irony with minstrel humor. The result is Berryman's "deadly-in-earnest" comedy. (pp. 174-77)

According to Wittke, the minstrel show came to be divided into two parts—the "first part" and the "olio." The first part featured colorful costumes and gaudy sets. It focused on the comic repartee between end men and interlocutor and interspersed grotesque jokes with lovely lyrical ballads. The second part, or olio, often began with a parodic stump speech or sermon and then featured solo performances of dances and songs and parodies of well-known people and poets.

Although the parallels are not exact, ***The Dream Songs*** do seem to reflect the general structure of the minstrel show.

Like the minstrel show, Berryman's poem is divided into two parts. The first part features repartee between Henry/Mr. Bones and an unnamed interlocutor, juxtaposing ribaldry and lyricism. In **Dream Song #26**, for example, Berryman says of Henry, "his loins were & were the scene of stupendous achievement," the kind of boastful claim Mr. Bones characteristically made of himself. And in **Dream Song #27** the focus shifts abruptly to a lovely lyric of the sort that punctuated minstrel repartee:

> I'll die;
> live you, in the most wild, kindly, green
> partly forgiving wood,
> sort of forever and all those human sings
> close not your better ears to, while good Spring
> returns with a dance and a sigh.

The second part of ***The Dream Songs,*** like the second part of the minstrel show, focuses a variety of individual performances, with references to well-known political figures as well as poets like Frost and Stevens. Indeed, Berryman may have gotten the idea for the opening of his second part from Wittke's reference to a typical mock sermon delivered by Dan Emmet at the beginning of the olio:

> Suppose, frinstance, dat yoa eat yoa full ob possam fat an' hominy; yoa go to bed, an' in de mornin' yoa wake up an' find youseff dead! Whar yoa speck yoa gwine to? Yoa keep gwine down, down, down, till de bottam falls out!

Perhaps it shouldn't have been so surprising when Berryman began the second part of his ***Dream Songs*** with Henry's death and resurrection. He had a clear precedent in the minstrel show.

The structure of ***The Dream Songs*** thus loosely resembles that of the minstrel show. It also reflects the typical comic structure. . . . in "Song of Myself" and "The Comedian as the Letter C." All three poems begin with a version of the poet's self—an aspiring clown-poet, a boaster and egotist—who, after a series of misadventures with the self and others and his own art, suffers a ritual death (Whitman in Texas and with John Paul Jones, Crispin at sea and in the Yucatan, Henry in the underworld) and recovers to new life. Whitman is reborn as a kind of comic God; Crispin and Henry settle for a comfortable, shady home with daughters. As do Whitman and Stevens, Berryman draws on both Meredithian exposure comedy and Shakespearean romance comedy for his plot, first exposing Henry through his own excesses and finally integrating him into domestic life. Although Berryman said that he modeled his poem on Whitman's, his method is really closer to Stevens's. Unable to share Whitman's transcendental convictions, Berryman and Stevens affirm his exuberance through parody.

The patterns of traditional comedy thus inform the structure of ***The Dream Songs.*** And the patter of the American minstrel stage gives Berryman's comedy its unique resonance. Negro minstrelsy appealed to Berryman for several reasons. By putting on blackface Berryman could identify with the Negro as outsider, as member of a long-suffering and abused race. He could tap into that long history of grief and sorrow which characterized the Negro experience in America, using it as a metaphor for his own sense of personal pain and frustration and powerlessness. More importantly, the blackface role enabled him to make fun of himself and of the very excesses of sorrow and fear that he wanted to express. As Imamu Baraka points out, originally "the cake-walk," a popular dance in the minstrel show, was a "Negro parody of white high manners in the manor house." Baraka muses, "I find the idea of white minstrels in black-face satirizing a dance satirizing themselves a remarkable kind of irony." The white minstrels were unaware that in satirizing the blacks they were really satirizing themselves. Berryman is clearly aware of it and thus becomes both victim and victimizer. Henry/Mr. Bones, on the other hand, remains ignorant. Berryman notes in an interview with Richard Kostelanetz, "Now Henry is a man with, God knows, many faults, but among them is not self-understanding." Berryman himself does have the fault of self-understanding, seeing that "we were all end men, end men and interlocutors." And he uses those characters as metaphors for the human predicament in a world that seems at best arbitrary and at worst consciously hostile to our needs and aspirations. Berryman's minstrelsy becomes a means of gaining perspective and distance on himself, a means of "rebuking fear," excess, and foolishness, while at the same time expressing them.

With the minstrel background clearly in mind, we can look more closely at Henry, Berryman's end man and everyman. Like his minstrel ancestors, Berryman's Mr. Bones exaggerates his terror, ineptitude, and mistreatment; he boasts about his sexual and literary endeavors; and he is capable of insult and attack while undercutting himself or being undercut by his friend and antagonist, the interlocutor. (pp. 178-80)

Whitman exaggerates his joy and happiness and health; Berryman exaggerates his fear and sadness and wretchedness, reflecting Walter Kerr's speculation about the future of comedy: "What if despair is the new heroic posture, the new pretense to greatness? What if there is, after all, an aspiration open to ridicule: contemporary man's aspiration to be known as the most wretched of all beings?" Thus Henry is Berryman's heroic posture. Boaster of loss and braggart of deficiency, Henry aspires to be the most wretched of all beings. "Come & diminish me," he pleads in **Dream Song #13**, "& map my way." In exaggerating his griefs comically, Berryman makes Henry into both noble hero and egotistical fool.

Dream Song #29 is one of the bleakest of the sequence, describing Henry's existential angst in terms so painful that the small residue of humor almost gets lost completely:

> There sat down, once, a thing on Henry's heart
> só heavy, if he had a hundred years
> & more, & weeping, sleepless, in all them time
> Henry could not make good.
> Starts again always in Henry's ears
> the little cough somewhere, an odour, a chime.

The depression (caused, one suspects, by [Berryman's] father's suicide) is a kind of monstrous entity that sits parasitically on Henry's heart, keeping him eternally down. The final stanza extends the notion of a suffering caused by objectless existential guilt, while adding a thin note of humor that makes the pain bearable:

> But never did Henry, as he thought he did,
> end anyone and hacks her body up
> and hide the pieces, where they may be found.

> He knows: he went over everyone, & nobody's missing.
> Often he reckons, in the dawn, them up.
> Nobody is ever missing.

The motiveless guilt is so hard to bear that Henry longs for a reason to feel guilty. Humorously, it would be better if he had killed someone (his father, perhaps, whom he does disinter and hack up later in **Dream Song #384**), so that he would at least know why he felt so bad. Unfortunately, nobody is ever missing. The reversal has just enough comic edge both to intensify the horror Henry feels and to keep it just short of a crucifixion. Berryman himself said of the poem, "Whether the diction of that is consistent with blackface talk, heel-spinning puns, coarse jokes, whether the end of it is funny or frightening, or both, I put up to the listener." (pp. 181-82)

The tone of melancholia prevails in poems like **Dream Songs #29** and **#76,** but Berryman often goes to rowdier lengths to expose Henry's pretensions to wretchedness. **Dream Song #50** is a good example. . . . The poem begins with Henry exaggerating his fearful and dangerous position in melodramatic terms that immediately establish the comic context. He is now the victim of intergalactic forces. The stars go out in a comic apocalypse, and Henry studies his weapons system—an incongruous catalogue if ever there was one: grenades, for modern infantry combat; the portable rack, a medieval torture, its portability humorously modern; the anthrax ray, a futuristic science-fiction device; and his sharpened pencils. The catalogue is comic in its juxtaposition of modern, ancient, and futuristic weapons, preparing Henry for all kinds of foes. The addendum of pencils, with the detail about their being sharpened, may elevate the power of the pencil, but it also deflates the catalogue of weapons.

Despite his elaborate preparations, Henry knows that the battle can go only one way: he must die. At this midpoint in the poem the interlocutor enters to deflate Henry's pretensions, serving as *eiron* to Henry's *alazon*: "Mr Bones, your troubles give me vertigo, / & backache." In stanza three the interlocutor switches to blackface in an effort to jolt Henry out of his fatalistic fantasies. The interlocutor/Tambo wants to remind Henry of the joys and beauties of life: "roses," "dawn," "green," "spring," "maidens." But the images are clichés and can't be asserted with any power or meaning. The only way to assert such traditional affirmations is to do it comically. "Yup," he mocks, "you is such bad powers that you've banished the roses and dawns and pearls and greennesses and springwater and ladies." By mocking Henry, the interlocutor is able to assert the old values in the face of Henry's paranoia. The last line, "you is bad powers," is both satiric and literal. "You sure are a tough guy and we're all scared of you," the interlocutor mocks. But at the same time he means it; Henry *is* powerful enough to destroy himself (and consequently his world). The interlocutor may also be reminding Henry (in the sense that *bad* means *good* in black dialect) that Henry has the potential to be a power for good, if only he will forgo his morbidities. (pp. 183-84)

Comedy is thus a means for Berryman to confess his inadequacies and fears and humiliations without being enmired in self-pity. When Henry gets too low, comedy pulls him up. Conversely, when Henry gets too high on himself, comedy pulls him down to size. Two areas in which Henry and his traditional minstrel counterpart boast superiority but perpetually get their comic comeuppances are love and fame, or more characteristically for Henry, lust and ambition.

If Henry/Mr. Bones is the world's greatest sufferer, he is also the world's greatest sexual athlete. "His loins were & were the scene of stupendous achievement." He exercises by climbing "trees, / & other people's wives." He is perpetually interested in women's "tops & bottoms / & even in their middles" and is prepared to exploit them for both his physical and literary satisfaction: "He published his girl's bottom in staid pages / of an old weekly." For Whitman, sex is evidence of cosmic continuity. For Henry it is more often an arena of conquest and personal triumph. His lust for Miss Boogry in **Dream Song #69,** for example, "would launch a national product / complete with TV spots & skywriting / outlets in Bonn & Tokyo / I mean it."

Throughout *The Dream Songs* Henry's lust, like his suffering, ultimately renders him grotesquely comic. The appellation *Mr. Bones* may itself be a dirty joke. And for all his aspirations to sexual godhood and dionysiac frenzy, Henry remains rather pussycatish and harmless, lusting from afar:

> Filling her compact & delicious body
> with chicken páprika, she glanced at me
> twice.
> Fainting with interest, I hungered back
> and only the fact of her husband & four other people
> kept me from springing on her
>
> or falling at her little feet and crying
> "You are the hottest one for years of night
> Henry's dazed eyes
> have enjoyed, Brilliance." I advanced upon
> (despairing) my spumoni.—Sir Bones: is stuffed,
> de world, wif feeding girls. . . .

The juxtaposition of sex and food, romantic ecstasy and chicken, worship and animality, is comic. The only "advances" Henry is able to make are on his spumoni. And the interlocutor's appellation, "Sir Bones," caps off the incongruity between Henry's inflated lust and his pretensions to courtly love. Late in *The Dream Songs* Henry is further reduced to envisioning not woman as food, but food as woman: "Melons, they say, though, / are best—I don't know if that's correct— / as well as infertile, it's said."

Without the comic perspective, Henry's lust would be merely outrageous or offensive, alienating the reader. Treated comically, the lust participates in a more affirmative comic tradition as well. Traditional comedy is rooted in sexual urges and energies, sometimes civilized into respectable images of marriage, spring, and festivity as in Shakespearean comedy, and sometimes allowed to take a more Dionysian form as in Aristophanic comedy. Contemporary comedy more often strips the social forms away to deal with the basic urges themselves. The Henry of *The Tropic of Cancer* and *The Tropic of Capricorn,* for example, comically rejects sexual taboos, satirizing a repressed society and affirming joy and life. Although Berryman's Henry isn't so affirmative an example of sexual energy, his lusts are both farcical and transcendent, undercutting him while elevating him as well. Laughing at the way sexual urges and energies control him, Berryman is able to assert their importance.

Similarly, Berryman is able to assert his ambitions, his "spellbinding powers," by exaggerating and undercutting them. . . . [In **Dream Song #71**] Henry boasts his transcendent powers as poet to hold spellbound "by the heart & brains & tail, because / of their love for it" exactly four followers. The small number of followers, juxtaposed with the almost religious faith in himself and his powers, is a comic, but nevertheless serious, affirmation of his art. [In **Dream Song #75**], Henry stops preaching on the steps of the market and puts "forth a book." "No harm resulted from this," jokes Berryman with a deadpan face, though not all the critics were respectful:

> Bare dogs drew closer for a second look
>
> and performed their friendly operations there.
> Refreshed, the bark rejoiced.

Even if the critics pissed on the book, Berryman will see their "operations" as "friendly." At least it makes the book and the critics feel better, "refreshed." Eventually, "surviving Henry" gets the last laugh as his book

> began to strike the passers from despair
> so that sore on their shoulders old men hoisted
> six-foot sons and polished women called
> small girls to dream awhile toward the flashing & bursting
> tree!

If Henry has been crucified, he will rise again.

Berryman satirizes himself, using exaggeration and deflation to ridicule and assert his claims of being the wretchedest of all men and the greatest of poets and sexual athletes. He also uses satire as a mode of attack, ridiculing attitudes or people he finds wanting. "I ask for a decree / dooming my bitter enemies to laughter advanced against them." He satirizes other poets both by name and more generally: "Yvette's ankles / are slim as the thought of various poets I could mention." And since Coleridge, Rilke, and Poe have died, "Toddlers are taking over. O / ver!" He satirizes political figures, as in the punningly titled **"The Lay of Ike"**:

> This is the lay of Ike.
> Here's to the glory of the Great White—awk—
> who has been running—er—er—things in recent—ech—

He dismisses Iowa as a place so low that people "get the 'bends' " coming from there. But Berryman's most consistent satire is reserved for the literary profession, the critics and scholars who will eventually determine the worth of his work. It is the critics, "the Professional-Friends-of-Robert-Frost" who turn literature "abrupt" into "an industry." Berryman has "a sing to shay" about the Modern Language Association, the phrase suggesting both his drunken rowdiness in the solemn surroundings and the appropriate vehicle (a shay) for conveying so flimsy an organization. . . . And yet, even here, Berryman implicates himself in the satire. He is, after all, himself a critic and professor of literature ("my o'ertaxed brain . . . even keeps an office hour"), and although he ridicules the annotators of his work, he covets them as well. In **Dream Song #373** he asks, "Will assistant professors become associates / by working on his works?" The question laughs at the whole institutionalization of the critical enterprise, but at the same time expresses the hope that readers will become *his* associates by reading him. Comedy enables

Berryman to be arrogant and humble at the same time, both attacking his enemies and exposing himself.

The dramatic play between end man and interlocutor, between *alazon* and *eiron,* that prevents *The Dream Songs* from degenerating into self-pity or self-aggrandizement is evident (as it was in Whitman and Stevens also) in the language itself. As we have seen, Berryman wanted to express his sense of personal suffering, disintegration, and pain without self-pity or mawkishness or cliché. By comically exaggerating his difficulties, Berryman renders Henry's pretensions to wretchedness both ridiculous and heroic. Treating the clichés of alienation, despair, and angst comically, he is able to use and renew them. Berryman's language itself reflects a similar strategy. Just as Henry claims to be the most wretched of men, so the language itself seems crippled, struggling helplessly and heroically along on its rubbery legs, confined in its arbitrary three-stanza form, the form in which, according to Howard Nemerov, most jokes are cast. Language, for Berryman, doesn't merely *report* a self, it *is* a self. Quirky, funny, sad, it breaks prescribed codes of behavior, offends good sense, and continually asks for sympathy. Just as Henry exposes his inadequacies, language exposes *its* inadequacies, tripping over itself, evading understanding, confusing pronouns, reversing word order, making grammatical mistakes, and dissipating into baby talk and nonsense.

Like Henry, Berryman's language is crippled and wretched. Like Henry, it is also comic, its juxtapositions of high and low style and its surprising incongruities keeping its pretensions in check. When Berryman's language gets too lugubrious, it picks itself up much the way the interlocutor picks up Henry, with a put-down or a sudden shift of pace and tone. In **Dream Song #175** when Henry, that "merry old soul," concludes that neither his pipe nor his bowl nor his fiddlers three will ever heed his call, the scene is set for despair. But true to the nursery rhyme opening, the language intrudes to make a joke that rights things:

> This world is a solemn place with room for tennis.

The juxtaposition of "solemn place" and "tennis" and the subsequent slant rhyme of "tennis" and "anus" prevents the potential solemnity from taking over. Similarly, when Henry fractures his arm, "no joke to Henry," the language refuses any sympathy, making a joke instead. Berryman explains that the arm is "fractured in the humerus," the pun defying Henry's pain. The world that boasts "the ultimate gloire" is often caught in its "underwear."

Just as language itself comically deflates Henry's claims to wretchedness, it can also elevate Henry's celebration. As we have seen, Berryman wanted to affirm romantic love and bardic power, two old notions that neither he nor his contemporary readers could take quite seriously any longer. By viewing Henry's parallel aspirations comically, exaggerating love into lust and bardic power into bathetic pretension, Berryman could celebrate what would otherwise have been sentimental, egotistical, or clichéd. Berryman's language, too, reveals a desire to celebrate the romance of its own power while exposing its limits and inadequacies simultaneously. Like Stevens, Berryman laughs at the clichéd language in order to use it. To say that humor is "fatal to bardic pretension" as Berryman does in **"Images of Elspeth"** is only half the story. By parodying its romantic tendencies, language is able to use those

tendencies. Parodying bardic pretension is a way of being bardic.

Dream Song #171 provides a good example:

> Go, ill-sped book, and whisper to her or
> storm out the message for her only ear
> that she is beautiful.
> Mention sunsets, be not silent of her eyes
> and mouth and other prospects, praise her size,
> say her figure is full. . . .

The poem is a parody of Waller's "Go Lovely Rose" (or perhaps a parody of Pound's parody of that poem), using the language and assumptions of the traditional love song by parodying them. The juxtapositions of the formal and idiomatic, the intrusion of the unromantic into a romantic context, and the humorous elaborations of the theme all add to the comedy. The courtly love elevation of woman as goddess (she is "beautiful," "heavenly," "modest," "excellent," and "fair") is undercut by the poet's evident carnality (he is drawn to her "mouth and other prospects," "and all her splendours opened one by one"). The archaic, even biblical language ("maketh," "forget not," "be not silent," "bound them fast / one to another") collapses under the deflating juxtaposition of the colloquial ("storm out," "yatter," "mention sunsets"). The syntax, the gags, the colloquialisms, and the tag phrases, here and elsewhere in *The Dream Songs,* enable Berryman to use language that would otherwise seem too sentimental, abstract, romantic, and conventional.

Finally, the playful language, in its vitality, nonsense, and buffoonery, strives against the power of despair and nightmare that permeates the whole of *The Dream Songs.* The comedy of the language may not neutralize the horror, but it qualifies and distances it. The clowning play of language, like the clowning drama between Berryman's minstrel characters, is Berryman's way of dealing with his most threatening antagonist—death. *The Dream Songs* are pervaded by death. Henry is smitten with the deaths of friends and colleagues and obsessed by intimations of his own impending death. If the name *Mr. Bones* refers to a minstrel character and to a sexual obsession, it is also a kind of *memento mori,* an image of death which the interlocutor constantly places before Henry. By calling Henry *Mr. Bones,* the interlocutor takes on another identity, one about which Berryman left some rather cryptic clues.

Most critics have accepted Berryman's explanation in the *Harvard Advocate* interview of the origins of Henry's name. Berryman explains, "One time my second wife and I were walking down an avenue in Minneapolis and we decided on the worst names that you could think of for men and women. We decided on Mabel for women, and Henry for men. So from then on, in the most cozy and adorable way, she was Mabel and I was Henry; and that's how Henry came into being." True or not, the explanation has drawn attention away from Berryman's challenge to readers to discover the name of the unnamed interlocutor. Later in the same interview Berryman refers to Henry's "friend": "He is never named; I know his name, but the critics haven't caught on yet. Sooner or later some assistant professor will become an associate professor by learning the name of Henry's friend." In his book on Stephen Crane, Berryman notes, "The names authors give their characters seldom receive sufficient attention unless the significance of a name is immediately striking." And in an interview in *Shenandoah* Berryman reveals, "One has secrets, like any craftsman, and I figure that anyone who deserves to know them deserves to find them out for himself." Berryman's three comments seem to fit together as a kind of challenge to the reader. He says that he has secrets a worthy reader will discover; names are more important than most critics think; the interlocutor's name is one of Berryman's secrets, the discovery of which will effect the promotion of some assistant professor to the rank of associate.

Although I am already a full professor, and therefore perhaps not qualified to guess the friend's name, I would like to suggest a possibility. Henry and Mr. Bones are variant names for a single character in *The Dream Songs,* a character who, despite Berryman's protestations, quite closely resembles Berryman. In fact, *Henry Mr. Bones* is almost an anagram for *John Berryman.* If one sets *Henry Mr. Bones* and *John Berryman* side by side and deletes all of the letters they have in common, three letters remain: *JAS. J. A. S.* are the initials of Berryman's father, John Allyn Smith (Berryman adopted his stepfather's surname), whose suicide when Berryman was eleven informs the tone and themes of *The Dream Songs.* Although this may be purely coincidence, it may also provide a clue to the identity of the unnamed "friend."

If Henry's friend is his dead father, then Berryman is participating in an old comic tradition. Aristophanes, for example, has Dionysus bring his poetic "father," Aeschylus, back from the dead in "The Frogs"; Dante relies on Virgil to guide him through hell in his *Divine Comedy;* and most recently, James Merrill calls on his poetic father, Auden, to help him in his own *Divine Comedies.* Further, I have suggested that the relationship between Henry/Mr. Bones and the interlocutor/Tambo resembles the relationship between the members of the comic film teams like Martin and Lewis, Abbott and Costello, and Burns and Allen. These teams are also based on father-child relationships, with Martin, Abbott, and Burns serving as father figures to Lewis, Costello, and Allen, who are clearly childlike.

In any case, Henry's friend in *The Dream Songs* does seem to function much like a father figure for Henry. Throughout *The Dream Songs* the friend intrudes to remind Henry that he is mortal, human, and comic, three important things (signified by the name Mr. Bones) that Henry is constantly in danger of forgetting. In poems like **Dream Song #25, #36,** and **#256,** for example, the interlocutor reminds Henry that he will die, something a dead father does by example: "Fate clobber all," he intimates in **Dream Song #25;** "Sah. We hafta *die.* / That is our 'pointed task," he insists in **Dream Song #36;** "Mr Bones, the Lord will bring us to a nation / where everybody only rest," he explains in **Dream Song #256.** And the friend appears in four of the "Opus posthumous" poems that begin the second part of *The Dream Songs.* What better friend could Henry talk with in the grave than a dead father? (pp. 185-93)

Whether we assume that the friend is Henry's father or not, it is clear that he focuses the central theme of *The Dream Songs* and of much of the comic poetry discussed in this book—death. Death for Whitman was an illusion or a blowhard; for Dickinson it was a terrible numbness, a trivial fly, or a kindly suitor; for Frost it was a seductive force, best avoided; for Stevens, it was an end of motion

and change. Death for Berryman is a fascinating horror. In his *Harvard Advocate* interview he defines his attitude: "There's a wonderful remark, which I meant to use as an epigraph, but I never got around to it. 'We were all end-men.' . . . Isn't that adorable?" For Berryman, Henry and all of us are "end" men, comic and condemned to death. Rather than evade the fact with Frost, who sneaks out the back window while death knocks on the lockless door, Berryman "called for a locksmith, to burst the topic open."

Berryman's "complex investigations of death" discover extremes. Sometimes, as for Whitman, death is for Berryman "lucky," a "happy ending." In **Dream Song #26,** for example, death provides Henry with an escape from discontent: "I had a most marvelous piece of luck. I died." And in **Dream Song #86** it frees him from guilt, as the mock lawyer of this Opus posthumorous poem argues at the final judgment that Henry cannot be held guilty for any crimes committed after he died. Henry is "Not Guilty by reason of death." In **Dream Song #319** the amputation of a leg provides the same comic protection from guilt and pain that the amputation of a self does: "*there* was one leg no more could happen to— / I thrust a knife into it, it doesn't hurt." Death is merely the "top job" to be "undertaken."

Death as the happy escape from suffering is counterbalanced by death as the ultimate horror. Berryman can rage at the death he sees around him, feeling his own utter helplessness to stop it: "The high ones die, die. They die." As it is for Sylvia Plath, death is for Berryman "a German expert." Henry's grief and outrage over his father's death lead him, as they led Plath before him, to a ritual revenge. In **Dream Song #384,** laughing and raging like a madman, Henry visits his father's grave. "O ho alas alas" he raves:

> I'd like to scrabble till I got right down
> away down under the grass
> and ax the casket open ha to see
> just how he's taking it, which he sought so hard
> we'll tear apart
> the mouldering grave clothes ha & then Henry
> will heft the ax once more, his final card,
> and fell it on the start.

Succumbing to despair over his father's suicide, Henry wants to murder the man who started Henry's own painful life and thereby condemned him to death.

If Berryman thus ranges to extremes in his attitudes toward death, both welcoming it as lucky and attacking it as a horror, he more characteristically combines the extremes, making death a character in the grand minstrel show. Death is a kind of straight man or interlocutor, a humorless reminder of mortality. Berryman, as end man, will keep death off balance with one-liners, comic reversals, and distracting antics while looking it straight in the face: "He stared at Ruin. Ruin stared straight back." As in a silent film comedy, Berryman's language and characters move quirkily, in fast action. They continually get knocked down and rumpled and continually bounce back up brushing themselves off, adjusting their bowlers, and fiddling with their neckties, their attitude one of surprise, consternation, and comically outraged dignity. When "he went to pieces. / The pieces sat up & wrote."

The "Opus posthumous" poems . . . provide a good example of Berryman's method. These fourteen poems read something like a minstrel end-man monologue, with appropriate interpolations by Mr. Interlocutor, Mr. Bones's friend and nemesis. The whole sequence is centered on Henry's outrageous claim, the kind of absurd claim that characterized the humor of his minstrel predecessor—he is dead. In the first of the series, **Dream Song #78,** Berryman recounts how Henry "sheared / off" down to his minimal self, a residue of Whitman's "orbic flex," Crane's "pain," and Henry's "powerful memory." With his "parts . . . fleeing" (the comic terminology undercutting any solemnity here), Henry knows that "His soul is a sight," and he broods on what is to come:

> the knowledge that they will take off your hands,
> both hands; as well as your both feet, & likewise
> both eyes,
> might be discouraging to a bloody hero.

It might be, but isn't finally for Henry. In **Dream Song #81** he reasons that the body "wasn't so much after all to lose, was, Boyd?" but is reminded by Mr. Interlocutor that "Mr Bones, you needed that." In **Dream Song #82** Henry discovers that God isn't around, the "great Uh" is a fiction left back above ground, and "we was had." But from the "cozy grave" he will "rainbow . . . scornful laughings." Although he does regret the lack of typewriters in the grave with which to sing his new knowledge, he is glad to be rid of deadlines that have become "ancient nonsense— / no typewriters—ha! ha!—no typewriters— / alas!" The indecorous "plop" of the earth falling on his coffin makes him feel like a lobster in a pot, as the enormity of his situation begins to trouble him. But he describes the lobster so well that Mr. Interlocutor intrudes, willfully misunderstanding Mr. Bones as is the traditional interlocutor's wont: "Sound good, Mr Bones. I wish I had me some." In **Dream Song #85** Henry poses Dickinson's punning question "How will the matter end?" and engages in her kind of speculations: "Who's king these nights?" Nevertheless, he keeps a Stevensesque perspective on his plight. Like Badroulbadour he knows the "Worms are at hand" and jokes "I daresay I'm collapsing. . . . I am breaking up." In this poem, the midpoint of the sequence, although he vaguely recalls the minstrel summons ("Go in Brack man de day's yo own"), he reaches bottom, coming to a "full stop" where even language is a closed system: "The cold is cold." By **Dream Song #86,** however, he has been judged "Not Guilty by reason of death," and it is rumored that he will, like Christ and Whitman and Crispin before him, do what Frost only threatened to do—return from the dead "in triumph, keeping up our hopes." But he puts his remaining time in the underworld to good use, visiting the dead and picking their brains, even having a bevy of female companions, his coffin "like Grand Central to the brim / filled up." "The Marriage of the Dead" represents for him but "a new routine," reminding us that this is just a stage show after all, with its own lovely visions: "O she must startle like a fallen gown." Before making his comeback he envisions an afterlife where "In the chambers of the end we'll meet again." The poems that follow his resurrection day show Henry recovering from illness, then drinking, breeding, and celebrating himself once again.

The "Opus posthumous" sequence, revelling in one-liners, puns, and self-deprecating and self-aggrandizing jokes, thus resembles the minstrel stage, and death itself becomes a kind of minstrel figure. (pp. 194-96)

Berryman's ambivalence about death is paralleled by his ambivalence about God and religion. On the one hand, Henry rejects God as his "enemy." He is "cross with God who has wrecked this generation." God is a "slob" who should be "curbed." God is full of morbid surprises "like / when the man you fear most in the world marries your mother." Like Whitman and Stevens, Berryman would prefer to dismiss this Dr. God, this "great Uh," the "high chief," "that abnormally scrubbed and powerful one" from the whole picture, and to substitute something else. But like Dickinson and Frost, Berryman is not so sure of himself and his own power. Henry and his world are just too flimsy to go it on their own, and Henry continues to ponder religion's place in the scheme of things: "Hankered he less for youth than for more time / to adjust the conflicting evidence, the 'I'm— / immortal—&—not' routine." (p. 198)

Berryman's fervent but disenchanted piety is evident throughout *The Dream Songs,* but his most impressive religious poetry appears in his next book, *Love and Fame,* a book that provides an interesting contrast to *The Dream Songs.* Indeed, the failure of the first sections of *Love and Fame* helps to clarify the success of the final section and provides an instructive contrast by which to measure Berryman's comic method in general. Like *The Dream Songs, Love and Fame* is a kind of spiritual autobiography of the poet. But while the comic strategy of *The Dream Songs* is continually to qualify and undercut Henry's excesses of lust and ambition, *Love and Fame* allows the excesses to go unchecked. Lacking the minstrel voice of *The Dream Songs, Love and Fame* becomes a noisy self-indulgence, glorifying the young Berryman's monstrous ego. Berryman's annoyed insistence that the ironical religious prayers in the final section of the book are meant to serve the *eiron* function by putting the protagonist's boasting and posturing in a comic context, and his reference to ironies in the first parts of the book, are intriguing but ultimately unpersuasive. The ironies he claims for the first sections simply are not there, and the prayers at the end are too far removed from the narrative to undercut it successfully. Trying to pull off Whitman's technical coup (investing his *alazon* hero with such confidence, energy, and exuberance that he overcomes all conventional responses and triumphs over society's and the reader's restrictions and hesitations), Berryman fails, and we are left with a protagonist who seems merely sophomoric and boorish, a protagonist who watches Marx Brothers and Chaplin films but learns nothing from them.

The concluding eleven prayers are another matter entirely. In his **"Eleven Addresses to the Lord,"** although they are certainly more muted and quiet, Berryman returns to the comic strategy of *The Dream Songs,* using parody to enable him to say what he could not say otherwise. Berryman remarks, "You know, the country is full of atheists, and they are really going to find themselves threatened by those poems." If not threatened, the modern reader might at least be bored or put off by straight conventional prayer as he is bored and put off by the straight boasting in sections 1-3 of *Love and Fame.* By parodying the language and sentiment of the prayer, Berryman is able convincingly to pray. The first poem in the sequence is a good example of the religious longing that had been evident as an undercurrent in the wilder and more painful *Dream Songs:*

> Master of beauty, craftsman of the snowflake,
> inimitable contriver,
> endower of Earth so gorgeous & different from the boring
>   Moon,
> thank you for such as it is my gift.
>
> I have made up a morning prayer to you
> containing with precision everything that most matters.
> "According to Thy will" the thing begins.
> It took me off & on two days. It does not aim at eloquence.
>
> You have come to my rescue again & again
> in my impassable, sometimes despairing years.
> You have allowed my brilliant friends to destroy them-
>   selves
> and I am still here, severely damaged, but functioning.
>
> Unknowable, as I am unknown to my guinea pigs:
> how can I "love" you?
> I only as far as gratitude & awe
> confidently & absolutely go.

The juxtaposition of levels of diction sets up the linguistic comedy. Colloquial phrases like "different from the boring Moon" and "It took me off & on two days" undercut the more elevated conventional religious diction, enabling Berryman to use it. The tone is loving but also wry, as Berryman manages to inject some of his doubts about God's goodness into the ostensibly humble invocation. As in *The Dream Songs,* but without their accusing tone, Berryman notes that God has allowed Berryman's brilliant friends to destroy themselves and has used Berryman (and all people) as guinea pigs. Thus Berryman still can't "love" God or truly know him, and he remains somewhat dissatisfied with God's inscrutable program. But he accepts God now and is able to express awe and gratitude. All eleven of the poems are similarly lyrical and comical. They are some of the most persuasive modern prayers we have, incorporating faith, doubt, humility, and ego into a parody of the conventional form.

The prayers, and Berryman's last two books in general, have not met with the kind of critical acclaim afforded *The Dream Songs,* which will continue to be regarded as Berryman's comic masterpiece. Full of profound truths and divine aberrations, eloquent insights and absurd obsessions, lyrical high-mindedness and nonsensical hanky-panky, and mawkish self-aggrandizement and witty self-deprecation, *The Dream Songs* succeed in offending, disarming, shocking, seducing, cajoling, wheedling, tickling, charming, slapping, joking, jostling, and caressing the reader into acceptance. Combining the flamboyant language and banter and dance of Whitman and Stevens with the sadness and doubt and pain of Dickinson and Frost, Berryman uses his comedy as a means of facing fear, dread, and anguish without seeming lugubrious or self-pitying, a means of facing ruin and going to pieces while affirming the self and its absurd aspirations:

> Why then did he make, at such cost, *crazy* sounds?
> to waken ancient longings, to remind (of childness),
> to make laugh, and to hurt,
> is and was all he ever intended.

(pp. 199-201)

*Ronald Wallace, "John Berryman: Me, Wag,"
in his* God Be with the Clown: Humor in American Poetry, *University of Missouri Press, 1984, pp. 171-201.*

Luke Spencer

Can it be apt, or even quite decent, to speak of the politics of so personal a poem as John Berryman's *Dream Songs*? What about all those 'confessional' glimpses of Berryman's private life—his drinking, his womanizing, his literary friendships, his anxieties and obsessions? With such an ample warrant for unpicking the poem as an autobiographical Gordian knot, why look for strands of public protest or debate? One answer would be that Berryman's experience was not confined to booze, sex and scholarship, however much at times he might have wished it to be. As a mid-twentieth century American intellectual his mental and moral universe encompassed the Depression, the Second World War, McCarthyism, the Cuban Missile Crisis, Vietnam, the Civil Rights movement and scores of other major national and international events. A simple enumeration of references to these things in *The Dream Songs* would suggest a greater degree of public awareness than Berryman is usually given credit for.

The Dream Songs is shot through with grief at the loss of much of the talent that emerged in the 1930s when he, Robert Lowell, Randall Jarrell, Delmore Schwartz and Theodore Roethke began to publish. There were some of that generation, like Karl Shapiro, who were not (to use Shapiro's own phrase) 'drunks and suicides', but the toll among its major figures was heavy enough to make a word like 'wreckage' seem entirely appropriate when Richard Kostelanetz interviewed Berryman in 1970. What is particularly interesting about the following extract from that interview is not Berryman's implicit endorsement of Kostelanetz's word, but his explanation of the phenomenon it describes:

> You ask me why my generation seems so screwed up? . . . It seems they have every right to be disturbed. The current American society would drive anybody out of his skull, anybody who is at all responsive; it is almost unbearable. It doesn't treat poets very well; that's a difficulty. President Johnson invited me to the White House by ordinary mail, but the letter reached me in Ireland, a few weeks after the ceremony. From public officials we expect lies, and we get them in profusion. The protests are going to get worse and worse and worse for years. Perhaps Sylvia Plath did the necessary thing by putting her head in the oven, not having to live with those lies.

Berryman might have been expected to hint at his generation's many and glaring psychological problems; but instead he blames only the corruption and philistinism of American public life. This is a familiar theme in the essays of Jarrell and Schwartz and one that sometimes comes too readily to hand as an extenuation of defeatism. Joel Conarroe dismisses the whole statement as 'interview rhetoric' and continues:

> Berryman was not equipped, by talent or by disposition, to suggest solutions to the problems of civilization . . . He was a spiritual historian, and his great poem, like Whitman's, was mainly the outcroppings of his own emotional and personal nature . . . It was not because of the lies of public

officials that he was 'screwed up', nor were such lies the cause of his death. The shape of a man's life, as of his death, has sources that are more complicated, more mysterious, and it is these, and not the corruption of politicians, that his brave songs explore. Berryman's subject is Henry House, not the White House.

Henry House or the White House: it is a very simplistic way of characterizing the relation between personality and politics; but Berryman himself has supplied the terms of the formula which Conarroe uses to evade the deeper issues. Suppose we acknowledge all Berryman's self-pity, his Romantic agonizing and that peculiarly American resentment at the nation's reluctance to take its poets to its heart; is the explanation that so private a poet as Berryman could not discuss public matters without triviality or inflation? Such a judgement merely underwrites Berryman's own crude self-versus-society model. If, on the other hand, we treat his statement as an example of a false-consciousness that was common to that whole poetic generation's perception of its relation to the social relations of post-war America—if we treat it, that is to say, as a piece of ideological mystification—then its very contradictions become productive of meanings which in turn can help us understand the tensions and contradictions of *The Dream Songs* itself.

To take an example: the statement lurches from high-minded, impersonal outrage to the pusillanimity of the White House anecdote. Berryman's hankering for some kind of cultural centrality (as disinterested commentator or exemplary victim) gets easily sidetracked into frustrated attention-seeking. Such abrupt movements from public discourse to private complaint become a structural imperative of many individual Songs and of their deployment within the whole sequence. Berryman admits the contrary pull of these extremes in **Dream Song 78:**

> . . . one block of memories.
> These were enough for him
> implying commands from upstairs & from down,
> Walt's 'orbic flex', triads of Hegel would
> incorporate, if you please,
> into the know-how of the American bard
> embarrassed Henry heard himself a-being,
> and the younger Stephen Crane
> of a powerful memory, of pain,
> these stood the ancestors, relaxed & hard,
> whilst Henry's parts were fleeing.

This Song stands at the very beginning of **His Toy, His Dream, His Rest** and is the first part of the 'Opus Posthumous' section. It attempts to stake out the limits of Henry's poetic ambitions from the vantage-point of a post-mortem. Since Henry is at all points Berryman himself, what we are reviewing here is Berryman's absolute and final failure to become the public poet he wanted to be. Despite having Whitman, Hegel and Crane as his mentors, prompting him to accept and consolidate a bardic role, his ambitions have been defeated by a sense of inadequacy and disintegration. Whitman's confident expansiveness; Crane's passionate social concern: even under the auspices of the Hegelian dialectic these could not be reconciled with Henry's collapsing ego. Berryman's songs of himself everywhere prove this true: they do not assimilate the public world, as Whitman's do; they incorporate it only as an occasional object of the ego's fretful grasping at reality, its

hoarding-up of each eighteen-line victory over disintegration and death. Martin Dodsworth makes the best case he can for this *pis aller* of embattled selfhood in his comparison of Berryman with Robert Lowell:

> As much as Lowell, Berryman is concerned with the health of America today, but where Lowell fights to keep poetry in the arena of public debate, Berryman with draws into contemplation of the universal human, of each man's apprehension of death, for example; his subject is the individual at those moments in his life when he experiences what all must feel sooner or later.

This amounts to a claim that Berryman's preoccupation with the individual is, via the 'universal human', no less socially committed than Lowell's 'public debate'. The wrong-headedness of such a proposition is exposed if we ask how 'the health of America today'—which I assume means the moral condition of contemporary American society—could be critically examined, let alone improved, by a concentration on 'what all must feel sooner or later'. Here, as so often in critical discourse, the 'universal' is given priority over historical actuality, with the result that Berryman's fear of a public stance can be characterized as a productive 'withdrawal' into the more truly (because, of course, more universal) human. Though Berryman more often than not shared this flattering view of himself, it is also to his credit that—unlike Conarroe and Dodsworth— he sometimes registered his uneasiness at its limitations.

Both the limitations and the uneasiness can be traced back to what Delmore Schwartz called 'the class of 1930'. That nickname for Berryman's poetic generation helps to explain why its members were worried about their real or imagined social function. They all came to maturity during the Depression, in the high noon of Auden's influence and at a juncture when many American intellectuals were making a serious, though short-lived, attempt to create a radical politico-literary discourse in and around magazines like *Partisan Review*. As a result, their intense psychic drives and the bardic tradition bequeathed them by Whitman got tangled up with the idea of social commitment, though that idea was invariably confused and often a-political. Berryman's own confusion comes across in several episodes recorded in John Haffenden's biography of him. In a list of interests prepared when he was a student at Columbia, Berryman put 'politics' at the bottom, just before 'etc' and after everything else from 'driving' to 'dancing' and 'bridge'. Years later, horrified by the A-bombing of Japan, he wrote an editorial for *Politics* magazine in which he completely failed to grasp the power relations in America itself that made the bombing possible. . . . A late Dream Song from the politically explosive year of 1968 offers a strikingly similar picture of other-worldliness:

> His friend wrote on incomprehensibly,
> the Viet war hottened up horribly,
> Nixon is back in sight.
> Shall willing Henry study art history
> or Number or write letters or test the text
> of *The Merry Wives* tonight?

Examples such as those I've given—of indifference, superficiality or only half-hearted commitment—add up to a picture of someone deeply uncertain about the political implications of his cultural situation. . . . Berryman regarded himself as a version of Philoctetes in Edmund Wilson's interpretation of the old myth, a social outcast waiting for society to recognise its need for his special sensibility. Thus a willingly or fatalistically accepted alienation could be substituted for critical social dialogue. By not understanding how far such an attitude conspired in the marginalization of the creative mind Berryman, like most other members of 'the class of 1930', was obliged to try and live out contradictions that no amount of purely psychological analysis could resolve. In fact it was Saul Bellow, a novelist and close friend of Berryman, who came closest to recognizing the ideological basis of that generation's tragic dilemma. His portrait of Von Humboldt Fleischer draws heavily on his first-hand observation of Delmore Schwartz's slow collapse. . . .

It is plain to Bellow that apparent conflicts between the artist and society, between public and private identities, have an integral function in the organisation of capitalist culture. Art is ideologically indispensable, but only so long as its rebels and martyrs testify to the omnipotence of 'America reality'. Assigned his individual pack of Romantic agony with its Chattertonian self-destruct mechanism, the poet becomes what Bellow calls 'a hero of wretchedness' at whom the prevailing commonsense can point with tolerant condescension. Art is not only marginalized but also neutralized by the sort of specious respect embodied in double-column obituaries and White House invitations. Berryman's 1970 interview statement fits this diagnosis exactly. It shows that he, like Schwartz, had accepted a factitious image of his importance that prevented him from recognizing his actual, subordinate, ideologically-determined position within post-war American society. A closer look at *The Dream Songs* will reveal the depth at which this false consciousness was imaginatively assimilated and expressed.

As early as **Dream Song 3** Berryman condemns deliberate withdrawal from the public world:

> Rilke was a *jerk.*
> I admit his griefs & music
> & titled spelled all-disappointed ladies.
> A threshold worse than the circles
> where the vile settle & lurk,
> Rilke's. As I said—

Previous references in this Song to Klement Gottwald and Joe McCarthy give these final lines an unmistakable political dimension: they insist that it is better to choose a social inferno peopled by real human-beings, even unsavoury politicians, than to retreat into Rilke's brand of solipsistic disengagement. The 'As I said—' that open-endedly ends the Song suggests a matter-of-fact return to the main business—but what *is* the main business for Berryman? The Song's whole movement of thought has been towards a renewed encounter with the public world. Instead of that the very next Song offers us an amusingly inconsequential account of Henry's lusting after the body of a woman in a restaurant. It is that characteristic shift of focus from public to private that I discussed earlier. Though quite a few Songs pay their dues to public horrors and scandals, as soon as Berryman gets a serious political issue in his sights his attention is distracted by a welter of reminiscence. Much of that reminiscence is sincere and compelling, but it does not disguise Berryman's failure to achieve the kind of bardic stance he himself adumbrated in **Dream Song 78.**

His inability to break free from the prison-house of the alienated ego finds its most appropriate expression in **Dream Song 66:**

> All virtues enter into this world:')
> A Buddhist, doused in the street, serenely burned.
> The Secretary of State for War,
> winking it over, screwed a redhaired whore.
> Monsignor Capovilla mourned. What a week.
> A journalism doggy took a leak
>
> against absconding coon ('but take one virtue,
> without which a man can hardly hold his own')
> the sun in the willow
> shivers itself & shakes itself green-yellow
> (Abba Pimen groaned, over the telephone,
> when asked what that was:)
>
> How feel a fellow then when he arrive
> in fame but lost? but affable, top-shelf.
> Quelle sad semaine.
> He hardly know his selving. ('that a man')
> Henry grew hot, got laid, felt bad, survived
> ('should always reproach himself.

A self-immolation in protest at the Vietnam War; the Profumo affair in England; the death of Pope John XXIII: these public dramas are recorded in unfractured syntax and simple diction: they enter the poem as largely undigested chunks of reality, prompting nothing but exasperation, 'What a week'. Then the Henry-style begins to assert itself, but with mixed results: 'journalism doggy' neatly lays the blame for race-prejudice on the newspaper industry as a whole rather than on any of its individual lackeys, yet 'coon' clumsily endorses the very bigotry it is out to expose. Nature puts in a slightly incongruous appearance with the sun and willow, symbols of renewal and eternity, before the final shift takes place to the problem of how to cope with the sort of social prestige that brings neither self-confidence nor effective power. Henry's 'affable, top-shelf' demeanour cannot conceal from him the inadequacy of his position, though he may try to distance himself from public events by high-brow flippancy ('Quelle sad semaine'). His inability to give existential significance to his life ('selving'—a continuous project) makes him angry, lecherous and guilt-ridden. The best that can be said for him is that he survives; but it is survival with no resolution of his problem.

To the above account we must now add the quotation from a fourth-century Desert Father that begins and ends the Song and is intercut with its other statements at crucial stages. Fragmented and deployed as it is, the quotation calls attention successively to: a) the need to find one's moral bearings in the public world; b) the paramount importance of individual virtue for worldly survival; c) the need for constant self-criticism. More than this, there are the ways in which quotation-fragments are made to qualify, or be qualified by, the context in which they occur. 'All virtues enter into this world' is unbracketed at the beginning but not at the end, so that the bracket, when it arrives, more sharply demarcates the boundary between precept and practice in the real world. The rest of the quotation is either sandwiched between references to debased public communication (journalism) and private communion with nature or it is left to wriggle out from under the weight of personal desperation. The final 'should always reproach himself' thus becomes simultaneously an open-ended acceptance of life's difficulty and a complacent excuse for Henry's continuing alienation. Because Berryman had not settled the issue of commitment for himself, he was unable to decide which view of Henry's situation we should take. By leaving the matter undecided Berryman allows us to condemn Henry for evading his social responsibilities or sympathize with him for surviving an identity-crisis. Yet how gutless Henry appears. If his ontological insecurity is the direct result of his inability to cope with the public world, it is not to be waved away with such a trite formula for self-improvement however sagely ironic the tone in which the formula is served up. The only way forward from the impasse that Henry has reached would be by means of a clear-sighted commitment to the unavoidably public—and undeniably difficult—situation which the modern writer is in. But Berryman's idea of the poet as an outcast, condemned to a lonely subjectivity, precludes such a commitment. He therefore ends up in a similar position to that of Sylvia Plath, for whom public events existed only to supply stage properties for her agonised private psycho-drama. (pp. 38-44)

As we move through *The Dream Songs* we can see the tragic relevance of a quotation from Gottfried Benn that Berryman puts at the end of **Dream Song 53,** 'We are using our own skins for wallpaper and we cannot win'. As private pain pushes social conscience to the edges of Berryman's mind there is a growing sense of self-defeat. Instead of an attempt at dialogue about public issues, there is a falling-back on the crudest clichés of Cold War nationalism. Even expressions of serious political concern come to sound hollow when they are as glibly paraded as in **Dream Song 162.** . . . 'Unimaginable . . . disgusting . . . definite . . . colossal'; the adjectives alone suggest the limpness of Berryman's imaginative grasp—and the imaginative limpness is exactly co-extensive with the political one. What we witness here is, in fact, a failure of the political imagination. The acknowledgment of mass slaughter in the second stanza yields immediately to a piece of grisly strategic logic that would not disgrace a Pentagon general. The enormous civilian casualties involved in a strike on targets 'near eighteen Chinese cities' are justified by the crass comment 'That would make them think'. Also the world would be made safer for international capitalism: this is only a 'quarter-lie' and therefore a tolerable one to use in justifying the strike. We can hardly be surprised that the mind that could think this is bereft of inspiration when trying to find an adequate rhyme for 'enemy' in stanza one. It is easier for Berryman to drop the whole subject and offer us next the display of childish self-pity in **Song 163** ('Stomach & arm, stomach & arm / Henry endured like a pain-farm').

Only once in all the Songs (and I include those in *Henry's Fate & Other Poems*) does Berryman manage to sustain a single political theme from one Song to the next. Numbers **180** and **181** share the same title and are treated as two parts of a continuous utterance. The occasion is the victimization of a poet, Joseph Brodsky, by the Soviet legal system. After a cautious opening ('Henry rushes not in here. The matter's their matter . . . '), Berryman has decided by stanza two that 'It's Henry's matter, after all . . . '. He then briefly condemns 'the Soviet world / in their odium of imagination' before focussing on Brodsky's skill as a linguist who

Translated not just Pole but Serbian

(a tough one, pal—vreme, vatre, vrtovi)
& Cuban: O a bevy!

They flocked to him like women, languages.
Bees honey but wound—African worst—Pasternak
bees . . .

The writer-translator's love affair with words can get him into trouble, though a Pasternak ('whom they not dared to touch') may keep some degree of freedom. The women and bee images are strong, but Berryman almost nullifies them by pieces of gratuitous erudition. His knowledge of Serbian and the characteristics of bee-strains is allowed to intrude at the very moment when the Song is developing its best imaginative expression of the murderous attraction and difficulty of the writer's situation in a totalitarian society. Once again it is Berryman's political imagination that lets him down. How else can we explain his frivolity in face of so serious an issue?

In Part II this momentary lapse becomes a full-scale retreat into clumsy posturing. First there is sentimentality ('Henry is dreaming of society, / one where the gifted & hardworking / young poet is cherished, kissed as a king / to come . . .') and then, more damagingly, a crude attack on the idea of equality:

I snuff the proper vomit of a State
where every tree is adjudged equal tall,
in faith without debate.

I beg to place in evidence, vicious mother:
That in the west of my land tower Douglas firs,
taller than others.

Thus the defence of creative freedom degenerates into an apology for American-style competitive individualism. Comparison of the bee-metaphor in Part I with the tree-metaphor here shows the imaginative cost of switching the mind to automatic pilot. The less screwed-up among Berryman's poetic generation learned to do this quite complacently when obliged to notice the existence of the public world at all. The others—Bellow's heroes of wretchedness—never managed to do it and remain at peace with themselves. (pp. 44-6)

American intellectuals *en masse* were guilty, after World War II, of what Christopher Lasch has called a 'wholesale defection . . . from social criticism' which—in the words of another commentator—kept American society 'provincial and decentralized . . . without a center of cultural intelligence and sanity'. This is not the place to examine the historical reasons for such an enormous collective failure. All I have tried to do is show that *The Dream Songs,* like the life it so closely reflects, is haunted by the ghost of the public poet Berryman might have been, if American reality had not proved to be too much for him. (pp. 46-7)

Luke Spencer, "Politics and Imagination in Berryman's 'Dream Songs'," in Literature and History, *Vol. 12, No. 1, Spring, 1986, pp. 38-47.*

Bruce Bawer

His real name was, of all things, John Smith, and he was born in 1914 in McAlester, Oklahoma, the elder son and namesake of a man who, after failing miserably both as a small-town banker in that state and as the proprietor of a modest Tampa, Florida, eatery, shuffled off this mortal coil in 1926 by means of a self-inflicted bullet wound. (p. 19)

One cannot, of course, make causal connections with absolute certitude, but the fact is that by his teens Berryman had developed a self-destructiveness as real as his father's: he attempted suicide at prep school, and threatened to kill himself at various times over the ensuing years. In [Eileen Simpson's memoir, *Poets in Their Youth,* she writes], suicide was throughout his adult life "a kind of undertow, sucking at him, sometimes feebly, sometimes with terrifying strength."

And it was poetry, during Berryman's early adulthood, that provided him with the chief means of resisting that undertow. Amid the torment of muddled memories and turbulent reflections, poetry represented a principle of order, a means of curbing unstable tendencies. T. S. Eliot, of course, had explained it all years earlier. In "Tradition and the Individual Talent" (1919), Eliot had proclaimed that "[p]oetry is not a turning loose of emotion, but an escape from emotion; it is not the expression of personality, but an escape from personality." Eliot was, needless to say, the premier literary authority not only for Berryman but for his entire generation; but to the haunted and fervently Anglophilic young poet from McAlester, Oklahoma, the eminent London literary man who had managed to put the Eliots of St. Louis behind him and to transform himself magically into an Englishman must have made an especially powerful impression. Certainly Berryman brought to his art the high seriousness that Eliot demanded: as Simpson recalls, "[t]he important thing, the real thing, the *only* thing was to write poetry. All else was wasted time." And Berryman's early poetry makes it clear that he took Old Possum's famous pronouncements on poetry as gospel (and took them, it might be added, even more literally than did Eliot himself), dutifully heeding Eliot's directive, in "The Metaphysical Poets" (1921), to "be *difficult,*" to "become more and more comprehensive, more allusive, more indirect." Published in *Five Young American Poets* (1940), *Poems* (1942), and *The Dispossessed* (1948), Berryman's early lyrics—almost all of which are formal and impersonal, elevated in diction and ambitious in range of reference, and preternaturally somber—patently reflect the earnest and arduous effort of a young man eager to be the most comprehensive, allusive, and indirect poet around. But these poems reflect other influences, too—notably those of W. H. Auden and William Butler Yeats (the latter of whom Berryman idolized). The most characteristic of Berryman's early poems, indeed, read like agglomerations of stylistic tics and pet phrases from all three of these elder poets, the poems' very titles alternately suggesting Eliot (**"Rock-Study with Wanderer," "World-Telegram"**), Yeats (**"Ceremony and Vision," "The Animal Trainer"**), and Auden (**"1 September 1939"**).

Yet to say that the young Berryman's stylistic and formal choices were heavily influenced by Yeats and Auden is not to say that he shared their ideas about poetry. The difference between, say, Berryman's **"1 September 1939"** and Auden's "September 1, 1939" (aside from the amusing fact that the Anglophile Berryman used the British system of date notation, and the English expatriate Auden fol-

lowed American practice) is instructive: for all its concern with international events, Auden's poem represents a direct, colloquial, and personal response to the Nazi invasion of Poland. . . . (pp. 19-20)

Berryman's poem, by contrast, begins by eliminating the human dimension of the events of September 1. . . . The differences between [Berryman's] poem and Auden's are striking: whereas Auden's reads like a profoundly felt response to the German attack, Berryman's reads like the work of an ambitious young poet who has self-consciously chosen a towering subject and is out to be as clever about it as he can. If Auden, in other words, draws straightforward connections between the invasion and real people in the real world, Berryman attempts to make ingenious metaphorical connections in the manner of the Metaphysical poets, representing bombs as rain, a continent as a piece of cellophane, two totalitarian states as a pair of animals. Yet one would hardly confuse this poem with anything by Donne; its imagery comes off not as fresh and witty but as pretentious and derivative—its title adapted from Auden, its eight-line stanza borrowed from Yeats, its rain metaphor and at least one turn of phrase ("His shadow / Lay on the sand before him") reminiscent of *The Waste Land.*

The impersonal route, then, wasn't very well suited to the tragic personal history and the idiosyncratic gifts with which fate had outfitted Berryman. There are, to be sure, several fine poems in these early collections; but the best tend to be those in which he rejects secondhand methods and grandiose themes and chooses not to escape emotion but to embrace it. One thinks particularly of **"World's Fair"** and **"Fare Well,"** in both of which he allows himself to vent disturbing thoughts of his father: "Suddenly in torn images I trace / The inexhaustible ability of a man / Loved once, long lost, still to prevent my peace, / Still to suggest my dreams and starve horizon." In form as well as manner, both poems seem to anticipate *The Dream Songs,* which he began writing in 1955. Even more suggestive of Berryman's celebrated long poem is a sequence of three-stanza, eighteen-line poems called **"The Nervous Songs,"** in which Berryman tries on a variety of whimsical, eccentric personas—a young Hawaiian, a demented priest, a tortured girl. The chattiness, the regular but flexible form, and the attempt at playfulness and irreverence all foreshadow *The Dream Songs;* but these early songs are just not very absorbing, perhaps because the characters and their stories were too removed from Berryman's own life to arouse in him the wit and pathos and urgency that characterize the finest of the *Dream Songs.*

All poetic careers that stretch out over decades undergo conspicuous modulations of some kind or another—changes in style, in tone, in subject matter. But the phases of Berryman's career are more distinct than most. His first major transition took place in 1947, when, over the course of a brief, intense extramarital affair, he composed a sequence of over a hundred sonnets that would not appear in print until twenty years later, under the title *Berryman's Sonnets.* In the newly published *Collected Poems,* these poems are labeled *Sonnets to Chris,* marking the first time that the pseudonymous lover "Lise" of the 1967 book has been given her real name. These are odd poems: Berryman's tone swings from the elevated to the vernacular (and, not infrequently, the bawdy) and back again, all within the rigorously heeded constraints of the Petrarchan sonnet form. Read from a four-decades-later perspective, these poems strike one mainly as warm-ups for *The Dream Songs*. Yet their speaker—though plainly tormented by life and love in the same way as Berryman's *Dream Songs* alter ego, Henry—is a good deal more mindful than Henry of conventional literary etiquette; poetry remains, for him, something of a shield against the self-destructive impulse. At times, indeed, one has the feeling that the only thing standing between Berryman and outright lunacy is his all-subsuming desire to finish off the sonnet at hand with a firm, coherent sestet.

It is clear, in any event, that Berryman the sonneteer was still mostly in thrall to the Eliotic idea of poetry. The sonnets are dense with exotic verbiage, with Metaphysical conceits, and with imitations and parodies of other poets (among them such masters of the form as Shakespeare, Wyatt, and Petrarch). They are dense, too, with highfalutin historical, cultural, and literary allusions, some of which seem thematically pertinent and some of which seem extraneous and mechanical. (The affair, he writes, began in "middle March"—an allusion to George Eliot that has no purpose other than to look clever.) Frequently the sonnets appear to be straining in two opposite directions: straining, that is, to sound cultivated and ingenious, and straining also to seem eccentric, funny, spontaneous, chockablock with personality. And there are times, alas, when the straining is all that one notices.

What's more, Berryman's apparent intentions notwithstanding, the sonnets rarely strike one as having much to do with love—unless, of course, one means a deeply neurotic self-love (which is balanced, as it were, by an equally deep and equally neurotic self-hatred). Too often, in these poems where the *I*s and *me*s typically outnumber the *you*s, Berryman comes off as glib, insincere, self-dramatizing, his putative devotion to Chris merely a handy excuse for reckless emotional excess and for the mass production of sonnets. And too often the inverted syntax that would become a familiar (and generally engaging) characteristic of *The Dream Songs* seems, in the sonnets, to be deployed largely for purposes of meter or rhyme:

> I lift—lift you five States away your glass,
> Wide of this bar you never graced, where none
> Ever I know came, where what work is done
> Even by these men I know not . . .

In **sonnet 47**, Berryman speaks of "[c]rumpling a syntax at a sudden need." This skill would figure importantly in his art. But at the time of the sonnets' composition it was a skill that he was still in the process of developing.

Berryman's only volume of poetry in the Fifties was *Homage to Mistress Bradstreet* (1956), a meticulously crafted, tightly packed poem of 456 lines that was five years in the writing, and that Edmund Wilson hailed upon its publication as "the most distinguished long poem by an American since *The Waste Land.*" The poem consists mostly of a monologue by the colonial New England poet Anne Bradstreet, whom Berryman imagines himself summoning, as it were, from out of Spiritus Mundi: "Out of maize & air / your body's made, and moves. I summon, see, / from the centuries it." Cosmic communion having been established, Berryman's voice gives way in the fifth stanza to Bradstreet's, and she proceeds without further ado to describe her existence in the New World: the ruggedness of life on the edge of an alien wilderness, the joys and tribulations of marriage and motherhood, the succor of Christian belief ("God awaits us"), and the composition of poetry ("quaternion on quaternion, tireless I phrase / anything past, dead, far, / sacred, for a barbarous place"). At one point Berryman interrupts to engage her in a dialogue, wanly contesting her faith—"I cannot feel myself God waits. . . . Man is entirely alone / may be"—and declaring his love for her. It is he, too, whose voice closes the poem:

> O all your ages at the mercy of my loves
> together lie at once, forever or
> so long as I happen.
> In the rain of pain & departure, still
> Love has no body and presides the sun,
> and elfs from silence melody. I run.
> Hover, utter, still,
> a sourcing whom my lost candle like the firefly loves.

This stanza—which, like the fifty-six that precede it, strictly follows the intricate, exacting eight-line form that Berryman devised for the poem—is typical of *Homage*'s lyricism as well as of its frequent obscurity. The poem swarms with recondite words, with nouns and adjectives used as verbs ("One proud tug greens Heaven"), with trimmed-down adverbs ("Women sleep sound"), and with taut, sinewy, heavily punctuated, and syntactically contorted sentences. Berryman also incorporates snippets of Bradstreet's own poetry, though the voice in which she speaks is very much his own creation. It's a remarkable poem, impressively and beautifully crafted, and represents the closest that Berryman would ever come to the controlled passion of, say, Lowell's *Life Studies* or Jarrell's *The Woman at the Washington Zoo* (to name books by two of Berryman's contemporaries and closest friends). But its control, unlike that in Lowell's and Jarrell's books, seems hard won; it *reads* like a poem that took five years to write, a poem that from the outset was intended to be nothing less than "the most distinguished long poem by an American since *The Waste Land.*" It also reads, after Berryman's early lyrics and sonnets, like a last, monumental attempt to be a rigorously formal and impersonal poet. Berryman claimed to have fallen in love with Bradstreet while writing the poem, and the fact that lines from his sonnets reappear in *Homage* addressed to the Puritan poet makes one suspect that *Homage* was, in part, the product of an obstinate desire to find a more impersonal way of making poetry out of what Berryman must then have considered to be the overly personal materials of the sonnets. What is telling, however, is that Berryman could not help but inject himself into the poem, however briefly; and his fleeting declaration to Bradstreet of his love and despair seems to anticipate the tone and persona of *The Dream Songs* more surely than anything he had yet published.

It was at about the time of the publication of *Homage to Mistress Bradstreet* that Berryman began writing *The Dream Songs*. He would continue writing them for the rest of his life, much as Whitman kept revising *Songs of Myself* and Pound kept adding to the *Cantos*. The comparison is fitting because, like those poems, *The Dream Songs* is a personal epic with a decidedly American personality; to read it on the heels of Berryman's earlier poems is to get the impression that the poet, after trying for so long to bring objective order to his verse, finally accepted—as did Pound in the *Cantos*—the fact that he could not "make it cohere." This is not to suggest, of course, that Berryman abandoned the idea of form. Though *The Dream Songs* as a whole can hardly be said to have a pre-ordained shape, the individual songs themselves observe a form that, while making specific demands of the poet, is at the same time considerably more elastic than, say, an English sonnet. The typical song consists of three six-line stanzas, in each of which the first, second, fourth, and fifth lines usually approximate iambic pentameter, and the third and sixth lines tend to be shorter; there may be rhymes or slant rhymes within each stanza, though no particular scheme predominates.

The quality of the songs varies enormously. Too often, the humor shades into cuteness, the wit into easy flippancy, and the childlike candor into infantile display. At their best, however, the songs are singularly moving. Abounding in clever, seemingly effortless, and often nearly imperceptible patterns of rhyme, the most estimable of them reverberate with life and feeling, their splendidly supple style capable of conveying humor in one line and pathos in the next with what often seems the greatest of ease. It should be mentioned that while the songs are highly intimate, Berryman insisted that they were not about him at all. . . . But this is nonsense: as Joel Conarroe has written in his book-length study of Berryman, "anyone who reads the songs carefully will reject the assertion that they are about an imaginary character—some details, of course, are invented, but the sequence adheres closely to the facts of the poet's life and mind."

Why, then, did Berryman insist on Henry's separate identity? One reason may be that, as an impersonal poet of long standing, Berryman felt more comfortable hiding behind a persona, however transparent; the invention of Henry, in other words, may well have made it easier for him to be himself—to be, by turns, maudlin, obnoxious, charming, paranoid, poignant, and embarrassingly confessional, continually addressing us as "pal" or "friend," like a chummy, garrulous, dipsomaniacal stranger in a bar. (Indeed, the usual tone of Henry's monologues might fairly be described as a cross between drunk talk and baby talk.) The stranger can, at times, be wildly funny, whether he is parodying the halting oratory of President Eisenhower in **"The Lay of Ike"** ("Here's to the glory of the Great White—awk— / who has been running—er—er—things in recent—ech—") or making fun of the annual MLA convention (for which "[w]e are assembled here in the capital / city for Dull"). . . . (pp. 20-4)

But he is mostly depressed, and the poem that he proffers, while volubly addressing such themes as love, fame, and God (and even, now and then, recording cherished moments of joy and tranquility), is predominantly a poem of loss, of mourning. Henry mourns his poet friends Delmore Schwartz, Randall Jarrell, and R. P. Blackmur; he mourns the literary masters Yeats and Frost and Eliot; and, as Conarroe writes, he's "in mourning for his own disorderly life." Then there is his late father, who is the object of both extraordinary rancor ("I spit upon this dreadful banker's grave / who shot his heart out in a Florida dawn /. . . / When will indifference come, I moan & rave") and genuine compassion:

Also I love him: me he's done no wrong
for going on forty years—forgiveness time—

I touch now his despair . . .

I cannot read that wretched mind, so strong
& so undone. I've always tried. I—I'm
trying to forgive
whose frantic passage, when he could not live
an instant longer, in the summer dawn
left Henry to live on.

                                                                (p. 24)

Aside from illustrating the striking degree to which Berryman bares his soul in *The Dream Songs,* this passage provides a good example of the poem's stylistic eccentricities. The seeming omission, in its closing sentence, of the one or two extra words that would make it sound like ordinary prose (i. e., "I'm trying to forgive *the man* whose frantic passage . . .") is typical of *The Dream Songs.* Whether calculated or not, such shorthand locutions can be oddly expressive and touching. . . . (pp. 24-5)

Then there are the songs in which Berryman shifts tone with what can only be called mastery. For example, **Dream Song 15,** in which Henry reflects that women are emotionally stronger than men and offers, by way of support, an obscenely funny anecdote about a "haughtil & greasy" wench overheard in a bar, comes to an unexpectedly moving conclusion with two statements, the latter of which plainly refers to his father: "Some [men] hang heavy on the sauce, / some invest in the past, one hides in the land. / Henry was not his favourite." And there are songs that surprise one with their lyricism, with an unforgettable line or two: "Life, friends, is boring. We must not say so. / After all, the sky flashes, the great sea yearns, / we ourselves flash and yearn. . . . "

Yet the songs can also be sloppy, slack, overly dependent on cheap shock value or on bad puns. (In one song, for instance, the bar-happy Henry speaks of himself as being "past puberty & into pub-erty.") And then there's what one may call the race question. Henry, in Berryman's own words, is "sometimes in blackface," which is to say that at times his chatter has a minstrel-show flavor. Why? Perhaps because, having made the Atlantic crossing with Anne Bradstreet and discovered himself to be not a pseudo-Englishman like Eliot but an American poet like Whitman and Pound, the ever-alienated Berryman found it appropriate, upon starting in on *The Dream Songs,* to identify his alter ego with the most isolated segment of American society, namely the black subculture. But *minstrel-show* talk? It is no surprise that Berryman has been accused by some critics of racial insensitivity, and one wouldn't want to have to defend him from the charge. But this insensitivity, if such it is, is only part of a larger problem with *The Dream Songs:* namely, that Berryman is almost invariably so engulfed in his own emotions that the feelings of other people—black or white, male or female, poet or non-poet—don't even enter into the picture. The songs teem with evidence to support the judgment of Allen Tate—one of the poet's closest friends—that Berryman "never grew up"; and anyone forced to read *The Dream Songs* from cover to cover can well understand Jeffrey Meyers's complaint in his book *Manic Power* that they "are simply paranoid projections of childhood manias and obsessions."

To put it somewhat more gently, if Berryman's early poems represented, for him, a means of resisting the "undertow" of suicide, by the time of *The Dream Songs* poetry had become rather a means of recording his struggle with it. "The older you get," he observes in **Dream Song 185,** "at once / the better death looks and / the more fearful & intolerable." "Can I go on?" he asks in **Dream Song 159.** "Maybe it's time / to throw in my own hand." But he has an answer to his own suggestion: "there are secrets, secrets, I may yet— / hidden in history & theology, hidden in rhyme— / come on to understand."

History and theology are, in fact, the twin quarries in which Berryman goes prospecting in *Love & Fame* (1970), the first book of his poetry to appear after the extraordinary success of *The Dream Songs.* Yet it's a messy, disorganized expedition: if *Homage to Mistress Bradstreet* had taken five years to write, the composition of the much longer *Love & Fame* is said to have occupied only five or six weeks' time, and after reading the book one can only wonder that it took that long. The first three of the book's four sections consist mostly of narrative poems about Berryman's life at Columbia, at Cambridge, and in later years, and virtually all of these poems are composed in appallingly slack, conversational free-verse quatrains. There is little artfulness in the selection of words or details; it is quite clear that these rambling and diaristic poems aspire, above all, not to an ideal of consummate artistry but to one of unmitigated honesty. Accordingly, some of them consist largely of pallid alumni-magazine reminiscences, studded with book titles and the names of friends, professors, intellectual heroes:

> I began the historical study of the Gospel
> indebted above all to Guignebert
> & Goguel & McNeile
> & Bultmann even & later Archbishop
> Carrington. . .

Other poems, meanwhile, contain gratuitous and vulgar locker-room anecdotes: Berryman tells how many women he slept with during his early manhood, tells about a college friend's meager genitalia, tells (in a flippant parenthesis) about his own illegitimate child. The general point of all this, when there seems to be one, is to underline the hopelessness of love, the futility of fame. (The book's title probably derives from the last line of Keats's poem "When I Have Fears": "Till love and fame to nothingness do sink.") But for the most part there doesn't seem to *be* a point to these poems: if in *The Dream Songs* there is the slightest vestige of an intention to make a universal statement about man and art, or life and death, Berryman manages in *Love & Fame* to write poems in which such a motive is well-nigh inconceivable. (pp. 25-6)

When Berryman is drinking, threatened with separation, and possessed by reflections on suicide and his father, all he can think of to say is—well—exactly that: "Reflexions on suicide, & on my father, possess me. / I drink too much. My wife threatens separation." As these lines suggest, this is a grim book, especially in Part Three—which concerns Berryman's post-Cambridge years, and whose poems have titles like **"Damned," "Of Suicide," "Death Ballad,"** and **"Purgatory"**—and in Part Four, **"Eleven Addresses to the Lord,"** in which the increasingly erratic Berryman, who claimed to have undergone "a sort of religious conversion" in the spring of 1970, offers his doubts and prayers up to God:

> If I say Thy name, art Thou there? It may
> be so.

Thou art not absent-minded, as I am.
I am so much so I had to give up driving.

Whatever Berryman's intention in these lines, their effect is both ludicrous and distressing. And in fact, as one reads through the post-*Dream Songs* collections, Berryman's poems seem less and less the spirited, imaginative record of a struggle against the undertow of suicidal impulses, and increasingly the stark whimpers and cries of a drowning man. The irony is sharp: *The Dream Songs* had won every major poetry award—a Pulitzer Prize, a National Book Award, a Bollingen—but once that work was past him, the now less-than-vigorous Berryman (who was hospitalized for alcoholism treatments several times between 1967 and 1970) appeared not to know what to do next. The posthumously published *Delusions etc of John Berryman* (1972) finds the poet still dwelling morbidly upon his earthly father's suicide, and still addressing his heavenly Father in a baffling and borderline delusionary way. The only thing that seems worth saying about the supposedly religious poems in this haphazard assortment—and, for that matter, about those in *Love & Fame*—is that they appear to be about God in precisely the same way that the *Sonnets to Chris* are about Chris. One hesitates to question the sincerity of anyone's religious ardor, but it must be said that Berryman, in his supposed enthusiasm for God, looks very much like a man grasping at a handy excuse to indulge himself in candid confession, in litanies of loss and longing, and in untempered, self-dramatizing apocalyptic rhetoric. Berryman's poems are at once too slipshod to be characterized, the way one would characterize the poems of Donne or Herbert, as beautiful objects created to the greater glory of God, and too flat and earthbound to be categorized as mystical or visionary.

The most provocative item in *Henry's Fate and Other Poems* (1977)—an assemblage of Berryman's previously uncollected poems and fragments—is less of literary than of biographical interest. It is a Dream Song that Berryman wrote on January 5, 1972, two days before leaping to his death from the Washington Avenue Bridge in Minneapolis:

> I didn't. And I didn't. Sharp the Spanish blade
> to gash my throat after I'd climbed across
> the high railing of the bridge
> to tilt out, with the knife in my right hand
> to slash me knocked or fainting till I'd fall
> unable to keep my skull down but fearless. . . .

The undertow had gotten him at last.

It should not, of course, have surprised anyone. "The artist is extremely lucky," Berryman had once quipped in an interview, "who is presented with the worst possible ordeal which will not actually kill him." While there is some truth in this remark, it also bespeaks a neurotic compulsion, on Berryman's part, to abuse his brittle nerves, to make a fetish of intensity, to dive deep. (It would seem to have been the second great tragedy of Berryman's life— the first, naturally, being his father's suicide—that he inherited both his father's fragile nervous system and his temperamentally hardy mother's stubborn tendency to overburden it.) And while it could be argued that there was something truly heroic in Berryman's ability to create powerful imaginative works in staunch defiance of the urge to self-destruct, the tendency among many critics these days, alas, is to romanticize those self-destructive attitudes themselves. (pp. 26-8)

Bruce Bawer, "Dispossession, Dreams, Delusions: The Poetry of John Berryman," in The New Criterion, *Vol. 8, No. 4, December, 1989, pp. 19-28.*

Brad Leithauser

Along with Robert Lowell, Elizabeth Bishop, Randall Jarrell, Delmore Schwartz, and Theodore Roethke, Berryman belonged to what is sometimes called the Tragic Generation. It's a melodramatic classification—one can imagine how the poets themselves would have bridled at it—and one trusts that posterity will find a designation that properly focusses on the triumph of the work rather than the trials of the life; but there is no gainsaying that "tragic" fits a group so ravaged by suicide, domestic violence, psychoses, fugue states, alcoholism, drug dependencies, failed marriages, incarceration. Yet even among such surpassingly troubled people Berryman stands out as an anguished soul. If his "lows" were no lower than what the others weathered, he apparently suffered such periods more often and with fewer respites. The lament he wrote to his mother on his thirtieth birthday—"my talent lost, like my hair, sex crumbling like my scalp . . . Every day I wish to die"—was both heartfelt and typical. By my lights, he had the grimmest life of the lot. . . . (p. 109)

Given the immediacy of his poems, the social role Berryman played while composing them seems surprisingly distant. His generation was notable as well for inhabiting a milieu that appeared not only to expect but to welcome outrageous behavior from its poets. They might have taken their cues from Dylan Thomas (predictably, a friend of Berryman's), who, in his notorious tours of American campuses, was counted on to tell filthy stories in mixed company, start fights, pinch the dean's wife on the bottom, relieve himself on the floor, and so forth. One is struck . . . by the routine forgiveness Berryman received after writing a letter to his absent girlfriend to inform her that he'd taken a new lover merely as protection against fainting spells brought on by sexual abstinence, or making spurned advances to a friend's girlfriend and then claiming she was the instigator, or spreading false reports that a woman who had rejected him had syphilis, or hitting a young man over the head with a Scotch bottle when he objected to Berryman's running a hand under his fiancée's skirt. This is the poet at large in a pre-feminist world. One is similarly struck by the clemency with which organizers of various colloquiums and lecture series dealt with his lurching drunkenness.

Since so much good poetry flowered in this free-for-all atmosphere, one hesitates to condemn such outlandishness on aesthetic grounds, but on the personal level the effect was unmistakably malign. Berryman constantly felt himself prodded toward just those patterns of excess which turned him, in time, into an alcoholic, an amphetamine abuser, an absentee father, a wayward employee, and an impossible husband in three marriages alike remarkable for the forbearance of his wives.

Not that he needed much prodding. For most of his life, Berryman instinctively endorsed the demons that undid

him. It was unlikely that he would abandon what he called his "forest of bottles"—and the transparent humiliations of the falling-down drunk—so long as he saw in alcohol a means . . . to "recover his creativity." Indeed, he was unlikely to alleviate his own or his family's suffering while espousing the credo he put forth in an interview a year before his death: "The artist is extremely lucky who is presented with the worst possible ordeal which will not actually kill him." To the outside observer the lives of others in the Tragic Generation retrospectively reveal self-destructive promptings, but these are generally of an inchoate, unrecognized nature. Berryman was perhaps alone in forthrightly equating catastrophe and good fortune, in explicitly welcoming what might be called the boon of affliction. (pp. 109-10)

[Only] at the close of Berryman's life did he begin to acquire a healthier outlook. His involvement with Alcoholics Anonymous encouraged a reënvisioning of himself and his society. He was greatly affected by the sight of people from all stations of life partnered in a desperate need to emancipate themselves from an addiction, and the duties he undertook with membership (writing sympathetic letters to those who had "slipped," visiting prisons to discuss alcoholism) were a corrective and a blessing. Religion permeated his last years, a preoccupation reflected in the final section of poems—**"Eleven Addresses to the Lord"**—of *Love & Fame,* which was published in 1970, and in most of *Delusions, Etc.,* which arrived in 1972, some months after his death. If, as these poems show, Berryman's journey toward God was a solitary affair, he probably came as close as he ever could to feelings of universal brotherhood in his A. A. meetings. In a painful irony—and most of the ironies in his life were of the painful sort—Berryman finally did win out over alcohol: with a minor lapse or two, he was on the wagon for the last year of his life. This period was both emotionally excruciating and creatively tepid. It was as though his forebodings had come true—as though, all along, drink had been the combustible fluid that fuelled him, that kept his artistry firing. In his eyes, no doubt, his victory over booze—like most of his other triumphs, in a career garnished by honors and awards to an extent matched by only a handful of American poets in this century—came to look hollow. (p. 110)

For all the intelligence, beguilingly harsh music, and mastery of form in Berryman's early poems, they are a strikingly uninviting lot. The opening lines of **"Fare Well,"** taken from *The Dispossessed,* are characteristic:

> Motions of waking trouble winter
> 　air,
> I wonder, and his face as it were forms
> Solemn, canorous, under the howled
> 　alarms,—
> The eyes shadowed and shut.

The Dispossessed, Berryman's first full-length collection, came out in 1948, but it was actually preceded by a singular project, a sequence of more than a hundred sonnets, written in the summer of 1947. These were not released until twenty years later, under the title *Berryman's Sonnets.* The delay in publication was a gesture of discretion: the sequence is addressed to a woman with whom he had a passionate but short-lived adulterous affair. (She was called Lise when the sonnets first appeared, but in the *Collected Poems*—the need for discretion having perhaps buckled under the weight of so many subsequent improprieties—the sequence is renamed **Sonnets to Chris.**) These poems are dense to the point of murkiness in places, and oddly bloodless throughout. Maybe because they feel so deliberately worked—the outcome of so effortful a grapple with language—they fail to convey what no successful sequence of love sonnets lacks: an outward-flowing passion. Too much of the energy is channelled inward. As Berryman contends with Berryman (the emerging poet of the freewheeling **Dream Songs** tussling with the receding poet of the straitened **Dispossessed,**), his beloved Lise/Chris gets nudged aside.

What Berryman was laboring toward in the sonnets was a living language of dislocation, a freshening of discourse by means of a wholesale dismantling and reconstruction. He succeeded sufficiently, in any event, so that we accept as all of a piece his archaisms and old-fashioned inversions, his grammatical irregularities and punctuational quirks, his British spellings and recherché diction. As was true for Ransom and Hopkins, two sonneteers he profoundly admired, he found that continual, programmatic rule-breaking allowed him a liquid ease with rhyme, and, like them, he naturally gravitated toward the stringent rhyming requirements of the Petrarchan sonnet rather than the less taxing Shakespearean form. His rhymes are clean; he rarely needed to stretch for an off rhyme. From a prosodic standpoint Berryman's sonnets are a curious feat: surely our language's longest Petrarchan sonnet sequence whose rhymes do not feel forced. (pp. 110-11)

[The] sonnets gave way, in 1953, to his first long poem, **Homage to Mistress Bradstreet**—an immense advance, even if a work so rigidly forbidding as to be easier to commend than to love—and **Mistress Bradstreet** gave way, after eleven years, to **77 Dream Songs,** the first installment of what would be his masterpiece.

If Berryman began his career with a line too stiff in its diction and metre to offer entrance to his queer humor and jazzy volatility, he concluded it with a line gone too slack in its music to support the burden of his titanic sorrows and yearnings. In his final years, he turned chattily anecdotal, and was at times both trivial in the tale and listless in the telling. While reminiscing over college days in **Love & Fame,** he demonstrated (in a passage that stands for me as his artistic nadir) that, though often blind to his own transgressions, he was capable of nursing a grievance over a lifetime:

> I must further explain: I needed a B,
> I didn't need an A, as in my other six
>   courses,
>
> but the extra credits accruing from
>   those A's
> would fail to accrue if I'd any mark
>   under B.
> The bastard knew this,
> as indeed my predicament was well
>   known
>
> through both my major Departments.

In the quarter century between **The Dispossessed** and **Love & Fame** lay an exciting interval during which Berryman the lyric poet sometimes managed to get things exactly right. This was the period of the liminal rhyme music of **"Note to Wang Wei,"** some hauntingly hopeless fragments about the Holocaust ("Lift them an elegy, poor you and I, Fair & strengthless as seafoam Under a deserted sky"), and, on the occasion of the birth of his son, what is surely his finest short poem, **"A Sympathy, a Welcome,"** here set out in its entirety:

> Feel for your bad fall how could I
>   fail,
> poor Paul, who had it so good.
> I can offer you only: this world like
>   a knife.
> Yet you'll get to know your mother
> and humourless as you do look you
>   will laugh
> and all the others
> will NOT be fierce to you, and
>   loverhood
> will swing your soul like a broken
>   bell
> deep in a forsaken wood, poor Paul,
> whose wild bad father loves you
>   well.

Stylistically, this is Berryman operating where Berryman is best—on the edge of excess. In a remarkable number of ways, given the brevity of the poem, he is always courting collapse: in the immediate, uncushioned clamor of its pararhymes (feel / fall / fail), the near-thing silliness of "loverhood," the hint-but-no-more of roguish self-congratulation in "wild bad father," the whimsically exclamatory capitalization of "NOT." (If the poem calls for such walloping emphasis, wouldn't you expect the stress to land on "all" instead?) What serves not merely to redeem the poem but to ennoble and glorify it is its overflow of something rare in Berryman's verse: a tenderness so capacious that, for a moment, Berryman the man—with all his tensions and griefs, his constant, unprofitable musings—stands small beside it.

"A Sympathy, a Welcome" leaves the reader wondering what sorts of lyric poems Berryman might have produced if at mid-career he had thrown himself into their creation. But when this little verse was written, in 1957, he had already embarked on **The Dream Songs,** a project so encompassing that he never quite got extricated from it. He had found his stanzaic form at last—a process that, by Berryman's own figuring, took about two decades. Most of these Songs are self-contained poems of eighteen lines, composed of three six-line stanzas. In prototype—from which Berryman deviates frequently, and often broadly—the metre is iambic, with each stanza conforming to a 5-5-3-5-5-3 stress configuration. Three such stanzas add up to a poem of a hundred and fifty-six syllables—very near the hundred and forty syllables of the archetypal sonnet—and many of the Songs carry a sonnet-size packet of information, and, in their individual stanzas, evoke the tone and flow of a Petrarchan sestet.

But in the form's diverse freedoms—its license to rhyme or not, its extensible and reducible line lengths, and (perhaps most important for a poet given to echoing his forebears) its structural novelty—Berryman's imagination found a deliverance that the sonnet could probably never have provided. Only in the Songs was Berryman able to illustrate how potent was his special gift for juxtaposing incongruities. He was forever paring from his verse the bridging phrase, the mediating observation. The Songs document the chiefly internal life of a man named Henry, who—in the most startling of these juxtapositions, at least initially—may be referred to in the first person in one line and in the second or third person in the next. . . . With similar abruptness, Berryman places baby talk beside theological musings, etymological puns beside vaudevillian black-face, prayer beside obscenity, sweeping political punditry beside minor physical complaints. The effect often looked like nothing that anybody had ever done before. . . . (pp. 111-12)

What is possibly most winning about *The Dream Songs* is how true to themselves, to their self-set mode of evolution and disclosures, they remain. Berryman was originally tempted to work with and refine traditional models, and traces of this impulse are found in the finished poem; the "Op. posth." lyrics of Section IV, for instance, in which Henry briefly dies, recall the journey to the Underworld which the epic hero customarily embarks upon. But by and large Berryman let his poem design itself. One is reminded of a contemporaneous sequence, Roethke's "Lost Son" poems, which also trafficked in nursery rhyme and baby talk, and also stubbornly refused to take shape from, as it were, above. In both sequences, the structure was meant to come from below, from the depths of consciousness, and both trailed off rather than risk the falseness of some tidied culmination. . . . (The two poets also shared a supernatural or mystical link, each forming so intense an affinity with Yeats as to meet his ghost in a sort of waking visitation.)

Although Berryman had a strong, at times hectoring, streak of didacticism in him, perhaps the most instructive lesson of these Songs is never explicitly stated. They show us that writers who seek a voice closer to everyday speech needn't necessarily move closer to everyday speech. Berryman in *The Dream Songs* fulfilled every poet's ambition: he managed to import something authentic and untapped from the language of his time into his nation's verse. And he accomplished this through consummate artificiality. No one talks the way Berryman, in his different personae, talks. Children don't babble as artfully as he babbles in his child mode ("Henry is weft on his own"); blacks don't speak like Henry when he speaks in blackface ("Maybe you both, like most of we"); scholars don't declaim as Henry has them declaim. But the music springing from this motley chorus is our music; Berryman glides and skids, boasts and blusters to cadences that are indubitably American.

What is it about *The Dream Songs,* then, that touches one with an unexpected regret? I doubt whether I am alone in finding them in some regards more compelling as symbol than as experience. Theirs is the special poignancy that attends an opportunity lost or misbegotten. For they are only superb, merely wonderful—and they might have been a good deal more than that. Are they one of the few significant long poems our country has produced in this century? Certainly. But it seems equally certain that they are not what their keenest supporters would have them be—a monument destined to hold a place in the second half of the century comparable with what "The Waste Land" and "Four Quartets" command in the first.

One is left to consider what might have been—the poem that, in some altered world, could have been constructed by a poet wielding Berryman's awesome energy and origi-

nality but liberated from his psychological occlusions. As a creation, this one-man-chorus Henry—a. k. a. Mr. Bones and Henry Pussycat and Henry House and Henry Hankovitch—has the good, haunting stuff of greatness in him. But, to begin with, the poem is much too long. Berryman initially envisioned a group of thirty poems, but over the years, in his obsessive industry, he extended the work beyond all reckoned boundaries. . . . And because the poem is, like most of what Berryman wrote, candidly self-absorbed, it gradually gives birth to a paradox: the larger it grows—the farther one reads—the more confining and claustrophobic it feels. Although Henry is followed all over the globe—to Japan, India, Spain, New York—none of these places have any visual or tactile sharpness. There is no Nature even in the nature poems. Nothing is real but Henry's fragile sensibility. (Although Eliot also dealt with mental dissolution, he was always capable of etching, with darkly biting acids, a street, a ship, a room.) (pp. 112-13)

No poet, however generous of spirit, hopes to enrich posterity by living out a cautionary tale, but this seems John Berryman's fate. His career, particularly in its final years, presents a bleak illustration of the bankrupting effects of having the self serve as one's exclusive subject. The writer who does not hear what others are saying may contrive, provided he is a brilliant enough monologuist, to flourish all the same, but he imposes a sizable burden upon himself—and additional burdens were the last thing Berryman needed. (p. 114)

> *Brad Leithauser, "Glass Forest," in* The New Yorker, *Vol. LXVI, No. 11, April 30, 1990, pp. 109-14.*

FURTHER READING

Bloom, Harold, ed. *Modern Critical Views: John Berryman.* New York: Chelsea House, 1989, 182 p.
      Collection of critical essays by such critics as Denis Donoghue, John Bayley, and Joel Conarroe.

Davis, Kathe. "The Freedom of John Berryman." *Modern Language Studies* XVIII, No. 4 (Fall 1988): 33-60.
      Examines Berryman's poetry according to standards set forth in his posthumous collection of critical essays, *The Freedom of the Poet.*

Gilmore, Thomas B. "John Berryman and Drinking: From Jest to Sober Earnest." In his *Equivocal Spirits: Alcoholism and Drinking in Twentieth-Century Literature,* pp. 119-43. Chapel Hill, NC: University of North Carolina Press, 1987.
      Detailed examination of Berryman's commentary on his alcoholism in *The Dream Songs.*

Gustavsson, Bo. *The Soul under Stress: A Study of the Poetics of John Berryman's 'Dream Songs'.* Stockholm: Uppsala, 1984, 135 p.
      Analyzes Berryman's use of postmodern techniques in *The Dream Songs.*

Haffenden, John. *John Berryman: A Critical Commentary.* New York: New York University Press, 1980, 216 p.

Critical complement to Haffenden's biography of Berryman.

———. *The Life of John Berryman.* Boston: Routledge and Kegan Paul, 1982, 451 p.

First full-length biography of Berryman.

Halliday, E. M. *John Berryman and the Thirties: A Memoir.* Amherst, Mass.: The University of Massachusetts Press, 1987, 222 p.

Draws upon Halliday's friendship with the poet during the period 1933-43 to illuminate the "Henry" persona of *The Dream Songs.*

Heffernan, Michael. "John Berryman: The Poetics of Martyrdom." *The American Poetry Review* 13, No. 2 (March-April 1984): 7-12.

Examines structure and theme in *The Dream Songs* as symptomatic of Berryman's personal and poetic crises.

Hofmann, Michael. "Single Combat." *TLS,* No. 4540 (6-12 April 1990): 363-65.

Brief overview of Berryman's life and career.

Kelly, Richard J. "John Berryman: A Ten Year Supplemental Checklist." *Literary Research Newsletter* 7, Nos. 2-3 (Spring and Summer 1982): 65-115.

Bibliography listing all materials by or about Berryman published since 1972, along with earlier works discovered after Kelly's original *Checklist* appeared in 1972.

Mariani, Paul. *Dream Song: The Life of John Berryman.* New York: Morrow, 1990, 519 p.

Biography.

———. " 'My Heavy Daughter': John Berryman and the Making of *The Dream Songs.*" *The Kenyon Review of Arts and Letters* n. s. X, No. 3 (Summer 1988): 1-30.

Recreates the events of 1962, when Berryman worked intensively on *The Dream Songs.*

Mazzaro, Jerome. "The Yeatsian Mask: John Berryman." In his *Postmodern American Poetry,* pp. 112-38. Urbana, Ill.: University of Illinois Press, 1980.

Traces the influence of Yeats' poetry throughout Berryman's career.

McGuire, Jerry. "John Berryman: Making a Poem of the Self." *Modern Poetry Studies* 10, Nos. 2-3 (1981): 174-89.

Analyses Berryman's use of "fluid characterization."

Pandey, K. S. "Some Comments on Berryman's First Dream Song." *The Literary Endeavour* 111, Nos. 1-2 (July-September 1981): 16-24.

Provides a close reading of Dream Song 1 as a key to understanding *The Dream Songs.*

Provost, Sarah. "Erato's Fool and Bitter Sister: Two Aspects of John Berryman." *Twentieth Century Literature* 30, No. 1 (Spring 1984): 69-79.

Explores *Homage to Mistress Bradstreet* as a sublimation of the affair that inspired *Berryman's Sonnets.*

Siegel, Muffy E. A. " 'The Original Crime.' " *Poetics Today* 2, No. 1a (Autumn 1980): 163-88.

Applies transformational-generative linguistic theory to Berryman's syntactic choices in *The Dream Songs.*

Thomas, Harry, ed. *Berryman's Understanding: Reflections on the Poetry of John Berryman.* Boston: Northeastern University Press, 1988, 259 p.

Collects interviews with Berryman as well as remembrances and criticism by others. Includes a chronology of the poet's life.

Thornbury, Charles. "John Berryman and the 'Majestic Shade' of W. B. Yeats." *Yeats: An Annual of Critical and Textual Studies* III (1985): 121-72.

Recounts Berryman's early encounters with Yeats and analyses their effect on Berryman's poetic development.

Vance Bourjaily

1922-

(Born Vance Nye Bourjaily) American novelist, short story writer, journalist, dramatist, critic, screenwriter, and editor.

Bourjaily is a prominent novelist often associated with the generation of American writers that rose to prominence immediately following World War II. This group, which included Norman Mailer, Gore Vidal, and Truman Capote, was designated "after the lost generation" by John W. Aldridge due to their use of literary techniques employed by Ernest Hemingway, F. Scott Fitzgerald, and other "lost generation" authors of the post-World War I era. Bourjaily, who was initially hailed by Ernest Hemingway as "the most talented writer we have under fifty," has garnered praise for his stylistic experiments and examination of the divisive consequences of war on American society and the individual. Although reviewers generally agree that Bourjaily has not attained the stature of his peers, usually noting either a lack of a unifying novelistic vision or an overreliance upon existing literary models, most consider Bourjaily an important contributor to postwar literature, and his accurate dialogue and exuberant style are consistently applauded.

Bourjaily was born in Cleveland, Ohio, the son of Barbara Bourjaily, who wrote popular romances under her maiden name of Barbara Webb, and Monte Ferris Bourjaily, a Lebanese-born journalist who became a prominent newspaper editor and publisher. Bourjaily's parents divorced while he was still a child, and he was largely raised on a dairy farm in Virginia by his mother and stepfather. After briefly attending Bowdoin College in Maine prior to World War II, Bourjaily became a volunteer ambulance corpsman for the American Field Service in Egypt, Libya, Syria, and Italy. From 1944 to 1946, he served in the United States Army, returning to Bowdoin College after the war and graduating in 1947. The same year he published his first novel, *The End of My Life*, a semiautobiographical work about Skinner Galt, a cynical, twenty-two-year old ambulance driver serving in Africa and Italy. Skinner's offhand decision to take an American Army nurse on a tour of the front results in her accidental death, prompting Skinner to contemplate his nihilistic attitude and lack of values. The novel attracted scant critical attention and was unfavorably compared to Hemingway's *A Farewell to Arms*, yet Skinner was deemed a representative symbol of Bourjaily's generation. The book's popular reputation escalated following the appearance of John W. Aldridge's study *After the Lost Generation* in 1951, in which he commented: "No book since [F. Scott Fitzgerald's] *This Side of Paradise* has caught so well the flavor of youth in wartime, and no book since *A Farewell to Arms* has contained so complete a record of the loss of that youth in war."

Bourjaily's second novel, *The Hound of Earth*, focuses on the final days of an atomic research scientist who is apprehended by the United States government years after he assimilated into mainstream American society. His decision

to leave his wife and family stems from his guilt over having unwittingly contributed to wartime research that led to the creation of the atomic weapons used in Japan during World War II. Working temporarily as a stock room clerk in a San Francisco department store, the protagonist is discovered as a result of his decision to stay and help others during the Christmas season. Although some critics maintained that Bourjaily failed to integrate the moral dilemmas of his protagonist with those concerning the use of atomic weapons, the novel was commended as one of the few postwar works to deal with the impact of nuclear weaponry on society. John J. Maloney called *The Hound of Earth* "a good book, provocative, thoughtful, crisply written and thoroughly worth reading." *The Violated*, an ambitious work that covers forty years of history and contains more than fifty characters, was also praised for its focus on difficult postwar issues. This book revolves around a group of nihilistic characters unable to communicate or to achieve worthwhile goals following World War II. Although several commentators observed that the book lacked a clear sense of statement, Granville Hicks lauded the *The Violated* as "a sad, beautiful novel of exceptional merit." Hicks added: "The novel is not 'well-made' and the author quite obviously doesn't want it to be. But to the end it retains its vigor and strangeness. It is the work of a man of unusual creative power and deeply compassionate insight."

Bourjaily's next novel, *Confessions of a Spent Youth,* is regarded as among his most experimental works. Avoiding moral commentary or judgment in the manner of the documentary, Bourjaily focuses on the attempts of a youthful narrator to obtain friendship and self-awareness amidst experiences with sex, drugs, and crime. Harris Dienstfrey called *Confessions of a Spent Youth* "a long, complex novel, naturalistic yet quietly lyrical, in which the experiences of one young man from 1939 to 1946 comprehend features of American life which have been decisive for the past twenty years." *The Man Who Knew Kennedy,* published after the assassination of President John F. Kennedy, centers on Dave Doremus, a charismatic man who is destroyed by his inability to fulfill his potential and by the disintegration of cultural and ethical codes in the post–World War II era. While the book achieved commercial success, several critics accused Bourjaily of opportunism, citing his inability to provide a meaningful parallel between the demise of his protagonist and the national loss brought on by Kennedy's death.

Bourjaily's next novel, *Brill Among the Ruins,* combines many thematic and stylistic techniques common to postwar fiction. This work concerns Robert Brill, an alcoholic, womanizing lawyer and former crusader. Disgusted with his small-town existence, Brill undertakes a trip to Oaxaca, Mexico, where he attains self-knowledge and then returns home to help his emotionally-disturbed wife. While some reviewers faulted the stylistic experimentation in Bourjaily's next novel, *Now Playing at Canterbury,* as superfluous or unnecessary, William McPherson called the book "an exuberantly eclectic aggregation of prose, heroic couplets, comic strips, operatic libretto, fantasy and fictional set pieces striving to contain itself in what we more and more loosely term the novel, which for purposes of this book should be defined as a work of the imagination." In this work, the premiere of an opera provides the subtext for an eclectic group of individuals to gather and recite their stories in the manner of Chaucer's *Canterbury Tales.*

A Game Men Play combines elements of the war novel, the espionage thriller, the historical novel, and the character study. This work focuses on C. K. "Chink" Peters, an honorable man who investigates the murder of the daughters of his former commanding officer despite the fact that the man previously seduced his wife. Shifting between intricate plots and settings, this novel was faulted by some critics as uncohesive but was lauded by Raymond Carver as "a long and profound, sometimes pastoral meditation on the human condition" and a "compelling and relentlessly authentic work of art." A similar complexity of plot characterizes *The Great Fake Book,* in which Charles Mizzourin analyzes incomplete sections from the autobiography of his father, Mike, who died while he was an infant. These memoirs provide insights into Mike's pursuit of a singer from a local club and his obsession with jazz following World War II, which led him to obtain a coronet and a "fake book," a plagiarized compendium of popular songs that enables musicians to "fake" songs without paying for sheet music. Mike's autobiography uses popular song titles for each chapter heading, finally emerging as the freely-improvised "fake book" of the title. John Seelye called *The Great Fake Book* "a tour de force of consider-

able complexity and craft" as well as "an enjoyable, exhilarating experience from start to finish."

From 1953 to 1955, Bourjaily edited *discovery,* a literary periodical he cofounded with John Aldridge in 1951 that featured the work of such authors as Norman Mailer, William Styron, and Saul Bellow. In addition to serving as the first drama critic of *The Village Voice,* Bourjaily also taught at the Writers Workshop at the University of Iowa from 1957 to 1958, where he later became an Associate Professor. In addition, Bourjaily has written *The Unnatural Enemy,* a nonfiction book on hunting, and served as an American specialist on North American literature on cultural missions of the U.S. State Department to South America in 1959 and 1972.

(See also *CLC,* Vol. 8; *Contemporary Authors,* Vols. 1-4, rev. ed.; *Contemporary Authors New Revision Series,* Vol. 2; *Contemporary Authors Autobiography Series,* Vol. 1; and *Dictionary of Literary Biography,* Vol. 2.)

PRINCIPAL WORKS

NOVELS

The End of My Life   1947
The Hound of Earth   1955
The Violated   1958
Confessions of a Spent Youth   1960
The Man Who Knew Kennedy   1967
Brill Among the Ruins   1970
Now Playing at Canterbury   1976
A Game Men Play   1980
The Great Fake Book   1987

OTHER

The Quick Years   (play)   1954
The Unnatural Enemy   (nonfiction)   1963
$4000 [with Tom Turner] (opera libretto)   1969
Country Matters: Collected Reports from the Fields and Streams of Iowa and Other Places   (nonfiction) 1973

Iris Barry

Short of organized eavesdropping, the best way to find out what young people today are thinking and saying is to study the new novels by young writers. And [*The End of My Life*] by twenty-five-year-old Vance Bourjaily seems to be a particularly revealing sample, not only because the conversations it includes have a most convincing ring. Beyond this, it combines a distinct maturity with youthful irreverence, is serious to a degree that would be terrifying if it were not so honest, yet at the same time embraces a disarming humor.

The hero of the book is serving as a volunteer ambulance driver with the British army in Syria and, later, in Italy— as, for that matter, the author himself did for two years. The experiences of Skinner Galt and his companions are so excellently well documented that they furnish what seems, in the reading, like a fresh experience of that kind of unwarlike wartime existence. The chief interest of the novel, however, is an analysis of the nature and moods of four young men—Skinner himself, Rod, the café pianist; serious Benny and a somewhat dim but pleasant boy called Freak. To say that none of them is idealized is understatement: they and life itself are observed with a shrewd and keenly sensitive eye and the spectacle is a harsh if fascinating one. It is indeed possible that many of the attitudes to life as expressed will horrify some and that scenes described and expressions used may send an eyebrow or two upward. On the other hand, there is certainly no intention to shock, and the tone of the book as a whole is astonishingly civilized, earnest and illuminating.

One of the four agonists finds the anonymity of his work with the ambulance corps insufficient. . . . [The] memory of the love affair which had embellished Skinner's last week in New York has faded into cynicism and cerebration: finally he ceases even to write unkind letters to his girl. The reason he does not commit suicide is a curious one. He ends up in prison in a state of strange listlessness. None of these young men seems to have any urge to save the world or any illusions, though all of them betray a considerable disgust both at man's inhumanity to those weaker than himself and at life in any kind of army whatsoever. If indeed they are typical of their generation, some one is going to have a hard time marshaling their contemporaries to follow any pipe or jump on any bandwagon, for they are noticeably wiser and cooler and more analytical than their fathers and less prone to self-deception. Which is not to say that they are incapable upon occasion of thoroughly enjoying themselves.

> *Iris Barry, "Irreverent Humor of War-Time," in* New York Herald Tribune Weekly Book Review, *August 24, 1947, p. 3.*

Merle Miller

Both his publishers and Mr. Bourjaily himself have quite honestly mentioned his debt to that older, better known author Mr. Hemingway, and those of us who admire *A Farewell to Arms* will find in **The End of My Life** a startling, at times uncomfortable resemblance to that earlier, more skilful novel of the first global war. Primarily, Bourjaily writes about four Americans who drove ambulances for the British in Africa and in Italy; Skinner Galt is twenty-two and bitter without illusions and left college to join the corps; Rod Manjac is a musician and a fine one, but he is also confused, and he is troubled by a sexual maladjustment that leads, eventually, to his self-banishment; Benny Berg is an idealist, an intellectual, an unquestioning admirer of the Soviet Union, and Robert (Freak) Lacey, the least successfully portrayed of the four, is a naïve, rather simple-minded young man who played good college football. There are tenderness and violence in Mr. Bourjaily's story, the genuine, not the movie-advertisement kind, and there is much more than that. There is a lot about a generation that is without much hope, that has never known stability, that found, even in the war we recently finished, not much to inspire a thinking man. Once Skinner sums it up pretty well. "I want a nice, small war, Jeff," he says, "with clear-cut issues. There should be a lot more than just a villain you hate. There should be a side you can love, too." I hope a lot of people will read **The End of My**

Life; I'm sure almost everybody will enjoy it, despite its faults, which are numerous and obvious, and I'm equally certain that Bourjaily is going to write other and better novels. He has done an almost first-rate job with this one. (pp. 17-18)

> *Merle Miller, "One for the Money," in* The Saturday Review of Literature, *Vol. XXX, No. 35, August 30, 1947, pp. 17-18.*

John W. Aldridge

[The process by which young men have] discovered the truth of war in the midst of war has been suggested in a dozen good novels over the last few years, but the full history of the process, from its beginning in the era between World Wars I and II to its climax in the futility of the period between World Wars II and III, can be traced in only one of them, Vance Bourjaily's **The End of My Life,** the most neglected but, in many ways, the most promising of them all.

To the generation who entered college in the first year or two of World War II, left college for the war in the third or fourth year, and came out of the war in the fifth or six, **The End of My Life,** in spite of its occasional callowness and crudity, will always have a special charm; for it is uniquely their story. No book since *This Side of Paradise* has caught so well the flavor of youth in wartime, and no book since *A Farewell to Arms* has contained so complete a record of the loss of that youth in war. Actually, Bourjaily has written the one-volume, contemporary equivalent of both. His Skinner Galt is at first a wiser and far more self-destructive Amory Blaine, and later a counterpart of the Frederick Henry who left everything behind and walked through the rain into nothingness after the death of Catherine; and his Cindy is a younger and much more innocent Catherine—strong, courageous, devoutly in love, and also fated to die, as all the truly living and loving, the very good, the very gentle, and the very brave, are fated to die in a futile and loveless world. But this is not to say that Bourjaily has attempted to reconstruct the world of either Fitzgerald or Hemingway. Rather, he has recaptured the flavor of a world that existed twenty years after Fitzgerald wrote *This Side of Paradise* but that Fitzgerald would, nevertheless, have understood; and he has written of a war experience that Hemingway never knew but that Frederick Henry's loss foreshadows. If much of his novel seems to fit more into their tradition than into the tradition of his contemporaries, it is perhaps because it has its roots in a time that was very much like theirs, a time that ended with the war and that remained outside the range of the other war novels. But **The End of My Life** is the last of that tradition. The lyric emotion and romantic irony of its early sections quickly give way to the black horror with which it ends and which is one of the distinctive trademarks of the literature of this war.

The long flash back to Skinner Galt's college life and his love affair with Cindy, which is introduced midway through the novel, belongs to the prewar time and the old tradition. It is dominated by a Fitzgeraldian fever-glow and a muted frenzy not unlike that of *The Sun Also Rises.* The time is roughly 1942, and even though the war has already begun for Americans in Africa and the Pacific, it has not yet really touched the college campuses. Its immanence, however, is everywhere. (pp. 121-22)

Skinner Galt is an extreme symbol of its neurosis. Born in the Twenties, he is the product of denial even though he has never known the values that were denied. Brought up in the Thirties, he remembers the tragedy of the Depression but not the prosperity which preceded it. Faced with war in the Forties, he knows only that he was taught to be cynical about war and that the books he has read have given a bitter picture of war. If Skinner were a writer he would write like Hemingway. If he wants to make a point in conversation he is likely to quote Eliot. But he has absorbed what Hemingway and Eliot have had to say without having had their experience. He has never known the innocence which made Hemingway bitter; and if he had ever felt the indignation which is behind *The Hollow Men,* he would have been afraid to admit it even to himself. The last refuge for him and those who are like him is casual indifference. "We've figured that as soon as we replaced all the illusions with defenses we'd be mature." But the defenses are effective only so long as there is something to defend; and in a generation without values, without hope of values, the defenses are likely to conceal only emptiness.

Yet there is something about Skinner's cynicism in these early stages of his story which neither he nor Bourjaily seems to understand but which has great bearing on his whole development. To Skinner cynicism is, as he later says of suicide, "an intellectual position." It is an attitude toward life, a philosophical compromise with the problem of belief, and as long as he holds to it, it keeps him from being hurt—"You've got to tear things down . . . before they get a chance to fall on you, and you don't get hurt." It is the philosophy of a disillusioned absolutist, one who will believe nothing if he cannot believe wholly; and it is the product of an age which has wrecked more than it has built. But for Skinner denial is itself an absolute; without it, he could not possibly survive. This, then, is the significant fact. As an intellectual position, cynicism for Skinner amounts to an act of faith. Like the Lost Generation's belief in *nada,* it has nothing to do with his emotions except to free them, and like Frederick Henry's early belief in the war, it gives him the sense of security he needs to live fully and exuberantly.

The tense excitement, daring, and essential confidence of that first year or two of the war have never been more clearly illustrated than they are in Skinner, and they are perhaps the most significant qualities of his story; for they show, if Skinner is typical, that for a brief moment before they were all caught up in the war this generation was secure. Their deep concern over the prospect of war was rationalized by their belief in the meaninglessness of the war. Their very uncertainty, along with the sense they had of coming to the end of something, became, in a way, a certainty which released their minds from all further concern and left them free to live intensely in the time they had left. Although they had arrived by a different road, they were as near to the Lost Generation at this point as they would ever be. The war had not yet turned their cynicism to horror, transformed their intellectual position into paralyzing emotionality.

This atmosphere of certitude-amid-chaos can be felt throughout the flash-back sections of *The End of My Life.*

It is present in the frenzied college parties, the drinking, and the love-making, and it is very much present in the bacchanalian revels, the wild orgies of negation, of Skinner and Cindy in New York. These scenes make it vividly clear that at least at the beginning the cynicism could be an exhilarating game and part of a restless search for thrills.

A few days before Skinner is to leave for the war, he, Cindy, and their friend Benny Berg fall into a discussion of belief. Benny is a Communist and has, so Cindy thinks, "a nice, reassuringly affirmative answer to this question of whether life is . . . worthwhile."

> "Most of the people who say 'Yes,' " Benny says, ". . . base it on one central belief. There are even some people who think the whole thing through, and can't find a central belief, who say yes anyway, just for the joy of saying it. They do all right."

> "But what are the other things you can base it on?" Cindy asks.

> "Oh, religion. Art. Belief in mankind. Lots of things. If your belief is political, it probably boils down to belief in mankind."

> "But why don't any of these things work for Skinner?" she wants to know.

> "Well," Benny replies. "You can take the simple explanation and say he's a masochist, and doesn't want any of them to work. But that's too easy. I figure with those guys, it's a case of there being two ways of believing. If you're an objective believer, if you have to be sure something is true first, before you believe it, you'll never find anything that will satisfy you for long. You have to believe subjectively, believe because you find it satisfying, believe by faith without requiring proof. A cause or principle is just as true as the amount of devotion you give it. If you wait for it to become true because it's undeniable, you wait forever."

The outcome of this discussion is a chart which the three of them gleefully draw up, showing how the great writers and thinkers of the past and present would look as two rival football teams representing the affirmative and negative views of life. Lincoln, Lenin, Cindy, Twain, Franklin D. Roosevelt, Falstaff, Christ, D. H. Lawrence, Marx, Wolfe, and Heywood Broun make up the "Yes" team, and Andreyev, Swift, Hemingway, the early Huxley, Freud, Voltaire, Waugh, Henry Miller, Hart Crane, Fitzgerald, and the early Eliot, the "No" team. Skinner is the ball, Johnny Walker the referee, and the timekeeper is Death. (*The End of My Life,* incidentally, is the only new novel which gives to books their true importance as source material for this generation's ideas and attitudes. It will probably never be known how deeply our responses to the second war were affected by the novels of the first war or how differently we might have thought, felt, and written if we had never read Hemingway, Fitzgerald, Eliot, and Wolfe.)

But this does not satisfy Cindy. She has already learned from observing the progress of Skinner's denial of life that "there is one final and unavoidable conclusion at which those who hold that life is basically intolerable must arrive to be consistent," so she asks Benny for another kind of answer.

> "He," Benny replies, pointing at Skinner, "is a pre-

war neurotic. Same symptoms, world-weariness, enlarged death-wish, tendency towards self-pity. . . . You see, we've all been involved in this war unconsciously, ever since we were old enough to know what the word inevitable meant. It was so clear that it was coming. All of us are pre-war neurotics to some extent—Skinner almost a perfect one. The pressure was terrific, Cindy. Every time we read a book about the last war, we were fighting this one."

At this point Skinner, who has been trying throughout the scene to turn the conversation away from the tender subject of himself, solemnly dumps the contents of his liquor glass over the top of his head. Benny's mouth drops open and he begins to laugh; Cindy, half shrieking, half whooping, springs out of her chair and throws her arms around Skinner's neck; and the whole affair dissolves into a fantastic, drunken dance of death. Benny has just finished saying that "the pattern of reaction was taking chances, being amoral, doing anything for a laugh," and now the situation becomes an outlandish parody of his words. Cindy begins to choke Skinner and he sinks, crucified, to the floor. "Again we kill Christ," Benny cries, pounding at Skinner's hand with his empty glass. . . . Finally they collapse, exhausted and purged, having courted death and found her willing. The "pattern of reaction" has been asserted, but asserted with action and an exuberant willingness to live.

Skinner's war service is, in most respects, ideal. Unlike the vast majority of his contemporaries, who either entered one of the college training programs or were drafted directly out of college into the Army and Navy, he leaves college and joins the British Field Service. As an ambulance driver serving with a foreign army, he is one of the very few American gentleman volunteers of this war. Even his attitudes toward the war assert his kinship to the old privileged tradition of Hemingway's Frederick Henry and Dos Passos' Grenadine Guards and set him apart from his contemporaries. . . . Skinner is still "in it for the laughs," still living out "the pattern of reaction." But the years separating him from Frederick Henry also separate him from the old kind of war. Skinner had said in the beginning that he wanted "a nice, small war . . . with clearcut issues. There should be more than just a villain you can hate. There should be a side you can love too." But the nice, small wars belong to the past, the issues that were once simple are now complex, and this time there are villains to hate on both sides.

The fact is made clear to Skinner in the sudden desertion of his friend Rod Lujack, an incident which divides *The End of My Life* into two distinct parts, almost exactly as the retreat from Caporetto divides *A Farewell to Arms,* and which prepares the way for Skinner's destruction. The material dealing with the early phases of his war service and leading up to Rod's desertion really belongs with the flashback material dealing with his prewar experience. Not only is it dominated by the same lyric emotion—so much like that of Hemingway and Fitzgerald—but it shows Skinner as still essentially unaffected by the war. There has, of course, been the brutal episode at the "Glass House," that chamber of military horrors to which men are confined for obscure disciplinary reasons and which they will do anything to escape. But even that has been largely canceled out by the exuberant nonsense of those nights in Beirut, particularly the one when Skinner disturbs the careful propriety of a British Army brothel with a cleverly faked sadistic orgy. He and his friends are not yet working in a combat area. Their ambulance runs are short, pleasant, and widely spaced, and they have plenty of time to drink, make love, and explore the city.

But Rod's desertion introduces a new element. Rod, the frustrated musical genius, had been, before the war, a piano player in nightclubs and bars. Between engagements, when short on funds, he had been the paid lover of countless rich and unattractive women whose vulgarity had disgusted him. As a result, he had turned to part-time homosexuality and had had an affair with one of the men in the ambulance unit. Now he sees no alternative but to desert. Skinner tries to persuade him to ask for a transfer to another unit, but Rod realizes that he will always be a "pushover for any fairy, anyplace." If, before, the war had been "a big joke" to Skinner, it now begins to be "a bad joke," part of a vast and impersonal system of evil which is capable of striking down one's self and one's friends at any moment. The effect on Skinner is to bring back his old sense of helplessness, his deepening remorse. (pp. 122-28)

By now, Skinner's position closely parallels Frederick Henry's immediately after Caporetto. Through Rod, the war has hurt him personally, threatened his detachment, and turned his self-possession to self-doubt. By touching him directly, it has made him aware, for perhaps the first time in his life, of human values. But cynicism has become so advanced in Skinner, so much a part of his being, that a violation of those values, instead of rousing him to indignation and protest, merely confirms in him his old conviction that life is indecent and that "war is the most grossly indecent thing of all."

This is revealed in the next episode of his story. As a result of Rod's desertion, the ambulance unit is broken up and Skinner is sent to an isolated camp where he serves with a regiment of African Bechuanamen and their British officers. His hatred of the cruel treatment the men receive soon makes him an outcast in the camp and turns him in on himself; and his resentment becomes a weapon of spite which he uses against Cindy in his letters to her.

> There existed a compulsion he did not try to understand, which made him inspect all the bright things they had had together for signs of tarnish. It almost seemed that he could not go to sleep easily at night until he had picked a favorite incident and turned it over and over until he found the weak spot that allowed him to see it as sordid.

First, there had been the war, then Rod, and now Cindy. And when Cindy could no longer be made to take the blame, there was himself. The "one final and unavoidable conclusion" which Cindy had feared had at last been reached.

> For me suicide is an intellectual position, the inevitable result of thinking things through to the end. It is the final stink, in a way, the only way of finally proving to myself that I don't actually care.

But like all Skinner's intellectual positions, suicide fails in the execution. As he walks through the camp gate with an automatic hidden in his shirt, he does not respond to the sentry's command to halt and narrowly misses being bayoneted before he is recognized.

He had been guilty of gross self-deception, had figured something so thoroughly wrong that it was no
longer permissible to act on it. He had not tried to
avoid the sentry's charge with the bayonet. So suicide was not an intellectual position. It was pure
emotionality, after all.

While Skinner's failure to avoid the charge is probably not
the best way to describe the thing that is happening inside
him, it is apparently intended to illustrate his loss of conscious control (therefore suicide is *not* an intellectual position) and to lead him to the conclusion that he has been
guilty of "gross self-deception." But we feel, in spite of the
imperfection, that the changes which have been occurring
within him throughout his war experience are, at this moment, fully climaxed. The paralyzing events of the last few
months—the horror of the "Glass House," the injustice
of Rod's desertion, the brutality of the camp—have finally
broken through the walls of his detachment, undermined
his confident cynicism, and brought him into naked and
uneasy contact with life. The "intellectual position" has
become "pure emotionality," and the change has reminded him of his basic humanity. But it has also swept away
the last of his props and prepared him for the final emergence of the destructive impulse which has been driving
him steadily toward ruin.

Not long after this, Skinner's unit is sent to Italy. There
are months of combat duty and finally a short leave during
which he meets Johnny, an American Army nurse, who
persuades him to take her on a tour of the front.

It was screwy, he thought, but why not? He could
drive past Capua, around the artillery position he
had passed two days before, and they could hear
the guns go off in comparative safety.

But it is not to be that easy. They reach the artillery position safely, but on the return trip, their ambulance is
strafed by a German plane and Johnny is killed. Skinner's
urge toward negation is thus ironically realized; the bad
joke is on him. (pp. 128-30)

The story of Skinner Galt, then, is the story of the "war-
born," the generation that grew up without a childhood,
without values, and with only an inherited disbelief between themselves and ruin. In many ways, it is like a postscript to the story of the Lost Generation. Skinner's arrival at that final state of negation, which is as near to death
as the living can come, is the furthermost evolution of the
process which Frederick Henry and John Andrews began.
But Skinner carries their loss beyond loss, to the utmost
meaninglessness and futility, and the final cancellation of
self.

In literary terms, *The End of My Life* stands as a transitional novel squarely between the two generations. Its
early lyricism that is so much in the spirit of the old war
writing gives way to the dead futility at its end that anticipates the spirit of the new war writing. The development
of Skinner through the novel, from the confident cynicism
of his prewar attitude to the self-destructive horror induced in him by the reality of war, sets the pattern of the
new writing as surely as if he had written it himself. It
shows how the discovery of war's truth carried this generation beyond the narrow but highly effective literary frame
of simple disillusion and left them with an acute but essentially inexpressible awareness of the complex ills of their

time. They witnessed the defeat of human values in the
midst of war and were sickened. But they were able only
to present the gigantic zero of what they saw, for they
never had the hope and the essential faith they needed to
make an effective protest. The greatest failure this generation has suffered, the thing that has left its stamp upon the
weaknesses of all their novels, has been the failure in their
time of a basic belief in the dignity and goodness of man.
The sense of his tragic yearnings, his endless struggle to
attain the perfection of a god, has been bred, analyzed, or
frozen out of them and been replaced by a dazed contempt
for his corruption and folly. In this respect, Skinner Galt
is their first and best ambassador; for he represents their
experience and contains in himself the seeds and the justification of their failure. (pp. 131-32)

> *John W. Aldridge, "Vance Bourjaily: 'The
> Two Worlds of Skinner Galt', "in his After the
> Lost Generation: A Critical Study of the
> Writers of Two Wars, McGraw-Hill Book
> Company, Inc., 1951, pp. 117-32.*

Paul Engle

[In *The Hound of Earth,* a] scientist, Allerd Pennington,
who had worked on an aspect of the atomic bomb without
knowing the real purpose of his job, disappears on the day
the bomb is exploded over Hiroshima. When he discovers
that he has contributed to the most stupendous moment
of destruction in the world's history, and has, in a sense,
been tricked into his contribution by not being told in advance the ultimate purpose toward which he and the other
scientists at the laboratory were working, he feels that he
must take his stand on the side of humanity. So he flees.

But why should he disappear into the dreary life of an
anonymous fugitive (he was in the army at the time of his
flight, and therefore was actually a deserter), instead of
making a public protest? At the book's end, when he is
waiting for his arrest, Pennington (known now as Al Barker) explains that he was fleeing not from this one action
only, but from science itself, which he felt had betrayed
him and the world. When he found that [instead of working for knowledge], science was working "for nothing
more than nationalities, I remember thinking: 'Science is
dead, now,' and I had no loyalty left for anything."

But was he not betraying at least his own wife and children
by his flight? His answer was: "As long as I stayed and
worked at the only work I knew, I was betraying them and
all wives and all children." What he tried to do in abandoning not only his job but his family was to abandon the
whole rational structure of the modern world, and make
himself into an unskilled worker, doing menial jobs. But
this novel has a more complex theme than the repudiation
of a machine age based on science. In the end, Al Barker,
once the intelligent scientist Allerd Pennington and now
stock room clerk in a department store, rushing toys to
counters in the pre-Christmas rush, is trapped by his own
humanity, the same generous impulse which led him to
leave his job originally. Because he permits himself to become involved in the private lives of the people with whom
he works, he is committed beyond his intention:

. . . caught at last. He had tried to run and, weary
of running, rested; and resting, been unable to re-

ject forever and ended by accepting them all; his love for Nickie, his pity for Finn, his responsibility to Tom, his fascination and compassion for the horror of Dolly, the impulse to oppose M'nerney—the need to take his stand. These things had held him, involved him, chased and trapped him, deprived him of his freedom to live alone with guilt—the hound of earth had caught him. No man, no matter what his time, his country, his condition, training, heredity or philosophy, forever escapes that hound, his own humanity.

That is the theme of this novel. But such a statement does little justice to one of the strongest forces in the novel: all of the action is set over against the bizarre rush of Christmas business. The characters in the store are amusingly and convincingly drawn: the hard-faced Dolly, a Lesbian who kills herself by drinking strychnine in warm milk from a nursing bottle, after having been discovered in her violation of a salesgirl at her counter; the hearty Finn, who runs the toy department as if it were an athletic contest. There is much humor and much vitality, and a large exuberance in the prose.

But the book has two restraints. One is the vagueness of Allerd Pennington. Mr. Bourjaily has chosen not to show the struggle Al had with his conscience, but to take up the driven man's life after he has been wandering for some years. The result is that the reader must take on pure faith so dramatic an act as Al's flight from job, army and family. He is a warm and attractive person in the book, but the struggle of mind is not revealed, save when he must decide whether to flee from San Francisco, when he has reason to believe that he is being watched, or stay and help the men and women who need him.

Another flaw in the book is the occasional falsely literary tone of the prose:

> Even the few customers who hurried in seemed to catch the general mood of feckless exhilaration which followed as tension drained away; they would slow their shopper's pace, smile as if caught in a harmless folly, and drift bemused about the department. . . .

But there are fine insights here also: "the well-dressed man wears a cluster of nerve-ends in his buttonhole"; "Society wanted to punish me for the impulse of decency"; they were "shoppers among the soiled goods in the eternal clearance sale of the world."

The liveliness of the department store events and people is so diverting that often one forgets the actual over-riding intent of the novel. But in the end there remains a solid sense of a human issue dropped down in the midst of decent people, an issue which is as close to all of us as the morning paper. (pp. 18-19)

Paul Engle, "A Scientist's Dilemma," in The New Republic, *Vol. 132, No. 8, February 21, 1955, pp. 18-19.*

John J. Maloney

About eight years ago, Vance Bourjaily published a novel called **The End of My Life.** It was one of the first of a spate of books about World War II, and while it was not, perhaps, the best of them, still it did, I think, more than any of the others, succeed in capturing the aura of reckless dedication and spurious gayety, worn almost raffishly by so many of the young men who left college to go, with a strange wizened kind of gallantry, into such hell holes as Guadalcanal, or Anzio, or Omaha Beach, certain, at last, that here was a war worth fighting, a war in which, finally, the true enemy had dared to show his face.

Since then, Mr. Bourjaily, like most of the rest of us, has had reason to ponder further the identity of the true enemy, and in his immensely readable and often significant second novel, entitled **The Hound of Earth,** he has come very close to unmasking him. Who is the true enemy, he asks? Why, the true enemy, of course, is you and it is I. It is we who fight the only war, the one, as his hero puts it, "fought steadily with only occasional exhausted pauses since Cain and Abel, the war between you and me."

Now supposing we have a sensitive, decent man highly trained in certain special skills, a young scientist, say, who hadn't been fully aware of the terrible nature of the project he was working on—mightn't he, on Hiroshima day, suddenly assume a great and possibly disproportionate share of guilt in the war between you and me? . . .

That, at least, is what Mr. Bourjaily's hero, 1st Lt. Allerd Pennington, does. Changing his name to Al Barker, he deserts his top-secret installation, cuts himself off from his wife and children, and becomes a "wandering gentile," crossing and recrossing the United States, pursued always by the F.B.I.

Yet **The Hound of Earth** is not, for all of this, a standard novel of suspense, climaxed by "the big chase." To be sure, there is a chase, but as you may have suspected from the title, it is more in the nature of a metaphysical one. The author does not try to keep any one guessing about the outcome, but concentrates, rather, on an almost allegorical treatment of Pennington-Barker's last four weeks of flight from the law and from humanity and from himself.

The time is Advent: the place is Santaland, the overgrown toy department of one of San Francisco's largest stores where Al Barker has got a Christmas job. Al is in charge of the stockroom and, one by one, the other employees of Santaland come to confide in him as they stop by the stockroom for a break. There is Sally Malinkrodt, the pretty young blonde who is disgusted with her ineffectual husband and is quite openly on the make. There is Hub Finn, the big jovial buyer, an ex-pitchman and an anachronism in the era of modern merchandising, secretly worried about losing his job. There is Nickie Moore, a beautiful college girl who is working to pay for an abortion. And there is Tom Vanderbeck, earnest high school athelete, who has been ordered to spy on Al by Dolly Klamath, the service manager and terror of the department.

Against his will, Al becomes involved with each of them, and this involvement is his downfall, or, if you wish, his salvation. He tries to comfort Sally, fight for Hub Finn, love Nickie and save poor mad Dolly, and in so doing he is enmeshed beyond escape and eventually captured. So, early on Christmas morning, the long flight ends. The "hound of earth" has run him down at last and he has rejoined the human race.

Surprisingly enough, in spite of the essential seriousness

of its theme, the most engaging feature of the book is its wit, which can be wise and gentle as well as perverse and mordant. Occasionally this humor descends to the mere wisecrack and now and then one gets a sense of strain, but for the most part it is penetrating and original and possessed of the sort of whimsical despair that the situation demands. Yet somehow it is this very quality, this despair, that makes the hero seem too absorbed in wry self-pity to move us quite as much as we should be moved by such a character and such a theme. Nevertheless *The Hound of Earth* is a good book, provocative, thoughtful, crisply written and thoroughly worth reading.

> John J. Maloney, "A Young Scientist in Flight," in New York Herald Tribune Book Review, *March 6, 1955, p. 4.*

Joseph H. McMahon

Important moral and human considerations lurk in the background of Mr. Bourjaily's second novel [*The Hound of Earth*], like invited but suddenly unwanted guests. The author's interest in them, though, is secondary to his sense of exploitation. The pattern of intention is inconclusive, burned out on the embers of lost creative fire; the insights do not have depth and wear, rather, the one-dimensional mantle of a failure to understand; the writing, suffering already from the above inadequacies, is unclear. Everything points to total inconsequence. The inconsequence, however, could not be total; it is the yield rather than the deposit, for the points of departure are of very grave moment indeed, since we in this novel are in an atomic age. . . .

Nobility suggests itself in the proud extremism of the protagonist; it is reduced to absurdity by the inability of the author to express emotion compellingly. The problem, once posed, surpasses Mr. Bourjaily's competence and fades away one clear Christmas night on the essentially insufficient comments of a man unable to understand the results of an intuitively enacted and cunningly sustained action: the negation, through flight, of his participation in the research that led to the discovery of the atom bomb. The title suggests an understanding of the meaning of flight; but the hero does not grasp it. One suspects his energies were exhausted in that moment of decision. Reflexes instead of reason are in the saddle, riding mankind.

Few demands are made upon a novelist: to sustain the key in which he poses the theme of his novel is one of them. But what is the theme here? Major questions are dismissed in minor key. The understatement is used so frequently that it loses its ability to shock, hollowed on the echo of embarrassed laughter. The lower depths of human degradation miss the inference of suffering. The mood is the edge of tragedy, the loss of personality, the inability to react; the treatment is inadequate. Only one character—the investigator pursuing the hero—emerges clearly, with an awareness of the possibility and the meaning of human action. He alone grasps the significance of the protagonist's flight. But the basis of his judgment is not satisfactory, for the two letters he finds in the hero's handwriting give no real insight into his initial motivation. They are straight from the school of social criticism genre 1930 and have no *particular* meaning in the aftermath of a smoldering Japanese city.

Mr. Bourjaily's insouciance is distressing. . . . Hiroshima was a rather grave event in the life of modern man and seems to have little direct connection with the sexually tormented, uselessly confused characters of *The Hound of Earth.*

> Joseph H. McMahon, "One Man's Revolt," in The Commonweal, *Vol. LXI, No. 24, March 18, 1955, p. 639.*

Carl F. Keppler

Probably nothing is quite so rare and welcome in any kind of writing, especially the kind we call creative, as the genuinely good central idea; and a pearl without price is the great one. It is such a pearl, in the mind of this reviewer, that Vance Bourjaily . . . has got hold of in *The Hound of Earth.* Like every idea it has of course been used before; playfully by Poe, for example, in "The System of Dr. Tarr and Professor Fether"; grimly by Chekhov in *Ward No. 6;* profoundly by Shakespeare in *Hamlet* and *Lear:* to a society that is ill, what can symptoms of health appear but illness; to a world gone or rapidly going mad, what can deviations towards sanity seem but the most flagrant madness? The question is neither new nor old but a timeless one, and this timelessness Mr. Bourjaily has combined with the timeliness of today's headlines, the headlines at once most sensational and most exigent.

For the hero of *The Hound of Earth* is a figure whose ideal worth has been preached with such enthusiasm and whose actuality has been found, in recent years, so acutely embarrassing: the scientist who has taken seriously the humanitarian embroidery of his education, who insists on evaluating for himself the results of his own skill. On the day Hiroshima disappeared, so did one Allerd Pennington, an Army first lieutenant and capable young scientist whose researches had contributed to the development of the atom bomb.—Unknowingly contributed, for like most of his associates he had had no notion of the purpose of his work; the project was a secret one, "a big pure research problem," he had assumed in his innocence. When the nature of its purity was made clear by the breaking of the Hiroshima story, Pennington, horrified not only by the perversion of his scientific efforts but even more by his tiny flash of pride and gratification at the thought of his part in the holocaust, had recourse not to the "inelegant fuss" of taking his own life but to a different sort of suicide: a life of fugitive anonymity. . . . (pp. 272-73)

At the time we meet him he has become Al Barker, the wandering gentile, friendless (for he cannot afford friends), homeless, working at odd jobs only to move on after the first payday. Behind him, by now far behind, moves the F.B.I. investigator Casper Usez, a comparatively sensitive young man with the imaginative capacity to think at times, almost, with the mind of his quarry—almost but not quite; the most telling irony of the book lies in its account of Usez's efforts to unravel the motives of the man he is pursuing; to interpret as Communist, as criminal, as psychopath, a man whose actions, from his own viewpoint, have been dictated by nothing more mysterious than outraged conscience. In his directionless flight Barker-Pennington has drifted to San Francisco; the time is the Christmas shopping rush, and he has installed himself briefly as stockroom man in the toy department of Mainways Department Store. His gentleness and resignation are set against the background of selfish bickerings, petty treacheries, dingy lust of an orthodox sort and the still dingier if somewhat more imaginative excursions into heterodoxy: a cross-section of the humanity in the name of which he has made his vows as a priest of science, and from which he has sought to escape. These people are the representatives of his culture, the American culture which to him, in its strange foreshortened course, has become, while still in what should have been its late childhood, senile and decadent; yet not comfortably decadent, since its impulse to decadence has appeared before its impulse of pioneer morality has vanished, with the result that one finds in the Greatest Nation on the Face of the Earth what Barker-Pennington analyzes as perhaps the first neurotic nation in history. But for all their illness, indeed just because of all their illness, he finds that he is not so successfully detached as he had supposed; in his living suicide there is not enough death for genuine withdrawal; and his final gesture of surrendering himself to his pursuers is an effort to solve the problems of these fellow-wretches and help them escape the various rods to which they have made themselves subject; the Eternal Scapegoat in the rather strange setting of Mainways toy department, he broadens his sense of guilt to include theirs, and takes upon himself not only his own sin of participation in mass-murder, but the more ignoble sins of the humanity he has tried to reject. He has been captured, not by "beagle-nosed" Casper Usez, but by his involvement in the web of human passion and misery, by his own capacity for pity and love. (pp. 273-74)

Such is the book that I believe Mr. Bourjaily has intended to write; it is the book *in posse,* the outlines of which emerge hazily through the book *in esse,* and are clarified by Mr. Bourjaily's helpful exegesis at the end. . . . But the story that is told, unfortunately, is something quite different. Instead of exploiting his superb idea, the author has run from it in very much the same jaded but successful fashion in which Barker-Pennington has run from the F.B.I. For a story whose point lies in major crisis within the soul of man must, one would suppose, take that soul as its main theatre of operations. But for the soul of his hero (or of anyone else in the book) Mr. Bourjaily shows the most incomprehensible distaste. With the exception of two or three excerpts of letters and a few snatches of conversation we know nothing whatever of the inner workings of Allerd Pennington. We know that he is a likeable sort, with a pleasant whimsical humor; we know something about his extra-marital loves and his taste in dogs, music, and bourbon. From such things the author apparently expects us to infer monumental developments in the realm of spirit. Now it is quite true that the reader of any book worth reading has always a job to do, but his ability to do it depends on the writer's having first done *his* job, and in *The Hound of Earth* this essential first job—a coming to grips with, a presenting in some living fashion of, what we are asked to believe—has not been done, has not even been attempted. Once or twice Mr. Bourjaily seems to approach it, only to recoil abruptly into what appears to be, after all, his true interest: the crowded toy counters at Mainways, the burping and diaper-wetting dolls with their doll-faced nymphomaniac guardian Sally Malinkrodt, the bespectacled pansy Hugh Harris, the religious fanatic-pervert Dolly Klamath, the alcoholic Santa Claus John Charles Evans, and their hardly less colorful associates. And so the great idea, timeless and timely together, is forgotten or at least evaded, smothered almost before it can draw breath under busy shovelfuls of that "realism" in which the germs of so many good modern novels lie buried: verbal photography of things as they really-truly-grimly are; brilliantly klieg-lit dramatically angled shots of a discovered pimple on the skin of life. As photography it is not bad, so long as it remains sufficiently irrelevant. We are convinced by the honest coarseness of Hub Finn, the infantile innocence of "Winnipeg" Robertson, the petty sadism of Dolly Klamath. It is when these people depart from their everyday drabness and nastiness, when they reveal deep-seated emotional disturbances, qualities of soul to capture the fugitive soul of Barker-Pennington, that almost without exception they ring false; the infatuated Nickie Moore, the drunken Sally Malinkrodt stealing toys and railing at her ineffectual husband, are as unconvincing as Dolly Klamath suckling herself to death on a bottle of strychnine in the arms of the murdered Santa Claus. That the personnel of Mainways' toy department comprises a pretty sorry lot Mr. Bourjaily establishes without question, and we have every reason to sympathize with the hero in the distance at which he keeps them and the air of apathetic mockery with which, on the whole, he treats them. But that anything warm or appealing, anything capable of becoming the teeth of the Hound of Earth, comes through this sorriness we are not convinced, and we have a strong suspicion that neither is Al Barker-Pennington convinced: that his final surrender to Usez has nothing to do with having been *won back* to humanity and everything to do with having been incurably wearied by it, with a boredom too tired for further action, even for active disgust. To be sure Mr. Bourjaily, in an eloquent passage at the end . . . , assures us of the opposite. But he is asking us to take his word for the fact, and in art we take nobody's word for anything; we insist on its *happening,* to us. In *The Hound of Earth* it doesn't. The book remains, in a very real sense, a half-baked one. About the best one can say is that given more "baking," more thought, more creative sweat and blood and tears, it might have turned out a great novel or at least a good one. As it stands it is neither. (pp. 274-75)

Carl F. Keppler, in a review of "The Hound of Earth," in Arizona Quarterly, *Vol. 11, No. 3, Autumn, 1955, pp. 272-75.*

Harding Lemay

With his third novel, *The Violated,* Vance Bourjaily joins that select band of writers equipped with antenna-like perception enabling them to project the heart and pulse of their generation. Under admirably controlled scrutiny here are those who grew up during the depression, attended college as war-clouds burst in Europe, and patrolled the streets of ancient cities and the beaches of distant islands before returning to civilian life, shaken beyond total recovery by what they had seen, in themselves and others.

Mr. Bourjaily's theme is chilling in its implication for all of us: that the violated, as he calls them, are crippled from within by a slackness in contact with others which turns to ashes the promises of their youth. To his theme, as to his characters, Mr. Bourjaily brings an urgent sense of what is missing and what is needed.

A children's performance of *Hamlet,* Shakespeare's classic study of lost innocence, opens the narrative in a deserted Brooklyn mansion. In the audience are three major characters in this heavily populated novel: Ellen Beniger Walls, whose daughter, Sheila, plays Hamlet; Ellen's younger brother, Tom, and his friend, Eddie Bissle, a taciturn farmer from Long Island. Across the bridge in Manhattan is a fourth central figure: Guy Cinturon, a wealthy Mexican whose college friendship with Tom and Eddie has lasted twenty years.

Mr. Bourjaily leaves his adolescent players on stage for several hundred pages while he traces, in absorbing detail, the life these four have shared, from the origins of their discontent in high school days, through college, and through the war (in sections written with a brilliance rare in our war-weary fiction), bringing them all together again at the close of the war.

As *The Violated* moves into its second half, skipping fourteen years to bring us back to *Hamlet* and to the present, we come face to face with this generation, uncommitted to anything dangerous (and exciting), safely repeating unsatisfactory patterns over and over, with the exception of Tom who fumbles at one thing, then another, and ends up in that catch-all of vagrant intellects, television. The pulse that beats with fervor in the early pages, slows down, flares in a final senseless explosion of violence, and then slows again, leaving center stage to the young people who may, or may not, follow the patterns set by their elders.

The Violated is a long, ambitious novel, shrewdly organized and written in precise, clean language by a man who knows what he means to say and creates, in his statement of it, a disturbingly pertinent work of fiction. Even if Mr. Bourjaily's violated are individual figures of tragedy, the cool, clear light he throws upon them is reflected, in startling illumination, upon most of their contemporaries.

> Harding Lemay, *"A Generation Acutely Seen," in* New York Herald Tribune Book Review, *August 24, 1958, p. 7.*

James Finn

With *The End of My Life* and *The Hound of Earth,* Vance Bourjaily established a strong claim to critical attention. While neither of these works received the acclaim given to many other post-war novels, they revealed an author who had knowing control over his material. They suggested a solidity and a basis for development absent from the more immediately impressive novels of his contemporaries.

The Violated extends further Mr. Bourjaily's initial claim. It is a large ambitious novel, a capacious, embracing work of a kind that is rare in American fiction. While the center of the novel is occupied by the four principal characters who are brought from childhood to maturity (and who are exact contemporaries of those now in their middle thirties), there are ever-widening circles of those whose own lives impinge, in varying degrees, upon these four. There are parents and children; schoolmates, teachers and employers; lovers, husbands and wives; close friends and casual, fleeting acquaintances.

As the lives of these four—Tom Beniger and his sister Ellen from Tennepin, Connecticut; handsome, wealthy Guy Cinturon from Mexico; and rough, insecure, unattractive Eddie Bissle from poor Long Island—cross, veer away, again come together and inter-twine, they become increasingly weighted with experiences of the last several decades. The author's range of interest and knowledge is everywhere evident and impressive. The silly, meaningful chatter of the high school, the easy obscenity of college and army, the stylized idiom of theater and T.V. studios, and the broken exchanges of close but estranged friends are all caught and set down with authority. The same sureness is apparent in the evocation of feelings associated with a particular place, whether it is a small town or Greenwich Village.

Not all, certainly, but many aspects of life in America are here present. There is a rich varied background for the characters, a dense medium to offer resistance to their best efforts. That is, where there are best efforts. . . . [Some] people live out their days, but they have no goal; they neither believe in, seek nor find a meaning.

What of those who make the effort? Tom and Ellen start with the high uncertain goals of adolescence, but these dwindle and pale when exposed to the unsparing demands of adulthood. Guy Cinturon is one of those who have clear, obtainable goals; his endures but proves increasingly less meaningful. As for Eddie Bissle, he is one of those who scarcely had a chance.

To these four there are analogues and parallels. For the other characters, too, fall under the general classification of the title. No character emerges whole; each suffers some violation of his being. It is primarily the act of violation which places these people in their universe. Though the violation frequently drives them apart from each other, it unites them in a common predicament. And it manifests itself in many, frequently violent, ways—in emotional detachment, alcoholism, both latent and active homosexuality, in Don Juanism, in sado-masochistic relations, in homicide and suicide.

And it is finally the over-all vision of the book which eventually tempers and weakens one's response. Or, rather, the feeling that a strong vision is lacking, that what should be vision is framework, an intelligently devised framework and quite extensive, but improperly limiting. It is not that we lack knowledge about the characters. We know very much. But we seem to know all that is to be known. There seems to be no reservoir from which further information could be drawn. There is room, thus, for the unexpected, but not real surprise; for problem but not for mystery. This universe is incomplete.

In his comments on the novel, Frank O'Connor says that "one can recognize the true realist by the very small area of unpleasant experience which he can comfortably handle." By this standard Mr. Bourjaily may well be a true realist, for the area of unpleasant experience which he handles comfortably is small. But his intentions, it is clear, would have carried him beyond that small area. Huxley attached to *Point Counter Point* Fulke Greville's "Oh wearisome condition of mankind . . . " And this could be a proper response to this book. But there is always a danger for the realist that he will become the sentimentalist and arouse the feeling one has for "Oh world I never made . . . " *The Violated* approaches this line of danger asymptotically.

In spite of reservations, however, there is one large section of the book that is stunning. It is a tour de force that is capable of redeeming many lapses, of absorbing the otherwise unacceptable detail.

After the uses to which *Hamlet* has been put in both criticism and fiction, it is a passing brave writer who once again places it in service. But Mr. Bourjaily has made a childish production of the play almost the pivot of his book. Young Sheila Walle, Ellen Beniger's daughter, produces, directs, stages and stars in the production. Her own dedication and the response she evokes in others, both players and audience, become high points of the book. The tensions and weaknesses, desires and strengths of the various characters are high-lighted by the actual production. For this achievement, alone, *The Violated* is valuable.

There are minor technical annoyances. The *Hamlet* section is impressive but Mr. Bourjaily presumes upon it too early. For the first section of the book (which opens, as Shaw would have said, in the imperative) plumps us down in the middle of the performance and surrounds us with the array of mature characters before it swirls us back to their beginnings. It reads as if the author, in search of a good beginning, wrote it last and tacked it on. And, in spite of the evident knowingness displayed, there is an intrusive handling of narrative techniques. But if *The Violated* does not completely fulfill expectation, neither does it disappoint. (pp. 550-51)

> *James Finn, "A True Realist," in* The Commonweal, *Vol. LXVIII No. 22, August 29, 1958, pp. 550-51.*

Harry T. Moore

The people who inhabit Vance Bourjaily's third novel [*The Violated*] are physically or spiritually violated by circumstance or by one another. Yet they are equipped with few of the trappings of their Beat Generation contemporaries, who would see them as squares, sticking to their bourgeois environment, rather than as hipsters rebelling against it. These specimens of the Violated don't associate with junkies or messiahs with dirty ankles, they don't live in what the Kerouac world calls pads, and they don't become noticeably engaged with values. Perhaps it is worse, at least more nullifying, to be among the Violated rather than among the Beat, who at least attempt to triangulate their own position. The people in this novel, on the other hand, pass through school, war and city life without seriously trying to discover meaning in such institutions or in themselves.

Their group includes a flashily rich Mexican, seduced in childhood, who blooms into an American Don Juan; a married woman who drifts into alcoholism and masochism; her sadist lover, who half-deliberately kills her brother; a classical scholar earning poor pay as a TV writer; a zany minor actress; and a homosexual TV director. The story of these people and their acquaintances is a disjointed one, with occasionally remarkable episodes. The most important of these deals with a production of *Hamlet* featuring the alcoholic woman's adolescent daughter. When the girl and her supporting cast of brilliant and eager chil-

dren startle their parents by performing tragedy in a condemned house in Brooklyn, adult treachery brings on a raid by police and firemen just after the play-within-a-play scene.

This "violation" ironically mixes real and unreal as in parts of Mr. Bourjaily's earlier novels. In *The End of My Life,* for example, he projected the fantasy of a football game in which famous men of past and present opposed each other in a contest between affirmatives and negatives. And in *The Hound of Earth,* he dreamed up a grotesquely symbolic toy department crowned by a drunken Santa Claus. Imaginative touches of this kind, bizarre or comically horrible, have become a Bourjaily trademark.

The inspired children in the present story, staging their black-market *Hamlet* with the insight of the innocent, disturbingly point up the essential loneliness of the bewildered and defeated adults in their audience. But, like so much else in this novel, the children's performance loses force because it is too painstakingly described. This applies also to an elongated drinking party, neither relevant enough nor fresh enough in treatment to warrant all the space it is given. Mr. Bourjaily is working on a larger scale than he has attempted before, but he has not yet learned to organize mass. And his characters don't develop in depth as they grow older; he is far better at detailing the mechanics of sex and football than at suggesting the magic of change in human beings.

Written in today's hard idiom *The Violated,* like so many recent novels that may be classified as good, seems at times to have a kinship with those one-shot ventures, the TV shows. When they're over, they're over, and even though memories of their better moments linger, time marches on to present the next attraction. It is the streaks of fantasy in Mr. Bourjaily's writing that often give it an attractiveness beyond the range of the more consistently realistic members of the literature-for-the-moment school. (pp. 6, 12)

> *Harry T. Moore, "To the Beat They're Square," in* The New York Times Book Review, *August 31, 1958, pp. 6, 12.*

Irving Howe

The interest and perhaps importance of Vance Bourjaily's new novel [*The Violated*] lies in the fact that he is one of the few serious young novelists who has tried to go directly toward the center of post-war experience. Not circuses that are to be taken as emblems of the modern world, nor picaresque tales about cocky boys from Chicago, nor nostalgic retrospects of down-and-outers in the thirties, but an enormous realistic narrative about four ordinary people who reach adulthood in the Second World War—this is Mr. Bourjaily's battlefield.

The Violated seems to me a failure, but an interesting one, if only because of the way in which Mr. Bourjaily's courage and ambition lead him to repeated troubles. He has chosen to write one of those full-scale, lavishly detailed narratives composed of parallel and intersecting levels. Such a technique, borrowed from the social novel of the early years of the century, assumes that society is distinctly, even rigidly stratified; that its component classes are intrinsically interesting and worth observing; that a novelist can arrange a conflict between members of these classes which will be dramatic in its own right and representative of larger issues; and that thereby the narrative can finally be brought to a coherent climax.

But for the material Mr. Bourjaily has chosen—the lives of pitiful and bewildered drifters during the past two decades—these assumptions do not operate with sufficient force. His central characters are not distinctive enough, either in social or personal qualities, to warrant separate strands of narrative. As they collapse into each other's lives, the successes of one indistinguishable from the failures of the other, they create a smudge of sadness at the very point where the novel demands tension and clarity. Like the post-war society they reflect, these characters are too much of a sameness, so that one wearies of their presence almost as quickly as one credits their reality.

Still, it might be said that Farrell and Dos Passos, in their early work, persuade us to find meaning in the lives of characters no more estimable or interesting than those of *The Violated.* Yes; but there, for writers of Mr. Bourjaily's generation, seems to be the rub. What keeps one absorbed in *USA* and *Studs Lonigan* is not so much their characters as the driving passion, the anger rising from a hurt of spirit, that lies behind these naturalistic novels and makes us finally indifferent to any awkwardness of idea or language. Mr. Bourjaily has presented some of the accumulative ardor of the naturalistic novel, but he lacks—and how can one expect him to have?—the social force of the early Dos Passos or early Farrell. The volcano of naturalism remains on the horizon, but it no longer smokes.

Yet I found myself admiring Mr. Bourjaily's decision to face directly the emptiness and wastefulness of much American life. There are some fine sections in his book, notably one on the inner happenings of a television show. Whenever the social world of *The Violated* allows itself to be pressed into some sort of shape, whenever Mr. Bourjaily can persuade us that his characters form part of a knowable and charted environment, his work comes alive. (p. 17)

> *Irving Howe, "Novels of the Post-War World,"*
> *in* The New Republic, *Vol. 139, No. 19, November 10, 1958, pp. 16-18.*

Martin Tucker

Although the subject matter [of *Confessions of a Spent Youth*]—youth, its bitter, maturing experiences, and its never-ending relevance—has been handled in thousands of novels the world has been heir to, Vance Bourjaily has turned out a work different from any of its predecessors. His novel is in the tradition of the young man looking back, and if his hero will undoubtedly be compared to Wolfe's Eugene Gant, Hemingway's Nick Adams, or James Jones' Prewitt, the references are of little importance. The major fact is that Bourjaily has created a new American Adam fed by experience to the bursting point, and searching not for his lost innocence but for the meaning of what he has gained.

Bourjaily's hero, U. S. D. Quincy (whom his friends call Quince), is twenty-four when the book opens, and through a series of "confessions" he tries to come to an understanding of the events that have totalled his life. He is con-

fessing the truth because in his own words, "I'm sure of this, that truth has value, even if I'm not altogether sure just what value and why."

Quince searches most strongly the memories of his sexual experiences, because it is in this province he reveals himself. Each man is a tourist in many worlds, Bourjaily is saying, but the one in which he belongs is the home he makes out of his journeys. That is the reason for Quince's confessions—he is re-crossing the country of his past, and especially his favorite provinces of memory—in order to arrive home with himself.

Although Bourjaily gets his title from De Quincey's famous diet of opium (as well as his hero's name), his real debt is to the post-Dostoievsky tradition of exploiting psychic disability and self-conflicts. For Bourjaily, this is an old story. From his first novel, he has been investigating the conflicts that destroy people. . . .

Bourjaily's fourth novel [*Confessions of a Spent Youth*] is undoubtedly his best, his most controlled piece of work, and up to this point, his most optimistic view. His hero Quince is not one who turns from life, even though he stops long enough to examine it. Quince's adventures are full of a rare kind of excitement and hilarity—from his first sexual experience with a lame girl while an older, exhausted couple look on, to his forays with a self-centered, nasal-twanged girl who makes a desperate attempt to swindle him into marriage. In between are moments of loss and passion, which Quince, being as honest as memory allows him, attempts to detail. . . .

Quince's sexual exploits include other girls too, the most important of them Jeannie Childress, the girl from Scarsdale who couldn't give of herself so she gave herself very often to men. Jeannie, the beautiful, the weak, the desperately-alone girl, is the female who touches Quince most deeply, but he does not save her. She, along with all his other girls, is left to work things out by herself.

At twenty-four, after a stint in an advertising agency, an abortive college education, and service in the Ambulance Corps and the U.S. Army, Quince returns home to define himself. That he accomplishes his mission is good news for all intelligent readers, for this novel of cathartic confession is one of the richest, tenderest, funniest, most shocking and disturbing books in years. Bourjaily illuminates Quince's well-spent youth, and though he may be an ordinary hero, as Quince claims for himself, he has indulged his experiences to the fullest. Thus he has never lost anything; he has always gained a sense of life.

> *Martin Tucker, "The Fruit of Knowledge: An*
> *American Adam and His Eves," in* Lively Arts
> and Book Review, *November 20, 1960, p. 31.*

Janice Davis

On an early page of Vance Bourjaily's *Confessions of a Spent Youth,* we are told that the real reason he "confesses" is because he wants to "tell some truths" and that he believes "the truth has value." These early pages lead us to expect that we are to be taken on a journey of considerable significance, that the themes are the great ones of "thinking about the war, about time, about love, about myself." But I wonder if many readers whose sympathies are thus engaged will not read on with ever-growing disappointment. The real subject matter of this book is not the war or time and it is certainly not love. It is the familiar, obsessive, American one of sexuality—driven, unhappy, meaningless sexuality.

Let us hasten to say that my quarrel is not with this subject matter itself. My quarrel is with the author's tacit assumption that the mere detailing of a variety of lurid sexual activities is enough to make a novel interesting and important. That quite a few people will agree with him, however, is obvious. How else explain the popularity, even among "serious" readers, of novels whose chief distinction is a sort of quaint, post-pubescent exhibitionism? (p. 17)

The oddest thing about these *Confessions* is that, despite this monotonously inescapable aura, the book does not hang together well. I do not think this is the fault of the picaresque form in which it is cast, for the episodic can still have unity. Some fault must be laid to the fact that many of the sections have appeared previously in a number of different magazines—the sharpest break is in "The Fractional Man," where suddenly the novel turns into one of those politely stylized I-had-an-exotic-grandmother recollection pieces. Even so, the real cause, I suspect, is a deeper one and is related to the author's going beyond his range. He is at his best with naturalistic description and straight-forward narration. When he sticks to these he often manages isolated scenes that are powerful and impressive and sometimes wonderfully funny, like the one in which the Scarsdale temptress, Jeannie Childress, goes through some memorable antics with a kitten. Even the descriptions of male undergraduate life and the agonizingly boring scatalogical conversations among these young men, each lavishly characterized from the outside but each somehow indistinguishable from all the others, have authenticity.

It is with the inner life that Mr. Bourjaily has trouble, and, unfortunately, this leads him to take up certain poetic and meditative postures. They are never more than postures, for the poetic lies outside his range, and the result is a disturbing pretentiousness. The narrator-protagonist is named Quincy; this and the frontispiece quotation from *The Confessions of an English Opium-Eater* are meant evidently to suggest a connection with De Quincey's erratic masterpiece. But except for the minor matter of a shared love of the sensational there is no connection. De Quincey's intellectuality, his language, his revelatory capacities—there is no suggestion of these. A few reefers in Cairo, a few more at the end of the book, interspersed with some unbelievably stilted dialogues about Bop Jazz, do not make a De Quincey out of a Quince.

But what, to give him his full name, is U. S. D. Quincey—be advised that the "U" stands for Ulysses—really like? Evidently he is like the boy next door, if Mr. Bourjaily and certain other writers are to be believed. Perhaps only history, or that very post-war generation which is now coming to its maturity and of which the novel insists Quince is an emblem can decide whether he is or not. Quince in the novel is "directionless," inclined to resent a world he never made and to rebel against it, but not with any purpose. Although he is in many ways passive, he asserts his masculinity in the hurly-burly of repeated sexual conquest. Very rapidly he learns a prodigious amount about sex, but he remains vastly ignorant about love in any of

the various forms in which it may be experienced. What is so astonishing is that Quince, at nearly forty (as he narrates these matters), seems remarkably to have retained the point of view of Quince at eighteen. Equally astonishing is the gap between the story he is telling and the story he thinks he is telling. He is never struck by how little joy his priapic adventures bring him (shades of Tom Jones or Felix Krull!), nor by the interesting fact that the girls he knows, albeit cooperative, do not much enjoy themselves either. (pp. 17-18)

The real difficulty is that Mr. Bourjaily is essentially a materialist (his last and highly praised novel, *The Violated,* elicited from one reviewer a comparison with Dostoevsky—no comparison could be more far-fetched); as such he evokes, often vividly, the accurately observed surface of his world—it is wholly recognizable, and it is immediate and "real." But he is seldom able to go beyond that surface to find and suggest those intenser realities that give his world its being, that set it in motion and people it. "The confusions of the heart," to use his own term, are what really matter, but it is just these which he is so reluctant to approach. . . .

On the last page of Mr. Bourjaily's long and labored novel we are asked to regard it only as a "specimen account of how a contemporary youth was spent—not misspent nor well-spent, merely spent." This reader at least was only too inclined to agree. (p. 17)

Janice Davis, "The Materialism of Vance Bourjaily," in The New Republic, *Vol. 143, No. 26, December 19, 1960, pp. 17-18.*

Thomas Curley

Since a number of people whose opinions I respect like Bourjaily's work, I'm going to say briefly why I cannot like this novel. *Confessions of a Spent Youth* is a story, told in the first person, of the life, from seventeen to twenty-four, of a man named Quince. His final and most important motive for writing is simply stated: "I confess because I want to tell some truths." At the end of his story, some four hundred pages later, he asks his reader if he was one of the great sinners and sufferers. In his judgment he was not; just average; a specimen of how a contemporary youth was spent. In between we read of his introduction to sex, his later loving and whoring and drinking, his experiences with marijuana, with the Ambulance Corps in Africa and Italy, and with the Army in Hawaii and Japan, after which we spend a few post-war months with him in Virginia and New York. That Quince told the truth I've no doubt; that he wrote nothing more than a documentary, I've also no doubt.

> The unity of a plot does not consist, as some suppose, in its having one man as its subject. An infinity of things befall that one man, some of which it is impossible to reduce to unity; and in like manner there are many actions of one man which cannot be made to form one action. One sees therefore, the mistake of all the poets who have written a Heracleid, a Thesied, or similar poems. *They suppose that because Heracles was one man, the story also of Heracles must be one story.* (My italics.)

I know that Aristotle was speaking of tragedy, not epic,

much less of the novel, but I emphasize the last sentence because I think Bourjaily and many others disagree with it. Behold a man: look at him, listen to him, repeat what he thinks and says, record what he does and what is done to him, and you have a novel. I disagree. You have the truth but you don't, in the best and literal sense of the term, have a story.

Quince would like to think of his confessions as a specimen account of how a contemporary youth was spent. . . . That, in itself, is a gratuitous assumption: I am not at all sure that most youths do not experience special depths of degradation and special heights of intellectual or sensual joy.

And without doubt representative characters in fiction do. Holden Caulfield and Huckleberry Finn do; as do Jake Barnes, Jay Gatsby, Joe Christmas, Anna Karenina and Hester Prynne. You start with the ordinary; you do not remain in it. To be representative, a character (or a book) must achieve individuality, that is to say, a kind of isolation. Quince does not. He neither achieves nor fails to achieve. Having said that, I must quote the end of Quince's story where, it seems, he does achieve something: courage.

> I'd remind myself of the way I'd stood there on the country road, bawling my lusty *No's,* with Hal grinning and pounding me; I'd feel that cool air again, and hear the shrill, crazy noise of the rooster crowing, and I'd catch enough of the spirit that came over me that early morning in Dayport to go on with my simple packing and avoid telephones. The spirit was a strongly physical thing—I felt it as a current in my legs and spine and in the back of my neck; it felt like courage, and it felt good.

Immediately afterwards, with characteristic honesty, Quincy remarks that he might have ended on an equally abrupt but negative chord, "as readily available and no less true." That is what I can't like. No book should end until it has to. *Confessions of a Spent Youth* is a long introduction to the story of Ulysses Quince. (pp. 641-43)

> *Thomas Curley, "One Man's Story," in* The Commonweal, *Vol. LXXIII, No. 25, March 17, 1961, pp. 641-43.*

Harris Dienstfrey

The four novels of Vance Bourjaily have not received much attention, partly, I think, because they have not been properly understood. The first of them, *The End of My Life* (1947), was discussed very favorably by John Aldridge in his book *After the Lost Generation* [see excerpt above]; and though he saw in it "occasional callowness and crudity," Aldridge wrote that "no book since *This Side of Paradise* has caught so well the flavor of youth in war time, and no book since *A Farewell to Arms* has contained so complete a record of the loss of that youth in war." In commenting on the main character's change from "the confident cynicism of his prewar attitude to the self-destructive horror induced . . . by . . . war," Aldridge isolated a theme that has remained central to all of Bourjaily's novels: each of them (while revealing increased control) has continued to relate the war's "self-destructive" effect to larger contexts. Now, in *Confessions*

of a Spent Youth—Bourjaily's best book, I think—he has written a long, complex novel, naturalistic yet quietly lyrical, in which the experiences of one young man from 1939 to 1946 comprehend features of American life which have been decisive for the past twenty years.

There are, at the outset, two general points to be made about Bourjaily's work. The first refers to its preoccupation with a concern which also serves to distinguish most current American fiction from the fiction of the fifteen or so years that followed World War I. In various degrees, all of these earlier novels were infused by the sense that the American dream, whatever it was, had been lost. Whether lost because of a group's willful malice, or by natural death, or by some mysterious and intangible process, and causing in turn sorrow or bitterness or cynicism or compassion—whatever the reason or the response—the novels that came out of the First World War all testified that the dream was gone. (p. 360)

But the ambience of today's fiction comes from a loss which belongs to individuals, not to a nation: the loss of the ability to feel. Saul Bellow's Eugene Henderson plunges into Africa in the hope of finding something to satisfy an inner voice that cries *I want, I want, I want;* Ralph Ellison's "invisible man," after putting his faith in one con-man after another, plummets into a manhole for a first chance to glean his own commitments; Norman Mailer's Sergius O'Shaugnessy returns from Korea to look for a good time "two hundred miles from the capital of the cinema," hoping to regain "the strength to try again." Each of these men, emotionally drained or filled with a kind of hysterical energy, is sustained mainly by the knowledge of his own emptiness and the one chafing desire that still abides—to feel again, honestly and with confidence. None of these novels—*Henderson, Invisible Man,* or *The Deer Park*—are similar in tone or content; and I only want to indicate here a basic theme around which they all focus, and which is even clearer in Bourjaily's books, the absence of emotion and emotional certainty. (pp. 360-61)

The way that Bourjaily has chosen to portray this loss of feeling in his latest novels, *The Violated* and *Confessions of a Spent Youth,* points to the second important generalization to be made about his work. Since World War II, most American fiction has gotten at American life indirectly. The "regional" novels, such as those of Wright Morris and Flannery O'Connor, carefully delimit a particular landscape or geographical location, and then treat that setting and its inhabitants as a metaphorical construct of America. Other novels, somewhat like didactic fables, offer characters who are meant to break through to an ideal concept of behavior or belief that is hidden or harshly denied by the circumstances of modern America— *Henderson the Rain King* is one example, or Mark Harris's *Something About a Soldier,* or Jack Kerouac's *The Dharma Bums.* In a third type of novel, the main character looks for a career, considers or briefly engages in several, and so cuts through certain cross sections of American life which are meant to stand for the whole of it; this is the approach of *Augie March,* of *Invisible Man,* and of *The Deer Park.*

It is in this sense that Bourjaily's first two novels were also "symbolic." The main character in *The End of My Life,* a volunteer in the Ambulance Corps in Africa, is made to stand for an entire generation. As he gradually comes to lose all his feeling for other people, and thus all his desire for life, he represents in extreme, as Aldridge noted, the effects of the war. *The Hound of Earth,* Bourjaily's second novel, takes place in a department store during the ten or so days before Christmas. Its main character is an American physicist who, hearing of the blast at Hiroshima, instantly realizes that this is the end result of the secret project on which he even then is contributing some relatively minor work. In a paroxysm of guilt and shame, he deserts his family and wanders from city to city and job to job, always avoiding connection, hunted by the FBI, until, at the store, after a series of complicated developments during the Christmas rush, he finally overcomes his horror of action, and allows himself to feel again.

But Bourjaily's last two books have made every attempt to eschew these metaphorical devices, and for this reason they stand apart from most American fiction. The four main characters of *The Violated,* three men and a woman all born after the First World War, represent no particular minority, neither Jews nor intellectuals; and as they grow up and live through the war's ensuing prosperity, the depression, the Second World War, and the curious peace which follows, the novel always urges that the problems and opportunities the characters face are in no sense out of the ordinary. Now, in *Confessions of a Spent Youth,* although Bourjaily has returned to the material of *The End of My Life,* he continues to approach it as he did the material of *The Violated,* naturalistically, as if it had meaning only because of its complete usualness. "I was only average . . . " the main character of *Confessions of a Spent Youth* says, "give or take some variety in the times my luck was good, yours bad," vice versa. With this average man as hero, the novel explores America.

Confessions of a Spent Youth is U. S. D. Quincy's first-person story of his life from 1939 to 1946. He is seventeen when the novel begins and twenty-four when it ends; and he has three particulars to tell about: "Sex, friendship, the war which became my world." . . . His story begins when he has completed high school; a series of revelations follows—concerning his first girl, his first love, almost two years of college (fraternity life and drinking), almost five combatless years of war (first as a volunteer in the Ambulance Corps, then as a draftee in the army), and finally, all his friends and friendships during these various times; it ends shortly after the war with Quincy's recognition that he had "better open up some possibilities for [himself], find a direction, make a commitment." (pp. 361-62)

The characters, events, and ideas in *Confessions of a Spent Youth* are held together by a tone of detached yet committed inquiry and by a conversational style that moves easily from quiet humor to unobtrusive lyricism. "I do not mean to be mock-eighteenth century or mock-Germanic, or mock-anything," Quincy says about midway through his long, loosely-structured narrative, "—only direct and truthful—when I say I thank you for your attention this far, and that I hope I can continue to engage it as you read on." Though the book's dialogue is awkward at times, and some of its characters are drawn too broadly, these faults are only minor distractions; for *Confessions* is not meant to be a series of stunning moments that rush together in overpowering brilliance. Its aim and achievement lie in a story that is consistently interesting, some-

times comic, and always intelligent. I intend only praise—no slight to anyone—when I say that *Confessions* comes on like a friend rather than a man possessed.

As background for many of Quincy's "confessions," providing a sort of counterpoint, are some newer additions to American folklore. Quincy explains, for example, that the prevision of his first sexual encounter was stimulated by those realistic American novels whose scenes of sexual initiation "took a form so stereotyped as to be almost mythic." And Quincy can, in fact, report that "not Eugene Gant, nor Ima Fool, not Ivan Tonowhi nor Nick Adams nor even Studs himself ever had it so sordid, so perfectly sordid." But quite unlike these others, Quincy does not feel shame or disappointment with his "myth made flesh." "Inwardly," he recalls, "I am strutting, revelling, romping, ready to go again, and I am neglecting to feel the guilt, the melancholy, the sense of loss." (p. 362)

The chapter on Quincy's college life is called "Quincy at Yale." But Quincy promptly notes: "I did not, by the way, go to Yale . . . so my title for this confession is traditional and, I hope, evocative." No part of the college myth is relevant—"Whiffenpoofs, blue sweaters, briar pipes, and Albie Booth"—college was none of these.

> Here is the image I intend: a stripling, sitting in the dark, on the steps of a Gothic library building, at one A.M., drunk and alone, hiccuping as light snow falls on his insentient shoulders from the cold night sky of a New England spring.

But Bourjaily intends these confessions to be more than semi-comic jabs at some assorted fancies of the American dream life. Like Bellow, Ellison, and Mailer, he is describing an American education, and he means Quincy's narrative to serve as an assessment of that education and of the time and country which gave it.

In most American novels the main character stands alone. He may attach himself to a surrogate father (against whom he will eventually rebel), but he is essentially isolated: at the beginning because society rejects him, at the end because he rejects society (or has set himself to transform it). In *Confessions of a Spent Youth,* however, Bourjaily is attempting something else (as was Bellow in *Adventures of Augie March*)—not the single crucial friendship that changes one's life, but the many friendships of varying intensities and kinds, typically provisional, that a young man ordinarily experiences as he grows older. Quincy explains that at college it was his friend Jeff "who persisted in liking me and even in trying to protect me from the results of my perverse, sophomore expedition towards oblivion." When Quincy enters the Ambulance Corps and makes "the closest friend I'd ever had," he thereby finds the "spores" of his mind "shook loose." Later, the victim of an apparently incurable form of gonorrhea, tormented and despairing, Quincy is again helped by a friend, who almost by chance leads him to recognize "that it is never properly himself to whom a man extends his deepest sympathy."

Though the friendships end, and the friends are capable of betraying each other, the characters here (unlike Bellow's) mainly draw their emotional support from friendship, and only friendship gives them a sense of common cause. . . . This single possession and comfort implies all those others which a community or a culture might provide . . . yet of these the careers of Bourjaily's characters are all bereft. It is from friendship alone that Quincy gains the strength and the chance to grow.

But what of the comforts of sex, the importance of love? As Quincy relates his adventures and those of his friends, he aims to illustrate a bitter proposition: that the experiences of love and lust in "our twentieth century, in America," exclude one another. "Where did it come from," he asks, "that polar incompatibility of sex with deep affection in my schoolboy mind?" The wounding and comic question that ends Quincy's first love, platonic by his choice, speaks for the influence of America. His girlfriend puts it to him: " 'Can a girl who necks keep a boy's respect? . . . I've been wondering about that.' " It is the voice, Quincy knows, of the American teenager; he knows also that it is the other half of the decision he himself had made for "love." "I knew then, that this first, best innocence was gone for Joan, and that it was my own clumsy teaching, now taking its delayed effect, which had destroyed it."

A few of the characters set themselves to achieve a wedding of these emotions, but none achieve it. "If love . . . means the preferring of one object above all others, then I loved Cynthia Ann all right, and what a sad and silly reason for marrying her that would have been." And the book closes upon Quincy's difficulty accomplished, but self-achieved release from a relationship sustained solely by the press of his desire: "It was as bad a moment as I'll ever have." (pp. 362-63)

Quincy's decision to "find a direction, make a commitment" is cast against all the dead weight of his truncated feelings. The ability of *Confessions of a Spent Youth* to reveal the exertion of self-will (and even willful cruelty) that lies behind this decision is a measure of the book's success and its significance. So, similarly, is its portrayal of the loss of feeling that gradually occurs in the typical life represented by U. S. D. Quincy. For if, finally, the events of that life are not altogether typical, the loss they led to is. (p. 363)

> Harris Dienstfrey, "The Novels of Vance Bourjaily," in Commentary, Vol. 31, No. 4, April, 1961, pp. 360-63.

Vance Bourjaily and Harry T. Moore

[*The following interview with Bourjaily was originally conducted by telephone on April 27, 1964, as part of an interinstitutional conference conducted by Dr. Harry T. Moore at Stephens College, Southern Illinois University. In the following excerpt, Moore fields questions from faculty members of Stephens College and five other institutions.*]

[Moore]: *Mr. Bourjaily is in Mexico on an archaeological expedition. . . . You don't need any further introduction so we'll ask Mr. Bourjaily to come in and speak to us for about ten minutes, perhaps telling us what he is doing as well as commenting on his own work. Mr. Bourjaily.*

[Bourjaily]: All right. Let me start, because you can hear me but not see me, by telling you what I look like and then I will describe where I am and so on. I am a forty-one-year-old man, about five feet seven inches tall, blue-eyed. I think of myself as having a pleasant manner. I don't think of myself as being a particularly polished speaker, but how speaking to you over the telephone will affect my relative degree of polish as a speaker I don't know. (p. 202)

[The] process of writing fiction is not a matter of describing directly a reality that one sees. It's much more often a matter of re-creating a reality which one recalls perhaps imperfectly which one remembers as having been in some way moving, and one almost has to re-create it in order to discover why it is that it still moves one to think about it.

Let me see if that doesn't lead us into a word or two about *The End of My Life.* That, again, was a book which I did not write immediately during the war, although I made a kind of start at it—I think it must have been in 1943 in Italy. I wrote what is now the next to the last chapter—the chapter in which Johnnie, the nurse, is killed—as a short story practically the day after a particular experience had suggested their story to me. This is something perhaps worth describing because this too has to do with how material becomes fiction. In this case I had done much what Skinner does in the book. I had met a nurse and she wanted to see the front so I drove her up a little way in my ambulance. We got somewhere around the artillery position and then I said, "Hey, let's turn around and go back," and she said, "Yeah, let's," and so we turned around and went back and nothing happened.

We went to a party that night and it wasn't until the next morning, waking up somewhat hung over and somewhat displeased with myself, that I began to have this masochistic fantasy of what might have happened, how things could have gone wrong. It became real to me. It really did. In a way the fantasy was more real than the experience of the day before had been. I kept torturing myself with these images of what might have happened to a point where I felt a kind of need to write it as a story, to write the fantasy as a story, which I then did. However, it wasn't a particularly good story and didn't lead anywhere at that time, and I put it away.

About three years later, in 1946, when I was finally discharged from the army I wanted to write a novel and I re-read this, by then, old story about that old, by then, experience, and saw that in order to explain Skinner and the thing he did and the circumstances in which he found himself I would have to fill in a great deal more than simply what had happened on that particular day. That gradually led to the writing of a full novel about that character culminating in that particular experience. (pp. 204-06)

Now the book that came out of the war, *The End of My Life* which you have been reading and which was written seventeen years ago—eighteen years ago, I suppose—is a certain kind of book. I think very much a young man's book. It's a book in a mood of romantic nihilism, I suppose, which is an appropriate enough mood for the age I was when I wrote it (twenty-four or twenty-five; I think I probably had a birthday while I was writing it so I was both twenty-four and twenty-five). The mood, then, still seems to me true. *The End of My Life* seems to me a reasonably accurate description of the way we felt about ourselves and the way we felt about that experience at the time. It doesn't seem to me an accurate book in the picture it gives of the war and of that kind of experience in an objective sense. It's a highly subjective book and like any highly subjective book, I think, limited. It was for that reason, the feeling that while I dealt with the emotional quality of the material, I hadn't really dealt with the war material in a way that satisfied me, that along about 1959 or 1960 I began to write *Confessions of a Spent Youth* in which I use the same material all over again. I think I use it in a very different way and in a very different tone. In my mind it wasn't until I had finished *Confessions* that I had really dealt with the war in a way that pleased me. In that sense *Confessions of a Spent Youth* could almost be read as a work of commentary on American first novels. What I tried to do throughout that much later book was to examine those experiences which are the standard—the set pieces—of American first novels; to hold the set pieces (I felt I had written some of them in *The End of My Life*) up against experience as recalled accurately and without the glow of romance and try to compare the convention with the reality. Having done this finally in *Confessions,* I felt that I was at last through with that particular body of material—the war, youth, and so on—and ready to go on and write novels about more mature experiences. (p. 206)

Moore: *Thank you very much for a fascinating presentation. . . . We will now get to the questions, and the first question is from Jackson State College.*

Jackson: *This question concerns itself with the title of the novel* [**The End of My Life**].

Did you say the title?

Jackson: *With the title, yes. Must we assume that Skinner's death in prison was inevitable; that he also had already died spiritually at the end of the book?*

Well, I think I was certainly thinking in terms of spiritual death. The core of the human being was in some way exhausted and would have no further vitality. The particular personality which this human core had constructed in order to meet the war situation was no longer of use and I meant to imply a kind of rebirth. The Skinner who had lived through the events with Benny and Freak and Rod and so on was a useful enough personality with which to grow up and meet the war and endure it. But at the time of his emergence from prison he would have to be some different kind of man in order to be able to endure or even enjoy the different sort of world conditions which, you know, were then in the making.

Morehouse: *I am of the opinion that the* **Confession** *can be seen as a sequel in a thematic sense to* **The End of My Life.** *If this is so, what major conclusions have you come to as to which book you like better in terms of thematic development, style, imagery, general accomplishment, development of character, and so on?*

All right. I think the two books are finally so different that I couldn't make a choice between them in terms of which I like better. First novels are like first loves, one is never able to reread them without becoming reinvolved in some way in the mood in which they were written. However, I think I feel that, for me at least, rereading *The End of My Life* is something that, when I do it, I have to make certain allowances for myself and my youth. I don't think I understood a great deal technically about fiction when I wrote it. And, in fact, most first novels are written within a kind of naïveté about the form. The stylistic influences and the conception one has of what a story is and how to tell it are much closer to the surface in a first novel than they are in later ones. I think that the two commanding figures were Hemingway and Fitzgerald for me. I felt both presences when I reread *The End of My Life.* It does, on the other hand, have a certain unity of effect it seems to me, because of the total predominance of that mood of romantic nihilism. It has a unity of effect which, I think, is a good quality and which I could not hope to reproduce again at this time, simply because it is no longer my own predominating mood.

I hope *Confessions* is a wiser book, a subtler book, a more profound book. It certainly is a far more experimental book in form. It's conceived almost as a series of essays. The relationship of one chapter to the next in the way time is handled in that each overlaps the other. Any given chapter may start anywhere in time—that is, at any point in the hero's, or the protagonist's, life in which a particular subject becomes of interest to him. This chapter internally will then progress in time to a point which leaves the book a little more advanced than did the end of the preceding chapter. However, the organization of each of these chapters is topical. That is, there is one particular topic dealt with in each of these chapters and all the relevant experiences to the topic are contained in that particular chapter and excluded from the others. So that in this way, the book seems to me somewhat experimental in form, but I don't think I would be the appropriate person to comment on how successful the experiment is. The experiment probably caused me to lose some of the pure narrative drive of *The End of My Life* which is all written consecutively and in which the story is told in a rather straightforward way. There are no particular devices used except flashback. So that is the way that I would compare the two books. *(laughs)* I guess I will just refuse to make a choice between them.

Langston: *This question is in two parts. First of all, none of the characters [in* **The End of My Life**,*] except Benny, completed his college education before volunteering his services for the armed forces; yet all of the characters are portrayed as very intellectual. This is particularly noticeable in the dialogue used, though at times they tend to display a youthful irreverence. There is an implication, too, that the protagonist, Skinner, is in search of an escape from something and there is an implication that he desires to identify himself with something. I would like you to comment on these factors.*

Yes. Well, let me take the education question first and then perhaps we can get the part that deals with values. The war itself was perhaps our junior year in college for many of us. (Incidentally, I think that most of the people I had in mind when I wrote *The End of My Life,* or the base characters, did get back to college after the war and finished their education.) In the experience of going abroad and hearing other languages spoken there was a good deal of involuntary educating of oneself that went on. Even more important, however, in being thrown into war, into very intimate contact with a group where, from almost desperate necessity, one makes very close friends of one's own age but of somewhat different backgrounds, there was a kind of interchange among friends which perhaps takes place in the junior or senior years of college but which took place for us removed from educational institutions. However, we weren't removed from books and we weren't removed from the cultural experience of traveling and so on, and we taught one another. I think this must have happened quite commonly. In the group I was writing about for lack of any other teacher I suppose Benny becomes the teacher. I don't think I made much of this in the book. Benny was the teacher because he could draw upon his experiences in some ways; Rod is a teacher because he can draw upon a different kind of experience. And then Skinner has a somewhat teacherlike function in the group in that he becomes the mocking critic of the other teachers. What happens in a very imperfect way, I think, in such situations is that the educational situation which we institutionalize in colleges is simply reproduced within a little group of people of educable age; it is an imperfect way but not a way that fails to produce any results at all. I would guess that the same kind of educating even goes on in a group of men thrown together in prison. It must go on certainly in the army or abroad. It may not be all desirable education but it is what we mean by education nevertheless. Now, about the value question, can we find out a little more about what they want to know about that?

Langston: *Was Skinner seeking an escape or some kind of identification with particular values?*

Well, I don't think he knew. I think he probably felt that he was trying to find values but that's really too abstract a way of putting it. I think Skinner was trying to find somebody *to be*. We use the phrase a search for identity about novels fairly often. It's not a very accurate phrase in my mind because it assumes that identity exists and that somehow one can find it as an accomplished and developed thing. Obviously identity doesn't exist somewhere to be found; identity—the feeling that one has achieved "self"—is something that develops very slowly perhaps through many years and through all one's youth. And identity is finally achieved, I think, from within rather than found somewhere without. Meanwhile, one is trying various systems of value; various ways of judging experience, various ways of estimating himself. These are suggested by the people we meet and the books we read and the things that happen to us and the things we cause to happen. I think Skinner in the book is probably ten years away, still, from finding himself in this sense. The book is only a partial record of his search for values or his search for identity, to fall back on those two phrases again. (pp. 207-11)

Tougaloo: *Two students of ours have asked whether Skinner's nihilism is really genuine. One suggests that his concern for people suggests not, the other suggests that he is just punishing himself. Would you comment on this?*

Well, I'll try. I'm not sure that I can successfully. Skinner's nihilism is genuine in that he seems, to himself, to feel that way. I think looking at him (if I could) as somebody else's character, I would say that there is a perfectly obvious contradiction in his feeling that way. After having adopted the pose and having said "Life sure is a dreary affair," he is capable of going out and having a marvelously good time. However, while this contradiction exists in the character, it seems to me to exist as a kind of fraternal feeling in characters of that age and that temperament. Right down through history each generation exemplifies very much the same thing. It seems to me that you can go back

decade after decade after decade and find this manifestation of the same combination: a kind of romantic nihilism and, at the same time, a considerable exuberance for life not only in its sensual aspects but in its intellectual aspects too. The fact is, when Skinner and his friends sit around contemplating how lousy life is, then, in a way, they are having a very good time. This is something I believe I dealt with in *Confessions.*

Now, on the other hand, there is a point in the book at which Skinner becomes, I think, genuinely hopeless and with cause. That's the point at which he joins the pioneer regiment of Africa and this certainly is indicative of the situation to which these particular soldiers are subjected. It occurs in a much different way; in a way that he doesn't enjoy. Instead of being a kind of glowing melancholy, he is really severely depressed, genuinely without hope. Does that answer the question?

Tougaloo: *Yes, thank you.*

Drury: *Do you mean to suggest that the kind of exuberance that dominates most of the scenes in the flashbacks is no longer possible for the Skinner who, in some kind of way, is going to be reborn at the end of the novel?*

Yes, that's a lovely question. As life implies death and happiness implies sorrow and so on, perhaps the nihilism and exuberance are really dependent on one another in a way. Therefore, when Skinner reemerges and is no longer the victim of one, he will no longer be able to produce the other. I think this quite possible.

Moore: *Thank you again. I think we are all greatly indebted to Mr. Vance Bourjaily for a most illuminating morning. Thank you and good-bye.* (pp. 212-14)

Vance Bourjaily and Harry T. Moore, in an interview in Talks with Authors, *edited by Charles F. Madden, Southern Illinois University Press, 1968, pp. 201-14.*

Webster Schott

The man who knew Kennedy [in Bourjaily's novel *The Man Who Knew Kennedy*] didn't know him very well. I'm almost as intimate with Lyndon Johnson. I met him once. . . .

[Bourjaily's protagonist, Dave Doremus], was laid up in a hospital with Jack Kennedy briefly during the war—and once ran as an anti-McCarthy Republican against his Massachusetts machine. Having known Kennedy makes no difference in Dave's life. He ends it with a hose connecting the exhaust pipe to his car window. Inside, Dave and his super-swinger girl friend, Sunny, follow a stupid relationship to a dumb ending.

Bourjaily's response to John Kennedy's death is to gag on the poison in our culture. He cries against the insane assassination—it occurs at the start of the novel—by describing the destruction of another attractive American, who should have flourished and enriched lives near him if our culture were safe for good men. It ought to be, the evangelist in Bourjaily says. And then the fatalist in him says, dammit, make do.

One keeps wishing the artist in Bourjaily were more in evidence to show us, not tell us, how people come apart. Pill-popping and sex-play, revries of Anita O'Day and uniformed Lee Harvey Oswalds threatening nice girls at U.S.O. dances don't explain why the century is out of joint. Bourjaily seems hung up on nostalgia, anti-nihilism, lost innocence. To convince us of the human price he believes our culture extracts, he must reveal people feeling the shakedown. We must share in the transactions of pain, anger, despair. Unfortunately, instead of changing characters we get reports on changes. The author has too much cool for what ought to be a very hot novel.

He tells two stories simultaneously. One is about Barney James, who runs a Connecticut hardwood factory, is married to a woman who quarrels for recreation and seduces to stay young. He has three children to remind him of life's purpose: continuity.

Barney plays the game of business seriously and the game of women cautiously. He has negotiated a sanity settlement with life.

The second story, about Doremus, is told through Barney. Bourjaily spins an idyl of youth for the pair, interrupts it with the war that matures them, and then follows Dave's downward spiral. From Harvard Law School, society marriage and flashy management consultant, Dave goes to failed speculator and emotional bankrupt.

The crash threatens during a long Caribbean cruise that Dave, Barney and their spouses take in a rented schooner. Sea-going group therapy is supposed to shake the depression of the assassination and celebrate Dave's third marriage. But Dave proposes a wife swap and generally acts nuts. Suddenly he leaves the cruise to haul back his dope-addict mistress from her incest-crazy brother. The chance of losing Sunny is one assault too many. All Dave's post-war failures—wrong wives, bad deals, misalliances—disappear in a cloud of carbon monoxide.

Barney buries him at Arlington. Another man who was handsomer, smarter, more engaging than most—Barney's personal equivalent of Kennedy—lies lost among the white headstones. One of evolution's drop-outs, Dave should have been among its fittest survivors. As the author says, we've all known Kennedys. They're born to succeed. Destroyed or failing, their lives become part of Macbeth's "tale told by an idiot . . . signifying nothing."

Bourjaily cannot explain the loss of beautiful, favored men except through the absurd. One instinctively accepts that: we live in Samuel Beckett's world of mud. Dave sinks in it. But in a novel distinguished by bravura reveries, visions of sea and forest and belief in love's redemptive power, why can't the author split Dave's mind to bare the hostility and heartbreak of suicide? Why does Dave seem a statistic instead of a casualty? Because Bourjaily forces his novel beyond fiction into the mists of social psychology. The story of one man within the story of another man within the frame of John Kennedy's assassination becomes a set of Chinese nesting boxes with labels.

It makes for a tiny last box: Dave Doremus. *The Man Who Knew Kennedy* is a problem novel all right. First problem: Will the real Dave Doremus please step forward?

Webster Schott, "A Statistic Instead of a Casu-alty," in The New York Times Book Review, *January 29, 1967, p. 4.*

Robie Macauley

Perhaps Mr. Bourjaily's new novel [*The Man Who Knew Kennedy*] ought to be scrutinized under the provisions of the truth-in-packaging act recently passed by Congress. In a time when revelations about the late President's life and death seem to be the most popular product on the market, it is probably inevitable that we should get some quite dubious advertising tie-ins—but it is surprising to find one with the respectable Bourjaily trademark on it. *The Man Who Knew Nixon* or *The Men Who Knew Harry S. Truman* would have had just about as much bearing on the essential story Mr. Bourjaily has to tell but, obviously, both of those are missing a certain kind of appeal.

To be fair about this, I should say that the author does, at times, try for a nominal amount of thematic justification. His narrator begins by saying that the story is an attempt to "straighten out my feelings about Dave Doremus. . . . Dave was, among my friends, the man who knew Kennedy. Knew him, off and on, all of his life." Nevertheless, the evidence for this friendship is rather thin and incidental, and it is hard to see how the relationship affects Doremus' life in any important way.

It is true that Doremus, like quite a few other Americans, bears something of a resemblance to John F. Kennedy—Doremus is a man with an attractive personality, a New Englander, a World War II hero, a sailing enthusiast and (to make one more tenuous connection) the son of a man who once worked for Joseph P. Kennedy. Unless I am missing some camouflaged or secret parallels between the two lives, that is the amount of it.

Likewise, there is a natural but somewhat hazy kind of 22nd-cousin affiliation between all of the other characters and Kennedy. . . . Throughout the story, they speak of him with nostalgia and admiration, regard him as something of a symbol of their generation, and have a genuine feeling about his loss. It is hardly enough to vindicate the pretensions of the title and the beginning.

Once that is put aside, however, *The Man Who Knew Kennedy* is a deft and persuasive novel. It is largely made up of accounts of two small-boat cruises—the first just after the war when Doremus and the narrator, Barney James, take a sloop for the summer and pick up two willing girls. That voyage represents the last days of youth and, even though the reader has little trouble in predicting all the carefree incidentals (nude bathing, happy lovemaking, a few lessons on the trombone, plenty of camaraderie), the story conveys a real sense of ease and pleasure.

The second cruise, which takes place some 17 years later, when both men are married and having their troubles, is a much more complicated and nervous time. The enjoyment of sailing is still there, but neither the men nor their wives can ever quite free themselves of their land-born anxieties again. There is a good deal of plot business about Doremus' involvement with a girl singer who has become an addict and about James' problem with an unfaithful wife, but the real shadow is that old you-can-never-recover-it feeling. There is nothing that ages us faster than a re-enactment of our youth; all the discoveries of our middle years are unwanted ones. This is more or less the tenor of the second voyage.

Before it is over, the wives have deserted the schooner and Doremus has taken a plane home to try to do something to help the singer. When James finally reaches port, he is greeted by the news that Doremus, overcome with his troubles, has killed himself and his girl.

Mr. Bourjaily is not a writer who generalizes very coherently, but I suppose if there is any generalization in his story it is that one about middle age. Life begins to end at 40; our powers decline and our problems grow insoluble; good men are driven to commit suicide. When a writer advances such an aphorism, it seems to me, he must do it well enough to inspire a kind of there-but-for-the-grace-of-God recognition in his readers. This is hardly true in the character of Dave Doremus, who manages his life with such unfailing ineptitude that we can hardly blame his years for his sorrows.

It is on this point that the whole machinery of Kennedy-symbolism seems to move off into absurdity. On one side optimism, vigor, confidence, success, a relish for looking ahead. On the other side failure, disillusion, and a fatal attraction for self-harm. Whatever minor characteristics Doremus may have had in common with Kennedy scarcely seem to matter. In fact, Mr. Bourjaily doesn't even convince me that they actually did know each other. What would they have to talk about?

> Robie Macauley, "Middle-age Spread," in Book Week—World Journal Tribune, February 5, 1967, p. 17.

Don Crinklaw

The jacket of [*The Man Who Knew Kennedy*] is red, white and blue, and its design is uncomfortably similar to that of *Profiles In Courage.* One is momentarily reassured to see that the author is Vance Bourjaily who wrote two very good—and undervalued—novels: *The End of My Life* and *The Violated.* But he also, in *Confessions of a Spent Youth,* took us through 400 anxious pages without creating a single moving line. And then Mailer's snap about Bourjaily's "nice gifts as a politician" comes to mind. Is *The Man Who Knew Kennedy* one more main chance item?

One begins to read with an air of waiting in ambush, ready to pounce upon the first fashionable tirade about our guilty society, the first yard of soggy, worshipful prose. But they never come. A mood of reflective sadness lingers over the book, and if the author does not completely squelch the critical impulse, he presents a tasteful and intelligent picture of the generation that came of age with Kennedy, wondered at his Presidency, and felt personally bereft at his death. Also—and this for me was the book's most interesting achievement—as the interplay between the characters progresses we are allowed glimpses of the elements in us which would elevate a Kennedy and, in a dark moment, bring him down.

Sinclair Lewis, in more ways than one, is the animus behind the novel; it was his bad, lively *The Man Who Knew Coolidge* which defined that President's charm for the electorate: "Maybe he isn't what my daughter would call

so 'ritzy.'" the main character says, ". . . he may not shoot off a lot of fireworks, but you know what he is? HE'S SAFE." Kennedy, of course, suggests a rather different description, and the man who knew him—Bourjaily's Dave Doremus—is totally unlike Lewis's preposterous Lowell Schmaltz. Doremus is rather, in fact, more like Kennedy.

We know Doremus through the eyes and memories of his friend Barney James, the head of a New England wood-products industry. The two came together in a St. Louis high school, and in the first flashback subtle parallels begin to appear. His charm and "magnetism" made him easily the most popular student, yet: "He was his own man, poised and wilful, capable of withdrawing when it seemed right to him." As the years go by, events in Kennedy's life find their echo in Dave's: both are Harvard and Navy men, both bear scars from the war (they are ward-mates in a naval hospital), and while Dave finds his *métier* in business rather than politics, his manner is suggestive: "I like a day with fifteen crises in it," he tells Barney. (pp. 373-74)

But Dave expends his gifts without calculation, and this "softness" renders him vulnerable to a wild, hopeless business scheme and two predatory wives. Suicide—a few months after the assassination—follows the total collapse of his fortunes, and his fate and the President's would appear to have radically different origins. But Barney James is with his friend often in the final weeks and his speculations, and those of others he records, are worth considering.

He ponders the kinship his generation felt for Kennedy, and suggests reasons for his success:

> We all knew Kennedy, didn't we? . . . Wasn't Kennedy the particular upperclassman in the fraternity, poised and cool but not unfriendly? It was the poise that made a freshman uncomfortably awed by him; and the grooming. His jackets were never too short this year, because he'd grown in the last six months. . . . You never thought in terms of having him on your side, only of being permitted to be on his.
> (p. 374)

Sinclair Lewis was known to brood on the problem of making ordinary people fictionally interesting, and his solution was an exasperated retreat into exaggeration and satire. Bourjaily confronts the same problem but seeks a different end: to epitomize the men of Kennedy's time, a Babbitt will clearly not do. Barney James' value is his conventionality, yet he must be able to sustain a novel, and it is Bourjaily's special skill to make skating on such thin ice seem almost effortless. As Barney leads us through the details of his business and family life, and through the memories of his generation—depression, war, and lighter memories of swing bands and liquor and cigarettes—we feel we are in the presence of an alert, sympathetic, though not especially distinguished mind, and this is surely proper.

Still, the author appears not to completely trust him, and to cover this uncertainty Bourjaily has manufactured—there is no other word—traits that make Barney something of a Renaissance-ordinary man. He speaks a conventional public-school argot yet rereads Shakespeare and discourses on lyric poetry. He shows a craftsman's concern for the products of his plant though his hands never touch the wood (but he does work at remodeling his house) and while he takes pride in his business ethics he is casual about his adulteries (no one is perfect). Plus: he is an athlete, an amateur musician, a photographer and a pilot. Perhaps Lewis' dilemma has no solution.

Other complaints can be brought against the novel: some of the scenes seem to be just revised versions of episodes in the earlier books—the sexual idyll in the beginning is too similar to "The Poozle Dreamers" section of the *Confessions*—and the author's dips into sophomoric humor can be downright infuriating (what is an overdose of soft drinks? "Pepsilepsy"). But the book easily survives its faults, and at the end one is aware of having been entertained and impressed. (pp. 374-75)

> *Don Crinklaw, in a review of "The Man Who Knew Kennedy," in* Commonweal, *Vol. LXXXVI, No. 13, June 16, 1967, pp. 373-75.*

Robert Garis

Vance Bourjaily's title, **The Man Who Knew Kennedy,** sounds opportunistic, and his novel may have failed to win readers for that reason. This instance of the manipulated public's striking back has its sad irony, for I am perfectly convinced that this novel comes out of a disinterested need to account for the impact and to discover the meaning of Kennedy's death. The question is explicitly posed by one of the characters on the day of the assassination: "What kind of people are we?" Mr. Bourjaily's "answer" is the story of the destruction of a smaller man, but a man of some real power, Dave Doremus, who had occasionally run across Kennedy. This upside-down version of the strategy of *The Republic*—look at the small letters and then check to see whether the big letters aren't the same—seems promising. And Mr. Bourjaily undoubtedly meant us to do most of the checking by ourselves, while and after reading. But he has confusingly done some himself—confusingly because his taste forced him to speak of Kennedy's death in almost entirely external terms, so that the question comes to be "What kind of people could allow or cause this death?" instead of the larger question "What did Kennedy's death mean about *him* and his relation with his and our way of life?" On the other hand, anxiety to give the smaller Kennedy stature leads Mr. Bourjaily to overweight the other side of the structure by making Doremus' destruction almost entirely self-destruction. This miscalculation actually impedes the hoped-for connection between the public world and the private world, and the result is that the novel does after all seem not entirely unlike an attempt to cash in on the Kennedy name. Furthermore, and worse, Mr. Bourjaily's scheme required him to cast about for a suitably representative private American tragedy, and I think it was this necessity that blinded him to the extraordinary trashiness of the story he finally concocted. I can find no other explanation for the sudden deterioration in the work of an interesting writer whose earlier novels, though notably middle-of-the-road in technique, insight and emotion, have always seemed genuine.

Dave Doremus has brains, looks, the capacity for hard work, and we are told explicitly that he has glamor; there are the ambitions to match. His financial, moral and physical self-destruction is initiated by the bitchy upper-class wife who represents his drive for power; it is violently consummated by his obsessed pity for a cheap doped-up nightclub singer who represents his yearning to express responsible love and also perhaps his unacknowledged yearning to cop out; this obsession makes it impossible for him to be saved by the love of his new wife, one of those familiar physically clumsy "real women" who are unconscious of their powerful sexual appeal. Now these stereotypes do of course owe something to Fitzgerald and O'Hara and other more or less serious writers, but what astonishes the reader is to discover that Mr. Bourjaily's story is virtually identical with the story endlessly repeated in the current high-class junk-fiction of writers like John D. MacDonald. I cannot believe that Mr. Bourjaily really wanted to play in this league, in which his taste and seriousness are obvious liabilities. MacDonald sermonizes appallingly, continually and confidently about American materialism; Mr. Bourjaily tastefully refrains but seems to be giving us the same sermon subliminally. MacDonald's lurid images show the unquestioning faith with which he inhabits his fantasy world and the sheer practice he has had in representing it; Bourjaily's soft-pedalling, since it doesn't amount to serious criticism of the images, seems timid, inept, and may seem even dishonest. And so on. But I prefer to forget the quiet banality of **The Man Who Knew Kennedy**—a somewhat unusual artistic effect—as an accident, just another confusion in the aftermath of the assassination. (pp. 327-28)

> *Robert Garis, "Varieties of the Will," in* The Hudson Review, *Vol. XX, No. 2, Summer, 1967, pp. 325-39.*

James R. Frakes

Vance Bourjaily belongs to an unfortunate group of American novelists who have been for too many years, like Leopold Bloom, "almosting it." Generally favorable reviews, an occasional thin analytic article, an alphabetical listing in an index of "promising" postwar fiction-writers. Their names are familiar, all honorable craftsmen: Wright Morris, Calder Willingham, Walker Percy, Frederick Buechner, James Drought, Herbert Gold. Too often their talents are referred to as foils for larger reputations like those of Malamud, Bellow, Styron, Capote.

I have seen Bourjaily used as reflector to enhance Mailer, Hersey, Fitzgerald, Dos Passos, Faulkner, Bowles, Kerouac, Ellison and Vidal. His first novel, **The End of My Life** (1947), and his third, **The Violated** (1958), received unusually responsive critical reception, but even in these works, it was implied, Bourjaily did well what others had done better. There must be times when a man treated like this feels that even total neglect would be preferable.

One of the troubles is that Bourjaily asks for such put-down comparisons in every work. I think that **Brill Among the Ruins** is his most finished, most wholly satisfying novel—but, even here, he seems to shout "Compare me!" There's a duck-shoot in the first chapter of **Brill** that will send you back to Hemingway's framing-account of the same activity in "Across the River and Into the Trees"; I happen to think that Bourjaily does it better here than Papa did, but go convince Field and Stream. The small-town legal involutions in Rosetta, Ill., happen to be just as authentic as, and trimmed more neatly than, the Cozzens labyrinth in *By Love Possessed,* but Cozzens, of course, did it first. You may certainly care more about Bourjaily's 48-year-old lawyer-hero, Bob Brill, but he still lives in the clammy shadow of Cozzens' Arthur Winner.

When Brill turns archeology-buff and enlists as site-surveyor on an academic field-trip to Mexico, he inevitably carries with him the reader's richer memories of Lawrence and Malcolm Lowry. And when, in one of Brill's marvelously sustained reveries about an Aztec handball game, the players observe that the "new jackrabbit ball" will "ruin the game," we're plummeted back into Faulkner's "Red Leaves" swamp with Louis Berry and Three Basket.

See how temptingly easy it is? Bourjaily makes himself more than fair game, and apparently there's no legal limit—except, maybe, the reviewer's integrity. One should at least try to match the integrity of big Bob Brill himself, who refuses to admit his generation has lost anything except just a little vitality and hair, a modicum of enthusiasm and relevance, and clean air and water. . . . Still, as the youngest and hippiest of his many mistresses tells him, "Existential pain. You carry more of it around than anyone I ever knew . . . your desperation is so quiet it's unconscious."

The pain consists, in unequal parts, of a long-dead male cousin, an alcoholic wife, a C.O. son turned professional soldier, a murdered friend, a cheating law-partner, pollution and a dying red elm. Brill also drinks a lot. An awful lot. He also projects himself out of this "time of the dangerous clowns" into the far past—as a caveman hunting a mammoth, as a sexy coelacanth, as a Mixtec-Zapotec stripling. Quirky, tough, witty, compassionate, Bob Brill is a man very much worth your attention. . . .

To keep the integrity pitch, however, I must point out that this novel breaks too suddenly in the middle, that the Midwest "country" complications fall apart from the Mexican anthropology; the tax evasions, moral mushrooms and deer-hair crawdaddy lures split too violently from the stratigraphic pits, tope maps and coprolites, despite Bourjaily's noble efforts to patch the wound with cross-references, resemblances and thematic parallels. The historical playlets are often over-clever, lumberingly playful, not sufficiently cooled by the self-mocking tone. The tricks with point of view, though fascinating to watch, remain tricks. The last-minute resolution, in which Brill realizes he has made "all the old bargains human life is based on" and flies home on wings of good faith, is too neat—not a moral cop-out but an esthetic one.

I wish *Brill Among the Ruins* would promote Vance Bourjaily out of the ranks of the also-rans. He has earned much more than a nod in passing. He matters.

> *James R. Frakes, in a review of "Brill Among the Ruins," in* The New York Times Book Review, *November 1, 1970, p. 5.*

John Leonard

[The title character of *Brill Among the Ruins*] is a lawyer, as were his father and his grandfather before him, in Ro-

setta, Ill. (pop. 32,800). He owns a farm, where he raises food for his own table. He hunts and fishes for the same purpose. He has a wife, who loves the sherry bottle more than life, and two children—a girl in high school and a boy who sought first to evade the draft by decamping to Montreal and then went to Vietnam and became a professional soldier. Brill does his own share of drinking, with vodka instead of coffee for breakfast, a can of beer between his knees while he's driving, a bottle in the back seat and a bottle in the office desk. Brill drinks because he is in a constant state of rage. . . .

This is not your average Middle-American rage against muggers and long-haired freaks and campus radicals, for Brill defends the freaks and radicals in court, and there isn't much mugging in Rosetta. Brill's rage is against the people who wage a poisonous war abroad, and the people at home who cheat farmers, subdivide the land for tract homes, pollute the rivers and fix the elections. His rage is *for* something else—a meaning; an escape from a failed self; a middle-aged version of the young man who flew to Yucatan in his own plane in search of the mother who deserted him; a decency gone out of the world of engineers and killers.

To Vance Bourjaily's considerable credit, he reopens the old question of specificity in fiction. Brill's rage does not derive from that epistemological discrepancy between subject and object—existential ennui, the substitution of *angst* for tuberculosis—with which so many modern novelists begin and end their verbal artifacts. (Gee, if empirical statements can't be proven true then the situation, *any* situation, is hopeless, isn't it?) His rage is rooted in the observable, in the family he came from, the family he lives with, the town he lives in, the self he might have been. Mr. Bourjaily pays his dues, thereby earning Brill's credibility for the reader. Here is how the political system works in Rosetta; what it's like hunting ducks; which remarks trigger which memories; who did what to whom, and why.

Specificity. Mr. Bourjaily has an appetite for details and a talent for organizing them that adds up to a savage accuracy. We are prepared, then, for Brill's second flight to Mexico, his experiments with archeology, his re-imagining among the ruins of his own life and the ruins of pre-Columbian cultures the way it might have been. Brill has a running fantasy in Mexico of a young man's struggle to survive in the time before Cortes; it is a marvelous mixture of the colloquial and the historical, hilarious and moving and fatalistic; it is, as well, a skillfully constructed dream version of Brill's own situation, full of the sacrifices, cruelties, damages, compunctions and consequences he has known.

But all the while the fantasy is running, Mr. Bourjaily tells us also what archeology is about, its procedures and excitements. Who, what, when, where, why and how—the whole burden of information the New Novel is supposed to discard on its way to being a poem or a string quartet—gets told; and told, moreover, in the service of a presumption that heroes are still possible. There are still some heroes, like Brill, who try to do "the right thing" and actually succeed in doing it more often than not. Learning why they do the right things, and what happens afterward, is a hundred times more interesting and entertaining than those long hours reviewers are obliged to spend with young writers who profess to find a tragic significance in the ambiguities of adverbs.

Information. Entertainment. Heroes. Intelligence. Consequences. Social and moral contexts. The world of work. The bourgeois novel. A *story*. Mr. Bourjaily shouldn't have to bear the excess baggage of all those modern theories about fiction that he has chosen to ignore; nor should he have to apologize to Hemingway, D. H. Lawrence, Malcolm Lowry and Sinclair Lewis, whose turf he has invaded. The author of *The Violated,* once more at the top of his form, demands only to be judged by the single standard relevant to the game of one-on-one between writer and reader.

Which is: When was the last time you wanted to argue with a novel's resolution, when you had sufficient data (provided by the author, of course) and sufficient empathy (likewise a gift) and sufficient absorption (a miracle) to disagree with what the hero decides to do? Such arguments have to do with imaginative worlds that have been realized; such disagreements are with characters in whom we believe and for whom we care. To learn something and to care about someone are precisely those experiences that make living worth the sweat, blood and confusion. Brill matters.

> John Leonard, "Would You Believe a Hero?" *in* The New York Times, *November 10, 1970, p. 45.*

James Kelly

In Robert Brill, the nature-loving, fist-fighting, hard-drinking, womanizing, deeply honest and deeply sensitive pivotal figure of Vance Bourjaily's new novel [*Brill Among the Ruins*], we have a viable image of today's fallible decent man at bay in a world he barely recognizes.

As Brill makes his way through the tangled undercurrents of a medium-sized Illinois town to find a tenuous escape amidst the Mixtec-Zapotec-Aztec-Olmec ruins of southern Mexico, his story becomes a sort of doomsday chronicle, full of human churning. There are vivid minor characters in *Brill Among the Ruins*—the alcoholic wife reduced to the role of noncontender, the biddable law partner and beddable women, the town bosses and union leaders, and of course the idealized best friends of boyhood and middle age—but they exist mostly as navigation points in Brill's headlong rush to nowhere.

As might be anticipated, the author draws freely upon his store of knowledge as outdoors enthusiast (the mandatory scenes of duck hunting and stream fishing are present), his lengthy field trips during the early Fifties to Oaxaca's antiquity sites (the second half of the book narrowly skirts becoming a how-to manual for the amateur archeologist), and his admiration for Mr. Hemingway in matters of content and stance. . . .

Regrettably, though, for present storytelling purposes Mr. Bourjaily has adopted a breezy shorthand style that at times threatens to become windblown or, worse, to drift into a jazzed-up flippancy. For example, Brill fancies himself as a character in a running Olmec or Aztec soap opera, with everybody expressing sonorous ancient thoughts in hippie jargon. And Bourjaily's impressive fund of scholar-ship concerning Mexico's melting-pot past and the archeological techniques for discovering it is laid upon us in vintage "cool" language that occasionally takes on a little pre-Columbian flavor of its own.

Bourjaily expertly depicts a campus demonstration, the endless shrewd vagaries of a small-town law practice, the inner mores and sociological by-play of Midwesterners struggling on their own sheets of flypaper, and the essence of man-woman sensuality, about which he has found some new, non-cliché things to say.

Above all, Mr. Bourjaily (through Mr. Brill) is concerned about what is happening at this point in history, and makes us think about the glum choices ahead. "Innocence is child's knowledge that he will never die," he tells us.

> Most of the energy in the world for getting things made came from this true innocence; after you lost it, you might get things done, but you would never get things made again. Except out of the true opposite of true innocence, which was a man's accumulation of despair on the long downhill drift toward his death. Brill thought that when a nation realized it could die, it, too, probably lost its energy for making things. . . .

Here is a novel for people puzzled by abrasive, contemporary life; for vicarious adventurers sick of desk, domestic responsibility, the whole damned spectrum of trifling choices, and for those who would like a fictional look at what it would be like to be a free agent (Brill) on life's highway. That Brill himself—a decent man with all guilts and responsibilities intact—watched the heady quality of his own freedom turn to an aimlessness which finally sent him full circle is neither here nor there. The concerned reader could always have handled things differently, couldn't he?

> James Kelly, in a review of "Brill Among the Ruins," in Saturday Review, *Vol. LIII, No. 49, December 5, 1970, p. 40.*

William McPherson

Question: What does *Boy's Life* have in common with *North American Review, Phoebe* with *Esquire, Dude* with *The Iowa Review*? A more disparate collection of journals one would be hard put to conjure up, right?

Answer: Over the past 12 years they have all run portions of Vance Bourjaily's long-running and long-awaited *Now Playing at Canterbury,* an exuberantly eclectic aggregation of prose, heroic couplets, comic strips, operatic libretto, fantasy and fictional set pieces striving to contain itself in what we more and more loosely term the novel, which for purposes of this book should be defined as a work of the imagination, of a certain length, told mostly in prose and more or less centered around a single event.

The event is the production and world premiere of an opera, *$4,000,* to open a $10-million cultural complex in the corn belt. If State University in State City is not the University of Iowa where Bourjaily teaches in the Writers' Workshop, it is a reasonable facsimile thereof. (Bourjaily actually wrote the libretto to an opera of the same title produced in Iowa City in 1969.) The opera tells a rather improbable story of passion, murder and greed set in and around a construction camp in backwoods Georgia in 1949. We are given the entire libretto but left to imagine the score.

To this cultural shrine come, like Chaucer's 14th-century pilgrims to Canterbury Cathedral, a host of very 20th-century characters, pilgrims now in the service of art instead of Christ. They come from New York and California, from State University faculty and students, from all ages and segments of society. "Here we go," Bourjaily begins, echoing with gusto the prologue to *The Canterbury Tales.* (p. H1)

So they begin to tell their stories: of campus protests, of orgies in the Wisconsin woods, of racial strife; of childhood, youth and age; tales of farm and town and city; of campus beer parties, faculty cocktail parties, pot parties—the whole episodic panoply of our life and times.

The art of the novel after Flaubert has mainly been an art of exclusion—a paring away of extraneous detail, a honing down, a concentrating of energy. But Bourjaily's mode is one of inclusion, which may explain why at 54 . . . he remains respected but not widely acclaimed. He tries to encompass everything—*Boy's Life, North American Review, Esquire* and *Dude.* His voice is exultant and his creative energy enormous, holding this Noah's Ark of a novel together and keeping the reader going even when his own energies, his own attention begin to lag.

Chaucer wrote after the terror of the Black Death, a time of upheaval at the end of the Middle Ages and the beginning of the modern era. Bourjaily writes in another time of shifting certainties, the response to which is an easy and fashionable despair. But that is not Bourjaily's response, nor was it Chaucer's. Then there was the Church, now the arts, and always the flux of the seasons and the variety of life. Chaucer's cathedral is Bourjaily's cultural center; it is not the architecture that counts but the purpose it serves. As with Chaucer, the transcendant high seriousness of the cause does not preclude an abundance of frivolity along the way.

Given all this, and a cast of hundreds, need one ask for a simple plot? And given all this, the wonder is not that *Canterbury* succeeds as a novel, which decision will be left for another time, but that it succeeds at all, which it assuredly does. It may be short on plot, but it is long on life.

As Dylan sings, the times they are a-changing, and change breeds confusion, a state of affairs faithfully recorded in *Now Playing at Canterbury.* It is enough to say, this is how it is, and to celebrate it; perhaps too much to ask the writer to tell us, this is what it means. It means what it is: a tapestry of our times, with flashes of brilliance, interludes of boredom; with its sentimentality, its longueurs, its absurdities and pomposities, its inflated rhetoric and bombast, its vulgarity and excesses, and, yes, its nobility.

The novel ends on a poignant, lovely note. The nomadic stage director—Bourjaily's Chaucer—imported from the East for the production is traveling again,

> empty again. Ready to be filled with stories, again. To make stories, again. Old Billy Bigears, with an empty seat beside him: Take it. There's a story you could tell to pass the time as the lovely, polluted California seascape passes. So could we all, every man his own Homer, blind, caught in the endless

wonder of the words, of the cries, of the shouts, of the laughter, of the tears of the things of the stories of our lives. There we go.

(pp. H1-H2)

William McPherson, "Chaucer Redux," in Book World—The Washington Post, *September 12, 1976, pp. H1-H2.*

Stanley Kauffmann

[In *Now Playing at Canterbury*], a professor of English, conducting a seminar on Fitzgerald, admonishes his students: "And remember, the form itself, the novel as an American expression shaped to the times, wasn't all laid out for him as it might be for one of you. It still had to be developed." One can easily argue with this proposition (Melville and Hawthorne and Mark Twain and Crane floundered for form? Were inexpressive of their times?), but it helps to explain Vance Bourjaily's view of his own work. For thirty post-Fitzgerald years, Bourjaily has been publishing novels that have tried hard for contemporary expression and that have relied on the belief that Fitzgerald, along with Hemingway, laid out the forms—more specifically, the available styles.

For the past twelve of those thirty years, Bourjaily has been working on *Now Playing At Canterbury.* One sees by the title that his model here is not American, and he underscores that fact by writing fourteen pages of the book in Chaucerian verse. Presumably he knows Nevill Coghill's comment that the Prologue of *The Canterbury Tales* "is the concise portrait of an entire nation," and Bourjaily has moved from that idea to make his group of tales a less concise portrait of a much larger nation. But even though the armature of the book derives from fourteenth-century England, the styles are still the styles of Bourjaily—the skimming of Fitzgerald, the long march with Hemingway.

His Canterbury is State University, in State City, in the Midwest. . . . Not all of the many characters who tell their tales in the course of the book are literal pilgrims to the place; some of them live and work there, but they are all brought together by one event—the first production of an opera written by two teachers at the university. (p. 26)

As in *The Canterbury Tales,* the book deals predominantly with the past lives of its many characters. Relatively little of consequence happens in the present other than a surprising stand of honor by the seedy little vagabond stage director. Past lives are usually recounted in first-person narratives, again as in the *Tales,* and deal with a cross section of major moral-social evolutions in the last twenty years, with such salient social-political issues as racism, Vietnam, and student radicalism. Taken together, these narratives, in their "present" context, are the purpose of the book—again as in the *Tales:* they are intended to provide an overview of and an insight into America weaving through the recent past into the future. (First line of the book: "Here we go." Last line: "There we go.") But the book falls into a familiar pitfall of American novelistic gigantism: Bourjaily thinks that by presenting a *lot* of experience, he is deepening our perception of it. I doubt that many readers will find their knowledge or understanding of contemporary matters much enlarged by winding along through the elaborate schema of this long novel.

Still, Bourjaily merits discussion if only because he is one of the last of a literary line. To examine his new book is to discern something of the changes in American writing in the last thirty years—a probably unwitting statement that he has made on his theme of "expression shaped to the times." Bourjaily's first novel, *The End of My Life,* published in 1947, deals mainly with an American who volunteered for the British ambulance corps during World War II and served in the Middle East. In the year of its appearance, it seemed to me a patent but moderately gifted attempt to continue the literary service that Hemingway had done to World War I, and it was interesting for that very reason. Hemingway's terse style and "doomed" tone seemed fitting to a young author after a much different war: *The End of My Life* seemed to say something about and to the author's contemporaries, as if its mannerisms at least provided a way to deal with experience in a relatively barren time. Looking through the book again before reading this new one, I could see only the mannerisms, no residual pertinence. This wouldn't matter, obviously, except that the mannerisms persist in this new book. And even that wouldn't matter if those mannerisms seemed truly *his,* ingested and controlled, pliant and directly mediative.

But the genuinely shocking point is that, after all this time, after seven intervening books (including a novel longer than this new one), Bourjaily's style still seems merely imitative and therefore stagnant. There are patches of lyricism that seem to have filtered down through several carbon copies of Fitzgerald, such as his description of the conductor at the premiere: "He is . . . neither man nor musician but seventy-eight instruments. . . . His mouth is reeds and mouthpieces, his skin tympani, his bones cymbals, glocks, and triangles." Most of the dialogue is so slavishly Hemingway as almost to be parody—clenched-teeth, we-happy-few-who-understand-one-another stuff. (Plenty of examples, but to represent adequately one of those telegraph-message exchanges would take up too much space.) Bourjaily's one personal contribution to style, as in his first novel, is recurrent undergraduate facetiousness. A woman in bed asks her lover to pass the champagne, and he says, "It's flat, I'm afraid." She says, "Such a dear, skeptical Columbus, oh, I'm sure it's round." (Matters are worse when, from time to time, Bourjaily seems embarrassed by the feeble jokes and treats them as if they were the characters' and not his.)

Now this assortment of devices, besides the artistic inadequacy, has the added burden of seeming passé. I can't think of a serious novelist under fifty who suffers from these particular defects. It's not a question of fashion-mongering, of maintaining that Bourjaily would be better if his stylistic model were Pynchon or Percy, Barth or Barthelme. The issue is a style that began as overt imitation and has remained overt imitation through thirty years, and it's the overt imitativeness itself that dates it. The English professor in this novel fulminates against the word "generation" as not being a true critical term. Perhaps not, but it is a historical one; and when Bourjaily describes student radical protests and drug busts of the 1960s in a style that evolved in the 1920s and gives us only worn mi-

mesis of that style, the effect is that of a middle-aged TV performer using rock jargon.

The dated quality is abetted by the loads of facts, of two kinds, that are dumped frequently on these pages. First, "manly" facts. For decades it was thought that details of occupation and milieu, hard and "real," would legitimate fiction in a country that had, or assumed it had, a pragmatic temperament. We had a range of "professional" novels about every kind of occupation from soldiering to literary agenting and beyond, and when they weren't loaded with details of a profession, they were loaded with details about guns or boats or bullfights or anything else that proved the author was not a mere writer. Bourjaily serves up a great deal about automobiles and tennis and the preparation of animal testicles as human food and much, much more.

The second kind of fact is interwoven. He splices in (as Hemingway did) culture material to show he's no mere brute: encyclopedia tours, for example, of Haydn, Adolphe Appia, operatic *castrati* (a quite different view of the testicle). These two-fold displays of data, which lie on the book like undelivered freight, reflect kinds of ambition and uneasiness that don't afflict writers any longer. They underscore the feeling that, despite its subject matter, this novel is at least twenty-five years old, that its author is a stubborn survivor.

I won't dwell on the tricks in the book. The Chaucer imitation is only one. There is much typographical horseplay. There are letters reproduced (supposedly) in the handwritings of the senders. There are many, many pages of comic-strip balloons in which the tale of the Japanese-American is given. (I assume that this device—meant to suggest *The Green Hornet?*—is to let a pop form comment sardonically on popular race prejudice.) The effect of all this razzmatazz is only to weaken characterizations that smell of glue anyway.

Still, in criticizing Bourjaily—or almost anyone else, for that matter—one must avoid the implication of reproof, as if he were just being naughty, as if he could see deeper and write better if only he would try. On the contrary, this new book shows again how hard he is trying. His trouble is not—certainly not—sloth or triviality of intent but simply an insufficient talent still mired in its first adorations. One chapter, called "Fitzgerald Attends My Fitzgerald Seminar," epitomizes this book. It begins promisingly as the dead author, unseen by anyone but the teacher, enters and seats himself. But the idea is not used to any purpose; it's just a gimmick on which to hang commonplace material. The whole novel, under its Chaucerian blazon, suffers the same way as that chapter. The title and the idea are the best things about it. (pp. 26-8)

Stanley Kauffmann, "This Side of Canterbury," in Saturday Review, *Vol. 3, No. 25, September 18, 1976, pp. 26-8.*

L. A. Walker

Reviewers are instinctively wary when a publisher makes extravagant claims for a novel. They are even more suspicious when the work being touted blatantly invokes classic literature. But they become most defensive when innovation—generally a desirable quality in fiction—turns out to be gimmickry. And Vance Bourjaily's *Now Playing at Canterbury* bears all three burdens: oversell, pretentious literary allusions and a phony newness.

"Nothing like this has ever been written," declares a wholly serious press release from Dial, whose editor-in-chief is quoted as saying that *Now Playing at Canterbury* is "one of the most important books Dial will ever publish." Indeed, we are given to understand, the search for a modern *Canterbury Tales* is over—and modern is better.

The Chaucerian connection, of course, is Bourjaily's doing. Like the original, his novel is about a group of people working toward a common goal. Instead of a pilgrimage, though, his entourage is preparing the premiere of an opera (a very bad one, incidentally) that will open a midwestern university's performing arts center. Each of the participants relates a story about his life to some of the others, with the present and the opera popping in from time to time. As in Chaucer, the tales are alternately humorous, serious and off-color, and are told by stereotypes (albeit quite up-to-date ones—a gay, a bubble-headed young actress-singer, a black with identity problems, a humble Japanese).

A final resemblance to Chaucer is Bourjaily's striving for innovation. *The Canterbury Tales,* as every college freshman knows, included a number of firsts; Bourjaily has attempted to do the same. In his case, however, the novelty consists mainly of rather empty technical devices designed to add freshness to his story and style.

Admittedly, some of the techniques have merit. For example, the author effectively eliminates the word "said" in rendering dialogue; to denote speech he merely gives the character's name followed by a period. The device is simple, unobtrusive and dramatic. Less successful, yet often skillfully employed, is cinematic scene juxtapositioning—having the action or dialogue switch back and forth between two periods of time or sets of characters. Unfortunately, this can degenerate into near chaos, so that parts of the novel seem to be modeled after *Easy Rider,* with all its jumbled banterings.

It is Bourjaily's flair for the cinematic, in fact, that leads him to silliness and prompts the feeling that his innovation is sheer gimmickry: He makes some pages look like the Sunday morning comics, some like manuscripts complete with proof-reader's marks, and some like scraps from notes and letters. The strangest use of graphics comes about when the brilliant but naïve Japanese composer tells the story of his formative years in America. All conversations in the tale are encased in cartoonist's bubbles (without the cartoons), giving the entire section an eerie, Roy Lichtenstein-like appearance.

At this point, the serious reader feels cheated: He is no longer reading a novel; he is experiencing an extension of the broadcast media. And since there does not appear to be any legitimate stylistic reason for the graphic games, the inevitable impression is that the publisher's packaging has been allowed to move too far into the realm of literature. In newspapers, headlines are meant to arouse interest; in fiction, that is supposed to be a function of the story.

Ironically, the frantic contemporary air about the book is likely to cancel out its readership. The television addict or pulp-fiction fan who might be amused by the print pyro-

technics will not appreciate the weighty thematic allusions to Chaucer; the purist will rankle at the spectacle, viewing it as perhaps mildly interesting but mostly as demeaning the venerable notion that good writing, not showmanship, is the compelling force in literature.

Which brings us to another of Bourjaily's pet devices, a conscious use of bad writing: The opera at the center of the action—about poker players in a Georgia construction camp—is horrendous. He also includes long digressions on such topics as castrati. Both ploys are ultimately purposeless, for bad writing and silly tidbits are like bad singing and babbling—funny and inoffensive for a second, but afterward merely tiring.

His lapses in judgment aside, it should be stressed that Bourjaily is an accomplished craftsman. Each of the individual tales is in essence engrossing and unique: the drag-racing sequence, the tale of the old woman who lives with dozens of cats, the story of lost innocence. The yarns themselves have a good feel for the nature of contemporary American life and make for pleasant reading.

Yet Bourjaily's final faux pas is deadly. He should have ended the book with the scene that has the opera's director riding out of town on opening night with his true love, who tells him the fates of the rest of the cast. Instead, we are suddenly thrust into another tale, of the young stage manager, a woman whose cello-fingering hand has been permanently damaged: She is killed by the American bombings on Hanoi on Christmas, 1972. The event—undeniably tragic—has absolutely nothing to do with *Now Playing at Canterbury.* It is one more trick, a deceitful one that plays upon the reader's sympathies for no reason except to attach a melodramatic finish to a confused book.

"Novel" means new, and one should by no means reprove Bourjaily for the experimentation he began in *Brill Among the Ruins.* Still, in searching for ground-breaking effects in *Now Playing at Canterbury* he is trying to play to too many people. His earlier novels, like *Confessions of a Spent Youth,* reveal a truer voice because the projected readership is better defined. Vance Bourjaily should remember that only a circus has something for everyone. (pp. 21-2)

L. A. Walker, "A Bundle of Tricks," in The New Leader, *Vol. LX, No. 2, January 17, 1977, pp. 21-2.*

Anatole Broyard

When Vance Bourjaily was editor of *Discovery,* he was very good about helping the young writers he published in the magazine, showing them how to pull together their sprawling enthusiasms and comb out their clichés. In *A Game Men Play,* he appears to have forgotten his own lessons.

It is difficult to determine what this novel is trying to do. Filled with improbable violence and all-too-probable sentimentality, it vacillates between seriousness and sensationalism, between a morality play and a portentous thriller.

Chink Peters, the hero, is a wrestler, boxer, champion rider, crack shot, fencer, polyglot, James Bond agent, veterinary, lover, altruist and a few other things. When *A Game Men Play* opens, this high-powered man is inexplicably taking five mediocre horses to Australia as a job for pay.

Mr. Bourjaily knows quite a bit about horses and he shares it with the reader in several authentic-sounding passages. But when Chink Peters talks to the horses and tells them the story of his life, one feels that he is imposing either on the horses or the reader. It is one of the peculiarities of the book that the only living creatures Chink gets along with are horses.

Wally, Chink's best friend, steals his wife, and Chink packs his saddle and his painting by Seurat, which was a wedding gift, and hits the road. He gives the painting to a museum, as if to announce that there is no longer any place for beauty in his life.

In spite of a long history of betrayal, Wally calls on Chink for help when he is in trouble, and Chink responds without hesitating. Wally's two beautiful grown daughters have been murdered in their Greenwich Village apartment. One of them, whose body was mutilated, was barefooted when she died, and Chink, in his grief, says, "She never would wear shoes." Mr. Bourjaily ought to know how dangerous it is to write a line like that.

Wally asks Chink to live in the apartment where the girls were murdered. Chink goes into the bathroom, kneels on the floor and "presses his forehead against the cool white enamel." When he was editing *Discovery*, Mr. Bourjaily would have blue-penciled that line for a cliché.

Chink is always fighting. In one fight, Mr. Bourjaily writes, he "went under the first big, wide punch to bang the solar plexus with four good jabs." This is not boxing writing. When you are fighting seriously, as Chink is, you don't jab to the solar plexus: you hook. And it is highly unlikely that you would throw four consecutive lefts unless your right hand was broken. Mr. Bourjaily, the editor, would say, "Write about what you know."

After she leaves him, Chink's former wife says, "You have the fairest, strongest, most generous mind of anyone I'll ever know." That, apparently, is why she had to leave him, and the reader sometimes feels tempted, too. Chink is just too good to be true. . . .

Mr. Bourjaily is a serious novelist who seems to have forced himself to write a thriller. And as Yeats said, when the will attempts to do the work of the imagination, rhetoric results. There are all kinds of rhetoric in *A Game Men Play.* A young black killer says, "If existence precedes essence, then simply change roles quickly and constantly, and you elude dull essence forever." Even Sydney Greenstreet could not get away with that line.

Sentimentality is one of the difficulties in the book. When an author cannot love his characters, he is likely to be sentimental about them. But although sentimentality can sometimes be an endearing fault, it isn't here, because the reader has to work too hard over the novel to be in a forgiving mood.

A Game Men Play is more complicated than an existential novel, in translation, by a Paris-educated South American symbolist. Perhaps, Mr. Bourjaily feels that, in a thriller, anything goes. But it doesn't. In fact, anything never goes.

Anatole Broyard, "Anything Never Goes," in The New York Times, *January 19, 1980, p. 21.*

Raymond Carver

The publicity release for [*A Game Men Play*] would remind us that Vance Bourjaily is one of America's major writers. I don't think this claim can be taken lightly. The proof of the matter lies in this compelling and relentlessly authentic work of art, *A Game Men Play.* It's his finest novel since *The Violated,* which up to now has been his best, and best-known, work.

A Game Men Play is a big book and one charged with acts of violence and dismay: You couldn't begin to count all the murders and "re-locations," the double and double-double dealings that occur in its pages. But, surprisingly, it is also—and this is more to our purpose—a long and profound, sometimes pastoral meditation on the human condition. . . .

The novel is Conradian in its entanglement of motive and its intricacy of plot. It is filled with lore of all sorts: the raising, training, and racing of horses; soldiering, mostly behind-the-lines guerrilla stuff; covert CIA activity; and as complete an inside look at the vile pursuits of terrorism as you'd ever want. But since I can only touch on the story's main lines, which will not begin to tell you what the novel is *about,* I want to say that it has to do with the not insignificant matters of courage, loyalty, love, friendship, danger, and self-reliance, and a man's lifetime journey of self-discovery.

The hero of this remarkable novel—and he *is* a hero, praise be—is a man of integrity and deep complexity; he has character, in the oldest and truest sense of that word. His name is C. K. "Chink" Peters (nicknamed because of the slightly slanted eyes he inherited from his mother, a Mongolian), and he is far and away Bourjaily's best fictional creation to date.

During World War II, Peters gained prominence as a young OSS agent tagged "Der Fleischwulf" (The Meatgrinder), and after the war found himself in the nascent CIA—the Agency, as it's called. Peters has written a small book on guerilla warfare, and the book as well as its author have come to assume some fame in underground circles, mainly a radical IRA group whose members are fanatical but suave terrorists with European and Middle Eastern connections. Now 49 and free from involvement either domestic or Agency related, Peters is living in a rooming house in San Francisco when the novel opens. He is about to sail for Wellington with a group of horses destined for a New Zealand breeder when he sees a television news account of the murders of Mary and Wendy Difenbach in their New York apartment. He has not seen these girls since their childhood when their father, his friend, neighbor, and wartime commanding officer, Walden Difenbach, took away Peters' wife. Difenbach is now a UN ambassador-at-large, often mentioned as a potential secretary of state. Peters sends a telegram asking if there's anything he can do, waits, then goes ahead and sails.

Peters spends a lot of time talking to his horses, believe it, on the way to New Zealand; and so, in long flashbacks, we have the story of his life. Moving from past to present, this way and that, using the freighter as both metaphor for a journey and real ocean-going vessel, we follow him through prep school, where he goes on a wrestling scholarship but studies foreign languages, then enlistment in the military, Army and Agency service. He later attends Yale and takes a degree in German medieval history. Happily married, he settles on the Eastern Seaboard to breed and race horses with Difenbach as his country squire neighbor. This Difenbach is a Machiavellian character with plenty of charm and intelligence who runs up against the IRA, whose agents set out to bring him down. Through a dreadful foulup, his daughters become the victims instead.

In New Zealand, a cable from Difenbach reaches Peters asking if he can come to New York and lend a hand in this horrible affair. What happens when Peters moves into the murdered girls' New York apartment takes up the second half of the book.

I've seldom read a novel that's offered up such rigorous and lasting pleasures. The people who populate this fine book will strike you not so much as characters but rather as common and uncommon men and women going about their lives, doing those things that may damn them forever—or that could raise them to something they might otherwise have not been capable of in this imperfect world, or in the hands of a lesser novelist.

Of course I won't give you the novel's ending. I can tell you that the plot turns, and then turns, and turns again. Until the last pages it has you, as they used to say, on the edge of your seat. For me, a discussion of the book brings to mind F. Scott Fitzgerald's invocation: "Draw your chair up close to the edge of the precipice, and I'll tell you a story."

Vance Bourjaily is a writer of great gifts and originality, hard at work, as always, and in the fullness of his powers.

> *Raymond Carver, "A Gifted Novelist at the Top of His Game," in* Book World—Chicago Tribune, *January 20, 1980, p. 1.*

Larry McMurtry

Vance Bourjaily has a tendency to be tempted by the big novel that more or less says it all about American life in our time. His most successful effort in that line was, in my view, *The Violated,* a large, convincing book that never seems either awkward or swollen.

Unfortunately, even America has not been subject enough for Mr. Bourjaily [in *A Game Men Play*]. In following his hero, Chink Peters—a competent, if reluctant, adventurer—we traverse 30 or 40 years of this troubled century, as well as most of the globe. The action ranges from New Zealand to the Russian steppes, from Thailand to Argentina. In our travels with Chink we also cross a number of genres: one moment we are reading a thriller, then a war novel, then a panoramic social history and, finally, an exhaustive character study of a man whose character is on the whole rather buttoned down and unexpressive. *A Game Men Play* is a flawed, intermittently interesting novel that quickly runs aground on its own ambition.

Chink Peters—the son of a Russian cavalryman and a Buryat princess—is in fact an all-too-familiar character:

the man with a code of honor that dooms him to be always slightly out of step in these codeless times. In the fiction of our time, most such men seem to end up working for the Central Intelligence Agency. Chink does just that, for the most part as an assassin, but because he is a world-class horseman and a competent farmer he sometimes performs services of a more pastoral nature.

Men with codes such as Chink's confront the novelist with a small but treacherous array of stylistic options. One can risk sounding like Hemingway at his worst, like Ian Fleming at his slickest, or like Graham Greene at his most portentous. Mr. Bourjaily circles all these bases several times; the effect at times is that of a kind of merry-go-round of pastiche, though when we are asked to attend solemnly to the loneliness and spiritual plight of such a man, the dominant echo is that of Hemingway at his worst.

When we first meet Chink he is about to board a slow boat to New Zealand, as the custodian of some fine horses. . . . As Chink slowly crosses the Pacific with his horses, we ourselves take a colorful if lengthy voyage through his experience. The liveliest parts of this trip involve commando action in Yugoslavia during World War II, whereas the least lively focus on horse breeding and marital upheaval in Virginia after the war. There are also loves to be pursued and men to be killed in Egypt, the Virgin Islands, Argentina: wherever the sinister finger of the agency happens to point.

When Chink finally decides to go back and help his old friend—now a distinguished ambassador—unravel the mystery of his dead daughters, he finds that the girls were incidental victims of a naïve and unsuccessful terrorist plot aimed at the ambassador, a man without a code who proves to be the book's most skillful and most malevolent gamesman.

Far from limiting itself to a consideration of the big game of life, or the corrupt and labyrinthine game of international politics, *A Game Men Play* devotes its most intense and most readable pages to precise and knowing descriptions of various lesser games. Chink Peters is very good at certain demanding physical games: riding, wrestling, boxing. Insofar as war is a game involving an extension of these physical skills, he is good at war. In emotional games, however—whether those that friends play with friends, that commanders play with subordinates, or that women play with men—he is far less adept. He shares with the Hemingway hero a yearning for a world in which the true and the good can be reached through clean physical action. Naturally, he is almost constantly disappointed, and his response to disappointment is invariably stoic. We feel that we have met him before, in the world of Hemingway, Fleming, Greene and le Carré—all, on their various levels, creditable fictional worlds, but a long way from the realities of the American Middle West, of which Mr. Bourjaily now writes so well. (pp. 14-15)

> *Larry McMurtry, "Assassin's Story," in* The New York Times Book Review, *January 27, 1980, pp. 14-15.*

Hilary Masters

[Bourjaily's novel], *The Great Fake Book,* follows the familiar trek that Natty Bumppo first blazed to discover his importance, if any, to a society that simultaneously overwhelmed him as it expelled him. That skepticism about the individual's place in the American landscape was an important ingredient of Bourjaily's earlier novels, and his subsequent pessimism generated huge social documentaries, such as **The End of My Life, The Violated** and **Confessions of a Spent Youth**—to name three—all of them recalling similar enterprises in naturalistic fervor from Europe like Jules Romains' *Men of Good Will.*

If their "case history" approach to the American experience owed more to O'Hara than to Hemingway, the nihilistic flavor of Bourjaily's novels caught the temper of that post-World War II era for many and, along with the work of other veterans turned novelists, probably laid down the pattern for a generation of younger writers all the way from the White Horse Tavern in New York to that workshop in Iowa City. But what happens when the subject matter for the naturalistic novelist runs out? What happens when the particular personal experience, in Bourjaily's case the horror and awful ecstasy of World War II, gets sucked up and extruded into trivialities: G.I. Joe dolls and television skits? What happens when the novelist is left to his own esthetic devices, in a time when irony is commonplace?

This new novel suggest some answers to these speculations. Charles Mizzourin, an aide to a congressman from Iowa, initiates an exploration into his father's past, including his death, by way of correspondence and telephone conversations but, mostly, through a journal the father kept during his early years in the South and New York as an incipient, self-taught jazz cornet player and journalist. This journal uses the form of a "fake book," a publication for professional musicians that provides the key chords for popular songs so that an orchestra can improvise—fake—arrangements without paying fees or royalties.

Entries from this fake book are segmented through the novel's ongoing action, which includes the protagonist's involvement with his employer's upcoming reelection being challenged by a member of the Mizzourin family in Iowa; his involvement with a jazzy Washington call girl; his involvement with some Middle Eastern terrorists, and so on. The father's history reads much like that of many of Bourjaily's earlier heroes, all fresh from World War II. The titles of songs in the fake book—such as "Am I Blue," "Two Sleepy People," "Wang Wang Blues"—are matched up, more or less, with the tone or circumstances of the events in the senior Mizzourin's life. It is a device at once ingenious and gratuitous.

These days, it may not be proper to question an author's intentions, but one wonders if Bourjaily intended the title and the device to be a metaphor for the novel itself, in which the reader is given the main chords of the story through the exchanges that Charles Mizzourin has by phone, letter and the journal and is then supposed to fake the rest of the book's substance—even make up characters. This technique only distances the reader from the subject, for all of the novel's information—whether about character or incident—comes second-hand through phone-chats and letters and recorded memos. We are told everything, never shown anything, which violates—if we are to speak of irony—the cardinal rule of all writing workshops.

The conversations even ring false, as if the author cares as little for their authenticity as he does for the depth of the characters who mouth the lines. This is especially true of the dialogues young Mizzourin has with the congressman and his secretary, who is a spin-off from Sam Spade's feisty Effie. They talk in a hip, trendy lingo that no one in politics has ever had the mind or inclination to use, and this reader has had considerable experience talking to politicians of all kinds. This incredible dialogue undermines belief in the rest. Curiously, it is the fake book, the old journal kept by the senior Mizzourin, that sustains a believable narrative. The episodes recounting the young veteran's attempts to relate to a post-war America no less brutish and intolerant than the tyrannies he had just helped put down have a ring of truth to them. Bourjaily makes these excursions into the past come alive; his ability to evoke the aura of this time is admirable. Consequently, one becomes impatient, frustrated and eventually bored by the artifices that trick out the journal segments.

All the plots are neatly tied up at the end, if only through long-distance. . . . [The protagonist] learns the circumstances of his father's death and then goes back to his callgirl—she of the small breasts and golden heart, a mythic figure writers of Bourjaily's generation seem destined to perpetuate. After all this, a reader is tempted to place a call of his own. Hello, Central, hello—any messages?

Hilary Masters, "Looking for Dad," in Book World—The Washington Post, *January 11, 1987, p. 6.*

Richard P. Brickner

[Bourjaily's recent novel] has the storytelling and linguistic exuberance one expects of this writer. **The Great Fake Book** is colorful and varied. It is also affectionate. (It is about different kinds of affection.) It is capable of delighting. But it would have been better if it were more straightforward.

The Great Fake Book has many plots, the dominant one involving Charles Mizzourin's research into the life of his father, Mike, who died in 1950, when Charles was an infant. Charles, now (in the early 1980's) a Washington aide to a liberal Iowa congressman, encounters one day, in the Library of Congress microfilm room, a woman who once worked for the editor of the newspaper where Charles's father had been a reporter. Charles writes to the editor, John McRae Johnson, retired in Colorado; Johnson sends Charles sections of Mike's private autobiography, which for some reason the editor has preserved. Mike's account of his late youth comprises much—and the best—of the novel.

The autobiographical sections are **The Great Fake Book** itself. (A fake book is an illegal compendium of the choruses of popular songs—melody and lyrics—accompanied by chord indications, that enables a musician or a band to play any song in the anthology without having to pay for the sheet music.) Mike, jazz-obsessed and just released from the Army, in Faraday, N.C., after World War II, is given a fake book and a cornet in exchange for a valuable fluegelhorn he has filched from the Army discharge center. Each of the autobiographical episodes is headed by the title of a popular song.

Mike's adventures in Faraday, as the lover of Evaun, an enchanting but down-to-earth young backwoods woman who sings in a local club, and among resident lowlifes, some of them dangerous, are satisfying. But the book's structural fussiness lessens the glow of the Faraday sections. When the novel isn't being Mike's fake-book memoirs, a lot of it is transcripts of phone calls his son has with Johnson, the retired editor, about the memoirs, or with others about other matters; or it is letters or reports, or notes—unwieldy documentary pieces. The book's overly intricate form can clog the narrative, while its inventiveness is sometimes so exuberant as to be uncloggable.

The story, when it doesn't concern Mike in Faraday in the 1940's, is about his son in the 80's, helping the congressman he serves run for re-election in Iowa against Charles's right-wing uncle—Mike's brother, no less. . . . The coincidences in this novel do not strike home as truthful surprises.

Still, the book's charm and energy are never extinguished. Its inventiveness is impressive when its events are not incredible. The book has many winning moments of fresh prose. The sexual passages describing Mike and Evaun together are lyrical without being solemn. At its sustained best, as in Mike's account of a Faraday jam session, the book shows unusual vitality, concentration and persuasiveness. . . .

Though *The Great Fake Book* obstructs itself with technical problems, it frequently succeeds in being original and enjoyable.

> *Richard P. Brickner, "Young Man with a Fluegelhorn," in* The New York Times Book Review, *January 18, 1987, p. 35.*

John Seelye

The Great Fake Book is a tour de force of considerable complexity and craft. It is the story of the search of Charles Mizzourin for his father, Michael, presumably killed in an auto accident in 1950, when Charles was less than a year old. Charlie, a *wanderkind* of the '60s and '70s, who has dabbled in college, carpentry, the Peace Corps and liberal politics before signing on as a congressman's aid (the story takes place in 1980, during the Iran hostage crisis), is initially inspired to trace his paternal roots because of a dispute involving a will, but his attempts at first are frustrated by his mother and uncles and by the wife of the man for whom his father was working (as a reporter) when he died. But by means of pages from the titular *Fake Book*, a diary kept during his last years by Mike Mizzourin and sent piecemeal by the editor for whom Mike had worked, we eventually learn what there is to know about his history.

The story is told through this diary and by means of letters, telephone conversations and memos kept by Charlie, documents which add up to a new-fangled version of the old epistolary novel. The cast of characters includes Mike's uptight but ultimately sympathetic mother (a former model who strives to hold on to her good looks), his jovial if preppy stepfather (who sounds like George Bush's classmate), a lovely young Brit of dubious morals, a Washington madame of admirable cast and her lover-politician-lobbyist, as well as the liberal, McGovernish congressman for whom Charlie works and his snarling but gutsy Republican opponent.

This multiple cast of '80s characters is amplified by the people encountered by Mike Mizzourin during the months following his discharge in 1945 from the U.S. Army, a period when he learns to play the cornet and performs in a small combo in a smaller North Carolina town.

As in the other Great Fake Books which Mike early in the story acquires, . . . this novel is made up of some very familiar tunes. But, like a skillful musician, Bourjaily does some marvelous things with old material, commencing with his documentary manner, from which the authorial point-of-view is entirely missing. As with familiar songs, the effect is one of shared knowledge played upon skillfully, with many intimate winks between performer and audience. What Bourjaily has managed to do is segue skillfully from the '40s to the '80s, juggling a complex cast of comic-book characters and at the same time slowly weaving and then (with a few tugs on vital threads) suddenly unweaving an equally complex but (finally) wonderfully simple plot.

Legerdemain is what we are talking about here, and even the story itself has a fairy-tale quality being that most ancient of mythic fables, the search of a son for his father. I found Bourjaily's latest novel an enjoyable, exhilarating experience from start to finish.

> *John Seelye, "There's Nothing Phony About Vance Bourjaily's 'Fake Book'," in* Chicago Tribune—Books, *February 15, 1987, pp. 6-7.*

FURTHER READING

Aldridge, John W. "Vance Bourjaily's *The End of My Life.*" *The Centennial Review* XXVIII, No. 2 (Spring 1984): 100-05.
  Updates Aldridge's comments on Bourjaily's first novel originally presented in 1951 in his *After the Lost Generation* (see excerpt above). Aldridge posits that in comparison to authors of the World War I era, Bourjaily's generation faced the crisis of war with cynicism rather than disillusionment. *The End of My Life* thus "represents an early and tentative effort to confront the condition of malevolent nihilism which in recent decades has become a central subject of such novelists as Pynchon, Vonnegut, and Heller."

Critique: Studies in Modern Fiction XVII, No. 3 (August 1976): 64-110.
  Special issue devoted to Bourjaily and John Hawkes. Contains essays by William A. Francis, John M. Muste, William McMillen, and Daniel Towner on Bourjaily's novels *The Hound of Earth, Confessions of a Spent Youth, The Man Who Knew Kennedy,* and *Brill Among the Ruins,* as well as a comprehensive bibliography.

Muste, John M. "The Second Major Subwar: Four Novels by Vance Bourjaily." In *The Shaken Realist: Essays in Modern Literature in Honor of Frederick J. Hoffman,* edited by

Melvin J. Friedman and John B. Vickery, pp. 311-26. Baton Rouge: Louisiana State University Press, 1970.

Analysis of Bourjaily's novels up to 1967 focusing primarily on what Muste considers the author's major works: *The End of My Life, The Hound of Earth, The Violated,* and *Confessions of a Spent Youth.*

Shakir, Evelyn. "Pretending to Be Arab: Role Playing in Vance Bourjaily's 'The Fractional Man.'" *MELUS* 9, No. 1 (Spring 1982): 7-21.

Evaluation of a short story that became a chapter in Bourjaily's novel *Confessions of a Spent Youth,* in which Shakir suggests that Bourjaily's protagonist, a rootless, second-generation Lebanese-American, discovers his native roots by adopting a variety of ethnic roles.

Kazimierz Brandys

1916-

Polish novelist, memoirist, short story writer, editor, dramatist, and essayist.

Among the most distinguished Polish writers of the post-World War II era, Brandys is best known to Western audiences for his novel *Rondo* and two volumes of his memoirs, *A Warsaw Diary, 1979-1981* and *Paris, New York: 1982-1984.* Lauded as trenchant introductions to Polish culture, these works examine the nation's recent history, its uncertain present, and its resilient national character. Replete with images of an aggrieved but dignified Polish populace, Brandys's writings often combine elements of fiction and nonfiction to illustrate personal reflections and philosophical concerns. A former Communist who became a dissident and eventually emigrated to France, Brandys is representative of the political vicissitudes of his literary generation.

Born into a Jewish family in Łodz, Brandys studied law at Warsaw University before World War II. His first novel, *Drewniany koń,* contains grotesque and ironic elements, demonstrating his interest in the avant-garde movement of the years between the world wars. Following World War II, Brandys, like many leftists of his generation, espoused Socialist values, producing unequivocal novels that employed the techniques of Socialist Realism to support the governing regime. For example, Brandys gained official accolades for his novel *Obywatele* (*The Citizen*), which features heroic high school students who report their teachers' unorthodox views to authorities.

In the mid-1950s, however, Brandys joined other major writers in reassessing his political allegiance. Joseph Stalin's totalitarian rule disillusioned many Central European intellectuals, who eventually rejected such socialist ideologies as collectivism. According to several critics, Brandys's skepticism, evident in his short fiction of the period and in his working-class novel *Matka Królów* (*Sons and Comrades*), constituted an important element of the cultural "thaw" of the 1950s. As his opposition to government policies increased, Brandys began to probe the relationship between illusion and reality in an authoritarian state. To simulate authenticity, Brandys's fiction incorporates such seemingly nonfictional forms as letters, interviews, and memoirs. The first of his generically ambiguous works, the multivolume *Listy do pani Z.* (*Letters to Mrs. Z.*), is a sequence of semi-fictional essays in epistolary form that is widely considered a Polish classic. Brandys's stylistic experimentation culminated in his dazzling, untranslatable novel *Wariacje pocztowe,* which is comprised of a series of letters that recount a family's history and evoke centuries of Polish language and culture.

Denounced for allegedly misrepresenting Polish history in *Wariacje pocztowe,* Brandys was castigated by authorities who derided his Jewish ancestry and labelled him an "enemy of the people." Brandys then repudiated his affiliations with the Communist party and Socialist Realism, producing works that openly accuse totalitarian regimes

of perpetrating mass deception. Framed as an extended interview with a Polish theater director, Brandys's novel *Nierzeczywistość* (*A Question of Reality*), for example, scrutinizes modern Polish consciousness. Asked to complete a questionnaire by an American sociologist seeking a profile of a "typical Polish intellectual," the director responds with a lengthy humanist monologue, inveighing against social generalizations that subvert individualism and foster a state of psychosis in entire societies, both capitalist and Communist.

In the internationally acclaimed *Rondo,* the same protagonist offers further commentary on the nature of reality under authoritarian rule. Ostensibly a letter to a historical journal, the text attempts to debunk the legend of Rondo, a secret resistance group created during World War II by the narrator, Tom. To refute a historian who had exalted Rondo's heroism, Tom reveals that the organization was actually an ineffectual ruse he devised to occupy the acting talents of his credulous lover, Tola. Tom then lost control of Rondo when too many would-be partisans tried to join, and the dissolution of this fiction caused the ruin of real lives. After Stalinist officials persecute Tom for his association with this clandestine organization, Rondo's renown increases until, despite Tom's protests, scholars of the current regime knowingly deem Tom's fiction a historical reality. Western reviewers lauded *Rondo* for its complex portrayal of a postwar Polish culture so effectively manipulated by Soviet censorship and propaganda that it deliberately embraces unreality. Philip Lopate observed: "[In *Rondo* there] are so many Big Ideas, levels and dichotomies being worked out constantly—theater versus life, historical reality as a hall of mirrors, unity versus multiplicity of self, . . . the ethics of change and stasis—that it gets rather feverish. But I'd still rather have Kazimierz Brandys's lush, caloric, Polish generosity and mental excitement than most slenderized comtemporary fiction."

A prominent dissident in the 1970s, Brandys helped to found the uncensored literary journal *Zapis* (*The Record*), a respected underground periodical for which he wrote personal essays. Contemplative and imagistic, these essays relate Brandys's observations of Warsaw in the late 1970s, as intellectual dissent and labor strife helped kindle the Solidarity movement. Later published covertly in Polish as part of a multivolume memoir series, these pieces are collected and translated in *A Warsaw Diary, 1979-1981*. Several reviewers commented that Brandys's journal displayed a jaundiced impression of Western life; according to some critics, he is at once unrealistic in his adulation of democratic freedoms and overly harsh toward Westerners who remain quiescent to Poland's fate. Most commentators agreed, however, that Brandys's diary provides an arresting portrait of Warsaw life. Charles Gati concluded: "[While] there are fine scholarly expositions about the momentous events that took place in Poland before and during Solidarity's heyday, none can match *A Warsaw Diary* in perspicacity; none conveys as effectively the ambiguities and uncertainties of mood, the doubts, the ambivalence, the ups and downs of hope and despair."

The third volume of Brandys's memoirs was published in English as *Paris, New York: 1982-1984,* a title that reflects the author's inadvertent exile. Abroad for a visit in late 1981, Brandys and his wife were stranded in New York when martial law was imposed by a Polish regime that listed him among its targets for persecution. In the United States and in Paris, where he later settled, Brandys composed essays that elicit his sense of alienation and his concern for his country's future. Although critics expressed some disappointment over the volume's translation, most agreed with M. G. Levine, who termed *Paris, New York* "a wise and beautiful book about the conjunction of personal life and historical forces."

PRINCIPAL WORKS

NOVELS

Drewniany koń 1946
Miasto niepokonane 1946
Miedzy wojnami 4 vols. 1948-1952
Obywatele 1954
    [*The Citizen,* 1954]
Matka Królów 1957
    [*Sons and Comrades,* 1961]
Nierzeczywistość 1978
    [*A Question of Reality,* 1980]
Rondo 1982
    [*Rondo,* 1989]

OTHER

Obrona Granady (novella) 1956
Listy do pani Z. 3 vols. (essays in epistolary form)
    1957-1961
    [*Letters to Mrs. Z.,* 1987]
Czerwona czapeczka (short story collection) 1956
A Warsaw Diary, 1978-1981 1984
Paris, New York: 1982-1984 1988
*Segments of Brandys's multivolume memoir that was
    originally published in the Polish underground press.

Alan Ryan

A Question of Reality poses a few questions of reality of its own. It's not exactly a novel, not exactly autobiography, not exactly philosophical or sociological speculation, not exactly political polemic—though it's evidently a fiction with all those things in it. It is a deft and spirited piece of work, which treats the reader with something of the same irony that its fictional narrator uses against his fictional interlocutor. The fiction on which the whole work hangs is that a Polish intellectual, an academic and theatre director, is asked to fill in a questionnaire for a Polish-American sociologist he has met at a conference in a Scandinavian seaside town. Although he luxuriates in the chance to discover who he thinks he is, with nobody but a tape-recorder to hear him, he neatly sidesteps every suggestion that his replies will disclose the 'typical Polish intellectual'—and Kazimierz Brandys provides him with a degree of inventiveness, as well as a sweetness of character, which surely aren't typical of any sort of intellectual. How many members of the Resistance set up fake cells shuttling harmless suitcases full of books across Poland, in order to give enthusiasts something to do which would bring them to no harm?

Of course, what is intriguing about *A Question of Reality* is just those questions which the narrator makes it hard to answer. Is the fate of Poland peculiar, or are there more similarities between loss of freedom there and in the West than we like to think? Does the political oppressiveness of communist regimes make intellectual life more interesting and more serious, or does it wreck it? The narrator's urge to frustrate our desire for a simple answer stems from a kind of deep anti-nationalism which runs through everything and makes him want to deny Poland's 'specialness'. Brandys is the sort of humanist who thinks that patriotism is a threat to each individual's need to think about his own life and death. And, of course, he is more than ready to invoke a plague on both right-wing and left-wing patriotism: prewar Poland was 'independent' but illiberal, anti-Semitic and incompetent, postwar Poland sees the Party encouraging the same old anti-Semitism.

Brandys's narrator goes on a good deal about the dangers of mass society. It's not only the dead hand of party ideologists which prevents people thinking about life, death, liberty and justice. Any society devoted to equating the good life with the full belly will go the same way. It is peculiarly absurd that freedom under socialism should degenerate into a question of whether there is meat in the butcher's shops; but the American obsession with the indefinite postponement of death and the lifelong accumulation of the goods of this world is a pretty wry commentary on the Founding Fathers' moral commitments.

He is also energetic in denying that intellectual life is made more vivid by political pressure. 'The Organised Lie' dominates everything, so that a pastiche of intellectual life is possible, but anyone who wants to think seriously has to do so privately—a claim which is backed up by some marvellously droll little anecdotes about the narrator's friend 'Icz', who spots a bandwagon when it is barely a puff of dust on the horizon.

Most striking of all, though, is the way *A Question of Reality* ends with an all-out and straightforward defence of human rights. . . . Freedom needs a genuine public life and room for discussion, all of which is impossible unless individuals have the right to speak up. Too much emphasis on the nation, too much emphasis on solidarity, abolishes this public life and creates claustrophobia instead. . . . [Brandys's narrator states]: 'I am *not* an exception: many people in Poland live and think like me.' I hope they find him persuasive when they read him.

> Alan Ryan, "Polish Individuals," in The Listener, *Vol. 105, No. 2705, March 26, 1981, p. 414.*

Ivan Sanders

The word Polish, as a qualitative adjective, probably figures more importantly in the literature of that West-Slavic nation than similar ethnic labels do in other national literatures. An outsider may be put off by the vagueness, the parochialism of these terms; he may wonder, for instance, about the mysterious qualities that make a work written in Warsaw or Cracow "typically Polish" or "intensely Polish." Yet, the obsession with national identity does make more sense if one knows something about the checkered history of the country, or even the general region, in question. In [*A Question of Reality*], his new "novel of Poland," which, incidentally, could not be published there, Kazimierz Brandys becomes acutely aware of this supercharged national consciousness; indeed he apologizes for it. His hero, a Polish intellectual responding to a neatly professional, earnest, and under the circumstances, woefully inadequate questionnaire prepared by a Polish-born American sociologist, admits ruefully toward the end of his meandering comments that he has been dealing with "local problems, Polish problems." . . .

If Brandys's book were only an eloquent albeit constricted apologia for a Polish thinker's excessive preoccupation with Polishness, it would be of limited interest to non-Polish readers. As it is, the novel is not likely to appeal to those who still believe that an intellectual must always rise above local prides and prejudices, who consider "the question of reality" to be, of necessity, a larger, more universal question. But fortunately the author has much to say about the drawbacks of a fixedly national point of view, thereby illuminating the dilemma of an independent-minded intellectual who is thwarted in his efforts to remain his own man not only by an authoritarian state, but by his own deepest impulses as well by a collective unconscious that colors his every response to the world. Brandys's hero remarks at one point that many of his compatri-

ots behave "as if the individual in Poland had no psychology of his own, as if there were only a national psychology.". . . The narrator knows only too well how useful, how comforting, how indispensable this overriding ethnic sensibility has always been to his people. He reminds us, for example, that the present "internationalist" Communist leadership is just as fond of romantic idealizations of the Polish past as were the discredited, chauvinist regimes of the pre-war era. But he knows, too, that there is a price to pay for illusions of national greatness—and the price is individual freedom. Nationalism impedes freedom, it fosters conformity. To be Polish, and to be free, is the greatest challenge faced by Brandys's hero. (p. 186)

[The] narrator becomes a well-known stage director, a university professor, and for a time, a member of the new cultural establishment. In his responses to the survey he alludes to the subtle and not so subtle ways in which he compromised his principles during his rise to fame. (It's worth noting that in the early fifties Kazimierz Brandys himself published a number of novels which contain every clichéd requisite of socialist realism; the works he wrote after the Thaw, on the other hand [e.g., *The Defense of Granada*] are painful reappraisals of the Stalinist years. In 1966 Brandys resigned from the Communist party, which he joined twenty years earlier.) By the 1970s Brandys's hero is a disenchanted, though not quite desperate, man. Marxism has lost its appeal for him, but nothing has taken its place. The whole matter of political *engagement* has become much more complex. He is fully aware now that there are ills which have nothing to do with, cannot be explained away with, politics. He finds it oddly revealing that "the perpetuation of Marx's social ideas is now the work of the developed capitalist countries, while we, instead of building our socialist superstructures as Marxists, are the ones who yearn for metaphysics." Ultimately, the narrator breaks with the establishment, gives up his position and privileges, and opts for the life of a dissident, an outcast. He does this not because he has found something better to believe in, not even because he is convinced that the system he lives under is that corrupt. He simply values intellectual freedom. "A man under a cloud begins to see more clearly," he says.

A Question of Reality is not an easy, nor always satisfying, book. Though its hero makes repeated references to his relationship with friends and family members, there is no plot to speak of; the work is not so much a novel as a long essay, a monologue. The critic John Aldridge has written that the great strength of the modern European novel is that "in it ideas are as important as physical sensations and may even be experienced with all the force and acuteness of physical sensations." In this sense *A Question of Reality* is an engaging example of a novel of ideas. What it lacks is sustained narrative interest, and that, it seems, is something not even the most sophisticated practitioners of the form can do completely without. (pp. 186-87)

> Ivan Sanders, "To Be Polish & to Be Free," in Commonweal, *Vol. CVIII, No. 6, March 27, 1981, pp. 186-7.*

Charles Gati

What makes *A Warsaw Diary* . . . authentic is that it goes

beyond the simple "we-they" dichotomy so familiar to both residents and students of Communist police states. True, Mr. Brandys affirms the basic validity of the dichotomy. In his imagery, the police state is deeply divided between the people and the proprietors of power. No concessions by the regime, no process of "liberalization" can change the essential characteristic of the relationship, for even when concessions are granted, they can never be *taken* for granted. One month Mr. Brandys is denied a passport to travel abroad, a few months later he gets one. But in neither case do the authorities offer an explanation. The law is what "they" say it is.

Yet even as the author's rejection of the police state itself is all but absolute, his portrayal of people coping with everyday political and moral dilemmas—people on both sides of the Great Divide—is nuanced, his judgment tolerant. "Heroes and cowards—I don't trust such divisions," he writes. "Two intellectuals, a scientist and a film director, were once asked to sign a protest. One refused: 'I can't. I have a son.' The other unscrewed the cap of his pen: 'I have to sign, because I have a son.'"

While insisting on the need to understand those who are quiescent, Mr. Brandys also knows that "they"—the authorities, members of the political elite—are not all alike either. At one point he relates the gruesome techniques used by the police to intimidate him and his friends, quoting a letter mailed to him from the town of Sosnowiecz: "Mr. Brandys, here, near Sosnowiecz, a Polish policeman shot and killed a certain Jew, Icek Brandys, in 1942. Was he perhaps a relative of yours?" Yet at another point, having observed a young guard in front of the apartment house where an unofficial literary meeting is to take place, he wonders about the young policeman's motives and choices. . . .

That Mr. Brandys can wisely combine stark images of the system with shaded pictures of the people that system has produced is all the more refreshing because of his background. One of Poland's foremost novelists, he was a "true believer" in Communism for two decades after World War II. Like many other Eastern and Western European intellectuals, he joined the Communist Party out of devotion to its professed causes.

So deep was his commitment that long after he had resigned as chairman of the Warsaw committee of the National Unity Front, . . . after he had turned in his party card and even after the ugly, regime-sponsored anti-Semitic campaign of 1968—after all that and more, he still believed as late as 1968 that "the party would extricate itself from the muck and blood." It did not, of course, but Mr. Brandys has emerged as a high-minded, straight-shooting opponent of his past, for the most part attuned to his own impulses and quite capable of keeping an open mind about the vicissitudes of Polish society.

The bitter legacy of Mr. Brandys's experiences nonetheless reveals itself, particularly when he deals with the West and with Western attitudes and policies toward Poland. His judgments seem hasty, if not ill-informed. Too often, his praise is extravagant, his criticism excessive.

Indulging in what he himself calls "exaltation and overstatement," Mr. Brandys paints a very flattering picture of Western life, one that may be as accurate from his Polish perspective as it is unduly rosy by the West's own high standards. The West has achieved, he writes, "the most authentic form of life"; even its "illnesses and calamities" are signs of normalcy and health. (pp. 9-10)

Coupled to this envious admiration for Western freedoms is a blistering attack on the West's irresponsibility and its indifference to Poland's plight. Conforming in this respect to the widely held American stereotype of East European former Communists, he claims Western intellectuals do not understand either the totalitarian threat or Poland, and he ridicules their preoccupation with such causes as the feminist movement and the rights of homosexuals. He decries the agreements that Franklin D. Roosevelt made with Joseph Stalin at Yalta in 1945, and he pleads for "some game plan" that would alter the map of Europe.

Writing before the declaration of martial law in Poland in 1981, he urges Westerners to form clubs and associations dedicated to the cause of aiding his country and committed to keeping the issue of Poland in "the world's memory." Such involvement, he feels, will make Westerners "spiritually stronger." "instead of coming to us to hunt and fish," he writes, "try to understand our countries and exert your minds to create if not a common existence, then at least the concept of one." And to the skeptic he replies, "Perhaps the least naïve thing of all is to push against this massive division of the world until it petrifies or breaks apart."

Perhaps so. The failure of Western governments to place the issue of Poland and the rest of Eastern Europe on the agenda of East-West negotiations is beyond serious dispute. So is the hypocrisy of Western governments in substituting rhetoric for diplomatic initiatives. And so is their inability to develop and sustain an effective carrot-and-stick policy to influence the fate of Poles and other East Europeans.

On the other hand, it is a fact that some Western governments entered World War II to defend Poland (and, of course, themselves). It is a fact that for more than two decades after 1957, the United States and other Western countries extended massive economic aid to Poland to encourage a process of liberalization. Moreover, if Mr. Brandys can understand those Polish intellectuals who refuse to sign a protest, why not extend the same understanding to those Western intellectuals who, guided by their own concerns, address their own priorities or prefer to remain quiescent? If Mr. Brandys can be open-minded enough to condemn Polish anti-Semites without indicting the Polish intellectuals or the Polish people who tolerate them, why overgeneralize about all Western intellectuals?

It may be that the source of Mr. Brandys's blurred vision of the West and the source of his illuminating depiction of Poland's recent tragedy are one and the same. That source, it seems, is the agony of his defeats—the defeat of his people, the defeat of his old faith. For, while there are fine scholarly expositions about the momentous events that took place in Poland before and during Solidarity's heyday, none can match *A Warsaw Diary* in perspicacity; none conveys as effectively the ambiguities and uncertainties of mood, the doubts, the ambivalence, the ups and downs of hope and despair. Mr. Brandys's considerable skills as a writer have helped, of course. In the end, though, what makes this book so disturbing and memorable is his portrayal of his own agony—pride and distress over his Polishness, sorrow and relief at having finally rid himself of his faulty ideological compass and the burden of being seen as a Jew without really being one—combined with his portrayal of the collective agony of a people destined to live in a good country located in a bad place. (p. 10)

> Charles Gati, "Personal and Collective Agony," in The New York Times Book Review, March 11, 1984, pp. 9-10.

The New Yorker

[*A Warsaw Diary, 1978-1981*] is not an account of the great political events of the period—the rise and fall of Solidarity—but a series of reflections of those events in the life and thoughts of a subtle, original, civilized man. The thoughts are far-ranging and unfailingly interesting, but most inspired, perhaps, are the descriptions of the precise moods of collective existence—of meetings, of crowds, of the whole country. When, in January of 1979, a blizzard hits Poland, the public, acclimatized to ambiguity and falsehood by its government, is hard put to it to take in a fact as simple and unequivocal as a big snowstorm: "We ask ourselves, Is this our snow? Are we under any obligation to shovel it? For there is some question as to whether this snow might not be *theirs,* imposed on us by the Russians in the framework of friendship, and so—shouldn't they remove it themselves?" And, on the evening before John Paul II makes his historic first visit to Poland as Pope, Brandys goes out into the streets of Warsaw, where, to his astonishment, instead of finding either fear or defiance, he finds "a crowd of children and grandmothers, with ice-cream cones and dogs, not directed from without, a colorful, summer crowd that had come in from all the city's districts simply because it had wanted to be there." In this "peculiar vividness and seriousness" and "concentrated festivity" the diarist of Warsaw finds the true meaning of the recent Polish revolution: "the city living a real life." (p. 134)

> A review of "A Warsaw Diary, 1978-1981," in The New Yorker, Vol. LX, No. 7, April 2, 1984, pp. 133-34.

Neal Ascherson

In 1978, when Polish intellectuals grew tired of playing games with the censors and launched an independent, "unofficial" literature, there appeared the first number of the journal *Zapis.* Among the mass of *samizdat*—the smudgy bulletins of opposition groups, the academic monographs cobbled into book shape which looked like volumes of amateur pornography, the typed manuscripts read so many times that the paper had been fingered down to a texture like cotton—there was plenty of good thinking and good writing. But *Zapis* stood out from the rest—it was a literary periodical, a place for the discussion of cultural and political history, a forum for every sort of argument about the nation's future. And, perhaps, a confessional. . . .

One of the most important and moving features of *Zapis* was the regular extract from the diary of Kazimierz Brandys, a large part of which is now published in [*A Warsaw Diary, 1978-1981*]. . . . A distinguished middle-aged novelist, Brandys belonged exactly to the generation of intellectuals that had been most acutely humiliated by history. His parents were Jewish; he had been a left-wing but not communist student in Poland before the war, and had witnessed the rabid anti-Semitism and brutality of Polish fascist gangs in the universities. After the war, he supported the new regime, joined the Party, and rose to some eminence in the Stalinist cultural world. His books were published in enormous editions just as he was becoming disillusioned by the system. In the upheaval of October 1956 in Poland, which overthrew the Stalinist leadership and brought Gomulka to power, Brandys became a prominent "revisionist"—or liberal communist.

His disillusion went on growing. From being a privileged and approved writer, he became a critic and protester, a signer of petitions, a victim of censorship, and finally a nonperson whose books and articles remained unpublished. Brandys resigned from his Party jobs, and eventually from the Party itself. For a time, even then, he continued to believe that the Party was still capable of regeneration. . . .

During the Seventies, while Edward Gierek ruled Poland, Brandys finally lost this remaining shred of faith. The Party, its ideology and its personalities, proved incurable. But when he looked about Poland to see where salvation might come from, Brandys fell into a mood of hopelessness. Close to him was a tiny group of civil-rights dissidents and publishers of underground literature, the handful who formed the Committee for the Defense of the Workers, who ran the "Flying University" courses, who held hunger strikes in churches. But they seemed to him candidates for martyrdom rather than—as they proved to be—forerunners of revolution.

Brandys during this period felt strongly pessimistic about the Polish masses; everywhere he looked he seemed to find evidence of a deep, deliberate, corrupt materialism. It was at this time that *Zapis* was founded, and began to run fragments of his diary. "Sovietism is a spiritual phenomenon," he noted in April 1980, only two months before the wave of strikes that were to evolve into Solidarity at the end of the summer.

> It is not so much a machine spewing forth a mass society as it is, primarily, a loss of memory, it makes us forget who we are and what we wanted to be. . . . I see time and again mental and ethical erosion in people, a blurring of their sense of the boundary between good and evil. I'm speaking here of the limp tatters to which we have reduced those ideas and concepts, that mankind used to call freedom, happiness, brotherhood.

Buried in this lament for a morally dead nation is a plain nostalgia for those "ideas and concepts" that can no longer be a basis of faith. Brandys wrote as an agnostic, as a homeless socialist, very much as one of those whose God had failed. But around him was a generation in its twenties that had discovered, or was rediscovering, a much older God. (p. 7)

[There] slowly appeared a very different form of opposition, based on the ancient values of Catholic faith and of the nation but selecting from them the new Catholic emphasis on human rights and social justice, and the idea of the nation as a righteous and responsible community (instead of resurrecting the older Polish chauvinism, which simply identified national independence as the single cause above all questions of morality). For this generation—and most of Solidarity's leaders were under thirty—the remorse and doubts of Brandys and his contemporaries were irrelevant. They respected him as a writer and as a conscience, and looked eagerly for each installment of the diary, but they saw Poland—especially after the Pope's visit in 1979—as a sorely oppressed but mature society with the patience and strength required to take its destiny into its own hands.

So the Solidarity revolution of 1980 hit Brandys as a dazzling surprise. For all his delight, he remained surprised, often detached, noticing the discords and absurdities as well as the heroic main theme. This is the value of his record. At times, he surges forward on the wave of national confidence. He speculates that Poland in the seventeenth and eighteenth centuries may not have been a dying polity but—on the contrary—the only healthy society on a continent where the absolutist empires were growing up around it. The hideous climax of the mid-twentieth century could be seen as the inevitable end of "a spiritual illness that afflicted Germany and Russia to the greatest extent and Poland to the least."

But then, writing in late 1981, Brandys looks down into the street where the worst economic crisis to strike a European country for forty years is taking place: a scene which is anything but one of national rebirth. . . . Strange but striking parallels occur to Brandys:

> the deeper kinship between the histories of the Jews and the Poles. Small, stubborn Judea with its God who tested it so cruelly, a crazy nation that would not kneel down before the superpowers. Its misfortune was accelerated by groups of youths who pelted the Roman cohorts with stones at the gates of the city.

And yet he sees a darker side of Poland emerging alongside the splendor and the hunger: peasant avarice and indifference as the cities starve, lightning-flashes of anti-Jewish madness even within Solidarity itself, petty outbursts of horrible selfishness in the food lines. "The miracle has become a reality, astonishing by the very fact of its existence but, at the same time, morbidly entangled and incomplete."

Brandys, like many other Polish intellectuals, nurses violently ambivalent feelings about the West. He considers Poland a "Western" nation, and yet shares that extraordinary and utterly un-Western Polish belief that his country has nothing in its history to apologize for. (A sense of guilt about at least some episodes in a country's history is surely a defining trait of Western consciousness.) But there "has probably been no other country in the history of Europe that has committed so few blameworthy acts against the world. . . . Between Germany's schizophrenic power and the deranged void that is Russia, Poland tried to live, a nation that for a long time took seriously mankind's noble ideas."

Brandys admits to sharing both the Polish instinctive faith in the West, especially the United States, and the nation's bitter cynicism about the West's capacity to understand and assist the Poles. "Does Warsaw always have to believe in the perfection of the West, which does not think about us?" . . . In 1980, Brandys is almost amused by his own fury at the failure of President Carter's raid to rescue the Iranian hostages. He assumed, in spite of Vietnam, that American military power was invincible, or at least immune to technical failure. "I think I am like many people in Poland in my grandiloquent idea and vision of the United States. They associate America with high-minded convictions in spite of remembering that it was that very country that thirty-five years ago decided to abandon the Poles to Russian domination."

In the end, Brandys is revealing here the ultimate terror of the Poles: that they will be forgotten. That fear runs high again today. The flow of parcels and trucks with medical aid is slowing to a trickle; the Western press is much more interested in Mrs. Thatcher's visit to Hungary than in, say, the latest chapter in Lech Walesa's war of words with General Jaruzelski. A miserable sense of abandonment is closing in. At times, Brandys allows himself frantic outbursts of accusation which seem out of any proportion, beyond justice.

> At one point, with an unpleasant sense of surprise, the people of the West received the news that a man from [Poland] had been elected Pope. For it is not we but they who have a besieged-fortress mentality, and it is they who are drawing down the iron curtains within themselves. The very thought that in Poland today something has arisen that is newer and more important than the Western synthesis of Luxemburg-Marxism and anarchoterrorism, or the self-repairing regulators of the Western economies, infringes on their mental zone, for the young neo-Marxists, the bank directors, housewives, and the editors of *Le Figaro* and the *Frankfurter Allgemeine* all share a dislike for experiments conducted in an area of strategic importance to the Soviets.

This absurd but absolutely authentic tirade comes from a man who spent long periods living in the West, even in some of the Solidarity months. Indeed, General Jaruzelski's coup caught Brandys and his wife in New York. The last entry in the diary, on December 13, 1982, runs: "News that martial law has been declared in Poland. All communications cut." (pp. 7-8)

> *Neal Ascherson, "The Surprise of Solidarity," in* The New York Review of Books, *Vol. XXXI, No. 7, April 26, 1984, pp. 7-9.*

Zdena Tomin

> Yesterday, in front of a grocery store in Gdynia, I saw two pensioners thrashing each other with their canes in a line of about 30 people waiting for butter . . . What I am talking about here is not filmable; there are some things camera and film cannot capture. And it is precisely that sort of thing that I most wish to describe.

Here is a book it is essential to read. In his **Warsaw Diary,** Kazimierz Brandys, one of Poland's leading contemporary writers, gives us that long and painfully missing link to Poland and its people whom we've been watching on our television screens over the past few years and never really knew. (p. 26)

And how he does it! The language is exquisite; the images

of people in everyday situations are painted with an almost Japanese brush; the personal, historical, philosophical and political reflections flow from page to page without embarrassing or intimidating the reader; the search for truth and for a glimmer of hope is both severe and sad.

A great amount of information about the history-making 'Polish events' can be gleaned from the book by fact-hungry readers; but primarily, it's a book that offers those extremely rare commodities—insight, understanding, material for true compassion. I have learnt more about Polish history from *A Warsaw Diary* than perhaps from any other book, because Brandys approaches it through the Polish people's consciousness *today*.

Brandys does not hide his passionate love of Poland, the kind of love hardly experienced by people of great, historically invincible nations; but neither does he cover up for the failures, sins and unlovable features of the Poles, including the deeply rooted anti-Semitism. He does not exclude himself from responsibility as one of the 'makers' of today's Poland; he does not offer apologies or ready answers either. His writing is almost painfully honest—and almost painfully beautiful.

And I don't remember a book that had me so scared, that left me in such deep anguish for the fate of Europe. I am one of the hopeful inhabitants of this divided continent; I believe that a 'healing process' (as E. P. Thompson calls it), though it will not come overnight, is not only necessary for our survival, but also possible. Brandys has reminded me of how terribly difficult a process it is going to be, of how far away the two 'halves of Europe' have drifted, or rather been torn apart, from each other: 'They . . . [the Westerners] . . . with their colourful pyramids of food . . . their banks hushed like cathedrals . . . their regal footwear galleries . . . They live in a civilisation; we live in a drama.' (pp. 26-7)

Each of us will have to contribute to the healing of Europe. As Brandys says, 'Individual human answers decide the sort of life we have on earth. As if the future of the world really did depend on us . . . This is good news; let us rejoice in it.' (p. 27)

Zdena Tomin, "Living in a Drama," in The Listener, Vol. 112, No. 2870, August 9, 1984, pp. 26-7.

Timothy Garton Ash

Kazimierz Brandys's *Warsaw Diary* contains a very good book and a very bad one. The very good book is a subtle, beautifully observed, *engagé* yet self-critical account of the author's experience in Poland through the electric years 1978 to 1981. The very bad one is a wild, slap-dash, even hysterical account of his experience abroad in the same period. This extraordinary split says something important—and sad—about contemporary Polish intellectual life.

In Warsaw, he records the flowering of *samizdat* literary magazines and independent publishers in the late 1970s, but also what seems to him, even in October 1979, the *isolation* of the "dissidents". "Society will not risk the little it possesses" for "ideas and ethical concepts", he notes in March 1979. Two years later, at the height of Solidarity, he observes—with characteristic honesty—that he was

wrong. Yet he is sharply critical of the crasser Polish myths and self-images. He knows what it was like to be a Jewish student (confined to apartheid benches at the back of the lecture-hall) in pre-war Poland. He heard what Poles said about Jews, even during the war. After recalling all this, he yet reflects on "the deeper kinship between the histories of the Jews and the Poles. Small stubborn Judea with its God who tested it so cruelly, a crazy nation that would not kneel down before the superpowers."

What Solidarity won for him personally was the chance to travel to West Berlin on a writer's fellowship, after having been denied a passport for several years by the Polish authorities. In West Berlin he finds the West Germans reacting to the Polish revolution with *angst*-ridden incomprehension:

> "As has already occurred several times in the past," declared the commentator on Berlin television yesterday, "the Poles' lack of consciousness of their own situation may cause them a rude awakening." This he said with the fatuously wise look of an uncle warning children not to play with matches.

At this, he is justly angry. But then goes wild:

> If you listen and read carefully, you can hear the West's faint-hearted recognition of its own biological weakness; they know their fatigue, the exhaustion of an old race that has to preserve carefully what strength it has.

Solzhenitsyn, Spengler and Darwin, all in one. . . .

How can this distinguished writer, so sensitive, sceptical and just in describing the intellectual condition of his own country, be so insensitive, simplistic and inaccurate in judging "the West"?

Any Westerner who thinks that "the West" does have much to learn from the experience of central and eastern Europe will be driven to distraction by his hectoring self-righteousness. It is as if Brandys was deliberately trying to sabotage his own message to the West. Indeed, he himself sees this. "Thus I carried on inwardly," he writes, "And I know there was exaltation and overstatement in that shouting to the conscience of the West. I know that I have fallen into the pathos of the preacher and that a complex is speaking through me." Yet on the next page he is off again: "We mean nothing to Westerners . . . Ireland and Chile mean more to Poles than the events of the last six months means to people in the West." He—*even* he—cannot leap over his own shadow, cannot escape from this Polish complex. And so long as writers like Brandys stay locked inside it, so long as they misunderstand as much as they are misunderstood, their message will not get through.

Timothy Garton Ash, "Warning Shouts," in The Times Literary Supplement, No. 4252, September 28, 1984, p. 1098.

M. G. Levine

[*Paris, New York: 1982-1984*] is a captivating example of what has become a very popular genre in Central Europe—the extended essay composed of meditative fragments that arise from the author's daily experiences. Not quite a diary, not quite a memoir, it is on one level a record of the author's life as a reluctant exile from Poland, forced by the December 1981 declaration of martial law to make a new life abroad. . . . [Brandys] brings to the dreary adventure of exile the keen powers of observation of an accomplished novelist and short-story writer who has lived through much of the turbulent history of this century. He writes, with a mixture of avid curiosity and bemusement, of life in Paris and New York as he observes it on the streets, in the university classroom, in intellectual circles. Poland's problems are always at the center of his consciousness, but this is not a camouflaged treatise on politics. It is a wise and beautiful book . . . about the conjunction of personal life and historical forces.

> *M. G. Levine, in a review of "Paris, New York: 1982-1984," in* Choice, *Vol. 26, No. 7, March, 1989, p. 1167.*

Stanislaw Baranczak

Imagine yourself as a writer in your mid-60s who has just arrived for a brief visit to a Western metropolis, half a world apart from your small and exotic homeland. As you set foot on the foreign pavement, you learn that a military coup was staged in your country and all your friends were arrested. You can't return. You are stranded with your elderly wife, your two suitcases and your frail health on the shore of an alien continent. You have no command of the language, no source of income in sight, no literary recognition to speak of, and no Social Security benefits to soothe your old age. The only thing you can count on is your writing skills. But you write in a language that almost nobody around understands.

This, give or take a few details, is what happened to the prominent Polish novelist and essayist Kazimierz Brandys when he arrived in New York at the end of 1981 [as described in his memoir *Paris, New York: 1982-1984*]. Like many of his fellow Poles who had the misfortune—or good fortune, depending on your point of view—to be visiting the West exactly when martial law was imposed on their country, he had no other choice than to stay put and wait for new developments. Any attempt to go back would have been foolish: After all, over the previous two decades Brandys had been one of the best known representatives of dissent in Polish literature, and indeed his name immediately sprang up as one of the favorite targets on the hit lists of martial law propaganda.

It is relatively easy to live out of your suitcase and wait for the dust to settle in your faraway country if you are young and strong enough to carry that suitcase. For Brandys, who could see that the situation in Poland might not improve within his lifetime, the very sense of being stranded indefinitely outside his country, language and culture was tantamount to a personal disaster.

Not that he was completely unknown in the West. On the contrary, Brandys has ranked for many years among the most widely translated contemporary Polish writers, though his output is not as readily available in English as it is in French, German or Italian. (p. 16)

In the West, however, he is merely one of those numerous, more or less intriguing writers from Central Europe. In Poland, he was himself, Kazimierz Brandys, a writer with his own clearly defined personality, his individual history of complicated political and artistic evolution, his sharply delineated circles of admirers and detractors, his particular place in his native literature. That is not the kind of baggage that you can pack for a trip on an intercontinental airline.

No wonder the focus of Brandys' memoir is not really New York or Paris (where he eventually settled and feels more comfortable). Neither is it Poland, even though his comments on the events in his country, and reflections on their historical roots and cultural contexts, form a large part of the book. The memoir's focus is actually the author's all-pervading sense of alienation: the alienation of an Eastern European in the West, the alienation of an old man amid the young, the alienation of someone who still dares to hope in a world that seems to have given up on hope. . . .

[In Poland in the 1970s, Brandys was] deeply involved in the rapid fermentation of intellectual dissent that directly preceded the emergence of Solidarity. In 1976 he cofounded the first uncensored Polish literary journal, *Zapis* (*The Record*), and his books, more and more indigestible for the censor, soon afterward began to be produced by underground publishing houses. One such book was *The Months,* his memoir, or rather personal chronicle, of the fateful late '70s in Warsaw, published in English as *A Warsaw Diary.* Since his decision to stay in the West in the wake of martial law, Brandys has been busy continuing to write *The Months,* three volumes of which have so far been issued by both émigré and Polish underground presses. *Paris, New York: 1982-1984* is the English version of the third volume.

The last sentence puts this reviewer in a state of mental torment: As someone who happens to have read both the Polish and English versions, I am torn between gratitude to Random House for having made Brandys' illuminating work available to the American reader, and resentment that it has been mutilated so terribly and inexplicably. For *Paris, New York: 1982-1984* is not simply a translation of the original book; it is a heavily edited abbreviation, and this fact is not mentioned on the cover or anywhere else. Only about a half of the full text has been preserved in this edition, and regardless of whether the cuts were made with or without the author's consent, they did the book a disastrous disservice. . . .

Based on the reading of this edition alone, one would have a hard time trying to reconstruct even what happened to Brandys between 1982 and 1984 in New York and Paris, let alone the entire system of his opinions and arguments. It would be deplorable yet still understandable if Brandys' book had been made shallow, if the editor's scissors had cut out anything that was difficult. As matters stand, however, it appears the editor's instrument here was not a scissors but a paper shredder. (p. 17)

> *Stanislaw Baranczak, "Out of a Shredder," in* The New Leader, *Vol. LXXI, No. 22, December 26, 1988, pp. 16-17.*

Wanda Urbanska

Fifty years after the Nazis stormed into Poland starting World War II, Polish writers continue trying to make sense of that brutal war in which 6 million Poles were gassed, bled or starved to death.

A quirky conceit is the linchpin of Kazimierz Brandys' [novel **Rondo**]. In Nazi-occupied Warsaw, protagonist Tom fabricates an underground organization—which he calls Rondo after a Chopin piece—for the sole purpose of providing an off-stage, cloak-and-dagger role for his lady love, Tola, whose spectacular acting career has been forced by the war into hibernation. Tom's every action is scrutinized by others, as the tall, redheaded former law student is rumored to be the illegitimate son of Poland's former leader, Marshal Jozef Pilsudski. In the eyes of others, the imaginary group becomes real. And so, before war's end, this organizational mirage has been "overtaken" by ambitious partisans, trying to make names for themselves in the Polish underground.

The novel is framed around a corrective letter Tom writes to a journal years later, responding to a "scholarly" account of Rondo's war activities. Brandys—who was born in 1916 in Lodz and lived through the war in Warsaw—uses this letter as a take-off and landing point for a discursive, first-person reminiscence of Tom's life, which is woven into a complex, heavily allegorical plot. The novel spans a 40-year period from the young man's coming of age in the 1930s—when "Warsaw started to resemble an affluent city"—to his advancing age in the 1970s. . . .

His passion for Tola—emotionally unrequited though it is—helps Tom survive the war, providing what contemporary commentators might call the necessary "coping mechanism." "If one gave up the personal sphere of existence, the last barrier against insanity would fall. . . . This was the source of my endurance: my laboriously built honeycomb." . . .

Tom's scheme to provide Tola her greatest role works, at first. He fills borrowed suitcases with used books which he assures her are written in code and dispatches her on trains to cities around Poland, where she deposits them in lockers. "She returned from her first trip radiant, almost euphoric." For a time, Tola worships Tom. Then the worm turns. When she accuses him of poisoning the man she loves, Tom reveals that Rondo is a hoax. The truth unhinges Tola. After a mental breakdown, she checks into a sanitarium.

Rondo is strikingly similar in tone and approach to the recent work of Tadeusz Konwicki. As in Konwicki's *Moonrise, Moonset,* Brandys intercuts between past and present, refusing to hold to strict linear time in his narrative. And Brandys' narrator intervenes in the text, commenting on the storytelling, apologizing for digressions and slow spots.

Light weekend reading **Rondo** is not. Because the plot is so far-fetched and the characters surreal, it is hard to read the novel as anything other than an allegory—rife with ruminations and philosophical musings, many of which are original and provocative. For example, "Who conceived of the idea that good struggles with evil?" Tom's father asks. " 'Only evil can fight with evil. Good cannot fight. . . . God is neither good nor evil,' he said quietly. 'He is our possibility of a good or evil choice. And they [the Nazis] have abolished that possibility.' "

And this: "The idealization of women is in my opinion a less dangerous thing than the cult of masculinity," Brandys writes. "The search for the Relentless and Visionary Leader who would substitute for conscience and reason begins when values and ideas are in ruins and when spiritual emptiness has set in. If I had to express it in the shortest possible way, I would say that real men need a woman-saint."

Rondo offers an important lesson—that the truth cannot be trusted to historians, to partisans, to victims or even to writers. This is worth bearing in mind as the generation of Polish writers including Brandys, Konwicki and Czeslaw Milosz, who survived the war and have reached or are approaching old age, attempt to leave their marks on the canon of memory, folk tale and written document about World War II.

It would seem that Brandys' own attitude toward the truth is paradoxical. Tom's history is itself a testimony to truth, and yet its telling proved the undoing of his beloved woman-saint, Tola. In **Rondo,** Tom quotes a friend: "A wise man knows what he says. A foolish man says what he knows." One cannot help but wonder what Brandys is holding back.

Wanda Urbanska, " 'Real Men Need a Woman-Saint'," in Los Angeles Times Book Review, *October 8, 1989, p. 2.*

Stanislaw Baranczak

In Polish, the word *rondo* means several different yet similar things: a hat brim, a traffic rotary, cursive writing, a musical form based on a repetitive refrain. Each of these has to do with roundedness, circular shape, cyclic movement, spherical self-containment. Kazimierz Brandys's novel **Rondo** is about what happens when someone attempts to create such a self-contained, closed-circuited niche of fictitious reality in real life. Though artificial and therefore seemingly safer than the angular and dangerously open world outside, the fabricated realm that his protagonist creates is marred by one deadly drawback: it can turn with astonishing ease into something terrifyingly real.

Brandys wrote the first draft of his novel in 1974. . . . Three decades of dealing with thematic restrictions and trying to outsmart censorship had left Polish fiction with a dubious legacy of allusions and disguises. Conceived to get one's message past the censor's eye unharmed, the devices ended up harming the integrity of the message even more than the red pencil would have. There was a powerful need for a more direct presentation of Polish experience. There was a thirst for the real.

At this early stage in literature's return to simple truths and straightforward realism, to jump one step further, as Brandys did, and discover unreality as the most real presence in Polish life required a paradoxical mind indeed. But then, the complicated course of Brandys's own career had prepared him well to cope with all the paradoxes involved in the clash between fact and fiction. One of the most popular Polish writers in 1974, by that time he had already shed several different novelistic styles as the political world around him changed, and his views of literature's relation to reality changed along with it.

He launched his career with the novel *A Wooden Horse,* written in Warsaw under the Nazi occupation and published in 1946, a work that owed a great deal to the pre-war novelistic avant-garde with its penchant for grotesque irony. Shortly afterward, Brandys's writing turned deadly serious, and anything but equivocal. Switching from his pre-war vague leftism to communism, in the early postwar years he joined the growing ranks of Socialist Realists. A skillful and prolific writer, he began to turn out novels that bore all the required stamps of official ideology, and then some (p. 37). . . .

Yet the true believer in Brandys turned quite abruptly into the equally true skeptic, an about-face familiar to many Polish writers at the end of the first postwar decade. The short stories and novels he published during the mid-1950s, some of them even preceding the official "thaw," may strike us today as somewhat naive in their political diagnoses. . . . Still in the early phase of his career, Brandys drew on his personal experience with the Stalinist "new faith" to explore the ethical conflicts produced by the pressure of collective beliefs, from totalitarian ideologies to nationalistic dogmas.

It was also at this point that the tension between fact and fiction began to appear in his works. Since the publication in 1958 of his first volume of *Letters to Mrs. Z,* a sequence of half-fictional essays in epistolary form, Brandys has been a certified master of making fiction pretend that it isn't. His numerous books published over the past 30 years may be viewed, in fact, as a series of experiments to that end. Narrative prose is variously disguised in conspicuously non-fictional genres and forms of discourse: a letter sequence, a writer's diary, an interview. We are dealing, to be sure, with a wider novelistic trend of our times, which to the cynical eye may look like novelists' panicky response to losing their readers to memoirs and biographies.

Still, in Brandys's best books the device has an interesting, individual twist, as personal as it is Polish. The novel *Postal Variations* (1972), an untranslatable firework of stylization, is a highly amusing collection of fictitious letters in which the history of one Polish family over several centuries—and by extension, the history of Poland itself—is offhandedly presented, while the author has a wonderful time imitating the stylistic flavors of the language of consecutive epochs. Unbelievably enough, this flash of literary brilliance provoked an ugly act of political mugging. After the publication of the novel in Poland, the regime's trusted critics staged a campaign of slander, accusing Brandys (not without unmistakable hints about his Jewish descent) of ridiculing Polish history. The pretense of non-fiction was, in a sense, taken at face value and turned against its creator. Brandys's artistic unreality began to function as something unexpectedly real.

Without delving too deeply into psychological motivations, one may safely assume that the idea of *Rondo*—which Brandys started in 1974, then dropped, turning instead to another novel, *Unreality* (published in English in 1980 as *A Question of Reality*), then picked up again and finished—had a good deal to do with the reception of *Postal Variations.* In Brandys's life, the writing of this pair of novels coincided with the beginning of his open participation in the rapidly growing intellectual dissent of the mid-1970s. In 1976 he was one of the editors of *Zapis*

(The Record), the first uncensored literary journal in Poland. His own books, increasingly free of self-censorship, came out in the late 1970s mostly through the newly founded underground publishing houses or émigré presses in the West.

The device of a non-fictional genre no longer served the purpose of literary experiment; it was simply the most direct and effective way of writing about contemporary events, which in Poland over the past dozen years have certainly been stranger than any fiction. This is the case, certainly, with *The Months,* Brandys's major work-in-progress, his multi-volume writer's diary or personal chronicle of events and reflections. Begun in Warsaw some ten years ago, Brandys continued it in New York, where he was caught by the news of martial law in Poland, and then in Paris, where he moved soon afterward and now lives. (Out of four volumes of *The Months* published in Polish so far, the first has appeared in English as *A Warsaw Diary,* and the third, unfortunately in heavily truncated form, as *Paris, New York: 1982-1984.*)

Both *Rondo* and *Unreality*—they are, in a sense, twin novels—make use of an ostentatiously non-fictional device. *Rondo* is, or at least begins as, a polemical letter written to a historical quarterly to rectify false information in an article; *Unreality* takes the shape of a series of tape-recorded responses by a Polish intellectual to a questionnaire handed to him by a Western sociologist. Overlapping details in the respective plots make the two novels a sort of tandem, linked by the figure of the protagonist: the same man who explains an episode of his wartime past in *Rondo* tries to explain how People's Poland works (or, more accurately, does not work) in *Unreality.*

Two variations on the theme of Polish unreality, *Rondo* is, true to its title, a self-contained whole in a way that its twin, in which plot loses out to explanation, is not. More than self-contained: it is based, like a musical rondo, on the compositional principle of close-circuited self-sufficiency. The recurring thematic refrains and the narrative method of circling around key events instead of presenting them in a linear fashion convey a claustrophobic impression of a determined world in which nothing is left open-ended, in which fate cannot be averted. Once events are set in motion, nothing can stop them. Once unreality is created, nothing can undo its very real existence.

This is precisely what *Rondo's* protagonist tries to explain in his letter to the editor of the historical quarterly. The letter, which soon evolves into a long narrative, has been inspired, we learn, by a pretentiously titled article, "A Chapter in the History of Struggle" by one Professor Janota, which offered a totally falsified account of the wartime activities of an underground fighting unit called Rondo. The protagonist knows all about the strange truth of Rondo for one simple reason: he was its sole creator. He is the only person who can certify that Rondo never existed in reality.

Didn't it? Or perhaps it did exist, but in another kind of reality, one where fictions become hard facts. Brandys's narrator is familiar with this transformation of unreality into reality from his provincial childhood, thanks to persistent gossip that made him a natural son of the national hero, Marshal Pilsudski. The gossip makes even wider rounds when, as a law student in pre-war Warsaw, he is accidentally seen by a friend at the entrance to Belweder, Pilsudski's official residence.

The unbidden notoriety turns into unbidden charisma when the war breaks out and many people start viewing the narrator—a man in whom nothing is in fact out of the ordinary save his "insane normality"—as a possibly providential leader. Meanwhile, he develops a powerful attraction to theater, drops out of law school, and makes his living as an extra in one of Warsaw's troupes. This settles his fate: he falls in love with a young actress named Tola, a woman as oversensitive and chaotic as he is calm, collected, and reliable. When they become lovers, it dawns on him that the only way to keep this impossible relationship alive is to make Tola's life a "role," of which he will be the invisible "director."

After the Nazis come in and theaters are closed down, the narrator's concern is to keep not merely their relationship but Tola herself alive. . . . While listening to Chopin's Rondo at a clandestine concert, the protagonist strikes upon a brilliant idea of saving Tola both from herself and from the Nazis: he will create a nonexistent clandestine organization and make Tola work for it as a secret courier.

Thus Rondo comes into being. Tola is sworn in, given instructions, and periodically sent out with suitcases containing secret messages that are in fact old newspapers and books. She has a role to play, but at the same time she is protected from any real danger. But the danger becomes real very soon. The news of Rondo's supposed existence inevitably begins to spread. Even its accidental name is deciphered as an acronym for a direct military extension of the Polish underground commander in chief. The myth of Rondo's exploits, combined with the narrator's unwanted charisma, attracts people who—much like Tola—need a role to play in order to fill their own spiritual void with some semblance of meaning and purpose.

Among the recruits is the protagonist's former schoolmate and the Mephisto of his life, Wladek Sznej. A highly intelligent mind, Sznej nevertheless has no inner resources of his own. He lacks any moral principle; his personality portends the future of Poland, which will soon be ruled by his "tribe of middlemen." . . . (pp. 37-8)

Before the war, Sznej's conscience finds an endorser in the ideology of right-wing nationalism; after the war, in communism. (This kind of evolution is not a farfetched fantasy. People's Poland has had a share of real-life Sznejs.) In the wartime interim, he grasps at the straw of Rondo's supposed existence with fanatical determination, forcing the protagonist to induct him, too, and immediately pressing him to broaden the base of the organization (which at this point already includes several young people whom, like Tola, the narrator tries to protect from real involvement).

Rondo quickly acquires an increasingly tangible existence. Conceived to save lives, it endangers them more and more. In the end, the roof of the whole structure of unreality falls in for real, burying all of the narrator's hopes. A rival guerrilla group messes up the execution of a traitor and instead someone else dies—a famous older actor who happens to have been Tola's idol and one-time lover. Convinced of the protagonist's omnipotence in murky dealings of the underground, Tola cannot be persuaded that he had nothing to do with the victim's death. Her mental illness

is just one disastrous consequence of Rondo's nonexistent existence.

There are others. Even after the war ends, Rondo never ceases to cast its long shadow on the lives it once touched. As a bitter irony of fate, the narrator spends several years in a Stalinist jail, accused of, and interrogated about, his wartime membership in an organization that arouses even more suspicion by having been so perfectly undercover that nothing is known about its activity. The all-pervading unreality of communism absorbs this instance of individual unreality with the greatest of ease.

As the narrator writes his letter, he has been free for many years; but even though he hopes to reunite with Tola, who is about to return from emigration, evil has already been done and lives have been ruined irrevocably. Professor Janota's article, which ultimately mythicizes Rondo's history and confirms the everlasting power of unreality, is the final insult—especially since, as we learn near the end of the novel, Janota's true name is Wladek Sznej. (pp. 38-9)

Thus *Rondo's* circular structure comes to its ultimate fulfillment: from the last page we must return to the first. From the first words of his letter, the narrator was aware that Janota was in fact Sznej. While ostensibly trying to defend the truth and to denounce unreality, he knew all along that his explanation would fall on the deaf ears of someone for whom "there is no such thing as the truth of reality." *Rondo* is a novel about what happens when someone or something, an individual or a political system, acts on those chilling words. (p. 39)

Stanislaw Baranczak, "Wake Up to Unreality," in The New Republic, *Vol. 201, No. 15, October 9, 1989, pp. 37-9.*

Phillip Lopate

In a more just—or at least more inquisitive—literary society than exists in America today, we might be much better acquainted with the name of Kazimierz Brandys, one of the major Polish novelists of the postwar period. . . . The West knows his writing principally through his recent memoirs, *A Warsaw Diary: 1979-1981,* and *Paris/New York: 1982-1984.* He is one of those writers who seems to have saved his best work for his full maturity. His novel *Rondo* (first published in Polish in 1982), and the previous one, *A Question of Reality* (1977), are the kinds of books that can only come as the summation of a lifetime's struggle for understanding, so packed are they with penetrating wisdom and worldly experience.

Rondo is an idiosyncratic, inclusive novel, which, through the story of one man, reflects on many classically Polish themes: romanticism, the cult of women, conspiratorial politics and the dramatization of history. It tells the story of a young law student who falls in love with an actress, Tola Mohoczy, and gives up his career, becoming an extra just to be near her. Tola, disliking the narrator's first name (which we never learn), renames him "Tom." . . . She herself is hopelessly in love with the theater's star, Cezar, and she warns Tom, in her acerbic fashion: "His least gesture would be enough to make me cut off your head and sell it to the butcher." The perfect *cavalier,* Tom reflects: "I understood two things: always, everywhere, and despite all circumstances, I shall fulfill her every wish, and never, under any conditions, shall I really matter to her, although she may need me." Somehow Tom accepts these conditions, remaining on call to receive the crumbs of love she throws him from time to time, partly because it gives him a role in life and helps him "to realize his first person singular." He is aware that he has invented this obsessive passion out of a need for self-definition and subtle control of the loved one: "If I acted in a discreet, careful, and skillful manner, I had a chance of becoming *the second director* in her life."

It is one of the many paradoxes of Tom that he embraces a modest role with a certain touchy vanity. He observes that in certain cafes, "I enjoyed . . . a certain popularity reserved for well-mannered eccentrics, patient listeners, and people free of fervent ambitions." He also sticks out by virtue of his red hair and the persistent rumor that surrounds him—that he is the illegitimate son of the Polish national hero, Marshal Pilsudski. Finally, his very calm and abhorrence of extremes is seen as a sign of "pathological normality" by his theater companions. Though there are playful hints that the narrator may be unreliable, essentially Tom seems to be a trustworthy if intensely quirky witness—the scion of those grandly self-conscious "I" 's found in European fiction, from Diderot's *Rameau's Nephew,* through Dostoyevsky's Underground Man and Italo Svevo's Zeno—protagonists whose relentless analytical activity carries with it a whiff of self-mockery.

Once the Nazis occupy Poland, the theater is shut down and everyone is forced to find a hustle of some kind; Tom himself finds a job as a cloakroom attendant in a restaurant. (pp. 30-1)

Tom engages in a number of illicit activities, becoming a sort of art dealer, while working for the Polish underground. But, realizing that Tola is sinking into depression for lack of theatrical opportunities, he invents an organization called Rondo, and uses her as a courier to deliver valises full of old Sherlock Holmes books, which he pretends are encoded. Not only does this give her a new "role" to play, but it elevates Tom romantically in her eyes. . . . Eventually, Rondo attracts more and more volunteers and takes on an independent life of its own; the fabrication turns into dangerous reality and wriggles out of Tom's control.

The novel assumes the playful form of a letter to the editor of a magazine, written by Tom 40 years after these events, in response to the quarterly's article "A Chapter in the History of Struggle," by a Professor Janota. Janota has purported to tell the history of Rondo, and our narrator is at pains to set the record straight. But in order to do so, he must drag in so much background that the letter expands into a full-length *apologia pro vita sua,* zigzagging between past and present and recounting the events in anything but a straightforward manner. The title, ***Rondo,*** is a triple pun referring not only to the organization's name and its subconscious inspiration, Chopin's "Rondo," but to the cyclical method of the narration, with its multiple foreshadowings, red herrings and suppressions of key facts.

To some extent this hide-and-seek, self-reflexive modernist machinery is unnecessarily complicated—especially for a novelist whose strong suits seem to be his humanistic de-

cency, sparkling character descriptions and swift insights. . . . However carefully the plot may be worked out, this is essentially one of those books one reads for the provocative digressions that swell out the paragraphs. The author's sentences are energetic and epigrammatic; he tosses off lovely asides on styles of acting, Warsaw ("that city of drafts and speeding streetcars"), good and evil ("Who conceived of the idea that good struggles with evil? Only evil can fight with evil. Good cannot fight. Maybe good is merely a trace of some primordial civilization that lost its battles millions of years ago").

He is particularly penetrating on the shifty opportunism of ideologues, like Tom's nemesis, Wladek Sznej: "There are people who torment themselves to death if there is a party in town and they are not invited. . . . He was tormented by the thought that he was not invited to the new epoch." Sznej is the weathercock changing with each breeze of historical necessity, while Tom sees himself as a "closed circuit," relatively impervious to external sanctions. "My hearing is attuned to myself rather than to what surrounds me: the times, public opinion, the future, historical milestones, etc." One can understand how such a stubborn consciousness can have developed in the stress of 20th-century Poland; still, there are times when being stuck in the "closed circuit" of Tom's meditations begins to feel slightly claustrophobic. There are very few dramatized scenes, and Mr. Brandys's restless, commenting intelligence, delightful as it is, sometimes threatens to overflow the margins of the story. Because the author is willing to entertain any speculation, with the synthesizing openness of a much younger person, the texture of his mind seems alternately sophisticated and naïve. There are so many Big Ideas, levels and dichotomies being worked out constantly—theater versus life, historical reality as a hall of mirrors, unity versus multiplicity of self, illegitimate paternity, truth versus fiction, sanity and madness, the ethics of change and stasis—that it gets rather feverish. But I'd still rather have Kazimierz Brandys's lush, caloric, Polish generosity and mental excitement than most slenderized contemporary fiction.

Toward the end of ***Rondo,*** the narrator observes poignantly:

> Questions concerning my past force me to re-create my past role. On such occasions I feel ill at ease and my performance is less than convincing. The explanation is rather simple: I lack the old stage design, the setup. My partners have long since left the stage. The audience is different. This last element is perhaps the most important one: an audience that does not understand the plot of the play. How can I explain my epoch to someone who lives in a different time? Totally impossible.

And yet, those adventurous American readers willing to try this novel by a masterful, relatively unknown foreign author will discover that Kazimierz Brandys has done the impossible. (p. 31)

Phillip Lopate, " 'I Shall Fulfill Her Every Wish'," in The New York Times Book Review, *November 19, 1989, pp. 30-1.*

Anthony Burgess

1917-

(Born John Anthony Burgess Wilson; has also written as John Burgess Wilson and under pseudonym Joseph Kell) English novelist, essayist, critic, dramatist, translator, editor, scriptwriter, short story writer, author of children's books, and composer.

A prolific writer who examines a vast range of topics, Burgess is considered among the most important novelists in contemporary literature. He frequently applies his knowledge of music and linguistics to his fiction, and his fascination with languages is particularly evident in his best-known novel, *A Clockwork Orange*. In his work, Burgess often explores the conflict between free will and determinism. Although his fictional worlds are sometimes disordered and Burgess remains pessimistic about the state of modern society, critics generally agree that his inventive humor and wordplay serve to temper his cynical vision. While Burgess's large canon is regarded by many critics as uneven, most acknowledge his significant contribution to modern literature.

Burgess enrolled at the University of Manchester in 1936 to study musical composition but soon switched to the study of English literature and various languages. After graduating in 1940, Burgess enlisted in the British Army. His assignments included a tour as a musician with a mobile entertainment unit and surveillance work in Gibraltar. Following his discharge in 1946, Burgess worked at a variety of jobs, serving as a piano player in a jazz band in London and as a grammar school instructor teaching various subjects, including English literature. In 1954, Burgess accepted a position in Malaya as an education officer for the British Colonial Service. His experience there supplied material for his early novels, *Time for a Tiger, The Enemy in the Blanket,* and *Beds in the East.* Following the adventures of Victor Crabbe, a young British teacher living in Malaya, the books examine the demise of British rule and present a detailed portrait of the conflicts between the British colonists and the diverse indigenous populations. Robert K. Morris stated that the novels offer "a continuing drama of change; how one man encounters and experiences it, founders upon and succumbs to it." These novels were published collectively in Great Britain as *The Malayan Trilogy,* and in the United States as *The Long Day Wanes: A Malayan Trilogy.* Burgess returned to England in 1959 when he was wrongly diagnosed as having a brain tumor. Given less than a year to live, Burgess produced five novels during that period, including *The Doctor Is Sick,* which relates his experiences while undergoing medical treatment.

A Clockwork Orange, Burgess's most popular and widely discussed work, was reportedly influenced by an assault on his pregnant wife and by his trip to the Soviet Union in 1961. The novel takes place in a near-future city dominated by lawless juvenile gangs. Burgess's proficiency in linguistics is evidenced by his invention of *nadsat,* a crude combination of Russian and Cockney slang spoken by juvenile delinquents that underscores the cultural fusion of

Eastern and Western cultures in the novel. The protagonist, Alex, is a maladjusted youth who, after committing a series of violent crimes, becomes the subject of a government-sponsored behavioral experiment. He is given drugs that induce severe physical pain and nausea whenever he has sexual or violent thoughts, thus denying him free will. After the treatment is completed, Alex is released from prison, unable to attack society yet also helpless to defend himself, and is subjected to attacks of revenge by his past victims. Several critics have suggested that in his portrayal of Alex's experiences Burgess is protesting similar experiments performed by behavioral scientists during the 1960s. *A Clockwork Orange* was adapted for film in 1971 by Stanley Kubrick, and many critics regard the popular movie as the catalyst for Burgess's subsequent rise to literary prominence.

Burgess has also written a series of humorous novels centering on the exploits of F. X. Enderby, a moderately successful lyric poet whom some critics view as Burgess's alter ego. Although written as entertainments, the Enderby novels seriously examine the role of the artist in contemporary society. *Inside Mr. Enderby,* written under the pseudonym Joseph Kell, introduces Enderby and places him in several ridiculous situations. The middle-aged Enderby is portrayed as a latent adolescent who can create poetry only in the privacy of his bathroom. His adventures continue in *Enderby's Outside,* and in *The Clockwork Testament; or, Enderby's End,* the hero dies of a heart attack. *Enderby's Dark Lady; or, No End to Enderby* marks the return of Enderby. Critics noted similarities between Enderby's resurrection and Sir Arthur Conan Doyle's restoration of Sherlock Holmes. Structured as a story within a story, *Enderby's Dark Lady* presents the hero engaged in writing the libretto for a musical based on the life of William Shakespeare.

In *Earthly Powers,* a novel dense with themes relating to philosophy and theology, Burgess further examines the nature of good and evil and the necessity of free will. This novel, which took Burgess ten years to write, follows the intertwining destinies of a homosexual British novelist and a charismatic Italian cleric through world events spanning fifty years of the twentieth century. As participants and observers of human cruelty and degradation, both characters conclude that God has created evil to preserve humanity's freedom of choice. *Earthly Powers* was acclaimed by critics and is considered Burgess's most ambitious recent work. *The End of the World News,* which consists of three separate narratives, was described by Burgess as "an entertainment" that is "all about the end of history as man has known it." The first story is a fictional biography of Sigmund Freud; the second section is a musical based on Leon Trotsky's visit to New York in 1917; and the third story is a fantasy about a cosmic disaster in the year 2000. *The Kingdom of the Wicked,* a historical novel chronicling the early years of Christianity, elicited a mixed reception, though critics acknowledged Burgess's thorough research into the writings of the Twelve Apostles and of various ancient Roman historians. *The Kingdom of the Wicked* was the basis for Burgess's script for the television mini-series "A.D."

The Pianoplayers, a novel with autobiographical significance, recounts the downfall of a pianist—a figure based on Burgess's father—who supplies musical accompaniment to silent films. When his livelihood is threatened by the advent of sound films, he seeks to better his fortunes with a publicity stunt that involves playing his instrument continuously for thirty days; however, he dies in the attempt. *Any Old Iron* is a picaresque novel of ideas that explores the role of individuals in twentieth-century history through the exploits of two eccentric families of Russian and Welsh descent. A side plot concerns the search for Excalibur, the sword of King Arthur and the subject of the book's title, which one character considers a symbol of justice, truth, and beauty. Susan Fromberg Schaeffer interpreted *Any Old Iron* as a study of "the two warring and fundamentally irreconcilable imperatives of human nature. One is the desire for something absolute, unchangeable—if not God, then something like God. . . . This imperative is opposed by the human need to survive simply, as the animal among other animals that man is."

Burgess is highly regarded for several scholarly works of criticism, including *Here Comes Everybody: An Introduction to James Joyce for the Ordinary Reader.* He has also published many textbooks on English literature and has earned renown as a translator, particularly for his 1972 adaptation of Sophocles's drama *Oedipus Rex.* Burgess has also written biographies on William Shakespeare, D. H. Lawrence, and Ernest Hemingway.

(See also *CLC,* Vols. 1, 2, 4, 5, 8, 10, 13, 15, 22, 40; *Contemporary Authors,* Vols. 1-4, rev. ed.; *Contemporary Authors New Revision Series,* Vol. 2; and *Dictionary of Literary Biography,* Vol. 14.)

PRINCIPAL WORKS

NOVELS

Time for a Tiger 1956
The Enemy in the Blanket 1958
Beds in the East 1959
The Right to an Answer 1960
The Doctor Is Sick 1960
The Worm and the Ring 1961
Devil of a State 1961
A Clockwork Orange 1962
The Wanting Seed 1963
Honey for the Bears 1963
**Inside Mr. Enderby* [under pseudonym Joseph Kell] 1963
Nothing Like the Sun: A Story of Shakespeare's Love-Life 1964
A Vision of Battlements 1965
Tremor of Intent 1966
**Enderby Outside* 1968
MF 1971
Napoleon Symphony 1974
**The Clockwork Testament; or, Enderby's End* 1974
1985 1978
Man of Nazareth 1979
Earthly Powers 1980
The End of the World News 1983
Enderby's Dark Lady; or, No End to Enderby 1984
The Kingdom of the Wicked 1985
The Pianoplayers 1986
Any Old Iron 1989

OTHER

The Novel Today (criticism) 1963
Here Comes Everybody: An Introduction to James Joyce for the Ordinary Reader (criticism) 1965
The Novel Now: A Student's Guide to Contemporary Fiction (criticism) 1967; revised, 1971
Shakespeare (biography) 1970
Joysprick: An Introduction to the Language of James Joyce (criticism) 1973
Ernest Hemingway and His World (biography) 1978
Flame into Being: The Life and Work of D. H. Lawrence (biography) 1985
Homage to QWERTYUIOP (essays) 1985; published in the United States as *But Do Blondes Prefer Gentlemen?*
Little Wilson and Big God (autobiography) 1988
The Devil's Mode (short story collection) 1989

---

*These works were published in Great Britain in 1964 as *The Malayan Trilogy* and republished in the United States as *The Long Day Wanes: The Malayan Trilogy.*

**These works were published in 1982 as *Enderby.*

Terry Teachout

Anthony Burgess has written approximately fifty-four books. . . . None of his books has stood up to even the modest test of time provided by a decade or two; no re-evaluation of his burgeoning *oeuvre* appears likely. The problem clearly goes deeper than mere logorrhea or the absence of a definitive masterpiece. Why has Anthony Burgess failed to make a more lasting literary impression? *But Do Blondes Prefer Gentlemen?: Homage to QWERTYUIOP and Other Writings* . . . goes a long way towards answering this vexing question.

Burgess's candid preface makes a very modest case for the publication of this book, a 608-page collection of occasional pieces most of which were originally occasioned by the urgent request of a checkbook-wielding literary editor for a thousand-word review:

> The reading and reviewing of books which, in the covenant I have always insisted upon, have been selected not by myself but by a literary editor, keeps my mind open to fresh ideas in both literary creation and criticism. . . . You are to open the book at any page and take what comes. The author took what came in living his journalistic life, and it would be pretentious to suppose there was a pattern in it.

A book which can be opened with profit at any page is eminently suitable for bedside use, and *But Do Blondes Prefer Gentlemen?* holds up reasonably well on this score. Burgess is, for instance, very sharp on feminism. ("Women don't believe there are neutral zones: what males call neutral they call male.") Some of his literary criticism like this offhand comment on John Steinbeck and Ernest Hemingway, is genuinely penetrating:

> Steinbeck was always luckier than Hemingway in his film adaptations. He loved the medium . . . because he had a gift for dialogue but no corresponding talent for a modern kind of *récit:* in film, *récit* is left to the camera. Hemingway's dialogue is less realistic than it looks, but his *récit* is nerve and bone and very original and new.

But there is not nearly enough substance to this collection. Graham Greene once called Burgess "an avid if undiscriminating reader," and he is all too clearly willing to write about anything he is sent, from *Selected Letters of James Thurber* to *The New Grove Dictionary of Music and Musicians* to Edmund Wilson's *The Forties.* The results are, to put it mildly, careless and superficial. The editors of *Ernest Hemingway: Selected Letters 1917-1961* and *Shaw's Music* are separately described as having done "the expected fine job of editing." A review of a volume of Dickens's letters starts off "The energy of the man!" *Ancient Evenings* is praised, *The Executioner's Song* panned. For every flash of insight there are a dozen unreliable summary judgments.

This book is littered with hints of why Anthony Burgess is so ineffectual as a critic. One of them can be found in the preface: "And the need to keep within the limit of a thousand words or so is, as with the composing of a sonnet, an admirable formal discipline. When I have typed three pages of typescript and a bit over, I know that my allowable quota has been filled." . . .

It is possible to write on demand and produce an *oeuvre* of lasting interest. G. K. Chesterton (on whom Burgess writes briefly and well) did exactly that. To succeed, though, it is absolutely necessary to have something to say that goes beyond the compass of the object of criticism proper. The occasional pieces of Evelyn Waugh, for instance, have a weight and gravity which derive from Waugh's underlying preoccupation with the permanent things. By comparison, the occasional pieces of Anthony Burgess—Irishman, lapsed Catholic, and Joyce addict—are little more than well-worded fluff. His artistic credo comes from Mallarme: "Literature isn't made with ideas, it's made with words." Mr. Burgess has no larger ideas; his criticism consists solely of point-to-point responses cloaked in words galore. Wilfrid Sheed, writing in *Max Jamison,* speaks of "the dreary business of accreting an opinion." Mr. Burgess has it backward: his opinions are excreted, and in volume. . . .

Comparisons to Chesterton are not *prima facie* ridiculous, but this book suggests an altogether less comforting analogy. "It is no use being angry with Connolly," Edmund Wilson once wrote of Cyril Connolly, another prodigiously gifted Irishman who started out as a serious author and ended up a *feuilleton* machine. "Whatever his faults may be . . . he is one of those fortunate Irishmen, like Goldsmith and Sterne and Wilde, who are born with a gift of style, a natural grace and wit, so that their jobs have the freshness of *jeux d'ésprit,* and sometimes their *jeux d'esprit* turn out to stick as classics." Connolly managed to write two or three books of lasting value; Anthony Burgess, in a career infinitely more prolific, has had no such luck. Even *Earthly Powers,* a book clearly meant to serve as clinching masterpiece, was fumbled through garrulousness. Though *But Do Blondes Prefer Gentlemen?* is a far more modest undertaking, it is every bit as revealing of the witty, flawed artist within.

> *Terry Teachout, in a review of "But Do Blondes Prefer Gentlemen? Homage to QWERTYUIOP and Other Writings," in The American Spectator, Vol. 19, No. 3, March, 1986, p. 43.*

Valentine Cunningham

It was a happy day when Anthony Burgess put himself to school at Joyce's fiction. No one has re-written and lived off *Finnegans Wake* more productively. *The Pianoplayers* is in Burgess's most dazzling post-*Wake,* I'll-be-Shem-the-Punman mode: language-games, history, religion, art and sex remain his preferences.

His narrator is Ellen Henshaw, gossipy confider to the cassette-player of a wandering musical journalist. She is in retirement in France, notorious for founding Schools of Love that teach men how to play women, to do Hamletian things to their stops and their heartstrings just as if they were musical instruments. The clue for using musical lessons as the basis for instruction in lovemaking came from her father, a piano player, silent-movie accompanist, marathon musician, copious inventor of his own tunes, deft exploiter and adapter of other people's tunes, who taught his daughter to play the piano in no time at all and invented a Violin Method for the very young (since pinched by a wily Jap).

Billy Henshaw is Burgess's most congenial kind of consciousness, a capacious one which will take any amount of whatever his author chooses to pour into it in the way of obsessions, likes, dislikes, facts, philologies, knowledge of all sorts, Joycean quashed quotatoes, current puns and so on. Henshaw is a most likeable musician and womanizer, a virtuoso of extraordinary productivity and technical variety. Sweating away cheekily in the dark of his occupational orchestra-pits, he can accompany any film whatsoever, in any key. . . . He's a virtuoso, too, with words, done out of business by the talkies but in his own person a one-man talkie, a producer of dizzying arpeggios of words and words about words (including, naturally, words about the root meaning of the word *arpeggio*). "Language, girl, language", are his last words to his daughter from the floor of the Star Cinema's piano enclosure, on to which he has slumped dead-drunk after a hilarious send-up of Sid Schwartz and Emmanuel Rubinstein's C-of-E-sanctioned version of *The Light of the World*. And like her father, and the novel that contains them both, Ellen Henshaw minds nothing if not her language.

Billy's omnivorousness licenses the attractive eclecticism of Ellen's musico-sexual life's work, and the bustling opportunism of her narrative. Through her, Burgess is able to bang on gloriously about mothers-in-law, Eyeties, Catholic priests reading the racing pages in the confessional, Blackpool food, Prots who always talk of RCs, films, seduction, songs and music-hall turns. The resulting ragbag is as enjoyably comic-operatic in its farce and mayhem as are the various set-piece scenes in which father, daughter, landlord, landlady, seducers and seducees of either sex clash noisily on and off the public stage.

Teaching and lessons are the stuff of this fiction. Billy teaches piano and etymologies; Ellen's instructions are the sexual ones her paying customers get. They're also the education she hands out to us through the cassette-recorder, in things like the shape of pre-War Concert Party programmes or the diet of the northern poor that she was brought up on. Mainly, though, Billy, Ellen and Anthony Burgess join pedagogical forces to show how verbal marathons are made, how inventions can be sustained, words and text spun out.

Many key pages of this novel are taken up simply (or rather, complicatedly) with listings of the titles of numbers Billy plays on his attempted Marathon. The manner is Burgess's most direct tribute here to *Finnegans Wake*. Serious, joky, made-up, historically accurate and apt to their times, or anachronistically before their time, the titles are poured out, just like the reams of verse, rhymes and ditties, that Ellen can recite or Billy can remember. Billy can keep his show going, he can churn them out. Billy, we're told, "was never stuck". Nor, all this is a way of demonstrating, is Burgess. . . .

What Burgess's confident practice of naming and misnaming demonstrates is the power of names. Whatever their status, historical, intertextual, accurate, mistaken, real, unreal, they can sustain the unlikeliest of worlds in being. The sheer generative power of words was the *Wake*'s most potent lesson: a lesson, it is implied here, that is much bet-

ter for the young, though less easy to follow, than the Yamasaki Violin Method, stolen from Billy, that deludes you into thinking any kid can get to play Mozart in just a month.

Valentine Cunningham, "The Music-Marathon Man," in The Times Literary Supplement, *No. 4352, August 29, 1986, p. 933.*

Gene Lyons

Compared with such vast and erudite Burgess productions as *Earthly Powers* or *MF, The Pianoplayers* seems a relative trifle. . . .

In Mr. Burgess's work, however, trifles are rarely so playful as they may at first appear. Specifically, *The Pianoplayers* comes equipped with overtones of parable and hints of autobiographical significance that make it clear it's a little tale with a purpose. The difficulty lies in discerning just what that purpose may be.

Narrated by an English courtesan tastefully retired in Provence . . . the novel tells the story of her long-dead father's sad demise. Ellen Henshaw's dad was a professional piano player. . . . Ellen's dad, exactly like Mr. Burgess's own, earned his pittance providing musical accompaniment for silent films in the author's native Manchester. As La Belle Hélène, our narrator "was a professional too, just like my dad, but I was more the piano than the player, and I was usually played on by players who could hardly manage chopsticks. Still, they paid for their bit of a tune." . . .

[The] most memorable of the novel's modest charms is its vivid re-creation of the humble joys of working-class Manchester and Blackpool during the 1920's: HP sauce and chips, pork sausages, tea with condensed milk, but above all music and song. Mr. Burgess summons up wonderfully corny music hall routines featuring the Cockadoodle Doos and the long-legged soubrette Maggie Paramour. Best of all are the song titles: "You've Worked All Your Life for Me Mother Now Go Out and Work for Yourself" and "She Was as Pure as Snow and She Drifted."

But silent films put an end to burlesque, and the talkies, as the world knows, to live musical accompaniment in theaters. Again like Mr. Burgess's own father, our narrator's dad does his poor little career no good by breaking into "For He's a Jolly Good Fellow" during a reverent cinematic portrayal of the Resurrection of Christ, and "I'm a Girl What Works Hard for Her Living" at the appearance of Mary Magdalene. Not to mention, in another familiar Burgess theme, playing Roman Catholic hymns despite the admonition that only the Church of England's were acceptable.

But it's when the talkies arrive and dad's career—such as it is—appears doomed that the novel's didactic side begins to undermine its playfulness altogether. To her father, our heroine recalls, movies were unnatural, and even one-time music hall comedians like Stan Laurel and Charlie Chaplin "became ghosts, my dad would say, and even the big money they earned was a kind of ghost money." As an author who has been victimized by Hollywood (see *The Clockwork Testament*), Mr. Burgess has surely earned the right to say so.

But few readers will know what to make of the novel's climax, in which Ellen's desperate dad hires on with a promoter for a piano marathon—30 days of nonstop music or die. It is not possible, short of giving away a good deal more of the plot than is fair to author or reader, to indicate just how mechanical the tale becomes. Genius aside, I doubt there is a novelist alive who doesn't fear that movies and television are killing off books for good. Taken together with the autobiographical hints, the effect, if one may be forgiven putting it this way, is rather like that of a player piano tinkling out a song called "He Worked Like a Dog and They Fed Him on Scraps." Unconvincing, that is, and faintly embarrassing.

> Gene Lyons, " 'She Was as Pure as Snow and She Drifted'," in The New York Times Book Review, *November 2, 1986, p. 7.*

Erica Jong

[*The Pianoplayers*] masquerades as the not quite literate (let alone literary) first-person account of her life by a retired courtesan/call girl, the unsinkable Ellen Henshaw, (who, in our day, might have become the Mayflower Madam). Ellen Henshaw rises from humble beginnings to complete happiness because she recognizes—in a direct, uncomplicated Wife-of-Bathish sort of way—the power of lust in our lives and how it relates to pianoplaying. The daughter of a hack piano player who, when he works, accompanies silent movies, Ellen is raised in seedy rooming houses and what the British call "bed-sitters" by her loving, drunken, brawling dad. Though he is no "Paderooski," as he himself would be the first to admit, he loves music as perhaps only a third-rate musician can; he knows and admires what he cannot do. He tries to pass this gift on to his daughter, who is pretty hopeless as a pianist but who finds another application for his lessons and dedicates her life to teaching men to play the keyboard of a woman's body.

So much for the rudimentary plotline. The happy ending I will not divulge; suffice it to say that the *The Pianoplayers* is, among other things, a spoof of what publishers like to call a "generational saga" and it takes us through four generations of "pianoplaying" of various sorts. The analogy between sex and music is elaborated in a variety of ways, both satirical and touching.

Among the many delights of this novel are its literary music lessons and the colloquial voice of the narrator-heroine, who is dictating to and simultaneously arguing with a young man, a writer, whom she has captured to play Horatio to her Hamlet. A kind of generational war goes on between Ellen and her amanuensis Rolf Marcus, and through its skirmishes we come to see the worlds of the '20s, '30s, and '40s and how they differed from our own both in style and content. I know of no other modern writer, except Joyce, who has used the metaphor of music so successfully and wittily in fiction. There is one whole chapter here dedicated to the rudiments of the piano, and it is a tribute to Burgess' humor and sense of language that this chapter is as amusing as the chapters on Ellen's adventures in high-class brothels. (pp. 1, 6)

If you have read none of his novels, *The Pianoplayers* is as good a place to start as any. It is breezy, entertaining, funny with a center of considerable substance. It also contains some of the most delightful comic characters to lurch through recent fiction, characters worthy of Smollett or Dickens.

If I have any quibble with *The Pianoplayers,* it is the same minor quibble I have with certain classics like *Moll Flanders,* in which a male writer impersonates a female heroine yet inadvertently glosses over some of the most wrenching passages of a woman's life: maternity and child-rearing. Picaros both, Ellen and Moll are rather flippant about maternity—flippant in ways I imagine only a male writer could suppose women to be. Only in novels do women drop babies with never a backward remorseful glance. Obviously Burgess intends Ellen Henshaw to be the male ideal of a lusty woman, determined to live like a man despite her biological predisposition to loyalty, Angst and longing. Bored by babies, Ellen nevertheless has strong dynastic feelings, and eventually she must triumph as the unconventional matriarch of an unconventional clan. Like most women of great strength and *joie de vivre,* her life comes to exemplify the proverb "living well is the best revenge." The details of this good living I leave for the delighted reader to discover.

Anthony Burgess is not only one of the most versatile artists of the English language but he is truly wise about the ways sex and music bind and harmonize our lives. [*The Pianoplayers*] should be both a cause for celebration and an excuse to go back over his amazing oeuvre and trace the evolution that brought him to this ebullient display of his extraordinary gifts. (p. 6)

> Erica Jong, "Anthony Burgess and the Music of Love," in Book World—The Washington Post, *November 16, 1986, pp. 1, 6.*

Robertson Davies

There is a danger that [*Little Wilson and Big God*] may not be received with the seriousness it deserves—though it is far more important than the usual literary autobiography. An author's life is rarely adventurous, and if he has a personal story to tell it is of the inner journey and the struggle with art. This first of a projected two-volume autobiography ends just as we have come to the beginning of Anthony Burgess's story as a writer. He is already 42 and has written seven novels and a novella, but he regards those as byworks thrown off by a man who was really a composer. He has received what appears to be a sentence of death from a physician, and the time has come to get down to business and provide as best he can for the wife who is to be his widow. A serious man, under great stress, and something more—something that makes the story of this provocative English novelist and man of letters turbulent and gripping: he is a man of faith and strong moral conviction.

Not by any means, however, a Holy Joe, clinging to the Old Rugged Cross. He is a rebel Roman Catholic, always in hot water with his superiors. The title of his book comes from an encounter he had with the principal of Xaverian College when he was 17. He was being thoroughly blown up for heresy, because he had said that the sacraments were nothing, and love and right living everything. Father Myerscough would have none of that talk, which sounded (and sounds) like left-wing Protestantism. Later the principal was heard to tell a colleague that it was "a sad business, a matter of 'little Wilson and big God.' " . . .

There are elements in the human spirit of which sociologists know nothing, for who could have foreseen that little Wilson would teach himself to write music by studying scores, would devour as much of that useless English literature as he could lay hands on and become an expert in the science of English speech? Who would have expected him to emerge from such intellectual and physical squalor without a violent class prejudice of the sort that fueled the Angry Young Men until they themselves achieved a degree of fame and prosperity? Who would have expected him to deplore the lack at Manchester University of those Epicene Exquisites who added so much spice to life at Oxford and Cambridge? This is a man of extraordinarily capacious and generous intellect—except in one area.

That area is the Catholicism against which he rebelled and against which he tirelessly inveighs, but which he insists is the one true faith. Lambaste the church as he will, he insists that there is no salvation outside it. He declares the church to be "a bad mother" and sometimes merely "a rough bludgeon for knocking the Protestant Midlands." But the Roman Catholic Church is the only church, and his contempt for the Church of England is total—total as it can be only in one who will not permit a fair crack of the whip to Erasmus and Archbishop Laud.

The nub of the matter seems to be this: the great achievement of the Protestant Reformation was to take the soul of mankind out of the keeping of the church and deliver each man's soul into his own hands, to be lost or found through his own striving toward God. Anthony Burgess seems to be very much a Protestant in this respect, but he cannot cut the umbilical cord that unites him to the Great Mother, and her promise to make all well in return for perfect obedience. But out of this fierce tension comes the energy that makes him a vastly prolific, adventurous and high-spirited novelist (***A Clockwork Orange, Earthly Powers***), one of the very few whose books, in the present day, one can pick up with the certainty that they will not contain another load of fashionable grief.

The work under review is a good example. It tells of deeply serious and sometimes tragic things, but it tells of them with an ebullience, a rapidity and an overflowing, joyously deployed vocabulary that makes it a delight to read. In his preface, Mr. Burgess calls the book his *Confessions,* in the manner of St. Augustine and Rousseau, but there is nothing in it of the minatory gravity of the saint or the self-indulgent egotism of the romancer. Here there are high spirits in abundance, but not a word that could mislead an innocent mind. A truly innocent mind, of course; not the pink vacuity of a ninny.

The life of a man up to the age of 42 must, of course, include most of his sex life. Mr. Burgess's adventures strengthen the impression that sex, which is an imperative in any life, is not an end in itself, the richest of all pursuits and the fountain of spiritual fulfillment. He approached it with all a boy's enthusiasm and romanticism, and it is greatly to his credit that enthusiasm and romanticism remain after a good deal of rough-and-tumble and a first marriage that was at the farthest remove from idyllic. It is a grim moment when a letter to an English doctor, from

a colleague in Malaya who had been examining Mr. Burgess and had decided that he was suffering from an inoperable brain tumor, says casually, "His wife is a chronic alcoholic." The disintegrating marriage ended only with his wife's death. It is no wonder that Mr. Burgess speaks of the shallowness of those who do not take the great, grim doctrine of hell seriously.

Autobiography is a remorselessly demanding literary form when it is undertaken seriously. Not the self-justifying blatherings of politicians, not the "as-told-to" popular works in which a film star's life is invented by a hack with a turn for sensationalism, but the true attempt to come to terms with one's own life is the test for an artist and a man of principle. Nobody succeeds completely, for nobody can be fully objective about himself. Mr. Burgess, weighted with a Catholic conscience of which any Calvinist might be proud, speaks endless ill of himself in his character as a man of principle, but the artist who does the writing gives us constant assurance that these judgments are too severe. Bad men do not give such unfailing literary pleasure, so many hearty guffaws, so many illuminations of wit as Mr. Burgess offers in this first volume of his story. The test is that we await the next volume with high expectation.

Robertson Davies, "Confessions of a 'Useless Man'," in The New York Times Book Review, *February 22, 1987, p. 9.*

Robert M. Adams

Early on in [*Little Wilson and Big God*], Burgess pays tribute to the Manchester of his youth by describing some typical Lancashire jokes—sour, all of them, with a thick flavoring of disgust, and turning inevitably on death. He was born into a lower-middle-class family; his mother and only sister died when he was young, and though his father—a professional drinker—soon remarried, neither the stepmother nor anyone else in the extended family ever gave a tinker's damn for little Johnny. He is quite cool and judicious about the matter; he does not specify maltreatment or neglect, but a cold and callous indifference that, he says, left its mark on his work. It certainly left its mark on this autobiography.

Covering about 40 years of John Wilson's life—only toward the end of the book does he start to think of himself as Anthony Burgess—the present volume describes an unbroken string of struggles after the most marginal forms of success. It's a record of crucial examinations failed or inadequately, narrowly passed, of dreary job-applications denied, of truculent quarrels with disdainful authorities, of rejections and humiliations, accompanied by a recurrent overtone of physical squalor—drunken binges, whoring around, plus a heavy dose of direct stench, filth and putrescence. A good deal of this seems to have been deliberate; Burgess made a point, during the war, of staying in the ranks, from what he indicates was class loyalty. But it was less love of the working class, to all appearances, than a blistering, blighting, blasphemous contempt for the Establishment.

And yet from the first, he was evidently a man of remarkable talents. Two of his four gifts were verbal; though he could fail Latin examinations of no great difficulty when passing them would advance his career, he really had an extraordinary gift of tongues, and could pick up, in addition to Greek, Russian, German, French, Spanish and Italian, several dialects of Malaysian. He was a poet of standing, and an immensely inventive comic/macabre novelist. He was a musician, not much more than a barroom performer on the piano, but a composer with several symphonies to his credit, as well as numerous smaller pieces. And he had a gift for drawing which might have led to a career as a painter had he not been utterly and incurably color-blind. Jack-of-all-trades and master of none, he was driven for years on end into a succession of marginal civil-servant jobs, teaching assignments of the most disheartening and disagreeable sort. Meanwhile he suffered through the vicissitudes of a terrible marriage with an openly promiscuous, frequently hysterical and ultimately alcoholic wife, whom Big God apparently forbade him to divorce or even leave decisively. The few embarrassed and belated words about love that appear in the book are spoken, almost elegiacally, about Lynne. They weigh on the heart like lead: the *poor* bastard.

No life divides more sharply than Anthony Burgess' into two volumes. This first one ends with him back in England after being kicked out of a final tropical assignment, hospitalized with an undiagnosed ailment which turns out to be an incurable cerebral tumor and left with a prognosis of one more year of life at most. His wife is scarcely better off than he is. Foreseeing that she will soon be a widow, he anticipates that she will need something to live on, and sits down to write in his year as many novels as possible. Among them, the reader may anticipate, will be his first major success, *A Clockwork Orange.* After that will be another story, to be told in the next volume.

It's a colorful canvas that Burgess has had to fill, from the provincial life of ignobly decent Manchester, to student highjinks at Manchester University, to service in the propaganda and education units of the British Army; from wartime duty on Gibraltar to ragtag journalism in London to temporary jobs in Malaysia and Brunei as they prepared for independence. Why then doesn't Burgess make a more readable book out of it? For one thing, in these 40 years of his life he doesn't seem to have encountered anyone, including his wife, who couldn't be reduced to a caricature. Nobody seems to have anything like an interior. There is an enormous amount about boozing with casual companions, wenching with faceless girls and run-ins with contemptible authorities, academic and military. But everything flickers past like a movie projector out of control, outline figures capering across a blank screen till they fatigue the eye. Several mannerisms in particular contribute to this effect. Burgess is given to private allusions, unexplained dialect jokes in his many languages, military abbreviations familiar to him but to nobody else. He has at best what the French call *le style plat,* and in this book he hasn't taken much trouble with his sentences. . . . (pp. 3, 8)

One enters the book with a considerable interest in, and sympathy for, Little Wilson; one puts it down with the dismaying sense of having been blocked into the corner of a pub, horribly deprived of a closing hour, by a self-absorbed old monologist with an undying grievance. (p. 8)

Robert M. Adams, *"The Confessions of Antho-ny Burgess,"* in Book World—The Washington Post, *March 1, 1987, pp. 3, 8.*

Gore Vidal

Little Wilson and Big God, "Being the First Part of the Autobiography" . . . , long as it is, takes [Burgess] only to the age of forty-two in 1959 when he was told that he had an inoperable brain tumor, and a year to live. In order to provide for [his wife] Lynne, he started turning out books at a prodigious rate, and now, twenty years after her death, he still, undead, goes on. Incomparable British medicine ("In point of fact, Dr. Butterfingers, that's *my* scalpel you're standing on") is responsible for the existence of easily the most interesting English writer of the last half century. Like Meredith, Burgess does the best things best; he also does the worst things pretty well, too. There is no other writer like him, a cause of some alarm to others—him, too. Now, in the sad—the vain, I fear—hope that once we've known the trouble he's seen we will forgive him his unfashionable originality and prodigiousness, he makes confession not to merciful God but to merciless us.

The subject of the first part of the autobiography bears, I should guess, very little resemblance to the man who wrote it, who, in turn, bears no resemblance at all to the John Wilson that he was born and continued to be until his relatively late blossoming as a novelist. It is not that he bears false witness; it is, simply, the problem of recalling past time as it occurs to someone in a present where "I have trouble with memory, especially of names." Also, this testament is not extravagantly and carefully shaped like one of his novels; rather, it is doggedly improvised (from diaries? There is a single reference to a diary).

Burgess tells us that in 1985, he was in New York's Plaza Hotel, waiting for a car to take him to the airport. Suddenly, like Gibbon on the steps of Santa Maria d'Aracoeli, he decided to tell this story. But when he started to write, I don't think that he had a clue where he was going or how he was going to get there. Fortunately, he has not the gift of boredom. He can make just about anything interesting except on those occasions when he seems to be writing an encoded message to N. Chomsky, in celebration not so much of linguistics as of his own glossolalia, so triumphantly realized in his screenplay for *Quest for Fire.* (p. 3)

Three themes emerge in the course of the autobiography. The first, religion. What it means to be lower-middle-class Roman Catholic in the English mid-Midlands; what it means to lose—or lapse from—one's faith; what it means to be forever on the alert for another absolute system to provide one with certainty about everything. At one point, in Southeast Asia, Burgess was tempted to convert to Islam. But Islamic bigotry distressed him; and he backed away. Now,

in old age I look back on various attempts to cancel my apostasy and become reconciled to the Church again. This is because I have found no metaphysical substitute for it. Marxism will not do, nor will the kind of skeptical humanism that Montaigne taught. I know of no other organization that can both explain evil and, theoretically at least, brandish arms against it.

This is bewildering to an American of the Enlightenment; but as the twig was bent. . . . Also, to the extent that Burgess has any political ideas at all, he's deeply reactionary, and capable of such blimpisms as, "In February the Yalta Conference sold half of Europe to the Russians."

The second theme is sex. After the glut of the salacious sexy Seventies and the hysteria of the anxious AIDSy Eighties, it is hard for those who grew up after the great divide—World War II—to realize that just about the only thing any of us ever thought about was getting laid. Burgess went into the British army at twenty-three in 1940. Three years later, at seventeen, I went into the American army. Each got out of the army in 1946; each with the nei-ther-fish-nor-fowl rank of warrant officer. Although Burgess was for all practical purposes married to Lynne when he was scooped up by the army, he, too—like the rest of us—was introduced to a world of sex where every tradi-tional barrier had fallen with a crash. There was a general availability unknown to previous generations of Europe-an—much less American—Christendom. Those of us who joined the orgy in our teens often failed, in later life, to ac-quire the gift of intimacy. Burgess himself had other prob-lems; innocently—always innocently—he tells us about them, unaware that an autobiography is no place for truth as opposed to the true: Augustine's sententious nonsense about those pears should have taught him that.

Because Burgess had no mother, he writes,

> I was not encouraged to express tenderness. I was reared emotionally cold. . . . I regret the emotion-al coldness that was established then and which, apart from other faults, has marred my works.

At least one dull American book-chat writer thought that this was really insightful stuff; and moved Burgess several rungs down the literary ladder. He cannot love; *ergo,* he cannot write. He is not warm; *ergo,* he is not good. He is cold; *ergo,* he is bad. Burgess is very conscious of his re-viewers but I do not think that he has ever quite grasped the deep ignorance of the average American book-chat writer, who is in place to celebrate obedience and confor-mity to that deadly second-rateness which has character-ized our garrison state for the last third of a century.

Recently a television documentary on one of our public schools was screened for the local school board. The board was near rapture. But when the public saw the film, the board realized that what they had admired, the successful attempt to destroy individuality in the young, did not play so well with the TV audience, hardly themselves nay-sayers. Since power not sex is true motor to human life, the powerless often prefer to die. That is why today's young do not eat goldfish. They kill themselves.

Burgess's thirty-year marriage is more harrowing to read about than, perhaps, to have lived. At first, he was obliged to share Lynne with a pair of well-off brothers, one of whom might bring her the money that he could not. Then Burgess attended the party that was World War II. Final-ly, Lynne and the brothers parted and the open marriage of the Burgesses gaped anew. Postwar, Burgess taught in Malaya and Brunei. He and she each drank a bottle of gin a day. She made love to a number of men; he to women. She fought with everyone; demanded a divorce; was rec-onciled by the publication of his first books. Fortunately, he enjoys being humiliated by women, a theme that runs through the novels, giving them their sexual edge (see the final Enderby volume). Fascinating; but mysterious—like Grace. Anyway, he loved her, he tells us, for thirty years.

Religion, sex, art—three themes that, unlike the Trinity, never become one. Finally, despite the distractions of the first two, it is the third that matters because that is all that's ever left. Burgess himself does not seem quite to know what to make of his novels. Wistfully, he goes on and on about music and the structure of language but, in the end, he is a writer of prose, a novelist, a sometime movie and television writer. There was a time whenever a producer came to me for a script on Jesus or the Borgias, or even Jesus and the Borgias, I'd send them on to Bur-gess, who would oblige. Today, he is the best literary jour-nalist alive, as V. S. Pritchett is the best literary critic. (pp. 6, 8)

This is not the place (nor does space afford, as Henry James would coyly note, having filled his review of some dim novel with a series of glittering false starts) to describe the twenty-eight novels of Anthony Burgess. So I shall stick to what he himself has to say about them in his mem-oir. One thing becomes clear: like so many highly serious brilliant men, he has no natural humor or comic sense as opposed to verbal wit. In thrall to Joyce's *Finnegans Wake,* he dreamed of the marriage of high literature to high music. When he wrote his first novel, about wartime Gibraltar, he gave it to an editor at Heinemann. "It was, he said, funny. I had not, in fact, intended it to be funny, but I assumed the right posture of modesty on this revela-tion that I was a coming comic novelist." Dutifully, seri-ously? he wrote several more novels set east of Suez; and each turned out comic, even though he was writing of sad exotic places, and people; but, of course, he was writing about the painful untidy lives of Anthony and Lynne in far-off places where, as Horace (no, not Greeley) so pithily put it, "People change their skies, not their feelings, when they rush overseas." The "rush" is often funny while "overseas," for the Brits, always is. Thus, tragedy turns out comedy.

Of Burgess's fourth novel (***The Right to an Answer***) he writes, it "was almost entirely invention. That I could in-vent was the final proof, to me, that I had not mistaken my vocation." For the Burgess reader, the great break-through came after his death sentence, when he was furi-ously writing and inventing. In 1944, the pregnant Lynne had been robbed and beaten up in a London street by four American soldiers. She aborted. Burgess turned this true story into a novel that he has small regard for because the world at large has such a high regard for the film version, done by another, of ***A Clockwork Orange.*** Burgess hurls the story into a future London where four local louts have been Sovietized and speak a new vulgate, part London prole, part Russian. The result is chilling; and entirely other. When Burgess moves away from his own immedi-ate life, his books come most startlingly alive, if ink mark-ings on mute paper can ever be called a life form or even its surrogate.

In the light of his three obsessions, Burgess wanted to bring God into the novel in a big way, with Berlitz-cum-Joyce symbolism, and resonating like a struck cymbal with atavistic Lorenzian blood myths. Happily, he failed. Of an early novel, he writes, "The realism overcame the symbolism. This usually happens when the novelist pos-

sesses, which Joyce did not, a genuine narrative urge."
One detects a regret here, an acknowledgement that the
Wilsonian passion for *Finnegans Wake* has no place in the
Burgessian novel. But then, "I see that the novel, an essentially comic and Protestant art form, is no place for the
naked posturing of religious guilt." He means of course
the English novel in this century. A twentieth-century
novel each of us admires, *Doctor Faustus,* has roots in the
human bloodstream (spirochete-ridden as it is) in a way
not allowed by our meager culture and overrich language.

If Burgess is obsessed with sex in his memoirs he uses sex
judiciously in his novels and in the best (he will not agree),
"The Enderby Four," as I call them—*Inside Mr. Enderby, Enderby Outside, The Clockwork Testament, or Enderby's End,* and *Enderby's Dark Lady*—he uses his obsession much as Nabokov did in *Lolita* to make a thousand
and one points about literature and life and their last
human sanctuary, the motels of America. On the showing
of the fugitive poems in the autobiography, Burgess himself is not much of a poet but his invention, the poet Enderby, on the showing of *his* poems is one of the finest of
contemporary poets and ought to be anthologized as himself, with symposia devoted to his art, and no reference to
either Wilson or Burgess as amanuensis. There is no invention quite so extraordinary as that which surpasses, at
inventing, the original inventor. Baron Frankenstein's creation just hangs out. But Enderby's poems have the effect
that only the best writing can have on a reader who also
writes. They make him want to write poems, too; and sur-
pass self.

The Burgess who doubts his comic sense or, rather, was
slightly appalled that his "serious" works made others
laugh must know by now that the highest art, which is
comedy, is grounded in obsession. With a bit of luck (a
Roman Catholic education?) Melville might have created
a masterpiece in *Moby-Dick.* As it is, we laugh—though
not enough—at Captain Ahab (*Pierre* is funnier). But Burgess was wise enough to allow *his* obsessions with religion,
sex, language, to work themselves out as comedy. Also, he
has been able to put to good use his passion, rather than
obsession, for language and its forms, and his lively restless inventions have considerably brightened the culturally flat last years of our century. How he managed to do
this is implicit, if not always explicit, in the pages of *Little
Wilson and Big God,* which might better be called *Little
Wilson and Big Burgess,* who did it his, if not His, way.
(p. 8)

> *Gore Vidal, "Obsession," in* The New York
> Review of Books, *Vol. XXXIV, No. 8, May 7,
> 1987, pp. 3, 6, 8.*

Robert O. Evans

Two of Anthony Burgess's early novels, *A Clockwork Orange* and *The Wanting Seed,* present an inverted vision of
society at some date in the not-too-distant future. Thus
both are dystopias or anti-utopian novels in the broadest
sense. Burgess himself prefers the term *cacotopia;* "it
sounds worse than dystopia," he says in a much later
work, *1985.* Both the early novels appeared in the same
year, 1962, suggesting that Burgess became interested in
an anti-utopian approach to literary structure somewhat
before that time, had his fling, and went on to other, possi-

bly better, subjects. Then, several years later, in 1978, he
returned to the earlier interest with *1985,* which is both
a fictionized essay on the subject of cacotopias, the language *Newspeak,* and Orwell's *1984,* and a novella in the
same spirit. The essay part of *1985* tells us a good deal
about Burgess's preferences in the genre, making clear a
good many things about the earlier novels that had been
matters of speculation among the critics. For instance,
1985 is firmly rooted in Orwell and pretty much ignores
Aldous Huxley's *Brave New World,* that other famous English dystopia from the era. Orwell dealt primarily with
a society constructed in denial of freedom and personal
liberty, subjects close to Burgess's heart; Huxley was more
concerned with the loss of pleasure. (p. 253)

Both earlier books and *1985* deal with what might be
called relevant social matters, reflecting concerns of their
generation. *The Wanting Seed* might be considered an
essay on the population explosion—almost a Malthusian
document—while *A Clockwork Orange* deals primarily
with teenage violence and amorality. *1985* presents a larger canvas, freedom in the modern world (to borrow a
phrase from Maritain). A still later work, *The End of the
World News,* only a third of which is properly a dystopia,
deals with the end of the world, or, more precisely, how
people might behave in the face of a planetary cataclysm.
There we find Burgess expanding his range of interest immensely, not simply using anti-utopian machinery to discuss still another aspect of twentieth-century society. Both
earlier novels are heavily larded with violence, so much so
that, were they not set in the future, and identifiable with
a number of other works with similar concerns, such as
Eugene Zamyatin's *We* or Orwell's *1984,* one might suspect Burgess of borrowing a page from the French *nouveau roman* and hanging his two 1962 books on fictive
structures dependent on violence for their very shapes. (p.
254)

[Of] what does *A Clockwork Orange* warn us? Social conditions over which we have no control? It is rather—I
have argued the point elsewhere—an expression of disgust
and revulsion about what has happened to society in our
lifetimes. It does not warn us to be careful not to follow
a certain political course, as do most of the other books
in the convention. It is, to be sure, a subtle work, often
pointing a finger at what Burgess considers to be the cause
of our situation. The climate of violence, of which Alex is
the teenaged exemplar, exists in a Britain in the near future, and the possibility exists that it is man's fallen nature,
in conjunction with his institutions, that has brought
about this dreadful situation. The book does not deal with
the consequences of political action. It is not an attack on
a Soviet-like system, though one can hardly doubt that the
author had little use for a Russia that could send Siniavsky
and Daniel to a concentration camp, and Sakharov to exile
and psychological rehabilitation, for speaking the truth as
they saw it. Neither is it an attack on the permissive society of the United States, though Burgess implies that at
least part of the fault in the England he depicts can be
blamed on the two giant superpowers. The violence of the
young gangsters is generally considered to be an American
trait; the language they speak has close relations to Russian, as I have also said. Burgess tells what he thinks about
the superpowers: "As for America, that's just the same as
Russia. You're no different. America and Russia would
make a very nice marriage."

The Wanting Seed deals in different themes. The subject of this book is man's natural desire to live and perpetuate himself, more particularly the results in some not-too-distant future of the population explosion. We are given a glimpse of a society in which motherhood is not honored, in which love as an encouragement to reproduce is evil, where homosexuality is approved, and where stupid, meaningless war is not a Malthusian catastrophe but an accepted means of keeping the population in balance with the food supply. (One may be reminded of some of the remarks made by pacifists about the American adventure in Vietnam, though Burgess wrote before that time.)

The book grows more disgusting, or more disgusted with human nature, with every chapter, finally turning to cannibalism as a solution for hunger. It is not the events on which the fable is hung that especially concern the reader, but rather the fact that this portrait, too, while outwardly dystopian, is not calculated as a warning—any more than *A Clockwork Orange* is. It is more an expression of vast loathing over what the author, a realist of no mean talent, makes us believe may almost be inevitable. It shakes us as Malthus, in quite a different way, shook the roots of his society. But it does not attribute the troubles of the world to political actions nor to instructions about which we might still do something. No, the worst has already happened. Man has outproduced the food supply. Even the most stringent controls can do nothing to alleviate the situation. From there Burgess predicts a sort of cyclical social progression (which I hardly believe we should take seriously), as hopeless in one phase as it is in another.

Neither *A Clockwork Orange* nor *The Wanting Seed* really fits the dystopian convention Burgess inherited. He borrows some of its devices, but at heart his statements are different. In these novels it is the statement about mankind, not the fictive structure in which it is embedded, that matters. If we search a little deeper, we may conclude that Burgess in these books is really closer to Jonathan Swift than Orwell or Zamyatin. We may discover, if we push matters a bit, that he is really closer to Milton's *Paradise Lost* than any of his predecessors in the dystopian convention. What Zamyatin is saying is that if we persist on the Soviet political course we may destroy something in our society and in ourselves which is precious (though a racial memory may remain). Burgess is saying that because of what we are (translate because of man's fallen nature) something dreadful is bound (or at least likely) to happen and happen quite soon—we can already see the beginnings (especially in *A Clockwork Orange*). In *1985,* in the essay portion, Burgess makes a rough division of mankind into Pelagians and Augustinians. "Bakunin believed that men were already good; Pavlov believed that men could be made good. . . . This was the ultimate Pelagianism." But he reserves his strongest disapproval for B. F. Skinner, appalled by Skinner's title *Beyond Freedom and Dignity*. In such works Burgess found the dissolution of virtually all worthwhile social values: "It was the sense of this division between *well* us and *sick* them [emphasis added] that led me to write . . . *A Clockwork Orange*." The tale that follows the essay portion of *1985* is by way of illustration. He does not say there is anything we can do about this situation, though I hasten to add I am not accusing him of cynicism. (There is, I suppose, a sense in which every writer—I almost said every decent writer—who draws such portraits hopes that his readers will understand them as object

lessons.) All Burgess says about his hopes and intentions is that the business of the novelist is to earn a living (see *The Novel Now*), beat the tide of life; that is, get the next story out while one is still in good health and has avoided the statistical accident. Not that he is entirely pragmatic; he does admit that "critics say there are certain persistent themes in my novels—the need to laugh in the face of a desperate future; questions of loyalty; the relationships between countries and between races."

In *The End of the World News* (1983) Burgess focuses his themes a little more strictly. This is a very unusual book, one which relates three disparate stories, a musical comedy about Leon Trotsky's visit to New York, a life of Sigmund Freud, and a science-fiction tale about the end of the world, or rather the end of our planet Earth. It is in the latter that he borrows from the dystopian convention, and then not heavily. The world does not come to an end because of what man has done politically or socially within his institutions. It does not end because he has unwisely produced a population in excess of the food supply, as in an earlier novel; but rather Earth disappears because of a cosmic accident. A planetlike structure called Lynx (appropriately) breaks into the solar system and finally into our orbit, and collides with Earth, destroying it. All this is foreseen by the astronomers and takes a certain length of time. What Burgess examines is the actions of men and women as they prepare for the inevitable, their idle hopes, and the very limited attempts to preserve the race in some sort of spaceship. For that he needs the machinery of science fiction, but his main interest seems to be partly psychological and partly theological. No one has a right to live. God made no promises of eternal life in the sense of mankind perpetuating himself through the generations forever. The solar system had a beginning, and it must have an end. What Burgess does is push that end into the not-too-distant future once more. Theologically his positions are traditional. The fictions in which he presents them are what we find unusual. We should not forget that Burgess is, after all, a Catholic.

Should we then dismiss his books as latter-day examples of the dystopian convention cut rather finer than the predecessors? Not quite, I think, for though he rather obviously uses the convention, he is not playing Cassandra for his audience. Burgess is certainly not a conventional artist, and he has perhaps been much misunderstood. Some critics and many readers take him for an *avant-garde* liberal, but if we dig deeply into what he has to say, that is exactly what he is not. He has little sympathy for theories of progress or the perfectibility of mankind. He is much more traditional in a Christian sense, closer probably to William Golding than to George Orwell despite his pervasive interest in the latter. He strives to express the truth, as he sees it, in the most original way he can. He is an experimenter, in the sense that Shakespeare was, a writer never content with something he had produced no matter how nearly perfect it may seem to the reader. He is in constant struggle to find a form (and a language) for the truth he expresses.

In that respect he reminds us again of Zamyatin. One of the charges levied against Zamyatin and the Serapion Brethren was that they were too much concerned with form—they were, in an age which denigrated not only form but even good writing, formalists (though strictly speaking we reserve that term for the school of criticism that grew up in Russia beginning before the Revolution). This is not the place to discuss Zamyatin's "functional expressionism" that he preached to his followers nor the "mother image" on which his works often hang. But there is a resemblance between what he tried to do with his writing and what Burgess seems to wish to accomplish. Both strive, as genuine artists, for a means of expression equal to the subjects which to them are serious, important, and quite unpleasant in terms of the societies in which each lives. I once wrote that Zamyatin is by far the better writer, that his books have a polish and subtlety of technique beyond Burgess's power, but that they share an impudence of expression. In *The Islanders* (1918), for example, Zamyatin creates an English vicar, Dewly, who is the author of a book called *Precepts of Compulsory Salvation.* Burgess can be equally impudent. He may not construct well-made novels. He sometimes seems to forget what he started out to accomplish, as in *Tremor of Intent,* which begins as super spoof of the James Bond or Eric Ambler sort of story and runs away from him; but he nearly always manages to shock his audience or somehow sting it into wakeful alertness. "It is not always easy," he has said, "to become a great novelist." But when I wrote that he lacked the stature of Zamyatin, Burgess had not written *1985, The Napoleon Symphony, Earthly Powers* nor *The End of the World News,* to mention only some of the bigger works. I rescind what I said then. If only for their language and techniques these books make him a great novelist.

He is even more so an experimental novelist, more than Zamyatin, more than Robbe-Grillet and the other writers in the school of the *nouveau roman,* more (perhaps because he is so indefatigable) than any other writer in English today. He has sought since his very early book *A Vision of Battlements* (in which, he says, he simply set out to recall his wartime experiences in Gibraltar) to find new ways of expressing devastating truths, not perhaps so subtly as the French novelists but quite as deliberately. His force is language while theirs perhaps is structure. This is the light, then, in which I think his dystopian works should be read. We may fault him on several grounds, primarily for not having always written well-made books, but not for any ambiguity of intention. His dystopian works are not calculated as warnings but rather as expressions of what he considers to be the truth of the human condition. (pp. 261-65)

Robert O. Evans, "The 'Nouveau Roman', Russian Dystopias, and Anthony Burgess," in British Novelists since 1900, *edited by Jack I. Biles, AMS Press, 1987, pp. 253-66.*

Malcolm Bradbury

Burgess is one of our most likeable writers, and one who is well entitled by now to claim all the freedoms of pastiche and prolixity he likes to claim. The Enderby books are perhaps a special clue to him, a sequence of tales about a poet-lecher much tormented by sex, death and literary misfortune, where the surrogate role of the author figure seems more nakedly used than usual. These playful literary romps are normally founded on what nowadays is called an intertextual relation with previous literary works, with Burgess parodying his reading not only in other writers but reconstructing and recalling work of his own. Thus *The Clockword Testament, or Enderby's End,* not only allows him to reconsider the critics in print and life who raged at his finest novel, but allowed him to bring Enderby to his end in a death of complicated sexual torment. Typically in Burgess, ends, though they matter much, simply breed new beginnings, text being about life but staying text. In due time there came *Enderby's Dark Lady or No End to Enderby,* which resurrected the hero, took him off to an American campus, had him write the book to a musical of Shakespeare's life, gave him a real dark lady, as well as the chance to do lyrics, and permitted several crucial textual interpretations and interpolations to be introduced, the whole thing being done in a modern ragbaggy way of writing that shows the author as literary clown. And that Burgess is; what is striking is that the literary clown can also deliver, through methods not dissimilar, works of a striking substance.

An interesting case is the later Burgess novel *Earthly Powers* (1980)—big book Burgess at his most expansive and ambitious, and it brings out both the prolixity and the underlying creative force. Not surprisingly it teased the critics, and enraged some of them, being what it is, a cross between an Enderby romp and a novel of managed concern with major issues of morality, evil and violence, the issues that gave their force to *A Clockwork Orange.* It is the narrative of Kenneth M. Toomey, a very famous homosexual, lapsed Catholic English writer of middlebrow persuasion who, at the age of eighty, sets down the events of his sexual, religious and literary life across the spread of our violent, morally horrific and sexually neurotic century. Toomey acknowledges himself as in all things something of a compromiser, and a mildly evasive, sentimental writer whose books would, "from the technical angle, have seemed unremarkable when Arnold Bennett was a boy". But Burgess has devised his role to cross with the lives of many of the major literary figures of the century: Havelock Ellis and Norman Douglas, Ezra Pound and Aldous Huxley, Ernest Hemingway and Rudyard Kipling, James Joyce, Gertrude Stein and Alice B. Toklas all make brief appearances. Often their roles seem curiously statutory (Hemingway shadow-boxes and Pound says "Make it new"), but it is that encompassing grasp, that fullness and often learnedness of reference, that readerly and writerly largeness, that Burgessian grandeur that brings off most of this side of the book. Toomey may be a machine to work a fiction, but he crosses with the best and most revealing literary-historical locations—expatriate Paris and also the exotic Orient in the 1920s, Hollywood and also Hitler's Germany in the 1930s, and the Euro-American literary and media circuits of the 1950s and the 1960s. This is the amusing face of the book, played somewhere between pastiche and parody. It's comic and sometimes overdone, somewhat too ready to suggest that modernism was a fashionable idiocy, the bulk of modern writers pederasts, and literary creation always something hastily fitted in between endless sexual encounters—a truth, in my own experience, only very partially true. But it constructs a writerly history of writing that gives the pastiching freedom of fiction which nowadays Burgess regularly likes to claim, and there is much more than this to the novel, which is laying groundwork for a deeper purpose.

Toomey's personal struggles start in the pederastic Celtic

twilight—he is youthfully initiated into homosexuality in a Dublin hotel on what has to be the first Bloomsday, in 1904—but they develop to cross with the violence and sexual extremism of suicidal Paris, homicidal Nazi Germany, disordered modern America, disordered black Africa. And early on in the book he becomes embroiled with the Italian family Campanati, from Gorgonzola, the seat of the cheese, so to speak. He comes to know the priest of the family, Carlo Campanati, who is evidently *papabili* and indeed at last ascends to the Supreme Office, after various interventions from fate or the Divine Will. Fictional popes may be a well-used literary device from the decadence, which is where Toomey undoubtedly belongs, but Carlo is indeed the triumphant characterisation of this novel— an extraordinary figure of ecumenical leanings, superb digestion, divine fortune at the card-table. It is his belief that man is sinless, and evil exterior to us. He is a great performer of exorcisms, and at one point achieves the miraculous—indeed it is the recording of this that is the proferred occasion for Toomey's narrative. He is a deft negotiator of the modern historical world of pain, violence and holocaust—an adversary of Mussolini, a partisan smuggling Jews out of Italy to freedom. Through his story, and Toomey's own, we are taken through the world of modern evil, from solitary agonies and deaths to the collective genocides of the German concentration camps, and from the perverse gay ghettos of California to the new religious settlements where murderous gurus mount guards at the gates to keep the faithless firmly out and the faithful firmly in. The world of the book reaches from Kipling to Goebbels, Gertrude Stein to Himmler, and the loose autobiographical web that holds it together becomes a strange fable exploring the relation of literature to faith and history.

If later Burgess has an open and sometimes slapdash way of writing, it is because he writes still with a patent fertility of ideas and inventions. And the book, on one level amusing for its international historical record, its ranging scenario of settings and moods, turns into a good deal more. For Burgess is not only a buoyant and comically inventive writer, a great player with texts, but an urgent one. And the subject here reveals its largeness, its concern with the deepest of all paradoxes: the relationship between the local acts of good and evil we perform, and the larger plot of the world, which we call history. Like his own Enderby, or like his Toomey, Burgess is not all gold, and he says so. But he is fecund, pained, intelligent, and morally honest, and we must be very grateful for him.

Earthly Powers, for all its pastiche, is clearly intended as a serious modern novel. In this it compares interestingly with its successor, *The End of the World News* (1982), which is, we are advised, an "entertainment". It takes its punning title from the close-down announcements of the BBC Overseas news service, much listened to by expatriates like Burgess, who lives in Monaco. Or we may hope he does, for the book is presented as the posthumous papers of the author—who was, we are told, stirred to write it by seeing a photograph of President and Mrs Carter in the White House, watching three television channels simultaneously. The same dead author also believed that the three most important events of modern history were Freud's discovery of the subconscious, Trotsky's doctrine of world socialism, and the invention of the space rocket. These are the subjects of his three tales, happily put into some sort of order by a certain scholarly John B. Wilson, who reassures us in another way—for informed rumour tells us that Wilson is none other than the real name of the pseudonymous Anthony Burgess. And in fact the tales all mesh nicely, each being apocalyptic, about the ending of one world or another. In *Earthly Powers,* Burgess offered a tale that manages to be an intercontinental record of modern history, a massive literary memoir, a religious fable about the papacy, and a moral fable of our insufficiency in defining the powers of good and evil. In effect only apocalypse itself was missing; now *The End of the World News* collectively provides it.

Thus the story of Freud tells of the progressive advancement of his theories, his struggles with Viennese anti-semitism, with cancer of the jaw, and with the heresies of supporters like Jung and Otto Rank, reaching its apocalypse with Freud's expulsion from Austria by the Nazis. Burgess tells us all this in the form of a dramatised historical narrative, good on political events, rather weaker on evoking the significance of the subconscious for our modern awareness, and inclined to popular dramatic cliché. The Trotsky tale is about Trotsky's visit to New York in 1917, when he encounters the alluring New World just as revolution breaks out in Russia. Here the form is that of the Broadway musical, with much bouncy lyric-writing that somewhat mutes the sense of historical urgency. The spaceship story is a tale of a planet that comes from elsewhere and collides with our own as the century ends; as the sea-quakes rage and the cities tumble, fifty people go aboard an American spaceship to take a remnant of mankind into space. Now the method is SF, a genre Burgess clearly has a taste for, and does well. Like most SF, it is a parody of other SF, but it opens up to other Burgess territory, the world of the moral fable. *The End of the World News* is a book of pleasurable fertility, a virtuoso enterprise in switching styles and registers and modes of storytelling. The seriousness returns, as the spaceship leaves, and Burgess asks what we should save from the detritus of modern history. The answers are predictable, if one has been reading Burgess for long: a fragment of faith, a passion for gambling, some science and technology, some remnants of art. But above all, if the race is to continue, what it will need is a storyteller or two. It is not hard to believe that what Burgess would indeed take out into space is more, and more, and more stories. (pp. 337-40)

Malcolm Bradbury, "Busy Burgess," in his No, Not Bloomsbury, *Andre Deutsch, 1987, pp. 336-40.*

Richard Eder

It is good news that with *Any Old Iron* [Burgess] has found a roomy and resplendent vessel—well, it does yaw sometimes—for his acerbic unquietness. He gets all his polymath's baggage aboard: his scholarship, his fascination with history, his knowledge of music, his stubbornly eccentric characters, his gaiety and gloom and a rowdy crowd of Burgessian alter-egos.

Any Old Iron, to put it briefly, is the history of our century, told through the fortunes of seven highly individual members of a family that is Welsh and Russian in one generation and Welsh, Russian and Jewish in the next.

It contains, by way of prospectus: Joseph Conrad, the Titanic, World War I and World War II, the Spanish civil war, Stalin, Chaim Weizman, the establishment of Israel, a discursive band of Welsh nationalists, the pianist Artur Schnabel and King Arthur's sword, Excalibur.

Sailing, limping, stomping or sneaking through all this is the Jones family of Gwent (formerly South Wales) and the Jewish brother and sister—he, a terrorist and philosopher; she, a tympanist—who attach themselves to it. It may give a notion of the energy involved that the philosopher/terrorist is the blandest of the lot, possibly because he is the narrator and has the burden of reflection.

This narrator, Harry Wolfson, begins with a scholarly discussion of whether a sword sneaked out of the Soviet Union years before by his brother-in-law, Reg Jones, could have been the Arthurian Excalibur. As Harry tells his story, the sword will reappear from time to time, both as historical symbol and as a comically prosaic bit of plot.

Harry then goes back to the rich and picaresque history of Reg's father, David Jones, who ran away to sea after his own father caught him masturbating over an illustration of Belshazzar's Feast in the family Bible.

On one of David's first ships, the first mate is Joseph Conrad, who tells him forebodingly of the fragility of large passenger vessels. Sure enough, David finds himself working in the galley of the Titanic when it goes down. Surviving, he finds a cook's job in a Russian restaurant in Brooklyn, where Ludmila, the owner's beautiful daughter, chooses him for her husband.

They return to Wales, and David goes off to war, where he is repeatedly wounded and at one point, given up for dead. Ludmila, always decisive, goes to St. Petersburg in time to be injured in the first rioting of the Russian revolution. She returns home upon hearing that David has survived. They convalesce together, move to Manchester, and start a flourishing restaurant frequented by politicians and artists.

One of these is the pianist Schnabel. Burgess brings him on only long enough to pay a hackneyed compliment to Ludmila. He trots other renowned figures on and off in the same way. It is one of his signals that the Joneses are living in history.

Such a device can be deadly; yet Burgess' playfulness is so compelling that it works very well indeed. The author is having fun with us; and so are we; but it is armed fun. It is hard to convey the special success of this alternation of humor and seriousness, of droll individual stories with the deadly movements of nations. *Any Old Iron* is both merry and grave.

The story of David and Ludmila, told dryly and with a touch of Welsh musicality, is only a prologue to the stories of their children, Beatrix, Reg and Dan; of Zipporah, the tympanist, who marries Reg; and of Harry, who loves Beatrix, mostly in vain.

Each is sharply, outrageously individual, yet each has a link to history. Beatrix, a cool lover of many men, becomes a Soviet specialist and works in the Foreign Office. Harry will leave Manchester for Israel and teach bombs and assassinations to the country's "black" services, before returning and switching to philosophy.

Dan, slightly backward, is enamored of fish. He becomes a fishmonger after a rough time in World War II. Dan has a kind of second sight; it is he, who by chance and premonition, traces the passage of the Excalibur relic from the Benedictine abbey at Monte Cassino to Germany to the Soviet Union.

The central figure is Reg. Burgess has made him funny and human; he has also made him the Don Quixote of his time. He goes to Spain to fight for the Republic—or more precisely, being a small-nation Welshman, for Catalonia—and is imprisoned and beaten so savagely by Soviet agents that he loses his sense of smell.

Stationed in Gibraltar in World War II, he slips across to neutral Spain and, following Churchill's policy of total war, knifes a German in a bar. This produces a major military-diplomatic embarrassment, which Burgess handles wonderfully well. "I mean you don't conduct war in that manner," Reg's superior splutters. "The enemy's faceless and impersonal, if you see what I mean."

Reg is flown out under detention; he is to be sent to the bloodiest fighting in Normandy in hopes that he will get himself killed. Beatrix intervenes; he goes, instead, as an interpreter—all the Jones children speak Russian as well as Welsh—to an internment camp for Russians taken prisoner in Germany.

They will all be turned over to Soviet authorities, and most of them executed. Reg's quixotic efforts to intervene land him briefly on a ship bound for Odessa and, for a while, in a British sanitarium.

For some years, he practices private life uneasily. In a final complex and far-fetched venture, he manages to steal the Excalibur sword from the Hermitage Museum in Leningrad.

The Excalibur exploit is protracted and plotty; so are a number of other episodes. The book, in fact, suffers from padding and more ambitiousness than it can always carry.

Nevertheless, it is one of the best that Burgess has written in recent years. Reg, in particular, is a shining and memorable figure. His obstinate simplicity and perpetual betrayal by the causes he believes in recall Guy Crouchback in Evelyn Waugh's war trilogy.

Putting aside its wit, its fireworks and its ponderous exfoliation, *Any Old Iron* has the feeling of a memoir. Harry's final comment about Reg, who retires grumpily to Israel where he will live quietly and be unhappy, has a radiant sadness to it. It sounds like an author's farewell to a certain kind of arms.

> What he wanted, I think, was negative: not to have been reserved for the life of this century. Or he wanted, as we all do, reality transcending time. . . . The Roman ruins we stumbled through told us all about injustice that could never be avenged. The citrus fruits outlived them as they would outlive the law of Moses. It was a pity that Reg had lost his sense of smell.

> *Richard Eder, "Rags and Old Anthony," in* Los Angeles Times Book Review, *February 5, 1989, p. 3.*

John Crowley

The central family of [*Any Old Iron*] is that of David Jones, a Welsh runaway, sailor and cook, who survives the sinking of the *Titanic,* a piece of luck so extreme that he thinks it may have drained all such good luck from the rest of his life. He and his strong, beautiful Russian wife, whom he inherited from the owner of a Russian restaurant in Brooklyn where he washed ashore, produce three Russian-Welsh-English-speaking children: Reginald Morrow Jones (named for a Welsh nationalist writer his father admired), a boy fierce, visionary, a little mad; his brother Dan, not bright but greatly strong; and their sister, the beautiful and even stronger Beatrix.

These three are bound up with a brother and sister, Jews of Manchester, the stolid dark-minded Harry (who narrates this novel, though in Burgess' unmistakable voice) and Zipporah, percussionist, beautiful and strong. . . . Reg Jones marries Zipporah; Harry is once commanded to bed by Beatrix, and loves her without return ever after.

Together and apart, in Wales, in Manchester, Gibraltar, Petersburg (and Leningrad)—nearly round the world—these families act and suffer through not only the *Titanic* disaster, but the First World War, the Russian Revolution, the Spanish Civil War (Reg volunteers), the Second World War (Dan walks from a prison camp in East Germany to Odessa), and the foundation of Israel (Harry becomes an expert in terrorism and bodyguard to Chaim Weizmann.)

This sort of immense buffet of historical anecdote, great men encountered briefly, turning points of the century witnessed and horrors endured, is of course offered in dozens of thick books published every year and never read again. The difference is that Burgess is not a leaden slogger through Our Times, but a man born under Mercury, natal star of writers and liars; his love of words and what can be found inside them and built out of them is deep and infectious, and his characters share it to an unlikely degree. The characteristic Burgess novel is a series of set-pieces, constructed like floats out of linguistic arcana, historical facts and fancies, evocative place-names, all connected by a swift and supple prose that stops for little and yet is so fully-packed nothing seems left out. (Almost nothing: inevitably the Burgess cast can seem somewhat chivvied along by Burgess' verbal energy, and undergo transformations or reversals too sudden to be digested, by them or the reader.)

In a review of a new edition of the *Oxford Companion to English Literature,* Burgess showed how an entire novel might be constructed out of the entries on two facing pages of that wonderful miscellany. . . . The brightest and strangest thread in this big loose fabric is just such a yoking of unlikelihoods: a story of resurgent Welsh nationalism, at once poignant and preposterous, and the discovery of what might be the sword of King Arthur and the stone from which it was drawn. The sword once belonged to Attila the Hun; the Benedictines took it for safekeeping to Monte Cassino; the Nazis shipped it to Germany with other plunder and the Russians stole it from them and put it in the Hermitage. A string of outlandish and wholly absorbing adventures returns the sword to Wales from exile in Russia, to the Jones family pub in Gwent.

The Welsh nationalists, a band of incompetents too de-

cently ordinary even to be very harmful (at least by the time the book ends; the same could once have been said of the Irish insurgents), are only the vivid fictional instance of a general truth Burgess wants to affirm: The past cannot be avenged. The crime is in the past, and the punishment is in the present, qualitatively different; it cannot be justice to inflict it, however compelling to the heart vengeance can be.

Reg Jones, a man thirsty for vengeance of several kinds, in the end returns the supposed sword of Arthur to the unknowable darkness where it belongs: he throws it (of course) into a lake. His brother Dan, who goes with him, disposes of the family burden of luck good and bad in the same water. It is one of the most moving scenes Burgess has written, dark as a dream, yet luminous with that wisdom about common things that age is supposed to bring and rarely does.

> *John Crowley, "That Old Welsh Magic," in*
> Book World—The Washington Post, *February 12, 1989, p. 5.*

Susan Fromberg Schaeffer

[Anthony Burgess's *Any Old Iron* is] a satiric, picaresque novel of ideas, in which the author looks at human destiny and finds it fashioned (and usually twisted) by the two warring and fundamentally irreconcilable imperatives of human nature. One is the desire for something absolute, unchangeable—if not God, then something like God; a desire that, when expressed, takes the name of romanticism, idealism, nationalism or justice, and which, when frustrated, turns to violence and leads to war. This imperative is opposed by the human need to survive simply, as the animal among other animals that man is—to eat magnificently, to smell the many fragrances of the earth, to beat swords into, as Mr. Burgess would have it, knives and forks.

"We have too many selves. . . . History is all about the other selves. Not the selves that eat and make love and play music. O God, kindly deliver us from our other selves." These lines are spoken by Reginald Jones, a member of the romantic and idealistic Welsh family of magnificent cooks and eaters whom we see quite literally driven crazy by these warring desires, and the words provide a kind of anthem for *Any Old Iron.* The book looks at recent history through the lives of the Jones family, asking whose spirit animates our century: Karl Marx's or Groucho Marx's? Mr. Burgess believes both do, and *Any Old Iron* undertakes the enormous task of setting the dialectical cycles of Karl Marx spinning in the lunatic manner of the Marx Brothers.

This intention underlies and determines the sequence of events in the novel—it explains, for example, why the book presents not one but *three* wars (possibly four or five, if we count the struggles of the Welsh nationalists and the birth pangs of the new state of Israel); why the novel opens with David Jones sailing on the Titanic, "a perfect exhibition of the modern blind trust in mere material and appearances," and why he survives the disaster (which he regards as "a judgment on the rich"), an experience that leaves him more or less immune to the charms of capitalism but does nothing to quench his terrible thirst for absolute knowledge, which, he is convinced, will give his life the sense of meaning he deems essential to survive.

Jones enlists as a private in the First World War so that "public death [can] have another go at him, otherwise he might be kicked to little private death by a drayhorse or choke on a mackerel bone." He wants, in short, a *significant* life, and although he would not have the words to say it, he believes, as Blake does, that the only true world is the world of symbols. In war, he finds only disillusion and bitterness ("Food's what matters, people will always eat and always have done when history's kindly permitted them to. Melt the sword down and make knives and forks out of it"), but the desire for the absolute symbol persists. "I wanted one thing from [my children's] education and I did not get it. . . . What I wanted was an explanation . . . of the kind of world we are living in." He is bitter and disgusted when he is told that "education's there just to show you that the knowledge that you really want is unobtainable." In David Jones, as in everyone, the desire for the pure and the absolute persists because it is a human appetite—as powerful as any other, if not more so. And since appetites do not learn from experience, but must be regularly fed, his war can never be the war to end all wars.

And so we see his son, Reginald Jones, once again in pursuit of an absolute (this time justice), enlist in the Civil War in Spain and then again in the Second World War, where his experiences repeat, with little profit, those of his father; when demobilized, he is caught up in the Welsh nationalist cause, the Groucho Marx of wars, and while he is at it he discovers and rescues Excalibur from the Hermitage in Russia. Indeed, the entire Second World War seems to exist in order to allow Reginald to find this legendary sword, the "any old iron" of the title, the symbol (to Reginald) of justice and truth and beauty. . . .

Any Old Iron is, finally, less a novel than a meditation on the individual in history, its characters sprinkled on its surface like cloves. Many of Mr. Burgess's ideas are fascinating. He is wonderful at demonstrating how events transcend reality, become myth, then revert once more to mere events. The novel is also, at times, funny, often hilariously so, as when the author decides to skip the rest of the Second World War, remarking, "You know all about that remote war, having seen it enacted by pacifist actors on television," or when his narrator observes that the phrase "He's not my type" will be eventually understood to mean, "He does not belong to the range that will in time, though I doubt it, be revealed as containing the one and one only with a totally matching set of chemicals." And it would be a mistake not to acknowledge Mr. Burgess's vision of individuals as bits of matter flung hither and yon throughout the universe, killing and interbreeding and eating, driven by their instinct to survive and to find meaning even when survival and meaning seem impossible.

Ultimately, however, all sinks beneath the tide of unassimilated commentary and authorial exposition. By the time Reginald Jones comes to his senses (three of them—as a punishment for his rabid romanticism, he has been deprived of his sense of smell, and thus his sense of taste) and literally sinks the two major symbols of the novel (his father's lump of gold ore and Excalibur)—*Any Old Iron* opens and closes with the sinking of symbols—the reader may be considerably enlightened, but he is exhausted. And

this is a pity, because the reader cannot help feeling the author's desire to convey *all* he knows, and this is a noble attempt, well worth saluting.

Susan Fromberg Schaeffer, "Beware of Justice, Truth and Beauty," in The New York Times Book Review, *February 26, 1989, p. 12.*

Nicholas Wroe

[*Any Old Iron* is Burgess's] Welsh novel about Welsh nationalism, Welsh language and Welsh people. And Jewish people, and Russians. And war and ideals and terrorism and the 20th century. And all the other centuries.

We're back in the land of *Earthly Powers,* as the author sweeps us through the first half of this century in the company of a Welsh-Russian family and a Manchester Jewish narrator. From the Titanic to the Bolshevik revolution, from the first war on to Spain, then the second war and the creation of Israel, history is laid before us in the lives of flawed individuals.

Despite his aversion to novelists who rewrite the one book, *Any Old Iron* fits into the Burgess canon as snugly as any Anita Brookner into hers. All the familiar themes and techniques are there. The belief in essential oppositions—that duality is the ultimate reality: individuals and the state, violence and non-violence, good and evil. The use of a myth as backbone and motif—this time it's Excalibur—and, of course, language. Lovely words and sounds and meanings to gulp in great drafts so as to saturate the blood and the brain. . . .

So where does it all go? All the words and ideas and the skills and the artifice.

Well, it's an attack on the result of the conference at Yalta. It's a warning that ideals, if strongly held, or sometimes if not, will transform themselves into violence. That "destruction, best expressed in this age . . . as terrorism, is truly there for its own sake, but the pretence of religious or secular patriotism converts the destructive into the speciously creative". That the oppressed, in fighting the oppressors, use the same methods as their enemy. That "there's no absolute crime and no absolute justice".

But this isn't really the point. With Burgess you know what you get and you get a lot to the pound. He expounds on some important themes both thoughtfully and imaginatively but the real tale is in the telling, in the craft of the writing and the sheer brio of its presentation.

Nicholas Wroe, "Same Old Burgess," in New Statesman & Society, *Vol. 2, No. 40, March 10, 1989, p. 35.*

Lionel Abel

The novel requires a particular bent, which a particular writer, no matter how gifted, may just not have—or if he does, may choose not to call on. I would suggest that essential to the novelist is at least one trait of the poet: a readiness to see the whole in what is apparently a part of it. Flaubert saw all of middle-class France in the affairs of Emma Bovary; Joyce saw in 24 hours of Dublin life the whole of our century.

[In *Any Old Iron*], Anthony Burgess has chosen not to do anything of the sort, and in fact to attempt the very opposite. He has chosen to limit his interest to clearly demarcated bits of experience, never trying to fit the rest of life into these bits. Mr. Burgess begins his novel with the sinking of the Titanic, touches (briefly) on World War I, then on the struggle in Spain, and only after that takes up World War II. As if this were not history enough, he traces the experiences of two families, one Welsh, one Jewish, and ends his novel with his Jewish family in Palestine, observing the birth pangs of the state of Israel. There also is this ideological note: The war might have ended, and probably should have ended, in Mr. Burgess's opinion, with Wales, like Israel, an independent state. Both of the two families—related by marriage—would then have found their proper homelands.

Just as the incidents of the wars do not add up to anything like a moving event, so too the incidents of personal experience here do not add up to passions or purposes that I can find of moral moment. Reg Jones, the Welshman (married to a Jew), is stationed at Gibraltar toward the close of the war. He finds himself drinking with a German who justifies and even recommends the Nazi policy of murdering Jews. Jones, offended, manages to kill the German for this, but not in a way that shows he is morally motivated. They walk into an alley and the German stops to urinate. Jones, having shown not one sign of hostility, promptly stabs the man in the back. He is sent off to England by the British Army, whose officers fear an investigation of the affair by the Spanish police. Returning home, Jones surprises his wife in bed with a stranger.

Now in this whole account we are not made to feel Jones's passion in killing the German, or his understandable jealousy in finding his wife with another man. So what purpose does the whole story serve? Any of us can imagine painful situations; it is far more difficult to convey the pain essential to their reality. The talent to do this Mr. Burgess has not called on.

But I think he must have felt some dissatisfaction with his decision to isolate bits of experience, separating them like islands. (Is this a typically British idea?) In any case, Mr. Burgess seems to have felt some anxiety about it. For in a further recounting of Jones's sad experience, this time by his Jewish brother-in-law, a comparable case of jealousy is called up: Othello's "Put out the light and then put out the light," and Blake's approval of "the lineaments of satisfied desire." Now why these literary references? Can it be that Mr. Burgess felt it unconscionable to leave this incident of infidelity unconnected with others like it? And in that case, what about all the other happenings, which Mr. Burgess has chosen not to connect with the rest of experience, or even with comparable instances of oddity or misfortune?

The fact is that too much happens in this novel for anything that happens in it to take on emotional power.

I assume that Mr. Burgess's project in writing *Any Old Iron* was to record the unmeaning hazards of individual destinies against the chaos and unshapeliness of historical fact. Let me grant here that I have no right to set any limit to this writer's talents. But I do have the right to criticize his having limited the range of his invention. No doubt ideology played some part in this. Mr. Burgess is for the small and against the large, for the part and against the whole, for the British Isles and against the land mass of Europe and Asia. But why does he have to treat experiences as if they were essentially separate, like islands off life's continent?

Lionel Abel, "Individuals, Adrift in the Sea of History," in The Wall Street Journal, *March 17, 1989, p. A13.*

Denis Donoghue

Any Old Iron is crowded with incidents. . . . The narrator, we are told off-handedly on page sixty, is Harry Wolfson, son of a Manchester Jew who was a Reader in biochemistry at Manchester University. Harry has been a student of philosophy at the same university, and when the novel ends he is getting ready to go back there to teach. While the book lasts, he sees much and suffers many disappointments, but he is a survivor, as narrators tend to be. On the first page, without yet disclosing his name, he describes himself as "a retired terrorist and teacher of philosophy." How he got to be a terrorist is part of the story; how he found himself in philosophy is an incidental motif.

But the main story involves Harry's friend Reg Jones and Reg's sister Beatrix, with whom Harry has been unsuccessfully in love; unsuccessfully in the sense that she slept with him but, in the end, marries a dissolute American soldier who is trying to write a novel. Going back a bit, we are asked to believe that Reg's father, David Jones, ran away to sea, turned himself into a cook on board, and may have served with a dour Pole named Korzeniowski who wrote novels under the name Joseph Conrad. After further adventures, David joined the crew of the *Titanic,* but was rescued when it sank, got to New York, and married Ludmila Petrovna, daughter of Piotr Likhutin, owner of the Nevsky Prospect restaurant in Flatbush. David inherits, from his father in Wales, 324 sovereigns and a gold nugget weighing thirty-eight pounds. In May 1915 he and Ludmila sell the restaurant and sail for England, narrowly escaping the mischance of booking passage on the *Lusitania.* David joins the British Army, Ludmila settles down in Abergavenny and learns Welsh. When the Easter Rising breaks out in Dublin in 1916, David is one of the soldiers sent to pacify the rebels. Later he serves in France, and is reported dead.

The report is erroneous. David survives, and in fairly short order he and Ludmila produce a family of three children, Beatrix, Reginald, and Daniel. Most of the novel deals with these three, and their diverse involvements with Harry Wolfson and his sister Zipporah. There are many changes of scene: Abergavenny, London, Petrograd in the first weeks of the Russian Revolution, France in the Great War, Italy during the Italian Campaign in World War II, Gibraltar, New York, Odessa, Leningrad, Spain during the civil war, Tel Aviv, and the new state of Israel.

There are also two heavy symbols: the gold nugget inherited by David Jones, and the sword Caledvwlch or Excalibur, said to be associated with Attila the Hun and now prized as a symbol of Welsh nationalism. The gold nugget is hardly worth its weight in the story. It is mostly a treasured nuisance, cause of strife between Reg and Beatrix, and in the end is chucked into a deep pond by the dimwitted but heart-wise brother Daniel. The sword is exhibited in Russia, at the Hermitage no less, and is stolen by a Russian defector at Reg's behest, an episode of notable derring-do. The last days of the sword are dismal, and its end is such that no one but an extreme Welsh nationalist will mourn it. If the gold nugget symbolizes the nuisance of money, the sword mainly testifies to the lethal character of every political myth.

It is not clear how a community would manage without a myth, or whether or not Burgess would be content to see people living their lives without a story to enhance them. The novel contains a great deal of verbal whispering about fish, *Belshazzar's Feast,* an imputed consanguinity between Wales and Russia, and the historically complex fate of being a Jew. Burgess is evidently content to brood upon the significance of such things, in the character of a linguist or a historian, but he gets sour when other people start taking them seriously or acting upon them.

The matter is complicated by Burgess's narrative procedures. Sometimes he lets Harry Wolfson do all the work, telling the reader what he needs to know about Welsh nationalism, the nature of the sword Caledvwlch, how radiocarbon dating works and why it doesn't work on metal, the difference between an epithalamion and a prothalamion, and the gist of *Belshazzar's Feast.* Harry's tone is that of an old duffer who's been around, knows a thing or two, and is ready for a highbrow joke. . . .

Sometimes Burgess takes over the narrative duty and becomes an omniscient narrative voice, as if he couldn't rely on Harry for the precise nuances. (p. 35)

Burgess has always liked a fancy style, or at least to have such a style close by. In *Any Old Iron* he doesn't need to invent a special argot, as in *A Clockwork Orange* with its droogs, goloss, rassoodocks, chellovecks, and other veshches well viddied. The normal style in *Any Old Iron* is middle-range speech, reduced to military expletives and the usual fighting man's obscenity when occasion offers. But Burgess goes fancy when he wants to. Ludmila doesn't wash her eyes, she laves them. The Hallé Orchestra "toured and discoursed beauty in northern town halls," a truck failing "coughed itself to sleep." When Zipporah arrived at Cranford Lodge, "it was a wet day and the greenery lisped in the wet wind." When soldiers at sea vomited, they "gargoyled into the foamy green." Of Beatrix: "Her pubic mane was rich gold leaf." Leaves on a chestnut tree "shushed at the window." A train engine came to a stop "and sighed out its steam."

I assume that these opulent phrasings are Burgess's way of keeping himself free from the mess he describes. The intricacies of a language, or of several languages, have always provided him with pastoral consolation; at least there, if nowhere else, one may find peace and stimulation. Elsewhere and pervasively in *Any Old Iron,* the tone is world-weary, dismissive, the irony ready even to shrug itself off. "Merlin's long gone under and there's no magic anymore," Reg tells Dan near the end of the novel, when it has become impossible to think of Malory and *Morte d'Arthur.* The sentiment provides a motto for the entire book. Burgess sounds like Dryden at the end of the seventeenth century. Thy wars brought nothing about. Thy lovers were all untrue. 'Tis time an old age were out. The implication of *Any Old Iron* is that nothing has been

achieved. The Great War and the Peace of Versailles made the Second World War inevitable. The Russian Revolution led to Stalin. Versailles led to Hitler and the Holocaust. The Spanish Civil War was a mess. The world is divided between Russia and America, six of one and half-a-dozen of the other. The Jews who survived got to Israel; but look at the Middle East now. Harry's father was working as an engineer in Palestine in 1928, "when the failed Schofin Letsipren project was initiated: this was to be a triumph of metallic tension, the thinnest building in the world":

> I remember in 1929 the eruption of the riot over the Wailing Wall, and, young as I was, realising that the future lay in terrorism. . . . Destruction, best expressed in this age in which I write as terrorism, is truly there for its own sake, but the pretence of religious or secular patriotism converts the destructive into the speciously creative.

Harry should know, because he learned in the British Army during the Second World War the skills he has practiced for the Israelis after the war, not only in the Middle East but in London. He shows no particular misgivings about training young Israeli men and women to kill their enemies. Tired of fighting now, he seems fairly content with the prospect of being a teacher of philosophy. Beatrix is in Manchester, but Harry does not expect any joy from her. Reg and Zipporah and their new child are to live in a kibbutz near Caesarea. At the end, about to leave Israel, Harry ascribes to Reg a desire he might justly ascribe to himself: "not to have been reserved for the life of this century."

If the Burgess of *Any Old Iron* finds peace only in his extravagant sentences, what corresponds to that peace at large is the plenitude of the natural world—landscapes, horizons, clouds, the smell of oranges:

> The Roman ruins we stumbled through told us all about injustice that could never be avenged. The citrus fruits outlived them as they would outlive the law of Moses.

If what I hear from environmentalists is true, citrus fruits are just as vulnerable as the law of Moses or Harry Wolfson's philosophy. Not that Harry takes his pastoral gestures very seriously. In an early conversation with Reg, he mentions *La Nausée,* describing it as a novel "about a man who is appalled by the fecundity of a chestnut tree. All that excess, that teeming ghastly life contradicting the human desire for refrigerated simplicity." Harry claims to see Roquentin's point. So, it appears from *Any Old Iron,* does Burgess: he is determined not to be appeased. In the beginning, if there is natural plenty, he enjoys it and is willing to see it spread by the force of analogy into personal and social life. But in the end he calls it surfeit, and longs to be rid of it. (p. 36)

Denis Donoghue, "The Revel's Ended," in The New York Review of Books, *Vol. XXXVI, No. 5, March 30, 1989, pp. 35-6.*

Bill Marx

Any Old Iron begins with Welshman David Jones surviving the wreck of the *Titanic* and follows him and his eccentric family through the late '40s. The fractured storyline zigzags in and out of a couple of world wars and various nationalistic battles, among them the fight for Welsh independence and the founding of the state of Israel.

As usual, Burgess skips through history with entertaining ease, slowing down for episodes of addled heroism, mouth-watering epicureanism, and robust sexual escapades. But Burgess's need to produce a grand historical summing-up almost sinks *Any Old Iron;* the book's symbols, which include King Arthur's sword, hang around its neck like lead weights.

Among those enamored of the legendary power of Excalibur is Reginald Jones, David's first son and a typically hapless Burgess hero—he's cuckolded and driven insane because of his obsession with cleansing the world of sin and evil. Like his family, Reginald is enslaved by the myth of uncorrupted justice; he enlists in the army during the Spanish Civil War and during World War II, only to witness rather than prevent barbarity. His fury at the horrors committed by all sides (in one of the novel's most powerful scenes, England sends Russian deserters back to the motherland and certain death in exchange for British prisoners) whips up a maddening desire to avenge crimes against war's innocent victims and inspires a madcap robbery of Excalibur from a Russian museum.

Burgess shares with such Catholic novelists as Heinrich Böll and Muriel Spark a view of the world that has a few lambs struggling, usually feebly, with packs of wolves. By the end of the book, Reginald realizes the absurdity of turning himself into a knight-errant whom God doesn't want. History's a quagmire, law "is no good," justice "is no good," and the blade is "any old iron." The widening rift between good and evil reflects Burgess's belief that the traumas of modern times have split us into schizophrenic creatures. Virtue issues from passive forgiveness—anything less means becoming part of the forces of sinful violence and irrational ideology. . . . In *Any Old Iron,* man's yearning for perfect justice, rather than earthly pleasures, yields the Devil's work.

Though Burgess's archly Manichaean sensibility can be intriguing ("This is very much the modern age. . . . *Because it's embedded in the past*"), it's just shoveled in large chunks onto his epic story line. A little too light on its narrative feet, *Any Old Iron* hops from graphic descriptions of English soldiers marching across the Polish tundra to comparisons of Welsh and Israeli nationalism to windy speculations about the weaponry of Attila the Hun, the storage habits of Benedictine monks, and the ancient wars between the Celts and the Anglo-Saxons. Cram in Harry (a friend of Reginald's who trains Israeli terrorists), Reggie's sister Beatrix (a cool sexpot who marries a Jewish war novelist called Irwin Roth), and brother Dan (a fishmonger whose stench could stop traffic), and you have the novelistic equivalent of the stateroom scene in *A Night at the Opera.* Since there's so little connective tissue binding the novel's lavish detail and its abstract conclusions, the story's philosophical structure sticks out like the ribs of a starving man. Burgess has written a book that manages to be both undernourished and overstuffed.

But even amid the clamor and confusion, his ambitious prose is enough to make the paradox pleasing—how often, after all, does a book come along that has too many ideas?

> *Bill Marx, "Knight Life," in* The Village

Voice, *Vol. XXXIV, No. 17, April 25, 1989, p. 49.*

Helen Benedict

A book like this story collection by Anthony Burgess [*The Devil's Mode*] makes one consider the dangers of a long writing career. Here is a man who has now produced more than 50 books . . . and whose articles and reviews appear with relentless frequency. Yet his first collection of short stories reads as if he had dashed them off in his bathtub. It makes one wonder if there is such a thing as writing too much.

This is not to say that Mr. Burgess has forgotten his craft. He is a linguistic gymnast; his stories are courageously playful, abounding in literary and historical allusions; and he is often funny. But he tends to sacrifice the authenticity of plots and characters to the pursuit of quirky ideas, with sometimes shallow and unconvincing results.

The Devil's Mode consists of a novella and eight stories; only three of these pieces have previously been published, one in English, one in French and one in Spanish. The best tales share a familiar Burgess device: in a series of imaginary events, real-life characters meet one another—and think, act and lust—in various historical settings. Thus, in the amusing, if self-conscious, story **"A Meeting in Valladolid,"** Cervantes and Shakespeare spar over whether suffering enhances art. In the most human and moving of the stories, **"1889 and the Devil's Mode,"** Claude Debussy travels to England on a typically gloomy day. . . . Debussy goes to a Dublin brothel with Stéphane Mallarmé; he also meets Christina Rossetti, who smells "of gin and peppermint," and Robert Browning, who is obsessed with guilt, as Mr. Burgess imagines it, at having murdered his famous wife. And in the novella **"Hun,"** an account of the life of Attila told by a crotchety imperialist who teaches patrician boys, the warrior meets his adversaries in a gripping story of merciless violence.

These historical tales are clever and, when the cleverness is not trumpeted too loud, they work. But most of the other stories are facile and hollow. . . .

The trouble may be that Mr. Burgess cannot resist showing off. His versatility and his knowledge of history, music and language have long been recognized. But rather than allow this erudition quietly to inform his stories, he flaunts it like an acrobat swaggering before his audience. . . .

Mr. Burgess's pirouetting is not helped by the misogyny and racism of many of his characters. "Rosemary was very black," a white Englishman muses, "a girl of twenty-five, of extreme beauty, the features totally Aryan, the naked body superb." Of a Malay lover, he says, "She had learnt one lesson from the black Rosemary and, a brown mare, she rode me."

Such observations, echoed throughout *The Devil's Mode,* make the book's overall narrative voice sound pompous and snide. In the end, one longs for a view from someone who has stepped down from the pedestal of privilege or fame. One longs for moments that are more compassionate than learned, more sympathetic than clever.

> *Helen Benedict, "Shakespeare Meets Cervan-*

tes," *in* The New York Times Book Review, *December 10, 1989, p. 38.*

FURTHER READING

Aggeler, Geoffrey. *Anthony Burgess: The Artist as Novelist.* University, Ala.: The University of Alabama Press, 1979, 245 p.
    Biographical and critical study covering Burgess's career through *Napoleon Symphony.*

Coale, Samuel. *Anthony Burgess.* New York: Frederick Ungar Publishing Co., 1981, 223 p.
    Biographical and critical study covering Burgess's career through *Earthly Powers.*

Modern Fiction Studies 27, No. 3 (Autumn 1981): 427-536.
    Special issue devoted to Burgess featuring essays by Samuel Coale, Geoffrey Aggeler, and Philip E. Ray. Includes an interview with the author and a selected bibliography.

Ray Cooney
19??-

English playwright and scriptwriter.

Cooney's plays are exemplary of the "Whitehall farce," which was made popular in the 1950s and named for the famous London theater where it originated. These works broadly satirize the sexual urges of British middle-class marriage and society. Featuring dubious plots, numerous double entendres, and cases of mistaken identity, Cooney's plays appeal to British audiences, but the distinct cultural humor has sometimes puzzled American reviewers. Cooney, who left school at the age of fourteen to become an actor, often produces, directs, and acts in his own works. He founded the Theatre of Comedy, a London repertory company that performs his farces as well as classic comedies and innovative commercial plays.

Cooney's first work, *One for the Pot,* which he wrote in collaboration with Tony Hilton, takes place at a midsummer's eve party at a country house outside London and revolves around the desperate attempts of drunken revelers to claim an enormous inheritance by posing as heirs. One of Cooney's first popular plays was *Not Now, Darling,* written with John Chapman. Set in a London furrier shop, the work features a highly complicated plot that involves many characters, including Mrs. McMichael, a young woman who agrees to have an affair with the shop owner in exchange for a fur coat. Realizing that her husband will become suspicious if his wife wears a fur coat he himself did not purchase, the furrier plots to sell it at a bargain price to Mr. McMichael. However, when Mrs. McMichael's husband buys the coat, he gives it to his mistress. In Cooney's plays, as in other Whitehall farces, rampant sexual desires are never satisfied.

Cooney's next work, *Run for Your Wife!,* focuses upon a bigamist's efforts to keep his two wives from meeting one another. Taxi driver John Smith enjoys his double life until the fateful summer morning when he rescues an elderly women from muggers. Despite Smith's frenzied attempts to evade both his wives and the incompetent authorities, his illegal lifestyle is ultimately discovered. While *Run for Your Wife!* was impugned for homosexual stereotypes, critics praised its dual setting; Smith's two apartments in the Wimbledon and Streatham suburbs of London are positioned side by side, allowing the audience to observe simultaneously the wives and action in each flat. *Two into One,* a satire of British Parliament, takes place in a posh hotel where several libidinous House members are eagerly anticipating sexual trysts. When a personal assistant is told to arrange a rendezvous, he unwittingly botches the alias his boss told him to use, and chaos ensues. A critic from *Variety* commented: "Doors open and close at an alarming rate, trousers drop and assignations are never fully consummated. But that's the essence of the British bedroom sex farce, and Cooney delivers with well timed double entendres, bright flippant chatter and a generous serving of sight gags."

PRINCIPAL WORKS

PLAYS

One for the Pot [with Tony Hilton]   1961
Not Now, Darling [with John Chapman]   1967
There Goes the Bride [with John Chapman]   1967
Run for Your Wife!   1983
Two into One   1984
**An Italian Straw Hat*   1987

*This piece is a revised version of the original play by Eugene Labiche.

John Chapman

Some time during the first half of **Not Now, Darling** . . . [the character Arnold Crouch] stepped to the stage apron and exclaimed to the audience, "Oh, what a tangled web we weave!"

He wasn't saying the half of it. It gets more and more tangled, for it is a farce, with people—mostly scantily clad girls—scampering thither and hither. It is an English farce, but it has been redirected by George Abbott, and it follows the old Abbott formula. In farce, George said years ago, you get a man up a tree then you throw rocks at him and then you get him down.

In the case of the new play—which has had 699 performances in London—there are two men up a tree. . . . I don't predict 699 more performances here for *Not Now, Darling,* but I enjoyed last evening's monkeyshines. It was good not to have to worry about anything for a change.

The authors are two Englishmen, Ray Cooney and John Chapman. The latter is no relative of mine, but I wouldn't disown him.

The plot? Well, there is this expensive furrier's shop maintained by . . . [Arnold Crouch and Gilbert Bodley]. Into it come various young women, all eager for a mink and willing to pay for one in kind. There also are assorted husbands, not to mention lovers, and there are two big closets for people to hide in.

That's enough about the plot. There isn't any more, anyhow.

If you see *Not Now, Darling,* you can check your mind at the door—which is fun.

> *John Chapman, " 'Not Now, Darling' Is a Now & Nubile Farce," in* Daily News, New York, *October 30, 1970.*

Richard Watts, Jr.

The English have a wonderful theater, but they have a perverse way of turning out foolish comedies calculated to distress Americans. The latest depressing example is *Not Now, Darling,* written by Ray Cooney and John Chapman, fortunately not the New York drama critic, which apparently was a considerable success in London. . . . [But at] its first Broadway performance, it seemed singularly flat, lugubrious and lacking in humor.

Not Now, Darling is described in the program as "a romp," and there is no denying that its eager and industrious actors romp through it. It has to do with activities of one kind or another, chiefly concerned with non-marital sexual urges, in the salon of what is called "an exclusive London firm of furriers." Without indulging in nudity, this enables the women of the cast to strip down modestly before returning in expensive-looking wraps.

I'm afraid I can't tell you a great deal about the plot because it seemed to me confusing without ceasing to be simple-minded. . . .

The fun simply isn't steadily forthcoming. There is the tagline to one of their jokes that goes, "I never trust those washing machines," and I'm still brooding about it. I can't remember the speech that leads up to that laugh line, and, for the life of me, I am unable to think of anything that could serve as the preliminary to that smash conclusion and make it hilarious. Unfortunately, most of the play's striving for humor struck me as equally alien.

Since the famous French farces of [Georges] Feydeau go in for door-slamming and people rushing in and out of closets, the authors of *Not Now, Darling* have evidently imagined that the same sort of frenzy would provide their play with the required amount of hilarity. But it calls for something more than mere physical energy and darting on and off the stage to keep the humor going, and here I think the two English playwrights have failed to work successfully.

> *Richard Watts, Jr., "A Day in a Furrier's Salon," in* New York Post, *October 30, 1970.*

Clive Barnes

Critics are masters of pretense. (Some of us are also masters of pretentiousness, but that comes as a special bonus offer to our readers.) We pretend that all plays are of equal intrinsic interest to us—but dear friends, they are not. We each know the plays that we would, individually, be prepared to pay good green money to see, sight unseen.

As a matter of course, I would pay to see any new play by, say, Harold Pinter or Edward Albee, or, for that matter, Arthur Miller or Terence Rattigan. But I cannot envisage, in any circumstances, paying to see a sex farce starring the British comedian Norman Wisdom.

Not Now, Darling, which . . . is a sex farce, by the way, starring the British comedian Norman Wisdom—lived up to the most deadly of my prejudices. However, I freely admit that a lot of people—many of them much smarter than myself—get a great deal of pleasure from this kind of play. So please read between my lines and remember that I despise this particular form of theater. I would prefer to watch *I Love Lucy* on television—and there are few activities of which I could say as little.

The authors of this typical example of the British West End farce, Ray Cooney and John Chapman, describe *Not Now, Darling* as a romp. A romp—why, it's not even a play! It is set in the salon of a firm of London furriers. . . .

The plot concerns one furrier who is trying to seduce a young and only comparatively attractive woman. To secure his designs on her, he is prepared to pay £4,500. Or rather—for he is a man of infinite ingenuity—he is prepared to sell the young woman's husband a mink coat worth £5,000 for a mere £500. The plot goes on from there—but not very far.

Husbands, wives and underclothes—the eternal triangle of British sex comedy, which for my taste is never comic or sexy enough. They order these things so much better in France—and even then they are pretty poor things.

However if *Not Now, Darling* is the kind of thing you like, you might very well like it. A fairly typical joke seemed to be: "98 per cent of mankind are born unfaithful—the other 2 per cent are born liars." The authors are full of jokes like this, and the cumulative effect is quite jovial. And it is suggestive rather than dirty. . . .

What more can I say? I bear the play no positive ill will. But why import this kind of thing to Broadway? Do we not have hungry American writers just as bad as Messrs. Cooney and Chapman, who could have provided the selfsame lamentable product just as well?

> *Clive Barnes, in a review of "Not Now, Dar-*

ling," in The New York Times, *October 30, 1970, p. 33.*

Michael Richmond

We have by now become accustomed to characters in farces behaving like idiots, not noticing what is staring them in the face, not hearing what is being spoken loud and clear, not understanding what is very obvious. They are obliged to—that's what keeps the plot moving. The plot of **Not Now, Darling,** not only expects such things of its puppets, but expects it again and again and again. The only reason for anything to take place is that the characters behave as if they were blind or deaf or moronic. With sufficient reason we are prepared to believe anything of a character in a farce. Look what motivates *Rookery Nook.* [The playwright] Ben Travers knows that an innocent person trying to extricate himself from a guilty-looking situation is stronger and funnier than a guilty person trying to make himself seem innocent. The greater the threat, the more extreme are the lengths the character is prepared to go to in order to clear himself. Lacking sufficient motivating impulse, **Not Now, Darling** has no internal motor, and often seems to be grinding to a halt. The amount of energy being provided by the actors manages to keep it on its feet. Fuelled by a gigantic amount of panic from the protagonist, the contrivances of the plot might not have been so noticeable. Subtext is as appropriate to farce as to any other kind of play. Stanislavsky didn't only direct Chekhov, he directed farces successfully.

The situation that the authors have contrived for Gilbert Bodley is this. He wants to have an affair with Mrs McMichael, but she will only sleep with him if he gives her a mink coat. If he gives her the mink coat, then Mr McMichael will wonder where she got it. So Mr Bodley plans to sell the coat to Mr McMichael very cheaply. ('It's going cheap.' 'I can't hear it.') Mr Bodley, who owns the West End Fur Salon in which the action takes place, will pay the rest of the money himself. Unfortunately, when Mr McMichael buys the fur, he gives it to his mistress. How can Mr Bodley get the coat back and gives it to Mrs McMichael so she will sleep with him? His efforts involve his partner, Arnold Crouch and his secretary, Miss Tipdale. (pp. 32-3)

[Mrs McMichael] spends most of the play naked under the mink. We don't *see* that she is naked—it's not that sort of play. Mr McMichael's mistress spends much of her time in her undies. We do see her in her undies—undies are funny. It's *that* sort of play. . . .

Genuine desire is not in evidence. Sexual activity is referred to as 'It', which gives rise (if you'll pardon the expression) to a number of double entendres. Such as 'If I don't get it, you won't get it.' The first 'it' refers to the fur coat. Get it? . . . If you can laugh hysterically at exchanges like 'You will always have my odium.' 'I've always wanted one of those'—then you'll have a good time. Certainly the play seemed to give pleasure to the majority of the audience. So don't take any notice of me, I only used to be Brian Rix's dresser. Perhaps I've grown accustomed to your farce. (p. 33)

Michael Richmond, in a review of "Not Now,

Darling," in Plays and Players, *No. 315, December, 1979, pp. 32-3.*

Peter Roberts

Ray Cooney's farce [**Run For Your Wife!**] which he has directed himself (as well as being its presenter) begins extremely promisingly in an Alan-Ayckbourn-meets-Philip-King manner. There is a dual set of a Wimbledon and a Streatham flat with the wives of both establishments simultaneously on view and cross-cutting one another's dialogue which will make Ayckbourn fans think happily back to *How the Other Half Loves.* Taxi driver John Smith is a bigamist who successfully keeps two homes running on a tight schedule until he meets with an accident. The play charts his increasingly desperate efforts one summer morning at preventing the two households from meeting. The best of the evening concerns the police's gradual discovery of his guilty secret—although it soon becomes clear that Mr Cooney is no Ayckbourn when it comes to extracting the ripe comedy of the nuances of English class consciouness from such a situation. . . .

The trouble is that about one third of the way through the evening Mr Cooney runs out of ideas—again so unlike Alan Ayckbourn who in *Relatively Speaking* spun out the basic situation so ingeniously it took your breath away. To fill up the evening Mr Cooney embarks on dramatic queer-bashing by introducing us first to the broken wristed caricature homosexual straight out of *The Crazy Gang* era. He then involves the bigamist taxi driver in pretending to be gay to deceive his wives and the Cooney line is that bigamy is really terribly manly and admirable thing to try to get away with but that homosexuality—seen only in parody form—is fit only for scornful guffaws. If Mr Cooney had filled up his play with similar treatment of Jews or Blacks he would certainly have been prosecuted for racial incitement but in **Run For Your Wife!** queer bashing in this post-Wolfenden era in England is obviously a very profitable occupation in which you can attract quite distinguished actors and an applauding and paying audience to join in.

Peter Roberts, in a review of "Run for Your Wife!," in Plays & Players, *No. 362, November, 1983, p. 23.*

Rosalind Carne

Ray Cooney knows how to make people laugh. He also knows how to make money, lots. Playwright, actor, director, producer, scriptwriter, he's the kind of maddening success you'd love to hate but can't. He's too nice. Hence the immediate enthusiasm among showbiz friends when he first mooted his ambitious plan to lease the 1300 seat Shaftesbury Theatre as a base for a new company, the Theatre Of Comedy. He would be artistic director, and the idea was to attract star names and capacity audiences for limited runs of comedy classics and commercially viable new plays. (p. 15)

But it wasn't just the charismatic Cooney that aroused interest. His idea struck a chord in many actors, worried about the gradual demise of West End theatre and conscious of the gulf between the performers and the businessmen who own and manage the theatres. Without the constraints of a resident repertory, the Theatre Of Comedy could offer them something like a home, a place to which they could return, as well as a potentially profitable financial investment in the world they knew and loved. They also shared the view that making people laugh was not only worthwhile, but a great challenge, a supreme test of the actor's skill. 'It looks easy but these things are rehearsed and rehearsed, to do these kinds of plays you need good actors at their best,' says Cooney.

Another incentive was the growing feeling that the best writing talents were being syphoned off into film and TV. Understandably, as Cooney admits. 'The money's good, and it's easier to do the half-hour slots. Stage plays mean being confronted with the need for two-and-a-half hours of continuous action, and that puts tremendous demands on a writer.'

Nevertheless, he has been responding to those demands without respite since his writing debut, **One for The Pot** which opened in 1961 for Brian Rix's company at the Whitehall Theatre. From that day he has cherished the idea of founding a company of his own, supported by his friends in the profession.

> For a long time I've had the feeling that we've got the best comedy writers in the world. The RSC and the National get the awards and the publicity, and of course they deserve them, but the general public don't go to those plays. I wanted to present truly popular plays of high quality. Also, I'd been disenchanted by the way theatre staff treat audiences. I knew if we were to have a better relationship between audiences and front of house, we'd have to have our own theatre. Most theatre owners are just landlords.

Always an astute operator, he was careful not to let his enthusiasm lead him into a foolhardy enterprise and he spent over fifteen years waiting for the right play to launch the project. There were plays he was proud of like **Move Over, Mrs Markham** and **Not Now, Darling,** but **Run for Your Wife!** has something more than the complex mechanics and crescendo of humour you expect from the sex comedy genre.

It has the marked theatricality of the divided set, showing the Streatham and Wimbledon homes of its bigamous hero. It also has an instantly identifiable bunch of characters the taxi driver, his unemployed neighbour, the loving anxious wives, all exuding an attractive whiff of ordinariness, and hovering around the lower middle class social rung where most of us have at least a toe hold. And the homosexual complications give a strong contemporary flavour, even if all that camp redecorating is a little too exaggerated for some tastes. (pp. 15-16)

With his uncanny sense of what the public wants, and his ability to produce it when the time is ripe, the outlook is bright for Cooney. He has just completed a screenplay of **Run for Your Wife!** for Columbia, transposing the action to the unlikely setting of New York. With characteristic inventiveness, he hit on the notion of placing one wife at each end of the Brooklyn Bridge. And of course the comic potential of the New York cabbie is legendary.

Anyone who takes on so many tasks at once needs oodles of charm and enthusiasm in order to win devoted follow-

ers, and this Cooney clearly has. Yet his enthusiasm is tempered with caution, he thinks carefully before he speaks and exhibits the actor's sensitivity to criticism, rather than the tough hide of the entrepreneur. Still, he knows how to ward off adverse comments. When one critic interrupted her otherwise favourable review of the Guildford try-out with the note that his performance lacked sex appeal and he looked like a 'wet old fish', she received a courteous letter in reply, thanking her for her kind notice, explaining that he was merely understudying the lead, and adding that his wife, Linda, thought he looked too young for the role. (p. 18)

Rosalind Carne, "Funny Ha! Ha!," in Plays & Players, *No. 364, January, 1984, pp. 15-18.*

Carole Woddis

Human nature—and Tory Ministers—being what it is and they are—adulterous afternoon goings-on in Westminster hotels are bound to be par for the course when it comes to farce. Ray Cooney, who mines the sexual proclivities of upper middle class marriage with some of the same gleeful abandon Ayckbourn was wont to rifle the storecupboard of lower middle class life before he became becalmed, reminds me in **Two into One** of the magician who, thrilled with pulling one bunch of coloured flowers from his sleeve, goes into manic over-drive, unable or incapable of knowing how to stop.

It's a shame. **Two into One** has all the makings of being rather a good dig at our ruling masters and their tumescent desires. . . . But Cooney settles instead for the more serious business of farce for its own sake with its steadily descending spiral of improbabilities, collapsing finally into unfortunate fag-baiting.

Those pursuing alternative life styles will therefore find little to comfort them in **Two into One.** They may well still marvel however at Cooney's dizzying ingenuity that keeps the Rt Hon Richard Willey in ever increasing sexual frustration (like all good British farces, the afternoon's activities remain unconsummated: the excitement is all in the hunt) dashing in and out of a bewildering number of bedrooms . . . in pursuit of a bit of nooky with one of the Prime Minister's secretaries—whilst busily avoiding discovery from his equally randy wife, herself trying to arouse the passions of Willey's . . . [secretary], the reluctant and beguilingly bumbling George Pidgen given to dropping verbal inversions more readily than his trousers but, with a gift for inspired improvisation. Entrusted with the job of fixing up Willey's assignation at their Westminster hotel, Pidgen, in a moment of blind panic, transposes Willey's pseudonym from Charles Easter of Chichester into the newly minted guise of Dr Noel Christmas from Norwich. Of such slips are giant fiascos made.

Carole Woddis, in a review of "Two into One," in Plays & Players, *No. 375, December, 1984, p. 26.*

Kenneth Hurren

There is, as the ancient Chinese sage remarked, a time for fishing and a time for drying the nets. What he was getting at, I daresay, is that there is a time when a cautious management might risk putting on a classic French farce and a time when it should not.

Such matters are generally beyond me but not, I should have thought, beyond an astute fellow like Ray Cooney. However, on the question of reviving Eugene Labiche's **An Italian Straw Hat** he blew hot and then cold, and only his proven commercial acumen, which is demonstrably greater than mine, precludes my saying that his indecision will lose him his shirt—or, anyway, somebody's shirt.

The sequence of events went like this. Back in mid-September, Mr. Cooney's Theatre of Comedy announced its production of the Labiche item, a legendary work by the man who was virtually the founder of French farce. A new version had been commissioned from Simon Moore, 'an exciting young writer.' Tom Conti was to star and rehearsals were about to begin under the direction of Anton Rodgers, who had himself played the lead in an earlier day and looked just the man for the job.

Forget most of that. At some point during the ensuing three months, Mr. Cooney evidently decided that the time for a classic French farce was not, after all, now. The show that opened a week before Christmas had the same title and Tom Conti was still the star, but Moore and Rodgers had vanished, the billing said it was 'written and directed by Ray Cooney' and it bore little resemblance to anything Labiche might have written or, indeed, to any classic French farce. (p. 20)

This doubtless accounted for a certain touch of bewilderment in . . . [the] performances on opening night, though it is hard to say how great the differences between the two scripts were. The scene on the Eiffel Tower, for instance, was probably there all along—not in Labiche's day, of course, for it wasn't built then, but these things can't be designed and run up overnight. On the other hand, the wan double entendre referring to 'this erection' sounds very much a Cooney inspiration, and there was a gag related to the position Placido Domingo had taken on seat prices that might have been incorporated only the day before.

These bits are more or less typical of the verbal tone and texture of what has replaced Labiche's frothy and felicitous confection. A scampering frolic somewhere became a lumbering trudge. . . . (pp. 20-1)

The work you think you remember . . . [it was done in the Fifties and Sixties], provides a mere outline: that is, there is still that amorous lady's straw hat, hung on a bush and munched by a passing horse, thus causing the horse's owner, a young bridegroom, to spend his wedding day haring around Paris in search of a duplicate to save her reputation.

All else is changed—beginning with the bridegroom who has become an Italian. . . . Gone, too, is the bride's amiable father who once bumbled along in the bridegroom's wake; instead, he has a fearsome, music-hall mother-in-law accompanied by a family posse of gormless yokels, apparently from Yorkshire (more funny accents).

The night ground on. I haven't even mentioned the bridegroom's turning up at the wrong church and briefly attending a stranger's funeral before getting to his own wedding. Then there is the Italian tenor, which leads to the

Domingo joke. And there is the Parisian tart with whom the hero's valet is involved, which leads to . . . [the character Felix] running across the stage now and then with his trousers around his ankles. Laugh, I thought I'd die, but there are no such consoling cop-outs in this business. (p. 21)

Kenneth Hurren, in a review of "An Italian Straw Hat," in Plays & Players, *No. 401, February, 1987, pp. 20-1.*

Howard Kissel

Run for Your Wife! is what is known in the trade as an Audience Show.

What this means is that it is so witless and inane that no self-respecting critic can possibly endorse it, but audiences enjoy it tremendously.

Run for Your Wife! has the level of taste and humor of, say, Benny Hill or *Hee Haw*. The point is that these you can get at home for free. Whether you want to pay Broadway prices for such humor is another matter.

Run is about a taxi driver who has two wives. He keeps to a rigid schedule, allowing him a reasonable amount of time with each wife. His double life is threatened when he is injured in a street incident and the police have to investigate him.

Farce begins in the real world and proceeds by slightly askew bits of logic into a daffy realm of its own. **Run** is unsatisfying because it never proceeds far enough. It's too farfetched to happen in a real setting and not farfetched enough to qualify as genuine farce. It's somewhere in the middle, like a gelatin mold that won't set.

Playwright-director-star Ray Cooney's humor runs toward musty sexual innuendo. When a detective, for example, figures out the cabby's complex living arrangements, the driver says all he wants is "peace and quiet." The cop's reply is, "I reckon you've got some little piece here you want to keep quiet."

Broadway used to have its own comedies that capitalized on people's uneasiness about sex. Presumably the Sexual Revolution put an end to such nervous humor. It apparently bypassed the people chortling around me.

Much of the second act is devoted to coy jokes about homosexuals. The humor is as offensive as it is stale.

As a performer, Cooney seems to have a gift for making vulgarity bland. He directs his work with flair. His charms as a writer and actor totally elude me.

Howard Kissel, "Don't 'Run'—Wait for the Video," in Daily News, *New York, March 8, 1989.*

Clive Barnes

First a warning: This review may be injurious to some playgoers' pleasure.

Ray Cooney's fantastically popular London farce **Run For Your Wife!** opened . . . last night and, at the final preview

I attended, it was greeted by the audience with virtually continuous and obviously genuine laughter, ranging from chuckles to chortles, from giggles to guffaws, from belly-laughs to sniggers.

I was not particularly amused by it, but I should confess to a prejudice against this kind of post-war British farce—what is often called the "Whitehall" farce, in recognition of the theater where it originated and first flourished, Brian Rix's Whitehall Theater.

How prejudiced am I? Well, **Run for Your Wife!** has been running in London (now it's actually moved to its spiritual home, that Whitehall Theater!) for more than 2,500 performances. During all that time, although I go play-visiting in London two or three times a year, I have never troubled to see it. That prejudiced, or rather that totally disinterested.

I have another difficulty with **Run for Your Wife!** There is in British music hall humor—from which this kind of farce stems—a certain, some would say robust, smuttiness that has always left me, as well as many averagely sensitive people in Britain, uncomfortable.

Certainly I would go to the stake (or nearby) for people's right to be as smutty as they like—but these jokes, whether they are ethnic, racist, sexist or, as here, wildly homophobic, make me first uneasy and then angry. Other people are obviously less queasy.

Now that you know where I stand, let me say that **Run for Your Wife!,** which has been staged with frenetically unavailing energy by Cooney himself, seems to be an unusually feeble example of a genre scarcely notable for its strength. This tall story of a bigamous taxi driver and his machinations to avoid discovery by the police and his wives with his madly accumulating pile of lies helped along by his crony lacks likelihood.

Or rather, it lacks the precious possibility of likelihood. A classic farce—by, say, Feydeau, or even Ben Travers—moves with the inevitable grandeur of a man in a top hat slowly slipping on a banana skin. Here the premises of the joke are ramshackle, its convolution arbitrary and its conclusion quite remarkably inconclusive.

The results are shabby, with the actors busting a gut for laughs, rather like a TV sitcom going down for the third time without a script.

The one originality of Cooney's contemptible little play is a device, presumably borrowed from the vastly inventive Alan Ayckbourn, of having the play's action take place, at times simultaneously, in two different apartments roughly represented by the same miserably suburban stage set. . . .

England has in this century alone produced some great farceurs, from Aldwych to the team of Ralph Lynn, Tom Walls and Robertson Hare onwards, but in such company Cooney is less than a rabbit.

> Clive Barnes, "Run from 'Your Wife'," in
> New York Post, *March 8, 1989.*

Mel Gussow

Every season, at least one British farce takes a long lease on a West End theater under a marquee festooned with effusive comments ("I loved it!" *Daily Mail*). One can tell almost everything about the plays from the apparently interchangeable titles: *No Sex Please, We're British,* **Not Now, Darling, Move Over, Mrs. Markham** and **Run for Your Wife!** The last three were written or co-written by Ray Cooney.

Last night, **Run for Your Wife!** opened . . . in a production directed by Mr. Cooney heading a cast composed primarily of English actors. This is the show as tourists might see it in London (the original production has just passed its 2,500th performance in the West End). On Broadway, **Run for Your Wife!** puts America's fondness for British comedy to a stress test.

Accepting the ground rules for allowable contrivances in farce, the play is still burdened with blind alleys, limp jokes, forced puns and troubled entendres. Even the four doors on stage are not used to farcical advantage; they are locked or blocked rather than slammed.

In this comedy about bigamy, a dull man turns out to have a hyperactive romantic life. That is the beginning and the slowly approached end of the evening's tomfoolery. John Smith, a London taxi driver, maintains two separate households, one in Wimbledon, the other a few minutes away in Streatham. Because of an accident too complicated to explain, his worlds collide, and the police are called in to investigate.

With increasing ineptitude, the taxi driver tries to keep one wife from learning about the other. To extend his comedy, Mr. Cooney uses every subterfuge in the joke book, including the pretense of his being homosexual. Whenever possible, the play makes fun of stereotypes (dumb cops, swishy gays and prefeminist women who think only of getting their man into bed).

The central idea has comic possibilities, as was proved years ago in the Alec Guinness movie *The Captain's Paradise,* but Mr. Cooney's play founders while rushing between ports. The sole attempt at ingenuity is to have both homes on stage at the same time, so we see the wives simultaneously though they remain invisible to each other. Alan Ayckbourn used this device with panache in *How the Other Half Loves.* Mr. Cooney uses it inattentively. The double occupancy comes and goes at whim.

To complicate the plot, almost everyone is mistaken for someone else, one wife for a nun, the other for a transvestite, and that leads to two more subjects for ridicule. Sex appears to be on everyone's mind, though there is an ingenuousness in that department. Much of the confusion derives from the cute terms of endearment characters use for their mates. It does not pay to ask questions—to wonder why the two policemen are so incredibly gullible, and why they are devoting so much time to a minor case, or what the two attractive women see in the colorless cabdriver. . . .

As a playwright, Mr. Cooney carries on a tradition created in the 1950's by Brian Rix. Since that time, there has been a revolution—and a revitalization—in British comedy on stage and in movies and television, led by Joe Orton, Tom Stoppard, Michael Frayn and the members of the Monty Python troupe, among others. In contrast, **Run for Your Wife!** aspires to mediocrity and achieves it.

Mel Gussow, "Farce in the British Tradition of the 1950's," in The New York Times, *March 8, 1989, p. C17.*

Doug Watt

The very existence of **Run for Your Wife!** can be explained only by the insatiable English appetite for this sort of thing.

For the record, it might be worth mentioning that Cooney has also been responsible, in his capacity as producer, for such worthier efforts as the original production of *Whose Life Is It, Anyway?* and the London mountings of *Children of a Lesser God* and *They're Playing Our Song.*

Having managed up to now to avoid **Run for Your Wife!** a farce which has been attracting susceptible Britishers and innocent tourists to London's West End for six years, I finally fell into this bundle of trash when it was dumped on Broadway last week.

While I sat through the first act in a deepening gloom, I was aware of almost constant cackling throughout . . . [the theater].

What were these devoted playgoers chortling over? Well, it seems this middle-aged taxi driver, who might pass unnoticed but for a bandaged head and his central role, is a bigamist, and the evening was spent in attempting to keep each of his two wives in ignorance of the other.

To accomplish this, the author, Ray Cooney, also the director and star, has invented far-fetched excuses and filled the air with double entendres.

The rest of the play is spent on foolish byplay. Two detectives, one from each of our man John Smith's districts, evidently have nothing more pressing to look into than, first, the source of the man's accident and, after that, his double life.

Explanations of the latter, which consume most of the second half, involve pretensions of homosexuality, suggestions of transvestism, and a steady stream of gags about "pansies," "queers" and such, along with crude references to sex organs, both real and counterfeit.

Doug Watt, in a review of "Run for Your Wife!," in Daily News, *New York, March 17, 1989.*

John Simon

Ray Cooney's **Run for Your Wife!** is an English farce hit that aspires only to low, old-fashioned, simpleminded, funny tomfoolery. It succeeds admirably in the first three categories and not all that badly in the fourth. The comic fulcrum is bigamy. John Smith is a taxi driver who has been living happily with a tall brunette wife in a yellow flat in Streatham and a short blonde wife in a blue, but otherwise identical, flat in Wimbledon. They are only four and a half minutes apart as the cab flies, and the strange shifts cabdrivers have to work facilitate marital shiftiness. But one good deed—coming to the rescue of an old lady beset by muggers—lands Smith in the hospital and then under scrutiny by two detectives (from Streatham and Wimble-

don, respectively), and pretty soon the cabbie's paradise comes tumbling down.

This despite the help of his upstairs neighbor and friend, Stanley, whose supportive schemes makes matters elaborately worse; next, Bobby, the flaming pederast from above the yellow apartment, adds his two farthings' worth to the chaos. There are jokes galore to offend feminists, homosexuals, Alan Ayckbourn (two flats' simultaneously occupying the same stage space is a crib from him), and probably all delicate souls, but not us belly-laughers in the crass majority. And bigamy being the favorite wish-fulfillment fantasy of timid, uxorious creatures for whom casual promiscuity is too frightening even to contemplate, **Run for Your Wife!** has a ready-made forum. (p. 80)

John Simon, "The Bug and the Bugged," in New York Magazine, 22, No. 12, March 20, 1989, pp. 78, 80.

Mimi Kramer

[The purpose of the British sex farce] is to confirm the prejudices of the middle class while catering to its baser instincts. You know these plays, even if you've never seen one. They generally have titles like *Diamonds in the Buff* or *Take My Trousers . . . Please!* and they run for years. They tend to involve an uninteresting and commonplace hero in a series of mixups and misunderstandings that provide the occasion for a lot of scantily clad women to parade around, and they usually contain a figure of authority—a mother-in-law or a member of the vice squad—whose prudish suspicions add to the confusion. You wouldn't think of attending one of these plays yourself on a visit to London—you'd be too busy planning your trips to the National and the R.S.C. (p. 88)

Run for Your Wife! was written and directed by Ray Cooney. It has been playing in London for the last six years. It has a bigamous hero (a cabdriver, played by Mr. Cooney himself); two wives (one dark, one fair), who live in adjacent suburbs of London, and one of whom we get to see in her bra; and two police detectives, neither of whom knows how to use a phone. It also has a single set representing two living rooms. This means that four doors represent six doors, which seems to me rather stylized for a sex farce.

The plethora of doors in several recent productions that call themselves farce suggests that door-slamming—i.e., door-closing—is held to be essential to the form. But in **Run for Your Wife!** door-slamming serves only to punctuate scenes; what carries with it the expectation of laughter is the *opening* of doors. This is because what actually lurks behind the doors is a series of funny performances. Not one of the lines in the play is actually witty; few would provoke even a wan smile were they not being delivered by a collection of pros. . . . What they are doing is pure genre acting: it's the acting of the *Carry On* films and silly movies like *Doctor in the House*—a style that culminates in the frenzied rages of John Cleese in *Fawlty Towers.* (pp. 88-9)

In order to enjoy the performances in **Run for Your Wife!** you have to suspend all your finer feelings and better judgment; this is, after all, a play whose chief targets are women, wives, and homosexuals, a play in which a reference to a pregnant Mrs. Thatcher passes for political satire. Here "funny" equals gay and gay equals funny. There's even a stereotypical stage fag, singsong-voiced and lavender-clad.

Run for Your Wife!—which is vulgar, crass, and downright disgusting, and also about fifteen minutes too long—assumes that homosexuality is more laughable than marital infidelity or bigamy, yet the curtain line, which suggests the opposite, is pure Joe Orton. Actually, *Run for Your Wife!* may prove to have a certain camp appeal, finding its audience in a younger segment of the public than that for which the producers intended it: the Nick at Nite crowd. After all, it isn't really any more offensive on the subject of women than an episode of *I Love Lucy* or more offensive on the subject of homosexuality than an episode of *I Love Lucy* might have been. (p. 89)

> Mimi Kramer, in a review of "Run for Your Wife!," in The New Yorker, *Vol. LXV, No. 5, March 20, 1989, pp. 88-9.*

Moira Hodgson

In *What the Butler Saw*, [Joe] Orton was sending up English farce in the style of Ray Cooney (Cooney's *Not Now, Darling*, written with John Chapman, was running in London's West End at the same time as Orton's play, in 1969). His *Run for Your Wife!* has been packing them in at the West End for the past five years and ironically, when the show opened on Broadway recently it provoked accusations of bad taste, as did Orton's work in the 1960s. This farce, with jokes like "My husband's been acting queer lately," is rooted in the Palladium school, which thinks gays, nuns and policemen are equally hilarious. It resembles those British seaside postcards with their awful double-entendre jokes and perennial cast of stereotypes—scrawny husband, fat overbearing wife and dithering busty blonde.

Like *What the Butler Saw*, *Run for Your Wife!* starts with one deed that provokes an irreversible chain of events. A taxi driver has two wives, Barbara and Mary. When he helps an old woman who is being mugged and lands in the hospital, the police and some reporters become involved, and suddenly his carefully worked-out marriage schedule falls to pieces, threatening the stability of his ménage.

The set (which borrows from Alan Ayckbourn's *How the Other Half Loves*) shows the living rooms of the husband's two houses onstage at once, but the wives remain invisible to each other. . . . *Run for Your Wife!* has something to offend everybody—and has them "rolling in the aisles" to boot. Cooney, though, has failed to notice that things have changed since the 1950s. . . .

> Moira Hodgson, in a review of "Run for Your Wife!," in The Nation, *New York, Vol. 248, No. 15, April 17, 1989, p. 534.*

Henry Dumas

1934-1968

American short story writer and poet.

Considered an author of extraordinary talent, Dumas did not achieve critical recognition until after his death. The short stories and poems contained in his posthumously published collections, including *Ark of Bones* and *Play Ebony, Play Ivory,* emphasize the African heritage of black Americans while chronicling their divergent experiences in the rural South and the industrial North. Commentators laud the complex symbolism in these works, as Dumas synthesizes elements of nature, music, African mysticism and Christian mythology. His deft balancing of artistic and political concerns and his stylistic virtuosity are also praised, and many critics regard Dumas's fiction as an important stylistic link between that of early twentieth-century black writers such as Jean Toomer and contemporary African-American authors, including Alice Walker and Toni Morrison. Darlene Roy asserted: "Dumas's writings are so stirring, penetrating, and unsettling that, at times, the reader feels swept up into a full-force tornado where one encounters whirling thoughts, flashing insights, and thundering emotions. Dumas psychologically transports the reader through Afro-culture, Afro-time, and Afro-dreams."

Dumas was born in Sweet Home, Arkansas, before moving with his parents to Harlem at the age of ten. In 1953, he entered City College, but interrupted his formal education to join the air force. Upon being discharged, he enrolled in Rutgers University where he studied theology, entymology, and sociology before settling upon English as his major area of study. However, Dumas's growing responsibilities as a father of two sons, coupled with his increasing commitment to the civil rights movement, forced him to leave the university without completing his degree. Described by family and friends as a man of boundless intellectual and physical energy, Dumas regularly took clothing and supplies to tent cities in Tennessee and Mississippi while writing and working as a print machine operator in New York City. He later became involved in the publication of such small magazines as *American Weave, Freedom Ways,* and *Hiram Poetry Review* before accepting a teaching position at Southern Illinois University. On May 23, 1968, Dumas was shot and killed in a New York City subway station by a white transit policeman. While labeled by authorities as a case of mistaken identity, the circumstances surrounding his death remain unclear. Concerning Dumas's life, Toni Morrison wrote: "He was thirty-three years old when he was killed, but in those thirty-three years, he had completed work, the quality and quantity of which are almost never achieved in several lifetimes. He was brilliant. He was magnetic, and he was an incredible artist."

The protagonists of Dumas's short stories, collected in *Ark of Bones, Rope of Wind,* and *Goodbye Sweetwater,* are often southern youths who endure racism by drawing upon their African heritage and its legacy of inner strength and mystical kinship with the natural world.

"Ark of Bones," for example, springs from African legends as well as the biblical narratives of Noah and the prophet Ezekiel. In the story, Headeye, a mysterious youth, takes his friend, Fishhound, to a fantastic ark floating in the Mississippi River where ancient men retrieve the bones of slaves and their descendents who were lynched and then discarded into the river. At the narrative's climax, Headeye is initiated into the ranks of those who tally each sacred relic and ensure the dead will be remembered. A complex vision of African-American suffering and spiritual resilience, "Ark of Bones" is considered one of Dumas's most successful short stories. Similiar pieces, including "Fon," "Double Nigger," "Boll of Roses," and "Rope of Wind," garnered critical accolades as well. In "Rope of Wind," the protagonist, Johnny B, learns that Reverend Westland is about to be kidnapped and lynched by whites. Powerless to prevent these events, Johnny B nevertheless summons superhuman intuition and physical strength to follow the kidnapper's car on foot to the remote spot where they hang the preacher. After saving the body from mutilation, Johnny B sets out to tell family and friends where to find the corpse. He completes his mission, but the intense strain of his efforts kills him. Like "Ark of Bones," "Rope of Wind" confronts the reality of violent death, yet celebrates the invinciblity of the human spirit through the character of Johnny B.

In addition to his mythical evocations of life in the South, Dumas also presented the experiences of African-Americans in northern cities, particularly New York. His urban characters, alienated from the vital energy of the natural world, often lack the moral certainty of his rural protagonists. "A Harlem Game," for example, portrays an unemployed father who, hardened by his many disappointments since arriving in New York, psychologically abuses his son when he asks for money. In other stories, however, men unexpectedly discover sources of spiritual strength in the city, as in "The Voice," where Central Park becomes an emotional refuge for a young jazz quartet devastated by the death of their leader.

Music—from African folk rhythms to blues, jazz, and gospel—also exudes a power similar to that of nature in Dumas's urban narratives. A student of Sun Ra, Dumas expressed that jazz artist's cosmic vision of African-American music in "Will the Circle Be Unbroken?" This story focuses upon Probe, a jazz musician playing in a New York City club that bars whites due to the "lethal vibrations" of Probe's afro-horn, an instrument embodying the ancient power of Africa. When three white men surreptitiously gain entrance, they are killed instantly by the force of the music. Evaluating this and other stories by Dumas, Amiri Baraka commented: "Dumas's power lay in his skill at creating an entirely different world organically connected to this one. The stories are fables; a mythological presence pervades. They are morality tales, magical, resonating dream emotions and images; shifting ambiguous terror, mystery, implied revelation. But they are also stories of real life, now or whenever, constructed in weirdness and poetry in which the contemporaneity of essential themes is clear."

In addition to his short fiction, Dumas left the unfinished novel *Jonoah and the Green Stone*. Born John, the title character, is christened Jonoah at the age of six after he is found floating in a boat during the worst flooding of the Mississippi River in modern times. His will to survive, first tested during this natural disaster, sustains Jonoah when he succumbs as an adult to the lure of the underworld in Harlem. While lamenting the fragmented nature of the work, critics lauded *Jonoah and the Green Stone* as a complex moral fable of the struggle between good and evil. Dumas's only collection of verse, *Poetry for my People*, republished under the better known title *Play Ebony, Play Ivory*, addresses many of the same themes outlined in his fiction. Poems such as "Son of Msippi" and "Root Song" evoke the spiritual affinity between rural African-Americans and the land, while "Jackhammer" and "Machines Can Do It Too (IBM Blues)" confront the destruction of the inner self by the impersonal, mechanized city. Clyde Taylor observed: "Dumas aspired to the oldest, most honored version of poet, that of poet / prophet to his people. He sought to incarnate their cultural identity, values, and mythic visions as well as to codify and even reshape those myths into modalities of a more soulful existence."

(See also *CLC*, Vol. 6; *Contemporary Authors*, Vols. 85-88; *Dictionary of Literary Biography*, Vol. 41; and *Black Authors*.)

PRINCIPAL WORKS

NOVELS

Jonoah and the Green Stone   1976

SHORT FICTION COLLECTIONS

Ark of Bones and Other Stories   1970
Rope of Wind and Other Stories   1979
Goodbye, Sweetwater   1988

POETRY

Poetry for My People   1970; also published as *Play Ebony, Play Ivory,*   1974

John Deck

There is a shape to this posthumously published collection [*Ark of Bones*] lent by the order in which the stories occur. Beginning with a simple, stunning fantasy of two black youths who are taken aboard an ark in the "Sippi" river, the imagination of the author moves steadily through a series of ideas that are more complicated, characters who are richer and better defined, all within the realm of black experience in the rural South and the urban North. The final story, **"Fon,"** returns to a traditional Southern situation—the seemingly "uppity" black youth confronting rednecks. But nothing about it will tolerate comparison to its predecessors. Dumas had a rich and varied talent, and he was foremost an original.

In **"Ark of Bones"** Headeye, the owner of a "mojo bone" and a local misfit, is ordained by the priest of the ship, who presides over a hold filled with bleached bones, which are handled with reverence and delicacy by attendants. "Son, you are in the house of generations. Every African who lives in America has a part of his soul in this ark." Fishhound, the more literal minded of the two, can't participate as fully in the vision, just as the boy in **"Echo Tree,"** who was raised in the city, is terrified by the rites and beliefs that were a part of his dead brother's life. When civil rights workers come to the fields where a boy picks cotton in **"Boll of Roses,"** he quickly discovers that he has nothing in common with an attractive Northern girl except for race, and that isn't enough.

"Harlem Game," is a savage piece of realism, an incident in which a son witnesses and suffers for his father's humiliation by his mother. One of the other two stories with urban settings contains a horn that literally kills non-blacks who hear it.

Henry Dumas, at 33, was killed by a policeman in Harlem in 1968. . . . [*Ark of Bones*] will be around a long time to remind us of who he was, how good he was.

John Deck, "A Rich Talent," in The New York Times Book Review, *October 24, 1974, p. 36.*

June Jordan

I am riding the subway with his book of poetry in my hand. The subway is where they killed him: they, a white cop, shot and killed my fallen brother, Henry Dumas, the gentle, dreaming Black poet who is now dead. . . .

Henry Dumas, poet unknown to his time, poet obscure and buried for the past six years of incalculable changes in our consciousness. It was, that murder of this Black man back in '68, a case of "mistaken identity" according to the police who told the tale. But anyone reading the poems of Dumas will know that there was no mistake he was, incarnate, the Black man America meant to eliminate from among the possibilities of Black manhood altogether; he was a survivor, one whose loving, tender spirit, whose fantasies of music and light, whose savoring of pride in history, whose smiling at the very moments of existence could not be otherwise destroyed by the racist distractions of hatred and violence. . . . They murdered Henry Dumas, a Black poet who is only now acknowledged, recognized, honored as a Black man who lived and laughed and sang his songs of beauty, here, in these united states of ash and dirty rivers.

On the subway, I am standing in front of a white woman who sits looking merely curious at the backflap photograph of Dumas: she must see how handsome, how softly engraved by years, his face still seems on paper. My impulse is to take away the reasons for her hands loosening on her lap: to hide his photograph from her eyes. But then I read his words:

> In due time these arms will
> embrace the earth.
> I will not lessen their love.

Reading him, Dumas, I cannot violate the generosity of his willingness, his hope: I let the woman look as long as she likes. Besides his poetry has captured my attention, quite completely:

> Let us have new wings
> among my people!
> Let us ride the wind
> into the high country.
> Let us have eagles.

What was happening to us, when he wrote those lines? Was that the night of Birmingham, when the dogs and the ferocious water hoses struck my people down like so much courageous debris?

> Strike the island!
> Strike the sun!
> Strike the eye of evil
> No power can stay the mojo
> when the obi is purple
> and the vodu is green
> and Shango is whispering,
> Bathe me in blood
> I am not clean.

Listen to the music of him! He was here, yes, among us, this Black man, a poet America meant to erase from our imagery, even the poems speak in a strange way in a far voice, to the demolition taking place, to the sickening exposure, revelation of the '60s. His is a counterpoint, a contrapuntal effort, a long reach to ritual rhythms, conceivably mythic formulations of a psychic underground that

opens into a wide and beautiful continent that is a home for Black people, a safety, a big space, space enough for one to concentrate upon the being of another one: "Each tear that fell / from the crushed / moon of your face / stabbed me / broke and split / into a thousand pains / But I held out my arms / and not one did I miss . . . if I don't let you seep / deep into me / and teach me / then you can cry / in the morning to the sun / and tell him to rise up and burn me away."

Much of the poetry is experimental: what else, for this one, Black man for whom all proven, known things of his actual country amounted to rejection of his swift foreshortened days? The technical range of his interests is expansive from incantational pieces to street dialect engagement, to pure lyric. . . . In his work, Dumas tried to form and keep a difference. He has left us much to cherish in his poetry. His stories *Ark of Bones* suggest the promise of a second, if you can imagine this, a second *Cane*. But, except for the first two, they remain clearly unfinished, as was his original and rising life: unfinished.

> *June Jordan, "To Keep Them Alive," in* The Village Voice, *Vol. XIX, No. 46, November 14, 1974, p. 44.*

Barbara Smith

There is a black folk tale that tells of a group of slaves who were able to return to Africa because they could fly. Once there was a day so searingly hot that slaves were dropping in the fields. The overseer whipped anyone who fell, but he didn't know that one of the slaves, the son of a witch doctor, knew powerful magic. This magic man passed a secret word around, and the next time the overseer raised his whip, the word was spoken and his victim flew into the sky and out of sight. When another slave collapsed, the same thing occurred. As the overseer turned on the magic man, everyone said the word, dropped their hoes, and flew away back home to Africa.

For several reasons Henry Dumas's writing in [*Ark of Bones* and *Play Ebony Play Ivory*] . . . brings this legend to mind. Dumas's work reflects a strong sense of the African past, a yearning for roots that have been involuntarily severed. In the poem **"Afro-American,"** he expresses the duality of Black identity:

> I am growing in the bosom and in the loins
> of America
> born and knitted in the soil, when I finish growing
> you can pick me up as you would a rare and fabulous
> seed and you can
> blow Africa
> on me as you would a holy reed.

Another link with the folk tale is that several of the stories in *Ark of Bones* are, themselves, mysterious collisions between the everyday world and the supernatural. And finally in all Dumas's work, both poetry and prose, there is a spirit of resistance that does not permit dehumanization even in the most dehumanizing circumstances.

In one of several poems entitled **"Thought"** Dumas writes:

> Lord, how I wept when I came upon
> a land whose people thought that they
> could make boats sail the stormy

ocean between the color of my skin
and my humanity.

In another **"Thought"** he warns:

Hate is also creative:
it creates more hate.

Bitterness and compassion are not mutually exclusive. Neither are artistry and commitment. Dumas's writing is marvelously and inventively black. Not only does he incorporate the traditions of African and southern folk experience, but there is also homage to black music—gospel and the blues—including 20 original blues lyrics of his own.

Another level of tradition comes from Dumas's roots in Afro-American literature itself. There are echoes of the poets Jean Toomer, author of *Cane,* and Langston Hughes. The wonderful way he captures both the language and landscape of the rural South in his stories recalls the work of Ernest J. Gaines who wrote *The Autobiography of Miss Jane Pittman.* Dumas writes: "He wasn't chilly. He wasn't cold. He saw a star. He saw the moon, far over from that head-whoopin sun. He looked at the faint profile of the bushes and the trees, bending, bowing, swaying, back and forth, dancing, a whole field of cotton in the night waiting for the morning, waiting for the morning. . . ."

This passage is taken from my favorite story **"A Boll of Roses."** Like many of the others in *Ark of Bones,* its protagonist is an adolescent boy who, in this instance, suffers the pangs of deliciously impossible love. Layton Fields skips school to pick cotton so he can earn money, but also so he can catch glimpses of a pretty civil rights worker named Rosemarie Stiles. Of course Rosemarie doesn't know he's alive and when his chance finally comes to speak to her, he acts like a smart-aleck because he doesn't know what else to do. This is a beautiful story, delicately told, although its resolution comes too abruptly. In it, Dumas's poetic gifts are most apparent.

Dumas is at his best when he celebrates Black life and his sense of near mystical communion with nature. . . . (pp. 52-3)

In poems that are more identifiably "protest," Dumas seems less comfortable and creative. This is not because social and political commentary do not make good art, but because Dumas expresses gentleness more expertly than wrath.

Because he is Black, however, violence is a reality that is unavoidable. In the haunting story, **"Fon,"** one of several legends in a modern setting, Dumas describes the confrontation between Nillmon, a white deputy sheriff, and Fon, who is not the Black "boy" he appears to be. Dumas writes:

Nillmon squeezes the pistol butt. This boy ain't no half-wit. Nillmon knows he is going to break him now. The nigger is trying to act bad. Maybe he'd break him later. Maybe Gus and Ed would want a piece of him. He looks at the youth and he can't decide whether he is bad or not. He hates to see a fool-headed nigger get it. No fun in it.

Like the slaves who could fly, Fon resists his attacker through seemingly supernatural means, or through what

might be called spiritual force. Although he did not choose it for his own life, Dumas knew the potential of hate just as surely as Robert Frost did when he wrote "I think I know enough of hate / To say that for destruction ice / Is also great / And would suffice." (p. 54)

All that we will have of Henry Dumas already exists. His life and work have become a part of the "precious tradition" of Black people that so concerned him. The tragedy in all of this is deep. At least we have his words:

For thirty-one years he planted roses,
until the withered structure of the house
became thorned flesh.
At night he would lie
exhausted and crucified.
For thirty-one years he had planted.
From the road I could see only
a mountain of roses growing wild.
"Why don't you train the stems
to bow?" I asked.
"The wind is the better teacher," he said.
"Why don't you trim their arms?"
"In due time these arms will
embrace the earth.
I will not lessen their love."

(pp. 54-5)

Barbara Smith, "Combining Traditions of the Black Experience," in Freedomways, *Vol. 15, No. 1, first quarter, 1975, pp. 52-5.*

W. Francis Browne and J. Launay

In his introduction to the short stories, Eugene B. Redmond, the editor of *Ark of Bones,* has said that the readers "are, afterall, viewing . . . several slices of black life." While this is true, there is, nevertheless, a seemingly invisible thread which unites each story in the collection. This fine but strong thread reaches into the secret places of a particular black view of reality, while connecting itself to the plight, the hopes and visions of all humanity. Yet, there is a tone of Africana underlying both the stories and poems. One senses a longing for African roots, the languages and customs, throughout these books.

Each of the nine stories that comprise the *Ark of Bones* has a different narrative presentation, which shows Dumas's technical versatility. Prose and poetry are juxtaposed in such a way that one feels Dumas's vision harking back to the past, as he looks for his roots. One "voice" speaks through various characters in an effort to communicate "messages" to the contemporary world, while another "voice," emanating from recurring images, projects itself into the future. His dominant images are the wind, rivers, boats, trees, lights, and music (spiritual-gospel in the South; blues-jazz in the North). The book's focus is on the young in both parts of the country, South and North. The few "old" people we meet—at least, in the southern stories—are, for the most part, sympathizers with the aspirations of the young and their spiritual advisers. If the older persons are in the North, where life is much more brutal, they are portrayed as "instructors" in the harsh realities of life. What one has then is the characteristic concept of the uncle or surrogate father of the extended family, as opposed to the "natural" father of the immediate family, who is often absent.

The impression a reader tends to get from these stories is that, instead of just "slices" of black life, there is a symbiosis of black experiences which all blacks share with one another—some knowingly, others unknowingly. For Dumas, they are comprehensive experiences with implications extending beyond the narrative borders of the stories themselves.

The fiction volume is separated into stories of the South and of the North. The southern stories are especially dependent upon memories, memories extending back to a heritage deeply rooted in an African past. One is reminded that Dumas, the New Yorker, spent his childhood in the South and is forever clinging to his African roots. His stories reflect the transmission of experiences of the elders to the young. For the young people, these memories are associated with the vital natural forces surrounding them. Their daily lives are in constant communication with "spirits" of the land, of nature and religion. The young are shown as seekers, keeping alive the colorful "magic" sounds of music and rhythm that teach them how their forefathers—so long gone—continue to inhabit the "winds," "streams," "rivers," "trees," and other "sounds" of life. Underlying these stories one hears the sensuous sounds of the African chants found in the spiritual and gospel music of the southern black.

The distinguishing quality of Dumas's collection is the simplicity of his style—his use of the vernacular which blends smoothly with the poetic narrative, giving the stories a freshness that works on the reader at various levels. The effect after one has finished reading them is similar to a psychological "after-image"—the impression remains on the senses:

> "Don't you know that spirits talk, 'n they takes you places?"
> "I don't believe about . . ."
> "Careful what you say. Better to say nothin than talk too loud."
> "Did you and Leo always come this far?"
> "That's right. Me 'n him."
> *The wind fans up a shape in the dust; around and over the hill.*
> *Out of the cavity of an uprooted tree, it blows up fingers that ride the wind off the hill down the valley and up toward the sun, a red tongue rolling down a blue-black throat. And the ear of the mountains listens . . .*

> . . . . .

> ". . . 'n he taught me how to call . . ."
> "What you bring me up here for?"
> ". . . how to use callin words for spirit-talk . . ."
> "What?"
> ". . . Sish-ka abas wish-ka. Saa saa aba saa saa."
> "What's that?"
> "Be quiet. I'm gettin ready . . ."
> *The wind comes. Goes. Comes again. Across the sky, clouds gather in a ritual of color, where the blue-black, like muscles, seems to minister to the sides of the sun.* (from **"Echo Tree"** All Ital. Dumas's)

In this excerpt, also, the conjuring up of "spirits" and the cryptic narrative give the sense of ritual. This scene gradually builds to an explosive climax which recalls the supernatural, but without any sense of terror. There is, instead, a kind of sensuous immersion into secrets of the past. The impression received from the experience remains with the reader even as he moves on to the next story, and to the next, until his perception of reality encompasses a broad emotional and spiritual range.

Another source of strength in these stories comes from the Bible. The pairing of the Hebraic Diaspora with the many generations of blacks brought over from Africa is part of what makes the Bible an inspirational source for black people. This "paralleling" of experiences with the Biblical stories, which blacks have incorporated, is shown in the opening story of Dumas's collection, **"Ark of Bones."**

"Ark of Bones" is a story about time—past, present and future. The narrator is a young man, whose name, "Fishhound," suggests both the closeness of the water and of the hunter, or searcher. Fishhound and his friend, Headeye (which suggests forward-looking) are wandering near a river, and they mysteriously "see" a huge ship floating toward them. They are encouraged to come aboard. We realize that the mysterious ship is a "spiritual" (ghost) slave ship, which for hundreds of years has been roaming the waters collecting "bones" of black people from the depths of the seas. The blacks are those who had died, jumped overboard or had otherwise been killed during the infamous Middle Passage.

In the course of the story, Headeye and Fishhound come to recognize, in fact, what they had always sensed in their young lives—their connection with the plight of all blacks. Eventually Headeye is recognized as someone with a special vision by the "old black captain" of the vessel. Fishhound comments on the captain, that "If that old fellow was Noah, then he wasn't like the Noah I'd seen in my Sunday School picture cards. Naw, sir. This old guy was wearin skins and sandals and he was black as Headeye and me . . . On them pictures Noah was always white with a long beard hangin off his belly." Headeye is anointed a "prophet" by the captain of the "ark," and his mission is given in a "chant"—a manner reminiscent of the African call. . . . (pp. 47-9)

Although the story is a moral exemplum, of sorts, told with humor, its tone is that of a serious religious experience, but without didacticism. Fishhound and Headeye have an experience that will change their lives, and, in a way, their experience alerts the reader to the kind of mental and physical "pilgrimage" on which the author intends to take him. (p. 49)

There is a special quality attached to names such as "Headeye" and "Fishhound" in **"Ark of Bones,"** or to "Greasey," "Blue," and "Taterhead" in **"Double Nigger,"** which make them unique. To those closest to them these names stress an intrinsic relationship to nature in ways that the usual common names, such as "John Henry Smith," "George Jimmy Johnson," or "Frank Jones," seldom do. These names are also terms of endearment that "belong" to the special person. Outside of the closed brotherhood, "Headeye," "Fishhound," and "Greasey" more than likely resume their "given" names, as part of their "double" personalities. This enables these men to face the public, the general society, where no one really sees beyond what you "look" like or what you can do "for" them. However, should some "stranger" just happen to have overheard someone refer to these young men as "Headeye" or "Fishhound," and carelessly vary the terms by referring to their owners as "Eyehead" or "Fishface," the *faux pas* might be resented.

In the five stories located in the South, Dumas concentrates on the legends, truths and cultural realities which "link" blacks in this country to something at once solid and spiritual—their African heritage. This doesn't mean, however, that Dumas's world is free from the potential for violence. But what passes for violence is raised to the level of symbol, such as is seen in **"Double Nigger,"** when Greasey, Fishhound and their friends are threatened by an irate farmer who suspects the boys of having trespassed upon his land. Also, symbolized violence is shown in **"Fon,"** which turns a bigot's hatred upon himself when confronted with the spiritualized force of a god. The more overt expressions of violence occur in the stories which take place in New York's Harlem.

The shift North in the stories, specifically to Harlem, represents for blacks, and for Dumas, a radical disruption of the roots of the South. It's like immigrating from one country to another: the affinities that blacks have with the soil, the "spirits" of nature, the indigenous values imbedded in them through their common experiences, had been fragmented. The North, like a kind of personified Circe, or some other magnetic Siren, had "charmed" masses of blacks into uprooting themselves in response to a "call" or vision of a new life. Instead, the change tended to wrench the faith of many black migrants and to threaten their spiritual homogeny. For instance, each of Dumas's Harlem stories, **"A Harlem Game," "Will the Circle Be Unbroken?"** and **"Strike and Fade,"** portrays an aspect of the callousness of the city. Nature is replaced by materialism, alcoholism and poverty—spiritually, as well as physically. Each story is a reminder of Dumas's nostalgia for the South, and his sojourn in the North becomes a kind of spiritual exile.

In **"A Harlem Game"** the names of the characters are hardened and abstract depictions, which contrast significantly with the mellifluent names of their southern counterparts. And while the *feelings* attached to "Mack" and "Jayjay," as names of affection, are ties which bind the boys, their names reflect the concrete urban world in which they live, a world of emptiness and futility.

The story concerns a young boy, Mack, who, along with his friend, Jayjay, wants to go to a movie. Mack must borrow the money from his mother, who, along with his father, is "entertaining" friends in a somewhat languid card game. Mack is hesitant about asking his laconic mother for money while his father's monolithic presence hovers nearby. The scene is devoid of the filial closeness that we see in the southern stories. The boy's father looms "like a bull" before him, a huge barrier which illustrates the distance between the children and their parents in the impersonalized city. Mack's father exemplifies the urban stereotype of the northern parent who is frequently absent, often terrifying and drunk, and nearly always unemployed. Yet, despite this bleak environmental picture, Dumas is *not* representing a total disconnection; instead, Mack will be taught a bitter lesson in urban survival by his father.

Mack's father, whose "body was like a steel beam bent by some force," instructs the youth in the dubious "art" of "conning." One notices the indifference on the mother's part, and that of her friends, as the father bullies his son:

he cons the boy out of the money his mother had given him for the movies. Force and violence underlie the meaning in Mack's "lesson.". . . ["**A Harlem Game"**] graphically illustrates the harsh realities of city life—notwithstanding the father's brutal and insufferable arrogance. Still, the child must learn to survive in this concrete-neon world; there is no room in it for sentimentality. It is certain that Mack was intimidated by his father and that he "wanted to punch out at the big man or use a knife . . . *But he was alone.*" (Ital. mine) When he finally leaves his home, Mack has nothing but a quarter remaining from the "give n' take" lesson in survival. He is bitter, yes. His frustration is displaced in a burst of self-flagellation:

> He slumped to the stoop, wiping his face. Punk, punk, punk, punk. When he got bigger . . .
>
> He stood up and touched the iron spike. He wanted to scream out and curse, but he didn't. He jerked the coin from his pocket and stared blankly at it. Then he slammed it down at the spike, which momentarily dug at the metal, then skidded off and gouged deep into his palm.
>
> Blood spurted from the hole and he ran off up the street beside his shadow. . . .

There are no tears, even though there is pain. Mack runs off into the "neon" shimmer of the city to meet his "shadow" face to face.

The city tales are told with the same simplicity as that of the rural tales; but they hit the reader harder because of their starkness—a starkness devoid of nature's influence on the sensuous visionary language found in the southern tales.

In the story, **"Will the Circle Be Unbroken?"** the author examines the mystification underlying jazz as a unique form of black city music. As the title shows, it too is linked to the spiritual cohesiveness—and, perhaps, exclusiveness—of a people's ancestral ties to religion. The protagonist, a jazz musician, named "Probe," uses his saxophone as a medium—along with his ancient "afro-horn," of which there are only "three in the world"—to connect the modern black man with his past, "like a bridge." Probe is portrayed as a "holy man," the *Magus* of his people, who had been in a self-imposed exile, and whose instruments have extracted secrets from the past which will transform black people. It is a "special sound" which Probe brings back and he "had chosen only special times to reveal the new sound."

The "outsiders" in this story are three white sympathizers who want to "crash" this "special session" at the "Sound Barrier Club." They have been warned that the "spiritual" message of Probe is only for "brothers and sisters," and might pose a danger to them. After some pressure, and the watchful eye of a "cop" they were reluctantly allowed in.

The presentation of Probe and his performance on the inscrutable "afro-horn" exemplifies the miracle of sound and rhythmic force of the black cultural heritage. It is the music of the ages, the special improvisations of spiritual sounds emitted in an incantatory "secret" Presence, reminding blacks that they must, in order to be saved, return and confine themselves to the "circle":

[Probe] heard the whistle of the wind. Three ghosts, like chaff blown from a wasteland, clung to the wall . . . He tightened the circle . . . Movement began from within it, shaking without breaking balance. He had to prepare the womb for the afrohorn. Its vibrations were beyond his mental frequencies unless he got deeper into motives. He sent out his call for motives . . .

. . . . .

He moved to the edge of the circle, rested his sax, and lifted his axe, (i.e., his afro-horn) (Ital. Dumas's)

The vibrations, sweeping over the ages, emit a power that is too much for the "visitors," the three "ghosts," who have attempted to "break the circle." Mysteriously, the three are "punished," i.e., symbolically killed by the vibrations of Probe's "special sounds."

Dumas apparently wants to show how, even in the urban "wilderness," spiritual values may be sustained; that black people have the force of their heritage to call upon. But they must be willing to listen to the "voice" inherent in the music, which is always available to comfort, cheer and encourage them.

"Strike and Fade" is a partial revolutionary tract revolving around a truncated fanatic, "Tyro," an ex-Green Beret in Viet Nam. He carries a "message" to the disturbed "brothers and sisters" in the large cities across the nation which have become battlegrounds. Tyro recounts how the "VC" miraculously spared him after he and his friends had been ambushed, in order to "come back and tell you." Tyro may be Dumas's reflection of America's negligence and hypocrisy toward its minorities—and its youth. Tyro says:

> America is gonna have to face the yellow race. Black and yellow might-have to put their hands together and bring this thang off. You cats out in the street, learn to fade fast. Learn to strike hard, but don't be around in the explosion. If you don't organize you ain't nothin but a rioter, a looter . . . Strike and fade, then strike again, quick. Get whitey outa our neighborhood. Keep women and children off the streets. Don't riot. Rebel. . . .

While there are obvious elements in this "message" for which the young men and women are urged to "kill," it underscores a sickness in America that Dumas intimates not only destroys the body but breeds a kind of insanity. This sickness may very well wind up destroying the country.

It is, however, in Dumas's collection of poems, *Play Ebony Play Ivory,* where his mastery, his poet's sensitivity, is best revealed. In his poetry we get the full force of his power—his love, his grace and charm. As a fiction writer, we are made aware of Dumas's poetic sensibilities. Both his stories and poems turn away from the despair of the '60's, the literature of recrimination that characterized so many of the writers of the last decade, to sound a note of hope and love for his people. His was one of the new voices among the younger writers of New York.

Often the poems reiterate an allusion or complete a statement made in the stories. For example, the Bible and faith in **"Ark of Bones"** and in **"Fon,"** the church and affirmative action in **"A Boll of Roses,"** and chaos in **"Strike and**

Fade" are picked up in many of the poems, such as **"Mosaic Harlem"** and **"Genesis on an Endless Mosaic."**(pp. 49-53)

The poetry volume is divided into sections, beginning with a series of poems grouped under the title poem **"Play Ebony Play Ivory."** A middle grouping includes: **"A Natural Man," "Where the Sidewalk Ends," "Blues Songs," "Thoughts/Images"**; a final section is grouped under three variations of the arabic terms for pleasure and religion: **"Kef," "Ikefs,"** and **"Saba."** From these divisions one can see how wide and diverse is the range of the poet's interests. The style variations demonstrate Dumas's remarkable grasp of poetic technique: he makes use of a spectrum of tones, imagery, imitative musical patterns and hortatory religious sentiment. Also, there are some fine examples of conventional poetic forms which lift the language to heights as significant as those found in the best linguistic manipulators of English verse in our time.

The title poem, **"Play Ebony Play Ivory,"** encompasses the whole of the black experience in a curiously rhythmic manner. The unifying image is the piano, which functions for blacks as a percussion instrument that, strangely, recalls the sonorous sounds of African drums and their connection to the spiritual-gospel-blues-jazz tradition in America. This poem envelops a people with a magic coat of love; yet it infuses one with a spirit which, at once, inspires and releases blacks from the multitude of burdens threatening to smother them. . . . (pp. 53-4)

By juxtaposing people with the piano image, Dumas does several things. Among them is the capturing of the world of music in black American culture—the spiritual-gospeljazz-blues heritage. The poem also serves to probe into the secret corners of the black psyche and open the world to the reader—a world of awe which explodes in the poems that follow:

> Let us have eagles!
> Let us have eagles
> among my people! . . . (from **"The Coming of the Eagles"**)

This excerpt suggests the "calling" for the "spirits," or the Messiah, as was seen in **"Ark of Bones"** and in **"Echo Tree."** When the poet speaks of poverty, the "teacher" is evident, as in **"Son of Msippi"**:

> Up
> from Msippi I grew.
> (Bare walk and cane stalk
> make a hungry belly talk.)
> Up
> from the river of death.
> (Walk bare and stalk cane
> make a hungry belly talk.)

The sound of the "worker," the oppressive weight of city life, is heard in the exacerbating drilling of **"Jackhammer."** Its pounding suggests breaking up of the old to make way for the new, while, at the same time, it becomes synonymous with the "breaking" up of men. . . . (p. 54)

Dumas's poetry is like a great symphony of rhythm and sound, diversified, but steady, each movement compelling the reader to "listen," as well as to read. The variety of moods that one finds in these poems express the diapason of our modern "moods"—the conflicts and changes of circumstances we meet in life; yet there is always a center, a "corner" to grasp hold of. The singularity of his works, his excellence, is proven by the fact that, even though many of his poems are written with a specific audience in mind, they retain a universal freshness and appeal. Both stories and poems address themselves to hope for the future, frustrated love, faith, sibling rivalry, friendship, hostility, rage, rural-urban conflicts, family closeness and estrangement, ritual and convention.

In the poems, however, there are shades and echoes of many "voices" from American verse, among them Whitman, Emerson, Hart Crane, and Sandburg. But there are deeper shades of Langston Hughes, Sterling Brown, Jean Toomer and other black poets of America and elsewhere. Above all, there is the distinctive "voice" of Dumas himself, dominant, lyrical, plaintive, angry, mystic. For these reasons, the sadness is heavier that the poet is no longer here to perpetuate his music. Nevertheless he did leave us all a fine legacy. (p. 55)

> *W. Francis Browne and J. Launay, "Henry Dumas: Teaching the Drunken Earth," in Centerpoint, Vol. 1, No. 3, Spring, 1975, pp. 47-55.*

Gordon Burnside

The black civil rights movement was profoundly anti-individualist, and therefore subversive of both dominant American culture and the novel as a literary form. Henry Dumas, who grew up in Mississippi and Arkansas in the '40s and then went north to become a poet and black studies teacher, demonstrated this fact in a tragic way. In 1964—four years before his mysterious death at the hands of a New York subway cop—Dumas began work on *Jonoah and the Green Stone,* a vast novel of the South. The surviving bits and pieces of that book . . . show it cracking up after a strong start because Dumas had lost his grip on his individualist hero.

Jonoah, a seven-year-old boy, is orphaned by and takes his name from the Mississippi River flood of 1937. The river, indeed, is Dumas's most memorable character:

> And all the land seemed to sense a bad year. Rabbits and squirrels ran off somewhere. Mama used to say they were looking for the Ark. People got a bit friendlier, and everybody knew it was because deep down inside no one wanted to move. But there was nothing you could do about it when the river rose. . . . When that river broke over the mud line and climbed up over the levee and headed toward the farms and town, there wasn't much even the Federal Government could do but obey the river and move.

Adrift in a johnboat, Jonoah takes aboard the Masterson family and, a little later, the poor white, Dog Whitlock. These will be the book's commanding figures—or rather would have been, if Dumas had found a way to keep them going.

Whitlock is a frightening creation, aimless rage personified. "God aint have to do that," he tells Papa Lem Masterson:

> He done took everything in this flood except me,

> and I aint forgettin it. When this rise drops, I'm changin my religion, from a backslider to a nothin. And, nigger, you better do the same.

And if God must persecute Whitlock, then Whitlock will do the same to his benefactors, simply because they are close to hand and black. The ensuing struggle for control of the boat ranks with the river stories of Twain and Faulkner. Papa Lem cowers helplessly at the tiller; his wife Mamada and little Jubal resist, and are thrown overboard; Lili Masterson goes mad, and Jonoah, watching all this, learns how terrible, more terrible than a flood, the power of white skin can be.

So ends the one successful long fragment of Dumas's novel. A middle section, concerning Jonoah's youth with the Mastersons, is mostly notes: characters raised and abruptly dropped, memories shading off into dreams, snatches of sermons and poetry, a jumble. We are told that Jonoah leaves his adopted family to go north, where he becomes a sort of minstrel on the periphery of the Movement. We are also told that the Mastersons, who have remained in the Mississippi Delta to fight segregation directly, consider him a deserter. That ultimate black separatist—an individual outside his community—Jonoah is plagued by guilty nightmares.

The last long section of the book is itself scattered and surreal, more obsession than narrative. For one thing, *all* of the characters are on the verge of disappearing. The evil Dog Whitlock, now a sheriff, is mentioned but not seen. Jubal Masterson, who has since become a Bob Moses-Meridian Hill self-abnegating organizer, may or may not be dead. Jonoah gropes his way back down the river, is hunted by murderous whites, and crosses a hallucinatory burnt and bombed landscape that is more like Vietnam than Mississippi. He finally reaches home, and a Masterson step-sister—but she has been blinded and can't see *him.* (pp. 284-85)

[In an important sense, *Jonoah and the Green Stone* is not a novel] as we generally understand the term. It is impossible to know what Dumas might have made of his book if he had lived to complete it, but a reintegrated Jonoah—one able to stand with one foot in his community and one foot out—might conceivably have told a great Tolstoyan epic about his people in the 1960s. Or perhaps not. . . . Epic novels require epic selves to write them, and it was away from mere selves that the Movement always meant to go. (p. 285)

> *Gordon Burnside, in a review of "Jonoah and the Green Stone," in Commonweal, Vol. CIV, No. 9, April 29, 1977, pp. 284-85.*

Herman Cromwell Gilbert

[*This essay was originally presented at a celebration for* Goodbye, Sweetwater *held May 22, 1988 at Chicago's Guild Books.*]

Occasionally, an experience becomes so pinpointed, so isolated, and so peculiarly one's own, that it seems as though nothing else of equal significance could possibly be taking place at the same time in the world. For years, I felt that way about the "high water" of 1937, when the women and children, black and white, of hundreds of families were moved from their homes in Cairo, Illinois, and surrounding farms, and taken to a junction called Olive Branch, about fifteen miles north of Cairo, to live in railroad boxcars. The purpose of the pilgrimage was to escape the ravages of the flood that was pillaging the Mississippi River valley all the way to the Gulf of Mexico. (p. 238)

Through the years I remembered those weeks with such pride, and with such a sense of uniqueness, I became certain in that region of the mind reserved for special things that nothing of equal importance could have been happening during that precise time to another boy anywhere in the world.

But now that feeling has been shattered. I have just finished reading Henry Dumas's powerful novel *Jonoah and the Green Stone,* which begins with Jonoah's memories of that same flood, a few hundred miles to the south of where my own experiences were taking place. Only, whereas I flirted with the girls and awaited word of danger to others in selfish anticipation, Dumas's alter ego, Jonoah, suffered physical and spiritual scars that would live with him all the days of his life. In recreating the flood, Dumas has rendered such a soulful evocation of his character's experiences that I know my memories of the time will henceforth take second place to his.

The story of *Jonoah and the Green Stone,* in summary, is basically a simple one. John (later to become Jonoah), a six-year-old boy, is separated from his parents (who apparently drowned) in the great Mississippi River flood of 1937. He is rescued from a raft by a makeshift family of blacks composed of an oddly estranged husband and wife, the wife's strong-willed sister and her son and daughter, and another stray boy. Also joining this crew on the raft is an evil white man, determined to exercise his superiority despite the ever-present dangers of the flood. After the waters subside, the black folks who escaped by way of the raft remain together as a family, and the white man becomes their tormentor. To a certain degree, all the members of the black family become associated in leadership roles with the just aborning Civil Rights Movement—all, that is, except Jonoah, the parentless boy, now a young man, who is the teller of the tale. Because he cannot connect with his past, Jonoah wanders through his present, leaves the South and goes up north, remaining on the periphery of the struggle. But he is drawn back home by his guilt and his restlessness, ostensibly to find out if his foster brothers and sister need him, yet spiritually searching for the Green Stone, a dream-like symbol of identity that has eluded him all of his life.

Although the story is clear, details are missing that Dumas would have included had he lived—details such as more fully developed relationships among the characters and a more sharply drawn story line. Yet, in editing the novel, Eugene Redmond has positioned the pieces of the story so expertly that the vision of Dumas comes through intact. There is even a possibility that the novel is better because Dumas didn't get a chance to fill in the details. Partly because of the missing parts, the haunting power of myth and legend are present, teasing the reader with the wonder of things just beyond the reach of knowing.

Dumas clearly belongs to that genre of African American writers in whose works myth and reality engage in a shifting, ritualistic dance along the ghostly corridor separating Africa and America. But he has the perspicacity not to shun the material while embracing the spiritual, for he understands that they are equal parts of the same world.

In his fiction, rich with the lyricism of his poetry, one is conscious of the rhythms associated with the best writings of African American women. There is much of the reaffirmation of heritage found in Paule Marshall's *Praisesong for the Widow,* something of the uncontrolled sense of adventure and freedom which marks Zora Neale Hurston's *Their Eyes Were Watching God,* and a lot of the mysticism and desire for retribution inherent in Toni Morrison's *Song of Solomon.*

His writings also remind one of James Baldwin's and John Edgar Wideman's. However, to me, his fiction has a softer edge than Baldwin's and is less self-consciously penetrating than Wideman's. His message is not so despairing as Baldwin's, less filled with hopelessness. Neither does he enter so deeply as Wideman into the bowels of rejection. Also, I do not sense in him as much self-hate as that which flows from either Baldwin or Wideman. He rides the spirit of lost souls, to be sure but, nevertheless, *is* the spirit that he rides. In many ways he and John Killens are blood brothers in revolution, regardless of the differences in the symbols and styles of their writings.

In telling the story of *Jonoah and the Green Stone,* Dumas creates a glorious allegory of a boy's, then a man's, and possibly a people's, search for salvation in a place and time where the past is hidden, the present confused, and the future dark. Having been cut off from the legends of his past, Dumas seems determined to create new ones. He appears to realize that it is not sufficient merely to release old legends from rediscovered texts and transplanted voices—too much has been lost—but that life resides in the continuity of the legend, passed uninterrupted through the generations.

So this, then, is our task: to create new legends of identity; and from the legends, new philosophies of hope; and from the philosophies, new strategies of survival; and from the strategies, new tactics of growth; and from the tactics, deeds of creativity and power.

Such is the road to salvation.

It is the lesson of Dumas.

It is Jonoah finding the Green Stone. (pp. 238-40)

> *Herman Cromwell Gilbert, "Henry Dumas and the Flood of Life," in* Black American Literature Forum, *Vol. 22, No. 2, Summer, 1988, pp. 238-40.*

Eugene B. Redmond

That Henry Dumas felt and thought deeply about his people—and the global flock—is evident in the abundance of sensitivity, love and insight embedded in *Goodbye, Sweetwater,* a magnetic collection of tales and visions. Dumas's territory—read laboratory—was wherever the imagination could roam free. Within such a limitless sphere of folk and fantasy Dumas projected his powerful fictional universe, an Afro-centered mirror-world that included fascinating fables and frame states for which he has become—one can't say "famous"—idolized and emulated by a growing diasporan tribe of storytellers, critics, multiculturalists, Africanists, folklorists, mystics, students of the occult, linguists, songifiers, ethnomusicologists, and poets. In my introduction to *Ark of Bones* I noted that, "already he is being compared to . . . Jean Toomer and Kahlil Gibran."

For some time following his violent death—which occurred deep in a Harlem subway on the night of May 23, 1968, at the hands of a New York City Transit policeman—factual components of Dumas's own life merged with those of his fictional characters, producing a bizarre grapevine of tales ominously immersed in government conspiracies and witch hunts. Indeed, many who knew about Dumas's constructs for ideosound, designed to wage "spiritual" combat against Big Brother, found easy connections or parallels between his death and what was perceived as the counterrevolutionary mission of an oppressive and trigger-happy "system." The fact that this young Black male, then not quite thirty-four years old, was shot by a white policeman, under what still remain unclarified circumstances, was all the more reason why many in the Movement waxed "suspicious." The precedents were all there, had been there—in fact and fiction: from the FBI's covert Cointelpro operations to the CIA-engineered murder of an Afro-American writer in John A. Williams's *The Man Who Cried I Am,* a best-selling novel of the late 1960s. Given Black people's history of "healthy paranoia," as some scholars put it, and in view of that tension-pregnant and anxiety-armed era, one needed very little imagination or coaxing to conclude that Dumas's awesome abilities as a seer-sorcerer had been deemed dangerous enough to destroy.

Dumas himself was ever mindful of this "threat"—so widely believed that it is discussed as "fact" among Black activists, writers and intellectuals. The broader theme of Black male vulnerability, which one hears and reads about everywhere these days, is one of the vital thread-messages in Dumas's fictional quilt. (pp. xi-xii)

But what of Henry Dumas? Friends and colleagues testify that his electric personality, intellectual energy and creativity drove him at an almost dizzying speed. And yet, ironically, he seemed to have time for those close to him. His widow, Loretta Dumas, recalled that his artistic intensity was so all-consuming that he appeared to be wide-awake even when he was asleep. Another observed that being Black prompted Dumas to "live the way he lived, to become so wide and wise, and certainly it 'helped' him to die the way he died." Hale Chatfield, author of that statement and coeditor of the Southern Illinois University editions of *Ark of Bones* and *Poetry for My People,* also said of Dumas:

> He was complex, intricate, variable, wise to innumerable ways of life, eclectic in his interests, and at ease in almost any company. Or at least he had acquired the appearance of these qualities, so that any of us who were his friends had to feel ultimately that at best we knew only facets of the entire man, had access, at best, only to those elements of his being that were available to us as individuals somehow more specialized, more restricted, in our perspectives. Nobody I know fails to feel or hesitates to affirm that Henry Dumas exceeded him in the breadth of his experience of human situations.
>
> (pp. xii-xiii)

[Jay Wright's] description of Dumas is a picture of order-centered hurriedness, of a disciplined and calculated rush:

> Henry Dumas lived very rapidly, and very slowly. We could never seem to keep up with him, or catch him, or hold him when we did. It wasn't that Dumas avoided any of us. There was simply so very much to do. He had so many friends . . . During the time he was an on-again off-again student at Rutgers University, he spent a great deal of time trying to organize informal readings, or starting or promoting small publications, or persuading one or another of his friends to go to a gospel concert. It was very hard to figure out just when he had time to write. But he did write, and quite a bit. Whenever he appeared, he had stacks of new poems, pages of a novel, articles, prose poems, sketches for a play. To conclude that he lived in an absurd swiftness would be a mistake. For Dumas had heavy roots, in his people, in the land. . . .

Although he later speaks about Dumas's poetry, Wright's observations nevertheless provide brilliant insights into the broader cosmos of Henry Dumas, writer, and the Afro-American creative mind in general:

> Dumas asserts that the language you speak is a way of defining yourself within a group. The language of the Black community, as with any group, takes its form, its imagery, its vocabulary, because Black people want them that way. Language can protect, exclude, express value, as well as assert identity. That is why Dumas's language is the way it is. In the rhythm of it, is the act, the unique manner of perception of a Black man.

In 1964, Dumas staked out the arena in which he would construct his religious-folkloric-literary frames of references. In a letter to George Hudson, he exclaimed that:

> I was born in the south (rural Arkansas) and come quite definitely from the rural elements. . . . My interest in Gospel music coincides with my interest in folk poetry, and the folk expression. There is a wealth of good things to be developed in our heritage. The Gospel tradition is among a few.

In a biographical note accompanying his contribution to *Black Fire,* the late-1960s anthology edited by LeRoi Jones (Imamu Amiri Baraka) and Larry Neal, Dumas admitted: "I am very much concerned about what is happening to my people and what we are doing with our precious tradition." The statement echoes his earlier call for "full-time, devoted scholarship" designed to establish a proper perspective on the Black heritage and simultaneously to create appropriate vehicles for utilizing traditional folk forms in the service of serious literary expression. His research, which represented a major undertaking, had hardly been completed at the time of his premature death. But Dumas had come far enough along that one could easily touch and enjoy with him his wonderful and multi-storied world. For as Jay Wright reminds us, "Dumas is there. The rhythm is the perception. The language is participation in the act."

According to Jay Wright, who brings righteous vision to the greatness of Dumas's craft:

> Dumas found this rhythm of perception most readily, as others have, in music. And he brooded a lot about musical structure. The blues and gospel music, particularly, were his life breath. Dumas

haunted gospel concerts, photographing, when he could, the singers and the action. For him, the songs and the style of the singers linked him to the land, pinpointed that sense of dispossession that he felt, living in the alien, crass and prejudiced cities, where too many people ignored what he was as a Black man, and too few cared enough to learn or honor him because of it. His singers [and poets-storytellers] have the wisdom of African priests. The music is more than gospel; it is mythic gesture and indicative of a social structure.

Henry Dumas was born into the racially segregated but culturally pluralistic world of Sweet Home, Arkansas, on July 20, 1934. At the impressionable age of ten he was taken to the even more segregated world of Harlem in New York City. There, in the Upsouth, he attended public schools, completing Commerce High School in 1953, and enrolling at City College that same year. Ever the searcher, the adventurer, the inquirer, Dumas broke off his college studies to join the Air Force. He was stationed at Lackland Air Force Base in San Antonio, Texas, and later spent one year in the Arabian Peninsula, this latter experience helping to generate his interest in Arabic language, mythology and culture. Selections from *Jonoah* and the awesome story, **"Goodbye, Sweetwater,"** seem to recall some of the experiences he may have had in the south.

On September 24, 1955, midway through his four years of military service, Dumas married Loretta Ponton. The year following his 1957 discharge, Dumas's first son, David, was born. Enrolling at Rutgers University around this same time, Dumas began a full-time pursuit of courses in etymology and sociology before discovering his natural habitat in English. Two years were apparently all he was able to devote to a full-time college program, having to work, as it were, assume responsibilities of father and husband, write, organize on the little-magazine circuit, and involve himself in America's great sociological practicum—the civil rights movement. A part-time student at Rutgers over the next seven years, Dumas finally quit the university in 1965 without finishing his degree. His second son, Michael, was born in 1962; and homebound responsibilities, coupled with a widening interest/involvement in the civil rights movement, detoured Dumas from his most passionately pursued subject—religion. He juggled his role as a part-time student and husband-father with his job as an operator of printing machines at IBM from 1963 to 1964. In this vortex of student, writer, wage earner, organizer, activist, father and husband, Dumas still managed to find the time and means to cart clothing, food and supplies to inhabitants of tent cities in Mississippi and Tennessee. From *Ark of Bones* through *Jonoah* through *Rope of Wind* through *Goodbye, Sweetwater,* there exists an oxymoronic constellation of hope and drudgery, pride and dispossession, advancement and setback, Black strength and resilience against omnipresent racism and degradation. It's all there in some phase or form—from racial volcanoes, covered by pretty wavy cotton fields, to Paul Laurence Dunbar's human mask that "grins and lies."

In my introduction to *Rope of Wind,* I engaged in a debate with certain critics and aestheticians, especially some who had suggested that a particular ideology—say Black nationalism—was the highest state of Afro-American fiction. My response was:

> When one considers that mothers, fathers, and children make up a community, however, one must search beyond ideology, contemporaneity, or hysteria. All of these foregoing elements are, of course, a natural part of Black writing, but a reader must be given a full "gulp" in order to savor the entire work of the "cook." Hence, Dumas's preacher in **"The Map of Harlem"** tells his audience that "the soul of the black man is an unexplored region."

Hence we enter, with Dumas, "the world of . . . surrealism, supernaturalism, gothicism, madness, nightmarism, child-men [girl-women], astrology, death, magic, witchcraft, and science fiction." I personally like the word comfortable when I'm thinking or talking about Dumas's work. Comfortable in the sense that he is not filtering his words and thoughts through some mechanical censor. He is not playing to the tube or the microphone. His is not a Top 40 prime-time rap. Instead he gives us interior songs, stories from the viscera. Therefore, the hippest way to "bop" with Dumas is to let yourself go "down-home"—to those down-home blues, with funky fictional arias, with low-down fables duffing through infinity. And, yes, this earth language and rhythmized way of seeing reach across the spectrum of these stories.

But while Dumas's fictions may appear to be "new" in the literary sense of that term, they are ancient in origins, archetypes, meanings and structures. This item was particularly arresting in the 1960s when a proliferation of "media"—conscious artists occurred. For, as Baraka saw and felt:

> Dumas's span shows a feeling (again!) for *all of our selves* or *all* of our self—the large black majestic one. A truly *new* writer (in the sense that the nationalistic consciousness all of us need is here) as a *true art form* not twenty "Hate Whitey's" & a benediction of sweaty artificial flame, but actual black art real, man, and stunning.

Such, too, were the exuberant echoes in Clyde Taylor's searching and unselfish ode to Dumas in "Henry Dumas: Legacy of a Long-Breath Singer," which appeared in the September 1975 issue of *Black World* (*Negro Digest*), where Dumas's fiction and poetry had been published in the 1960s [see excerpt above]. Earlier pithy reports on Dumas's vision and technical virtuosity were confirmed by Taylor. . . . Dumas's ambitious and successful undertakings as a 1960s Black writer, according to Taylor, included avoiding the pitfalls of transient hipness, or microphone mentality, and reintegrating Black literature into natural processes—or nature. This observation could not have been truer coming from Dumas himself. (pp. xiii-xviii)

In his earth lore, his cultural reclamations and his creative far-reach, Dumas is reminiscent of James Baldwin, Ernest Gaines, Alice Walker, Toni Morrison, Ralph Ellison, Sherley Anne Williams and Lance Jeffers. However, there is a mellowed-down "freshness" in Dumas, that one looks hard to find in Black or, for that matter, any current writing. Thus he is both ancient and contemporary.

I first met Dumas in 1967, when he came to Southern Illinois University's Experiment in Higher Education, where I taught, to take a position as teacher-counselor and director of language workshops. (pp. xviii-xix)

During the ten months or so that he lived in East St.

Louis, Dumas's life continued to be hurried and productive. He vigorously overhauled old things and wrote new ones. He loved to visit the Celebrity Room, a local hangout for activists, poets, dancers, intellectuals and street denizens. The bar featured jazz, great conversation, poetry readings, fashion shows and other cultural events. It was there that Dumas first read his great poem, **"Our King Is Dead,"** an inspiring but frightening elegy to Martin Luther King, Jr. Dumas also spent countless hours walking, driving and talking in East St. Louis and he was especially fond of Naomi's, a soul food restaurant, which he frequented with Sherman Fowler, Joseph Harrison and myself. I took him to the South End and to Rush City, sections of East St. Louis in which I spent my childhood, and he exclaimed about how "southern," "real," and "basic" the people and the land were. That was Henry Dumas: eternally observant, thoughtful, peripatetic. . . . Whenever we had been away from Dumas for a few days, he never failed, upon his reappearance, to favor us with a reading of fresh work or to give us photocopies of new creations, usually signed and often dedicated to one of us. (p. xix)

During those electric and trying years of arts and activism, I doubled as an editor of the *East St. Louis Monitor,* a weekly newspaper owned by the late Clyde C. Jordan. Henry Dumas became a familiar figure around the *Monitor* offices and when news of his death was received, the staff of the paper expressed grief and shock. The *Monitor* published a loving obituary and my editorial, entitled simply "Henry Dumas Poet: 1934-1968." I drew some loose parallels between Dumas's and Dr. King's death—noting that in **"Our King Is Dead,"** Dumas had ironically and prophetically cried: "I am ready to die." In that same poem, he admonished Blacks for allowing too many of their "kings to be sent to the volcano," even as he himself was headed for that very same fate. The editorial, which appeared in the June 6, 1968, edition of the *Monitor,* spoke of Dumas's "instinctive communication with the spirit and soul of blackness, his remarkable insight into, and understanding of, the sources of Afro-American poeticism, his undying love for humanity and his insatiable quest for truth."

Such were the lives and times of Henry Dumas, who picked up his gauntlet, carried it with grace, funk, speed, seed and honor, and then passed it on to us. And what a grandiloquent baton! Dumas always, always insisted that we *listen,* a request he often followed with the communal exhortation, "Man, let's just *tell* it!" (p. xx)

> *Eugene B. Redmond, in an introduction to* Goodbye, Sweetwater: New & Selected Stories *by Henry Dumas, edited by Eugene B. Redmond, Thunder's Mouth Press, 1988, pp. xi-xx.*

Amiri Baraka

Dumas's power lay in his skill at creating an entirely different world organically connected to this one. The stories are fables; a mythological presence pervades. They are morality tales, magical, resonating dream emotions and images; shifting ambiguous terror, mystery, implied revelation. But they are also stories of real life, now or whenever, constructed in weirdness and poetry in which the contemporaneity of essential themes is clear.

"Fon" is strange, exuding a fantastic aura of ancient mystery and a quality almost Biblical, yet the story moves around a kind of black liberation motif which sees would-be lynchers killed. **"Will the Circle Be Unbroken?"** connects black art with anti-white black nationalism. A mysterious black musician will play the afro-horn. Whites are warned to leave, staying at their own risk. The solo is described in a brilliant poetic intensity; when it is finished, a white man slumps dead. The resistance motif in *Poetry for My People* exists in the dynamism of Dumas's imagery—plus an electric persona of black folklore, history, language, custom.

The strangeness of Dumas's world resembles Toni Morrison's wild, emotional "places." Both utilize high poetic description—language of exquisite metaphorical elegance, even as narrative precision. But language *tells* as well as decorates. Both signify as powerfully as they directly communicate. The symbols *sing,* are *cymbals* of deeper experience, not word games for academics.

The world of *Ark of Bones,* for instance, shares a black mythological lyricism, strange yet *ethnically* familiar! Africa, the southern U.S., black life and custom are motif, mood and light, rhythm, and implied history. Zora Neale Hurston, Jean Toomer, Toni Morrison, and Henry Dumas are the giants of this genre of African American literary Afro-Surreal Expressionism. Jacob Lawrence, Vincent Smith, and Romare Bearden are similar in painting; Duke, Monk, Trane, Sun Ra in music. Dumas, despite his mythological elegance and deep signification, was part of the wave of African American writers at the forefront of the '60s Black Arts Movement.

The Black Arts Movement was a reflection and important element in the '50s-'70s social upsurge of the Civil Rights and Black Liberation Movements. In each of the major upsurges of the African American freedom movement— the anti-slavery movement, the Harlem Renaissance, and the '60s Black Liberation Movement—, an accompanying artistic outreach shaped by and endowed with the energy of black rebellion would also emerge! (The whole nation is *inspired.*) (pp. 164-65)

The Afro-Surreal Expressionism of Dumas and the others mentioned unfolds the Black Aesthetic—form and content—in its actual contemporary and lived life. MUSIC (drum—polyrhythm, percussive—song as laughter or tears), preacher and congregation, call and response, the frenzy! The *color* is the polyrhythm, refracted light! But this beauty and revelation have always existed in an historically material world. The African masks are shattered and cubed. Things float and fly. Darkness defines more than light. Even in the flow of plot, there are excursions and multi-layered ambiguities. As with Bearden, Dumas's is a world in which the broken glide by in search of the healing element, or are tragically oblivious to it.

The very broken quality, almost to abstraction, is a function of change and transition. It is as though the whole world we inhabit rests on the bottom of the ocean, harnessed by memory, language, image to that "railroad of human bones" at the bottom of the Atlantic Ocean.

But in this genre the most violently antagonistic of contradictions, colors, shapes animates the personalities, settings, language of the work.

History and culture are expressed through detail and emotion. Real and unreal, it would seem, defining the disintegration and the "crossed Jordan" of wholeness or liberation, are contending themes and modes. At the same time, they are naturally twained, as fall and rise, tragedy and transcendence, slavery and freedom—parameters of the Black Aesthetic: Africa and African American, Death and Birth and Rebirth. And because so much of our collective feeling is invested, the "meanness" of the genre is literal! (pp. 165-66)

> Amiri Baraka, "Henry Dumas: Afro-Surreal Expressionist," in Black American Literature Forum, *Vol. 22, No. 2, Summer, 1988, pp. 164-66.*

Eugenia Collier

To settle down to read *Goodbye, Sweetwater,* the new collection of Henry Dumas's stories, is to embark upon a spiritual journey, for the stories reach into deep recesses of the psyche, speak to profound levels of the self. The stories dip into wellsprings of historical racial experience and become more than stories. (p. 192)

Collected and edited by poet/critic Eugene Redmond, the stories are powerful portrayals of struggle, often violent struggle, usually seen through the perceptions of a young boy. Although the names of the youths differ, as do their ages and residences, each is a child initiated, through the experience of the story, into a new level of maturity. Usually the experience is agonizing, even tragic. The young protagonist learns a bitter lesson, faces life thereafter with new and bitter wisdom. Almost always his pain is balanced by increased strength.

Often the protagonist is an adolescent on the brink of manhood. From this vantage point Dumas reveals the mythic experience, the rituals of blackness. There is no loss of innocence, for innocence is the luxury of the protected: This youngster is already aware that his motherland would destroy him if it could; buffered by his community, he has developed the toughness of spirit which enables him to endure. He is, from birth, a man/child, the focus of racist America's fears, the center of white America's nightmares. Dumas's choice of the young boy as protagonist is wise, partly because he is able to utilize his own memory of what it was like, but mostly because this acutely sensitive point of view enables Dumas to portray most forcefully black people's tragic experience and the spiritual force which is ever available if one would but acknowledge it.

The stories take place in both rural Arkansas and Harlem—the Southern homeland and the Promised Land whose promise is corrupted by the same racism which propelled black people northward in the first place. Most of the stories are set in the South, where Dumas had strong roots. It is in the South, where bare feet tread the soil and where rain nourishes the fields, that one is in contact with the ancestral spirit, the place where extreme brutality is met with collective strength and wisdom. In the squalid city, where the soil is smothered by cement and the skies yield cold and impotent snow, that spirit is remote. In the

South, for example, Headeye undergoes the mystic initiation into the timeless company of the ancestors in **"Ark of Bones."** It is in the South that the mysterious Fon, armed with little beyond the power of the spirit, defeats white Nillmon (nil/man) and his cronies, who wantonly terrorize and murder blacks. It is Harlem which is wrecked by riots, the wreckage reflecting the spiritual wreckage of a racist society. It is in Harlem that young Mack, in **"A Harlem Game,"** suffers emotional abuse by his parents, who are themselves ravished by poverty and degradation. Mack is left with a physical wound, a bloody puncture of the palm—a symbol, perhaps, of gratuitous suffering. Yet my generalization does not entirely hold up, for it is in Harlem in **"Will the Circle Be Unbroken?"** that the spiritual power of black music is so strong that whites who listen to it actually die. And it is in Harlem that the teenage quartet the Expressions, bereft by the death of their lead singer and spiritual core, find strength in unity and learn that death is not the end. These mythic areas of black America are the backdrop for the action in Dumas's stories.

The language in which the stories are executed flows from the setting. Dumas fully utilizes his poetic genius in rendering both the language of the black folk and that of the literate narrator. The language is lean and sinewy yet easy flowing and full of imagery. The recording of black folk language is ever a challenge to the writer. . . . In Dumas's work you actually hear the rich folk voice, and through it you enter the world of the black grassroots people, the nuclear people who undergird our culture. Consider, for example, Fishhound's witness:

> I come up on a snake twistin toward the water. I was gettin ready to bust that snake's head when a fox run across my path. Before I could turn my head back, a flock of birds hit the air pretty near scarin me half to death. When I got on down to the bank, I see somebody's cow lopin on the levee way down the river. Then to really upshell me, here come Headeye droopin along like he had ten tons of cotton on his back.

The voice of the literate narrator is equally compelling. Jonoah, for example, grown now, recalls the devastating flood which, when he was seven, destroyed his world:

> The current was getting stronger as the river continued to rise. The tops of trees barely showed now above the vast sea in front of us. . . . The trees that were able to hold to the ground looked like the shaking fingers of a swimmer clutching the air in that momentary period before going down to the bottom, and the floating trees—caught in the muscles of the river current—were helpless ships, drifting toward the edge of the world.

Dumas's world is peopled with archetypal characters, timeless figures who embody the essence of the black experience. The names he has given his characters plunge into the heart of their meaning, and critics need to study the symbolic value of these names. There is Headeye, for example, in **"Ark of Bones."** As his friend Fishhound explains, "Well, on Headeye, everything is stunted cept his eyes and his head." The name *Fishhound,* too, is symbolic. Christian symbols abound in Dumas's work, and one is here reminded of the old Christian symbol of the fish and the reference to the Fisher of Men. Jonoah, after a symbolic death and rebirth in the flooding Mississippi, is renamed a combination of his old name John, after the gentle Disciple, and Noah, who administered the death and rebirth of the world. Some names recur. Layton Fields in **"A Boll of Roses"** seems doomed to repeat the lifelong drudgery of picking cotton; yet Layton Bridges in **"Goodbye, Sweetwater"** realizes that his mother, living in the city, will never be able to send for him; he prepares to leave the oppression of the South with no resources but his own grit and—somehow—the will to make a way. Names are vital in Dumas's work, as they were to our ancient ancestors. In each story the names reveal important aspects of character and plot. Dumas's system of naming—places as well as people—needs further study.

Perhaps the most revealing—and challenging—aspect of Dumas's work is his symbolism. The deepest reaches of the self—both individual and collective—can be plumbed only through symbolism. Dumas's symbols are complex and not subject to easy "translation." Some have meanings which seem consistent, but most have numerous shadings and shiftings. Some of Dumas's stories are, in fact, full-blown allegories which need to be analyzed and interpreted.

A major symbol pervades **"Ark of Bones,"** the story with which Redmond wisely begins the volume. The symbol is *bones*—the bones of our ancestors. The story itself brilliantly combines Old Testament and ancient African references to deliver a powerful message. The boy Headeye finds a bone which he claims is a mojo bone—" 'a keybone to the culud man. Ain't but one in the whole world'." Even his schoolmates sense the bone's power. A few days later Headeye and his friend Fishhound, the narrator, whom Headeye brings as witness, enter an eternal dimension of the spirit, where Headeye undergoes a mystic initiation. The initiation occurs on an ark, which Fishhound at first thinks is Noah's Ark but which Headeye recognizes as a " 'soulboat.' " Headeye explains the symbol of the bones through the Biblical account of Ezekiel in the valley of the dry bones—but with an interpretation which predates the world of Ezekiel. Headeye quotes the words of God, " 'Son of man, these bones are the whole house of thy brothers, scattered to the islands. Behold, I shall bind up the bones and you shall prophesy the name'." The ark, where the boys enter the world of the ancestors, is strewn with bones, arranged ritualistically. Headeye must make his way through the bones, there to take the oath, pledging on his own bones that from his oneness with the ancestors he will strike for the freedom of black people.

The bones link past, present, and future; the physical world and the spiritual world. For bones are the nitty-gritty—they, like spirit, are what remains when flesh is gone. In Dumas's story the bones ironically symbolize hope—no, promise. The ancestors are still with us, are an ever-present resource. The bones are constantly replenished, for even as Headeye is being ordained, the mystic crewmen are pulling bones from the river. And even then, as Fishhound learns when he returns home, whites were lynching a black man, whom they threw into the river. More bones. The symbol of the bones is an important vehicle in Dumas's work, for it appears in his poetry as well as in his fiction. This symbol should receive further study.

Intensive critical analysis is needed, too, of Dumas's symbolic use of the elements—earth, air, fire, and water. These, the ancients believed, are the timeless things, the

foundation of the universe. Virtually all of Dumas's stories employ combinations of these elements, not merely descriptively but also as means of interpretation.

Earth in Dumas's stories is a shifting symbol. Bare feet walk the Southern earth, often tread carefully to avoid stumbling over roots or stepping on snakes. The mud between the toes is evidence of the link with the natural world and a subtle reminder that racism—man preying upon his own kind—is unnatural, perverted, evil. Earth is also the things that grow from it. In **"Echo Tree"** a magnificent tree is the axis in which the worlds of the flesh and the spirit meet, in which sounds *"come from the earth and the red tip of its tongue"* and echo *"voices—remade, impregnated—screaming out to the world."* In Harlem the three boys mourning their dead friend turn to the earth—to Central Park—to seek meaning in their loss.

Perhaps the earth symbol is most powerful in the staggering **"Rope of Wind."** Here the earth is the vessel which receives the sacrificial blood of the lynched Ukie: "Ukie Dodds was found shot fifteen or twenty times on his storefront veranda, and the blood ran all the way out into the year. . . . Johnny was standin in the place where Ukie lay and all his blood soaked into the ground." It is from this earth that Johnny is re-named Johnny B. And later, having borne witness to the lynching of the minister, Mr. Westland, and having run pursuing the murder car and then back to bear witness to the community, having run until his heart burst, Johnny B was laid on the very earth "over which Ukie's blood had flown" until "the blood burst out of his mouth" and mingled with the welcoming earth.

Air, for Dumas, is the wind, ever in motion, speaking, underscoring mood and action, carrying messages from the invisible to the visible world. It is the wind which carries the spirit sound from the Echo Tree to dead young Leo's brother and his friend: *"The wind, the wind. All of a sudden it sweeps across the top of the hill like an invisible hand swirling off into the darkening sky. Whispers echo from the valley throat, and all motion becomes sound, words, forces."* In several stories the wind is the messenger, unseen but palpably present, the witness of other dimensions of being.

Fire in Dumas's fiction is sometimes literally fire, as in **"Fon,"** when the white men, bent on destruction, set fire to black homes and then light torches to facilitate their intended lynching of Fon. Here the puny fire of the torches is contrasted with eternal fire: "High in the heavens now, a star comes into view from the clouds. A thin glow from a hidden moon peeps ominously from a horizon of clouds." The torches go out one by one as the would-be lynchers are shot with arrows fired by an unseen archer. Again the symbol of fire is vital as Fon, stamping out the torches with his bare feet, thinks, *"That was mighty close. But it is better this way. To have looked at them would have been too much. Four centuries of black eyes burning into four weak white men . . . would've set the whole earth on fire."* Sometimes fire is the sun, sometimes lightning flashes which illuminate significant action. Through many of the stories Dumas uses the symbol of fire.

Water, too, is a major symbol. In the stories set in the rural South, the Mississippi River is both a lifeline and a threat. The rising water presages destruction. Yet it is to the river that Headeye and Fishhound go (at Deadman's Landin) to await the arrival of the Ark of Bones. The river, which has no beginning and no end, is the agent of death and of rebirth. In *Jonoah,* the river has many meanings. On a literal level, a flash flood has devastated the area, leaving six-year-old John (later Jonoah) orphaned and facing the raging waters, naked and feverish, with only an unstable boat between him and oblivion. Acquiring first a ravished black family and then a brutal white man, who still considers himself king, Jonoah survives. Poling to maintain the precarious balance, they all survive. But as a symbol of the dangerous world of blacks in a racist society, the river is extremely effective. Water is a many-faceted symbol. Sometimes it is the rain, purifying, washing Ukie's blood into the earth. Sometimes rain, like the wind, brings messages. . . . (pp. 192-97)

In Dumas's stories (as in life) the elements must be balanced or there is chaos. Earth without water is dust. Water in excess is flood. Sun nourishes, but without rain it is fire upon the people in the fields and drought to the farmers. All of these elements as symbols need explication and interpretation.

Perhaps one of the most pervasive symbols in Dumas's work is music. It is apparent (from his poems as well as his stories) that Dumas loved black music and found in it the strength, the ancestral tie that black people have always found. Music, like the river, ties us to the generations who labored and sang out their sorrow and looked to each other and to their religion for sustenance. In several stories music is a reminder of collective strength, as in **"A Boll of Roses,"** and as a commentary on the action, as in **"The White Horse,"** in which Lili, driven mad by white brutality, sings ominously that "Pharaoh's army got drownded." Music becomes a central symbol in **"Will the Circle Be Unbroken?"** in which the spirit in black music is so strong that whites are warned not to listen, and when they do, they keel over dead. And it is through music that the teen quartet the Expressions touches infinity.

In Dumas's work symbolism blossoms into profound levels: allegory certainly, but more profoundly, myth and ritual. He probes into our collective soul-self, into levels not reached by the lyncher's rope or the subway policeman's bullets. These aspects need serious study.

Goodbye, Sweetwater leaves the reader shaken. For Dumas has portrayed black realities on so many levels. On a literal level, the life of the black folk is hideous. They are trapped in poverty which they barely survive through herculean effort. From children who ought to be in school to old people who ought to be at ease, all labor under the cruel sun to pick cotton to enrich the white man. White people—even the most economically degraded—are free to cheat, humiliate, rape, torture, and murder blacks with impunity. In Harlem, blacks are just as trapped but removed from their roots; they are confused and sometimes prey upon each other. The deplorable condition of blacks is no random occurrence: It is the predictable consequence of the racism which is supported by government at every level.

Moreover, Dumas is merciless in showing us our own inadequacies. He shows us how our blind faith in charismatic leaders has failed to reach the depths of our need, how we confuse "higher education" with real wisdom, how we become duped by the false, cruel promise of American technology, how even religion foolishly and unquestioningly pursued is deceptive. Dumas makes us uncomfortable by showing us our collective agony and our own cooperation in prolonging it.

Yet he also shows us our strengths, which can, if we use them, make us free. Mainly, Dumas tells us, we have the strength of the spirit. Dumas's black people, especially the Southern folk, are tough-spirited people whose history extends to the beginning of mankind. The racism which has diminished whites and robbed them of their humanity has not extinguished this psychic resource, for time is an endless chain in which each generation is a link forging the next link. Dumas reminds us of the force of the ancestors not only in **"Ark of Bones"** but also in his portrayal of parents and grandparents. Older women are especially strong: the old people going to the cotton fields, still knowing who they are and still riding herd on the youngsters: Jonoah's Mamada, whose dogged strength saves them all from the flood of the Mississippi and the flood of racism; Layton Fields' mother, who works with the Civil Rights workers; Layton Bridges' grandmother, who encourages him to go to the city although she, old and in dire need, will be left alone. All. Our own past, Dumas tells us, is our key to the future.

Shorn of past delusions and using past strength and wisdom, Dumas assures us, we can prevail. But he does not necessarily advocate nonviolence. Headeye pledges:

> Aba, I consecrate my bones.
> Take my soul up and plant it again.
> Your will shall be my hand.
> When I strike you strike.
> My eyes shall see only thee.
> I shall set my brother free.
> Aba, this bone is thy seal.

Not only on a psychic level but also on a physical level, the battle must be waged. Dumas does offer solutions.

It is these solutions, I am convinced, that resulted in Dumas's lifeblood's ebbing away not in the earth, like Ukie's and Johnny B's, but on the cold concrete of a New York subway.

This Fact, this inescapable Fact, is not irrelevant—indeed, is central—to serious analysis of Dumas's work. Critical analysis is not an academic exercise in pedantic isms but a serious attempt to link literature with life, with solutions, with human striving. John O. Killens used to say that the task of the writer is to change the world, and Toni Cade Bambara has said that the task of the black writer is to make revolution irresistible. These, not any empty academic standards, are the measures by which we must assess the achievements of black writers. By these standards, Henry Dumas, as demonstrated by *Goodbye Sweetwater,* is the quintessential writer, the long-distance runner—in Killens' words, the ultimate warrior—who, like Headeye, pledged his bones to free his people. (pp. 197-99)

Eugenia Collier, "Elemental Wisdom in 'Goodbye, Sweetwater': Suggestions for Further Study," in Black American Literature Forum, *Vol. 22, No. 2, Summer, 1988, pp. 192-99.*

Arnold Rampersad

The temptation in writing about authors who have died young is to concentrate on the tragedy of their premature passing and on what might have been, rather than on their actual achievement and on the fact that the future is a mystery about which we can only guess, usually with great uncertainty. In Henry Dumas's case, in particular, we should not concentrate on what might have been and in the process underestimate what he has in fact left behind him, especially in such works of fiction as *Ark of Bones, Jonoah and the Green Stone, Rope of Wind,* and *Goodbye, Sweetwater* and in his poetry. These books command our attention by their high quality. In addition, there are aspects to his body of work that show conclusively that his talent, far from being a fleeting matter, was as deeply rooted as that of many writers who have become household names in literature. (p. 329)

In the first place, and in common with the finest writers and other artists, Henry Dumas exhibited a strikingly organic rather than a contrived or spasmodic sense of composition. Rather than being forced out by the factory-like exigencies and ambitions of many of our writing schools, which increasingly have affected American literary artists for the worse, his fiction seems to have grown naturally, luxuriantly out of an inexhaustible core of inspiration. That core probably would never have completely lost its fertile power, no matter how much it had been depleted by time. Dumas was, in other words, a natural and extremely gifted writer. Character and situation, plot and landscape—all the essential elements of creativity in fiction seem intertwined in his world, even in those pieces that are obviously unfinished, mere drafts of fully realized stories.

This does not mean that there was no effort to Dumas's art. Another tendency in treating young writers, and especially those stopped too soon by death, is to see them as innocent of technique, naïve and even blissfully ignorant of the demands of art. Not so with Dumas. . . . [We] see that Dumas worked extremely hard to shape his craft, changing this and that, noting what needed to be revised and augmented. Clearly Henry Dumas was something of a perfectionist, searching for the perfect word in the exalted tradition of discipline we sometimes associate with Flaubert. All the while, on the other hand, Dumas was maturely also well aware that art is basically process, and that perfection of craft is finally an unattainable goal.

There may be a fascinating link here between the author and his subject. Dumas wrote about people who worked hard, who were made to work hard and expect little reward—and he himself obviously worked hard at his writing. In a sense, he worked alongside of his key characters, as if he, too, were a sharecropper, and expected little reward beyond the satisfaction of a job well done. He worked hard at his writing in spite of this limited expectation of reward from a culture that generally ignores and even despises the minority artist—and especially the black artist. If Dumas were at all alienated politically by racism, as he must have been, then he was aware of himself as a writer in an essentially foreign tongue which he nevertheless believed he had to master. He attempted that mastery. Remarkably present in his writing is the quality of eager wrestling with the word, in a mixture of rage and almost erotic delight, that one finds in the work of so many very good writers, of all races, who find themselves in a state of permanent and irreconcilable tension with a dominating and essentially hostile culture.

As a writer, too, Dumas had an extraordinary and rather different sense of place. It matters little whether this place was specific and rooted in his actual experience, or a fusion of various places he had known, or a fusion of the actual and the imagined, or of the actual and the literary. The fact is that, reading Dumas, one is convinced by the authenticity of his regional American setting, as one is convinced by writers as different as William Faulkner, Eudora Welty, Ernest Gaines, and Richard Wright. There was a difference in Dumas, however. Perhaps more than any of these writers, he was eager to suggest not only an authentic, verifiable identification of place but at the same time a surreal, intensely symbolic spatial element which opens up his fiction beyond the limits of realism and naturalism toward further symbolic and surrealistic complication.

In the basic landscape depicted in his fiction, nature—not industry or the city—predominates. The woods and fields are challenged only tentatively by human settlements, and everything is dominated by the big river, which operates . . . as a dominating and retributive God, implacable and fatalistic. The land is fertile but demanding, the crops rich but bitter, the atmosphere humid and erotic but lethal and forbidding—as before a cyclone. Time takes on a different character and function in Dumas's world, at least when his fiction is most powerful. Time seems to join space in detaching itself from the grounding context of realism and naturalism.

The most fascinating aspect of his work may well be the tension between his interest in realism and his interest in the surreal. Side by side with his concrete, tactile sense of reality is Dumas's imaginative determination, fed no doubt by his interest in Eastern culture, to render the world and experience in a mythic and symbolic sense. While many, perhaps even most, readers will find this approach among the least satisfying of his ventures in fiction and poetry, Dumas's experiments in this area unquestionably broaden our sense of his range of vision, as well as his intellectual and philosophical depth. What holds the sometimes conflicting elements of his art and thought together is Dumas's reverence for black life and his respect for the vagaries of black experience both historically, as concerning Africa, slavery, and Afro-American neo-slavery, and on a daily basis. To some extent, the marked degree of this reverence and respect was typically of the nineteen sixties, when much of his fiction was written. Sometimes, the theme of black dignity is developed against a background of the Civil Rights Movement. But Dumas eventually transcends the particulars of his decade. The feeling for black character, the avoidance of the sensational or the stereotypical, of trite situations and hackneyed phrases—these qualities have to do with a deeply internalized affection for black culture and a feeling of comfort and security within it. Human beings in Dumas's world testify by their sweat and their suffering, as well as their efforts to transcend both, and by the eloquent terseness of their language.

All these elements finally come together into a whole. Dumas, in a remarkable achievement—given the brevity of his career and his few books—, has succeeded in creating a world in which the reader recognizes new characters

CONTEMPORARY LITERARY CRITICISM, Vol. 62

as one would recognize distant relatives, because they emerge almost inevitably after a while from the basic text of the author's imagination. While no one can claim persuasively that the fictional world created by Henry Dumas is as well defined and as memorable as, say, William Faulkner's Yoknapatawpha or Thomas Hardy's Wessex, he shares with these and certain other great writers a rare gift—to be able from early in his career to see his fictional domain, both written and as yet unwritten, as in a lordly overview. In other words, Dumas seemed to know where he was going from the start; he seemed to be aware of what was going on in different places at different times within his imagined world, and where the whole was heading. This prescience has to do with the fact that a consistent intelligence—reflective, brooding, illuminating, commanding—informs virtually all the work, even the abbreviated or unfinished pieces, or those apparently immature.

Not least of all in importance in understanding Dumas is his sense of security with himself as a black writer. If he felt, as other black writers have felt, alienation from the English language, he seemed to harbor no confusion whatsoever about the validity of his role as an artist committed to writing about the Afro-American experience. The fact that Dumas was committed to politics, fascinated by a solemn mode of the surreal, and also prepared to indulge a notable comic sense (about which more needs to be written, I would suggest) underscores our sense of his confidence that he had an almost guaranteed place as a writer in Afro-American culture. This confidence will finally be shared by anyone who approaches Henry Dumas's writing with an open mind and an open heart. (pp. 329-32)

Arnold Rampersad, "Henry Dumas's World of Fiction," in Black American Literature Forum, *Vol. 22, No. 2, Summer, 1988, pp. 329-32.*

FURTHER READING

Black American Literature Forum 22, No. 2 (Summer 1988).

Special issue devoted to Dumas which features articles by Gwendolyn Brooks, Ishmael Reed, and Eugene Redmond among others. In addition, this issue features several of Dumas's poems and an interview with his widow, Loretta Dumas.

Jackson, Angela. A review of *Ark of Bones, and Other Stories.* *Black World.* Vol. XXIV, no. 3 (January 1975): 51-2.

Laudatory review in which the critic praises Dumas's characterizations and vibrant use of language.

Morrison, Toni. "City Limits, Village Values: Concepts of the Neighborhood in Black Fiction." In *Literature and the American Urban Experience,* edited by Michael C. Jaye and Ann Chalmers Watts, pp. 35-43. Manchester: Manchester University Press, 1981.

Brief treatment of rural and urban life in Dumas's fiction.

Taylor, Clyde. "The Poet's Work." *Black World.* Vol. XXIV, no. 11 (September 1975): 4-16.

Positing that "Afro-American literature will be recognized as the first line of defense of Afro culture," Taylor views Dumas as a major figure for his confidence in rendering language, themes, and identity pertaining particularly to African-American culture.

Ilya Ehrenburg

1891-1967

(Born Ilya Grigoryevich Ehrenburg) Russian novelist, poet, short story writer, journalist, memoirist, and nonfiction writer.

Among the Soviet Union's most prolific and widely read twentieth-century authors, Ehrenburg alternately ridiculed and glorified the political and social conditions of his country. A bold satirist during and immediately following the 1917 Revolution, Ehrenburg escaped Josef Stalin's persecution of Jewish intellectuals by publicly supporting the Soviet leader, a stance he abruptly recanted after the dictator's death. Reflecting upon his survival, Ehrenburg stated: "I lived in an era when the fate of man resembled not so much a chess game as a lottery." While critics generally dismiss the novels Ehrenburg published under Stalin's regime as turgid examples of state sanctioned "socialist realism," his works written before the advent of rigid controls are often lauded as incisive syntheses of melodrama and satire. Glem Struve observed: "It is [his] corrosive, all-pervading nihilistic cynicism, apparent in all his best work, that is Ehrenburg's principal attribute as a writer. All the rest—his enthusiasm for Soviet achievements on various fronts . . . or his patriotic effusions during the Soviet-German war—are mere pose. And yet behind this cynical, wholesale negation one senses the tragic dualism of a man whose real roots are in that very civilization he so ruthlessly yet lightheartedly exposed."

Born to middle-class Jewish parents, Ehrenburg joined the Bolsheviks in his early teens and was imprisoned for five months following the failed Revolution of 1905. He withdrew from political activity in 1909 and emigrated to Paris, where he associated with such artists and writers as Pablo Picasso and André Malraux before briefly entering a Benedictine monastery. At this time, Ehrenburg also published his first poems, which were largely unnoticed. After the outbreak of World War I, Ehrenburg became a correspondent for the Russian newspapers *Birzhevye Vedemosti* and *Utro Rossii*. His volume *Lik voiny* (*The Face of War*) collects many of his dispatches from this period. Ehrenburg returned to Russia in 1917 following the overthrow of the tzar, but was disillusioned by the ensuing chaos of civil war. He expressed his sorrow over the revolution's "release of evil spirits" in *Molitva o Rossii* (*A Prayer for Russia*), his best known volume of poetry.

In 1921, Ehrenburg attempted to return to Paris, but French officials refused him entry, erroneously believing he was a Bolshevik spy. He travelled instead to Belgium, where he wrote his first novel, *Neobychainye pokhozhdeniya Khulio Khurenito i ego uchenikov* (*The Extraordinary Adventures of Julio Jurenito and His Disciples*). This satirical work revolves around Julio Jurenito, a mystical Latin American whom, some biographers claim, Ehrenburg modeled after his friend, Mexican artist Diego Rivera. Julio travels through France, Mexico, Italy, and Russia, cynically preaching anarchy and nihilism to his diverse following, which includes an American brothel owner, a bourgeois Frenchman, and a Russian Jew named Ehren-

burg. Generally considered Ehrenburg's greatest achievement, the novel transcends cultural and class distinctions in its scornful indictment of modern life. Erik de Mauny asserted: "[*Julio Jurenito*] is a fireworks display of wild inventiveness, a ferocious orgy of wit and black humor, which has lost none of its corrosive bite over the years; and although Ehrenburg subsequently directed his satiric barbs at various aspects of modern civilization, he never quite rivalled it in any of his later works."

Permitted to reenter France in 1924, Ehrenburg continued to compose novels contemptuous of both capitalism and communism. Following his novel *Liubov Zhanny Nei* (*The Love of Jenny Ney*), the story of a Frenchwoman and her liaison with a subversive Russian communist, Ehrenburg published *V Protochnom pereulke* (*A Street in Moscow*). Considered among the most comprehensive portrayals of its social milieu, this work follows shopkeepers, beggars, orphans, and former aristocrats as they struggle to survive in a Moscow slum during the aftermath of the revolution. Ehrenburg's next novel, *Burnaia zhizn Lazik Roitschwantz* (*The Stormy Life of Lasik Roitschwantz*), lampoons Western and Eastern European society in its depiction of a poor Jewish tailor and his comic misadventures while wandering across the continent. Vera Alexandrova observed: "Lazik wanders from city to city, from prison to prison, from country to country in search of the small but eternal truth—man's right to happiness—and ultimately comes to the conclusion that happiness is 'only an antiquated word in a mighty language'."

With the rise of the Nazi party in Germany during the 1930s, the focus of Ehrenburg's writing altered radically. Virulently anti-fascist, Ehrenburg became a dedicated supporter of the Soviet government and abandoned his satirical style previously condemned by authorities in *Julio Jurenito* and *A Street in Moscow.* He instead adopted the official literary form of socialist realism, which resulted in such works as *Den' vtoroi* (*Out of Chaos*). Concerning the building of a steel mill in Siberia, *Out of Chaos* chronicles the complex relationships between Kolka, a dedicated construction worker, Volodia, a suicidal intellectual, and Irina, Volodia's lover who, in rejecting him, renounces all ties to the czarist past. Western critics often disagreed in their assessment of this and other novels Ehrenburg wrote in the 1930s, including *Moskva slezam ne verit* and *Ne perevodia dykhaniia.* Routinely dismissed as a propagandist, Ehrenburg nevertheless garnered praise for his kaleidoscopic portrait of the Soviet people.

While living in Paris, Ehrenburg also worked as a journalist for the Soviet newspaper *Izvestia,* reporting on such events as the Spanish Civil War and the movement of Nazi troops into Austria during 1938. After the invasion of France by Germany in 1940, Ehrenburg returned to Moscow, where he wrote *Padenie Parizha* (*The Fall of Paris*), which couched his strong opposition to the Nazi-Soviet pact of 1939 in an emotional portrayal of his beloved city's surrender to the fascists. Although Soviet publishers initially rejected the novel, *The Fall of Paris* went to press days after a telephone call by Stalin to Ehrenburg in which the communist leader expressed his respect for the work, a change in attitude that foreshadowed the rift between the Soviet Union and Germany. Outside the U.S.S.R., critics labeled *The Fall of Paris* a political diatribe yet praised its sensitive evocation of a society in turmoil. During World War II, Ehrenburg became a correspondent for two Soviet newspapers, *Kransnaya zvezda* and *Pravda.* His vivid journalistic style, coupled with his loathing for Nazism resulted in pieces immensely popular among Soviet soldiers. These wartime efforts eventually won Ehrenburg his country's prestigious Order of Lenin, and several Soviet military leaders later indicated that his agitation was instrumental in the success of their campaign against Germany. Yet Edward Crankshaw recalled: "When I knew [Ehrenburg] in Russia during the war it seemed to me that the vitriolic hatred of the Germans that came pouring out in the extraordinary flow of daily articles which made him a popular hero was nourished not only by his rage and horror at what the Germans were doing to his country but also by his pent-up hatred of Stalin and himself."

Following the war, Ehrenburg continued to publish novels under the auspices of his government. *Buria* (*The Storm*) won the Stalin Prize in 1949 for its story of a Russian emigré's disillusionment abroad and subsequent return home. Ehrenburg also received critical accolades in the Soviet Union for *Deviatyi vai* (*The Ninth Wave*), a novel often grouped with *The Fall of Paris* and *The Storm* as a three volume chronicle of the relationship between France and the Soviet Union. Leigh White's review of Ehrenburg's

nonfiction work *Dorogi Evropy* (*European Crossroad: A Soviet Journalist in the Balkans*), sums up general Western opinion of Ehrenburg's post-war efforts under Stalinism: "[Ehrenburg writes] in a style that is perfectly adapted to the demands of Soviet censorship. His book, as a result, is superficial, inaccurate, maudlin, and unenlightening." Following Stalin's death in 1953, however, Ehrenburg astonished the Soviet literary establishment with his novel *Ottepel* (*The Thaw*), which repudiated his well-publicized conservatism. A portrait of a drab Russian factory town and the frustrations faced by its inhabitants, *The Thaw* openly addresses such previously forbidden subjects as squalid housing conditions, food shortages, and favoritism among party members. While Western critics questioned its literary value, *The Thaw* ignited international debate concerning artistic freedom in the U.S.S.R. and prompted communist leader Nikita Khrushchev to publicly condemn the novel as subversive.

In the last years of his life, Ehrenburg continued to support the liberalization of government policies toward the arts and championed the official rehabilitation of such banned authors as Isaac Babel and Osip Mandelstam. His literary output following *The Thaw* consisted primarily of his six volume memoir, *Liudi, gody, zhizn* (*Men, Years, Life*), which moves from his early years in Paris to the final days of Stalin's dictatorship. *Men, Years, Life* is often regarded as Ehrenburg's attempt to redeem his standing in intellectual circles outside the Soviet Union and to resurrect the experimental vitality of his early prose repressed by his work as a propagandist. While many critics faulted Ehrenburg for not directly addressing his capitulation to Stalinism, *Men, Years, Life* is nevertheless considered a sincere reflection of a tumultuous age. Michael Scammell concluded: "The melancholy fact is that [Ehrenburg] lived through a period of unparalleled ferocity in modern Russian history, which caused special hardship in the arts. The Soviet experience produced new categories of horror for writers to endure, and Ehrenburg's tortured career testifies to the terrible price exacted from those who weren't strong enough for heroism or martyrdom, but who tried to preserve at least some shred of integrity."

(See also *CLC,* Vols. 18, 24; *Contemporary Authors,* Vol. 102; and *Contemporary Authors New Revision Series,* Vols. 25-28 [obituary].)

PRINCIPAL WORKS

NOVELS

Neobychainye pokhozhdeniya Khulio Khurenito i ego uchenikov 1922
[*The Extraordinary Adventures of Julio Jurenito and His Disciples,* 1930; also published as *Julio Jurenito,* 1958]
Liubov Zhanny Nei 2 vols. 1925-1926
[*The Love of Jenny Ney,* 1929]
V Protochnom pereulke 1927
[*A Street in Moscow,* 1932]
Burnaia zhizn Lazika Roltshvanetsa 1928
[*The Stormy Life of Lasik Roitschwantz,* 1960]
Desiat loshadinykh sil 1929
[*The Life of the Automobile,* 1977]
Moskva slezam ne verit 1933
Den' vtoroi 1934

[*Out of Chaos,* 1934]
Ne perevodia dykhaniia   1935
Padenie Parizha   1942
   [*The Fall of Paris,* 1942]
Buria   1948
   [*The Storm: A Novel in Six Parts,* 1948; also published
      as *The Storm,* 1949]
Deviatyi vai   1953
   [*The Ninth Wave,* 1955]
Ottepel   1955
   [*The Thaw,* 1955]

POETRY

Stikhi o Kanunakh   1916
Molitva o Rossii   1918

SHORT FICTION COLLECTIONS

Trinadtsat trubok   1923
Ispanskii zakal   1938

OTHER

Lik voiny (nonfiction)   1920
Voina, iiun 1941-aprel 1942 (nonfiction)   1942
   [*Russian at War,*   1943, also published as *The Temper-
      ing of Russia,* 1944]
Dorogi Evropy (nonfiction)   1946
   [*European Crossroad: A Soviet Journalist in the Balkans,*
      1947]
Luidi, gody, zhizn   6 vols. (memoirs)   1961-c. 1967
   [*Men, Years, Life*   6 vols.   1961-1966; also published
      as *Men, Years, Life*   4 vols. (revised edition),
      1962-1967]

The Nation, New York

[In *A Street in Moscow,* the] citizens who live in "the"
Protochny Street, near the Moscow River, do not argue
the principles of Marx and Engels. Kulaks, hunchback
fiddlers, broken-down aristocrats, betrayed maidens, misfit journalists, dismissed Latin instructors, hangers-on,
"abandoned" children—they are the backwash of the revolution and spend most of their energy keeping alive. Mr.
Ehrenbourg's purpose in writing about them is not to tell
a story, though he helps himself freely to the devices of
narration; his purpose is really to reveal his encyclopedic
knowledge of slum life in the U.S.S.R. Like his characters,
he is not a Communist himself, though we are told that
the Communist chiefs, including Stalin, read him for the
sociological information that his work contains. Artistically this book is not interesting, being a mixture of superficial brilliance, sentimentality, hokum, and Grand
Guignol horrors. But as a piece of fictional journalism it
is exceptionally informative.

> *A review of "A Street in Moscow," in* The Na-
> tion, *New York, Vol. CXXXIV, No. 3489, May
> 18, 1932, p. 578.*

Joanna Cannan

There are many people who make a point of refusing a
Russian novel, suspecting a melancholy outlook or a
string of proper names and the trouble of remembering
"vitch is vitch"; to these I would recommend *A Street in
Moscow* as an eminently readable and not uncheerful
book. Its author, Ilya Ehrenbourg, is a true artist; he has
his "pivot of repose"; and though he writes of Moscow in
1926, of cruelty and poverty and oppression almost unbelievable to the English mind, in his mean Protochny Street
there blossoms, with the abrupt beauty of a Russian
springtime, the wisdom and nobility of the beggared
schoolmaster, the love of the hunch-backed violinist, the
deathless idealism of the girl Tanya; and the story ends on
a note of pure and reasoned joy.

> *Joanna Cannan, "Hugh Walpole and Others,"
> in* The Bookman, *London, Vol. LXXXIV, No.
> 499, April, 1933, p. 62.*

Gertrude Diamant

It is an interesting aspect of a novel like *Out of Chaos,* and
true for most of the novels reflecting the industrial epic in
Russia, that psychological realism in the treatment of
character persists along with the journalistic presentation
of those specific and transitory problems that have arisen
in the Soviet Union. In a sense the Russian novelist has
no choice but to become a propagandist. The terrific import of the revolution and the fact that few aspects of Soviet culture have become crystallized and static inevitably
impose on him an orientation toward the themes of indus-
trialization and the conflict between the old and the new.
It is the nature of things, and not any political fiat, that
has deprived the Soviet novelist of autonomy; and his
problem at the moment would seem to be not so much the
relation between propaganda and art as the problem of
conserving character portrayal, and other aesthetic elements of the novel, within the framework of a topical
theme and a journalistic rapidity of narration. Politically,
Out of Chaos is a sympathetic yet not uncritical picture
of the building of a giant steel plant in Siberia. Aesthetically, it is a detailed and convincing study of the psychological evolution of three characters: Kolka Rzhanov, a young
shock-brigader who identifies himself wholly with Soviet
construction; Volodia Safonov, the intellectual who passes
from doubt and skepticism to suicide; and Irina, who in
renouncing her love for Volodia rejects all that is identified with the old order, all indecision and defeatism. (p.
681)

Chaos in the spiritual world; in the physical world a confusion of barracks, blast furnaces, steam shovels, cranes,
and hoists; death from freezing and typhus—this was the
reality of the Five-Year Plan at Kuznetsk. This was the
embattled world in which Kolka Rzhanov found the answer to his boredom, a complete way of living, the integration of his personality, and an outlet for all his aggressive
instincts. At the same time, in the Soviet university at
Tomsk, Volodia Safonov observed the inhumanity, the
crassness, the terrific power and buoyancy of the revolution, and yet remained aloof. He found that his comrades
could not "speak like human beings, making mistakes,
stammering, with fire . . . of that which is personal." Volodia did not believe that a blast furnace was more beautiful than Venus, he did not "explain Dr. Faust's boredom
by the peculiarities of the period of initial accumulation

of capital." Though he was too young to remember the old regime, he suffered from the "hereditary illness" of introspection. He lacked faith and optimism; his sensibilities were still individual and aesthetic. He could not adapt himself to a world that recognized action as the only form of behavior, and he found in suicide the one gesture of self-assertion left to him.

Technically, the novel borrows from the cinema. In order to show the chaos of the revolution, the simultaneity of conflicting occurrences, the eye of the author ranges over all Russia, catches an event in sharp, visual impressions. Frequently the attention of the reader is concentrated wholly on things, on objects in motion, as a symbolism for building up both mood and background. There are thirty-two characters in all, some represented only by short biographies. But wherever he deals extensively with a case history, Ehrenbourg notwithstanding his sympathy with the ultimate aims of communism, reserves the novelist's prerogative—that is, he shows the complex, subjective motivation under the new, socialized sensibilities of his characters. (pp. 681-82)

> Gertrude Diamant, "Soviet Kaleidoscope," in The Nation, *New York, Vol. CXXXVIII, No. 3597, June 13, 1934, pp. 681-82.*

Kate O'Brien

To commit a novel, which by its form asserts itself to be a free work of imagination, outright from before its first appearance to the uses of propaganda, is to offend against it seriously, some writers . . . will think; but Russian novelists have accepted the harnessing of their talents to the State and to its expediencies, and so it is possible that Ilya Ehrenburg will find nothing odd in the presentation this week to English readers of his new novel, *The Fall Of Paris.* It is the Stalin Prize Novel of 1942, it comes to us crowned and blessed by M. Maisky, and was ushered in by the B.B.C. in the eight o'clock news on the morning of Premier Stalin's birthday.

Now all of this may be very nice and courteous, but it is irrelevant, and tells the average intelligent reader nothing of what he really wants to know about a new piece of creative writing. In any case, there is no doubt that *The Fall Of Paris* will do very well on its own steam, for it is a very good novel, and it comes to us in a period of bad novels; it is like a swallow in winter, and will receive all the consideration due to such a visitant. Moreover, it deals on a large scale, and as no other novelist of any nationality has yet tried to, with the most gigantic of contemporary tragedies—the collapse and humiliation of France. It is a very ambitious book, and, without resorting to hyperbole, it can be said to justify a large measure of its ambition. It opens in *Rue Cherche-Midi* in the studio of an obscure and peaceful painter in the early spring of 1936, and it ends in the same studio on 14th July, 1940. Within that crowded span of time it takes us all over Paris and here and there in France, up and down the agitated social scale; it shows us the public actions and the private anxieties, sins and dreams of a great crowd of characters; and in close relation to these picked machinators and victims, it endeavours to reveal to us in its process that decay and "dilapidation"—to use *de Saint Exupéry's* word—which

hereafter we must view as one of the bitterest calamities of all history.

The book is packed, as it had to be, with disaster, disillusionment and sorrow; and if it contains the seeds of a faraway, general hope—in its simple presentation of the courage and the detached generosity of some of the young, some of that generation hitherto supposed by its elders everywhere to be no good, to be "degenerate"—it attempts no personal consolations. It is nowhere cheap, and it is not sensational. What the author has seen and has to record surpasses comment and exclamation; he lets events and people speak faithfully for themselves—and it is indeed wonderful that, standing still so near his enormous theme, and writing necessarily out of fresh and painful emotion, he manages to be so honest, so steady, and so fair, almost kind, to those terrible personal weaknesses and dishonesties which brought down ruin on the most civilised and intelligent people in the world.

There are a great many excellent character sketches; as it deals closely with historical events, it is to some extent a *roman à clef,* and those public men who, disguised, are impressed into the text of the story, are presented with a just restraint, with an understanding of their sentimentalities, their blindnesses, and their fatal French individualism which is firm and effective, but also merciful. But with the obscure characters who are the tragedy's real victims—the works engineer, the actress girl, the two children of the successful politician, the detached, peaceful painter—the author is at his best, although with them, particularly with the last, he loses a little his sense of French character, and reveals himself as a Russian novelist, thereby gaining certain variations of mood and thought which enrich the whole work. So that although, one is reminded sometimes, by the book's shape and its theme, of the later work of Roger Martin du Gard, and sometimes of Jules Romains, such comparison would be mainly technical, for psychologically the book reflects light that is not French, and lacking something of French precision, immediacy, and penetration, is compensatorily gentle and touched with lyricism. But if the author is not French, he knows and loves Paris through and through; and Paris shines, living and lovely, on page after page, even to the very end, in her bedraggled desolation. "German flags were everywhere. German soldiers were marching along the quay: right-left, right-left. Grey-green uniforms. . . . And all around was blue—the sky, the Seine and the houses." This is a good book indeed. . . . (pp. 604, 606)

> Kate O'Brien, in a review of "The Fall of Paris," in The Spectator, *Vol. 169, No. 5974, December 25, 1942, pp. 604, 606.*

Queen's Quarterly

[*The Fall of Paris*] is the tale of the disintegration of French politics and army command from 1935 to the occupation of Paris. With the background of the author, there is no wonder that the communists come out best. But not only they: the younger people at large prove better politicians because, at heart, they are better, more enlightened patriots than the older men of 'l'entre deux guerres'. The book presents a panoramic picture of moving events. We have the first stay-in strike, the elections that brought in the Front Populaire and the political manoeuvres that made it ineffective, the war in Spain and the intrigues to prevent any military help being sent to the Republicans; the 1938 mobilization; the the 'phony' war and the excruciating débâcle; then Bordeaux, then Vichy and the strangling of the French constitution by the mandataries of the people: "It was hara-kiri . . . we declared ourselves dead and then applauded. There were 569 corpses and 80 impudent ones. That's all." Then Paris occupied and the killing of people by Germans who cannot but feel that they are out of place there.

Two generations are pictured. Among the older men we find Picart, the general concerned above all with the measures that will keep the 'rabble' in its place; Dessert, the financier and industrialist, born in the well known, solid, French lower middle class. He strives to keep the traditions of the French republican liberals and finds no way out but to kill himself after his failure; the sinister fascists Breteuil and his younger colleague Grandel, both of whom turn collaborationists and traitors; Joliot, the journalist utterly rotten; Tessa, the Deputy who sells his conscience and betrays his party to keep his seat and later becomes a Minister. Some of their wives see through them, but most remain passive or pleasure-seeking. And contrasted with all these are the younger people: Tess's children: Lucien, supremely intelligent and perfectly amoral, and Denise, who becomes a communist; Pierre the engineer, and his wife Agnès, the teacher, who both die; André the painter, in whose studio the book begins and ends, as the symbol that art in France always survives.

And as a setting against which these actors move there is Paris, a familiar Paris which Mr. Ehrenbourg knows and loves well. Some of his pictures stand out with a nostalgic beauty: a street in the suburb of Belleville, la rue du Cherche-Midi, "the grimy houses of the Ile St. Louis, the waters of the Seine, mysterious as Lethe, the dimly perceived pale sky . . . "

At times one regrets a somewhat melodramatic streak: Breteuil's little son dies on the same day as young Jeannot, the apprentice killed in the strike by stooges; or the death of Jennette, the stupid, good and beautiful woman whom Dessert and André love. It is difficult to understand how Lucien, after his swim to reach a boat at Dunkirk, finds his death inland, later on when he is taken for the bandit he is not. The idea of the descent of the working men to the Champs Elysées on the 14th of July recalls a tale by Jules Romains. And the style, at times, makes one think of Dos Passos in his *1919*: vivid flashes, with a good deal of power and life.

And the beautiful end, and the faith in the common people of France, Michaud, the serious, young communist engineer, Denise's mate, speaks the author's conclusion:

> Michaud and Denise sat silent with their arms round each other. Then Denise freed herself and said: "You don't know what it's like in Paris now. Yesterday I saw a German club a workman on the head with a revolver. The man fell down but the German didn't even look back. They arrested Gémier for listening to the London radio. They tortured him two days running. A German officer said to Marie: "Your father's jacket is blood-stained. Bring a new one." She brought it. The officer took the jacket and went away with it. Then he came back and said: 'You're still here? What are you

> waiting for? Your father is already in the English heaven.' Michaud, are they human beings?"

> "No. They're Fascists. I've seen just the same. They killed a child. No, I won't talk about it. But there's going to be happiness, Denise, a great happiness! Don't you believe it? You must realize we're going to win. It's as simple as day after night or spring after winter. It can't be otherwise. What fine people we've got! They're ready to lay down their lives. But who have the others got? Robbers. Or degenerates. We're bound to win! And then there will be happiness. How the people have longed for it! Big, simple happiness, the simplest happiness even—to live and breathe, not to fear the sound of footsteps, not to hear the wail of sirens, and to fondle children and to love, just as you and I . . . It will be happiness . . . "

This was written in 1940-41. (pp. 214-15)

> *M. T., in a review of "The Fall of Paris," in* Queen's Quarterly, *Vol. L, No. 2, Summer, 1943, pp. 213-15.*

Soviet Literature

There is the breath of war in this collection of Ilya Ehrenburg's poems [*The Tree*] which contains the best of his verses written in the past seven years. Whereas Ehrenburg's newspaper articles tend to convey the heroic deeds of his fellow citizens, the wrathful voice of conscience, his verses are expressions of love and sorrow. And so, in his poems, Ehrenburg speaks in a voice that is quiet and subdued, yet most penetrating.

The book's title comes from the first poem, a landscape of the war. The grass lies flat and the last lark has deserted a solitary tree that remains on guard as though to defend the eminence alone. When the tree perishes in the shelling, the moment is as solemn and poignant as the death of a man.

This symbol is well expressive of the contents of the book. War's devastation of nature, of cities, art and culture, the creations of man, is the sombre theme of the poet.

The book begins with a series of poems dedicated to the Civil War in Spain. Barcelona, Madrid, the Spanish battlefield, the first open struggle against fascism are treated laconically. Then follows Paris, a peaceful city in 1938, but overrun and occupied by the Wehrmacht in the summer of 1940. The final poem, one of the best in the book, describes a city that has vanished and died, forgotten by all. The poet here compares occupied Paris with fallen Rome. The element of protest is not long lacking, as he exclaims "it was not for this that Balzac wrote," not to hear "the iron tread of alien troops." "It was not for this," repeated again and again, resounds like an oath, an appeal not to be subdued by the enemy, an appeal harbouring the conviction that Paris shall rise again. . . .

Three poems might be mentioned as characteristic of the entire collection. In the first, **"Kiev,"** that city arises as a fighter, as a living thing, "Kiev rent apart its bridges and shed its stone," says the poet. The second, called **"Europe,"** is a hymn to European civilization which nurtured the poet and expresses his longing for the shaded halls of the Louvre, for Praxitiles. Mentioned side by side here are the names of the German poet Heinrich Heine and the Russian publicist Gleb Uspensky. **"The Ghetto"** is the third of these poems and it begins a series dealing with the most fearful and monstrous pages of World War II, the annihilation of the Jewish people by the fascists. These verses are biting, wrathful, imbued with a great sorrow.

The collection concludes with a poetic legacy in which Ehrenburg writes: "When I am gone you will remember the rustle of newspapers, the year that was terrible and yet dear to us all." He exhorts the reader to think then not only of the thunder of Stalingrad, but also of the barely audible whisper of the trees, of nature which he loves, which he looks on as a symbol of constancy and to which he has dedicated his verses.

> *"Ehrenburg's Poems," in* Soviet Literature, *No. 3, 1947, p. 52.*

Russell Kirk

Ilya Ehrenburg, one of the most influential of Soviet writers, tried . . . [in 1954] to express in fiction the mildest of criticisms and the faintest hint of ridicule of the Soviet state. He and his novel, *The Thaw,* came off badly within a few months, being denounced late that summer by the Union of Soviet Writers, and Ehrenburg was forced to defend himself against the attacks of Simonov and other pillars of Soviet orthodoxy when the Second Congress of Soviet Writers met at the end of the year. He gave ground, but he did not recant wholly; and his novel was not officially suppressed. Possibly Ehrenburg thought some show of sincere opposition safer than abject contrition and confession; while Simonov and his colleagues may have thought it the part of discretion to rest content with Ehrenburg's imperfect apology. Some of Ehrenburg's allies were reprimanded or punished; but at least they did not die or vanish, like Gorki and Babel.

This episode, closely related to the silent struggle for power in the Soviet Union after Stalin's death, may have a sequel. It is part of the long contest between the Soviet state and the presumptuous man of letters, which recurs from decade to decade. . . . But possibly more important than the political significance of this tempest in a samovar is the novel itself. I do not mean that it is a good novel: it is dull and formless. The characters in *The Thaw* do not live; it is no better than Ehrenburg's earlier work. To say that Ehrenburg is one of the best writers surviving in Russia is only to damn him with faint praise. Yet, however timidly and ineptly, Ehrenburg attempted in this book to break with the orthodox 'Soviet realism' and to represent real human beings and real problems of life. 'You read novels where everything is in its place,' he said in his own defence before the Congress of Soviet Writers, 'every detail of the machines and of production meetings is properly described . . . but where's the human soul?' (pp. 249-50)

Now I think that *The Thaw* tells us a good deal about the frame of mind at present dominant among the administrative and intellectual orders in Soviet Russia—and gives us some understanding of the prospects of that society. I think, also, that it unintentionally reveals the ruinous condition of serious literature under a totalist state, and the impossibility of reviving humane letters in a collectivistic society.

'Realism, n. The art of depicting nature as it is seen by toads. The charm suffusing a landscape painted by a mole, or a story written by a measuring-worm.' This is Ambrose Bierce's definition, from *The Devil's Dictionary.* Now *The Thaw* is a genuinely realistic novel—which is a far cry from conventional 'Soviet realism'—but it has little enough in common with the 'realism' of Zola, say, or James T. Farrell. It is much closer to the realistic novel written by the garret-scholar in Gissing's *New Grub Street,* who trails a butcher and his wife about London so as to miss no dull detail of their conversation. What Ehrenburg has endeavoured to do is to examine candidly the decent drabness of existence among very ordinary and obscure middle-class Russians of the new order. These people have no grand passions and no overweening aspirations. Ehrenburg is no toad; but the analogy of the measuring-worm is apt enough.

I repeat that the society of *The Thaw* is restricted middle-class society. Nothing to come out of Soviet Russia since the triumph of Stalin—except, possibly, for two or three films, and those unintentionally—better establishes the fact that the classless society is only a phrase in modern Russia. The characters in this novel—characters ineptly drawn, and possessed of no living personality, but nevertheless marked with the stamp of authenticity—are reasonably well off, secure, and even smug, displaying many of the virtues commonly called bourgeois, and few of the vices. They go to the theatre and the opera; they have their little parties; they fret about self-advancement; they slip into love rather languidly, and slip out of it again. They know next to nothing of the political oligarchy which governs them—only an occasional dreaded reprimand or summons from Moscow disturbs the placid round of domestic duties and factory production and lectures and amusements. And the life of the labouring classes is nearly as remote from them as is the life of the upper ranks of Party and bureaucracy. . . . The managerial class, with its literary and artistic appendages, is what interests Ehrenburg. There are some brief conventional glimpses of a *kolhoz* presided over by a matriarch; yet of what life really is like in such a collective we are given few hints. White collar and business suit seem to be the marks of a distinct status far more in this Russian town than they are in Birmingham or Chicago.

Ehrenburg is writing, then, of the pillars of society, of the people who read books and form local policy and keep the production-system of the Soviets reasonably efficient. Almost all of them are well-meaning little people, civil and decent, the people who buy Ehrenburg's books. They must have been surprised and gratified, after a literary diet of Socialist Realism, to find themselves represented without distortion in *The Thaw.* That they are not the real masters of Russia, the fate of this novel demonstrates; yet probably we have here a truthful description of the bulk of the intellectual and administrative classes which have settled down into a decent routine a generation after the triumph of the Bolsheviks. These are not Bolsheviks; they do not think of world dominion, nor of the future terrestrial paradise; their own round of small duties, and their private problems, loom much larger than the old catch-phrases of the class struggle. None of these characters has any intention of leading a crusade. (pp. 250-51)

Out of the disjointed conversations of this novel comes the impression—never expressed clearly by Ehrenburg himself—that all these people are on the verge of asking themselves, 'What are we here for?' And some of them are almost as close to asking themselves a question yet more significant, 'Is life worth living?' Are these petty intrigues, these flirtations, these arguments about housing versus the new precision-casting bay, these worries about promotion or demotion, these headaches and anxieties, the whole end and aim of being? Is this the New Order for which millions of lives were expended? In this book are symptoms of a deep-seated disillusion: the triumph over the Germans, for instance, seems scarcely anything more than an unpleasant business in which some of these people lost friends or lovers. These are not men and women who want a revolution or a restoration. They are looking, rather, for some clue to the meaning of life; but, cut off from the Past, they find it difficult and even dangerous to carry their curiosity very far.

It is not fear, however, that these people commonly suffer from: it is boredom. Now and then some gargoyle face peers out of Ehrenburg's pages, as when a tenth-grade girl is expelled from the Comsomol on vague charges, or when Juravliov is removed by the Head Office. ('Where was Juravliov? What had become of him? Not a living soul remembers. A storm comes, gives a lot of trouble and passes over; who remembers it once it has stopped roaring?') There is no mention of the secret police or the Siberian camps. Yet probably we would fall into error if we were to treat Ehrenburg's picture of an administrative class comparatively secure and placid as mere sham. It has now been more than three decades since the end of the Russian Revolution; and fanaticism, with its spies and purges, weakens in that length of time, in defiance of all the endeavours of a ministry of propaganda. Any quasi-reasonable political régime, once all effectual opposition is eliminated, will endeavour to rule by custom and persuasion, not by terror. The heartless struggle for power, with its conspiracies and betrayals, will continue among the people who lust after power, in the upper reaches of Party and Army and Bureaucracy and Police; yet to the placid shallows of provincial towns and conveyor-belt factories will return some considerable measure of peace and toleration, lacking which even a Marxist society cannot get its day's work done. The people in *The Thaw* are somewhat nervous: the possibility of a reprimand from central authority, a transfer to unknown regions, an irremediable blight to a career, a denunciation by a committee, never is quite thrust out of consciousness; but they may expect, by and large, to get on in their world, if they conform to the slogans of the moment and do not trouble themselves with speculation. Volodya the painter knows how to walk discreetly and how to paint factory-directors likely to succeed. Writers aren't paid to have ideas, he says. 'All that happens to you with ideas is that you break your neck. What you're meant to look for in a book is ideology. If it's there, what more d'you want? It's lunatics that have ideas.' The Second Congress of Writers echoed him.

Ideas abjured, these middle-class comrades may sleep reasonably sound. Escape from less tangible anxieties, however, remains difficult. Those vexatious questions, 'What are we here for?' and 'Is life worth living?' have a way of creeping back into the mind of the most orthodox Communist. They plague especially the administrative and artistic classes which Ehrenburg describes, possessed of just enough comfort and just enough leisure to make them inquire whether comfort and leisure are all that life ever can afford. These people, by the triumph of the Revolutionary doctrines from which none of them venture to dissent, have been deprived of nearly all the old motives to integrity which have governed mankind since men entered upon the civil social state, and of nearly all the old rewards. These people are fed; they are housed; they enjoy some idleness; but that is all.

Though theirs is not a society in which love lies dead, still love is very sick. In its ancient meaning, love is intensely private. The Soviet state is inimical to real privacy. Ehrenburg hints at the conflict between personal loyalty and the demands made by the production-consumption society, in which everyone (as in *Brave New World*) belongs to everyone else. Not that the lovers of *The Thaw* are promiscuous: with one or two exceptions, they are almost Victorian in their proprieties—though still too free for the Congress of Soviet Writers. At the back of these lovers' difficulties, rather, seems to be a feeling that something is wrong with tenderness—possibly it is anti-social. Everything in life is supposed to contribute to the material betterment of the masses: well, what is love good for, and what is marriage good for? In the Soviet society, marriage is simply a union for physical satisfaction and procreation in the interest of the state. Lacking spiritual sanction, or any aspiration towards continuity and immortality in the classical and Christian tradition of family, love is truly blind in this new domination. These people do not defy the state by secret indulgence in lust, like the rebels in Orwell's *1984:* lust of any description is no strong factor in their lives; they merely ask about love, as about most other things in life, 'What is the meaning of all this?' And no one gives them an answer—certainly not Ilya Ehrenburg.

If the sense of meaning in life that comes with enduring love is difficult to attain in this modern Russian society, the sense of meaning that comes with lasting achievement is in worse plight: for under the cloak of collective benevolence this society has been atomized, and that delicate growth which constitutes true community has been destroyed. The provincial town in *The Thaw* seems no better than a collection of barracks and impermanent flats, in which men and women exist after the fashion of what Burke called 'the flies of a summer', generation scarcely linking with generation, family reduced to the most tenuous of bonds between husband and wife or mother and son, state disciplines and decrees substituted for that complex of affection and common interest which made the old Russian family—even at its worst, as in Gorki's novels—a great power for good. The instinct of the stronger and better natures in every generation to pass on some tangible advantage or permanent possession to their children has been thwarted in obedience to Marxist dogma. Even the successful intriguer cannot spend his money in any way very satisfactory to himself. Volodya, musing on how he will use the fat fee from his latest politic portrait, says to himself, 'Shall I buy a "Victory"? Nice to speed on the road, everything flickers past, you haven't time to notice anything. Not worth it, perhaps, better give half to Mother . . . ' Everything flickers past. The Revolutionary Utopia, after three decades, has faded away to this boredom with the present and this indifference to the future. Nearly fifty years ago, Graham Wallas, in his *Human Nature in Politics,* while confessing it possible that a desire for property might be ineradicable in human nature, speculated as to just how little and how abstract this property might be made without outraging the instinct. The society which Ehrenburg describes seems to have passed that limit of discretion long ago. The salaried administrative and 'intellectual' circles with which he is familiar enjoy many comforts and even luxuries: but they have been deprived of the possibility of enduring accomplishment, either in the sense of material possessions or of family continuity. Thus they languish in an apathy which dismays Ehrenburg himself.

Tanechka the actress, thinking of the approaching summer with a sodden resignation, expresses this whole mood of futility, somehow more depressing than nearly anything in Gogol or Dostoievski:

> She would apply to go to Zelenino, that suited her purse. But she could see it all in advance: conversation at lunch on the benefits of steamed cutlets for those who were taking the cure; picking worm-eaten mushrooms in the afternoon; somebody getting drunk at dinner and making a scene which everybody else would go on chewing over; then the crossword from the *Ogoniok,* with twenty people torturing themselves over a mineral of six letters starting with B.

Boredom of this description is not peculiar to modern Russia; but one of the oppressive and significant revelations of this disturbing novel is the fact that very little *except* this boredom is left to active natures under the Soviet régime. Those at the very top, it is true, may console themselves with the great and terrible game of power, what Orwell called 'stamping forever on a human face'; the rest find even lively conversation beyond their abilities, because the principal topics of interesting talk are either dangerous or else accepted as being for ever settled by official Soviet philosophy. The Old Bolsheviks thought they were opening illimitable vistas to humanity; in fact, they were sealing up every avenue of escape from a technological prison. *The Thaw* constitutes a confession that no radical political or economic device can succeed in liberating mankind from the ills to which flesh is heir. (pp. 251-55)

No counter-revolutionary shows his face in Ehrenburg's portrait-gallery. Yet the very ennui which disheartens the better men and women in *The Thaw* may give some promise of a Russian regeneration. Smugness, far more than positive oppression, is a common cause of the fall of tyrannies. No régime ever was smugger than the Soviet political power, or more inimical to a liberal understanding. Boredom with the featureless uniformity of Russian life may penetrate even to the ruthless little knots of men who play the grim game of power, so that they may grow weary of the whole vast undertaking. And there is this, at least, to be learnt from *The Thaw:* the heart seems to be gone out of the party of proletarian revolution, so that, supposing the Western world can hold its lines against the present physical power of Russia for some years or decades, the forces of traditional society and morality may hope to win the battle for men's minds against a fanatic ideology, an armed doctrine, already far sunk in decadence. (pp. 255-56)

Russell Kirk, "The Death of Art: Ehrenburg's 'Thaw'," in The Dublin Review, *Vol. 229, No. 469, third quarter, 1955, pp. 249-61.*

Harrison E. Salisbury

It seems to be Mr. Ehrenburg's misfortune that, at least in recent years, he has been presented to the American public for reasons that have not too much to do with the works being published.

This was true several years ago of Mr. Ehrenburg's *The Thaw.* In many ways *The Thaw* was the most important Soviet novel of the immediate post-Stalin era. Not only did it give a title to the atmosphere of the creative world in the first years after Stalin's death but it also broke important ground. It was the first work, for example, to mention anti-Semitism in the Soviet Union, to discuss concentration camps and the hardships of ordinary life under Stalin. But the book was presented as an "exposé" (which it was not) and its few American readers must have wondered what the point of it all was.

Now another Ehrenburg novel [*The Stormy Life of Lasik Roitschwantz*] is published. It is advertised as "suppressed by Soviet censorship" and "never published in the Soviet Union."

Those who pick up this book expecting sensation and revelation will, again, be sadly disappointed. It is impossible to say at this time why the book was not published in Russia. But it is very likely that the changing taste of the times, as well as that of its author, had something to do with it. For *The Stormy Life of Lasik Roitschwantz* is a genre novel and not a terribly good one at that.

Ehrenburg was living in Paris when he wrote this book. It was published there and, in 1929, in Berlin. It is a picaresque satire of life in the Soviet Union, very much in the style of the late Nineteen Twenties. The hero, Lasik Roitschwantz, is a Jew from Gomel in Byelorussia. He is fated to be the fall guy. Wherever he goes, whatever he does the blame falls on him. He is the one who winds up in prison while those with whom he is associated go on to glory or to riches.

The setting is the N. E. P. (New Economic Plan) period in Soviet Russia, the time when private enterprise was encouraged and the wildest kind of private speculation ran riot. The era and the atmosphere are those of the most famous of Soviet realistic satires of the day—of Ilf and Petrov in their *The Little Golden Calf.* Lasik Roitschwantz is a blood cousin of Ostap Bender, the Ilf-Petrov hero who wandered over Russia, eternally swindling and eternally getting away with it. Roitschwantz is the little man who didn't get away with it.

Ehrenburg lived in France during most of the Nineteen Twenties and was widely traveled in Western Europe. He takes his hero abroad and lets him continue his misfortunes in Poland, Germany, France and England. But everywhere the result is the same. The miserable Roitschwantz winds up beaten, robbed, swindled and jailed.

The novel is hardly typical of Ehrenburg's work. It is presented in what seems to be a retranslation of a German translation of the original Russian, which hardly improves its literary quality. If, however, the publication of this virtually forgotten and discarded tale should focus some interest upon Ehrenburg then the effect will have been only to the good.

Ehrenburg has gone through many phases as a Soviet writer. He has been a Western cosmopolite and, later, a sycophant of Stalin. But today he has become one of the world's most eloquent spokesmen for the freedom of the writer—freedom to dream, to create, to write with only his conscience as his guide. His essays on Stendhal, on Chekhov, on French Impressionism, upon the tragic Russian poet, Maria Tsvetayeva, should be read by every American who thinks that truth, no matter how crushed, cannot find its way upward into daylight through the matted weeds of Marxist dictatorship.

> *Harrison E. Salisbury, in a review of "The Stormy Life of Lasik Roitschwantz," in* The New York Times, *August 12, 1960, p. 17.*

Vera Alexandrova

[The future place of Ilya Ehrenburg is not] clear. Today he enjoys great fame as a writer who has participated actively in Soviet literature at its various stages of development. As he himself says in his autobiography (1958), he has always been involved with the "present."

This absorption in the events of the day was particularly evident during World War II. Ehrenburg was fully aware that the works devoted to the war were "not immortal tomes, not marble, but rather wax." . . . "The great books about the great war," he said, "will come later." But while "the lines written today may be forgotten in a day or a year, that which prompted their writing shall not be forgotten." And yet, much of what Ehrenburg produced, even before the war, is now forgotten. Who remembers such books of his as *The Love of Jeanne Ney, The Life and Death of Nikolay Kurbov,* and many others?

Ehrenburg's personal biography is as complex and tortuous as his literary career. He was born in 1891, in a well-to-do Jewish family in Kiev. When he was five, his parents moved to Moscow, where his father managed a beer brewery. The future writer received his secondary education at the Moscow Gymnasium. At first he was an excellent student, but soon, as he wrote in an early autobiography (1928), he "got out of hand," "escaped into the revolutionary movement," and was even arrested. After six months in prison he was released on bail, and left for Paris in 1908. There the young Ehrenburg shared in the enthusiasms prevailing among many of the younger European intellectuals on the eve of World War I. These included medievalism, Catholicism, mysticism, and the works of the famous fifteenth-century French poet François Villon (Ehrenburg translated many of his poems).

The traces of Ehrenburg's many enthusiasms are easily discernible in his first book of verse (*Poems,* Paris, 1910), published when the writer was only nineteen. The poems are not original either in form or content, but they show an undeniable poetic flair. As he wrote recently in his recollections (*People, Years, Life,* 1960), Ehrenburg was drawn to poetry because he understood that "in verse you can say things that cannot be expressed in prose." One rather interesting example of his early verse is a poem about Russia. The poet feels guilty because he fled from Russia, because he had not been able to live by her "holiness"; but he believes that, if his destiny should ever bring him to his homeland:

> I shall know how small and poor I am before Thee,
> How much I've lost in all these years.
> And then perhaps I'll gather up again
> What still remains of childhood, of my own,
> And give Thee what is left of former powers,
> What by some chance was hidden and preserved.

The war of 1914 put an end to Ehrenburg's restless spiritual quest. He became a war correspondent for the large Petersburg newspaper *Birzhevye Vedomosti* (Stock Exchange News). When the revolution broke out, he was irresistibly drawn back home and returned to Russia in July 1917, during the days of the first Bolshevik attempt to seize power. But he was not at that time with the Bolsheviks; nor was he with them after the October coup. It is scarcely necessary to dwell at length on his well-known **"Prayer for Russia"** (1917), which was copied and circulated from hand to hand, and which he later repudiated. The character of this **"Prayer"** was such that the Whites published it in Kiev during the Civil War. He rejected the **"Prayer,"** but it is difficult to ignore the fact that recantations have always come somewhat too easily to Ehrenburg.

After wandering over the land, torn by Civil War, Ehrenburg arrived in Moscow from Georgia in late 1920 or early 1921. But he stayed there very briefly, leaving again soon for his beloved Paris, where he began his first novel, *The Extraordinary Adventures of Julio Jurenito and His Disciples* (1922). In his first autobiography (1928) Ehrenburg confesses that this was his "only book in earnest." In *Julio Jurenito,* he says further, "neither the critics, nor the readers, nor I myself can determine exactly where the wry grin ends."

The initially reserved or even negative response to the October revolution was not limited to Ehrenburg alone. It was characteristic of a large number of young writers who had begun to write on the eve of World War I. Ehrenburg, however, was the first to discern the *national* elements in the revolution. As early as 1920, living in the Crimea, which was then under White occupation, Ehrenburg wrote in a poem dedicated to Russia and the revolution that those who saw death in Russia's "delirium of travail" were wrong. (pp. 127-29)

[The action of *Julio Jurenito*] unfolds in Paris, Mexico, Rome, Moscow, and the provincial Russian town of Kineshma, during the war and the early years of the revolution. Julio Jurenito is a Mexican and, in the author's conception, a Mephistophelian character. But he might, perhaps, more properly be regarded as a representative of the international artistic Bohemia that is found in all the capitals of the world. Ehrenburg himself appears in the novel as one of the seven disciples of Julio, who has come into the world in order to destroy it by his own powers. Julio, "The Teacher," "indigent and great, did not possess even the ordinary man's meager capital: he was a man without convictions." The hidden paradox of the book is that this Teacher, who flaunts his lack of convictions, is in reality fanatically in love with the future, while his disciple, Ehrenburg, who pretends devoted allegiance to his Teacher, believes in nothing and proudly parades the philosophy of a renegade.

Enamored of the idea of destroying the old world, Julio welcomes the world war "as the first day of typhoid fever, from which a man will either come out regenerated, or will die." In the same spirit he welcomes the Russian revolution. The ideas about the revolution are, in fact, the most interesting element in the book. Underneath the chaff of the anecdotes and absurdities, the book contains a number of serious appraisals and prognoses. Julio is convinced that the outbreak of the revolution has initiated a period when the land must go through "the blackest, the sweatiest purgatory." Finding himself in the Cheka [the secret police], Julio lectures the Chekists: "You have a great and difficult mission—to train man to such an acceptance of shackles that he will come to think of them as the tender embraces of his mother. . . . You must create a new mystique for a new slavery."

With this appraisal of the implacable tasks of the national revolution, neither Julio himself nor his disciple Ehrenburg are especially tempted to take part in its work. Julio is murdered in the street by thieves who take his boots, and Ehrenburg, his disciple and creator, leaves Moscow in 1921 for the cafés of Paris.

Julio Jurenito is still interesting, not only as testimony of the moods of a certain portion of the young Russian intelligentsia of the early revolutionary period, but also as an aid to the understanding of Ehrenburg the writer. In the preface to his book of poems *Eves,* Ehrenburg anticipated the reader's reproach for his "inner dissonance" by openly admitting that, "like all the children of our fateful age," he had "two faces, two loves, two sorrows." This self-characterization is helpful in understanding Ehrenburg; the unsuccessful effort to overcome this duality runs through *Julio Jurenito* and through a number of subsequent works. In a certain sense Ehrenburg's books are not novels in the old meaning of the word, but lyrical reportage about the writer's time.

It was Ehrenburg's fundamental approach to the October revolution as a national revolution and his acute sense of being *déclassé* that gave birth to the sudden "left-ness" that marks almost all of his works of the NEP period. The writer's own sense of being *déclassé* seeks and finds expression in *déclassé* heroes. The Chekist Nikolay Kurbov (*The Life and Death of Nikolay Kurbov,* 1923) is the son of a "saintly" prostitute; Mikhail Lykov (*The Grabber,* [*Rvach*] 1926) is the son of a waiter; Sakharov (*Protochny Lane,* 1927) is *déclassé* through his marriage to an aristocrat. Of course, the prototypes of these characters existed in reality; wounded from childhood by their social "alienation," they frequently "escaped into the revolution." But Ehrenburg's tendency to overcrowd his works with such misfits lends his books an unhealthy, feverish glow and seems to verge on affectation, making the reader somewhat wary of the writer's observations and appraisals. Thus, for example, Nikolay Kurbov, an entirely unconvincing character, is interesting only as the first attempt in Soviet literature to create the image of the "saintly Chekist."

More convincingly motivated is Mikhail Lykov, whom the author invested with some features of his own childhood. Muddled, unstable, enamored of success, with eyes that are "deep, almost angelic in their sorrowful goodness" and hands that at times seem touching in their helplessness and "inertness," and at other times become "strong, prehensile, and desperate," Mikhail starts with sincere enthusiasm for the revolution, then plunges into speculation and ends his days in prison. Yet, Ehrenburg is fond of him until his last breath: "We love our hero. Let us, too, be judged for this."

Ehrenburg is also fond of Olga, Mikhail's wife. While he lent Mikhail certain incidents from his own childhood, he gave Olga a number of details of his own life abroad. Olga is the daughter of the owner of a match factory; the revolution has not only taken her wealth; it has freed her of the need for spiritual questing—of "aestheticism, urbanism, Catholicism, Nietzscheanism, Montparnasse, Sicily," and so on. Now she is "carried away" by the revolution. "Sympathy with the revolution has become her current camping ground. And the revolution attracted Olga precisely because it had no room for her."

More important than these central figures is the background of the novel. Ehrenburg's observations are keen, with a trace of ironic melancholy. And he is right when he says that "neither Wells, nor any other known writer of utopian novels has ever invented anything more unreal than the life of any Russian city" during the revolution. "As in the best of utopias, everyone lived by rations and endurance. . . . Sometimes the Cheka arrested men born without a shirt for speculation in benzine or kinship with a Left Socialist-Revolutionary. The Cheka shot people. But the Chekists called their prisoners "Comrade.'" It was "an astonishing time, and what we want to do now, looking back upon it, is not to laugh, but to honor its magnificent absurdity." The pages of *The Grabber* abound in such lyrico-political digressions, glorifying the harsh, hungry days of the revolution when people lived and breathed "catastrophically," showing unexpected heroism, frequently studying, greedily and chaotically, and, of course, starving.

In *The Stormy Life of Lazik Roitschwantz* (1928) Ehrenburg painted a picture of this "magnificent absurdity" as seen through the eyes of a meek little "gentlemen's tailor" from Gomel. This tailor is able to discern in Soviet reality both the arrogance of those in power, and the shocking abrogation of rights and justice for the individual. . . . Unable to transform his heart into "a thundering speech," Lazik wanders from city to city, from prison to prison, from country to country in search of the small but eternal truth—man's right to happiness—and ultimately comes to the conclusion that happiness is "only an antiquated word in a mighty language."

It is significant that Ehrenburg not only tends to choose his heroes from among the *déclassé,* but that these *déclassé* are frequently the carriers of genuine social truth. In *Protochny Lane* (1927), a novel that depicts the lower depths of the NEP period, the bearers of social truth are the former Latin teacher who has become a beggar, the little Jewish musician Yuzik, and the homeless waifs. They all wander the dark byways of life, where "only the snow creaks underfoot, the snow of fields and steppes, reminding the heart how great our land is, how rich, how poor, and how terrible."

The basic idea of the novel is that the revolution is over, and the upper hand has been won not by anything new that came out of it, but by the old, brutal right of the strong . . . In this new life that is now entrenching itself, there is no trace of the things of which Olga had dreamed in the novel *The Grabber.* The country is now likened to a gang of homeless children:

> And it seems to me it is our own Russia walking there—just as childish and homeless, dreamy and embittered, without a corner of her own, without anyone to give her love or care, an infant country, but one that has already experienced everything—walking . . . down a parched empty road, amid other people's fields, other people's wealth. . . . And the heart goes numb, and does not dare to ask: will she reach it, will she reach her goal?

The picture of the October revolution as it was synthesized by Ehrenburg's creative vision out of his immediate impressions of the early revolutionary years was shaken by the realities of the NEP period. Seeing the triumph of the "old" amid the ruins of heroic yesterdays, Ehrenburg nostalgically gave himself up to tenderly ironic reminiscences of the "magnificent absurdity" of the first years. The official critics dealt harshly with him for this "weakness." They barely tolerated his patronizing affection for the days of War Communism, but his revelation of the "renascence" of the manners and customs of the old regime was entirely unforgivable.

Constant critical attacks compelled Ehrenburg, as they did many other Fellow Travelers, to abandon contemporary themes. Ehrenburg could do this easily, since he had already written historical fiction (the stories in *Thirteen Pipes*) and novels of adventure. At this moment of crisis he turned once more to historical subjects, producing the novel *The Conspiracy of Equals* (1928), devoted to Babeuf. Into this story of the French revolution, Ehrenburg transposed the atmosphere of another great revolution in its expiring days. His intimate contemporary knowledge helped the writer to reveal in simple and moving words the tragic solitude of Babeuf, the Left-wing revolutionary, amid the weariness and indifference of the Paris of his time.

It is difficult to assess the direction that Ehrenburg's political and artistic development might have taken. His lively sympathy with Babeuf might well have led him into the camp of the Left Opposition. He was saved by the new world crisis which began in Europe and America in 1929, and by the first Five-Year Plan in the Soviet Union. Ehrenburg summed up the hopelessness of the crisis in the destinies of a group of residents of Mont Blanc, a small Paris hotel, with its tiny musty rooms, and its water closet—"ancient and brutal like the human conscience," in which life "stinks without shame" (*Moscow Does Not Believe in Tears,* 1930). The only vital and optimistic person in this hotel is the Russian artist Mey. The secret of his optimism is his feeling that he has behind him a large, young country lying outside the sphere of the deadly crisis. The novel concludes with his departure for Russia.

Since the end of the 1920s, this theme of the final and hopeless crisis of the West has been assiduously preached by Ehrenburg the publicist (*White Coal, or the Tears of Werther,* 1928; *Ten Horsepower,* 1929; and other works). He has thus been squarely in the mainstream of that Left-wing European fellow-traveling intelligentsia whose radicalism is confined to the painting of constant gloomy images of a dying Europe and eulogizing the Soviet Union and its economic achievements.

In fiction Ehrenburg's acceptance of the policy of Five-Year Plans and the official line of the Soviet government found expression in two novels, *The Second Day* (1932) and *Without Pausing for a Breath* (1935). The former deals with the construction projects in the Kuznetsk Basin. Ehrenburg, who lived in Paris, came to the Soviet Union for a visit to collect material for his novel. *The Second Day* contains more reportage than the writer's other novels, especially in its background picture of the construction work. Amid the cold and hunger of a remote Siberian wasteland, a vast construction project is being launched by human will. Animals retreat before the bitter climate; even rats cannot endure the grim conditions. Only insects "remain true" to man. . . . Much later, in 1958, Ehrenburg wrote in his autobiography that, working on this novel, he came to realize "the necessity for truth in art," adding in elucidation: "Truth is frightening only to the decrepit old; and if it sometimes frightens adolescents, that is mostly because of their insufficient understanding."

Among the many lesser characters sketched in the novel, several claim particular attention. They are the director of the project, the Bolshevik Shor, and the foreign experts who marvel at "the enthusiasm, the lice, and the frosts." The foreigners live apart from the rest of the construction personnel; they have their own housing, they eat in separate dining rooms, and their salaries are paid in dollars. The central figures in the novel are the shock worker Kolka Rzhanov, who starts as a backward, ignorant country lad and wins local fame for his high output, and his antithesis, the student Volodya Safonov, a young man of intellectual parentage who is presented as the negative hero.

Ehrenburg's ideological reorientation had brought about a change of attitude toward the "negative hero" as well. Formerly, Ehrenburg preferred Mikhail Lykov to his "Correct" brother Artemy; he was fond of the shiftless musician Yuzik and the other "superfluous people" who found no place in the revolution. But now he treats Volodya Safonov like a disliked stepson; he fears Volodya, and it seems at times that the thing he fears in him is his own former voice and self. Unable to reply convincingly to Safonov's criticism, Ehrenburg hastens to blacken him morally. Safonov is outraged most of all by the enforced *conformism,* the standardized falsehoods, the official optimism and obligatory "enthusiasm" which are imposed upon the people. (pp. 129-36)

Safonov dreams of standing up at a meeting one day and saying publicly all that he thinks: "Some people are silent because you have intimidated them; others, because you have bought them. Simple truths demand affirmation. As in the days of Galileo, they can be uttered only from a bonfire. You want to discuss the problem of culture. But it is unlikely that any of you understand what culture is. You have eliminated all the heretics, dreamers, philosophers, and poets. You have established universal literacy, and equally universal ignorance." Dreaming of this speech, Safonov even becomes "more animated and younger-looking." But when he gets the floor at the meeting, he loses his nerve. In the end he commits suicide.

The second novel of this period, *Without Pausing for a Breath,* contains nothing essentially new. After its publication Ehrenburg seemed to become subdued, and wrote no fiction of any length for several years. He did write two books about Spain; the second, dealing with the Spanish Civil War, appeared in 1937. The latter 1930s were a period of the "great purge" and the subsequent triumph of conformism, brought to its ultimate degree and particularly dangerous to people of Ehrenburg's psychological make-up. Ehrenburg successfully weathered these dangers while living in Paris, until the Second World War opened before him new opportunities to expand.

In Ehrenburg's life the Second World War, especially after Hitler's invasion of the Soviet Union, was a period of extremely fertile literary activity in many forms. In 1940 he returned to live in the Soviet Union, where he soon wrote his novel *The Fall of Paris.* The first part of the novel had already appeared in the magazine *Znamya* when Hitler attacked the Soviet Union. Ehrenburg quickly shifted positions and transformed the French Communists, who had asserted in the early pages of the novel that this "is not our war," into virtually the only genuine French patriots. Nevertheless, there is something in the novel that leaves a lasting impression. This "something" is Ehrenburg's sense of history: the nineteenth century, he says, ended throughout the world with the outbreak of the First World War; it "died a timely death," and only in France, and particularly in Paris, "it overstayed its day." As one of the characters in the novel explains, "in our country generally the old are in no hurry to die." The occupation of Paris in 1940, and the entire situation under which it took place, signaled the end of nineteenth-century France. But at the moment when he realized this, Ehrenburg, the skeptic dabbling in radicalism, was moved momentarily by sincere regret for the old, dying France: "Like the knick-knacks on the table of one newly dead, the monuments of Paris moved one to tears. Its poets clutched their silent lyres. Its marshals galloped on dead horses. Its bronze orators conversed with the pigeons." (pp. 136-38)

Ehrenburg gained great prominence during the war as a publicist. He wrote widely for newspapers, and in 1943 his articles were collected in a book, *The War* (April 1942-March 1943). Of his numerous articles of that period it is important to mention **"We and Europe."** In it he wrote: "But we never drew any line between European culture and ours. We are linked with Europe not by rails or wires, but by our very bloodstream and the convolutions of our brains. We have been both the diligent pupils and the teachers of Europe. . . . Throughout the last century the leading minds of Russia shared Europe's passions, hopes, and griefs. They brought into the European consciousness Russia's passionate temperament, her truthfulness and humanity. . . . We do not look at Europe's tragedy from the sidelines. . . . "

The sincerity of these lines is beyond question. But we must also note, not only that such feelings were attacked by many official Soviet journalists, especially after the war, but that Ehrenburg himself was often disloyal to them.

More sparingly, but with greater conviction, Ehrenburg came forward again at the end of the war as a poet. Poetry occupies a special place in Ehrenburg's literary biography: he turns to it when he tires of his own grandiloquence. Characteristic among the poems he published soon after the end of the war (*Novy Mir,* October 1945) is the one dedicated to Paris. As if replying to the words of an unknown friend, the poet writes:

> With jealousy and with reproach
> You say I've fallen silent. . . .

But, almost apologetically, he speaks of his continuing love for Paris, which he likens to a "forest of stone':

> Forgive that I lived in that forest,
> That I experienced everything, and yet survived,
> That I will carry to my dying day
> The looming Paris twilight.

But on the whole, the poems deal with the theme of victory. In his autobiography of 1958 Ehrenburg admits that "the victory has turned out differently from what we dreamed of in dugouts and shelters." In a poem dedicated to victory the poet speaks of meeting her: "We did not recognize each other." (pp. 138-39)

Of Ehrenburg's postwar works written before Stalin's death, two must be mentioned: they are his novels *The Storm* (1947) and *The Ninth Wave* (1951-52). When he began the serial publication of the latter, Ehrenburg wrote that these two novels were parts of a trilogy which began with *The Fall of Paris.*

The Storm is a summing up of Ehrenburg's impressions of World War II. Its action begins in Paris and is later carried into the Soviet Union. The opening chapters, describing the Paris of 1938-39, have many elements in common with *The Fall of Paris:* the "atmosphere" of Paris is the same in both, as is the underlying feeling of doom. This feeling is expressed most deeply by the uncrowned king of France—the financier Desser. He is convinced that the "climate" of the world has changed and that nothing can save the old-fashioned provincial France, "with its anglers, village dances, and Radical Socialists." The same feeling is voiced in *The Storm* by the Soviet engineer Sergey Vlakhov, who comes to Paris on an official mission at the end of 1938. Sergey, the son of old *émigrés* who left Russia before the First World War, was born in Paris, but returned with his parents to Russia soon after the beginning of the revolution. Coming back to Paris as an adult, Sergey feels that the city casts a spell upon him. He falls in love with the wan, mysterious Seine, the cool narrow streets.

But *The Storm* also contains some new notes: in *The Fall of Paris* Ehrenburg was silent about the reaction of the various French social circles to the Soviet-German pact of 1939. When he was writing *The Storm,* a spurious official myth was already firmly established, and Ehrenburg manipulated his picture of events to fit the myth: naturally, "the bourgeois and philistines" are indignant over "Moscow's betrayal," as is the manufacturer Lancier, whose daughter Madeau loves Sergey and longs to go to Russia. She hastens to the Communist sympathizer Lejean to speak to him of her anxiety. For a moment, he too was shaken by the pact, but he has rapidly oriented himself to the "situation" and now explains to Madeau: "Our Russian comrades have done the right thing—they are gathering strength. If Moscow holds out, France will also live." But generally, he intimates that the pact is a payment "for the sins of others"—"for Munich."

Another feature of *The Storm* is its continual stressing of the idea that a wide gulf separates Soviet life from life abroad. These are "two worlds" which have no common language. This idea is illustrated in the destinies of the Alper family. The tailor Naum Alper, a native of Kiev, has long dreamed of emigrating abroad. Shortly before the war of 1914 he realizes his dream. He goes to France and settles in Paris with his older son, Leo; his wife and younger boy, Osya, temporarily remain in Kiev. The outbreak of war prevents their departure. Naum Alper is killed in the war (he enlisted in the French army); Leo makes his way in the world, becoming an engineer. Shortly before World War II he succeeds in visiting the Soviet Union and searching out his relatives. Osya has become a Communist and treats Leo as if the latter were a Rothschild or a Deterding.

All the positive and negative qualities of Ehrenburg's work may also be found in the third part of his trilogy, *The Ninth Wave.* This novel is linked with *The Storm* by the presence of many of the same characters, but most of them are there merely to serve as mouthpieces for the author's ideas. The artist Samba, whom the reader knows from *The Fall of Paris,* is worth mentioning here. During the war and the first two postwar years Samba painted a number of Paris landscapes. One of his friends, examining his works, tells Samba: "How strange, you have virtually no people here, and yet I see the Paris of those August days. . . ." This remark may in a sense apply to Ehrenburg's novel as well. It often seems that all its journalistic welter is used by the writer merely as a pretext for returning in imagination to the old Paris which has been his lifelong love.

Among the new notes sounded in *The Ninth Wave* is its clearly expressed anti-Americanism, which infects most of its French characters. The keenly observant Ehrenburg was one of the first writers to discern the anti-American feelings which were just then emerging in many European countries.

As a literary work, the trilogy is one of Ehrenburg's artistic failures, and it is not by chance that it lacks a unifying title. The novels are unified only by the feeling that the old world is ending—a feeling first voiced by the writer in *Julio Jurenito* almost forty years ago. The sense of the old world's doom has haunted Ehrenburg throughout most of his life, although at different stages of his literary biography it was given different expression. (pp. 139-41)

However, the "new world" did not turn out to be as new as the young dreamers of the great "eves" had expected. And although he was slow to see it, Ehrenburg, too, had finally come to face this truth. Hence the role he assumed soon after Stalin's death, taking up the defense of creative freedom in his article **"About the Writer's Work"** (*Znamya,* October 1953). This new direction found its sensational continuation in the novel *The Thaw* (*Znamya,* April 1954) and its sequel *The Spring* (*Znamya,* April 1956).

Late, in "the deep autumn of his life," Ehrenburg has found strength to face many of the fatal errors of his earlier literary activity. Perhaps he has not said all that he might have, and has not spoken with the full voice of his talent, but on many occasions during the post-Stalin years Ehrenburg has championed creative freedom. During this period Ehrenburg has for the first time in his life taken up a position not only as an individual writer, but as a man

exerting an influence on the formation of social moods among the literary milieu, and thus affecting in some measure the development of literature as a whole. . . . [In his essay, **"The Lessons of Stendhal,"** Ehrenburg] confesses that for him these "lessons" are contained above all in Stendhal's "absolute veracity": "This is perhaps the most important thing to us—not only to writers, but to all men of mid-twentieth century: the more passionate the attractions and revulsions of our time, the more insistently our conscience and our reason demand the truth." (pp. 141-42)

> *Vera Alexandrova, "Ilya Ehrenburg (1891-),"
> in her* A History of Soviet Literature, 1917-
> 1964: From Gorky to Solzhenitsyn, *translated
> by Mirra Ginsburg, 1963. Reprint by Anchor
> Books, 1964, pp. 127-42.*

Galina Belaya

The new 9-volume collected works of Ilya Ehrenburg is a carefully conceived and planned publication quite different from his collected works of the twenties or his 5-volume selected works of the fifties.

It includes the author's most representative works, most of which were out of print by the early sixties. They are: *The Unusual Adventures of Julio Jurenito and His Disciples, The Grabber, The Summer of 1925, In Protochny Lane,* and others. Now they are once again available to the reader; they have left the niche of "literary history," as it were, and have become part of our contemporary literature.

The author's choice of books for this new collection is worth noting, not only on account of what is included but also of what is excluded. Absent from the new collection are, for example: *Without Pausing for Breath,* which Ehrenburg now sees as a repetition of the plot of *The Second Day; The Ninth Wave,* which the author regards as a superficial treatment of a vital theme—man and the history of society's spiritual development; and the second part of *The Thaw,* as the author believes that the theme of the book has been exhausted in the first part of the work.

The new collection enables the reader to observe the growth of certain basic themes in Ehrenburg's works. Most readers of Ehrenburg know that his books are populated by individuals with destinies of their own who are, nevertheless, subject to influence exerted by the social conflicts of the time. Ehrenburg's heroes lead different lives and have different experiences from one another, and yet they are all involved in the drama of world history and represent one or another stage of its development. Such is the pattern to be found in *Julio Jurenito* (vol. 1), *The Second Day* (vol. 3), *The Fall of Paris* (vol. 4), and *The Storm* (vol. 5), four of the most important works of Ehrenburg.

But what lies behind this intense effort to delve into the complex relations of man with the world, to extend the scope of human life by dealing not only with the ties between one individual and those around him, but also with the invisible threads that link isolated individuals into one whole—humanity? How does Ehrenburg go about portraying the individual's relation to humanity as a whole? What are the means by which he demonstrates the undeniable fact that the destinies of men have become so closely interwoven that the history of one man is no longer an isolated event but a part of the history of society?

In this new collection the reader has an opportunity to trace Ehrenburg's philosophical and aesthetic views and observe their development. The nine volumes represent the fruits of fifty years of creative work, and by considering them as a whole, we can see that the question of the relationship between the individual and society has long troubled Ehrenburg. We can also see the changes in Ehrenburg's view on this question. In *Julio Jurenito,* for example, man is seen as depressed, downtrodden, and crushed by society. There the relationship between man and society has disintegrated. In the *Chronicle of Our Time* (vol. 7) Ehrenburg came to recognize the economic base of human relations. And finally, in *The Fall of Paris* and *The Storm* Ehrenburg shows an understanding of the fact that the history of one man has become organically fused with the history of society.

It is characteristic of Ehrenburg to evaluate social phenomena through the eyes of individual men. The latter's outlooks and attitudes constitute for Ehrenburg the basic criterion for accepting or not accepting social changes. For Ehrenburg, who strives to understand the "meaning of the passions and sufferings of men in the course of what we call 'history,'" society is to be judged according to the extent to which it provides for the spiritual self-realization of man. It is likewise important to Ehrenburg to understand the forces that unite men, the forces that draw them together despite their different nationalities, professions, and convictions.

In the twenties, these forces appeared to Ehrenburg to lie in a general-humanness, which is a natural, inborn, and vital power that draws men together despite all the difference in their ideas. In those years Ehrenburg regarded the strict discipline of the new society as unjustifiably harsh in respect to man's aspirations for love and happiness. This abstract aesthetic approach, however, was inadequate in dealing with the complex social contradictions of the twenties. In some of Ehrenburg's novels, for example, *In Protochny Lane,* such contradictions were seen as contradictions between man and society.

Nevertheless, Ehrenburg's conception of the general-humanness was extremely broad. Though it introduced certain weaknesses into his philosophical and aesthetic outlook, it also had its strong points, which may be observed in Ehrenburg's works in the twenties. For one thing, it had compelled the author to compare and to analyze deeply the lives of different countries and peoples (*Julio Jurenito* and *Thirteen Pipes*), which came to be a peculiar trait of Ehrenburg's creative vision. Gradually, Ehrenburg's conception of general-humanness began to lose its abstract quality. . . . The general-humanness came to assume a concrete and specific form, the form of anti-fascist struggle.

In this connection, one may point out another feature of Ehrenburg's artistic thinking, which may be described as a striving towards synthesis or, to borrow the words of Fedin, an attempt to "reach through separate individuals the people as an entity." Already in *Julio Jurenito* (1921) the question of the "evils of society" was examined on a "universal scale." In the breadth of its scope, in its closeness to the type of a survey-novel, and in the freedom of

the narrative which suggested the potential cinematographic possibilities of the novel, its readers saw at the time the birth of a new prose form.

In *Julio Jurenito* one can observe a shifting of the "centre of gravity": the classical novel is, as a rule, based on the history of characters but in *Julio Jurenito,* though attention is drawn to individual characters, there is no attempt to trace in detail the history of their formation. However important is the image of Julio, the reader rightly senses that the pivotal idea of the novel lies in something more general and more powerful than the destinies of separate individuals. In the centre of the novel, as Ehrenburg himself has noted, lie the "destinies of humanity in time of peace, war, and revolution." The same can be said of *The Second Day* (vol. 3), *The Fall of Paris,* and *The Storm.* In *The Second Day* Ehrenburg conveys the rhythm of socialist constructions under the First Five-Year Plan and portrays the masses being awakened by the hopes of building a new life and united not only in their common tasks but also in a sense of shared aspirations and aims. In *The Fall of Paris* and *The Storm* Ehrenburg shows how the lives of people are isolated from one another only in appearance but are in fact subject to the influence of worldwide trends and conflicts.

It is clear, then, that the chief characteristic of Ehrenburg's works lies, not in the numerous facts, colourful episodes and picturesque portraits, but in that long-evident quality which, as Ehrenburg once wrote to Bryusov, is the quality of the "general" and the "monumental."

In this respect Ehrenburg may be considered as a follower of Zola. In the opinion of many scholars, the series *Rougon-Macquart* is based not so much on portrayals of characters typical of the time, as on general ideas, social themes, and "philosophical thoughts," on the author's view of the historical forces of the period.

But despite this similarity between Ehrenburg and Zola, there is also an important difference between the two writers. Ehrenburg is more subjective; his personality is reflected in his images to a much greater extent than is the case with Zola. In Ehrenburg's "look" at the world there is invariably a large element of personal feeling. The logic of thought is inseparable from a lyrical feeling, which imparts an emotional tone to Ehrenburg's works. This combination of the lyrical with the philosophical may be said to be the underlying pattern of all Ehrenburg's works.

A good example of such a pattern may be found in *The Fall of Paris.* The emotional power of this novel lies not only in the depiction of the political tragedy of France, but also in the revelation of the psychological implications of the national catastrophe. Ehrenburg saw that "betrayal, like rust, has corroded the people." The French government's policy of "peace at any price" has not only led to the betrayal of Spain; it has left a trauma on the psychological state of the average Frenchman. This view on the fall of France, expressed in tragic tones, underlies the plot of *The Fall of Paris.*

The new collection also includes a large number of poems. This is significant, not merely because Ehrenburg began his literary career as a poet and in fact has never stopped writing poems, but because poetry has always been for Ehrenburg a kind of reconnaissance of reality, which has always anticipated prose works.

Ehrenburg's poems reveal the poetic core of his creative art in general, his skill in fusing the universal historical meaning of life with its concrete embodiments. Generalized and at times abstract portrayals of events and the states of human spirit are created from the mosaics of genuine, concrete, and extremely precise spiritual features. That is why the "general" and the "monumental" do not turn Ehrenburg's works into coldly speculative and rational exercises. On the contrary, Ehrenburg is able to see the world in terms of fine gradations of feelings, though he cannot limit himself to one "private" point of view. Thus the hero of Ehrenburg's poems is Spain and the heroes of his novels are Paris (in **The Fall of Paris**) or the war which towers above the fates of individual characters (in **The Storm**).

The last two volumes in the new collection are the author's memoirs, **People, Years, Life.** Here Ehrenburg does not claim to be objective. He regards the past in the light of retrospection. The memoirs contain many reservations about the long and difficult past of the author which is not free of errors. Naturally, not everything said in these memoirs is indisputable, but they are written with an intensity of feeling and passion which holds our interest and attention. One may disagree or take issue with the author on this or that point, but one cannot help being impressed with the richness and the variety of events described in the volumes, the colourful portraits of literary and other outstanding figures with whom the author came into contact, and with the author's phenomenal memory and his deep concern and feeling for the destinies of his epoch and his contemporaries. (pp. 184-86)

> *Galina Belaya, in a review of "Collected Works," in* Soviet Literature, *No. 8, 1967, pp. 184-86.*

Anatol Goldberg

[Ehrenburg's] life was one of constant movement, and often fraught with danger: apart from his early experience of Tsarist gaols, he was at various times expelled from France, and detained during his travels as a suspected foreign agent; and in 1947, at the height of Stalin's anti-Jewish campaign, he expected at any moment the fateful knock on the door that would signal his arrest. Indeed, it is difficult now to grasp the all-pervading atmosphere of fear and foreboding which gripped virtually every section of the Soviet intelligentsia at that time. Yet in spite of all these external pressures, Ehrenburg managed to pour out a flood of books, some sixty in all, including poetry, novels, plays, short stories, translations, and some thirty volumes of collected essays and newspaper articles, to say nothing of the six-part memoirs.

Inevitably, such a huge output was bound to be uneven in quality, and this is especially noticeable in the novels. At their best, they recall some of those brilliant polychrome posters produced during and just after the Revolution. At their worst, they are either woodenly propagandist or saccharinely sentimental. Among his contemporaries, there were certainly better novelists and poets.

On the other hand, Ehrenburg knew and understood the West far better than any of his contemporaries, and he was incomparably the most brilliant journalist of his time in the Soviet Union, with the born reporter's sharp eye for tell-tale detail. Let me cite just one example. In early 1935, *Izvestia* sent him to cover the Saar Plebiscite:

> I arrived in Saarbrucken in the evening. Coloured lights glimmered through the fog. In the main street, the window of a big delicatessen was adorned with a swastika made of sausages; passers-by paused to look and exchanged enraptured smiles. At my hotel, the proprietress, a stout, apoplectic woman, shouted down the corridor: 'Don't forget—I am German!' Out in the street, loud-speakers were broadcasting martial music . . . I slept badly. During the night, shots rang out. I half-opened my door. The hotel boots was collecting shoes to be cleaned. 'They probably caught another traitor . . . ' he said by way of explanation.

In any survey of Ehrenburg's voluminous output, certain works stand out as landmarks. The first among these is the satirical novel which he wrote in Belgium in 1921, entitled **Julio Jurenito. . . .**[It] is a fireworks display of wild inventiveness, a ferocious orgy of wit and black humour, which has lost none of its corrosive bite over the years: and although Ehrenburg subsequently directed his satiric barbs at various aspects of modern civilization, he never quite rivalled it in any of his later works.

But the sheer destructive zest that animates **Julio Jurenito** raises an interesting question. Even while still in his adolescence, Ehrenburg made an existential choice: he was to be a European first and foremost, and so he would remain to the end of his life. This did not contradict his Russianness, since he felt that Russia's rightful place was firmly within the orbit of European culture. Nor did it spring solely from his early infatuation with the life of the Paris boulevards and cafés, although that obviously counted. At a deeper level, he was drawn to the whole European cultural tradition, and as a young man he assiduously made pilgrimage to a number of its venerable sites, monuments and holy places. Indeed, the extent to which he immersed himself in that tradition may be shown by the fact that at one point, under the influence of the French Catholic poet, Francis Jammes, he even toyed with the idea of joining the Benedictine Order! That impulse turned out to be short-lived, but his interest in religion persisted for some time afterwards, and a curious streak of what one can only call religiosity crops up unexpectedly in some of his later writings.

There was, however, another side to the coin. In the First World War, visiting various sectors of the Western Front as a correspondent, he watched with revulsion the spectacle of Europe tearing itself apart in the slaughter of the trenches. But what shocked him even more, on his return to France after the war, was to witness what seemed to him a hedonistic pursuit of pleasure, in which former war profiteers revelled, and in which everyone was bent only on forgetting the lessons of 1914-18. In short, wherever he looked, he seemed to detect signs of the apparently irreversible decadence of the West; and this must go some way to explaining his decision, from the early thirties onwards, to throw his weight behind the Soviet regime.

It is at this point that one should perhaps briefly examine his attitude towards Stalin. Like much else in Ehrenburg's life, this did not follow a consistent pattern, but was shot through with ambiguities. He first saw Stalin during one of his visits to Moscow in the mid-thirties. The occasion was a ceremonial meeting of Stakhanovite shock workers in the Great Hall of the Kremlin.

> Suddenly, everyone stood up and began fiercely applauding: and out of a side door which I had not noticed came Stalin, followed by the members of the Politburo . . . The applause went on for a long time, perhaps ten or fifteen minutes. Stalin was also clapping. When the applause began to die down, someone shouted, 'Hurrah for the great Stalin!' and it all burst out once more. Finally, everyone sat down, and then a woman's voice, desperately shrill, rang out: 'Glory to Stalin!' So we all sprang to our feet and started clapping all over again.
>
> By the time it ended my hands were sore. It was the first time I had seen Stalin and I could not take my eyes off him. I had seen hundreds of portraits of him, and I recognized his double-breasted tunic and moustache, but he was less tall than I had imagined. His hair was very black, and he had a low forehead, but his eyes were lively and expressive. At times, inclining his head slightly to right or left, he laughed softly; at others, he sat motionless, surveying the hall, but still with the same animated gleam in his eyes . . .
>
> Returning home, I had a sense of uneasiness. Of course, I thought, Stalin is a great man, but he is a Communist and a Marxist: we talk of our new culture, but we resemble worshippers bowing down before some shaman . . . Then I caught myself up: I was probably reasoning like an intellectual. How many times had I heard that we intellectuals had got things wrong, that we did not understand the demands of our age!: 'highbrow', 'fellow-traveller', 'rotten liberal' . . . But what of those incomprehensible epithets: 'All-wise Leader', 'Genius of the Peoples', 'Beloved Father', 'Mighty Helmsman', 'World Transfigurer', 'Artificer of Happiness', 'Our Sun' . . . Yet still I managed to persuade myself that I did not understand the psychology of the masses, that I judged everything merely from an intellectual standpoint . . .

This dichotomy in Ehrenburg's view of Stalin persisted for the next two decades. Having been shocked by the signing of the Nazi-Soviet Pact, he was equally dismayed by Stalin's manifest unpreparedness when the German Armies launched their assault on the Soviet Union. But then, as the Soviet Armies regained control of the situation and the tide of battle gradually turned, he seems, like so many others, to have seen Stalin in an increasingly heroic light as the chief architect of victory; and this clearly paved the way towards that period . . . in the early fifties, when for a time he showed almost complete subservience to the all-powerful ruler in the Kremlin. He could hardly disregard the brutal repressions of the postwar years, however, and he did not profess to fathom the tortuous workings of Stalin's mind. (pp. 3-6)

Nor could Ehrenburg turn a blind eye to the fate of his fellow Jews, so many of whom perished in Stalin's postwar anti-cosmopolitan campaign, although on his visits abroad, he—the arch-cosmopolitan—pretended to be in ignorance of what was happening. This was certainly the most dubious episode in his entire career, and one which is explored in some detail in the following chapters. On the other hand, despite an allegation published in an Israeli newspaper, there is no evidence to suggest that he person-ally played any part in the betrayal of other Jewish intellectuals. He could, of course, have spoken out against the wave of arrests and executions, in which case he would almost certainly have joined the victims: as it was, he chose to remain silent. As he put it much later in his memoirs: 'Yes, I knew about many crimes, but it was not in my power to stop them . . . Far more influential and better informed people than I were unable to stop them . . . Silence for me was not a cult but a curse . . . ' In any case, on other occasions he showed no lack of courage. . . . (p. 6)

On various occasions he came to the defence of people in trouble, as in his letter to Alexei Adzhubei requesting the reinstatement of a girl student expelled from the Komsomol. And if, at the end, his reputation was still not entirely free from the lurking wisps of earlier suspicion, this was no doubt due to the very fact that he had survived when so many others had perished. His own explanation of his survival hinged on the element of pure chance. As he put it: 'I lived in an epoch when man's fate resembled not a game of chess but a lottery.'

Ehrenburg spent some five years writing his last major work, ***People, Years, Life,*** which can perhaps best be described as a sustained effort to set the record straight. It is true that on some matters, he shows a certain reticence. He says, for example, that he is not going to talk about 'affairs of the heart' . . . ; and in the case of certain political relationships and encounters (as with Bukharin, or with Trotsky in Vienna), official censorship, even after all these years, compels him either to remain silent, or to restrict himself to the merest veiled allusion. Nevertheless, he does manage to say a great deal on a multitude of themes, including many I have not had time to touch on here—such as his vigorous defence of modern art, as opposed to so many drab products of socialist realism ('like fifth-rate coloured photographs in splendid frames'). Above all, for the younger generation of Soviet readers, he opened up undreamt-of horizons: and for that reason alone, ***People, Years, Life*** remains a uniquely valuable document. (pp. 7-8)

> *Anatol Goldberg, in her* Ilya Ehrenburg: Writing, Politics and the Art of Survival, *Weidenfeld and Nicolson, 1984, 312 p.*

FURTHER READING

Austin, Paul M. "An Interview with Ilya Ehrenburg." *Soviet Studies* XXI, No. 1 (July 1969): 93-8.
> Combines the substance of two conversations with Ehrenburg in January and February of 1966.

Erlich, Victor. "Ilya Ehrenburg Takes a Bow." *Problems of Communism* XIV, No. 5 (September-October 1965): 72-4.
> Review of the final installment of Ehrenburg's memoirs.

Johnson, Stowers. "Lunch at Ilya Ehrenburg's Moscow Flat." *Contemporary Review* 217, No. 1254 (July 1970): 34-42.

An informal, state supervised interview with Ehrenburg in his home.

Narovchatov, Sergei. "Ilya Ehrenburg, Poet." *Soviet Literature,* No. 12 (1978): 138-41.
Evaluates Ehrenburg's verse in relationship to his achievements as a journalist and novelist.

Ortenberg, David. "The War Years." *Soviet Literature,* No. 6 (1981): 155-64.
Reminiscences concerning Ehrenburg by the former chief editor of the Soviet Army's newspaper *Krasnaya Zvesda,* whom the author worked for during World War II.

Slonim, Marc. "From the Five-Year Plan to Socialist Realism." In his *Modern Russian Literature: From Chekhov to the Present,* pp. 375-79. New York: Oxford University Press, 1953.
Brief overview of Ehrenburg's life and career.

Treadgold, Donald W. "Ehrenburg's Partial Truth." *The New Republic* 158, No. 11 (16 March 1968): 30, 32.
Discussion of the autobiographical volume *Ilya Ehrenburg: Post War Years, 1945-1954.*

John Fuller

1937-

(Born John Leopold Fuller) English poet, novelist, critic, author of children's books, and librettist.

Fuller is respected for his skillfully crafted verse, which offers witty observations and poignant satire on ordinary life, art, love, and the relationship between humankind and nature. Featuring elegant language arranged in intricately patterned cadences, rhymes, and meters, Fuller's verse has been linked with a tradition of British poetry—spanning from the Augustan Age to the works of twentieth-century poet W. H. Auden—distinguished by amusing insights, strict poetic forms, and exploration of moral themes. Accommodating a variety of tones, ranging from comic to haunting, colloquial to scholarly, Fuller presents a moral vision that addresses unsettling and disordered aspects of existence as well as beauty and harmony. Michael Hulse commented: "Fuller has insisted by example that lightness and wit and technical expertise are perfectly compatible with moral and intellectual seriousness."

Fairground Music, The Tree that Walked, and *Cannibals and Missionaries,* Fuller's first three volumes of verse, immediately established his reputation as a poet of technical virtuosity, wittiness, and ornate language. Employing such conventional forms as sonnets, rhymed couplets, songs, dramatic monologues, riddles, and ballads, Fuller frequently examines themes relating to art and contemporary life. Critics noted tension in these pieces, deriving from a sense of menace, obscurity, and terror rendered in graceful language and forms. Fuller's concern for orderliness, often presented within the context of struggles or games, is reflected in "The Labors of Hercules," an elaborately structured sonnet sequence that examines love, motivation, and the artistic process. Fuller's talent for light verse is evidenced in *Epistles to Several Persons.* Consisting of letters to five acquaintances, these pieces comment on a variety of topics and contain esoteric references, parody, decorous language, and slang. Critical reception was mixed as to the effectiveness of Fuller's use of this august verse form. In *The Mountains in the Sea,* his next collection, Fuller abandons his adherence to formal poetic devices while examining mental processes, nature, and death.

Fuller returned to his characteristic emphasis on strict forms in *Lies and Secrets,* which focuses on the nature of language and the pursuit of meaning. Many of the poems in this volume are concerned with games, including chess, children's amusements, and sporting competitions, which are likened to quests for significance in life. *Lies and Secrets* is considered Fuller's most accomplished collection by several critics, including Andrew Motion, who stated: "The dazzlingly finished constructions aren't allowed—as they occasionally were in the past—to become an end in themselves and a replacement for thoughts which proved unmanageably difficult or painful. Instead, formal dexterity is continually regulated to suit the demands of content, and the result is [Fuller's] best and most serious book yet." Fuller's next volume, *The Illusionists: A Tale,* is a nine-

part verse narrative rendered in the stanzaic form employed by Alexander Pushkin in his verse novel, *Eugene Onegin.* Informed with moral themes concerning art and culture, this work details the experiences of a young man from his university days to his work in the London art world. As the young man encounters love, forgery, and disillusionment, narrative digressions featuring comic events, satire, word games, and self-conscious investigations of the artistic process extend the scope of the story to an indictment of modern culture. Fuller's later verse is collected in *The Beautiful Inventions,* which contains many elegant and strictly formal poems rendered in assorted tones and vernaculars to evoke a sense of beauty and mystery, and *The Grey Among the Green,* in which reflections on family life and human concerns are juxtaposed with observations on nature.

Fuller has also authored a respected critical study, *A Reader's Guide to W. H. Auden,* and three novels. *Flying to Nowhere,* the first of these, is set in a monastery where an investigator arrives to examine the disappearance of several pilgrims. The novel is rich in imagery and allusions to Christian beliefs concerning death and rebirth, the soul, and the mysteries of the body. *Tell It Me Again* centers upon the relationship between an English composer of ballets and an American jazz singer. Artistic obsessions and transformations of personality are prominent themes in this work. *The Burning Boys* is set in London during World War II and concerns two protagonists, a boy attempting to survive German bombardment of the city, and an anguished pilot, who significantly impact each other's lives.

(See also *Contemporary Authors*, Vols. 21-24, rev. ed.; *Contemporary Authors New Revision Series*, Vol. 9; and *Dictionary of Literary Biography*, Vol. 40.

PRINCIPAL WORKS

POETRY VOLUMES

Fairground Music   1961
The Tree that Walked   1967
Cannibals and Missionaries   1972
Epistles to Several Persons   1973
The Mountain in the Sea   1975
Lies and Secrets   1979
The Illusionists: A Tale   1980
The Beautiful Inventions   1983
The Grey Among the Green   1988

NOVELS

Flying to Nowhere   1983
Tell It Me Again   1988
The Burning Boys   1989

OTHERS

Herod Do Your Worst: A Nativity Opera   (libretto) 1968
A Reader's Guide to W. H. Auden   (criticism) 1970
The Spider Monkey Uncle King: An Opera Pantomime for Children   1974

P. N. Furbank

[John Fuller's first collection *Fairground Music,* is] a puzzle. It seems to be a try-out for various styles and kinds of poem; which will be his right direction I can't guess, and nor perhaps can he. One can divide the poems perhaps into the ones that are 'about' something and the ones that merely present—though even that distinction doesn't work entirely. One or two of the poems have definite themes, *e.g.,* the stony ideal versus the living flesh. Leontes in **"Leontes, Solus"** secretly wants Hermione to remain a statue and not to come to life; in **"The Statue"** the serene humanity of the Greek sculpture begins to look inhuman and sadistic beside a living human face. Other poems merely work by juxtaposition and montage: for instance **"Band Music."** Baby among the cabbages is frightened by cows; Betty runs to comfort him, while Ernest shoos the cows away. Brass bands play from the cottage radio. Cabbages and cottages and bandsmen and Betty's blouse melt into one tableau. It is like an animated Victorian scrapbook, or perhaps a zoetrope. In the title poem, **"Fairground Music"**, the form of which is itself designed to spin like a zoetrope, King Cyrus's cavalry melt into roundabout horses and his warriors into the whirling figures of

'a turning box'. Elsewhere Fuller uses the techniques of another 'turning box', the cinema. The curious and striking **"Morvin"** is like a flash-back sequence from a Bergman film. Idling in some southern resort, a statesman, exiled by a populist *coup d'état* is reminded by a fireworks show of the flames and shots of revolution—a visual simile of a thoroughly cinematic kind. It is a brilliant and evocative poem, rich like Bergman's films in hints of significance, and no more substantial I think. The verse-handling in this collection is often distinguished and attractive:

> And Earth with rooks and bell-ropes swinging make
> Bright Sunday mornings in her antique style

But what is Fuller, I wonder? A fabricator of toys, a sort of poetical Fornassetti, or something much more considerable?

> *P. N. Furbank, in a review of "Fairground Music," in* The Listener, *Vol. LXVI, No. 1705, November 30, 1961, p. 943.*

Robin Skelton

Opening John Fuller's book [*Fairground Music*] I felt at first that he . . . had taken his laurels from the public park, but the browsing eye betrayed me. For one thing, he has a good deal more craftsmanship than the common run of young poets. For another, his poems have a gaiety and a clarity that are invigorating. He has an eye for detail. He sees the dog walking "sideways on his mistress' lead", and notices, as it crouches, the "coiling excrement". He looks out of a legend at "the smug church" and the "fat squashy cows". He is not afraid of archetypal imagery, and makes deft and witty use of fairy stories and legends, but the poems are not merely clever. In a splendid poem called **"Florizel's Complaint"** he shows how "The moon appears as snow smudged on a glass of blue". Some of these poems are, admittedly, a little too tricksy; one or two look like practice-shots at temptingly novel targets. But in **"The Ballad of Lord Timbal"** (a gay, delightful, romantic-ironic, thrust at La Dolce Vita), and in **"Fairy Tale"** there is evidence of a talent quite beyond the ordinary. I'm not going to say that this poet will turn out to be a major one, but I am certainly not going to say he won't. I'm only going to pray that life allows him to keep his powder dry, and doesn't betray him by means of his own abilities.

> *Robin Skelton, in a review of "Fairground Music," in* Critical Quarterly, *Vol. 3, No. 4, Winter, 1961, p. 376.*

George Macbeth

John Fuller is twenty-four. *Fairground Music* is his first book, though he has been appearing for some years in the best poetry-publishing magazines. It seems to me very clearly a young man's book, by which I don't mean a novice's or an amateur's book. The attitudes have a kind of Byronism about them in the way that the attitudes of his contemporary, Dom Moraes, have a kind of Shelleyism. Mr Fuller's persona has a tough, rather aristocratic, even fancy-waistcoated quality which I personally find very congenial. Quite often this persona seems to be used as a mask is worn at a ball, to create a style appropriate to a romantic but rather artificial situation. In **"Morvin"** the persona suggests a more effervescent Thom Gunn. . . .

In **"Fairy Tale"** it suggests the Hans Andersen side of Auden. . . .

In **"Snapshot"** it reminds me of William Plomer:

> Roger, fresh from soap and razor,
> Approaches in his candy blazer

And strokes his Maupassant moustache:

> 'This July sun is really *harsh!*'

The best poem in the book for me is the last one, **"The Ballad Of Lord Timbal,"** where the Byronism seems to be recognized and gently taken off, though the glamour of the pose is still allowed full value. The poem describes the life and death of a young English exile ('a gentleman / And of the richest kind') who grows disillusioned (or bored?) with his way of life and sails away in his 'brass expensive yacht' to be drowned off the coast of Spain. *Fairground Music* seems to me to be the best first book of poetry by someone under twenty-six since Thom Gunn's *Fighting Terms* came out in 1954. This is a smaller claim than it might sound, since poets tend to publish first books much later than they used to. Nevertheless, Mr Fuller's work is worth studying and it will become more so if he can gradually discard his persona and reflect his experience more directly.

> *George Macbeth, in a review of "Fairground Music," in* London Magazine, *n.s. Vol. 1, No. 10, January, 1962, p. 91.*

Julian Symons

John Fuller's second book [*The Tree that Walked*] gives the pleasures of wit, ingenuity, a continuous freshness of phrasing and observation. Freshness: he sees toasted kidneys like new pigskin purses, elevators rising like bubbles, tyre treads squeezing out perfect diamonds, Niagara as braided ropes of crystal. (These last three images come from a series of poems about American scenes which are the best in the book.) His characteristic method is to build and fantasticate an idea to make a final point which may be familiar but comes newly in its context. So the great meal eaten in **"The Cook's Lesson,"** 'a biological history of food', leads to the observation that food is never really dead:

> The bland liquids slid over our tongue as
> Heartbeats under crust, mouthfuls of feathers.

If admiration of poems like this one, and **"An Exchange Between the Fingers and the Toes"** must be qualified, it is largely because of a deliberate personal detachment, as of an amused benevolent spectator, that is inevitably limiting. Yet few poets today write so wittily, or have such a nice awareness of exactly what they are doing.

> *Julian Symons, "Cooked and Raw," in* New Statesman *Vol. 74, No. 1897, July 21, 1967, p. 87.*

The Times Literary Supplement

A few years ago, in a series in *The Times* called "Pleasure in Reading", John Fuller ended his essay on his enthusiasms in literature with the words: "For me, form can be the be-all-and-end-all of art (remote, or trivial, perhaps, but always interesting). Feeling never." Mr. Fuller's first book, *Fairground Music,* showed a precocious elegance of form and wit, a sprightly sophistication in which one could see the varied influence of Wallace Stevens, the later Auden, and, to be blunt, the poet's father, Roy Fuller. It seemed that several of the poems, such as **"Fairy Tale"** and **"The Ballad of Lord Timbal"**, had been written in Mr. Fuller's teens, yet there was nothing gauche, half-baked, or uncertain in the whole book. What it lacked was, precisely, feeling.

If one wanted to make a damaging attack on Mr. Fuller, one could say that there are enough glib, smart verses in [*The Tree That Walked*] to sink anyone with less sheer formal talent: **"An Exchange Between the Fingers and the Toes," "Revolution", "The Safety-Valve", "The Thousand and One Nights"**, and a few others. That rather dashing cleverness, so nimble that the eye can hardly stay still long enough to take it in—is it really anything more than *Oxford Poetry* of the late 1950s served up warm? But Mr. Fuller could survive such an attack, because *The Tree That Walked* contains a range of work which shows that his talent is altogether more solid, less modish. Nothing here is less than well made, and at a time when the well-made poem is often greeted with contempt this is heartening. Mr. Fuller has a true poet's primal delight in language, in words, so that his vocabulary is wide and curious without being barbarously onomatopoeic or stuffed with neologisms; there are none of Auden's exotic verbal blooms here, though clearly Auden is a poet who has meant a great deal to Mr. Fuller. What Mr. Fuller has developed is a voice and an intelligence that carry great authority; a phrase-making eloquence that works itself into the memory ("Everywhere sap stiffens into bark / And I am sick for something to believe"); an assured command of cadences. And the most striking poems here, such as **"Alive and Dead", "Green Fingers", "Now and Then"**, and **"Goodbye to the Garden"**, are much more the products of feeling than Mr. Fuller's remarks in *The Times* would have led one to believe: their controlled movement does not disguise a disturbance that is never self-indulgent or appealingly winsome. One would like to see Mr. Fuller extending this territory, and also a greater willingness to be open to clarity. The ambitious sequence of ten quatorzains, **"Out of the Wood"**, has the bewildering and fogging effect of being convincingly lucid at any single point, but taken poem by poem or as a whole it seems to add up to nothing but disjunction and confusion. And one would like to see Mr. Fuller trusting feeling a bit more and the skill of the equilibrist a bit less.

> *"Formal Feelings," in* The Times Literary Supplement, *No. 3415, August 10, 1967, p. 726.*

The Times Literary Supplement

[John Fuller and James Fenton] can, and no doubt will, be represented as crusaders in the War for Standards—troops raised by Wit in its campaign against neophile

Dullness. This is part of the story, but not the most important part. Each poet is as much an innovator as any English experimenter looking Westward. Mr. Fuller's poem **"Ghost Village"** [in *Cannibals and Missionaries*] is new to all classifications, the spirit of Auden inhabiting but not possessing it: Mr Fenton's "The Kingfisher's Boxing Gloves" [in *Terminal Moraine*] is original enough to baffle the intelligence while delighting the imagination.

Of course, the ingredients of these books are familiar, even traditional, but they are arranged in highly personal patterns. Mr Fuller is as skilled as an Old Master—there is not a flawed poem in his book, though there are some which tread water instead of getting anywhere.

Mr Fuller has one poem where his technical address is self-defeating. **"The Labours of Hercules"** is a sonnet-sequence in a progressive Hungarian form which recently overwhelmed George MacBeth. (It consists of fifteen sonnets, Nos 2 to 14 each beginning with the last line of its predecessor, the last line of No 14 also being the opening line of all, and the final sonnet made up of all fourteen repeated lines. Needless to say, No 15 has to be specially constructed and tends to get written first.) Mr Fuller follows the twelve labours dutifully if cloudily and fits them out with some amusing anachronisms (of the labour concerning the carnivorous Stymphalides, he writes, "the sixth was for the birds"), but there is nothing in the sequence to take it beyond a technical exercise. Imagination should know what to refuse when sheer skill comes to tempt it. But this is the one failure: there are many successes. **"Scenario for a Walk-On Part"** has an ease of movement which supports its theatrical self-awareness perfectly. Most of us are aware of an alter ego who is as rusty as he is superfluous. In the last stanza, the dramatis personae leave this stooge to his fate.

> The sexy minister reclaims his scarf,
> A girl in denim runs to meet a train,
> Mrs Jocasta bastes the fatted calf,
> The guests have taken to their beds again:
> I hold the floor but nobody will laugh,
> Nobody is there to kiss if I complain.
> I enter only in the second half,
> Unwilling, underwritten, used to pain.

"Aberporth" is accomplished but also warmly human. It is a landscape with figures, the sort of descriptive poem which opens inwards with a series of fine rhetorical flourishes. Above all, the musical handling of the language is eminently satisfying:

> The sea is much visited here, whose colours are cooler
> And life uncertain as well it might be in
> The earth's tears. Gulls on the sand look sharp.
> Without anxiety the jellyfish is hideously still.
> And the same could be said of the cliffs where wind carries
> The loves of freewheeling crickets across a haze
> of sun-baked blackberries.

The strangest poem is **"The Two Sisters"**, whose Mary and Martha polarity gives Mr Fuller the chance to compose a chain of hard aphorisms. The story is baffling, but the atmosphere grows more oppressive as you read. To create so sombre an effect in such stately verse is a real achievement. The songs and pieces for music are much simpler. **"London Songs"** succeed where so many urban song-cycles fail—they put their place names and Betjeman details into a convincing metrical harness. The slight-

ly Surreal tone of much of **"Cannibals and Missionaries"** suggests that Mr Fuller is changing his poetical stance. The perfect technique now reflects a disturbed world, making these his most impressive poems to date.

> *"Wit on the Offensive," in* The Times Literary Supplement, *No. 3665, May 26, 1972, p. 607.*

David Harsent

John Fuller is a poet of formidable intelligence and skill; he is also rewardingly susceptible to the oddities of experience: the strange lesions in our lives around which lines of poetry accrete. His two previous collections, **Fairground Music** and **The Tree That Walked,** are books one goes back to repeatedly for their wit, their depth and their sheer entertainment value. *Cannibals and Missionaries* displays all those qualities, and contains some very good poems, but there are times when the most pleasing of virtues lead to vice. Now and then that's just what happens in Fuller's new book, especially when the poems seem not so much *invested* with his intelligence as laden with its full weight until the bones creak.

Wit and entertainment are certainly to be had. **"The Art of Love,"** a long poem in octosyllabic couplets, takes a well-timed and fetchingly donnish swipe at the lantern-jawed Aunt Sally, Contemporary Sexual Mores, though the donnishness is renegade and never circumlocutory:

> *Dr Johnson* and *Dr Masters*
> Excluded obvious disasters,
> Turned from their scientific eye
> The weird, incapable or shy,
> And steered around a public storm
> By sticking firmly to the norm.
> Yet who if he is really normal
> Could stand an atmosphere so formal?
> What decent girl would choose how thick
> She'd like her perspex camera-prick?

Third-raters have got a novel out of that notion without making the point so well. **"God Bless America"** uses humour to attack, assuming our partisanship and getting it wholeheartedly:

> When they can be happy without noise, without knowing
>   where on earth they've been,
> When they cease to be intellectual tourists and stop wanting to be clean,
> When they send their children to bed at the proper time
>   and say just what they mean . . .

The flaws creep in, though, not least when the form appears to stretch the content, making a poem run woodenly on when its force seems spent.

> With one thin strand of hair loose from her head
> Falling in its tiredness, cedar red,
> Across the bent and pale half-humorous face,
> Hair like precious garment of the dead
> Tucked now behind the ear into its place,
> An automatic gesture yet with grace
> To make a ceremony of her task
> When fingers smoothing dows the finished lace
> Are answered by the question that they ask
> Of labour's quiet satisfaction, such
> As simply sanctifies the sight and touch.

The final seven lines there push the effective and resonant

lyricism which precedes them into the background, though it's the poem's lyrical power that makes the narrative line compelling.

The balance and strength at Fuller's command are best demonstrated in **"Her Morning Dreams,"** in which a brutal commonplace—the desolation following a failed affair—is transformed by the actions and distracted recollections of the poem's protagonist (not incidentally, the poet) into a unique and irresistible history: the language resists banality, promotes needle-sharp images and perceptions, and finally allows the poem to come beautifully to rest:

> I shall sit it out, here by the misty glass,
> Till I can face the morning's empty graces,
> The window sill becomes an abacus.

Perfect judgement, and not a syllable gloated over. The bad news is that the occasional gloat is to be found: there's a flexing of intellectual muscle which looks daunting but pointless, and Fuller comes close to tearing a ligament in **"The Labours of Hercules"** which takes the Hungarian form (used previously by George Macbeth) in which a sequence of fifteen sonnets link by taking the last line of the sestet for the first line of the next octet and end by making those lines, together with the first line of the first octet, which is also the last line of the penultimate sestet, add up to a final sonnet. It's undeniably clever, and the effect is a bit like beating your head against a wall—it's so nice when you stop. (p. 135)

> David Harsent, "A Collection of Poets: Fuller, Mahon, Fenton, Sexton, Smith," in The Spectator, Vol. 229, No. 7517, July 22, 1972, pp. 135-36.

Douglas Dunn

Cannibals And Missionaries is John Fuller's third book. What he has gathered in skill he seems intent on reducing by being mandarin, chasing after a personal *summum bonum* of rhyme and metre. He is, at 33, the indisputable master of all poets under 40 (and most over) in matters of traditional versifying with confidence. He sometimes reads like a poet of inclination rather than necessity; it's almost as if some of his poems at least are the result of a failure to resist yet another exercising of his remarkable technique, like a gigolo who doesn't like the girl but is, well, a gigolo. . . . Pressure of feeling in his work always seems distant. Emotional intensity as a requirement of contemporary poems has been overstated; even so, Fuller's poems are too cool. It would hardly do to advise a poet to reveal more of his private life; I merely note the fact that Mr Fuller has thought it unwise or unnecessary to do this.

Several poems are poised over personal crises to a greater extent than my remarks indicate. In these, significantly enough, he subdues his formalist passions, and is more concerned with proving the truth of observations and confrontations with sights and feelings. This may be chancing my arm with too thumping a generalisation; but I think it is preferable for a contemporary poet to prove his authority from personal experience, rather than impress with ingeniously and perfectly made surfaces and outsides of poems.

Fuller is not a show-off; but he does reach the point where displays of skill attain the appearance of bad taste. If this behaviour is a reaction to sloppy standards, it is a bad reaction. An example is **"The Labours of Hercules"**, a sonnet sequence in which the 15th sonnet is composed entirely of the first lines of the preceding 14, and each sonnet begins with the last line of the one before. It reads like a game played out of dedication, a poem about the labours of Fuller as well as Hercules, and perhaps about the life of art. Enthralling technical wizardry of that order is not altogether a waste of effort, but my suspicion is that it comes dangerously close to intricate fiddling while the world burns.

There are enough examples to show that Fuller finds poetry in modern life. What I consider the best poem in the book—**"Her Morning Dreams"**—proves this. A monologue by a woman attempting to begin again after the finish of a brief but important affair, it gives Fuller opportunity to use colloquial language important not for the formal excellence in which it is contained, but because the subject is of the present time, the role of the character assumed with powerful imagination.

In the pugnaciously sub-Augustan long sprint of **"The Art of Love"**, he surveys contemporary erotic manners. The iambic tetrameters are incisive; but he is sometimes cynical, too "normal" and well-balanced. The style of Auden's *New Year Letter* was probably Fuller's model, and he is recognisably present in the acceptable conclusion of the poem:

> Love has no watch, no train to catch,
> No lingering, no plot to hatch;
> It is the current not the cog,
> It is itself, no pedagogue:
> Love's unseen affirmative
> Is all the teaching it can give.

(pp. 58-9)

> Douglas Dunn, "To Still History," in Encounter, Vol. XXXIX, No. 5, November, 1972, pp. 57-64.

The Times Literary Supplement

Light verse bears close affinities to self-abuse: it may not be the real thing, but it has its own peculiar satisfactions. To begin with, poet and reader enjoy the surmounted difficulties of form. John Fuller's testing form is the "standard habbie", taken from Burns and so called by Allan Ramsay after Robert Sempill's "Life and Death of the Piper of Kilbrachan or, the Epitaph of Habbie Simpson". From it Mr Fuller extracts some dazzling rhyme sequences (incognito-SEATO-*Quito*-pardons-*Emperor Hirohito-Kew Gardens*) as witty as, say, Auden's "Akureyri-very dreary" or MacNeice's "gaffelbitar-Rye-vita". The Master, however, remains the master.

The danger of light verse (as of self-abuse) is that it can seem private. One recalls Auden's in-joke in *A Letter to Lord Byron*—"documentaries by the GPO"—which refers to "Night Mail", written for Grierson's documentary. Or, worse, the arcana of the MacNeice-Auden joint composition, "Last Will and Testament", which rivals in obscurity the Villon it parodies. To take an example from

Epistles to Several Persons, one wonders what an American would make of this:

> Managerial boobs
> And answers that you won't take no for
> From *Fine Tubes.*

Presumably, the innuendo will be lost as *Fine Tubes* fails to ring the door chimes. . . . Mr Fuller has turned to advantage the danger of privacy. The compiler of *Nemo's Almanac* (a literary quiz of impossible difficulty, designed to keep the most learned academic busy for a full year) has mined his new volume with references. But the references are calculated to baffle the merely academic: thus, granted the knowledge that Luigi Nono is an Italian composer and Charles Ives an early American experimentalist, will the same person know that Olga Korbut is a Russian Gymnast or that Paul Newman played Eddie Fingers in Robert Rossen's film, *The Hustler*? How many people know that "Rolling Down to Rio" is a Kipling shanty set by Edward German *and* that Frank Bough is a BBC sports commentator *and* that Dave Wottle is the be-capped United States and Olympic 800 metres champion?

In addition to this competitive quiz element, there is the pleasure to be derived from Mr Fuller's play with decorum—something he perhaps learnt from Burns. Burns begins with an uneasy mixture of Lallans and the educated neo-classic style reserved for moments of high seriousness. It is a mélange which ruins "The Cotter's Saturday Night" and "The Vision", but eventually Burns used high-style reference for comic purpose. . . .

In the same way, Mr Fuller's elevated references (Pablo Sarasate, Stockhausen, Deuteronomy) are deliberate breaches of light verse decorum, particularly when they occur in the splendid isolation of the short last line, with all the arhythmical force of a clerihew.

But nothing will convince the person who instinctively loathes the "crambo-jingle", the "spavet *Pegasus*", as Burns put it. Despite its long history, the verse letter has never really been accepted: Burns's Muse, "the tapetless, ramfeezl'd hizzie", has never been welcome in literature's polite drawing room. . . .

Mr Fuller often reminds one of Pope. In the letter to Angus Macintyre, for example, there is a surreal fantasy about bringing Oxford's academic procedure to the countryside: it is as good as Pope's fantasy in the *Epistle to Bathurst* about the abolition of all currency. And there are genuinely evocative moments:

> an interrogator's cigarette
> Quietly glowing.

The problem of the "form that's large enough to swim in" is insoluble and will remain so. Chaff and grain lie side by side, demanding a catholic response from the reader. Mr Fuller's mixture is not, finally, as potent as Pope's. There are too many empty stanzas (created by the impetus of his ornate form) for the comparison to be sustained. But ***Epistles to Several Persons*** will be welcomed for its skill by all who like light verse, while those who do not may retort, like Thom Gunn, that

> It's better
> To go and see your friend than write a letter.

"Private Pleasures," in The Times Literary Supplement, *No. 3750, January 18, 1974, p. 51.*

Clive James

John Fuller, though we haven't as yet
In the narrow how-do-you-do sense met,
You heard me lose in a verbal set-
-to early this Winter
A wrangle I should sooner forget
With *Harold Pinter.*

Unfit for struggling through the press
Afterwards with a view to es-
-tablishing rapport, I'm less
Distraught today,
And so with sang-froid if not finesse
Let me roundly say

How deucedly much I have enjoyed
Your bundle of verse letters, buoyed
Up by the skill you have employed,
Your glib bravura:
That your tongue is platinum unalloyed
There is nothing surer.

Your form's from *Burns,* plus the brio *Auden*
Praised when he addressed *George Gordon
Lord Byron:* in you, all three co-ordin-
-ate their roles.
With, I'm afraid, a whiff of the *Warden
Of All Souls.*

But the speed, the grace, *che sprezzatura!*
It goes like a rabbit drawn by *Dürer.*
I expect, in trying to ape so pure a
Style, mockery:
There ain't no kudos for *disinvoltura*
If one drops the crockery.

But a cat may look at a king. Though you
And I are in no way spiritu-
-ally allied like the younger *Schu-
-bert* and *Rossini,*
We're as closely meshed in at least one view
As the *Arnolfini.*

You like Art it takes *nous* to make
And can't quite, even for pity's sake,
Smile when a dolt thinks he's being *Blake*
By just doing his thing.
However sincere, the Crass is Fake—
That's the song you sing.

Right on. Small wonder that, gem-like, *James
Fenton's* eyes throw adamant flames:
He matches you in these verse-form games
Strophe for strophe.
The boy's so quick I suspect his name's
On the *Schneider Trophy,*

And that Mirandolian erudition!
An exophthalmic Man-With-A-Mission
(The wits of *Trotsky,* the looks of *Titian*),
He's bound to get famous.
He's a lengthened, scholarly edition
Of *Martin Amis.*

Ian Hamilton also receives your blessing.
Saying how I agree would entail digressing
For fifteen pages, as well as confessing
My depth of debt—
Which to see declared he would find distressing,

On that I'd bet.

So let's just say that you've sent a letter
To *guru numero uno.* Better
Minds there may be but I've not met a
    Single example.
(The dunces, victims of his vendetta,
    Would say none's ample.)

At *The Pillars of Hercules,* in the bar,
He holds his court, half monk, half Czar,
Reminding his men true letters are
    Not mere marked paper
But a much more life-and-death by far
    Species of caper.

Reminding *you,* too, *John:* for I
Reluctantly must identify
Such apogees of Look-Ma-I'm-Fly-
    -ing in these pages
That despite their enchantment for ear and eye
    My spirit rages.

Fascination of what's difficult?
OK, but why this terrific cult
For stanzas pressure-packed like a mult-
    -iple *M1* pile-up?
Is the aim to bring, as a vivid result,
    The reader's bile up?

Your Greek and Latin, with the aid of cribs,
He might just manage, but his schooling jibs
At *Welsh,* for *Christ's* sake! Come on, no fibs:
    Are you a *Druid?*
Or a second-home don with the yen (and dibs)
    For vacs unsewered?

To *insist* on being misunderstood—
What an *Oxford* conception of the good!
This book's as twisted as *Hollywood,*
    Only in reverse:
In some departments bent, I should
    Say, even worse.

Bereft of sweetness and of light
Mass Man, you gaily mourn, has blight
For Art: for Life, perpetual night.
    In your gloomy joy
You sound up-tight and out of sight
    Like your father *Roy.*

                           (p. 187)

John, down here somehow the Truth
Survives. That whoring after Youth
Is a sure-fire way to blow my couth
    You needn't warn
(*Ich habe heimweh* as bad as *Ruth*
    In the alien corn)

And how cardio-cerebral growths like Art
Are dialogues between Mind and Heart,
On that we agree—but where we part-
    -'s over your conviction
That they natter together like *Beauvoir* and *Sart-*
    -re, in *Mandarin* diction.

Well, I think that's just about it.
I've dug the dirt, I've slung the . . . Bit
By bit I've squandered my penn'orth of wit
    In this Verse Epistle:
The secret's in knowing when to quit.
    Time to blow the whistle

And bellow SON, IT'S A BRILLIANT BOOK!
(I'd have been more cheeky than you might brook

Had I said, while spurning the path you took,
    That this stuff you do
Can't be as clever as you make it look
    If I can do it too.)

                           (p. 188)

*Clive James, "To John Fuller: An Epistle in
Reply," in* New Statesman, *Vol. 87, No. 2238,
February 8, 1974, pp. 187-88.*

Patricia Beer

Epistles to Several Persons left me feeling like a cross between Adrian Mitchell and the heathen who said that the
story of the Virgin Birth would be quite interesting if you
knew the people. I have often felt like the heathen, but
never before like Adrian Mitchell. John Fuller converted
me to this new sympathy in the course of an afternoon,
and from then on Mitchell's often-expressed view that
most people don't care for poetry because most poetry
doesn't care for people began to seem luminous in its wisdom.

Mr Fuller turns his back on his readers. He is talking to
five of his friends—James Fenton, Bryan Kelly, Angus
Macintyre, Ian Hamilton and David Caute; and we can
listen, if we like, and if we think we can follow. Traditionally, this stance has not been essential to his purpose. It
has always been possible for poets, from the sonneteers of
the 16th-century to that great in-grouper, W. H. Auden,
to address individuals—friends, lovers, even enemies, or
especially enemies—without excluding the reader. But
perhaps it is hardly fair to mention Auden, in view of his
outstanding talent for the private address which is also
fully open to the public. . . .

The *Epistles* are not open to the public. Where they contain serious messages, we do not get them; we overhear
James, Bryan, Angus, Ian and *David* (*John*) getting them.

    I see you smile. All right, it's late.
    But, *Angus:* though it lies in wait
    With terrible reproaches, fate
        May yet forgive
    Our scared retreats, both small and great,
        And let us live.

When there is danger, in the shape of bad poets lurking,
we do not get the warning; the alarm bells are ringing for
him and his pal.

    For they are all still with us, *James,*
    Fiddling among the flames,
    Brandishing the brittle fames
        They soon arrive at.
    It's better not to mention names:
        They'll wince in private.

Mr Fuller likes people to wince. Perhaps we identify with
the wincers.

It is not that Mr Fuller's references and allusions are particularly cliquish or esoteric. In fact, they are much less
so than Auden's. Few of the names he sprinkles are outside the range of most people's general knowledge or powers of supposition: *Lord Longford, Roger Woddis, Teresa
Hayter.* And if some of them are no longer as modish as
they were—*Father Illich* is rather old biretta by now—

that is not Mr Fuller's fault, as the poems were written in 1972. . . .

It is the ineffable superiority of John Fuller's tone, and actual comments, that causes the alienation which possibly he was aiming at—which he has achieved, at all events. Superior in one sense, of course, he really is. The inventiveness, ingenuity, wit and technical skill of these verses are far beyond what most poets today could effect.

Like the heathen I mentioned at the beginning, I don't know the people, the ones he is writing to—personally, that is; I know the work of three of them quite well. It is difficult to know to what extent one can include the recipients of letters in comments about the writer. In one sense they are not responsible, in another they are: like murderers' victims. . . . On the other hand, a great many persons addressed in poetry may have loathed the image they were given. Mr W. H. may not have seen himself in the slightest as a summer's day, even though more lovely and more temperate, and indeed he was almost certainly not like one. But at least one can say that all these men *sound* just like Mr Fuller: superior and exclusive. So, watch the wall, my darling, while the Gentlemen go by.

> Patricia Beer, "Fuller's Worthies," in The Listener, *Vol. 91, No. 2353, May 2, 1974, p. 575.*

Douglas Dunn

Verse is still a preoccupation of some of the most talented of younger poets. John Fuller, for instance, persists with verse as if it was a hobby. He chases stanzas as Nabokov does butterflies. His *Epistles to Several Persons* is written in a stanza known to him as Burns's, known to experts as "Standard Habbie", named for the hero of Sir Robert Semphill's "The Piper of Kilbarchan," written about 1630, though Alexander Scott had used the same verse in a less rumbustious manner before 1590.

Comparison with Burns is out of the question. Anyone familiar with Burns's use of the verse will be struck by Fuller's insipid transformation of what, in Burns, contains some of the liveliest language ever written, forceful, genial, scathing, vulgar, and gratulatory as the subject demanded. Fuller's competence is certainly of a high level, though at times the clarity and power of the stanza is cruelly revealing. To James Fenton, another poet faithful to light iambic verse, he writes,

> Much of the Left we can ignore
> (Sheer anarchy I don't adore).
> The trendy educate the poor
>   In greed and fear. . . .

Where, apart from the hasty moral contempt—as trendy as what it tries to oppose—a word like "adore" is itself enough to indicate the politely laconic lack of substance which verse instead of mind tends to encourage. What we are reading is *verse,* a dose of cleverness. Towards the end of the poem Fuller writes,

> Some day I'll join you in the street
> Where suffering and truth must meet:
> It isn't easy to feel effete
>   This side of anguish,
> When those who can't choose what to eat
>   Don't speak our language. . . .

and the unfortunate effect of the verse is that he just doesn't mean it. Re-reading the lines, however, makes it clear that honest turmoil, guilt, self-effacement, doubts, are being squandered for the sake of a style that not only converts the ostensible form of verse-letter into thematic failures, but which lends serious subjects an ease, a sense of being amenable to prompt decisions, which is assuredly not the case.

In three of the five *Epistles* (the word itself is verse), Fuller ruminates on politics with his mind far from made up, though the decisive style pretends otherwise. Writing to a friend who like Fuller owns a rural retreat—though grander than Fuller's—he says,

> Aren't we fakers
> Pacing about our fenced-off acres?
> Aren't we the economic Quakers
>   In a cold war
> Between the strikers and strike-breakers?
>   What are we for?
>
> A rustic view in Coed-y-Brenin?
> A waste to keep a cow or hen in?
> What about all the jobless men in
> The National Parks?
> (I make no reference to Lenin
>   Or Karl Marx.)
>
> The unemployed are twelve per cent
> In Blaenau where the rain squalls dent
> A century's slag, a broken tent
>   Of splintered slate.
> I wonder where the profits went,
>   And who to hate.

Wonderings—Fuller, bemused, has tapped a core of political resentments in the wrong metre. It sounds, to my ear, like Mozart's Clarinet Concerto played on a referee's whistle. Like Young, and like Plomer, he is drawn towards a specifically imagined Englishness, sufficiently expansive in its liberal attitudes to include rich and poor, capitalist and socialist, owner and tenant, under the one tolerant umbrella. Is it possible?

Epistles to Several Persons contains many examples of Fuller's political discomfort. He appears guilty of his circumstances and education. They seem to have put him in a position from which he can recognise his own ambivalent outlook on left-wing politics with a certain amount of anxiety. On the whole this is an honest response to contemporary conditions. However, a writing of deeper imaginative turbulence would have appeared more in the mainstream of contemporary poetry than the 18th-century verse-form which Fuller has preferred. (p. 86)

> Douglas Dunn, "Secret Countries," in Encounter, *Vol. XLIII, No. 3, September, 1974, pp. 82, 84-7.*

Peter Ackroyd

There is a great divide in English poetry, not that you would notice it if you read the literary weeklies and the intellectual monthlies. Here, to begin with, are two books: John James's *Striking the Pavilions of Zero*—a somewhat odd and abstract title, perhaps—and John Fuller's *The Mountain in The Sea* which has a more familiar and a more 'poetic' sound to it. Mr James's book is published by a small press; its design and its typography are unfamiliar, and it has a colourful print on its cover. Mr Fuller's book is produced by a large London firm of publishers, and its cover is the simple and standard one they use for their poetical products—the point being, no doubt, that no one could possibly buy one by accident. Mr James's book has a note: "Some of these poems first appeared in *The Anona Wynn, Collection, The Curiously Strong, The Park, One, Second Aeon* and *Sesheta.*" Mr Fuller's acknowledgements are: " . . . some of these poems first appeared in *The Cellar Press, Encounter, The Listener,* the *New Review,* the *Observer, Outposts* and the *Times Literary Supplement.*"

And there you have it: the great divide. On the one side, magazines which are not the staple diet of the 'reading public' and poems which are not read or discussed by our poetry 'critics', whoever they may be nowadays. On the other side, the familiar parts of the literary soft machine. John Fuller's poems have become a standard feature of the cultural prints, and you will generally find them tucked away at the bottom of a column (where an article by John Carey or Jonathan Raban has just stopped, alas, a little too soon). You would find it much harder to come across the collections of John James, or of Andrew Crozier, or of Jeremy Prynne but all the fuss about *Poetry* not being read (even the literary editor of the *Times* has been raising his voice for the proper distribution of *Poetry*) is not about these poets at all; it is only about the John Fullers, the Douglas Dunns and the Vernon Scannells: in other words, *Poetry* in its familiar and domestic guise, that English *voice*—that *tone*—we have come to know and love.

John James has, quite deliberately, moved out of this context. *Striking The Pavilions of Zero,* in other words, breaks up the conventional, formal limits of 'the poem', it attends instead to the discrete line of the verse—that single, specific instance and its possible harmonies. John Fuller, in *The Mountain in The Sea,* adheres strictly to small forms in which the lines are, characteristically a vehicle for gnomic 'thoughts' and wry 'feeling'. But to press poetry into the service of reflection and observation is to make it, I think, inexpressive:

> Here warmth is transmitted.
> Your idle hand reaches
> And grasps a myriad boulders
> Of impossible size.

And it is this monotone which characterises the volume. James's freer use and more open development of the language allow for a much greater range of effects. . . .

Mr Fuller's poetry, where every word is heavy with the weight of implied reference, cannot quite manage this variety of tones. It is significant that the best poems in his book—like **"Wild Raspberries"**, for instance—are attractive simply because they have a momentum which breaks free of syntax and small form. . . .

I could put it another way by noting that, ordinarily, Mr Fuller employs the same syntax and the same range of voices as the current social novel in England; the problem with the now sacrosanct division of prose *Poetry* is that it reduces the difference between them to the level of simple content and treats only in passing the language which is actually being used. Where the novel concerns itself with the romance of individual life, Mr Fuller concerns himself with the romance of pre-individual life: the mountain, the sea, ancient settlements and the other poetical emblems of early twentieth century verse.

> Peter Ackroyd, "Verse, and Worse?" in The Spectator, *Vol. 235, No. 7695, December 20, 1975, p. 793.*

David Bromwich

From the *Letter to Lord Byron*-esque **Epistles to Several Persons** Mr Fuller now proceeds, forward in his own career and backward in Auden's work, to the style of *Poems 1930.* His new collection [**The Mountain in the Sea**] has its dwelling in a world of vague menace and jagged stone-age wonders. The atmosphere is, on the whole, attractively inhuman: over it all, understanding but not divulging, presides the author. Mr Fuller is a good poet and more than a good pasticheur, and his progress has been extremely odd. Influence at this level is mysterious. One can only say that something deep in Mr Fuller responds to something deep in Auden, and the more he writes like Auden, the more assured his poetry gets.

He opens with a tour de force: a long, "talky", and highly idiomatic meditation on the sublime entitled **"Up and Down"**.

> This is where it begins:
> A cairn marks the place
> Where sky negotiated
> A hasty truce.
>
> Thrown up like apophthegms
> Of a phlegmatic culture
> During some geological
> Tedious prologue
>
> They shoulder for position
> While offering their profiles
> Like notables at a spa
> Grouped for the lens.
>
> They have settled into age
> With fear of being alone.
> Such gaunt tranquility,
> A herded peace!

The third stanza has an effect of not quite sinister animation (Mr Fuller can make a geological deposit as eloquent as a bloodstain). And the reader who is arrested by *thegmphlegm* will soon meet *nanunculous,* be told of the exploits of "that old enemy" (Supreme Antagonist?), and finally settle down to the poem's slow and grand peroration, which allows some comfort from the spectacle of composure amid the flux:

> Privacy of worlds
> Not wasted but perpetual,
> Tons and tons of indifference,
> Lightness of heart.

Mr Fuller is frighteningly adept at the almost-echo—of himself and of Auden—and he knows how to impart to ordinary things a sense of impenetrable ritual: "Hat in hand, a wave from the shoulder / A shift of plane, colour catching the light, / Fanning of sheep or delay of shot." Sometimes he is a little too close to what used to be home; hearing of "the drill of seeds, the hill coming down", anyone who has loved *Paid on Both Sides* will think: "But surely he means 'The ice-sheet moving down, / The fall of an old house'." At the same time Mr Fuller is a strong enough poet to make one feel that his conscious tribute is often simply a case of shared temperament—the predilection for, as his jacket note agreeably explains, "ruined buildings of several periods".

The "we" of these poems, which is familiar rather than conspiratorial, grows steadily warmer through the book. Now and then Mr Fuller speaks not as an exceptionally subtle reader of poetry but as "one of us"—a peculiarly observant and marvelling one—and his verse, without warning, begins to breathe a different air. He can write, in **"Caer Arianrhod"**, of a "village in the sea" as it rises up from

> The gaze and gossip of those generations
> For whom a map could never end at the shore
> Where livelihood begins, that salt harvest
> To be shared with busts of seals who come to dine
> Alone, like emperors, in the black waves.

These lines are the loveliest moment in **The Mountain in the Sea.** With one conjuring look Mr Fuller takes in the large expanse of a theme that preoccupies him: the solitude of man in nature and the solitude of nature without man. He is indeed a student of the nostalgias, preferring, to what the present helplessly knows, all that the past chose not to know.

Fluency over the long stretch and, over the short, the poetic equivalent of "perfect pitch" are Mr Fuller's overriding virtues. Three poems here—**"Up and Down"**, **"Evening Signs at Gallt-y-Celliog"**, and **"Boundaries"**—seem wholly satisfactory on their own terms. Why is it, then, that one continues to think of him as a poet of local felicities? Why is it that the lines quoted above have more individual life, more imaginative *pace,* than any extended piece of writing he has done since **"The Two Sisters"**? A poet as directly influenced as Mr Fuller runs the risk of producing an undifferentiated patchwork of his favourite author's mannerisms, and he can afford to remind himself that no one has ever scaled the heights while reading a map. In the best passages of this collection, there are signs that he is becoming a creature you would mistake for no other, as well as that unnaturally cultivated thing: a natural poet.

> David Bromwich, "Under the Influence," in
> The Times Literary Supplement, *No. 3859,*
> *February 27, 1976, p. 215.*

John Matthias

The publication of poetry is . . . a chancy matter of waiting an all-too-often indefinite length of time while the unhappy publisher tries to raise the requisite funds or balance his books, and the protracted delay of reviews compounds a poet's justified irritation with the whole miserable machinery in terms of which the existence of his work is to be called to the attention of prospective readers. Fuller's epistles [in **Poems and Epistles**], for example, were written in 1972, and a couple of hours ago I turned at random to a stanza on Olga Korbut just as a fourteen-year-old Rumanian girl dethroned the now-ageing Russian gymnast in the present Olympic extravaganza. (That gets today more or less on the calendar.) In the world of films—an art the public is willing to pay for—one is arrest-

ed by the lightening speed of response to events. *All the President's Men* helped to create some of the incidents it depicts; and now Warner Brothers has announced that Steve McQueen has gone to work on their movie about the Israeli commando raid at Entebbe which happened just a few months ago. The reviews of that one will come faster than Idi Amin's press releases. But we must also serve who only stand and wait and will, alas, from time to time procrastinate.

That's a John Fuller rhyme. Well, not quite. Try these for the real thing: "fifty coolies / Pierre Boulez", "go all goosey / Claude Debussy", "something terser / vice versa", "off their hinges / Celtic fringes", "Coed-y-Brenin / jobless men in", "Smith to Yale / Texas gaol", "one excuse is / gastric juices", "purely mental rapes / Apollonian sour grapes", "liar's quinsy / Dr. Kinsey", "etcetera / blah blah blah." (It's hard to stop this once you really get going.) The knockabout idiom developed in Fuller's epistles via the Burns stanza has its immediate source in W. H. Auden's *Letter To Lord Byron,* one of the few successfully sustained comic poems between *Don Juan* and the early work of Kenneth Koch. The enduring influence of Auden, in fact, can be seen, with and without anxiety, in [Peter Porter's *Living in a Calm Country* and Elizabeth Jennings's *Growing Points*], as well. All three poets share with Auden a commitment to an anti-Romantic, anti-Modernist poetics; Ms. Jennings writes him an elegy, complete with the carpet slippers and the "leather skin", and Porter borrows the syllabic organization of *Spain,* the approach to a cultural occasion of *Metalogue to the Magic Flute,* the *paysage moralisé,* the ironic political song in trimeter quatrains (rhyming "Fanon" with "sine qua non", "Brechtwerk gay" with "Ethnic Shadowplay"), and other characteristic procedures. But it is Fuller, who has published a discerning *Reader's Guide to W. H. Auden,* who writes a book approaching something like a systematic dialogue with that fussy shade which, if not appropriate to the heaven of Blake and Bloom, is just right for that part of Soho where Ian Hamilton edits the *New Review.*

> If *Ian Hamiltons* galore
> (Offhand, I can distinguish four
> Or five. I hope there are no more)
>   Think it's addressed
> To them, too bad. You're tooth and claw
>   Above the rest.

Tooth and claw, indeed. But what is the American reader, uninformed about or uninterested in the London literary-political scene, to make of it? . . .

It's quite impossible not to like this, and I *do* like it, and yet one must run the risk of being thought a bore and say straight out that several of the very things mocked in the passage constitute the chief strengths of modern British poetry, such as it is, and *guess* that even John Fuller himself, not to mention Ian Hamilton, may suspect this from time to time. But who, as I say, could possibly dislike it? And who, pills / bills / frills, would not be pleased to learn—unless he should be someone so insensitive as to value experiment and to want to see it supported—that much of the patient's share of the Arts Council coffers has been paid in doctor's fees, some of it, one hopes, to cover malpractice insurance. In an *Epistle* to James Fenton (who is also the recipient of some *Baroque Quatrains* in Porter's book; it's a small world, folks), we are invited to read

Colin Falck (whose name Fuller has the decency to rhyme with "body talk") instead of all the "foul-mouthed transatlantic spivs / Wooing *Trigram*"; further—winding up for the pitch with *Flecker, trekker, Mecca, verum pulchrum*—"I'm glad, of course, that you're with *Secker* / And not with *Fulcrum*." Written in 1972, that. While we're busy laughing at it, the sad thing is that Fulcrum is now inactive, that Trigram is hopelessly overburdened, that Cape-Goliard has closed down, that *Agenda* has lost much of its original energy and purpose, that many of the most innovative English poets have had to go to America for publication or employment or both. Leaving the world to darkness and to thee, Colin Falck. English poetry threatens to return to the tedious sterilities of the 1950s.

But I mustn't get solemn; one is meant to be having a good time here. Indeed, one *does* have a good time here. Too good, perhaps, to keep one's values wholly intact. Along with Hamilton and Fenton, the letters are addressed to Angus Macintyre, an Oxford colleague of Fuller's (who gets at unpronounceable *Achaglachgach* a letter from unpronounceable *Llanaelhaiarn*); Bryan Kelly, the composer with whom Fuller has often collaborated; and David Caute, the novelist and historian. All of the epistles are full of the characteristic throwaway rhymes, and edgy with an equally characteristic throwaway wisdom. They are funny, flippant, nervous, awkward, nervy, elegant, couth and kulchured, irreverent, irrelevant, opinionated, learned, allusive, longhaired, longhorned, smug, smutty, philistine, mock-philistine, bored, lively, livid, friendly, fierce and fighting, fat-assed, worried, wearied, committed, timely, public, private, pubic, political, anti-political, stimulating, irritating, anti-academic, donnish, dapper, dotty, and so on by turns. My personal favorite is the long and wonderfully prejudiced piece on music addressed to Kelly which takes, as it happens, as in nearly all of the other letters too, opinions quite contrary to my own on nearly all conceivable issues related to the subject. This has its own strange pleasures, as any reader of good polemic knows. If the spiritual home of the epistles is at the gossipy center of literary London, their actual place of composition was far-away Wales, where Fuller was on leave from his university. Both the distance and the leisure put him in a position quite like Auden's in Iceland when he wrote *Letter to Lord Byron*. He can comment on even the most horrendous events—during a year, as he says in his note, of hijackings, IRA bombs, and the tragic Munich Olympics—without quite taking them seriously. For the most part, anyway. When the tone does suddenly change, it can be very moving. In the letter to Macintyre he has been writing about respectable middle-class (specifically, middle-class academic) compromise, escapism, and complicity in political and social injustice—another favorite, if not *the* favorite, theme of the early Auden. It ends like this:

> We need some vision to achieve,
> A heart to wear upon our sleeve,
> We need a holy spell to weave
>   Some sacred wood
> Where we can teach what we believe
>   Will do us good.

> I see you smile. All right, it's late.
> But, Angus: though it lies in wait
> With terrible reproaches, fate
>   May yet forgive

> Our scared retreats, both small and great,
>   And let us live.

To David Caute (who plays Fuller's Isherwood), he writes: "Your novels are at least committed. . . . You show what forces pull the triggers / While still creating living figures. . . . You are the man we want to read, / The kind of writer that we need." . . . All of these emotions are appropriate enough to a time in which Fuller finds, reversing Auden's "ironic points of light" of *September 1st*, "Random flares of evil" in the "massive darkness". The range of tone in the epistles is more considerable than a first and inevitably rapid reading suggests. Still, one should read them chiefly because they are funny. Taken together, they constitute a rare tour de force, a small comic masterpiece. (pp. 340-45)

The poems which make up the other half of Fuller's volume are various and, for the most part, successful and interesting. There are a few failures here, like the stridently unfunny and predictable **"God Bless America"** (Adrian Mitchell's sort of thing), and an anti-academic academic sequence—Audenesque again with its "antagonist with whom / We ever contrive grandmaster draws"—which strikes one, as Sean Golden has said of something similar, as being more a part of the problem than a part of the solution. But the level of formal achievement is usually high in this part of the book, and often enough the effects are stunning. There is an impressive sonnet sequence, **"The Labours of Hercules";** there is a longish poem in tetrameter couplets, **"The Art of Love,"** which has the muscle and wit of the best parts of Auden's overlong tetrameter epistle of 1940 and which might also be profitably compared with Kenneth Koch's recent poem of the same title; there are poems in terza rima, in quatrains, in a wide range of other stanzas and meters; there are the songs set by Bryan Kelly, a riddle, a monologue, a footnote, and a poem in what I think is an invented form combining certain characteristics of the villanelle and the sestina. The intelligent, conscious, and effective use of Audenesque resources is consistent. This is exactly the kind of song Auden would have written had he been, like Fuller, the father of daughters:

> Dear girl, your bud unfolded
> And brought you to this peace,
> But my drab heart is still patrolled
> By its corrupt police.

>   · · ·

> My body's single, and my love
> A melancholy roar.
> The children hide their faces when
> I stand outside the door.

In **"Ghost Village,"** the Audenesque theme of exile and quest tosses up some equally Audenesque allegorical figures moving through the landscape: "Did Squire Tribute, coming from beyond the ridge / Where the harnessed pismire superb in its plumes of dust / Pretended to be a horse on a careless errand, / Judge?" Most interesting of all, perhaps, is Fuller's attempt to extend the possibilities of those early Auden poems in short lines, themselves deriving in part from Laura Riding, such as **"This Loved One,"** **"Never Stronger," "Easy Knowledge," "Too Dear," "Too Vague,"** and **"On Sunday Walks."** The title of the poem in question is **"The Wreck"**, and it seems to me to be one of the most suggestive and actually useful poems to have been written after a close reading of Auden since Ashbery's "Rivers and Mountains." It repays careful study (as does a shorter poem in the same idiom, **"Annotations of Giant's Town"**). At three hundred or so lines, it manages to sustain effects that Auden himself inevitably restricted to a context of between fifteen and forty lines. Partly parodic, it also looks sideways (with a little affection?) at a modernist alternative to Fuller's characteristic brand of neo-classical formalism. (pp. 345-46)

> *John Matthias, "Pointless and Poignant," in* Poetry, *Vol. CXXIX, No. 6, March, 1977, pp. 340-55.*

Edward Mendelson

In 1969 John Fuller published a sonnet-sequence called **"The Labours of Hercules."** This title referred to the poem itself as well as to its subject: the sequence consists of 14 Petrarchan sonnets, each beginning with the last line of the one before, and a 15th sonnet made up of the first lines of the preceding 14. Technical fireworks of this sort—especially in the sonnet form—had lit up Fuller's earlier career, but neither he nor anyone else writing in English had attempted anything comparably spectacular before. (There are similar sequences by Sidney and Donne, but these are technically less ambitious.)

Even more surprising than the formal acrobatics of Fuller's poem was its poetic excellence. Yet the poem is bitterly dissatisfied with itself. As it approaches its final sonnet, it looks back to review "All my great failures." It recognizes at last that its structures were put together for their own sake only. While claiming a more than formal purpose for itself, the poem knows that its claims are false—but that it is too late to change. (p. 32)

The sequence was evidently conceived as an allegorical address made by the conscious mind to the instinctive flesh, but in the writing it became a love poem of a very odd kind. (Possibly its ancestry includes Meredith's "Modern Love.") Each of the Herculean labors is modernized into a lover's emotional ordeal. The sequence speaks in that tone of bewildered defensive pride that, looking over the wreckage it has made of love, tries to evade its knowledge that its claims to generosity and concern are spurious, and had been spurious from the start. "I did all that I had to do for you"—but it never served your need. "Our continuing is what we share"—but it is all we share. "We shall never see the end of it"—for when it is ended, there will be no "we" to see it. The impulse in which the poem began may have been a loving one, but "In ignorance we break / What we love most." The poem—the labors—is, in contrast, knowing and unbroken, but the poem neither needs love nor gives it. (pp. 32-3)

Poetic virtuosity is a rare gift; it can also be a dangerous one. Fuller's virtuosity led him to write so many good poems from the start of his career that for a long time he hesitated to risk giving rein to a simplicity that might have led to even better ones. There had always been a layer of instability and unease beneath the polished surface of his work, some sense (as in **"The Cook's Lesson"**) that each poem might be his last, but his early work kept that instability under control. After the crisis intimated in **"The Labours of Hercules"** all this began to change. Recently Fuller has become not only the best poetic craftsman of his generation in England, but one of England's best contemporary poets by any standard. Before he could live up to his early promise, however, Fuller had to learn that his limitless technical skills had limits as means of writing poems. Only when he had in fact achieved the greatest possible control over his materials, as in **"The Labours,"** could he openly question the value of control itself. His doubts are earned, not easy ones.

The change in his work came at first through indirection. For a few years Fuller put aside received forms to experiment instead with complex structures of his own invention, as in **"Annotations of Giant's Town."** These experiments, more gnomic than dazzling, were still formal, but their edges were rougher than before, their landscapes more untamed, their manners less urban. (Much of their style derives from the premonitory archaisms of early Auden, as Fuller's earlier style descended from the more formal urbanities of Auden's later poems. Fuller has written a book on Auden, and his own career in many ways reverses the sequence of Auden's.) Fuller gathered these poems, together with **"The Labours of Hercules"** and some other poems, into his third book in 1972. This was *Cannibals and Missionaries.* Its publication almost but not quite marked the end of Fuller's technical apprenticeship; he was to permit himself one last formal fling.

In the summer of 1972 he wrote a series of five verse letters to friends, using the Burns stanza. This is much more difficult than it looks. The poems throw off sparks, but for all their technical razzle-dazzle, they are transitional poems which moved Fuller away from his old obsession with technique. First of all, they take themselves much less seriously than did the earlier poems:

> But ssch! you know and understand
> The way these verses have been planned,
> Gritty like little bits of sand
>   Not shining quartz,
> No interference from a gland,
>   Just random thoughts. . . .

In the uneasy period before Fuller renounced his virtuosity he was claiming his private privileges with a vehemence he would soon let subside. (And as for "collectives"—a few years later Fuller would collaborate on a long poem with the poet to whom this outburst was addressed, James Fenton.)

Fuller published these five poems as *Epistles to Several Persons.* The title sets them firmly within an Augustan frame. The poems are essays, in the Augustan sense of the word, on poetry, music, politics, and the condition of England; in the Augustan manner also, they are *occasional* poems whose references date them to their year of composition. Far from being private, these poems embody something new in Fuller's work, something which had long been unfamiliar in English poetry. They are—and this is possibly the most important point to be made about them—*public* poems. That is, they occupy that vast disused territory in the landscape of verse rhetoric between the intimate and the oratorical, between the domestic and the sublime. They address themselves to named individuals, but they are not concerned with personalities or passions: they take their cues from their recipients' public roles—journalist, composer, editor academic, historian. The poems bristle with references, but these are neither learned nor private; they coincide with the interests common to the educated, newspaper-reading audience which is the only audience modern poetry has.

An aggressive tone surfaces occasionally in the *Epistles,* a survival from Augustan satire. This led one or two reviewers—who certainly shared the poems' attitudes and assumptions—to misread them as exercises in snobbery. Their tone actually points to an underlying modesty. To write public poems on public issues, while neither hoping to turn the engines of the state nor feeling bitter about poetry's inability to do so, is to acknowledge that the powers of literature are limited, that prophetic and unacknowledged-legislative claims have always been self-deceiving. But if limited, the power of poetry is real. It has none of the powers the Romantics claimed for it, but it can, through formal balance and verbal precision, bring issues into sharper focus, cause a disturbing increase in its audience's knowledge of the world's relationships. This is a small accomplishment, but it is at least genuine and not self-proclaimed.

Fuller's consonance of aim and achievement in these *Epistles*—possible for him only after he turned away from futile Herculean labors—makes itself felt with greater seriousness in the poems gathered in his next and most recent book, *The Mountain in the Sea.* Here Fuller has come entirely into his own. His renunciations are complete. The book contains no sonnets, not even any rhymes. Fuller sounds relieved that he no longer feels a need to drill his subjects into parade-ground formation. He knows himself a visitor in the world of objects, not an artist-hero determined to master it. . . . (pp. 33-4)

These poems keep a cautious, cagey respect for their subjects, a willingness to leave them alone, never to sing their transformations on a blue guitar. Precisely because Fuller's latest poems know the limits of poetic language—a knowledge modernism tried to avoid, and foundered in doing so—they have become deeper and more disturbing than they were before. His most recent work, written after *The Mountain in the Sea* and not yet collected, includes some rhyming poems, but these lack the old glitter; Fuller's renunciation of formal brilliance was less a vow of asceticism than a sobered turn toward careful moderation. His poems recognize the border between poetry and the world of fact as a surface easily wounded, too complicated and uneven to be polished smooth: "The meeting place of all the made / And unmade" is "a point of old discomfort." His earlier work used rhetorical elegance to protect itself from the world around it; now "Such diplomacy / Can scarcely guard us / From greater intimacy." Nor can it guard us from intimacy's risks. "Frightening," he writes in **"Mushrooms"**—"but still we search and pick."

The Mountain in the Sea is Fuller's best book, but two years after its appearance in England it lacks an American publisher. Outside some early pieces in anthologies, Fuller is known here only through his two previous books, published by David R. Godine in a single volume of *Poems & Epistles.* The formal precision of the first of these books and the Anglocentric props and vocabulary of the second could hardly have helped the poems' reception among an American audience. Through most of its history, American poetry has found its strength in a *resistive* stance against old forms and old manners, while Fuller's Augustan recollections are *receptive* instead. American poets have always taken the custom of poetic form as one best honored in the breach. One needn't look back as far as Whitman, or to Williams and Pound with their rhetoric of "breaking" the forms; pinned to any page of Lowell and Berryman some venerable stanza may be found bloody and disfigured. It would have been kinder to have set the forms free years ago, instead of keeping them home for a weekly Saturday-night beating, but American poets tend to thrive best when locked in struggle with their literary ancestry. (p. 34)

[The American] tradition is a local version of the Romantic inheritance which extends most vividly in English from Blake and Wordsworth to Yeats and Stevens; some of its light is reflected from the European traditions of Mallarmé and Rilke. This is the line in which an imaginative transformation of the world is more important, more interesting, more worthy of honor than the world itself. For better or worse, in America this tradition is now in the hands of the heirs of Wallace Stevens. At their best (as in some poems by John Ashbery) the heirs seem not entirely happy with their legacy. Although critical supporters in the universities want to proclaim them pure Romantics, new pioneers of the American sublime (for readers of this journal, names needn't be named), their work is more ironic, more cautious—and less self-deceived about its powers—than the work of their predecessors had ever been.

Yet whether tempered by irony or not, romantic assumptions remain central to American poetry, as to American criticism even at its most "advanced." This tradition is however in the midst of its own crisis, and there are signs that it may be in terminal decline. An alternative tradition—it can usefully be called Augustan in contrast with Romantic—has recently begun to reemerge with unexpected strength after 200 years of underground passage. In light of this, Fuller's work is as important for its suggestions of change in the literary and cultural atmosphere as for its own merits. If a tradition like the Augustan one should emerge in American poetry—it has already triumphed in American fiction in the work of Pynchon—it will take a form very different from its English counterpart, but Fuller's work can still suggest some of its characteristics.

The recent recovery of Augustan traits—public, occasional, "kinetic" (to use as praise a term Joyce used for disapproval), collaborative, formal, receptive to tradition—was primarily the work of Auden in England and of Brecht in Germany. But Fuller has made his own contributions to the recovery of the public mode. The "we" in a Fuller poem (as in **"The Cook's Lesson"**) is unlike anything else in modern poetry. It is a choral "we": neither a false-modest version of "I" nor a limitless generalization of humanity. Fuller's first-person plural evokes a group similar to his audience, and similar to poetry's audience: small enough to recognize its own boundaries, large enough to be receptive to variety.

Fuller's own receptivity, like that of his tradition, is far from mere passive acceptance; it is a way of identifying—without narrowing—one's past origins and present responsibilities. This cannot be done without making exclusions, but these are more reluctant and less heated than the exclusions that define and limit Romanticism. Fuller's own early style, in the mid-'60s, was built partly as a defense against an American takeover of English poetry which then appeared imminent. In the years when Fuller was finding his style, English poetry tended to think of itself as in disarray and decline, and began to look across the Atlantic for its models. Yet Fuller never tried to fake an American accent, even when he was most discontented with his own. (pp. 34-5)

What Fuller was shrewd enough to realize was this: American poetry found its vitality mostly in its own native tradition. If English poetry was to rise from its decline, it might be able to learn some construction methods from beyond its borders—as it had done in earlier periods of crisis—but its building materials would, as always, have to be native ones. If the coming years produce a new revival in English poetry, much of the credit should go to John Fuller. Not only will he have helped to build the new structure, he may also prove to have been the poet who discovered that the old building-stones were still sound, still capable of building strong walls with large windows. (p. 35)

> *Edward Mendelson, "The Poetry of John Fuller," in* The New Republic, *Vol. 176, No. 22, May 28, 1977, pp. 32-5.*

Andrew Motion

John Fuller's first four books of poetry were praised for their technical virtuosity—sometimes at the expense of their main thematic concerns. And when his fifth, *The Mountain in the Sea,* came out in 1975 the surprise of its uncharacteristically free forms dominated critical attention. His new collection [*Lies and Secrets*], although it reverts to earlier, stricter methods, doesn't let off meanings so lightly. The dazzlingly finished constructions aren't allowed—as they occasionally were in the past—to become an end in themselves and a replacement for thoughts which proved unmanageably difficult or painful. Instead, formal dexterity is continually regulated to suit the demands of content, and the result is his best and most serious book yet. From time to time there's a distracting whiff of the Poetry Comp. (in his Oxford Prize Poem on a Sacred Subject, for instance), but he usually manages to humanise the artifice associated with occasional verse, and always creates an impressive balance of objectivity and involvement.

"Annie Upside Down" is a case in point, suitably, because it's the first poem in the collection, and concentrates most of its major themes. The peculiarity of its heroine's plight—hanging upside down on a barbed wire fence like 'a wounded umbrella'—is prevented from remaining merely strange by Fuller's handling of detail. As Annie's indignation gives way to fear, he refuses to lose contact with her physical 'position', or permit its oddness to command all his attention. And what begins by seeming remote and faintly ludicrous ends by becoming intimate and tragic:

> The years fall out of your pockets, something comes in
> To your head like a passing thought
> And can't be set to rights once it's got inside your skin.
> There: you're caught.

A large number of images in "Annie Upside Down" are concerned, in one way or another, with children: sixpenny

magnets, pencilboxes, pantomimes and so on. These fulfil a variety of purposes, and one of them is to generate, during the course of the bizarre disaster, a sense of reality which is both familiar and half-forgotten. They are palpable but disturbing reminders of life, and Annie clings to them as the poem moves from describing her physical situation to retailing her reflections on nostalgia, anxiety and hope. Elsewhere, children officiate at many similar transitions from the particular to the general, and often introduce the same preoccupations. "Blind Man's Buff," "Musical Chairs" and "Charades" are three obvious examples. In all of them, Fuller uses party games to create a sense of disorientation which, to him, is as perturbing as Annie's, and which forces him to face life as 'a problem he must solve'. This emphasis on the riddling aspect of experience recurs throughout the book. As its title suggests, meanings, identities and pronouncements are usually lies or secrets or both. The human condition, whether intellectual or emotional, is always dauntingly complex because it is always 'a fiction carefully rehearsed'.

To puzzle over riddle and investigate fictions as diligently as he does is proof of Fuller's intelligence. And to realise that his endeavours cannot be finally concluded is testament to his integrity. He knows that character is too fluid and life too unpredictable for there to be much chance of finding absolute authenticity. His elegy "In the Corridor" and long (20 page) dramatic monologue "The Most Difficult Position" suggest that only mortality, sorrow and heartbreak can be relied upon to be repeatedly and harrowingly themselves. But these and other poems also insist on the power of hope to combat such certainties: whatever the threats, page after page turns to meet their challenge. (p. 686)

> *Andrew Motion, "Dazzling," in* New Statesman, *Vol. 98, No. 2537, November 2, 1979, pp. 686-87.*

Alan Brownjohn

Lies and Secrets seem, of course, qualitatively different in common usage. But John Fuller, in [*Lies and Secrets*], insists that the limitations of language *must* betray the truth, and that whatever his *personae* are saying it will be misleading; turning the world upside down, as in his opening poem about Annie, who is trapped in that position on a barbed wire fence. This volume is, indeed, more than ever a kind of teasing dance around the reader, a witty, delicate and haunting game. But it's of the nature of games played seriously to involve energies and motives which usually go with more important activities; and I don't take Fuller's jokes *un*seriously or regard his evasions as frivolous. The two finest set-pieces in a book largely *of* set-pieces are absorbing dramatic monologues (a form interestingly making one of its periodic reappearances); one, "Spirals", about (I think) the mutation of radical, rational beliefs into self-deluding mysticism, the other, "The Most Difficult Position", a brilliantly sustained study of obsession, in this case with chess, and scholarship, and self-esteem. The least satisfactory poems are those which circle too restrictedly in the pursuit of tiny games and devices: the poem wholly in words of three syllables, the batch of joky "Literary Observations." But the more elaborate the game, the more the hint of alarm breaks in: "Musical

Chairs" goes through the circling and the eliminations to end as a parable on the final hollowness of succeeding and surviving:

> And One is alone, for one is one,
> She blows a sigh for all you did,
> Stack the chairs and close the lid,
> Who can win when the game is done?
> For the music stops, and out you drop,
> And all you know is that you know
> There's nowhere to hope for, nowhere to go.

"Charades" is in the same vein, life being a children's game turned sinister, a pursuit of a meaning constantly denied until one is sent "out of the room" for the last time. *Lies and Secrets* also has Fuller's justly-praised **"In the Corridor"**, the one about the apparent return to life of the dead friend, the poet Francis Hope, to whom the book is dedicated—a poem that is very much for real. Intelligence, the power to move, and surface attractiveness are rarely combined in a poet, but Fuller has them all in a blend of spoof and dedicated seriousness which becomes more skillful with every new volume. (pp. 67-8)

> *Alan Brownjohn, in a review of "Lies and Secrets," in* Encounter, *Vol. LIV, No. 1, January, 1980, pp. 67-8.*

Alistair Elliot

John Fuller's taste for clear, colloquial and juicy English is well known to the readers he yearly entertains with his annual literary quotation competition, *Nemo's Almanac.* . . . If ever he gives up editing *Nemo,* his files would yield us a brilliant anthology of observant crystalline poems, sprinkled with carefully felt phrases and the occasional right rare word.

Fuller's own best work adds a riddling, equivocal element to these qualities. An excellent early example is **"Girl with Coffee Tray"** (a sonnet), in which slipping and falling indoors is described with cubistic fragmentariness as far as perception goes, but in standard sentences and with an image-over of falling into and down through the sea. My own favourite of this kind is **"Thing from Inner Space"**. . . .

When this poem was published in its context in *The Mountain in the Sea,* its head-start on my attention made it hard for me to see how good the other poems were. Now, the end of **"Morning"** has grown into a moving image of Fuller's world, and of his style: "At once precise and blurred. / Dew handprints on iron. / The valley filled with mist." And I can see, too, that the enigmas of **"Up and Down"** prefigure a method that has produced whole poems in other Oxford hands since: "They own everything, / Saddled with foot-thick wool / And a family resemblance / Like the first Marlboroughs. / . . . on misty mornings / Moving like ancient sofas / On castors over the gravel / They keep their watch."

The Mountain in the Sea was a collection of related poems (in unrhymed but roughly accentual forms) that seem to have originated from the same sabbatical summer of 1972 when Fuller wrote the sparkling letters of *Epistles to Several Persons* (in Burns stanzas). By contrast, the new book, *Lies and Secrets,* seems to contain most of, or even all, the poems Fuller has written since closing the file on

Cannibals and Missionaries (1972), itself an omnium-gatherum which also included words for music by Bryan Kelly. In spite of its generous size (62 type-pages of verse), the new book seems insubstantial. Surely these words for music will always seem weak on their own—like the slight and uninvolved poems about games (playing blind man's buff with his daughters is more or less thrown away over his shoulder), and the competition poems. They should at least have been protected, by an Auden-like partition, from contact with the stronger and less papery long poems about people, which are the sustaining thing about the book.

For, like James Merrill, though not on such a scale, Fuller has been writing first-person verse-narrative. **"Annie Upside Down"** opens the book with a crash of boisterous, even funny, stanzas (5-3-6-2-beat rhyming quatrains), the monologue of an old woman caught (presumably till she dies) on some barbed wire ("fastened to the tilted hill with kisses / I did not care for"). In isolation, such gallows humour is hard to recognize; the more so when compared with the smiling tribute to an older colleague at an American university (**"The Wilderness"**—loose unrhymed hexameters). **"Spirals"** (in rather Browningesque and sometimes very flat blank verse) is a slice of speech (seven pages long) beginning and ending with omission marks, from a tantalizingly unidentified character who in his old age (date "179—") is living by the Susquehanna and is seen refusing to be drawn back into politics. The question "Who is this guy?" continually interferes—as it does not in "Gerontion", say; and the poem itself does not resolve its theme. . . .

The final poem in the book, **"The Most Difficult Position"**—the chess-board before any move is made—has an epigraph from Goethe which means "A man who plays with life will never get anywhere; a man who cannot command himself will always be a slave". It relates the conflict between two actual nineteenth-century chess-masters, the Englishman Staunton (who narrates the prologue and the epilogue, in blank verse) and his would-be American challenger Morphy (who in loose hexameters with feminine endings describes Europe to his mother in New Orleans). The men never play their game, but both lose: Morphy his mind, and Staunton his beautiful young wife, whom he has neglected for chess and Shakespearean scholarship. Fuller plays with the ideas of success and seriousness. . . .

Fuller makes Staunton shock his wife by explaining that chess is unimportant, despite the time and thought and devotion he expends on it. The contrasting forms of American and English commitment and the complex of losses in this story allow Fuller to express a sense of passion that I cannot remember seeing in his work since that extraordinary sonnet in his first book, **"A Kiss in Galloway."**

> *Alistair Elliot, "Precisely Blurred," in* The Times Literary Supplement, *No. 4006, January 4, 1980, p. 4.*

Andrew Motion

Narrative poetry never had it so good as in the 19th century. In the 20th its popularity has decreased considerably—with a few shining exceptions to prove the rule. For one thing its potential audience has been distracted by alternative entertainments. For another, the modernists severely reduced confidence in the poetic tradition of 'realistic' story-telling. Interestingly, large numbers of English novelists have continued to produce work which conforms broadly to Victorian examples. English poets, though, in the last 50-odd years have often been driven to concentrate on lyrics at the expense of narratives.

In the last few years there have been signs that this trend is being reversed. As the influence of post-modernists has filtered into England from America, and as a new generation of English writers has become articulate, a strong pleasure in poetic fictionalising has reasserted itself. This hasn't necessarily meant a full-scale revival of the narrative tradition, but a more self-conscious form of story-telling.

In a verse Epistle to James Fenton, John Fuller once wrote: 'Poets hate to have directives: / They're on their own, not on collectives', but in spite of this assertion and although strictly speaking he belongs to an older poetic generation, Fuller's own work is also pre-occupied with various kinds of serious playfulness. His last collection, *Lies and Secrets,* illustrated and analysed it on almost every page, and in *The Illusionists* the same themes are writ even larger. The new book is a nine-part verse tale written in the stanza Pushkin invented for *Eugene Onegin,* and its ostensible narrative purpose is to follow the career of a young Camford graduate, Tim, once he has left university to work in a London art gallery. Here his ideals undergo a sustained assault—first as he competes with his colleague Nico for the attentions of a society belle called Polly Passenger, and latterly as he becomes unwittingly involved in the sale of a fake Hogarth. Eventually the painting's true nature is exposed, Polly is revealed as a man, and Tim's romantic illusions are shattered. It's a conclusion reached by comic ends to serve a high moral purpose, and as in all Fuller's poems the elegance and humour co-exist with a profound and restless melancholy.

The poem's most striking gravities and comedies are emphasised by another more hidden subject: its own creation. Fuller repeatedly parallels the duplicity of his characters with his own inventiveness—and thereby suggests that the supreme illusion is to suppose omniscience in any form:

> My characters have not been taught to
> Accept me as a hanger on.
> They hide their thoughts from me, refusing
> To share their hopes or be amusing,
> They change their minds or disappear,
> Or turn out not to be sincere.

The Illusionists is at its most fascinating when Fuller allows his subjects to comment on one another in this way. It is a rapprochement which enables him to include—among various other things—virtuoso literary games, and lengthy digressions, without jeopardising his structure. How can digressions be considered as such, when the poem is written about itself?

There are, however, indications that Fuller's faith in this process does not stay the whole course of his poem. The abundant self-deprecations ('If this chapter feints or lingers . . .', 'When will we get back to the point . . .?') do not always seem designed to make a virtue of free fictionalising, but to apologise for formlessness. And their modesties open a gap between traditional narrative methods and post-modernist ones, in which questions quickly spring up. Why should Tim sink so far and fast from sight? Why should the language sometimes be allowed to slacken? Why should some unimportant characters get pages of description while some important ones get almost none? These and other questions insist on emerging throughout the poem—and in the end they guarantee that, instead of achieving a kind of deceitful unity, it exists as a series of funny, sad, brilliant fragments. (pp. 22-3)

Andrew Motion, "Hating Directives," in New Statesman, *Vol. 100, No. 2594, December 5, 1980, pp. 22-3.*

Gavin Ewart

This short novel in verse [*The Illusionists*] is written (and very well written) in the rhyming stanza used by Pushkin in *Eugene Onegin.* Its English ancestors are *The Rape of the Lock* and, more particularly, Byron's *Don Juan.* The story, of fakes and illusions, is not important except as an opportunity to moralize about London life; it produces its own interest and expectations, however—the desire to know what will happen next never vanishes, but the proportion of narrative to digression and speculation is not high. Fuller, a beautiful writer of apt light verse, has no passages to rival Byron's fine account of the shipwreck in *Don Juan,* for instance. Yet he has the essential poetic quality of imaginative description: 'His cuffs shot pearls, and white gold drew / Rings that his fingers struggled through'. As well as Byronic asides and moralizings he very wittily uses Byronic rhymes (Hockneys / knock-knees), and ingenious Pope-like circumlocutions ('the lips' parenthesis' for the mouth). There are palindromes—dream characters called Enid Dine and Noel Leon, rare words like 'orectic' (a medical adjective that means stimulating appetite or desire). In the middle of all this deftness and ingenuity he is still master of fantastic exaggeration, as were Pope and Dryden: 'Famous careers at his behest / Were summarily re-assessed, / And when his merest qualms were quoted, / Rank upon established rank / Of reputations promptly sank' (this is of an art critic). Of its kind—and it is now a very rare kind—this poem could hardly be better, or more enjoyable. (pp. 244-45)

Gavin Ewart, in a review of "The Illusionists," in British Book News, *April, 1981, pp. 244-45.*

Peter Porter

The title of [*The Beautiful Inventions*] applies exactly to the poems it contains. It's a measure of Fuller's skill that of those two words, 'inventions' matters most. Many poets are good at the 'beautiful,' but Fuller is unrivalled in Britain today when it comes to contriving scenes, situations and stories.

There is no shade of disapproval over 'contrive,' as I use it here. A poem is like a painting or a piece of music; it is a made object. Feeling is as likely to come through the shape of the verse as it is through truthful observation. Fuller's verse is as precise as a digital recording. More important, his precision is the friend and sponsor of imagination.

Some poems in this book are tourist vignettes of a trip to

Turkey. They have a packed, haunting quality, like coming awake and remembering every detail of a dream. . . .

Inside his perfected forms, Fuller can afford to be mysterious and to employ an exotic vocabulary. **"Linda,"** for instance, written to be set to music, is a funny ballad of disillusion, as outré as Auden's "Miss Gee," but much gentler. His long poems in dexterous light verse—**"Amazing," "A Valentine"** and **"How Many Goodly Creatures"**—are indeed amazing. **"A Valentine"** catches the excitement of a good Broadway lyric, and **"How Many Goodly Creatures"** is as smooth as Praed and just as warmly social. . . . I don't enjoy his poems on cooking, though one, **"Sorrel,"** gets the better of my priggishness:

> Apologies to the snail
> For gathering his dinner
> And perhaps tomorrow's,
> With whom I have no quarrel
> As fingers search for sorrel.

Readers who let their sense of pleasure guide them will buy the new Fuller volume. He is a key figure in contemporary British poetry.

> Peter Porter, "Digital Watchwords," in The Observer, *April 10, 1983, p. 31.*

John Mellors

John Fuller has chosen as epigraph for his first novel [*Flying to Nowhere*] those five lines of nearly perfect verse by the Emperor Hadrian, beginning *Animula vagula blandula.* It is a hard act to follow, but few readers will feel any sense of anticlimax in the 80-odd pages of prose. *Flying to Nowhere* is written in a style at once richly colourful and vividly precise. There are scenes that suggest a detail from some crowded Pre-Raphaelite canvas: for example, girls scything grass 'moved together against the silent fullness of the field, skirts kilted up about their thighs, feet scratched and bleeding from the stubble'.

The Abbot of a monastery on an island apparently off the coast of Wales spends most of his time in a dank underground chamber dissecting bodies. If the soul is *hospes comesque corporis,* whereabouts in the body does it reside? Obsessed with his search, the Abbot sometimes fears that he will never succeed: 'The body was like a house, whose single inhabitant might be impossible at any one time to find. You could . . . be forever entering the chamber just vacated by the object of your pursuit'.

What is Fuller's answer to Hadrian's *quae nunc abibis in loca?* Does the soul go somewhere else when it leaves the body? Gweno tells the other farm-girls a bedtime story in which she is dying, 'wrapped up in a leaf'; then, she goes on, she is 'flying away . . . flying to nowhere. I'm just becoming myself.' The Abbot, it seems, is more sceptical. He tells the novices that every monk must put behind him 'the temptation to fly'; we cannot free ourselves from 'our soil and nature and the bed of our corruption'. However, his sermon finished, the Abbot feels ashamed, 'because he knew he had lied'. So what does he really believe? That the soul can leave the body and exist independently? That there is some sort of life after the body's death? *Flying to Nowhere* asks unanswerable questions, encouraging speculation and provoking wonder.

> *John Mellors, "Soul-Searching," in* The Listener, *Vol. 109, No. 2807, May 5, 1983, p. 27.*

John Mole

W. H. Auden once commented that there's no such thing as a pretty good omelette, and I'd guess that John Fuller agrees. He's undoubtedly one of the best cooks since Auden—his ingredients are carefully chosen, his mixes often surprising, and the resultant dishes invariably rare. The meal [in *The Beautiful Inventions*] is given a final stir for good luck, then served with decorum:

> Afterwards you may walk the block,
> Or collect your daughter from judo, noticing
> In the jut of lip and foot in the jostling
> For a fall, an equal determination.
> Then coffee, and music. And perhaps a cigar.

No perhaps about it. Definitely a cigar—and a toast to Auden. That flash of a world outside—collecting your daughter—partakes of the meal.

The *bonne bouche* is a paradigm of the good life: the grub *is* the ethics. And reading **"Steamed Carp's Cheeks"**—one of several poems in *The Beautiful Inventions* where cooking instructions emerge as a branch of moral philosophy, and where we're told to buy Chinese mushrooms if our grocer has them—I found myself remembering the ancient Chinese saying that you should govern a country as you would cook a small fish. Fuller is just such a fastidious emperor, issuing and acting upon instructions for the business of good government and craftsmanlike making. He has a delight in the workings of orderly little universes—beautiful inventions in themselves—which he sometimes recreates through the details of a protective rhetoric, as in **"Wasp Nest"**:

> Be careful not to crush
> This scalloped tenement:
> Who knows what secrets
> Winter has failed to find
> Within its paper walls?
>
> It is the universe
> Looking entirely inwards,
> A hanging lantern
> Whose black light wriggles
> Through innumerable chambers
>
> Where hopes still sleep
> In her furry pews,
> The chewed dormitory
> Of a forgotten tribe
> That layered its wooden pearl. . . .

The delicacy of this is admirable, and, in the main. I like *The Beautiful Inventions* best when it is at its most intricately riddling. There's nothing fussy or wilfully smart about Fuller's cleverness in such poems. Their small, exact occasions clear an ample space for tenderness and wisdom.

What I'm less happy about is some of the brilliant, rhymed displays of metrical footwork—*copious* inventions, certainly, and in their way amazing, but they're a kind of Ira Gershwin gone *nice:*

> I'd like to have your back to scour
> And other parts to lubricate.

Sometimes I feel it is my fate
To chase you screaming up a tower
  Or make you cower
By asking you to differentiate
Nietzsche from Schopenhauer.

There's a preciousness in this. It's like listening to the King's Singers going through their repertoire of jazz items—bending the notes so self-consciously with such knowing accomplishment—but if you like that kind of thing, no one does it better than John Fuller and there's plenty of it towards the end of the book.

The last poem, though, is the most remarkable, and one of the best that Fuller has written. **"The College Ghost"**, in which the poet meets and listens without protest or interruption to a spectre which is not unlike his alter ego, manages to be both disquietingly modern in its edgy questioning of the value of university life and traditionally donnish in the manner of M. R. James. It's a poem in which the void whispers beyond the dreaming spires, and in a book that is in so many ways accomplished and complete it seems somehow right that a ghost in the works should have the last word:

"Now I appear to you because at last
I have rejoined you for ever. Life has made
Its choice. My affairs are finally quite complete
And there is nothing left in the world to alter.
Whatever you teach will make no difference at all."

(pp. 69-70)

John Mole, in a review of "The Beautiful Inventions," in Encounter, *Vol. LX, No. 6, June, 1983, pp. 69-70.*

Edward Mendelson

Every so often two scientists working independently make the same discovery at the same time. A lucky coincidence of this sort has now occurred in literature. John Fuller's *Flying to Nowhere* is, among other things, a murder mystery set in a medieval monastery. It appeared in England at the same time Umberto Eco's murder mystery set in a medieval monastery, *The Name of the Rose,* appeared in English translation. . . .

Flying to Nowhere, a first novel by a 46-year-old English poet and Oxford don, is as rich and exciting as Eco's book, but deeper and more disturbing.

It is also a miracle of compression, each of its brief chapters displaying the density and precision of a Dürer woodcut. Its 80-odd pages begin as a murder mystery but end in a revelation of deeper mysteries of death and rebirth. Vane, the Bishop's emissary, arrives at an island monastery off the coast of Wales to investigate the fate of pilgrims who never returned. While he struggles for answers against the reticence of the Abbot and the enmity of the Manciple (or steward), a greater struggle between mortality and fertility takes place all around him. The Abbot, who seems part Dr. Frankenstein and part René Descartes, dissects dead bodies, suspiciously acquired, in a search for the location of the soul. Inadvertently, his experiments reveal a means of restoring the dead to life. Meanwhile, the stones of the monastery itself take on the attributes of a gigantic body, sweating and drying according to secret moods. . . . From the grass-fruits breaking free from their stems in the opening paragraph to the appalling vision of the resurrection on the final page, the book pulses with the rhythms and energies of organic life. The savor of mushrooms and the stench of disease vie continually in the island air.

This is a novel dense with transformations, both ordinary and miraculous. A young novice in the days before his ordination confidently translates vivid scenes into dry meditations. In the transforming ritual itself—it proves disconcertingly to have something to do with a naked young girl and an old woman bearing a knife and stone—he is reduced to shivering terror. A farm girl imagines herself metamorphosing into a winged soul, "flying to nowhere . . . becoming myself." Vane's horse, having perished in the attempt to disembark on the island, takes on a variety of new lives. . . . Bodies and buildings constantly exchange characteristics in this book. The Abbot searches the depths of his house like an intruding spirit, while he searches the depths of the body for the elusive soul.

As the transformations grow more mysterious, Vane's rational inquiries grow ever more futile. By the end they turn fatal also. Vane's name, like that of his doomed horse Saviour, serves as an element in the book's allegory. But that allegory, like everything else, undergoes transformations of its own, tantalizingly dissolving and reforming from one chapter to the next. The one constant element is Mr. Fuller's exact and vivid prose. His control of image and cadence remains firm, no matter how marvelous the events he describes. This feat of literary tightrope walking is impressive in itself—but Mr. Fuller surpasses it in two virtuoso chapters that transcribe, first, a letter from an uneducated pilgrim complaining about his body's disorders and, second, the Abbot's exalted sermon warning against the desire to escape the limits of the body through flight.

The book's most extraordinary moment is one that will occur at a different point for every reader. It is the moment when a reader understands that the book will not resolve all of its myriad puzzles but will end instead with something entirely unexpected—a mystery more revelatory than any solution.

Edward Mendelson, "More Murder in the Monastery," in The New York Times Book Review, *March 4, 1984, p. 9.*

Michael Hulse

The New Poetry, Al Alvarez's Penguin anthology that made 1962 the most important turning-point in post-War British poetry, ended with selections from John Fuller (born 1937) and Ian Hamilton (born 1938), at that time newcomers to British writing. . . . [Fuller] has gone from strength to strength, and a look at his work gives us a clue to much that has been happening in British poetry recently.

The poems Alvarez printed were from Fuller's first book, *Fairground Music* (1961), and a number of the poems in that volume remain among Fuller's best. [These include] a sonnet Alvarez didn't anthologize, titled **"In a Railway Compartment"**. . . . [The] oppressive variant on two themes in one—Death and the Maiden, and sexual initiation—harmonizes the anecdotal and the mythic into an unusual accommodation within the sonnet's stern but flexible form. A mysterious tension survives the harmonization, a tension which is more than the apparent incompatibility of the exact opening and the fantasized conclusion, but harmony remains in the fluent urbanity which leaves the reader quite literally in the dark with his fourteen-line puzzle. Elements familiar from *The Interpretation of Dreams*—the confined setting, "crimson", the boredom awaiting an interrupting action, "tunnel" and "tower"—are united with the context of childhood through fairy-tale images, the princess and the lion, introduced via the terminology of children's puzzle-comics. The effect of this exercise in the synthesizing capabilities of wit is to evoke a suffocating and—for all its coolness—convincing image of childhood bursting unwillingly into womanhood.

Perhaps it remains an exercise. Perhaps **"In a Railway Compartment"** is not finally a fully achieved poem: there is, after all, something a little too knowing in its smothered and sympathetic sense of menace. Still, it will serve to illustrate Fuller's typical strengths: a very pleasing formal competence, an alertness to the potential power that lies in yoking the disparate, an effect of relaxation in the imaginary museum, and, behind all the knowing Oxonian accomplishment, a genuine sensitivity to the people in his poems, however impersonal the work may appear. It is no accident that John Fuller is associated with Oxford (he has, in fact, been a Fellow of Magdalen College since 1966), since these particular qualities of his imagination link him both with the Auden generation and with those newly important poets—James Fenton, Craig Raine and Christopher Reid—who have followed Fuller at Oxford. What resemblance he might have to that literary generation of the late Forties and Fifties which included Larkin, Amis and Wain is perhaps less clear, but I think we can find it less in qualities of the imagination than in a cast of mind: careful, critical, cool, modest. Indeed, an Empsonian note of clipped reticence such as we might expect in early Wain can at times be heard in Fuller's third book of poems, *Cannibals and Missionaries.* (pp. 89-91)

Maybe James Fenton went too far in suggesting that Fuller has been "the decisive influence" for many younger poets, even if *The Mountain in the Sea* was clearly important for the Martians [Fenton, Raine, and Reid]; but certainly Peter Porter is right in finding Fuller "a key figure in contemporary poetry", for in all of these volumes Fuller has insisted by example that lightness and wit and technical expertise are perfectly compatible with moral and intellectual seriousness. In this he naturally reminds us not only of Auden but also of such contemporaries as Richard Wilbur and John Holloway, and looking beyond our own century we find that the poet Fuller most persistently brings to mind is Marvell, a comparison that was made by Martin Dodsworth when reviewing *The Tree that Walked* [see excerpt above]. . . . (p. 91)

Such a description prepares us for a poet of some urbanity, and the expectation is well met if we turn, for example to the verse letters with which (in *Epistles to Several Persons*) Fuller perhaps comes too close for comfort to self-congratulatory in-crowd chat, but nonetheless achieves some deliciously light effects in the Burns stanza, such as this—

> We're as incognito

> As is the CIA in SEATO,
> A worker Jesuit in *Quito*
>   Selling pardons
> or trilbied *Emperor Hirohito*
>   in *Kew Gardens*

—or this—

> Where has the living starlight gone?
> The owls are loud where once it shone.
> We see the archetypal don
>   Pen in his cloister
> A footnote to a footnote on
>   *Ralph Roister Doister.*

The *Epistles* contain a good deal of literary back-chat (three are addressed to writers—James Fenton, Ian Hamilton and David Caute) and Fuller expresses his distaste for any of the poetic trends of the Sixties and early Seventies, from Black Mountain to the confessional writers (a snide aside is aimed at those "of the Left" who are presented "Glossing the *Variorum Plath* / From *Krafft-Ebing*"). Prejudices make poor reading even when wittily expressed, but Fuller occasionally chooses to make a serious point in passing:

> The porcelain culture of the French
> Was founded on an Empire's stench:
> *Dien Bien Phu* was quite a wrench
>   Since fifty coolies
> Go to make up one übermensch
>   Like *Pierre Boulez.*

This is a typical stanza for its chatty manner, energetic rhymes and its wit, which, though trim, has an unpleasantly immature flavour and is clearly open to charges of blinkeredness: we long to hear a Frenchman ask Fuller if the British Empire couldn't have been described in similar terms.

These passages from the *Epistles* are also a good example of Fuller's inclination to approach poetry as a game. His *jeu d'esprit* leads him not only to exemplary use of the Burns stanza in the *Epistles* and Pushkin's in *The Illusionists* but also to a sonnet sequence (in *Cannibals and Missionaries*) called **"The Labours of Hercules"** in which lines recur through fourteen sonnets and the fifteenth is composed solely of these fourteen refrain lines. Why? You may well ask. For the fun of doing it, of course: why else? In *Lies and Secrets* there are poems called **"Blind Man's Buff"**, **"Musical Chairs"** and **"Charades"**, and a seemingly endless poem called **"The Most Difficult Position"**—a chess poem. A mood of mere jolliness seems often to inform Fuller's creative drive, as in his apparently new and irredeemably trivial method of rhyming in **"Secrets"** (from *The Beautiful Inventions*):

> Secrets certainly have a power to charm.
> In front of you, an ape; behind, a chasm.
> Keep it happy, keep it happy! Its fangs are hideous!
> You must be almost a day's trek from your hideout!
> A secret will make it pause. A secret amuses.
> Take off your skin. Do explorers have anuses?
> What a joke! Show it the other hole,
> The metal one. Bang. The point goes home.

Such passages make it plain that those who approach poetry with Arnoldian high seriousness in their thoughts are likely to feel sorely let down by John Fuller. His poetry is altogether social, light, convivial, companionly. There is nothing in it you couldn't let the children read (though of course there's a good deal of cleverness the children wouldn't understand).

I shall return in a moment to what I consider Fuller's best volume to date, *The Mountain in the Sea,* and shall attempt to show that, the damningly trivial lightness notwithstanding, the poet has claims on our attention; but for the moment let me press the case against him, against this games-playing notion of poetry as a post-prandial pastime. Clearly the chumminess of the *Epistles,* the donnishness of technical virtuosity, and the witty cultural allusiveness of **"In a Railway Compartment"** cannot accommodate much—indeed, hardly any—of the matter of great poetry. Where are the marvellous love poems? Where is the moving experience of transience? Where, for that matter, is there the smallest awareness that life has filthy sides undreamt-of in Oxford colleges? John Fuller can seem more faults than virtues if we approach him from this angle. His most serious fault is that his formal poise can lead either to over-smoothing of complex material or even to a kind of neo-Edwardian inconsequentiality, as in these lines from **"How Many Goodly Creatures"** in [*The Beautiful Inventions*]:

> When freshmen have thoughts of adoring
>   And tutors are keen to impress,
> When the wife of the provost starts pouring
>   And the chaplain begins to confess,
> When the poet has hopes of reciting
>   And the wine buff sets out to unscrew
> Who is it they think of inviting?
>   Miranda, my dear, it is you.

Very pretty. Poetry is note-taking and jotting, poetry as parlour game, poetry as travel marginalia, poetry as five-finger exercise: Fuller commits all the sins that make an accusation of triviality seem defensible, especially that typical Oxonian sin of complacency, of too self-satisfied an accomplishment. Any non-British reader who is presented with these poems will probably find all his fears of English unseriousness and smugness confirmed. Those who believe that poetry needs some manner of social or political awareness will frequently find Fuller deficient; he writes implicitly for the comfortable middle class, and there are no signs in his work of any struggle to vindicate this approach, of any soul-searching. The tendency can be toward too much smoothness and gentility; as Edward Lucie-Smith remarked, "the uneasier it becomes, the better Fuller's work appears," but all too often—particularly since *The Mountain in the Sea*—the unease has been smoothed out of Fuller's work, and his virtuosity has seemed more self-indulgent and unquestioning.

But the case against John Fuller, persuasive as it is, cannot reduce the significance of his contributions to the new line of wit in Britain, a line which has consistently given more emphasis to the world of things than to the world of the self, and which contextualizes those things in an erudite, humane, mild-mannered world-view which takes the stability of known culture more or less for granted. This new line of wit manufactures a poetry in which wisdom is compatible with jest, moral concern is united with linguistic zest, domestic seriousness goes hand in hand with man-about-town urbanity, and the whole is underpinned by a well-mannered avoidance of any kind of extreme. An im-

portant theoretical component of this new line is the rejection of confessional writing. . . . (pp. 92-5)

[The] permanent value of *The Mountain in the Sea* as well as of the finest of his other poems seems to me to lie in Fuller's ability to locate a quiet and credible language of celebration. If the *Epistles* or such poems as **"In a Railway Compartment"** are witty and allusive, other poems are strong because of their simplicity. **"Wild Raspberries"** is a good example from *The Mountain in the Sea*. . . .

Here the element of fairy-tale fantasy we have already noted in Fuller does no violence to his subject, but rather confirms the closeness of his observation. We feel here that a fine writer of the simple life has been lost in Fuller the sophisticated wit—but then, it is pointless to lament. In his latest collection, *The Beautiful Inventions,* this same vein is continued in a handful of attractive domestic lyrics, the most successful of which [is **"Sorrel"**]. . . . Here as elsewhere I think we should find it finally possible to agree with Peter Porter, that, whatever Fuller's shortcomings, the poet has a constant moral centre; it resides in his craft and his dedication. (pp. 96-7)

> *Michael Hulse, "The Poetry of John Fuller,"*
> in The Antigonish Review, *No. 57, Spring,*
> *1984, pp. 89-98.*

Peter Wolfe

Flying to Nowhere offers a rich bounty despite its brevity. It includes a mystery, a look into Church philosophy, a quest, and, radiating all, a prose that is pure and haunting without being overripe. . . .

The novel's opening combines incongruity and menace. A boat heading to a mysterious island-shrine has on board a tethered stallion who leaps to his death upon sighting land. That the horse's name is Savior and that horses symbolize man's animal vitality darken further the ominous mood building from the death. More storm clouds gather. Savior's owner, a man called Vane, has come from the mainland at his bishop's behest to investigate the possibility of foul play suffered by pilgrims who have sought health from the waters of the island's miraculous well.

Fuller's having named the investigator Vane portends defeat for the quest. Vanity first misled Vane into believing that he could transport his horse safely over choppy waters. Nor did he learn from his mistake. . . . How can such a man be expected to find the missing pilgrims?

Our doubts both multiply and deepen as the abbot in charge of the island's religious community keeps sidestepping Vane's questions. Then a local man goes mad after eating some grass sprouting near the well. Narrative structure enhances this bad portent. The central activity of the book's central chapter is the dissection of a body found decomposing in the well. Following this horrible apparition, basic questions of existence are posited and go unanswered. The abbot and a dying woman both wonder why their bodies determine the boundaries of their physical selves when, by contrast, their spirits move freely. Referring in general to the mind-body dualism, the question goes back specifically to Savior, the nonaquatic horse who died trying to swim. This kind of cross-referencing typifies *Flying to Nowhere.*

The doubling patterns made by the words uttered in a sermon (soil-soul, savor-savior, germination-generation) imply a unity of matter and spirit that redeems the ugliness described in the novel. But intuition, not reason, will tell you whether redemption and renewal brighten *Flying to Nowhere.* Any sensitive reading of the novel goes beyond polite, rational discourse. Here is a work that awakens our secret hopes and fears.

> Peter Wolfe, in a review of "Flying to Nowhere," in Prairie Schooner, Vol. 59, No. 1, Spring, 1985, p. 105.

Hugh Haughton

Peter Porter described [John Fuller] as a "key figure in contemporary British poetry" and James Fenton called him a "secret guru" for many younger Oxford-associated poets like himself, yet despite his eight books of poetry and the successful Booker short-listed novel *Flying to Nowhere,* Fuller has remained an elusive poet, with little representation in anthologies—influential certainly, but not widely read. The welcome publication of his *Selected Poems 1954-82* might bring him to a wider audience, though I rather doubt it. It certainly doesn't make him any less an elusive poet or curious phenomenon.

Fuller is an adaptable writer, a master of many manners and from first to last a contriver of "beautiful inventions", but it's hard to size up this academic Proteus as he switches from the Audenesque to the Ransomesque to the Rainesque, from academic sonnet to cosmopolitan verse-novel, don's diary to Victorian pastiche to Martian arabesque. The successful poems are miniature triumphs within their own terms, but they don't seem to establish resonances between each other or with the intractable world outside. This *Selected Poems,* for all its well-tempered virtuosity, doesn't seem to be more than the sum of its parts.

Nevertheless the parts give some idea why John Fuller should have played a significant role in maintaining the modern "line of wit" running from Auden to Porter and Fenton. He's a sophisticated, unashamedly intellectual poet, fascinated by the possibilities of playing with inherited conventions and poetic forms. He has proved influential by his example—Fenton declared his debts in the "Letter to John Fuller" which spoofed Alvarez's urgently suicidal poetics, while Fuller's verse in the 1960s showed a remarkable anticipation of both the Craig Raine manner and recent interest in poetic narrative—but he is also visibly a prey to the influence of others, Auden in particular. His poems aren't always easy to read, but it's often easy to know what he's been reading. He is an expert at pastiche, of course, best seen in **"The Most Difficult Position"**, a Nabokovian study of nineteenth-century chess grandmasters that rivals Auden's *Letter to Lord Byron* in its extended reference to poetic predecessors. Yet it's not always easy to know where pastiche begins and ends in his work. **"Ghost Village"**, for example, works up a cryptic, quasi-allegorical geography of inside and outside to evoke "the ghosts who must be faced / Who questioned the blind world", but is itself dominated by the Audenesque manner. . . . This looks less like a questioning ghost faced, than a bigger poetic voice submitted to.

Fuller may not have much to "say" either, but he has certainly learned to read, and it is the very arbitrariness of the "literary" that appeals to him. The first poem here is an ironic comment on the fairy-tale convention in sonnet form. . . . Another sonnet gives an Empsonian reading of Helen of Troy in old age as Lewis Carroll's pallid, scatty White Queen; another a riddling essay on Spenser ("clownish without armour") in the form of an inconclusive episode in Spenserian romance; a fourth elaborates a Victorian genre-piece about a little girl confronting Mr Dodgson with a "case of puzzles" in a railway carriage (from riddle to romance and vice versa), while a double-sonnet acts out a Marvellesque dialogue between fingers and toes. Such witty fables, with their parade of dexterity and allegory, celebrate the art of being for ever agile.

From the outset, then, Fuller was a master of the stylish bagatelle. In later books he includes more notation of circumstance and local detail, but he always insists on an elegant or perverse stylization. He writes with art on sleeve. **"Hedge Tutor"**, for instance, an account of a walk along a country lane with his small daughter, transforms the pedestrian by means of gentle but artful transposition of the kind associated with Raine: "Consulting the calendar of hedges / Banked up higher than your head / We seem to share the surprise of walking / On a riverbed", while **"Object Trouvé: Piazza San Marco"** ends with a surreal Firbankian apotheosis as he imagines "How Mark rose upwards through the air / Out of his feet left standing there", and "How round his pretty feet they built the square"— less an *objet trouvé* than a rather camp *objet d'art.* (p. 213)

Fuller's third book, *Cannibals and Missionaries,* represents him at his worst with its elaborately allegorical and elegantly "light verse" academy pieces—mannerist exercises about Oxford and his country cottage in Wales. When not turning out "light verse" of this kind, he was concocting stilted Audenesque topographical poems (like **"Ghost Village"**) and stiflingly opaque narratives like the sonnet sequence **"The Two Sisters"** or the hit-and-miss monologue **"Her Morning Dreams"** ("The unmade bed. Finger on my pink. / Dead as he groaned upon a linen ocean, / Who would have thought he had such little ink?").

After the playful virtuosity of the first books and the mannerist cul-de-sac of the third, Fuller seems to have found himself in his next four, from the witty verse-letters of *Epistles to Several Persons* (1973) to the Byronic narrative of *The Illusionists* (1980). These contain his liveliest and most interesting work, in touch with colloquial idiom and recognizable social realities, at home with his chosen literary conventions. The epistles (only one of which is included here) helped him find a voice with which to confront his subjects and audience directly and lightly. The **"Epistle to Angus Macintyre"** is a jokey light-verse commentary on his rural retreat in Wales which manages to accommodate a tough and buoyant range of tones and arguments. . . . The light-fingered virtuosity with which he uses the Burns stanza enables him to shift between self-criticism of this sort to genial self-celebration *à la* Byron. The poem is at home with laid-back academic jokes ("The academic's one excuse is / He knows about the gastric juices, / Suppression of the anacrusis") and the absurd *faits divers* of the newspaper ("We're as incognito / As is the CIA in SEATO / A worker Jesuit in Quito / Selling pardons / Or the emperor Hirohito / In Kew Gardens") but able to allow the concluding sober pleas for "some vision to achieve" and forgiveness for "Our scared retreats, both small and big". It is that kind of interplay between "small and big", intellectual and trivial pursuits, acted out in the tonal and allusive mobility of the verse, which characterizes the best in his next three books, but gets lost, to my mind, in his most recent two, **Waiting for the Music** (1982) and **The Beautiful Inventions** (1983), with their rather precious aestheticism.

The Mountain in the Sea (1975) is full of bucolic Welsh poems of place which are stylish exercises in intricate map-making. . . . Like Craig Raine after him, Fuller relies heavily on the Flash Simile.

Lies and Secrets (1979) is up and down too, starting with the absurd and touching portrait of an up-ended woman, **"Annie Upside Down"** ("It's the whole earth turned inside out like a sock / And me just hanging on") and ending with **"The Most Difficult Position"**, his three-part closet drama about two nineteenth-century chess grandmasters who never actually do battle with each other. He's generally a rather frustrating narrative poet since nothing much happens worth telling, and perhaps for that reason the poem about the mandarin discomforts of the legendary chess virtuosi Staunton and Morphy may be Fuller's most convincing performance to date. Morphy, a neurotic American tyro, a kind of Rimbaud of the chess world, arrives in England to challenge the established world champion Staunton, Shakespearean scholar and gentleman, and the poem explores their attitudes towards the great match that never takes place. Fuller portrays the inner drama of the two men by way of dazzling pastiche of the styles of the two grandmasters of Victorian dramatic monologue, Browning and Clough, those worldly and unworldly experts in trapped, secular self-consciousness. Morphy speaks in Clough-like hexameters of the fascination of arbitrary conventions. . . . (pp. 213-14)

I'm sorry there wasn't room in the **Selected** for more than one chapter of his Byronic (or Pushkinian) verse-novel comedy of manners about the metropolitan art-marketing world, **The Illusionists.** The one given is another virtuoso exercise in narrative self-consciousness, depicting a secretary's morning dreams and breakfast and taking on Pope and Eliot at their own game:

> Being a widow in East Pinner
> She didn't mention Distimuth
> Fearing that something was afoot
> Beginning with lifts, moving to dinner
> And after-dinner mints and verse
> And after-dinner-something-worse.

It makes great play with social stereotypes, journalistic cliché and consumer detail as it evokes secretarial dreams, the "Camford graduate grotesque" and the oily, lecherous art-dealer Distimuth ("Lifting eight fingers from the wheel / In unctuous emphasis"), but for all its nods and winks and (Clive) Jamesian high-jinks, and however accurately it inventories a modern handbag or a "Freudian" dream, its brand of light-verse narrative seems rather old hat—a pastiche of pastiche, as in the *Byronismo* of "Nico was half in love with failure / While Tim was twice in love with what? / With youth? with Love? but surely not / With Polly Passenger". Hang it all, there can be but one *Don Juan.*

The felicities of Fuller's most recent books seem a bit thin after the self-conscious social comedy of **The Illusionists.** They include many rather Martian postcards from abroad and notes on domestic music. So we have a flute being "the most surgical of the instruments" and a "telescope for a wind's song", a double-bass player acting as a "drunk leaning companionably / Against a lamp post" and a pianist enjoying a "banquet for one". The poem on "Ironing" has handkerchiefs "imposed in 16mo / and lastly collated", shirts laid upstairs in opened "coffins" and ties imagined as a "fatal noose". Though he's a skilled exponent of this manner and can use it to serve up the rumpled ordinary world in a smart, eye-taking fashion, Fuller doesn't have Raine's thrillingly luxuriant sense of the commonplace world, the domestic as a perversely utopian bower of bliss.

The poetry seems weakest when it attempts a strong voice (as in the portentous "Perhaps it was something the heart thought / Loud in its cave of blood. If so, what matter?") and strongest in the light-verse set-pieces like the *risqué* album-verse about pornography called **"Amazing"** ("So many jobs for the hands / And explored hinterlands / So many well-used glands / Saw I never") or the up-dated variation on romance-conventions in **"Valentine"** ("You are the end of self-abuse. / You are the eternal feminine. / I'd like to find a good excuse / To call on you and find you in") or the daintily Betjemanesque urban pastoral about a girl from a Reading biscuit factory ("Linda, Linda, slender and pretty / Biscuit girl in a biscuit city").

But even here, there seems to be something stilted about the idiom—maybe his sense of "light verse" is itself precarious and questionable, a thing of the past, less like that in Auden's many-mannered, socially promiscuous anthology than Kingsley Amis's collection of smoking-room ditties and gentlemanly jokes. When the College ghost in the poem of that name speaks in fluent Audenese ("Theories of diet dispersed tribes, infections / Accompanied stately truths like interpreters"), I find it hard to distinguish the poet's own voice, even as he confronts his own feelings of failure and betrayal in the last lines in the book:

> Thoughts too late to unthink; I had the feeling
> Of being betrayed by something of my choosing,
> Something I had connived at, something belonging
> To the projection of a long-suspected failing,
> Haunted by the forces it exploits.

Like **"The Most Difficult Position"** and the **"Letter"** **"The College Ghost"** takes a well-worked form, and through a mix of pastiche and projection, portrays an uneasy sophisticate's self-consciousness about his privileged fluency and "mastery". It's hard, reading Fuller, not to ponder Bloomian fantasies about the anxieties of influence, but is this a post-Modernist "ludic" triumph? Or the familiar compound ghost of Eng Lit? The ghost in the machine of this frequently subtle, funny poetry is often just the Oxford college ghost. (p. 214)

Hugh Haughton, "The Art of Agility," in The Times Literary Supplement, *No. 4326, February 28, 1986, pp. 213-14.*

Michael Wood

The most haunting image in John Fuller's first novel, **Fly-**

ing to Nowhere, is that of a strange resurrection of the natural world. The dead woodwork of an old monastery grows back into profuse forest; leather-bound books, cured of their curing, become bellowing herds devoted to "panic and rebellion". This reversion is ominous but also obscurely heartening, a reminder of chances of renewal.

Tell It Me Again, Fuller's second novel, similarly involves a flight to nowhere, a literal disappearance, and is much concerned with transformation. "He was transformed", we are told of the diffident hero, an English composer of witty, restrained and possibly too programmatic classical music, "as radically as the erotic transgression of the human boundary can transform us". That is a fancy way of describing the first stirrings of love, but "transgression" and "boundary" do catch this character's anxiety. His love-life till now, he feels, has been all "longing and botched experiment". We see him letting things happen for once, making less of a botch, but still not making much of a success. . . .

The figure for transformation in this subtle, reflective novel is jazz singing: the conversion of a merely agreeable, familiar tune and lyric into a feat of risk and invitation through shifts of speed and phrasing, inflections of scat, reorganization of melody, late entry of the solo, and so on. The composer, Hugh Howard, in New York for the première of his ballet *Beatrice and Benedick,* staying on to finish a violin concerto which is giving him trouble, meets Virginia Gerald, a black singer who is a sort of cross between Billie Holiday and Nancy Wilson. She specializes in the worldly, bitter-sweet songs of one Sammy West, who in turn is a sort of cross between Jerome Kern and Sammy Fain, an ancient survivor of old Broadway scores. Hugh takes off for Texas with Virginia, "this tender fragment of Manhattan", as he pictures her, a woman and talent born of a pile of myths about New York. Their idyll is a suspension of fear and complication, and a meeting of musics. Virginia learns what her singing means to a serious composer—she is not Sammy West's creation, she creates him by bringing new life to his songs—and Hugh learns about transformations. "Yeah, well", Virginia says. "So what *is* the song till someone sings it?" What if classical violinists thought this way about the material they played; if they were improvisatory geniuses rather than highly disciplined prodigies? This question (which is Hugh's) is not entirely fair, because he himself doesn't like jazz violins, feels they lack "the dangerous aura of smoke and liquor that belonged to jazz".

The idyll breaks and ends; the plot both thickens and gets more elusive. Not quite as much happens as you might expect, and there is great delicacy in the way the narrative skirts the world of the thriller. Sammy West's songs are evoked very engagingly for us:

> You can have anything on earth
> And every little glance is worth
> Its weight in gold.
> But if you touch it I say broken,
> If you break it I say sold.

—as are Virginia's singing ("a hectic scattering of slurs and swoops, a contrary of qualifying feeling, a kind of melancholy or critical drag") and its accompaniment ("The piano agreed, casting down its tender but terse clustered cadences like a losing hand at cards"). There are some sharply drawn characters (a teenage violinist, a *New York-*

er writer who is always eating, Virginia herself), and some memorable scenes. . . .

[Hugh] is a disappointed Narcissus, but even so he seems too small for the part the novel assigns him, tepid beyond the needs of the story. This excess of mildness—the novel doesn't have anything as gross as faults—is echoed in the sometimes over-talkative writing, which protests beautifully but too much. . . . I'm drawn to a novelist who is so obviously and so imaginatively interested in the world he has made for us, who is not afraid of elaborate musical discussion or of words like "susurration" and "abrupted". But one can detect a certain wishfulness in the performance, as if the flurry of words were reaching out for a rough and awkward world beyond their own mirror; as if there might be a lot of jazz beyond this classical appreciation of jazz's virtues.

> Michael Wood, "Transforming Cadences," in *The Times Literary Supplement, No. 440, May 6-12, 1988, p. 500.*

Anthony Thwaite

[John Fuller's Hugh Howard, in ***Tell it me again,*** is in his late forties] but acceptably an innocent abroad. Abroad is America. Hugh is an English composer, talented and successful, but a bit of a cold fish. In this sense, Fuller's is another version, cool, elegant, distanced, of that kind of novel which has observed the talented, effete, bewildered intruder from the Old World into rich and strange America: Bradbury's *Stepping Westward,* Hinde's *High,* Lodge's *Changing Places.*

It becomes a mystery story, in which the mystery is long in arriving, and which works on such a slow fuse that it almost seems over before it's begun. ***Flying to Nowhere,*** Fuller's earlier (and Booker-shortlisted) novel, was also mysterious, but it was constructed as if in a single breath of inspiration. ***Tell it me again,*** though not a long novel, drifts from moment to moment, from scene to scene, from reflection to reflection, without impetus. Yet, oddly, I felt that this teasing delay may have been part of what Fuller intended.

There is, on the one hand, Hugh Howard's grappling with music, with his composition: this struck me as convincing and interesting, an aspect of the life of art versus obsession interfering with art, as Hugh spirals down into his bewildered affair with Virginia/Gin/the Baroness of the Blues, the black singer of whom he reflects: 'He was in love with the embodiment of a romantic attitude.' On the other hand, there seems an imperfect grasp of the obsession itself: is it really to do with the exotic Virginia, or is it 'an adventure that took him even further from the calculated arc of his own ordered life'?

Fuller has shown himself, not only in ***Flying to Nowhere*** but, more relevantly, in his verse-novel ***The Illusionists,*** a cunning weaver of intricate tapestries, and, in his shorter poems, a craftsman who is inventive, intelligent, suave and teasing. Perhaps the greater length of ***Tell it me again*** has overtaxed his staying powers. It's a very oddly paced novel, as if Fuller didn't quite know how to build a work of some length; and in this—and if so—he's rather like his composer Hugh, who seems capable of turning his hand to anything, and yet who also seems (if one gropes below the text and beyond the itemisation of Hugh's successes) to have achieved less than he'd hoped for.

As for the fascination with sex which pervades the novel, the fascination is there without being the least bit erotic. Hugh appears to think a good deal about sex, but seldom allows it to be more than thought, just as Fuller's book seems to be fascinated with construction without being well-constructed. There's an edgy feeling of something percipient, not perceptive; calculated, not inevitable. And yet—too late to give it proper leverage—there suddenly breaks through something truly sharp and shocking: a letter from Daisy, Hugh's ex-wife in England, which shows how cruel and true John Fuller's art can be. I wish that his distrust of straight confrontation would relax and allow him more moments like this.

> Anthony Thwaite, *"Eyes and Ears,"* in London Review of Books, *Vol. 10, No. 12, June 23, 1988, p. 22.*

Neil Corcoran

"Variety" and "diversity" are words the blurb-writers and reviewers have often reached for when faced with John Fuller. Always technically adroit and manoeuvering casually between fantasy, narrative, dramatic monologue, verse letter, pastiche and a kind of anxious modern pastoral, Fuller has successfully eluded easy classification. To adapt a distinction made in another context by the American critic Dillon Johnston, he has his recognizable tones of voice, but no distinguishable *timbre.* His poems have been, in the title of one of his volumes, "beautiful inventions"—ingenious, witty, elegant, allusive—but have run the risk of seeming to lack depth or centre, refusing the greater pain or consolation of self-declaration, preferring the occasional, the unhurriedly discursive and the "light".

His new collection, *The Grey Among the Green,* has its instances of all these kinds: its **"Lines for a 21st Birthday"**; its long concluding quasi-Marvellian poem, **"The Grey and the Green"**; its Audenesque (or Cole Porteresque?) squib about love, **"Incident"**. In all of these, Fuller's touch is a little unsure. The **"Birthday"** poem is a very slight piece, and metaphorically laboured; **"The Grey and the Green"** ambles along entertainingly and always intelligently, but Fuller allows himself too large a space to wander in; and I hope it is not too po-faced to find the lines from which **"Incident"** derives its title—"Love is an incident at Newry / Love is the verdict of the jury"—almost affrontingly unfeeling; even in "light verse" words like "Newry" still carry a heavy weight, heavy enough to act as a millstone around this poem's neck in any case.

In some other respects, however, *The Grey Among the Green* does differ from Fuller's earlier volumes, despite its unwavering refusal to disrupt neo-Augustan decorums. For all its formal diversity, it has a marked unity of mood and preoccupation. It is hard to say exactly what this is, since being unable to say exactly what it is is the theme of many of the poems. Deriving from a strong sense of the human mutabilities consequent on ageing and an openly admitted fellow-feeling (in the poem **"Bud"**) with Pope's description of his life as a "long disease", some of these poems ache with those feelings we cannot ever quite put a name to. . . .

If these poems have their familiar Romantic velleities and regrets, however, the persona at their centre is, in the title of one of them, **"The Curable Romantic"**. In that poem the loved one is "his dear impossible", and "Imperfection" is "the truly loveable". The note of a less deceived self-rebuke accompanies a strong if muted sense of the improbability and absurdity of most human desire. This is given its strangest and most striking expression in the poem **"Daughter"**, where Fuller laments a never-conceived daughter (in a poem which admits that he has three others). The ungrateful preposterousness of the longing is the most naked instance in the book of a fallibility close to self-pity; and **"Daughter"** culminates with a stanza which implicates the art of poetry itself in consolatory fantasizing:

> Only the subject
> Of unuseful poetry:
> What never occurred.

This reflexiveness supplies a new element in a number of poems in the book, implicating Fuller more straightforwardly than hitherto in his inventions. . . .

The book's outstanding poem is one in which some of these preoccupations are mated with something tougher and less relenting: **"Wednesday"**, about the death of a pet rabbit. Skilfully avoiding sentimentality (a danger always in wait for Fuller in his more personal modes), the poem conjures a powerful sense of the absence that is death by first conjuring a vivid sense of the rabbit's living presence (its "scissored ears positioned like microphones", the poet's address to it as "Sturdy little president of the lawn!"), reminding us of Fuller's descriptive novelty, which is elsewhere in this book very subdued. Death itself is the thing that cannot properly or adequately be named in this poem; but it nevertheless prompts the volume's most memorable confrontation between self-deception and implacable necessity:

> We prefer to make of you a remembered image
> That accords with our myth of perpetual contentment,
> Of life as an unfolding
> Towards an unseen horizon. . . .
>
> And as night comes, the garden is suddenly empty
> Of a black shape in the blackness, coming from nowhere,
> Coming at an idle call
> Though never making a sound.

This is John Fuller at his best: quiet, unportentous, understated, speaking a common language that is also memorable speech.

> Neil Corcoran, *"The Elusive Thing,"* in The Times Literary Supplement, *No. 4449, July 8-14, 1988, p. 758.*

Peter Porter

If a poet has control of his technique, he can write simple poems which are never simple-minded. John Fuller is the omni-competent ringmaster of contemporary British poetry, and [*The Grey Among the Green*] finds him in relaxed and reflective mood. Not only are most of these poems easy to enjoy, but they rely very little on Fuller's more usual self-consciousness of virtuosity. Keeping out the banal and the maudlin is his insistence, and this he always manages to do.

The poems in the first part are generally domestic, reflections on family life, on photographs, music, gardens and the passing of time. They are full of a delicate moral melancholy which is nevertheless always hard-edged. Their emotional themes are displayed in everyday shapes, as in **"Lucy's Daffodil"**:

> Tissue lifts from the stalk knuckle.
> The baby bell is haunted, nowhere
> Else to turn. Its silent yell
> Is like a gasp for oxygen
> Claiming the whole room in the name
> Of an emotion still to be invented.
> What does the sun say? I can't hear.

The title poem is ambitious in scope and length, but remains lightly scored and exquisitely balanced. It is a sort of "Upon Appleton House", though necessarily more hesitant than Marvell needed to be, since we have lost the will to take morals directly from Nature. Fuller's stanza is more complex than Marvell's though his tone is not so intense. He considers the natural world from within the comforts of a house in rural Wales, equipped with a computer which plays chess with him, and with a full array, traditional and electronic, of reminders and satisfactions. The grey is man's world, the green is Nature's and the poem is their resolution:

> For flowers, mind is only touch.
> Green is the colour that began it,
> Green the sign of the cell's toil,
> A touch of sky, a touch of soil,
> The ladder of the planet.
> Green is the negative of stars,
> Green is the mirror of the sun,
> Green is the cooling of earth's fire:
> A height from which we have reached higher,
> But the best thing earth has done.

> *Peter Porter, "What the Sun Says," in* The Observer, *August 7, 1988, p. 41.*

J. K. L. Walker

Two powerful images illuminate the quiet surface of ***The Burning Boys,*** John Fuller's short but concentrated new novel, set on the seaside coast of Lancashire during the early years of the Second World War. Both are visions of ascent: the one, beatific, of white-clad gymnasts climbing daringly towards the light in the roof-beams of a great Tudor library, heralds the struggle back to life and consciousness of a badly burnt airman; the other, blazing forth in a transcendental conclusion to the book, is of burgeoning male energy, as a boy comes to adolescence moving upwards with a thousand companions through the vents and chimneys of an old house out into the night.

If the novel's cohesion is to be sought at this poetic level, Fuller offers teasingly few clues, as he alternates his narrative between his two protagonists, how—or if—events will in the end bring them together. Little but time and setting link these parallel but apparently disparate, not unfamiliar, wartime stories, of the London boy whose mother has been killed during the Blitz and of the disfigured one-time fighter pilot enduring protracted plastic surgery. Because,

though, the sense of place is strong—the mothballed resort with its trams and ice-cream kiosks and Palace of Pleasure hemmed in by miles of deserted sand-dunes, on the edge of which looms the Victorian Seaton Hall where the burnt airmen are reconstructed—the reader is prepared for an outcome of some kind.

Alternating chapters notwithstanding, the weight of the novel falls on young David Mullard's experiences in his grandmother's house. Life at 20 Viewforth Road is seen through the boy's eyes, a perspective which Fuller sustains with skill and affection, at the same time indicating enduring traumas. David hides underneath the dining-room table or in a cupboard high up in the kitchen, retreats from which he overhears puzzling gossip, particularly between his young aunt Jean, a mother-substitute, and her friend Phyllis, a nurse at Seaton Hall. On one such occasion, as he watches the two of them weighing their breasts on the kitchen scales, he is "wrought to the nervous pitch of a performer waiting to make an entrance". But, of course, "his role had not yet been written".

Nor can it be said to have been written by the end of the novel. Fuller plays fair and subtly by this wartime innocence, permitting no flood of awareness about the reasons behind Uncle Jacko's sudden marriage to Sylvia Elswick. Bestowing an "important" kiss on Sylvia to mark the announcement that she is pregnant, and receiving in his own mouth the sweet that she is dreamily sucking, is, however, David realizes, different from the fierce, dry kisses of Jill, Dr Simpson's daughter. Sylvia's kiss is "like something out of nature. It was like a glistening snail coming out of its shell and putting out horns." Embarrassed, he wonders whether he should have pushed the sweet back, like a game.

Like the snail's progress, this wartime growing-up moves unwaveringly: it isn't to be rushed by factitious incident. The war, that other game, is adumbrated, its effects on this ordinary Lancashire household seen chiefly in the departure of the street's young men into the Services, including Jacko, as his treasured illusion of working in a reserved occupation collapses. It is a stage in David's maturing when he realizes that he is more than just an onlooker, that Pearl Harbor actually occurred, and that the war is not merely "an undifferentiated public spectacle".

It is the pilot, Burroughs's, story, however, which energizes the novel. Despite the contrast between the airman's pain and sacrifice and the finely realized mundaneness of David's life there is no suggestion that Fuller is making *passé* points about the lot of soldier and civilian. These are separate circuits, across which sparks jump. When, towards the end of the novel, boy and airman meet briefly on two occasions, the significance for each remains ambiguous and to be found only in unspoken recognitions. David, visiting Seaton Hall, hurries guiltily past Burroughs, sensing the airman's gaze on him, and feels changed, for reasons that Fuller fastidiously does not elaborate—leaving ample room for speculation about the scene's meaning. As an outcome it won't quite do, even though the poetic charge of the narrative leaves the reader with a sense of circuits satisfactorily completed, of transfiguration and rebirth.

> *J. K. L. Walker, "The Ascent into Life," in*

*The Times Literary Supplement, No. 4500,
June 30-July 6, 1989, p. 714.*

Dinah Birch

[In **The Burning Boys**] David's mother is killed in the Blitz, and he goes to live with his down-to-earth grandmother and nubile young aunt. His life goes underground. David covertly observes the strange adult goings-on around him, approaching puberty through the ardour of school friendships, and at last moving into the place of the young men who are going to war. His hesitant coming to consciousness is paralleled by that of a fighter pilot who barely survives an appalling conflagration as his plane comes down on a mountainside. Grotesquely burned, the pilot's ruined face assumes the horrifying strangeness of the freaks that fascinate David in the local fairground. Like David, the pilot must construct an identity out of disaster. The two protagonists merge in the final words of the novel, becoming a single shining image of courage and hard-won release: 'on and on upwards, a thousand boys climbing, hair glowing, a determination in their eyes that could not be put out, climbing out into the night, a thousand burning boys.'

This is a poet's moment, and the assurance of this elegantly brief novel lies in its poet's eye. It is in simile that Fuller catches the creativity of a vanishing innocence. David's uncle has an astonishing motorbike 'like a dentist's chair mounted on a torpedo'. The pilot goes to a dance with an amateur band. 'It was like dancing to a public address stethoscope.' These glimpses of the incisive immediacy of what David and the pilot experience are a delight. But simile is a double-edged tool: it can distance what it illuminates. In one of the most winning passages in the novel, David and his friends watch the convalescent pilot with a group of fellow-patients:

> Some of the others stood about on the sand in a widely scattered group, as if placed to illustrate the solar system. They barely moved, or only moved if another moved. Venus crouched, looking at his toes. Uranus lifted his arms to his head, walked two paces to one side. Neptune hugged himself. Then almost all of them at once stooped slightly, as if a passing wind had brushed their backs. It was impossible to see if some signal may have been given. They seemed to have settled to these new positions wearily, as if they could barely give the matter their full attention. Nothing else happened.
>
> Then Mars, as if suddenly galvanised by physical discomfort, like Uncle Alfred and the wasp, started to stamp gently on the ground with both feet, lifting his knees higher and higher, finally flailing his arms and almost collapsing, doubled over as if in pain. At this, Venus lifted his clasped hands and turned to look sharply towards the sea, where Pluto was suddenly running along the tideline, as if to chase a wave before it broke slightly into flower.
>
> The figures sitting on the benches, and on the edge of the terrace, applauded.

As a Martian description of the oddness of beach cricket, that could hardly be bettered. But the fact remains that cricket by the sea, even when transformed into a pattern of strange and luminous grace, is a comfortingly nostalgic activity. Those sporting figures on the sand quietly evoke the rites of a world we have had to move beyond.

You don't have to have been alive in Hitler's war to feel that you have been within the covers of this book many times before. The skilful fluencies of its language finally insulate its readers from what might have been distressing: the pilot's anguish, David's loneliness. A radiantly poised expression of an imagined Eden remains, when boys burned with heroism and girls were peripherally enticing, if a little unreliable. Fuller's shapely writing allows his readers to retreat into a sanctuary of bygone values. The dust-jacket highlights the invitation, tempting the retrospectively-minded with a cunning collage of wartime memorabilia—a ration book, an identity card, newspaper headlines in which the solitary word 'Safe . . . ' is prominently positioned. For all its beauty, this is a book that is not prepared to take many chances. (p. 18)

Dinah Birch, "Other People," in London Review of Books, *Vol. 11, No. 13, July 6, 1989, pp. 18-19.*

FURTHER READING

Davis, Dick. "Mirrors and Moonshine." *The Listener* 105, No. 2697 (January 29, 1981): 151-2.
  Reviewing *The Illusionists,* Davis praises Fuller's wit and technical virtuosity.

Fuller, John and Mick Imlah. "An Interview with John Fuller." *Poetry Review* 72, No. 4 (January 1983): 25-30.

Furbank, P. N. "Knockabouts." *The Listener* 88, No. 2269 (September 21, 1972): 374-5.
  A review of *Cannibals and Missionaries* in which the critic praises Fuller's technical skill but finds him reticent in conveying meaning.

Gilbert, Harriett. "Ivory Tower, Ebony Basement." *New Statesman* 116, No. 2980 (May 6, 1988): 25.
  Assesses *Tell It Me Again* as a structural and thematic failure.

Mackinnon, Lachlan. "Loved Surfaces." *Times Literary Supplement* No. 4159 (December 17, 1982): 1399.
  Positive review of *Waiting for the Music* in which the critic praises Fuller's wit and technical skill.

Richman, Robert. "Them, Uz and Annie." *The New York Times Book Review,* November 28, 1987: 25-6.
  Attributes Fuller's success to his command of traditional poetic forms, which expands his subjective outlook.

"Poets in the Middle." *Times Literary Supplement* No. 3172 (December 14, 1962): 974.
  Review of *Fairground Music.*

Wesling, Donald. "Thinking in Poetry." *Parnassus: Poetry in Review* 3, No. 2 (1975): 280-88.
  Discusses the pieces collected in *Poems and Epistles.*

Lorraine Hansberry

1930-1965

(Born Lorraine Vivian Hansberry) American dramatist.

The following entry presents criticism on Hansberry's play *A Raisin in the Sun* (1959). For an overview of Hansberry's complete career, see *CLC,* Vol. 17.

The first African-American and the youngest woman to win the New York Drama Critics Circle Award, Hansberry is best known for her play *A Raisin in the Sun.* The story of a black working-class family and their decision to move into a white neighborhood, *A Raisin in the Sun* pioneered the acceptance of African-American drama by Broadway producers and audiences. The play provoked extensive debate during the early years of the civil rights movement. Although dismissed by some militant black critics as assimilationist, *A Raisin in the Sun* has nevertheless garnered praise as among the most sensitive and revealing portraits of the African-American family and its multi-generational struggle for equality. Anne Cheney observed: "A moving testament to the strength and endurance of the human spirit, *A Raisin in the Sun* is a quiet celebration of the black family, the importance of African roots, the equality of women, the vulnerability of marriage, the true value of money, the survival of the individual, and the nature of man's dreams. A well-made play, *Raisin* at first seems a plea for racial tolerance or a fable of man's overcoming an insensitive society, but the simple eloquence of the characters elevates the play into a universal representation of all people's hopes, fears, and dreams."

The daughter of a successful Chicago real estate broker, Hansberry was eight years old when her family moved into an exclusively white community, an act that violated the city's "covenant laws," which legally sanctioned housing discrimination. With the help of the NAACP, Hansberry's family took their case to the Supreme Court, which struck down the restrictive legislation as unconstitutional. During litigation, white neighbors continually harassed the Hansberry family; in one incident, a brick thrown through their living room window barely missed Hansberry's head. Despite their victory, Hansberry's father grew increasingly disillusioned by racial discrimination in the United States, and planned to relocate his family in Mexico, but died in 1946 before the move materialized. In 1948, Hansberry enrolled at the University of Wisconsin, where she first became interested in drama after seeing a production of Sean O'Casey's *Juno and the Paycock.* However, she left the university two years later and moved to New York City, where she joined the staff of *Freedom,* a radical publication founded by activist Paul Robeson. As a journalist and aspiring dramatist, Hansberry became increasingly aware of the prevalence of racial stereotypes in the popular theatre. She later revealed in a 1959 interview how she sought to answer the "cute dialect bits [or] hip-swinging musicals from exotic scores" with *A Raisin in the Sun,* a realistic drama which, like *Juno and the Paycock,* would universalize the experiences of an ethnic group without compromising its unique character.

Hansberry originally named her play "The Crystal Stair," after a line in the Langston Hughes poem "Mother to Son," but later changed its title to *A Raisin in the Sun,* an image taken from another Hughes piece, "A Dream Deferred." The bitterness and urgency pervading the play, reflect the poem's statement "What happens to a dream deferred? / Does it dry up / Like a raisin in the sun? / . . . *Or does it explode*?" Set in a modest apartment in Southside Chicago after World War II, the play focuses upon the Younger family: Lena, the matriarch; her son, Walter Lee, a chauffer; her daughter Beneatha, a college student; Walter Lee's wife, Ruth; and their son, Travis. In the opening scene, Ruth rouses her family on an early Friday morning. Hansberry describes her as "a settled woman," whose disappointment in life clearly shows in her demeanor. Walter, conversely, is a lean, intense man whose voice always contains "a quality of indictment." His second question of the morning—"Check come today?"—immediately reveals the central conflict of the play. Walter's father has died, leaving a ten thousand dollar insurance policy to Lena. Walter plans to persuade his mother to give him the money so that he, along with two other men, can invest it in a liquor store. Over breakfast, his wife dismisses the idea as one more impractical scheme, yet Walter reveals the extreme importance of his plan as he vents his frustration over Ruth's unwillingness to understand. "Man say: I got to change my life, I'm choking to death, baby! And his woman say . . . Your eggs is getting cold!"

The family conflict over money continues when Beneatha enters from the bedroom she shares with her mother. A gifted student, Beneatha hopes that the money will be used to allow her to attend medical school, but, unlike Walter, she acknowledges her mother's exclusive right to decide how the insurance check will be spent. Walter chauvinistically dismisses Beneatha's career aspirations and then attacks her for not contributing financially to the family, to which she retorts: "forgive me for ever wanting to be anything at all!" After Walter leaves indignantly for work, Lena enters. A commanding figure, she is an authoritative yet loving mother. When Beneatha rushes to the bathroom to get ready for school, Ruth unexpectedly approaches Lena concerning Walter's plans, hoping that the liquor store will alleviate the destructive tension within her marriage. Lena, however, rejects Ruth's plea, suggesting that she might buy a house for the family instead, something her husband, Big Walter, worked tirelessly for yet did not achieve in his lifetime. She also speaks about the pride and ambition they instilled in their children, a point integral to the climax of the play. The mood of the scene lightens, however, when Beneatha returns and conversation shifts to her many boyfriends and expensive pursuits, including horseback riding and guitar lessons. Hansberry later disclosed that she modeled Beneatha on herself at age twenty. While several critics consider Beneatha's upper-class tastes and attitudes to be inconsistent with her working class background, others perceive her as a young woman struggling to reconcile the ideas and opportunities shown to her by college with the reality of the ghetto. When Beneatha carelessly remarks that she does not believe in God, Lena slaps her, forcefully displaying the deep moral convictions that dominate her character. After Beneatha quickly departs, Ruth momentarily assuages Lena's fears for her children, yet collapses suddenly at the curtain.

Scene two takes place the next morning. Lena privately informs Beneatha that Ruth has gone to a doctor after Walter leaves on business concerning the liquor store. When Ruth returns, she despairingly tells Beneatha and Lena that she is pregnant. Lena fears that Ruth has consulted an abortionist, yet concern for her daughter-in-law's condition is momentarily diverted with the arrival of Asagi, Beneatha's Nigerian boyfriend. Critics often contend that the relationship between Beneatha and Asagi typifies Hansberry's ambivalent attitude toward the connection between American blacks and native Africans. Asagi brings Beneatha African robes and music, then gently mocks her straightened, "mutilated," hair and overly serious attempts at self-knowledge. He also accurately nicknames her "Alaiyo," which in his native language means "one for whom bread is not enough." When Asagi departs, Beneatha tries on her new clothes, then excitedly leaves "to become a queen of the Nile." When she has gone, the insurance check arrives in the mail. Walter returns as Lena opens the envelope, and a heated argument ensues. Insisting that only his venture will improve his family's circumstances, Walter jealously describes the powerful white businessmen he sees inside posh restaurants. Money, he shouts, is "only thing that matters!" Appalled

by his words, Lena tells her son that Ruth is pregnant and considering an abortion, but this news fails to divert Walter's attention from his own anger, and he storms out of the apartment. Visibly shaken, Lena leaves as well.

Act II opens that evening when, to Ruth's astonishment, Beneatha emerges from her bedroom dressed in the robes and headdress Asagi gave her. She puts on his record and begins to dance as she believes an African woman might. Walter, drunk, walks in the door and joins his sister, leaping onto the table and swaying to the music. As he dances, calling out to his black brothers, the comedy of the scene vanishes and Walter reveals an inner consciousness that momentarily overwhelms his prior selfishness. This mood is broken, however, when George Murchison, Beneatha's other suitor, enters. The superficial son of a wealthy black businessman, George embodies the negative aspects of the society to which Walter aspires. After speaking condescendingly to her brother, George is shocked when Beneatha takes off her headdress to reveal her now close-cropped, unstraightened hair. When he insists that she at least change into more acceptable clothes for their date, Beneatha, after considerable argument, acquiesces. Following their departure, Ruth tenderly approaches Walter, and the couple almost succeed in recapturing their closeness when Lena enters. When Walter asks where she has been, Lena tells him that she has used the insurance money to buy a house in Clybourne Park, an exclusively white neighborhood. Although she explains that she acted so that her family could "push out and do something bigger," rather than succumb to the squalor of the ghetto, Walter accuses her of destroying his dream and he departs.

The next scene takes place on a Friday evening a few weeks later. After Beneatha curtly rejects George when he admits that he desires a "simple" girl rather than a "poet," Mrs. Johnson, the Younger's intrusive neighbor, visits. In an episode previously excised from the original production, Mrs. Johnson maliciously predicts bombings in Clybourne Park, underscoring the gravity of Lena's decision to move. After she departs, Ruth confronts her husband, who has missed three days of work. Walter laconically dismisses his wife's concerns, telling her instead about the smoky bars and dimly lit jazz clubs he frequented while driving aimlessly through the city. Critics often contrast the demoralizing effect of this stagnate, predominately black environment upon Walter with the insipiration previously provided him by the white business world. When Lena hears of her son's wanderings, she realizes the effect of her decision upon his self-esteem. She gives him the money remaining after the down payment, sixty-five hundred dollars, with the one stipulation that he put thirty five hundred dollars in the bank for Beneatha's education. Revitalized by his mother's display of confidence, Walter rejoices, telling his son he now has the power to transform their lives.

One week later, the family packs for the move as Walter dances with his wife and jokes with his sister. Their revelry, however, is interrupted by the appearance of a white man at their door. He politely introduces himself as Karl Lindner of the Clybourne Park Improvement Association, but the Youngers soon realize that his intent, though never explicitly stated, is to induce them to abandon their plans by offering to buy their new home at a profit. He speaks of how his hard working white neighbors "dream of a kind of community they want to raise their children in"—an ironic reflection of the Youngers own aspirations. Although they angrily dismiss Lindner from their apartment, Walter and the others comically describe the incident to his concerned mother before presenting her with gardening tools and hat for her to use in their new backyard. Yet the good mood is destroyed when Bobo, one of Walter's business partners, arrives to tell him that Willy, their other associate, has disappeared with their money. Devastated, Walter informs his family that all of the remaining money, including Beneatha's college funds, is lost. Lena physically attacks her son, and the scene ends with her cry to God for strength.

Act III takes place an hour later as Asagi arrives to help with the packing and finds Beneatha alone in the living room. She cynically reveals what has happened, then announces her intention to give up medicine, which she now perceives as a futile attempt to improve an undeserving world. Asagi admonishes Beneatha, however, telling her that she must continue to struggle despite an unsure future. He then unexpectedly proposes marriage and for her to return to Africa with him. Confused, Beneatha asks him to give her time to think, and Asagi departs before the other Youngers enter the living room. Ignoring Beneatha's verbal attack, Walter rushes out of the apartment. Upon returning, he informs his family that he contacted Lindner, telling him to return so that Walter can accept his offer. All three women plead with him, but Walter, railing against "the takers" and "the tooken," ignores them as he affects the stereotype of the subservient negro. When he exits into the bedroom, Beneatha bitterly dismisses him as "no brother of mine." Yet Lena reprimands her in one of the most recognized passages from *A Raisin in the Sun,* telling her that she must "measure him right" and love Walter when the rest of the world cannot. Critics often point to this speech as a distillation of the play's theme of how individuals must re-examine their perception of others different from themselves. When Lindner arrives, Walter emerges from the bedroom, but, upon facing the white man, he falters. He speaks of his father's hard work and the dignified way in which he conducted his life. Then, drawing Travis to him, Walter rejects Lindner's offer. Stunned, the white man leaves, and with Ruth's cry "let's get the hell out of here," the family hastily gather their remaining possessions. The play then ends as Lena looks one last time at her apartment before shutting the door.

When *A Raisin in the Sun* first appeared on Broadway, New York reviewers generally praised it as an intelligent, enlightening portrait of African-Americans whose complex concerns and hopes transcend racial stereotypes. During the 1960s, however, several black critics derided the play as a clichéd melodrama that denies the reality of African-American life and promotes the materialistic values of white society. Subsequent commentators objected to this argument, contending that Hansberry's broad themes concerning the illusiveness of the American dream are inextricably bound to a black point of view as memorably realized in the character of Walter. Douglas Turner Ward asserted: "It is Walter Lee—flawed, contradictory, irascible, impulsive, furious and, most of all, desperate—who emerges as the most unique creation for his time and ours. It is his behavior throughout the play—his restless

impatience, his discontent with the way things are, his acute perception of societal disparities, his fury at status inequities, his refusal to accept his 'place'—which gives [*A Raisin in the Sun*] prophetic significance. . . . He remains the pivot of the play around which everything revolves. And no matter what we have experienced in the years since his entrance, the Walter Lees of the world have yet to be reckoned with."

(See also *Contemporary Authors* Vols. 25-28, rev. ed. [obituary], Vol. 109; *Contemporary Authors Bibliographical Series,* Vol. 3; *Black Writers; Dictionary of Literary Biography,* Vols. 7, 38; and *Concise Dictionary of Literary Biography: 1941-1968.*)

PRINCIPAL WORKS

PLAYS

A Raisin in the Sun   1959
The Sign in Sydney Brustein's Window   1964
To Be Young, Gifted, and Black   1969
Les Blancs   1970
*The Drinking Gourd   1972
*What Use Are Flowers?   1972

OTHER

The Movement: Documentary of a Struggle for Equality   1964; also published in Great Britain as *A Matter of Colour,*   1965

*Unproduced scripts published in book form.

Harold Clurman

A Raisin in the Sun by a young Negro woman, Lorraine Hansberry, might be called an old-fashioned play—which should not be taken to mean that it is not a good one. It may have escaped our attention that although American drama is very largely realistic, there has been a tendency in the past twenty-five years or so not only to veil our realism with a silk of poetry, a kind of disguised romanticism, but to extend it with a suggestion of social interpretation too bashful to be dubbed propaganda. Our new realism is something more than a picture of a concrete state of affairs. It is a generalization from a commonly known situation heightened by moral fervor and oblique lyric expression.

A Raisin in the Sun shows some of these latter traits but its inspiration is in a certain sense less ambitious and more plainly specific than that of the neo-realist writers, who usually are filled with a desire to express themselves and thus to produce art and literature. Miss Hansberry simply wants to say what she has seen and experienced, because to her these things are sufficiently important in themselves. This is what I mean when I call her play "old-fashioned."

She is right. While the drift away from naturalism in the American theatre is healthy, it is entirely false to assume that we have no further use for the old realism. . . . The poetic realism we have been cultivating in recent years often grows fuzzy or mushy. It needs the control of a severe probity in regard to reality and the exercise of discipline in language. The traditional realistic play needs genuine identification with its subject matter (the realist should never be an investigator in the slums) in addition to objectivity and heart.

A Raisin in the Sun is authentic: it is a portrait of the aspirations, anxieties, ambitions and contradictory pressures affecting humble Negro folk in an American big city—in this instance Chicago. It is not intended as an appeal to whites or as a preachment for Negroes. It is an honestly felt response to a situation that has been lived through, clearly understood and therefore simply and impressively stated. Most important of all: having been written from a definite point of view (that of a participant) with no eye toward meretricious possibilities in showmanship and public relations, the play throws light on aspects of American life quite outside the area of race. (pp. 301-02)

> Harold Clurman, in a review of "A Raisin in the Sun," in The Nation, New York, Vol. 188, No. 14, April 4, 1959, pp. 301-02.

Henry Hewes

In Lorraine Hansberry's *A Raisin in the Sun* we have at last a play that deals with real people. The fact that they are colored people, with all the special problems of their race, seems less important than that they are people with exactly the same problems everyone else has. The five human beings and potted plant who make up the Younger family live in a crowded, rundown apartment on Chicago's South Side. We meet them at the start of the day when everyone is feeling salty about the prospect of getting up, taking turns at the bathroom, and facing the day's routine. Their interfamily joys and anxieties are universal ones. . . . [The daughter-in-law, Ruth], is the essence of any wife who has the thankless task of having to raise her voice and nag, of having to watch the budget while her husband, Walter, acts affluent, of having to talk him down to his face, and up to everyone else, and of trying to preserve a good relationship with someone who is depressed about himself. As Walter says, "I am thirty-five years old, been married eleven years, got a boy who sleeps in the living-room and all I've got to give him is stories about how rich white people live."

The rest of the family consists of their ten-year-old son Travis, Walter's twenty-year-old sister Beneatha, who jumps too easily at new ideas, fads, and causes, and his mother, Lena. Lena is godfearing, unpretentious, and would do anything for her children. She loves her daughter-in-law too, but like any mother cannot keep herself from meddling in such simple things as Travis getting the right food for breakfast. She can say in one breath that she is not meddling and in the next go right on interfering. Yet she is completely unselfish, and when she collects the money from her late husband's life insurance, she takes the instinctively right step of buying a new house for her family. She explains, "I just seen my family falling apart today . . . just falling to pieces in front of my eyes . . . We couldn't of gone on like we was today. We was going backwards 'stead of forwards." . . .

At first [Walter] . . . has a friendly flippancy, then a hot and desperate anger at the world, when we see him as the representative of this generation of Negro, not satisfied with or proud of his parents' hard won but small progress. He wants to jump miraculously into money and dignity, or to escape his life away in bars. . . . But his finest moment comes when he tearfully and awkwardly talks to a white man who is trying to buy him off and prevent him from moving into a white neighborhood. "We are very proud and this is my son who makes the sixth generation of our family in this country and we have thought all about your offer and we have decided to move into our house because our father earned it for us."

The twenty-eight year-old authoress, whose first Broadway play this is, deliberately resists the heroic. At the moment when you'd expect the characters to work themselves up into a fight or a tirade, they melt into touchingly human, though cleanly unsentimental, acts. And it is on the basis of emotional impact and humor that this play must rest its case. Wisely, Miss Hansberry has avoided trying to solve all of the problems. The nearest she comes to a message is in a short speech by Mr. Asagai, a Nigerian revolutionist, who says, "I know that we cannot allow life to depend on accidents." And here we see a glimmer of condemnation of today's America in which life seems to abound with accidental successes and sudden acquisitions of wealth. In the past, the American Negro had less opportunity to fancy himself part of this illusion than he does now. Like the rest of us some will be destroyed by it. But *A Raisin in the Sun* would seem to suggest that when the bubble bursts the families with the most courageous pasts will be best equipped to pick up the pieces.

> Henry Hewes, "A Plant Grows in Chicago," in Saturday Review, Vol. XLII, No. 14, April 4, 1959, p. 28.

Lorraine Hansberry

Some of the acute partisanship revolving around *A Raisin in the Sun* is amusing. Those who announce that they find the piece less than fine are regarded in some quarters with dramatic hostility, as though such admission automatically implies the meanest of racist reservations. On the other hand, the ultra-sophisticates have hardly acquitted themselves less ludicrously, gazing cooly down their noses at those who are moved by the play, and going on at length about "melodrama" and/or "soap opera" as if these are not completely definable terms which cannot simply be tacked onto any play and all plays we do not like.

Personally, I find no pain whatever—at least of the traditional ego type—in saying that *Raisin* is a play which contains dramaturgical incompletions. Fine plays tend to utilize one big fat character who runs right through the middle of the structure, by action or implication, with whom we rise or fall. A central character as such is certainly lacking from *Raisin.* I should be delighted to pretend that it was *inventiveness,* as some suggest for me, but it is, also, craft inadequacy and creative indecision. The result is that neither Walter Lee nor Mama Younger loom large enough to monumentally command the play. I consider it an enormous dramatic fault if no one else does. (p. 7)

All in all, however, I believe that, for the most part, the

play has been magnificently understood. In some cases it was not only thematically absorbed but attention was actually paid to the tender treacherousness of its craft-imposed "simplicity." Some, it is true, quite missed that part of the overt intent and went on to harangue the bones of the play with rather useless observations of the terribly clear fact that they are old bones indeed. More meaningful discussions tended to delve into the flesh which hangs from those bones and its implications in mid-century American drama and life.

In that connection it is interesting to note that while the names of Chekhov, O'Casey, and the early Odets were introduced for comparative purposes in some of the reviews, almost no one—with the exception of Gerald Weales in *Commentary* [see Hansberry, *CLC,* Vol. 17]—discovered a simple line of descent between Walter Lee Younger and the last great hero in American drama to also *accept* the values of his culture, Willy Loman. I am sure that the already mentioned primary fault of the play must account in part for this. The family so overwhelms the play that Walter Lee necessarily fails as the true symbol he should be, even though *his* ambitions, *his* frustrations, and *his* decisions are those which decisively drive the play on. But however recognizable he proves to be, he fails to dominate our imagination and finally emerges as a reasonably interesting study, but not, like Arthur Miller's great character—and like Hamlet, of course—a summation of an immense (though not crucial) portion of his culture.

Then too . . . we must not completely omit reference to some of the prior attitudes which were brought into the theatre from the world outside. For in the minds of many, Walter remains, despite the play, despite performance, what American radical traditions *wish* him to be: an exotic. Some writers have been astonishingly incapable of discussing his purely *class* aspirations and have persistently confounded them with what they consider to be an exotic being's longing to "wheel and deal" in what they further consider to be (and what Walter never can) "the white man's world." Very few people today must consider the ownership of a liquor store as an expression of extraordinary affluence, and yet, as joined to a dream of Walter Younger, it takes on, for some, aspects of the fantastic. We have grown accustomed to the dynamics of "Negro" personality as expressed by white authors. Thus, de Emperor, de Lawd, and, of course, Porgy, still haunt our frame of reference when a new character emerges. We have become romantically jealous of the great image of a prototype whom we believe is summarized by the wishfulness of a self-assumed opposite. Presumably there is a quality in human beings that makes us *wish* that we *were* capable of primitive contentments; the *universality* of ambition and its anguish can escape us only if we construct elaborate legends about the rudimentary simplicity of *other* men.

America, for this reason, long ago fell in love with the image of the simple, lovable, and glandular "Negro." We all know that Catfish Row was never intended to slander anyone; it was intended as a mental haven for readers and audiences who could bask in the unleashed passions of those "lucky ones" for whom abandonment was apparently permissible. In an almost paradoxical fashion, it disturbs the soul of man to truly understand what he invariably senses: that *nobody* really finds oppression and/or poverty tolerable. If we ever destroy the image of the black

people who supposedly do find those things tolerable in America, then that much-touted "guilt" which allegedly haunts most middle-class white Americans with regard to the Negro question would really become unendurable. It would also mean the death of a dubious literary tradition, but it would undoubtedly and more significantly help toward the more rapid transformation of the status of a people who have never found their imposed misery very charming.

My colleagues and I were reduced to mirth and tears by that gentleman writing his review of our play in a Connecticut paper who remarked of his pleasure at seeing how "our dusky brethren" could "come up with a song and hum their troubles away." It did not disturb the writer in the least that there is no such implication in the entire three acts. He did not need it in the play; he had it in his head.

For all these reasons then, I imagine that the ordinary impulse to compare Willy Loman and Walter Younger was remote. Walter Lee Younger jumped out at us from a play about a largely unknown world. We knew who Willy Loman was instantaneously; we recognized his milieu. . . . Willy Loman was a product of a nation of great military strength, indescribable material wealth, and incredible mastery of the physical realm, which nonetheless was unable, in 1946, to produce a *typical* hero who was capable of an affirmative view of life.

I believe it is a testament to Miller's brilliance that it is hardly a misstatement of the case, as some preferred to believe. Something has indeed gone wrong with at least part of the American dream, and Willy Loman is the victim of the detour. . . . His predicament in a New World where there just aren't any more forests to clear or virgin railroads to lay or native American empires to first steal and build upon, left him with nothing but some left-over values which had forgotten how to prize industriousness over cunning; usefulness over mere acquisition, and, above all, humanism over "success." The potency of the great tale of a salesman's death was in our familiar recognition of his entrapment which, suicide or no, is *deathly*.

What then of this new figure who appears in American drama in 1958; from what source is he drawn so that, upon inspection, and despite class differences, so much of his encirclement must still remind us of that of Willy Loman? Why, finally, is it possible that when his third-act will is brought to bear, *his* typicality is capable of a choice which *affirms* life? After all, Walter Younger is an American more than he is anything else. His ordeal, give or take his personal expression of it, is not extraordinary but intensely familiar like Willy's. The two of them have virtually no values which have not come out of their culture, and to a significant point, no view of the possible solutions to their problems which do not also come out of the self-same culture. Walter can find no peace with that part of society which seems to permit him and no entry into that which has willfully excluded him. He shares with Willy Loman the acute awareness that *something* is obstructing some abstract progress that he feels he *should* be making; that *something* is in the way of his ascendancy. It does not occur to either of them to question the nature of this desired "ascendancy." Walter accepts, he believes in the "world" as it has been presented to him. When we first meet him, he does not wish to alter *it;* merely to change *his* position in it. His mentors and his associates all take the view that the institutions which frustrate him are somehow impeccable, or, at best, "unfortunate." "Things being as they are," he must look to *himself* as the only source of any rewards he may expect. Within himself, he is encouraged to believe, are the only seeds of defeat or victory within the universe. And Walter believes this and when opportunity, haphazard and rooted in death, prevails, he acts.

But the obstacles which are introduced are gigantic; the weight of the loss of the money is in fact, the weight of death. In Walter Lee Younger's life, somebody *has* to die for ten thousand bucks to pile up—if then. Elsewhere in the world, in the face of catastrophe, he might be tempted to don the saffron robes of acceptance and sit on a mountain top all day contemplating the divine justice of his misery. Or, history being what it is turning out to be, he might wander down to his first Communist Party meeting. But here in the dynamic and confusing post-war years on the Southside of Chicago, his choices of action are equal to those gestures only in symbolic terms. The American ghetto hero may give up and contemplate his misery in rose-colored bars to the melodies of hypnotic saxophones, but revolution seems alien to him in his circumstances (America), and it is easier to dream of personal wealth than of a communal state wherein universal dignity is supposed to be a corollary. Yet his position in time and space does allow for one other alternative: he may take his place on any one of a number of frontiers of challenge. Challenges (such as helping to break down restricted neighborhoods) which are admittedly limited because they most certainly do not threaten the basic social order.

But why is even this final choice possible, considering the everpresent (and ever so popular) vogue of despair? Well, that is where Walter departs from Willy Loman; there is a second pulse in his still dual culture. His people have had "somewhere" they have been trying to get for so long that more sophisticated confusions do not yet bind them. *Thus the weight and power of their current social temperament intrudes and affects him, and it is, at the moment, at least, gloriously and rigidly affirmative.* In the course of *their* brutally difficult ascent, they have dismissed the ostrich and still sing, *"Went to the rock, to hide my face, but the rock cried out: 'No hidin' place down here!'"* Walter is, despite his lack of consciousness of it, inextricably as much wedded to his special mass as Willy was to his, and the moods of each are able to decisively determine the dramatic typicality. Furthermore, the very nature of the situation of American Negroes can force their representative hero to recognize that for his *true* ascendancy he must ultimately be at cross-purposes with at least certain of his culture's values. It is to the pathos of Willy Loman that his section of American life seems to have momentarily lost that urgency; that he cannot, like Walter, draw on the strength of an incredible people who, historically, have simply refused to give up.

In other words, the symbolism of moving into the new house is quite as small as it seems and quite as significant. For if there are no waving flags and marching songs at the barricades as Walter marches out with his little battalion, it is not because the battle lacks nobility. On the contrary, he has picked up in his way, still imperfect and wobbly in his small view of human destiny, what I believe Arthur Miller once called "the golden thread of history." He becomes, in spite of those who are too intrigued with despair and hatred of man to see it, King Oedipus refusing to tear out his eyes, but attacking the Oracle instead. He is that last Jewish patriot manning his rifle in the burning ghetto at Warsaw; he is that young girl who swam into sharks to save a friend a few weeks ago; he is Anne Frank, still believing in people; he is the nine small heroes of Little Rock; he is Michelangelo creating David and Beethoven bursting forth with the Ninth Sympony. He is all those things because he has finally reached out in his tiny moment and caught that sweet essence which is human dignity, and it shines like the old startouched dream that it is in his eyes. We see, in the moment, I think, what becomes, and not for Negroes alone, but for Willy and all of us, entirely an American responsibility.

Out in the darkness where we watch, most of us are not afraid to cry. (pp. 7-8)

> Lorraine Hansberry, "Willie Loman, Walter Younger, and He Who Must Live," in The Village Voice, *Vol. IV, No. 42, August 12, 1959, pp. 7-8.*

Theophilus Lewis

At the end of every theatrical season, when the time arrives to award prizes and distribute ribbons of merit, at least one play becomes the subject of a controversy that lasts well into the summer. The usual issue is whether the prize-winning play deserved the honor or a more deserving play was denied the accolade. . . . This year the controversial play is *A Raisin in the Sun,* Lorraine Hansberry's drama of a Negro family struggling for survival.

The current annual hassle is as acrimonious as usual and is complicated by peculiar circumstances. The most coveted honors are the Pulitzer Prize and the Critics Circle Award. This year the Pulitzer judges decided that *J.B.,* a religious drama based on the Old Testament story of Job, was the outstanding play of the season while *A Raisin in the Sun* garnered the Critics Circle Award. Since both prizes were origially intended to reward the best play of the year, the donor's divergence of choice is a source of virulent dispute. Obviously there cannot be two best plays.

The day after the play opened, all seven of the critics who write for daily newspapers wrote favorable notices, some of them "rave reviews." Reading their reviews, one can visualize Atkinson and Kerr throwing their hats in the air. A few weeks later, however, when they assembled to decide on the best play of the year, not one of the reviewers for the dailies cast his ballot for *A Raisin in the Sun.* . . . The ballots that gave *A Raisin in the Sun* a plurality were cast by reporters for the wire services, writers for magazines, the astute critic for a socialist weekly and the reviewer for a horse paper. A switch of one strategic vote could have bestowed the award on either of the runner-up plays.

Performed by a brilliant cast, *A Raisin in the Sun* may easily be accepted as a great play. The action, which occurs in a shabby flat on Chicago's South Side, is packed with emotional tension that remains taut until the last line. The central character is Walter Younger, a Negro father who is worried because, at the age of thirty-five, he can see no way to give his young son a better start in life than his father gave him. Walter's problem, of course, is universal among fathers.

Walter and his family live with his widowed mother, a stalwart matriarch who is the real head of the household. In the opening scene the widow is expecting a $10,000 insurance check, the legacy of her deceased husband. Her relatives, of course, are all too eager to tell her how to spend it. Walter wants to buy a share in a liquor store, an obviously sound investment, while his younger sister, a pre-medical student, demands that a part of the money be set aside to finance her education. When the bickering gets too hot, the widow walks out of the house and does what she thinks is best for the family.

Her decision, though essentially sound, confronts the family with a problem more serious than the one she had hoped to solve. . . . Hoping to provide the family with more ample living space, the widow makes a down payment on a house in the suburbs. While the Youngers are preparing to move into their new home, their packing is interrupted by a white visitor who introduces himself as the representative of an organization known as the Better Neighborhood Association or a similar name. He explains that the house the Youngers have purchased is located in an all-white neighborhood, and that its residents fear the community will deteriorate if a Negro family moves in.

This partial synopsis, while it describes the characters and their motives and foreshadows the crisis, does not carry even a vague idea of the emotional impact of the play. Its reception on Broadway, among the lay audience as well as the critics was one of unrestrained enthusiasm. The play was an overnight hit. (pp. 31-3)

While there can be no doubt that the play owes much of its success, especially in the box office sense, to [the luminous performances of such actors as Sydney Poitier and Ruby Dee] . . . , it is no less true that the author has given the stars substantial roles that challenge their talents. Indeed, *A Raisin in the Sun* is quite likely to become a durable theater piece because actors like to play it. (p. 33)

What will concern serious observers of the theater is whether, aside from its popularity, the play has inherent significance that makes it a timely and permanent contribution to our national drama. While its permanence is for the future to decide, there can be little doubt that the play is a unique contribution to the contemporary stage. While some modernists will call it a throwback to an outmoded style of dramaturgy, mature observers are as likely to welcome it as a return to a more wholesome and intelligible era of dramatic writing. For the better part of a generation our stage has been deluged with psychological drama—plays in which the principal characters were motivated by hidden compulsions or childhood trauma. There are no Freudian implications in *A Raisin in the Sun,* no clinical motivation, no symbolism. It is a straightforward social drama, at least superficially, written in a naturalistic style that is refreshing in its simplicity.

Walter Younger, while obviously high strung and worried, is not a couch patient. He is mentally and emotionally upset, yes, but only as any sensible man would be in an economic blind alley. His young son shows no tendency toward delinquency as a result of Oedipus yearnings, and

his wife's only frustration is not enough money to balance the family budget adequately. His mother is a Gibraltar of emotional stability.

The Youngers are a rather representative Negro family, not as prosperous as the top fifth nor as penurious as lower layers of their race. Their only dependable income is Walter's pay as a chauffeur, eked out by his wife's occasional earnings as a day worker. They live in a dilapidated apartment in a rundown section of the city. Still, although incessantly bickering among themselves, their morale is high. While they are typically working class in income and surroundings, they are middle class in their thinking; and somehow manage to keep Walter's younger sister in college. If their skins were lighter they would be immediately recognized as a courageous American family striving for higher status, which they are.

The plight of the Youngers, enfiladed by economic insecurity from one side and by race prejudice from the other, offers the author obvious opportunities to indulge in propaganda for interracial justice. Miss Hansberry avoids a snare that has often tripped more experienced playwrights. Authors of social drama frequently make the mistake of dramatizing social injustice or crusading for its correction. Miss Hansberry wisely declines to usurp the function of the social reformer, the clergyman or the working politician. She merely holds the mirror up to life, as the greatest English dramatist advised, allowing her audience to supply the interpretation.

While the play has the structure and substance of social drama, the emphasis is on character. The Youngers are not guinea pigs manipulated to illustrate economic or racial inequity, although they are victims of both. They do not have to prove anything or conform to the author's thesis, if she has any. They are interesting people, each invested with distinctive personality; each one's conduct determined by personal motives. Observing them, we are never concerned with what will happen to the Youngers. Our interest is centered on what each of the several members of the family will do. We see them embroiled in an apparently interminable intramural quarrel, doubting that family loyalty can hold them together, and we breathe easier when they close ranks against an outside enemy. That is when the play, as social drama, reaches its crisis.

The real and decisive crisis is Walter's spiritual ordeal, when he has to make a decision for the family. We have seen Walter faltering and stumbling, and now he must make a fatal decision. Here is a study of Negro character under pressure. Indeed, we see Negroes under pressure throughout the play. They often bend but never break. If there is a message in Miss Hansberry's drama it is that Negroes have to be tough to survive.

The "message" is not underscored or forced on the audience. It is implied rather than explicit, and only those who are already socially alert are likely to recognize its significance. Socially naïve playgoers are more likely to become too involved in the Youngers' problems to discern their implications. The Youngers themselves, while they are intelligent and sensitive to economic pressures, seem unaware that they are engaged in a sociological race war. There is less social protest in the play (it is rather embarrassing to admit) than there is in this commentary.

In a capsule description, *A Raisin in the Sun* is a drama

of spiritual conflict, in the arena of Walter Younger's soul, with an obbligato of social awareness. Although the obbligato is muted, some observers will hear it more distinctly than the essential melody, while others will be too absorbed in the story to notice either the melody or the accompaniment. The different aspects of the drama will appeal to various tastes and temperaments for different reasons; but few will come away from a performance unmoved by its total impact.

A play that stirs the emotions of some observers, while pricking the conscience of others, *A Raisin in the Sun* has the distinguishing marks of first-rate drama. It carries an effective sermon for those who want to heed it without impairing its esthetic appeal. The critical honors and popular approval it has been accorded are well deserved. For it is a good play in its time and one we can be proud to bequeath to posterity. (pp. 34-5)

> *Theophilus Lewis, "Social Protest in 'A Raisin in the Sun'?" in* The Catholic World, *Vol. 190, No. 1135, October, 1959, pp. 31-5.*

Harold Cruse

The phenomenal success of *A Raisin in the Sun* has to be seen against the background of the temper of the racial situation in America and its cultural implications for American artforms. Broadway and the rest of the American theater has not been at all kind to the Negro playwright or performer. Miss Hansberry's play provided the perfect opportunity to make it all up, or at least assuage the commercial theater's liberal guilt. Of course, when *Raisin* burst on the scene with a Negro star, a Negro director plus a young Negro woman playwright everybody on Broadway was startled and very apprehensive about what this play might *say*. What obviously elated the drama critics was the very relieving discovery that, what the publicity buildup actually heralded was not the arrival of belligerent forces from across the color line to settle some long-standing racial accounts on stage, but a good old-fashioned, home-spun saga of some good working-class folk in pursuit of the American Dream . . . in their fashion. And what could possibly be thematically objectionable about that? And very well written also. We shall give it an award (A for effort), and so they did, amidst a patronizing critical exuberance I would have thought impossible in the crassly commercial institution of Broadway. Not a dissenting critical note was to be heard from Broadway critics, and thus the Negro made theater history with the most cleverly written piece of glorified soap opera I, personally, have ever seen on a stage. Only because it was about *Negroes* was this play acceptable, and this is the sobering fact that the aspiring Negro playwright *must* live with. If this play—which is so "American" that many whites did *not* consider it a "Negro play"—had ever been staged by *white actors* it would be judged second-rate—which was what the British called it, and what the French said of the film version. Why was it that *Raisin,* although it was hailed on Broadway, impressed no one in Europe, which has always been more appreciative and receptive to Negro art than American whites?

Here, the general attitude inspired by the success of *Raisin* was that the Negro in the theater had come of age, so to speak, and that the path was now clear for more resounding achievements. Lorraine Hansberry emerged like a Saint Joan of black cultural revival, sounding off in journalistic and television debates like a prophetess who had suddenly appeared carrying messages from the soul of the "people." The truth is that *A Raisin in the Sun,* far from being the *beginning* of anything, was the end of a trend that had been in process for a long time and had not been critically examined. *Raisin* was the artistic, aesthetic and class-inspired culmination of the efforts of the Harlem left-wing literary and cultural in-group to achieve integration of the Negro in the arts as first postulated by the Committee for the Negro in the Arts in the late 1940's. But this culmination was achieved in a very unique way. CNA had fought for the integration of the Negro in the theater without making the necessary distinction between Negro actor and Negro playwright, both of which roles represent different functions in terms of integration. Thus *Raisin* was not an integrated play of the type Negro actors strive for, but an all-Negro play supposedly passé—but with a difference: *It was an "all-Negro" play about a family in the throes of integrating into a white community.* In terms of American social and racial realities, this was a very good theme and exceedingly timely; but what all the so-called perceptive critics missed was that, from the very real standpoint of Negro urban class sociology, the author deliberately chose the wrong family for the theme.

As a poor Chicago Southside working-class Negro family, the Youngers were most atypical of poor families from the South. True to the socialist-realist tradition, the Younger family was carefully tidied up for its on-stage presentation as good, hardworking, upright, decent, moral, physchologically uncomplicated ghetto folk; poor but honorable, they had kept their heads above water and had not sunk down into the human dregs. There were no numbers-runners in sight, no bumptiously slick, young "cats" from downstairs sniffing after Mama Younger's pretty daughter on the corner, no shyster preachers hustling Mama into the fold, no fallen women, etc. (pp. 277-79)

Miss Hansberry had certainly come a long way from Robeson's "Freedom Family." This Younger family was, in 1959, not of a mind for Negro labor unity in the trade-union struggle for working class liberation; or for socialism in Robeson's world of all the oppressed peoples in the "age-long struggle of the Negro and Jewish people with the same heroes," etc. Lorraine Hansberry had definitely outgrown that poppycock to the extent of knowing that Broadway would not accept it. She was embarking on her phase of the "swirl and dash of the Camus-Sartre debate," but saving it for *Brustein's Window.* However, in the meantime, the Younger family had to be readied for something more immediately crucial and important—integration. Thus, the only working-class Negroes who are fit for integration are those who can be made to mouth middle-class values, sentiments and strivings: platitudes that are acceptable to whites of the middle classes. No wonder the Broadway audience responded to the buildup and embraced *Raisin.* "We really didn't think of it as a Negro play at all." "Why, after all, that Younger family was just like us." "Why *anybody* could have played those characters," etc. "Bravo! How wonderful for letting us know. Now here is your prize!" But nobody asked out loud some pertinent questions such as: "How could a poor ghetto family of Southern origins come by a $10,000 insurance policy and what Southern Negro insurance company would have covered it for this type of family?" "Since when does this type of Negro family have daughters in college studying medicine and where did the money come from to pay for it?" "How did the married son, a taxi driver, come by the connections and the inside political pull and the granting of credit necessary to purchase a liquor store?" All three of these circumstances in Negro life derive not from a working class status, but a lower-middle or middle-class family background. They represent the class advantages that are economic keys, guarding the very limited world of social privilege and advancement of the Negro petite bourgeoisie and bourgeoisie, a world jealously closed against black working-class penetration.

Taken historically, if all things social in Negro-white relations had been equal over the past twenty-five years, all the material in *A Raisin in the Sun* would have long ago been done on the radio, with several variations during the heyday of soap opera series. It was only the racial integration theme that added timeliness to an old-fashioned genre. But *Raisin* arrived on Broadway in the midst of something unheard of when soap opera was fashionable—the Negro middle-class social revolution. Consequently, the Negro working-class characters had to mouth middle-class ideology—witness the line about Mama Younger with her wide-brimmed hat: "She looks just like Mrs. Miniver." When the Younger family moved out of the slums at the play's end and walked out of their house, out went the "Negro" theme in serious theater; and also, as far as the playwright was concerned, out went even the integration of the Negro in the theater because Miss Hansberry as a writer had departed from the Negro scene long before her Younger family put their last piece of furniture in the moving van. It could easily have been forecast that her next play would be about white folks *and would not even be integrated, as Negro actors had hoped.*

Thus the pathetic illusions about the integration of the Negro in the theater were shown up as leading to a hopeless dead end. The profound differences between playwright and actor—one the *creator* and the other *interpreter*—had never been considered. If the creator integrates herself, as Lorraine Hansberry did, it implies the end of the Negro as a creative Negro being, for the Negro playwright has nowhere to go if *A Raisin in the Sun* is considered as the ultimate in the theater. He (or she) must either be left high and dry as a creative nonentity, or follow Miss Hansberry's lead and write about white people. But can the Negro playwright attempt to do this and survive? Does American culture really need him for that? As one Negro playwright said, the Negro writer must live with *A Raisin in the Sun,* for its arrival signalizes a profound cultural dilemma for the Negro in the theater. (pp. 279-81)

A Raisin in the Sun demonstrated that the Negro playwright has lost the intellectual and, therefore technical and creative, ability to deal with his own special ethnic group materials in dramatic form. The most glaring manifestation of this conceptual weakness is the constant slurring over, the blurring, and evasion of the internal facts of Negro ethnic life in terms of class and social caste divisions, institutional and psychological variations, political divisions, acculturation variables, clique variations, religious divisions, and so forth. Negro playwrights have never gone past their own subjectivity to explore the severe stress and strain of class conflict within the Negro

group. Such class and clique rivalries and prejudices can be just as damaging, demoralizing and retarding as white prejudice. Negro playwrights have sedulously avoided dealing with the Negro middle class in all its varieties of social expression, basically because the Negro playwright has adopted the Negro middle-class morality. Therefore, art itself, especially the art of playwriting, has become a stepping stone to middle-class social status. As long as the morality of the Negro middle class must be upheld, defended, and emulated in social life *outside* the theater it can never be portrayed or criticized *inside* the theater à la Ibsen, or satirized à la Shaw. In this regard it becomes the better part of social and creative valor to do what Hansberry did—"Let us portray only the good, simple ordinary folk because this is what the audiences want, especially the white audiences; but let us give the whites the Negro middle-class ball to carry towards the goal of integration. Beyond that very functional use of the Negro in the theater, of what other value is this thing, the so-called Negro play? None at all, so let us banish it along with that other parochial idea 'The Negro Theater.' We don't like this 'Negro play' category in the American theater anyhow, and we don't like to be told that we must write it, but we'll *use* it (as a starter) and then we'll go on to better things; that is, we'll become what they call human and universal, which in the white folks' lexicon and cultural philosophy means 'universally white.' "

But Miss Hansberry even went that theatrical strategy one better. Although in 1959-1960, she did not deny that *Raisin* was a play about a Negro family, in 1964 when *Brustein's Window* opened, Miss Hansberry denied that *Raisin* was ever a "Negro play":

> Some persons ask how it is that I have "left the Negro question" in the writing of this latest play. I hardly know how to answer as it seems to me that I have never written about "the Negro question." *A Raisin in the Sun,* for instance, was a play about an American family's conflict with certain of the mercenary values of its society, and its characters were Negroes. . . . I write plays about various matters which have both Negro and White characters in them, and there is really nothing else that I can think of to say about the matter.

Miss Hansberry was essentially right about many aspects of *Raisin* and its impact on white audiences but was also adroitly evasive about what her intentions were. She intended to write a Negro play because she could not make her stage debut with anything else. But what crept into *Raisin* was the author's own essentially quasi-white orientation through which she visualizes the Negro world. This was a matter of having one's "cultural" cake and refusing to eat it. However, one indication of Hansberry's intentions about *Raisin* was her choice of the play's title, which was a line taken from a poem by Langston Hughes called "A Montage of a Dream Deferred." Langston Hughes, however, would never have said that this poem was *not* about Harlem Negroes but about a vague species of American. *A Raisin in the Sun* expressed through the medium of theatrical art that current, forced symbiosis in American interracial affairs wherein the Negro working class has been roped in and tied to the chariot of racial integration driven by the Negro middle class. In this drive for integration the Negro working class is being told in a thousand ways that it must give up its ethnicity and become human, universal, full-fledged American. Within the context of this forced alliance of class aims there is no room for Negro art (except when it pays off). . . . (pp. 281-83)

This being the case, it is a foregone conclusion that Negro writers who are middle-class from birth will pass from Negro plays (which are not Negro plays) to writing plays which are universally human, before they will ever write a play that would have to portray some unpleasant truths about their own class. . . . [These writers have] achieved nothing more in print than an agitated beating of their literary breasts. They are lost sheep bleating to the God of Freedom for their deliverance. Sometimes they manage to get angry, and bleat all the louder—while snapping righteously at the white liberals. Meanwhile they analyze nothing and clarify less and heap confusion on top of confusion. Their literary or "cultural products" (Miss Hansberry's phrase) are, for the most part, second-rate because they reflect their creators' oversimplified and over-emotionalized views about their own ethnic group reality. (pp. 283-84)

Harold Cruse, "Lorraine Hansberry," in his The Crisis of the Negro Intellectual, *William Morrow & Company, Inc., 1967, pp. 267-84.*

C. W. E. Bigsby

Lorraine Hansberry's first play, *A Raisin in the Sun,* was awarded the New York Drama Critics' Prize for 1959-60. For all its sympathy, humour and humanity, however, it remains disappointing—the more so when compared with the achievement of her second play, *The Sign in Sidney Brustein's Window.* Yet it passes considerably beyond the trivial music-hall dramas of Langston Hughes and does something to capture the sad dilemma of Negro and white alike without lapsing into the bitter hatred of Richard Wright or the psychodrama of O'Neill's *All God's Chillun Got Wings.* Its weakness is essentially that of much of Broadway naturalism. It is an unhappy crossbreed of social protest and re-assuring resolution. Trying to escape the bitterness of Wright, Hansberry betrays herself into radical simplification and ill-defined affirmation. Like Saul Bellow she senses the validity of affirmation before she can justify it as a logical implication of her play's action.

A Raisin in the Sun is set in Chicago's Southside 'sometime between World War II and the present'. The Younger family live in a roach-infested building so overcrowded that they have to share the bathroom with another family while Travis the only son of Walter and Ruth Younger, has to sleep on a sofa in the living room. Yet the central factor of the play is not poverty but indignity and self-hatred. The survival of the family is dependent on their ability to accomodate themselves to the white world. Walter works as a chauffeur while his wife works as a maid. To both of them accommodation to the point of servility is required for the very right to work. James Baldwin has indicated the cost to the individual of accepting one's life on another's terms, 'one of the prices an American Negro pays—or can pay—for what is called his "acceptance" is a profound, almost ineradicable self hatred'. *A Raisin in the Sun* is primarily a study of such self-hatred, emphasised here, as Baldwin saw it emphasised in an article called 'Alas, Poor Richard', by a confrontation between the enervated American Negro and the dignified self-confidence of the African.

There is a story by Richard Wright called "Man of all Work" in which a Negro man dresses up as a woman in order to get work as a cook. His action emphasises what Baldwin has called 'the demoralisation of the Negro male' when his position as breadwinner is necessarily usurped by the woman. It is this agony with which Walter Younger lives. He has been desexualised and his dignity has been crushed. It is this knowledge which underlies his bitter disgust and self-contempt. 'I'm thirty-five years old; I been married eleven years and I got a boy who sleeps in the living room—and all I got to give him is stories about how rich white people live'. When a ten thousand dollar insurance matures on his father's death he has to watch the money pass into his mother's hands—a final blow to both his dreams and his manhood. '*You* the head of this family. You run our lives like you want to.'

Richard Wright, sensing the emasculation of the Negro trapped in the physical ghetto of Chicago and the cage of self-contempt alike, had seen in violence both the Negro's attempt to re-assert himself and an expression of white oppression. Bigger Thomas, who kills, decapitates and incinerates a white woman thereby achieves a measure of self-awareness which had previously escaped him. Hansberry's play is set in the same locale. Its sense of desperation is the same. Walter Younger's emasculation is pushed to the point at which he condones his wife's attempt to secure an abortion. Yet where Wright created in Bigger Thomas a hardening of the stereotype, which was in effect a springboard for an exegesis of communist doctrine, Hansberry, writing some twenty years later, is concerned with demonstrating human resilience. The gulf between the two writers is in part that dictated by the changing social position of the American Negro but more fundamentally it is indicative of Lorraine Hansberry's belief in the pointlessness of despair and hatred. Indeed Hansberry's play is essentially an attempt to turn Wright's novel on its head. Where he had examined the potential for violence, Hansberry sees this as a potential which once realised can only lead to stasis. Both works start with an alarm-clock ringing in the stifling atmosphere of Chicago's coloured ghetto. Yet whereas Bigger Thomas wakes up to the inexorability of his fate, Walter becomes conscious of the existence of other levels than the purely material. The sense of urgency presaged by the initial alarm is as much the key-note of Hansberry's play as it is of Wright's novel yet while the alarm functions as a threat in the latter it functions as a promise in the former.

The play's title is taken from a poem by Langston Hughes—a poem which expresses the sense of kinetic energy and tension which underlies the frustrations of the American Negro, an energy which can be turned into violence, self-destruction, despair or genuine realisation:

> What happens to a dream deferred?
> Does it dry up
> Like a raisin in the sun?
> Or fester like a sore—
> And then run?
> Does it stink like rotten meat?
> Or crust and sugar over—
> Like a syrupy sweet?
> Maybe it just sags
> Like a heavy load.

Or does it explode?

The dreams of the Youngers are sharpened and pointed by the indignity and self-hatred which is their racial inheritance. Walter dreams of owning a store and thus becoming independent of the system of which he is the victim, while his sister, impressed by the need for compassion, wants to become a doctor. Lena Younger, Walter's mother, however, is concerned only with the disintegration of the family. When the money arrives she places a deposit on a new house. The decision drives Walter into a despairing disaffiliation.

Walter Younger's sullen cynicism, which, like Willy Loman's confused mind, grants value only to wealth and power, is balanced by his sister's passionate belief in the feasibility of change and the need for compassion. Beneatha has a strong sense of racial pride compounded with humanistic commitment. Intensely aware of her racial origins she associates with Asagai, an African student, and steeps herself in the culture of her forbears. When Asagai gives her the nickname Alaiyo, 'one who needs more than bread', it is both an ironical comment on her intensity and an indication that Hansberry's concern is less with the poverty of the Youngers than with the need for spiritual replenishment which can only come with a return of dignity. Yet when Walter squanders the money which was to have paid for her medical training Beneatha lapses into despair and the compassion which she had shown evaporates as had Ruth's hope and Walters's ambitions. Like Sidney Brustein in Hansberry's second play, forced to confront present reality, she slips into the cant of nihilism. She projects her personal disappointments onto a universal scale and Asagai identifies the questions which obsess her. 'What good is struggle; what good is anything? Where are we all going? And why are we bothering?'

The personal and familial crises are finally resolved by the open challenge offered by the white world. Karl Lindner, whose name suggests non-American origins, is the representative of the white community into which the family had planned to move. He offers to buy the house from them at a profit. The insult is delivered with courtesy but it stings Walter into a response which simultaneously gives him back his dignity and commits him to an involvement which he had sought to escape. Thus in a sense this is a fulfilment of Asagai's prophesy. In speaking of his own political future in Africa he had said, 'They who might kill me even . . . actually replenish me!'

Yet while leaving the Youngers committed to 'new levels of struggle' Miss Hansberry brings about this partial resolution through something of a specious *deus ex machina*. Although she is as antipathetic towards a life printed on dollar bills as Odets had been, it is clear that the spiritual regeneration of the Younger family is ultimately contingent on a ten thousand dollar check, for it is only the money which makes it possible for them to challenge the system under which they have suffered. In making it the necessary prerequisite for their return to dignity and pride Hansberry would seem to demean the faith in human potential which she is ostensibly endorsing. Walter, again like Willy Loman, far from rejecting the system which is oppressing him wholeheartedly embraces it. He rejects the cause of social commitment and compassion and places his faith in the power of money. It is the unintentional irony of this play however that he proves to be right, 'You all want everybody to carry a flag and a spear and sing some marching songs, huh? You wanna spend your life looking into things and trying to find the right and the wrong part . . . There ain't no causes—there ain't nothing but taking in this world, and he who takes most is smartest—and it don't make a damn bit of difference how.' Without the insurance check not only would the dreams have been left to shrivel like raisins in the sun but so would Beneatha's compassion and Walter's courage. Indeed Walter's final conversion, or, as Hansberry would put it, the eventual realisation of his potential, is itself as unconvincing as Biff's similar conversion in *Death of a Salesman*. Her true declaration of faith is, however, embodied in the person of Asagai, the least convincing of the play's characters. This African revolutionary is used by Lorraine Hansberry as a point of reference—as the realisation of the dignity and commitment which exists in Walter only as potential. When Walter, returning home drunk, had leapt onto a table and shouted out the words of a defiant nationalism he had been establishing a contact with the African which served at the same time as a source of contrast and promise. Yet Asagai's self-assurance remains untested. His confident assertion of progress and redemption remains unreal precisely because we do not see him, as we do the Youngers, brought face to face with frustration.

The relationship between the American Negro and the African remains, as Baldwin had in part anticipated it would, a complex arrangement of subtle misunderstandings. Particularly in the nineteen-twenties' 'Negro Renaissance' Africa was seen as a pagan but innocent land [as seen in the poem "No Images" by Waring Cuney] . . . :

> She does not know
> Her beauty,
> She thinks her brown body
> Has no glory.
>
> If she could dance
> Naked,
> Under the palm trees
> And see her image in the river
> She would know.
>
> But there are no palm trees
> On the street,
> And dishwater gives back no images.

While this romantic view of Africa repelled both the Christian and the communist whose approach to that continent was coloured by their own ideology, it was a view which seems to have seized the imagination of many writers. It is certainly clear that *A Raisin in the Sun* accepts unquestioningly the validity of Cuney's symbol. Asagai has no validity outside of this convention. If Hansberry mocks the naïvete with which Beneatha tries to adopt African modes of dress and general culture she leaves unchallenged the assumption that those values stem from a purer source. Yet Asagai's vitality and enthusiasm spring from his own dreams which differ in kind from Walter's only in magnitude and in the fact that they are never put to the test. We see Walter balance his manhood against a dream of success but Asagai remains nothing but an oracle whose declarations make sense only to those who are faithful to the stereotype African of . . . Cuney, rich in wisdom and standing, like the noble savage, as a reminder of primal innocence. Asagai's declaration of the inevitability of change built on courage and compassion, a declaration which clearly represents Lorraine Hansberry's own faith, remains as unconvincing as do the circumstances of Walter's change of heart, 'things will happen, slowly and swiftly. At times it will seem that nothing changes at all . . . and then again . . . the sudden dramatic events which make history leap into the future. And then quiet again . . . And I even will have moments when I wonder if the quiet was not better than all that death and hatred. But . . . I will not wonder long.' (pp. 156-61)

Lorraine Hansberry's greatest achievement lies in her ability to avoid what Saunders Redding has called 'The obligations imposed by race on the average . . . talented Negro'. The obligation to limit one's scope to the immediate but parochial injustices of racial intolerance has for long sapped the creative energy of the Negro writer. Having paid her debt to this tradition with the poor *A Raisin in the Sun,* however, Hansberry achieves a significant break-through with *The Sign in Sidney Brustein's Window* which is clearly in the mainstream of contemporary drama. The Negro is no longer seen as the victim of a savage social situation but becomes an endemic part of a society desperately searching for a valid response to the human condition. Lorraine Hansberry's death at the age of thirty-four has robbed the theatre of the one Negro dramatist who has demonstrated her ability to transcend parochialism and social bitterness. As she has said in an article called "The Negro in the American Theatre", 'while an excessively poignant Porgy was being instilled in generations of Americans, his true-life counterpart was ravaged by longings that were, and are, in no way alien to those of the rest of mankind, and that bear within them the stuff of truly great art. He is waiting yet for those of us who will but look more carefully into his eyes, and listen more intently to his soliloquies.' Regrettably this remains as true in 1966 as it was in 1960 when Hansberry wrote it.

Camus has said that it 'would be impossible to overemphasise the passionate affirmation that underlies the act of revolt and which distinguishes it from resentment. Rebellion, though apparently negative since it creates nothing, is profoundly positive in that it reveals the part of a man which must always be defended.' It is clear that neither James Baldwin nor LeRoi Jones succeed in attaining to this affirmation for their protest never progresses beyond 'resentment'. Lorraine Hansberry's commitment, however, transcends the merely parochial for her rebellion is directed less against intransigent racialism than against the sterility of the absurd and the inconsequence of a theatre founded on distraction. Like Miller, Gelber, Albee and Bellow she clearly sees the dramatist's function as consisting in a compassionate statement of the need for human contact in an unattractive world. Indeed her faith in the need to face reality effectively bridges the gap between confrontation and commitment. (pp. 172-73)

C. W. E. Bigsby, "Lorraine Hansberry," in his Confrontation and Commitment: A Study of Contemporary American Drama, 1959-66, *University of Missouri Press, 1968, pp. 156-73.*

Doris E. Abramson

When Lorraine Hansberry was eight years old, her father bought a house in a middle-class white neighborhood just a few blocks away from the Negro Southside of Chicago. This move precipitated one of the NAACP's most celebrated housing cases: *Hansberry* v. *Lee* (311 U.S. 32). The Illinois Supreme Court had ruled that whites had the right to bar Negroes from their neighborhoods. Carl Hansberry, a wealthy real estate broker, challenged its decision. . . . On November 12, 1940, the Supreme Court reversed the lower court's decision, and the Hansberrys were permitted to occupy their property.

Lorraine Hansberry was born May 19, 1930, in Chicago. She attended Jim Crow grade schools, because, as she put it, "My parents were some peculiar democrats [who] could afford to send us to private schools, but they didn't believe in it." She recalled moving into the white neighborhood:

> My mother . . . sat in that house for eight months with us . . . in what was, to put it mildly, a very hostile neighborhood. I was on the porch one day with my sister when a mob gathered. We went inside, and while we were in our living room, a brick came crashing through the window with such force it embedded itself in the opposite wall. I was the one the brick almost hit.

Incidents of this kind contributed to her father's decision to leave the United States. Though he had been able to become a wealthy businessman and even a United States marshall, he never felt that he had true social freedom. When Carl Hansberry died in 1945, at the age of fifty-one, he was making preparations to move to Mexico. Though his daughter did not agree with "the leaving part," she did agree with her father's assessment of the United States. Several years after his death, she was quoted as saying:

> Daddy really belonged to a different age, a different period. He didn't feel free. One of the reasons I feel so free is that I feel I belong to a world majority, and a very assertive one.

This spirit led her to an early and lasting commitment to the struggle for civil rights.

Her choice of theatre as her medium came after she had moved from the Midwest to New York City, but it was influenced by earlier educational experiences. After graduating from Englewood High School, Lorraine Hansberry went to the University of Wisconsin for two years. At the university she saw plays by Strindberg and Ibsen for the first time, and later said that they influenced her. Earlier, on dates in Chicago, she had enjoyed productions of *Othello* and *The Tempest.* When she moved to New York in 1950, she began hanging around little theatre groups and discovered that "theatre embraces everything I like all at one time."

It is not certain when she began trying to write for the theatre, but in an interview in 1959 she referred to *A Raisin in the Sun* as her fourth and only finished drama.

> I wrote it between my twenty-sixth and twenty-seventh birthdays. One night, after seeing a play I won't mention, I suddenly became disgusted with a whole body of material about Negroes. Cardboard characters. Cute dialect bits. Or hip-swinging musicals from exotic sources.

Encouraged by her husband, Robert Nemiroff, a music

publisher to whom she was married in 1953, Lorraine Hansberry wrote *A Raisin in the Sun* and saw it produced on Broadway. (pp. 239-40)

[Perhaps] most important, Lorraine Hansberry lived up to a promise she had made earlier to her husband: "I'm going to write a social drama about Negroes that will be good art." Critics may still be divided on how good the art is, but most agree with Harold Clurman that *A Raisin in the Sun* is "an honestly felt response to a situation that has been lived through, clearly understood, and therefore simply and impressively stated." [see excerpt above].

A Raisin in the Sun is the first play by a Negro of which one is tempted to say, "Everyone knows it." Thousands of Americans have seen it on the stage in New York, in other large cities, on college campuses, and in community theatres. Many more thousands have seen it on the screen. And, finally, millions of American who might not seek it out have seen the movie on their television screens. (It is fascinating to speculate that the majority of white Americans have had Negroes in their homes *only* via television.) Americans who read could have read *A Raisin in the Sun* in hardcover, in a very inexpensive paperback, printed alone or in anthologies. (p. 241)

It hardly seems necessary, then, to analyze the play scene by scene in order to remind the reader/viewer of those elements that are reflections of American Negro existence. It will be sufficient to pull out moments in the play that demonstrate Lorraine Hansberry's use of Negro problems in creating a play that has become for many white people an introduction to the contemporary Negro.

Much has been written about *A Raisin in the Sun,* about Lorraine Hansberry (who died of cancer in 1965), and about the implications of her Broadway success, but neither the critics nor Miss Hansberry ever acknowledged her debt to Richard Wright's *Native Son* (novel or play), although surely one existed. Both plays are set in Chicago's Southside. Bigger Thomas and Walter Younger are both chauffeurs, black men who feel caged in a white society. And they both "explode" because of a "dream deferred." Walter's explosion, to be sure, is not so fatal as Bigger's, but it erupts from much the same frustration and confusion. Both plays even begin with the same sound—the ringing of an alarm clock. To press comparisons much further would not be fair; it is enough to say that the influences of *Native Son* on *A Raisin in the Sun* are striking. What the later play has that the earlier one lacked is warmth and humor as well as characters who never become categories.

The living room in which the action of *A Raisin in the Sun* takes place is scrupulously described by the playwright; she wants it to be known that the shabbiness comes from the fact that the room has had to accommodate "too many people for too many years." The Negroes who live here, like any other poor family, live with old furniture that reflects their own weariness and poverty. (pp. 241-42)

Three generations in three rooms can lead to various complications. It is soon evident, for example, that the apartment has always been Mama's, with the result that Walter is no more the "head of a household" than a much younger Bigger Thomas was in a meaner apartment in the same part of Chicago. Not much is made of it by the playwright, but the little boy, Travis, has no single authority figure,

and so he plays all three adults off against each other and is, as a result, "spoiled." This kind of domestic situation is common among the poor, black and white. There is, however, an added burden placed upon the Negro adult male; not only is he unmanned by the fact that frequently his wife and mother can more readily find work than he can, but he is also subject to a dominant white society that would keep him a "boy," keep him harmless and "in his place."

A Raisin in the Sun is set up to demonstrate the clash of dreams, a clash between generations, between men and women, and even—because for all its commonality with domestic dramas about white people, and in spite of Miss Hansberry's statement to the contrary, it *is* a Negro play—the clash between black and white. (p. 243)

Lena Younger is the old-fashioned Negro mother (we have already seen her in *Harlem,* in *Native Son,* and in *A Medal for Willie*) who has over the years worked hard, attended church, and made sacrifices for a family and a future in which she has always had faith. Early in the play Ruth tries to speak in favor of Walter's business plans: "Like Walter say—I spec people going to always be drinking themselves some liquor." . . . Mama tells Ruth that she will not be responsible for people drinking liquor; she has no desire to have that on her conscience at this late date.

What Mama wants to do with the insurance money is to put some of it away for Beneatha's schooling and then to make a down payment on a "little old two-story somewhere, with a yard where Travis could play in the summertime." Hers is a simple desire for a home that is the reward of her labors. And lest we think that she will capitulate easily to youth, there are two scenes that show Mama's strength as she stands up first to her daughter and then to her son.

Although Beneatha is a twenty-year-old medical student, she is quite adolescent in her behavior. She is fresh, full of talk about dates and "forms of expression." When she speaks of playing the guitar and riding horseback, one cannot help thinking more of the black bourgeoisie than of a lower-class family. Nor is it surprising to read that Lorraine Hansberry once said of Beneatha, "She's me eight years ago. I had a ball poking fun at myself through her." Beneatha calls her rich boy friend, George Murchison, "shallow" and dismisses her own brother as an "elaborate neurotic."

At one point, when Mama says that her daughter will be a doctor, "God willing," Beneatha answers drily, "God hasn't got a thing to do with it." At first Mama tries gently to get Beneatha to retract her statement, but the girl persists in saying that she is sick of hearing about God. Mama warns her that she is about to get her "fresh little jaw slapped," but Beneatha feels compelled to state her modern position. She assures her mother that she will not go out and commit crimes or immoral acts simply because she no longer believes in God. But she is tired of having God get all the credit for everything the human race achieves. As far as Beneatha is concerned there is only man, and he is the maker of miracles.

Mama slaps her daughter across the face and after a moment of silence, forces her to repeat, "In my mother's house there is still a God." Beneatha does as told, but when her mother is out of earshot, she says quietly to Ruth, "All the tyranny in the world will never put God in the heavens!" Commenting further on her personal relationship to Beneatha, Lorraine Hansberry said, "I don't disagree with anything she says. I believe science will bring more rewards for our generation than mysticism and all that jazz."

Beneatha takes her slap and goes her independent way. It is Walter who will inevitably clash with his mother. Medical school, after all, is more compatible with the Protestant ethic than Walter's highly suspect business adventure.

Some wonderfully warm, humorous scenes involve Beneatha and her African boy friend, Asagai. (Interestingly enough, much of the message of the play is embedded in the lighter speeches.) When she first tells her mother that an African student, an intellectual, will be coming by, Mama says that she has never met an African before. Beneatha is worried that Mama will ask ignorant questions because, like most Americans, she knows the dark continent only from seeing Tarzan movies. "Why should I know anything about Africa?" Mama asks indignantly. Beneatha reminds her not of her people's history but of the missionary work she has supported to save Africans from heathenism. Then, modern young woman that she is, she adds that they need salvation from colonialism, not from heathenism.

Asagai turns out to be a sophisticated young African who is delighted by Beneatha. He brings her a gift of colorful Nigerian robes and records of tribal music. Having draped the robes properly, he admires her, as he says, "mutilated hair and all." She tries to defend her straightened hair, but he reminds her that when they met she told him that she was looking for "her identity." To him she looks more like a queen of the Nile than like a Hollywood queen. She is both flattered and disturbed.

Beneatha protests when Asagai accuses her of being an assimilationist, and yet she seems disturbed by what he is awakening in her. She does not want to be "someone's little episode in America." He bursts into laughter, telling her that she is like all American women; white or black, they are not so liberated as they proclaim themselves to be. (pp. 243-46)

As soon as the check is an actuality, a check that can be held in the hand, Walter is frantic to get his mother to agree to his business plans. Mama is particularly adamant in her refusal because she not only has her old convictions on her side, but she also knows that Ruth has become desperate enough to plan the abortion of a baby Walter has had no knowledge of. To the old woman this is a sign of how ugly their life has become. To her way of thinking liquor stores could only make it uglier.

Finally, in an effort to make her see his dissatisfaction with his job—"Yes, sir; no, sir; very good, sir; shall I take the Drive, sir?"—Walter speaks to her seriously, but with little hope, he says, of being understood:

> Sometimes it's like I can see the future stretched out in front of me—just as plain as day. The future, Mama. Hanging over there at the edge of my days. Just waiting for me—a big, looming blank space— full of nothing. Just waiting for me. (*Pause*)

Mama—sometimes when I'm downtown and I pass them cool, quiet-looking restaurants where them white boys are sitting back and talking 'bout things . . . sitting there turning deals worth millions of dollars . . . sometimes I see guys don't look much older than me—

She interrupts him to ask why he talks so much about money. "Because it is life, Mama!" he says passionately. To which she answers, almost to herself, "Once upon a time freedom used to be life—now it's money." Walter disagrees, saying that it was always money, but "we just didn't know about it." (Psychologists have described the basic Negro personality as "a caricature of the corresponding white personality, because the Negro must adapt to the same culture, must accept the same social goals, but without the ability to achieve them.")

Although it accomplishes nothing, Mama tells Walter about the old days in the South when to stay alive was a goal. And for her it has been enough to work and save, to give her children the freedom allowed in the North. Walter cannot make her understand his frustration. Here, as in *Take a Giant Step,* the generations cannot communicate their different dreams. "The dream deferred is Walter's dream," Max Lerner once wrote, and then he observed:

> Examine it—the dream of getting away from his despised job, of setting up a business with a liquor license, of building it up big, of having pearls to hang around the neck of his wife, of enabling his young son to drive to school in a taxi—and you will see that it isn't particularly Walter's dream as a Negro, nor yet an intensely private one. It is a dream that comes out of the larger culture of the whites, in which Walter is caught up.

Not their disagreement about money or even his refusal to say that he will accept the responsibility of another child, but rather the events that follow persuade Mama to look at Walter in a different light. He stops going to work. If he is at home, he is drinking beer. When he is out, he drives around Chicago in a borrowed car or walks all over the Southside, just looking at Negroes—unemployed ones like himself.

In the midst of a drunken scene in which Walter stands on the table, swaying to Beneatha's recording of African music and speaking to a tribe that he can see in fantasy, George Murchison arrives. ("The Murchisons are honest-to-God-real-*live*-rich colored people, and the only people who are more snobbish than rich white people are rich colored people.") A completely convinced assimilationist, he would be the last one to understand a wild parody of African ritual. George calls Beneatha eccentric, and when she accuses him of being ashamed of his heritage, he reminds her that her heritage is "nothing but a bunch of raggedy-assed spirituals and some grass huts." Although she counters with a proud reference to the Africans "who were the first to smelt iron on the face of the earth," she does agree to change from her Nigerian robes for their date.

Walter has drunk enough beer and had sufficient discouragement about his business prospects to welcome a chance to attack the privileged young Murchison. First he makes fun of the college boy's clothes. Then he goes into a sardonic appreciation of George's "old man," someone who "thinks big." When he suggests that he and George should sit down for a talk sometime, the boy's skepticism and boredom are very evident. Walter is offended to the point of belligerence. He attacks George for not learning anything important in college, not learning to run the world, only to read books, to speak properly, and to wear "fairyish-looking white shoes." George, who has remained aloof until this time, cannot resist saying to Walter, "You're all wacked up with bitterness, man." Walter replies, through clenched teeth:

> And you—ain't you bitter, man? Ain't you just about had it yet? Don't you see no stars gleaming that you can't reach out and grab? . . . You contented son-of-a-bitch. . . . Bitter? Man, I'm a volcano. Bitter? Here I am a giant—surrounded by ants! Ants who can't even understand what it is the giant is talking about.

And soon after this scene Walter learns that his mother has made a down payment on a house in Clybourne Park, in what is a white, not a Negro, neighborhood. Walter turns on his mother then, accusing her of running her children's lives as she wishes. "So you butchered up a dream of mine," he says to her, "you—who always talking 'bout your children's dreams."

It is in response to his bitterness and the despair that she reads in her son's growing alienation from his family that Mama finally admits to Walter that she has been wrong. "I been doing to you," she tells him, "what the rest of the world been doing." Now she tries to make it up to him by giving him the $6500 left after the down payment on the house, for him to put in the bank—$3,000 for Beneatha's education and the rest for his own checking account. He is astonished to hear her say, "I'm telling you to be head of this family from now on like you supposed to be." This moment is a turning point in Walter's fortunes and in the play itself.

The crucial scene in Act II, a scene that begins with enthusiasm and ends in despair, introduces the one white character in the play, a middle-aged man named Karl Lindner. He interrupts a lighthearted scene in which the Youngers (all but Mama) are packing their things in anticipation of the move to their new home. As chairman of the New Neighbors Orientation Committee of the Clybourne Park Improvement Association, Lindner announces that he has come to see the Youngers in order to "give them the lowdown" on the way things are done in Clybourne Park. Commenting on the background of the members of the community, Lindner says that there is no question of racial prejudice. "It is a matter," he explains, "of the people of Clybourne Park believing, rightly or wrongly . . . that for the happiness of all concerned that our Negro families are happier when they live in their *own* communities." The welcoming committee turns out to be nothing more than an attempt to bribe the Youngers to stay out of a white neighborhood. . . . Walter, rising to his role as head of the family, orders him out of the apartment.

The young people are quite amused by the whole idea of the welcoming committee. When Mama is told of the white man's visit, she asks, "Did he threaten us?" Beneatha's answer serves to show youth's relaxed attitude toward what was and is very serious to their parents:

> Oh—Mama—they don't do it like that any more. He talked Brotherhood. He said everybody ought

to learn how to sit down and hate each other with good Christian fellowship.

The relaxed atmosphere of the early part of the scene is easily recaptured, but it is interrupted once again by a doorbell. (The playwright has a sure sense of the dramatic value inherent in shattering moods in this fashion.) When Walter opens the door, it is to admit a frightened little man named Bobo, who confesses to Walter before his astonished family that another partner has disappeared with their money.

Walter cries out in sheer madness now, praying and cursing, begging an absent Willy to bring back the money that was *"made out of my father's flesh."* He falls to the floor sobbing, and he is there when his mother goes to him to ask if all the money is gone. Lifting his head slowly he says, "Mama . . . I never . . . went to the bank at all." His money and Beneatha's, all of it is gone. When Mama has taken in the enormity of his act, she tells her children about their father, who worked himself to death for the money that Walter has given away in a day. Standing over her son, she prays, "Oh, God . . . Look down here—and show me the strength."

On the page this climactic scene seems both melodramatic and sentimental, but it is doubtful that many members of the theatre audience could resist the performance of Claudia McNeil [in the original production of *A Raisin in the Sun* in 1959]. (pp. 246-50)

Act III, in one scene, is short and still in a melodramatic vein. It begins quietly with an episode that further defines Beneatha and Asagai. She tells her African friend about Walter's treachery, and Asagai expresses his concern for her future. Beneatha tells him that she may have stopped caring about being a doctor, about curing hurt bodies. He questions her original impulse if she can so easily give up helping the ailing human race because of her brother's childish mistake. He wants to know why she does not continue to struggle for the future. Disillusioned, she turns the questions back to him and to the Africa of which he dreams; she wants to know what he plans to do about all the crooks and stupid men "who will come into power and steal and plunder the same as before—only now they will be black and do it in the name of the new independence."

His reply is that he is living the answer to her question by getting an education for leadership. And he acknowledges the fact that there will be retrogression before there is progress. Like a good revolutionary, he knows that even his own death could represent an advance for his people. When Asagai asks Beneatha to go home to Nigeria as his bride, she asks for time to consider his proposal. Something about her hesitation implies that she will not go "home to Africa." The tug toward the exotic was present earlier in the play, and while even now she seems flattered by his attention, Asagai remains, for Beneatha, a symbol of the past, not a portent of the future.

The balance of Act III belongs to Walter. It depicts his temptation to accept compromise and then a reversal that leads him into real nobility. At first he announces that he is ready to make a deal with Lindner's welcoming committee. As he explains to Mama, life is divided up between "the takers and the 'tooken.'" He has been among the "tooken," but he has learned to keep his eye on what counts.

One of the most moving statements in the play is made by Mama when she says to Walter in response to his decision:

> Son—I come from five generations of people who was slaves and sharecroppers—but ain't nobody in my family never let nobody pay 'em no money that was a way of telling us we wasn't fit to walk the earth. We ain't never been that poor . . . that dead inside.

Walter's only answer is that he did not make the world the way it is, and he does a heartbreaking imitation of a begging darky: "Yassssssuh! Great White Father, just gi' ussen de money, fo' God's sake, and we's ain't gwine come out deh and dirty up yo' white folks neighborhood."

And yet, by the time Lindner arrives, Walter has had time to consider his mother's words and his own humiliation, and he tells the astonished white man:

> We have all thought about your offer and we have decided to move into our house because my father—my father—earned it. . . . We don't want to make no trouble for nobody or fight no causes—but we will try to be good neighbors. . . . We don't want your money.

When Lindner tries to appeal to Mama's good sense, she says that her son speaks for all of them.

The play ends with Walter's coming into his manhood and the family moving on to a future that promises to be bright only because it is predicated on the strength of the characters as we have come to know them. It is interesting to note Robert Nemiroff's contention that *A Raisin in the Sun* does not have a happy ending, "only a commitment to new levels of struggle," an idea that he says escaped most of the play's critics in 1959. Such an oversight is understandable in view of the fact that critics had nothing but the play before them, not Miss Hansberry's political statements or social proclamations.

John Davis, executive director of the American Society of African Culture, has said that the Negro writer's basic problem has been that "he must write for a non-Negro market which often is also the object of his protest." It would be difficult to disagree with this general statement. He went on, however, to call *A Raisin in the Sun* "social protest" that is "such consummate art" that audiences applaud the very protest that is directed against them. A few observations should be made about both the art and the protest in Lorraine Hansberry's play.

In the first place, members of the Negro community supported this Broadway production of a Negro play as they had supported no other; there were nights, even in New York, when the audience was almost half Negro. This particular Broadway play, then, was not performed for the usual white middle-class audience. Also, the play is not what is generally termed a protest play. The values of white society may have warped Walter Younger . . . , but it is not a play overtly protesting those values. Members of the audience, both white and black, could appreciate the play because Walter's rebellion is meliorated by the conservative values of Mama. In fact, he is shamed into maturity by his mother, which is to say that he is persuaded to accept her version of middle-class values.

Henry Hewes [see excerpt above] felt that the nearest thing to a message in *A Raisin in the Sun* was spoken by Asagai, the Nigerian revolutionist: "I know that we cannot allow life to depend on accidents." But few Americans would hear in this statement, as the critic did, a condemnation of sudden success and overnight acquisition of wealth in our society. Hewes concluded that Negroes are becoming a part of the illusion sometimes called the American myth of success. "Like the rest of us," he predicted, "some will be destroyed by it. But *A Raisin in the Sun* would seem to suggest that when the bubble bursts the families with the most courageous pasts will be best equipped to pick up the pieces."

Other critics were less concerned with social commentary and more concerned with art. Brooks Atkinson [see Hansberry, *CLC*, Vol. 17] wrote that *A Raisin in the Sun* could be regarded as a Negro *Cherry Orchard*. No matter how different the social scale of the characters, he observed, "the knowledge of how character is controlled by environment is much the same, and the alternation of humor and pathos is similar." Kenneth Tynan's main reservation about the Hansberry play was in connection with its sentimentality, "particularly in its reverent treatment of Walter Lee's mother. . . . I wish the dramatist had refrained from idealizing such a stolid old conservative." But, like Max Lerner, he could compare the play favorably with those of Clifford Odets.

Some critics—Miss Hansberry agreed with them, according to a stage manager who knew her a few years after the original production of *A Raisin in the Sun*—called the play a soap opera. It abounds in types: Mama is a tyrannical but good-natured matriarch; Walter, a frustrated young man surrounded by too many women; Beneatha, a free-thinking college student; the African Asagai, a poetic revolutionary; and the one white man, a cliché-ridden suburbanite. The interest in them lies chiefly in the fact that the central characters are Negroes, which is something new to soap opera. Tom Driver [see Hansberry, *CLC*, Vol. 17] went so far as to say that this play would have done well to recover its investment if it had been written by a white woman about a white family. Of the play he concluded:

> As a piece of dramatic writing it is old-fashioned. As something near to the conscience of a nation troubled by injustice to Negroes, it is emotionally powerful. Much of its success is due to our sentimentality over the "Negro question."

After everything is said that can be said about the form and content of the play, one must agree with Harold Clurman about the importance of the Broadway production of *A Raisin in the Sun.* As he put it, "The play is organic theatre: cast, text, direction are homogeneous in social orientation and in sentiment, in technique and in quality of talent." (pp. 250-54)

> *Doris E. Abramson, "The Fifties," in her* Negro Playwrights in the American Theatre 1925-1959, *Columbia University Press, 1969, pp. 165-266.*

Lloyd W. Brown

Ever since the sixties the reputation and significance of several established Black American writers have become issues in the running ethnopolitical debates on Black

American literature. James Baldwin, Ralph Ellison, and LeRoi Jones, for example, have been at the center of confrontations between "militants" and "moderates," Black "extremists" and white "liberals," integrationists and Black nationalists, and so on. And it is increasingly evident that Lorraine Hansberry has joined this list of controversial writers, especially on the basis of her first play, *A Raisin in the Sun* (1959). On the anti-integrationist side, Harold Cruse [see excerpt above] deplores *Raisin* as "the artistic, aesthetic and class-inspired culmination of the efforts of the Harlem leftwing literary and cultural in-group to achieve integration of the Negro in the arts." In other words, it is a "most cleverly written piece of glorified soap opera," a "second-rate" play about working-class Blacks who "mouth middle class ideology." Moreover, the alleged shortcomings of Lorraine Hansberry's integrationist philosophy are linked, somehow, with her supposed inferiority as a dramatic artist. . . . (pp. 237-38)

On the other side of the debate, both C. W. E. Bigsby [see excerpt above] and Richard A. Duprey have praised Hansberry precisely because, in their view, she transcends those "special ethnic group materials." . . . In short, Hansberry's work has been caught up in the continuing conflict between the ethnic criteria of social protesters and the pro-integrationist's ethos of love and reconciliation. And when a critic such as Jordan Miller [see Hansberry, *CLC,* Vol. 17] is confronted with this kind of debate he responds with the art-for-art's-sake thesis. He refuses to discuss Hansberry's work "on the basis of any form of racial consciousness" or "in any niche of social significance," and insists instead on the critic's "obligation" to judge the dramatist's work as "dramatic literature quite apart from other factors."

These three representative viewpoints need to be emphasized here because, taken together, they demonstrate a continuing problem in the study of Black literature: the tendency, for one reason or another, to isolate questions of structure or technique from those of social, or racial, significance. Harold Cruse's reservations about *Raisin* begin with assumptions based, not so much on a searching analysis of the text, but on a jaundiced view of Hansberry's social background (Black middle class) and ideological activities (left-wing "in-groups"). Consequently, his allegations about her dramatic technique are really a species of non sequitur: Hansberry's play is a bourgeois integrationist work, *therefore* it lacks "technical . . . ability." At the opposite extreme Jordan Miller would have us concentrate on the play as a "dramatic structure"—to the esoteric exclusion of Hansberry's obvious preoccupation with "social significance" and "racial consciousness." But this erudite escapism does no more justice to Hansberry's art than Harold Cruse's ideological bias, for, once again, the artist's total achievement is being obscured by the critic's determination to treat technique and social content as if these are unrelated or mutually exclusive.

Bigsby does offer some analysis of Hansberry's dramatic techniques, but the attempt is limited by his preconception that *Raisin* is primarily an integrationist manifesto. The rhetorical design of Hansberry's title is a case in point. Bigsby assumes that the play as a whole incorporates all the thematic tensions (destruction versus fulfillment, despair versus self-realization) that dominate "Harlem," the Langston Hughes poem from which Hansberry takes her

title. And this reading of the play's title justifies the critic's view that the play "clearly represents Lorraine Hansberry's own faith" in the inevitability of change built on courage and compassion. But the fact is that the phrase, "a raisin in the sun," does not embody all of the thematic tensions in Hughes' poem. On the contrary, it is one of the ominous negatives which counterbalance positive possibilities in the conflicts of "Harlem":

> What happens to a dream deferred?
> Does it dry up
> like a raisin in the sun?
> Or fester like a sore—
> And then run?
> Does it stink like rotten meat?
> Or crust and sugar over—
> like a syrupy sweet?

In effect, the connotations of Hansberry's title establish an ironic context which is crucial to an understanding of the play's themes and design. Hughes clusters the ambiguities and tensions of his poem around the experience of a "dream deferred"—a deferred dream may simply end in the drying up of hope (like a raisin in the sun) or, paradoxically, the adversities of frustration may motivate the "syrupy sweet" realization of human potential. Consequently, when Hansberry selects the "raisin" phrase she limits the thematic relevance of Hughes' poem to her play: her themes are concerned, not so much with a fulfilled faith in inevitable changes for the better, but with the drying up of dreams. Hence the basic contextual irony of the title, and of the themes which flow from it, is based on an acceptance of the dream ideal—spiritual and material fulfillment in America—and, simultaneously, on a realistic recognition of those (like Walter Younger) whose dreams, or hopes, have dried up. The point is not that Lorraine Hansberry rejects integration or the economic and moral promise of the American dream, but that she remains loyal to this dream ideal while looking, realistically, at its corruption in the United States. Once we recognize this fundamental strategy, then we will begin to accept the ironic nuances of the play as intrinsic qualities of Hansberry's dramatic insights rather than as the "unintentional" irony that Bigsby attributes to the work. Indeed, there has been a curiously persistent refusal to credit Hansberry with any capacity for irony, and this has led critics to interpret thematic conflicts as mere confusion, contradictions, or as a rather insipid species of eclecticism. On the much-debated Pan-African theme, for example, Harold R. Isaacs finds it difficult to reconcile Hansberry's Black nationalist sympathies and her long-term ideal of human reconciliation. But the complex grasp of self-esteem and human solidarity as compatibles is no more "contradictory" than W. E. B. DuBois's famous and well-considered ideal of ethnic self-awareness coexisting with human unity. . . . Consequently, it is not really an exaggeration of her dramatic insights to assume that the romanticization of Africa, in the person of Asegai, goes hand in hand with the emphasis on the Youngers' American commitment. Indeed, Hansberry's ironic grasp of the Black American's duality enables her to portray (rather than merely succumb to) the African nostalgia which has been nurtured by the Youngers' dreams but which remains realistically counterbalanced by the inexorable facts of the Youngers' American identity (complete with the pervasive American dream). In short, we need to break away from the old condescension which assumes, arbitrarily, that perceptual conflicts within the play are merely reflections of Hansberry's personal confusions rather than reflections of her ironic insight into social and psychological ambiguities that already exist. And, in this connection, the need to reevaluate her themes is especially strong with respect to two interwoven themes: (1) the ambiguity of the American dream itself, and (2) integration as the Black American's means of realizing the dream.

The more familiar irony of the Youngers' poverty is obvious enough: their deprivations expose the gap between the American dream and the Black American reality. But, equally important, both the nature of Walter Younger's ambitions and the success of George Murchison emphasize another paradox. Ideally the promise of the American dream is aimed at the total personality of the individual: the dream is defined not only in moral terms—freedom, equality, justice, and self-realization—but also in material and socio-economic terms. However, in practice, the moral ideals of the dream are invariably subordinated to material criteria and ambitions. Hence the socioeconomic advantages of the affluent society have been culturally ennobled as the passport to spiritual fulfillment, in much the same way that the physical freedom of the slave is a prerequisite for the total realization of human dignity.

The dialectical materialism in which the American dream is rooted in the very staple of the society's cultural modes—as in the television commercials and billboard advertisements in which toothpaste, automobiles, or deodorants promise emotional and sexual fulfillment, or in which images of novelty justify built-in obsolescence by appealing to the dream ideal of inevitable change as improvement, newness as fulfillment, and modernity as achievement. And in Hansberry's play this intrinsic ambiguity of the American dream is demonstrated by the Murchison family, especially by George, whose bourgeois materialism illustrates the American propensity to confuse material achievement with the total promise of the American dream. Thus, however well intentioned, Bigsby actually reduces Hansberry's social insights to the level of idealistic naivete when he assumes that she dissociates the socioeconomic issue from "the need for spiritual replenishment which can only come with a return of dignity." And when critics such as Harold Cruse dismiss *Raisin* as bourgeois soap opera, they ignore the dramatist's fundamental ambivalence toward the American dream: having affirmed her faith in the human possibilities of the dream by deploring its deferment in the lives of some Americans (as indicated in her title), Lorraine Hansberry underscores the moral ambiguities that are inherent in the process of actually realizing the dream, in the lives of other Americans (like the Murchisons).

Moreover, when Hansberry dwells on the deferred dreams of the poor, she heightens the ironic paradox of all these ambiguities. For in the cultural psychology of the Youngers' community (and of Langston Hughes's Harlem) the deprived and the disadvantaged are like the affluent bourgeoisie in that they, too, view materialistic achievements as self-justifying, even self-redeeming, goals. The acquisition of material things (either across the counter in legal trade, or in the "revenge" looting of urban riots) is really a means of participating vicariously in the affluent society. This vicarious participation increases in value in direct ratio to the deprived individual's role of "outsider." And

Walter Younger is an outsider on two counts: he is both Black and poor. Hence Walter's unabashed obsession with the insurance money as a key to instant affluence fits the materialistic priorities of the outsider's dream. In presenting the moral conflict between the spiritual promises of the dream ideal and the frank materialism of the impoverished dreamer, Hansberry is being faithful to the cultural psychology of American poverty, and to the ironic basis of her thematic design. And, viewed in this context, the importance of the money in the Youngers' eventual choice—the purchase of a house in a white neighborhood—is not the unintentional irony that C. W. E. Bigsby condescendingly attributes to Hansberry. On the contrary, this emphasis on money as the key to moral and spiritual fulfillment is consistent with the playwright's ironic overview of the socioeconomics of the American dream ideal.

The ambiguous implications of the money are also integrated with the ironies which underlie Hansberry's treatment of ideological choices between integration or separation. The crucial factor in the presentation of these choices is the play's strong hints that the choices have already been severely limited by the negative emphasis of the "raisin" title. Given the pervasive connotations of dried up hopes and deferred dreams, then the very notion of choice, with all its attendant implications of free will, has been restricted to a set of ironically balanced alternatives. From the viewpoint of the integrationist ideal, Mama is commendable in her determination to use the insurance check to buy the house. And this choice, such as it is, offers its own advantages over Walter's crassly materialistic scheme to invest the money into a dubious liquor scheme. But if housing integration is praiseworthy on the ideal principles of the American dream, then it is difficult to accept the Younger venture into a determined and hostile neighborhood as a complete fulfillment of the dream ideal. The embittering realities of enforced housing integration in Hansberry's own family life is ample evidence that she was well aware that enforced or legal integration is rather different from the ideal concept of integration as the complete reconciliation of human beings. Once again, Hansberry has ironically juxtaposed the ideal possibilities of the dream with the limitations of the American reality. Mama's (and Walter's) moral triumph over white racists is real enough, and it is undoubtedly significant in the confirmation of Walter's self-respect. But as the humiliations and hardships of the Hansberry family demonstrated in a white Chicago neighborhood, the tactical defeat of individual racists is not, ipso facto, the destruction of racism. At best it is a self-ennobling start without the certainty of a satisfactory conclusion based on genuine reconciliation. Compassion and understanding may very well be the dominant social values espoused by *Raisin,* as Bigsby and Duprey argue. But a realistic, rather than ideologically subjective, reading of the play hardly supports their view that these qualities "transcend" (racist?) history. For it is obvious enough that compassion and understanding can only transcend conflict and division if such ideals are shared equally by all sides. And it should be equally obvious that the Youngers' new white neighbors are neither compassionate nor understanding. In other words, the integration which is eventually realized at the end of the play has been severely, and realistically, limited by Hansberry's awareness of the contradiction between the dream ideals of reconciliation and equality, and the social realities of hatred and unresolved conflict. So without debunking the integrationist ideal, Hansberry confirms the inexorable barriers and the frustrations represented by her dominant raisin symbol.

Conversely, the rebuff to Walter's liquor-store scheme is no more decisive, morally, than the triumph of Mama's integrationism. Admittedly, Walter is no businessman; and his scheme is motivated by a self-serving materialism which, as we have seen, is intrinsic to the moral and psychological ambiguities of the American dream itself. But the fact still remains that the long-term socioeconomic problems of the Younger family have not been solved by the final disposition of the money on behalf of Mama's crusade for integration and for the reclamation of (Walter's) Black manhood. The Youngers now own a house in a better (white) neighborhood, but Walter's prospects for even a moderate socioeconomic self-sufficiency remain bleak; and there have been no changes in the general economic frustrations which have left their mark on [the furnishings]:

> the furnishings of this room were actually selected with care and love and even hope—and brought to this apartment and arranged with taste and pride.
>
> That was a long time ago. Now the once loved pattern of the couch upholstery has to fight to show itself from under acres of crocheted doilies and couch covers which have themselves finally come to be more important than the upholstery. And here a table or a chair has been moved to disguise the worn places in the carpet; but the carpet has fought back by showing its weariness, with depressing uniformity, elsewhere on its surface.
>
> Weariness has, in fact, won this room. . . . All pretenses but living itself have long since vanished from the very atmosphere of this room.
>
> (pp. 238-45)

Despite the pride and ebullience with which the play concludes, it is difficult, even then, to escape the grim reminders of these furniture symbols in the opening scene—the more difficult because the concluding scene is dominated by the same pieces of furniture as they are transferred from the old apartment to the new house. The point is that Hansberry offers no easy promise that the old frustrations and "weariness" will be left behind, or that there will be inevitable change in terms of socioeconomic achievement and complete human reconciliation. For after we have duly acknowledged all the bourgeois excesses and the poverty-inspired expectations which encourage exclusively materialistic images of the American dream, among the Murchisons and the Youngers alike, it is still a fact that the American dream ideal seeks to fulfill both the material and spiritual needs of the human personality. And as long as material and attitudinal barriers persist there will be no complete realization of the American dream for the Youngers. What they do achieve at the end of the play is neither the transcendental social triumphs envisioned by Bigsby's integrationist ethic, nor the facile soap-opera resolutions derided by the pro-separatist Cruse. Their main achievement lies in an incipient (rather than full-blown) self-esteem; but within the ironic design of Hansberry's themes, this is still counterbalanced by the forbidding prospects for both material opportunities and social regeneration as a whole. The African student, Asegai, is really

an idealistic embodiment of that kind of self-esteem, but he is far from being the mouthpiece of Hansberry's ideology, as Bigsby argues. For his ringing rhetoric of optimistic self-esteem comes easily in an Africa already being swept by the now famous winds of anti-colonial change. But the uncertain future of the Youngers and the persistent "weariness" of that old furniture undercut, or qualify, this optimism in an American context. And this, surely, is the ultimate irony of the play: that moral malaise and spiritual weariness have tarnished the characteristically American optimism in dreams-for-change, change-as-improvement, and improvement-as-humanization; that despite all the hallowed myths of change and the cherished dream of ideals of human fulfillment, American society allows far less room for optimism about real change than do the despised societies of the so-called underdeveloped world. (pp. 245-46)

> *Lloyd W. Brown, "Lorraine Hansberry as Ironist: A Reappraisal of 'A Raisin in the Sun',"* in Journal of Black Studies, *Vol. 4, No. 3, March, 1974, pp. 237-47.*

Douglas Turner Ward

A Raisin in the Sun is history, but not just history. Contained in it is proof of why and how Lorraine's works still speak to us today. I refer to the prophetic quality of the drama expressed through the character of Walter Lee Younger.

Most interpretations of *Raisin* and of Walter Lee stress Walter Lee's "becoming a man" at the play's climax, as he refuses to cravenly "sell out" black integrity, legacy, values, etc. Inevitably, these analyses imply that previous to this denouement, Walter Lee has been merely the repository of all the negative, materialistic aspirations of American society—only redeemed in the end by his opting to "grow up." I consider this interpretation too tendentiously simplistic.

Lorraine's real triumph (and here I acknowledge my subjective relationship to the material, having interpreted the role as a performer) is the depiction of Walter Lee as a complex, autonomous character who thinks and acts not as an author's marionette, but as a harbinger of all the qualities of character that would soon explode into American reality and consciousness.

It is not Walter Lee's action at the end of the play, as meaningful as it is to his development and inspiring for the audience, but his central presence and thrust *throughout the play* that I would emphasize. As fully dimensional as the other characters are, compared to Walter Lee's openendedness, they are closed entities. Even though Mama Younger is a pillar of strength, ethical wisdom and moral rectitude, her manner is familiar; we have seen her before. As marvelous as Beneatha and Asagai are in exemplifying positive awareness and intellectual consciousness, they are not broadly typical.

It is Walter Lee, the bearer of aims and goals that have been conditioned by the prevailing values of the society, who is, dramatically, most representative. It is Walter Lee—flawed, contradictory, irascible, impulsive, furious and, most of all, desperate—who emerges as the most unique creation for his time and ours. It is his behavior throughout the play—his restless impatience, his discontent with the way things are, his acute perception of societal disparities, his fury at status inequities, his refusal to accept his "place"—which gives the play prophetic significance, for these traits are not embodied in an exceptional prototype but are the properties of an average person, a typical member of the broad black majority. Most of the 1959 audience, encountering this anger within such a prevalent type, felt threatened. He made them uneasy; he raised unsettling doubts; he was difficult to identify with. Where would all this raging frustration lead? Despite his fixation with America's pragmatism and dreams of success, he was, in his energy, an omen. That energy was soon to erupt into American reality with a vengeance.

I am not certain that, in creating Walter Lee, Lorraine was even fully cognizant of the extent of her accomplishment. Indeed, I think a close reading of the play reveals her ambiguity. A tendency exists in the writing to undercut the weight and seriousness of Walter's desperation by having other characters dismiss his behavior as being that of a headstrong tantrum-thrower. This tendency does not, however, negate his achieved stature. He remains the pivot of the play around which everything revolves. And no matter what we have experienced in the years since his entrance, the Walter Lees of the world have yet to be reckoned with.

This is the reason why *A Raisin in the Sun* still remains fresh, and why we continue to be able to discover new aspects of ourselves in the mirror of Lorraine Hansberry's art. (pp. 224-25)

> *Douglas Turner Ward, "Lorraine Hansberry and the Passion of Walter Lee," in* Freedom-ways, *Vol. 19, No. 4, fourth quarter, 1979, pp. 223-25.*

Helene Keyssar

When Lorraine Hansberry died in 1965 at the age of thirty-five, she was not only the first black playwright to have achieved significant national recognition but also one of very few American women playwrights to have been noticed at all by the general public. . . . Lorraine Hansberry's fame has been due almost exclusively to the resounding success of her first completed script, *A Raisin in the Sun*. . . . Winner of the Drama Critics' Circle Award for best American play of the 1958-59 season, *A Raisin in the Sun* went on to play 530 performances in New York City and had countless other presentations on stage both in this country and abroad. For many Americans, the play may be best known in its film version, which won a special Cannes Film Festival award in 1961 and has since been shown repeatedly on television. (p. 113)

The success of *A Raisin in the Sun* is important to the history of black drama; it is also notable in a larger historical context. *A Raisin in the Sun* is the best known of the black dramas that transform into theatrical terms the political strategy of integration. The play includes only one white person in its cast, and this person, Mr. Lindner, appears in only two brief scenes; yet *A Raisin in the Sun* is vividly a drama of "contact of black and white." Hansberry's strategy is an attempt to reveal to the white audience how much black and white people really are alike; she wants

the audience to desire the fulfillment of the personal dreams of the characters of the play. If white spectators can acknowledge both this likeness and the aspirations of the characters, they can abolish their fears; black and white people might then live together harmoniously. Because white people are not ordinarily in situations through which they can see the daily lives of black people, the play will provide this experience. Black spectators will find nothing seductive in the presentation of black characters living out their lives, but the play can provide the pleasure and the terror of a rare instance of public acknowledgement that this place and these people are important. (pp. 113-14)

Hansberry's own biography is remarkably coherent with both the historical period in which she grew up and the conflicted world reflected in her drama. Born in Chicago in 1930, Hansberry as a child saw her father fight the Illinois Supreme Court so that his family could live in a house they had purchased in a middle-class white neighborhood. Hansberry's father won the legal battle in the Supreme Court, but Doris Abramson quotes Hansberry as remembering the open hostility with which her family was met by their white neighbors [see excerpt above]. (p. 114)

Hansberry left Chicago to attend the University of Wisconsin for two years; she also took courses at Roosevelt College in Chicago and the University of Guadalajara in Mexico. In 1950, she moved to New York City, where she wrote for *Freedom* newspaper, lived in Greenwich Village, and came to know many of the black and white left-wing intellectuals of the period. During the 1950s, she began a number of playscripts, although *A Raisin in the Sun* was the first drama she actually completed. (pp. 114-15)

Both admirers and censors of Hansberry's dramaturgy agree that mainstream American is the appropriate location for her work and reputation. Although critical evaluations of *A Raisin in the Sun* vary considerably, there can be little dispute concerning what *A Raisin in the Sun* is about: The play dramatizes the efforts and frustrations of a family in pursuit of the American dream. The title of the play is itself an allusion to this theme. "A raisin in the sun" is an image drawn from a Langston Hughes poem that presents the basic rhetorical questions apparent in Hansberry's play. Hughes's poem, taken from the volume *Montage of a Dream Deferred*, is almost an outline of the events enacted in *A Raisin in the Sun*. . . . Perceived as a poem about black people, Hughes's verse takes on particular concrete meanings, just as the black characters of Hansberry's play specify the elements of the plot because of their racial identities. There is little question, however, that the substantive center of both works is simply a description of what happens to a dream deferred.

In *A Raisin in the Sun* what happens to the deferred dream is just as Hughes imagines it. The Younger family of Hansberry's play are industrious, working-class Chicago black people. The sixty-year-old matriarch of the family, Mrs. Younger (Mama), came north with her husband years before the play begins in order to fulfill the American dream for her children. Although the family has survived except for Mr. Younger, who died of overwork, dreams of leisure and prosperity have almost dried up when the play begins. Walter Lee Younger, Mrs. Younger's thirty-five-year-old son, has been working for years as a chauffeur and is disgusted with his demeaning labor and his inability to go into business for himself; his wife, Ruth, is weary of her work as a domestic but is most deeply troubled by her sagging marriage, which she bears "like a heavy load." (Hansberry exploits Hughes's line: Early in the play we discover that Ruth is pregnant.) Walter Lee's twenty-year-old sister, Beneatha, is a medical student who has developed her own tough intellectual "crust." She is too immersed in her own plans and fantasies to understand or tend to the sore festering in her family. (pp. 115-16)

In *A Raisin in the Sun,* the dream is not once but twice deferred. Indeed, as the play commences, the dream is not only being renewed but is tantalizingly close to becoming reality. A check for ten thousand dollars, the payment from Mr. Younger's life-insurance policy, is about to come into Mama's hands. Everyone in the family agrees that it is Mama's money to do with as she wishes, but each person, and Walter Lee especially, has his not-so-secret dreams of how to spend this sudden wealth. As we witness episodes during one month in the Younger household, we see the dreams revealed, suspended, destroyed, and renewed again. In the end, the Youngers will move into a new house that is the fulfillment of one fantasy and the beginning of others at the expense of many dreams deferred, and others blurred.

Doris Abramson has called attention to the similarities between the plots of *A Raisin in the Sun* and Richard Wright's *Native Son,* written initially as a novel and later made into a play. Abramson notes that in both works, the central male character is employed as a chauffeur and " 'explodes' because of a 'dream deferred.' " Those similarities do exist, but a more revealing comparison can be made between Theodore Ward's *Big White Fog* and *A Raisin in the Sun.* Both works are concerned with the aspirations and frustrations of black Chicago families and the individual members of each family play somewhat parallel roles within the family itself and the larger society. Both plays also raise questions about an African heritage, education, housing, marital relationships. These similarities suggest some congruence in at least the dramatic image of the black family in America. What is more provocative, however, is that both *Big White Fog* and *A Raisin in the Sun* reveal the potency of the American dream for black families while simultaneously showing that the dream evokes acute frustration and confusion for many black people. While there are skeptics in each instance, members of both families have lived as if it were indeed true that they had as good a chance for comfort and prosperity as any one else in the United States. These people still hope that good, honest labor will bear security as its fruit. In each play, the audience, at least, is led to perceive the fallacies of such a belief. Part of the frustration for each family occurs because the values and life-styles they embrace or aspire to are distinctly middle-class, but racial barriers that are in turn tied to financial and occupational limits not only prevent upward mobility but tend to push each family increasingly into the lower class. This descrepancy between class consciousness and actual participation in a class is both less severe and more directly confronted in *Big White Fog* than in *A Raisin in the Sun.* Neither play overtly employs the language of class identity or class conflict, but spectators for each play should be troubled by the distinction between what initially appears to be a fluid world and what is eventually revealed as a rigid class

structure. The important connection between *Big White Fog* and *A Raisin in the Sun* is that not only over the course of two decades has little changed in the explicit separations and injustices between black and white Americans, but the structure of the society that determines the nature of the contact of black and white has remained essentially the same.

To achieve such an understanding is not, however, ostensibly the main intent of either *Big White Fog* or *A Raisin in the Sun.* Indeed, the strategy of *A Raisin in the Sun* is almost opposite to that of *Big White Fog.* Whereas Ward attempted to show the flaws in any program proposed as an "answer" to the difficulties of black Americans in a white society, Hansberry writes to persuade a white audience to accept racial integration. The strategy Hansberry uses to effect her intention is exceptionally accessible to both reader and spectators. From the play's first lines through its last, Hansberry leads the audience to feel at home with the theatrical manner of *A Raisin in the Sun* and the world it presents. The realistic setting, characters, and dialogue of *A Raisin in the Sun,* bound to a linear plot that fixes the audience's attention by presenting a problem and withholding its solution until the last scene, are for a white audience comfortingly similar to the modes of American drama anthologized in paperbacks and seen yearly on Broadway. *A Raisin in the Sun* appears to be O'Neill without heavy symbols, Miller without allegory, Williams without flashbacks; from the moment the curtain rises on the customary box set, the audience feels reassured that this play will not assault its sensibilities or make disturbing demands on its relation to the stage.

Equally central to Hansberry's strategy, the specific characteristics of the people on stage and the problems they confront are recognizable and familiar. There is, of course, for white spectators one essential difference in the characters before them: They are all black. But this is, simply, the point. No spectator can ignore the blackness of the people onstage, but the white spectator is also led to perceive how much these people are like him and his family. The audience is drawn into the family onstage by the presentation in Act I of incidents so like those we are accustomed to in our own families, be they black or white, that we come to feel kinship with the stage family. Hansberry impresses us so consistently with our similarities to the people on stage that when, in Act II, a strange white man who is in no way connected to the family enters the room, he is an intruder to white spectators as well as to black spectators and those onstage.

Nor does Hansberry rest with showing likenesses. The black characters onstage not only arouse empathy through the ordinariness of their problems and behaviors, they are often admirable and, more frequently, witty and funny. The Youngers relieve anxieties in white spectators and reaffirm self-respect in black spectators, but they also delight and interest their entire audience. *A Raisin in the Sun* resists classification as a comedy or farce because of its persistently somber undertone and the frequent proximity of events to tragic resolution, but Hansberry does skillfully and consistently use humor as a kind of insurance for the success of her intention: The laughter that the dialogue incites is more frequently with the Youngers than at them. That laughter insures that we will like these people, that we will find their presence before us pleasing. If the white audience can find the Youngers pleasing in the theater, they may then accept them in their neighborhoods and schools. Each moment of the play not only amuses us or holds us in suspense, it also provides a stone that when laid beside or above all the others, will seem to make a firm wall for a house we can imagine inhabiting.

The set on which the curtain of *A Raisin in the Sun* rises is of a realistically detailed living room. The furnishings here suggest many years of use; the dwelling is crowded and therefore initially chaotic and oppressive for the audience. . . . The play begins in the quiet of early morning sleep. The stillness is broken and the play commenced by the annoying ring of an alarm clock. Those onstage and off are being told that it is time to wake up.

The opening scene can hardly fail to elicit some sense of shared experience between audience and characters. Ruth, the young wife and mother of the household, is stumbling around the house attempting to rouse her family from sleep. She clearly plays this role every morning, and it is a chore that we can recognize while we also sympathize with the annoyance of those trying to catch a last three seconds of sleep. We discover immediately that the bathroom is outside the apartment, across the hall, and this, with the worn furniture, supports the impression that the Youngers are poor. There is a no-nonsense, assertive air about Ruth's reveille, but she also nags from her first words. Her nagging is softened because it is not self-pitying; it creates an honest identification in the spectator. The sound of Ruth's language, spoken in a consistent but always comprehensible dialect, augments the sense of verisimilitude created by the set and situation. The omission of verb parts and vowels, the frequent lack of subject-verb agreement, the persistent use of "ain't" may not be an entirely accurate representation of Chicago's black-ghetto dialect, but these variances from "standard" English usage create the illusion of a specific and appropriate language for this place. . . . [The use of dialect] is part of Hansberry's strategy. The white spectator should eventually be able to admit that he understands what is being said, that if the differences between the language onstage and the language of the spectator do not create an impossible barrier in the theater, they need not create hostility in the world outside.

While the spectator is juggling all these immediate impressions of the place, Walter Lee enters and, though not yet quite awake, promptly informs the audience of the central object of conflict in the play: After two brief questions about the availability of the bathroom, Walter asks, "Check coming today?" Both the question and Ruth's answer that "they" said it wouldn't come until Saturday and that she "hopes to God" Walter is not going to start talking about money first thing in the morning provide important information about these characters' anxieties and the events of the play. The immediate mention of the check and the indication from Ruth that it is a constant subject of conversation make us curious about the check's source, and significance. We are made wary of Walter, to whom the check matters so much. There may also be some sympathetic recognition of Ruth, who seems weary of the subject of money.. . . . (pp. 116-20)

The audience is given another clue to tension between Ruth and Walter when Ruth asks Walter what kind of eggs he wants. Walter replies, "Not scrambled," and Ruth obviously proceeds to scramble eggs. This may stimulate laughter in the audience, but it also creates a slight antagonism toward Ruth and sympathy for Walter. Moments like this, in which we laugh at a line or action but then catch ourselves in an awareness that there is an underlying bitterness or sobriety, recur frequently in the play and are central to creating an experience for the audience that is felt as both troubling and pleasurable.

The next line locates the action in time for the audience and suggests the kind of news that interests the Youngers. Reading the newspaper, Walter says, "Set off another bomb, yesterday!" We know that the play is occuring sometime after World War II, and we are reminded that this is a time in history when many people vaguely feared this new form of holocaust. The dialogue goes on to reveal more of the tension between Ruth and Walter—Walter's friends are keeping Travis up too late—but then Ruth's nagging is suddenly interrupted by Walter's unexpected observation, "You look young this morning, baby." This is not only a surprising comment for the audience to hear, but it also draws us to Walter. His tender and sexual acknowledgment of his wife extends our sympathy for him as the victim of Ruth's complaints. We are then dismayed when Ruth refuses the compliment and pleased again by Walter's light retort: "First thing a man ought to learn in life is not to make love to no colored woman first thing in the morning. You all some evil people at eight o'clock in the morning." These lines illustrate cogently one of Hansberry's strategic devices: Walter makes the comment specific to "colored" women, but it is as true (or untrue) for white women as well. In the act of laughing at Ruth and Walter—at others—both black and white spectators can recognize themselves. The black spectator can respond directly with a "yea" or an "okay" to the articulation of a common experience; the white spectator will take an extra step of applying the assertion to the women he or she knows. Even such minor moments of self-recognition contribute to the important and distinct experience that theater can give us.

The next episode furthers our empathy with the family. Travis comes in to breakfast, asks about the check, thus reminding us of its imminent arrival, then asks for fifty cents and gets into a minor row with his mother. Everyone will recognize here a familiar morning scene, including Ruth's scoldings about her son's uncombed hair and the child's sullen politeness. As Travis leaves for school, however, there is suddenly more fun and affection displayed on stage than may be apparent in most homes. Ruth speaks what she knows Travis is thinking to himself: "Oh, Mama makes me so mad sometimes, I don't know what to do . . . I wouldn't kiss that woman good-bye for nothing in this world." Ruth has changed the mood for both her son and the audience. She is both funny and tender; we laugh at her and we like her. We can also recognize the game being played between mother and son, and we can probably associate with both sides. We may well go farther and admire Ruth, knowing that often we are neither as clever or as understanding or as honest in similar situations. As Walter did a moment earlier, Ruth has now become a particular and interesting personality; she is no longer any mother or wife in any household, but she is not so unique that she disorients us.

Hansberry's sense of timing here is perfect, for we are not

allowed to linger in this tenderness until it becomes maudlin. Travis breaks the mood by simply being a young boy. He exploits his mother's good humor by renewing his plea for money, which she again refuses to give, and it is now Walter's turn to gain his son's affection. In the first really troubling moment in the play, Walter hands his son fifty cents and then fifty cents more to "take a taxicab to school or something!" Both Ruth and the audience know that Walter is deliberately challenging Ruth's authority with her son and daring her to a confrontation. Walter has asserted his power to both his son and his wife, and although the audience may not feel the disgust that Ruth exhibits and may find Walter's gesture familiar, it also knows that what Walter has done is wrong for both his child and his marriage.

With Travis now departed, Walter gets the conversation back to the subject on his mind from the start of the scene: the check. Although our curiosity may have been diverted by the intervening dialogue, we are glad to find out more about this matter. Walter is quick to reveal his purpose: He wants Ruth to convince his mother to give him the money she is about to receive so that he, with two other men, can invest it in a liquor store. Ruth responds with some skepticism but mostly with disinterest. As she reminds Walter to eat his eggs, the eggs again become a source of humor and a more serious message. In a funny but bitter diatribe, Walter summarizes his frustration and his view of the condition of marital relationships: "That's it. There you are. Man say to his woman: I got me a dream. His woman say: Eat your eggs. Man say: I got to take hold of this here world, baby! And a woman will say: Eat your eggs and go to work. Man say: I got to change my life, I'm choking to death, baby! And his woman say— Your eggs is getting cold!" Verbal repetition and the juxtaposition of the sublime and the mundane lead us to laugh in response to Walter's scenario. Our laughter may be limited, however, by annoyance at his narrow vision of woman and by sympathy for the real pain breaking through his parody. We are meant to hear the plea for help in his words and feel disturbed for him. Hansberry makes it even more difficult to withhold pity from Walter when, as he continues describing his present sense of himself, Ruth does interrupt to tell him to eat his eggs. Ruth's defense is that Walter has said the same thing every day, and that it is nothing new that Walter would rather be his own boss than the white man's chauffeur. Her defense mellows our response to her, as does her final quip, "So—I would rather be living in Buckingham Palace." Our sympathetic laughter is cut off quickly, however, by Walter, who resumes his attack, this time specifying that he is talking about what is wrong with "the colored woman." What he argues is that black women do not make their men feel potent, that they are castrating through indifference.

The intentions of this series of speeches, and our reactions to them, are complicated and perhaps not clearly conceived by Hansberry. Walter's words can divide both men and women in the audience and black people from white people. One could perceive his attack as the somewhat didactic and well-known argument that, because of the conditions of slavery and its aftermath, the black man has been rendered impotent, and that the legendary endurance of the black woman, coupled with her easier access to jobs, have exacerbated rather than assuaged the black man's impotence. Those who disagree with this understanding of

history may be distanced from the world of the play, and even those who concur with Walter may feel uncomfortable with this "reality." Walter's words may also draw our focus to the differences between white people and black. But it is equally possible that the white audience may see Walter's assertions as remarking another point in common with black people. . . . [At least some white men in the audience might] be driven to protest Walter's belief that it is the *unique* plight of black men to be cursed with "women with small minds." This would be a trap fully in keeping with Hansberry's intentions to persuade white people of their likenesses to black people. The device could be especially successful because it would suggest further that black people, as well as white people, erroneously think of their problems as racially distinct.

Hansberry's wish to draw our attention here to sex-based roles rather than racial identities is substantiated in the very next scene. Beneatha, Walter's twenty-year-old sister, enters and is immediately engaged in a sarcastic and increasingly sharp exchange with her brother. We pay close attention to Beneatha because her responses to Walter's jabs and queries are quick, witty, and often very funny. Their repartee reveals Walter's anxiety about the claims of others in the family to Mama's check and thus makes us uneasy about Walter because of the suggestion of his selfishness. (pp. 120-23)

While we ponder the potential conflict over money, we are also being assaulted with an increasingly forceful impression of Walter's sexism. Walter's first remark to his sister is paternalistic; his second, "You a horrible-looking chick at this hour," will warn some spectators of his attitude toward women through his use of the word "chick." He proceeds from there to a more overt sexism, commenting— and the impression is that he has said this before—that it "Ain't many girls who decide to be a doctor." Finally, Walter is blatantly chauvinistic and demands to know why Beneatha couldn't just be a nurse "like other women—or just get married and be quiet." (pp. 123-24)

The blatancy of Walter's chauvinism suggests that Hansberry intends the audience to refuse both Walter's perception and his attitude. It is not clear, however, that some spectators, particularly in the late 1950s and still in the 1970s, might not cheer Walter on sympathetically. Hansberry's central intent that we recognize the characters as distinct but knowable people, with whom we share problems, will work whether we support or condemn Walter. Her attempt to "raise our consciousness" about sex roles is not skillfully controlled or clearly conceived but occurs as a repeated provocation throughout the play.

Just as in the previous scene with Travis, the heaviness of the confrontation of the man with the women is broken on the edge of a departure. Because Walter has given his son extra money, he now has no money of his own and must return to ask Ruth for carfare. Her teasing response, "Fifty cents?," when Walter asks for some money will elicit laughter and relieve anxiety about both characters.

Once Walter has left, it is time for Mama's entrance, and her imposing appearance makes clear that the stage needs to be somewhat emptied to allow the audience to receive Mama for the first time. Her first line and movement set up much of our response to her. The voice of authority and decorum sounds in her "Who that 'round here slamming doors at this hour?" We know this is a person who commands respect. But her immediate attention to a scraggly little plant trying to survive on the one windowsill in the apartment is a symbolic gesture that reveals the softness in Mama and leads us to expect, too, that her decisions will reflect concern for the vulnerable and the brave.

The following scene affirms our initial impressions of Mama. She is, foremost, a mother. As that role is overbearing, she arouses our impatience; as it is loving, she elicits our affection. . . . In her bickering with Ruth about the latter's rearing of the boy, it becomes clear that Mama behaves as the stereotypical interfering mother-in-law. This revelation arouses our antipathy for Mama and our sympathy for Ruth. The pattern of effect is continued when Ruth decides, somewhat to the audience's surprise, to plead to Mama Walter's case for his business venture. Mama's response to the request is more negative than was Ruth's initially, but Mama's grounds, although we may find them foolish, are not disputable; she feels drinking is wrong and a liquor business only adds a bad mark to her ledger in life. We don't dislike Mama for her refusal, but we may be disappointed by her obstinate refusal to consider Walter's dream. (pp. 124-25)

As in most scenes of *A Raisin in the Sun,* the weight of gloom is not allowed to rest for long. After Mama's refusal, we are given further reason for anxiety in Mama's observation that Ruth looks ill and in Ruth's affirmation that she is tired. Then Mama comes to the audience's rescue with quick-witted remarks about white people. She tells Ruth that she will call Ruth's employer and say she has the flu, and when Ruth asks, "Why the flu?" Mama responds, "Cause it sounds respectable to 'em. Something white people get, too. They know about the flu. Otherwise they think you been cut up or something when you tell 'em you sick." Amusement in response to these lines may be greater among black spectators than white ones, but it is difficult to imagine Mama's words offending anyone. The passage strikes at the absurdity of white people's assumptions about black people, but it does not suggest any unpardonable or unalterable sin. White spectators are urged to laugh at themselves in the way they might if a child reveals that she accurately understands something that adults have disguised because of the child's innocence. The passage also reminds white spectators of their responsibility to treat black people fairly. (p. 125)

The remainder of Scene i provides us with hints that arouse our curiosity [about how the money will be spent] and set up the possibilities for the rest of the play. Mama's talk of her dream as a young woman of owning her own house suggests that this is her fantasy about spending the money. Mama's descriptions of her deceased husband's virtues, which seem at this point to be a sentimental gimmick to arouse sympathy for the widow, actually set up a sense of heritage that will become crucial in the final scene of the play. Mama's memory of the baby she lost with much grief brings the idea of pregnancy onto the stage, and may lead some spectators to guess at the end of Scene i that Ruth's collapse is caused by a condition as ordinary as the flu or fatigue, but different from them. These various hints sustain our interest in the events of the play, but also add to a sense of Mama as a good and easily recognizable woman who has suffered much and should be relieved of some burdens.

Before Scene i ends, we are also given the most overt example thus far of Hansberry's strategy. Beneatha returns to the stage from the bathroom. She becomes involved in a row with her mother so typical of the disputes that occur between a mother and an almost adult daughter that one can hear spectators saying, "That's exactly like *our* family." Beneatha initially annoys her mother by using the Lord's name in vain. The spectator's sympathies here will probably vary according to his or her attitude toward religion. Beneatha then mentions her latest hobbyhorse, guitar lessons, and is accused by Mama and Ruth of "flitting" from one interest to another. Beneatha's outrage at not being taken seriously is both so typical of her youth and so clichéd in its expression that we have to laugh at her, as do Ruth and Mama. . . . The expense of Beneatha's "forms of expression" and their association with college life may indicate that these are ways of behaving that she has learned or imitated from white friends. As such, Mama and Ruth's laughter may be at Beneatha's unconscious imitation of white behavior as well as at the overly-serious manner in which she takes herself. Perceived as a satire of white adolescent behavior, the scene then allows the black spectator a laugh at white people and may find the white spectator suddenly realizing she is laughing at herself.

Sensing that Beneatha is not about to share in their laughter, Mama and Ruth then change the subject to Beneatha's latest boyfriend, a rich young man named George Murchison. This conversation returns us to the play's earlier concerns with stereotyped sex roles, and our sympathies are switched now to Beneatha. Ruth and Mama are pushing for George Murchison as a husband for Beneatha because he is rich, handsome, and comes from a "good" family, but Beneatha is not overwhelmed by these appeals. She makes clear that there is no marriage in sight for her because she is emotionally uninvolved with George. That she is able to reject such an eligible suitor because she neither loves him nor feels a need to be married is both romantically and rationally attractive. We are thus led not only to commend her but also to consider the possibility that marriage is not the only answer for women. During this scene, the fact that the people onstage are black is subordinate to the fact that they are female. If we miss the intended blurring of racial distinctions, Beneatha finally proclaims it:

> BENEATHA. Oh Mama—the Murchisons are honest-to-God-real-live-rich colored people and the only people in the world more snobbish than rich white people are rich colored people. I thought everybody knew that. I've met Mrs. Murchison. She's a scene!
>
> MAMA. You must not dislike people 'cause they well off honey.
>
> BENEATHA. Why not? It makes just as much sense as disliking people 'cause they are poor, and lots of people do that.

Beneatha's lines appeal because of their honesty; she is not trying to hide anything about black people or to set them up as better than white people. The message is clear: We should not dislike people because they are rich or poor, black or white.

Beneatha is not allowed to go off triumphantly, however.

She is still childlike in both her behavior and her role in this household, and she demonstrates that by attacking her mother on a subject about which Mama is very vulnerable: God. Beneatha's cry—"There simply is no blasted God—there is only man and it is he who makes miracles!"—raises such fury in Mrs. Younger that she forcefully slaps her daughter. The lightness of the previous scenes is broken; we are no longer amused, but made anxious by the intensity of this confrontation. We are made to know, probably with as much dismay as with respect, that Mama is the authority in this household, as Mama forces Beneatha to repeat, "In my mother's house there is still God."

The episode is too loaded for the audience's responses to be simple or unified. No matter what we think intellectually of the two women's beliefs, Beneatha arouses our impatience for not having learned when to remain quiet, and Mama elicits our sympathy for her pain. Some spectators may also feel dismay at Mrs. Younger's violent and authoritarian display, while others may respect Mama for asserting her beliefs and rejecting the insubordination of a child. Part of Hansberry's intention here is certainly to make Mama's character more specific. Her reaction to Beneatha establishes Mama's intense commitment to her values and clarifies for the audience the individuality of each person onstage. Mama's actions bring another dimension into this stage world; she shows us the older generation, devoted to religion, demanding that the children respect God and the laws, and dismayed by the cynicism of the young. Spectators of different ages and backgrounds will react differently to Mama's behavior in this scene, but she does serve to provide some audience members with a focus of recognition onstage that they might not find as readily in Beneatha, Ruth, or Walter. Whatever the location of our empathy, the scene should resound with almost too much familiarity. The episode is not a gratuitous histrionic moment; it is fully within the bounds and intentions of Hansberry's strategy. Who in the audience could justly say, "Oh, *those* awful people?"

On these discomforting notes, the scene nears its conclusion. Ruth calms the tension briefly by mediating between Beneatha and Mama, but then Ruth herself collapses, arousing new anxiety in the audience as the curtain comes down on Scene i.

Scene ii of Act I confirms suspicions aroused in Scene i and draws our attention momentarily away from the Youngers by introducing us to Beneatha's African boyfriend. Scene ii also gradually enforces and extends the hints of desperation in the lives of Walter Lee and Ruth. It is the following Saturday morning, the house is a chaos of cleaning, and Ruth is mysteriously "out." There is an air of expectancy; it is the day for the check to arrive. Within thirty lines we are led to expect more than the check: In a phone call to his business partner, Walter reveals that papers are being prepared; Ruth, we are informed, is at the doctor's; Beneatha invites a visit from "Asagai," whom she labels "an intellectual." Within minutes, all of the events of the scene are set up, and the audience is made anxious to see what will occur.

In an obvious maneuver and somewhat didactic message, Beneatha informs her mother of the correct pronunciation of Asagai's name and of his Nigerian heritage, and warns not to ask silly questions of the man, because "All anyone

seems to know about when it comes to Africa is Tarzan—" Beneatha's lesson is interrupted by Ruth's return. Ruth's demeanor and words tell more than we or the family want to know: She is pregnant, but that news has depressed her because it does not seem to her the time to bring a child into her world. There is an early hint that Ruth has actually not been to a physician, which, if heard, keeps the spectator uneasy for half the scene before Ruth admits that she has consulted with an abortionist.

As Mama takes a weeping Ruth offstage, and we are left puzzled and distraught, Asagai enters and shifts the mood and our attention. The scene between Beneatha and Asagai is meant to both amuse and inform the audience, although it may arouse some further annoyance with Beneatha, who, quickly forgetting her concern for Ruth, turns to the banter and gifts Asagai provides. Again, we are led to smile ruefully at Beneatha's adolescent behavior as she revels in her new African robes and repeatedly is unable to laugh at herself as Asagai gently mocks her "mutilated" straightened hair and her overserious assertions of her search for identity. Our respect for Beneatha is renewed when, detecting Asagai's romantic intentions, she tells him that more than one kind of feeling can exist between a man and a woman. Beneatha goes on to make emphatic Hansberry's intention to disturb the audience's assumptions about sex roles:

> ASAGAI. For a woman it should be enough.
>
> BENEATHA. I know—because that's what it says in all the novels that men write. Go ahead and laugh—but I'm not interested in being someone's little episode in America or—(*with feminine vengeance*)—one of them!

Beneatha almost defeats her argument by her angry self-consciousness, but she is ironically saved and the audience is relieved by Mama's entrance. Mama now attempts to act properly and retell all the "right things" that Beneatha has suggested earlier. We are not allowed to see Mama's behavior simply as comic, however. Although she does not know much about Africa, Mrs. Younger does know how to be compassionate to a young man away from home: As Asagai prepares to leave, Mama invites him to dinner sometime soon. Both Beneatha and the audience are being shown that there is more to being a decent person than having intellectual knowledge. The message seems to pass by Beneatha; as Asagai departs, Beneatha, dancing in front of a mirror, is imagining herself to be "queen of the Nile."

All this time, everyone has been waiting for the check, which finally does arrive. New anxieties quickly replace the old. Mama forces Ruth's admission of her visit to the abortionist, but even that is interrupted by Walter's excited arrival. His entrance and the ensuing arguments about the way the check is to be spent provide no surprises for the audience. Despite Walter's pleas that he needs this money, that his needs should be heard, Mama remains adamantly opposed to the liquor store enterprise. Walter is stunned when Mama tells him Ruth is pregnant and considering an abortion, but even this news does not shift his focus from his own despair. We may agree or disagree with Walter's cynical assertions that life is money, that money is all that matters, but we are certainly drawn to pity him in his anguish, to know the emptiness felt at the loss of a dream. Even if we respect Mama's stance, we can wish she would give him the money so we could believe that a man's dreams can in fact come true.

Hansberry's strategy is the same at the end of Scene ii as in Scene i. Both Walter and Mama depart, making us eager for the curtain to rise on Act II in order to find out where they have gone and what is happening. We are left again with a recognition of these characters as people whom we care about, whose troubles we can acknowledge.

Act II confirms the appropriateness of our anxiety, affirms the attitudes and insights of Act I, and fulfills the unfortunate possibilities suggested earlier. Although Act II, like Act I, alternates between moments that delight and moments that trouble, both our awareness of Walter's frenzy and our knowledge that something will have to be done with the check create a presentiment of impending doom.

The act begins with a scene that will amuse and catch the audience's attention. Beneatha appears, dressed in her African costume, and begins to dance to the African music Asagai has also given her. As she dances, genuinely enraptured with the whole experience, a very drunken Walter enters and joins her. . . . As drunken antics, Walter's act is surely funny for an audience, but he appears so persistent and obsessed that the spectator is also made to wonder if this may not be some mystical and strange self-discovery that should be taken seriously. Had Hansberry extended this scene, the black audience in particular might have had a fuller sense of Walter's struggles with his identity. Hansberry may have cut the scene short because it risked alienating the sympathies of white spectators by emphasizing the distinctive African heritage of blacks, which in turn would call attention to a potential difference between whites and blacks.

Our bewilderment is arrested and our perspective changed when Beneatha's date for the evening, George Murchison, the rich man, arrives. Instinctively, we see the scene for a second from George's eyes because we, like George, have been intruding on a private family ritual. But the moment George rejects Walter's fraternal hand-clasp (and thus rejects an act of comradery from Walter) and retorts "Black Brother, hell!" our hostilities are turned on George and our association with the Youngers becomes effective. George's condescension toward Beneatha demands to be thwarted. We may find Beneatha's behavior immature or clichéd, but George is an outsider who has no right to interfere. (pp. 125-30)

Thus, when neither Beneatha nor Ruth is able or willing to squelch George, we are delighted that Walter tackles the invader. Hansberry's strategy here in bringing George into the scene is to provide a contrast between Walter and another black man. Hansberry leads us, black or white, to prefer Walter, whose African heritage has just been acknowledged, to George, who affects the worst aspects of white society. . . . The attack on George is indeed inebriating for Walter and the audience, until Walter's drunken insights turn back on him, revealing the profound bitterness at the root of his antics and words. Once more, Hansberry has changed a light game into a potentially dangerous encounter. We are plunged into sobriety by the awareness of the depth of Walter's unhappiness.

As soon as George has left with Beneatha, now dressed "appropriately" in an evening gown, Walter begins to vent his anger on Ruth. We fear for another troubling scene. Ruth, however, calls forth all of her strength and love on this occasion. . . . The Ruth who speaks here should remind us of the woman who earlier asked Mama to help Walter out. Ruth is troubled about her marriage, about her pregnancy, about the tension in her home; that her anxiety is expressed in both anger and love makes her more rather than less believable. Thus, we feel a pleasant surprise at Ruth's gentle words and offer of hot milk to Walter. We sit hopefully watching their attempts to talk to each other, to recapture some lost warmth, when Mama enters. All of the spectator's anxiety returns; Walter and Ruth have been allowed no time for resolution.

We now find out where Mama has been all day. Her previous hints are confirmed for the audience: She has spent the afternoon buying a house. Ruth cannot hide her delight. The spectator is caught in that pleasure until Ruth's probe for details pushes Mama to reveal that the house happens to be in a white neighborhood. This information allows Walter finally to vent his anger; his silence was ominous while Mama told Travis and Ruth her news. To Walter's, "So that's the peace and quiet you went out and bought for us today," Mama responds that it was the nicest house she could find for the money; houses put up for "colored" cost twice as much. The black spectator may be glad that white spectators are learning the truth; Hansberry intends that white spectators be at least troubled if not ashamed by this account, although it is not certain that such a reaction will occur, because we must accept Mama's words as truth if we are to be disturbed by them. Ruth is able to put aside the worry this added detail creates, but, for Walter, it is the final blow. Now the money is actually gone, and his dream appears to be not only deferred but destroyed. The audience is torn between pity for Walter and relief for Mama and Ruth. We are thus caught in the strife of this family. We may enjoy an affirmation of belief in one well-shared portion of the American dream—the desire for a decent home—that has actually been fulfilled for the Younger family, but we should be wary that the contentment Ruth and Mama are seeking in the ownership of a home may be threatened by the house's location in a white neighborhood and by Walter's frustration.

The ambivalence set up for the audience at the end of Act II, Scene i, seems irresolvable. We can wish that Walter were less self-pitying, but it is still distressing to see a man so destroyed. Because it is Mama's decision that has directly caused Walter's present suffering, we are tempted to turn our pity for Walter into anger at her, but simultaneously our concern for Ruth is relieved by Mama's action. Scene ii leads the audience to feel a temporary reconciliation of these contradictory sympathies. The scene begins with a brief episode between George and Beneatha that is intended to inflate our dislike for George, who announces that he is only interested in Beneatha because she is physically attractive and sophisticated, not because she has interesting thoughts. George's remarks are so callous and stupid that we applaud Beneatha's curt dismissal of him and achieve a greater respect for her stance as an independent woman. The scene also sets up the opportunity to demonstrate Mama's compassion and wisdom: Instead of condemning Beneatha's rejection of George, as we might expect, Mama accepts her daughter's word that George is a fool and urges Beneatha not to waste her time on him. Beneatha thanks her mother for understanding her this time. Our appreciation of Mama's sagacity relieves us of some of the annoyance we may have felt toward her as the source of Walter's pain.

The further elevation of Mama occurs just a few minutes later. Walter's employer calls. It is revealed that because of his depression, Walter has not been to work for three days. Instead, he has been driving and walking around, drinking, listening to the blues, and watching "the Negroes go by." These signs of the depth of Walter's own blues convince Mama that she has made a mistake. She informs her son that only about a third of the money has been spent on the down payment for the house. She will turn the remaining sixty-five hundred dollars over to Walter's care, with the stipulation that three thousand dollars are to be put in a savings account for Beneatha's schooling. The plan seems amazingly simple and satisfying, even if the sudden disclosure of remaining money is a bit contrived. Clearly, Hansberry's strategy is to build up our concern for Walter and to lead us to believe that there can be an answer for him in Mama's decisions. But we may wonder why Mama did not do something like this from the beginning. (The explanation that she was trying to prevent the liquor store venture does not really suffice.) Our relief that the tension in the household seems finally resolved is heightened by Walter's marked change of mood. (pp. 13-33)

If there has ever been any suspicion that Walter's dream is somehow unique or unique to black people rather than the archetypal American dream, such doubts are dispersed in Walter's vision of the future presented to his son. Daddy, Walter tells Travis, is going to make a business transaction. The results of that transaction will mean cars that are elegant but not flashy, a house complete with a gardener whom Walter will address as "Jefferson," and a choice for Travis of any of the great colleges in America. . . . That Walter's thirty-five hundred dollars is not likely to fulfill such splendid fantasies is irrelevant at the moment. Hansberry's strategy is to lead the audience to believe that Mama's gift to Walter has solved all problems.

Scene iii of Act II introduces a new strategic element. It sets us up for a long, ironic fall through the display of Ruth's new contentment and her dreams for the future. . . . [Walter's] mood, though more boisterous, matches his wife's obvious joy. We cannot help but feel pleasure in their happiness.

We do not wait long before a shadow appears to dim the good cheer. The introduction of the play's only white character is set up with humor and deliberately ironic juxtaposition. Only a moment before the doorbell rings, Walter is imitating Beneatha, suggesting that at some future time she will be leaning over a patient on the operating table, asking, "By the way, what are your views on civil rights down there?" They laugh and we laugh as Beneatha goes to the door to allow the surprising entrance of a middle-aged white man in business attire. Walter immediately moves forward to confront the situation with an air of authority that amuses the women. The white man introduces himself as Karl Lindner, chairman of a "sort of welcoming committee" from the neighborhood into which the Youngers are about to move. Lindner's verbal and physical awkwardness and the deliberate vagueness of his language warn the audience from the start that this man's intentions

are suspect, but only Beneatha among the characters onstage seems immediately wary of this "friendly" white man. Lindner never faces the question of race directly, but piles one ambiguous and euphemistic statement onto the next, using one rhetorical device after another, in an attempt to gain the trust of his onstage audience; by the time he gets to his point, we know he carries a message of rejection, not welcome. Lindner has come to the Youngers to buy their new house from them at a profit for the family in order to keep black people out of the neighborhood. Hansberry makes Lindner's presentation of his mission dramatically ironic because everything we have seen of the Younger family defeats the "rational" core of Lindner's argument. His central point is that people are happier when they live in a community in which the residents share a "common background," and from his viewpoint, "Negroes" and whites obviously do not have that common background. But just before he articulates this conclusion, Hansberry has Lindner describe his community in a way that for the audience should clearly appear as a striking parallel to what it knows of the behavior and desires of the Youngers: "They're not rich and fancy people; just hardworking, honest people who don't really have much but those little homes and a dream of the kind of community they want to raise their children in." We might laugh at how well Lindner disproved his own point about "differences in background" were it not for the fact that his bigotry will harm others, will create pain and difficulty for people like the Youngers.

Walter and Beneatha are appropriately outraged. They firmly evict the man from the house. Even if the white spectator had privately shared Lindner's rationalized prejudices, Lindner's conniving dishonesty should provoke disgust at his behavior and applause for Walter's unhesitant refusal. Here, black spectators might feel fear for the Youngers, since black spectators would know what whites have done to the homes of blacks who have moved into white neighborhoods. Hansberry's purpose, however, seems less to arouse fear in black spectators than to provoke a recognition in white spectators. The white audience needs to *see* Lindner to know he is despicable; the black audience may have assumed that possibility.

The triumph of this scene is extended and relieved when Mama returns and is told of the event. Because the Youngers respond with humor rather than bitterness to Lindner's proposal, the audience can remain empathetic rather than pitying or ashamed. Through irony, parody, and exaggeration, Ruth, Walter, and Beneatha point out the absurdity of the segregationist position. They also note so openly and unthreateningly the fears of white people that such fears are reduced to foolishness. (pp. 133-35)

The audience is almost brought to believe that the play can continue in this vein indefinitely, when the levity is broken once again by the sound of the door bell. Remembering what that sound brought the last time, the audience should react on cue. Walter reinforces our response with a display of sudden tension, the motivation for which is unclear, but which does serve to focus our attention on him. Our anxiety turns out to be appropriate, although its object in the stage world would not have been foreseen. The newest visitor is one of Walter's business associates, Bobo, whose frightened demeanor vividly warns the audience that this intruder brings even worse news than did the last. Bobo, like Lindner, cannot tell his story straight-forwardly, but finally, in tears, he blurts that Willy, the third business partner, has vanished with all the money intended for the liquor store. Furthermore, Mama forces Walter to admit that this amount includes not only Walter's money but Beneatha's as well. (p. 135)

The problem with this newest denial of a dream for the Youngers is that it provides no real enemy, no clear object of hatred on whom we can vent our anger and thus purge ourselves of anxiety and dismay. Walter has been foolish and deceitful, but since it is *he* who has been most directly exploited, our anger must be mingled with pity. Lindner is a kind of enemy, but he is not responsible for this misfortune. Willy, the third "partner," is an abstract, unknown figure, and therefore a difficult target for cathexis.

The audience turns to Act III with no sense of how all this can be resolved, but with the anticipation well established throughout the play that by the final curtain the problem of that money will have to be confronted in some fashion. That problem has, of course, now been partially eliminated, but like the conclusions of previous scenes, Act II, Scene iii, leaves the audience with the question of what will happen to the money that remains, invested, as it is, in the house. Hansberry repeats in Act III a strategic device she has used earlier in the play. She keeps the audience in suspense about the major question—what will happen to the new house?—while drawing our attention to a subordinate problem. In this instance, the distraction is what has come to be the second most important concern of the play, or what might be called the subplot of *A Raisin in the Sun*: Beneatha's concern with her "identity," as defined particularly in her relations to men. The man at the beginning of Act III is Asagai, who has ostensibly come to the Youngers' house to help with the moving, but who seizes the occasion to propose marriage and a life in Nigeria to Beneatha. Asagai is suggesting going "back to Africa" as an answer, at least for Beneatha. Since the suggestion is not well developed in the play, the effect on the audience is to let them know that such a possibility exists.

Beneatha's bitterness about Walter's loss of the money has brought her to a high degree of cynicism such that she now considers even a life of healing the sick to be a futile gesture. We can perceive these new hesitations about her career as consistent with her flirtation with various fads, but her poignant description of an incident from her childhood, when another child was badly hurt but returned from the hospital almost as good as new, suggests a serious and long-lasting motivation for a career as a doctor. Hansberry's strategy here is not carefully developed. The passage may serve once more to erase a sense of difference in values between black and white people, but the combination of Beneatha's provocative anecdote with her rejection of medicine as a career makes the strategy at this point ambiguous. At the end of the scene, after Asagai's proposal, Beneatha admits that she herself is "all mixed up," and perhaps Hansberry intends that the audience respond to Beneatha with the same tolerance and understanding that have been elicited for the ambivalence of other characters, with an added measure of patience because of Beneatha's youth.

During the entire scene between Asagai and Beneatha there is no clear indication of whether or not the family still intends to move, but, after Asagai's departure, Mama suggests with resignation that someone should tell the movers not to come. Our hopes that things might still work out begin to tumble, but they are momentarily renewed by Ruth's desperate cry that she will work twenty hours a day with her baby on her back if they will stick with their plans to move. . . . Ruth's plea increases our admiration for her; her willingness to work so hard for what she wants fulfills the central ethic of American society. The intensity of her desire to move also should solidify the audience's wish that the Youngers still be able to acquire their house. . . . Mrs. Younger's resignation, while evoking some respect for her willingness to accept an alternative, should sharpen our disappointment and make acute our realization of the emptiness subsequent to the shriveling of the dream.

On this dismal note, Walter enters with his own resolution to the problem. His cynicism, like his sister's, has increased from his experience. To the horror of the entire family, Walter has called Mr. Lindner and asked the latter to come over so that they can now negotiate the sale of the house to the white man. Any hopes we may have had that the Youngers would have a new home are dashed. If the spectator is tempted to defend Walter's action on pragmatic grounds, Mama's voice intrudes to disallow such a response: "I came from five generations of people who was slaves and sharecroppers—but ain't nobody in my family never let nobody pay 'em no money that was a way of telling us we wasn't fit to walk the earth. We ain't never been that poor. . . . We ain't never been that dead inside." Mama's pride and her horrified understanding of the nature of Walter's action call forth our admiration for her and our dismay and pity for Walter. . . . Walter's call to Lindner is a sign of death. Mama's words do not berate her son; they are an expression of human dignity that tells us what dignity is—and what it is not.

Mama's proclamation also focuses our attention on Walter. Hansberry here has her strategy under remarkable control. Throughout the play, the author has developed our concern for each of the characters as individuals and for each of their dreams and frustrations. We have been shown three different women, not "the" black woman. Yet, in subtle ways, Walter has stood particularly apart all along: He was a man surrounded by women; his lows were nearer madness and his highs nearer ecstasy than the depressions and joys of the other characters. The Younger women did not have identical dreams, but they shared a desire for some greater sense of fulfillment, of comfort and simple pleasure. None of them, however, was struggling with the loss of self-respect that has been Walter's plight. What Mama's words lead us to recognize is that Walter has been striving for dignity—just what he lost with his call to Mr. Lindner.

What we want from Walter now is that he, too, recognize the challenge in Mama's words, and that he find in them the inspiration to recapture the dignity he has lost. But Walter's defense moves him in just the opposite direction: He falls to his knees in a hysterical imitation of the slave before the white "Father." Walter's behavior is painfully self-demeaning, but, if we feel a sense of disgust or condemnation, as Beneatha does, it is Mama who again leads us to the more complicated, more appropriate response. After Beneatha has said that Walter is no longer any brother of hers, that he is a "toothless rat," and that she despises any man who would behave this way, Mama tells her, and us, how and why that rejection is wrong:

> There is always something left to love. And if you ain't learned that, you ain't learned nothing. (Looking at her) Have you cried for that boy today? I don't mean for yourself and for the family 'cause we lost the money. I mean for him; what he been through and what it done to him. Child, when do you think is the time to love somebody the most; when they done good and made things easy for everybody? Well, then, you ain't through learning—because that ain't the time at all. It's when he's at his lowest and can't believe in hisself 'cause the world done whipped him so. When you starts measuring somebody, measure him right, child, measure him right. Make sure you done taken into account what hills and valleys he come through before he got to wherever he is.

It is not difficult to find in Mama's words the "message" of the play: When we measure someone, not just Walter, but any character on the stage or any person in any world, we must measure him right. To ignore this lesson is not just to put aside Mama's somewhat didactic sermon; it is to refuse the experience of the entire play. Mama's speech should ring true to the audience, not just because we respect her or because we find a romantic appeal in this passage, but because Hansberry has so constructed her strategy that to acknowledge the world of this play necessitates a re-examination of each of our modes of "measurement." It also means that we must accept differences between characters and ambivalences within characters: to "measure right" is partially to avoid stereotyping. If, for example, we judge Ruth in her moments of hostility toward Walter, we must alter that judgment when we witness her gestures of love (the play prohibits us from labeling her the nagging wife); if we judge Mama when she is being tyrannical, we must also do so when she is generous and understanding. Furthermore, Mama reminds us that Walter is not on his knees now because he is essentially a weak and cowardly person. He is on his knees, as we have seen, because he has been through too much, because the world has "whipped him so." Because Hansberry's strategy has so persistently been an attempt to make us accept the Youngers as ordinary people like ourselves, it would be false now to expect of Walter a strength we would certainly not presume in ourselves. We cannot condemn Walter for falling after a beating. A black spectator can empathize with Walter, while a white spectator may feel shame at being part of the world that is responsible for the whipping; any spectator should recognize in Walter's experience, however, the defeat of having struggled and lost.

A Raisin in the Sun could end with Mama's speech. Such an ending would leave us with a message and a vague depression. We do not have sufficient reason to condemn Walter, but neither do we have the reasons his family has to love him and feel a deep anguish at his defeat. We have also only seen Walter rehearse his humiliation; although we have no reason to hope that he or other characters onstage will change his behavior, we would be left without a sense of completion were we not to see Walter's encounter with Lindner. Yet we feel a sense of futility when Lindner does arrive. There appears no way for the characters onstage to aid Walter or alter the situation.

There is also the important frustration in being an audi-

ence member who wishes to aid the characters on stage but cannot because one is in a world separate from theirs. When the playwright creates such an effect, the intent is that we transport the desire to change behavior, either our own or someone else's, into the world in which we do or can act. Drama presents to the audience the limits of a world and arouses the desire that someone break through those limits. In tragedy, the hero is most often thwarted in his attempts to deny or destroy the boundaries of his world, but our sorrow for him relieves us of our own impotence and allows us to act anew in our world. In *A Raisin in the Sun* we are led to the edge of tragedy, from where we can see the abyss into which Walter is falling, yet we are finally led away from that edge because Hansberry does not intend us to remove ourselves from her characters. In traditional tragedy, we are meant to see the central character or characters as other and greater than ourselves: Their falls thus create anguish; and their struggles provide hope. In *A Raisin in the Sun,* we are meant to see ourselves as like these characters in all important ways. Thus, neither pity nor awe is wholly appropriate, for the former would lead to self-pity and the latter to egotism.

More than in our experience of many plays, when we arrive at the end of *A Raisin in the Sun* we feel that everything else in the play has been set up precisely to accomplish the final scene. One reason for this sensation is that we know we are being told a story, and we expect a story to have a beginning, a middle, and an end. We have also been led to recognize that this is, in an important way, Walter's story, and his tale is not yet complete. Once engaged in the final episode, its surprising reversal and its emphatic assertion of survival tend to erase our memories of earlier troublings much as the baby that arrives after labor dissolves the memory of the pain that brought it forth.

Our attention is all on Walter as the final portion of the play begins. Walter has "set this scene," and the other Youngers, like the audience, are witnesses. Lindner, the white man from the neighborhood committee, returns to the Youngers' home expecting, as we do, that Walter is about to sell the house to the white community. Just as Hansberry has played with our curiosity in previously unpredictable scenes with Lindner and then Bobo, she now elongates Walter's response to Lindner. In words that approach a parody of Lindner's earlier speech, while sustaining an air of utter sincerity, Walter speaks slowly of his family, of his pride in his sister's studies, and with increasing emphasis, of his father. Our attention is held rapt because this is not the role Walter has rehearsed; we have no reason not to expect him eventually to come to his deal, but the words he speaks suggest a sentiment and pride we have not seen previously in Walter. We are thus only vaguely prepared for Walter's sudden reversal. Crying unashamedly in front of "the man" Walter finally says that the Youngers will move into their new house, "because my father—my father—he earned it."

With these words, Walter pays a debt both to his parents and to the audience. The time and trust they and we have invested in him are now rewarded. He is behaving with the dignity we have had only glimpses of since the beginning of the play. (pp. 136-40)

If we contemplate Walter's sudden redemption, we will be puzzled by it. The only possible motivation we are given for Walter's change of mind is the brief appearance of Travis before Lindner's arrival. Perhaps we are to infer that the sight of his son jars Walter into understanding that it is not only he who will suffer humiliation and loss of a dream. But the script does not guide the audience to that conclusion. Rather, we are given no pause to search for an explanation of Walter's new behavior. The moment Lindner leaves, Ruth cries, "LET'S GET THE HELL OUT OF HERE!" The women become so hastily involved in other activities and conversations that they suggest that Walter's redemption is too fragile and too fortunate to be questioned. The bustle of activity at the end of the play prevents excessive sentimentality, but it also demands that the audience feel satisfaction without understanding.

If we look closer at that feeling of satisfaction, we will find in it the essence of Hansberry's strategy. We are pleased that Walter has behaved with dignity and relieved that the Youngers will go on, not in futile desperation but with a sense of a new world before them. They have not changed very much, nor did Hansberry lead the audience to demand or expect great changes. The conclusion of *A Raisin in the Sun* returns us to a world of buoyant wit, and our ability once again to share laughter with the Youngers reassures us of a shared vision of the world.

It is this very laughter, however, that prevents many spectators from perceiving the contradictions of the Youngers' world. Early in the play, our laughter relieves us from fully confronting the evidence that *A Raisin in the Sun* presents not simply the dreams of the characters but the complexities of "dreams deferred." Nor does the conclusion of the play make us ashamed of our good humor. The Youngers are back in high spirits. We can leave the theater happily persuaded that still another family has rightfully joined the infinitely extensive American middle class.

Such an experience of Hansberry's play is not a mistake; it may be what is essentially intended, but it is simply not whole. There is a confusion in the world of the Youngers, which Harold Cruse [see excerpt above] glimpses but finally misperceives: "The Younger family was carefully tidied up for its on-stage presentation. . . . There were no numbers runners in sight, no bumptious slick, young "cats" from downstairs sniffling after Mama Younger's pretty daughter on the corner, no shyster preachers hustling Mama into the fold, no fallen woman, etc." Such omissions may be glaring to some spectators, but can be understood as a decision not to distract a middle-class audience from their recognition of the Youngers as similiar to themselves. To gain the aura of authenticity for those who know the ghetto might mean to relinquish some contact with a middle-class audience. To untidy the Youngers might be to dishevel as well the audience's social and aesthetic security that allows it to recognize these people.

The difficulty with a genuine recognition of the world of *A Raisin in the Sun* is not that Hansberry lies to maintain order; it is rather that she is finally unable to lie. Her drama reveals more than the main intention of her strategy would wish. The Youngers are not moving into the middle-class when they move into their new house; they are simply and only moving into a house. For many Americans, the act of purchasing one's own house clearly signifies upward mobility and membership in the middle class. This signification occurs for at least two different reasons: In order to buy a house, the purchaser must present some assurances of stable income and occupation, and the act itself is one of choice. Since the dramatic structure of *A Raisin in the Sun* can exist only because a choice does exist, we can allow ourselves to believe that we are in the world of the middle class. But choice for the Youngers is poignantly and emphatically a singular event. They are only able to make a choice because the ten thousand dollar benefit from Mr. Younger's life insurance policy has suddenly appeared in their mailbox. Ironically, it is through death, not the nature of their lives, that they are able to choose to buy a house.

It is made amply clear that Hansberry cannot lie about the limitations of this move for the Youngers. Ruth recognizes fully that she will have to work herself to the bone to help keep up the mortgage payment, yet the early scenes of the play remind us that she cannot continue her pregnancy in health and harmony with her domestic work. And what will happen when Ruth does have a baby? If the implied assumption is that Mama will take over the rearing of another Younger child, this must also be an assumption of further internal destruction in the family, since the tensions caused by Mama's meddling in Travis's upbringing have been poignantly demonstrated. Walter Lee's situation is at least equally closed. Not only are there no new options for him to change his occupation, for him to find work less servile than that of a chauffeur, but the dream of going into business for himself has itself been muddied. The theft of his share of the insurance policy concretely removes his chance for starting a liquor business now, but it also suggests that ventures into the world of private business necessitate a kind of cunning, distrust, and encounter with corruption that calls the entire operation into question.

To turn to Beneatha or Travis only further reveals the imprisonment of the family. Beneatha may be able at the end of the play to return to her fantasies of getting married and going off to practice medicine in Africa, but the audience, at least, should remember that such notions are now even more fantastic than before, because Walter Lee has lost not only the money for his business but Beneatha's money for school. Travis may now have a room of his own, at least until the arrival of the new baby, but how will the family find the fifty cents (if it is only fifty cents out in the white suburbs) for school activities when there is no new income and the pressures of taking care of the house will create even greater financial burdens? . . . The bustle of moving may allow all members of the family to repress momentarily their fears and despair, but Beneatha's earlier words to Asagai, her African friend, are the only authentic description of where the family really finds itself: "Don't you see there isn't any real progress, Asagai, there is only one large circle that we march in, around and around, each of us our own little picture—in front of us— our own little mirage which we think is the future."

Hansberry has succeeded in persuading the audience to the legitimacy of the Youngers' aspirations, but she has simultaneously shown the extreme difficulty, if not impossibility, for this family of fulfilling their dreams of change, stability, and comfort. Hansberry directly undercuts the central middle-class American notion of "equality of opportunity" by presenting the white man, Mr. Lindner, who finally believes that opportunities for blacks should not be identical with those for whites, that blacks should not move into a white neighborhood; this is only one direct instance, however, of the limitations of opportunity for the Youngers. Mr. Lindner slams a door on the Youngers that may have appeared to have been open; other doors for the Youngers simply remain closed.

Perhaps despite her intentions, Hansberry's play takes one additional step to undermine a belief in one great middle-class world for all Americans: At crucial moments her characterizations and plot structure call into question the very nature of the values and opportunities being presented as shared.

> BENEATHA. (*hissingly*): Yes—just look at what the New World hath wrought! . . . There he is! *Monsieur le petit bourgeois noir*—himself! There he is! Symbol of a Rising Class! Entrepreneur! Titan of the system!
>
> . . .I look at you and I see the final triumph of stupidity in the world!

Walter's subsequent courage in rejecting Mr. Lindner's bribe prevents us from concluding that Walter is "the final triumph of stupidity in the world." But while we may be forced away from this particular conclusion, the first lines of Beneatha's attack may resound with accuracy. The world of *A Raisin in the Sun* is often affable, but the assaults on class identity for black people suggest a paradoxically coherent confusion.

That recognition may lead to at least small changes in the social and political worlds from which the audience comes. Woodie King and Ron Milner, strong contemporary proponents of a black theater, have urged in the introduction to their anthology of black drama that "*A Raisin in the Sun* reaffirmed in blacks the necessity for more involvement in black theater." Partially by the inclusion in its casts of such notable black theater artists as Lonne Elder III, Robert Hooks, Douglas Turner Ward, and Ossie Davis, the play "marked a turning point." These remarks emphasize the play as historical event rather than experience for an audience. It may well be that this is how *A Raisin in the Sun* will be best remembered, but the fact that it *is* remembered is inseparable from the play's ability to impress an audience. That impression may not have been as facile as it once appeared. *A Raisin in the Sun's* success raised the curtain for many subsequent productions of black theater; it may also have lifted the veil for some spectators to glimpse the complexity of black life in America. Even for black spectators who know that complexity in their daily lives, the act of witnessing its revelation, with all of the play's omissions and inconsistencies, can be important.

At the end of *A Raisin in the Sun,* Mama starts to leave, then symbolically returns for her plant. The plant, like the family, is still scraggly, but there is hope that it will flourish when cultivated in new soil. Although Hansberry wanted us to see that plant as representing the Younger family, some twenty years later it also suggests the place *A Raisin in the Sun* has found in the evolution of black drama. (pp. 141-44)

> *Helene Keyssar, "Sounding the Rumble of Dreams Deferred: Lorraine Hansberry's 'A Raisin in the Sun',"* in her The Curtain and the Veil: Strategies in Black Drama, *Burt Franklin & Co., 1981, pp. 113-46.*

Amiri Baraka

In the wake of its twenty-fifth anniversary, Lorraine Hansberry's great play *A Raisin in the Sun* is enjoying a revival of a most encouraging kind. Complete with restorations to the text of scenes and passages removed from the first production, the work is currently being given a new direction and interpretation that reveal even more clearly the play's profoundly imposing stature, continuing relevance, and pointed social analysis. At major regional theaters in city after city *Raisin* has played to packed houses and, as on the night I saw it, standing ovations. It has broken or approached long-standing box office records and has been properly hailed as "a classic," while the *Washington Post* has called it succinctly: "one of the handful of great American dramas . . . in the inner circle, along with *Death of a Salesman, Long Day's Journey into Night,* and *The Glass Menagerie.*"

For a playwright who knows, too well, the vagaries and realities of American theater, this assessment is gratifying. But of even greater significance is the fact that *A Raisin in the Sun* is being viewed by masses of people, black and white, in the light of a new day.

For *Raisin* typifies American society in a way that reflects more accurately the real lives of the black U.S. majority than any work that ever received commercial exposure before it, and few if any since. It has the life that only classics can maintain. Any useful re-appreciation of it cannot be limited, therefore, to the passages restored or the new values discovered, important though these are: it is the play itself, as a dramatic (and sociopolitical) whole, that demands our confirmation of its grandeur.

When *Raisin* first appeared in 1959, the Civil Rights Movement was in its earlier stages. And as a document reflecting the *essence* of those struggles, the play is unexcelled. For many of us it was—and remains—the quintessential civil rights drama. But any attempt to confine the play to an era, a mind-set, an issue ("Housing") or set of topical concerns was, as we now see, a mistake. The truth is that Hansberry's dramatic skills have yet to be properly appreciated—and not just by those guardians of the status quo who pass themselves off as dramatic critics. For black theater artists and would-be theorists especially, this is ironic because the play is probably the most widely appreciated—particularly by African Americans—black drama that we have.

Raisin lives in large measure because black people have kept it alive. And because Hansberry has done *more* than document, which is the most limited form of realism. She is a *critical realist,* in a way that Langston Hughes, Richard Wright, and Margaret Walker are. That is, she *analyzes* and *assesses* reality and shapes her statement as an aesthetically powerful and politically advanced work of art. Her statement cannot be separated from the characters she creates to embody, in their totality, the life she observes: it becomes, in short, the living material of the work, part of its breathing body, integral and alive.

George Thompson in *Poetry and Marxism* points out that drama is the most expressive artistic form to emerge out of great social transformation. Shakespeare is the artist of the destruction of feudalism—and the emergence of capitalism. The mad Macbeths, bestial Richard III's, and other feudal worthies are actually shown, like the whole class, as degenerate—and degenerating. (pp. 9-10)

Hansberry's play, too, was political agitation. It dealt with the very same issues of democratic rights and equality that were being aired in the streets. It dealt with them with an unabating dramatic force, vision, political concreteness and clarity that, in retrospect, are awesome. But it dealt with them not as abstractions, fit only for infantile-left pamphlets, but as they are *lived*. In reality.

All of *Raisin*'s characters speak *to* the text and are critical to its dramatic tensions and understanding. They are necessarily larger than life—in impact—but crafted meticulously from living social material.

When the play opened on Broadway, Lena Younger, the emotional adhesive of the family, was given a broad, aggressive reading by Claudia McNeil. Indeed, her reading has been taken as the model and somewhat institutionalized in various productions I've seen.

The role itself—of family head, folksy counsel, upholder of tradition—has caused many people to see her as the stereotyped "black matriarch" of establishment and commercial sociological fame. Carrying with them (or rebelling against) the preconceived baggage of that stereotype, and recalling the play through the haze of memory (or from the compromised movie version), they have not bothered to look more closely at the actual woman Hansberry created—and at *what* tradition she in fact upholds. (p. 11)

[In the recent New York revival of the play, Olivia Cole's reading of Lena] was revelation and renewal.

Ms. Cole came at the role from the inside out. Her Lena is a woman, black, poor, struggle-worn but proud and loving. She was in the world *before* the rest of the family, before many of us viewing the play. She has seen and felt what we have not, or what we cannot yet identify. She is no quaint, folksy artifact; she is truth, history, love—and struggle—as they can be manifest only in real life. (p. 12)

Similarly, the new interpreters of Walter Lee . . . are something "fresh," like our kids say. They bring a contemporary flavoring to the work that consists of knowing—with more certainty than, say, Sidney Poitier could have in the original—the frustration and rage animating the healthy black male, *post*-civil rights era. They play Walter Lee more aggressively, more self-consciously, so that when he does fall we can actually hate him—hate the frivolous, selfish male-chauvinist part of ourselves. And when he stands up at the finale and will not be beaten, we can cry with joy.

Part of the renewed impact of the play comes with the fresh interpretation of both director and actors. But we cannot stop there! The social materials that Hansberry so brilliantly shaped into drama are not lightweight. For me this is the test of the writer: no matter the skill of the execution—*what* has been executed? What is it he or she is talking about? Form can never be dismissed, to say the least, particularly by an artist. But in the contradiction between form and content, content must be the bottom line—though unless the form be an extension of (and correctly serve) that content, obviously even understanding of the content will be flawed.

Formalist artists must resort to all kinds of superficial aberrations of form because usually they have nothing to say. Brecht said how much safer the red is in a "non-objective" painting than the red of blood rushing out of the slain worker's chest. . . . And it is one reason why some critics will always have a problem with the realism of a Hansberry—and ignore the multilayered richness of her form.

A Raisin in the Sun is about *dreams,* ironically enough. And how those psychological projections of human life can come into conflict like any other product of that life. For Lena, a new house, the stability and happiness of her children, are her principal dream. And as such this is the completion of a dream she and her late husband—who has literally, like the slaves, been *worked* to death—conceived together.

Ruth's dream, as mother and wife, is somewhat similar. A room for her son, an inside toilet. She dreams as one of those triply oppressed by society—as worker, as African American, and as woman. But her dream, and her mother-in-law's, conflicts with Walter Lee's. He is the chauffeur to a rich white man and dreams of owning all and doing all the things he sees "Mr. Arnold" do and own. On one level Walter Lee is merely aspiring to full and acknowledged humanity; on another level he yearns to strut his "manhood," a predictable mix of *machismo* and fantasy. But Hansberry takes it even further to show us that on still another level Walter Lee, worker though he be, has the "realizable" dream of the black petty bourgeoisie. "There he is! *Monsieur le petit bourgeois noir*—himself!," cries Beneatha, the other of Lena Younger's children. "There he is—Symbol of a Rising Class! Entrepreneur! Titan of the system!" The deepness of this is that Hansberry can see that the conflict of dreams is not just that of individuals but, more importantly, of classes. Not since Theodore Ward's *Big White Fog* (1938) has there been a play so thoroughly and expertly reflective of class struggle within a black family.

Beneatha dreams of medical school. She is already socially mobile, finding a place, as her family cannot, among other petty bourgeois aspirants on the rungs of "education," where their hard work has put her. Her aspiration is less caustic, more attainable than Walter's. But she yearns for something more. Her name Beneatha (as who ain't?) should instruct us. She is, on the one hand, secure in the collegiate world of "ideas" and elitism, above the mass; on the other, undeceived by the myths and symbols of class and status. Part militant, part dilettante, "liberated" woman, little girl, she questions everything and dreams of service to humanity, an identity beyond self and family in the liberation struggles of her people. Ah, but will she have the strength to stay the course?

Hansberry has Beneatha grappling with key controversies of the period, but also some that had yet to clearly surface. And she grapples with some that will remain with us until society itself is changed: The relationship of the intellectual to the masses. The relationship of African Americans to Africans. The liberation movement itself and the gnawing necessity of black self-respect in its many guises (e.g., "straightened" hair vs. "the natural"). Written in 1956 and first seen by audiences in the new revivals, the part of the text in which Beneatha unveils her hair—the "perm" cut off and she glowing with her original woolly crown—precedes the "Afro" by a decade. Dialogue between Beneatha and her mother, brother, Asagai and George Murchison digs into all these still-burning concerns.

Similarly, Walter Lee and Ruth's dialogues lay out his male chauvinism and even self- and group-hate born of the frustration of too many dreams too long deferred: the powerlessness of black people to control their own fate or that of their families in capitalist America where race is place, white is right, and money makes and defines the man. Walter dreams of using his father's insurance money to buy a liquor store. This dream is in conflict not only with the dreams of the Younger women, but with reality. But Walter appreciates only his differences with—and blames—the women. Throughout the work, Hansberry addresses herself to issues that the very young might feel only *The Color Purple* has raised. Walter's relationship to his wife and sister, and Beneatha's with George and Asagai, gives us a variety of male chauvinism—working class, petty bourgeois, African.

Asagai, the Nigerian student who courts Beneatha, dreams of the liberation of Africa and even of taking Beneatha there: "We will pretend that . . . you have only been away for a day." But that's not reality either, though his discussion of the dynamics and dialectics of revolution—and of the continuity of human struggle, the only means of progress—still rings with truth!

Hansberry's warnings about neo-colonialism and the growth (and corruption) of a post-colonial African bourgeoisie—"the servants of empire," as Asagai calls them—are dazzling because of their subsequent replication by reality. As is, above all, her sense of the pressures mounting inexorably in this one typical household, and in Walter Lee especially, and of where they must surely lead. It was the "explosion" Langston Hughes talked about in his great poem "Harlem"—centerpiece of his incomparable *Montage of a Dream Deferred,* from which the play's title was taken—and it informs the play as its twinned projection: dream or coming reality.

These are the categories Langston proposes for the dream:

> Does it dry up
> Like a raisin in the sun?

Dried up is what Walter Lee and Ruth's marriage had become, because their respective dreams have been deferred. When Mama Lena and Beneatha are felled by news of Walter Lee's weakness and dishonesty, their life's will—the desired greening of their humanity—is defoliated.

> Or fester like a sore—
> And then run?

Walter Lee's dream has festered, and in his dealings with the slack-jawed con man Willie (merchant of the stuff of dreams), his dream is "running."

We speak of the American Dream. Malcolm X said that for the Afro-American it was the American Nightmare. The little ferret man . . . is the dream's messenger, and the only white person in the play. His name is Lindner (as in "neither a borrower nor a Lindner be"), and the thirty or so "pieces of silver" he proffers are meant to help the niggers understand the dichotomous dream.

"But you've got to admit that a man, right or wrong, has the right to want to have the neighborhood he lives in a certain kind of way," says Lindner. Except black folks. Yes, these "not rich and fancy" representatives of white lower-middle America have a dream, too. A class dream, though it does not even serve them. But they are kept ignorant enough not to understand that the real dimensions of that dream—white supremacy, black "inferiority," and with them ultimately, though they know it not, fascism and war—are revealed every day throughout the world as deadly to human life and development—even their own.

In the post-civil rights era, in "polite" society, theirs is a dream too gross even to speak of *directly* anymore. And this is another legacy of the play: It was one of the shots fired (and still being fired) at the aberrant white-supremacy dream that is American reality. And the play is also a summation of those shots, that battle, its heightened statement. Yet the man, Lindner, explains him/them self, and there is even a hint of compassion for Lindner the man as he bumbles on in outrageous innocence of all he is actually saying—that "innocence" for which Americans are famous, which begs you to love and understand me for hating you, the innocence that kills. Through him we see this other dream:

> Does it stink like rotten meat?
> Or crust and sugar over—
> Like a syrupy sweet?

Almost everyone else in the play would sound like Martin Luther King at the march on Washington were we to read their speeches closely and project them broadly. An exception is George Murchison (merchant's son), the "assimilated" good bourgeois whose boldest dream, if one can call it that, is to "get the grades . . . to pass the course . . . to get a degree" en route to making it the American way. George wants only to "pop" Beneatha after she, looking good, can be seen with him in the "proper" places. He is opposed to a woman's "thinking" at all, and black heritage to him "is nothing but a bunch of raggedy-ass spirituals and some grass huts." The truth of this portrait is one reason the black bourgeoisie has not created the black national theaters, publishing houses, journals, galleries, film corporations, and newspapers the African American people desperately need. So lacking in self-respect are members of this class of George's, they even let the Kentucky Colonel sell us fried chicken and giblets.

The clash between Walter Lee and George, one of the high points of class struggle in the play and a dramatic tour de force, gives us the dialogue between the *sons* of the house and of the field slaves. (pp. 12-18)

When *Raisin* appeared the movement itself was in transition, which is why Hansberry could sum up its throbbing profile with such clarity. The baton was ready to pass from "George's father" as leader of the "Freedom Movement" (when its real muscle was always the Lena Youngers and their husbands) to the Walter Lees and Beneathas and Asagais and even the Georges.

In February 1960, black students at North Carolina A & T began to "sit in" at Woolworth's in a more forceful attack on segregated public facilities. By the end of 1960, some 96,000 students across the country had gotten involved in these sit-ins. In 1961, Patrice Lumumba was assassinated, and black intellectuals and activists in New York stormed the United Nations gallery. While Ralph Bunche (George's spiritual father) shrank back "embarrassed"—probably more so than by slavery and colonialism! But the Pan African thrust had definitely returned.

And by this time, too, Malcolm X, "the fire prophet," had emerged as the truest reflector of black mass feelings. It was of someone like Malcolm that Walter Lee spoke as in a trance in prophecy while he mounts the table to deliver his liquor-fired call to arms. (Nation of Islam headquarters was Chicago where the play is set!) Walter Lee embodies the explosion to be—what happens when the dream is deferred past even the patience of the Lena Youngers.

Young militants like myself were taken with Malcolm's coming, with the immanence of explosion. (pp. 18-19)

We thought Hansberry's play was part of the "passive resistance" phase of the movement, which was over the minute Malcolm's penetrating eyes and words began to charge through the media with deadly force. We thought her play "middle class" in that its focus seemed to be on "moving into white folks' neighborhoods," when most blacks were just trying to pay their rent in ghetto shacks.

We missed the essence of the work—that Hansberry had created a family on the cutting edge of the same class and ideological struggles as existed in the movement itself and among the people. What is most telling about our ignorance is that Hansberry's play still remains overwhelmingly popular and evocative of black and white reality, and the masses of black people dug it true.

The next two explosions in black drama, Baldwin's *Blues for Mr. Charlie* and my own *Dutchman* (both 1964) raise up the militance and self-defense clamor of the movement as it came fully into the Malcolm era. . . . But neither of these plays is as much a statement from the African American majority as is *Raisin.* For one thing, they are both (regardless of their "power") too concerned with white people.

It is Lorraine Hansberry's play which, though it seems "conservative" in form and content to the radical petty bourgeoisie (as opposed to revolutionaries), is the accurate telling and stunning vision of the real struggle. . . . The Younger family is part of the black majority, and the concerns I once dismissed as "middle class"—buying a house and moving into "white folks' neighborhoods"—are actually reflective of the essence of black people's striving and the will to defeat segregation, discrimination, and national oppression. There is no such thing as a "white folks' neighborhood" except to racists *and to those submitting to racism.*

The Younger family is the incarnation—*before* they burst from the bloody Southern backroads and the burning streets of Watts and Newark onto TV screens and the *world* stage—of our common ghetto-variey Fanny Lou Hamers, Malcolm X's, and Angela Davises. And their burden surely will be lifted, or one day it certainly will "explode." (pp. 19-20)

> *Amiri Baraka, " 'A Raisin in the Sun's' Enduring Passion," in* 'A Raisin in the Sun'; *and*

The Sign in Sidney Brustein's Window, *by Lorraine Hansberry, edited by Robert Nemiroff, New American Library, 1987, pp. 9-20.*

J. Charles Washington

It seems incredible that *A Raisin in the Sun,* which opened on Broadway in 1959, has reached the ripe old age of twenty-nine and even more incredible that its creator, Lorraine Hansberry, who died in 1965 at the age of thirty-four, has already been gone twenty-three years, for she is still spoken of with passion and reverence by a younger generation of writers and critics whom she encouraged and influenced. . . . What has inspired them is not only the quality of her art, but also her courage and commitment. Hansberry was fearless and brash enough to declare that art does have a purpose, and that purpose is to change things. She was not afraid to write a play about social problems because she understood that "there are *no* plays which are not social and no plays that do not have a thesis."

In the eyes of some critics, however, *A Raisin in the Sun* was passé almost before it closed, because they saw it only as a protest play or social drama about a Black family's struggle to buy a house in a white neighborhood. In *Confrontation and Commitment,* C. W. E. Bigsby [see excerpt above] reflects this critical point of view: "For all its sympathy, humour and humanity, . . . [*A Raisin in the Sun*] remains disappointing. . . . Its weakness is essentially that of much Broadway naturalism. It is an unhappy crossbreed of *social protest* and reassuring resolution" (emphasis added). Even more damaging and unsound is the evaluation of critic Harold Cruse [see excerpt above] who, in *The Crisis of the Negro Intellectual,* observes that the play is "the most cleverly written piece of glorified soap opera" he has ever seen.

On the other hand, more perceptive critics, such as Julius Lester in his introduction to *Les Blancs,* early on recognized the play for what it really is: a work of art that contains universal and universally American themes that make it a significant contribution to American dramatic literature. In her recent biography of Hansberry, Ann Cheney writes that " . . . the simple eloquence of the characters elevates the play into a universal presentation of all people's hopes, fears, and dreams."

For Hansberry, there was never a conflict between the play's specific social value and its universal literary value because the latter was inextricably bound to and grew logically out of the former: "I believe that one of the most sound ideas in dramatic writing is that in order to create the universal, you must pay very great attention to the specific. Universality, I think, emerges from the truthful identity of what is." Regarding *Raisin,* Hansberry observed that, while

> . . . there are no waving flags and marching songs at the barricades as Walter marches out with his little battalion, it is not because the battle lacks nobility. On the contrary, he has picked up in his way, still imperfect and wobbly in his small view of human destiny, what I believe Arthur Miller once called "the golden thread of history." He becomes, in spite of those who are too intrigued with despair and hatred of man to see it, King Oedipus refusing

to tear out his eyes, but attacking the Oracle instead. . . . [He] is the nine small heroes of Little Rock; he is Michelangelo creating David, and Beethoven bursting forth with the Ninth Symphony. He is all those things because he has finally reached out in his tiny moment and caught that sweet essence which is human dignity, and it shines like the old star-touched dream that is in his eyes. [see excerpt above]

The dignity of Walter's character is present long before the end of the play, "when he marches out with his little battalion." However, the fact that Walter's dignity is somewhat obscured from view has led many readers, critics, and viewing audiences to misunderstand him and his true intentions. I agree with Douglas Turner Ward that "it is not Walter Lee's action at the end of the play, as meaningful as it is to his development and inspiring to the audience, but his central presence and thrust *throughout the play*" that should be emphasized. The overpowering personality of Lena Younger, particularly her moral rectitude and selfless nature, tends to overshadow Walter, and this accounts in part for the tendency of many readers and audiences to focus their attention almost entirely on her. Unfortunately, this violates the equal balance or proportionate share of the spotlight which each deserves and which the structure of the play calls for.

Some months subsequent to the play's opening, Hansberry regarded the lack of a central character as a flaw in **Raisin.** "I am not certain," writes Douglas Turner Ward, "that, in creating Walter Lee, Lorraine was even fully cognizant of the extent of her accomplishment. Indeed, I think a close reading of the play reveals her ambiguity" [see excerpt above]. There is room for disagreement here, with both the author and with Ward's concluding statement. There is no ambiguity in the writing itself, except for the play's ending where the author intentionally shifts focus from **Raisin's** primary to its secondary meaning in order to satisfy the needs of her Black audience. Rather, misunderstandings and misinterpretations tend to involve the inappropriate moral standards used to measure Walter's character. Our literary judgments, to a large extent, are determined by our own moral standards, by our adherence to the rules society deems appropriate. Generally, these standards differ according to the sex of the individual: A good man, for instance, is strong, aggressive—masculine—, whereas a good woman is sweet, gentle—feminine. It is a grievous error to assess Walter's character by a set of moral standards somewhat more applicable to his mother, whose actions rarely receive censure even though they are far less than ideal. The consequence is a diminution of Walter's strength and dignity, which are in every respect equally as great as, if not greater than, his mother's. Compounding this mistake is the common failure to distinguish between appearance and reality. Judging Walter on his surface actions, as opposed to his deeper, underlying motives and traits of character, one misses his real significance, which Ward has correctly identified: "Lorraine's real triumph . . . is the depiction of Walter Lee as a complex, autonomous character who thinks and acts not as an author's marionette, but as a harbinger of all the qualities of character that would soon explode into American reality and consciousness." To fail to see this complexity is to fail to see the essence of the play and, hence, its aesthetic value; for, as Ward also observes, Walter is both structurally and thematically the play's dramatic focal point: "It is Walter Lee, the bearer of aims and goals that have been conditioned by the prevailing values of the society, who is, dramatically, most representative. It is Walter Lee . . . who emerges as the most unique creation for his time and ours. It is his behavior throughout the play . . . which gives the play prophetic significance. . . ."

If one is able to discern this "prophetic significance," even though Lena overshadows Walter, the lack of a central character is of little consequence. In fact, the dual protagonists and the conflict centered on their differing ways of looking at the world are what give the play dramatic tension as well as intellectual and emotional appeal. In addition, this duality provides a structure that points to the primary meaning of the play—the tragedy of Walter's reach for the American Dream. The intent of this essay is to restore the proper balance between Lena and Walter by focusing on him and his mode of thinking, as well as on the American and Afro-American values which formed his character. "As Lorraine Hansberry always emphasized," but some critics are wont to ignore, "*A Raisin in the Sun* was not just a human document . . , but a play of ideas: a political and philosophical statement."

Ironically, the positive qualities of character which should lend dignity to Walter's character, such as his iron will, his high expectations of himself, and his determination to succeed, are those which often reduce him to the role of villain when he is compared to his mother. Hers may be a more positive image, but this is due to the fact that she must rely on, and fight with, Walter using the only tools available to her—patience, understanding, selflessness, and love—even though these may be, indeed are, genuine expressions of her character. Moreover, though it appears that she relinquishes her role as head of the household out of concern for Walter's welfare, she is no doubt quite happy to lay that burden down. Significantly, this occurs after she has taken a step toward the realization of her own dream by purchasing the house, an act which would seem to nullify Walter's dream. However, no real enmity exists between Walter and his mother, for though opposites in their ways of looking at the world and in their responses to it, they are character types united by love for each other and for their family; both seek to improve the conditions affecting their lives.

That Walter seems to many to possess an inordinate degree of self-respect and to expect too much out of life for himself and for his family may have more to do with viewers' perceptions than with Walter's actions. If one has been conditioned to expect little, as many Blacks have been through racism, or to believe that Blacks deserve and are entitled to little, as some members of society have been led to believe, then the demand for any degree above this "conditioned less" will seem excessive. For such viewers Lena Younger's dream appears much more "normal." There is a logical explanation for Lena Younger's behavior. According to the findings of Black female scholar Claudia Tate, editor of *Black Women Writers at Work*, Lena's posture reflects not only racial but gender conditioning: "The black heroine seldom elects to play the role of the alienated outsider or the lone adventurer in her quest for self-affirmation. This does not mean that she is unconcerned about her self-esteem . . . , but rather that her quest . . . has different priorities and takes place in a different landscape. . . . she is usually literally tied down to her children." Because Lena Younger's children, though fully grown, and family come first, her purchasing the house they need so badly may seem to viewers of the play a much more sensible idea than Walter's wanting to open a business.

Yet the root of the conflict between them goes deeper than this. Lena Younger's thinking is restricted by time. Hers is the thinking of a Black woman born near the turn of the century in a racist American society, and she does not understand the modern ways and thinking of her children. "Something has changed," she tells Walter. "You something new, boy. In my time we was worried about not being lynched and getting to the North if we could and how to stay alive and still have a pinch of dignity too . . . Now here come you and Beneatha—talking 'bout things we ain't never even thought about hardly, me and your daddy. You ain't satisfied or proud of nothing we done. I mean that you had a home; that we kept you out of trouble till you was grown; that you don't have to ride to work on the back of nobody's streetcar—You my children—but how different we done become." As this statement makes clear, racial conditioning has had as profound an impact on her life as that of gender. Her experiences with discrimination as a young woman in the South affected her thinking. While they did not destroy her self-esteem, they did color her outlook on life, narrowing her perspective and restricting her beliefs about what a Black person could reasonably expect to achieve in American society. The only way a Black person could escape discrimination in the South of that time was to move to the North. Though it was a compromise, the action she took meant that she was a fighter who took the step that many of her generation did in order to make a meaningful change in her life. In fact, she is still a fighter, and she proves it by buying the house to bring about the change she now feels is needed for her family's welfare. . . . Her belief in this change, which is her version of the American Dream, sets her at odds with her son Walter. Like her earlier move to the North, the purchase of a suburban Chicago house reflects a compromise or acceptance of less than she deserves or is entitled to. Hers is, in short, not the true American Dream, but a second-class version of it reserved for Black Americans and other poor people. Considering all the obstacles she has had to face as a Black woman, one can hardly fault her for what she does. Nevertheless, her dream is unacceptable to Walter, who will have nothing less than the complete American Dream, since her version of it only amounts to surviving, not living in the fullest sense.

Unlike his mother, Walter has managed to escape almost completely the crippling inferiority that destroys many Blacks, men in particular. In order to help determine how he managed to acquire the strength to dream his dream, one might examine what is most American about Walter and his thinking, for it is his acceptance of American values, rather than stereotypes, myths, and untruths about Blacks, that enables him to dream and act in a typically American way. As Hansberry has stated, " . . . Walter Younger is an American more than he is anything else." Foremost is his belief in the value which holds that, in the land of opportunity, anyone can become anything he wants to be. While the play contains no explicit evidence to support this conjecture, the fact that this democratic ideal is the most cherished of those which form the American consciousness—indeed, is synonymous with the freedom that America stands for—means that Walter would be affected by it, as all Americans are. Believers in this myth let nothing stand in their way, as he does not. For him, this includes racism, which he barely considers until he is directly confronted with it in Act II, Scene 3, in the person of Carl Lindner, who tries to bribe the family in order to keep them out of his white neighborhood. Even then it has no real effect on his dream or his plans.

Another source of Walter's strength is the fact that he is male. As Lena Younger's world view and range of possibilities are restricted by her femaleness, Walter's are enlarged and enhanced by his maleness. Another source of strength lies in his belief in himself and in his ability to do what other successful Americans have done. He sincerely believes that he is cut out for better things. . . . This strong faith in himself is the basis of his typically American self-reliance and rugged individualism.

Ironically, the influences of his own Black family and the values they believed in and lived by prepared Walter to accept mainstream American values and to strive to reach his goal; however, he was also influenced by outside forces existing in the society at large. These delicately balanced value systems both coexist to provide a particular individual and form the basis of the biculturality which characterizes the Afro-American. At the same time, this fact of biculturality underscores the two levels of universality inherent in the Black American experience: The dreams, hopes, and fears of the Younger family are universal reflections of those shared by people of all races all over the world, and these are universally American aspirations.

These family influences are of two kinds and produce two significant results. First, the love Walter received from his parents during his childhood led to the development of his strong sense of self-esteem, enabling him fully to accept American values and giving him the confidence to pursue his dream. Second, the example of courage and dignity invested in his parents' valiant struggle to overcome adversity, provide for their children, and teach them to be better than ordinary resulted in his love of his race and his pride in his heritage. The stronger of these influences as it relates to his self-esteem is that which came from his mother, although his father's contribution was important as well. The similarity between Lena and her son, which ironically she fails to recognize, is clearly revealed in her words about herself: "Lord, ever since I was a little girl, I always remember people saying, 'Lena—Lena Eggleston, you aims too high all the time. You needs to slow down and see life a little more like it is. Just slow down some.' That's what they always used to say down home—'Lord, that Lena Eggleston is a high-minded thing'." Walter's father also played a meaningful role in his life, as seen in Lena's statement that Big Walter "sure loved his children. Always wanted them to have something—be something. That's where Brother gets all these notions. . . . "

Because he is "high-minded" and wants to "be something," Walter readily accepts the American value which holds that owning one's own business is the primary path to economic success and prosperity. His acceptance of this value contrasts with Lena's belief in the efficacy of hard physical labor like that which killed her husband and which she still does. Hers is an attitude based on a kind of reverse elitism which imbues hard work with a respectability and dignity that business does not possess. It seems to spring from the kind of thinking reflected in the old adage "Money is the root of all evil," which is at odds with the American Horatio Alger myth, as well as with the historic tendency of Protestantism to combine "an extraordinary capitalistic business sense . . . with the most intensive forms of a piety." Her feelings about the moral superiority of work and the contempt she holds towards business are made clear in her comment that "we ain't no business people, Ruth. We just plain working folks." (pp. 109-16)

This facet of her world view arises from her own particular Protestant religious beliefs, and it is very likely that her attitude toward hard work is a residue of the cultural conditioning Blacks received during slavery when the Bible was used to convince them to be satisfied with their lot. In fact, Lena Younger gives manual labor a kind of mythical, almost Biblical meaning: As Jesus gave his life for man, Big Walter gave his life for her and his family. In other words, work itself, as well as the sacrifice of the worker, is given a higher meaning than the financial and material rewards it was intended to bring. Of course, this reaction is in part a psychological defense mechanism. So little of a material nature remains of Big Walter's life, aside from the $10,000 check, that his sacrifice and the love it represents are all she has left and the only meaning she can find in it. This attitude has an unfortunate effect on her life. While it may make her dying more peaceful, it makes her living more difficult.

Walter, on the other hand, shares neither her attitude toward hard work nor her worry about transgressing God's laws. In fact, other than his having been taken to church "every Sunday" as a child, he is not a religious person. This is not, however, to say that he is immoral. Indeed, in light of the parental influences on his life, especially those of his mother, it would be almost impossible for him to have abandoned moral values completely. The separation of moral values from religious dogma, however, is seen in his sister Beneatha's modern attitude toward God, an attitude which approximates his own and which is antithetical to his mother's: "Mama, you don't understand. It's all a matter of ideas, and God is just one idea I don't accept. It's not important. I'm not going out and be immoral or commit crimes because I don't believe in God. I don't even think about it. It's just that I get tired of Him getting credit for all the things the human race achieves through its own stubborn effort. There simply is no blasted God—there is only man and it is he who makes miracles!" Unknown to her, and possibly even to him, Beneatha's faith in man is borne out in the dreams and strivings of her brother, who in his own way attempts to make his own miracle.

Walter's dream of success was nurtured by a young white man whom he saw in town and sought to emulate. He has not modeled himself after his father, whose death and sacrifice assume a meaning for him which is radically different from that which his mother has given them. His image of his father matches the old stereotype of the hardworking, long-suffering Black male who literally worked himself to death. As Lena says, "I seen . . . him . . . night after night . . . come in . . . and then look at me . . . the red showing in his eyes . . . the veins moving in his head . . . I seen him grow thin and old before he was

forty . . . working and working and working like somebody's old horse . . . killing himself. . . . " There is no way Walter could forget this image, and the check becomes the symbolic representation of the senseless waste of his father's life. Other tangible signs of it are the cramped, roach-infested apartment, the shabby furniture, and the worn out rug on the floor. No matter how much he may have loved his father, it would be unthinkable to want to replicate his father's life. For this reason, the young white men his age personify for him the true American Dream, a dream he knows he is worthy of: "Mama—sometimes when I'm downtown and pass them cool, quiet-looking restaurants where them white boys are sitting back and talking 'bout things . . . sitting there turning deals worth millions of dollars . . . sometimes I see guys don't look much older than me."

The stimulation that he gets downtown from seeing the young white men is quite different from that which he gets from the Black musicians at a Southside Chicago bar called the Green Hat: "You know what I like about the Green Hat? I like this little cat they got there who blows a sax . . . He blows. He talks to me. . . . And there's this older guy who plays the piano . . . and they got a sound. . . . They got the best little combo in the world in the Green Hat . . . You can just sit there and drink and listen to them three men play and you realize that don't nothing matter worth a damn, but just being there." The former source of stimulation invites action, while the latter induces inactivity. The actions of the young white men stimulate him to hope, dream, think, even scheme. Black music, on the other hand, becomes for him a kind of drug or narcotic that lulls him into a state of listlessness which allows him to escape depression.

His reliance on white models does not mean that he hates himself or his blackness. Rather, it is a sign of his pragmatism and confirms his self-love: He believes he can do what they do and that he deserves to have what they have. (pp. 116-18)

Strong, aggressive, ambitious, ruthless even, like the men he imitates, Walter reaches for the complete American Dream. It is natural that he would, for the freedom that America grants an individual holds the possibility of unlimited riches, both spiritual and economic. What Walter dreams of and aggressively pursues is the power that money brings, power being the essence of the only kind of manhood he is willing to accept. Of course, some degree of self-aggrandizement is attached to the American Dream; many of those who attain it, such as captains of industry, do become great American heroes. However, Walter's personal stake in his dream must be balanced by the primary purpose for which he seeks it—a radical change in his family's living conditions. This change is much wider in scope than Lena's planned move from their cramped apartment to a larger suburban home. It means a wholly different and improved standard of living: a substantial move up the socio-economic ladder, the complete abandonment of poverty, the chance to live the kind of life most Americans dream of living. The selflessness and nobility of this dream are what give Walter's character its dignity and spiritual dimension.

Long before he receives the money from his mother, near the end of Act I, Scene 2, Walter demonstrates the selfless nature of his dream. When Lena tells him, "There ain't going to be no investing in no liquor stores," Walter replies: "Well, *you* tell that to my boy tonight when you put him to sleep on the living-room couch . . . Yeah—and tell it to my wife, Mama, tomorrow when she has to go out of here to look after somebody else's kids. And tell it to *me,* Mama, every time we need a new pair of curtains and I have to watch *you* go out and work in somebody's kitchen. Yeah, you tell me then!" The same selflessness characterizes the long fantasy he spins at the end of Act II, Scene 2, after Lena has given him the money, which he plans to invest in the liquor store without her knowledge: His main concern is not for himself, but for his wife and son. Finally, his altruistic purpose is seen near the play's end, when he tries to explain the reason for the action that led to his losing the money. Unrepentant but on the defensive, he says, "Hell, yes, I want me some yachts someday! Yes, I want to hang some real pearls 'round my wife's neck. Ain't she supposed to wear no pearls? Somebody tell me—tell me, who decides which women is supposed to wear pearls in this world. I tell you I am a *man*—and I think my wife should wear some pearls in this world!"

Because the legitimate pursuit of financial security and prosperity can so easily become the immoral acquisitiveness that leads to materialism, it should be emphasized again that Walter's goal, as seen in his fantasy, rests on a morally sound foundation. Modest by comparison to the status of many middle-class Americans, his dream of a lovely home with a gardener, two rather expensive cars, and the choice of the best schools for his son's education could not be called an example of rampant, conspicuous consumption. A further clue to its moral soundness is that in Walter's eyes he would be repaying a debt owed to his father; he would be making his father's dream come true by actualizing his prophecy: " 'Seem like God didn't see fit to give the black man nothing but dreams—but He did give us children to make them dreams seem worth while'." Moreover, in his own way he would be heeding his mother's admonition to "push on out and do something bigger," words she had uttered when telling him why she had made a downpayment on the house. Finally, possessing wealth is not inherently wrong or immoral. The poor do not have a monopoly on morality. As Walter knows, money is not the root of evil; it is what evil people do with it that leads to immorality.

Walter realizes that it requires a great deal of money to live the kind of life his family deserves. Thus, his action is a pragmatic one based on the reality of life. At the end of Act I, Scene 2, when Lena asks him, "Son—how come you talk so much 'bout money?" Walter replies, "Because it is life, Mama!" The dialogue between them which follows this exchange further illustrates their conflicting world views:

> LENA. Oh—So now it's life. Money is life. Once upon a time freedom used to be life—now it's money. I guess the world really do change . . .
>
> WALTER. No—it was always money, Mama. We just didn't know about it.

The pronoun *we* refers not just to the Younger family, but to Blacks in particular and to the American people in general. The more fundamental difference between the world views of Lena and Walter, then, turns on their respective meanings of *freedom* and their efforts to attain it. The freedom that Lena seeks, the struggle for which has dominated the social and political history of Blacks in the United States, is freedom from racism and discrimination or the unfinished business of slavery. In contrast to Lena, Hansberry, whose prescience remains uncredited, pointed out through Walter in 1959 a much more important kind of freedom, economic freedom, which, with few exceptions (most notably Marcus Garvey in the 1920s), Black leaders and intellectuals only began to discuss a decade later. . . . Often treated like a mental cripple by members of his family, especially his sister Beneatha, Walter is astute enough to recognize the power of money as the source of both social and political freedom in America. He knows that money is the best remedy for the twin evils of racism/discrimination and poverty, and that only with this kind of freedom can one speak of having realized the American Dream.

While the freedom the individual enjoys in America provides for opportunities, it does not guarantee success. Walter's dream remains only that not because of defects in the American system but because of basic flaws in his own character. His recognition of the responsibility for his own fate marks him as a tragic hero.

Though in Act III he indulges in self-pity after he has lost the money, railing about the "takers and the 'tooken' " as he tries to escape the blame for his failure, Walter had indicated earlier, in Act II, Scene 3, that he was aware of the danger his plan entailed. Speaking of his plan to George Murchinson, Walter remarks, "Invest big, gamble big, hell, lose *big* if you have to. . . ." He knows that the possibility of failure is also a vital part of the American success story. Though as viewers of the play we know this too, we are nevertheless deeply affected by his failure because of the nobility of his dream and the vigor and intensity with which he pursues it. We have sympathy for him in spite of the fact that he bullies his wife, ridicules his sister's dream, deceives his mother, and attempts to bribe state officials in Springfield in order to get a liquor license for the business. Even more serious than these defects in his character as they affect his dream, and hence the welfare of his family, is his flaw in judgment; he considers Willy Harris a successful businessman when he is really an untrustworthy con man. In regard to the likelihood of Walter's success in business, an even greater flaw would be his lack of knowledge of how a business is run. This is not to say that he requires a Harvard M.B.A., for another vital part of the American success story is the great number of individuals lacking formal education who with raw talent, intelligence, drive, and luck have succeeded in establishing and running their own businesses. At the same time, Walter fails to see the potential value of education. This attitude is evident in his disparaging remarks about his sister's plans to become a doctor, although they also reflect stereotypical male chauvinism regarding the careers women should or should not pursue. . . . Walter has disdain for education not only because he feels it is a waste of time, but also because the sensitive, intellectual types who pursue it do not correspond to his conception of manhood. For him, the only "real" men are the powerful ones who manage America's businesses. His mistake lies not only in his false conception of manhood but also in his failure to see that some kind of education, formal or otherwise, is a necessary requirement for his goal, particularly as there is in his community no cultural basis of business ownership comparable to that in mainstream American communities through which he could learn what he needs to know about business management. Finally, while his initial contact with young white males was positive, inasmuch as they supplied him with the inspiration for his desperate attempt to escape poverty, his casual contact with them could not provide him with the hands-on experience he needed to attain his goal. Even if he had been able to acquire the business, his chances of success would have been affected by both his lack of knowledge and his lack of experience. While Walter himself is largely responsible for his negative attitude toward education, his lack of experience, over which he has no control, points out the need for positive business contacts or role models in his own Black community.

Although the end of the play supplies conclusive proof of the soundness of Walter's character as he comes to appreciate a concept of manhood based on love rather than power and accepts the consequences of his actions by refusing to exchange his family's racial pride and dignity for money, it does not resolve the family's economic plight. They remain in the same depressed economic condition. Before discussing this idea, however, I must comment on the specific nature of the change Walter undergoes, for it has often been misunderstood, leading to a distortion of his character and of the primary meaning of the play. As I have attempted to show, the play's meaning is a tragic one, as Walter reaches for the American Dream but fails to achieve it. Grafted onto this meaning and running parallel to it is a secondary meaning. Realistic in form, it lies in Walter's symbolic representation of Black people's struggles and triumphs, and it is this secondary meaning and its resolution in transcendence that elicit tremendous emotional responses from audience members, especially Black ones, who view the play.

Rather than relying solely on the cathartic resolution the play's tragic meaning was capable of producing—an option available to her—, Hansberry vitiated the power of her main theme by making allowance for a more traditional "happy ending" that Black audiences could readily identify with and appreciate. To her credit, the stage business she added to accomplish her goal fits logically within the context of both the primary and secondary meanings of the play. Walter's final action does not represent a renunciation of American values or of his belief in the rightness of his dream of opening a business. That would have required a specious *deus ex machina* or illogical outcome of what the play had consistently shown throughout about Walter and his thinking. On the contrary, his final action represents a strong and unqualified repudiation of American racist "values," and of his own threatened immoral conduct—he had planned to accept Lindner's bribe as a desperate means of recouping the loss of his money. While Walter never admits explicitly his own responsibility for the loss, this frantic effort to recover it must be taken as his acceptance and recognition of his culpability. This act of an Uncle Tom, which he has rehearsed for his mother, complete with grotesque dialect and gestures, and which instills fear in the audience and primes them for his change, would have meant debasing his own and his family's honor, pride, and dignity. . . . It is natural, then, that his refusal to play the Tom would cause Black audience members whose lives are characterized by the same kinds of struggles to be swept away in a tremendous outpouring

of emotions and that, as an unfortunate result, his heroic reach for the American Dream and his tragic fall—the primary meaning of the play—might tend to be ignored.

Another factor contributing to this view might be wishful thinking on the part of some members of the Black audience. Those who believe that Walter's goal is purely materialistic and therefore immoral are content to see his supposed renunciation of American values as an expression of the moral superiority they believe Blacks possess. Finally, Lena's comment to Ruth that "he finally come into his manhood today . . . " compounds the problem. True, Walter is forced to re-accept this concept of manhood, which he already knew well because he had learned it from his father; however, his reversion to it does not necessarily mean that he believes any less in the American concept of manhood as money or power—an understanding he prefers. Because Walter is the product of two cultures whose character is shaped by the permanent possession of two different sets of values, his tenacious adherence to the mainstream American values that he believes are morally sound is no less surprising than the seemingly sudden and unexpected resurgence of the Black values his parents had instilled in him. While the overwhelming majority of the audience applauds him for this victory, which was not his alone because "it drew on the strength of an incredible people . . . ," very few have appreciated his heroic reach for the American Dream, which required even greater strength, precisely because he had to do it alone, unaided by a similar kind of inner cultural resource.

Viewers of *A Raisin in the Sun* can be moved by a tragic hero who is elevated by his growth from ignorance to knowledge, and deeply affected by a realistic hero whose transcendence involves a tremendous sacrifice—at the play's end, Walter and his family are as poor and powerless as they were before. The new house provides a "pinch of dignity" that allows them a bit more breathing and living space, but their lives are essentially unchanged. Without the greater financial rewards the business could have produced, they must all continue working at the same menial jobs in order to survive and pay for the house. In fact, they may be even worse off, since the birth of Ruth's second child will mean an extra mouth to feed. Walter and Ruth have made no substantive economic progress; their current life is a modern version of the life of Lena and Big Walter. The principal hope that Ruth and Walter have is the one Lena and Big Walter had and which people everywhere have always had—that some day in the future their children will be able to make their parents' dreams come true.

Considering that this sobering reality should provide a cause for despair would involve a serious misunderstanding of the author's intention and a grievous contradiction of her faith in the perfectability of humanity based on her conviction that humankind will "do what the apes never will—*impose* the reason for life on life." Moreover, this small but significant hope, as well as the characters who embody it, offers perhaps the best example of the universal materials the play abounds in, giving Hansberry's art its distinguishing mark and enduring value. Illustrating her ability to see synthesis where others could only see dichotomy, Hansberry discovered the basis of this universal hope, indeed of her faith in humanity, in the Black experience: " . . . if blackness brought pain, it was also a source

of strength, renewal and inspiration, a window on the potentials of the human race. For if Negroes could survive
America, then there was hope for the human race indeed."
(pp. 118-24)

> *J. Charles Washington, " 'A Raisin in the Sun'
> Revisited," in* Black American Literature
> Forum, *Vol. 22, No. 1, Spring, 1988, pp. 109-
> 24.*

FURTHER READING

Baraka, Amiri. *"Raisin in the Sun's* Enduring Passion." *The
Washington Post.* (16 November 1989): pp. F1-3.
　　Reappraisal of *A Raisin in the Sun* that affirms its stature
　　as "an esthetically powerful and politically advanced
　　work of art."

Brown-Guillory, Elizabeth. "Black Women Playwrights: Ex-
orcising Myths." *Phylon* XLVIII, No. 3 (Fall 1987): pp. 229-
39.
　　Compares *A Raisin in the Sun* to dramas by Alice Chil-
　　dress and Ntozake Shange.

Carter, Steven. *Hansberry's Drama: Commitment amid Complexity.* Champaign-Urbana: University of Illinois Press,
1990. 216p.
　　A biographical and critical overview of Hansberry's ca-
　　reer.

Cheney, Anne. "Measure Him Right: *A Raisin in the Sun.*"
In her *Lorraine Hansberry,* pp. 55-71. Boston: Twayne Pub-
lishers, 1984.
　　Detailed explication of *A Raisin in the Sun.*

Davis, Arthur P. "Lorraine Hansberry." In his *From the
Dark Tower: Afro-American Writers 1900-1960,* pp. 203-07.
Washington, D. C.: Howard University Press, 1974.
　　Brief overview of Hansberry's career.

Dedmond, Francis. "Lorraine Hansberry." In *American
Playwrights Since 1945,* edited by Philip C. Kolin, pp. 155-68.
New York: Greenwood Press, 1989.
　　Provides a brief assessment of Hansberry's career as well
　　as an overview of the play's production history and a
　　bibliography of secondary sources.

Hooks, Bell. *"Raisin* in a New Light." *Christianity and Crisis*
(6 February 1989): 21-3.
　　Contends that Hansberry and her work continues to in-

spire African-Americans thirty years after the debut of
A Raisin in the Sun.

*Lorraine Hansberry: The Black Experience in the Creation of
Drama* 16mm, 35 min. 1979. Distributed by Films for the
Humanities, Inc., Princeton, N.J.
　　Short film tracing Hansberry's life and career from her
　　early childhood in Chicago to her death at the age of 34.
　　Features her own previously recorded comments as well
　　as excerpts from productions of her work.

Freedomways 19, No. 4 (1979).
　　Special issue devoted to Hansberry that includes essays
　　by James Baldwin, Nikki Giovanni, and Alex Haley.

Nemiroff, Robert. Introduction to *A Raisin in the Sun,* by
Lorraine Hansberry, pp. ix-xviii. New York: Signet / New
American Library, 1987.
　　Reappraisal of *A Raisin in the Sun* by Hansberry's for-
　　mer husband that focuses upon sequences removed from
　　the original production and restored in a recent revival
　　of the play.

Norment, Lynn. *"Raisin* Celebrates Its 25th Anniversary."
Ebony XXXIX, No. 5 (March 1984): 57-60.
　　A production history of *A Raisin in the Sun* featuring
　　photographs of the original staging.

Olauson, Judith. "1950-1960." In her *The American Woman
Playwright: A View of Criticism and Characterization,* pp. 77-
99. Troy: The Whitston Publishing Company, 1981.
　　Analysis of the play that focuses upon Hansberry's char-
　　acterization of Walter and Lena.

Peerman, Dean. *"A Raisin in the Sun*: The Uncut Version."
The Christian Century (25 January 1989): 71-3.
　　Discussion of the play focusing upon material excised
　　from the original production that clarifies its social and
　　political themes.

Wilkerson, Margaret B. *"A Raisin in the Sun*: Anniversary
of an American Classic." *Theatre Journal* 38, No. 4 (December 1986): 441-52.
　　Article celebrating the enduring qualities of *A Raisin in
　　the Sun.*

Wilkerson, Margaret B. "The Sighted Eyes and Feeling
Heart of Lorraine Hansberry." *Black American Literature
Forum* 17, No. 1 (Spring 1983): pp. 8-13.
　　A brief biographical and critical survey of Hansberry's
　　career, centering upon *A Raisin in the Sun.*

Tony Hillerman

1925-

(Born Anthony Grove Hillerman) American novelist.

Critically acclaimed for their accurate and dramatic evocations of contemporary Native American life, Hillerman's mystery novels are set in the "Four Corners"—the Southwestern region where the borders of Colorado, Arizona, New Mexico, and Utah intersect. Most of Hillerman's works focus on Navajo police detectives Joe Leaphorn and Jim Chee, whose investigations cover the Navajo, Hopi, Apache, and Zuñi reservations. Educated at universities but cognizant of Navajo customs, the two protagonists personify sharp contrasts between the majority and minority cultures of the Southwest. Constantly mediating between Native American groups and numerous white law enforcement agencies, Leaphorn and Chee solve mysteries through a judicious blend of the white man's logic and the Navajo's nature-oriented metaphysics. Most reviewers esteem Hillerman's novels less for their conventional detective plots than for their illumination of Indian cultures. Robin W. Winks observed: "[Hillerman] has developed his own niche in mystery and detective fiction . . . by turning the mystery and its solution upon the intricate social and religious life of the Indians of the American Southwest. These books could exist nowhere else, they are authentic, and the resolutions grow out of the character of an entire people."

Raised in a German-American family that settled among the Pottawotomie, Blackfoot, and Seminole tribes of Oklahoma, Hillerman developed an early appreciation for Native American traditions. After retiring from a career in newspaper reporting, he became a professor of journalism at the University of New Mexico, where he wrote his first novel, *The Blessing Way*. Focusing on the apparent murder of a young Navajo by a wolf spirit, this novel introduces police Lieutenant Joe Leaphorn, a reserved, logical, and partially assimilated Navajo who tracks down the killer. Leaphorn investigates Zuñi tribal rites in *The Dance Hall of the Dead*, which earned Hillerman the Edgar Allan Poe Award from the Mystery Writers of America. This second Leaphorn mystery begins with the murder of Ernesto Cata, a Zuñi boy in training for the ceremonial role of the fire god Shulawitsi. Suspicion falls on Cata's Navajo friend, George Bowlegs, who longs to become a Zuñi and spends his time chasing the *kachinas,* lake spirits who could admit him to the tribe. When Bowlegs is killed, Leaphorn discovers the actual murderer is a white archaeologist, who, after "salting" his excavation site with artifacts that would support his theories, killed the Indian boys to keep them from exposing his counterfeit practices.

In Hillerman's next novel, *Listening Woman,* detective Leaphorn meets Margaret Cigaret, a traditional Navajo healer who discerns the cause of illnesses by listening to the wind. After Margaret leaves the *hogan,* or dwelling, of the ailing Hosteen Tso to hear the wind, Tso and Margaret's niece are killed inside. The healer's testimony leads Leaphorn to discover that Tso had broken a tribal taboo by attempting to preserve his sand paintings, sacred draw-

ings intended to be ephemeral. Of Hillerman's first three Leaphorn novels, Newgate Callendar remarked: "[Each] has been a model of its kind: well plotted, full of Indian lore and the feeling of the desert, never condescending, beautifully written." *People of Darkness* introduces Hillerman's second detective, Sargeant Jim Chee of the Navajo tribal police. Younger and more immersed in traditional Navajo beliefs than Leaphorn, Chee is a part-time tribal ceremonial singer who occasionally considers adopting an American lifestyle in order to join the Federal Bureau of Investigation. In Chee's first adventure, a burglary in a wealthy white man's house leads to an examination of an oil-rig explosion that occured thirty years earlier. In *The Dark Wind,* Chee pursues criminals involved in a cocaine ring who have killed several Navajos. Chee's specialty, tracking criminals across the desert, combines his high-tech police training with the intimate knowledge of land that is instilled in most Navajos. Hillerman's next work, *The Ghostway,* takes Chee to Los Angeles in search of two Navajos who steal luxury cars. When one of the thieves returns to the reservation, he is killed in his uncle's *hogan.* Chee notices that whoever prepared the body for burial neglected the ceremonial ritual of washing the dead man's hair in yucca. While Chee's Navajo heritage helps him to solve the mystery more quickly than the federal agents to whom he is assigned, it also isolates him from his lover, a white schoolteacher who wants him to leave the reservation.

Leaphorn and Chee unite to probe four murders in *Skinwalkers,* a novel that begins when Chee's trailer is battered by a shotgun blast. Skeptical of Chee's involvement in Navajo shamanism, Leaphorn suspects his younger colleague of consorting with criminals. Although their temperaments and convictions differ, the two develop a grudging alliance, and ultimately deduce that the murderer thought his victims were *skinwalkers,* or Navajo demons. Jean M. White commented: "Once again Hillerman evokes the haunting sense of place with the arid, harsh Southwest landscape. This hard land is as much a character in *Skinwalkers* as the Navajos and their world of ancient rites and beliefs. It is difficult to believe that Hillerman is not a Navajo himself." At the beginning of *Talking God,* a lawyer for the Smithsonian Institution's Museum of Natural History opens her mail and finds two human skeletons. A note identifies them as her New England grandparents. The anonymous sender, who is protesting the museum's refusal to return Native American ancestral remains to descendants, insists the Smithsonian display these skeletons instead. Both Leaphorn and Chee, involved in separate investigations on the reservation, unearth clues that lead them to Washington, D.C. While some critics noted minor errors in Hillerman's depiction of the city, most lauded the novel's unique, Navajo perspective and praised Hillerman's diverse and astute characterizations. Jane S. Bakerman stated: "[Hillerman's mysteries are] telling commentaries upon American life in the Southwest, for in addition to beautiful nature imagery and remarkably clear and effective glimpses into Native American life, they offer vivid accounts of the difficulties of operating in a multi-ethnic society."

(See also *Contemporary Authors,* Vols. 29-32, rev. ed. and *Contemporary Authors New Revision Series,* Vol. 21.)

PRINCIPAL WORKS

NOVELS

The Blessing Way 1970
The Fly on the Wall 1971
Dance Hall of the Dead 1973
Listening Woman 1977
The People of Darkness 1978
The Dark Wind 1981
The Ghostway 1984
Skinwalkers 1986
A Thief of Time 1988
Talking God 1989

Allen J. Hubin

In-depth explorations of sub-culture are not often found in detective fiction. In fact, only one example comes to mind: the illuminating and evocative novels by Arthur W. Upfield about Inspector Napoleon Bonaparte and the aborigines of Australia. Mr. Upfield's death in 1968 repre-

sented a great loss to our genre, and no one appeared on the detective horizon to take up his mantle. Now, though it is certainly too early to suggest that Tony Hillerman, with his first novel *The Blessing Way* will do so, some promising flickers come through.

Mr. Hillerman was raised and schooled among Indians, and now lives in New Mexico. Although the protagonist of his story is a Caucasian—Dr. Bergen McKee, educator and researcher on Navajo tribal witchcraft—greater appeal for me lies in the well-developed, spirited presentation of Indians: policeman Joe Leaphorn, called Law and Order; Luis Horseman, on the run from a criminal charge and from an enemy he does not know; the Navajo Wolf, the legendary wielder of witchcraft, rumored now to be abroad with death in the hills. It will be interesting to see what Mr. Hillerman does with this milieu in the future. (p. 36)

> *Allen J. Hubin, in a review of "The Blessing Way," in* The New York Times Book Review, *April 19, 1970, pp. 36-7.*

A. L. Rosenzweig

Locale is of key importance to the thriller writer. It's often the prime mover of the story; it's more often there, alas, for the production value, to dress the background and throw off an exotic odor. . . .

Tony Hillerman, who teaches journalism at the University of New Mexico and grew up with the Navajo, not unexpectedly chose an Indian reservation as setting for *The Blessing Way.* He has created an intriguing Indian sleuth in Joe Leaphorn of Law and Order, but I wish there had been more Leaphorn and less cultural anthropology. The plot turns on the apparent witch murder of a young Navajo delinquent in a lost stretch of land near enough a government radar installation so that certain conclusions can be drawn rather early in the proceedings. Witchcraft lore comes thick and fast with the appearance of a college professor looking for source material on primitive legend. Hillerman is a dab hand at evocative topological description, hunting songs and Navajo orthography, but he's unfortunately weak on twanging the nerves in his first offering.

> *A. L. Rosenzweig, in a review of "The Blessing Way," in* Book World—The Washington Post, *May 10, 1970, p. 14.*

The New Yorker

[*The Blessing Way* is a] thriller set among the mountains and deserts and labyrinthine canyons of the Navajo reservation in northeastern Arizona, and enriched by the matching spiritual complexities of the Navajo Way and a chorus cast of Scalp Shooters, Stick Carriers, Hand Tremblers, Listeners, and Singers. The action has to do with the murder of a young Navajo named Luis Horseman by a manifestation of the Navajo Wolf (or werewolf), and it is most satisfyingly resolved by a Blue Policeman called Lieutenant Joe Leaphorn.

> *A review of "The Blessing Way," in* The New Yorker, *Vol. XLVI, No. 16, June 6, 1970, p. 136.*

The New Yorker

"The fly on the wall" is Walter Lippmann's depiction of the ideal newspaperman—observant, objective, uninvolved. [In *The Fly on the Wall*] Mr. Hillerman introduces us to one John Cotton, an experienced political reporter at the state capital, who is just such a newspaperman. Cotton stumbles into a situation that leads him to the discovery of some high-priced corruption in the state highway department and elsewhere. A moral question then arises: publication of the story will hurt a good politician and profit a crooked one. This draws us quickly and inescapably into a thriller that is not merely thrilling (with a stunning manhunt high in the mountains north of Santa Fe and another in the midnight corridors of the statehouse) but also a provocative ethical conundrum. (pp. 142-43)

> *A review of "The Fly on the Wall," in* The New Yorker, *Vol. XLVII, No. 32, September 25, 1971, pp. 142-43.*

Newgate Callendar

Ethnic mysteries, when well done, have always attracted a wide audience. . . . Tony Hillerman's *Dance Hall of the Dead* is a fine example of the sub-genre.

This time, it is the American Indian culture that is examined. A few white men appear, but the main characters and the ambience are Indian. Two boys are missing from their New Mexico reservation. One of them may have been murdered. Police Lieut. Joe Leaphorn, a Navajo, is the investigating officer. The trail leads him into Indian religious rites, anthropology and drugs.

It will be a dull reader who has not figured out the murderer halfway through—but that, somehow, is not important. Hillerman knows his background well, and is skillful enough to make it an integral part of the action. He has created an altogether believable set of characters. Never once is there an indication that he is slumming or in any way feels superior.

> *Newgate Callendar, in a review of "Dance Hall of the Dead," in* The New York Times Book Review, *November 25, 1973 p. 49.*

Newgate Callendar

Unlike the two-a-year wonders, Tony Hillerman seems to spend time writing his books—and it shows. . . . [In 1970] he started a series about a college-educated Indian policeman in New Mexico. There have not been many books since then, but each has been a model of its kind: well plotted, full of Indian lore and the feeling of the desert, never condescending, beautifully written. Now Lieut. Joe Leaphorn is back, in *The Listening Woman.*

The basic ingredients and some of the leading characters are much the same. Leaphorn, himself a Navajo, can naturally work with the reservation people much more sympathetically than white law officers, and he can also understand nuances that would be undetectable to those without Indian blood. In *The Listening Woman,* several elements are tied together: the murder of an old Indian and a young Indian girl, the disappearance of a helicopter, a Wells Fargo robbery, Indian political activists and a killer who operates with a huge, savage dog. At the end there is a climax involving Boy Scouts held as hostages.

There is plenty of good, action-packed detective work in this book. And, as in the previous books, there are insights into the way Indians today think and function. Mr. Hillerman, who lives in New Mexico, obviously has done a great deal of research into Indian customs and religion. Above all there is the country—hot, forbidding, with its own austere kind of beauty. *The Listening Woman* ranks even with Mr. Hillerman's *Dance Hall of the Dead,* and that is praise indeed.

> *Newgate Callendar, in a review of "The Listening Woman," in* The New York Times Book Review, *May 7, 1978, p. 26.*

Jean M. White

The desert land of New Mexico with its Indian lore and traditions has been magnificently evoked in Tony Hillerman's four earlier novels. In *People of Darkness* he returns with a new hero, Sgt. Jim Chee, of the Navajo Tribal Police, who soon must decide whether to join the FBI or become a tribal singer with his people.

Hillerman has written another superb mystery with character and background deftly interwoven around a complex plot that ends with a spine-tingling, cat-and-mouse chase after a hired killer over the desert wastes. Chee tracks down clues that lead to a 30-year-old oil-rigging explosion and an unusual number of cancer deaths among Navajo workmen who were members of a peyote cult.

Hillerman sensitively explores the cultural identity crisis of the modern American Indian through the relationship of his Navajo policeman and a feisty young graduate student teaching at an Indian school. As Chee speaks of the "strange ways" of the white man, we learn that his tribal beliefs may also be strange to others. (p. 7)

> *Jean M. White, in a review of "People of Darkness," in* Book World—The Washington Post, *November 16, 1980, pp. 7, 8.*

Robin Winks

Tony Hillerman's fifth mystery (and fourth set in the midst of the Navajo nation), *People of Darkness,* is his best. While his series figure, Navajo policeman Joe Leaphorn, plays a tiny role here, the action centers on Sergeant Jim Chee, of the Navajo Tribal Police, who is pursuing a relatively simple burglary of an Anglo's house. At the same time he is trying to decide whether to take up an offer of promotion to the East, where he inevitably will take on the Anglo ways he has already begun to learn while studying at the University of New Mexico, or to pursue the path of traditional healing and spiritual care among his people, for which he has been training as well. Hillerman always has used Navajo tradition as an integral part of his mystery, letting the problem grow directly from the culture, but here he is especially skillful and oblique. Though the reader will solve the formal mystery some pages ahead of Sergeant Chee, the human mystery remains: how do Anglo values differ from Navajo values?

> *Robin Winks, in a review of "People of Darkness," in* The New Republic, *Vol. 183, No. 24, December 13, 1980, p. 40.*

The New Yorker

[In *People of Darkness*] Mr. Hillerman continues to imagine the most disturbing and diverting monkey business in and around the great Navajo reservations in northern New Mexico, and he introduces us here to still another attractive (and redoubtable) member of the Navajo Tribal Police, one Jim Chee. Chee's problem is manifold. Who stole a little box of keepsakes from the home of a white uranium millionaire? And why? Why have so many members of the Charley family, all of them peyote preachers, died of cancer? And why is he being stalked by a white professional assassin? The Indian lore that is always an engaging part of Mr. Hillerman's thrillers is somewhat less closely integrated into the action this time, but it is here, and, as always, it gives the story an extra edge.

> *A review of "People of Darkness," in* The New Yorker, *Vol. LVI, No. 45, December 29, 1980, p. 74.*

Ellen Strenski and Robley Evans

The most important character in a detective story is the detective. He or she has special sensitivities that make possible the discovery of "who did it." Identifying the murderer is, of course, essential. But even more important is the process of careful observation and reflection whereby the detective comes to understand why, as well as how the murder happened. . . . Tony Hillerman's Navajo detective successfully fulfills the aesthetic and ethical demands of the genre. His stories, dependent on folklore motifs and a western setting, also merit attention for their place in a tradition of American literature by and about Indians.

Modern American Indian literature often features a correlation between the manifest world of human experience and the latent world of the spirit. The manifest world, usually one of conflict between white and Indian values, gives way to the elemental and spiritual vision of the Indian, as the protagonists in such works, alienated members of native societies, are returned to spiritual health through what is essentially a religious conversion to tribal values. . . . This religious element in American Indian fiction is an idealized vision, both in the novelists' creation of a perfected community of mankind living in nature, and also in the spiritual healing of the alienated member of the community through visions, suffering, and ritual procedures. In novels by [Frank Waters, Leslie Silko, and N. Scott Momaday] and others, the tribal Edenic world of the Indian, more valuable for its spiritual milieu than its deserts and barren mountains would at first suggest, has been lost to the rootless outcast, caught between inherited values he cannot believe in, and the acquired soulless vision of the white man. He must be redeemed from spiritual death by being taught to read the symbolic or latent elements of the world correctly, a formulation which has become a convention of American Indian fiction.

Interest in the ceremonial and visionary elements in American Indian life, stereotyped or not, continues in Tony Hillerman's three detective novels featuring a Navajo policeman, Joe Leaphorn, modeled on a real Jicarilla Apache tribal policeman whom Hillerman met while a crime reporter. Leaphorn's "beat" is the Navajo reservation. For him, the Navajo sense of pervasive connections between the natural and supernatural worlds is spiritually meaningful and provides the essential pattern of "clues" for solving crimes, sometimes directly, more often through analysis of correspondences. That is to say, Leaphorn acts upon intimate knowledge of his own people's culture to discover the patterns that either lead him directly to the criminal or provide analogies by which such patterns can be deduced. Hillerman writes about crimes and their causes. But he is also concerned with men caught between cultures, thereby moving his novels, for all their detective story conventions, towards the field covered by novelists like Waters and Silko. Leaphorn is a cross-cultural figure who operates in part with shortwave radios, pickup trucks and the "un-help" of the FBI. But his larger acts of detecting are guided by his Navajo belief in the metaphysical nature of the universe in which what is "evil" is "unharmonious," *not* beautiful in the Navajo sense. As a mediator between worlds who believes in the symbolic system of correspondences which men will either honor or betray, Leaphorn is an important contribution to the class of fiction using Native American material.

Like Silko and Momaday, Hillerman sets his stories in the post-World War II period when Indians returned from the war tainted by contact with the white man's soulless vision. Ceremonies described in their novels represent spiritual security for the members of the community, and it is the men returned from the corrupting outside world who are the disrupters of harmony. If such men are not Indian—and usually they are half-breeds, symbolic figures of mixed blood—they are corrupt white men who either live alone, or are parasitic on the spirit of community which the stable Indian society represents. In one Hillerman novel, *Dance Hall of the Dead,* a commune of hippies gathered in an abandoned hogan suggests that the alienated can be white as well as red. Hippies, alienated tribal rejects, half-breeds and renegades, are not only pattern breakers, but also searchers for a place in the pattern as well.

Joe Leaphorn develops through the three novels as a cultural mediator. Because he is a detective who must figure out the criminal's mind and motives, Leaphorn can thus translate the requisite spiritual values of the Indian vision into more practical and immediate terms than is the case where dreams and visions express the protagonist's suffering and return to harmony, as in Silko's *Ceremony.* A man centered in a culture with a deeply rooted spiritual sense of itself, Leaphorn does not go through the process of alienation and return suffered by other figures in American Indian fiction. However, he is a fictional detective and, according to the demands of the whodunit genre, responsible for restoring a state of grace or harmony. So as a kind of secular priest, Leaphorn must suffer too. Apart from experiencing regret and distress, Leaphorn also suffers from cold, fatigue, isolation from his family, lack of food, and racist slurs. His deprivation is partly a deliberate technique to heighten his empathetic understanding of the criminal's mind. From the critical viewpoint associated with W. H. Auden and others, this suffering can also be appreciated, to some extent, as expiation for the disruption caused by the crime, a test for spiritual health in Indian protagonists fleeing from the white man's guilt-fostering society.

Hillerman's procedure is to set up an alienated figure and play him off against the ceremonial life in which tribal members find identity and meaning. The lore connected with the protective and healing ceremonials of the Navajo, for instance, provides much of the metaphysical context in his fiction, suggesting both threatened disruption and recovery. The criminal's perverse ceremonies of disruption, in turn, are negative or parodistic versions of the proper versions. . . . The villains in Hillerman's whodunits are perverters of true belief and true health. It is Leaphorn's calling to probe beneath such parodies to the truths they reveal through their perversion.

Each of the three novels begins with an Indian who has become alienated from his own people, and yet who turns to ceremonies implying healing in traditional ways. In *The Blessing Way* (1970) Luis Horseman, described as a "lost soul" by Leaphorn, hides from justice in the Navajo reservation. Forced to live off kangaroo rats, he desperately tries to remember the correct prayers for good hunting. But he remembers the wrong prayers (for deer), and is himself killed by the true criminal of the story. In *Dance Hall of the Dead* (1973) George Bowlegs, a Navajo from an outcast family, wants to become a Zuni, to join another, more spiritually rewarding nation. And in *Listening Woman* (1978) an old man who has corrupted symbolic sandpaintings is murdered. The criminal slips into this introductory pattern-breaking. In *Dance Hall of the Dead* he is a white man, but in the other novels he is an Indian, alienated or corrupted.

In *The Blessing Way,* Hillerman's first Leaphorn story, the victim, Luis Horseman, is killed by "Big Navajo," the product of enforced emigration of Navajos to Los Angeles during the Depression. Without the benefit of tribal training, this misfit ends up as a "Relocation Indian," bought by the Mafia to recover a MIRV projectile and its data secretly from a desolate crash site on the reservation. Jackson, the murderer, knows his lore only from books (e.g., "*Case Studies in Navajo Ethnic Aberrations,* by John Greersen," a parody title). He frightens off inquisitive tribesmen by disguising himself as a Wolf Man, wearing a dog skin over his head and maiming livestock. Beyond this disguise is his implied metamorphosis into an "unnatural" or "unharmonious" being—a witch, as he is perceived by other Navajos. Onto the scene stumbles Horseman, who therefore has to be eliminated, and others, including Bergen McKee, a white anthropologist researching witches.

In this way, Hillerman can introduce lore associated with the Navajo fear of witches, "Wolf Men" who traditionally have been cast as werewolves killing sheep (the basis of Navajo wealth), sprinkling "corpse powder" on victims, engaging in incest, and hoarding wealth. As anthropologists with a psychological bent have noted, witches provide the Navajo with outlets for anger against family and fellow-tribesmen. Hillerman, interestingly, uses the fear of Wolf Men as a way to hide the villain and make him seem ominous; moreover, he is thus "unnatural." No Navajo would kill as he does: "You've put it together—a lot of money and a killing. It's not natural, and it's not Navajo!" (pp. 205-10)

For Leaphorn, Navajo ceremonials provide meaningful clues to the sources of evil. In *The Blessing Way,* the Navajos conduct an "Enemy Way" ceremony to cure a man "bothered" by the witch. But the Enemy Way is conducted for those who have been in contact with strangers outside the tribe; therefore, the murderer could not have been Luis Horseman. Leaphorn admits that ignoring tribal wisdom had cost him lives in a case he mishandled early in his career. He means this in a psychological sense, for fear of the witches had driven the Navajos involved to murder and suicide. It is this touch that makes Hillerman's use of the motif of lore unique because Leaphorn does not reject the cultural suppositions upon which personality and action are based. He knows the traditional source for witchery in the history of Navajo origins, and when a healer in *The Blessing Way* asks him if he believes the story of First Man and First Woman and Snake, Leaphorn answers laconically, " 'My grandfather,' he said, 'I have learned to believe in evil,' " a comment making Leaphorn more than the usual secular detective. (p. 210)

Leaphorn's sense of "evil" has been conditioned by his immersion in his own culture, one which is supra-intellectual in its powers, and knowledgeable in terms of its own psychology. He knows how Navajos or Zunis will act; he is correct in guessing that the ceremonies of healing will reveal clues and motives, however indirectly, given the unified nature of existence. The largest value of the "native" element lies in this learned sense that there is an "order" to events, "order—the natural sequence of behavior." Deviations from the normal are "unnatural and—therefore—unhealthy." This sense of something false in the pattern presented makes Leaphorn uncomfortable, and forces him to work out the logic of cause and effect until he can explain, and so reveal. . . . The point here is his deep immersion in the emotionally meaningful lore of his people, and his consequent belief that the "only goal for man was beauty, and that beauty was found only in harmony." In turn, this harmony is expressed as a "pattern" in which man must learn "to live with evil, by understanding it, by reading its cause."

In terms of characterization, then, Hillerman cleverly exploits appropriate Indian beliefs to build up his detective, Joe Leaphorn, in such a way as to fit the conventional requirements of one kind of fictional detective. Hillerman's accommodation of Indian material to the mystery genre successfully produces a detective who fits the formula and is also an attractively exotic figure in his own right. Especially happy is the coincidence in Indian culture and the mystery genre of the hero's powers of close observation. Mystery buffs, responding to traces of mud on a shoe, or the precise chiming of a clock in the library, from Sherlock Holmes on, have always been noted for their "eagerness . . . to take pleasure in the special activity of observation." How extremely satisfying for readers to watch Leaphorn literally track his prey across the desert, guided by a displaced pebble or snapped twig on a creosote bush. Given the harsh exigencies of the nomadic Navajo people's life, Leaphorn's ability is credible, and also perfectly congruent with an important aspect of the detective fiction formula. Although Hillerman often gives major action to others, like Bergen McKee in *The Blessing Way,* it is still in the mental evolution of Leaphorn's search for the pattern that the latent meaning is fulfilled. No book is exactly patterned like a particular ritual, but the detective's search for meaning and the ritual development of the cures with their return to harmony nonetheless correspond. (pp. 211-12)

This pattern of correspondences is carried out most fully in *Dance Hall of the Dead* where the first victim of murder is a young runner training for his role as the little fire god, Shulawitsi, in the Zuni Shalako ceremony. "Running" becomes a motif of the book, in fact, for the supposed murderer "runs" from the police, the real murderer, and Leaphorn. He is a young Navajo, George Bowlegs, who wishes to become a Zuni, and spends most of the novel out of sight, searching for the kachinas or spirits who like in a lake, according to Zuni belief, and who will give him admittance to the tribe. The true murderer, an archaeologist "salting" the dig of his student to support his theories, runs or drives wildly from place to place. A hippie girl, Suzanne, runs, too, or actually, hitchhikes away from her problems. And, of course, Leaphorn drives in his pickup truck, when he isn't walking. The novel is built on these correspondences. George Bowlegs' father is a drunk. His mother, like some other mothers in Indian fiction, was a whore and a drunk. Demoralization of Navajo children under such conditions may even be suggested in the distance away from the rest of The People the Bowlegs live. The son steals evidence of the archaeologist's wrongdoing, and the professor pursues him disguised in the mask of the Salamobia, one of the punishing Zuni kachinas or spirits. The headdress of the figure both disguises the criminal, as the dog skin does Jackson, and also suggests the spiritual quest which the Shalako ceremonies embody at the novel's close. Hillerman uses a group of hippies as red herrings in the plot, and as foils for tribal values: they comprise an artificial community, decadent and corrupt.

What is missing in the lives of these misfits, white and Indian, is the satisfactory involvement in the harmonious order that animates Zuni life in this novel, a pattern that is again held up as a model by the Navajo Leaphorn: "In all things a pattern, and in this pattern, the beauty of harmony." It is Leaphorn who serves both as the raisonneur, and as the mediator of human values, making the connections between the analytic or Western mind and the idealized tribal mind with its symbolic formulations, a kind of Hermes figure crossing boundaries that are metaphysical as well as physical.

[*Dance Hall of the Dead*] is filled with ceremonial references and rituals. More skillfully than in his first novel, Hillerman merges the detective formula with the mythic traditions of the hunt, death, and rebirth. The detective becomes the prey of the hunter-murderer, and a living part of the ceremonial organization of the work. For instance, Leaphorn is shot with an arrow containing a substance for putting animals to sleep without killing them, paralyzing him. He thus serves as a substitute for the intended victim of the hunt, and in mythic terms is "reborn" with increased knowledge. . . . Myth comes alive as well in the figure of the Salamobia who is the personification of anger introduced into the Zuni ceremony so that it may be exorcised. . . . Through specific symbols expressing a communal and theological vision, and through mythic references, Hillerman maintains correspondences between the "evil" of the detective story, its exorcism, and the ceremonial values of the tribal world with its essentially religious vision of the world's natural harmony.

The final work of the series, *Listening Woman,* follows Hillerman's pattern of interlacing detection with descriptions of ceremonial renewal and affirmation. Again the connections between the ceremonials and the detection are both literal and symbolic. A sick man, Hosteen Tso, soon to be murdered to protect a corrupt secret, is being diagnosed by a Navajo diviner, Mrs. Cigaret, whom the Navajo call Listening Woman. "Listening," like hand-trembling and star-gazing, is practiced to determine the cause of illness, the assumed break in the harmonious pattern by the sick man. By going into a trance, as Hillerman describes it, Listening Woman, who is also blind, can "see" into the earth and "read" the vision. She is able to look into the Fourth World and see a symbolic representation of past disruption of harmony. The divination ceremony here at the beginning of the novel suggests correspondences with the forthcoming story of the detection. What Listening Woman sees is a cave and sand-paintings, among other things, and Old Man Tso in a rocking chair, beyond help. The sick man has indeed committed a "crime" by trying to "fix," that is, make permanent, sacred sand-paintings, and there will be a cave, revealed by Leaphorn, in which these sand-paintings exist, and where a gang of half-breed Indians—a band of the alienated—are in hiding. Anarchists, they rob banks (hence one association with Navajo witches who hoard treasure) and plot the overthrow of law and order. Even as Listening Woman is in her trance, her niece and Old Man Tso are murdered, bringing Leaphorn into action. Listening Woman both sees and does not see.

At the center of the story is the lengthy description of the Kinaalda, a ceremony for a girl initiated into womanhood, which Leaphorn attends in order to interview his fellow Navajos, including Mrs. Cigaret. Here he is played off against the white man's FBI which ignores the "superstitions of the natives." As in other Hillerman uses of ceremonies, the ceremony's patterns evoke correspondences and meanings that are more than specific "clues." For instance, Leaphorn tries to discover why Listening Woman had prescribed a Black Rain Chant, an "obscure ritual," for healing Tso. In a myth, Coyote, the Trickster god of so much Indian mythology, steals fire; when the land begins to burn, however, Hosteen Frog, inflated with water, "produced black rain to save Dinetah" (Land of the People). The dead man, Tso, killed a frog, Mrs. Cigaret reported; and he had therefore broken a taboo. The connections between myth and natural experience in the Navajo vision overlap, and Leaphorn guesses that Tso had been in a cave with the questionable cave-paintings where frogs might be found. And so he looks, as it turns out, in the right place, because the criminal band is there, too. Hillerman is linking the thinking detective with the natural world in which myth is being both exploited by criminals and given new life by the believing community of Navajos. Leaphorn goes through an elaborate pursuit sequence with mythic overtones: trapped by fire set by the enemy, he escapes into a cave like that seen by Mrs. Cigaret in her vision, and is reborn with a baptism in Lake Powell. In an apocalyptic blowing-up of the cave, the sand paintings, which were to preserve the secret of how to renew the earth after destruction, are destroyed, the detective bringing together in his detection both tribal legend and white man's knowledge. He has righted the "perverted" or unnatural worlds of both Indian and white man. More than a successful detective, Leaphorn is a culture hero whose concern for pattern as defined typologically by The People gives him a spiritual strength and insight not available to the alienated criminals and misfits who die without finding the appropriate kachinas.

This structural interlace of myth and detection reveals Hillerman's reliance on the conventions of the detective story milieu as implied by Auden and others: a deeply conservative society in which change is evil, a move towards chaos, the failure of the identifying formulae in which the members of the community can know their world. The taboo-ridden Navajo world provides deeply-experienced guidelines for identification. Leaphorn, descended from a line of Singers, has available to him all the intricate, multi-layered mythology and the complicated, lengthy rituals for curing, of a tribal society which lives a life of the mind with its rich inheritance. (pp. 213-16)

> *Ellen Strenski and Robley Evans, "Ritual and Murder in Tony Hillerman's Indian Detective Novels," in* Western American Literature, *Vol. XVI, No. 3, Fall, 1981, pp. 205-16.*

Ralph B. Sipper

Until someone I trust praised Tony Hillerman's fiction, I had not read any of his mystery novels featuring a Navajo policeman. The detective as gimmick—be he blind, wheelchair-bound or homosexual—usually portends a one-note performance with everything hinged to the differentness of the gimmick being exploited. Such superficial invention usually means the reader is in for a long night.

Not so with *The Dark Wind,* a convincing argument for examining each case on its own merits, for not filling in the quick pigeonhole. Hillerman's book works on the levels a good mystery should. It is a compact story that engages, an implicit commentary on the Indian society it portrays, a mini-study of arcane subjects that bear directly on the plot.

Jim Chee becomes involved in solving several murders tied to a cocaine shipment hidden in the Southwestern high desert country he patrols. Though his jurisdiction does not extend beyond Indian borders, Chee commits himself to finding out who killed on his turf and why.

As in better police procedurals, we learn, concretely, how professionals work. Chee's forte is tracking—thorough hands-and-knees stuff that requires an intimate knowledge of the terrain and those who live on it. He knows just how high the sun must be for the slanting light necessary in reading the faintest of tracks. Nor is Chee's talent a cultural hand-me-down only. He has learned modern methods to discern differences of tire treads quicker than you can say Mark C. Bloome.

Chee's investigation takes us into Navajo and Hopi communities where poverty is indexed by hard facts. The nearest movie is 100 miles away; there is little electricity; the Indian telephone book encompassing a territory larger than New England can be carried by Chee in his hip pocket.

When he is troubled, this modern-day detective falls back on his cultural heritage. . . .

Language as well as philosophy melds with narrative, as in the scene when Chee asks a woman about her son:

> 'You are hunting for him,' she said. Navajo is a language which loads its meanings into its verbs. She used the word which means 'to stalk,' as a hunted animal, and not the form which means 'to search for,' as for someone lost. The tone was as accusing as the word. Chee changed the verb. 'I search for him,' Chee said.

Throughout, the language is equally precise and plain as befits its subject and stoic protagonist. Chic phrases and flashy metaphors are for faraway places like Santa Fe or Las Vegas, places Jim Chee does not know.

Like his Navajo policeman, Tony Hillerman never loses his sense of place.

> *Ralph B. Sipper, "How High the Sun and Other Tracking Clues," in* Los Angeles Times Book Review, *July 25, 1982, p. 6.*

Robin W. Winks

The Dark Wind is Tony Hillerman's best book in an already strong series. A professor of journalism by trade, Hillerman knows the Navajo, Hopi, and Apache cultures intimately, and has developed his own niche in mystery and detective fiction, much as James McClure has done with his novels based on apartheid in South Africa, by turning the mystery and its solution upon the intricate social and religious life of the Indians of the American Southwest. These books could exist nowhere else, they are authentic, and the resolutions grow out of the character of an entire people.

This time Jim Chee, Navajo tribal policeman, has three mysteries to solve: the identity of a murdered man who has had the soles of his feet and his fingertips removed; the reason why a vandal is damaging a windmill on the Navajo/Hopi tribal border over and over; and the cause of a small private plane's crash just beyond Oraibi Wahs. For someone who knows this country from the ground—and I do—the sense of place is enormously appealing, but one need never have been to the Hopi mesa-top villages to be there with Hillerman. Of course the three puzzles prove to be related, and in his careful, slow way Chee, with a bit of help from the Kachina spirits, brings the mystery to a resolution satisfying to Hopi and Navajo theology alike. (pp. 43-4)

> *Robin W. Winks, in a review of "The Dark Wind," in* The New Republic, *Vol. 187, Nos. 12 & 13, September 20 & 27, 1982, pp. 43-4.*

Newgate Callendar

For the last 10 years or so Tony Hillerman has been writing mysteries featuring Indian cops on reservations in New Mexico or Arizona. He takes his time on these books, and *The Dark Wind* is only the fifth of the series. This one features Jim Chee of the Navajo Tribal Police, who suddenly has a lot on his plate: a mutilated corpse, vandalism at a windmill, a plane crash in the desert, dead bodies and every indication that a big drug ring is operating in the area.

Chee finds himself under suspicion, and he has to do a lot of fancy footwork to clear himself. The phrase is used literally; Chee is an expert tracker who can read minute signs in the desert and arrive at a coherent picture. As in all the Hillerman books, a great deal about Indian lore is introduced, and all of it is germane to the plot.

The Dark Wind is, in its way, a traditional mystery, despite the exotic locale, and one of the best in the series.

> *Newgate Callendar, in a review of "The Dark Wind," in* The New York Times Book Review, *October 17, 1982, p. 41.*

Jane S. Bakerman

Tony Hillerman, journalist, academic, and novelist, has earned high praise for his detective fiction. Five of his mysteries compose the two brief but compelling series for which he is best known. *The Blessing Way* (1970), *Dance Hall of the Dead* (1973), and *Listening Woman* (1978), feature an officer of the Navajo police force, Joe Leaphorn; and *People of Darkness* (1980) and *The Dark Wind* (1982) center upon Leaphorn's younger colleague, Jim Chee. All of the novels are carefully wrought mysteries, satisfying for mystery fans as well as for critics. They are also, however, telling commentaries upon contemporary American life in the Southwest, for in addition to beautiful nature imagery and remarkably clear and effective glimpses into Native American life, they offer vivid accounts of the difficulties of operating in a multi-ethnic society.

Each of the novels poses an interesting and taxing puzzle for its protagonist-detective, and each problem involves at least one murder. Joe Leaphorn's cases require him to find the killers of Luis Horseman, a man who has compromised his tribal identity; of Ernesto Cata, a youngster murdered during his preparation for an important role in a Zuñi ceremonial; and of Anna Atcity and Hosteen Tso who are killed during a ritual directed toward healing, not death. Jim Chee's first assignment, tracking the killer of the head of the Peyote Church, also forces him to solve a much older crime, and his most recent case focuses upon the identification of a mutilated corpse—and of its killer. All five plots are informed by the religious faiths or ethical obligations of the characters; all examine the problems generated by overweening ambition or greed; and, very importantly, all are complicated by the tangled web of jurisdictional conflicts between various segments of the multi-ethnic society in which Officers Leaphorn and Chee work.

In the detective novel, it is common practice for the author to exploit assumed tensions between various law enforcement agencies and even sometimes between departments within the same agency. In Hillerman's novels, this tradition is observed regularly. (pp. 17-18)

Useful in themselves, these complications are further intensified in the Hillerman novels by a constant underlying awareness of the racial tensions which inform them. Though many non-Navajo characters are admirers or students of Navajo culture, and though others, who are strangers, are often open, friendly, and seemingly unbiased, still others are unfriendly or dangerous. (p. 18)

It would be easy to dismiss overtly racist acts by unattractive characters as atypical behavior, to assume that most people would abjure it. When, however, one of these unattractive characters represents the power of the political order, the social commentary cannot be dismissed; it must be reckoned with. . . .

Benjamin Vines, a major villain in the earlier Jim Chee novel *The People of Darkness,* is an abusive person. Though he does not represent the United States Government, he does represent the power structure, for he is immensely wealthy and is a strong economic and political force in his community. Enamoured with wealth, arrogant with power and his own cleverness, he embarks on a self-protective, long-term plot. Quite simply, he is systematically (and, one must admit, inventively) silencing every member of a group of Native Americans who pose a danger to him—they know too much, but they are, for the most part, unaware of their dangerous knowledge.

Under the general guise of friendship to the Peyote Church, a subcult of Navajo-Christian belief, and specifically under the guise of friendship of the original leader of that congregation, he plots and manipulates. He also operates under the underlying assumption that the victims are "just Indians"; indeed, one victim, buried on Vines's property, has been designated "A Good Indian" on his tombstone. Misunderstood by some as testimony that the two men were such good friends that they could turn a racial slur, "The only good Indian is a dead Indian," into a joke between them, the epitaph actually, as readers come to realize, is both a statement of motive and an openly racist comment. (p. 19)

Here again, Hillerman extends the psychological portrait of an unsympathetic character by welding racist thinking and other equally dangerous habits of mind into one powerful, effective motivation. Vines's racist attitudes so mirror the attitudes pervasive in his society that for many years—and many pages—it is difficult to identify him as the profoundly villainous character he is, and this pattern is a very useful plot complication as well as good evidence of careful characterization.

In *Dance Hall of the Dead,* an antagonist violates his own professional ethics and sacrifices the lives of two children, a Navajo and a Zuñi, in order to serve precisely the motivations displayed by Vines. Here, too, is the strong implication that despite his training as an anthropologist, Reynolds sees anyone outside his tight, white world of the senior academic as expendable, and he exacerbates the horror of murder by engaging in sacrilege as well. . . . [He] is enabled to strip away his customary mask of civility, education, and professionalism because his victims and the cultures they represent are, for him, merely artifacts. They are, in a very real sense, convenient tools to use in order to advance his career.

No reader can be unaware of the underlying racism in the attitudes of figures such as these, but it is, I suggest, a major factor in Hillerman's appeal (and testament to his skill) that even his despicable characters do not indulge in overtly racist speech. Instead, Tony Hillerman dramatizes the presence of racist behavior in our society by consistently showing its effects as they are linked to other traits of character and social behavior. By developing his characters in this fashion, Hillerman deepens characterization and strengthens his social commentary in one sophisticated, effective stroke. Useful as it is to both plotting and to his social commentary, however, this "I am white; I have might; I am right" brand of racism and exploitation is far from Hillerman's most frequent or even most effective treatment of the problems of prejudice within our multiethnic society. Instead, the author presents most of his social commentary from the point of view of the protagonists and other sympathetic characters.

Both Leaphorn and Chee studied anthropology as undergraduates; both now study "the white man" as symbol of an alien and puzzling culture. This effort to understand the dominant culture is essential to their work—they must try, for instance, to grasp the concept of vengeance, a desire which motivates many Belacani [white people]. A concept absent from Navajo thought, revenge is puzzling to them. One cannot function well personally anymore than one can function well professionally within a culture whose values remain wholly mysterious. (pp. 20-1)

The detective's "intuitive leap" of imagination which, coupled with careful investigation, is so dear to the hearts of mystery fans would be unavailable to Leaphorn and Chee were they not earnest students of the societies around them, and the novels' popularity would also suffer markedly. Thus, their extended analysis of their multiethnic society, like most of Hillerman's devices, not only intensifies the social commentary but also enhances the plots in these novels.

Leaphorn and Chee are practical men who recognize reality and who then strive to operate effectively within it. Their realistic pragmatism is also clearly revealed in their attitudes toward situations which have developed from the government's manipulation of lands and people. Chee, for instance, assigned to discover who is vandalizing a windmill located on land recently and arbitrarily transferred from Navajo to Hopi control, doesn't evaluate the justice or injustice of the transfer; he recognizes the parameters used by the Bureau of Indian Affairs and proceeds with his job.

Similarly, Leaphorn, who has puzzled throughout a difficult case about the unpredictability of one character who seems to be a Navajo but who behaves counter to the Navajo Way, understands that behavior when he learns that the suspect is a Relocation Indian, moved from the Southwest to California, separated from the People and thereby deprived of the opportunity to absorb their values and practices. Leaphorn, like Chee, recognizes the injustice involved but does not ponder it much; he wastes little time over situations which he cannot alter.

Occasionally, however, each protagonist allows himself a moment of angry—or at least self-protective—reflection upon generalized racist attitudes toward his culture and toward himself. At one point, Leaphorn, having survived great danger and pain in order to solve a case, contemplates its final irony. A site sacred to the Navajo and the secret hiding place of a huge sum of money has been rendered inaccessible in the course of the chase, and the policeman wonders if access to the sacred relics will be restored. The money, he concludes, will prompt action, for it is money which counts; sand paintings, no matter how great their meaning, how deeply they are revered by the Navajos, would not matter much in the face of the vast effort and expense necessary to salvage them. (pp. 21-2)

These moments of bitterness or defensiveness enhance and humanize the characterizations of Hillerman's protagonists. Capable of the heroic action called for in almost every plot, they must also reveal some vulnerability to meet the demands of most modern detective fiction fans, and their very human responses to ignorance and prejudice aid in that process. Though both officers' pragmatic acceptance of and occasional reactions against the complexities of life as minority group members serve the novel very well, Hillerman's *most* effective treatment of prejudice arises from biases Leaphorn and Chee themselves reveal and cope with day by day.

The fact that both Joe Leaphorn and Jim Chee clearly recognize that they must *themselves* guard against behaving in prejudiced fashion deepens their characterizations considerably. Most of their biases arise directly from the multicultural society in which they live and work. Important to their work, as well as to their personal relationships with the dominant culture, is, for instance, the necessity for retraining their eyes. Both men look very carefully at Belacani strangers, for both are educating themselves out of the habit of thinking that—and behaving as if—all white men look alike.

This detail serves a number of purposes, including adding a bit of sardonic humor, as do the equally complex problems the Navajo policemen face in their professional and personal interactions with members of other Native American cultures. Just as intruders (often perpetrators) penetrate the Navajo culture, so do Leaphorn and Chee penetrate other cultures, and sometimes during those moments of intrusion, they risk violating the beliefs and practices of their neighbors.

To solve one of his cases, Joe Leaphorn must analyze the personality of George Bowlegs, a Navajo youth who yearns to become a Zuñi because the Zuñi way of life and belief appeals to him enormously. As a result of living near Zuñis all his life, of talks with a college roommate, and of his study of anthropology, Leaphorn knows something of Zuñi culture. But he is uncomfortable with Zuñi people. This latter complication is foolish, he understands, and it arises directly from prejudice. (pp. 22-3)

During his investigation, however, Leaphorn must take two steps which, at least momentarily, assuage his old hurt and, perhaps, move him toward a sounder, warmer, more informed understanding of the Zuñi. The case forces him to work with—and around—Ed Pasquaanti, Chief of the Zuñi Police, who controls the investigation on the Zuñi reservation, while Leaphorn, of course, works in Navajo territory. The early stages of the inquiry are marked with reserve and some tension between the two men; at one point, Leaphorn even allows himself to think, scornfully, that he can "find tracks where a Zuñi couldn't," and the thought is, in large part, still another reaction to what he, himself, dubs a "silly inferiority complex."

Later, however, Leaphorn and Pasquaanti must hold a

difficult conversation which touches upon secret matters. Leaphorn's developing theory about the fates of the two youngsters requires him to ask delicate questions about a Zuñi ceremonial; he does so with tact and discretion. (p. 23)

Soon after, the case takes Leaphorn (amid a host of other observers) to Shalako, the ceremony. There, in a hot, crowded room, the mystery and majesty of the ritual touch him deeply, and for an instant, he sees "Shalako, the courier between gods and men" as the Zuñi see him. This moment of union allows readers a brief, revealing glimpse into the spiritual side of Leaphorn's nature, and coupled with the conversation with Pasquaanti, it also clarifies the Navajo policeman's motivation for the surprising action he subsequently takes toward the killer. Empathy, even should it prove fleeting, helps him to serve justice over law, and in doing so, he also serves his Zuñi neighbors.

Jim Chee's penetration into another culture also results in the solution of a crime and in the application of rough but appropriate justice; yet its implications are very different, and his behavior, while redemptive rather than destructive, is alarmingly similar to that of Reynolds, the villain-anthropologist. Chee, too, must seek information about another culture in order to piece the clues he has been gathering into a useful pattern. . . . Early in the novel, for instance, Chee asks about a shrine he has discovered near the site of a crime. . . .

Chee uses this knowledge to slip into the tiny Hopi village of Sityatki during Astotokaya, Washing of the Hair, "sort of an initiation ceremony into the religious societies of the village." The community is completely barred to visitors on this night, and Chee's secret presence is a serious intrusion. While this violation of custom and confidence serves justice and helps save Chee's career—perhaps even his life—it is, nevertheless, a profound infringement on Cowboy's friendship and upon the rights of the Hopi villagers. Chee, usually introspective, does not address this problem, largely, perhaps, because action rather than contemplation wholly occupies both his and the reader's attention from the time of the penetration to the conclusion of the plot. Still, Chee's unusually exploitative behavior extends and deepens his characterization even as it underscores the complexity of human relationships in a society composed of smaller societies so numerous and so diverse.

Hillerman's use of racial and cultural differences and the prejudices they engender clearly, then, enhances his portraits of antagonists and protagonists alike. As it simultaneously complicates and clarifies motivation, this device also strengthens the plots and, in a very real sense, alters readers' perceptions of the books. The Hillerman novels, fine entertainments in the tradition of the best detective fiction, also make serious, effective social comments, pointing out that prejudice and its consequences—distrust, discomfort, and exploitation—are endemic in our society.

A major difference between hero and villain in Hillerman's work is an awareness of one's prejudice and a willingness to combat it in oneself. If even the heroes, as Jim Chee demonstrates in *The Dark Wind,* occasionally slip into exploitative behavior toward other cultures, readers—ordinary, non-heroes like most of us—learn that they, too, must always monitor their own behavior as much as they must guard against racism in others. This is a serious lesson, and it makes its point well. It also teaches us that Tony Hillerman is a serious novelist who raises entertainment fiction to the level of valid social commentary without for a moment sacrificing either objective. (pp. 23-5)

Jane S. Bakerman, "Cutting Both Ways: Race, Prejudice and Motive in Tony Hillerman's Detective Fiction," in MELUS, *Vol. 11, No. 3, Fall, 1984, pp. 17-25.*

Jean M. White

One of the consistently superior—and definitely distinctive—mystery series of the last 15 years has come from Tony Hillerman. *The Ghostway,* which brings back Sergeant Jim Chee in this sixth outing with the Navajo Tribal Police, more than meets Hillerman's high standards. . . . [It] doesn't seem foolhardy to predict it will be one of [1985's] best.

The Ghostway is a tense mystery-thriller with the runaway action of a western. It is also a sympathetic, yet levelheaded, examination of the clash of cultures and the anguish this can bring to two people sincerely in love. This is the overriding theme in this carefully-crafted book with the Hillerman hallmarks: pursuit over the desolate land of New Mexico, the beautifully-evoked sense of place with slopes of snakeweed and buffalo grass, great open spaces, arching skies, dazzling desert sunsets, and abrasive windblown sand, the background of Indian lore with tribal rituals, beliefs, singer's chants.

In *The Ghostway,* Chee takes one of his rare trips off the Navajo Big Reservation to travel to Los Angeles. There he learns that Albert and Leroy Gorman, two lapsed Navajos who have gone the white man's way in the big city, had been high-class car thiefs stealing Mercedes and Caddies on order for an importer to deliver overseas.

Albert had come back to the reservation, looking for his brother, when he was wounded in a shootout outside the local laundromat. He had driven away, leaving a dead hit man from Los Angeles.

Chee, assigned to the local FBI agent and told not to ask questions, tracks Albert's car to the abandoned hogan of his uncle, Hosteen (a title of respect for elders) Begay. The chimney is plugged, the single door sealed, and a "dark hole" chopped in the north side to let out the chindi, or evil spirit of the dead. Chee finds nearby Gorman's body laid out in ceremonial fashion, shoes reversed to confuse pursuers, cornmeal and water for a four-day journey to the underground world of the dead.

But why, Chee wonders, was not the corpse's hair washed in yucca suds for purification? And why had Hosteen Begay not taken his kinsman outside to die in the open rather than infect a hogan on a prime site near a meadow and stream?

Only a Navajo cop would pick up these clues, but Chee must tread carefully because of the secretive FBI agents. Again, it is Chee, the Navajo policeman, who thinks to ask about the cottonwood tree in a Polaroid snapshot. It leads him to the trailer where Albert's brother may be hiding. Yet the owner denies he is Leroy Gorman. . . .

The trail takes Chee back to the reservation for a corker of a confrontation with the villains. It comes at a ghostway—a five-day curing ceremony for Margaret [Hosteen Begay's granddaughter] after her exposure to the evil spirit in the hogan where Gorman died. Chee, again with Margaret to the rescue, must face the vicious hit man and another villain who has slipped into their midst under a false identity.

University-educated Chee, who has chosen to stay with his people and is studying tribal rituals, is constantly tugged between the Navajo and white man's way.

Hillerman catches the quandary as Chee hesitates outside the deserted hogan and debates whether to enter to search for evidence:

> To the Jim Chee who was an alumnus of the University of New Mexico, subscriber to *Esquire* and *Newsweek,* an officer of the Navajo Tribal Police, lover of Mary Landon, holder of a Farmington Public Library card, student of anthropolgy and sociology, 'with distinction' graduate of the FBI Academy, holder of Social Security card 441-28-7272, it was a logical step to take.

Yet this Chee is also a Navajo taught to avoid chindis, the evil spirits that inhabit hogans if people die there:

> But from this talus slope, in the dying light, the dead stillness of this autumn evening, the rationality of the universe was canceled.

Throughout his investigation and pursuit, Chee is haunted by his quarrel with Mary Landon, the white teacher at one of the reservation schools, who was introduced in an earlier Hillerman novel. For both Chee and Landon, their love has deepened. He sees only Mary as the mother of his children. She wants him to take a job with the FBI, leave the reservation, and send their future children to better schools.

There are times when Chee sounds self-righteous in his disdain for the white man's ways. The Navajos, he observes at one point, do not hide people away in hospitals to die. Yet he embraces the belief that takes a mortally ill man out of his house to die in the open to avoid contagion of his evil spirit. It is an irony that Hillerman, in his respectful and unremitting admiration for the Navajo way, probably never intended.

Mary, who appears only in Chee's thoughts in *The Ghostway,* has asked him: "What gives you the right to be so superior?" In the end, she returns to Wisconsin, leaving a note that she needs time to think but has decided "not to force my Jim Chee to be a white man."

> *Jean M. White, "The Navajo Way of Death,"
> in* Book World—The Washington Post,
> *March 17, 1985, p. 10.*

T. J. Binyon

[*The Ghostway* is another] of Tony Hillerman's ethnographically exact detective stories set in an Indian reservation of the American west. Here Jim Chee, of the Navajo Tribal Police, is alerted to the possibility of something odd going on when he finds a corpse that has been buried with its hair unwashed. *The Ghostway* is more wide-ranging than the earlier books—Chee gets as far as Los Angeles in search of a Navajo girl who has vanished—and the introduction of some elements from more ordinary crime novels is perhaps a mistake, but it's still a solid, well-written, interesting and original piece of work.

> *T. J. Binyon, in a review of "The Ghostway,"
> in* The Times Literary Supplement, *December
> 27, 1985, p. 1478.*

Robley Evans

Tony Hillerman has been writing a series of murder mysteries using Navajo Tribal Police as detectives, first Joe Leaphorn, and lately Jim Chee. Chee's life in two worlds parallels the usual situation in Hillerman's plots, but conversely: the criminals are usually not Native Americans, or if they are, they've been alienated from the tribal world by removal to Los Angeles, like Leroy Gorman of *The Ghostway.* They pick up enough Navajo lore to cover them and hide out in the Navajo Reservation where Chee must travel long distances to turn up bodies and clues. What Hillerman concentrates on, of course, is Sergeant Chee's Navajo intuition and his knowledge of the clan links, the lore surrounding the hogan where a man has died, the way a Navajo thinks. The usual murder mystery, translated to Navajo country, can be solved by contrasting the way a "false" Navajo would do it with the methods and motives of the Dinee. In this latest mystery, Hillerman adds Chee's own conflict: Should he let his love for an "outlander," Mary Landon, carry him away to the White Man's world, or should he stay on the reservation to preserve his spiritual heritage? (p. 63)

The carefully-wrought ingredients for cross-cultural detection are all here. The story, however, is not up to earlier thrillers like *People of Darkness,* partly because there isn't enough lore significantly used. Hillerman has turned to death and burial customs before; in *The Ghostway* they seem almost accidental, given the complexity of the plot, partly because the search Chee makes through the sleazy streets and development sites of the city is long and rather thin in "event," as well. Finally, too much may be made of Chee's role as a character; here he thinks about Mary Landon, but she is not present in the action. (She took an active part in *People of Darkness.*) Much of the problem-solving, with speculation about complex relationships and their details, goes on in Sergeant Chee's head. We miss the wild action of *The Blessing Way* or *Dance Hall of the Dead.* Probably the effort to turn a detective into a human being who thinks and has a private life not involved in solving that murder is a mistake. The gentle Navajo who becomes a *yataalii* will want to heal rather than hound. (pp. 63-4)

> *Robley Evans, in a review of "The Ghostway,"
> in* Western American Literature, *Vol. XXI,
> No. 1, May, 1986, pp. 63-4.*

Newgate Callendar

[Tony Hillerman] has published some of the best, and certainly most unusual, mystery novels of the last few decades. . . .

[*Skinwalkers* brings Hillerman's two detectives, Joe Leaphorn and Jim Chee,] together for the first time. Each has been the main character in previous books of the series. *Skinwalkers* starts with a bang; somebody tries to bushwhack Chee as he is sleeping in his trailer. He doesn't know why, much less who, and that bothers Leaphorn. Could Chee be lying? Could he be mixed up in something nasty?

Another thing on Leaphorn's mind is quadruple murder. Four Navajos have been killed. Leaphorn has a tidy mind. There must, he thinks, be a connection, but try as he can he is unable to figure one out. At first, anyway. Later, working with Chee, he develops a "skinwalker" theory.

In Navajo lore a skinwalker is an evil being, a witch who can run faster than a bullet, fly, change into an animal. Could it be that the four people were murdered because somebody believed them to be skinwalkers? So we get the expected examination of many aspects of Navajo life and religion. We also meet some ripe, unusual characters, white as well as Indian. This is, after all, basically a police procedural, exotic as its locale may be, and it is told in sensitive prose that once in a while approaches poetry.

> *Newgate Callendar, in a review of "Skinwalkers," in* The New York Times Book Review, *January 18, 1987, p. 23.*

The New Yorker

Agile as ever, reflective as ever, absorbing as ever, Mr. Hillerman [in *Skinwalkers*] returns us once again to the Navajo otherworld of skinwalkers (Evil) and listeners, hand tremblers, and singers of the Blessing Way (Good), and to Lieutenant Joe Leaphorn and Officer Jim Chee, of the Navajo Tribal Police. The case that occupies them is once again a slippery one—a series of seemingly unrelated murders (and an attack on Chee) in widely separated parts of the great reservation complex of New Mexico—Arizona—Utah. The motive or motives that eventually reveal themselves are rooted in the dominant white world, but the murders have their roots just as deeply in the still powerful forces of Navajo culture.

> *A review of "Skinwalkers," in* The New Yorker, *Vol. LXII, No. 50, February 2, 1987, p. 102.*

Jean M. White

What more can you say about Tony Hillerman's Navajo mysteries? *Skinwalkers,* the latest and eighth in the series, is superb and pure pleasure to read.

As a reviewer who has watched Hillerman's talent mature and break new ground over a decade and a half, I find that I only can repeat an earlier assessment: "one of the consistently superior—and definitely distinctive—mystery series of the last 15 years."

In *Skinwalkers,* Hillerman, for the first time, brings together his two series characters, Lieutenant Joe Leaphorn and Officer Jim Chee. He beautifully handles the interplay

between these two Navajo tribal policemen: the older, more worldly Leaphorn, who has rejected the shamanism of his Navajo culture, and the younger, better-educated but more mystical Chee, who is learning the old ceremonial rituals to become a practicing shaman under his uncle's tutelage.

When Chee barely escapes a shotgun blast that pierces the aluminum skin of his trailer, Leaphorn is suspicious of Chee's activities. There have been complaints about his shamanism, and, after all, people don't shoot at cops without a reason.

Leaphorn also has other worries. He is awaiting a doctor's report on his wife's loss of memory (he fears Alzheimer's disease). And there have been a string of unsolved murders with overtones of the dark world of Navajo witchcraft and "skinwalkers," who turn the Navajo rituals to evil purpose.

Once again Hillerman evokes the haunting sense of place with the arid, harsh Southwest landscape. This hard land is as much a character in *Skinwalkers* as the Navajos and their world of ancient rites and beliefs. It is difficult to believe that Hillerman is not a Navajo himself.

> *Jean M. White, "Esprit de Corpse," in* Book World—The Washington Post, *February 15, 1987, p. 4.*

Jean M. White

If you read only one mystery this summer (pity!) let it be *A Thief of Time.*

This is vintage Tony Hillerman: a suspenseful, compelling story that moves across an authentic background of Southwest Indian culture and arid scenery and involves memorable people who engage the reader's emotions and intelligence.

Hillerman transcends the mystery genre without betraying the elements that have special appeal for its followers. First, he tells a good story.

A Thief of Time opens with stunning impact as a solitary figure—a woman anthropologist—backpacks along a remote cliff ruin in search of Anasazi Indian clay pots.

> The moon had risen just above the cliff behind her . . . Sometimes when the goat trail bent and put the walker's profile against the moon, the shadow became Kokopelli himself. The backpack formed the spirit's grotesque hump, the walking stick Kokopelli's crooked flute . . .
>
> If an Anasazi had risen from his thousand-year grave in the trash heap under the cliff ruins here, he would have seen the Humpbacked Flute Player, the rowdy god of *fertility* and lost people. But the shadow was only the shape of Dr. Eleanor Friedman-Bernal blocking out the light of the October moon.

It is the disappearance of Dr. Friedman-Bernal that involves Lt. Joe Leaphorn of the Navajo Tribal Police, who appeared [in 1970] in Hillerman's first novel, *The Blessing Way.* Also featured is Sgt. Jim Chee, Hillerman's other series character. It is an uneasy, wary collaboration. The younger, more mystical Chee is training to be a Navajo singer. He respects but does not really like Leaphorn. Leaphorn does not practice the old rituals and has a legendary reputation among the Navajo tribal policemen.

Leaphorn is on terminal leave. "Just tired," he tells his superior officer when he hands in his letter of resignation after the death of his wife, Emma. Nothing seems to interest him, and he decides to try to find the missing woman rather than sit in an empty apartment.

Meanwhile, Chee is chasing the Backhoe Bandit, who has stolen heavy digging equipment from a police parking lot. He finds the stolen backhoe, and two corpses, at an illegal digging site. The diggers are pothunters, "thieves of time," seeking to take advantage of soaring auction prices.

The threads of the separate investigations by the two Navajo policemen are pulled together in the finale, which is literally a cliffhanger.

The question is: Why hasn't Hollywood filmed a Hillerman novel?

Hillerman's characters are etched in the mind—Houk, the powerful rancher-politician who manages a quick note ("Tell Leaphorn she's still alive") before he is murdered; the effete New York collector who relishes the bloody history behind the artifacts he collects; the Indian who has become a born-again evangelist, financing his tent revivals with sales of clay pots; the arrogant anthropologist with an Ivy League background who collects jawbones with a genetic flaw of a surplus molar in the left mandible.

[*A Thief of Time*] is one of the best Hillermans.

> *Jean M. White, "Just the Artifacts, Ma'am,"*
> in Book World—The Washington Post, *June 19, 1988, p. 8.*

Mark Harris

Recently I read that Somerset Maugham said of Georges Simenon, "There's more atmosphere than detection in his stories." Did Maugham intend this as compliment or complaint?

Tony Hillerman's new novel, *A Thief of Time,* is rich with detection. . . .

The hero, or central character, is Joe Leaphorn, a figure well-respected by readers of Hillerman's earlier mystery writing. Leaphorn is a lovely, quiet, slow-moving, thorough man of good heart, who has undertaken the case on the emotional rebound from his wife's death. His task is to find a woman who is missing, perhaps dead. It would be the wish of his late wife, Leaphorn reasons, that he rescue the woman.

Dr. Eleanor Friedman-Bernal, an anthropologist, had been digging for "pots" up there in the Four Corners country of New Mexico. She had made the remarkable discovery of a kind of artist's signature among the ancient artifacts she unearthed. . . .

Thrilling as this may be to Dr. Friedman-Bernal, her success inevitably arouses the jealousy of her colleagues and the avarice of fortune-hunters who dig pots for money—thieves of time, as they are called. As we follow Leaphorn we learn of three murders. . . .

When a novel of mystery rises above its mere classification—"mystery"—and becomes a fine literary work it offers that dimension of atmosphere Maugham mentions. Detection is not enough. Detection satisfies the left brain only. The other side of the story, like the other side of my brain (I am told), must make me feel the thing I feel when *A Thief of Time* is at its best—not detection but landscape. In this case, it is the sense the author imparts of the sparseness, the spaciousness, the silence, the poverty and the ancient sullen Indian presence in this haunted wild country where the action occurs.

Almost all mystery novels focus on detection at the sacrifice of atmosphere, which is why they so seldom enrich our interior lives in the way of memorable literature. In literature, great mystery is all—not the standard mystery of a murder, but questions and mysteries of life lying beyond solution by detection.

The thing most marvelous, and somewhat unbelievable, about the people created by Hillerman for *A Thief of Time* is their extreme left-brained power to retain and report precisely those details of life that serve Lieutenant Leaphorn as clues. Hillerman's principal focus tends to be not upon character but upon clues. He gives each character a little setting of his or her own, a personal identification, eccentricity or idiosyncrasy.

Thus the people of this novel think always small, never big. If I am to follow their thinking I must turn off my right brain in order to divert my gaze from questions of the mind's landscape to questions of muddy footprints and low motives.

I am told on good authority that Hillerman carries sound background and information into this tale set within the Navajo culture of which he is a part. Convincingly, in this book, he knows the people, the topography, and the footing both from his own experience and through his learned knowledge of the findings of anthropologists—like his Dr. Friedman-Bernal.

He employs his breadth of comprehension to create a novel of detection. For the reader who prefers detection to atmosphere this book is another in an abundant setting.

> *Mark Harris, "A Mother Lode of Detectives,"*
> in Chicago Tribune—Books, *June 26, 1988, p. 6.*

Michael Dorris

It takes nothing away from the genre of mystery writing, or from Tony Hillerman's masterly way of telling a rousing story, to say that *A Thief of Time* is also a skillful, provocative novel. Like the best work of Ruth Rendell, P. D. James and Sir Arthur Conan Doyle, Mr. Hillerman's new book transcends the conventions of the simple whodunit and plunges the reader into a fully realized world, populated by complex, fascinating characters.

Swept along by the light, sure touch of an author both steeped in and delighted by his material, we become enmeshed in Navajo life, language and social conventions. Before we realize what's happened, or quite how, we have crossed cultural boundaries, developed a quick familiarity with a new set of perspectives and are emotionally and intellectually involved with a group of people whose usual stereotypes are left in the dust.

The Native Americans in *A Thief of Time* are a paradoxical mix of the traditional and the contemporary, informed by systems of ancient belief yet also, for example, avid readers of *The New Yorker*. . . . They are thoughtful and intelligent, funny and depressed—and always humane, wholly believable and compellingly interesting.

Readers of Mr. Hillerman's previous books will already be familiar with Lieut. Joe Leaphorn and Officer Jim Chee of the Navajo Tribal Police, who combine forces here in the search for a missing archeologist, Prof. Eleanor Friedman-Bernal. A specialist in Anasazi pots, she's on the verge of a major breakthrough—the identification of a specific artist, dead a thousand years—when, beneath a full desert moon, she seems simply to vanish. The trail of clues leads Leaphorn and Chee through a maze of distinctive characters. . . . The action never flags, the complicated plot moves constantly forward and the conclusion is, if not startling, satisfying.

In *A Thief of Time* unlike most mysteries, a sense of place and character often takes precedence over the story. The Southwest setting is beautifully, graphically rendered. . . .

Mr. Hillerman is similarly attentive to descriptions of his characters. Thus Leaphorn mourns his deceased wife, Emma, in a thousand little ways. ("He had turned the bed ninety degrees so that his eyes would open in the morning to the shock of a different view. That broke his lifelong habit, the automatic waking thought of 'Where's Emma?' . . . He had moved from his side of the bed to Emma's.")

Mr. Hillerman also makes good use of the practice by which people on the reservation relate to one another in ways that uniquely derive from their complicated kinship. And so, Robert Bates of the San Juan County Sheriff's Office was "married to a Navajo, who happened to be 'born to' the Kin yaa aanii—the Towering House People—which was linked in some way Chee had never understood to his grandfather's To' aheedlinii—the Waters Flow Together Clan. That made Chee and Bates vaguely relatives." Therefore, Chee gets extra cooperation in his police investigation.

Mr. Hillerman plays with ironic juxtaposition as well. (The young Chee, for instance, is more involved in traditional Navajo beliefs than the elder Leaphorn.) Furthermore, Mr. Hillerman manages to make a potentially dry subject like the classification of pot fragments exciting to the nonspecialist reader—a feat few anthropology professors can accomplish even with their graduate students. Most important, Mr. Hillerman's picture of modern American Indians is never patronizing, never hokey, never precious. We finish *A Thief of Time* with the impression of having visited, vividly though briefly, a place and a people unlike any other. That a mystery is astutely solved as well seems almost a bonus.

Michael Dorris, "She Vanished Under a Full Desert Moon," in The New York Times Book Review, *July 3, 1988, p. 6.*

Herbert Mitgang

Tony Hillerman, the author who created the American Indian policier, adds a dividend for the reader in his latest novel, *Talking God.* In addition to setting his story in familiar Hillerman country—the Navajo Reservation and its environs in New Mexico—this time he includes Washington, a venue with its own mysterious tribal rites.

It's a sign of Mr. Hillerman's powers of observation that he (or rather his appealing main character, Lieut. Joe Leaphorn of the Navajo Tribal Police) sees things that even seasoned Washington observers might overlook. One of his nonmystery novels, *The Fly on the Wall,* also had a Washington locale; the author recognizes that there are shamans in the capital, too. So it's interesting for a follower of Mr. Hillerman's detective fiction to watch how he joins two different worlds to form his mystery.

The point of contact is the Smithsonian Institution's Museum of Natural History in Washington. A Smithsonian conservator who is part Navajo sends a coworker bones of two "white Anglo types" to protest the museum's policy of not returning ancestral remains to American Indians. The Navajo conservator is arrested by Lieutenant Leaphorn's younger sidekick, Officer Jim Chee.

Mr. Hillerman uses Chee to good advantage in his mysteries: the experienced hand and the protégé play off each other while exchanging detective lore and wisdom. Readers will remember the pair from his previous book, *A Thief of Time.* They make a fascinating team. . . .

Lieutenant Leaphorn and Officer Chee are in the capital pursuing separate matters. Leaphorn is there because of a homicide; an unidentified corpse has been found near Gallup, N.M., with a note mentioning an Indian ceremony. The trail takes Leaphorn to what J. Edgar Hoover in his correspondence grandiloquently called the "Seat of Government"—the late F.B.I. Director's name comes up several times in Mr. Hillerman's mystery—where he obtains some help from an old G-man. Officer Chee is tracking down a ceremonial mask, the title's "Talking God," the maternal grandfather of all the Navajo gods.

Along the book's journey to resolution, there are the usual fine scenes of the Navajo countryside and customs—Hillerman I.D.'s—as well as keen views of the capital. Officer Chee says he would like to ride New York's subways sometime but settles for Washington's. . . .

Awareness of differences of race and privilege are never far from the eyes and minds of Mr. Hillerman's Navajo characters. There is also a scene of homeless people living in cardboard boxes in the shadow of the Washington Monument. A couple of comments about the late F.B.I. Director are woven quite naturally into the story. . . .

Two uncooperative young F.B.I. agents talk stiffly, using phrases like "at this point in time." Contrasting them with Leaphorn and Chee, the reader senses that the author is making a point he has made before: official bias exists against American Indians.

There is a political twist at the end of *Talking God* that gives the mystery another dimension—far from the immediate lives of the people on the Navajo Reservation. It involves the Chilean dictatorship of Gen. Augusto Pinochet and its long reach and killing ways, even in the United States. Somehow, the elements all come together.

To sweeten *Talking God* and give the two Navajo Reservation officers more rounded personalities, Leaphorn is grieving over the recent death of his wife and Chee is nearing the end of a love affair. These side attractions don't get in the way of the mystery; rather, like George Smiley's wandering wife who hovers in the background of several John le Carré stories, they add elements that enrich the book. It is touches like these, and political sophistication, that make the difference between a routine and a masterly genre writer.

> Herbert Mitgang, "Hillerman Adds Tribal Rites of Washington to the Navajos'," in The New York Times, *June 10, 1989, p. 15.*

Timothy Foote

[In *Talking God* the] story starts with a starchy female lawyer for the Smithsonian Institution receiving a pair of human skeletons in the mail. A note explains that they are the bones of her aristocratic New England grandparents. The sender suggests the Smithsonian should put them on display, in turn releasing "the bones of two of my ancestors so that they may be returned to their rightful place in Mother Earth."

As everyone knows these days, aggrieved Indian tribes are seeking Federal help in retrieving their aboriginal skeletal remains from museums all over the country, while embattled anthropologists lament the potential loss of priceless information about ancient tribes and cultures. . . .

It would not be unreasonable, therefore, if a neophyte reader of Tony Hillerman's fiction concluded that the author intended to plunge headlong into this painful question. Not so. By trade and perhaps temperament, Mr. Hillerman is a narrative circler. Besides, as fans familiar with his engaging mix of lethal doings and tribal lore know, the Navajo have a "fierce religious aversion to corpses and everything associated with death." And isn't it a bit odd that the giver of the grisly gift is a Smithsonian curator who claims to be one-quarter Navajo?

Indeed it is. Before you can say Yeibichai, the Navajo name for the Talking God of the title, the scene shifts from the nation's capital to Mr. Hillerman's literary preserve, some 25,000 square miles of Navajo turf in Arizona, Utah and New Mexico. Once again, Lieut. Joe Leaphorn of the Navajo Tribal Police is on the job, beginning to wonder just how a man with pointed shoes wound up dead beside

some railroad tracks. His younger colleague, Officer Jim Chee, meanwhile, is staked out on a totally different problem. He is watching a Night Chant curing ceremony, with orders to arrest some kook named Henry Highhawk who wants to become a full Navajo, but (Aha!) has been charged with "desecration of graves" back East.

In mystery writing there is no shortage of heterogeneous violent acts yoked by ingenuity together. Mr. Hillerman's method is brilliant, though. Leaphorn and Chee more or less leapfrog each other, trying to sort out what appear to be separate puzzles. . . . Because they don't communicate with each other much, the reader, privy to both searches, is often ahead of them in putting it all together. Curiously, this sometimes creates more, rather than less, suspense. One kind is pure mystery—simply wondering what will happen next. The other, more subtle, is the suspense of waiting to learn exactly how and when what you roughly know has to happen actually does happen.

With the success of Mr. Hillerman's earlier novels, including *A Thief of Time,* a best seller, Chee and Leaphorn have achieved some national fame. . . . As regular players in Mr. Hillerman's long running show-and-tell course in Navajo language and culture, the two help illuminate the range of small truces a college-trained Navajo must make between tradition and the modern world. Leaphorn, with an advanced degree in anthropology, is more skeptical about religion than Chee, who is practicing up to conduct Talking God's nine-day curing ceremony as a freelance shaman. . . .

Mr. Hillerman, too, seems a bit more at home on the reservation than in the murder capital of the nation. Yet except for the standard tourist misspelling of Silver Spring, Md., as Silver Springs, and turning E Street into E Avenue, his background use of Washington is breathtaking. Real and false masks of Indian deities, an attempted political assassination—at a gala in the Smithsonian's National Museum of Natural History—and a short course in how to murder a man and keep it secret for a month, are all included in *Talking God.* So is the creation of a curiously winsome Dickensian character, an urban hit man who knifes his victims with surgical skill but spends his off-duty hours trying desperately to find a nursing home willing to keep his savagely obstreperous mother.

> Timothy Foote, *"Inside the Beltway with Chee and Leaphorn," in* The New York Times Book Review, *June 18, 1989, p. 9.*

Margaret Laurence

1926-1987

(Born Jean Margaret Wemyss) Canadian novelist, short story writer, memoirist, essayist, editor, and translator.

A prominent figure in contemporary Canadian literature, Laurence earned international acclaim for realistic fiction that focuses on the individual's quest for self-actualization. Admired for the evocative power of her depictions as well as for her passionate valorization of quotidian Canadian life, Laurence was revered by her compatriots, many of whom agree with David Stouck's assessment: "The first writer to create a feeling of tradition among Canadian novelists is Margaret Laurence." While her earlier fiction is set in Africa, Laurence's most respected and popular works feature protagonists from fictitious Manawaka, Manitoba, a small Scots-Irish community on the Canadian prairies that Laurence derived from her native town of Neepawa. The Manawaka series, comprised of four novels and a short story collection, examines the interwoven relations of four generations of the town's families, concentrating on five women who seek literal and metaphorical escape from the stifling values of their forebears. Although Laurence's fiction generated controversy in the 1960s and 1970s—notably for her advocacy of women's independence, her relatively frank discussion of sexuality, and her defense of the rights of Canadian Indians—her works are now considered integral to the Canadian canon and are widely studied in high schools and colleges.

Critics often observe that the events of Laurence's own tumultuous life inform her fiction. Born in Neepawa to a pianist and a lawyer, she was four years old when her mother died of a kidney infection. The death compelled Laurence's maternal aunt, Margaret Simpson, to leave her Calgary teaching position and return to Neepawa to care for her young niece. When Laurence was five, her aunt Margaret married Laurence's father, Robert Wemyss, who died of pneumonia four years later. An orphan at age nine, Laurence was raised by her aunt in the home of her maternal grandfather, a stern, dominating man upon whom Laurence modeled the strict grandfather of the autobiographical stories collected in *A Bird in the House*. In 1944, after earning a scholarship, Laurence left Neepawa for Winnipeg's United College, where she wrote short stories, became involved with social reform issues, and met Jack Laurence, a civil-engineering student whom she married in 1947.

After spending two years in Canada, the couple travelled to England and then to Africa, where they lived from 1950 to 1957. While Laurence's husband directed a dam-building project for the British Protectorate of Somaliland (later Somalia), she explored the oral narratives of the Somalis, who had no written language until 1973. This endeavor led Laurence to translate *A Tree for Poverty: Somali Poetry and Prose,* the first collection of Somali works to appear in English. From 1952 to 1957, Jack Laurence continued his engineering work in the Gold Coast (later Ghana), and Margaret Laurence investigated African culture and cared for the couple's two small children. The

Gold Coast became Laurence's setting for her first novel, *This Side Jordan,* and a short story collection, *The Tomorrow-Tamer.* Probing the implications of personal and political independence, these works depict African communities whose members are torn between cultural inheritance and Western modernization but united by their distrust of white imperialists. Although praised for its perceptive and evocative portraits, Laurence's African fiction is more often studied for the insights it yields regarding her literary development. Based on diary entries from her sojourn in Somalia, Laurence's travel memoir, *The Prophet's Camel Bell,* was completed a decade after the events it analyzes. This work discusses how Laurence's study of African colonialism helped to shape her literary objectives, stimulating her interests in racial equality, women's emancipation, and the promotion of the national literatures of emergent nations, including Canada.

In 1957, the Laurences returned to Canada, settling for five years in Vancouver, where the author completed her African fiction and began her first Manawaka novel, *The Stone Angel.* After separating from her husband and moving with her children to England in 1962, Laurence finished this novel, which is widely hailed as a Canadian classic. A first-person narrative, *The Stone Angel* is ninety-year-old Hagar Shipley's intimate account of the last days of her life. Cantankerous and befuddled, the old woman feels trapped by her debilitated body and overwhelmed by memories, including her privileged childhood as the daughter of Manawaka's only merchant, her defiant marriage to a simple-minded farmer, and the death of her favorite child. Hagar's obdurate nature ensures her survival but isolates her from meaningful human contact. When her remaining son threatens to consign her to a convalescent home, Hagar flees to an abandoned cannery, where recollections flood her consciousness, driving her to an epiphany of honest self-appraisal. "Pride was my wilderness," she concludes, "and the demon that led me was fear." Commonly assigned in Canadian high schools, *The Stone Angel* is also used by instructors of geriatric nursing, who value Laurence's illumination of the mental and physical impairments associated with aging. While many critics praise the novel as a trenchant analysis of Christian doctrines regarding sin and death, most assert that it proves more memorable as a potent character study. S. E. Read commented: "At times vicious and vulgar, irascible and prideful, stubborn and independent, [Hagar] is by no means lovable; but she is capable of profound feelings and in the end demands respect . . . I'll not forget [her]. I may even see her from time to time—on the street, in a bus, or in a hospital ward; for she is timeless and the world is her home."

Like *The Stone Angel, A Jest of God* focuses on a Manawaka woman whose small-town Christian values have instilled in her a paralyzing fear of social censure. Rachel Cameron, a thirty-four-year-old elementary teacher, lives with her demanding mother in the flat above her late father's funeral parlor. Lonely and emotionally confused, Rachel longs for affection, but strikes her favorite pupil and rejects her only friend, an eccentric coworker whose affection she distrusts. When an awkward liaison prompts Rachel's first sexual experience, she attains a measure of self-confidence that is quickly obscured by a dread of pregnancy. Yearning for a child yet horrified by the social ostracism that accompanies unwed motherhood, Rachel suffers a crisis. After discovering that her supposed pregnancy is a benign tumor, she gathers enough strength to leave provincial Manawaka. Most commentators praised *A Jest of God* as an indelible portrait of anxiety bordering on madness. Patricia Morley concluded: "In Laurence's handling Rachel's plight becomes an analogue for human alienation and isolation, a crisis which finds its solution in the woman coming to terms with the jests of God, coping with difficulties, and growing stronger in the process."

As *A Jest of God* chronicles a woman's inner turmoil, Laurence's next Manawaka novel, *The Fire-Dwellers,* focuses on the violence of the outer world. A housewife and mother who lives near a large city in the late 1960s, Stacey Cameron McAindra has achieved the conventional life to which her sister, Rachel Cameron, aspires. Stacey, however, finds little serenity in a seemingly self-destructive world that appears intent upon its own eradication. Bombarded with news images of mutilated people in riot-plagued cities and napalm-blasted villages, Stacey suffers a nightmarish anxiety that she is powerless to protect her children from senseless brutality. She receives no comfort from her husband, who has grown sullen after twenty years of carrying the family's financial burden, nor from her young lover. Although Stacey considers suicide, she

eventually ends her affair and resolves to endure her predicament, determining that "there is nowhere to go but here." While *The Fire-Dwellers* relates an individual's concerns about aging, parenthood, war, and nuclear proliferation, it is widely considered Laurence's funniest work, for its black humor addresses the banality of suburban life, satirizing New Age vitamin therapy, women's magazines, cosmetic make-overs, and Tupperware parties. Through the use of such typographical devices as irregular indentations and italic print, Laurence incorporates Stacey's thoughts and conversations directly into the third-person narrative, evoking the immediacy of Stacey's experience but maintaining an authorial distance. These techniques proved controversial among critics, but most reviewers deemed Laurence's examination of suburban angst disturbingly accurate.

While writing the first three Manawaka novels, Laurence also published seven short stories, which she linked with one other previously unpublished work in the collection *A Bird in the House.* Ordered chronologically, the stories depict pivotal episodes in the youth of Vanessa MacLeod, who lives with her mother and aunt in the home of her autocratic grandfather. Recognized as Laurence's most autobiographical work, *A Bird in the House* chronicles young Vanessa's evolution as a writer; the first-person narrative infuses the girl's observations with the commentary of the mature writer examining her past. Laurence described her double perspective: "The narrative voice is, of course, that of Vanessa herself, but an older Vanessa, herself grown up, remembering how it was when she was ten . . . The narrative voice, therefore, had to speak as though from two points in time simultaneously." Though Laurence conceded that the collection resembles a novel, she contended that, unlike chapters in a novel, these stories are complete, independent structures. While some reviewers faulted as hollow Laurence's sparse characterization of her narrator, a girl who calls herself a "professional eavesdropper," others commended *A Bird in the House* as Laurence's most technically proficient volume.

At the 1974 publication of *The Diviners,* Laurence announced that this novel, considered her most ambitious, would be her last. The culmination of her literary career, *The Diviners* is Laurence's *Künstlerroman;* although the protagonist's experiences differ from Laurence's own, the volume constitutes what the author called her "spiritual autobiography." Struggling to complete her latest novel, forty-seven-year-old Morag Gunn meditates upon her turbulent life and its sundry participants: her long-forgotten parents who succumbed to polio when she was five, her eccentric garbageman stepfather and his reclusive wife, her restrained and repressive English husband, and her ardent but erratic Native lover, with whom she bore a rebellious daughter. Like *The Fire-Dwellers, The Diviners* employs typographical devices to differentiate its two narrative lines. Morag's digressive inner dialogue, which includes extended flashbacks, imaginary conversations, and personal ruminations, is thematically integrated into the novel's unfolding present. Considered a significant literary achievement, *The Diviners* also serves to complete the Manawaka cycle. As strong as Hagar but more emotional, Morag endures anxiety and adversity that might disable Rachel and Stacey, yet she survives to achieve personal fulfillment through the cultivation of talents similar to those of young Vanessa. In addition, the social issues that permeated Laurence's fiction—women's individuation, equality among Canada's racial groups, and the literary validation of Canadian experience—find their resolution in *The Diviners*. Morag, whom some critics contend symbolizes Canada itself, investigates and mythologizes her Scottish heritage and matures under the domination of her English husband, but she eventually rejects him for the authentic love of a Canadian Indian, who begets a feisty personification of the racially and culturally unified Canadian future.

(See also *CLC,* Vols. 3, 6, 13, 50; *Contemporary Authors,* Vols. 5-8, rev. ed., 121 [obit]; *Something about the Author,* Vol. 50; and *Dictionary of Literary Biography,* Vol. 53.)

PRINCIPAL WORKS

NOVELS

This Side Jordan   1960
The Stone Angel   1964
A Jest of God   1966; also published in England as *Now I Lay Me Down* and *Rachel, Rachel,* 1968
The Fire-Dwellers   1969
The Diviners   1974

SHORT FICTION COLLECTIONS

The Tomorrow-Tamer   1963
A Bird in the House   1970

CHILDREN'S BOOKS

Jason's Quest   1970
The Olden Days Coat   1979
Six Darn Cows   1979
The Christmas Birthday Story   1980

OTHER

A Tree for Poverty: Somali Poetry and Prose [editor and translator] 1954
The Prophet's Camel Bell (travel memoir) 1963; also published in the United States as *New Wind in a Dry Land,* 1964
Long Drums and Cannons: Nigerian Dramatists and Novelists 1952-1966 (criticism) 1968
Heart of a Stranger (critical and autobiographical essays) 1976
Dance on the Earth (memoir) 1989

Clara Thomas

Many Canadian writers have carried characters or settings from one novel to another, among them Hugh MacLennan, Mordecai Richler, Roch Carrier, and Mazo de la Roche. Many others have used the small town as a setting—so many, in fact, that a "Dictionary of Canadian Mythology" would contain a very large entry under "Small Town." . . . But no town in our literature has been so consistently and extensively developed as Margaret Laurence's Manawaka. Through five works of fiction, it has grown as a vividly realized, microcosmic world, acting

as a setting for the dilemmas of its unique individuals and also exercising its own powerful dynamic on them. Manawaka is also specifically, historically, and geographically authentic, dense with objects and true to its place and its development through time. (pp. 173-74)

The towns of Canadian literature provide us with illuminations of a major strand of our tradition, which is both historically and artistically true to our experience. For many Canadians a town was the matrix of social growth, the point of departure into a wider world and, inevitably for many, a point of no return. (p. 175)

But no writer has been in any doubt of one thing: the power and the influence of the town's corporate personality on its people, be they its heroes or its victims. The isolation of small groups of people in a vast land was one of the factors in the growth of a town's personality; in English Canada the other factor was the drive to build a progressive, successful, and Protestant community. Ideals of godliness and business enterprise were inextricably meshed and individuals were expected, both by commitment and from need, to adapt and to give evidence of their partnership in the community ideals by unremitting work, or to fall short of the corporate ideal at great personal loss and social peril. The town was our tribe—not, primarily, a network of kinship and family, but a powerful structure of hierarchical social relationships. (pp. 175-76)

The community assigned roles to its people too; in the eyes of the town, individuals were often seen only in relation to their assigned roles. Generations of writers have realized that the town provides them with a setting that is both authentic and manageable, and also highly complex, highly dramatic, and ripe for explorations in the ironical distance between man as he seems to be and man as he really is. [In *The Diviners*] Christie Logan plays the part the town expects of him up to the hilt—and every town had its clowns—but the energy that brings Christie to life on the page lies in Margaret Laurence's successful fusing of his public and his private voices, clown and seer. (p. 176)

Margaret Laurence's Manawaka world is Everyman's and Everywoman's, but its particularities are emphatically Canadian. Grounded in a small western town, her people move out into the wider world, but they carry Manawaka with them, its constraints and inhibitions, but also its sense of roots, of ancestors, and of a past that is living still, both its achievements and its tragic errors. A past so rooted, geographically and socially, is within the memory of many Canadians, and it is within the imaginative range of all.

The voices of Manawaka speak a Canadian vernacular, retained and recalled by Margaret Laurence and heightened according to the demands of her characters, but retaining its typical idioms and figures of speech, and particularly its irony of tone. . . . [The] self-mocking voice of Hagar and the self-saving humour of Stacey are as truly authentic to Scotch-Irish Canadians, and Margaret Laurence's combination of ear and talent have recorded them.

Manawaka incorporates the general geographical and physical features of the town of Neepawa [Margaret Laurence's Manitoba birthplace]. Riding Mountain is Galloping Mountain, Clear Lake is Diamond Lake, and Manawaka's river is the Wachakwa. The town is not, strictly speaking, a prairie town, for it is still in the treed area. . . . Manawaka has neither the flatness nor the unvegetated bleakness of Sinclair Ross' fictional Saskatchewan town of Horizon, for instance. The river, the hill on which the cemetery stands, the poplar bluffs, and the mountain in the distance provide major diversifications to its landscape, and its entire natural surroundings in their precise detail are often described in vignettes as beautiful, not ugly. . . . Margaret Laurence often sets a natural beauty in contrast to a planned one; Hagar's memories of the scent of cowslips in the cemetery, the "tough-rooted . . . wild and gaudy flowers," stubbornly cancelling out the "funeral parlor perfume of the planted peonies," sets up and demonstrates the dichotomy between the works of man and nature that is basic to her description of Manawaka and to its deepest meaning.

Manawaka is the supply-centre for a farm region that is well cultivated and fruitful, except for the years of drought in the thirties. Even as it was described in *The Stone Angel* and *A Bird in the House,* the area was never completely barren. . . . (pp. 177-78)

Galloping Mountain to the northwest symbolizes a kind of frontier of civilization and cultivation—and the possibility of freedom. It is there that Pique Tonnerre goes at the end of *The Diviners* to stay with her Uncle Jacques who has made a home for his own and all the other lost children of the Tonnerre family. Beyond the mountain is "up north," a land that belongs to another geography and seems as different as another country or another planet. (p. 178)

Manawaka's climate is one of extremes, the enervating heat of Rachel Cameron's summer holidays, or the blizzard in which a man might lose his life or lose, as Bram Shipley did, the horse that might have meant the fulfilment of his dreams. Ordinary weather is rarely described and almost never seen as being compatible to human comfort, though a mellow day can be used to point up the granite qualities of such a character as Grandfather Connor: "It was a warm day, the leaves turning a clear lemon yellow on the Manitoba maples and the late afternoon sun lighting up the windows of the Brick House like silver foil, but my grandfather was wearing his grey-heather sweater buttoned up to the neck."

Powerful though the town is in its effects on its people, Manawaka has no power over the cataclysmic events that batter them. The Depression and two wars simply and starkly happened *to* its people. Control is not in their hands, but as remote, as ominously and terrifying mysterious as the God of Wrath himself. People leave Manawaka and the land around it to go to "the west coast," to go to "the city," to go to the world wars, to go to the ladies' college in Ontario. Each of these destinations seems equally remote, as if on another planet. There is no idea or imagining, no warm encircling dream that joins Manawaka to any place outside, nor any important physical manifestation of joining in the way that the railway-networks are triumphant, almost magical, physical symbols of uniting far distances in the works of Thomas Wolfe and of Willa Cather.

In contrast, Manawaka's railroad runs *through* the town and west to Vancouver, the city that is the goal of hope and escape for many of the townspeople, and for some a place of final despair. Hagar went to Vancouver when she left Bram Shipley, and in a Vancouver hospital she finished her life. John Shipley faced himself in Vancouver in a way that his mother could not yet do, and he realized that his real place was in Manawaka with his father. Stacey Cameron couldn't wait to leave Manawaka for Vancouver, but at forty, trapped and desperate as she feels, Vancouver has become the very epitome of "The City Of The End Of Things" to her. To Rachel, Vancouver represents hope and a positive decision. She takes her mother and goes there to take her chances at living independent of the physical familiarity of Manawaka, at the same time recognizing that she carries the town always within her. (pp. 179-80)

After five books, the town of Manawaka can be specifically mapped. Its geography is precise and consistent, and there are now many landmarks in the town. At least two-score businesses and institutions have accumulated; some of them—Doherty's stables, Jarrett's bakery or the Queen Victoria Hotel—are simply reference points necessary to the setting, and others—Currie's General Store or Cameron's Funeral Home, later the Japonica Chapel—are essential focuses for the action of the various books. River Street runs south to the Wachakwa and north to the CPR tracks and Main Street intersects it. The Camerons live on Japonica Street, and Rachel, walking home from school, turns at River Street. (p. 180)

The cemetery, the garbage dump, and the valley where the Tonnerres have their shacks are all on the outskirts of Manawaka. The stone angel stands in the cemetery on a hill overlooking the town. Christie Logan is garbage collector for Manawaka and his "Nuisance Grounds" are not so very far from the cemetery. This dump is the repository of the town's rubbish, its discards and, sometimes, its awful secrets. In the cemetery, death is set apart, kept within bounds in "the beautifully cared-for habitations of the dead," as firmly and regularly as rubbish is cast out and dug under in the "Nuisance Grounds." Like death and garbage, the Métis family of Tonnerres are outside the pale of Manawaka. The valley near the dump where Piquette Tonnerre burns to death with her children is a place of horror for Morag Gunn, who was sent there by Lachlan McLachlan to cover the story for the *Manawaka Banner.* But earlier, in her encounters with Jules (Skinner) Tonnerre, the valley was also its own world apart, an exotic place where Morag and Skinner explored making friends and making love.

Out over the railway tracks is the trestle bridge where John Shipley and Arlene Simmons died in a dare, and further out from the town to the southwest is the Shipley farm. There Bram Shipley dreamed of founding his dynasty and establishing his horse ranch, and there Hagar worked, loved, despaired and dreamed of changing Bram into the mould of her father, Jason Currie, a founder and pillar of Manawaka. About three miles to the west of the town is the prosperous dairy farm of Nestor and Teresa Kazlik, Ukrainian immigrants whose past is almost lost to their children as Rachel Cameron's Scottish past is almost lost to her. Morag Gunn's parents, Colin and Louisa, also had a farm outside of Manawaka, but when they both died of polio in the thirties, the farm and all their other possessions had to go up for auction to pay off their mortgage.

When Hagar Currie was a child in the 1880's, Manawaka

was still close to its beginnings, with board sidewalks, oil lamps, a few successful businesses such as Jason Currie's store, institutions such as the well-cared for cemetery, the ever-present undertakers and the churches, especially the Presbyterian church. . . . The Methodists, Baptists, Congregationalists, and all the other sects who established their churches in the small towns of Canada, carried with them religions that balanced far more towards fear than love. Certainly, everything men and women found in pioneer experience would confirm an impression that their God required hard service before rejoicing, as the land demanded battle from them and did not repay love. The God who presided over such a bleak experience must have seemed to the pioneers remarkably analogous to the Old Testament Jehovah, God of War and Wrath and Judgement.

Manawaka's was a swiftly forming social system, based on thrift, hard work, pressure to conform to the patterns of respectability, and, above all, financial success. In the beginning there werc a few men, like the lawyer Luke McVitie and Jason Currie, who were "God-fearing," as Aunt Doll Stonehouse impressed upon Hagar, but who were even more emphatically "self-made." Jason Currie's pride impelled him to have Hagar educated in the faraway Ladies' College in Ontario and then to refuse to allow her to teach, insisting instead that she stay at home and be his lady-housekeeper. There were many other citizens of the town who saw and emulated such patterns, Lottie and Telford Simmons, for instance, who tried to wrap up their daughter Arlene in a cocoon of polite appearances and so lost her to John Shipley and death.

It was in the early days that the social map of the town was made with the "right" people and "the others" and, in geographical fact, a right and wrong side of the tracks. On the side farthest away from the railroad tracks there were a few big houses like the Currie's and many more modest, but eminently respectable ones. Near the tracks where land was cheap, or had been claimed simply by squatters' rights, were the houses and shacks of the poor, those who, like the Winklers, the Shinwells, and the Logans, were what the town called "shiftless" or simply unlucky. Three generations after its founding, in the twenties and thirties, when Stacey, Rachel, Vanessa, and Morag were children, the old standard in Manawaka remained. Rachel and Stacey Cameron lived above the funeral parlor where their mother, desperate to keep up appearances, had become a harping hypochondriac, and Niall Cameron, their father, drank to forget that he lived more closely and more easily with death than with life. At the beginning of *A Bird in the House* Vanessa and her mother and father are living with Grandmother MacLeod whose house is among the few big houses of Manawaka. Grandmother mourns ceaselessly for the relatively luxurious and, by Manawaka's standards, even ostentatious way of life that vanished with the twenties. . . . (pp. 181-84)

There are five major and interacting family connections in Manawaka and these now stretch over four generations: the Curries and the Shipleys; the Camerons and the Kazliks; the Connors and the MacLeods; the Gunns and the Logans; and the Tonnerres. Many others—Henry Pearl and Luke McVitie, Doctor Cates and Lachlan McLachlan, Lottie Simmons and Eva and Vernon Winkler among them—come in and out of two or more of the works with

brief but vivid impacts. Manawaka's timespan comes up from the early 1880's, the childhood of Hagar, to the present; Pique Tonnerre is four generations on from her great-grandfather, Jules Tonnerre, as Stephen Shipley, Hagar's grandson, is from Jason Currie. In *The Diviners,* however, it is made clear that the townspeople incorporate in their bones and blood a far longer span of history than the town's, one that comes down from the time of the Highland Clearances and from before the settlement of the West, and is landmarked by battles—Batoche, Bourlon Wood, and Dieppe.

Manawaka is a fully realized, three-dimensional, imagined town of length, breadth, and depth, and of history and corporate personality. We can orient ourselves to its social structure, as to its streets and buildings. Through the stories of its people, we can make connection with the present and the past of the people of Canada, their aspirations and failures—and our own. Manawaka also possesses, implies, and constantly reveals beneath its surfaces the fourth dimension of time and the timeless, of men and women as the victims and prisoners of the institutions they have made for their own survival, and of the endless, stumbling pilgrimage of the Tribe of Man towards God. (p. 187)

> *Clara Thomas, in her* The Manawaka World of Margaret Laurence, *McClelland and Stewart Limited, 1975, 212 p.*

Barbara Hehner

[*The Diviners*] is overflowing with ideas about life, about life in Canada, and about life in Canada as experienced by a woman. Laurence has been quoted as saying, "Now the wheel seems to have come full circle—these five books [the Manawaka fiction] all interweave and fit together." (p. 40)

Laurence has been quoted as saying that she will probably never write another novel, and one can almost feel, while reading *The Diviners,* the pressure on its author to make a final important statement about Life and Art. It seems to have been Laurence's ambition in this novel, dense with themes and symbols, complex in structure, but meandering in plot, not only to clarify the ideas expressed in her earlier books, but to express all those ideas for which she never previously found a suitable fictional embodiment.

In the earlier Manawaka books, Laurence explored such themes as the difficulty of achieving genuine communication between individuals, and the limits placed on personal freedom by family and ethnic background, in ways that critics have come to identify as distinctively "Canadian". Her female protagonists merely survive rather than triumphing, and they grow up in a community which displays the "garrison mentality" in its need for rigid conformity and its fear of spontaneity and sensuality. But in *The Diviners,* Laurence has overturned the negativism of these Canadian literary themes. Morag is no Philip Bentley: she has published five novels. She is in touch with the needs of her body as well as her mind, and has striven to satisfy both. She has freely chosen a loving relationship with the Métis, Jules Tonnerre, and borne a child by him who seems to symbolize the healing of the division between culture and nature in the Canadian psyche.

At times *The Diviners* seems almost too self-conscious in its reworking of Canadian literary clichés. As just one example, Margaret Atwood has defined the "Rapunzel Syndrome" in Canadian literature: imprisoned by the repressive attitudes of the society around her, the woman passively awaits rescue by the prince. Atwood points to Rachel in *A Jest of God* as a typical victim of this malaise. In *The Diviners,* Morag, caught in a stifling marriage, sees *herself* as Rapunzel: "Maybe tower would be a better word for the apartment. . . . The lonely tower. Rapunzel, Rapunzel, let down your hair." To Morag, however, "letting down her hair" does not mean waiting helplessly for the prince to save her; it means taking a first step towards freeing herself, by defying current standards of chic and letting her straight black hair grow out.

Cultural nationalism and women's liberation dovetail nicely here. Morag's marriage to the Englishman Brooke, whose taste and intellect she considers superior to her own, can be seen both as the outcome of the "colonial mentality," which considers indigenous culture inferior to that of the mother country, and as the result of growing up in a society that assigns housework to women and intellectual achievement to men. *The Diviners* comes to grips with currently-debated issues much more explicitly than Laurence's previous fiction: the search for a Canadian identity, the discrimination encountered by women, the unjust treatment of native people, and even ecology, find a place in the novel.

The Diviners also uses the most sophisticated narrative technique Laurence has yet attempted, and an examination of this technique provides a suitable introduction to the novel, since both its virtuosity, and the unfortunate outcome of this virtuosity, its obtrusiveness, exemplify the strengths and failings of the novel as a whole. In *The Diviners,* Laurence not only attempted to refine the narrative devices she had used before, but, as with other aspects of this novel, to stretch her story-telling abilities in new directions.

The recurring narrative device used in *The Stone Angel, A Jest of God,* and *The Fire-Dwellers* is the first-person, present-tense narrator who is also the central character of the book. . . . Paradoxically, the first-person technique provides Laurence as a writer with the feeling that she is sharing another person's mind while, by strictly limiting the point of view of each novel, it conveys to the reader Laurence's conviction that human beings are hopelessly isolated from each other.

The Stone Angel presents the reminiscences of ninety-year-old Hagar Shipley. The novel's present, revealed to us by Hagar speaking in the present tense, covers only a few days, as she "rages against the dying of the light." But Hagar's memories, in the past tense, range over her whole life. Laurence exercised great care in providing both the time and the motivation for these memories in the novel's present. . . .

Laurence wrote in **"Ten Years' Sentences,"** a 1969 article, of her pride in being able to recapture the idiom of her grandmother's day:

> Yet Doris never cared a snap about that pitcher, I'm bound to admit. Well there's no explaining tastes, and ugliness is pretty nowadays. Myself, I favour flowers . . .

but she also allowed Hagar some unlikely flights of rhetoric, whose equivalent is not to be found in her next two novels:

> I now think she must have been carved in that distant sun by stone masons who were the cynical descendants of Bernini, gouging out her like by the score, gauging with admirable accuracy the needs of fledgling pharaohs in an uncouth land.
>
> (pp. 40-2)

In *A Jest of God* and *The Fire-Dwellers,* which portray much younger women, memories play a much smaller part than in *The Stone Angel.* Thus Laurence was able to present these memories out of chronological order without fear of confusing her readers. And she continued to take great care that these reminiscences seem to be called up naturally by events in the novels' present. . . . (p. 43)

A Jest of God marks Laurence's most sustained use of the first-person, present-tense narrative, and the technique produces a *tour de force* recreation of a troubled and often divided mind:

> And Mother nods and says yes it certainly is marvellous and Rachel is a born teacher.
>
> > *My God. How can I stand—*
> > Stop. Stop it, Rachel . . . Get a grip on yourself now.
>
> and
>
> > *Crack!*
> > What is it? What's happened?
> > The ruler. From his nose, the thin blood river. . . .
> > I can't have done it.

These dramatic effects are, however, offset by the equally striking limitations of Laurence's chosen technique. As Robert Harlow wrote of *A Jest of God,* shortly after it was published, "What is lacking is . . . objectivity, distance, irony. . . . One yearns for the third person point of view and the omniscient author—old-fashioned techniques for an old-fashioned story." Harlow complained particularly about the presentation of the other major characters in the novel, which, apart from Rachel's impressions of their appearance and manner, relies on what they reveal about themselves in conversation with her. "Both Nick and Calla suffer from having to explain themselves . . . dialogue cannot be successfully used in place of narration." While it is true that we are never provided with the depth of characterization which would unify for us Calla's flamboyant untidiness, her devotion to the tabernacle, and her lesbianism, she is warm-blooded enough for the size of her role in the novel. (pp. 43-4)

But the characterization of Nick Kaslik is indeed a problem, since it is Laurence's plan to make him a major character in *A Jest of God.* Although his roots are in Manawaka, and many of his growing-up experiences parallel Rachel's, he is a stranger to her. Thus Nick has to tell Rachel (and us) everything Laurence wants us to know about him, during those few evenings he and Rachel spend together. Despite all Laurence's efforts to give verisimilitude to these briefing sessions (Rachel is rigid with shyness and someone must do the talking), the novel falters whenever Nick begins to reminisce. Although Laurence stoutly defended the narrative method of *A Jest of God* in **"Ten**

Years' Sentences," she abandoned the strict first-person point of view in her next novel, *The Fire-Dwellers.*

The Fire-Dwellers is a type-setter's nightmare. Stacey's story is told in blocks of third-person present-tense narrative, flush right and left; paragraphs of first-person present-tense thinking by Stacey, indented with a dash; passages of dialogue, without quotation marks, indented about an inch from the left margin; memories of Stacey's childhood, in third-person past tense, with smatterings of present participles (conversation within these memories is indicated by italics); and the interruption of radio and television broadcasts in block letters. Although this complexity can be confusing, it is well-suited to the portrayal of a harassed middle-aged housewife with little time for reflection and little gift for articulating her feelings:

> You missed your calling, Mother. You should've been in the army. . . .
> Nuts to you. So long, Katie. 'Bye, kids.
> 'Bye.
> Slam. . . .
> —Quick, coffee or I faint.
> EIGHT-THIRTY NEWS BOMBERS LAST NIGHT CLAIMED A DECISIVE VICTORY. . . .
> Stacey . . . switches off the radio.
> —I can't listen. . . . Listen, God, I know it's a worthwhile job to bring up four kids. . . . But how is it that I can feel as well that I'm spending my life in one unbroken series of trivialities?

Apart from the news broadcasts and the staccato bursts of conversation, however, the novel stays as close to Stacey's mind as the entirely first-person narrative of *A Jest of God.* As Allan Bevan points out in his introduction to the New Canadian Library edition of *The Fire-Dwellers,* this limited point of view conveys the "terrifying isolation" of the characters. Stacey's conversations with her husband, as we know from sharing her mind, communicate a little of what she feels for him. . . . And her uncommunicative husband's thoughts are as great a mystery to her as they are to the reader. . . . (pp. 44-5)

On the other hand, the scenes involving the most relaxed figure in the book, the young, happy, self-reliant Luke Venturi, have the same jarring falseness as Nick Kaslik's monologues in *A Jest of God.* (p. 45)

Before turning to the narrative problems Laurence faced in her most ambitious novel, *The Diviners,* it is interesting to look briefly at the almost perfect narrative form of her most modest Manawaka book, *A Bird in the House.* As Laurence sees it, the motivation for a short story is quite different from that for a novel:

> With a novel the main characters come first, they grow slowly in the imagination until I seem to know them well. . . . Most short stories I've written seem to be triggered off by some event, either in my own life, or something I've observed or read about.

Perhaps because Laurence did not have such a desperate need to portray a single dominant character in all her complexity (although often at the expense of complexity in the other characters), her narrator, Vanessa, is perfectly and delicately poised between retrospective omniscience and her role as a child participant in the events she describes. In the early stories, particularly, Vanessa is an almost transparent recorder of the difficult inter-relationships of her parents, Aunt Edna, and her grandparents. Only an occasional passage, such as the one describing Vanessa's dissatisfaction with a clothespeg doll she is dressing while eavesdropping on an adult conversation, characterizes the narrator as a little girl. There is some humorous exploitation of the gap between Vanessa the character's limited understanding, and Vanessa the narrator's adult awareness:

> My grandmother was a Mitigated Baptist. I knew this because I had heard my father say, "At least she's not an unmitigated Baptist . . . "

but such "cuteness" is used sparingly.

In *The Diviners* Laurence brought to bear all that she had learned in her earlier fiction about the advantages and drawbacks of various narrative devices. Again she was faced with a problem she had encountered when writing *The Stone Angel.* She had decided that Morag's life story, like Hagar's, would benefit from being told in a series of extended flashbacks. A novel that maintains a continuing tension between past time and present, the past moving rapidly and the present moving slowly, until the past catches up with the present, may appear to the reader to be more "manipulated" by the author than an equally craftsmanlike beginning-to-end narrative. Laurence had been aware of this in her analysis of the flaws in *The Stone Angel.* On the other hand, if *The Diviners* began with Morag's childhood and worked its way through her life to the present, it would lose the heightened contrast and modest suspense achieved by the flashbacks. (pp. 45-6)

In *The Diviners* Laurence made extensive use of a technique that she introduced in *The Fire-Dwellers:* a third-person narrative which is so intimately connected to the protagonist that, on first reading, one is left with the impression that the story has been told in the first person. But the third-person narrative form of *The Diviners,* although it reveals only Morag's point of view, is far more flexible than the first-person narration of *A Jest of God.* At times it approximates a train of private thought:

> The postcard from Pique yesterday. No address. Mustn't think of it. . . . But a somewhat more newsy letter would be appreciated. Idiotic. How many newsy letters had Morag written to Prin and Christie, after she left Manawaka? That was different. Oh really?

But at other times the third-person narrative is free to use flowing sentences and elegant turns of phrase which, while recording Morag's perceptions, do not masquerade as transcriptions of her thought. . . . (pp. 46-7)

A few first person passages, in italic type, indicate Morag's thoughts, but there are far fewer of these than in *The Fire-Dwellers.* This is partly a result of the character being portrayed. Stacey is afraid to express herself honestly, either because what she really thinks is too vulgar or sarcastic for the social situation she finds herself in (the Polyglam party), or because, within her own family, her efforts at genuine communication are rebuffed (Mac's arrival home in Chapter I). Thus Stacey's thoughts, in the first person, are a rebellious and often anguished protest against the falseness of her wife-and-mother façade. The mature Morag, however, usually says what she means. . . . Usually the italicized passages are used to highlight a particularly significant realization on Morag's part, and if these are to have their proper impact, they must be used sparingly:

> Would Pique's life be better or worse than Morag's? *Mine hasn't been so bad. Been? Time running out. Is that what is really going on, with me, now, with her? Pique, harbinger of my death, continuer of life.*

Laurence's choice of tense for the narration of *The Diviners* was apparently just as carefully considered as her choice of person. *The Stone Angel* made what seems to be the obvious grammatical distinction between Hagar's present situation and her memories: the former are related in the present tense, and the latter in the past tense. But in the later books Laurence explored for herself the effects that can be created by different tenses. The present tense puts us *in media res* in both *A Jest of God* and *The Fire-Dwellers.* Both Rachel and Stacey are women with severe problems in their present lives, and we feel that we are sharing their struggles with them.

In *The Fire-Dwellers,* Laurence experimented with the present participle in place of the verb in some of Stacey's memories:

> Stacey, swimming back to shore, coming up for air intermittently . . . thinking already of the dance she would go to that evening, thinking already of the pressure on her lake-covered thighs of the boys

Although this innovation was not followed through consistently, the passages in which the participle was used suggest that these memories are still an active part of Stacey's image of herself: she has not yet come to terms with the fact that she is no longer a carefree young girl.

In Chapter Eleven of *A Jest of God,* which is basically a present-tense narrative, Rachel describes her decision to take control of her own life in the retrospective tranquility of the past tense. Similarly, the aura of serenity in *A Bird in the House* seems to result from its consistent use of the past tense: all the hurts felt by Vanessa have been healed by the passage of time, and her insight into, for example, her father's (**"A Bird in the House"**) and her grandfather's (**"The Mask of the Bear"**) true natures has already been achieved. Although Laurence has said that the writing of *A Bird in the House* was a process of self-discovery for her, we do not share the process, only the achievement. The fact that the adult Vanessa is an unknown quantity, the most faceless of Laurence's narrators, adds to the effect of calm detachment.

In *The Diviners,* Laurence's protagonist is, for the first time, a woman who has already found a measure of fulfillment, whose present life is busy and, by and large, satisfying. Thus Laurence's seemingly perverse decision to write of Morag's past in the present tense, and of Morag's present in the past tense, is the right one. The past tense narrative, in much of Laurence's work, suggests an achieved personal equilibrium, and this Morag possesses. On the other hand, Morag has experienced a difficult journey to her present autonomy, and she vividly recalls her earlier struggles; indeed, she feels that she is constantly reworking her past, even embellishing the events, in order to link her past life to her present life in a meaningful way:

> What happened to me wasn't what anyone else thought was happening, and maybe not what I thought was happening at the time. A popular misconception is that we can't change the past—everyone is constantly changing their own past, recalling it, revising it. What really happened? A meaningless question. But one I keep trying to answer, knowing there is no answer.

Laurence's Canadian novels, whether narrated in the present tense or the past, in the first person or the third, have always been constructed so that we share the consciousness of a single dominant female character. In each novel Laurence has seemed to move closer to her own experience, and in *The Diviners* she has carried the parallels between herself and her protagonist farther than ever. Morag is, like Laurence, a divorced writer, author of a number of successful novels, who, having once made a romantic pilgrimage to England, settles down to work in a cabin by a quiet river in Ontario. Even Morag's smaller quirks are shared by her creator, as the many profiles of and interviews with Laurence have made known to her readers: for example, Morag chain smokes and refuses to learn to drive.

One is tempted to think, while reading *The Diviners,* that Laurence resorted to the numerous irritating ways in which the narrative, as Robert Fulford put it, "untactfully draws attention to itself," in an attempt to distance herself from her material. Perhaps these devices are the evidence of her struggle to create a fictional past for a character who, in the novel's present, bears such a close resemblance to herself. Morag's reminiscences are presented as a series of "Memorybank Movies," which break into the narrative flow, and whose often satirical titles undercut the emotions portrayed in them. (pp. 47-9)

This obtrusive technique is particularly jarring in the early sections of *The Diviners,* when Morag is recalling her early childhood. Laurence's three earlier Canadian novels showed increasing skill in simulating the stream of consciousness. Hagar's reminiscences, although capturing the idiom of her generation convincingly, are expressed in well-formed sentences, suggesting written memoirs rather than thoughts. By the time she produced Stacey, Laurence was attempting to recreate the free associations and near-incoherence of the inner voice. But in *The Diviners,* for the first time, Laurence sought to reproduce the thoughts and speech patterns of a very young child.

Mercifully, she did not follow Joyce in returning her protagonist to the crib. Morag's earliest memories are expressed in adult vocabulary, as Morag examines a number of faded photographs. Successive Memorybank Movies portray Morag at five, six, seven, nine, twelve and fourteen, her development at each age distinguished not only by her opinions and her degree of awareness but, with great care on Laurence's part, by her vocabulary and syntax. Six-year-old Morag's first day at school is described this way:

> Girls here. Some bigger, some smaller than Morag. Skipping with skipping ropes singing. . . . And oh
>
> Their dresses are very short, away above their knees. Some very bright blue yellow green and new cloth, new right out of the store. You can see the pattern very clear, polka dots flowers and that
>
> Well oh

This is almost concrete poetry, suggesting an immature mind bombarded with new sights and sounds, while making it quite plain to the reader that this is Morag's first experience of her low social status. Morag at twelve is a vulgar little tough:

> The girls yell at her, but Morag doesn't care a fuck. They can't hurt her. The teachers hate her. Ha ha. She isn't a little flower, is why.

but at fourteen she tries to be ladylike, while fuming at the social ostracism she now fully recognizes:

> . . . no one will say *Good Morning* to Morag and Prin. Not on your life. Might soil their precious mouths. . . . They're a bunch of—well a bunch of so and so's. Morag doesn't swear. If you swear at fourteen it only makes you look cheap.

This writing, at its strongest, becomes almost transparent, as the reader experiences the illusion that he is sharing Morag-the-child's thoughts. Then a wry Memorybank Movie title pulls him back to the surface of the page. As was noted earlier, in *A Bird in the House,* where we are constantly aware that the adult Vanessa is giving form to her childhood perceptions, a little cuteness goes a long way. In the early sections of *The Diviners* there are long passages of childlike thought which, when we are suddenly reminded of the author guiding our responses to Morag, become forced and un-heartwarming:

> At four o'clock Morag can go home. She still does not know how to read. . . .
> But knows one thing for sure.
> Hang onto your shit and never let them know you are ascared.

MEMORYBANK MOVIE: MORAG, MUCH OLDER

As Morag matures, the narrative reaches one further stage of complexity in the Innerfilms: Morag's fantasies in the past. These tend to be extended self-mockeries. . . . But Morag is portrayed as a strong-willed woman who has made a decent life for herself against heavy odds, and thus we become impatient with a negativism not supported by the novel's plot. Laurence has always given her protagonists a portion of self-deprecating humour, but in *The Diviners* this humour is beginning to seem more like the undisciplined voice of Laurence's own "Black Celt."

To be fair, some aspects of Morag's personality and development are deftly and convincingly portrayed, particularly her sensitivity to the power of language, both in its inhibiting aspect, as a social indicator, and its liberating aspect, as an exquisite medium through which an artist can communicate. Even at the age of seven, Morag notices the grammatical lapses of her guardian, Prin. . . . She relishes vivid colour and rich texture, even though they are found in bizarre forms in Christie's hovel, and puzzles over the proper way to describe them. . . . Both aspects of language continue to play an important part in Morag's life. Her concern for "proper usage" epitomizes her feelings of inferiority in her relationship to Brooke. . . . (pp. 49-51)

The mature Morag of the novel's present is no longer concerned with the social niceties. She has also come to doubt her earlier belief that language can accurately convey sensual experiences, although she remains convinced of the value of the effort. . . . (p. 51)

Laurence has been quoted as saying, " . . . it's one of the most difficult things to do, writing about a writer. But I had to. At first I made her a painter, but what the hell do I know about painting?" However, her believable portrait of the artist as a harassed Canadian woman is one of the most successful aspects of *The Diviners.* Morag experiences many of the barriers that can stand between a woman and creativity, including a husband's ego, morning sickness, and sleeping children.

But in her presentation of the internal doubts that beset Morag as a writer (and which surely afflict Laurence as well), Laurence comes perilously close to sinking her novel under the weight of its self-consciousness. Morag agonizes, in true Calvinist fashion, about whether spinning tales may not simply be a form of telling lies:

> A daft profession. Wordsmith. Liar, more likely. Weaving fabrications.

Elsewhere, Morag wonders whether, as a writer, she most resembles Christie Logan the scavenger or Royland the diviner. Does she simply "tell the garbage," by fictionalizing other people's pain, or is she, like Royland, the possessor of a special gift, which allows her to reveal to others basic truths that they could not see without her help? She comes to the tentative conclusion that fiction *is* her truth. . . . (p. 52)

And she seems to have concluded that this truth-telling is impeded by some of the ordinary conventions of novel-writing. Although this realization does not make Laurence's "distancing" narrative devices any more successful, it helps us to understand why she chose them. Hagar's and Rachel's first-person narrative is abandoned for the third person in *The Diviners* because, after all, Morag is not *really* telling us her own story. Similarly, Memorybank Movies are substituted for a smooth transition into reverie, because no one has memories so detailed and complete, with all past conversations intact. Here, as with Morag's difficulty in describing colours, the novel seems to comment on its own technique. Laurence has Morag draw attention to the "fictional" quality of her reminiscences. . . . Later Morag muses that "everyone is constantly changing their own past." Apparently Laurence's Memorybank Movies are not simply, or even predominantly, the result of her effort to distance herself from her material, but are meant to illustrate her belief that every person, writer and non-writer alike, makes a fiction of his past truth, and by doing so, transmutes it into new truth. And the new truth is myth.

A major theme in *The Diviners* is the process of myth-making, and in particular, the application of this process to the needs of the Canadian imagination. In discussing this theme, we must consider the other characters in the novel. The presentation of the supporting players has always caused Laurence considerable difficulty. Because of her determination to limit herself to the point of view of her protagonist, these characters either succeed or fail on the believability of what they say. Laurence has had particular difficulty in devising realistic dialogue for male characters, and for characters considerably younger than herself: the two problems came together disastrously in her characterization of Luke Venturi in *The Fire-Dwellers.* Her most believable male characters, such as Bram and Mac, have been relatively taciturn, the motivation for their action largely supplied by the woman protagonist, who explains in her own idiom why they may have behaved as they did. (pp. 52-3)

In the past Laurence has given mythic dimensions to otherwise rather sketchy characters by suggesting that their relationships to the protagonist re-enact a biblical situation. Thus *The Stone Angel's* Hagar (like the biblical Hagar) lives in exile from her husband Bram (Abram), and her son John, like Ishmael, is also an outcast. In *A Jest of God* Laurence developed the parallels between Nick Kaslik and the biblical Jacob, not only in his relationship to Rachel (who, like her biblical namesake, demands of him, "Give me my children"), but also in his relationship to his twin brother Steve, the brother who (like Esau), was disinherited.

In *The Diviners,* Laurence takes the essential elements in these myths: exile and dispossession, and reworks them in Canadian terms. These experiences are not limited to Canadians: Brooke has lost his boyhood India forever, and Dan McRaith, the Scotsman, knows no Gaelic. But Brooke retains his language; he still has an identity as an Englishman, and McRaith retains the land, journeying back to Crombruach to renew his creative powers. The Canadian characters have lost both their language. . . . and their land. . . . (p. 54)

Morag's life is an illustration of what will and will not heal the pain of these losses. Morag loves, in turn, three men: the Englishman, Brooke Skelton; the Scot, Dan McRaith, and the Métis, Jules Tonnerre. Only the relationship with Jules bears fruit, a child who carries the blood of the two people who possessed the land before them. Brooke represents the cultural inheritance that attracts many Canadians to England ("I guess there's something about London, as a kind of centre of writing," says Morag), but makes them feel that their own country is inferior. Dan McRaith represents the country from which Morag's ancestors, too long ago for her to know their names, set out for Canada. But the value of these cultures for her, Morag comes to realize, is mystic and not literal.

In *A Jest of God,* particularly, the demands of the myth with which Laurence was working made the realistic level of the novel less effective. All Nick's Jacob-like revelations are made to Rachel in the course of normal conversation, and, as has been pointed out, these monologues are not only boring but unconvincing. Laurence avoided this failing in *The Diviners* by striving less for a continuous narrative flow. Christie Logan, Morag's guardian, is the first spinner of tales in the novel, and his stories of Piper Gunn, Morag's mythic ancestor, are set off both typographically and stylistically from the rest of the text. Although Christie is always a colourful speaker, the language in the tales has an archaic sonority:

> *Christie's First Tale of Piper Gunn*
>
> It was in the old days, a long time ago, after the clans was broken and scattered at the battle on the moors, and dead men thrown into the long graves there, and no heather grew on those places, never again, for it was dark places they had become and places of mourning.

(pp. 54-5)

Jules Tonnerre, Morag's lover, is also a teller of tales, about his Métis ancestors, Rider Tonnerre and Old Jules.

As with Christie's tales, the point is made that their value does not lie in historical accuracy. . . . Jules' stories stand even farther apart from the text than Christie's. After Morag first goes to bed with Jules, they have a brief conversation about his family as he walks her home. Although we are invited to assume that Jules told Morag his stories then, they are grouped together, each with a title, several pages later.

When Morag incorporates these tales as well as Christie's into her mythology, she has come to terms with what Margaret Atwood calls the "ambiguity" of Canadian history, for in Christie's tales Riel is a villain, and in Jules' he is a hero. "Canadians," writes Atwood, "don't know which side they're on." So, the proper response is Morag's when, in relating these stories to her small daughter Pique, she takes neither side.

The gift of myth-making, like the gift of divining, is "finally withdrawn to be given to someone else." There comes a day when the adult Morag requests a story about Piper Gunn and Christie is unable to remember one; when Jules, whose myths had reached a further stage of refinement when he recast them as folk songs, develops throat cancer and sings no more. But Pique is also a folk singer and will continue the myth:

> Would Pique create a fiction out of Jules, something both more and less true than himself, when she finally made a song for him, as she would one day, the song he had never brought himself to make for himself?

At the end of the novel, Pique, whose restless search for identity has, as the time scheme of the novel allows us to see, paralleled Morag's own, is making a journey back to her father's people, with her grandfather's knife as a talisman. But she also wants to carry a Scottish plaid pin of her mother's, and Morag assures her that, when she is "gathered to her ancestors," Pique may have it as well. And then, symbolically, Pique will recover the birthright that Lazarus Tonnerre and John Shipley, the original possessors of the knife and the pin, and both exiles in their own land, had traded away.

Laurence's *The Diviners* is a noble work with obvious flaws. In it, Laurence probably touches on most of the ideas she wants to express, most of the values she wants to affirm before she falls silent, but at a cost. The novel contains far too many characters, some of them, like McRaith, important to the theme of the book, but dull as individuals. It has far too many obtrusive narrative devices, and while they were no doubt carefully considered, they produce a book much less impressive than the novel Laurence now considers naive in narrative form, *The Stone Angel.* But Laurence will probably not be surprised if the critical response to *The Diviners* mixes respect for the scope of her effort with disappointment at its flaws:

> Sure I'm ambitious . . . *extremely* ambitious, because—Heavens, let's not deceive ourselves—to try and get down some of the paradoxes of the human individual with everything that has gone to influence their life—their parents, the whole bit about history, religion, the myth of the ancestors, the social environment, their relationship with other people and so on—even to *attempt* it means attempting the impossible.

273

and she concludes, quoting Graham Greene:

> For the serious writer, as for the priest, there is no
> such thing as success.

(pp. 55-6)

*Barbara Hehner, "River of Now and Then:
Margaret Laurence's Narratives," in* Canadian Literature, *No. 74, Autumn, 1977, pp. 40-
57.*

Ildikó de Papp Carrington

The Diviners, Margaret Laurence's fifth novel and the
final work in the Manawaka series, is fiction about fiction;
its multiplicity of narrative forms is a result of this fact.
Although recognized before, this point has not been explored in its full complexity. In *The Diviners* Morag
Gunn, the novelist-narrator, recalls her own life story. Orphaned at five, she is adopted by Christie Logan, the
Manawaka garbage collector. Growing up during the Depression and World War II, Morag attends college, marries and divorces her English professor, bears an illegitimate child fathered by a Métis lover, and swiftly becomes
a successful novelist. *The Diviners* is about her
novels. . . . Like her creator, Morag writes five novels,
and all within the time span covered by *The Diviners.* At
least three of them are clearly autobiographical, the other
two contain autobiographical elements, and all of them
have important internal relationships to *The Diviners.* (p.
154)

The first of Morag's five novels in *The Diviners* is *Spear
of Innocence.* It is followed by *Prospero's Child, Jonah,
Shadows of Eden,* and her fifth novel, which she finishes
in the last sentence of the book and which is obviously *The
Diviners. Spear of Innocence* is not directly about Morag,
but Lilac, its heroine, aborts herself just as Eva Winkler,
Morag's childhood friend, did. Morag begins writing this
novel because her husband, Professor Brooke Skelton, will
not agree to their having a child. Barred from the future
she wants, she writes about a past which she has witnessed
at close hand and which in the second section of the novel
she has already narrated in long flashbacks to the reader,
but not to Brooke. Her improbably swift success in getting
the novel published contributes to the breakup of her
marriage. . . . Morag feels that staying married to
Brooke will mean being "chained forever to that image"
of herself "which he must have and which must forever
be distorted" because, fourteen years older than she is, he
condescendingly insists that she has "no past."

Morag's second novel, *Prospero's Child,* is clearly the story
of this dissolved marriage and as such an act of literary exorcism. She feels that her memories of her husband are a
"shed skin of another life," and that while writing about
him, she is "living . . . in" this "husked-off skin." In a letter to a friend, she summarizes the plot of *Prospero's Child,*
a plot very much like her "Memorybank-Movies" about
Brooke in the third section of the novel. At first "the
young woman . . . virtually worships" her husband, but
"then . . . has to go to the opposite extreme and reject
nearly everything about him . . . to become her own person." A review of this novel, quoted by Morag, describes
how

the character of Mira shows an interesting develop-

ment from a child-like state to that of a limited independence and the eventual possibility of spiritual
maturity.

Although the name "Mira" is short for "Miranda," Prospero's child in *The Tempest,* it also bears some resemblance to "Morag."

Brooke is Prospero in several ways, both literary and political. By denying Morag's past, he insists that the world *be*
new to her, as it was to Miranda. Before their marriage he
is his wife's teacher, as Prospero is Miranda's "schoolmaster." After their marriage he continues to treat Morag like
a child. He calls her "child" and "little one," prescribes
her coiffure, and before making love to her, always asks
her if she has been "a good girl." This question reduces
intercourse to a lollipop from Daddy. Most humiliatingly,
however, he is Prospero because he treats his wife the
same way that Prospero, who can be seen as a "colonial
imperialist," treats Caliban and other "natives." This political element is recognized by another reviewer of *Prospero's Child:* he describes Brooke's character as "a perceptive study of authoritarianism." (pp. 156-57)

Brooke is the typical "colonial" in two ways. First, he was
born the son of an English schoolmaster in India. He still
feels "a kind of muted and concealed homesickness" for
his childhood India where, just like the English boy Mat-
thew in **"The Drummer of All the World,"** he had a much
closer and more loving relationship with his native nurse
than with his sickly, ineffectual mother. This homesickness manifests itself in Brooke's persistent dreams about
his Hindu nurse. Falling asleep in the arms of his young
wife, he dreams not about her, but about the embraces of
his *ayah,* who, he tells Morag, "would get into bed beside
me, and hold me in her arms and stroke me . . . all over.
I used to have an orgasm or . . . [its] equivalent in a child,
and then I'd go to sleep." Second, like his father before
him, he is an English schoolmaster in what he considers
a colony: he is a professor in a Canadian university. Educated in England and bearing the names of two English
poets, Brooke Skelton plays Prospero to Morag's native
Canadian Miranda. In *New Wind in a Dry Land* Laurence
says that Prospero the colonial is sympathetic, but that his
"sympathy" leads him to see "people not as they really are
but as the beholder feels they ought to be." Thus Brooke
is convinced that Morag does not have a past, does not
need a baby, and should not take her writing more seriously than the punctual preparation of his dinner. At first
Morag is enchanted by her magician's arts, which are
mainly verbal and sexual, but gradually she begins to feel
[a need for independence]. . . . As this ambivalence is
gradually resolved, the results are Morag's first novel, her
baby by Jules Tonnerre, her divorce, and finally the fictionalized record of the whole process, *Prospero's Child.*

Yet when Brooke visits Morag after the publication of
Prospero's Child, she wonders whether the book has hurt
him: *"Brooke, forgive me."* This silent plea shows that her
thoughts about him and their marriage do not remain permanently fossilized in her second novel. [Clara] Thomas
argues that "Brooke is both remote and two dimensional—but this is the whole point." It is not. Morag does not
leave untouched her Portrait of the Professor as Male
Chauvinist Villain. In recent years there has been a flood
of almost identically plotted feminist novels in which
wives leave husbands who are complete monsters; their

multitudinous sins are catalogued with vindictive relish; they are not granted a single saving scrap of grace. Laurence does not let Morag fall into this fashionable pattern, because Laurence is writing fiction about fiction: a novelist separated from her husband is writing about a novelist separated from her husband who has written about a woman separating from her husband. When Morag's divorce becomes final, Laurence divorces Morag from Miranda, too. Having depicted Prospero, Morag takes up her palette again and paints in different colors: "she can remember only the good things that happened between herself and Brooke." And when she recalls him in the present, she wonders how *he* would remember their marriage. "Not the same, obviously. A different set of memories from Morag's." By admitting that there were "good things" and that his memories must be different, she admits that neither her view nor his could be the only valid one. Hence at this point Laurence develops three characters, not only the exorcizing young novelist, frantic to be free, and the middle-aged narrator judging that younger *ego,* but also Brooke, the failed enchanter, not completely understood but at least recognized and pitied in the "solitary confinement" of *his* ego. Morag wonders if Shakespeare's Prospero could really relinquish his magic power. *Her* Prospero has lost his, and when Morag leaves him he weeps.

Morag's third novel, symbolically called *Jonah,* is about her relationship with another man, Christie Logan, her garbage-collector stepfather. The Memorybank-Movies have already familiarized the reader with Morag's agonies of adolescent embarrassment about his job. Now *Jonah* tells the story of a disreputable "old man" and "his daughter Coral, who resents his not being . . . reputable. . . . " This description of the novel is immediately followed by another fictionalization of the relationship, "Morag's Tale of Christie Logan," a story she tells her daughter Pique: Christie "used to wear the same overalls, always, and that embarrassed me and I used to think he stank of garbage . . . " As with *Prospero's Child,* the title is another clue to the autobiographical nature of the novel. The Biblical Jonah was literally an outcast in two different ways. During a storm at sea the sailors on his ship cast him overboard to appease the wrath of God. The whale swallowed him and sea "weeds were wrapped about [his] head." He prayed to God, Who "spake unto the fish, and it vomited out Jonah upon the dry land." After being cast out of the whale's belly, Jonah must have been redolent of seaweed and whale-vomit. So Christie the stinking social outcast begets Jonah, and the embarrassed Morag, his daughter Coral.

Christie is also the indirect inspiration for Morag's fourth novel, *Shadows of Eden.* When Morag was a child, Christie entertained her with tales of Piper Gunn, her mythical ancestor, the charismatic leader of the Sutherlanders who emigrated to Canada. When the adult Morag is in Scotland she decides that she doesn't need to visit Sutherland, the home of her ancestors, because "the myths," Christie's tales, "are my reality." *Shadows of Eden* is a historical novel, but it is about the same period of Canadian history as "the tales Christie used to tell of Piper Gunn, and the Sutherlanders." Although Piper Gunn "never lived in so-called real life," Morag feels that he "lives forever" because "Christie knew things about inner truths that I am only just beginning to understand."

Just as Prospero, Mira, and Jonah are symbolic names, so is Morag, the name Laurence gives her narrator. An ancient Gaelic name, it not only links the narrator with the world of Scottish history and old Scottish lays and legends associated with Christie but also emphasizes the many forms that Morag assumes as narrator and protagonist in her novels within the novel. When Morag visits Scotland and the train passes through Culloden, she is deeply moved; the place-name evokes echoes of the terrible defeat that destroyed so much of Highland culture. After Culloden some of Prince Charles' followers fled to Loch Morar in the west. And according to an old Scottish lay, Loch Morar is inhabited by a monster named Morag.

> Morag, Harbinger of Death,
> Giant swimmer in deep-green Morar,
> The loch that has no bottom . . .
> There it is that Morag the monster lives.

This early tradition about the monster gradually developed into a firmly established legend about a much more complicated creature. "The *Mhorag* . . . or 'Morag' in its Anglicised form . . . was the spirit of the loch." It was "something . . . like a mermaid," but "capable of appearing in different forms," as "spirit, omen, mermaid and water monster." . . . This polymorphous creature most appropriately gives her name to a narrator who appears in many shapes—as a child, a young girl, and a middle-aged woman—and as characters in her own novels. Morag often imagines "another younger Morag," and "the many versions of herself, combining and communing" in her mind and in her works.

Her fifth novel, presumably about her life after her divorce, is the one Morag finishes at the end of ***The Diviners,*** but, as I have shown, it is preceded by four other published novels dramatizing Morag's life in one way or another. A friend remarks, "I get this feeling sometimes of living too many lives simultaneously," to which Morag replies, "I know. Jesus, do I ever know." This remark and Morag's fervent assent aptly describe the way in which Morag recalls her past to the reader, turns segments of her past into a series of novels, and lives and narrates her present—all simultaneously. ***The Diviners*** is like a nest of Chinese boxes, stories within stories. Beginning with *Spear of Innocence,* Morag is remembering, writing, living, and turning her living into writing all at the same time. (pp. 157-60)

[It] isn't only Morag who remembers or divines; there are many other diviners. In the brief opening section of the novel, which is in the present, Morag recalls that she used to believe that "words could do anything. Magic. Sorcery. Even miracle. But no, only occasionally." In the second section, entitled "The Nuisance Grounds," she introduces Royland, an old diviner, who asks her why she is "so interested in divining," and takes her along when he goes divining for water. Royland is successful, but Morag, he says, doesn't "have the gift." She thinks, "He was divining for water. What in hell was she divining for? You couldn't doubt the value of water." In these passages Laurence begins to do two things: to raise the question of the value of fiction, and to establish the metaphorical equation of writing with "magical" activities such as divining.

This question is tentatively answered through the expanding symbol of the Nuisance Grounds, the Manawaka town dump. Thomas describes the dump merely as "the repository of the town's rubbish, its discards and, sometimes, its awful secrets." (p. 160)

The dump is the scene of Christie Logan's divining activities. Smelling of "rotten eggs" and nicknamed "the Scavenger," he mocks himself by telling Morag that he has "the gift of the garbage-telling." As he sorts through the garbage, he explains, "By their christly bloody garbage shall ye know them in their glory . . . ". . . . Christie, as well as Morag, is a scavenger in the metaphorical sense. Thomas calls Christie Morag's "first and greatest diviner." His skull is full of invented memories, and in the section entitled "The Nuisance Grounds" he tells Morag his fantastic tales of Piper Gunn, which inspire her first childish attempts to write. When she meets Jules Tonnerre, her Métis classmate, who, like her, is "looking" and "collecting" in the dump, she retells some of Christie's tales to him; but he dismisses them as "crap" and starts telling *her* stories *his* father has told him, only to break off and call them "all crap" too. At the time Morag is both frustrated and indignant, but when she has graduated from high school she also decides that Christie's tales are "all a load of manure." . . . (p. 161)

In the novel's third section, after Morag has married Brooke and published *Spear of Innocence,* she meets Jules again. When she takes him home for a drink, Brooke insults Jules by remarking to his wife, "Your past certainly *is* catching up with you. . . . Anyway, I thought it was supposed to be illegal to give liquor to Indians." Morag leaves with Jules, and they immediately become lovers. In spite of their earlier, unconsummated relationship as teenage sweethearts, this union is accomplished with improbable speed. But of course Jules is a symbolical rather than a realistic character, and it is at this important turning point in the plot that his symbolical function as a diviner is established. It is two-fold. After intercourse he says to Morag, "You were doing magic, to get away. . . . I'm the *shaman,* eh?" This ironically self-conscious word emphasizes his power as an Indian. . . . [She] clearly needs a second magician to free her from the sexual enchantment of the first. She trots right home the next morning to tell Brooke what she has done. And later it is also made graphically clear that Jules lets Morag take the sexual initiative: with him she is an aggressive lover, not Daddy's little girl. So Jules is Brooke's foil, both ethnically and sexually. In addition to Jules' supernatural power, he, like Morag, is a scavenger in the past. But instead of writing fiction, he has been composing and singing his own songs, a form of expression Morag secretly envies. Both the lyrics and the music are given in the "Album" at the end of the novel. "Maybe they're crap," Jules says, "but at least it's my own crap." Through repetition this vulgarism becomes symbolic: Jules' songs, like Morag's novels, are about his indestructible accumulations, his personal and historical past, events in his own life and tales about the Métis narrated to him by his father, Lazarus. Morag deliberately bears Jules' illegitimate child, and to their daughter, Pique, she retells both the tales Lazarus told Jules and the tales Christie told her. This combination endows Pique with the double heritage of her two parents, and thus makes her, symbolically, a quintessential Canadian.

After Morag has written *Jonah,* her novel about Christie, she returns to Manawaka to Christie's deathbed and recognizes that like Jonah, Christie was a prophet. In her interior monologues after his death, she clearly relates divining, doing magic, tale-telling, and novel writing. . . . And again, as in her comments about Brooke after the divorce, Laurence has Morag make anti-mimetic distinctions between the three Christies she has created: the two fictional Christies—the character in her orally narrated tales for Pique and the character in *Jonah*—and the "real" Christie, who of course is also fictional. . . . She wonders whether she is a scavenger or a diviner or whether they are "the same thing." When Jules, stricken with cancer, commits suicide, Morag also wonders if Pique, who shows signs of becoming a singer like her father, will write a song about him: "Would Pique create a fiction out of Jules, something more and less true than himself, when she finally made a song for him . . . ?" At the end of the novel, when Royland tells Morag that, rather like still another Prospero, he has lost his divining ability, she thinks of him as "an ex-*shaman,*" and, just as she did at the beginning of the novel, she contrasts the value of his divining with the value of hers. . . . So the shape of the novel, as Thomas notes, is essentially circular, though labyrinthine would perhaps be more accurate: after writing five novels, Morag is back where she started, asking her question and only tentatively answering it.

And just as there are many diviners—Brooke, Royland, Christie, Lazarus, Jules, Morag, and Pique—their divinations take many forms. Discussing two of these forms, Morag's photographs and the Memorybank-Movies, [Leona M.] Gom points out that the photographs of Morag as a child are paralleled by photographs of Pique as a child and that both sets of pictures introduce flashback movies. (pp. 161-63)

In addition to these Memorybank-Movies, however, Morag's mind, which she refers to as "the projector," imagines two other kinds of films. The Memorybank-Movies are long narrative sequences of events which Morag remembers, events which actually occurred, though not, of course, always exactly as remembered. Morag also remembers very short, rapidly flashing scenes in moments of emotional crisis, such as Pique's hospitalization after a "bad trip." . . .

Morag also thinks of other people's memories in visual, cinematic terms. When Brooke tells her about his lonely childhood, she is conscious of "not being able to see the pictures that grow inside his head when he talks of it." When Jules becomes her lover, she thinks of "everything he knows, everything he has seen, the films there in his head—all unseen by her." Both men have repeated nightmares about their past. As I have already shown, Brooke tells her about his; Morag imagines Jules'.

Jules is a veteran of Dieppe. After the fiasco of the tragic commando attack on Dieppe, Morag reads the long Canadian casualty lists and the newspaper articles full of the abstract, inflated diction rejected by Hemingway after World War I. (p. 164)

Jules' harrowing personal memories of Dieppe, as contrasted to the patriotic propaganda of the newspaper stories, are closely paralleled by Christie's earlier memories of the Battle of Bourlon Wood in World War I, as contrasted to the official version of this battle in *The 60th Canadian Field Artillery Battery Book.* After reading the impersonally factual description in the *Book,* Christie exclaims, "Oh Jesus, . . . don't they make it sound like a Sunday School picnic?" What he remembers are "the mud and slime and shit and horsepiss," the "screaming" of horses drowning in mud, and the air "filled with . . . bleeding . . . guts." At this point he begins to shake so hard that he cannot finish his story.

The two veterans' similar memories are the products of their particular experiences in time and space; they have amply earned the right to say with authority, "This is how it was for me." But both of them also tell Morag tales of events which culminated in a battle in which neither participated, the Battle of Batoche in Saskatchewan in 1885. And their strikingly different versions of these events are conditioned by their experiences in different cultures. Since Morag has read about the events in school, she knows the so-called historical facts and is therefore in a position to see how the Scots narrator's tale differs from the history books and also from the Métis narrator's version. It is at this point that Morag's function as "a professional listener" becomes especially significant for the purpose of *The Diviners.*

Morag listens to "Christie's Tale of Piper Gunn and the Rebels," and after several skeptical interruptions from her, Christie reluctantly concedes, "Maybe the story didn't go quite like I said." Soon after, Jules tells her three tales of his own about the same series of events. As befits oral narrative his chronology is vague, but one central point is vivid: his grandfather, Old Jules, fought under the Métis leader, Louis Riel, in 1885 and told his story to his son Lazarus, who, in turn, told *his* son Jules. This oral tradition culminates in the third generation, in Jules' tales and ballads. Jules tells Morag, "My dad's version was a whole lot different." Like Christie, he is willing to concede a point: "I don't say Lazarus told the story the way it happened, but neither did the books. . . . " Predictably, Christie's version denigrates the Métis and glorifies the Scotsmen. Christie says that "the halfbreeds . . . got very worked up" and "decided they was going to take over the government. . . . " And naturally he gives the Scotsmen who participated in the battle the credit for the victory. In dramatic contrast, Jules insists that "the government men" were planning "on getting the Métis land, all of it." He describes Riel as a hero, "a very tall guy," and refers to him as "the Prophet" of "our people." . . . At the end of the novel, Morag, trying to sort out some of the facts in these two conflicting tales about historical events, decides that Jules' grandfather borrowed some names for his narrative, but "that's okay" because he "had a right to borrow them. I like the thought of history and fiction interweaving." This interweaving makes Jules' tales and ballads the colorful ingredients of epic. Thomas points out how *The Diviners* incorporates "epic conventions: the stories of heroes and their battles" and "the transposition of the oral into the written." (pp. 165-66)

Shortly after Jules tells his tales to Morag, his insistence that the Métis were defenders of "their fathers' lands," not rebels, is once again refuted by the dominant culture. When his sister Piquette and her children accidentally burn to death in their shack, Morag the reporter writes up the story for the Manawaka paper and "mentions . . . that Piquette's grandfather fought with Riel." But the editor deletes this fact from her article because his readers "would still consider Old Jules . . . had fought on the wrong side." Jules' racial memory is thus officially stamped "Invalid." His disappearing family has no history. The thematic significance of this point is emphasized by another event in the plot. On one of his infrequent visits to see Morag and their child, Jules tells her that his brother Paul, "working up north as a guide," has disappeared. The two American tourists he took into the bush came back alone to report that "his canoe overturned at some rapids. At least, that was the story." But Jules insists, "I'm pretty damn sure it wasn't what they said happened," because "Paul was the best hand with a canoe I ever saw." The unsolved mystery of Paul's disappearance parallels the editorial deletion of the reference to Old Jules in Morag's newspaper story because the American tourists make their report to the Mounties, who take their word for it, and that's that. What happens to "halfbreeds"— whether they fight in famous battles or disappear in the bush—does not really matter. They are deleted. As Vanessa MacLeod remarks in **"The Loons,"** "the year that Riel was hung . . . the voices of the Métis entered their long silence." They are "barbarians," so their voices are not heard, let alone recorded or interpreted, except by the novelist.

Scattered among these many ingredients of narrative record—photographs, movies, nightmares, book reviews, newspaper articles, history books, oral tales, ballads, and letters—there are passages which can be classified as miniature plays. These consist of short scenes and dramatic dialogues between Morag and actual characters in the novel, and sometimes between Morag and Catharine Parr Traill, the author of *The Canadian Settlers' Guide.* In the case of dialogues with actual characters, such as Morag's first Vancouver landlady, the device of printing the characters' names as in the text of a play seems merely a typographical gimmick. In the case of Mrs. Traill, the device is a way of objectifying her as a kind of *alter ego.* Like many people living alone, Morag talks out loud to herself; one of the many functions of these imaginary dialogues with Mrs. Traill is that Morag creates a sounding-board for herself as she struggles to understand why she feels compelled to live by "wrench[ing] up her guts and heart" and setting "these carefully down on paper . . . " This highly dramatic description of the writing process as a kind of psychological *hara-kiri* further reinforces the autobiographical nature of the fiction contained within *The Diviners.* (pp. 166-67)

So, although *The Diviners* circles back upon itself and answers the question of the value of fiction only tentatively, surely faith in anything can only be tentative today. But the achievement of this novel lies in its technique, not in its theme. The emphasis is on tales in the *telling*: this gerund denotes not a completed structure but a continuing action. Laurence dramatizes in detail the creative processes by which "facts" become fictionalized, by which life, lived and remembered, is not simply recorded but intellectually and emotionally reinterpreted in successive stages of time and imaginatively transmuted not only from one narrative form to another but also from one point of view to another. For although Morag is always the self-conscious narrator, she is never the narcissistic protagonist. She confronts the multiple versions of herself in the mirror of her mind and speaks in her changing voices, but at the same time she always sees the reflections of others and grants each one of them his many shapes and plural tongues. Thus, there are her Brooke and *his* Brooke, and three different Christies telling tales and rewriting history. But most significantly, there are the reflections of those who have not been reflected before: Laurence makes the image of the dispossessed, inarticulate, and invisible Indian as dramatically real and solid as her own. (p. 168)

Ildikó de Papp Carrington, " 'Tales in the Telling': 'The Diviners' as Fiction about Fiction," in Essays on Canadian Writing, *No. 9, Winter, 1977-78, pp. 154-69.*

George Woodcock

Margaret Laurence has published only one travel narrative in the conventional sense, which is *The Prophet's Camel Bell,* and that book, produced a decade after the period of life in Somaliland which it narrates, she has described as the most difficult of all her works to write. The difficulty is not evident in the finished version, which is one of the finest and most evocative travel books ever written by a Canadian, and the existence of difficulty at any time in connection with this book in particular seems at first a little surprising, since the creation of a natural setting and the placing of human drama in that setting (which is the main content of *The Prophet's Camel Bell*) are prime constituents of all Laurence's writing. Her novels are all in a sense travel books, vividly descriptive in terms of environment, involving a great deal of journeying, both inner and outer, and coming at the end to those self-transforming realizations that are the destinations of all internal voyagings.

I suspect that a great deal of the difficulty incurred in the writing of *The Prophet's Camel Bell* arose from the fact that, while it is a narrative in which an inner journey and arrival at a personal destination run parallel, as in the novels, with a great deal of external and physical journeying through a dramatic landscape, in this case the inner journey is not that of a fictional persona; it is the journey of the author herself. *The Prophet's Camel Bell,* in other words, is much more than a mere narrative of exploration; it is an autobiographical document, a guide book to a large area of the mental world in which the novels, from *This Side Jordan* to *The Diviners,* were conceived.

The Prophet's Camel Bell is not the only piece of travel writing Margaret Laurence has done. The first book she ever published, *A Tree for Poverty,* is to all appearance a brief treatise on Somali oral literature, with selected translations of poems and stories, but even here the experience of a traveller is evident, as it is in Laurence's only book of literary criticism, *Long Drums and Cannons,* concerning the work of West African novelists who emerged during the 1950s and 1960s. More directly relevant, however, are the occasional pieces collected in her one volume of essays, *Heart of a Stranger;* these, as the title suggests, are largely concerned with the places that have been significant to Margaret Laurence in both her life and her writing. They cover the important periods of the life, from childhood in Manitoba, through the crucial experience of Africa, and on in later years to the Scotland she visited in search of her ancestry, and back to the Ontario where she now lives, in full consciousness that the land of her birth has more significance for her than the land of her forefathers, of which she has neither direct recollection nor even

a vicarious memory transmitted through immediate relatives. Perhaps, indeed, one can describe the final effect of *Heart of a Stranger* as an arrangement of personal myths in their order of relevance. (p. 3)

[One can] turn to *The Prophet's Camel Bell*—that narrative of fact so strange and so startling in its impact that Margaret Laurence never seems to have had any desire to turn it into fiction—and find touches that were later melded into the fiction of other places. The marble angels which Margaret Laurence saw with such astonishment in the Staglieno cemetery at Genoa on her way to Somaliland not only appear in the short story **"The Perfumed Sea"** in *The Tomorrow-Tamer,* but also, of course, provide the most commanding image in *The Stone Angel.* The child prostitute encountered in the Somali desert reappears in the West African child Ayesha in **"The Rain Child."** The double solitude of Italians in Somaliland, isolated from both the native people and the British overlords, is reflected in the predicament of the Italian hairdresser, Mr. Archipelago, in *The Tomorrow-Tamer.* Diligent readings can disinter many echoes and links of this kind without in the least detracting from the essential imaginative autonomy of Margaret Laurence's novels, and clearly the importance of *The Prophet's Camel Bell* and *Heart of a Stranger* lies in another direction, in what they reveal of the state of mind out of which Margaret Laurence's novels and stories emerged.

There is no question of the experience of Somaliland having started Margaret Laurence in the career of writing, though all her publications postdate it. Indeed, it may have beneficially delayed the maturing of a talent—and on this point there is no reason to doubt the autobiographical nature of *A Bird in the House*—which she had already begun to develop as an assiduous scribbler during her Manitoba childhood. Obviously the early experience of Somaliland, and particularly as member of a moving camp in the drought-ridden desert, produced the kind of culture shock which often makes it hard for a writer to say anything immediately about a country in which he has moved as "a stranger in a strange land," and forced Margaret Laurence into a salutary re-examination of her own character that prevented her writing more about the country at the time than the rather brief descriptive paragraphs which are part of the introductory material to *A Tree for Poverty.* Her literary activity in Somaliland was restricted to translating the poems and stories that appear in *A Tree,* and this was perhaps excellent work under the circumstances, since it brought her into contact with a number of Somalis through their own literature and traditions and so gave her an insight into the land and its people no merely external observation could have produced, as well as providing a temporary substitute for more originative writing. (p. 4)

The Prophet's Camel Bell is in fact a much more complex work than the travel narrative it may appear at first sight to be. In the Laurence chronology it stands after *This Side Jordan* and *The Tomorrow-Tamer,* and we have to view it with this experience of fiction-writing in mind. While much of the basic content may indeed have been provided by the original diary, the shaping is that of an experienced novelist, and if we see *The Prophet's Camel Bell* as representing an intermediate genre between the novel and the ordinary travel narrative, we appreciate most fully what the book has to offer.

There are really three levels on which **The Prophet's Camel Bell** moves forward. A landscape is described, with the kind of vivid feeling for the surface of the earth that had already become evident in her West African fiction, and on that bizarre terrain—usually barren but at times bursting into fantastic blossomings—a people is observed which has created a way of life and an accompanying philosophy as specialized and as closely adapted to survival in an extreme environment as that of the Eskimo. Like so many Canadian writers, a generation or so away from the pioneers, Margaret Laurence was interested in the theme of survival long before Margaret Atwood made it the subject of a perhaps excessively celebrated book. . . . (pp. 4-5)

At the second level, **The Prophet's Camel Bell** provides a series of rounded character vignettes, with four of the Somalis being given a chapter each, and chapters being devoted to the Italian workers with whom Margaret Laurence and her husband associated in the course of their dam-building project and also to "the imperialists," including many kinds of Englishmen in Somaliland. Finally, on the third level, it is a study of the author's own mental development, and of the transformation of her reactions to a strange world during the two years she lived in Somaliland; this process of unfolding self-revelation runs through the book from beginning to end, and is not only its profoundest theme but also its main structural connection.

The construction of the ballehs or earth dams which was entrusted to Jack Laurence took place in the Haud, the arid inland region of Somaliland that Margaret found "so seemingly remote that one almost doubted the existence of the rest of the world." It was a place of drought, broken by rare and violent periods of rain, of which there was only one during the Laurences' term of service; one was enough, for they only narrowly escaped disaster in the flash floods that tore down the dry watercourses. At the time of their arrival there, the Haud was in the grip of one of the great prolonged droughts known as *Jilal.* (p. 5)

[Laurence] saw the Somalis in the *Jilal* as "a dying people in a dying land. The dust filled their nostrils like a constant reminder of mortality." Yet as a people they did not die:

> They were not a passive people. They struggled against terrifying odds to get through to the wells. But always in their minds must have been the feeling that if Allah intended them to make it, nothing would prevail against them, and if he did not intend them to go on living no effort of theirs would be of any use. This fatalism did not weaken them. On the contrary, it prevented them from wasting themselves in fury and desperation.

Margaret Laurence finds herself as unable as Ivan Karamazov would have been to accept with Islamic calm the fate of the innocents in such a world, yet is forced to recognize the relevance of such a religious attitude to the realities from which it emerges. . . . (pp. 5-6)

With most of the Somalis who lived that hard life and professed that faith of resignation, Margaret Laurence's encounters were necessarily fleeting, and limited by the lack of a common language or anything in the way of a shared

view of existence, yet often they had the epiphanic quality which only such brief encounters can acquire, and it is a measure of Margaret Laurence's artistry that she recognized their value as revelations. Encounters of this kind punctuate her book, and constantly strengthen its authenticity as an account of a strange and stark culture. (p. 6)

[These] vignettes tell of communities, of the temporary halting places in the desert or the old and decaying towns on the coast, where only vestiges remain of the flamboyant past of Arab merchants and slave traders, of pearl divers and warring sheikhs whose exploits have been magnified in tribal legend. Such a place was Zeilah, where they stayed in a Residency haunted by the ghost of an English administrator who had killed his wife and then shot himself. There was something ghostly also about the people of Zeilah who [lived] in memories of their past as traders and pearl divers.

The Somalis whom Margaret Laurence got to know reasonably well were already men between two worlds, the servants and tractor-drivers who retained some links with their tribes, but who had already been affected by their contacts with the modern world. . . . All these people come alive, not only in their actions, but also through Laurence's extraordinary ear for eccentricities of speech, so that she can convey a twist of Somali character in the very way a man speaks brokenly the alien tongue of English.

The gradual recognition of the complexity of Somali motives and the ambiguities of relationships with these people was as much part of Margaret Laurence's self-transforming education as the horrors and harshnesses of life in the Haud during the famine of the *Jilal.* She learnt how excessively simplified had been her assumptions about a nation of tribal peoples who nevertheless adhered to one of the world's great civilizing religious traditions. (p. 7)

Essentially, it is the experiences of foreignness, of the special self-recognition that comes to exiles, of the difficulty of communicating over cultural barriers, that carry forward from Margaret Laurence's Somali experience into her later work and make **The Prophet's Camel Bell** so important as a key to understanding her writing. As late as 1976 she called her very personal book of essays **Heart of a Stranger,** and the phrase dates from the very beginning of her Somali experiences when, lacking reading matter on the voyage out, she read for the first time in her life the five books of Moses—in a Gideon Bible.

> Of all the books which I might have chosen to read just then, few would have been more to the point, for the Children of Israel were people of the desert, as the Somalis were, and fragments from those books were to return to me again and again. . . .
>
> [The] verse that remained with me most of all, when at last and for the first time I was myself a stranger in a strange land, and was sometimes given hostile words and was also given, once, food and shelter in a time of actual need, by tribesmen who had little enough for themselves—*Thou shalt not oppress a stranger, for ye know the heart of a stranger, seeing ye were strangers in the land of Egypt.*

The last sentence lingered on, echoing through Margaret Laurence's career, summarizing much of her experience as a stranger, and taking on a new relevance when she found that "my experience of other countries probably taught me more about myself and even my own land than it did about anything else." Certainly the Somali experience, as it affected Laurence herself and other Europeans, underlies the preoccupation with exile, from one's own land, from one's adopted land, even from a traditional way of life, that is so prominent a theme in *This Side Jordan* and *The Tomorrow-Tamer*. . . . Always behind these stories about exiles or misfits or people thrust out of their traditional ways by the forces of change, there looms a deeper strangeness, which comes from the difficulty of human communication of any kind, and it is perhaps appropriate that Margaret Laurence should have drawn out this point in her 1968 book on African writers, *Long Drums and Cannons.* (pp. 8-9)

Surely the difficulty and yet the necessity of communication is not only the major theme of such novels as *The Stone Angel* and *A Jest of God* and *The Fire-Dwellers,* but is also a leading preoccupation of the principal characters in each of these works. In *The Diviners,* Morag Gunn's special gift and so her special reward is her capability of understanding—of divining—more than other people the hidden strangenesses of the human heart, including her own. And so we understand what Margaret Laurence means when she says at the beginning of *The Prophet's Camel Bell* that "the strangest glimpses you may have of any creature in the distant lands will be those you catch of yourself" and, at the end of the book, "and yet the voyage that began when we set out for Somaliland could never really be over, for it turned out to be so much more than a geographical journey."

As I hope I have shown, *The Prophet's Camel Bell* is a book that lies at the centre of Margaret Laurence's achievement, partaking of many of the characteristics of fiction (for the character sketches often read like stories and the book has a novelistic kind of structure), and many of the characteristics of autobiography, dealing with a key phase of the author's personal life, in the form of a travel book. It was, one now realizes, a difficult book to write, but one that demanded writing, for nobody returns to an experience after ten years unless there is some special inner reason to give it the permanence of recording it, and in so doing to understand its real significance.

Margaret Laurence's other travel writings, the essays which form the greater part of *Heart of a Stranger,* are largely occasional pieces, produced on commission. . . . Like any tale of experiences, these narratives do tell us a certain amount about the writer and the way she sees her world. Other essays like **"The Poem and the Spear,"** about Mahammad 'Abdille Hasan (the so-called Mad Mullah of Somaliland), and **"The Epic Love of Elmii Bonderii"** (about a Somali poet) must really be read as supplements to *The Prophet's Camel Bell* and *A Tree for Poverty,* deepening our view of the breadth of Margaret Laurence's sympathies, but not really telling us much that is new about her or her work. (pp. 9-10)

The geographical pieces in *Heart of a Stranger* that, in a more or less direct way, bear a relationship to Laurence's fiction similar to that of *The Prophet's Camel Bell* are two essays, **"A Place to Stand On"** and **"Where the World Began,"** relating to her origins in Manitoba; **"Road from the Isles,"** which tells how she came to terms with her Scottish ancestry and its mythical implications; and two pieces, **"Down East"** and **"The Shack,"** which relate to the parts of Ontario, formerly associated with Catharine Parr Traill, where in recent years she has chosen to live.

Curiously, at first sight at least, Ontario seems to be the only place she has been able to set in fiction while she was experiencing it. She only wrote successfully of Africa when she had reached Vancouver, but, as she says in one of these essays, "I always knew that one day I would have to stop writing about Africa and go back to my own people, my own place of belonging." But going back is in the mind, and not a physical return, for as Margaret Laurence also says:

> Living away from home gives a new perspective on home. I began to write out of my background only after I had lived some years away.

And one can follow the removes by which Margaret Laurence makes sure, after she has finished writing of Africa in Vancouver, that she is still distant enough to write with fictional detachment about the worlds of her past. Going to England, she writes of Vancouver in *The Stone Angel, A Jest of God, The Fire-Dwellers,* and locates the present tense of two of the novels there. Even more in these novels and also in the stories of *A Bird in the House* she writes of the mythical small town of Manawaka, where the past of all the novels, and the present of *A Jest of God* and *A Bird in the House* are set. (p. 10)

[In **"A Place to Stand On,"** Laurence] remarked that: "Writing, for me, has to be set firmly in some soil, some place, some other and inner territory which might be described in anthropological terms as 'cultural background.'" In the Canadian novels as much as in the African novels, this sense of an outer territory every bit as sharply apprehended as the inner territory of the mind is vividly present; I know of no living novelist—and very few in the past—who have quite so marvellously balanced the two necessary landscapes of fiction.

I think the relationship of *The Diviners* to what Margaret Laurence has to say about the role of place in her novels is in some ways a major key to her work, certainly as it has been manifest during the past fifteen years. (pp. 10-11)

[One has the feeling] that she regards her coming to literary maturity as being connected closely with her being able to express in convincing fictional and almost mythical form her perceptions of her own country, and this gives a profound significance to the shifting terrain of *The Diviners,* which she has told us (unwillingly as we may hear it) is her last novel. Morag Gunn's beginnings are in Manawaka, intimately linked through her scavenger guardian Christie Logan with the town dump, known, as in Margaret Laurence's native Neepawa as

> "the nuisance grounds," a phrase fraught with weird connotations, as though the effluvia of our lives was beneath contempt but at the same time was subtly threatening to the determined and sometimes hysterical propriety of our lives.

In Vancouver Morag has her child, Pique, sired by the Métis Jules Tonnerre, last of a line of descendants of Riel's warriors, whose presence long troubled the consciences of Manawaka people. And in Scotland, like Margaret Laurence, Morag comes face to face with the real meaning of her ancestry, and could have said, as her creator does in **"Road from the Isles"**: "But this, my first view of Scotland, was in some strange way also my first true understanding of where I belonged, namely, the land where I was born," i.e. the Canadian prairie. (p. 11)

The Diviners, as I have said, goes beyond any of Margaret Laurence's other books by including the region where she is actually writing and a simulacrum of the river she looks out on while she works. Experience and its transmutation, in other words, have drawn together in terms of time and place, and this is the kind of encounter one can understand a writer facing with awe, perhaps even regarding as creatively terminal. Yet though *The Diviners* contains the artistic transfiguration of all the experience that relates to Margaret Laurence's ancestry and youth—the memories that make her the kind of writer she is—Africa is dropped out. Unlike Laurence, Morag Gunn never goes to Africa, or anywhere outside Canada except to Britain. At this point, one has the feeling that Africa played in Margaret Laurence's writing the cathartic role, teaching her the necessary distance between experience and its imaginative reconstruction, teaching her the value of the stranger's role, preventing her—as she remarks—from writing an autobiographical first novel about her prairie youth that would have been "too prejudiced and distorted by closeness," and giving her the subject matter out of which she could write her early fiction (too fine to be classed as apprentice work) and the magnificent farewell of *The Prophet's Camel Bell.* After that she was liberated to attempt the great task of her life up to the present, the Manawaka tetralogy. Perhaps one can end a survey of the significance of her travel writing no better than with some sentences from the final pages of *Heart of a Stranger,* which for me express with a vividness I have rarely encountered elsewhere the importance, to novelists of Margaret Laurence's kind, of a link approaching the closeness of symbiosis between the creative sensibility and the living environment:

> The land [Canada] still draws me more than other lands. I have lived in Africa and in England, but splendid as both can be, they do not have the power to move me in the same way as, for example, that part of southern Ontario where I spent four months last summer in a cedar cabin beside a river. . . . (pp. 11-12)

> This is where my world began. A world which includes the ancestors—both my own and other people's ancestors who become mine. A world which formed me, and continues to do so, even while I fought it in some of its aspects, and continue to do so. A world which gave me my own lifework to do, because it was here that I learned the sight of my own particular eyes. (p. 12)

> *George Woodcock, "Many Solitudes: The Travel Writings of Margaret Laurence," in* Journal of Canadian Studies/Revue d'etudes canadiennes, *Vol. 13, No. 3, Fall, 1978, pp. 3-12.*

Melanie Mortlock

During an interview in 1966, Margaret Laurence confessed: "I'm stuck with writing about the Scots Presbyterians, God help me." Such has been her lot ever since she ceased to write about Africa. Since 1960, Laurence has had five novels published, all of which have female protagonists who are born and bred in Manawaka and have Scots-Presbyterian backgrounds. Every one of these women is compelled to struggle with her religious heritage in an attempt to come to terms with her past. A chronological study of the novels reveals that each protagonist moves one step further along a spiritual continuum leading towards a truly gratifying form of religious assent. In *The Diviners* this goal is finally realized.

English-Canadian fiction is replete with professed atheists who suffer direly from the obscure psychological remnants, the conditioned emotional reflexes, of a Calvinist heritage. Hagar Shipley, of *The Stone Angel,* is an archetypal "secular" Calvinist. A religion which emphasizes the Old Testament and promises damnation to all but the predestined few forces man to fall back on his own reserves and to develop the spiritual pride and awesome strength which can issue from the fear of being utterly rejected and alone. For Hagar's father, a pioneer battling for survival against a hostile wilderness, this religious ethos resulted in material success. But the strength Hagar inherits from her father is her weakness; the independence, her bondage. . . . Quite simply, in an act of self-protection, she denies the God she fears. In the final weeks of her life, however, by wayfaring and warfaring—through the Puritan methods of pilgrimage and battle—Hagar manages to move away from the Old Testament and towards the New by acknowledging the possibility of redemption and grace. Her tragedy is that her guilt-ridden Calvinist character prevents her from totally accepting the good news that God is not Fear but Love. Being incapable of forgiving herself, she is never quite able to forgive Him or to accept her fate in life. Having felt deserted by a cruel God for ninety years, she is unable to bring herself to beg forgiveness, even from the more merciful deity she manages to conceptualize in her final days.

Laurence's second Manawakan protagonist, Rachel Cameron, is two generations younger than Hagar. It is not surprising that the spiritual resolution of *A Jest of God* is distinctly modern in tone by comparison. Rachel is able to gain the ground which Hagar could not quite grasp. By making the decision to have her "baby," Rachel manages to overcome her fear of being a fool, that same fear which Hagar finally perceived as leading to the wilderness of pride. By taking her life into her own hands, Rachel moves from the deterministic mode of predestination into the realm of free will. In so doing, she discovers that God is not to be feared as an all-powerful, untrustworthy force but is to be—if anything—pitied for having the weaknesses of man; the most dangerous of these is spiritual pride, that quality which precludes wisdom. In exchanging her fearful pride for wise foolery, Rachel is able to project—more in a horizontal than a vertical direction—a truly merciful God who embodies the force of fate and is as illogical and inconsistent as Rachel knows herself to be. When God's supernatural powers are no longer assumed, when prayers become wishes and He is no longer expected to perform the impossible, God ceases to elicit and manifest fear and begins to embody the love, wisdom and mercy of humbled man. In calling for "God's pity on God," Rachel mercifully buries Hagar's fearsome, cosmic deity and substitutes her own more human image.

As Rachel's sister, Stacey, struggles to come to terms with her religious heritage [in *The Fire-Dwellers*], she realizes that her God is a cultural echo from the past, a severe and chastising voice of conscience and duty. He is also a companion to converse with and confide in, one that can be magically summoned at will. No longer an external projection, Stacey's God resides completely within her psyche. He is a dim reflection of the old Calvinist God, a mere echo within her head: He has become both morally passé and spiritually impotent. At this stage of thematic development in the Manawaka series God moves into eclipse.

Eight years passed between the publication of *The Stone Angel* and *A Bird in the House.* Until this point Laurence had not embodied in fiction any truly meaningful solution for the sense of indirection and disintegration which was afflicting so many members of her generation of Scots Presbyterians. In this autobiographical set of short stories, Laurence again retraces the past back to Hagar Shipley's generation.

As members of Vanessa's family fall victim to the depression, disease, and war, the young girl surmises that God has entirely withdrawn Himself from human vision. Her many Calvinist character traits are not engaged as Hagar's had been—as a buttress against the wrath of a vengeful but living God. Instead they marshall Vanessa's defense against the psychological collapse that can result from contemplating a totally empty universe—the collapse experienced by her cousin Chris. In her concentrated attempts to come to terms with the past, Vanessa manages to grope towards the possibility of constructing a new religion: the disassembled materials of the old faith become the potentially rich raw materials for a new religion based on her heritage. This possibility, however, is only fully realized in *The Diviners*; here, a surrogate, personalized religion emerges to illuminate the darkness which fell when God, having once incited fear in Hagar, pity in Rachel, and duty in Stacey, finally withdraws, in Vanessa's understanding, from human conception or relevance.

When Vanessa claims in **"Jericho's Brick Battlements"** that her grandfather is "immortal" in ways it has taken her "half a lifetime to comprehend," she means more than that she is his cultural descendent. In times of spiritual stress she has fallen back on him, recalling his sayings and asking herself what he would have done in similar crises, just as a Christian falls back on the words and deeds of Christ. Vanessa finds that in a new way Timothy Connor has regained the stature he held for her when she was a child, the stature of the old-fashioned "God" he, like Hagar, had struggled endlessly and with such profound feelings of failure to be. Just as Hagar eventually points the way towards Rachel's final religious stance, Rachel towards Stacey's, and Stacey towards Vanessa's, the grown Vanessa's last reflections concerning her deceased grandfather anticipate the slowly acquired religious outlook of Morag.

The Manawaka series reaches a natural conclusion in *The Diviners* by arriving at a clear explication of a modern-day religion. The theme being examined comes full circle, inverting itself during its orbit: Hagar Shipley's revelation is, in essence, that her ancestor's religion has been her own true heritage; ten years later in Laurence's time, and two generations later in fictional-historical time, Morag Gunn takes on her entire ancestral heritage as her own personalized religion.

Like her creator, Morag Gunn uses her pen as a vehicle to travel into the past and divine truths lying hidden from view. In the novel's time-present sequence, Morag is writing her fifth novel and hoping to mitigate the gloom and confusion she feels over her daughter Pique's growth into womanhood and corresponding demands for independence. Like the other four Manawakan protagonists, Morag is "a professional worrier," and the spiritual pilgrimage she takes into her past is a subconscious effort to discover some partial solutions to her present emotional problems. Morag examines her past in minute and painful detail, recalling it creatively, never knowing what are memories and what are fabricated memories of memories. . . . (pp. 132-34)

Morag's pilgrimage into the past at the age of forty-seven is also a spiritual quest for the meaning of her heritage. This quest is symbolically manifested in the search by an adopted child for her dead parents, the loss of whom grieves her more in her forty-seventh year than ever before: *"Perhaps I only want their forgiveness for having forgotten them?"* . . .

For the most part, Morag's life history is an attempt to run away from her past, and for years after leaving Manawaka she refuses to look back. When Jules acts as her shaman, freeing her from her marriage to Brooke, she believes that she has paid off "some debt or answer to the past." In reality, she is refusing to learn from Jules that one must struggle painfully with the past to accept it finally, that one *has* to go home again, in one way or another. Instead of doing this she continues to create one island after another, first in Vancouver and later in England. But her past keeps catching up with her. In Vancouver Jules reminds her that she should be tending to Christie's needs. In England Dan McRaith divines a Presbyterian in Morag and nicknames her "Morag Dhu," or the Black Celt.

By observing Dan's own furtive and futile attempts to escape from the past, Morag comes to realize that an acknowledgement rather than rejection of one's heritage may well be the true road to self-awareness. . . . What she learns is that Scotland is not the true land of her ancestors; instead, "Christie's real country"—the land of her birth—is. (p. 135)

Having finally learned where she belongs, after Christie dies Morag settles near a town similar to Manawaka. . . . She suspects that the local water diviner, who looks as "old as Jehovah," is soon to become her new shaman. She feels "about to learn something of great significance from him, something which would explain everything," the mystery of "his work, her own, the generations, the river." This spiritual quest pursued in the novel's time-present is its main forward thrust. Morag is aware that she must prepare her mind for what Royland may have to teach her, and one can observe her religious growth as she writes each section of her autobiographical novel and learns both from what she is writing and the events taking place around her.

As a child, Morag feels rejected by, and lives in fear of, a God who tolerates injustice. Like Hagar she feels that God neither cares nor understands. When she is eighteen she decides that "God does not actually see the little sparrow fall," echoing Vanessa's religious negations after her father's death. By the time Christie dies, however, Morag has come to appreciate the symbolic power of religious rituals despite her disbelief. . . . Morag expands her spiritual horizons still further when she imaginatively canonizes Catherine Parr Traill. While writing her fifth novel, Morag attempts to resolve her problems through imaginary conversations with C.P.T., in much the same way as Stacey debates with God. (p. 136)

Royland takes his divining on faith, believing that he need not understand it but simply must do it while he can. Morag, however, has never been able to take her art on faith, and early in the novel she seriously questions the value of her work. . . . What Morag has subconsciously been divining for is faith itself, and by the end of the novel she realizes that writing *has* to be taken on faith, for, as in the case of water divining, there is no explaining it. . . .

This affirmation is the positive result of the religion Morag has discovered on her voyage into the past. Always having fended for herself without the aid of God, Morag had lived in awe of her mythic ancestor, Piper Gunn, who, unlike her, possessed "the faith of the saints" and "the strength of conviction." As a teenager Morag had thought: "The Gunns have no crest, no motto, no war cry. . . . Just as well. It's all a load of old manure." But this, of course, had been a defensive pose. Morag eventually learns that what she has always wanted is a past, ancestors. Her writing had taught her years ago that "fiction was more true than fact. Or that fact was in fact fiction." She had learned to apply this knowledge to Christie's tales of her ancestors, and by divining the truths in his lies, she had come to realize that he had "left a place to stand on" (epigraph of the novel). (p. 137)

Morag's final words to her daughter before Pique boards the train moving west after leaving Gord and Dan—just as Morag herself had done after leaving Brooke and Jules—are: "So long. Go with God, Pique." Just as Piper Gunn had lived, died and been reborn in Morag's mind over the years, Morag once again has come to believe in God, but in a different way than she had as a child: Piper is not the only hero "who probably never lived in so-called real life but who lives forever." In Morag's mythology the Christian God becomes a symbol of the searching human spirit.

Morag has recently learned to accept humbly life's many gifts (or, in mythic terms, God's grace): her final lesson is to learn—as Jules does at his death—to relinquish them willingly. When Jules dies blaming no one for his fate, Morag realizes how difficult it would be for him to have Pique see his pain. This realization closes a gap in Morag's understanding which had reinforced her proud Calvinist fear of rejection: she now perceives that her dying parents "had wanted to see her; they had not wanted her to see them." When Morag is home again Royland arrives at her door with the news that he has lost the ability to divine water. She is upset at first, but Royland cheerfully informs her that others can learn his trade if they can only overcome the desire to explain it, if they can simply accept it on faith. . . . (p. 138)

Morag's new religion teaches what any religion worthy of the name teaches its adherents—to accept death, to see it as part of the continuum of life: *"Pique, harbinger of my death, continuer of life.".* . . Morag now sees that she too will have a place in the future when her gift for writing has been withdrawn to be given to someone else, when her talisman passes to Pique and Morag is gathered to her ancestors. In joining this group she will become one of the voices from the past that speak to the inheritors, just as Piper Gunn, Christie Logan, Catharine Parr Traill, and the ancient Currie family have each spoken to her. Morag manages to render death meaningful by this immortality of sorts, her personal metaphor for Christian salvation.

Morag's mythological religion, based on the concept of heritage, gains much of its broad-reaching scope from her contact with Jules. A consistent pattern in the Manawaka series is that each protagonist acquires a more distanced, objective, and revelatory perspective on her religious heritage by coming in contact with someone from a different cultural and religious background. Murray F. Lees performs this catalytic function for Hagar, Nick Kazlik for Rachel, Luke Venturi for Stacey, and Piquette Tonnerre for Vanessa. Morag is the most successful of the five in gaining insight from this type of experience.

The factual contradictions between Lazarus' tales of his ancestors and Christie's tales of hers are so striking as to compel Morag to rise above the facts to the level of myth if she is to achieve the synthesis that her spiritual marriage to Jules ordains. Morag has learned that, at the literal level, every diviner divines his own unique truth and there is no such thing as a "true" story at all. But at the mythic level there is, for the tales of Lazarus and Christie are identical if seen as myths. They are tales of the heroic bravery of the individual who fights to save his tribe from annihilation.

Because Morag's religion is formulated as myth, it is capable of reaching beyond the boundaries of her own specific heritage and of drawing on the religious basis of Jules' Indian heritage. Morag's religion entails a metaphorical return to magic, nature worship, shamans, and animism. So-called primitive religions originate with superstition and magic, with the belief that certain specific actions taken by man have certain unforeseen but specific effects upon the natural world. Morag acknowledges the analogical or mythic truth of this belief as she watches an endangered blue heron fly towards the death of its kind. Her nature worship is, of course, not literal, but now that the land is being engulfed by the cities, Morag stands in renewed awe and reverence of nature's majestic and vulnerable beauty. In her modern philosophical religion a shaman is still a living priest (Christie, Jules, Dan, Royland) who, through mysterious means, cures the sick, divines the hidden, controls events and foresees the future. But the shaman's magic is understood by Morag as secular divination, or unusual intuitive insight. The gods are still the ancestors in Morag's conception of animism. But they are not believed to be capable of truly supernatural actions. They do, however, perform the god-like function of instructing life's sojourners as to the rules of physical and psychological survival—Morag promises to remember C.P.T.'s advice, and she cherishes the faith and strength of Piper as well as the pride of the Curries.

As his name clearly implies, Morag's god (or ancestor) incarnate is Christie. Like Christ, he sacrificed himself for the sins of others. Christie's parables, proverbs, and preachings furnish Morag with a way of life to follow. As an ancestral god *and* a Christ figure, Christie himself symbolizes the blurring of distinctions that characterizes the myth-making process at which he was so gifted: he represents both major sources of Morag's religion—animism and Christianity. It is no doubt significant that his worth was the one thing Jules and Morag could always agree upon.

It is only by looking *"ahead into the past and back into the future"* that the inheritors in Morag's religion can learn what the mythic and real ancestors—especially those who lived longer in the past than the surviving generation has yet lived in the present—have to tell their descendents, through word, song, and deed, about how to survive with dignity in the future: the river flows both ways. Mystery and religion, Morag seems to imply, persist in the modern world because it is extremely difficult to see to the bottom of the river of life, particularly as the accumulation of years draws one further away from the shore: "You know a whole lot you won't know later on" (prophecy of C. Logan).

The critical consensus on *The Diviners* seems to be that it is an ambitious work with some serious stylistic flaws. It undoubtedly lacks the compelling forcefulness that the powerful character of Hagar brings to *The Stone Angel.* And yet, with its reflective and somewhat wistful tone, *The Diviners* comes closer than any of Laurence's other Canadian novels to achieving her artistic goal. (pp. 138-40)

Hagar shows us how an outdated religion can thwart the life of someone for whom it is no longer entirely relevant. Morag demonstrates that with sufficient temporal and psychological distance from an old religion, it is possible to re-interpret it without having to forsake one's heritage. As Laurence explains, one must first get away from one's heritage and "go through the process of learning about the rest of the world" before returning, at least mentally, and "coming to some kind of terms with your roots and your ancestors and, if you like, your gods." Again, it is Morag who is most successful at this task.

As a writer Morag shares her preoccupation with mythology—or what she calls the interweaving of history and fiction—with her creator. The compounded effect of this double concern is a work of fiction or a myth about the nature of myth and the myth-making process. . . . As in the case of Morag's heritage, fiction necessarily takes over where history leaves off: "Beyond your great-grandparents . . . the ancestors become everybody's ancestors. . . . It all becomes myth at that point." Because this is so, Morag finds it possible to adopt Hagar's ancestors as her own, thereby shaping the final link which renders the Manawaka series a unity, and the Manawaka people a tribe.

Laurence seems to believe that the process of myth-making is ultimately inevitable for every tribe of people. . . . Religion, she might have added, is man's most ubiquitous, comprehensive, and meaningful form of historical fiction. Morag's religious mythology is particularly broad because she views herself in relation to a multicultural world. Why, one might ask, is Morag so preoccupied with fashioning a new religion with the outdated remnants of the old? It is possible because Laurence believes that none of us can "live without myths. Man is a myth-making animal who knows he must individually die but who cannot bring himself to believe it." (p. 141)

Melanie Mortlock, "The Religion of Heritage: 'The Diviners' as a Thematic Conclusion to the Manawaka Series," in Journal of Canadian Fiction, No. 27, 1980, pp. 132-42.

Angelika Maeser

The four Canadian novels of Margaret Laurence—*The Stone Angel, A Jest of God, The Fire-Dwellers,* and *The Diviners*—present to the reader a provoking and timely exploration through a central female character of the process of individuation. The experience of autogenesis or self-creation constitutes the core of Laurence's stories about the lives of women, ranging from the aged pioneer Hagar to the modern late-sixties Morag, and Laurence thereby provides us with insight into the complex psychic interaction between the personal and collective aspects of history. From such a perspective we can critically examine the structures of consciousness and their symbolic forms as projected by the imagination. Such an approach proves useful since these forms determine psycho-social reality and are the basis of a culture pattern, tradition, and belief system which can facilitate transcendence, liberation, and integration for the individual. Laurence's novels reveal that the struggle for wholeness and freedom is a spiritual one that engages the characters in an initially disturbing but ultimately rewarding journey toward self-discovery and renewal. The social, not solely personal, aspects of these works are significant because it is through the gradual discovery of the link between form and reality that the imaging self is freed to become the creator of its own forms and to stand in an active shaping relation to the traditional "givens", or the symbolic forms socially legitimized.

In the course of individuation each heroine undergoes a quest for spiritual and worldly affirmation which invariably leads into an acute conflict with the existing social forms and myths of the dominant culture. The structures of the existing forms of so-called reality, characterized by moral blindness and sanctioned biases, prove too narrow and repressive for these women who attempt to discover where the cause of their bondage lies. As they endeavor to re-form themselves, they confront the arch-representative of the prevailing cultural and social order—the God of patriarchy in his religious and secular guises. In defining themselves anew they must wrestle with the symbolic form of ultimate reality as male-gendered and with all that this representation implies—both socially and culturally—for woman. It is in the pre-patriarchal form of the Absolute, the Great Mother, that these women discover the Ground of Being, their own inner spiritual and creative depth. (pp. 151-52)

The first of the four Canadian novels, *The Stone Angel,* opens with Hagar Shipley's reminiscence of her mother's grave in the Manawaka cemetery.

> Above the town, on the hill brow, the stone angel used to stand. I wonder if she stands there yet, in memory of her who relinquished her feeble ghost as I gained my stubborn one, my mother's angel that my father bought in pride to mark her bones and proclaim his dynasty, as he fancied, forever and a day.

The remainder of the narrative deals with Hagar's sporadic flashbacks into the worlds of her childhood, adolescence and adulthood, in the course of which she frees herself from the restrictions that have prevented her from leading a more satisfying existence. Although it is too late to relive her life, she can and does reshape it imaginatively by coming to a realization of the forces which conditioned and bound her.

Hagar's entire life was dominated by the authority of the father—Jason Currie, a Scots-Presbyterian pioneer whose values of thrift and work were set long before he came to the new land. The patriarchal god who reigns as a supreme, if at times philanthropic, dictator over the lives of his underlings is a symbol under whose aegis the European consciousness was shaped and then superimposed upon North American soil. (p. 152)

In the course of Hagar's reflections, there emerges an image of a woman who was hampered psychologically by her father's standards and creed to the point of chronic inability to display love and affection to husband, sons, and other people. Her emotional reactions and superficial mental outlook were determined by the world-view expressed by the father's example and reinforced by punishment.

> *The devil finds work for idle hands.* He put his faith in homilies. They were his Pater Noster, his Apostles' Creed. He counted them off like beads on a rosary, or coins in the till. *God helps those who help themselves. Many hands make light work.*
>
> He always used birch for whippings. That's what had been used by his father on him, although in another country.

These values were, moreover, enshrined and sacralized in her society's structure, which adds support to the personal father's claims upon the daughter's loyalty and obedience. Rebellion against and rejection of the father thus assumes larger cultural proportions, for it is the Father in a collective value-system that Hagar unconsciously opposes when she marries the ne'er-do-well Bram Shipley. The death of the personal mother, then, becomes a symbolic motif in the story, pointing to a larger issue, the death of the Mother principle in the Protestant religious and secular ethos.

The pathos of both father's and daughter's lives emerges more clearly as Hagar matures, for neither of them can adequately express the repressed emotions of the maternal-feminine side of a complete human nature. . . . Currie's inability to link himself sensuously to Nature and his emphasis on rigid self-control is evidenced in his reluctance to remarry and in Hagar's adolescent memory of him in the company of a woman on the town's outskirts. . . . Eros, here as in later novels, is depicted as being "out of bounds", not within conventional limits of respectability and antithetical to social moral codes and religious regulations. The victory is that of the grave, of death, and of snow and cold marble.

In regard to her own conjugal and child-bearing experiences, Hagar failed to bring the quality of love and thus received no satisfaction or joy from them; too late she mourns: "oh, my lost men". Paradoxically, before finally coming to a reconciliation with herself and her fate, Hagar fled domestic confinements three times: from her father, from her husband, and lastly from her eldest son, Marvin.

In these escapes she sought to find herself, but each time she came face-to-face with her original problem: the Father in his personal, social and religious aspects. It is no surprise that her attitude toward the stone angel in the cemetery and to religion remained ambivalent; the symbols of transcendence in the patriarchal religious myth excluded the expression of the instinctual, life-supporting, and more humane qualities of Eros. The union of Justice and Love, the mysterious conjunction of opposites in the God-Reality, is the integration that Hagar must personally experience before she can be transformed from her father's chosen image, and hence society's definition of woman, into a compassionate flesh and blood woman. (pp. 152-54)

She has discovered that the patriarchal God-image of law and order, reinforced by punishment and exile, alone is insufficient to save and does not really represent true justice. By her name she is linked to the Old Law and, specifically, to the outcast woman, the mother of the Ishmaels of life, of those who do not belong lawfully in the ruling mythology. She is the mother of peripheral wanderers, the oppressed, and the outcasts like herself. However, as St. Paul's commentary on Sara and Hagar makes clear, the works of the Law do not themselves effect justification, and it is only through the self-discovery in compassion that a total divine image is experienced.

Rachel and Stacey, respectively the heroines of Laurence's next two novels, *A Jest of God* and *The Fire-Dwellers,* also undergo transformation through contact with the repressed contents of their souls. As in Hagar's case, these contents have primarily to do with the biological instincts of nurturance and sexuality. The novels expose the conflict between the sectors of civilized existence, within town or city boundaries, and of Nature, beyond city or man-made limits. Psychologically, this territorial demarcation corresponds to the socialized segments of self-identity and to the hinterland of the unconscious. Outer and inner landscape mutually interact in a symbolic exchange of meaning as the stories unfold. The confinements or parameters of so-called civilized social life and patriarchal culture are in each instance inhibitory for the woman's full expression of her powers—powers which, significantly, are untapped, unexperienced, and consequently turned destructively against the self. (pp. 154-55)

Rachel is a thirty-four year-old elementary school teacher who lives with her aged demanding mother above the Japonica Street Funeral Parlour, once operated by her father, Niall Cameron, but now owned by Hector Jonas. Associated with the father's occupation is an atmosphere of psychic as well as physical mortification. In his personal aspect he haunts Rachel's memory and the basement underworld below the familiar occupied quarters, and in his collective aspect he represents social values, rules, religious and secular norms. . . . In order to confront death and society's norms courageously, asserting her own life power, she must strengthen, express, and expand her feminine side. Before she can effectively deal with the Father, she must find the power of the Mother within herself. This expansion of self is paralleled by a widening of physical territory. At the beginning of the novel, Rachel's mobility is restricted to the key sectors of home, school and church. All three represent varying modes of repressive and sadistic social forms which institutionalize the values of the dominant class of Manawaka.

Religion, as the novel stresses, has become either the refuge of the living dead or else the final hope of those who seek some manner of social acceptance in an alienated community. The church and mortuary have become unified in a socio-cultural merger; in both sectors genuine life has vanished or else decays in protracted stages of macabre paralysis. The contrast between the high church of Rachel's mother and the evangelical domination, represented by the unusual Calla, becomes the spotlight of tension in Rachel's development. Neither type of religious statement can satisfy Rachel, who is in a painful vaccum of meaning and engaged in an ontological struggle for survival. . . . In order to find a resolution to her dilemma, the neurotic split between the surface layers of the socialized mind and the deeper strata of the soul wherein Nature's life-furthering instincts reside, Rachel must undergo two decisive experiences: firstly, an initiation into love, and secondly, an initiation into death. The first of these is mediated to her through Nick Kazlik, with whom she has her first short-lived affair, and the second through Hector Jonas, resident mortician-humorist.

The experience of Eros effects for Rachel the connection with the instinctual and spiritual need to feel the maternal source of life from within. This drive for self-actualization is expressed in the forlorn cry, echoing her Biblical namesake, "give me my children". Nick cannot give her that child which would symbolize her own rebirth; desiring and fearing pregnancy, Rachel must come to terms alone with the creative powers of mature womanhood—here symbolized by the sexual function and physical procreation. Thus she takes the next step of her journey to wholeness, through death experienced psychically as a descent to the underworld of the funeral parlour—the taboo unconscious terrain where life and death are one. In the funeral parlour with Hector Jonas, Rachel undergoes a Jonah-type experience of "death by water", an introversion into the unconscious after which she emerges charged with new power gained from assimilating the formerly unavailable or lost contents of psyche. Like Jonah, who is charged with power to speak the Word of God after his release from the belly of the whale, Rachel assumes a new mastery over her life and gains a new stable sense of her place in the universe. (pp. 155-56)

Death in life, represented by grotesque and distorted forms of existence, recurs as a fundamental theme in *The Fire-Dwellers*. Set in Vancouver where Stacey MacAindra lives out her roles of housewife and mother, this novel presents perhaps the most terrifying indictment of contemporary social structures, particularly those of the bourgeois family and competitive labor, which are alienated from substantial power to alter the fate of repetitive consumer patterns. The primary alienation, however, to which the other forms are subsidiary, is the separation of a patriarchal society from its base in a spiritual consciousness that is life-respecting. Woman, in this culture, has become the victim—as has Nature—of the projection of the shadow side of the rational masculine mentality that leans ever more toward violence and sterility as it separates itself from its ground in *matter*/matter.

Stacey attempts to survive the imprisonment of the traditional structure without succumbing to a nervous break-

down, madness, or other pathological symptoms—examples of which the author furnishes abundantly. The drug culture, the global wars raging everywhere, television's programmed violence for entertainment, sexual sado-masochism, alcoholism, and the slow deaths of those people on our cities' skid rows are indices of the more fundamental problems Laurence tackles in this novel: the fragmentation of the human soul, the mass media's proliferation of commercial and artificial images of identity, the denial of life-fostering instincts or their manipulation into pathological avenues of expression, conformist adaptation to the *status quo,* the destruction of the physical environment, and the loss of community among men and women.

The woman, because she is living on the periphery of the power-structures that determine her life, is able to have the ironic vision; she is the victim but also the potential rebel against the institutionalized inhumanity of her society. Stacey's discontent and ironic vision are on target but she has not yet understood how she can turn them to her advantage and use them as conscious weapons in the interest of more humane values and the creation of a different type of society. Consequently she suffers the pangs of all victims who live on the periphery rather than at the centers of action and self-direction; she sees herself and others imprisoned in the destructive structures but does not know how to escape, how to articulate her dilemma clearly to others, or how to express her intuition in a form which can be effectively shared with others. Thus her surplus creative energy is turned against herself. The woman turns to alcohol, to drugs and to tranquillizers, to an endless redecorating of her home and herself to match the images of "the good life" served up to her by the advertising media and magazines, to a diversion in night school classes, to excessive over-protectiveness of her children, or to the last resort—an affair. (p. 157)

Stacey is, unlike the two previous heroines, a mother in the spiritual sense; she is in touch with her compassion and senses the distortions with which she must deal daily, but her despair comes from the fact that the maternal principle has no voice in the system. She is a reluctant puppet whose strings are pulled by the powers she never sees. What these powers are, finds expression in her monologues with God whom she calls "Sir" and in her science fiction fantasies about the "Spirit Sires" who are projected hostile extra-terrestrial powers. Both signify the abstract mental forces of the imagination constellated as an oppressive tyrannical force threatening to destroy the earth and its inhabitants—either in an Armageddon of the Judaeo-Christian Judgement Day when the Elect are separated from the damned or in an annihilation by invaders from other galaxies. Her dreams are nightmares either foreshadowing a fascistic control sweeping over society or depicting the head of woman severed and bloodied. . . . (p. 158)

This novel is a pessimistic one insofar as it ends on the note of repetitive monotony; routine prevails and tomorrow will be the same as yesterday for Stacey. A few things will change in minor fashion, of course, but basically the structures remain intact. Stacey's attempt to escape briefly into an affair with a younger man was, as she always knew, a desperate but doomed attempt to live out her deepest desires and dreams. A clue to the nature of the latter is given in the allusion to the Zorba dance which Stacey cannot yet perform in real life, only in the privacy of her basement when she is alone with her despair and the bottle. The claims of the humane imagination for an integrated body/mind, for a genuine reason reborn from the maternal source of life and organically linked with Nature, cannot be satisfied in existing culture forms but wait to be realized, hopefully, some day. In the meantime, "the Fire-Dwellers" perpetuate their holocausts because they cannot rid themselves of the memories of war and violence. Insofar as Stacey had the courage to find her father's gun from the war and to throw it out of the house forever, there is yet hope that feminine values will eventually overcome the death-orientation of patriarchal culture and that all the children will be safe in a house that has ceased to burn.

Themes explored in the foregoing novels are reworded in **The Diviners** into an aesthetic resolution comparable to the individuation process represented in varying degrees by each heroine. If Stacey remained imprisoned within the symbolic forms and alienating structures of her society, it was in large measure due to her inability to appropriate the power aspect of the feminine archetype. . . . Whereas Stacey fantasized about alternate life-styles but remained stuck in the frustrating dichotomy between fantasy and reality, Morag Gunn develops to the stage of the creative imagination which is intimately linked to the ontological affirmation of the I AM, the spiritual center in consciousness that has the power to give form. Laurence, its seems, is attempting to come to terms with the collective myth structure of patriarchal culture and to discover, through Morag, a creative resolution to those problems left unresolved by the previous novels and specifically posed for woman.

Stacey's persistent recognition of her own and others' dilemma was overshadowed by a sense of global doom and personal impotence in face of the unknown outer forces—whether tyrants in the heavens or on earth. Laurence left her in the position of a tragi-comic anti-heroine, similar to Beckett's absurd but human characters who wait for tomorrow to bring something better. Laurence picks up this thread and depicts the sterility and violence of modern existence upon a larger background of the conflict between Nature and civilization. Morag is situated on the borderline, physically and psychically—neither of the world nor out of it. At McConnell's landing, a home on the land not too far removed from civilization, she has found a temporary island refuge and resting place for her soul after much wandering; here, like Prospero, she must confront the nature of the human heart and proceed with an alchemy of integration.

The opposing claims of city and country, civilization and Nature, have been a perennial feature of our Western tradition and correspond to the male/female polarization and to the hierarchization of functions according to male-assigned values. The city has been identified as the creation of the male principle, rationality, and the assumed ethical imperative has been to subjugate Nature for the greater glory of the masculine god. Woman and Nature have consistently been identified with the land, to be possessed and conquered. Upon both the male builds his dynasty, eventually to be represented in the city meant to embody the triumph of the rational principle over the irrational. The city-builders are the patriarchal myth-makers who always tend to ignore the underside of their myth; it is the exploration of this lower and rejected side that Laurence has undertaken here through Morag. (pp. 159-60)

As secular symbol the city has, since the Renaissance, stood for the triumph of the earthly, de-sacralized order ruled by men's reason; however, the obvious failure of that enterprise, based on the suppression and punishment of the fallen realm and its projection upon woman as the cause of that original sin, has resulted in the more usual depictions of the city as hell. The psychological problem at issue here, enacted culturally in mythic form, becomes even clearer when we look at the allusions, frequently made by Morag, to Shakespeare's *The Tempest.* . . .

As *The Tempest* shows, there is no place where one can be isolated from evil or from the monsters that lurk within the soul. Morag also attempts to come to terms with her inner demons. For Shakespeare, Caliban—the shadow of Western patriarchal reason—sums up in his abhorrent shape all that the divided consciousness fears about its own unredeemed depths. Caliban's mother, the witch Sycorax, is a projection of "the darkest continent" and its offspring. The dark or black one, therefore, lends itself through the projection mechanism to an ingrained cultural racism directed against all those native peoples who inhabited the lands of uncivilized Nature before colonization by Western culture-heroes. The Old World humanism, based as it was on the patriarchal myth-structure, bears the seeds of its self-destruction within it and might do well to listen to the speech of Caliban which could also be that of the outcasts in **The Diviners.** (p. 161)

Laurence's heroine has the formidable task of discovering her identity not in the elect and chosen of the world, but in the feared and shunned who are represented by the native Indians, the Métis, and Christy Logan, the garbage collector. Even more centrally related to her identity as woman, she must come to accept the Black Celt—the dark, suppressed and feared power-aspect of the feminine archetype of the Great Mother. . . . Whereas Sycorax and Caliban were the outcasts within the patriarchal mentality, here in the matriarchal schemata the converse holds true, and they have respect and recognition. It is Jules, as native earth son, who—with his outcast stigma—ultimately triggers Morag's decision to leave Brooke and the world he represents, a world that she had once wanted to be part of but of which she had eventually discovered the sterility and indifference.

Submerged rebelliousness, a motif that has run through each of the four novels, finally surfaces here with full force and explosiveness; the pent-up dynamic of the repressed unconscious's contents have added power due to the cultural components which are mixed with the personal. Rebellion against the existing order is touched upon rather playfully in the scenes with Ella Gerston who carries a volume of Marx while Morag carries Milton. . . . For Morag and her development into an autonomous woman, this issue is symbolically resolved through a union with Jules—that is, a union with the most despised element of the prevailing culture, with the dark or black aspects, the shadow side of her society. Furthermore, when she returns to Christy whom she had somewhat disowned in her younger pursuit of social acceptance, he is acknowledged as her "father". The one who had examined society's garbage, its discarded things, its refuse, is given primary value after the integration of the outcast elements has taken place. The refuse heap—in the Bible, Gehenna, the garbage dump outside city limits later designated as hell—functions as the secularized symbol of alienation within a society built on false values. Preoccupation with ritual purity has ended in self-righteousness and in building a heaven on others' misery. When Morag can stand proudly with the outcasts and rebels, with those who "see with the good eye" and feel "with the heart of a child" as do the Piper Gunns of Christy's legend, she is closest to the center of transcendence within. (pp. 162-63)

The over-emphasis on analysis, rationality and activity directed outward is a hallmark of Western culture, and what this novel tries to achieve is a balance between the perceived opposites, whether these be expressed through sexual differentiation (qualities traditionally associated with maleness and femaleness), or through cultural values of hard work, competition, industry and profit-making. Simply to be, to experience one's unity with the cosmos at an organic level of awareness, to contemplate as well as to toil: these are spiritual values Morag expresses as she matures and engages in "river-gazing". The balancing of opposites cannot, however, occur until she has previously found the power of the feminine depths within herself. Through the symbols of egg, serpent, well, heart, spear, wand, pin, knife, and river, Laurence creates a new androgynous imaginative framework, or symbolic structure, that is more accepting and wholistic than the one she has been examining in its effects throughout the novels. (p. 163)

The symbol of containment, of holding something precious and divine, appeared in the first novel as the bedpan/Grail (union of profane and sacred) and in this final novel as the well and the heart. With the latter two symbols go the divining rod and the spear of innocence. Feminine and masculine qualities of reception and penetration blend to create an integrated pattern of psychic functions. Finally, the Currie plaid pin and the Tonnerre knife are variants of this symbol structure, the pin representing the round and the knife the piercing object. In the Christian mysteries of Mary, the Christ-bearer, the pierced heart assumes a highly important place in the devotee's transformation; although Morag has had an aversion to pierced hearts throughout the novel, it is not insignificant that, through the experience of Our Lady of Sorrows in the rosary prayers, woman undergoes the mourning phase of the feminine archetype. This is precisely the meaning of loss—particularly loss of men—in Laurence's four novels, and this Pieta aspect of the Great Mother, woman who mourns the death of her offspring, is a thread running throughout Laurence's works. Her offspring are not only the children of her personal womb, but—from the universal or cosmic standpoint—all living forms. . . . With the integration of the shadow side of her culture, the self-discovery of the power of the Feminine as Absolute and not Other, and the balancing of male/female polarities, Morag Gunn has completed the work of individuation. Just as Hagar's story had ended on the request for a glass of water, so too does Morag end looking out at the river; the blockages to growth have been washed out, so to speak, and the repressions that were culturally inherited and made part of character structure have been released. A flowing quality, a dynamic of *Tao* almost, supervenes at the conclusion of *The Diviners*.

Certainly these novels can be read and appreciated separately, but thematically they comprise a quaternity and it is in understanding their intrinsic connectedness and preoccupation with the above-discussed issues that a sense of unity, of a holistic imaginative pattern, is gained. The blend of solidity (earth—"a ground to stand on"), and fluidity (water) achieved by the last novel reflects the concern with tradition and change on personal and cultural levels of being. Through the heroines' struggles to partake of that process, and in so doing to find the creatrix Mother, they have become permanent parts of a larger structure of symbolic meaning than the one in which they began. Perhaps we may say the same for the reader. (pp. 163-64)

Angelika Maeser, "Finding the Mother: The Individuation of Laurence's Heroines," in Journal of Canadian Fiction, *No. 27, 1980, pp. 151-66.*

Patricia Morley

Manawaka, as Laurence has frequently stated, is both an amalgam of prairie towns and her own private world. It is a mythic territory, mapping universal human experience, and a Scots-Canadian subculture in the Canadian West. Laurence has emphasized that societies need their own myths, generated by their own artists, in order to understand and fulfill themselves as communities. Of Manawaka/Neepawa, Laurence says: "in raging against our injustices, our stupidities, I do so *as family,* as I did, and still do, in writing about those aspects of my town which I hated and which are always in some ways aspects of myself." (p. 77)

The Stone Angel is Laurence's best known and most deeply respected work, a novel hailed as a Canadian classic. Ninety-year-old Hagar Shipley of Manawaka is the stubborn angel, a defiant woman filled with a "rage" for life. Her story is presented in two separate but interlocking strands, with present events triggering memories of the past. The two periods gradually converge.

Time present is Hagar at ninety, needing hospital care but stubbornly refusing to leave her home. Time past begins with the memories of six-year-old Hagar Currie, whose father Jason owns the general store. Time past moves through Hagar's marriage to Bram Shipley, a marriage that takes her out of her social class and isolates her from her family; through the birth of two sons, her desertion of Bram, and the deaths of Bram and the favorite son John; to her life in a West Coast city with her son Marvin. As her health fails, Hagar makes a desperate attempt to evade the hounds of fate by a secret journey to the nearby Shadow Point. This jailbreak is a descent into Self which is healing. The novel ends with a death which is also a birth. Hagar achieves a measure of self-knowledge, freedom, and joy: the objects of her life's quest.

Hagar has the speech, the values of Laurence's grandparents. She is clearly a person from the same kind of prairie Scots-Presbyterian background and yet, at the same time, is "an old woman anywhere," forced to come to terms with death. Hagar may indeed be everyone's grandmother. But in a deeper sense, we recognize in her not our grandmothers but ourselves: proud, stubborn, selfish, generous, fearing love, needing love. Seeking freedom, Hagar forges more chains. Seeking community, she builds psychic walls. Her final self-knowledge accompanies the breaking of these bonds, as Hagar is released into love, death, and the new life suggested by images of rebirth and transformation. (pp. 78-9)

The universality of the theme, and the intricacy of the images, make *The Stone Angel* a novel that readily lends itself to textual analysis along New Critical lines. Students are sometimes surprised by questions on Hagar's prairie environment, as if it were irrelevant. But Hagar is a Scots-Presbyterian from the Canadian West, and her perceptions grow from these roots. The starkly beautiful Manitoba land becomes the analogue for her conflicts. Manawaka's cemetery, for example, holds formal peonies and "upstart" ants; wildflowers encroach on its tenuous order. The theme of pride as an isolating wilderness is caught in the class-structured guest lists of Manawakan parties. Japanese porch-lanterns, hung from wooden gingerbread trim, are ironic reminders of the exclusion of Orientals from full participation in Canadian society, an exclusion which is the indirect source of Hagar's West Coast job as housekeeper.

By juxtaposition, Laurence establishes subtle parallels between the town's social hegemony (shanties and brick houses), its harsh climate (sweltering summers, and winters "that froze the wells and the blood"), and human pride, masked as meekness and charity. Jason Currie's pride in the size of his contribution to the new Presbyterian Church is echoed in Hagar's six-year-old pride in her new gloves, while the hymn speaks of longing for salvation. (*A Jest of God* strikes the same note of longing, in the opening chant.)

Contrasts in prairie environment suggest paradoxes in human nature. These include muddy farmyards awash in urine, skeletal machinery, and lilacs, "a seasonal mercy." Chokecherries sting sweetly. The "heedless and compelled" sap of Manitoba maples suggests Hagar's sexual attraction to Bram, but the pride which makes her conceal her enjoyment of their sexual relation acts, once again, to isolate her. (p. 82)

Hagar's rebelliousness is expressed in the novel's epigraph ("Do not go gentle into that good night. / Rage, rage against the dying of the light") and the title image. The latter metaphor, like Dylan Thomas's injunction to "rage" against death, catches much of the paradoxical quality of human existence. Hagar's rage, which involves the pride that prevents her from rejoicing, is also her stubborn love of life, her courage, her fighting spirit—qualities lacking in her brothers. The tragic aspect of her experience, her alienation, is thus inseparably united with her admirable fighting spirit. Like the wounded gull in the cannery, Hagar's strength is both her glory and her doom. There is no place for quietism in Laurence's creed.

The image of the stone angel unifies the novel. The actual angel marks the grave of Hagar's mother, who died in giving birth to her stubborn daughter. Purchased to proclaim the Currie dynasty, the angel is "doubly blind," carved without eyeballs by cynical stonemasons (Hagar thinks) who accurately gauged "the needs of fledgling pharaohs in an uncouth land." Like Jason's church contribution, the statue is pride made visible, blind to the needs of others and to the deepest needs of self. As the proud product of an Eastern finishing school, Hagar is "Pharaoh's daughter reluctantly returning to his roof." As she leaves the town and her husband, Hagar sees the stone angel in the cemetery, sightlessly guarding emptiness and death. Bram's senility fills her with anger at fate, or God, "for giving us eyes but almost never sight." John, who has his own blindness, wrestles with the angel in the cemetery while Hagar looks on. Later, it stands crookedly over two men's graves. The irascible Hagar, prisoned by flesh and pride, waits "stonily" for poor Mr. Troy. In this paradoxical image, the stone half (bondage) is more prominent than the linked suggestions of light, love, freedom, and life. The latter culminate in the closing scene: "Can angels faint?" Laurence had difficulty finding the title, despite its apparent inevitability. (pp. 84-5)

[In *The Stone Angel*], as in the Manawaka cycle as a whole, the beauty and wit of Laurence's language, and the use of setting as human analogue, serve to develop character. Laurence's special talent is the creation of vital individual characters within a vividly realized social group. George Woodcock calls Laurence "a Canadian equivalent to Tolstoy," not in terms of "literary gigantism" but rather "in such terms as a writer's relevance to his time and place, the versatility of his perception, the breadth of his understanding, the imaginative power with which he personifies and gives symbolic form to the collective life he interprets and in which he takes part." Both writers, Woodcock argues, have a panoramic sense of space and history, an ability to preserve lost times and worlds so that outsiders can imaginatively apprehend them. . . . (pp. 87-8)

Hagar Shipley is the first in a series of memorable women. In five closely connected works of fiction Laurence presents universal concerns in terms of Canadian experience over four generations. She allows us to see into the hearts of her individual characters; their society; and ourselves.

Fear is the dominant force in *A Jest of God,* as was pride in *The Stone Angel.* Rachel Cameron's story is a study of anxiety bordering on madness, and of the society that nurtures these fears. Sinclair Ross, a Canadian whose prairie fiction Laurence read during her teens, describes "the exacting small-town gods Propriety and Parity." Manawaka's gods are very similar. As Sandra Djwa notes, "Laurence and Ross share a central vision—a sense of the ironic discrepancy between the spirit and the letter of the religious dispensation. . . ." Manawakan values are work, devotion to duty, "decency," and respectability— above all, respectability. Rachel has incorporated these values, often against her will and better understanding. The town is all-pervasive but is seen at one remove, through Rachel's eyes and through its effects upon her.

Rachel is a lonely teacher who has taught primary school for fourteen years in the Manitoba town where she grew up. The death of her father cut short her university career and necessitated her return to Manawaka to care for her mother. Rachel is afraid of what the townspeople think; afraid of her mother's weak heart and subtle bullying; afraid of the authoritarian school principal; afraid, in essence, of herself and of life. A summer romance with a high school teacher from the city leads to Rachel's conviction that she is pregnant. Her agony of fear and indecision climaxes in an operation to remove a benign tumor and in Rachel's decision to remove herself and her mother to the West Coast city where her sister Stacey lives.

Rachel's quest, like Hagar's, is a search for freedom and joy, caught here in a phrase from the Psalms which runs through Rachel's mind as she is leaving Manawaka: "Make me to hear joy and gladness, that the bones which thou hast broken may rejoice." She wins a partial release from fear, a new understanding of her relation to her mother, and an acceptance of the mystery of human personality. . . . (pp. 88-9)

A Jest of God has been criticized as "a very inturned novel." [Laurence] defends the use of the first person and the present tense as the logical and indeed inevitable method for presenting a protagonist who is a very inturned person. (p. 89)

Robert Harlow criticizes the use of the first person and the present tense in the novel: "Her milieu is a small town, a cramped set of quarters, and her view of the world is correspondingly, and necessarily, narrow. . . . What is lacking . . . is objectivity, distance, irony. One simply gets tired of listening to Rachel taking pot-shots at herself." Harlow misses the multiple voices of Rachel, who thinks and voices a very complex self. Rachel is sometimes unconscious of the incongruity in her self. At other times, painfully conscious, she is embarrassed by her condescension, prudery, and hypocrisy. Sentimentality issues in her "Peter-Rabbitish voice." A falsely egalitarian ideal pronounces the verdict "Splendid" on all class drawings, even the worst. Rachel, adopting her mother's voice, wonders how the Tabernacle worshippers can bear to make public fools of themselves. She perversely condemns the Tabernacle decor as gaudy, and the Anglican as insipid good taste. She seesaws between longing for a life of her own and condemning herself for begrudging her mother care: "Oh—can I possibly be this mean?" Most horrible to Rachel is the sound of her own voice raised unconsciously in the Tabernacle crying the emotions that are taboo to Manawaka's middle class.

The first-person point of view subsumes the many voices of Rachel, while the larger fictional form contains an ironic, implicit commentary through event, image, juxtaposition, and the reactions of the other characters. H. J. Rosengarten acknowledges this corrective distance within the novel's voice, "the moral perspective that is provided by Rachel's dual consciousness"; confinement to Rachel's consciousness does not, he argues, limit the novel's meaning: "The theme of individual aspiration conquered by social convention and personal guilt is all the more forcibly conveyed by this intense concentration on the single sensibility." George Bowering, another critic who finds that Laurence chose wisely with regard to voice and verb tense, praises her "uncommon courage" in making the novel "confront social and deep personal stupidities and fears in the womb of her narrator."

Like other protagonists in the Manawaka cycle, Rachel perceives three worlds with herself caught in the middle, "a weak area between millstones." The remark has psychological and social analogues. Psychologically, the first "world" (Rachel's word) belongs to her pupils and the apparently self-confident teen-agers they so rapidly become. The third world belongs to her mother and the mores of Manawaka. Both worlds exclude Rachel, and isolation generates fear.

The children fear authority figures. Their eyes mirror Rachel as a demonic parody of God, "the thin giant She behind the desk at the front," the one with power. Rachel is intimidated by glamorous adolescents, whose piled and lacquered hair (the beehive style of the sixties) suggests a race of strange creatures, Venusians, to whom the planet belongs. She is further intimidated by their easy acceptance of sexuality. Haunted by the memory of a young couple in the deep grass by the river, Rachel is forced to subscribe to the view of her mother, her doctor, and her neighbors that she has no sexual needs.

In the world of Mrs. Cameron and her friends, unmentionable subjects include sex, age, and death. Their world, internalized by a harsh superego, sits in constant judgment of Rachel: "What a strangely pendulum life I have, fluctuating in age between extremes, hardly knowing myself whether I am too young or too old." She does not accept her mother's view, but cannot act on her own. Rachel sees herself as an anachronism, sole survivor of an extinct species; a fantasy in the mirror; or an invisible woman. She thinks the children look through, not at her. Her cruel self-portraits constitute an attempt to deal with the limbo she inhabits. Rachel sees herself as a skinny sapling servicing a dog, a scampering giraffe, gaunt crane, lean greyhound on a leash, cross of bones, and inhibited ostrich walking carefully through a formal garden.

This fearful suspension between other states perceived as real is depicted in grotesque and macabre images, as Rachel tries unsuccessfully to sleep. The night is a gigantic carnival wheel turning in blackness; glued to the wheel, a paper Rachel is powerless to stop its pointless circling: "I see scratch of gold against the black, and they form into jagged lines, teeth, a knife's edge, the sharpened hackles of dinosaurs." The world is microcosm (every detail magnified) or macrocosm, a phallic apocalypse full of pouring, piercing, arching forms.

Rachel's story, and all the Manawaka works, dramatize the plight of women in a male-oriented, chauvinistic society where both sexes are often unconscious of bias and social conditioning. Hagar's experience could be transposed into a male key with relatively minor alterations, but Rachel's is inescapably female. Her basic insecurity and passivity, her financial anxiety, her sexual vulnerability in the event of pregnancy, and her responsibility for her mother (a situation called by some feminists "the compassion trap") are all traditional female dilemmas. (pp. 89-92)

After the apprentice novel, *This Side Jordan,* Laurence's central characters are female. [In *A Jest of God*] Nick remains a shadowy figure with mysterious problems. Rachel is flanked by her carping mother and her lesbian friend, Calla. (p. 93)

Rachel's relation to Calla is marred by fear, as are her other relationships. (Hagar has no close friend; only in *The Diviners* does Laurence portray mature female friendship.) The stocky Calla, with her scorn for female fashion, her religious fervor, and her independent spirit is a perfect foil for Rachel. In Jungian terms, Calla is both Animus (beloved) and Shadow (the feared and despised), embodying qualities in Rachel that have yet to mature. This does not mean that Rachel has latent lesbian qualities, but that her fear of touching, of tenderness in any form, is part of her prison. At Calla's Tabernacle Rachel tried to make herself narrower, to avoid brushing against her neighbor: decent people should keep "themselves to themselves." A kiss, provoked by her confession of fear, sends Rachel running down the street in flight from Calla, and from herself. Rachel turns back to her friend in time of trouble. Calla's non-judgmental acceptance, unqualified offer of help, and shared strength help Rachel to discover her own strength. (pp. 93-4)

The title [of *A Jest of God*], rich in ambiguities, relates to an image-pattern of fools, clowns, jesters. The silent dead on Camerons' first floor [a funeral parlor] wear clown masks. Mrs. Cameron and her bridge-playing friends have clown voices. Rachel continually sees her tall, awkward body as clown-like, grotesque. Nick's father was Nestor the Jestor to the local children when he delivered milk; senile, and mourning for his dead son, Nestor's plight suggests the black joke of a cruel deity.

Laurence's fiction, like Patrick White's, hints at a dark god whose ways are not only mysterious but cruel. One of White's images for this concept is the vivisector. In the novel so named, White depicts human suffering as a kind of vivisection, a cruel surgery which becomes a stage in our transmutation into a more desirable state. Rachel thinks that God, if He exists, must be some kind of brutal joker. She sees her plight as a "knifing" reality, "grotesque, unbearably a joke if viewed from the outside." Her life is one long fight with God; she prays, with no certainty of being heard; and speaks of God to her mother, wondering if this is a partial triumph or the last defeat.

The fool pattern modulates from the demonic to the apocalyptic form. Calla reads from St. Paul: "If any man among you thinketh himself to be wise, let him become a fool, that he may be wise." The word *God* recurs four times in the novel's last short paragraph, composed of thirteen words. The circular sentence structure of the very last sentence, and of the paragraph that contains it, brilliantly identify God with mankind as Divine Fool. They are joined by mercy/grace/pity, the three verbs of the closing sentences. This is the culmination of an intricate pattern on the folly of fear and the fear of folly. Wrestling with it, Rachel is ready to smile at "that fool of a fear, that poor fear of fools"; "I should be honoured to be of that company." (pp. 95-6)

Stacey's story [*The Fire-Dwellers*] concerns violence and its many masks. Hagar Shipley and Rachel Cameron are relatively unusual characters, but *The Fire-Dwellers* presents an ordinary housewife with whom many women will identify. Her world is the frighteningly familiar one of a postwar North American city. This is a manipulative society characterized by brutality and deception: masked violence. Stacey's fears, both personal and social, are generated largely by her society: "Doom everywhere is the message I get."

Stacey MacAindra is Rachel Cameron's married sister who has grown up in Manawaka but escaped early. The novel covers several months in Stacey's thirty-ninth year, ending on the eve of her fortieth birthday. Events include her husband taking a sales job with Richalife ("Not Just Vitamins—A New Way of Life"), the death of Mac's best friend, Buckle, and Stacey's brief affair with Luke, a young

writer. Much of the action takes place inside Stacey's head as she struggles with herself, her husband, their four children, and their society, to wring a modified victory from besetting difficulties. Without the irony of the narrative voices and the honesty of vision this material would be melodrama. As it is, the novel's ending parodies a serialized soap opera, anticipating the possibilities for the next episode: will the city return tomorrow? We suspect it will, with very similar difficulties.

The violence that blares from radio and television is not simply outside the MacAindra home. Violence, sometimes latent or concealed, permeates their relationships. Stacey's "fortress" harbors a Trojan horse. She is slow to recognize her own capacity for violence and, when she does, is terrified by the idea of hurting her own children: "God, don't let me. Stay my hand. I scare the hell out of myself when I think this way." Simultaneously, she remembers a newspaper story of a divorced mother found in a catatonic state beside her dead child. (pp. 99-100)

Mac, her husband, is less prone to physical violence, but his icy calm is a different (and perhaps worse) form of rage. Ian inherits Mac's tight-lipped control. He craves his father's approval, yet is suspicious of him: they "knife" one another with words. Mac's Puritan restraint has been bred in him by his clergyman father, who used the whip of iron will and moral superiority to shame his son's exhibition of rage.

Mac is seen through Stacey's eyes and through his own words and actions—never from inside. His chief fear is financial. Stacey suspects that this heavy family responsibility has driven Mac "underground" into silence. Guilt at being part of his financial burden is a gun aimed at her head. Mac counters Stacey's objection to the advertising methods of Richalife's manager with the reminder that she wants their children to be able to go to university. Fear breeds guilt, in both Mac and Stacey. He must juggle the claims of personal integrity with financial responsibility. Mac has left an earlier sales job which went against his conscience, but he eventually finds a workable compromise for the problems posed by Richalife.

Violence represents one type of communication, and the failure of other types. One of Stacey's chief fears is of being unable to communicate, or remaining trapped in her skull. The difficulty of peaceful communication, the alternative to violence, becomes a dominant theme. The problem preoccupies Stacey. She moves from the naive view that it can be solved by an honest voicing of thoughts and feelings, to the understanding that whereas this may be a partial solution, silence and concealment are also necessary in human relations, and communication does not depend simply on words. (pp. 100-01)

After nearly twenty years of marriage, Mac and Stacey find it difficult to communicate. Stacey resents Mac's silences. After a day spent alone or with children (the typical situation for the housewife), she looks to Mac to bring her something of the outside world. But he responds to questions with the demand to be left alone. Stacey fears he no longer takes her seriously or finds her attractive. . . . Her imagination connects Mac's willed isolation with his fear of pain, and with some ancient or Edenic crisis. (p. 101)

[In *The Fire-Dwellers,* private] fears echo public horrors.

The epigraph from Carl Sandburg's "Losers" speaks of fiddling to a world on fire, and hints that action is meaningless. This epigraph, and the children's rhyme ("Ladybird, ladybird, / Fly away home; / Your house is on fire, / Your children are gone") reflect the characters' fears. In Stacey's society, death takes many forms: suicide, automobile accident, police bullets, bombing, maiming, napalm. Her city assumes, for an instant, the form of "that other city" (Hiroshima), "glass and steel broken like vulnerable live bones, shadows of people frog-splayed on the stone." A gull is admired for its simple knowledge of survival. Stacey thinks her children will need to know the violence of the city's core.

Newspaper headlines chase through Stacey's mind as backdrop to family activity: " 'Seventeen-Year-Old on Drug Charge.' 'Girl Kills Self, Lover.' 'Homeless Population Growing, Says Survey.' " The radio blares disaster at frequent intervals: NINE O'CLOCK NEWS PELLET BOMBS CAUSED THE DEATH OF A HUNDRED AND TWENTY FIVE CIVILIANS MAINLY WOMEN AND CHILDREN IN. . . ." A story of an ex-soldier with murderous reflexes suggests we have been conditioned into monsterdom. Everyone lives dangerously, Stacey tells Luke; we are all fire-dwellers in a world gone mad. Niall's revolver provides an escape fantasy which she finally abandons. Even the children fear death, having lost one friend in an auto accident.

Lesser anxieties concern the need for a university education; the need to look beautiful and elegant; the need to be "free" in some unspecified way; and the need to be a perfect spouse. Popular journalism feeds the "tapeworms of doubt" in the social body: "Nine ways the Modern Mum May Be Ruining Her Daughter"; "Are you Castrating Your Son?"; "Are You Emasculating Your Husband?" Conversation at parties reveals the fears of many women at the prospect of an empty house after the children are all at school.

Since people prefer not to see the disasters they help to create, society develops deception to a fine art. The con man is king. Mac's new employer illustrates our will to be deceived. Richalife, promising rejuvenation through vitamin pills, is a secular parody of the religious vision of the Promised Land: "Both Spirit and Flesh Altered." The parody extends from the obvious pun in the name to evangelical testimonials at rallies by those who believe the pills have altered their lives. Thor Thorlakson is the prophet of this pseudo-religion, preaching the good news that "the shackles have been lifted.". . . Laurence's parody of high-pressure religious evangelism is extremely funny. (pp. 102-03)

Laurence's ironic technique includes Stacey's silent dialogue with a God in whom she does and does not believe. This dialogue is at the core of Stacey's personality. The image of God fluctuates from an authoritarian, omnipotent being to one who shares in our helplessness. Talking with God is also talking to the unmasked self; questions remain largely unanswered but can be faced with some degree of honesty. God is connected with the destructive aspect of time passing: contemplating her present shape, Stacey decides God has "a sick sense of humour." She attempts to bargain with Him for the safety of her children, like Jacob wrestling with the angel. (p. 104)

Time, as humans experience it, is one of Laurence's continuing concerns. In *The Fire-Dwellers*, she examines the breakdown in communication in terms of the ways in which we experience time. Stacey wonders if time has imposed layers of masks over too-tender truth (like the circles that tell the age of a tree), or stripped them away. Time passing has turned Mac from a confident extrovert into an anxious, silent introvert. Stacey's change, from a vivid teen-ager who seems to have existed five minutes ago into a plump, dowdy housewife, seems "some monstrous injustice." Yet the vivid young woman survives within the housewife: "*Is* time? How?"

Throughout much of the novel, time appears to Stacey as a negative, hostile phenomenon. Her inner self is masked by fat; stretch marks on thighs and belly appear as silver worms, an image of death and putrefaction. Her intelligence has also altered for the worse. Evening courses bore and humiliate her: "Where have I gone?" "Once I was different." (p. 105)

The Fire-Dwellers points implicitly to the force of social conditioning on women's consciousness. Stacey has no thought of getting work outside the house; she has neither time nor strength for such aberrations. When Mac suggests that the solution for the painful nervousness of the beautiful girl who testifies at a rally is the lasting love of a good man, Stacey agrees. There is no irony in this encounter, no suggestion that the woman has needs beyond those which might be satisfied by marriage and a family.

The comic narrative structure is buttressed by many techniques for humor, from puns to juxtaposition. *Jen* suggests *genuine; Polyglam,* synthetic or false *glamor;* "fishwife, fleshwife, sagging guttily"; "No recriminations. No un-merry-go-round of pointless words." Something unendurable is "Not to be borne. Not to be born would be not to have to die." Laurence's wit and love of language runs throughout her work, but *The Fire-Dwellers* is perhaps her funniest novel, albeit the humor is black. (p. 106)

An imaginative use of typography indicates Stacey's different voices, and separates these from third-person narration. The latter, represented by ordinary type, advances the narrative, and sometimes provides oblique commentary. Stacey's practical thoughts, factual and ironic, are introduced by a long dash, whereas her poetic and romantic daydreams are in italicized passages with regular margins. Memories of newspaper events are in ordinary type, with deep indentation. Snippets of radio news come in unpunctuated capitals like telegrams. Open-ended remarks, without terminal punctuation, accurately reflect verbal patterns, while Stacey's longer inner monologues are in stream-of-consciousness form. As Allan Bevan notes, in his Introduction to the New Canadian Library edition, the introductory dash is essential in conversations interlaced with Stacey's thoughts, and there is constant interaction of memories, thoughts, fantasies, conversations, and actions.

Laurence made three or four false starts on *The Fire-Dwellers* over a ten-year span. She was seeking a form to convey a sense of simultaneity and complexity: "Narration, dreams, memories, inner running commentary,—all had to be brief, even fragmented, to convey the jangled quality of Stacey's life." No single voice could convey the disparity between the inner and outer aspects of her experience, and the frequent contrasts between her thoughts and speech. Problems of voice, Laurence adds, were compounded by the multiplicity of interlocking themes, all inherent in Stacey's situation: the marriage relationship after many years; the relation between generations; the relation with an incendiary world; and the relation with Self, which includes coping with aging and death. (p. 107)

Stacey is one of Laurence's survivors. She wrestles a modest victory from a society which she finally accepts on her own terms. She enjoys debunking hypocrisies propagated by Richalife, Polyglam, and other advertisers. Violence remains, but "there is nowhere to go but here." Stacey learns that the trap is the world, not her four walls, and that it is not without its compensations and pleasures.

The eight stories that compose *A Bird in the House* reveal a society through its precocious product and critic. All but the last story have been published separately and are, on one level, self-contained. The collection forms an unconventional novel, linked by character, setting, narrative voice, and structure. Taken together, and in order, the stories trace Vanessa MacLeod's growth to maturity, depicted as an understanding of herself and her heritage.

Laurence says the net effect is "not unlike" a novel and that the stories were conceived from the beginning as a related group. She believes the stories are "totally unlike" a novel, structurally, but by this she means that it is unlike a conventional novel or her other novels. She describes themes and events in the average novel as a series of wavy, interlocking, horizontal lines: "The short stories have flow lines which are different. They move very close together but parallel and in a *vertical* direction. . . . Nevertheless, the relationship of time and the narrative voice can be seen just as plainly in the stories, as in a novel.

Vanessa is ten in the first three stories, and eleven or twelve in many others. In briefer incidents she is a small child, an older adolescent, or young adult. The first-person narrative voice in *A Bird in the House* is technically brilliant. It is multiple, representing Vanessa the child and Vanessa the remembering adult. Ingenuity and sophistication blend unobtrusively. Laurence shows us what the child sees, and what she does not see because of her inexperience: "I did not know then"; "I had at the time no idea how much it cost him." . . . Vanessa's love of writing is another ingenious aspect of the voice. Because she thinks of herself as a writer struggling to understand people, Vanessa is a "professional listener" who eavesdrops unashamedly in plain view or from various posts such as a bedroom air-register. This helps to solve one of the problems of first-person narration, the need for the observer's omnipresence. Vanessa's writings are tragic, romantic, and melodramatic. As she begins to understand the real passions around her, she despises her compositions. Her stories and flamboyant fantasies are ironically juxtaposed with family events so as to serve as indirect commentary. They also allow Laurence to parody popular Canadian romances of the late nineteenth and early twentieth centuries, such as *Annette, the Métis Spy.*

The stories are unified by a steady progression in the type of suffering depicted. The first deals with social exclusion and loneliness; the second, with a past death and painfully aborted dreams. The birth of a baby boy, a new Roderick, effects a bittersweet mood. The third concerns Grand-

mother Connor's death, the family's grief, and Aunt Edna's lost love. The death of Dr. MacLeod in the fourth story precipitates Vanessa's loss of religious faith. The fifth, sixth, and seventh stories relate individual suffering to massive social failures: economic breakdown, world war, poverty, class friction, and racial discrimination. Laurence shows a development in Vanessa's ability to comprehend both human suffering and the limitations of her understanding in this regard. (pp. 109-10)

Brick House, bear, battle, bird, horse, song: the key images here are central to the collection. Grandfather's house, like his person, is dwelling place, monument, and embattled fortress in a heathen wilderness. The opening metaphors hold the ambivalence Laurence has frequently expressed towards her heritage. It is "sternly protective" (like the sweeping spruce branches), yet also threatening and inhibiting. Warlike images include a lawnmower beheading stray flowers. In the last story, opposing Grandfather is like batting one's head against a brick wall. (p. 112)

The image patterns converge in the last story, where the brick battlements are invaded by suitors, grandfather's auto becomes Vanessa's retreat for writing, and the bear of a man is laid to his final rest. The Brick House is prison, and fortress against winter storms. Vanessa's mother feels trapped but her children will escape. Edna finds it "dungeon" and "refuge." "The absolute worst wouldn't happen here, ever. Things wouldn't actually fall apart." (pp. 112-13)

As a feminist statement, *A Bird in the House* is subtle, never didactic. It shows three generations of women coping with inherited myths and changing conditions. Vanessa's mother, who stood first in the province in high school graduation, was denied a college education. She and the indomitable Aunt Edna remain admirable models. "Escape" for their generation usually meant marriage. In the last story Vanessa sets out for college and the city feeling *less free* than she had expected: higher education is no panacea. Laurence's female protagonists continue to wrestle with difficulties in the battle that is life. As Robert Gibbs notes, the real freeing is still in process where the book leaves off.

The Diviners is a sprawling, brawling epic with tremendous energy and power. It expresses a mature and profound understanding of human nature and destiny. As local reaction indicates, it is disturbing. What great novel is not? A strong case can be made that this novel, rather than the universally appealing narrative of Hagar Shipley, or the beautifully crafted stories of *A Bird in the House,* is Laurence's masterwork.

Novelist Marian Engel, who reviewed *The Diviners* for *Chatelaine,* remembers reading the proofs with the excitement that is generated by a major work. . . . Engel discovered that some of the local academic critics were reluctant to review the book: one called it "big and sloppy" in comparison with the "almost perfect" *A Bird in the House.* Engel concludes that Toronto critics are terrified of the monumental, particularly in the works of women. Unlike the Vanessa MacLeod stories, *The Diviners* is untidy: "There are signs in the text of blots and erasures, spilled ink, thumbprints and tears. Tut, tut, Ms. Laurence, girls should be neat. It is unladylike to achieve apocalypse."

Clara Thomas also finds the structure epic in intention and techniques. Laurence's longest, most complicated prose narrative incorporates traditional epic conventions such as stories of heroic battles, lists, heightened descriptions, oral techniques, "and one magnificent epic simile."

The essential unity of technique and vision has been discussed by critics as diverse as Jean-Paul Sartre and Wayne Booth. *The Diviners* illustrates this literary axiom particularly well. The creative vision that underlies the work is located in Laurence's understanding of the way in which humans experience time. Simple-minded notions (such as the one-way flow of time, or the idea that individual pasts consist of clearly verifiable sets of events) are invalidated. In *The Diviners* the technical brilliance of voice and place, the handling of narrative, and the structuring of human experience are correlatives for the vision: an understanding of time as a living river incarnate in human generations, *a river which flows two ways.*

The narrative joins history to myth. *The Diviners* is the story of forty-seven-year-old Morag Gunn, a writer from Manawaka. It is the story of her lovers, her daughter, her neighbors, and her inner growth. Morag moves from the small prairie town to Winnipeg, Toronto, Vancouver, London, and McConnell's Landing, an Ontario town even smaller than the Manitoba town of her childhood. On one level, the novel is a *kunstlerroman,* the story of the education of an artist. It is also the story of two peoples whom destiny has brought together in Canada, the Scots and the Métis. Each has its own ancestors, gods, and inspirational myths. Morag's daughter, fathered by Métis Jules Tonnerre, carries in her veins a heritage that she does not yet understand but is unwilling and unable to reject.

The novel is framed by the river seen from Morag's desk, a river whose current runs counter to the prevailing wind, and which thus appears to flow both ways. The phenomenon fascinates Morag, and becomes the central metaphor for the way in which we experience time and life itself. As the novel opens, this phenomenon introduces Pique's departure, and the apparent contrast between her daughter's way of life and Morag's own. At the beginning of Part 4, the two-way flow is linked with Morag's sense of order, and Pique's reversal of this order by staying up at night and sleeping by day. Pique's reversal is also expressed through her unsettled nature, her difficulties in finding a vocation, and her lack of what Morag's generation would call ambition. At the novel's end, the river has cumulative force. The water at its edge is clear, while beyond, it deepens and keeps its life hidden. River depths suggest mysteries in time for individuals, generations, and nations. The novel's ending, like its beginning, evokes the mysterious core of human experience, and its unity in diversity.

For individuals, the two-way flow means that relationships are being continually altered as events are reinterpreted. This can be frightening and painful, yet carries with it creative possibilities for growth. Morag's neighbor, an old man with the gift for water divination, tells her of his early married life. Royland's story incorporates several voices or viewpoints, all of which are Royland's at different times. His transformation from a self-righteous, aggressive evangelist, who unwittingly destroys his wife, into a kindly grandfather-figure is credible and touching.

History and legend merge in Morag's pictures of herself as a small child with her parents. The faded photographs are jumbled together in a large envelope lifted from the dump. Morag's skull is another container for Louisa and Colin Gunn, whose people came to Canada during the Highland Clearances. Morag remembers herself as an older child composing the interpretations of her parents and herself which answered to her emotional needs.

Strangely suggestive is the adult Morag's desire to converse with her dead mother, coupled with the realization that she is now more than ten years older than her mother was when she died: "she would seem so young to me, so inexperienced." *A Jest of God* effects a similar reversal, as Rachel realizes that she is now responsible for her mother. Morag remembers their deaths, not their lives: "yet they're inside me, flowing unknown in my blood and moving unrecognized in my skull."

Despite its brevity, Part 1 establishes the middle-aged Morag, loving, anxious, ironic, defiant, "born bloody-minded"; the succeeding generation's rebellion; the preceding generation's battle with poverty, drought, and disease; their ancestors' trials in the Scottish Highlands; and the river metaphor, identified with the generations, genes, instinct, blood, memory, cultural values, and individual experience. (pp. 119-22)

Morag is adopted by Christie Logan, the town's garbage collector, and his obese wife Prin. They live on Hill Street, which the adult Morag remembers as the Scots-English equivalent of the other side of the tracks. As the adopted child of a couple despised by the establishment, Morag experiences blatant discrimination. Like Adele Wiseman's *Crackpot,* *The Diviners* portrays class prejudice in an ostensibly democratic society. Attempts to humiliate Morag only encourage her inner toughness. She hates the Logans for exposing her to pain, and hates herself for her failure to respond adequately to their goodness. Pique's mixed feelings for Morag are paralleled by Morag's for Christie and many others.

The long second part juxtaposes Pique's current rebellion with Morag's childhood in Manawaka. Morag reminds herself that Pique sees differently, that time changes not only one's relation to others but to oneself: "What happened to me wasn't what anyone else thought was happening, and maybe not even what I thought was happening at the time. A popular misconception is that we can't change the past—everyone is constantly changing their own past, recalling it, revising it. What really happened? A meaningless question. But one I keep trying to answer, knowing there is no answer."

Morag's unfinished university career and her marriage to Brooke Skelton are related in Part 3. Its ironic title suggests the idealistic hopes with which the average girl approaches marriage. "Halls of Sion" chronicles the birth, growth, and bitter failure of this relationship, as Morag's strength grows. . . . Brooke considers his bride a child, an attitude Morag accepts initially as romantic but which becomes intolerable. His refusal to have children and, worse, his inability to take her writing seriously stem from this misconception of Morag as child and princess. She becomes a trapped princess in an elegant apartment tower in Toronto. Adultery with Jules, after Brooke has insulted him, is a joining that is also a severing of the chains which have separated her from part of herself.

Morag's leaving is a desperate necessity and a kind of death. She and Brooke will continue to inhabit one another, a sexual metaphor which covers feelings and parallels the continuation in Morag of her Manawaka experience. As she heads west, the prairie winter reflects her emotional state, and hints at rebirth. Small, tough prairie trees survive terrible winters: "a determined kind of tree, all right." Prairie flowers are similarly sturdy. Morag thinks that strangers would find the landscape dull, bleak, empty: "They didn't know the renewal that came out of the dead cold."

Part 4 takes Morag through the next two decades, covering Pique's birth and growth to young adulthood, Morag's development as a writer, and her growth towards self-acceptance and the hard-won maturity that is in the narrative voice from the beginning. Its title gives an ironic turn to a phrase from anthropology which is usually applied to ceremonies where an adolescent, after undergoing rigorous rituals, is accepted as an adult member of the tribe. Morag's rites must be discovered by her, and extend over her adult life.

Royland's gift for water-divining is linked with Morag's writing, and with the songs and ancestral tales of Christie and Jules. Art, like the ability to locate water, is a mysterious gift which is given for a time and may be withdrawn. Both the Old Man of the River and Morag are very conscious that they hold their gifts by grace, that "things remained mysterious, his work her own, the generations, the river." (pp. 123-25)

Royland's divining, Morag's writing, Christie's gift for "garbage-telling" and ancestral tales are all analogues. The Scavenger's booty includes the Highland tales, and a Gaelic Bible rescued from the "Nuisance Grounds." The implicit parallel between the dump, with its euphemistic name, and the subconscious, seen by Freud as a dump of repressed childhood memories, is witty, like Marshall McLuhan's dictum that art is formed from the garbage of the past.

Christie—grimacing clown, fool, hero, and religious prophet—is a complex creation, one of Laurence's best. His adages include "One man's muck is everyman's muck," and "By their garbage shall ye know them." His view of life has been shaped by his profession, or his profession chosen (after the carnage of World War I) because it concurs with his views. He tells Morag that people of any class are "only much"; the remark is illustrated in the cruel scenes that follow. . . . (p. 126)

Laurence is conscious of an affinity between her fiction and that of Chinua Achebe and Patrick White. Nowhere is the link with White so clear as in the figure of Christie Logan, the Good Fool. His name, little Christ, underlines Laurence's intention. The loving simpleton, or foolish sage, points to the limitations of reason and to a supra-rational vision. The fool figure, in White and in Russian novelists such as Dostoyevsky, is generally a mystic, whose simplicity and honesty is interpreted by conventional society as stupidity, even madness. Blewett calls Christie "one of the greatest fools in modern literature, but for that reason a channel and an image to divine grace." The fool is also a prominent device in *A Jest of God,* where Rachel and Calla are God's fools. (p. 127)

Despite its deep religious humanism, *The Diviners* has been attacked as pornographic. The controversy centered, in 1976 and 1978, in attempts to have the novel removed from Ontario's Grade Thirteen English curriculum. The 1976 attack was organized by the Reverend Sam Buick of Peterborough's Dublin Street Pentecostal Church. Reverend Buick and his Citizens in Defence of Decency appeared to see in the novel little but blasphemy, immorality, adultery, and fornication. (p. 130)

Morag Gunn and the novel which embodies her attitudes constitute a threat to many people. *Her sexuality is threatening, her independence is threatening; and her language is threatening.* (p. 131)

Morag's sexuality offends ancient, firmly entrenched stereotypes of women as much less highly sexed than men. The well-bred Victorian woman had to conceal hunger for food, let alone sexual appetite. Morag's need for sex, her frank enjoyment of it, the ease with which she climaxes and her means of solitary relief are attributes of women that have become topics for public discussion only in the last decade, in conjunction with a new wave of feminist writings. Morag's brief encounter with Chas during her lonely Vancouver years is doubtless one of the passages that attracted Reverend Buick's yellow pencil. Yet this encounter, prompted by her sexual hunger, is ethical *within context.* Chas's sadism, and Morag's fear of becoming pregnant by a man she despises, should be nemesis enough for the moralists. Morag determines that this will never occur again. She has learned that body and spirit cannot be divorced, and that her flesh carries responsibilities. The earlier encounter with Harold is black comedy, as two solitudes attempt mutual consolation. As Marian Engel observes, Morag's attempts at casual sex are disastrous because she is not a casual person.

Sex and power: Morag's inner growth is partly a coming to terms with her own strength. She learns early that weakness attracts bullies. Her humiliated friend Eva, sterilized by a bungled abortion, illustrates what happens to a lower-class girl without Morag's determination: "Morag is not—repeat *not*—going to be beaten by life. But cannot bear to look at Eva very often."

Eva attracts boys at dances because her conversation consists of monosyllables designed to flatter. The adolescent Morag is torn between pride and the longing to be popular with boys. She succumbs to peer pressure and wears make-up, which separates her from herself. At university it is not loneliness that makes it unbearable to lack dates, but the sense of being "down-graded, devalued, undesirable." One Morag, the product of North American social conditioning, wants to be glamorous and adored, get married and have children; another Morag wants something not yet fully understood: "All I want is everything."

So Morag marries her prince, and the relationship becomes a prison and a lie. Symptoms are Morag's eager agreement to go out with Brooke when she feels like writing; her attempt to conceal her black moods; her acceptance of his demeaning game before they have sex: "Have you been a good girl?" Repressing knowledge of the lie adds to her feeling of being separated from herself. It is only when the decision to leave is irrevocable that Morag can acknowledge the chains, now broken.

Brooke has felt that he *owns* his wife. When she leaves, he wants legal proof of what is and is not his property. Morag makes no financial claims. The novel depicts, with ironic humor, the high cost of independence. It also shows that psychological and economic independence are closely linked. One suspects that it is really this portrait of a woman who does not need male shelter, financial or emotional, that disturbs many readers of both sexes. Yet Morag is no superwoman, no monster of self-sufficiency. Catharine Parr Traill's innumerable talents make her feel inadequate. But Morag copes. She survives, with a little help from her friends.

In connection with the 1976 Peterborough School Board affair Laurence spoke to John Ayre of her intention in the novel: "One of the major themes, of course, is the maturing of a woman, to show how she ultimately becomes an independent person, not just in an external way but how she eventually achieves a sense of inner freedom. In that sense, Morag moves further ahead than any of my women characters. I think it is an extremely positive book." (pp. 131-33)

[Morag's language] is offensive to many readers. One obvious defense, if such were needed, would be that her vocabulary is in character: it is realistic for someone with her background. (p. 134)

Language reflects values as well as class. People swear *by* what is important to them. For the postwar generation, the switch from religion as a source of obscenities to sexuality indicates changing social values. Morag's language draws on both areas. Moreover, people swear *at* what is important to them. Morag and Pique, like rebels in the 1960s who termed the Vietnamese war an obscenity, are repelled by human suffering and degradation. This concern sometimes finds expression in four-letter words. Jules's oaths, similarly, express anger over the mistreatment of his people, or the ironies of fate which facilitate their self-destruction. Christie's language is an intimate part of the man.

Indecent language is also a source of black humor. Six-year-old Morag conveys fear, courage, and defiance in her "Hang onto your shit and never let them know you are ascared." The adult Morag's explosive anger, when her husband insists on treating her as a child, issues in some of Christie's choicest terms. Just prior, her grief and guilt over Prin's death and Christie's loneliness induce in Morag "the mad and potentially releasing desire to speak sometimes as Christie used to speak, the loony oratory, salt-beefed with oaths, the stringy lean oaths with some protein on them, the Protean oaths upon which she was reared." Normally, Morag's language is strong and ironic, but far from obscene.

Language as the expression of character is illustrated by Morag's dialogue with Catharine Parr Traill, a nineteenth-century pioneer who lived and wrote in the Peterborough-Lakefield area which inspires the fictional McConnell's Landing. Catharine's formal language, innocent of humor, contrasts comically with Morag's inner voice: "In cases of emergency, it is folly to fold one's hands and sit down to bewail in abject terror. It is better to be up and doing" (*The Canadian Settler's Guide*, 1855). Traill serves as a model of women's experience in an earlier century, just as Pique suggests future generations. Again, myth and history join hands. Morag takes what she needs from

"C.P.T.," mythologizing the historic character. (pp. 134-35)

Like the river, [Morag's daughter] Pique is drawn in two directions. She inherits two mythologies. Her ancestors, represented by Jules's songs, and by Christie's tales as retold by Morag, contain her future and her past. Music is the medium for Pique's generation. She treasures the Métis ballads from her father, and writes one of her own that begins "There's a valley holds my name." She was named after Jules's sister Piquette, who died in the shack fire. At the novel's end, Pique intends to join the communal life of her Métis uncle's family at Galloping Mountain. This journey "home," like the rest of life, is a backwards/forwards process. Pique hopes to share in their life, and contribute to it, for an unknown period. Her generation accepts unstructured situations.

Women and Métis, two central concerns in *The Diviners,* are natural partners in a modern Canadian setting. An American equivalent of politically disadvantaged groups might be women and blacks. The Métis were actually called *black* in the nineteenth century by some Scots settlers in the Red River Valley. Pique is the child of Canada's founding races (Indian, French, Scots, and English) and symbolizes Canada's future. The symbol might easily have been melodramatic, forced, or pat. In Laurence's handling it is none of these. As a Manitoban, Laurence grew up in the area where Métis had hunted buffalo only a few generations earlier. There were Métis in her town, her school. Her experiences in Africa, and her experience as a woman and a writer, made the themes in this novel natural and inevitable.

The Manawaka novels as a whole contain a composite portrait of four generations of Canadian women, of their problems, challenges, aspirations, and achievements. They range from the ordinary to the extraordinary, from housewives to artists. *A Bird in the House* and *The Diviners* depict woman as artist, in youth and maturity. (p. 137)

The Diviners is Laurence's most political novel, and her most spiritual one. She is writing, here, about the disinherited, the dispossessed. She is writing of psychic and economic alienation; of struggle, growth, and hope. In his editorial for the Margaret Laurence Issue of the *Journal of Canadian Studies* [see Further Reading list], Michael Peterman objects to what he calls the "explicit political qualities" of the novel. Peterman's argument owes more to his observation of Laurence's activities in the 1970s, and to his implicit conviction that good novels avoid political issues, than to any concrete analysis of *The Diviners.* (pp. 137-38)

The critical consensus is that Laurence does balance the elements of art and politics. Indeed, the novel's success *as* art is inseparable from the very human social concerns (political in the widest sense) that animate it.

In the Manawaka cycle Laurence creates a continuous, multidimensional world, an entire society, complete with hegemonic patterns. This portrait of a society is one of the great values of her fiction. It follows from her method of allowing characters to gestate in her mind for years, and of rooting them solidly in the society she knew so well. Laurence has said that she would like the five Manawaka works to be read, essentially, as one work. This is understandable since all five are religious pilgrimages: "the affirmation of faith and the finding of grace," as Clara Thomas describes *The Diviners.* In a similar vein, Denyse Forman and Uma Parameswaran [see Further Reading list] speak of "sacramental overtones" in the cycle's first three novels, of a search for identity which is also an indirect search for a relation to God. (p. 138)

Manawaka was Laurence's time and place, and she set herself to get it "exactly right." Her success fulfills the prophecy of the closing line in one of her undergraduate poems: "this land will be my immortality."

Two of Laurence's essays, collected in 1976, deal directly or indirectly with the Canadian Métis, whose problems occupy an increasingly important place in her fiction throughout the Manawaka cycle. **"Man of Our People"** reviews George Woodcock's biography of Gabriel Dumont, the Métis military leader in the Northwest Rebellion of 1885. On the dustjacket of Woodcock's book, Laurence speaks of repossessing, through knowledge of the Métis and their tragic confrontation with white civilization, "a crucial part of our past." . . . Laurence notes that many of the settlers who came to Canada came as oppressed or dispossessed people. She urges readers to become aware of the "soul-searing injustices" done to the Indians and Métis.

Some background to the tragic history of the Métis in Manitoba and Saskatchewan may help the reader to appreciate Laurence's concern. Indians originally provided much of the labor force for the fur trade in the Canadian West. Gradually, white traders and *voyageurs* began to marry ("after the fashion of the country") with the native population, principally the Cree, the Salteaux, and Assiniboine. The mixed-blood population increased, and acquired a sense of cohesiveness. When fur traders were discharged, many remained in the Northwest with their Indian wives and families. Because of their dark complexions, the French half-breeds often called themselves *boisbrules* (literally, burnt wood), but generally the French group was referred to as *Métis* and the English, as *half-breeds.* The Métis were largely migratory or nomadic, whereas many of the English half-breeds settled down to agricultural pursuits.

For nearly two hundred years prior to 1869, Rupert's Land, the vast drainage basin of Hudson Bay, was ruled like a feudal fiefdom by the Hudson Bay Company. Their charter gave them complete control, political and economical: one citizen of the Red River Valley, writing in 1856, called the Company an incubus which had buried the area in apathy. By 1869, a sizable group of half-breeds, French and English, lived in the Valley near Fort Garry (now Winnipeg). Their livelihood centered on the buffalo hunt, an enormous enterprise which required a military type of organization and which supplied the dried meat and pemmican on which the traders depended.

Indian and Métis had common bonds, including languages; and both claimed territorial rights as aboriginal people. But the Métis, unlike their Indian cousins, were never accorded legal status by the Canadian government. Faced with overt discrimination and violence, they were forced to abandon the name of Métis; politically, they were nonexistent. They inherited all the Indian problems; and their tragedy "climaxed and epitomized the whole struggle of red man, or brown, against white."

In 1869, the Hudson Bay Company, without informing the people of the area, surrendered their charter and sold the Canadian West to the government in Ottawa (newly confederated, two years before). White settlers had been slowly increasing for half a century, and trade between the Métis and the Americans, just to the south, was rapidly increasing in the 1860s. The Métis feared for the security of title to the lands on which they lived, on the banks of the Red and Qu'Appelle Rivers, while the Canadians, in central and eastern Canada, feared for the security of Rupert's Land against American encroachment. Louis Riel led the Manitoba Métis, first in passive resistance to the Canadian surveyors, and finally in an armed rebellion. His provisional government stopped entry of the Canadian representatives in December, 1869, seized Fort Garry, and composed a list of constitutional demands, most of which were made law the next year when Manitoba became the fifth province to enter the Dominion of Canada.

For Riel and his people it was a Pyrrhic victory. His provisional government had executed Thomas Scott, an Ontario Orangeman, after a court-martial. This act, and Riel's unfortunate links with American supporters, were largely responsible for the military force which took Fort Garry in the spring of 1870, and forced Riel into exile in the United States. As for the Manitoba Métis, some received title to their farms and subsequently lost it to unscrupulous land speculators and white settlers. Ontario settlers (Laurence's ancestors among them) poured into Manitoba in the next few decades and altered its social makeup from a large proportion of French-speaking Roman Catholics (the Métis) to a predominantly Protestant, English-speaking majority. The Métis were the tragic heirs to centuries of hostility between these groups in Canada.

After 1870, many of the Manitoba Métis moved westward to the area of Batoche on the South Saskatchewan, where the Dumont family had lived, and helped to lead the buffalo hunt, for two generations. Between 1870 and 1885 (the second rebellion, and the one which sealed the fate of this people), the Saskatchewan group was enlarged by Métis who had lost their land in Manitoba or who preferred the greater freedom of the Northwest Territories and access to the remaining buffalo. It was a tortured time for Indian and Métis alike, as Joseph Kinsey Howard writes: "—a time of war, famine, disease, moral dissolution. It was a time when smallpox, whiskey, prostitution and the slaughter of the buffalo did more to win an empire than bullets could; and perhaps the bullets could never have done it alone."

The disappearance of the buffalo, and the inevitable spread of white settlement westward, doomed the way of life of Métis and Indians, both of whom depended on the buffalo for food and other necessities. By the late 1870s and early 1880s, the Saskatchewan Métis were in fear for their land rights, while pleas on their behalf from white intermediaries and their own petitions went unanswered by Ottawa.

The Métis story leads deep into the heart of Canadian history and the Canadian psyche. Other major writers, especially the Western Mennonite novelist Rudy Wiebe, have made these events the basis of fiction and drama. Excellent biographies of Riel and Dumont, the central figures in the events of the 1800s, are Howard's *The Strange Empire of Louis Riel* (1952) and George Woodcock's *Gabriel Du-*

mont (1975). But readers of these biographies will find the neglect and delays by the Canadian government almost incomprehensible, even in terms of self-interest. A third biography balances the picture and makes that neglect comprehensible in terms of another culture and another dream, an English-Canadian dream of a united nation from sea to sea—a British North America. Riel's vision of a Métis nation ran aground on the shoal of Sir John A. Macdonald's vision of " 'an immense confederation of free men, the greatest confederacy of civilized and intelligent men that had ever had an existence on the face of the globe.' "

Donald Creighton's two-volume biography of Canada's founding father and greatest political leader explains the forces in central Canada which doomed the Métis to extinction as a people for the next eighty years. Sir John A. Macdonald, from his early years in a border community which had been threatened by American raiders in 1838 after the rebellions in the Canadas, and again in the 1860s by Fenians after the American Civil War, had a lifelong fear of American encroachment. As a lawyer, Macdonald had played a leading part in the military trials which followed the 1838 invasion and battle, near Kingston; as a politician, he had felt the weight of American pressures through two generations. The Métis fell between the Scylla of a vision of a British North America, and the Charybdis of American Manifest Destiny.

Macdonald held consistently to four policies. These were, first, the need for a strong central government, and the desirability of maintaining the British connection as the only realistic counterweight which might ensure Canada's survival as an independent nation; after confederation in 1867, he envisaged the settlement of the West with white immigrants and the building of a transcontinental railway. The latter made the former possible. Only settlement, and the railway, could tie British Columbia to the federated eastern provinces of Canada, and defend the entire Northwest against encroachment from the south.

The British connection was more, of course, than a political counterweight. It was also a deeply held ideal. For Macdonald, British institutions and culture were the epitome of human development. Ethnicity was not a Victorian value; military valor was. The Métis *as a separate people* were almost literally invisible to Sir John, and were doomed by the forces that had formed him. He and his colleagues saw the Canadian West as empty, with the exception of the Indians who had been conveniently consigned to reservations by a series of treaties with their chiefs. Yet Macdonald was no bigot. He stoutly opposed Protestant extremists who attacked French Catholic interests. His moderate coalition policies made confederation possible, and held the country together through half a century of political crises.

Ironically, the neglected Métis and their armed rebellion in 1885 solved the financial crisis of the Canadian Pacific Railway Company and Sir John's government. By using the unfinished railway to get troops to Saskatchewan to put down the rising led by Riel and Dumont, the central Canadian provinces were convinced of its value, and a previously balky parliament voted money for its completion. A flood of patriotic enthusiasm in the East temporarily united its warring factions. (pp. 139-43)

The state of the Métis, after 1885, was pitiable: "not only had many Métis not received the land grants which the government had promised, but after their defeat many of them were so poor that they had neither the means nor the heart to cultivate any land that they might be graciously given." Many retreated north (their ancient pattern in the face of a threatening white civilization) to marginal lands where some semblance of the old free hunting life could be maintained. (Pique's Uncle Jacques, in **The Diviners,** represents this trend.) Others became unwilling, impoverished farmers. All had become "a people without standing in the new world of the future, and without rights in the old world of the past. . . . "

Laurence's fiction accurately depicts the general contempt with which the Métis were regarded in the latter part of the nineteenth century, and the twentieth. In a primitive or frontier society their invaluable abilities won the Métis a fair degree of social acceptance. As the fur trade declined, white civilization spread westward, and the buffalo became almost extinct, Métis usefulness to white society declined, and with that change came a growing contempt for an illiterate, nomadic group.

With typically imperial arrogance, the whites saw the Métis as not merely uneducated but *improvident.* One is reminded of Laurence's jibe at the British in Somaliland, who found the Somalis stupid because they did not speak English fluently. What Woodcock and Howard see as evidence of generosity, hospitality, and general disrespect for money, was seen by Victorian travelers (and by the thrifty Scots settlers of Manitoba) as prodigal.

The Métis maintained a strong sense of individual liberty and egalitarian democracy, such as existed among the great Indian tribes of the plains. Alexander Ross, an early nineteenth-century historian, praised the splendid organization of the buffalo hunt, where mutual aid and mutual restraint was necessary if the animals were not to be frightened prematurely. Woodcock describes the Métis attitude as one of anarchic egoism, tempered by mutual respect among the strong and by generosity towards the weak. The "uneducated" Métis could often speak half a dozen languages (French, English, and different Indian languages). They could ride and shoot better than their Indian cousins. They were superb hunters, trappers, guides.

In their prime Métis helped to protect the white settlers of the Red River Valley from hostile Indians; and constituted a formidable antagonist to the Canadian militia in 1870 and 1885. One is inclined to agree with Woodcock's thesis, that if Dumont had been allowed the free exercise of his military judgment at that time, the Métis, by guerilla warfare tactics, could have brought the confrontation to a stalemate and consequently won infinitely better terms for their people. Such was not to be. Nor was Riel's dream of a new nation in the Northwest, where Métis would live in harmony with a united Canada.

After roughly eighty years, Métis reappeared as an ethnic group in Manitoba. In the 1960s the political climate was particularly favorable to the kind of pressures the group could bring to bear, and group cohesiveness could be used to improve conditions for its members. Modern Métis are radically different from the prairie horselords of the 1800s. Joe Sawchuk, who worked with Métis in Manitoba in the 1970s, objects (like Laurence) to the kind of Social Darwinism that sees European culture as superior to primitive cultures and thus entitled to preempt the "inferior" people's land. Sawchuk speaks of a "white settler mentality" which helped to destroy the Métis sense of self-worth. Laurence's fiction depicts their struggle against this psychic aggression.

One of the political structures that has helped the Métis in the 1960s and 70s is the Manitoba Métis Federation, a nonprofit, voluntary organization dedicated to achieving recognition of the Métis and their problems, to educating them in social action, and to bettering their economic position. This new political process is very different from that manifested by the nineteenth-century Métis who stressed their independence and organized around a feeling of separateness. Since this is no longer possible in Canada, their current political strategy has been described as "fighting the white man with the white man's weapons," the weapons of institutionalized political process. In the 1800s the Métis were organized around the buffalo hunt; today, they are organized around a lack of occupation and the need to improve their social and economic position.

Laurence's review of Woodcock's biography closes on three main points: along with the injustice done to Métis and the necessity of redressing that injustice, she stresses their "rediscovered sense of self-worth and the ability to tell and teach the things needed to be known". By the latter, Laurence means the Indian respect for and closeness to the earth and its creatures, an intimacy lost by the greed and exploitative nature of industrial culture. We have forgotten, she says, our need to pay homage to the earth and its creatures. Pre-industrial societies were not ideal, "nor can we return to them, but they knew about living in relationship to the land, and they may ultimately be the societies from whose values we must try to learn". In *The Diviners* the haunting ballads of Jules Tonnerre, Lazarus, and Piquette catch the pain of this prairie people, while through Pique, child of Morag Gunn and Jules Tonnerre, Laurence expresses her belief that white Canadians are inextricably joined to Indians and Métis in Canada's future as in her past. (pp. 143-46)

Patricia Morley, in her Margaret Laurence, *Twayne Publishers, 1981, 171 p.*

Michel Fabre

Critics have adequately analysed Margaret Laurence's last volume in the Manawaka cycle as an experiment in "voice and pictures" which attempts to convey the quality of experience through an "audio-visual" narrative process. Still, it remains that *The Diviners* is patterned as much as a pilgrimage along epic lines as a *Bildungsroman*, and that Morag Gunn's archetypal quest for salvation and meaning is linked, through fable and dialogue, to an insistent theme: that of writing as a creative and communicative process indissociable from the problematic relationship between fiction and reality, between the Word and the World. Evident as it is in the programmatic title, *The Diviners,* the rendering of the exploratory process inherent in both experience and writing deserves more than a mere decoding of allusions because it proposes at the same time an exhaustive, coherent inquiry into the verbal creative process and a mimetic, self-contained symbol of whatever "divining" may be.

By professional, more than religious, definition, diviners at first appear to be somewhat different from wordmakers, creators, and even readers. The story provides explicit answers to the question: what is it to divine? The professional diviner is, of course, Royland, a water-diviner who makes a living finding springs and wells underground with the help of a Y-shaped willow wand. Although one must have the gift, he concedes, this is no magic trick but only a process which works most of the time even though it cannot be explained. His character, however, is endowed with more than the usual professional and even human attributes. His name makes him the "king of the land," the Prospero of McConnell's Landing, the genius of inland and underground waters. He also is a fisherman, "the Old Man of the River" (as Pique likes to call him), a sort of river god or Fisher King who brings Morag offerings of pickerels. . . . Even more than his long, grey beard, his "terrible eyesight"—he is too stubborn to wear glasses—marks him as gifted with "some other kind of sight," the visionary powers of a seer. Thus, Royland is not only a "diviner," through unseen vibrations, of water, but also a prophet from whom "Morag always felt she was about to learn something of great significance . . . which would explain everything . . . his work, her own, the generations, the river."

Morag is linked paradigmatically to Royland, not only as a substitute daughter (since he considers Pique his granddaughter), ready to welcome his wise teachings, but as an antithetic equal: she is 47 and he is 74; he is nearly blind, she is terribly myopic. They are companions in many ways, although she apparently does not have his gift. As she remarks: "She wasn't surprised. Her area was elsewhere. He was divining for water. What in hell was she divining for?" You could not doubt the value of water, she implies, the way you can doubt the value of words and literature.

"Old as Jehovah," "ancient," Royland embodies an inexpressible, archaic force. He is

> Old Man River. The Shaman. The Diviner. Morag, always glad to see him, felt doubly glad. He would, of course, not tell her what to do. Not Royland's way. But after a while she would find she knew.

Royland's gift as a soul-diviner duplicates his ability to release earth-locked water; he releases pent-up spiritual resources from others' innermost beings. He does not create them, however, and when Morag speaks of his Celtic second-sight he answers that *she* is the Celt, not he. Gradually, they exchange roles, or with time his powers at least seem to be transferred to her. One day, when he comes to see her, he says he has lost his divining abilities. He insists it is not an uncommon occurrence, rather a rule as one gets older and "by no means a matter for mourning." And as he loses his power, he imparts a lesson to Morag—maybe not the secret she expected, but one that enables her to hope:

> It's something I don't understand, the divining . . . and it's not something that everybody can do, but the thing I don't usually let on about is that quite a few people can learn to do it. You don't have to have the mark of God between your eyebrows. Or if you do, quite a few people have it.

The elect are more numerous than is believed. Royland's

power (or faith) can be acquired by trying hard and, especially, by not attempting to understand and explain. And the gift can be transmitted:

> The inheritors. Was this, finally and at last, what Morag had always sensed that she had to learn from the old man? She had known it all along but not really known. The gift, the portion of grace, or whatever it was, was finally withdrawn to be given to someone else. . . .

Contrasting Royland's true achievements, to which existing springs testify, Morag doubts her own "magic tricks . . . of a different order," because the reality of her achievement—communication—cannot be gauged: "She would never know whether they actually worked or not, or to what extent. This wasn't given to her to know. In a sense, it did not matter. The necessary doing of the thing—that mattered." Such is the answer to her earlier, anguished question: "Why not take it on faith, for herself, as he did. Sometimes she could, but not always."

The second character who comes to mind as a diviner is Christie Logan. Their appearances, as well as their ages, point to a parallel between Christie and Royland. There is something clownlike about both—Royland is "a loon" and Christie laughs like a "loony"—and both are brothers to the mythical Piper Gunn. When Royland performs, he stalks the ground "like the slow pace of a piper playing a pibroch. Only this was for a reverse purpose. Not a walk over the dead. The opposite. . . ." This recalls the pibroch piped at the funeral of Christie and his tales of Piper Gunn. Also, structurally, both men stand in the same relationship to Morag as adoptive fathers and as spiritual guides and mentors.

Christie is early characterized as another type of diviner—a garbage reader. Like Royland, his appearance marks him as one of the elect. He "looks *peculiar*," slightly misshapen with bobbing head and "cloudy" eyes. He is soon revealed to be a clown, a jester, a sacred idiot. When he acts for the children, he is possessed, in a sort of drunken ecstasy. He becomes, by physical similarity, a "redskin," i.e., a "natural" man or shaman, and utters his divining words, "By their garbage shall ye know them." Christie yells like a preacher, a clown preacher: "I swear by the ridge of tears and by the valour of my ancestors, I say unto you, Morag Gunn, that by their bloody goddamn fucking garbage shall ye christly well know them." Christie prophesies, in biblical language as befits his role, and interprets men's "monuments in muck, reading their lives from their garbage—a true fortune-teller." (pp. 60-2)

Moreover, his name and his favourite swear words ("Jesus" and "christly") make Christie an incarnation of Christ. Indeed, he takes upon himself the physical and moral muck of the Manawaka community, making the Nuisance Ground homologous to a peaceful cemetery. His symbol is a heart pierced by a passion nail, not unlike the image of the Bleeding Heart of Jesus Morag can see on the wall of Lazarus's shack.

A later episode develops "Christie's Gift of Garbage Telling":

> "DId I ever tell you, Morag, that telling garbage is like telling fortunes? . . . You know how some have the gift of second sight? . . . Well, it's the gift of garbage telling which I have myself, now."

Telling, in this sense, is richly ambiguous again since it means deciphering and recounting, interpreting and handing down to others through oral tradition. This is in part what Morag attempts as a novelist. Several years after Christie's death, she wonders: "Would there be a special corner of heaven, then, for scavengers and diviners? Which was Morag, if either, or were they the same thing?" And again, nearly despairing of emulating him, she proclaims her spiritual and vocational relationship to Christie just as she had to Royland:

> Christie, tell the garbage—throw those decayed bones like dice or like sorcerer's symbols. You really could see, though. What about me? Do I only pretend to see in writing?

Then, at last, Morag regrets that she could only see "too late" the beauty of Christie and his love for her. And she grieves at her lack of response: "I told my child tales about you, but never took her to see you. I made a legend out of you while the living you was there alone in that mouldering house." Indeed, literature is a pale substitute for life, words for feelings. One should keep legends for the time when death has taken our relatives, for myth-making cannot equal the giving of love.

This may be one of the secrets Morag was incapable of guessing, the message associated with her river- or bird-watching, or with the cry and flight of the geese, themselves associated on one occasion with Royland's divining. The flock sounds a "deep drawn resonant raucous cry that no words can ever catch but which no one who ever hears it will ever forget." Through this indescribable, yet unforgettable and eternal sound, divining and memory are associated. The river and the geese also become spatial equivalents through their north-south dynamic movement: the river seems to flow simultaneously in two opposing directions, while the geese twice-yearly ply their route between the arctic cold and the milder south. These movements can be watched and their meaning read by Morag. Part diviner, she is a bird-watcher and a river-gazer, still fascinated by the apparent contradiction, "even after the years of river watching." (pp. 62-3)

Divining thus amounts, in many senses, to being able to read the meaning inscribed in the world, in nature, and in events by the hidden hand of God. It is the ability to discern a design or a "pattern." The word significantly recurs in the novel, calling to mind the Jamesian metaphor of "the figure in the carpet." When Morag scans snapshots of her parents, she cannot "discern the pattern" in her mother's dress; in another snapshot "you can see the pattern quite clear." At school, the visibility of a dress pattern similarly serves as a criterion for the value and social standing refused Morag. "Pattern" refers to the used, worn-out condition not only of garments but of words, while the dress itself, according to the metaphor in Carlyle's *Sartor Resartus,* is the visible manifestation of essence and being. The metaphor of meaning is thus compellingly pursued when Morag, wearing glasses for the first time, can discern the patterns of leaves on the trees, thus reading what Whitman called "leaves of grass" as she would the leaves of a book.

To discern word patterns and to wield language is tantamount to creating some degree of reality. Practically all references to words in *The Diviners,* from Morag's early attempts at school to her later hesitations as a novelist at work, point to this. Words generate words through sound combinations, it seems: "they are dumb, dumb-bells, dumb bunnies!" They generate images which give the illusion of being visually real: "Morag thinks of the sparks, the stars, and sees them again inside her head. Stars! Fire-stars! How does it happen?" Metaphors, born from words, change appearances in a funny way: "The blinds are pulled down the front-windows of the houses to keep out the heat. . . . The windows are the eyes, closed, and the blinds are the eyelids, all creamy, fringed with lacy lashes. Blinds make the houses to be blind. Ha ha." Very soon Morag masters the meaning of new words—"principal," "strap," or "recess" at school, and "gaelic" or "scavenger" out of school. From denotative, functional meaning she accedes to plural senses and connotations. When Prin calls her a "mooner," she superimposes her (preferred) new meaning, that of a child from a fabulous planet like the moon, on that of "daydreamer." She perceives the scandalous situation of a term whose morphology is at odds with its referent: "The flies are *blue-bottles.* How come they got this nice name given to them? They're ugly." A name is thus felt as emblematic of its referent and the reality link between signifier and signified is vindicated as a rule. Whereas Prin is a big, fat, slovenly woman in the novel, her "real Christian name is Princess. Morag thinks this is the funniest thing she has ever heard." Of course, such textual incidents or remarks must be read as pointers to the way in which the narrative should be decoded, not only as steps in Morag's discovery of words or of the fact that certain things, like the face of Botticelli's Venus, cannot be described for lack of them. (pp. 64-5)

The writer's attempt at properly reading and expressing the pattern of life is an attempt at reducing chaos, dispelling ambiguity, eliminating "the blue" in vision. Some forty years later, Morag is still struggling with the same problem of rendering referential reality in words:

> How could that color be caught in words? A sort of rosy peach color, but that sounded corny and was also inaccurate.
>
> *I used to think that words could do anything. Magic, Sorcery. Even miracles. But no, only occasionally.*

As she reflects upon her "trade" as a writer, the protagonist is aware that she must aim both at mimesis and at respecting the prevalent cultural code; she must be neither inaccurate nor "corny." As a result, she is always compulsively looking for the right word. Speaking of "creases" to evoke the effect of wind on water, she catches herself: "Naturally the river wasn't wrinkled or creased at all—wrong words, implying something unfluid, like skin, something unenduring, prey to age." The right word is most difficult to find in the case of images, precisely because the link between the referent and the connotation is so tenuous. And words are always ambiguous because intent can modify meaning. Maybe the only occasion when Morag could be sure of the match between intent and meaning was when Christie (who often used "blessed" as a swear word in order to express surprise or indignation) answers, "Well, I am blessed" from his death bed with clear purpose and joy, as Morag thanks him for having been a father to her. (p. 66)

There are times when words come too late and are ineffec-

tual, times when some other means of communication should be established between living people; yet this does not negate the value of the word, in the form of the Book, within the larger context of the world.

The Book: the Bible. Throughout Morag's life, books are essential. In the family setting evoked by a snapshot of her at age three, she places "stacks of books" in the closet under the stairs, with leather bindings and "the names marked in gold." Books recur, though in less fine form, among the items rescued from the Nuisance Grounds and displayed in Christie's sitting-room. . . .

Here, the book [a Gaelic Bible] is, significantly, in another language, which implies that it should be translated and deciphered, and which introduces the theme of different and/or lost languages, an important topic in the novel. When the school children sing "O Canada," rendering the second line, in roughly phonetic French, "Teara da nose ah yoo," it always makes them titter: "They know it means the land of our forefathers but that is not what it seems to mean." French is perceived as possibly ludicrous through mispronunciation. Yet, when Morag listens to Christie reading Ossian and he shows her the Gaelic words but cannot say them, the "old language" is highly valorized. . . . (p. 67)

[Language] creates kinship and a sense of belonging, tradition and identity. At school, when Skinner Tonnerre does not join the children singing "The Maple Leaf Forever," Morag concludes: "He is not singing now. He comes from nowhere. He is not anybody." In fact, Skinner refuses to sing because the song does not belong to his cultural tradition. Of course, he should be able to speak French and Cree, but he only remembers scraps of these tongues. Morag's remark that Christie pronounces "Ossian" "aw-shun" and Skinner's remark that Morag pronounces "Jules" "jewels" point to translinguistic homophony, but they mostly emphasize lack of communication or language as obstacle. When Pique sings Louis Riel's song, which she has learned from a book, in French and then in English, she acknowledges: "I only know how to make the sounds, I don't know what they mean." Here, the non-French-speaking reader is in the same position as the non-Gaelic-speaking reader was when spelling out the stanza from Cuchullain's ballad. (p. 68)

This need to recapture one's lost linguistic heritage and the inability to magically have access to it explain Morag's frustrated urge to look up the Gaelic nickname Dan McRaith has given her—Morag Dhu, Morag the black—in the Gaelic glossary in *The Clans and Tartans of Scotland:* "It says *dubh, dhubh, dhuibe, dubha,* but omits to say under what circumstances each of these should be used. Morag Dhu. Ambiguity is everywhere."

Again, words and books are not enough. There exist dictionaries, catalogues, lists of recipes and sets of tools and terms, but these must be reinterpreted, put in context, recreated by reader and writer alike. More interesting than Margaret Laurence's attempt at "audio-visual fiction" in **The Diviners** is her repeated reaffirmation that reading and writing are not only complementary but also homothetic or homologous activities. Just as a professional writer encodes in a text his reading of other books, including the Book of Life, so does a reader recreate the book he reads, or rewrite it in his specific idiom. From the genesis of fiction, the emphasis is thus displaced to reading as an active form of communication, most textual incidents in *The Diviners* being evident metafictional reflections on and hints at this process.

In the course of the narrative, the writer is defined not only as a diviner, with all the connotations the word assumes, but as a craftsman, in a coupling which evokes the "Tinker, tailor, soldier, sailor" rhyme:

> Wordsmith, liar, more likely. Weaving fabrications. Yet, with typical ambiguity, convinced that fiction was more true than fact. Or that fact was in fact fiction.

The crux and truth of *The Diviners* may thus be found in its demonstration that fact and fiction are indistinguishable in appearance and may well be alike in essence.

Practically all of Morag's activities, past and present, tend to prove this truth. At five she would surround herself with imaginary creatures like Blue Sky Mother and Old Forty Nine, drawn from songs she had heard; she would project herself into blonde Peony or her true alter ego, Rosa Picardy, who slayed dragons and polar bears and was Cowboy Joke's mate. At forty-seven, she is still engaged in repeating the recreation of imagined memories from a handful of photographs in which, as in a pack of tarot cards, she guesses her past and future. Although she can recognize that some memories are "totally invented," she cannot stop elaborating upon scraps from her half-forgotten past, not only in a compulsive attempt to compensate for her being able to remember only her parents' deaths "but not their lives," but because a distinctive mark of the creative imagination consists in elaborating ancestors, in giving voice to a presence which, Morag feels, is "flowing unknown in my blood and unrecognized in my skull." (pp. 68-9)

Ambiguity again characterizes the snapshots which are preserved not so much for what they reveal as for what they conceal, "not for what they show, but for what is hidden in them." They are monuments to memory, totems, items to be deciphered without one ever being certain of their meaning and of the reality of the past.

The narrator presents a skeptical view of man's power to establish meaning and order:

> Morag put the pictures into chronological order. As though there were really any chronological order, or any order at all if it came to that. She was not certain whether the people in the snapshots were legends she had once dreamed only, or were as real as anyone she now knew.

More than one of Morag's psychological hang-ups, this is a clue, indicating how the novel should be approached and stressing the undefined, changing relationship between the real and the fictive.

One has to look for answers to the question of the status of fiction in the novel itself. Christie is unambiguous. Just as the Bible is the archetypal book and the blue heron is the archetypal bird, he establishes Ossian as the archetypal poet. . . . Not only in his mind, but also in Morag's and in the reader's the existence of the bard and the authenticity of the poems are established as truth. His "act of faith" (embodied in the "Strength of Conviction" motto) duplicates the reader's "willing suspension of dis-

belief" usually required by tale-telling. This is a magical practice rooted in belief which, not unexpectedly, connects Morag and yet another ancestor-diviner, Old Jules Tonnerre. (pp. 70-1)

The characterization of divining as second-sight, or seeing through people, is developed in several scenes in which one character looks at the other intently, as though seeing the deeper truth and reality behind his appearance. This face-to-face reading of the other comes to a climax in the perfect understanding brought about by love. Not only is it referred to in John Donne's lines about two lovers seeing as one, which Morag explains at the university, but it is dramatized in the tête-à-tête between Skinner and Morag.

Second-sight or the good eye serves as a powerful talisman when the time for action comes. Thus, the strength of Louis Riel as a "prophet" is rooted in his strength of conviction, as evidenced in "Skinner's Tale of Rider Tonnerre and the Prophet." . . . Here, although he is recounting a tale handed down by tradition, Skinner is also sketching, making up, creating the portrait of an archetypal religious and military leader, endowed with clearsightedness, with a sense of being invincible and with religious faith which enable him to rally people to his cause. His cross is only a material sign for his faith, just as the fact that people believe he can actually stop bullets is sufficient, even if contrary to actual fact. And Riel is also cast as a "very tall man"—tall not only in actual height but in mythical size—a hero out of the "tall tales." In the following episode, the tale of "Old Jules and the War Out West," the Prophet is defeated, less because of the sheer military superiority of the English than because, instead of attacking, he "is walking around with his big cross, waiting for the sign . . . a bit too long, because by that time the big guns begin." Defeat comes to those who wait for omens too long or who cannot read them properly at the right moment.

Piper Gunn stands in very much the same relationship to Morag as Old Jules Rider Tonnerre stands to Skinner. In "Christie's Tale of Piper Gunn and the Rebels," Gunn plays a role comparable to Riel's as a leader. He finds his people, the Sutherlanders, "sitting on their butts and [doing] nothing," just as Riel found the Métis. And Gunn arouses them to battle through the power of his music. . . . (pp. 71-2)

The most evident characteristic of these two tales is the fact that each one stems from an oral tradition which runs counter to the other; each one presents a version of the past which apparently negates the antithetic version of the other insofar as each side may claim to have been the only heroic one. But the two traditions also are complementary, just as the Gunns and the Tonnerres are needed to converge and create Pique. When Christie tells the tale of Piper Gunn and the Rebels, Morag has not yet heard Skinner's tale of "Old Jules and the War Out West." Yet she has learnt about the Canadian past in History class, and her heart is on the side of the Métis, partly because of her attraction to Skinner. She reacts accordingly at the end of the tale:

> (I liked him, though. Riel, I mean.)

> That so? Well, he had his points, no doubt.

> (The book in History said he was nuts, but he didn't seem

so nuts to me. The Métis *were* losing the land—it was taken from them. All he wanted was for them to have their rights. The government hanged him for that.)

Métis, huh?

(Halfbreeds)

Well, well, hm. Maybe the story didn't go quite like I said. . . .

(p. 72)

More important than Christie's willingness also to consider the point of view of the Métis as an antithetical variant is Morag's measuring a story (tale or legend) against the yardstick of History. It is commonly assumed that what is printed in history textbooks and taught at school is true. Indeed, it is consecrated, official "truth" but nothing more. Rather, truth is not reality but the interpretation of it by and for a given person or group at a given moment. Such recognition is implied in Morag's remarks about the official, national characterization of Louis Riel as a "mad" rebel and her own conviction that he was not. A further example of how partisan truth enters into history is provided by Lachlan McLachlan when Morag's report on Piquette's death mentions that "the deceased's grandfather fought with Louis Riel in Saskatchewan in 1885, in the last uprising of the Métis." Lachlan just deletes the sentence, saying "that many people hereabouts would still consider that Old Jules fought back then on the wrong side." If truth is nothing more than individual conviction or group consensus, it ensures that history and legend, factual report and fiction, are on the same footing. This is the point of Morag's interruptions when she listens to Christie's later stories or to Skinner's tales. Earlier Morag was only able to respond to the unlikelihood of certain details—"Did they eat *foxes*?" or "They walked? A *thousand* miles? They couldn't."—which caused the teller to reduce the scale of epic descriptions in order to achieve a sense of verisimilitude. In the later stories, Morag intervenes as a critic, an intellectual, full of bookish knowledge, in order to re-insert legend into history, to sift myth from fact, or at least to distinguish clearly between the two. When Christie tells about Piper Gunn and the Rebels, her acceptance is mitigated ("You are romantic, Christie") or skeptical. (pp. 73-4)

The teller is forced to compromise on unimportant points ("this Reel or Riel, however you want to call him") and to acknowledge the possibility of different versions. . . . As a consequence, truth is defined explicitly as what the teller of the legend says it is, here and now, because this is necessary for the telling to function and the tale to exist. The teller may know (rationally or by having read volumes of nonfiction) that certain historical events took place, but the telling of the tale demands another truth, not so much a different version as a different *kind* of truth whose criteria are not to be found in fact but in language. Later in her life, when writing fiction about the same episodes, Morag discovers that legend and history mix, indeed, in an unbelievable and inextricable fashion. . . . She then readily accepts and even welcomes "the thought of history and fiction interweaving."

It thus appears that the criterion for evaluating the success of a story is not the measurable degree of truth it contains but the "agreement"—both as pleasure and mental or spiritual adhesion—it can evoke in the audience: "I liked it fine" is Morag's ambiguous appreciation.

Evidently, such dialogues and episodes of story-telling as we find in *The Diviners* have to be read as parables of the writer's situation and the way literature functions. They also point at the difference existing between oral text and written literature. The gestural or verbal response of the audience while the tale is being performed and told, as well as the comments which express pleasure or displeasure after the telling, are clear signs of success or failure. . . . But, in the case of fiction, the audience is absent; the person reading a tale is separated from its teller by time and distance. This probably entails more creative participation on the part of the reader, but it also leaves Morag at a loss as to how she can measure her success as a novelist. In spite of the bunch of review clippings she receives from her agent at the publication of each novel and of the statistical reaction they more or less adequately express, she continues to wonder about the way in which her novels are being read and about the degree of communication she has achieved. . . . Literally, no writer can gauge how his books will be read, deciphered and understood by readers.

To revert to the ambiguous relationship between tale (or fiction) and truth, a further step towards reversing the status of history as official record and the status of personal versions or visions of it is provided by the Battle of Bourlon Wood episode. As in the case of Ossian's poems, the bibliographic reference to a real, extra-textual book, *The 60th Canadian Field Artillery Battery Book* (1919), the reproduction of its complete Table of Contents and a partial listing of its illustrations all serve to authenticate and establish its existence as fact. Christie only has to read what the book "says"—an 18-line, third person, matter-of-fact, condensed report of military operations in the Bourlon Wood section on September 26th. Since he actually was on the battlefield with Morag's father, Christie can comment, "Oh Jesus, don't they make it sound like a Sunday school picnic?" Consequently, he feels moved to tell his eyewitness version of it: "Well, d'you see, it was like the book says, but it wasn't like that, also. That is the strangeness. . . ." His is a story of fire, mud, and slime, guns pounding, horses dying, noise, and a man blown to pieces, and such fear that it left him "shaking like a fool" at the time and still leaves him shaking as he evokes the events again.

"It was like the book says and it wasn't like that, also. That is the strangeness." Such is the Janus-faced appearance of reality and/or literature. Not lies, as Morag-the-novelist first thought, but ambiguity. Ambivalence, rather monumentally symbolized by the apparent contradiction with which the narrative opens, as opposing dynamics arrest the river in statuesque stasis:

> The river flowed both ways. The current moved from north to south, but the wind usually came from the south, rippling the bronze-green water in the opposite direction. This apparently impossible contradiction, made apparent and possible, still fascinated Morag even after the years of river-watching.

The first paragraph not only introduces the theme of "the River of Now and Then," the possibility of a simultaneous journey back into the future and ahead into the past; the complementary action of the two elements, air and water, also serves as a superlative paradigm or emblem cast in bronze, of the ambivalence of reality couched in words and "divined" in fiction.

Only thus can the dilemma of the writer be solved and can Morag accept what she at first half-ironically called her "trade" as a worthwhile vocation. . . . Morag meditates that she could fail and that she cannot write a novel in such an intentional fashion, possessed as she often is by her characters: "They'd been real to her, the people in the books. Breathing inside her head." Word-beings are therefore akin to the old, long-lost languages "lurking inside the ventricles of the hearts of those who had lost them" or to one's real or imaginary ancestors. The writer is possessed like a shaman, chosen as a vehicle or voice for spirits to speak through. . . . Again, the narrator refuses to act as a critic, to analyze the nature of character and of so-called inspiration, but fully accepts the role of the writer as "possessed" (in a fashion comparable to Christie moved by the spirits) while claiming the responsibilities attached to it.

The writer is thus defined as an interpreter of the past, a transmitter of tradition in a relevant and usable form to new generations, as well as a diviner of the pattern of the world. Again, art and belief are reconciled in action; for, like divining, writing has to be taken on faith because it sometimes, magically, works and sometimes does not. Morag's letter to Ella concerning *Prospero's Child* contains a paragraph which is another way of answering this question:

> I have always wondered if Prospero would be able to give up his magical advantage once and for all, as he intends to do at the end of *The Tempest.* That incredibly moving statement "—what Strength I have's mine own. Which is most faint—" If only he can hang onto this knowledge, that would be true strength. And the recognition that the real enemy is despair within and that he stands in need of grace, like everyone else—Shakespeare did know just about everything.

Of course, Morag is speaking for herself, alluding to the magical island she has tried to build in order to fend off harsh reality. And her enemy is her own despair at not coping with her responsibilities as a twentieth-century Canadian woman, mother, and writer now that she has definitely asserted her own worth in the face of Manawaka and achieved recognition. She still stands in need of love and grace and security, however. And she finally learns from Royland's loss of his divining powers the lesson that she, too, can be an inheritor and have inheritors: "The gift, the portion of grace, or whatever it was, was finally withdrawn to be given to someone else." She can experience this "now," at the end of her career and of the narrative, which has been an exploration or incantation leading to such epiphany and self-realization.

Also, she has been able to see the sign (the Great Blue Heron's rising) and to accept the token. The token is the plaid-brooch of the Shipley family which, properly traded against the knife of Lazarus Tonnerre (whose hieroglyphic mark is at last read for what it means, a half-inverted "T"), provides Morag with the symbolic weapon she needed to slay the Grendels of doubt, "an arm in armour holding a sword." She also receives (adopts?) a motto blessing her with what she lacked, the Strength of (religious) Conviction: "My Hope Is Constant in Thee." Finally, her war cry, "Gainsay Who Dare," allows her to assert herself as well as to create a possible meaning and order in a world where she could see no pattern. "Everything is improbable. Nothing is more improbable than anything else," explicitly applies to the coincidence of the knife finding its rightful owner but also refers, by extension, to the not improbable, hence possible—it is a matter of faith—design of a superior order or providence.

With the buying of the house at McConnell's landing, the protagonist has found her roots: "Land. A river. Log house nearly a century old built by great pioneering couple, Simon and Sarah Cooper. Ancestors." She has accepted her ancestry to be, not of pre-revolutionary Scottish stock but of post-immigration Canadians, "here and now." She has allowed the half-breed line of the Tonnerres to blend with a line of Scottish descendants to make a truly Canadian offspring, whole in the flesh and spirit of Pique. She duplicates this creation in life and blood with a creation in words by writing *Shadows of Eden,* which follows the trek of the Sutherlands to Hudson Bay and York Factory. She thus allows history and fiction to blend. . . . (pp. 74-7)

All passion spent, and confidence—however fragile—restored, the quester/writer at middle-age thus brings to a close her spiritual pilgrimage, the wiser for knowing the limits of her ignorance, the more secure for having experienced the presence of a pattern and meaning in the Book of the World. She can finally proceed to return to "the house, to write the remaining private and fictional words and set down her title." The phrasing is ambiguous and broad enough to duplicate literal meaning—the final words and title of a novel (possibly *The Diviners*) in the process of completion—and the connotation of a life to be continued and a title to be claimed, be it that of inheritor through heraldry and tradition or that of diviner through clear vision and deliberate faith. (p. 78)

Michel Fabre, "Words and the World: 'The Diviners' as an Exploration of the Book of Life," in Canadian Literature, *No. 93, Summer, 1982, pp. 60-78.*

Timothy Findley

This memoir [*Dance on the Earth*] is a book about being a woman. It is also a book about being alive and about the giving of life; a book about being a mother—and having a mother.

Dance on the Earth is the last of Margaret Laurence's books, which for some will lend a sadness to their reading of it, a sadness that will not be justified and should be discouraged from the outset. That we have a book at all is reason to be anything but sad. That we have this book, which is filled with celebration, is reason for celebration in itself. It was written while Margaret Laurence was dying. That fact, though pertinent to the quality of every reflection she cast upon its contents, is not reported in a single sentence.

What Margaret Laurence has to say in this book is always of interest and, often, it is a challenge. It also provokes meditation on the lives of those to whom we are most indebted and those whose lives are touched by our own. It is a thoughtful book, though never philosophical. It also provokes in other ways. But then, it wouldn't be a book by Margaret Laurence if it didn't.

In an early paragraph of *Dance on the Earth*—a memoir principally concerning the women in her life—Margaret Laurence cautions her readers never to speak "as though there were only one set of responses in the entire male population." "No generalization," she writes, "should be the rule for either women or men." She adds that she often finds it "excruciatingly difficult" to adhere to this principle. And, indeed, there are moments in this book that will leave male readers feeling as if they belong to a sex that is universally dedicated to acts of stupidity, thoughtlessness, violence, and meanness of spirit. At one point, following yet another parenthetical putdown of the male sex, I said out loud, "Oh, come on, Margaret Laurence—give men *some* credit!"

A few lines later, she did. And, for whatever reason, the sense of this unLaurence-like disparagement was lifted. Perhaps it was simply that her focus had been pulled from the general to the particular. Perhaps it was because she had turned her eye towards individuals and away from group portraits.

At any rate, it seems important to draw attention to these factors in *Dance on the Earth* because it would be a pity if this book about being a woman went unread by men simply because they were offended by what appears to be a bias in its early pages.

All that being said, the reading of *Dance on the Earth* moves forward with increasing pleasure and intrigue. This is a memoir that tells what Margaret Laurence revered in the lives of the women who shaped and contributed to her own life. She sets down these lives (and also her own) as being collectively the lives of women who were mothers first and all else second.

She tells the stories of the women who mothered her: her birth mother, her adoptive mother, her mother-in-law, and her aunts. She also tells of her friend Adele Wiseman, of Wiseman's mother, of her English publisher's mother, and of Sylvia Plath. The cross-lines are numerous: sometimes amusing, but, far more often, angry-making and desperate. Every one of these women was presented with the choice of motherhood as sublimation of self or motherhood as survival of self. All of them, including Laurence, chose motherhood also as a means of expression. But for most of these women, the choice of motherhood meant giving up—to some degree, or entirely—all hope of becoming "the maker of works." Being "the maker of works" was exclusively a male activity, and men had devised a hundred ways to keep it for themselves. "What every writer needs," Margaret Laurence once said (she may have been quoting), "is a good wife!" This, as she points out in *Dance on the Earth,* is what Virginia Woolf found in Leonard. But it is not, on the whole, what the majority of women writers have found. Those who do find it are accused of being "man-eaters" and "ball-breakers." Relationships based on this seeming reversal of roles are often under such heavy stress that they disintegrate from the sheer force of public pressure, from the blind stupidity of sexist perceptions. (pp. 9-10)

Margaret Laurence's mother, Verna Simpson, was dead by the time Laurence was five. "My mother was my long-lost child," Laurence said, in her adult years. She barely remembered her—the most telling picture being the indelible image of Verna on her deathbed. Thereafter, Margaret Laurence was raised, in the motherly sense, by her mother's sister, Marg—or "Mum," as Laurence called her. . . .

[Marg Simpson] never remarried; she devoted herself entirely, despite her ambitions to write, to raising young Margaret and the son who had been born during her marriage. The sacrifice of her Mum's personal ambitions was a sacrifice Laurence never forgot, and with her portrait of Marg Simpson she gives a voice to those thwarted ambitions and honour to the woman who endured their thwarting on Laurence's behalf.

Margaret Laurence's mother and aunts were known—to their great displeasure—as "the Simpson girls." Their lives were first explored in Laurence's book of interconnected short stories, *A Bird in the House.* Verna, Ruby, Velma, and Marg Simpson are all, one way or another, central in that book, just as they were in Margaret Laurence's life. *A Bird in the House* is the only Laurence fiction she would acknowledge as being more or less "biographical." Margaret Laurence was rightly adamant about this. Far too many readers, including many critics, have claimed (as if they knew better than the author) that her novel *The Diviners* was autobiographical. Laurence denied it categorically, and turned an effective phrase in the course of that denial. *The Diviners,* she said, was her "spiritual autobiography"—not the detailed story of her life.

This distinction between actual and spiritual biography is an important one for writers of fiction, and it is especially telling here, when *Dance on the Earth* is balanced in the scales with *The Diviners* and *A Bird in the House.* For readers of all three books, the reading of one must necessarily affect the reading of the others. The facts seem to jibe; the circumstances are often precisely similar—the houses that are lived in, the people who are encountered, the incidents that illustrate the progress of the given lives—and they all seem to be the echoes and the shadows and the mirrored images of one another. How can they not be the same?

They cannot be the same because, in the first place, fiction is organized in such a way that the lives and events it portrays unfold in a patterned fashion that allows the reader to find a path from beginning to end. In biography, there is no pattern; there is only progress. Whereas, in *auto*biography, a pattern can be superimposed on that progress to provide a story line. Reflections on a life, however, are not the same as the life itself. And the business of all three modes of writing—biography, autobiography, and fiction—is the business of providing divergent reflections. This way, an absolute distinction can be made as Margaret Laurence tells her "story" in *A Bird in the House,* in *Dance on the Earth,* and in *The Diviners.* The distinction is worth exploring. The eye that is central to all three tellings was an eye with matchless powers of observation and matchless integrity. . . .

[*Dance on the Earth*] is a vibrant reflection of a vivid life. It is also a tribute to the women who shared that life—and a powerful augmentation of our understanding of motherhood. (p. 10)

Timothy Findley, "A Vivid Life," in Books in Canada, *Vol. 18, No. 6, August-September, 1989, pp. 9-10.*

George Galt

When Margaret Laurence was born in Neepawa, Manitoba, in 1926, children could still, as she notes in [*Dance on the Earth*], "safely drink out of brooks." In the North and on the fringes of the West, Canada remained a pioneer country. The prairie provinces were still overwhelmingly rural. For many people in the country's industrial heartland of Ontario and Quebec, where the urban population had by 1914 overtaken rural dwellers, life on the land was still a fresh memory.

Even among good writers Laurence's extraordinary talent and strength of will set her apart, yet her middle-class upbringing in a quiet Canadian community typified the experience of a large part of her generation. A religion-infused childhood, tight local relationships, a chafing small-town narrowness softened by a sustaining small-town intimacy, and then the flight from home at an early age: all have been common features of many lives that joined the waves departing from Canadian farms and towns for the cities when Laurence was young. In her four Manawaka novels she was able to articulate these experiences through characters who were unique yet quickly recognizable as Canadians shaped (and sometimes misshapen) by the values of pioneer self-reliance, United Church moral rigour, and small-town community ties. The people she invented, particularly her powerfully realized women, gave voice to the fears, exasperations, and joys of mid-twentieth-century English-speaking Canadians in such a convincing way that they will remain pillars of our literary mythology as long as the country exists. There were some excellent Canadian novels before she began to publish fiction, but few written by and about women. None of them could claim Laurence's complex cycle of interrelated characters, her acute ear for everyday Canadian language and richly drawn vision of place. Like her forebears who left Ontario and rode to Manitoba in a Red River cart, she broke new ground. (p. 73)

[Like other writers of her generation], Laurence left the country, first for Africa, and then later, when she separated from her husband, for England. Canada must have seemed an inhospitable backwater to these young writers attempting to launch their careers in the late 1940s and the 1950s, when a Canadian novelist was regarded either as an oxymoron or a genetic freak. . . . In her memoirs, *Dance on the Earth* . . . she wrote that England was where she imagined, "wrongly as it turned out, there would be a literary community that would receive me with open arms and I would at least have the company of other writers." Instead she lived almost entirely outside London literary life in a country cottage in Buckinghamshire with her two young children. There she completed three novels, *The Stone Angel, A Jest of God,* and *The Fire-Dwellers,* and a collection of linked short stories, *A Bird in the House.* All of these books were set in her mythical prairie town of Manawaka. Her decade in England, the work suggests, was spent mainly thinking about home.

Those English years apparently provided little material for fiction, although Morag Gunn, the protagonist of *The Diviners,* Laurence's last novel, is a single mother and a writer whose emotional life must have been modelled to some degree on the author's own. Still, since none of her books is set in England, those who didn't know her have no clear picture of her life there. We might expect to find that picture in her memoirs, but *Dance on the Earth* is a curiously uninformative book. It certainly won't add to Laurence's literary reputation; it confirms the sad truth that her best work ended with *The Diviners* in 1974, when she was only forty-seven. (pp. 73-4)

[Apparently] there weren't many interesting figures, apart from her daughter and son, who sustained her in those English years. "Loneliness was an almost constant part of my life . . . ," she writes. "I severely missed having a mate." . . . She felt deprived but, as she puts it, "my priorities were clear: the kids and the work, the work and the kids." This overriding sense of moral duty characterized much of her life.

It must have been partly her notions of ethical rectitude that rendered her memoirs so circumspect. The author's daughter, Jocelyn, mentions in the preface that her role as editor "was simply to smooth out some portions and eliminate any repetitions." She also notes that her mother was dying of cancer as she prepared the second draft of the manuscript. Perhaps Laurence's own pain left her even less inclined to inflict hurt on anyone else. In any case, she took great care not to tread on other people's lives in this book, but too often traded any possible offensiveness for dullness. Her novels bristle with insight, but the memoirs are an earnest litany of biographical fact sprinkled with passionate outbursts on the social evils against which she spoke out increasingly in her last years. The diatribes aimed at war, pollution, the slaughter of wildlife, and discrimination against women inject a hectoring tone into her narrative that will irritate some readers and perhaps by their excess embarrass others. "How dare we call our species *homo sapiens*?" she lectures in one passage about war. "The whales and dolphins, whom we are rapidly destroying, are surely superior in every way that counts." These shrill, blunt messages bear little resemblance to the subtle, many-sided observations of the human predicament that she wove into her novels. Her memoirs don't answer many questions, but they certainly pose one: what happened to Margaret Laurence's talent in the dozen years between *The Diviners* and her final illness?

Dance on the Earth does offer some clues to this puzzle. Laurence grew up in a mutually protective, nurturing clan that had a deep respect for family ties, hard work, and social justice—the strongest part of her memoir focuses on these early years. . . . As an orphan Laurence must have developed a strong sense of the frailty of life, as well as a compelling sense, from her stepmother, of how determined effort can surmount adversity. (p. 74)

Along with her moral and religious convictions, Laurence was endowed with an obsessive, penetrating intelligence and an emotional empathy that impelled her to invent people and tell their stories. From the beginning her novels were driven at least in part by her moral passion. (*This Side Jordan,* her first work of fiction, was a vehicle through which she could express her anti-imperialist, anti-colonial views.) But successful novels aren't merely moral arguments. Paradoxically, it was her almost clairvoyant, amoral writer's eye and ear that allowed her to re-create in such credible detail the cast of characters that gave her novels their rare vitality and depth.

A carefully examined morality is one sort of truth; an unblinking eye absorbing the chaotic details of everyday reality yeilds another. The novelist in Laurence wouldn't settle for anything short of palpable life on the page, no matter how unattractive or disturbing. She mentions Virginia Woolf as an early literary model, but adds that in her late twenties, "I began to feel that her writing lacked something I needed. . . . Her characters were beautifully, ironically drawn, but what was lacking was ordinariness, dirt, earth, blood, yelling, a few messy kids. Virginia Woolf's novels, so immaculate and fastidious in the use of words, are also immaculate and fastidious in ways that most people's lives are not." Laurence's mature work succeeded in incorporating the grit of everyday life into narratives that never shied away from the dark side of human nature yet were always underpinned by her unbreachable moral sense.

It was, I suspect, that moral sense and the acute distress it summoned that stalled and ultimately silenced her as a writer of fiction. A serious novelist's work must be one of the most difficult of human endeavours. A writer of realistic fiction has, in some way, to live inside the skins and experience the lives of her characters. She has to confront in every detail not only their capacities for love and generosity but also their malice, rapacity, and fear. This cannot have been easy for a sensitive woman with such highly developed standards of goodness.

In the end, Laurence's moral outrage at the human greed and destructiveness she saw demonstrated in her time on the planet seems to have overtaken her artistic commitment to depicting life in all its low sleaze, comic hubris, and costly struggle. In her final years the harassment she had to withstand from fundamentalists who sought to ban her books can only have exacerbated her anger and bewilderment. **Dance on the Earth** takes every opportunity to lash out at the forces she detested. The evocative remark about children being able to drink out of brooks in her day, for example, is the sort of telling observation she might have used in a novel. But in the memoir this elegiac note is quickly shattered by a furious outburst of didactic excess: "I do not say this with any sentimental nostalgia. I say it with enormous rage and anger at the chemical pollution by commercial firms committed to making money (never mind anything else) that now makes it almost impossible for anyone to drink from or even bathe in natural waters. All this in the name of making a buck."

There's bald truth in her assertions, but nothing that can't be found in dozens of banal speeches on the threatened environment. Perhaps the series of sermonizing asides in her last book was meant as a final testament to Laurence's strong views as a social activist. These plain-spoken messages, unoriginal in thought and language, are certainly proof of her moral toughness. But her enduring testament will remain the rich, full world she added to the Canadian imagination before her powers as a novelist deserted her. (pp. 74, 76)

George Galt, "Morally Bound," in Saturday Night, *Vol. 104, No. 10, October, 1989, pp. 73-4, 76)*

Morton Ritts

A young Toronto journalist once met Margaret Laurence leaving one of that city's trendiest hairdressers. Flustered by her unexpected meeting with the famous Canadian writer, the journalist blurted out that she admired her work. To which Laurence replied: "Gee, kid, it's good to hear that. Back where I come from, they call me the whore of Lakefield." That anecdote—referring to Laurence's painful censorship battles over her books in her adopted home town near Peterborough, Ont.—sums up the qualities of feisty courage, patient endurance and earthy wit that marked both the author and such memorable fictional creations as Hagar Shipley in **The Stone Angel** (1964) and Morag Gunn in **The Diviners** (1974). Indeed, during a 30-year writing career that included novels, short-story collections and children's books set in Africa and in Canada, Laurence—who died of cancer in 1987 at the age of 60—helped redraw the map of Canadian literature.

But the rich complexity that typifies Laurence's best fiction is largely missing in her posthumously published memoir, **Dance on the Earth.** The book is a nobly inspired effort to set down the author's "feelings about mothers and about [her] own life views" on issues ranging from politics to feminism and the environment. Yet it is also, at times, preachy, mawkishly poetic and unforthcoming. . . .

Laurence's description of her 22-year marriage is more protective than revealing, and Jack Laurence is a shadowy figure at best. More satisfying is the author's account of her father, Robert Harrison Wemyss, a gentle, highly respected lawyer in the small Prairie town of Neepawa, Man., where Laurence grew up.

That setting provided much of the material for the five "Manawaka" novels that are the foundation of her international reputation. Although her father died when she was 8, Laurence's memories of him are fond and clear. "He was by nature a builder, not destroyer," she writes, though he was scarred by his experiences in the First World War in ways he could never talk about. That war— and the tragic sacrifice of innocent young men—provokes Laurence to rage against a creaking patriarchy of "the old statesmen, the old politicians, the old military men, who talk of 'megadeaths' and 'acceptable losses.' "

Few readers will have difficulty endorsing Laurence's attacks on war, the nuclear arms race, despoilers of the environment and "torturers . . . and purveyors of brutality and racism" everywhere. But most have heard that and similar pronouncements from others. Laurence's great gift was for fiction. The Bible and her Scots background attuned her to the music of speech and the allusive power of images. The deep core of humanity that runs through all her work is also part of her uniqueness. But after the publication of **The Diviners** in 1974, Laurence's fictional voice fell silent except for a few children's books. She became active in social causes and was the recipient of many honors—from a second Governor General's Award to the chancellorship of Trent University.

At the outset of her memoir, Laurence says, "there were

areas I wasn't prepared even to set down." That may be one reason why **Dance on the Earth** gives few clues about the reasons for its author's post-*Diviners* silence. For revelations about that and other difficult matters, readers might have to rely on the fiction itself. Indeed, the characters there seem more real than the ones in the memoir—which may simply be another example of those ironic jests of God that Laurence understood and appreciated so well.

> *Morton Ritts, "A Diviner's Life: Margaret Laurence's Memoir Bares Her Roots," in* Maclean's Magazine, *Vol. 102, No. 43, October 23, 1989, p. 70.*

FURTHER READING

Bailey, Nancy. "Margaret Laurence, Carl Jung, and the Manawaka Women." *Studies in Canadian Literature* 2, No. 2 (Summer 1977): 306-21.
   Examines the influence of Jungian theories concerning self-individuation on Laurence's depictions of psychologically developing women.

——. "Fiction and the New Androgyne." *Atlantis: A Women's Studies Journal* 4, No. 1 (Fall 1978): 10-17.
   Maintains that Morag Gunn reaches full artistic maturation in *The Diviners* through the integration of the masculine and feminine elements of her personality.

Bennett, Donna A. "The Failures of Sisterhood in Margaret Laurence's Manawaka Novels." *Canadian Literature*, No. 93 (Summer 1982): 26-41.
   Analyzes the failure of Laurence's prairie women to establish supportive female bonds.

Birbalsingh, Frank. "Margaret Laurence's Short Stories." *World Literature Today* 56, No. 1 (Winter 1982): 30-6.
   Introduction to the themes of Laurence's short fiction with a discussion of its place within Canadian literary traditions.

Blewett, David. "The Unity of the Manawaka Cycle." *Journal of Canadian Studies* 13, No. 3 (Fall 1978): 31-9.
   Argues that characters in the Manawaka works share a metaphysical approach to the events of daily life.

Capone, Giovanna. "A Bird in the House: Margaret Laurence on Order and the Artist." In *Gaining Ground: European Critics on Canadian Literature,* edited by Robert Kroetsch and Reingard M. Nischik, pp. 161-70. Edmonton: NeWest Press, 1985.
   Explores themes present in Laurence's short story collection.

Demetrakopoulos, Stephanie A. "Laurence's Fiction: A Re-visioning of Feminine Archetypes." *Canadian Literature,* No. 93 (Summer 1982): 42-57.
   Interprets the Manawaka women as modern incarnations of such mythological figures as Aphrodite and Artemis.

Dombrowski, Theo Q. "Who Is This You?: Margaret Lau-

rence and Identity." *University of Windsor Review* XII, No. 1 (Fall-Winter 1977): 21-38.
   Posits that Laurence's fiction displays an "increasingly articulated and coherent view of the nature of consciousness and identity."

Forman, Denise, and Parameswaran, Uma. "Echoes and Refrains in the Canadian Novels of Margaret Laurence." *The Centennial Review* XVI, No. 3 (Summer 1972): 233-53.
   Analyzes characteristics common to the protagonists of Laurence's first three Manawaka novels and concludes that the novelist presents a unified vision of the "feminine mindscape."

Gunnars, Kristjana, ed. *Crossing the River: Essays in Honour of Margaret Laurence.* Winnepeg: Turnstone Press, 1988, 213 p.
   A *festschrift* anthology of criticism organized shortly after Laurence's death.

Hales, Leslie-Ann. "Spiritual Longing in Laurence's Manawaka Women." *English Studies in Canada* XI, No. 1 (March 1985): 82-90.
   Investigation of the fragile religious faith evidenced in Laurence's characters and by the novelist herself in various interviews.

Johnston, Eleanor. "The Quest of *The Diviners.*" *Mosaic* XI, No. 3 (Spring 1978): 107-17.
   Discusses Laurence's repeated use of the metaphor of psychological divination.

Kearns, Judy. "Rachel and Social Determinism: A Feminist Reading of *A Jest of God.*" *Journal of Canadian Fiction,* No. 27 (1980): 101-23.
   Considers the subtext of *A Jest of God* as an exploration and rejection of sexist social conventions.

Keith, W. J. "Margaret Laurence's *The Diviners:* The Problems of Close Reading." *Journal of Canadian Studies* 23, No. 3 (Fall 1988): 102-16.
   Contends that careful readers of Laurence's last novel will discover flaws related to the author's ambitious attempt to simultaneously chronicle a writer's development and tie together narrative threads from other Manawaka works.

Labonte, Ronald N. "Disclosing and Touching: Reevaluating the Manawaka World." *Journal of Canadian Fiction,* No. 27 (1980): 167-82.
   Examination of critical reactions to Laurence's works, concluding that her oeuvre is not high art, but it can be valued for the psychic catharsis it provides.

Laurence, Margaret. "Ten Years' Sentences." In *The Sixties: Canadian Writers and Writing of the Decade,* edited by George Woodcock, pp. 10-16. Vancouver: University of British Columbia Press, 1969.
   Laurence analyzes her personal and artistic development during the pivotal decade in which she established her literary reputation.

——. "Ivory Tower or Grassroots?: The Novelist as Socio-Political Being." In *A Political Art: Essays in Honour of George Woodcock,* edited by William H. New, pp. 15-25. Vancouver: University of British Columbia Press, 1978.
   Laurence discusses the artist's duty to incorporate contemporary social concerns into one's work while avoiding didacticism.

————. "My Final Hour." *Canadian Literature*, No. 100 (Spring 1984): 187-97.

Reprint of Laurence's 1983 address to the Trent University Philosophy Society. The author outlines her political, spiritual, and literary opinions and accomplishments.

New, William H, ed. *Margaret Laurence: The Writer and Her Critics.* Toronto: McGraw-Hill Ryerson, 1977, 224 p.

Anthology of critical essays about and interviews with Laurence.

Osachoff, Margaret. "Colonialism in the Fiction of Margaret Laurence." *Southern Review* (University of Adelaide, South Australia) XII, No. 3 (1980): 222-38.

Probes Laurence's fictional examination of "the psychological damage that imperialism and the colonial spirit has left behind" in Africa and Canada.

Pesando, Frank. "In a Nameless Land: The Use of Apocalyptic Mythology in the Writings of Margaret Laurence." *Journal of Canadian Fiction* 2, No. 1 (Winter 1973): 53-8.

Links images of natural predation, suffering, and death in Laurence's African fiction to parellel visions in her Canadian works.

Rocard, Marcienne. "The Dispossession Theme in Margaret Laurence's *The Diviners*." *World Literature Written in English* 21, No. 1 (Spring 1982): 109-14.

Traces the leitmotif of alienation and repatriation throughout the last Manawaka novel.

Rooke, Constance. "A Feminist Reading of *The Stone Angel*." *Canadian Literature*, No. 93 (Summer 1982): 26-41.

Declares that the subtext of *The Stone Angel* justifies Hagar's self-defeating pride as a reasonable psychological response to a prefeminist, patriarchal society.

Wainwright, J. A. "You Have To Go Home Again: Art and Life in *The Diviners*." *World Literature Written in English* 20, No. 2 (Autumn 1981): 292-311.

Explores the implicit and explicit connections between Morag Gunn's personal experiences and her compulsion to create.

Woodcock, George. "The Human Elements: Margaret Laurence's Fiction." In his *The World of Canadian Writing*. Seattle: University of Washington Press, 1980, 306 p.

An introduction to Laurence's work in which Woodcock asserts that, in terms of perception and breadth of understanding, Laurence is Canada's equivalent of Leo Tolstoy.

————, ed. *A Place to Stand on: Essays by and about Margaret Laurence.* Edmonton: NeWest Press, 1983, 301 p.

Collection of analytical essays written by the novelist and major critics.

Howard Frank Mosher

19??-

American novelist and short story writer.

Mosher's novels and short stories are set in the fictional county of Kingdom, which is based on his birthplace in rural, northern Vermont. His colorful, folkloristic protagonists are significantly influenced by the rugged environment in which they live. Stoic and quietly accepting of life's adversities, their dispositions are analogous to their natural surroundings. Mosher infuses his works with factual sketches of Vermont history, detailed imagery, and authentic rendering of Vermont dialect and landscape. In a review of his first novel, *Disappearances,* Thomas LeClair observed: "[Mosher] knows how to mix comedy with moving remembrance, suspense with local lore, the authentic past with the tourist present."

Disappearances is a nostalgic homage to fatherhood. Narrated as a series of flashbacks by "Wild Bill" Bonhomme, the book loosely revolves around a three-day bootlegging excursion he undertakes with his father, "Quebec Bill," during the Depression. A resourceful and cheerful jack-of-all-trades, Quebec Bill assumes the mythical qualities of a folk hero in the admiring eyes of his adolescent son, who nonetheless relates the story pragmatically forty years later. Many critics commended the work's blend of folklore and realism, maintaining that Mosher was lamenting a disappearing American lifestyle in an optimistic manner. His next novel, *Marie Blythe,* ostensibly offers a detailed family history of a French-Canadian family. Soon after they move to Vermont, both parents die, and their eight-year-old daughter, Marie, is raised by gypsies. At fourteen, she is raped and bears a stillborn child. The rest of the work concentrates on Marie's subsequent relationships with men, her travels through Vermont, and her many hardships. Ever the survivor, Marie remains optimistic despite her adversities, epitomizing the staunch New England spirit of Mosher's protagonists.

Mosher's next novel, *A Stranger in the Kingdom,* examines the primitive fears of "civilized" society and illuminates the motivation behind human cruelty and prejudice. Mosher again employs an adolescent narrator, this time drawing parallels between the youth's coming of age and the changes and concerns that irrevocably alter life in Kingdom County during the turbulent summer of 1952. While the village has a mélange of eccentric citizens, Kingdom County is generally a peaceful, wholesome place where "high school soccer is the most violent activity." Thirteen-year-old Jim Kinneson, the son of the editor of the town's weekly newspaper, lives a life reminiscent of Mark Twain's Huckleberry Finn. When a black minister named Walt Andrews and his family arrive in this French-Canadian town, they are met with overwhelming intolerance and bigotry. Jim, however, befriends the minister's son. Several days after they bring an impoverished, wayward girl to the parsonage for refuge, she is shot to death with a bullet from Andrews' pistol, and prejudice and circumstantial evidence lead authorities to identify the minister as the prime suspect. Jeffrey A. Frank asserted:

"Mosher is clearly smitten by the complexities, appealing and otherwise, of small-town life, and it is one of the novel's virtues that he conveys these with subtlety and compassion."

The short stories in Mosher's acclaimed collection *Where the Rivers Flow North* are also set in northern Vermont, and frequently explore tragicomic elements of obsession. For example, in "Kingdom County Come," Henry Coville, a recurring character in Mosher's fiction, attempts to commit suicide in an absurdly methodical way that generates both sadness and personal pride. The book's title novella revolves around Noël Lord, a logger adamantly opposed to development, who doggedly attempts to travel to Oregon with his companion, an Indian ex-prostitute named Bangor, in search of virgin forests. Reviewers lauded the dynamic characterizations in the volume, as well as Mosher's detailed descriptions of nature.

PRINCIPAL WORKS

NOVELS

Disappearances   1977
Marie Blythe   1983
A Stranger in the Kingdom   1989

SHORT FICTION COLLECTIONS

Where the Rivers Flow North   1978

Kirkus Reviews

Never mix, never worry-it applies to genres too, and this coming-of-agerama *cum* folk-tall-tale *cum* symbolic fantasy *cum* family chronicle, [*Disappearances* by Howard Frank Mosher], though written throughout with a likable, evenhanded calm, isn't quite talented enough to bridge the gaps in credibility, time frame, and momentum. But talented it is, especially when narrator Bill Bonhomme (inappropriately called "Wild Bill" by his father, "Quebec Bill") concentrates on the bootlegging, train-hijacking, canoe-sinking family adventures that were the highlight of his Depression-era youth in Kingdom County, Vermont—near the Canadian border and nothing much else. "I always try not to romanticize him," Bill says of his relentlessly optimistic and resourceful father ("Ain't it all wonderful, Wild Bill?")—and promptly proceeds to show Quebec Bill in Paul-Bunyanesque, roguish action: cajoling brother-in-law Henry and young Bill into doomed confrontations with cutthroats, swilling monks, decapitated Mounties, and Texas longhorns; swimming, fiddling, lying, fleeing, and, finally, dying—all with staggering proficiency or endurance. The gaps arise when bloody, violent deaths are rolled right into the cheer—and when the already desultory telling is interrupted for clan history (back to the picaresque 18th century) or for a jarring flash-forward to 1967, when Wild Bill's son Henry crosses the border to evade the draft ("Is Henry rejecting his country or is his country rejecting him?"). Worst of all, the rather murky theme of sons haunted by disappearing fathers culminates in a final, cymbalic, utterly unintegratable tableau: Quebec Bill's mortal enemy, the unkillable fiend Carcajou, turns out to be Q. Bill's own long-lost father. Timber! . . . What almost triumphs over these serious overreachings, however, is the detailed, cold-river sense of place, the woodsy chunks of character (like Bill's unshakable, Greek-teaching aunt), and the unforced exuberance when Quebec Bill, Henry, Wild Bill, and their demolished white Cadillac really get going.

> *A review of "Disappearances," in* Kirkus Reviews, *Vol. XLV, No. 19, October 1, 1977, p. 1064.*

Thomas LeClair

Disappearances by Howard Frank Mosher is a rare celebration of an endangered species, the good father. "Wild Bill" Bonhomme, a Huck Finn boy now a Faulknerian lawyer, recalls the real wild Bill, his father "Quebec Bill," a 1930's Vermont jack of all trades, innocent outlaw, and eternal optimist. Centering on the Bonhommes' three-day adventure smuggling Canadian liquor into Vermont, the novel is also an unsentimental initiation and a meditation on the disappearance of this marvelous father, the family whose traditions he embodied, and a way of life that created mythic fathers. (pp. 796-97)

Mosher [also] remembers the other Vermonters—the Canuck adventurers, farmers, and monks who lived in cold woods with a crazy joy. Mosher also knows how to mix comedy with moving remembrance, suspense with local lore, the authentic past with the tourist present. The Bonhommes were for a time Goodmans; the translation reminds us what they are. (p. 797)

> *Thomas LeClair, in a review of "Disappearances," in* Commonweal, *Vol. CIV, No. 25, December 9, 1977, pp. 796-97.*

Frances Taliaferro

[*Disappearances*] is a vigorous and peculiar novel. The setting is Kingdom County in northern Vermont, as close to Canada as possible; the year is 1932. Insofar as the plot can be described, it relates the bootlegging adventures of Quebec Bill Bonhomme and his young son Wild Bill as they attempt to run a heroic amount of whisky across the border. The tales are tall; the cast of characters is numerous and eccentric. Aunt Cordelia, ninety years old and six feet tall, is both schoolteacher and sibyl; at moments of general passion she is likely to read aloud from *Urne Burriall,* and she can shoot a musket as straight as she quotes Milton. Carcajou, the villain, master of disguises and reappearances, is a figure of chaos and old night. . . . There are also lesser albinos, bootlegging monks, fur-trapping voyageurs, a beloved Cadillac called White Lightning, a horny, anorexic maiden whom Wild Bill mistakes for the Tooth Fairy, and a whole old people's home full of hermaphrodites and pawky senior citizens. This book will inevitably be described as rollicking, boisterous, sprawling, and lusty. It is all of these at times, and it is highly entertaining as long as Carcajou is the antagonist and whisky is the issue. Mosher seems to be after bigger game, however; *Disappearances* has some philosophical pretensions as it slips in and out of past and future, fusing generations and identities. Allegorical thoughts spring to mind: is this book simply a good read, or is it a crypto-Bicentennial novel that celebrates the wonders of a disappearing America? Mosher leaves us uncertain and uncomfortable. (pp. 86-7)

> *Frances Taliaferro, in a review of "Disappearances," in* Harper's, *Vol. 256, No. 1532, January, 1978, pp. 86-7.*

Sheldon Frank

Howard Frank Mosher's first novel, *Disappearances,* is an annoying mixture of genres—a puzzling combination of family saga, tall tale and nature reverie focused on the coming of age of a 14-year-old, Vermont-raised French-Canadian. It is a novel that just can't seem to decide what it is and what it is trying to say. Now novels don't have to be just one thing—in fact, the combination of disparate genres can often produce the most intoxicating fictions—but the abrupt changes in tone and direction that riddle *Disappearances* leave the reader far more befuddled than entranced.

Set in the far northern part of Vermont, near the Canadian border, a desolate land that even the Indians ignored, the novel is largely the story of a wild, passionate, lackadaisical French-Canadian farmer, fiddler and ex-whisky smuggler; it is told by his not-very-wild son, "Wild Bill" Bonhomme. The heart of the novel takes place in 1932, when father, son, brother-in-law and hired hand go on a completely disastrous, often quite brutal, often quite maniacal smuggling run. It is a last-ditch effort by the ne'er-do-well father that ends as a rite of passage for his teen-age son.

Mosher's prose is competent at best, with a persistent tendency to stiffness. The early parts of the novel are rather slow going, and while the tall-tale smuggling catastrophe has a number of nicely lunatic moments, . . . the reader's attention is continually deflected by the odd snatches of family history, awkwardly juxtaposed flashbacks and flash-forwards, and the arbitrary and unnecessary coincidences that Mosher plops into his narrative. A very peculiar book that disappeared from this reader's memory in a matter of hours.

> *Sheldon Frank, "A Mix of Tall Tales," in* The New York Times Book Review, *February 5, 1978, p. 22.*

Kirkus Reviews

The *Saturday Evening Post*—at its best—would have been a snug crib for Mosher's short fiction; the stories [in *Where the Rivers Flow North*] have a quiet confidence, uncomplex plot, and are set in a beautiful and strange place: Kingdom County, rural upper Vermont. The characters are pithy and determined. Life is lovely and very, very hard. The title novella fleshes out these felicities.

Noël Lord, an ex-logger now in his seventies, shares camp upstream with Bangor, his Indian "housekeeper," also old. The land they're on was leased to Noël's father, himself a legendary logger, but now a dam will be built that will flood them out. The dam-builders offer him $5,000, a lot of jack for 1927, but Noël holds out instead for a stand of pines along the mountainside: he wants—and gets—*them.* He means to cut them down, sell the wood, and use the receipts to take himself and Bangor out to Oregon, where lumbering (so says a magazine he's got) still flourishes in the old style. It doesn't work out, which you instinctively know from the start. But Mosher wraps you so easily into the cranky dignity of these two old heroes that their tenacity and orneriness and foolishness seem natural as plant life. The descriptions, the feel, of the land and water and trees all around is superb; the book appears now and then to be written on bark, captivatingly close to its natural setting. Plain and stately storytelling—eye-poppingly vivid and deeply attractive. (pp. 967-68)

> A review of "Where the Rivers Flow North," in Kirkus Reviews, *Vol. XLVI, No. 17, September 1, 1978, pp. 967-68.*

Publishers Weekly

Mosher's first novel, *Disappearances,* received high praise, and this collection of short fiction—six stories and a novella—shows that this is no flash-in-the-pan writer. . . . [In *Where the Rivers Flow North,* he] has made Jay Peak country, that stark, roughly beautiful bit of Vermont that touches the Canadian border, his own—the landscape, the people. Existence there is uncertain, circumscribed, hard. Lives are shaped by the land, the seasons, solitude, the mixture of French-Canadian, Indian, Yankee temperaments. In the short tales we meet Alabama Jones, who sings with her brother's traveling show; Burl, now near death, whose father gave her away to care for another man's 13 children; Eben, whose cousins come in hunting season; a tall dying man who raised and now has lost a peacock. Kingdom County and the history of one of its families are explored in the novella, *Where the Rivers Flow North,* about Noël Lord, the last of the line, the holdout against progress. Mosher captures the place and the people in these strong, elemental, finely worked fictions that are New England through and through, from snows to mud seasons, to rushing waters and flaming leaves.

> A review of "Where the Rivers Flow North," in Publishers Weekly, *Vol. 214, No. 13, September 25, 1978, p. 128.*

Geoffrey Wolff

This fiction writer has come out of nowhere—Vermont's Northeast Kingdom, his home and his subject. Howard Mosher's novel *Disappearances* was published a year ago; it evoked this primitive region he calls Kingdom County, where most are poor and many are luckless, where seasons change with brutal speed and the circumstances of life shift glacially.

Disappearances, nominally about running liquor across the Canadian border of this region, is told in the mid-

1970s but set during Prohibition and the Depression. Typically out of sync with the rest of America, Kingdom County enjoyed an exuberant moment of opportunity during the Depression (because of Prohibition), and Mosher's prose has more of celebration than gloom about it. Nevertheless, the narrator of *Disappearances* meditates on the central question of this second book of fiction (the title novella and six stories): "Kingdom County—it remains a wonder to me that it was settled under any conditions."

Mosher's second book advances past the limits of his first good novel, and the novella is lovingly crafted, economical with scenes but lavish with a sense of lives being lived. Like the stories, and like *Disappearances, Where the Rivers Flow North* is about the consequences of climate and geography on people with the imagination to leave Kingdom County (but without either the means or the desire), and people who have bent to Kingdom County's implacable, bleak givens.

Mosher writes about the place with loving attention; but he knows how mean it is. As in *Disappearances,* he writes about its unlikely exploration and settlement (who would want to see more of it, having seen a little?), about its terrible nature. . . . (p. 85)

The novella [*Where the Rivers Flow North*] tells of a logger, Noël, connected by family with Kingdom County for many generations, proud, willful, skilled, huge. To the people sitting around the town common swapping stories as night falls, feeding the legends and keeping the history going, Noël "became in their talk a kind of apotheosis of himself and his family, already in his own lifetime aggrandized into something more than an elderly ex-riverman who had outlived his profession."

This passage achieves a distance (short of condescension) from Noël's realities, and imitates the enhancing power of stories. In truth, Noël and his companion, the Indian ex-whore Bangor, *are* bigger and better, fuller of the juices of life, than characters I have encountered in any other recent American fictions. They are loved relentlessly by their creator, but Mosher knows that his love is not enough to provoke our love, so he gives them a wonderful story to live. It is a story about two people trying to horsetrade their way to the virgin timber of Oregon, fighting the power company, hunting a panther, cutting down a huge stand of white pines, fighting with each other, prevailing almost to the end, making their presence felt. To read about Bangor and Noël is to know someone has been here, forever.

This novella gathers Mosher's preoccupations from his looser first novel and his six stories, and knits them tight. He is obsessed with obsessions, especially when they achieve harmony between comic extravagance and grandeur of intensity. In the story **"High Water,"** a wife tells of her husband's almost insane determination to race his car at a track in Canada, despite awful rain, a broken bridge and a closed racetrack. The couple, accompanied by her father, who loves bad fortune, undertake an odyssey that resembles in its assortments of singlemindedness the burial journey in Faulkner's *As I Lay Dying.* In **"Burl,"** told by a woman cursed with a man's name by her father, she will not ease up on her hatred of her father and brothers: "It has been a comfort to me in hard times to think of them roasting on Satan's spit in Hell."

The dominant quality of Mosher's fictions is an almost aggressive acceptance of what is. This can include death, which quickly takes Burl's two husbands; she turns bitter, and then feels the bitterness lift: "Then I saw, or thought I saw, that there was nothing more life could do to me because there was nothing more I cared for." Or it can show the would-be racer staring at his ruined car sunk beneath many feet of muddy, roaring water, holding a chain to haul it out and begin again. Or it can be the wife in **"The Peacock,"** about to be widowed, telling her husband to stop talking about a job next year in the local mill: " 'You wouldn't be able to stand it.' There was no rancor in her remark. It was simply true." Or it can be Henry Coville (who appears in *Disappearances,* and in the novella), about to kill himself in the best of the stories, **"Kingdom County Come,"** a kind of coda to Hemingway's "Big Two-Hearted River."

Here, as in Hemingway's best piece of fiction, a man travels alone through barren land, and fishes a river, and faces a treacherous bog. Like Hemingway's hero, Mosher's has been hurt in World War I. Hemingway's hero is young, and lives to fish the swamp. Coville is at the end of everything, yet there is more sense of discovery in Mosher's story. Coville enters a deserted beaver lodge to finish a bottle of whiskey, and cut his wrist. He has carefully sunk his canoe. He is old, has lost one lung in the war; now the other one is going. "Nothing surprised Coville now and he was puzzled by nothing. He understood that everything that had happened had helped prepare him for this time in this place."

The people of these fictions achieve such nobility of acceptance by the exercise of meticulous rituals. Hemingway would have understood these people, and so would have Faulkner. Here the survival of the race depends on the fitness and regularity of acts. Coville dresses his last day on earth "with the concentration of a man who had learned as a boy of twelve to concern himself with small things such as properly lacing his boots in the early morning before going to the woods." In the story **"First Snow,"** a brother turns against his brother for encouraging friends to shoot a doe, when there is no season on does, and where the hunters were not welcome to hunt. This was the violation of rite, and the outraged brother calls the game warden to assert his "right to own private property and obey the law on it."

Everything counts, every small act: "No matter how fatigued he was Noël always washed after a day in the woods." As hardship temporarily wears him down, he begins to let himself go, and then finds a dream to obsess himself with, and brutal work to do. He recovers his balance; and this is signaled by the resumption of a simple ritual: "He began to shave every morning as he had never neglected to do when running a crew."

I wish I could suggest all of the wonderful properties of this novella. Many times in the reviews I write for this magazine I have asked readers, with implicit urgency, to share with me what I have just experienced. Usually I trust my characterization of a book to leave a sense of it full enough to suggest to you whether you wish to share it. On behalf of this novella, I want to do more. I want you to know that there is a love story—about a balding, gumless ex-whore and a logger who wears a hook where his hand should be—that I am afraid to crush in summary.

I want you to know that the novella is at once noble and savagely comic, and so tightly constructed that I cannot pick at this or that thread without unweaving the whole thing.

Where the Rivers Flow North deepens Mosher's exploration of stoicism ("Your father is what he is"), and the complicated ways people endure what seems to be misery. Bangor loves to fish, and never catches fish: "Luckless and ebullient, she fished on into the rainy afternoon." She loves misfortune, too, because it can be depended upon. "So long as all was wrong with the world, Bangor was content." For all this, she is joyful beyond words, or almost beyond words. She wears a red dress when she kills herself, and she buries Noël as rain turns to snow, and does it the right way, carefully, without resentment, having watched him fight death unto death, loving him for that, and glad to have lived for a time. On behalf of this novella, just this once, let me dust off the hack reviewer's tag line: Please read it. (pp. 85-6)

> *Geoffrey Wolff, "Kingdom County Has Come: Welcome," in* New Times, *Vol. II, No. 12, December 11, 1978, pp. 85-6.*

Dean Flower

Howard Frank Mosher tells stories of Vermonters up near the Canadian line, where he lives, and writes with such authority as to suggest he's recording contemporary history. The first sketch in . . . [the short story collection *Where the Rivers Flow North*] describes a girl hitch-hiking who turns out to be a hillbilly singer from Alabama. The issue is whether her magnetism will outpull the beautiful mountains, trees, home. It doesn't. Another story concerns a boy whose passion to race his '49 Chevy leads him to heroic battle against every obstacle of man and nature. Mosher seems to be . . . celebrating the character of our contemporaries who are closer to nature and the knowledge of survival than we are. Wallace Stegner is quoted on the dust jacket in praise of Mosher's voice: "it's new—nobody ever did these people or this country before." The implication is misleading, however; the material isn't new. As one reads into the collection it becomes clear that the references to recent things—like black bikinis and '49 Chevys—have quietly disappeared and we find ourselves amongst bootleggers, loggers, truck drivers and lumberjacks during the drought of 1927. Nor is that year very important: these are changeless woods, the only time is seasonal, and death becomes natural transformation.

Mosher's characters are not really new either: they hark back through Faulkner's Ike McCaslin to Thoreau's coarse Indians and voyageurs in *The Maine Woods* and to Cooper's Leatherstocking ruffian. These old Vermonters are engaged in the most elemental and symbolic actions: proving courage in nature, rejecting the town laws, defying the whole Power Company and its hydroelectric dam, spurning every modern device, preserving the sacred laws of hunting and woodsmanship. Mosher's craft is to tell these familiar stories as if they were not romantic fables at all but purely episodes of local history. They are scrupulously made, clean of affectation as newly-planed boards, and subtly mortised and tenoned. Occasionally, through the restraint and humor, we can hear a romanticizing, Faulknerian voice:

The dawn after the day the ice went out of the pond, men and women came ten and fifteen and twenty miles in mud up to the hubs of their wagon wheels to stand in freezing rain or sleet or sugar snow on the bluff at the end of the country road, waiting in pearly-gray tableau for the terrific roar high in the notch signifying that the gate in the driving dam had been raised. . . . A wall of water would appear between the cliffs, cresting over the spring white water, followed closely by thousands of fifty-two-foot logs hurtling down out of the dawn fog.

Mosher's stories get their inspiration not from contemporary Vermont but from our all-too-favorite myths about American Adams, frontier simplicities, and renunciatory virtues. With that fine eye for landscape and an excellent ear for the dialects he knows, Mosher should stop looking backward and give his attention to contemporary Vermont. (pp. 297-98)

> *Dean Flower, "Picking up the Pieces," in* The Hudson Review, *Vol. XXXII, No. 2, Summer, 1979, pp. 293-307.*

Publishers Weekly

[*Marie Blythe*], from the author of *Disappearances* and *Where the Rivers Flow North* is the rich saga of a French-Canadian woman who as a child comes to live in northern Vermont in 1899. Soon after her family settles at Hell's Gate, a prosperous village-factory enclave owned by Abraham Benedict, her father is killed in an accident and her mother dies of tuberculosis. Marie is taken in by gypsies (stonecutters by trade) and raised by them for a time. Eventually a place is arranged for her in the Benedict household. It is here that she serves her apprenticeship and bears a child at 14 to the Benedicts' son. Mosher follows Marie, a survivor, to logging camps and hospitals and schoolrooms and explores her relationships with men she loves and those she does not. His way with the north and the people who settle there is extraordinary, his tale of Marie and the Benedicts full of unusual twists and turns. A candidate for bestsellerdom.

> *A review of "Marie Blythe," in* Publishers Weekly, *Vol. 224, No. 9, August 26, 1983, p. 369.*

Pat Goodfellow

Marie, a young French-Canadian orphan, lives in New England at the turn of the century, in a wilderness and a time when survival is all. In [Howard Frank Mosher's *Marie Blythe*], a novel full of passion, vivid historical and natural detail, incident and irony, we follow the gypsy Marie, not only a survivor, but almost a life force. She prevails over sickness, the deaths of loved ones, betrayal, and a myriad of natural and human-engineered hardships. The writing is spare yet evocative of the textures of nature and the everyday life of the period; the characterization is varied, strong, and sure; the narrative drive never falters. *Marie Blythe* should find a home in every fiction collection, however small.

> *Pat Goodfellow, in a review of "Marie Blythe,"*

in Library Journal, *Vol. 108, No. 15, September 1, 1983, p. 1721.*

Bruce Allen

Howard Frank Mosher isn't one of your standard, brand-name American writers. Yet his 1977 first novel, *Disappearances,* compares favorably with the best ones of recent years.

In that book, Mosher told of a fractious French-Canadian family whose members vigorously resisted being tamed by contact with the 20th century. And he created the fictional territory of Kingdom County, a mostly wilderness area of northern Vermont near the Canadian border. This is a territory developed by way of fur trapping, logging, and—in its headiest day—bootlegging. *Disappearances* was fueled by what seemed boundless comic energy and spilled over with outrageous and wonderful tall tales, many of them worthy of Mark Twain.

A second book, *Where the Rivers Flow North* (1978), collected half a dozen nondescript short stories that appeared to be basically outtakes from Mosher's novel. Already it was evident he'd be revisiting and reexamining Kingdom County and its inhabitants in approximately the same way William Faulkner treated his invention, Yoknapatawpha County in Mississippi.

More important, the second book included the title novella—a rich regional tragicomedy about the relationships and the inevitable fates of an aging logger and his Indian housekeeper—hardy and stoical anachronisms alike. This is one of the best short novels of our time, a brilliantly detailed chunk of Americana that has the narrative density and emotional force of ballad or myth.

Now comes *Marie Blythe,* a big novel also set mainly in Mosher's Kingdom County. The story encompasses numerous people's lives and spans the quarter century from 1899 to 1925—and, I regret to report, it seems to go on forever.

At the outset, several French-Canadian families fleeing a smallpox epidemic travel south to work and live in Hell's Gate, a township owned and overseen by Capt. Abraham Benedict. His woodworking factory supplies office furniture to purchasers throughout the United States. The focal character is eight-year-old Marie Blair, who will soon be orphaned. She is menaced by various catastrophes, and left to shift heroically for herself.

To encapsulate: After the deaths of her parents, Marie spends two years on the road. She travels with a band of gypsies (one of whom renames her "Marie Blythe"), works as a chimney sweep, manages a decrepit trained bear, and (dressed as a boy) wrestles all comers. Returning to Hell's Gate, she becomes the Benedicts' housemaid and the pre-adolescent lover of young master Abie Benedict, an intemperate rakehell with a frightening streak of irrational cruelty in him.

Marie's illegitimate baby is born dead, in a swamp; she leaves again, tramps around northern New England for several years doing odd jobs and seeing the successive men in her life taken away by savage twists of fate. Stricken with illness, she eventually becomes a nurse. Finally learning to read and write, she next becomes the village school-teacher (back at Hell's Gate again).

Following his father's death, Abie, now a war hero, mismanages the township into bankruptcy and sells off its property at auction. Marie comes upon the late Captain Benedict's diaries and learns a secret that leads her to a final confrontation with Abie—just as an enormous fire (which has been repeatedly foreshadowed, almost since the novel's beginning) reduces Hell's Gate to ashes.

It is undoubtedly unkind to say so, but all I could think of during those climactic pages when Marie was racing through the forest alongside terrified minks and muskrats was the forest fire in Walt Disney's *Bambi.*

I trudged through this overcrowded story with gathering exhaustion and disbelief, looking for things to admire. There are just a few: nicely detailed pictures of men and women at work (Mosher has no peer at describing exactly how outdoor jobs of all kinds are done); background stories about many of the novel's secondary and peripheral characters—often more interesting than the main action; a vivid account of 10-year-old Marie stalking and killing a deer, filled with superb images of scene and weather and telling evidence of her natural instincts.

I could go on about the facile dramatic situations, impossible coincidences, hairbreadth escapes, and operatic emotions that possess this novel's people. But there's little point in judging this novel by standards that, clearly, don't apply to it. It's smooth and entertaining while you're reading it, but its characters have no depth, and its narrative no resonance. For all the wealth of period and local detail, it feels lightweight.

Why, then, is this novel of interest at all? Because Howard Frank Mosher is, I'd argue. And because it's always worth observing what a really first-rate writer is attempting. . . . If I thought he'd used up a storehouse of valuable material on this very unworthy conception, I'd be worried about Mosher's future. But I see no signs that his imagination is running dry. Perhaps if we'd all paid more attention to *Disappearances* and *Where the Rivers Flow North,* they'd have been followed by a book worthy to stand beside them, Perhaps *Marie Blythe* will earn a bundle and finance the writing of future novels comparable to Mosher's first one. I surely hope so.

Bruce Allen, "Read 'Marie Blythe,' But Only to Remember Its Author," in The Christian Science Monitor, *January 9, 1984, p. 20.*

Jeff Danziger

[Howard Frank Mosher's novel *A Stranger in the Kingdom* is a saga of] small-town New England life; young men coming to terms with their rural upbringing; the falling apart of an agrarian society; and the influence of outside elements. To these, Mosher has added racial violence.

His novel is set in the northeast corner of Vermont, not exactly the United States and not exactly Canada, a place dubbed "the Northeast Kingdom" by the state's legendary Sen. George Aiken, a place Mosher has written of before in *Disappearances* and *Where the Rivers Flow North.* This story is inspired loosely (if such a thing is possible)

by an incident of racial cohabitation in the town of Irasburg, Vt., back in the '60s, which revealed a streak of violence and baseless intolerance in that most unlikely of places.

Mosher likes to weave elements of Vermont history into his work, even if he has to rearrange a decade or two to make them fit. In this one he uses, among other things, the still-unsolved murder of Orville Gibson, a Newbury, Vt., farmer, so despised by his townsmen that no witnesses would come forward. Mosher may be the best writer on the French-Canadian culture (some would call it a subculture) in Vermont.

The young narrator's father owns the local newspaper and his older brother is a rough-hewn country lawyer. There is a good deal of bucolic philosophizing that goes on, which, after living 20 years, more or less, in Vermont I have never heard philosophized.

That, however, is about all that's wrong with *A Stranger in the Kingdom.* The setting . . . is endearing. This is because of Mosher's great affection for the Northeast Kingdom, a place that has gone gradually from woods to farms and back to woods again and has, says the editor's son, "remained free of significant news . . . for the past 150 years." Mosher deals frankly with the idea that prejudice results from fear of the unknown and unexpected.

The local church is assigned a new minister who turns out to be an erudite black man, a former Canadian Armed Forces chaplain, who despite his wise reticence, is drawn into conflict with the local yahoos. The conflict is intensified when a young, homeless Montreal girl arrives, answering a personal ad placed by a ne'er-do-well member of the narrator's family. The minister gives her shelter when no one else will, and at the same time gives his enemies the opportunity to arrange what looks like her murder by his hands.

Mosher has succeeded in placing an important and uncomfortable event in the state's history in a fictional setting Vermonters will recognize. They will also recognize the liberties he's taken with facts. For others, the story will still be a good one, told in a straightforward style with a plainly worded intensity characteristic of northern Vermont residents.

Jeff Danziger, "Novels Reveal New England Intensity and Alienation," in The Christian Science Monitor, *September 20, 1989, p. 13.*

Christine Watson

[In *A Stranger in the Kingdom*], the year is 1952. Small-town prejudice, especially against blacks, is an accepted if publicly bemoaned fact of life in the South—but in Kingdom County, Vermont, the townspeople pride themselves on their tolerance and their willingness to live and let live. That tolerance, and the underlying assumptions which support it, are tested to their limit in one disquieting summer. Reverend Walt Andrews, a black Presbyterian minister from Canada, comes to "the Kingdom" to take over a long-empty pulpit, all from the day he and his son Nathan arrive, they are shown in subtle and blatant ways that not all the residents of Kingdom County welcome them.

And when a young white girl is killed, and the Reverend is put on trial for her murder, the Kingdom and its residents are permanently changed.

The story of that traumatic time is told by Jim Kinneson, a thirteen-year-old boy who is initially far more interested in baseball and in tagging behind his idolized older brother than in any sort of social issues. All of that changes when he becomes friends with Nathan who, in spite of his dislike of small-town life, joins with him in playing baseball, watching a cockfight and, in an act with longer-reaching consequences, sneaking into a tent show where they encounter the terrified Claire LaRiviere.

Seventeen years old and desperate to make her way to "Holly-wood, where the movies are made," LaRiviere has come from Quebec in answer to a letter from Jim's drunken cousin, Resolved Kinneson, who has advertised for a "female woman companion." On her way, however, she becomes entangled with the proprietors of a traveling strip show, and it is while she is being forced onstage that Jim, Nathan and Charlie, Jim's brother, see her for the first time. Charlie rescues her, and she eventually takes refuge at the parsonage, where Reverend Andrews—against his better judgement, but seeing no alternative—gives her a place to stay. But it is her death, more than her short life, that will have an effect on the Kingdom; and when she is found to have been shot by a pistol belonging to the Reverend, it appears that even Charlie Kinneson's much-touted ability as a lawyer may not be enought to save him.

Mosher has done an outstanding job of story-telling here, using a narrator who is simultaneously coming of age himself and watching his hometown, neighbors, even family being irrevocably changed. Jim is not far from childhood, but tells his story with no trace of childishness, and we are drawn into a tangle of adult concerns almost before we have a chance to realize that it is not an adult who is taking us there. *A Stranger in the Kingdom* is a sensitive and beautifully-written book, and one which reminds us how shallow the veneer of civilized behavior can sometimes be. (pp. 20-1)

> Christine Watson, in a review of "A Stranger in the Kingdom," in West Coast Review of Books, *Vol. 15, No. 1, September-October, 1989, pp. 20-1.*

Jeffrey A. Frank

The "Kingdom" in the title of Howard Frank Mosher's new novel [*A Stranger in the Kingdom*] is a county in northern Vermont, and in particular a place where 13-year-old Jim Kinneson is introduced to some of the wicked ways of the world. It is 1952, the Red Sox are floundering, and it is not uncommon to find small communities where the stop signs say ARRET as well as STOP.

For Jim Kinneson, life is an American dream—or perhaps a dream of how America might have been. His father is editor of the *Monitor,* a local weekly, and older brother Charles has gone from being a star school athlete to being a defense lawyer on a winning streak. Kingdom County is described by one character as a spot "where hunting and fishing are the main sports and high school soccer is the most violent activity—even the time is an hour behind the rest of the country." The state capital, Montpelier, is commonly referred to as Most Peculiar.

Into young Jim's life come a parade of men and women who would today be described as colorful—among them an outlaw cousin; a mean-spirited sheriff; a French-Canadian girl who arrives with a traveling stripshow and the Dog Cart Man, a deaf-mute who wanders about repainting, in almost magical fashion, faded signs.

The world changes for Jim, and indeed for Kingdom County, from the day Walter Andrews, the new Presbyterian minister, comes to town. The Kingdom (as it is called by locals) prides itself on being a splendid place to live and raise a family, but in fact this proves to be so mainly for a certain class. Those with French blood have a tougher time than those of WASP descent, and the Rev. Andrews is set notably apart by the fact that he is black. Inevitably, the presence of Andrews and his son Nat (who becomes Jim's close friend) leads to developments of a tragic sort. . . .

A Stranger in the Kingdom is certainly an examination of the roots of prejudice, but even more it is an examination of a proposition stated by Jim's father: "I'll concede that a small town can be as nosy and sometimes as downright cruel as any place on the face of the earth . . . But what it all boils down to is this. Small towns can be extremely sympathetic, in a rough-hewn sort of way—if you *belong*—but the Lord help strangers who wander in needing help." Mosher is clearly smitten by the complexities, appealing and otherwise, of smalltown life, and it is one of the novel's virtues that he conveys these with subtlety and compassion.

A Stranger in the Kingdom has other fine qualities. It speaks to values most Americans cherish: tolerance, loyalty, courage, independence. And, particularly in the novel's second half, events carry the plot with lots of drama and energy.

But Mosher has difficulty sustaining the point of view of a 13-year-old, in part because the boy's language is unusually stilted, and in part because Mosher tries to have it both ways: now and then, he leaps forward in time to observe the boy's observations: "Still and all, I didn't see how she or anyone else could truly know how bad I felt and despite her assurances I was very certain, with all the certainty of my thirteen years, that I would never feel any different." The effect of this is to cheapen a literary device; where Mosher wants authority, naivete creeps into the narrative.

Finally, Mosher is simply unable to avoid something very much like nostalgia. It is easy to sympathize with the impulse; when he evokes the woods and streams, he does so in a mood close to reverence. But the sentimentality can be jarring when the events unfolding are meant to be unfolding years ago before the eyes of a boy.

Yet such keen nostalgia lets Mosher lovingly bring to life a world sadly distant from the shrinking villages and expanding malls to be found in much of modern rural America. It is obvious that he sorely misses many of the good folks and scamps who were part of his childhood; his fierce, honest embrace of the past becomes the special reward of reading *A Stranger in the Kingdom.*

Jeffrey A. Frank, "Murder in Vermont: The Secrets of Kingdom County," in Book World—The Washington Post, *October 1, 1989, p. 7.*

Lee Smith

Set in 1952 in remote northern Vermont, Howard Frank Mosher's third novel, *A Stranger in the Kingdom,* is a real mystery in the best and truest sense. The actual plot, with its familiar elements of race, sex, murder and long-held grudges, is compelling enough. But the real mystery lies, as it should, in motivation—what makes people do what they do? What pain, what secrets, can and cannot be held in the human heart?

A Stranger in the Kingdom is that rarity, both a "good read" and a fine novel. It is about deeply felt emotion, about prejudice, about the clash between the past and the present, the end of the frontier and of religious differences—all presented in a lucid, straightforward style that's a pleasure to read. (And, incidentally, nobody writes as well as Mr. Mosher does about trout fishing.)

Jim Kinneson, the novel's 13-year-old narrator, describes himself as "a daydreaming boy brought up on Robert Louis Stevenson and Mark Twain and Dad's wonderful stories of our own family's odd history." Actually he's a writer in the making, and so *A Stranger in the Kingdom* is also a fine portrait of an artist in the works.

Jim's parents read aloud to him from *The Ecclesiastical, Natural, Social, and Political History of Kingdom County,* which was written by a former slave named Pliny Templeton, who founded the Kingdom Common Academy many years earlier. This history is described as containing "whole chapters on such diverse and fascinating subjects as the wild animals and plants native to our corner of New England, the Kingdom's geological evolution and political history, and all kinds of curious legends, anecdotes . . . even a section of regional recipes like brook trout chowder and partridge pie." The same might nearly be said of Mr. Mosher's novel, which is both a suspenseful tale about the trial of a courtly black minister for the murder of a pregnant teen-age girl and, coincidentally, a compendium of lore about a little-known section of our country.

In Kingdom County, whose basic stance toward the outside world is symbolized by its refusal to leap forward into the newfangled daylight saving time, . . . a third of the farm families speak French at home. Returning to the county from a brief springtime trip with his father, Jim sketches a vivid portrait of the region's distinctive landscape:

> Heading down the mountainside toward the village of Kingdom Common, we might have been entering a much earlier part of the century as well as an earlier season. Rickety old horse-drawn hay loaders, some abandoned not many years ago, sat out in hedgerows between stony pastures. Most of the farmhouses still had faded brown Christmas wreaths hanging on their doors, a tradition meant to ameliorate the grueling dreariness of our seven-month winters, though by this time of year they seemed only to call attention to the fact that it was already late April with warm weather still weeks away. The houses themselves had long ago faded to the same toneless gray as their attached barns; and the few farmers and loggers we passed looked as old and weathered as their buildings.

A Stranger in the Kingdom is like a big easy chair, a book to sink into. Nothing minimal here, thank you. In fact, Mr. Mosher is happy to give us a page-long description of a diner or a long chunk of chapter detailing an idyllic day Jim spends with a wandering painter known as the Dog Cart Man, a section that charms and beguiles us and takes us back to those endless summer days when we, too, had all the time in the world.

Jim is struggling to grow up in a volatile household where his cantankerous newspaper editor father and his much older (and wilder) lawyer brother are prone to haggle "into the wee hours over which was the better pastoral poem, Thomas Gray's 'Elegy Written in a Country Churchyard' or Oliver Goldsmith's 'The Deserted Village' "—or whether a baseball "will truly curve." . . . They also argue about politics and the weather and the King's English. Father and brother, it seems, are "simply too much alike to be easy with each other for very long."

At the beginning of the novel, Charles Kinneson Sr. is mightily put out with Charles Jr., for reasons he explains to his younger son: "As you very well know, James, there's never been any real law and order in Kingdom County. Since your brother hung out his shingle, there's been less than ever. . . . The truth is that he goes out of his way to defend any scalawag who staggers down the road." But Charlie has his own explanation, perceiving himself as "a kind of specialized conservationist preserving a unique, threatened species." That species, the "vanishing outlaw breed," happens to include the Kinnesons' own outlaw cousin, Resolved, a cockfighter, moonshiner and poacher.

However, Charlie's talents are really put to the test when he undertakes the apparently hopeless defense of a much more respectable client, his father's friend the Rev. Walter Andrews, a black man newly arrived in town and accused of the brutal murder of the pregnant 17-year-old girl who has come to town as Resolved's mail-order housekeeper. All the characters in this unfolding drama are fully drawn, from the minister himself, a Luckies-smoking, erudite former serviceman, to his enigmatic son, Nat, to the unfortunate girl herself, the ignorant, pretty Claire LaRiviere, who wants only to be a movie star and ends up as everybody's victim. . . .

The minister's trial for murder ends in a dramatic courtroom confrontation that leaves the whole town—and especially Jim—forever changed. But one thing remains unaltered. As the novel closes, the Kinnesons are still cheerfully arguing, this time about fishing.

Lee Smith, "The Case of the Hopeless Case," in The New York Times Book Review, *October 29, 1989, p. 11.*

Grace Edwards-Yearwood

Growing up in Vermont in the summer of 1952, 13-year-old James Kinneson's major concerns [in *A Stranger in the Kingdom*] are trout fishing, baseball and whether or not he will grow an inch or two taller before school reopens in the fall.

James' village of Kingdom Gool, so remote that he and his farther, Charles, frequently drive for miles to the highest ridge in order to pick up the Boston Red Sox game on the car radio, is typical rural Americana.

The small farms and weathered barns, the kind seen on wish-you-were-here picture postcards, appear serene and stable, a reassuring contrast to the havoc unfolding in Washington where Joseph McCarthy is about the business of destroying lives and careers. The senator's mission, among the sorriest in American political history, has cast a pall over the nation, but with the exception of James' father, the crusty editor of the town's newspaper, the events touch the inhabitants of Kingdom County not at all.

Like most small and insular places, the town has its share of peculiar personalities: the dog cart man—an itinerant deaf-mute artist who appears mysteriously every summer to restore the outdoor paintings destroyed by the harsh New England winter. Under his hand, brilliant colored fish, cows and other figures spring to life on the sides of the weathered barns, the old bridge, a town monument and the wall of the quarry. When his work is finished, the artist—with his six dogs and supply cart—disappears as mysteriously as he had come.

There are peculiar names: Replacement Mari, the young girl left by the Gypsies in gratitude to Charles Kinneson's widowed grandfather; Welcome and Resolved, sons of Replacement Mari, cousins of James and Charles and an embarrassment to the entire town because of their slovenly ways and petty outlaw activities.

And there are peculiar habits, as Jimmy relates:

> My father and my older brother, Charlie, couldn't say two words to each other without getting into an argument. In and of itself, I don't suppose that their quarreling was so very unusual . . . what distinguished Kinneson-family arguments from most others is that once they got up a head of steam, Dad and Charlie refused to speak to each other directly. Instead they conducted their running verbal battles through the nearest available third person, who, more frequently than not, turned out to be me.

> Your father and brother agree to disagree, that's all, my mother told me a hundred times. 'Every family has its little peculiarities, Jimmy. Arguing is just the Kinnesons' special way of visiting with each other, I suppose.'

There are further degrees of dissension. Between families, within families, between friends, among the church members, and within the casual network of old-boy politicians that pass for power in the town.

So even the dog cart man's artistry cannot disguise the moral rot that comes to light when the Rev. Walter Andrews and his teen-aged son, Nathan, arrive in Kingdom County. They have come in response to an inquiry from the congregation that had been without a pastor for two years.

Rev. Andrews is Canadian-born, a former RCAF officer, a handsome athlete, and black.

His presence is a revelation. Young James is amazed that the minister's speech is so well modulated, "Not like Amos 'n' Andy or Rochester at all." . . .

Rev. Andrews takes over the church duties, institutes new programs and revives flagging attendance. He also begins to research the history of Pliny Templeton, a slave who had escaped to Vermont in 1860 via the Underground Railway and who founded the town's first academy.

Although Andrews fits easily into his pastoral duties, he remains a stranger in the kingdom, and to some of the inhabitants, his color and confidence are more than an irritant.

The town's false sense of serenity is further displaced when Claire LaRiviere, a girl of 17, arrives in response to an ad placed by Resolved Kinneson. The ad is misleading. Claire assumes she will be working for him as a housekeeper. Resolved—filthy, unkempt and a chronic alcoholic—has other plans for her. Horrified at the situation in which she finds herself, she flees to the parsonage. Resolved, vowing revenge, tracks her down but is challenged by Andrews. This triggers a confrontation with the town's ineffectual policeman, who demonstrates his own peculiar idea of maintaining law and order. What Resolved and the policeman cannot effect by force and intimidation soon is accomplished by rumor and innuendo, and the townspeople are divided by the scandal.

Then Claire disappears. When her horribly mutilated body is found, emotions fueled by latent bigotry boil up like lava through the cracks in a mountain. The minister immediately is charged with the murder, and Charles Kinneson Jr. steps forward to defend him.

The trial ends in a most surprising and grisly climax, but not before revealing more about the inhabitants of Kingdom County than about the accused. Jealousy, rage, hatred and hypocrisy come to light. There is legal chicanery, cover-ups and outright lies. But there also is a rock-hard integrity, a deep sense of loyalty based on enduring friendship, and a dogged willingness to find the truth in the most unlikely places.

In this fine novel, Frank Howard Mosher focuses an unerring eye on people caught in a web of fear and suspicion and develops them into whole persons capable of evoking sympathy and understanding. He avoids constructing larger-than-life heroes and avoids reducing the villains to stereotypical, bumbling bigots. Even Resolved, repulsive and evil-looking though he may be, exhibits on more than one occasion comic glimmers of humanity.

Grace Edwards-Yearwood, "Hidden Hypocrisy in a Vermont Idyll," in Los Angeles Times Book Review, *November 12, 1989, p. 9.*

Pablo Neruda

1904-1973

(Born Ricardo Eliezer Neftalí Reyes y Basoalto) Chilean poet, essayist, short story writer, editor, memoirist, and dramatist.

Widely regarded as the most important contemporary Latin American poet of the twentieth century, Neruda was noted for his innovative techniques and influential contributions to major developments in modern poetry, both in his native Chile and abroad. Due to the difficulty of accurately translating his works, only a small body of his poems have been rendered into English and often in multiple forms that prompt critical debate regarding their relative quality or accuracy. Although translations of his works have existed since the 1940s, Neruda remained relatively unknown to English-speaking readers prior to the appearance of several of his works in the early 1960s and his being honored with the Nobel Prize for Literature in 1971. Most critics arrange his *oeuvre* into different periods of development—ranging from the early, traditional works, to the spontaneous surrealist poetry of the 1930s, to the direct political poetry of his later years. Geoffrey Barraclough called Neruda "a one-man Renaissance . . . who has modified the outlook of three generations of Latin Americans. His roots are firmly planted in Chile . . . ; his appeal is to the whole continent."

Born in the agricultural region of Parral, Neruda moved with his family at a young age to Temuco, a rainy region of Chile that later figured in his poetry. Neruda commented: "Nature there went to my head like strong whiskey. I was barely ten at the time, but already a poet." He started publishing poetry at the age of fifteen under the pseudonym Pablo Neruda, and at the age of sixteen entered Chile's Instituto Pedagógico, where he majored in French. In 1921, Neruda entered a poetry competition at the annual Spring Festival in Santiago for which he received first prize. The poems in his first collection, *La cancíon de la fiesta,* which was published by the Students' Federation that had sponsored the competition, reflected the influence of symbolist poets, Walt Whitman, and Rubén Darío. In a traditional style, the poems in this collection address such topics as love and death. A similar blend of romantic and symbolist influences characterize *Crepúsculario,* a second volume that Neruda later dismissed as unsophisticated but which is often considered a classic of Chilean poetry.

At the age of twenty, Neruda began studying poetry in Santiago at the University of Chile; that same year, he established a promising reputation with *Veinte poemas de amor y una cancíon desesperada (Twenty Love Poems and a Song of Despair).* A highly popular best-seller, this work is considered to mark his transition from symbolist to surrealist poetry. Apparently chaotic and arbitrary in its enumeration of material objects and complex evocation of thought and sensation, the book features poems that convey personal emotion in mystical terms. Although these verses initially shocked critics with their colloquial language and lyrical yet explicit treatment of the joys and fail-

ures of love and sex, Neruda later asserted in his famous essay, "Sobre una poesía sin pureza" ("On a Poetry without Purity"), that poetry should be "corroded as if by an acid, by the toil of the hand, impregnated with sweat and smoke, smelling of urine and lilies." Since their initial appearance, Neruda's love poems have been variously faulted and commended for their dualistic celebration of woman as both the seductress of man and his vital link to mother earth and nature. *Veinte poemas* is widely regarded as a masterpiece of Hispanic erotic poetry, and the book's success inspired several later volumes of love poetry, including *Los versos del capitán (The Captain's Verses)* and *Cien sonetos de amor.*

Neruda broke further with conventionalism in *Tentativa del hombre infinito,* an experimental work that marks his first use of interior monologue and abandonment of traditional structure, rhyme, syntax, and punctuation. While contemporary scholars concur that reviewers have often misinterpreted this work's illogical surrealist images, resulting in critical neglect, the collection is now regarded as one of Neruda's major works. During the mid-1920s, Neruda further experimented with new constructions in *Prosas de Pablo Neruda,* a collection of prose, and *El habitante y su esperenza,* a volume of short fiction. In honor of his achievement, Neruda was appointed to the diplomatic service in 1927 as the Chilean consul in Burma, and later served in Ceylon and the Dutch East Indies. Neruda began writing the poems in *Residencia en la tierra (Residence on Earth and Other Poems)*, the first volume in a continuing cycle that established him as a leading figure in Spanish-language literature. Complex in structure and meaning, this work makes use of dense, hermetic language and introspective interior monologue to express a complex metaphysical vision of the earth in which existence is viewed as a continuous process of decay and despair.

Neruda returned to Chile from the Far East in 1933 and was reassigned to Buenos Aires, where he became friends with Spanish poet Federico García Lorca and others associated with the Generation of 1927. The second volume of *Residencia en la tierra,* written after his appointment as Chilean consul in Barcelona in 1934, features a lighter, declamatory style and a more direct approach to communication with his reader. In this work, Neruda reveals a more pragmatic view of world problems and expresses less anguish over his inability to resolve human contradictions. *Tercera Residencia, 1935-1945*, a third installment in the *Residencia* cycle written over ten years later, is less highly regarded than its predecessors due to its didactic espousal of ideological concerns. Following the onset of the Spanish Civil War, Neruda's life and poetry took an abrupt political turn. In *España en el corazón (Spain in My Heart)*, an impassioned tribute in verse dedicated to the cause of the Spanish Loyalists, Neruda's poetry became less personal and began to depict political concerns from a socialist perspective. In "Las furias y las penas," a later poem that was revised and incorporated into *Tercera residencia* following its original publication as a single work in 1939, Neruda stated that his poetry had changed to reflect the transformation of his life and the the world following global conflict and economic depression. While serving as secretary to the Chilean embassy in Mexico City from 1939 to 1941, and as a consul from 1941 to 1943, he became increasingly involved in leftist causes. *Nuevo canto de amor a Stalingrado,* a poem in which he praises the defenders of Stalingrad in Russia, led to his dismissal from his diplomatic post in 1943.

Although recalled to his country, Neruda instead traveled to France in 1943 to arrange for the passage of refugees of the Spanish Civil War to Chile. The same year he published his acclaimed poem *Alturas de Macchu Picchu (The Heights of Macchu Picchu)*, a work inspired by his 1943 visit to the Incan ruins of the title. This piece was later integrated into his epic work *Canto general de Chile,* a collection extensively revised between its original appearance in 1943 and its final version in 1950 that features 340 poems on Chile's natural, cultural, and political history. With this volume, Neruda renounced his work written prior to 1937 and proclaimed himself a populist poet. Writing in a direct, documentary style, Neruda treats each canto as an individual chapter, skirting the boundaries between political reportage, propaganda, and art to enlist reader support for his socialist values. While most critics have agreed that his Marxist view of Chile's history of poverty and tyranny results in a work of uneven quality, *Canto general* is often regarded as one of Neruda's major achievements.

Neruda returned to Chile in 1944 and was elected to the Senate in 1946. There he denounced the prevailing anti-communist stance of his government. In 1947, Neruda published letters in the Mexican and Venezuelan press charging Chile's president, Gabriel González Videla, with violating his country's constitution by betraying the national interest in collusion with the United States government. Indicted for treason, Neruda fled his homeland in political exile in 1949. In the next few years he traveled extensively, finished his revised *Canto general,* and completed an exposé. *González Videla, el Lavel de la América Latina.* During the early 1950s, Neruda received the Stalin Prize for literature as well as the Lenin Peace Prize and was permitted to return to Chile in 1953. In such works of political verse as *Poesía política* and *Las uvas y el viento,* Neruda employs a new, simpler style to communicate more directly with the common people, a goal that had eluded him despite his popular and political earlier poetry. His next major work, *Odas elementales (Elementary Odes)* is a cycle of poems free of political intent that humorously exalt banal objects and the mundane occurrences of everyday life. These short-lined poems, written in free verse and displaying such titles as "Ode to the Tomato" and "The Dance of the Artichoke," elevate fruits and vegetables to poetic stature while mocking the traditional ode. Fernando Alegría called Neruda's *Odas elementales* "a song to matter, to its dynamism and to the life and death cycles which perpetuate it. His concept of universality does not always refer to a philosophic order." Neruda later completed several additional volumes of odes, including *Nuevas odas elementales, Tercer libro de las odas,* and *Odas: al libro, a las Américas, a la luz.*

Most critics agree that *Estravagario (Extravagaria)* signals the last major development in Neruda's poetry. Like the *Odas elementales,* the poems in this volume are characterized by a flippant, self-indulgent tone and lucid style. Returning to the egocentrism of his earliest verse, Neruda employs self-parody to gently satirize his previous works and persona, particularly mocking his early stance of the poet as hero. His later poetry includes didactic political poetry, light, frivolous verse, and serious, prophetic works, often combining elements from all three styles. A member of the Chilean Communist Party since 1945, Neruda became a nominee for the presidency of Chile in 1970, but his name was withdrawn from consideration when the five parties that made up Chile's political left decided to endorse Salvador Allende. Under Allende's government, Neruda served as Ambassador to France prior to his death. In addition to his many works of poetry and prose, Neruda also completed *Fulgor y muerte de Joaquín Murieta (Splendor and Death of Joaquín Murieta)*, a stridently anti-American play about a Californian bandit and hero; *Memorial de Isla Negra (Isla Negra: A Notebook)*, a five volume autobiography in verse expressing reflections on his life and work; and *Confieso que he vivido: Memorias (Memoirs)*, a posthumous volume of reminiscences written in prose.

(See also *CLC,* Vols. 1, 2, 5, 7, 9, 28; *Contemporary Authors,* Vols. 17-20, Vols. 45-48 [obituary]; and *Contemporary Authors Permanent Series,* Vol. 2.]

PRINCIPAL WORKS

POETRY

La canción de la fiesta   1921

Crepúsculario   1923
Veinte poemas de amor y una cancíon desesperada   1924; definitive ed., 1932
   [*Twenty Love Poems and a Song of Despair,*   1969; also translated as *Twenty Love Poems: A Disdaining Song,* 1970; later tr., 1973]
Tentativa del hombre infinito   1925
El hondero entusiasta, 1923-1924   1933
Residencia en la tierra,   Vol. 1, 1925-1931   (poetry and prose)   1933
Cantos materiales   1935
Homenaje a Pablo Neruda de los poetas espanoles: tres cantos materiales   1935
   [*Tres cantos materiales: Three Material Songs,*   1948]
Poesías de villamediana presentadas por Pablo Neruda   1935
Residencia en la tierra,   Vol. 2, 1931-1935   1935
**España en el corazón: himno a las glorias del pueblo en la guerra (1936-1937)*   1937
Las furias y las penas   1939
Un canto para Bolívar   1941
Selected Poems   1941
Canto general de Chile   1943; definitive ed., 1950
Cantos de Pablo Neruda   1943
Nuevo canto de amor a Stalingrado   1943
Pablo Neruda: sus mejores versos   1943
Selected Poems by Pablo Neruda   1944
Nocturnal Collection   1946
Tercera residencia, 1935-1945   1947
   [*Residence on Earth,* Vol. 3, 1973]
Colección Residencia en la tierra: obra poética   10 vols. 1947-1948
Alturas de Macchu Picchu   1948; definitive edition, 1954
   [*The Heights of Macchu Picchu,*   1966]
Himno y regreso   1948
Que despierte el leñador!   1948
   [*Peace for Twilights to Come!,*   1950]
Dulce Patria   1949
Let the Rail Splitter Awake and Other Poems   1951
Poesías completas   1951
Cuando de Chile   1952
Poemas   1952
Los versos del capitán: poemas de amor   1952
   [*The Captain's Verses,*   1972]
Poesía política: discursos politicos   2 vols. 1953
Todo el amor   1953
Odas elementales   1954
   [*Elementary Odes,*   1961]
Regreso la sirena   1954
Las uvas y el viento   1954
Los versos más populares de Pablo Neruda   1954?
Nuevas odas elementales   1955
Los mejores versos de Pablo Neruda   1956
Oda a la tipografía   1956
   [*Ode to Typography,*   1964]
Obras completas   1957; rev. ed., 1962, 1967 (2 vols.)
Poesía   1957
Tercer libro de las odas   1957
Estravagario   1958
   [*Extravagaria,*   1972]
Algunas odas   1959
Cien sonetos de amor   1959
Navegaciones y regresos   1959
Odas: al libro, a las Américas, a la luz   1959
Todo lleva tu nombre   1959

Canción de gesta   1960
   [*Song of Protest,*   1976]
Oceana   1960
Las piedras de Chile   1960
Cantos ceremoniales   1961
Los primeros versos de amor   1961
Selected Poems   1961
Antologia poética   1962
La insepulta de paita   1962
Plenos poderes Buenos Aires   1962
   [*Fully Empowered,*   1975]
†*Memoríal de Isla Negra*   1964
   [*Isla Negra: A Notebook,*   1981]
Bestiary / Bestiario   1965
Arte de pájaros   1966
   [*Art of Birds,*   1985]
La barcarola   1967
Twenty Poems   1967
We Are Many   1967
Las manos del día   1968
Aun   1969
   [*Still Another Day,*   1984]
La copa de sangre   (poetry and prose)   1969
The Early Poems   1969
Fin de Mundo   1969
A New Decade   (Poems, 1958-1967)   1969
Las piedras del cielo   1970
Selected Poems   1970
Antología esencial   1971
Poemas inmortales   1971
Antología popular 1972   1972
Cuatro poemas escritos en Francia   1972
Geografía infructuosa   1972
New Poems, 1968-1970   1972
El mar y las campanas   1973
La rosa separada: obra póstuma   1973
   [*The Separate Rose,*   1985]
El corazón amarillo   1974
Defectos escogidos: 2000   1974
Elegía   1974
   [*Elegy,*   1983]
Five Decades, A Selection   (Poems, 1925-1970)   1974
Jardín de invierno   1974
Oda a la lagartija   1974?
Libro de las preguntas   1974
Elrío invisible: poesía y prosa de juventud   (poetry and prose)   1980

PROSE

Anillos [with Tomas Logo]   1926
Prosas de Pablo Neruda   1926
Chile os acoge   1939
Homenaje a García Lorca   1939
Neruda entre nosotros   1939
O Partido Comunista e a liberdade de criaçao [with Pedro Pomar and Jorge Amado]   1946
Los heroes de carcon encarnan los ideales de democracia e indepencia nacional   1947
La verdad sobre las ruputuras   1947
Viajes al corazón de Quevedo y por las costas del mundo   1947
Neruda en Guatemala   1950
Viajes   1955
Discurso al Alimón sobre Rubén Dario [with Federico García Lorca]   1959

Discursos del rector de la Universidad de Chile [with Juan Gomez Millas] 1959
Cuba, los obispos 1962?
Pablo Neruda y Nicanor Parra: discursos [with Nicanor Parra] 1962

OTHER

El habitante y su esperenza (short stories) 1925
La crisis democratica de Chile (essay) 1947
   [*The Democratic Crisis of Chile*, 1948]
Carta a Miguel Otero Silva, en Caracas (correspondence) 1948
   [*Letter to Miguel Otero Silva, in Caracas*, 1970]
González Videla, el Lavel de la América Latina: breve biografía de un traidor [essay] 1949
Fulgor y muerte de Joaquín Murieta: bandido chileno injusticiado en California el 23 de julio de 1853 (play) 1966
   [*Radiance and Death of Joaquín Murieta*, 1972; also translated as *Splendor and Death of Joaquín Murieta*, 1973]
Discurso pronunciado con ocasión de la entrega del premio Nobel de literatura, 1971 1972
   [*Toward the Splendid City: Nobel Lecture*, 1972]
Cartas de amor de Pablo Neruda (love correspondence) 1974
Confieso que he vivido: memorias 1974
   [*Memoirs*, 1977]
Pablo Neruda, Héctor Eandi: correspondencia durante "Residencia en la tierra" 1980
Passions and Impressions (poems, essays, and lectures) 1983

*These works were published in one volume as *Residencia en la tierra (1925-1935)* in 1944, and in English with other poems in one volume as *Residence on Earth and Other Poems*, 1946; later tr. as *Residence on Earth*, 1962; later tr., 1973.

**This work, translated as *Spain in the Heart*, appears in *Residence on Earth and Other Poems*.

†This work was originally published in five volumes: *Donde nace la lluvia* (Vol. 1); *La luna en el laberinto* (Vol. 2); *El fuego cruel* (Vol. 3); *El cazador de raices* (Vol. 4); and *Sonata critica*, (Vol. 5).

Jonathan Cohen

The history of Neruda in English begins just two years after his first book of poems, *Crepusculario* (*The Twilight Book*, 1923), was published in Chile. What seems to have been the earliest mention of "Pablo Neruda, with his unequivocal pictures of youth tortured by desire," appeared in the June 1925 issue of *Poetry* (Chicago), a special Latin American issue edited by poet-translator Muna Lee. Although it was only a brief note in a review of an anthology of contemporary Chilean poetry, Muna Lee, who presumably used the pseudonym "Pablo Matos" for this review, deserves credit for the historic first news in English of Neruda.

A few years later, in 1929, Willis Knapp Jones published a short review of the second Chilean edition of *Crepusculario* (1926), about which he said:

> In a 166-page book of awkward size (7 ¾ inches square) and with much blank space, Neruda, already known for two novels and a gift edition of poetry, reprints a three-year-old collection of love poems in various meters. He is at [his] least successful with his sonnets and most with his melancholy laments in rimed vers libre, and with one or two passional, sensual outbursts . . . Interesting as a sample from a country where every youngster writes poetry.

Here Jones, a translator and professor of Romance languages, gave the first critical response in English to a whole book of Neruda's poems. It was a review that sounded much like reviews written by Chilean critics at the time, politely reserved, but positive. Jones's notice appeared in *Books Abroad*, which would continue to discuss much of Neruda's work in the years to come.

Surprisingly enough, Neruda's poetry was noted in T. S. Eliot's magazine, *The Criterion*, the following year, by which time Neruda had already published several books. Eliot's reviewer of Spanish periodicals, Charles K. Colhoun, focused on three poems Neruda had published in Ortega y Gasset's magazine, *Revista de Occidente*, from Madrid. Colhoun felt that they presented "problems of versification and interpretation . . . made more palatable by the beautiful language in which they are written," and he compared Neruda's poem **"Galope muerto" ("Dead Gallop")** to Rimbaud's dark symbolism.

In 1932, Henry Alfred Holmes published an anthology titled *Spanish America in Song and Story*, with Spanish texts only, but with English commentary. This was the first time Neruda's poetry appeared in a volume published in the United States. Holmes chose a single poem, **"Un hombre anda bajo la luna" ("A Man Walks beneath the Moon"),** and he introduced it with the following note about the poet:

> 'In the midst of this latest generation a voice has been raised like a fountain jet which from the first instant should soar on high. The voice was Neruda's.' The critic, Donoso, assigns this young man a place in lyric poetry beside Gabriela Mistral.

The particular poem was a rather poor selection by Holmes, since it was such an early poem and not representative of Neruda's more mature style. Nonetheless, it offered an initial glimpse of Neruda to readers of Spanish-language poetry in the United States.

English translations of Neruda's poems were slow in coming, despite his growing international reputation as a major poet. A booklength collection would not appear in the United States until 1946, when New Directions published *Residence on Earth and Other Poems*, translated by Angel Flores. First, translations would be published in anthologies of Spanish American poets, in literary and political magazines, and in pamphlets, mostly during the Second World War.

G. Dundas Craig published the first verse-translations of Neruda's work in 1934. In his anthology titled *The Modernist Trend in Spanish-American Poetry*, Craig presented **"Arsenal by Night" ("Maestranzas de noche"),** a short poem, which may be the first poem of social protest Neruda ever wrote, from *Crepusculario;* and four of the twelve early poems from *El hondero entusiasta* (*The Ardent Slingsman,* not published in its entirety until 1933), which Craig grouped under the title, "Poems of Love." To Craig, even though Neruda was "one of the most interesting lyrical personalities in Chile" at the time, representing "one of the later phases of the reaction from the Parnassian and Symbolist schools" in Latin America, his poetry still embodied a corrupt sensibility; it was a poetry "quite in the Whitman manner." . . .(pp. 272-74)

Commenting on the poems he had chosen to translate, Craig admitted a dislike for Neruda's work in general. "There is no denying the power of these verses, but the power is so ill regulated that they frequently become merely incoherent," he said. His criticism took on a moralistic tone against Neruda, who "seems to have become obsessed by sex and sensual instinct; to be, in fact, a promising case for the psycho-pathologist." Craig concluded that "to judge by what Neruda has written, not only has the age of chivalry departed, but we have got back to the morals of the cave-dwellers or of some beings still more primitive." In short, Craig rejected Neruda's "brutal crudeness" which, he felt, would most likely shock an English-reading audience; and yet, he allowed Neruda a certain benefit of the doubt, saying "we may be justified in looking forward to something richer and more mellow as the years bring more matured judgment." Given the terrible mismatch of temperaments between poet and translator, it is no wonder Craig's translations were stiff and unnatural, filled with much poetic thee-ing and thou-ing, in addition to an archaic diction utterly alien to the original Spanish. . . . Here the attempt to render Neruda in English failed because the translator, with a miserable poetic sense, imposed his own frigid values on Neruda's passionate verse and gave a good example of translation at its worst. There was no critical response to Neruda's first appearance in English translation. . . . No other translations of Neruda would appear in the United States until the early forties.

When the experience of the Spanish Civil War (1936-39) widened Neruda's outlook and the range of his poetry, his English-reading audience also became wider. Of that time, Neruda has said: "The blood spilled in Spain was a magnet that sent shudders through the poetry of a great age." For Neruda the war was the turning point in his thinking. His newly awakened sense of social struggle led him to write an *engagé* poetry that reflected attitudes shared by the international Left.

In 1937, Neruda's poem **"To the Mothers of the Dead Militia"** (**"Canto a las madres de los milicianos muertos"**) appeared in the London-based magazine, *Left Review,* translated by his good friend, Nancy Cunard. It was one of the poems that would make up *España en el corazón* (*Spain in My Heart,* published later that year), and it was not merely a piece of political rhetoric or propaganda but rather a well-crafted symbolist elegy, in free verse, which begins:

> They have not died!
> they stand upright in the midst of the gunpowder,
> they live, burning as brands there.
>
> In the copper-coloured prairie

> their pure shadows have come together
> like a curtain of armoured wind,
> a barrier colour of fury
> like that same invisible breast of sky.
>
> Mothers, they are standing . . .

This was among the first of Neruda's poems translated into English as an act of true sympathy, unlike Craig's previous effort. The translator took certain creative liberties in order to sustain the poem in English. Nonetheless, her impassioned rendering was quite faithful to the movement, tone and imagery of the original verse, especially to the Nerudian music, and it read like real poetry in English.

Strange as it may seem, Neruda did not receive the attention he deserved in the United States until the early sixties, when translations of his poetry began to flourish. Then, translations of his work came to represent the interests of many poets in this country, as well as a new interest in Latin America. (pp. 274-76)

> *Jonathan Cohen, "The Early History of Neruda in English (1925-1937)," in* Romance Notes, *Vol. XXII, No. 3, Spring, 1982, pp. 272-76.*

Ronald Blythe

It has become an affectionate convention for the poets of the age, as it were, to be presented with a 60th birthday book of appreciations by thankful contemporaries. But must it be hubristic for a poet to appreciate himself at this milestone?

Not if he is Neruda. 'Little by little, and also in great leaps, / life happened to me'—and [*Isla Negra: A Notebook*], the five extraordinary volumes which set this life in sequences of autobiographical poetry, are the latest translations by Alastair Reid, Neruda's friend and English interpreter. Reid describes the Chilean writer as a 'sayer', a poet who communicates in a speaking voice, and believes that his essential duty as translator is to catch the tone of Neruda's voice. He reveals the poet by being entirely open-handed about his own technique and philosophy as translator, and by setting the original Spanish and his own understanding of it side by side.

The result is frequently heady and thrilling, like the total capturing of a composer's meaning by an executant. In order to feel this meaning and excitement, it is necessary to read *Isla Negra* right through from beginning to end, as one would a prose autobiography. Foraging for a word or two to describe my own reaction to seeing Neruda at such spiritual and physical close quarters, I thought of a sentence in Sir Thomas Browne's *Urn-Burial* which says that life is 'pure flame, and we live by an invisible sun within us'.

Written when Neruda was 59 and living in a small village on the Pacific coast of Chile, the Isla Negra of the title, these 100 or so poems are an imaginative unification of his existence as child, student, lover, political force, adorer of the natural universe, moralist and artist. Although frequently involved in fights against ideas which were enough to make any man born in 1904 accept that his was a century shorn of hope, he can truthfully admit that 'I belong to fruitfulness', and he refuses, as a communist, to be stuck with a grim outlook.

He sings his faith with early fervour—'We are the pure silver of earth / the true mineral in man . . . / A moment in the dark does not blind us.' Like Hazlitt, he does not grow out of his first convictions—'I am not one who comes back from the light'—and yet he insists on movement, development, 'so many poems about / the first of May / that now I write only about the second' Monsters of his era are gunned down—'Always those stucco statues / of the mustacheoed god with his boots on / and his immaculate breeches / ironed by real slavery'—this comment on Stalin. This is a note book full of the tang and mellifluence of one extraordinary man's days.

> *Ronald Blythe, "Pure Silver," in* The Listener, *Vol. 108, No. 2788, November 25, 1982, p. 28.*

Mark Abley

Nothing sustains a man through a complex life as well as simple faith. Although the great Chilean poet, politician and diplomat Pablo Neruda was intimate with the turmoils of history, he always maintained a passionate belief in language. "For human beings, not to speak is to die," he once wrote. Through words, they could rise above the indignities of history. "Poetry is indestructible," he wrote. "Poetry was born with man and will continue to sing for man." For his pride, his resilience and his matchless gift for song, Neruda was awarded the Nobel Prize for literature in 1971. And he has continued to provide inspiration around the world since his death in September, 1973. **Passions and Impressions,** a new collection of Neruda's speeches, prose poems, essays and elegies, is the sort of book that could easily have been a dusty homage. But Neruda's enthusiasm and his irresistible eloquence charge the snippets of prose with life.

No matter what occasion provoked the pieces, his rich, tireless voice echoes with inimitable force. He had no patience with any conception of literature as the preserve of a lucky minority. Having listened to the words of farmers, miners and fishermen, he pulled their struggles into his work, rejecting the surrealism of his early poetry in favor of heartfelt hymns to everyday life. Because of that, he became a national hero; the speech he gave in Santiago after receiving the Nobel Prize had to be delivered in the national stadium, the only place large enough to accommodate his admirers. His triumph was their own. "I have always wanted the hands of the people to be seen in poetry," Neruda declared. . . .

Like his poetry, **Passions and Impressions** is memorable when it is passionate and forgettable when it is merely impressionistic. Neruda delighted in art that was stained, scarred, wrinkled by experience. By the end of the book he may seem to be a larger-than-life character, some fantastic bard and orator from a Latin American extravaganza. But that is pure illusion. Pablo Neruda was never larger than life; he was only larger than most people permit themselves to be.

> *Mark Abley, "Passionate Words," in* Maclean's Magazine, *Vol. 96, No. 6, February 7, 1983, p. 50.*

Stephen Dobyns

Neruda's house, which is still owned by his wife, Matilde, stands on an acre of land on a small hill above the ocean [in the village of Isla Negra]. . . . Through the windows one can see dozens of ships in bottles, framed pages of Dante, African masks, ancient Tarot cards, bottles in the shape of fish, castles, cats and famous men. Everywhere there are books. In the room where Neruda wrote are photographs of Whitman, Baudelaire, Poe, Rimbaud and Mayakovsky.

These were the poets he considered his teachers. They led him to see his own work as "anti-literary," almost "a handicraft." Neruda was not a rationalist: that is, as a poet, he chose not to be a rationalist. He scorned those critics who tried to insert themselves between the reader and the text with their analysis and explications. In an article reprinted in **Passions and Impressions,** a collection of his prose, he wrote, on a volume of Robert Frost's prose:

> It is the book of a rationalist with a perfect library, a humanist. But also of a virtuoso of ideas, those ideas about poetry and metaphor that lead nowhere. I have always believed that a study of poetry by poets is pure ashes.

Neruda felt that rationalism could only measure the surface of things. Poetry, on the other hand, attempted to chronicle the epoch in which it was written, while great poets like Shakespeare, Dante and Whitman "help us discover ourselves: they reveal to us our labyrinths." For Neruda this also had a political aspect. "I have assumed the time-honored obligation to defend the people, the poor and the exploited." When he received the Nobel Prize in 1971, he wrote, in **"Poetry Shall Not Have Sung in Vain"**: "The poet must learn from his fellow men. There is no unassailable solitude. All roads lead to the same point: to the communication of who we are."

In regard to his own poetry, he called himself a potter, a baker, a carpenter. He took his poems not from ideas but from the "eternities at my disposal right outside my window." To be successful, he felt that a poet had to link himself to his country and his people. Neruda could not separate being a poet from being Chilean. In **"The Poet Is Not a Rolling Stone,"** he wrote:

> The first stage of a poet's life must be devoted to absorbing the essences of his native land; later, he must return them. He must restore them, he must repay them. His poetry and his actions must contribute to the maturity and growth of his people.

Some of Neruda's best prose is his travel writing. This is hardly surprising since as a poet he tried to let the world pass through him, pass through his five senses, to let all that he experienced be transformed into language, image, metaphor. It was through metaphor, not rational analysis and argument, that the mysteries of the world could be revealed. The poet had to approach the mystery, "the magic zone where we can dance an awkward dance," with a confession of ignorance. Neruda called himself "a humble collector of puzzles" and again scorned the rationalist for presuming to know.

The rationalist, he felt, tainted his subject with his own subjectivity and egoism. "The analytical dagger doesn't reveal the guts of the poet but the insides of the one who wielded the dagger." But the poet who tried to give a chronicle of his age had to be free of the need to put the stamp of his ego on everything he touched. He had to let the world pass through him in its entirety, without judging.

Neruda analyzed by metaphor, if such can be called analysis. He felt it was only through metaphor that the dimensions of the mystery could be indicated; only through metaphor that the world could be remade in the mind of a reader. He began one poem, "A day dressed in mourning falls from the bells." He was writing about rain, the first rain of autumn.

His prose also was full of such metaphor. In discussing a Rumanian poet, he wrote, "The lamentations that enveloped the Symbolist Bocavia like a mantle were stained with the smoke of the city and the blood of the slaughterhouse." . . .

But critics tend to be rationalists and Neruda is often criticized for his lack of rationalism. At times it is assumed that he wasn't a rationalist because he couldn't be. This collection of 50 years of his prose [*Passions and Impressions*] should partly correct that misconception. It shows Neruda both at his most metaphorical and his most rational. It shows him to be precisely analytical in his political writing as a Communist senator and cloyingly poetical in some dreadful eulogistic writing. It is a book that is in turn both wonderful and tiresome. It contains prose poems, travel pieces, elegies, political writing, newspaper articles, introductions, and acceptance speeches for his numerous prizes. At first I thought that the editors should have made a more careful selection; there was too much hyperbole, too much poeticizing. But then I decided that one needs it all. It is only with the whole mess that one gets a sense of Neruda with all his apparent contradictions. The book's only failing is that it needed an introduction to help the reader place these 120 separate pieces in some historical perspective.

What one comes to realize from these prose pieces is how conscious and astute were Neruda's esthetic choices. In retrospect at least his rejection of the path of the maestro, the critic, the rationalist was carefully calculated. In **"Latorre, Prado, and My Own Shadow,"** he wrote:

> We had to choose between appearing to be masters of things we didn't know, in order to be believed, or condemning ourselves to the perpetually obscure lot of common laborers, shapers of clay.

Neruda "fled the role of literary master" and chose to be a shaper of clay. In the same essay, he wrote:

> I somehow understood that my work should be of a form so organic and whole that my poetry be like the very act of breathing, the measured product of my existence, the result of natural growth.

This is very close to Whitman, whom Neruda called his "primary creditor." And it was partly by adopting Whitman's sense of being the reader's representative that Neruda was able to reject the poet as literary master or "little god" and instead chose "the difficult road of shared responsibility." . . .

What is most amazing about Neruda's house at Isla Negra

is the fence that surrounds it. On three sides it is made up of about 2,000 rough boards. At least 1,500 are covered with writing. Sometimes it is simply, "Hola, Pablo," or a name and a date. Sometimes just the words "paz" or "libertad" or "amor." Sometimes poems are quoted or statements like "your poetry will live forever." Thousands of messages written in charcoal that washes off each year, so that each year the messages are replaced by new messages written by the thousands of people who come to his house just to look at it, to see the place where he wrote his poems. One said, "Peace to the poet of the hippies." Another said, "I am red when I approach the place of your blood." Another said only, "Orgullo de Chile"—pride of Chile.

> *Stephen Dobyns, "The Prose of a Nobel Poet," in* Book World—The Washington Post, *February 27, 1983, p. 4.*

Charles Tomlinson

Pablo Neruda has written some of the best and worst poems of our era. He confronts the translator with two chief problems: an idiom which frequently has no easy equivalent in English—thus we possess no fully convincing version of his masterpiece *Las Alturas de Macchu Picchu*—and an oeuvre of extraordinary unevenness. The first of these problems stares in the face any would-be translator of *Las Alturas,* the second anyone who, like Alastair Reid, undertakes to give us, without picking and choosing, the whole of a work like *Memorial de Isla Negra*. . . .

Isla Negra is the village (neither an island nor black, as Enrico Mario Santi tells us in an Afterword) where Neruda had a house on the Pacific coast of Chile. This is the setting from which he looks back, as he is nearing sixty, over his entire life. *Isla Negra* consists of five books. The first of these is the most autobiographical. It runs from 1904-21 and the poet gives us many memorable pictures of his rain-drenched part of Chile, together with affectionate portraits of his step-mother, his father, his uncle. There is often a humour at play here which makes these poems doubly delightful. In one of them, two sexually precocious little girls give the infant Neruda a nest with eggs in it to distract his mind, while they proceed to undress him and study "with their great eyes / their first small man". English, with its lack of diminutives, can never quite equal here "su primer hombrecito". Book Two takes us from the beginnings of his poetry to the consular years in the Far East. In Book Three come the meetings with Lorca, Alberti and Aleixandre and the tragedy of Spain in the Civil War. Book Four centres on the theme of exile, but by this point in the *Memorial* the idea of a chronological development of biography has long since been abandoned. The ideological climax occurs in the fifth and final book, with Neruda's reaction to Khrushchev's "revelations" about Stalin: "What happened? What happened? How did it happen? / How could it happen?" Neruda hams up his feelings in a poem of twenty-nine sections in which he not very convincingly tries to get into Stalin's mind and now calls him "the mustachioed god with his boots on". This will hardly do from the poet who for years had praised the dictator. Not so long before, in his elegy to Stalin, **"En Su Muerte"**, he had declared, "Stalin is the noon / the maturity of men and of peoples". There is a moment of unintentional comedy towards the close of that poem when Neruda is roused from his sorrows by the words of a simple Chilean fisherman: "But Malenkov will continue his work now". Perhaps even Malenkov, exiled to his electricity project in Siberia, would see the joke by this point of time.

In *Isla Negra,* "The darkness was slashed with a golden knife"—that is, Khrushchev spoke out—and Neruda, having gone through the motions of a laboured penitence, decides that "we Communists" are all right after all:

> We are the pure silver of earth,
> the true mineral in man . . .
> A moment in the dark does not blind us.
> We will die with no agony at all.

Pure silver, golden knives, guitars, jasmine, honey, the sun come easily to Neruda, who has a sort of all-purpose manner which could be applied to nature, woman, birds, flowers and even to Stalin himself. Indeed, in one of his earlier poems, **"Jóyenes Alemanes"**, the flowers in the mouths of East German youth are "the word of Stalin / on millions of lips". Neruda has been praised for writing "with burning simplicity about the great issues of our time" (Robert Nye) and for "breaking away from the concept of an élite or minority poetry" and "using instead the arts of rhetoric" (Jean Franco). Yet when all is said and done, the burning simplicity and the arts of rhetoric too often serve politics of a dismal crudity. "Fiercely anti-intellectual", says Enrico Mario Santi of Neruda. Octavio Paz adds more dryly, "A man of few ideas"—this in a fascinating account of their relationship in *Vuelta* for September, 1982. Clearly, in his Mexican sojourn, Neruda could not but gravitate away from the non-partisan intelligence of a Paz who, thirty years ago—against much opposition—got into print in Latin America a dossier on the Soviet camps. The Losada *Obras Completas* contains a telling image of Neruda in Mexico, a photograph of him signing the first edition of *Canto general* seated together with the mural painters Diego Rivera and Alvaro Siqueiros, the three great egotists massively selfconscious beside one another. Neruda's "burning simplicity" was very much that of the world of their history paintings with its rather sentimental Indianism and its strip-cartoon Marxism—though Rivera had a softer spot for Trotsky than either Neruda or Siqueiros (Siqueiros, in fact, tried to assassinate him). . . .

There follow excellent poems like **"The Long Day Called Thursday"**, about Neruda's difficulties in getting up and putting his socks on, and **"Look to the Market"**, a celebration of the contents of Valparaíso market—the fish, birds, cheese, oranges, chestnuts, tomatoes, apples, wine. Once more, it is the humour of these poems that saves the day. Neruda can be funny about himself in the first of these and in the second he even seems to be mocking his own public manner:

> Atención al Mercado
> que es mi vida!
> Atención al Mercado
> compañeros!

One of the disconcerting things about reading Neruda is the way an air of generous ease, even a certain mockery of the self, gives way to an anxious self-regard. It was Whitman ("you / taught me / to be / American") who freed him from the alienated and artistically persuasive voice of *Residencia en la tierra* (1933). But as with Whitman's words to the prostitute, "Be composed—be at ease with me—I am Walt Whitman, liberal and lusty as Nature", there is something overbearing in the proffered generosity: "Let it be known that nobody / crossed my path without sharing my being". And how, for example, does one respond to such a tribute as that to the poet Homero Arce, who was for a time Neruda's secretary: "Here, once again, I give you (my thanks), because you have lived / my life for me as if it were your own . . . "? Neruda managed to arrange the passage aboard the Winnipeg of a number of refugees from Spain and we hear of this in the third book of *Isla Negra:*

> they came,
> summoned by my voice,
> Saavedra, I called, and the mason came,
> Zúñiga, I said, and there he was.
> Roces, I called, and he came with his serious smile.
> Alberti! I cried out, and poetry arrived . . .

Less tactful than in his dealings with the vegetables in Valparaíso market, he leaves us in no doubt about who is at the centre of all this. For as with that other apologist for the collective, Mayakovsky, all Neruda's songs were songs of myself. Translations like those of Alastair Reid give us a real incentive to go back through the works and reassess for ourselves what is of lasting value in the work of Chile's most remarkable poet.

> *Charles Tomlinson, "Overdoing the Generosity," in* The Times Literary Supplement, *No. 4173, March 25, 1983, p. 286.*

Alan Cheuse

[*Passions and Impressions* is a] new collection of essays, speeches both political and literary (though the two realms intertwine thickly by the middle of the poet's life), newspaper articles, prose poems and jottings from a lifetime of notebooks, prefaces and letters (both public and private, and here too the two realms coincide). . . .

Few people [in the United States] except scholars would normally be privileged to know as much as we do about the poet's mind after reading through these hundreds of highly charged pages, from the early prose poems of the eighteen year old Neruda ("The moon must be swaying above like the painted curtain on a stage. Winds of night, dark and gloomy winds!") on through his travel pieces for a Santiago newspaper published five years later, quite exotic prose poems in themselves. . . . There are many prefaces and introductions to works of poetry and fiction by friends and strangers who would become friends, brief essays on poets whose work he studied quite carefully, such as Whitman and Robert Frost, and a multitude of miscellaneous notations on poetry, politics, and his Chilean homeland. . . .

Thanks to the poet's widow, Matilde, and his friend Miguel Otero Silva, the Venezuelan novelist and newspaper editor, and translator Margaret Sayers Peden, English readers now have access to this varied collection and can trace the evolution of the young lyric poet from the south of Chile who grew with Santiago, travelled throughout the Far East, and Europe, found a politics in the rescue of refugees from Franco's Spain, and founded an epic school of art out of the vastness of his native continent.

In the late forties, Neruda, then a Communist Senator in his nation's legislature, went into hiding to escape imprisonment and possibly worse at the hands of an incipient dictatorship. The story of his trek across the snow-covered Andes is famous in left-wing Latin American political mythology, and the polemics he unleashed in his political struggle against Gonzalez Videla, the President of Chile who wished to extradite the poet and try him for sedition, are included in *Passions and Impressions.* Neruda threatened at one point during the speech he made in his own defense before the Chilean Senate, titled **"I Accuse,"** to attack his political opponent "in the vast poem entitled *Canto general de Chile* which I am presently writing, singing of our land and the episodes that formed it. . . . " This seems almost laughable compared to the charges he makes elsewhere in this speech about an apparent fascist attempt to burn his house in Santiago and place all those in opposition to the government in concentration camps. But with hindsight these accusations take on a frightening, portentous air.

> *Alan Cheuse, "Chilean Voices, Chilean Blood," in* The American Book Review, *Vol. 5, No. 4, May-June, 1983, p. 13.*

Jonathan Chaves

Prior to the posthumous publication of [*Passions and Impressions*] (the Spanish edition was put out in 1978), the primary example we had of Neruda's prose was his *Memoirs*. . . . [This] was one of the richest personal chronicles produced by a modern literary figure. The current work consists of a great many short prose pieces, few of them more than two or three pages in length. There is an early set of prose poems from 1922 and a number of others interspersed throughout the rest of the book that represent important additions to the existing corpus of Neruda's published poetic output. In them we see Neruda at his best, on the fine edge also occupied by Gabriel García Márquez, where sensuously experienced reality and dream-like fantasy intersect, as in **"The Hunter After Roots"** where Neruda evokes the nearly mystical connection between Chile and his life and poetry.

Other essays consist of criticism, and these vary in quality. At times one gets the impression that Neruda is heaping largely ceremonial praise on a figure for whom he does not actually feel too deeply. At others, when he is truly moved, he uses what might be called metaphoric criticism of a sort that academic critics would contemptuously label "impressionistic," but which often reveals more than the various modish schools of criticism (and which Neruda himself derides with accuracy and passion). For example, in the piece on the sculptor Alberto Sánchez, he tells us that the artist "was a tree, and high in his branches he harbored birds and lightning rods, wings for flight, and tempestuous magnetism." This mode of criticism has been successfully emulated in the United States by Robert Bly, and the extent of Bly's debt to Neruda is now clear.

There are disappointments in the book, however. The "Travel Images" of 1927 perpetuate embarrassing stereotypes of Africans and Orientals of the sort Edward Said

has convincingly lambasted in his book, *Orientalism.* Neruda has more real empathy for the sea creatures in the Madras aquarium than he has for the people of Singapore or Port Said. He even castigates the latter for being less exotic than their counterparts in the romantic novels of French author Pierre Loti.

Then there are the political essays and speeches. Some of these are worth having: Neruda's scathing dismemberment of the administration of Gabriel González Videla is definitive in its political acuity and moral outrage. The problem—and it is the major problem in Neruda as a whole—is his tragic blindspot with regard to the shortcomings of communist governments. Thirty years ago Czeslaw Milosz, himself one of the great poets of our time and like Neruda a Nobel laureate in literature, wrote in his book *The Captive Mind,*

> Revolutionary poetry becomes weak when it begins to extol the longed-for future as already realized, or in the process of realization, in a given part of the earth. To approve convincingly is difficult not because 'positive' values are incompatible with the nature of literature, but because approbation, in order to be effective, must be based on truth. . . . Let Pablo Neruda fight for his people. He is wrong, however, when he believes that all the protesting (i.e., anti-Soviet) voices of Central and Eastern Europe are the voices of stubborn nationalisms or the yelps of wronged reaction. Eyes that have seen should not be shut. . . .
>
> (pp. 61-2)

> *Jonathan Chaves, "A Major Voice of the 20th Century," in* Américas, *Vol. 35, No. 5, September-October, 1983, pp. 61-2.*

Paul Binding

One of the shorter, and later pieces in this generous anthology of Neruda's occasional writings [*Passions and Impressions*] is entitled **"Far-ranging Beetleology".** This begins with a poem in which Neruda expresses a wish that he had been born a beetle, had burrowed 'deep in dark and compact matter' and 'scrawled' his 'name in hidden patterns / in the agony of the wood'. Because, he imagines, 'Thus my name some distant morning, / would once again see the light of day, / emerging from nocturnal channels'.

These lines surely encapsulate the two dominant—and, more often than not, conflicting—qualities of Neruda's personality as he emerged from the figuratively nocturnal channels of his precocious youth: an instinctive veneration for the mystery of the natural world, and a total inability to lose sight of himself, particularly himself as public figure with mankind's admiring eyes upon him. (p. 20)

Passions and Impressions can be seen as an extensive gloss to Neruda's *Memoirs* (called in Spanish, much more revealingly, *Confieso que he vivido*—'I confess that I have lived') which demonstrate the same conflict and arouse—in me, at any rate—the same emotions.

One of the most interesting, and to the student valuable, sections of *Passions and Impressions* concerns those Spanish-language writers with whom Neruda enjoyed association. There are two obviously deeply-felt tributes to García Lorca, and a number of pieces on Lorca's Spanish contemporaries, the unparalleledly brilliant 'Generation of '27'. Unfortunately self-congratulatory rhetoric breaks out repeatedly to mar their validity as pictures or records. Of the complex surrealist Vicente Aleixandre: 'I set him apart from all other friends, because of the infinite purity of his friendship.' Of Rafael Alberti, close to Neruda in his attitudes to both art and politics: 'Rafael and I have been, to state it simply, brothers.' (Neruda appears to have had a great many literary 'brothers'.) And I turned with great interest to what Neruda had written about the enigmatic figure of Miguel Hernández whose poems meant so much to Republican Spain and who died in one of Franco's brutal gaols:

> My great friend, Miguel, how I love you, and how I respect and love your strong poetry. Where you may be at this moment, in prison, on the road, dead, is of no consequence.

It was, of course, of very great consequence—most notably to Hernández's bereft young widow and child! But then even the Spain these poets gave their lives for has too often contracted to a stage on which Neruda made his youthful star-performances.

For all his loftiness of mind, for all the undoubted beauty of his frequent apostrophes to Chile, for all that they are the work of the author of the splendid *Alturas de Macchu Picchu,* Pablo Neruda's essays are too often the effusions of a self-important windbag, who surely should have tried rather harder to expel the sham-mantic from his work.

But then one reads the sixth section of this book, **"The Struggle for Justice"**, and humbly recants one's exasperation. In 1946 Neruda, a prominent member of the Chilean Communist party, had directed the publicity campaign of Señor González Videla, who was duly elected President. González Videla had espoused a most impressive programme of constitutional and social reform, and had guaranteed the inclusion of Communists in his Assembly. Soon after his election he went back on all his promises, serving the interests of the US and the multinationals, allying himself with Franco's Spain (which he had formerly condemned) and unscrupulously repressing all resistance to his *volte-face* with shootings, sudden arrests, concentration camps.

Neruda's stand was unequivocal and exceedingly courageous. Indeed he had to flee the country on account of it. His two major public denunciations of González Videla make both vigorous and moving reading. Paradoxically, where one might expect rhetoric there is none. At these times of crisis Neruda forsook effusion for hard fact. And his literary powers were never more sympathetically revealed than in his descriptions of the wretched living conditions of the abused miners of Southern Chile:

> Official statistics show the horrifying figure of six workers for every bed. At the site they call Pachoco Rojas they operate a 'warm-bed' system. This system—which reveals the terrible tragedy of the Chilean people—consists of a regular turn to use a bed, with the result that for years on end a bed never grows cold.

The same unflinching adherence to humanitarian principle was displayed almost a quarter of a century later in Neruda's relationship to Salvador Allende, whose end almost certainly hastened his own.

So maybe he was entitled to some of his high self-regard after all. And in the tenth anniversary year of Pinochet's despicable regime, brought about by forces Neruda consistently and uncompromisingly attacked, he is worth honouring. No one believed more firmly than he in the cause of peace (to be served by nuclear disarmament), and no one loved his own country more passionately: 'Life and struggle and poetry will live when I am but a tiny memory in the radiant history of Chile.' (pp. 20-1)

> Paul Binding, "A Tiny Memory," in New Statesman, *Vol. 106, No. 2749, November 25, 1983, pp. 20-1.*

Florence L. Yudin

Pablo Neruda's **Third Residence** (1935-45) marks a sharp break from the **Second** (1931-35), heralding radical content and diction. At the same time, this volume in the trilogy also speaks with the desperate, angry voices which dominate Parts I and II. Within this context of transition, "Las furias y las penas" is a model text: it combines resemblance in tone and imagery to **Residencias I** and **II** with Neruda's new social perspective. Thematically, "Las furias y las penas" bridges earlier and later works by means of its hellish vision of individual violence motivated by social decay. What Neruda had previously expressed in terms of personal alienation, he projects from the nadir of collective bankruptcy and the imminence of gratuitous holocaust. Viewed as a whole, **Tercera residencia** illustrates a fluid coherence of innovation with retrospective, creativity with continuity, that would characterize Neruda's entire development.

In 1939, after the Spanish Civil War had propelled Neruda into the arena of commitment, the poet himself drew attention to his new course, singling out the human and artistic values which impelled a pivotal transition: his conversion from poet as outsider to people's rhapsode. (p. 55)

[During this period, Neruda discovered] Spanish Baroque poetry, whose champion he saw in Quevedo. René de Costa, one of Neruda's most thoughtful critics, has summarized pointedly the effects on Neruda of this "revaluation":

> Not uncharacteristically, he would eventually detail the circumstances of the changes in his work; and in a radio speech of 1939 ("Quevedo adentro"), he publicly acknowledged not only his admiration for the great Spanish poet, but also the catalytic effect the belated discovery had on his personal outlook, moving him from an attitude of anguished despair to a kind of social optimism. What most fascinated Neruda—besides Quevedo's condemnation of corruption, his civic spirit, and his intense passion for love and life—was his notion of 'la agricultura de la muerte'. . . .

Thus, two consciousness-raising events—Neruda's experience of the Spanish Civil War, his maturing affinity with the poetry of Quevedo—converged to produce major distinctive features in his poetic vision. "The new posture assumed is that of a radical nonconformist. *Tercera residen-*

cia must, therefore, be considered in this light, from the dual perspective of art and society, poetry and politics."

Despite its importance as a major transitional work, the third of the *Residence* volumes, is, according to de Costa, "the least studied and most maligned." Whatever the muddled pretexts for neglect, the biases are crystal clear: Neruda's controversial treatment of society, politics and sex. To put this differently, the contents, rather than their poetic expression, have been the real motive for rejection or silence. By default, Neruda's originality in *Tercera residencia* remains to be illuminated. I hope to invite fresh thinking with an analysis of **"Las furias y las penas,"** the longest poem in this volume and perhaps the one with the most extreme point of view.

As the epigraph to **"Las furias y las penas,"** Neruda quotes one verse from Quevedo's sonnet, "A todas partes que me vuelvo, veo." The line, "Hay en mi corazón furias y penas," opens the first tercet, in which the "I" blames passion's tyranny for his suffering and guilt. . . . What does Neruda do with his model? How large is his debt to Quevedo? Both questions are secondary to my purpose in this explication but they are basic to an understanding of Neruda's explosive originality.

"Las furias y las penas" is divided into twenty-four stanzas, varying in length from one to twenty-seven verses. Its proportions and chaotic expression contrast sharply with Quevedo's formalism. More importantly, while both poems share a related theme—male protest of love's psychic torment—Quevedo's complaint is traditional and cerebral, while Neruda's is unconventional and emotionally savage. Of necessity, Quevedo and Neruda selected from the literary tradition of the Furies those characteristics that suited their individual expressive modes—Baroque/Surrealism, respectively. If we examine the mythological sources, it is clear that Neruda preserves but attenuates key Roman contexts, whereas Quevedo omits the more negative and psychically damaging powers that were attributed to the Eumenides. (pp. 55-6)

Neruda's context is one of circular crime and punishment: *poenas* in the form of psychic torment, with concomitant rage, resulting in an even more violent action which, in turn, increases the despair. This vicious circularity derives from the need for and repetition of sex. . . . Like their ancient counterparts, Neruda's Furies are implacable. For the modern victim, they personify dehumanization and nihilism: an irrational rejection of the self and others. This is, I believe, the central metaphor of Neruda's sulphuric expression. With the quotation, "Hay en mi corazón furias y penas," Neruda confesses his indebtedness to Quevedo; throughout his poem, he elaborates on his own experience with Quevedo's inner torments—*fuego, Tirano,* and *culpa mía*—, intensifying Quevedo's implied human dilemma; then, Neruda makes of his model the pivot around which to construct a poem whose meaning and structure express devastating failure.

Why the nihilism? For what does Neruda need metaphors of violent sexuality? Mainly, I think, to work out, what was at the time of composition (1934), a truncated dialectic. From the subterranean point of view, sustained in *Residencias I, II,* personal blackout is the answer to institutionalized dissolution. Perceiving no escape hatch, no way to reach and join a community of unbrutalized others,

Neruda's protagonist reacts like a raging somnambulist in an infernal habitat. Drunken technology celebrates the reign of order, but fails to anticipate the obscene product of its renewal. From this extreme, volatile perspective **"Las furias y las penas"** takes its twisted momentum. The base image of society in the advanced stages of dissociation gives rise to the depiction of individuals as crazed primates.

Society's sickness is mirrored through Neruda's impotent dialectic. Even a surface reading of the text reveals that the wild contradictions go nowhere: like irrational fears, there is no letting go of the demons, no time or space for experiential adjustment, no resolution of antitheses; therefore, no dialectical base. In terms of his evolving *Arte poética,* it seems fair to say that Neruda had not yet reconciled personal contradictions with his social project. . . . By keeping in mind the brilliant synthesis of life with society he would soon achieve in *Canto general* (1950), we can gauge both the psychic and artistic distance he needed to travel before reaching a livable dialectic.

The opening lines of **"Las furias y las penas"** express sharply the dominant theme and convey the tone of the poem:

> En el fondo del pecho estamos juntos,
> en el cañaveral del pecho recorremos
> un verano de tigres,
> al acecho de un metro de piel fría,
> al acecho de un ramo de inaccesible cutis,
> con la boca olfateando sudor y venas verdes
> nos encontramos en la húmeda sombra que deja caer
>   besos.

It is unclear in the first seven lines who is the grammatical subject: is it "I" against myself—my Furies—or is it "I"/"You"? This ambiguity appears in other sections of the poem, sometimes marking "ella"/"enemiga," at other times projecting a divided self. With no holds barred, Neruda exposes the animal instincts of mutually destructive partners: enemies joined in the hunt for sexual gratification. (pp. 56-7)

It is useful to put into perspective the radical diction and naked referents in the poet's expression. Neruda pulled back the trappings of centuries of love poetry to unmask the beast; namely, his version of alienated sex. What remains of human relationship is a mere shadow: both partners abuse each other, in apparent disregard of their common humanity. Thus, whomever he meant to be the subject is antagonist and mirror image. . . . *Húmedo,* as a natural characteristic, usually carries positive connotations in Neruda's lexicon, as when he refers to the Chilean forest (*Memorias*), or in the context of reconnecting with natural sources ("Entrada a la madera," *Segunda residencia,* IV). But in **"Las furias y las penas"** even origins are negatively charged because the sex act is both re-birth and death.

Stanza II lashes out against the female antagonist, while it also establishes the fierce symbiosis between the lovers. . . . The progression of comparisons suggests unleashed fury, trampling whatever lies in its path, be it animate or inanimate. Mounting aggressivity and gigantism choke the environs. And like the symbolic inversion of *húmedo, campanas* announces a frightful menace, rather than the vitality which the term generally conveys in

Neruda's poetry. As if to signal the imminent onslaught, each imagistic pair in Stanza II contains a striking antithesis between human and dehumanized reality. . . . Alienated sex is like a re-enactment of one's elemental fears. Neruda suggests this paradigm in icily physical terms; alternatively, each can match the other's threshold of violence. . . . Whether such fusion of instinct and conscious ferocity are metaphors of a primal nature, they clearly reflect mutual hatred and the need to wound. What the speaker envisions as his own rapacious drive, he projects on the other, and magnifies the potential violence. As with the repeated criminal offenses of a single individual, there seems to be the knowledge that once you have crossed the threshold of violence, it is easy to do again and again. We recognize this inward and outward looking at cruelty as a radical trend in certain contemporary arts: "To involve oneself with violence can indeed compel one into thought about oneself and man and society, sometimes very painful and disconcerting thought" [as John Fraser asserted in his *Violence in the Arts* (1976)].

Having conceded brutalization as the erotic mode, the victim/victimizer depicts his female counterpart as a prehistoric amphibian, stalking the earth, and targeting her prey with polymorphous instinct. . . . Both the chaotic description and repeated qualifier ("aun más") suggest the inability of the speaker to define or adequately express the wildly irrational nature of his enemy. His is a dual failure, rooted in the dissolution of identity, bound to the sterility of mutual hatred ("tengo también tus ojos de sangrienta luciérnaga"). With the ghastly words, "adivinas los cuerpos," we view primitive behavior through the lens of surrealism. The chain of verbs that follows plots the course of animalism: "acechas," "rompes," "caes haciendo crepitar," "Adivinas los cuerpos." This is not sexual hunger but biological rapacity: a human being driven by antihuman instinct. . . . Yet out of such a totally negative context, Neruda's expressive art produces the beautifully alliterative verse which is the fourth stanza.

The ambiguity of identity, which we examined in the opening lines of this poem, intensifies to such a degree that it is now the male antagonist who points the way to vicious sex: "Mi odio es una sola mano que te indica / el callado camino." Like his mythical counterparts, enraged by the all-powerful Furies, the modern victim rails against himself, only to become the accomplice in a sickening spiral of prostitution. . . . (pp. 57-8)

From the anguish which gives first voice to this poem, a floodtide of alienating phenomena engulfs the antagonists. Their intercourse is a cholerically futile defense against despair. Their habitat is correspondingly inhospitable, a nightmarish admixture of Eros and the grotesque. . . . In this modern Armageddon, everything converges at the apex of hell: "y duras olas que suben la piel hacia la muerte." (p. 58)

Perhaps because it harks backward to *Residencias I, II* and pushes forward Neruda's social project, **"Las furias y las penas"** embodies the dilemma of an irrational dialectic and elaborates an unbearable prospect. If I am correct in taking "el odio" as the antecedent of "su estatua," the speaker is at dead center: exiled, devoid of feeling, self-destroying. Rejection of self and hatred of the devouring other preclude humanity. In the zones of radical negativity which Neruda explores, sex is not renewal; rather, like

a ricocheting missile, its destructive energy returns to knock down hunted and hunter. Hatred and despair, rejection and submission, oscillate to the rhythm of nihilism.

The "Furies and Punishments" of failed humanity feed on themselves in Neruda's subterranean vision. With no viable outlet, these irrational outbursts fixate on woman as whore. She is reduced to a single, emasculating function, wearing the scarlet brand of ire and perversity. . . . The speaker calls upon the Furies to impose punishment befitting sub-human criminality. . . . Isn't this threat the ultimate revenge a poet might conceive? Not to have speech, not to sing, to have one's voice pierced, this is the rhapsode's most bitter attack on his primal enemy. (pp. 58-9)

Stanza XV makes a transition in which the poem moves away from the particular (you/I) towards a generalization about life's emptiness. Through imagery that links abortive nature with human sterility, the narrator strikes a universally desolate chord: succession, whether in nature, individuals or time, atomizes. . . . (p. 59)

Disintegration, therefore the impossibility of continuity, formulates one of the poem's key metaphors. Alone, the "I" is spectator and actor in the drama of end-game. . . . He has wallowed on humanity's sordid bed, "cien veces ocupada por miserables parejas," retelling the story of incessant failure, of nowhere man and woman. . . . The deadness of love making is augmented by the inability to connect with other human beings, to bridge solitudes dialectically. Thus, efforts to find a way out of the black, to reverse stasis, end in pulverization. . . .

If there are no personal or temporal linkages, each action is a onceness, governed by chance, flat and ultimately absurd. Such is the common thread woven into the last eight stanzas of **"Las furias y las penas."** But unlike the majority of preceding sections, the final block of verses is characterized by more objective diction and certain rational statements. . . . As if wiped clean of memory, the speaker has only unmarked time—static continuity—and the fleeting recall of orgasm on which to make his moorings. . . . The sex act has no apparent climax, only a pathetic finality or an inconclusive dropping off. In this erotic hell, the partners are both loveless and incompatible, briefly joined in a doomed attempt at salvaging a shadow of identity. . . . They are irreconcilably separate, each one debasing the other as the agent of his/her unbearable frustration and total failure.

The mixed sequence of tenses in Stanza XVIII suggests that Neruda meant its verbal structure as a kind of summing up: "Era una sorda ciencia"; "he rodado a las grandes coronas genitales." The circularity, from where the speaker has been to where he is, defines both the content and literary form of **"Las furias y las penas"** (Stanza XIX). The poet explicitly draws attention to this alliance:

> Este es un cuento de puertos adonde
> llega uno, al azar, y sube a las colinas,
> suceden tantas cosas.

The main idea contained here telescopes the philosophical outlook of the entire poem. What makes up life's narrative ('cuento') are single, unconnected events, governed by chance, and meaningless ('suceden'). Man is out of control, like someone hallucinating one-night stands in sordid places. This statement and the one that follows provide the clearest outline of the thrust and power in **"Las furias y las penas."**

Stanza XX correlates the speaker's anguish with his sense of betrayal. . . . From the point of view which informs the violence and hopelessness of the poem, Neruda needed radical diction and esthetic nonconformity to carry his expression from wasteland to printed page. Therefore, I believe that it is faithful to the text to understand **"Las furias y las penas"** as an art of love, in diametric opposition to Ovid's *Ars Amandi.*

Echoing leitmotivs, Stanza XXI states in a low key the pain of illusions smashed. Both the kind and quality of desired realities have been banished and will remain locked out of the speaker's future. . . . The longed-for intensities, such as the experience of true passion, will be denied. He is hemmed in, totally isolated and without a spark of hope.

In contrast with the plea for repose, Stanzas XXII and XXIII mandate an ineluctable, berserk future: "corre," "corre," "corre," "golpea," "derriba." With the final image, this devastating wave of frenzy crests in frozen sexual assault. . . . (pp. 59-60)

In words more dreadful than Quevedo's most piercing *desengaño,* Neruda encloses *his* **"Furias y penas"** in the grip of death against life. . . . Thus, hunter and hunted come together in fatal stasis, and the tragedy of their defeat will be played out endlessly in the theater of the absurd. Like the best of Neruda's poetic codas, these lines are remarkable in their fusion of terrible import with beautiful cadence.

The poetic coherence of **"Las furias y las penas"** derives from its underlying dialectical fault. Like natural rifts, Neruda's is a metaphor of catastrophe. His male/female antagonism feeds on its own bitter divorce; blocked by psychic and moral bankruptcy, the possibility of union, through sexual or social action, could not find entry in his esthetic of dehumanization. (pp. 60-1)

The organic unity of Neruda's work shows a pattern of evolution plus revolution. In such a dynamics, even the occasional extreme perspective offers adequate textuality. Despite its failed dialectic, **"Las furias y las penas"** sustains a haunting beauty in meaning and tone. Thus, this major transitional poem bears the unmistakable signature of Neruda's originality and achievement. (p. 61)

> Florence L. Yudin, *"The Dialectical Failure in Neruda's 'Las furias y las penas',"* in Hispania, *Vol. 68, No. 1, March, 1985, pp. 55-62.*

Jack Schmitt

Chile, stretching some twenty-six hundred miles from north to south, averages but a hundred miles wide. Some of the world's most arid deserts in the north and agricultural lands in the central valley give way to the pristine temperate-zone rainforest extending toward the south. Pablo Neruda (1904-1973), the Chilean Nobel laureate, was raised in Temuco, roughly two-thirds of the way southward, where farming areas yield to timberlands. The capital of Cautín Province, Temuco is also the gateway to the spectacular Chilean Lake District, which lies between the towns of Temuco and Puerto Montt. Due to the extremely heavy precipitation from the Andean ridge to the coast, the valleys, set against the magnificent backdrop of the Andes, are blessed with snowcapped volcanic mountains, glaciers, countless rivers and lakes, and a lush, dense, impenetrable vegetation, an ideal habitat for the rainforest flora and fauna. According to Neruda, these are the lands that "sank their roots into my poetry . . . My life is a long pilgrimage that is always turning on itself, always returning to the woods in the south, to the forest lost to me." It is thus fact, not nationalistic pride, that motivates Neruda to claim that "anyone who hasn't been in the Chilean forest doesn't know this planet."

Emir Rodríguez-Monegal correctly asserts that the "last paradox" of Neruda, "a millionaire in books and personae, is that all his works originate and end in a single definitive image: the rain that 'a sad child like me' hears forever after." In the poetry of his maturity, Neruda insistently recalls the familiar markers of his childhood: Temuco and its surroundings, summer holidays on the coast (Puerto Saavedra, Imperial del Sur), horseback trips along the beach and through the forest to Lake Budi, his dramatic escape from Chile to Argentina many years later by way of Temuco, Ranco and Maihue lakes, through the forest and over the Andes on horseback to San Martín, and his obsessive catalogs of Mapuche placenames, the flora and fauna, the entire vast, humming nature of the southern rainforest.

In an interview with Robert Bly, Neruda said,

> Poetry in South America is a different matter altogether. You see, there are in our countries rivers which have no names, trees nobody knows, and birds which nobody has described . . . Our duty, then, as we understand it, is to express what is unheard of. Everything has been painted in Europe. But not in America. In that sense, Whitman was a great teacher . . . He had tremendous eyes to see everything—he taught us to see things. He was our poet.

To name an object is to identify and catalog it, showing how it differs from other things which superficially it may resemble. A scientific name always refers to the same plant or animal and may be used in any part of the world. It is thus significant that Neruda often gives both the Spanish and the scientific names for the flora and fauna closest to his heart, for there is just one correct scientific name for each animal or plant. In Chile, for example, the lapwing (*Vanellus* species) is known as the *queltehue,* a name of Araucanian origin. In Argentina, the same bird is called the *tero-tero.* "Everything exists in the word," says Neruda.

Birds are only a small, albeit important, aspect of Neruda's multifaceted evocation of nature, and nature imagery is a constant in his poetry from early on. He had quite thoroughly covered the subject of birds before he began to write the ***Art of Birds.*** Among the most beautiful of his more than two hundred odes are those dedicated to the birds: **"To the Birds of Chile," "To Bird-watching," "To the Oriole," "To Hummingbirds," "To the Gull," "To a Wandering Albatross," "To the Migration of Birds," "To September Wings,"** and **"To the Gulls of Antofagasta."** There are many bird poems and countless images and instances of figurative language relating to birds and flight in other books by Neruda.

Arte de pájaros was first published in 1966. . . . It is a brief but beautiful, charming, loving, and playful book in which the poet's passionate lyricism and powers of observation cannot but impress the reader. Of the fifty-three poems in it, thirty-eight are devoted to the "real" birds (*pajarintos*), twelve are riddles (*pajarantes*), and three longer poems (**"Migration," "The Flight,"** and **"The Poet Says Good-bye to the Birds"**) give cohesion and coherence to the entire book.

Neruda's impressionistic sketches are brilliant in capturing movement, light, the habitat, and the peculiar characteristics of the different species. The poems reflect a broad range of moods and feelings. Birds of prey and carrion birds are presented in an ominous or negative light, and Neruda the social critic emerges in a number of the poems. Several of the most painfully nostalgic poems are those dedicated to the birds of the Far South. The large and sociable black-faced ibis is synonymous with the rainforest lakes, rivers, marshes, and meadows, and Neruda situates it in the heart of the Lake District, "from Ranco to Lake Maihue / and the meadows of Llanquihue." He sees the flying formations of ibis in a reverie, perhaps from the streets of a foreign city, where he poignantly recalls "the fluvial waters," "the forest's secret sounds," "a silence of / bursting roots and seeds," the "pungent rainforest aroma, / feet sinking in leaves, / lakes like opened eyes," and the "smell of fallen cinnamon laurel." (pp. 9-11)

The elegant black-necked swan, perhaps the most important bird to the poet, receives the shortest (two mysterious lines) poem in the book. In one of the first chapters of his *Memoirs,* Neruda gives a moving account of his attempts to revive an injured swan that had been brought to him from Lake Budi to Puerto Saavedra. After twenty days of nursing it, he was carrying it back home from the river when he "felt a ribbon unrolling, and something like a black arm brushed my face. It was the long, sinuous neck falling. That's when I learned that swans don't sing when they die." A beautiful evocation of these swans in Lake Budi appears in his poem **"El lago de los cisnes" ("Swan Lake").** The poem on the Chilean pigeon, which is found in the heart of the forest, particularly in stands of araucaria pines, is unusually tender and poignant. This bird was attacked by Newcastle disease in the mid fifties and its numbers so reduced that it seemed doomed to extinction. Full protection of the species has fortunately resulted in its slow comeback. (p. 11)

Out of fairness to Argentina, it should be stressed that the Lake District, most of the birds, even some of the lakes are shared by these two beautiful countries and peoples. In the Argentine provinces of Neuquén, Río Negro, and Chubut, Andean Patagonia lies in the shadow of the Chilean rainforest and the birds move freely from country to country without visas, passports, work permits, or border inspections. I know Pablo Neruda always supported such freedom of movement for the peoples of this planet as well as the birds. Finally, I shall confess that these translations have been a labor of love, and I should like to thank the great Chilean poet for his generous legacy of beauty and love, his reverence for life, his plea for justice and equality, peace and goodwill, and his passionate commitment to the human enterprise. (p. 12)

Jack Schmitt, in an introduction to Art of Birds *by Pablo Neruda, translated by Jack Schmitt, University of Texas Press, 1985, pp. 9-12.*

James Finn Cotter

[*The Separate Rose*], Pablo Neruda's sequence of twenty-four poems about a visit to Easter Island in 1971, has been translated by William O'Daly and published in a bilingual edition. The poems, alternating between "The Men" and "The Island," contrast modern man's indifference, competitiveness, alienation, and guilt with the native genius that raised the stone figures in a spirit of cooperation, creativity, and religious awe. The poet finds himself caught between the two worlds, past and present, oceanic and urbanized, permanent and transient. Neruda, who knew he was dying of cancer at the time, never forgets that he is a tourist and visitor, yet he yearns to absorb the reality of the island and to be reborn. At the midpoint of the sequence, he glows "with new radiance":

> I want to touch, to know Oceania,
> stone and wind, to build and build again,
> to court on my knees the chastity of the sun,
> to dig out my destiny with poor bloody hands.

Disillusioned and ill, the poet found in the natural setting and mysterious statues a testament of lasting hope. Just as wind and water formed the island, the human spirit shaped these monuments of "moral radiance," "purity," and "truth." Some of the names he gives to the island ring with the beauty of a litany: "separate rose," "natural star, green diadem," "tower of light," and "navel of gold." However, when Neruda depicts his fellow tourists and the cities from which they come, he descends to name-calling; his presentation of contemporary life is utterly bleak and negative, unrelieved even by irony. Today's pilgrims "murdered / the five-masted ships" and arrive "in enormous aluminum geese, / seated correctly, drinking sour cocktails." The poet breaks away from the other travelers on the island to undergo his mystical transformation, but in the end he returns with them, a man "of our mournful professions and occupations." The pilgrim can only hope that the great sea will protect Easter Island "from our barren brutality." Nevertheless, the journey has been taken and has made a difference, at least to the poet:

> We went a long way, a long way
> to understand the orbits of stone,
> the extinguished eyes still gazing out,
> the gigantic faces ready to enter eternity.

(p. 160)

James Finn Cotter, "Poetry's Need to Name," in The Hudson Review, *Vol. XXXIX, No. 1, Spring, 1986, pp. 153-65.*

Peter Wild

Chilean poet Pablo Neruda may well go down in the literary histories as the Hemisphere's greatest poet of the twentieth century. This for his surreal leaps in *Living on Earth* and for his celebrations transcending political turmoil in his *General Song.* Ironically, in one way of looking at it, Neruda took over where our own Walt Whitman left off, refining the good, gray poet's exuberance even while turning it to modern ends. Foremost among other American poets, Robert Bly ingenuously acknowledges Neruda's mentorship, an influence widely seen in the "deep-image" poetry popular in the 1960s and 1970s.

One need not press Neruda's case beyond this. Students of contemporary American poetry have been saying as much for nearly two decades. However, most English-speaking readers know the South-American poet from the *Selected Poems,* translated by Ben Belitt, and perhaps from the less readily available but far more readable *Twenty Poems* decaled into English by Robert Bly and James Wright. These appeared in 1961 and 1967 respectively. This leaves us with a hiatus. For the Chilean poet kept publishing right up until the end, and upon his death in 1973 he left eight manuscripts on his desk. Two recent translations, *Still Another Day* and *The Separate Rose,* go some way in bridging the gap.

Despite the fact that Neruda devotes each to a different subject, he cuts them from like cloth, for in these writings we see the circumstances of his life. The poet was dying of cancer, and he knew it. In the early 1970s, he saw his country sliding toward a bloody welter climaxing in its President's violent death. As Neruda looks back on his own literary successes, he measures their context and senses, as one critic says of Emerson at a similar stage, that "the spiritual achievement he had formerly dreamed of . . . was not accessible to him or to any man." Hence, two lines from the first of these translations bracket both collections:

> . . . the portrait of bullet-riddled yesterday, the love of
> the
> unbearable earth. . . .

Neruda has not given up his lifelong faith in the redeeming florescence of the earth, but as a rational person he despairs over the shambles man has made of his terrestrial garden.

Or, rather, the shambles that technological man, the invader of the garden, has made of the earth. In *Still Another Day,* the poet evokes the rain-soaked forests surrounding his childhood town of Temuco. He recalls the mythology of the Araucano Indians while remembering the tribe's cultural dismemberment by the white man's takeover. Likewise, *A Separate Rose* results from a trip to Easter Island, a Chilean possession 2,300 miles west of the mainland. Here, on the last Pacific dot of lava settled by Polynesians, Neruda meditates on the gigantic figures for which the place is famous, "the stone larvae of mystery" erected by an ancient culture now shattered by asphalt and jet airliners.

It sounds gloomy, and of course it is. Yet the gloom serves as underlying structure for an overlying, glittering wit. As elsewhere, Neruda's allusions are not always clear. That is not the issue. Clear or obscure, drawing on private or public visions, they ring with their own poetic rightness. This holds true particularly for *Still Another Day* in which the writer caricatures the rough-shod conquistadors:

> Columbus passes with the first hummingbird
> (bird on the wrist), little lightning bolt,
> don Pedro de Valdivia passes hatless

and later returns, headless. . . .

In *A Separate Rose,* the poet displays a saving sense of imagery by sawing back and forth between descriptions of the giant stone heads and mockery at the expense of the gawking tourists. The former are "faces of hardened honey," monuments "of naked silence" so weighted with significance they are "ready to enter eternity." In contrast, the tourists arrive "in enormous aluminum geese" to "discover nothing more than the price of their drinks." Then, after their short stay, they return to "wheels ready to roll."

Together the works tend toward the carping, but it is good carping. In all likelihood the two books won't go down among Neruda's best, though they reassure us that the dying poet's feel for irony and his native earth remained rich to the end. (pp. 264-66)

> *Peter Wild, in a review of "Still Another Day"*
> *and "The Separate Rose," in* North Dakota
> Quarterly, *Vol. 54, No. 2, Spring, 1986, pp.*
> *264-66.*

Marjorie Agosin

Any posthumous poetry poses the question of whether the author has had the time to revise and put his writings in order. This is the case of the eight posthumous books of Pablo Neruda that were published almost simultaneously in 1973, and whose order is the following: *La rosa separada (The separate rose), Jardín de invierno (Winter garden), 2000, El corazón amarillo (The yellow heart), El libro de las preguntas (The book of questions), Elegía (Elegy,) El mar y las campanas (The sea and the bells)* and *Defectos escogidos (Selected failings).* However, this order, which the poet himself preferred, was altered after Neruda's death and therefore they appeared in different years. *El mar y las campanas* was the first to be published.

In this chapter, we will not follow the order of publication or the order chosen by the poet but treat the posthumous books according to thematic coherence, concentrating principally on *La rosa separada* (1973), *El mar y las campanas* (1973), and *Jardín de invierno* (1974).

The language used in the posthumous poetry becomes progressively more simple, taking on an even more prosaic quality than the *Odes* or *Extravagaria.* The rich metaphors of the early poetry and the transparency of the highly lyrical language are left behind. Throughout these poems we find no easily identifiable poetic unity, as there used to be in the *Residences,* the *Odes,* or the *Canto general.* These verses can almost be read separately, as if each book were made up of separate poems with no unifying theme. It is important to mention this, since Neruda is a poet of books and not poems. The reverse occurs in his posthumous poetry. It would seem that these books form part of an unconcluded collection, from which the ill-crafted poems have not been eliminated. Still, they too are important since they are the last work of the poet.

The dominant aspect of the posthumous poetry is introspection. Now near death, Neruda commences a process of hermetic self-contemplation in which his self is the essential poetic material to be rediscovered. This man who was for so many years the lyric spokesman of others, now fatigued, decides to seclude himself within the confines of his rapidly fading persona. He excuses himself for his omissions and bids farewell to all those who, for so many reasons, could not be part of his final verses. (pp. 112-13)

The poems of greatest relevance in Neruda's posthumous poetry are those in which . . . the realm of personal experience predominates over political ideology, the social poems of *2000,* and the varied poems of *El corazón amarillo.*

La rosa separada, El mar y las campanas, and *Jardín de invierno* form a trilogy with a common perspective: the aging poet nearing the other shore is delineated as a solitary figure seeking communion with nature, especially with the sea and the sand. The anticipation that the present will vanish because approaching death will return him to nature allows him to contemplate his mortality with serenity and acceptance.

These three books permit us to sketch the figure of Neruda, walking toward that same sea that beckoned to him so powerfully in all his poetry, and that will take him out of his suffering. Nonetheless, these books are not the tragic, morose work of a man near death but a man at peace with himself, his life, and his imminent end.

After his return from Paris in 1971, Pablo Neruda travels to Easter Island (Rapa Nui in the indigenous language), a remote site in the Pacific that belongs to Chile, where the gigantic and strange anthropomorphic sculptures planted on the green expanses of the island stand as a backdrop to the sea. In [*La rosa separada*], however, Neruda sees no fusion of man with nature but a fragmentation reflected in the book's division into "Los hombres" (The men) and "La isla" (The island). *La rosa separada* is a book of disjunctions between men and nature. "La isla" is purity, intuition, and uncorrupted earth. "Los hombres" are the awkward, heavy, inopportune creatures who crowd onto the island. . . . (pp. 113-14)

Throughout *La rosa separada,* men are defined as "pobres hombres," victims of their silent daily tedium and their colorless lives, who hope for promotions, publications, discussions, and acceptance by an elite of monotonous established values. The island is just the opposite of these humans. It is a separate rose in a garden, in a wild mythical surrounding made for and by the gods. The men prefer to remain separate from the island, which is metaphorically identified with primeval matter and the uncontaminated purity of nature. For this reason, the poet, like the rest, abandons this place:

> And that is my cowardice,
> I take my oath here:
> I was only capable of transitory
> buildings, and in this capital without walls
> made of light, salt,
> stones and thoughts,
> like the rest, I gazed and left,
> frightened by the luminous mythology
> the statues surrounded by blue silence.
>   ("Los hombres XIX" ["The men XIX"])

The poet, united with the alienated men he used to criticize, is seen here as indecisive, vacillating, and tangled within himself, alien to that universe of silent stones and mysteries, so he returns to the city, having learned nothing, enveloped in desolate sadness. . . . (pp. 114-15)

Rapa Nui and Macchu Picchu, two monuments in Latin American history, are seen by one poet, but through different prisms. Macchu Picchu in the 1950s represents the integration of a wild and beautiful nature and a personal credo sung by the poet. Rapa Nui is seen in its beauty and mystery, secluded but separate from men who in no way represent Latin America but rather a universal condition born of bourgeois shackles, tedium, and tourism. The poet, too, is part of that human mass that has arrived on the island only to invade and to increase the human pollution. In poem 3, the poet says to the ancient Rapa Nui:

> Ancient Rapa Nui, country without voice,
> forgive us bubblers of the world:
> we have come from everywhere to spit on your lava
>   ("La isla III" ["The Island III"])

Spittle, synonymous with violation and devastation by the men who bring to the island their conflicts and differences, is the very antithesis of the pure volcanic lava of Easter Island.

The poet's response to this conflict between men and the natural world is to take refuge in solitude and in contemplation of his experience, far from that modern world of bitter discussions, wars, and disease.

Silence and seclusion are the leitmotivs of *Jardín de invierno.* If he was "otoñabundo" ("autumnful") in *Extravagaria,* now he is in the winter of his life. He alludes to that last season just as the nocturnal images of *One Hundred Love Sonnets* anticipated it twenty years before. In the title poem we find the expression of awareness of the life cycle:

> I am a book of snow,
> a spacious hand, a meadow,
> a circle that waits,
> I belong to the earth and its winter.
>   ("Jardín de invierno")

In this stanza we find the characteristics we mentioned earlier as inherent in the posthumous poetry: the serene resignation of a man who knows that his days are numbered and that he will return to the eternal regenerating earth. Neruda associates death with the primitive doctrines that propound a return to those roots. Therefore, death is not an end but a continual rebirth. In another poem, **"Con Quevedo en primavera"** ("With Quevedo in spring"), we find the concept of a nature that germinates and surrounds all living things in juxtaposition to the poet who vainly seeks spiritual regeneration. This concept is described in terms of the night, the snow, and other metaphors associated with winter's passing. That longing indicates a continuous proliferation of infinite springs to come:

> External spring, don't torment me,
> give me today the slumber of the nocturnal
> leaves, the night of the dead, the metals,
> and the roots, And so many extinguished Springs
> that awaken each spring.
>   ("Con Quevedo en primavera")

The "extinguished spring" germinating once more in the precincts of death recalls previous poems in which spring gives life and love. Here we have one of the central aspects of *Jardín de invierno.* In this context death is only a passing state. In the posthumous poetry, Neruda does not depart from the poetic theme present in all his books: nature as a redemptive force and the integration of man with the universal cycle that intertwines life with death.

Another recurrent motif in this book is the desire for solitude not as an escape from other men but as a state of preparation for the union with nature. In this properly titled collection, the poet seeks to comprehend forces, like the sea and the earth, that will become part of himself. The first poem of *Jardín de invierno* exemplifies this state of mind. There he says:

> No one is missing in the garden. No one is there:
> only the green and black winter, the day
> wide awake like an apparition,
> > **("El egoista" ["The selfish one"])**

At the end of the poem he asks that no one intrude on his need for solitude, his only remaining refuge from "institutions, medals, and propositions."

Still, with that same desire for solitude and peace comes guilt, for in *Canto general* Neruda proclaimed himself the poet of communion with man. At the end of the poem his ambivalence becomes more evident and for a moment we glimpse the pained Neruda of the *Residence* cycle:

> And there is a scent of sharp solitude
> humidity, and birth water again
> what can I do if I breathe with no one,
> why should I feel wounded?
> > **("El egoista")**

In comparing solitude to water, humidity, and amniotic fluid, and linking man to the cycles of nature, Neruda comes full circle thematically. But the tour de force in this poem is that the same elements do not act as integrating forces but entropic ones. The poet's pain comes precisely from those elements in his poetry that earlier were its essential strength.

In a poem dedicated to the sea, **"Llama el océano" ("The call of the sea")** the poet, from afar, imagines and brings forth the sea of his country, since the poem is written while Neruda is ambassador to France. The expatriate Neruda refuses the alien sea of foreign cities and longs to die in his country, facing the beach at Isla Negra. It is a prophetic poem because his wish was fulfilled. (pp. 115-18)

This poem also presents a duality of the sea that awaits the poet near his native land and death that wants to pull him away. The sea, for Neruda, is a site of cosmic reconciliation and transubstantiation. Another important poem that alludes to the return to the sea and the homeland is **"Regreso," ("Return")**. The last stanza is particularly revealing:

> the earth wrapped in shadows and glimmers
> and the wineglass of the sea touching my lips.
> > **("Regreso")**

This poem has been analyzed both by Jaime Alazraki and Manuel Durán. For both critics the idea of the wineglass sea is related to the Nerudian concept of diving into his own being as if he were diving into the sea. Alazraki believes that the marine images of the poem refer to the concept of total unity of nature and man: from that unity peace filters through. For Neruda it is a peace that leaves him facing a deep well. The well might be death but that no longer matters. Life and the world have now been incorporated with the being that breaks itself like a crystal shell on the rock, and in the blow, as in a flash of lightning, life glimmers in its incommensurable unity.

When the glass is destroyed and spilled Neruda begins the entry into another stage of equal cosmic force—the death that, despite its potential for annihilation, can be regeneration.

Jardín de invierno keeps its essential unity throughout, centered on the personal reality of the poet and his destiny, with the exception of the poem, **"Otoño," ("Autumn")** in which he speaks of the last days of the Allende government. Here it seems that the political Neruda, the friend and defender of the people, returns from self-contemplation for a brief moment to denounce a new injustice.

The introspective poems, with their desire to be alone in the garden, are a way for the poet to prepare himself for merging himself with other men, with matter, and with the vast sovereignty of the sea: "Ya no hay más estrella que el mar" (Now there is no star except the sea) (**"La estrella," ["Star"]**).

Solitude, silence, and introspection are the recurrent motifs of this collection [*El mar y las campanas*] that, with *La rosa separada* and *Jardín de invierno,* comprises a thematic trilogy in Neruda's posthumous poetry. In addition there are also numerous associations with sound and music in *El mar y las campanas.* . . . (pp. 119-20)

The counterpoint to the theme of music is the theme of silence, that silence necessary for the comprehension of the flow of time. In the poem that begins the collection, we read:

> Man waits
> and only
> his bell
> rings above the others
> keeping in its emptiness
> an implacable silence)
> > **("Inicial" ["Initial"])**

Man can find his voice in meditative introspection.

In **"Salud decimos cada día" ("We say 'cheers' every day")**, there is another type of silence, the false one of empty and meaningless words:

> You hear it clearly, we exist,
> Cheers, cheers, cheers,
> to this one and that one
> and the other one
> and to the poisoned knife.
> > **("Salud decimos cada día")**

It is this atmosphere that the poet wishes to escape, that sonorous emptiness "como para cegar o ensordecer" (that can blind or deafen) ("Les contaré" [I will tell you]). Thus, in alluding to the false silence, Neruda says "Hace tiempo que no escucho nada" (I haven't heard anything for a while) ("Les contaré"). In "Quiero saber" (I want to know) again we have the desire for a perfect silence far from the wordly noise of men and to a certain extent, the desire not to speak. The poet opts for nonverbal communication or for saying nothing since speech only serves to "introduce merchandise," like the colonizers who "cambiando baratijas por silencio" (exchanged trinkets for silence) ("Quiero saber").

In *El mar y las campanas* there is sharp criticism of language that says nothing, that is filled with cavities and voids. Neruda proposes that one will realize himself in quietude and interior truth.

Pablo Neruda, at the end of his days, executes a profound critique of the craft of the word that only obscures communication, or words like nets that only entangle the content and lead to a vacuum, to nowhere. . . . (pp. 120-21)

The dimension of social and political solidarity and the continued commitment to meaning turns this posthumous poetry into a deconstruction of false premises and values. But Neruda always presents an alternative, a new possibility: individual examination of conscience.

The word, used before as a vehicle to denounce suffering and exploitation, becomes a defense of silence. Neruda in using such apparently contradictory images as a bell without sound or a submerged silence, is implying all this. *El mar y las campanas* goes in a direction chosen by many poets such as Mallarmé, whose search led to the concept of a music of silence.

"Se vuelve a yo" (**"A return to me"**) synthesizes not only the themes of *El mar y las campanas,* but all the highly personal and introspective posthumous poetry of Neruda, which uses the personal language of *Extravagaria* but without the playful spirit of that book:

> One returns to the self as if to an old house
> with nails and slots, so that
> a person tired of himself
> like a suit full of holes,
> tries to walk nude in the rain,
> he tries to take a dip in pure water,
> in elemental wind, and cannot
> but return to the well of himself.
>
> (**"Se vuelve a yo"**)

The tone of reflexive intimacy that predominates in *El mar y las campanas* is particularly evident in this poem. Neruda uses the symbology of the house, with its "tools and slots" to express a dual journey: the physical return to his parental home in Chile and a spiritual return to himself and the origins of his poetic impulses. The image of a suit full of holes, used previously in the famous poem **"I Explain a Few Things"** of the *Third Residence,* implies a casting off of old ways and creeds that leads the way to a new poetic and political ideology. Also in this poem, the suit full of holes reveals the desire to abandon the old garments of his previous poetry and begin afresh in "agua pura" (pure water). Neruda is in search of transparency and purity: "porque llueve / quiere el hombre mojarse en agua pura" (because it's raining, man wants to drench himself in pure water); yet he knows that the return to virginal immaculateness is a mirage, for one can only return "al pozo de sí mismo" (to the well of one's self).

Once more we see the encounter of man and his solitude, the poet's reencounter with his own essence and a new resurrection that is part of personal regeneration.

Though the theme of death appears in *El libro de las preguntas,* it is certainly not the prevalent one in this playful book, which, as the title suggests, is written in the form of questions. The style of the collection is brief and cryptic, full of interrogatives written with candor and childlike ingenuousness. The book conveys the vision of the poet in perpetual wonderment at the problems of humanity. There are questions about himself, about the weather, and about philosophy.

Each question corresponds to a certain vision or attitude toward the world such as when he asks himself how many churches there are in heaven. The organization of each poem is difficult to discern, and there are questions on the same page that apparently have nothing to do with each other. All of which gives this text a sense of naiveté, of continual playfulness that makes it delightful to read. In its deceptive simplicity it contains the great metaphors and themes of all times: death, life, rebirth, and all the questions that have no answers. The appeal of the book lies in the marvelous questions that mix the sophisticated poet with the child that he once was. . . . (pp. 122-23)

Defectos escogidos, 2000, and *El corazón amarillo* are three of the books of posthumous poetry that shall be mentioned but not discussed here, since the most important volumes are those already analyzed. *2000* is a collection of poems attacking the technological era, and *Elegía* is the recounting of a journey through the Soviet Union, a country that for years was the ideological center for the poet. It is interesting to compare some poems of this text with those dedicated to Russia in the *Third Residence,* like the **"Canto a Stalingrado."** *El corazón amarillo* is a collection of random poems that center upon the absurdity of social behavior and convention.

El fin del viaje (*Journey's end*) and *El río invisible* (*The invisible river*) are considered posthumous books in the sense that they appear after Neruda's death but many of the works in the books were written at all stages of his life and are simply collected here. Such is the case of *El río invisible,* a mixture of prose and poetry from the poet's youth. . . . *El río invisible* is a true jewel for those interested in the period of Neruda's adolescence because it contains the seeds of his conception of the world, tells of his relationships, and his reading.

El fin del viaje is also a collection of dispersed poems culled from a number of Chilean and foreign journals. The book enhances the poet's personality and identifies the people with whom he corresponded. For example, **"Elegía para cantar"** (**"Elegy for singing"**) is a moving poem dedicated to the eminent folklorist Violeta Parra, and the poem **"Mujer"** (**"Woman"**) is dedicated to the washerwoman, women workers, and wives of prisoners, a poem where we see women becoming involved in the social struggle and future political change.

The second part of the text of *El fin del viaje* consists of a section entitled *Paloma por dentro* (*Dove inside*), which is the original facsimile edition of some poems of *Residence on Earth* with illustrations by Federico García Lorca.

In *El libro de las preguntas* we find the following query:

> Isn't our life a tunnel
> Between two dim clarities?

The concept of a tunnel sinking into the self is the essence of this posthumous poetry, written largely in the winter of Neruda's life. But death is not feared but almost welcomed as a time for clarification and, at the same time, the commencement of a new existence where "one returns to the self as to an old house." The house is a space of reflection and introspection, necessary in order to enter into dialogue with the sea and with silence.

The shortcomings of the posthumous poetry are comprehensible if we remember that this is the story of a man tired of being chronicler of others. The posthumous poetry is a clear integration with nature, with that child of the southern forests, with that man who hopes to reintegrate himself with the roots that he believes will nourish him. Therefore the poetry is more personal than ideological. (pp. 124-25)

> *Marjorie Agosin, in her* Pablo Neruda, *translated by Lorraine Roses, Twayne Publishers, 1986, 157 p.*

FURTHER READING

Anderson, David G, Jr. "Pablo Neruda's Noncelebratory Elementary Odes." *Romance Notes* XXVI, No. 3: 226-31.
    Examination of Neruda's books *Odas elementales, Nuevos odas elementales, Tercer libro de las odas,* and *Navegaciones y regreso.* In opposition to many critics who view the poems in these volumes as works of celebration, Anderson asserts that many express denigration.

Belitt, Ben. "Pablo Neruda: A New Decade." In *Pablo Neruda: A New Decade (Poems: 1958-1967)* by Pablo Neruda, edited by Ben Belitt, translated by Ben Belitt and Alastair Reid, pp. i-vii. New York: Grove Press, 1969.
    A brief introduction to Neruda's later poems.

———. "The Laughing Neruda." In *Pablo Neruda: A New Decade (Poems: 1958-1967)* by Pablo Neruda, edited by Ben Belitt, translated by Ben Belitt and Alastair Reid, pp. ix-xvi. New York: Grove Press, 1969.
    Analysis of *Estravagario* in which Belitt asserts that the poems in this volume "represent, politically a kind of 'revisionism' " and serve to convey "both the irreverence and autonomy of Neruda's commitment to an ideology."

Bly, Robert (unsigned). "Refusing to Be Theocritus." Introduction to *Twenty Poems* by Pablo Neruda, translated by James Wright and Robert Bly, pp. 7-17. [Madison, Minn.]: The Sixties Press, 1967.
    Biographical and critical introduction to translations from Neruda's *Residencia en la tierra, Canto general de Chile,* and *Odas elementales* in which Bly calls the pieces in the first volume "the greatest surrealist poems yet written in a western language." Includes an interview with Neruda.

Costa, René de. *The Poetry of Pablo Neruda.* Cambridge: Harvard University Press, 1979, 213 p.
    Reassessment in which de Costa attempts to lay grounds for critical consensus regarding the significance of Neruda's major works. See excerpt in *CLC,* Vol. 28.

Durán, Manuel, and Safir, Margery. *Earth Tones: The Poetry of Pablo Neruda.* Bloomington, Ind.: Indiana University Press, 1981, 200 p.
    Gerneral biographical and critical study focusing on such topics as Neruda's love and nature poetry and posthumously published works. See excerpt in *CLC,* Vol. 28.

Figueroa, Esperanza. "Pablo Neruda en inglés." *Revista iberoamericana* 82-83 (1973): 301-47.
    Annotated bibliography of English-language criticism on Neruda and English translations of his works. Includes a critical analysis of English translations.

Hart, Stephen M. " 'Galope muerto' Revisited." *Hispanic Journal* 9, No. 1 (Fall 1987): 107-14.
    Interpretation of a poem from Neruda's cycle *Residencia en la tierra* that draws from the criticism of Amado Alonso, Alfredo Lozada, and René de Costa while centering on "ambiguous images which remain undiscussed by these critics."

Neale Silva, Eduardo. "Neruda's Poetic Beginnings." *Modern Poetry Studies* 5 (1974): 15-23.
    Neale Silva, who attended the Instituto Pedagógico with Neruda from 1922 to 1924, describes Neruda's early personality and ideology.

Perriam, Christopher. "Metaphorical Machismo: Neruda's Love Poetry." *Forum for Modern Language Studies* XXIV, No. 1 (January 1988): 58-77.
    Analysis of the critical tendency to deconstruct Neruda's works according to collective responses. Specifically focuses on sexist or chauvinist elements that are presumably expressed through metaphor in his love poetry.

Pring-Mill, Robert. "Preface." *The Heights of Macchu Picchu* by Pablo Neruda, translated by Nathaniel Tarn, pp. vii-xix. New York: Farrar, Straus and Giroux, 1966.
    Identifying this work as Neruda's "finest poem," Pring-Mill briefly discusses each segment in Neruda's acclaimed poem.

Riess, Frank. *The Word and the Stone: Language and Imagery in Neruda's "Canto general".* London: Oxford University Press, 1972, 170 p.
    Structuralist study of Neruda's poem in which Riess analyzes the poet's ordering of imagery as it derives from his personal experience.

Santí, Enrico-Mario. *Pablo Neruda: The Poetics of Prophecy.* Ithaca: Cornell University Press, 1982, 255 p.
    Study of rhetoric in Neruda's major works in which Santí aims "to probe Neruda's sense of prophecy as the significant metaphor for modern poetry."

Schade, George D. "Sight, Sense, and Sound; Seaweed, Onions, and Oranges: Notes on Translating Neruda." *Symposium* XXXVIII, No. 2 (Summer 1984): 159-73.
    One of the more accessible critical essays that analyzes the difficulties of translating Neruda's works into English.

Tolman, Jon M. "Death and Alien Environment in Pablo Neruda's *Residencia en la tierra.*" *Hispania* 51 (1968): 79-85.
    Attempts to resolve seemingly unconnected elements in Neruda's cycle by means of the themes of death and solitude.

Woodbridge, Hensley C., and Zubatsky, David S. *Pablo*

Neruda: An Annotated Bibliography of Biographical and Critical Studies. New York: Garland Publishing, Inc., 1988, 629 p.

Comprehensive bibliography incorporating biographical and critical studies on Neruda in both Spanish and English. The volume includes biographical information divided into different periods, criticism by Neruda's peers, essays on special topics, and studies on both individual works and general subjects.

Cynthia Ozick

1928-

American short story writer, novelist, essayist, poet, and translator.

Ozick is best known for her intricate prose style and use of magic realism to illustrate the appearance of metaphysical realities in ordinary lives. Much of her fiction concerns Jewish characters, many of whom discover the significance of, or are struggling to maintain, their heritage in a predominantly Gentile world. Ozick often embodies this conflict in the theme of a quest for identity, as in her first novel, *Trust.* Deborah Heiligman Weiner remarked: "Ozick sees the world divided in two, that is, with opposing forces pulling at each individual. Whether she terms it Nature versus History, Paganism versus Judaism, Pan versus Moses, or Magic versus Religion, she is talking about the same thing: the pull on the one hand of the easy life, and the pull on the other of order, sense and clarification." Although some critics fault Ozick's prose as overwritten and opaque, others praise her expertise with language and ideas as the most attractive element in her fiction.

The issues Ozick addresses obliquely in her fiction are more directly confronted in her literary criticism. In *Art and Ardor,* Ozick focuses on issues of Judaism, feminism, and the work of other Jewish writers. Ozick uses the Second Commandment, "Thou shalt not make unto thee any graven image," to explore the contradictions she finds inherent in being a Jewish writer. Her contention that literature is an idol—a "graven image"—radically undercuts her own identity as an artist and, some critics feel, puts her in a false position with regard to her own work. Ozick's early stories and her first novel explore this dilemma within fictional settings.

A tribute to her youthful obsession with the works of Henry James, *Trust* has been praised for its exceptional prose style. This novel revolves around a quest for identity that drives the unnamed, illegitimate protagonist to alternately adopt the lifestyle and values of the various father-figures her superficial mother presents her. Her mother's first husband, William, is a "pagan" in Ozick's critical terminology, defined as the non-Judaic, and characterized by worldliness and corruption. Enoch Vand, her mother's second husband, is William's opposite, a representative Jew, a student of history, and thus infinitely adaptable. The protagonist lends her allegiance first to one and then to the other of these extreme approaches to life before finding her biological father. Her confrontation with this womanizer—the male counterpart to her mother—provides the climax of this lengthy philosophical novel. *Trust* received mixed reviews from critics who admired Ozick's meticulously crafted prose but were dissatisfied with the vagueness of the plot and the static quality of her characterization. *Trust* does, however, provide a first glimpse of the issues Ozick was to continue to explore in her fiction.

The Pagan Rabbi and Other Stories successfully drama-

tizes the stylistic and philosophic qualities that garnered Ozick praise for *Trust.* In the highly acclaimed title story, Ozick utilizes magic realism to demonstrate her conviction regarding the temptation to replace love of God with love of art. Rabbi Isaac Kornfeld, the title character, is literally seduced by nature in the form of a dryad, a spirit embodied in a tree. Critics found Ozick's depiction of this seduction a masterful achievement of balance between fantasy and believability. The struggle between Kornfeld's soul, which belongs to Judaic law, and his flesh, which longs for the sensual beauty of nature, is one way in which Ozick embodies her ideas about what it means to be a Jew in America. "Envy; or Yiddish in America" approaches this issue from another angle. A Yiddish poet, Edelshtein, emigrates to New York City, seeking a translator for his works. His bitterness over his failure is focused on Ostrover, an undeservedly successful Yiddish writer whose fame and wealth Edelshtein craves and believes is due himself. Critics praised the energy and inventiveness in *The Pagan Rabbi and Other Stories,* as well as Ozick's concrete, finely detailed settings and believable characters.

Ozick's next collection, *Bloodshed and Three Novellas,* confirmed her reputation as an accomplished short story writer. This volume includes "Usurpation (Other People's

Stories)," a complex intertwining of narratives in which a writer seeks the source of a story that she feels belongs to her but has already been written by someone else. In "Bloodshed," a normally skeptical lawyer named Bleilip visits a community of Hasidic Jews and comes to yearn for the truth these people seem to possess. Then, during prayer-service, the rebbe forces Bleilip to empty his pockets, revealing both a toy gun and a real one in his possession. The rebbe announces that only the toy gun is dangerous because it is a symbol and thus, in some sense, uncontrollable. As in much of Ozick's work, her theme in this dark, complex story is the spiritual danger inherent in art. Paul Gray commented on Ozick's writing in *Bloodshed and Three Novellas:* "She demands nothing less of her prose than the ineffable, yet her language does not simply point a finger at prepackaged symbols or detachable interpretations. With remarkable success, it makes a fist around the unknown."

In the title story of Ozick's next collection, *Levitation: Five Fictions,* she satirizes the New York literary scene through a party given by two undistinguished novelists. The only unusual occurrence at this dull gathering transpires when one of the guests, a survivor of the death camps, begins to speak of his experiences and he and his listeners float up into the air. This variously interpreted event is deemed by some critics as an indication, typical in Ozick's work, of the moral superiority of Jews. The volume's two final pieces, "Puttermesser: Her Work History, Her Ancestry, Her Afterlife" and "Puttermesser and Xanthippe," are interrelated, witty fantasies concerning an unmarried civil servant with a rich dream life. In the first story, Puttermesser's study of Hebrew provokes a dream of a Jewish ancestor who helps her learn the language, and in the second, she inadvertently creates a golem. This mythological creature, Xanthippe, helps Puttermesser realize her ambition to become mayor of New York. Just as Puttermesser takes on god-like qualities in calling Xanthippe to life, she becomes New York's savior, magically resolving such problems as crime, garbage disposal, and political corruption. But Xanthippe, like other symbols of art in Ozick's fiction, escapes her creator's control, and Puttermesser is eventually forced to kill her. Robert R. Harris commented on the stories in *Levitation: Five Fictions:* "Ozick writes magically about magical events. But she distrusts sorcery, the stock in trade of fiction writing. This irony gives her work a thought-provoking dialectical quality. Her stories are elusive, mysterious, and disturbing. They shimmer with intelligence, they glory in language, and they puzzle."

Ozick's novel, *The Cannibal Galaxy,* has a more realistic plot, concerning Joseph Brill, the founder and principal of a school governed by a "Dual Curriculum," formed from European humanistic and Judaic traditions. Brill invents a test purportedly capable of predicting which of his students will succeed. However, Beulah Lilt, the daughter of a brilliant philosopher, unexpectedly tests badly yet becomes a recognized artist-genius as an adult, while Brill's own son, who tested very highly, eventually becomes a business administration major at a local junior college. For investing so much faith in a rigid educational system and for attempting to create ideal children—like works of art—Brill is guilty of idolatry in Ozick's terms.

In *Metaphor and Memory,* her second collection of critical essays, Ozick argues for a moral fiction and against the kind of journalistic, minimalist narratives she finds dominating the contemporary literary scene. Her next publication, *The Messiah of Stockholm,* expands upon her belief in writing as a moral act. This short novel concerns Lars Andemening, a beleaguered book reviewer for a small Swedish newspaper who believes he is the son of Bruno Schulz, a Polish writer killed by Nazis in 1942. Lars's quest for his father's lost masterpiece puts him in the hands of unscrupulous book-dealers, and his resulting confrontation with reality changes his view of literature and the world around him. In *The Shawl,* Ozick returns to the intense prose style and magical plot devices most often found in her short fiction. "The Shawl," the short story that forms the first part of the book, takes place in a concentration camp. Rosa, the protagonist, hides her infant daughter Magda from camp authorities within the folds of a magic shawl that somehow nourishes the starving baby. Magda's eventual discovery and brutal death are starkly portrayed. "Rosa," the story that completes this volume, takes place in Miami thirty years later, with the memory of Magda enshrined in the shawl itself and Rosa insane from unabated grief. Elie Wiesel, an eminent writer on the Holocaust, observed: "Rosa's impotent but overwhelming anger, her burning memories, her implacable solitude, her hallucinations, her shawl—Ozick speaks of them with so much tact and delicacy that we ask ourselves with wonder and admiration what has she done to understand and penetrate Rosa's dark and devastated soul. Non-survivor novelists who treat the Holocaust ought to learn from Ozick the art of economy and what the French call *pudeur* (modesty)."

(See also *CLC,* Vols. 3, 7, 28; *Contemporary Authors,* Vols. 17-20, rev. ed.; *Contemporary Authors New Revision Series,* Vol. 23; *Dictionary of Literary Biography Yearbook: 1982,* and *Dictionary of Literary Biography,* Vol. 28.)

PRINCIPAL WORKS

NOVELS

Trust   1966
The Cannibal Galaxy   1983
The Messiah of Stockholm   1987

SHORT FICTION COLLECTIONS

The Pagan Rabbi and Other Stories   1971
Bloodshed and Three Novellas   1976
Levitation: Five Fictions   1982
The Shawl   1990

ESSAYS

Art and Ardor   1983
Metaphor and Memory   1988

Janet Handler Burstein

Whether she is lecturing the literary establishment on its parochialism at the MLA convention, or pointing out to George Steiner the defects of his universalism, Cynthia

Ozick's is the most provocative of contemporary Jewish-American voices. Also one of the most disquieting, for she lifts up again and again the vexed and intricate tangle of Jewish attitudes toward art that many readers would rather not see so clearly. Embedded in a non-Jewish cultural tradition, schooled in techniques that help interpret that tradition, and accustomed to value art and artists as the finest achievements of our civilization, we listen to Ozick's misgivings with more than a little discomfort. Despite her own writing, for all her admiration of Henry James and George Eliot, Ozick's conviction that art is idolatrous for Jews announces itself in essay after essay; works of art can be redeemed, turned toward the service of God, only when they reveal "moral purpose." (p. 85)

As a teller of stories, Ozick not only explores the danger of idol-worship but also risks it and ultimately justifies her daring. Thus in the years that lie between **"The Pagan Rabbi"** (1966) and *The Cannibal Galaxy* (1983) Ozick's fiction seems to have cleared a path through the moral, philosophical, and social problems created for Jews by art.

The curve of this path is defined by her best known stories of three decades: **"The Pagan Rabbi"** (1966), **"Bloodshed"** and **"Usurpation"** (1976; 1974), and *The Cannibal Galaxy.* All these works explore the problems art brings to Jewishness and Jewishness brings to art—problems linked by Ozick's preoccupation with idolatry. Idolatry, the "abomination" forbidden to Jews by the second commandment, threatens all artists, even Jewish artists, because of the nature of their minds and work. This is the tragic nexus from which conflict often rises in Ozick's stories—this knot of the artist's inevitable implication in sin. Ozick rarely uses that old-fashioned word, which suggests both disobedience and moral reprehensibility. But her essays encourage one to conceive of Jewish artists as transgressors in a double sense: first, because they offend against the commandment to have only one God; and second, more literally, because they cross over boundaries that help us differentiate one kind of experience from another.

Ozick's essays indict the artist on four separate charges. First, she explains, the "artist as artist is not a moral creature"; her loyalties are too deeply divided for any simple obedience to moral imperatives. A writer must be responsible "solely to the seizures of language and dream." Because she depends entirely upon the sources of her inspiration, the artist sets aside responsibilities that would dilute this primary obligation.

Second, the imaginative power that makes art possible also draws the artist away from the paths sanctioned by religious law. "Imagination," Ozick points out,

> is more than . . . the power to invent. It is also the power to penetrate evil, to take on evil, to become evil. And in that guise it is the most frightening human faculty. . . . Imagination owns above all the facility of becoming: The writer can enter the leg of a mosquito, a sex not her own". . . .
>
> (pp.86-7)

Third, because of the imagination's capacity to transgress conventional boundaries and moral restrictions, the very freedom that art affords becomes "dangerous." Thus, for Ozick, the writer's gift is also her burden. "There is only one very old truth," she writes,

> as old as Sappho, as old as Homer, as old as the Song of Deborah, as old as the Songs of David—that the imagination is free . . . that when we write we are not women or men but blessed beings in possession of a Promethean art, an art encumbered by peril and hope and fire and, above all, freedom.

Both "blessed" and "encumbered" by freedom, Ozick's artist reflects an ambivalence here that will flourish fully only in the fiction.

Finally, Ozick's essays indict the artist most severely because the very sensitivities that nourish her power subvert simultaneously her exclusive worship of the one God. "The Jew has this in common with the artist," she writes:

> he means nothing to be lost on him . . . nothing that passes before him is taken for granted, everything is exalted. [But] if we are enjoined to live in the condition of noticing all things . . . in the condition of awe—how can we keep from sliding off from awe at God's creation to worship of God's creation?

This danger of "sliding" from awe of the world into worship of the world threatens both the artist—whose susceptibilities are particularly keen—and the reader, whose more moderate susceptibilities are intensified by the experience of art. Thus, "the story-making faculty itself can be a corridor to the corruptions and abominations of idol-worship," for both artist and reader may be seduced away from the worship of God. When we revel in the formal and technical achievements of art without seeing through them to the creator of the world, we are seduced into idol-worship.

The saddest part of these indictments for readers nourished abundantly by Western culture is Ozick's conclusion that art can yield to Jews only two, dubious fruits. Art can teach one "detachment" from one's own imaginations; or it can offer moral enlightenment. Both ends are potentially tragic, for both can be self-destructive. Detachment "made absolute destroys . . . individual imagination." And a morally redemptive literature, as Ozick knows, "must wrestle with its own body, with its own flesh and blood, with its own life." Ozick is speaking here, as consideration of her stories will show, about the subversive potential of figurative language, the "flesh and blood," so to speak, of narrative art. But not only, one notes, of narrative art, for figures are the language in which all of us think and dream and tell our stories.

Clearly, Ozick's essays offer little comfort to lovers of art. But her fiction amplifies the slight ambivalence that sometimes surfaces within her polemic. "Why do I, who dread the cannibal-touch of story-making, lust after stories more and more and more?" plaintively asks the narrator of *Bloodshed*'s "Preface." The stories develop far more fully than the essays the conflict this question reflects—yielding not only different insights but also a sense of movement through the problem of Jewish aestheticism described by the essays.

"The Pagan Rabbi" offers at the outset, for example, a familiar, traditional condemnation: "Idolatry is the abomination," argues Isaac Kornfeld, the protagonist for whom the story is named. But the tale itself deeply qualifies that simple given of Jewish law. Isaac is a serious scholar, "a man half-sotted with print." But the story traces his journey from traditional texts to romantic poetry, from traditional familial responsibilities to illicit sexual passion, from traditional restraints to freedom—and then to suicide. In the metaphor created by the story to describe Isaac's journey, he scales the "Fence of the Law" to "free his soul," and freedom first enraptures and then destroys him.

The fictional embodiment of Isaac's liberator, "a delicate young oak, with burly roots like the toes of a gryphon" and a seductive nymph for a soul, recalls in its metaphoric mixing of species the admonitions of Leviticus. The nymph herself, moreover, mixes in her own appearance the colors and textures of vegetables and flowers with animal and human characteristics. (pp. 87-9)

Her language also illustrates Ozick's concern with the transgressing of conventional boundaries, for the nymph's words come to Isaac not as sounds but as fragrances: "Whatever she said reached me in a shimmer of pellucid perfumes," Isaac remembers, and his words to her become like objects: "She either caught my words like balls or let them roll." Strong talk offends her not morally or temperamentally but physically; his unguarded cry causes a "white bruise" that disfigures "her petally lid." "Where you have pain, we have ugliness," she explains. "Where you profane yourselves by immorality, we are profaned by ugliness." In her multiple crossings of moral, sensory, and biological boundaries, the nymph illuminates both the seductive delights and the moral dangers that Ozick associates with art.

This association is reinforced by the narrator's own use of language in the story, for the narrator's words, like the nymph's and the pagan rabbi's, cross important boundaries by ascribing material existence to immaterial phenomena. For example, when the narrator listens to Isaac's wife Sheindel, he observes that "it was as if every word emitted a quick white thread of great purity, like hard silk, which she was then obliged to bite cleanly off." Though this description is clearly metaphoric, not literal, the likeness between what happens to language in narrative metaphor and in Isaac's actual conversations with the nymph suggests that metaphor may be a "corridor" to Isaac's sin, for metaphor allows the mind to transgress conceptually the boundary Isaac crosses existentially between different orders of reality.

His transgression, however, is unfruitful; once the nymph has freed Isaac's soul by beguiling his body into clinging to her, she rejects him, abandoning him to despair and then to suicide. Thus far, the story follows faithfully the line of argument formulated by Ozick's essays. As one would expect, given Ozick's condemnations of idolatry, Isaac's freed soul lectures him self-righteously as it leaves him: "If you had not contrived to be rid of me, I would have stayed with you till the end. . . . In your grave beside you I would have sung you David's songs. . . . But you expelled me . . . and I will walk here alone always. . . . " This self-righteousness, however, which appears in other characters as well, offers no satisfactory alternative to the transgressions represented by the nymph.

Sensitivity to Ozick's Jewish commitments should not blind readers to the ways in which this work undercuts its apparent commitment to traditional Jewish values and its

apparent bias against imaginative freedom. On one hand, the soul who speaks of the rewards of righteousness is sadly unbeautiful: "He is so sad! Such antique weariness broods in his face! His throat is striped from the whip. His cheeks are folded like ancient flags, he reads the Law and breathes the dust. . . . He passes indifferent through the beauty of the field. . . . His feet are bandaged, his notched toenails gore the earth." As the nymph's counterweight in the story's symbolic structure, this "ugly old man" embodies the absence of all her "virtues." The "truth" he speaks is the reverse of hers: she wishes only to be free; he wishes "only to be bound to the Law." But his desire denies the world instead of affirming it; in his love of Law he has lost the love of God's creation. Though he is faithful to the epigraph from *The Ethics Of The Fathers* that warns the pious student against susceptibility to the beauties of earth, Isaac's soul warns of the danger awaiting those who dwell within boundaries too narrow to do justice to the created world.

This undesirable alternative of ugliness to beauty, moreover, is complicated further by the story's negative portrayals of other characters who have chosen Law over freedom. The fathers of Isaac and the narrator, for example, are both rabbis who cleave to traditional pieties. But they offer no human alternative to the nymph's coldness. "They were . . . friends, but only in a loose way of speaking: in actuality our fathers were enemies. They vied with one another in demonstrations of charitableness, in the captious glitter of their scholia, in the number of their adherents." When the narrator marries a gentile, Isaac's father gloats while his "friend" mourns. The narrator's father ceases entirely to speak to his son after that marriage and dies, unreconciled and unforgiving. "Fathers like ours don't know how to love. They live too much indoors," Isaac observes. This inability to love marks symbolically the way of Law as no more promising than the way of freedom.

In Isaac's wife Sheindel, moreover, the story offers an even more troubling image of loveless piety and traditionalism. The narrator's attitude toward Sheindel changes drastically in the course of the story; he desires at first to court and marry her, remembering her beauty and vitality as a girl. But ultimately he leaves her, appalled by her lack of pity, her spitefulness, her "mockery and gall." (pp. 90-2)

Close reading of this story, then, discloses not only Ozick's familiar anxieties about imaginative freedom, but also her awareness that life may turn bitter, cold, and sterile in its absence. On the whole, **"The Pagan Rabbi"** is a tale as balanced as the oxymoron of its title between alternative visions of Law and imaginative freedom that cannot be reconciled. Ozick's stories of the seventies depart, however, from that precarious balance, moving decisively toward the negative view of art described by the essays. These are difficult stories, partly because they explore technical problems confronted by the Jewish writer as she "wrestles" with language, the "flesh and blood," the "life" of her own artistic work.

In the protagonist of **"Bloodshed,"** whose tendency to rely on images is contrasted with the literalism of his hasidic cousins, Ozick demonstrates both the danger and the inauthenticity engendered by figurative thought and language. Because Bleilip sees his cousins through a cloud of sentimental associations, he can neither perceive them as they are nor recognize his own negative feelings about them. He will end his visit confused, unenlightened, a virtual prisoner of his own projections and misconceptions.

The toy gun he carries in one pocket, moreover, helps him "get used" to the idea of killing and is, thus, more dangerous than the actual gun in his other pocket. "It is the toy we have to fear," the rebbe points out, for the toy serves—as images always serve—the mind's need to experiment with ideas. Images function this way in ritual also, but the rebbe insists that in the ancient ritual of the Temple images worked toward wholesome, divinely sanctioned ends. For example, in Temple ritual the idea of bloodshed was chastened, restrained by the image of a scapegoat accepted for sacrifice "instead of" a man. In the sacrifice, worshippers could watch the "miracle of life turned to carcass" and might, therefore, be kept from unsanctified shedding of blood. But in the absence of the Temple and its rituals, men use one another as animals: the rebbe displays his own mutilated hand as evidence, the once healthy flesh transformed into "toy fingers" in a "freezing experiment" at Buchenwald. Both Nazi savagery and Bleilip's weapons become consequences, then, of the loss of ritual imagery. The story suggests that the danger of violent transgressions is increased by unsanctified images which help us "get used to" the idea of shedding blood.

The power of this story lies partly, one suspects, in its subject matter: the bold defense of animal sacrifice startles and compels. But one is also moved by the profound distrust of image and metaphor that underlies the story's validation of literalness and ritual. Though artists have long distrusted metaphor and image, Ozick's condemnation of figurative language is extraordinarily radical, its anger fueled, one suspects, by the complicity of images in both the murderous experiments of the Nazis and the propaganda that helped people "get used to" the idea of such behavior.

In **"Usurpation,"** the most controversial story in this collection, Ozick particularly condemns artistic uses of language by exposing the nature of the artist, the work, and the "world" in which art becomes dominant. In the labyrinth of this story, the real protagonist is the narrator herself. Her peculiarities (like Bleilip's prejudices) dominate and distort the tale she tells. Both the nymph of **"The Pagan Rabbi"** and Ozick's preoccupation with the imaginative tendency to transgress boundaries offer an important clue to the nature of this narrator. She remains indistinct and faintly disturbing to us because her image is neither consistent nor coherent; her character obeys no law, but reflects only the capricious demand of imagination.

As incoherent and inconsistent as its narrator, the story embraces several narratives which the story teller clumsily attempts to fuse into a single tale. And as she speaks obsessively of her own biases and artistic difficulties, her story reflects her preoccupations and inconsistencies and makes us uneasy. In its self-centered self-enclosure, this tale becomes a perfect idol.

The fictional "world" this story depicts, therefore, is appropriately a world of idolatry: empty of God, forgetful of the covenant, fallen into incoherent, meaningless fragments. In the filthy debris of the "neighborhood" that is, now, empty of Jews, the narrator recalls the previous inhabitants: "mothers, fathers, children pressing library cards inside their pockets." The telling detail offers insight

into their faithlessness. Idolators, they have worshipped stories fashioned by artists; thus, the integrity of their world has eroded—like the character of the narrator—under the "lust" of imagination to "tear down meaning, to smash interpretation, to wear out the rational, to mock the surprise of redemption."

Ozick's ambivalence toward art gives way in these stories of the seventies, then, to a vigorous castigation of the devices, fruits, and agents of imagination. These stories do not qualify their vision of the ways in which art subverts what is wholesome for Jews. Nor do they countenance any possibility of reconciliation, synthesis, or creative tension between Jewishness and art, imaginative freedom and Law. (pp. 92-5)

The Cannibal Galaxy (1984) considers again the problem these earlier works explored but develops a new perspective. The novel announces in its epigraphs its preoccupation with the need of seeing past the dualisms that obscure vision and obstruct progress. From Emily Dickinson, Ozick borrows a passionate cry for a vision that will transcend time: "The rest of Life to *see*! / Past Midnight! Past the Morning Star!" And from Yehuda Amichai she recalls a more plaintive though no less moving demand to visualize the dreamed of future beyond the tight, dualistic antagonisms of the moment: "Half the people love, half the people hate. And where is my place between these halves that are so well matched? And through what crack shall I see the white housing projects of my dreams, and the barefoot runners on the sands, or, at least, the fluttering of the girl's kerchief, by the hill?" Both passages articulate the sense of being oppressed by what William Blake once called the "war of contraries," of being unable to see or to move beyond dualism: "halves that are so well matched," midnight and morning, love and hate. The work will address this inability and, to some extent, resolve it.

At the "crack" between opposing "halves," [*The Cannibal Galaxy*] places its protagonist—Joseph Brill, a man of the middle in all respects. Literally, he has been "born into the Middle, the sea of monsters that was—coup de hasard—his own time." A middle child, born into the middle of the century, landlocked in a school that "was of the middle and in the middle" of America, between lake and meadow, between intellectual distinction and academic disrepute. (pp. 95-6)

Perhaps the most salient feature of Brill's portrayal is his Dual Curriculum—a philosophical, pedagogical commitment that identifies him not only, as one reader has observed, as a representative of "American Jewish reality," but also as a symbolic response to the post-Enlightenment dualism experienced by all modern Jews. The idea for the Dual Curriculum arises from Brill's readings in traditional Jewish and non-Jewish literature. Alternating one day between Proust and the Talmud, he is suddenly struck by "the terrific truth of both passages. . . . How different they were! *And neither told a lie*" (Ozick's emphasis). From this moment of insight Brill emerges with a vision of a school "run according to the principle of twin nobilities, twin antiquities. The fusion of scholarly Europe and burnished Jerusalem. The grace of Madame de Sevigne's flowery courtyard mated to the perfect serenity of a purified Sabbath." Susceptible to the power of both traditions, "split" by two worlds in heart and mind, Brill neither chooses nor rejects but attempts—like many contemporary American Jews—to hold together two very different and often mutually antagonistic intellectual currents. (pp. 96-7)

Against the lure of unreliable human love and beautiful but dangerous and false images, this story opposes Brill's teacher of Talmud, Rabbi Pult. Unlike the rabbi-fathers of Isaac and the narrator in **"The Pagan Rabbi,"** Pult is a sympathetic figure—lost to the Nazis during the Holocaust. And unlike the burden of the Law borne in a giant sack on the sagging shoulders of the pagan rabbi's soul, a single volume of Talmud in an old briefcase is Rabbi Pult's most precious legacy to young Brill, who cherishes it through all the time of his imprisonment.

In Brill's Dual Curriculum, then, the symbolic balance between Jewish and non-Jewish texts is restored. But balance is not, as Brill had hoped, the same as "fusion" of the two traditions. In an anticipatory essay, **"Bialik's Hint,"** Ozick had called for an attempt to fuse post-Enlightenment ideas with traditional Jewish ideas as a way of resolving the dilemma of contemporary Jewish bifurcation and trivialization. From such a fusion, she hoped, would rise the possibility of fresh growth for Jewish culture. But from the pedagogical equilibrium of Brill's Dual Curriculum comes only stasis. Like the epigraphs, Brill laments his inability to move beyond the equilibrium created by the dynamic of his own life and intellectual commitments. (pp. 97-8)

He is deeply troubled by the stasis that grips him; year after year his students always look the same: "Nothing moved. Nothing altered. The first grade was always the first grade, the eighth grade always the eighth. This knowledge turned him cold. . . . The same, the same, always the same" he thinks. "Nature replaces, replaces identically, replaces chillingly." As he watches the waves on the lake he realizes "that he was dying of unchangingness." But where he attributes his sense of immobility to his situation, Hester Lilt—his opposite and antagonist—sees him as the author of his own predicament. "You don't proceed. You're glued in place. You're a man who stops too soon. You deduce the future from the present. . . . You're stuck," she insists.

In Hester Lilt and Joseph Brill Ozick gives us alternative responses to the cultural predicament suggested by the epigraphs, a predicament sharply familiar to contemporary American Jews. Both characters have been scarred by recent history. Between them, as Brill realizes, is "the bond of ravished Europe. Europe the cannibal galaxy." But these "victims" of cannibalism, like the "smaller-brother galaxies" devoured by a "sated ogre-galaxy, continue to rotate" within the devourer. While the forces that consumed them remain "motionless as digesting Death," Hester and Joseph are moving toward an as yet unimaginable future in very different ways.

Whereas Joseph is partly immobilized by his fidelity to the cultural and historical past, Hester, knowing "herself to be a flake of history," was "all future; she cut the thread of genesis." . . . Thus she chastises Joseph for clinging to the past, for trying to predict the future from evidence of "early performance," for trying to move forward in a straight line. Unlike Joseph, who marries and raises a child for the sake of continuing the dynamic of his own life, and unlike other mothers who are simply "rafts on

their own instinctual force," caught "in the pinch of nature," Hester is unconcerned with continuity. She seeks instead the transcendence of both past and present.

Hester and Joseph differ not only in their orientation to time but also—more importantly—in their work with texts. Joseph can draw discrete texts into conversation with one another, his mind preserving the distinct identities of each partner in the dialogue. His is the faithful scholar's mind. But he cannot see how one text may interpret another: "how the pinwheel cosmos," for example, "interprets pedagogy." Only in Hester's mind does a fusion of traditions take place, for in her lecture disparate insights of both midrash and modern astronomy address themselves to the problem of educating the young.

Her subject is profoundly appropriate, for the vessel of the transcendence Hester seeks is her daughter Beulah, a student in Brill's Dual Curriculum. Like Rebbe Akiva, who can laugh at the desolation of Jerusalem because he anticipates its future through the crack that prophecy opens in time, Hester sees past the inauspicious early school record of her daughter to a "seamless future." She disencumbers Beulah "of any remnant of history," making her, in Brill's eyes, "an orphan of the future." In time Beulah will throw off her early influences, rejecting both Brill's Dual Curriculum and her mother's ideas, to become a blindingly original artist. But Naphtali, Brill's son, will "sail on in a forward line," continuing—despite his early promise—his father's sad journey toward mediocrity.

In these two children—the scholar-turned-listmaker and the artist—Ozick considers again the dualism explored by her earlier stories. But here she considers the triumph of imagination from the perspective of a character who, like the narrator of Ozick's own essays, is "embittered" against it, simultaneously terrified and fascinated by it. Joseph Brill sees Beulah's canvasses as "phantasmagorical windows enclosed in narrow silver frames. . . . You could fancy amazing scenes in them: but when you approached, it was only paint." He knows these strange forms, significantly described even by this unsympathetic viewer as windows, are "thought to be a kind of language." He is alienated by it, but Ozick's readers will note that this language does not, like the words of the nymph, the imaginings of Bleilip, or the images of Ozick's narrators, transgress boundaries—it seems to transcend them. In the "vale of interpretation" to which Joseph Brill and all of us are bound, one cannot imagine "the purity of babble." But it is that "purity" which these uninterpretable forms achieve, and out of them—as even Brill realizes—"a flaming nimbus sometimes spread."

Perhaps, like Amichai's "fluttering of the girl's kerchief, by the hill," or like the second prophecy that engenders Akiva's laughter, that nimbus offers a token of a future redeemed from both the devouring past and the mediocre present of Jewish culture. If so, the image offers a vision of art more promising than any comparable image in Ozick's earlier work. This image recalls and realizes imaginatively the consequences of Bialik's hint, the "new alternative" to the hopeless stasis of our indebtedness to two incompatible traditions. Like that alternative, Beulah's work "opens out to riches: originality, the brilliance of the unexpected, the explosive hope of fresh form"—of a new language, to use the novel's metaphor, despite the fact that her canvasses are "only paint." Fiction here, like the jaundiced eye of Joseph Brill, insists on the telling defect—the inevitable disillusionment art engenders when its purely formal resolutions are translated directly into another order of being. But this misgiving is itself transcended in the novel by the expectation of fresh vision as the forerunner, perhaps, to more practical—perhaps even moral—resolutions.

Indeed, apart from the didactic moral purpose that Ozick has long demanded of art, perhaps this latest work suggests another way in which a work of art may justify itself, may compensate for the risk of subversion it presents to Jewish artists and readers. Perhaps artistic vision will be as vital as the study of Law to those who are, simultaneously, enriched and burdened by two traditions—trapped in middleness. One cannot say for sure. But the curve of Ozick's extended artistic engagement with the problem of Jewish aestheticism suggests that she has moved far beyond the simple condemnations of the essays, and that her stories may be opening a new perspective on the promises and transgressions of art. (pp. 98-101)

Janet Handler Burstein, "Cynthia Ozick and the Transgressions of Art," in American Literature, *Vol. 59, No. 1, March, 1987, pp. 85-101.*

Harold Bloom

Cynthia Ozick's brilliant new novel is dedicated to Philip Roth, a dedication that seems to me part of the book's meaning. *The Messiah of Stockholm* is a worthy companion to Mr. Roth's superb *Prague Orgy,* the epilogue to the comic trilogy *Zuckerman Bound.* In *The Prague Orgy,* Mr. Roth's surrogate, Nathan Zuckerman, seeks to obtain and remove from Prague the unpublished Yiddish stories of a fictional writer named Sinovsky, who was supposedly killed by the Nazis. But Ms. Ozick has taken as her true inspiration an earlier writer than Mr. Roth—Bruno Schulz, a Polish Jew and an extraordinary writer whom Mr. Roth himself brought to our attention.

Schulz was shot dead in a street of his native town of Drogobych by an SS man in 1942. He published two books of stories, *The Street of Crocodiles* and *Sanatorium Under the Sign of the Hourglass.* Both were brought out in the United States by Penguin Books in a series, "Writers From the Other Europe," edited by Mr. Roth. Schulz is believed to have written another work, *The Messiah,* which is lost. With a fine audacity, Ms. Ozick centers her story on the recovery of Schulz's lost *Messiah,* not in Poland or even in Prague, but in the unlikely locale of Stockholm.

Ms. Ozick's main characters are almost all Polish Jews who, though they bear Swedish names, are still obsessed with their origins. The most obsessed is "the Messiah of Stockholm," Lars Andemening, a not very successful book reviewer for a newspaper. Middle-aged, twice divorced, solitary and alienated, Lars has convinced himself that he is the son of Bruno Schulz. He learns Polish to read Schulz in the original, and he achieves a sense of reality only when he discusses Schulz with an old woman, Heidi Eklund, who runs a desolate bookshop that Lars frequents.

Lars is the most persuasive and poignant figure in a fiction by Ms. Ozick, surpassing even Edelshtein, the untranslated poet in her early masterwork, "Envy; or, Yiddish in America." The difference between Lars and her previous protagonists resides in the subtle internalization, in this book, of the author's preoccupations. Lars never thinks of himself as being Jewish and scarcely understands that his fantasy of being Schulz's son is a quest for a lost identity, for belonging to a people. Beyond question, and yet with superb, almost Jamesian, indirection, Lars is Ms. Ozick's surrogate, an emblem for her own maturation as an artist as she becomes a true daughter of Schulz, whose Jewishness, like Kafka's, is fascinatingly implicit in his writing.

Very little seems to happen in *The Messiah of Stockholm,* yet no one would wish it to be shorter. The only event, carefully prepared from the first paragraph on, is a deft conspiracy involving Mrs. Eklund, the bookstore owner; her enigmatic husband, Dr. Eklund, a dealer in manuscripts; and a woman purporting to be Schulz's illegitimate daughter (he never married) who calls herself Adela, the name of the formidable and sexually menacing housemaid in Schulz's stories. Adela comes bearing the supposed manuscript of her father's lost book, *The Messiah,* which the Eklunds offer to Lars, to read, translate and publicize. In the novel's most extraordinary scene, Lars reads through the manuscript in the presence of the Eklunds and Adela and then, in a rage, burns it. *The Messiah* goes up in smoke, a final sacrifice after the Six Million.

Even before that act of destruction, Lars has lost his sense of identity as Schulz's son, though he sees clearly that Adela is the Eklunds' daughter and not Schulz's. But was the manuscript a forgery? Each reader will have to decide. Lars is left in doubt, though mostly persuaded that Dr. Eklund, a forger of passports for refugees, himself wrote *The Messiah.* A close rereading might lead to other conclusions, but I will not spoil the mystery. What is more the critic's share is Lars's experience of reading the manuscript, which marks the central point in Ms. Ozick's writing to date, something of a culmination of her own quest after forbidden magic in order somehow to reconcile her need to create tales, idols of a sort, and her desire to continue as a truster in the covenant, a moral follower of Jewish tradition.

Ms. Ozick's vision of literature is conditioned by her anxiety about idolatry, her fear of making stories into so many idols. And her most profound insight concerns her ambivalence about the act of writing and the condemnation of the religion of art, or the worship of Moloch. This insight comes to the fore when she asks herself the combative question that governs every strong writer: "Why do we become what we most desire to contend with?" Her reply in her early critical essays was immensely bitter. In my judgment, she repeated the prime error of Christian moralizing critics like T. S. Eliot and W. H. Auden—a failing to see that there are only political or societal distinctions between supposedly secular and supposedly sacred literature. Her triumph in *The Messiah of Stockholm* reflects a developed awareness that her earlier view of art as idolatry was too severe. (pp. 1, 36)

Ms. Ozick has taken a large risk here—at first the book might not seem to be wholly available to a reader not familiar with Schulz's remarkable writing. In my judgment, however, even someone who has not read Schulz will be open to the full range of her achievement. The novel is a complex and fascinating meditation on the nature of writing and the responsibilities of those who choose to create—or judge—tales. Yet on a purely realistic level, it manages to capture the atmosphere of Stockholm and to be, at times, very funny indeed about the daily operations of one of the city's newspapers and Lars's peculiar detachment from everyday work and life. At the same time, Ms. Ozick has written a very Schulzian book, in substance as well as in spirit. I suspect that Schulz has enabled her at last to transform Malamud's influence fully into her own fiction. And although *The Messiah of Stockholm* is deliberately Schulzian in its fantasy and narrative procedures, it emerges powerfully on its own. Ms. Ozick clearly has gained her own fully achieved style, with Schulz as an exemplary catalyst.

A reader will take away from *The Messiah of Stockholm* the memory of a powerfully rendered person in Lars, who not only is a student of losses, but is himself a grand loss, a blighted version of what would have been an eminent Jewish critic but for the sorrows of history. Yet a sensitive reader will take away something more heartening as well. Ms. Ozick slyly has restituted us for Schulz's lost "Messiah" by composing her *Messiah of Stockholm.* The humor of that title is her wry commentary both on her own daring and on the problems of trying to maintain and extend Jewish literature in the post-Holocaust era.

Her successful effort to find a connection with Bruno Schulz is an imaginative act akin to Mr. Roth's poignant gesture of reaching out to Kafka in *The Prague Orgy.* In dedicating her book to Mr. Roth, she affirms the common nature of the enterprise that they, and perhaps only a few others, are carrying forward. They are helping to mature an American Jewish literature that may aid in the larger venture of seeking continuity in an authentic American Jewish culture. (p. 36)

> Harold Bloom, "The Book of the Father," in The New York Times Book Review, *March 22, 1987, pp. 1, 36.*

Anne Tyler

Novelists who write about writers run any number of risks. They may be accused of egotism, insularity, or—given the motionless life of the average writer—simple tedium. But Cynthia Ozick, never one to play it safe, has chosen to populate [*The Messiah of Stockholm*] with not one writer but two.

The first is Lars Andemening, a book reviewer for a Swedish newspaper. By preference, he restricts his reading to difficult, earnest works from obscure little foreign countries. "Prince of the Indecipherable," his colleagues call him. A typical piece of his begins: "Here is a universe as confined as a trap, where the sole heroes are victims, where muteness is for the intrepid only."

The second writer, taken from real life, is a Polish Jew named Bruno Schulz, who was murdered by the Nazis some 40 years before the story opens. Schulz wrote convoluted tales in which "savagely crafty nouns and verbs were set on a crooked road to take on engorgements and transmogrifications." For a sample of *his* style, try a sentence from one of his letters: "These are the mass instincts that eclipse within us a clarity of judgment, reintroducing the archaic and barbaric epistemologies, the arsenal of atavistic and bankrupt logic."

Small wonder that Andemening, an orphan smuggled into Sweden as an infant, has seized upon the notion that Schulz must have been his father. Smaller wonder still that both men should engage the attention of Cynthia Ozick, herself a writer who has always avoided taking the shortest path between two points.

Her subject matter generally reveals a cousinship to Isaac Bashevis Singer. Golems and dryads and dock witches scamper across her pages, and the Jewishness of most of her characters is central to their identity. But her prose lacks Singer's directness and simplicity. Great clots of turgid phrases pour forth; long sentences knot upon themselves and swallow their own tails. People are summed up from outside and from a considerable height. Physical descriptions seem oddly lacking in vantage point—oddly non-physical, in fact.

What most complicates her writing, though, is her backhanded approach to narrative. Why, exactly, does she choose such-and-such a beginning point, such-and-such a point at which to digress or to analyze? In her novel *The Cannibal Galaxy,* for instance, the plot wandered into view about halfway through the book. It happened to be a perfectly wonderful plot: a narrow, reactionary headmaster is baffled when his most unpromising pupil grows up to be a famous artist. The reader's response is, "Oh, *now* I see what she's getting at! In other words. . . . "

In other words; in plainer words; to make a long story short. . . .

The Messiah of Stockholm has some of the same backhandedness. A three-and-a-half-chapter synopsis of past events separates a man's arrival at a shop from the start of his business there, and this occurs at such a crucial moment that we have a sense of reading on with a thumb left behind to mark the detour. But the fact that we resent the interruption testifies to the story's pull. It's packed with possibility: Lars Andemening's entire, airless life is devoted to researching his putative father, Bruno Schulz. With the help of Mrs. Eklund, a book dealer who keeps miraculously locating various memorabilia from Schulz's native village of Drohobycz, Lars peruses old photos and letters, undertakes the study of Polish, and reads and rereads Schulz's two published books. He would probably be happy to continue in this vein forever, but one day events take a surprising turn. A woman named Adela shows up claiming that Schulz is *her* father, and with her she has a manuscript that she insists is Schulz's long-lost, unpublished masterpiece, *The Messiah.*

Partly, of course, Ozick's novel is a parable, complete with a morally instructive ending. The Messiah of her title is not Adela's manuscript but Lars Andemening himself, single-mindedly crusading (amid the constant, eerie smell of something roasting) to deliver from oblivion the writings of various vanished Eastern Europeans. As Mrs. Eklund puts it, somewhat bitterly:

> He took on everyone's loss; everyone's foolish grief. Foolish because unstinting. Rescue was the only thought he kept in his head—he was arrogant about it, he was steady, he wanted to salvage every scrap of paper all over Europe. Europe's savior!
>
> (pp. 39-40)

It is also part fairy tale, at least in the manner of its telling.

Lars lives in an apartment "no bigger than a crack in the wall," and the magical Mrs. Eklund is a "thick globular dwarf of a woman" who resembles a "forest gnome." One of the book's more significant objects is a jar like Ali Baba's, which, when its contents are set afire, chatters and boils, "battering the little table, dancing across it like a demon." And after Adela's arrival, Lars tells Mrs. Eklund that "there's no room in the story for another child. . . . You know the story as well as I do. There's only me." It's an *old* story, is what he's saying—a ritualistic, familiar story, like a folktale or a legend told many times before.

And here, at times, told vividly. Lars's walk through Stockholm on a snowy night can chill your bones, and a description of his writing process is convincingly feverish. ("It was as if his pen, sputtering along the line of rapid letters it ignited, flung out haloes of hot grease.") (p. 40)

Elsewhere, though, the prose is more opaque. It draws too much attention to itself; it brings to mind that bumper sticker from the '60s: ESCHEW OBFUSCATION. There are lengthy strings of adjectives—"crumpled, splotched, speckled, aged" and "buried, beaten, bruised, drowned" and "broken, beaten, hidden" (all these within a mere page and a half). Some of the images seem curiously askew, or just uncomfortable. For instance: "the merciless boil of a saving chimerical eye" and "those indecipherables that steam up from the stomach-hole of Central Europe" and "his old certainty, grown out of him like a fingernail. He chopped it off." (pp. 40-1)

As in *The Cannibal Galaxy,* there is a moment when you say, "Ah, yes, now I understand what this book is about." A belated moment, yes; but an admiring "Ah." (It is a haunting, provocative plot, no doubt about it.) The only question is, do you want to have to strain the story from a dense ragout of language, or don't you? And the question is not rhetorical. Some people do want to; they like conundrums. They like to take a certain distance from their reading—which is, finally, the issue at stake here. What you have to decide is not whether Cynthia Ozick is a "good" writer or a "bad" writer (clearly she is intelligent, skilled, and consummately serious) but whether you expect from your reading a visceral experience or an intellectual exercise. I vote for visceral experience, myself; but that is not to deny *The Messiah of Stockholm* its strengths. It does intrigue and entertain, and it does weave a tale that is richly, intensely imagined. (p. 41)

> Anne Tyler, "The Mission," *in* The New Republic, *Vol. 196, No. 14, April 6, 1987, pp. 39-41.*

Alberto Manguel

The theme of creation (who creates? what is created? how does creation take place?) runs through Ozick's work like a scarlet thread. It makes her wonder, in her superb book of essays *Art and Ardor,* how Virginia Woolf and Edith Wharton created their fictional worlds, one teetering on the edge of madness, the other condemned to riches. It leads her, like a photographer in a nightmare, to portray in exquisite long and short stories the visionary creations of her characters. It takes her, in her novel *The Cannibal Galaxy,* into the budding groves of parenthood and education. It forces her, in her latest book, *The Messiah of Stockholm,* to build an infinite progression of creations, of literary chickens and eggs.

In *The Messiah of Stockholm,* Ozick has invented the story of a man who invents his story: his name, his birth, his ancestry. He reshapes his daily life to make it unreal to others but real to himself. For Lars Andemening, the outside world is a person from Porlock. Lars is a dreamer.

He is also a book reviewer for a small Swedish newspaper. He never knew his parents—he is an orphan smuggled into Sweden during the Nazi terror—but he has convinced himself that his father was the great Polish writer Bruno Schulz, murdered by the SS in 1942. Lars has no proof of this parentage except his own conviction, which has made him a half-hearted misanthrope. His only confidante is a German bookseller named Heidi, a woman protected from both affection and pain by a cocoon of scorn. Heidi provides Lars first with a teacher of Polish, then with Polish books to learn the language of his chosen father.

Schulz's entire oeuvre consists of two volumes, *Sanatorium Under the Sign of the Hourglass* and *The Street of Crocodiles* (both available in English in Philip Roth's "Writers From the Other Europe" series, published by Penguin), plus a few letters and drawings. Missing is a novel scholars suppose to have been Schulz's masterpiece, *The Messiah.*

One day, Heidi tells Lars that a woman calling herself Adela (the name of a character in Schulz's books) has appeared out of the blue with the lost manuscript in a plastic bag; she says she is Schulz's daughter. According to Heidi and her husband, Dr. Eklund, *The Messiah* has returned. Lars's reality (and therefore his sanity) is threatened: "There's no room in the story for another child," he says to Heidi. "It's not feasible. It can't be." For Lars's story to make dramatic sense, there must be only one child, Lars himself. Adela must therefore be a fraud, and *The Messiah,* the long-awaited, much thirsted-for *Messiah,* must be a false one.

The choice of Schulz as Lars's father is not fortuitous: Schulz's work is inhabited, even possessed, by the figure of the Father, a man who does not believe that Creation is exclusively the prerogative of God. In a quote Ozick places at the beginning of her book, Schulz's Father says: "There is no dead matter. . . . lifelessness is only a disguise behind which hide unknown forms of life. . . . even if the classical methods of creation should prove inaccessible for evermore, there still remain some illegal methods, an infinity of heretical and criminal methods." Ozick the citizen, the Jew, must have watched in awe as Ozick the writer, the pagan, rolled out the following heretical chain of linked creations.

It is as if Lars stood between two mirrors. First, there is Ozick, who creates Lars, attributing him to "an indifferent maker" whose hand "had smeared his mouth and chin and Adam's apple." Then comes Lars himself, a reviewer, a creator—admittedly a secondhand one. Reviewers are envious readers who believe in surrogate parenthood, creating texts from someone else's seed; Lars, after devouring a book he must review, falls asleep feeling "oddly fat," as if pregnant with the words the writer had created. After his sleep, he can produce his piece almost in one draft. Lars is also the creator of his own name (in secret he calls himself Lazarus Baruch), of his own time (living much by night and sleeping in the afternoon, wringing two days out of one by dividing the day in two with a nap), of his own ancestry. In third place are Heidi and Dr. Eklund, who create around Lars's world a meaner, tawdrier reality. Finally, somewhere along this line of creator-creations, is God.

God provides the contrast. In the 17th century, Judah Loew ben Bezabel, rabbi of Prague, made an artificial man, a Golem who could, it was said, do a few menial tasks around the synagogue, like sweeping the floor and ringing the bells. But something was lacking in the Golem, and in the eyes of those who marveled at it, the creature was more like a thing than a person. In the end, its creator destroyed it. Lars's reality is like the Golem: to Lars it may seem more real than real life, but it lacks the ironclad immanence of a reality made by God. Lars knows this and refuses to see the last surviving person who had been part of Schulz's life: Jozefina, Schulz's Catholic fiancée, now living in London. Lars will not see her because his reality is far too fragile to bear confrontation. Schulz himself declared (as both Lars and Heidi quote) that "reality is as thin as paper and betrays with all its cracks its imitative character." Lars, like God, will admit no other reality than his own. "He's a priest of the original," says Heidi of Lars. "What he wants is the original of things." . . .

The Messiah of Stockholm is a web of creators and creations, each projecting itself in many directions at once. In some sections, Ozick echoes Schulz—his surprising choice of images, startling but exact, his rich and precise vocabulary. Here is the Stockholm that serves as a stage for Lars's alchemy: a "spired and watery town—at this lachrymose yet exalted hour," with gray steeples that "had the look of whirling Merlin hats." And the library of the Academy holding "rows and rows of superannuated encyclopedias . . . solemnly cradled, like crown jewels, in glass-flanked cabinets in a red-brick cellar." . . .

There are books designed to have no end: they are fathomless, they have the richness of unsolved mysteries. Every time we read through one of them and answer all the questions, more questions arise, and then more answers, which in turn lead to other questions. *The Messiah of Stockholm* is one such book. Its wealth, its wisdom, its humor, can, at least in part, be attributed to a Talmudic tradition of leaving no word idle, of pursuing each meaning to the marrow, as if the author were convinced that the entire Creation, including novels, was pregnant with revelations.

But there is more. When, at the end of the book, Lars comes face-to-face with his grief, as his phantom father vanishes "inside the narrow hallway of his skull" clutching the never-to-be-seen-again *Messiah,* we know that Lars's dream-world has been shattered, and we mourn for his loss—but we are left also with a curious sense of wonder. It is as if, in spirit of murdered writers and orphaned men, Ozick were showing us, halfway between bewilderment and belief, the ultimate beauty of the universe.

Alberto Manguel, "Paternity Suite," in The Village Voice, *Vol. XXXII, No. 16, April 21, 1987, p. 45.*

D. J. Enright

In *The Messiah of Stockholm* we have, for once, a truly intriguing mystery, quietly (and at times not so quietly) sounding those overtones or undertones of allegory or fable, of universality, without which no mystery will detain us for long. (p. 18)

Cynthia Ozick's character, Lars Andemening, although forty-two years old, is a conspicuously unfinished page, looking for an author to complete him; an "arrested soul" is how he sees himself. More specifically—believing himself to be an orphan of Polish origin adopted by a Swedish family—he is looking for his father, whom he has designated as Bruno Schulz, the Polish-Jewish author of two books of "peculiar tales" published in English translation as *Cinnamon Shops* (in the US, *The Street of Crocodiles)* and *Sanatorium Under the Sign of the Hourglass.* We hear that in one of these stories of "losses, metamorphoses, degradations" the father turns into a crab and the mother boils it and serves it up to the family. Schulz lived in the Galician town of Drohobycz, and was gunned down there by the SS on November 19, 1942.

Lars, who is most at home under his quilt, makes a thin living as the Monday book reviewer of the *Morgontörn,* not a good day for books, and not a very good newspaper. According to his fellow reviewers, Lars's trouble is Central Europe: he is "a Monday Faust," or "prince of the indecipherable," obsessed with people with names like Broch, Kiš, Musil, Canetti, Kundera, Schulz, inscrutable authors who hold little appeal for the healthy readers of the Wednesday and Friday culture pages. In return, though he cannot admire their intellectual tastes or literary principles, or lack of them, he loves in his colleagues "their maimed scribblers' odor, pale and dimly prurient, a fuminess skimmed from the *Morgontörn's* omnipresent staleness."

Lars's confederate and rival in the search for Schulz and Schulziana is Heidi Eklund, an aging German of dubious antecedents who once lived in the vicinity of a death camp. Now a bookseller, she contrives by uncertain means to procure rare Polish books for him, among them Schulz's translation of *The Trial.* (Lars isn't too pleased with this; he doesn't care to see his putative father "in the role of the dummy on Franz Kafka's lap.") Her husband—for a long time Lars believes she has invented him since he is always away on business—turns out to be a skilled forger of passports; he gets people "in" and "out," and likewise books and manuscripts. Heidi has also procured a Polish teacher for Lars, a refugee professor from Cracow, maybe a princess, maybe a Radziwill.

Lars, as the author states or understates, is "untouched by the comic muse." The editor of the *Morgontörn* tells him that readers are complaining: "Your reviews are practically theology." Theological is a harsher epithet even than existential or Faustian or surreal or Central European. All the same there is a lot of comedy here—as in fact there is a lot of everything except (unusually) sex, all packed into an unusually modest number of pages. The humor derives mostly, or most obviously, from the newspaper and from Lars's colleagues, vigorous Viking giants compared with the etiolated Lars, blasé philistines, "literary creatures who served, sidestepped, and sometimes sold out the Muses." Collectively they are a stewpot, and part of a larger stewpot, for "all over the world the great ladle was stirring, stirring. The poets, dreamers, thinkers, hacks. The ambitious and the meditative. The opportunists and the provocateurs. The cabalists and the seducers."

Lars's father shunned the stewpot; he lived in an obscure town, not in Warsaw or Paris, he never won the Nobel Prize though he would have done had he lived. And Lars will follow his example. "If you've never heard of it, leave it to Lars," says one of his colleagues. "Or if it's dead," another mocks. "If it never existed." "If you *wish* it never existed." Badinage of this sort, jocular, not exactly kindly, but not altogether wide of the mark, helps us to swallow occasional overwrought or overheated passages, in particular Lars's agonizings and his recurring vision of an alabaster egg—or a globe—or no, an eye, his own, but not his own, his father's murdered eye. When, as he feels, a "greased beak" carries him to high places, it is just as well that people touched rather heavily by the comic muse do their best to bring him down to earth. It is through such juxtaposition that Cynthia Ozick brings off effects comparable to those of Isaac Bashevis Singer, who can persuade the reader to believe the incredible. In *The Messiah of Stockholm,* where there is nothing that is quite incredible, the reader is released from irritable reaching after reasons and meanings. Only in the cold light of day are mysteries recognized as what they are. The physicality of the prose plays a part here:

> There was a bitter wind now, lording it over the black of one o'clock. The blackness went on throwing the snow into Lars's face, and he packed his scarf over his nose and mouth—how warm his breath was in the little cave this made! He hurried past the Stock Exchange and the Academy—not a lit bulb anywhere, or even the daub of a watchman's flashlight. Succession of whitening roofs: how easy to see into the thickest dark through a lens of snow. The spiraling flakes stuttered around him like Morse code. . . . The few cars with their sleepless headlights slipped by like slow cats. Stockholm, an orderly city, has its underlife, its hidden wakeful. Whoever owns a secret in Stockholm turns and turns in the night emptiness, but not in sleep.
>
> Under the screen of revolving flakes the steeples had the look of whirling Merlin hats.

If it never existed, leave it to Lars. Did *The Messiah,* Bruno Schulz's third and last and hence greatest book, ever exist? If it did, it must surely be dead now, must have perished somewhere in Drohobycz. However, the Eklunds find—or fabricate—a daughter of Bruno Schulz, and the daughter possesses the original manuscript of *The Messiah.* It came to her circuitously, but in a way circumstantially accounted for and hence feasible. Yet not feasible in Lars's eyes. He wants the book to exist, but not to have survived, to be there in front of him, thanks to someone who would be his sister, but can't possibly be since he was an only child. He is not prepared to share his father, not for anything, not even (it might seem) for *The Messiah.* We begin to see more point in Heidi's earlier remark: "Why don't you pick Kafka to be the son of?"

It is considered unseemly for reviewers to give away the ending of a fiction reckoned to be mysterious and thus spoil the reader's enjoyment. Yet I wouldn't wish to suggest that the present book is no more than a whodunit. So here goes.

Toward the end Cynthia Ozick falters, because there is nothing else she can do. She certainly cannot win. By now the reader positively wants *The Messiah,* and wants it to be a great work. And here, seemingly, it is, in an authentically battered but still readable manuscript. A new name is about to be added to the roll call of European giants; the work must be in the same class as Kafka, or at least rank with Gombrowicz. Cynthia Ozick will have to establish *The Messiah's* credentials more firmly, and present it to us in the Polish original and then in English translation. Which is rather a tall order. Her way out of the problem is anticlimactic and commonplace.

That there is a problem is her own fault; if *The Messiah of Stockholm* were less engaging, we wouldn't care about the fate of *The Messiah.* As it is, we must console ourselves with the thought that the manuscript was a fake (wasn't it?). Or else, judging by Lars's reactions on hurtling through it—"a waterless tract," "desert-dry all through," although about (if "about" anything) creation and redemption—and by the fact (albeit one mightn't hold this against it) that afterward he forgot practically all of it, we may incline to dismiss it as one of those great crazed works which are more certainly crazed than great.

In any case, the true mystery is that of Lars Andemening. Emerging from the holocaust (with a small *h*), he turns into a respectable reviewer (or an ordinary one), even taking on detective stories and autobiographies of film stars. He has "given up existential dread" and "those indecipherables that steam up from the stomach-hole of Central Europe." His colleagues see him as bruised and overthrown and humbled, and, after making merry, they embrace him as a comrade. He actually gets letters from readers; the editor asks him to write for Sunday and Tuesday as well as Monday; he acquires a word processor; his pay goes up. No doubt to be a haunted man is a distinction, but we are bound to feel some relief when such a person sinks at last into relative normality. The deflation was intimated halfway through the novel, when Lars called out in the office, "*The Messiah*'s turned up! Here! In Stockholm!" and a colleague explained to the others: "It's Lars Andemening. I think he's announcing the Second Coming."

Yet Lars is still haunted, if decreasingly, by a smell of burning, and by the vision of a man in a long black coat hurrying along with a manuscript under his arm. Since the mystery of Lars remains unresolved, the most vulgar of reviewers cannot give it away. (pp. 18-19)

> *D. J. Enright, "Visions and Revisions," in* The New York Review of Books, *May 28, 1987, pp. 18-20.*

Haim Chertok

That the idolatrous impulse fuels Literature, lies in wait in its very lap, may be discerned in Ozick's **"The Riddle of the Ordinary," "Toward a New Yiddish," "Bialik's Hint"**—indeed, as a background hum in almost all of her essays, but nowhere more frontally than in **"Judaism and Harold Bloom."** Here her position *in extremis* is that the phrase "Jewish writer" is itself oxymoronic. Before examining how Ozick misleads us over similar terrain in her fiction, **"Judaism and Harold Bloom"** is worth an extended pause.

The Second Commandment's curb on idols is for Ozick the very ground and substance of Jewish being: "The single most serviceable . . . description of a Jew . . . can be rendered negatively: a Jew is someone who shuns idols, who least of all would wish to become like Terach, the maker of idols." Idols are normalcy; such is current of the world. "It is the Jewish idiom that is in its deepest strain dissenting, contradictory, frequently irreconcilable." And the anomalous crux: "Literature, one should have the courage to reflect, is an idol."

Ahh! For someone of Ozick's grain, that is no small, inconsequential confession. It casts, in fact, a riddling haze over even the least of her fictional sketches. What can she possibly be talking about?

In her polemic on Bloom, Ozick abstracts four essential attributes of the idol and reveals their native congruence in Literature: 1) "The chief characteristic of any idol is that it is a system sufficient in itself"; 2) "the idol always has an ideal precursor on which to model its form"; 3) "it cannot create or alter history"; and 4) "an idol crushes pity." Only this final point seems to me not, once stated, self-evidential. What she means (citing Bloom *contra* Bloom) is that poems are revolutionaries that arise at the feet of predecessors and end by devouring them. (This is of a piece with the deconstructive critical impulse.)

Conclusion: "Based on Bloom's premises, it comes down to this: no Jew may be idolator or idol-maker . . . no Jew ought to be a poet." What could be clearer than that "the recovery of Covenant can be attained only in the living-out of the living Covenant; never among the shamanistic toys of literature." And yet about disingenuousness, with this stroke that earth beneath Ozick's well-wrought fables trembles. The edifice of her *oeuvre* wobbles. We have smacked against the barest bone of an iceberg. What rough, slouching beast, pen in hand, drifts toward its lusty birthday?

Not for a passing, wayward time has Ozick struck this startling counternote. On the contrary, it is fully in character. When on a recent trip to Israel Ozick was asked by a *Jerusalem Post* reporter what most excited her, she retorted it was the headless statue of some Roman deity at Caesarea: "Oh my, the world of nature, of plural gods. Oh it's yummy, the poetry of that." Her essay on Henry James reviews her lengthy thralldom to the Beast of Literature, how James had "ravished" her, how she indeed "had become Henry James, and for years and years . . . remained Henry James." To the same gothic point is the climax to her Preface to the short story collection *Bloodshed:* "Why do I, who dread the cannibal touch of story-telling, lust after stories more and more and more? Why do demons choose to sink their hooves into black black ink? As if ink were blood?"

A pallid but all-the-more instructive parallel to Ozick's linking of shamanism and literary lust as an occupational hazard occurs in Welsh-Jewish writer Dannie Abse's *A Strong Dose of Myself:* "I feel certain . . . I have written . . . poems which are more intelligent than I am, more witty than I am, feel more than I do, are wiser than I am. Despite this certainty, my ambition is still to write the next poem and then the one after that."

As usual, Ozick's rhetoric is sexually overdetermined (as well as more urgent), but *that,* I believe, is what she means. Abse finds no cause to agonize over his artist's condition—certainly not as a Jew, anyway. Ozick, however, is lust-tormented, demon-haunted. Her fictionalized selves fear and crave ambush, orgy, dybbukization, and despoliation. Such is the Hawthornesque texture of her imagination. Her tales are a self-tattling, not a rise but a plunge, a yielding to suck of the *yetzer horra.* Not for an instant may one wink at her linkage of blood to ink.

Ozick's strategy for straddling her writer-Jew oxymoron is to urge that the stories she plainly has labored over joyfully are her "toys," that they're not, after all, serious statements. As long as such patent self-duplicity works, only the over-precise may cavil. What still stands, however, is the riddle of how adequately to grasp and respond to the fictions of a writer who asserts in a dozen ways that they are precious but illegitimate, the bastards of her ravishing muse.

The contrast to her mentor Henry James is flagrant. His self-ironic tales and tale-telling seduce his characters and readers together; taken together, they comprise the testament of an artist's faith. Ozick's fictions are self-flagellant: she is at once both Clarissa *and* Lovelace. Her stories are always on the lam, fugitives at odds with her Jewishness, covert compromises with herself. It shows. They occupy a universe apart from that of James's psychological realism. They yield most, I suggest, as cautionary dialectics which exude in their very essence the breath of fantasy and allegory. The issues, the characters, the shapes of **"The Pagan Rabbi," "The Dock-Witch," "Puttermesser and Xanthippe"** devolve from Ozick's Jewish psychomachia, a tension between instant gratification (subsuming both Art and Passion) and the control conferred by abnegation (usually fictionally rendered as the need and the power *to wait*).

Ozick is nothing if not audacious: as God employed idolatrous Balaam as a means of conferring blessings on the Jewish people, she self-consciously uses intrinsically tainted, personally perilous fictions which, wiser than she herself, may possibly prove for her reader a blessing. But the reader had best be wary. Working (unlike James) against her natural grain, Ozick deploys layers of camouflage. She must pretend to mislead even herself in order to write at all!

Just because nothing within it incontrovertibly fantastic occurs, **"Shots,"** the centerpiece tale of her latest collection *Levitation,* is useful for charting Ozick's moral and psychological terrain. The narrator, 36 and virginal, is a typically tight Ozick type who falls in love with Sam, a historian expert on things Latin American. Seemingly, he is uneasy with his "terrific" wife Verity but cannot imagine leaving her. Photographer and historian walk and talk, but their affair hangs in suspense. In the end photographer, attired like a nun, takes a shot of Sam and Verity together, and muses. "Now they are exposed. Now they will stick together," which closes the story and puts the seal on the desperation of her passion.

It also returns the reader to the story's opening: "I came to photography as I came to infatuation—with no special talent for it, and with no point of view." At the age of 11 she had chanced upon a sepia photo of an adolescent (who would now be either a crone or decaying corpse), but the faded Brown Girl, as she fashioned her, was preserved. She kept it still. "What I had seen was time as stasis . . . the time . . . of Keats's Grecian Urn." But flawed nonetheless by human frailty: she had been photographed with the sun at her back. "The face faded out because death was coming." Time slides into timelessness.

What really here confronts us? The photographer is beguiled by the camera's power to fix the girl forever in her Grecian ripeness, a perpetual maiden. The photo overcomes time and death by producing a defiant artifact. Like Ozick by Henry James, narrator is ravished by the Brown Girl, *becomes* Brown Girl. It is the Ozick-James affair which provides the key to the relationship: "I chose Art . . . and this cost me my youth." Not a muddleheaded Art for Art's sake devotee (she informs us she is blind to "composition"), the narrator chooses the magical camera to make an idol in order to defeat death and time (or, in the well-known story **"Envy; or Yiddish in America,"** through permanence or fame). The narrator is, in short, a version of Ozick tempted into a vision of art as an alternative reality, a stop against historical flow and covenantal time.

The photo, however, is fading: Marvell supersedes Keats; narrator is at 36 still unattached. At a symposium, Sam on the platform, her attention is drawn by a simultaneous translator "tormented by bifurcated concentration. His suffering attracted me." At the precise moment he is shot by terrorists, she snaps her shutter. Astonished by the spurting blood she seems to have caused, her chief concern is not at all for the dying man but rather for her confiscated film.

The bizarre episode seems to testify to the magical power of art to affect history, as if the dolls of Terach after all *could* act. Jealous, unawares of the one who hung on Sam's every word (translator was described with the loaded image of seeming to kiss the microphone he caressed), she *shoots* him into permanence and oblivion, she replaces him: "whatever he said that was vast and public . . . I would simultaneously translate . . . into everything private and personal and secret . . . the tune Sam was moaning all the while: wife wife wife. He didn't like her. . . . His whole life was wrong. He was a dead man." Central here is that the creative act of taking a photograph issues in the taking of the very lives of others. Something destructive indwells in the very process. It is, Ozick unconsciously demonstrates with *The Cannibal Galaxy,* the same with a novel that feeds too closely on undigested life: An idol is pitiless.

The art of simultaneous translation bears further exploration. Its practitioners are those who are equally conversant with several cultures. For Ozick it is an assimilationist trope which recurs frequently in her work: Lucy and Feingold, the complementary couple (pagan and Jew) in **"Levitation"**; schizoid golem Leah and Xanthippe in **"Puttermesser and Xanthippe"**; Terach and Abraham in **"Judaism and Harold Bloom"**; priest-engendered Dual Curriculum in *The Cannibal Galaxy.* Everywhere in story, novel, and essay it is artifice and hoax, ploy and ruse.

Once only, in her essay **"Bialik's Hint,"** does Ozick see a hopeful flicker in cultural commingling—and this in the distant future. In the fiction—trust it!—no convergence is imaginable. Translator must die or, like Leonard Woolf in Ozick's essay on Virginia and malleable spouse, be himself translated. Scarcely concealed is the moralist-in-residence who continually threatens to pull the stopper on the fable-spinner bestriding her illicit idols like duplicitous Rachel on the stolen household goods of Laban, her father. Like the dolls of Terach, what after all are her yarns but "instant though illusory gratifications—namely, immediate answers to riddles. The answers may or may not be lies . . . but they are exceptionally poor at urging the moral life" (**"Judaism and Harold Bloom"**). The point is salient. Photographer *qua* photographer is fatally mistaken: it is not Sam who is dead; it is not *his* life that is botched.

Polaroid is of a piece with simultaneous translation—instant message. No waiting. Narrator at 36, like an errant Ozick fatally attending to a voice that cries "Live! Live!" in Henry James, temporarily abandons her normal apparatus and takes her shot at Sam. Tacky camera suits tacky situation. *Waiting* is an aspect of her genuine vocation. When later Sam asks why she doesn't use the Polaroid all the time, her reply is I'd wager bone and bone that of an Ozick herself: "You really have to *wait.* What's important is the waiting . . . between the exposure and the solution, history comes into being."

It is no small irony that the man of history, man of virtue, nincompoop Jew cannot fathom her. She finally resorts to a simplification that is a deception: "Photography is literal." Literal! The best gloss on this howler may be found in *The Cannibal Galaxy* when scholar Hester Lilt, unliteral author of *Metaphor as Exegesis,* delivers a lecture on the faith of Rabbi Akiva. When Akiva's rabbinic colleagues sat weeping at the destruction of the Temple, astonishingly the great rabbi laughed, for he looked not only to the despoliation but also to the prophecy of the future restoration. With perfect faith he could laugh and wait. Such in the novel is *not* the way of pedagogue Brill who puts *his* faith in a psychological tester whose job is to predict "infallibly" how well first graders will perform in the future. Generally adequate, he proves this time startlingly wrong. As Hester Lilt justly accuses, in both his profession and professions Brill stops too soon. Brill is a patsy to "Progress," a victim of Dual Curriculum.

Waiting entails both self-control and a sense of the purposes of history. It is for Ozick a heroic Jewish preoccupation and profession. In her tale **"From a Refugee's Notebook,"** she refers to Gershom Scholem, "that magnificent scholar of Jerusalem," whose historical sensitivity protected him from being enveloped by the very messianic demons he was actively investigating. (His alter ego is Freud, denier of Jewish selfhood, who was pursued by the very quarry he was seeking.) As she notes in **"The Fourth Sparrow,"** Scholem's masterwork details the cataclysmic upheaval of the Jewish world when it surrendered to the pretensions of Sabbatai Sevi, *when it grew tired of waiting for the end of days.* Messianism run amok is likewise the very center of fictions like **"Puttermesser and Xanthippe"** and **"The Sewing Harems."** Murder itself ensues.

What photographer knows and what she suffers run in contrary directions. At 36, Eros repressed is an arrow-sharp pain in the neck. This is not for Ozick a first encounter. Recall **"The Pagan Rabbi," "The Dock-Witch,"** even indeed poor Brill. The paradox is that the artist is seduced from a chaste pursuit of Art by dumb, good Sam who will never assuage her passion. The impasse renders her stupid: photography is *not* the same as life; she *will* be surprised. We may feel for her, but she is a crippled version of the fate Ozick describes herself as barely escaping under her misapprehension of Henry James. She cannot help but blunder.

Photographer's opposite is the almost insupportable Verity (perhaps "Truth" to Sam's "Goodness" to Narrator's "Beauty"?). She sews, she cooks, engages in a hundred projects, mothers superbly, is simply "terrific." Who, indeed, could manage to live with *her?* A glance at Ozick's early essay **"The Riddle of the Ordinary"** yields the clue to her thematic function. In it, Ozick opposes the Extraordinary of the aesthetic experience to the Jewish strategy of elevating the Ordinary. This opposition precisely clarifies the chasm between the two rivals. With her every motion, Verity infuses the normal, the daily, the humdrum with unsanctimonious sanctity.

In the story's final episode, Verity dresses the narrator in a costume of nunnery brown, and the narrator photographs the couple: "I shoot into their heads. . . . Now they are exposed." The photographer, a study in brown, has been fatally absorbed into her own filmic image: Brown Girl fixed forever in garb, pose, and guise. She holds her true lover between her palms. He is camera. Restive Sam will waver, but he is Verity's faithful husband. Not merely by virtue of the illusory power of the narrator's art do they stick (photographer again misconceives). Rather it is that Paganism and Judaism spin independent orbits, a fundamental lesson Brill-the-failed-astronomer missed to his life's pain but which Ozick unerringly spins again and again whenever the point is obscured by their fitful phrases of intersection. (pp. 6-12)

Haim Chertok, "Ozick's Hoofprints," in Yiddish, *Vol. 6, No. 4, 1987, pp. 5-12.*

Earl Rovit

Although Cynthia Ozick's production has not been voluminous—one long and two short novels, some two dozen short stories, and a generous assortment of occasional essays—the density, allusiveness, intellectual concern, and ambiguity which characterize her style impart a weight and imaginative breadth to that work which is markedly disproportionate to its modest size. Partly for this reason, it is a work which presents formidable difficulties for its readers. Ostensibly didactic in purpose—indeed, if Ozick's essay-voice can be trusted, even belligerently so—the typical Ozick tale is multilayered, deliberately skewed, and elusive in meaning. A rather narrow spectrum of recurrent themes and images confronts the reader. Ozick's fiction is obsessed with idols and idol-making; with artist-types who may be writers, rabbis, painters, philosophers, photographers, or teachers; with forgeries and plagiarisms; with the bewildering interplay between the hallucination which distorts and the vision which clarifies; with narrative focuses whose trustworthiness is always suspect; with characters who tend to be grotesques; and—although it is not usually noted—the whole enterprise seethes on a steady turbulence of rage.

I am not sure whether one can separate writers into those

whose approach to a reader is "user friendly" and those who choose more recalcitrant tactics, but if one could posit such a division, Ozick's work would certainly lean toward the more severe, if not more "unfriendly" side. In fact, she even provides us with what I take to be her notion of the ideal reader—a figure whose intensity and intelligence must surely make the common reader quake a little in the awareness of his ineptitude. I refer to the remarkable model of perusal which Hester Lilt presents in *The Cannibal Galaxy:*

> Every image, she said, has its logic: every story, every tale, every metaphor, every mood, is inhabited by a language of just deserts. We judge a myth by its practical influences, and are obliged to ask it practical questions: What do you intend? Who should respect you? What will you cause? What do you disclose about envy, cruelty, lust, hope, growth, power, choice, faith, pity? Whose mouth should receive you?

Accordingly, even without the sensitivity of Ozick's "imagistic linguistic logician," we are obliged to make an attempt to confront her work with Hester Lilt's questions: What do you intend? Whose mouth should receive you? What is your language of just deserts? At the same time, we would be best advised to proceed with considerable caution as we press our questions because we are likely to discover that for an ironist like Ozick, it will be the answers rather than the questions which are multiple-choice.

Thus, to begin on a kind of neutral ground, let us note in the story **"The Suitcase"** Mr. Hencke's description of his son Gottfried's exhibition of paintings.

> His canvases were full of hidden optical tricks and were so bewildering to one's routine retinal expectations that once the eye had turned away, a whirring occurred in the pupil's depth, and the paintings began to speak through their after-image. Everything was disconcerting, everything seemed pasted down flat—strips, corners, angles, slivers. All the paintings were in black and white, but there were drawings in brown pencil. The drawings were mostly teasing dots, like notes on a score. They hurtled up and down.

Within the context of the story—a somewhat bland and inconclusive satirical portrait of moral and esthetic hollowness in what purports to be a representation of the New York City "art-world," Mr. Hencke's disparagement of the exhibition seems justified. Aggressively nonrepresentational, Gottfried's work appears almost designed to compel the viewer to impose his own meanings on it, as though it were a public Rorschach test. . . . In terms of the story itself, it is clear that Gottfried's paintings are little more than avant-garde Kitsch and an opportunity for Ozick to present scathingly a milieu and a concept of art of which she strongly disapproves.

And yet I think the description of Gottfried's images is a little more complicated than Ozick intends. Except for the resolute avoidance of figural representation—and it is, admittedly, a large exception—Mr. Hencke's impressions might serve to define analogously one of the characteristic signatures of Ozick's own style. For her stories are frequently "bewildering to one's routine . . . expectations," "disconcerting," and often engender "a whirring . . . in the pupil's depth" after they've been read. Not uncommonly her fiction simulates two-dimensionality, flatness, an almost cartoonlike precision of edges and contours—a technique which seems to rest on the principle of employing severe contrast to assert certitude. To be sure, her stories have human characters and they depict or recount events which allude in a general way to the world of commonplace reality. But they often do this, it seems to me, in a manner similar to that of an animated comic strip. Let us examine a more familiar story, **"Bloodshed,"** for example—a story which many readers have admired, even as they have confessed to some confusion in interpretation.

The characters in **"Bloodshed"** are imaged in garishly vivid outlines and all their individuating features are presented in caricature. Bleilip's cousin Toby looks "freakish" to him: " . . . her bun was a hairpiece pinned on, over it she wore a bandanna . . . , her sleeves stopped below her wrists, her dress was outlandishly long. With her large red face over this costume she almost passed for some sort of peasant." Toby's husband Yussel "wore a small trimmed beard, very black, black-rimmed eyeglasses, and a vest over a rounding belly." . . . As the reflecting consciousness of the story, Bleilip himself is largely undescribed. We know he is forty-two and we know that his pockets are heavy. As in the sequence of actions in a cartoon, the frames move in the jerky rhythm of melodrama and the characters inhabit a series of frozen instants of time without the backgrounds of past histories or present entanglements unless divulged by dialogue or interior monologue. As frame follows frame, Bleilip is deposited by Greyhound bus and taxi at the hasidic community, he tours Toby and Yussel's house, he attends the *mincha* and *ma'ariv* services in the schoolhouse. Characters appear and disappear as needed; events explode with sudden unprepared violence.

As in cartoons, motives are reduced to single adrenal urgencies, personality is equated with blunt obsession, and the fluidity of normal human intercourse is grotesquely rendered in a series of collisions when a caricatured dread or desire comes into thudding impact against its immutable or immovable limit. Jules Bleilip, a self-proclaimed "secularist," pilgrimages to the hasidic community seeking a miracle. The Yiddish poet, Edelshtein (**"Envy"**), becomes the tortured personification of bitter raging frustration. The gentle rabbinical scholar, Isaac Kornfeld, fornicates with a tree (**"The Pagan Rabbi"**). The thick multilayered dimensionality of commonplace existence is flattened out to a vividly etched foreground of jagged spastic actions with just enough of an indication of background, as in a cartoon, to suggest that a milieu does exist. Also, as in a cartoon, a strong emphasis is placed on some few selected things which serve as objects of identification: Bleilip's pistols, the rebbe's "terrible hands," the silver crown in **"Usurpation,"** the photograph of the Brown Girl (**"Shots"**), the shawl in **"Rosa,"** Elsa Vaz's white beret (*The Messiah*), etc. Whereas animated cartoons typically place their accents on physical impact (BANG! CRASH! ZAP!), Ozick tends to mute the physical violence, transferring its brutality to a sometimes inspired monologue or dialogue of verbal execration. But even though actual physical violence, is minimized—the most violent action in **"Bloodshed"** occurs when Bleilip's yarmulka slips off and a stranger slaps it back on his head!—the typical Ozick story balances on the fulcrum of violent struggle, whether overt, disguised, or latent.

Such a style or "language of just deserts" inclines toward the comic and/or moralistic; it is punctuated by recurrent surprises, its action is frequently on or across the verges of the surreal, and one of its inherent functions is satirical. Secure outside the frames of the action, the reader can condescend to the mechanical victims caught in the mechanical precision of their cartoon-fates, and witness the incongruities and compulsions which become flagrant vice excessively punished or, at least, shamefully exposed. For surely a significant aspect of Ozick's power is that of a fierce moralist mercilessly skewering the world of middle-class affectation—most especially in its intellectual pretentiousness and its substitution of "feel-good" sloganry for the agonizing moil of human realities. This style tends to dominate some of the earlier stories (**"A Mercenary," "Virility"**), but it threads itself throughout Ozick's work from **"Levitation"** and the Puttermesser sequence to *The Messiah of Stockholm.* At its least effective, it gives the impression of being driven by an animosity or contempt grossly disproportionate to the materials under view; consequently, it runs the danger of being so heavyhanded and excessive as to be frivolous or tiresomely predictable. When it works reasonably well—and it often does—it invites the reader to join the author in condemnation of the attitudes paraded before him.

But of course Ozick's thought and artistry are not so simple as this. Balancing, as it were, Mr. Hencke's description of Gottfried's exhibition is a sort of companion-piece of esthetic appreciation: Joseph Brill's pained response to the acclaimed paintings of his onetime student, Beulah Lilt, in *The Cannibal Galaxy:*

> He looked through phantasmagorical windows enclosed in narrow silver frames. . . . It wasn't that all these curious windows were "abstract"; it might be that they weren't abstract enough. You could fancy amazing scenes in them: but when you approached, it was only paint, bleak here, brilliant here, in shapes sometimes nearly stately, sometimes like gyres. . . . Once, from four feet away, he thought he was gazing into a scarlet ditch, from hip to heel, in the haunch of a nude female: the ditch was crowded with two double-rows of fat human toes with coarse yellow nails. It unnerved him—but when he came near he saw it was again only paint. There was no nude, no ditch. . . .

Like Gottfried's paintings, Beulah's are also "nonrepresentational" and they too require the viewer to participate actively in the creation and reception of the images. But how radically different they are! Beulah's work stands in diametric opposition to what I called earlier the technique of certitude by means of contrast. Here the stress is on perspective, depth, color, and the cunning play of solid shapes emerging from and diffusing into the blended textures of paint. Here there is a denial of certitude and an espousal of evocation. Here I would suggest is a second language of just deserts which is designed for different functions and which elicits different responses.

The first style, in other words, invites the reader to assume the luxurious stance of objective analysis. From outside the text (**"A Mercenary"** or **"An Education,"** for example), the reader can treat himself to the illusion of overseeing its creation, of diagramming its rhythm and climaxes, of assessing this simulated life as a predictable set of episodes proceeding to an inevitable end. If we are moved to join with what I take to be Ozick's auctorial insistence that a clear line of demarcation can and must be drawn between Nature and Spirit (see **"The Pagan Rabbi"** or **"Levitation"**), then it is because that contrast has been articulated in the first language of just deserts. And this is what the style of Beulah Lilt's paintings precisely denies. Joseph Brill, not especially more sensitive than Mr. Hencke, but totally confident of his ability to draw distinctions—to discriminate, for example, between the mediocre and the exceptional—cannot keep himself out of Beulah's phantasmagorical paintings. Her visual language haunts him. "She labored . . . in calculated and enameled forms out of which a flaming nimbus sometimes spread." And whether that nimbus is created exclusively by Beulah or by Brill or some curious collaboration of the two, it flames unpredictably (thus destroying the "completion-complex of the schoolroom and/or the madhouse"), and as it spreads, it easily eludes the cool calipers of behaviorism, cocksure rationalism, and dogmatic moral judgment.

Thus, it seems to me, to answer Hester Lilt's difficult questions about the logic of images is to confront a peculiar problem. Is Ozick's work inhabited by one language of just deserts or, as I have implied, by two? If there are, in fact, two, are they compatible, complementary, contradictory? Perhaps a closer examination of **"Bloodshed"** may be useful in this inquiry. If **"Bloodshed"** is controlled by what I have described as Ozick's "cartoon-style," then the story should work to expose Bleilip as a curiosity-seeker, a potential idolater, a secularist who is uncomfortable when he cannot find something to mock and make a joke of, a man who is leading a mistaken life. On this level of interpretation, Bleilip can be securely identified with the goat destined for Azazel when the rebbe unerringly isolates him from the group and they collectively cast him out. But this comic paradigm becomes blurred in the rebbe's passionate exegesis of the parable and his even more passionate deflection of its meanings when he presumably intuits Bleilip's silent and sullen resistance.

That is, the ritualistic casting-out of the goat in the days of the Temple has been followed by an era of anarchic slaughter. With the destruction of the Temple, "everyone on earth became a goat or a bullock, he-animal or she-animal," and the whole world is Azazel. With the destruction of the Temple, two orders of existence have replaced the one unified reality; there is that which remains real—what the rebbe calls "capable"—and that which he (and presumably Ozick) regard as much more elusive and dangerous, that which imitates the real.

This, I imagine, is why Ozick gives Bleilip two pistols to carry around in his pockets, a real one and a plastic toy. The real one ("monstrous, clumsy and hard, heavy, with a scarred trigger and a barrel that smelled. Dark, no gleam") is "capable": in fact, it has killed a pigeon. But it can be dealt with in real matter-of-fact terms; it can be unloaded, it can be controlled, it can be guarded against. The plastic toy, on the other hand, incapable in reality, cannot be incapacitated because its symbolic potency is outside the jurisdiction of real physical principles. As an imitation of reality, it is—in Ozick's fabric of meanings—always capable of creating new meanings, of violating the Second Commandment, of purposely or inadvertently leading to the submissive worship of the cannibalistic Moloch. When Bleilip tries to defend himself by accusing the

rebbe of a willingness to slaughter anything to attain the restoration of the Temple, the rebbe tells him that he, Bleilip, is "as bloody as anyone." But his sin is not the killing of a pigeon; it is his desperate if only partly acknowledged desire to believe in magic and miracles.

I have tried to produce a reading of **"Bloodshed"** which recognizes the two languages of just deserts which somewhat contentiously inhabit that story. In trying to be fair to both the story and what I take to have been Ozick's intentions, I have probably distorted either or both. But, I believe, whatever my misreadings may be, ultimately there is a confusion in the story itself and this is a consequence of an irresolute clash between Ozick's two languages. The significant movement of the story is the transference of Bleilip's pistols to the rebbe's "terrible hands," and all the elements of the story must be subservient to that movement. We know why the rebbe's hands are "terrible" (the result of Nazi medical experiments) and we are willing, as readers, to equate the personality and the stature of the rebbe with the image of his hands, but I do not think we can accept the same equation for Bleilip and his pistols. I can try to explain why Bleilip has two pistols instead of one, but I am at a loss to account for his having one in the first place. Or, to put it in different terms, I think Bleilip's pistols are forged in the perspectiveless language of Gottfried's flat cartoonlike paintings (like the geometric-patterned dress of the Jewish mistress in the same story), while the rebbe's hands exude the emotional resonance of Beulah Lilt's craft. When these two languages come into conjunction at what should be the triumphant climax of the story, there is a small but crucial babble of confusion and misconnection rather than a confluence.

Ozick's cartoonlike style is blunt, didactic, comic, judgmental, often cruel, and severely moralistic. It is perfectly willing to consign poor Lucy Feingold to the "humanists" and the party-residue of cake crumbs and salted peanuts while her husband and the refugee and all the *real* Jewish remnant glide high in the air above the living room (**"Levitation"**). It is a style which dominates stories like **"An Education," "A Mercenary," "Virility,"** and the Puttermesser sequence where the funny names, the topical allusions, and the exaggeratedly outrageous episodes are clearly fashioned to instruct by ridicule, to enlighten by mocking castigation. Similarly, Ozick's sustained acidulous portrayal of the Edmund Fleg School of the Dual Curriculum, as well as of Lars Andemening's idolatrous worship of Literature (**"The Academy,** more sacred to him than any cathedral"), or of the hilarious, if somewhat sinister, confidence racket of the Eklund clan are unabashedly comic in their development and figuration. And yet, in both *The Cannibal Galaxy* and *The Messiah of Stockholm,* as also in **"Envy," "Usurpation," "Levitation," "Shots,"** and the two Rosa-stories, the cartoonlike style is shadowed and sometimes overshadowed by her second language, the style of "the nimbus" or, to use one of Ozick's favorite Jamesian notions, the *corona*-style.

The corona-style aims to evoke, connote, suggest, symbolize; its processes are predicated on a faith in creativity instead of the fait accompli of discovery. In the rebbe's terms, it is the dangerous language that has taken occupation over the time between the destruction of the Temple and the not yet arrived coming of the Messiah. It is a style which inclines toward originality rather than tradition; it nurtures the subjective voice of individuality, resisting the utterance of scriptural collectivity; and, for Ozick, it is associated with the lyrical rather than the comic/moralistic mode. Like Beulah's paintings, it is capable of creating a flaming nimbus; it can instill a fire of vitality into dead matter (mere paint), but harbored within its most intense spark is the omnipresent potentiality of fire to rage into holocaust. In one of her brilliant essays, Ozick calls attention to the distinction in Hebrew between *t'shuva* ("the energy of creative renewal and turning") and the *yetzer ha-ra* ("the Evil Impulse . . . that is said to be the source of the creative faculty"). In a series of remarkable images, she argues that imagination is its own most deadly and endlessly resourceful enemy, but she posits the hope that the "redemptive corona" can sometimes emerge from what appears to be virtually an Armageddon-like conflict.

For my more prosaic purposes—the distinction between these two languages of just deserts—let me cite Ozick's definition of "corona": it is "interpretation, implicitness, the nimbus of *meaning* that envelops story." What I have been indicating as her "cartoon-style" could hardly be more directly opposed. Instead of interpretation, it delivers judgment; in place of implicitness, it offers overt, heavyhanded assertion; and rather than the "nimbus of *meaning*" which presumably emanates from a story like an effluvium or aroma, the cartoon-style administers an axe-blow or the subtle slide of a stiletto. The purposes of the one are to come to a point, to make a point, to point with unwavering rectitude a direction, a meaning, a verdict. The purposes of the other are to atomize and diffuse a single unique point into auras of undefinable radiance. Point and nimbus: can the same mouth receive them simultaneously?

Thus, it seems to me that the central problem of Ozick's work is the existence of two languages whose generic structures incarnate different purposes which impel them in contrary directions. And that Ozick is keenly aware of some powerful impulse toward bifurcation at the very root of her creativity is quite evident. (pp. 34-42)

[As] has been evident in and since *Trust,* Ozick's imagination fervidly seeks out and revels in warring dichotomies of one sort or another: Jew and Gentile, orthodox and secular Judaism, Hebraism and Hellenism, Moses and Pan/Apollo, Torah and levity, male and female, fiction and the essay, short fiction and the novel, Hebrew and English, Nature and Spirit, Art and Life. It is as though the first instinctive quiver of Ozick's mind is to cleave as with an axe an uncompromising distinction between sameness and otherness—and to do this with a quasi-religious zeal for purity. Her two most comprehensive images, which encompass all the disparate smaller evils in her system of morality, are, I suppose, cannibalism and idolatry; and these, in turn, nudged one further notch up the scale of abstraction, merge into her concept of Moloch/Holocaust. Curiously, there is a scarcity of strong images of a countervailing Good in her work. But rather than trying to retrace the surges and counter-surges of her passionate debates, the changes and exchanges of ideas which boil in her fiction and which she records so eloquently in her essays, it might be useful to suppose that Ozick the fiction-writer thinks more in images than in ideas, and we might return to Hester Lilt's penetrating question: What does your work disclose about "envy, cruelty, lust, growth, hope,

power, choice, faith, pity?" What, in other words, can the reader take away from Ozick's fictional world? What are the practical influences of that world?

The first thing we must recognize, it seems to me, is that the weight of Ozick's passion is heavily focused on the portrayal of vice, not virtue. The manifestations of envy, cruelty, and lust are vigorously limned in the variety of their cunning guises. There is relatively little direct presentation of love, hope, growth, pity, or faith. More concretely, we should note that this is a fictional world peopled, for the most part, by unlikeable and unattractive characters. Those like Rosa Lublin or Edelshtein, who clearly merit not only our pity, but our most generous sympathy, repel it. Their condition is so far beyond reform or redemption—and their rage is so incontrovertible— that our pity can only be gratuitous and self-indulgent. The bulk of the dramatis personae of Ozick's world is composed of the weak, the greedy, the hypocritical, the intensely selfish. Characters like Isaac Kornfeld, Jules Bleilip, Pincus Silver, the Feingolds, Una Meyer, Stanislav Lushinski, etc. serve too pliantly the comic-morality roles of satirical target to be particularly likeable or sympathetic. This may be in part a consequence of the fact that they inhabit short stories where characterization tends to be reduced to a single gesture and stance. And it may partly reflect their functions as illustrations or examples in a didactic text. " 'Rabbi, I'm not an exercise, I'm not a demonstration—' " complains Bleilip, but of course he is—like so many of Ozick's characters, not just for the other members of the worship service, but for her readers.

In spite of the fact that **The Cannibal Galaxy** extends the short-story form and provides a larger space for the exploration of character, it does not seem to me that Ozick uses that space much differently than she does in the shorter form. Joseph Brill is an odd amalgam of comic target and aborted lyrical possibility. On the satirical level which dominates the novel, he and his pedagogical experiment suffer comic laceration to illustrate Ozick's disgust with "the completion-complex of the schoolroom," the torpid acceptance of rational determinism, and the cowardly rejection of *t'shuva,* the possibility of creative renewal. Sensitive enough to have responded to Rabbi Pult's injunction that "the world rests on the breath of children in the schoolhouses," and idealistic enough to have conceived of the Dual Curriculum which will fuse "scholarly Europe and burnished Jerusalem," Brill leads a long "mistaken life" in which he personally commits the sin of "stopping too soon," and professionally allows his school to fallow into a faddish mediocrity swamped in cant and cannot. (pp. 42-3)

The reader is disposed to admire Hester and Beulah; he would like to find in them some alternative models of value to set against the fiasco of Brill's career. Unfortunately, Ozick tells us too little about them to validate such claims. Each, in different ways, is a creature with no defining class, tradition, institution, or inner struggle; both act, as it were, like single erratic comets unresponsive to any terrestrial or celestial gravity. The novel ends with Brill oppressed by his sense of the implacable judgment implicit in "the flaming nimbus" which spreads from Beulah's language, but by this point, Brill has been so thoroughly debased as comic victim that his belated perception only certifies his utter failure. And since there is another level of connotation in the cannibal-image—the Holocaust of which Brill is a "dervish"-survivor—even an unsentimental reader may feel that the comic mechanisms designed to expose and punish vice have themselves become vicious in their instrumentality.

Finally, the interplay between point and nimbus in *The Messiah of Stockholm* may achieve a subtlety or muted compatibility rather new in Ozick's work. From an overly reductive view, Lars's story can be seen as another variation on and reversal of the "mistaken life" theme that we have noticed in Bleilip and Brill. Like the narrator of *Trust,* Lars is on a paternity quest, but his peculiar genius is to have fathered himself, choosing his name from a Swedish dictionary (as a refugee orphan, he is Lazarus Baruch). He has elected as his father Bruno Schulz, the Polish Jew exterminated in Drohobyzc, who left behind him a slender oeuvre and the rumor of a lost novel in manuscript, entitled *The Messiah.* Religiously obsessed with Literature at its most intensely symbolic (Kafka, Kiŝ, Musil, Broch, Canetti, Jabès, Gombrowicz, etc.), Lars strips himself of the trappings of life like an unwanted skin—two wives, one daughter, the quotidian furniture of domesticity. His aim is to pursue without distraction his role as suppliant-worshipper of the sacred words which, imitating reality, become, he believes, a greater Reality. Most particularly, he seeks the lost words of his putative father in what is for Ozick a demonically comic, curiously heroic, idolatrous action. The plot of the novel—an ironic consequence of the plotting of the Eklund clan to use Lars as the discover/introducer of the lost Schulz *Messiah*—works to release the forty-two-year-old Lars from his prolonged egglike boyhood, as he burns the manuscript, abjures his obsession with Schulz and Literature, and embraces mediocrity and commonplace existence.

My synopsis, of course, can hardly indicate the remarkably rich texture of the novel which—144 pages in my edition—is a nearly sustained and breathless stylistic tour de force. Narrated at a pitch of intensity which constantly scintillates into the surreal, which flashes back and forth in time-sequences like an electric storm, *The Messiah* has the pace of exponential acceleration. It is a little like a skyrocket which hurtles through frenzy into explosion and settles abruptly at the end into an evocative ashen acridity. Especially brilliant are Ozick's depictions of Lars's fevered impressions of Stockholm in the winter nights, the cool satire of the literary "stewpot" of the cultural department of the *Morgontörn,* and the assembled Eklund clan of conspirators—three outrageous caricatures, fully costumed and stage-propped for their roles in the animated morality-cartoon which Ozick presents. (pp. 44-5)

The cartoon action of the novel bursts into climax in the burning of the manuscript—a scene as hilariously choreographed as a Marx Brothers (or Three Stooges) movie sequence and as painful to watch as an epileptic seizure. Heidi throws water ineffectually into the flaming brass amphora, Olle storms around the room refilling the teakettle, and Elsa is huddled in a heap on the floor, "a bloody rip across the blade of her frail nose," from her father's brutal kick. Here Ozick permits her grotesque images to express the physical violence which is always potential in caricature, releasing both the characters and her readers from their efforts of restraint. Further, the surrealistic pitch of the novel's style has the effect of raising the

satirical burlesque to something very close to a lyrical cri de coeur—or, at any rate, to a level more compatible with the evocation of her second ("nimbus") language.

The role of the Eklunds as comic victimizers on whom the tables are violently turned allows Lars a measure of stature denied Brill, and this, in part, narrows the distance between the effects of Ozick's two languages. Lars is ruthlessly ridiculed for his obsessions, even though his obsessions have ennobled him. In fact, the most ironic turn in the novel suggests that when Lars finally perceives the plot into which he has been beguiled and accuses the Eklunds of being in competition with God—a recognition which parallels his similar complicity in the plot of his entire life—his ascent into health is also a precipitous descent into mediocrity. Paradoxically, the Lars in wild pursuit of his father and the pristine gods of Literature is a much more interesting and admirable person than the successful reviewer of popular fiction who closes the novel. In Hester Lilt's terms, perhaps it is not that he stops too soon, but that he has not gotten around to starting yet ("the completion-complex of the madhouse").

The leitmotif of chimneys, burning, and the smell of roasting meat that pervades the novel, coupled with the ubiquitous presence of the Holocaust (Lars's and the Eklunds' backgrounds, Nelly Sachs, and Bruno Schulz), provide the connotative rhythms with which Ozick's corona-style climbs and ultimately seeps over the comic action. The final image, itself a fictional invention of Elsa Vaz as part of the manuscript scam, becomes a dark searing nimbus that colors the entire novel in retrospect:

> When, less and less often, the smell flushed up out of the morning's crevices, Lars inside the narrow hallway of his skull caught sight of the man in the long black coat, hurrying with a metal garter box squeezed under his arm, hurrying and hurrying toward the chimneys. And then, in the blue light of Stockholm, he grieved.

Lars grieves for his own burnt-up life, he grieves for Schulz, he grieves for the millions who hurried unwittingly to their unappeasable deaths in wild actions, in burial pits, in innocuous shower-rooms, in the oven that had become Europe.

Let me try to summarize this analysis of Ozick's use of two languages. If I had to give a name to the most characteristic mood or feeling that prevails throughout Ozick's work—a sort of ground bass that has sustained itself at the very foundation of her fiction regardless of the melodic variations that distinguish her very different stories—I should call it *grief.* Her typical tale travels from rage to grief. Sometimes her main characters are aware of their detours and destination; sometimes they are not. But this is always the itinerary which Ozick lays out for her reader. Generally, her cartoon-style is energized by the rage, her corona-style by the grief. Traditional satire employs the cautery of its condemnation with the hope, however feeble or farfetched, of reform and redemption. Grief—or at least the kind of grief which is the final evocative note of Ozick's fictions—is terminal. One of the sources of the kind of confusion or frustration which many readers justifiably feel at the denouements of much of Ozick's work may be due to this. Satire, the literary mechanism which embodies and releases rage, traditionally implies a future. Uncontainable grief is expressed in a dirge which precludes the future tense; its dark music sounds in a permanent present without end. (pp. 46-7)

Earl Rovit, "The Two Languages of Cynthia Ozick," in Studies in American Jewish Literature, *Vol. 8, No. 1, Spring 1989, pp. 34-47.*

Michiko Kakutani

Two themes have preoccupied Cynthia Ozick throughout her career as a critic and as a writer of fiction: the dangers of idol worship (that is, the violation of the Second Commandment "Thou shalt not make unto thee any graven image"), and the difficulties experienced by the Holocaust generation in coming to terms with the compromises of contemporary American society. Both these themes lie at the heart of the two interconnected stories in [*The Shawl*], both of which won O. Henry Prizes after appearing first in *The New Yorker.* The two stories stand, at once, as dazzling philosophical meditations and beautifully crafted works of fiction.

In **"The Shawl,"** Ms. Ozick sets down, in short, intense takes, an account of what happened to Rosa Lublin and her baby daughter, Magda, during their internment in a concentration camp during World War II. Both of them, along with Rosa's niece, Stella, are starving. Rosa worries that Stella wants Magda to die so that she can eat her tiny body; she, meanwhile, tries to placate her baby's hunger by giving her a linen shawl to chew on. . . .

When Stella steals Magda's shawl, the distraught infant toddles out of the barracks—until then, Rosa has kept her alive by keeping her hidden—and she is spotted by a soldier who brutally murders her by throwing her into an electrified fence. Rosa simply stands there, "because if she ran they would shoot, and if she tried to pick up the sticks of Magda's body they would shoot, and if she let the wolf's screech ascending now through the ladder of her skeleton break out, they would shoot."

Fierce, concentrated and brutal, **"The Shawl"** burns itself into the reader's imagination with almost surreal power. In contrast, the story **"Rosa"**—which takes up Rosa's life some 30 years later—achieves its power through the accumulation of seemingly naturalistic details, immersing us persuasively in its heroine's new life.

Having survived the war and its aftermath, Rosa has been living in New York City. Recently, however, she has given up her antiques business—she made headlines in the papers by abruptly demolishing her own store—and moved to Miami, where she lives in an old people's "hotel," grudgingly supported by Stella. It is a squalid, circumscribed existence: she rarely ventures outside her room, rarely speaks to her neighbors. . . .

The present . . . holds no interest for Rosa. She dwells, obsessively, exclusively, on the past—on what happened to her and Magda so many years ago in Poland; on what happened to all the hopes and dreams she once cherished as a young woman.. . . .

The Proustian madeleine that summons up the past for Rosa is Magda's magical shawl. With the shawl, Rosa can actually conjure up Magda's presence: she will hold the shawl, cradle it, and suddenly the room will be "full of Magda." Sometimes Magda appears as a teen-ager, wearing one of Rosa's lovely sky-blue dresses. Sometimes she is a beautiful young woman of 30, a doctor married to another doctor with a large house in Mamaroneck. Sometimes she is a professor of Greek philosophy at Columbia University.

In Ms. Ozick's fictional world, Rosa's obsession with the shawl and her fantasies about Magda make her guilty of idol worship. Like Lars Andemening in *The Messiah of Stockholm,* like Ruth Puttermesser in an earlier short story, Rosa has created a fictional world of her own, a tiny solipsistic system of thinking that excludes everyone and everything else. As a result, she has cut herself off from reality, excluded herself from the mundane satisfactions of ordinary life, and in the process she has become a madwoman.. . . .

As a strict student of traditional Judaism, Ms. Ozick condemns what she has called the "corruptions and abominations of idol worship, of the adoration of the magical event," and yet as a fiction writer, she doubtless understands Rosa's love of fantasy, her need to create a private world. In the case of this story, that conflict generates both sympathy for Rosa, and horror at the consequences of her obsession. It is a measure of Ms. Ozick's mastery as a writer that she is able to communicate this dual vision to the reader, while at the same time grounding the theoretical implications of her narrative in a wonderfully supple and compelling story.

Michiko Kakutani, "Cynthia Ozick on the Holocaust, Idolatry and Loss," in The New York Times, *September 5, 1989, p. C17.*

Francine Prose

One thing Cynthia Ozick's characters do well is to evoke in the reader an instructive mix of sympathy and irritation. The headmaster in *The Cannibal Galaxy,* Puttermesser in *Levitation,* the minor poet in **"Envy, or, Yiddish in America"**—the modern golem is cranky, a loner, obsessive, bad at parties. Her characters push against our limits of patience and compassion, and it makes us feel somehow larger to care about these lives, up to and beyond the point of seeing some of ourselves in them.

In her remarkable new book, *The Shawl,* Ms. Ozick turns from these unquiet and disquieting souls to the more disturbed and disturbing and pulls off the rare trick of making art out of what we would rather not see. The experience of reading *The Shawl* is immensely troubling, especially if one pauses to think and feel and is not simply lulled by the pure pleasure that Ms. Ozick's wonderful sentences might otherwise occasion.

Though the two parts of this slim volume—[the short story, **"The Shawl"**] and the novella **"Rosa"**—were first published separately (both appeared in *The New Yorker*), they take on new resonance and weight from their inclusion here together. Images and incidents echo between the two sections, like signals sparkling across the hemispheres of a scarred and fevered brain.

The brain is that of one Rosa Lublin, who, in the explosive title story, watches her daughter, Magda, murdered by the Nazis. Never has the Holocaust so resembled the Brothers

Grimm: a claustrophobic, horrific fairy-tale world of evil, of cannibal children, of objects invested with the magic power to protect or destroy. [The tone of **"The Shawl"**] is a departure from the more cerebral, ironic voice of much of Ms. Ozick's fiction; its rhythms grow almost incantatory as Rosa witnesses her daughter's death. . . . (pp. 1, 39)

By the time **"Rosa"** opens, 30 years later, its eponymous heroine, now "a madwoman and a scavenger," has trashed her Brooklyn furniture store and moved to a corner of Florida that Dante might have described if he'd descended to the lowest circle of hell and discovered that it was Miami. In this infernal retirement paradise populated by "scarecrows, blown about under the murdering sunball with empty rib cages," Rosa, like so many of Ms. Ozick's characters, practices her own version of idolatry.

The object of Rosa's veneration is the lost Magda, whose death Rosa refuses to accept and to whom she writes eloquent letters in "the most excellent literary Polish." Rosa's niece, Stella, accuses her of being "like those people in the Middle Ages who worshipped a piece of the True Cross, a splinter from some old outhouse as far as anybody knew." And, in fact, Rosa's holy relic is the shawl in which she once wrapped Magda; she prepares to enter its presence with the solemnity of arcane ritual.

Here, as in *The Cannibal Galaxy,* Ms. Ozick explores the complex connections among idolatry, maternity and philosophy. Yet *The Shawl* is not a raking-over of familiar ground. Instead, Ms. Ozick goes farther to suggest that history too may be cast in the role of demiurge, that Rosa's idolatrous pantheon includes not only her daughter, but her own past, the war, the "real life" that, she keeps repeating, has been stolen from her by thieves.

It's excruciating to watch Rosa tear through Miami in search of a lost pair of underpants, but what keeps it from being depressing or numbing is the consolation of art, its power to mediate chaos. Rosa is brilliantly realized. Her dark night of the soul is lit by flashes of insight about memory, culture, old age, a welcome meditation on the euphemistic inadequacy of the word "survivor," and—as we've come to expect from Ms. Ozick—by humor. . . .

Jewish artists—Woody Allen is an obvious example—have made much of the notion that anticipating the worst is a Jewish tic, that metaphysical paranoia is part and parcel of the Judaic DNA code. *The Shawl* can be read, I suppose, as an exercise in imagining the worst: the Holocaust, a child's death, a stolen life, the reduction of a human being to a creature that can survive on "half a sardine, or a small can of peas" in a hellish Miami cubicle. But Ms. Ozick wisely reminds us that history has repeatedly proved to have a darker imagination and that there are lives, even in sunny Florida, that put paranoia to shame. (p. 39)

Francine Prose, "Idolatry in Miami," in The New York Times Book Review, *September 10, 1989, pp. 1, 39.*

Elie Wiesel

[*The Shawl*] is not a book about the Holocaust, but about men and women who have survived it. Therein lies its depth; therein one encounters its truth.

Normally, the survivors of such a catastrophe, which we call—so poorly—the Holocaust, should not be normal. Having seen the collapse of their universe, with its system of values and networks of cultural alliances and social loyalties; having approached the abyss where their existence was swallowed up, it is inconceivable that their spirit remained whole. How can they believe in the power of intelligence, while, for so long, they witnessed the triumph of brutality? How can they invest in the future while, together with the past, it is buried under ashes?

And yet. . . . After the torment, miraculously, men and women found the strength in themselves to affirm life, and the sanctity of life. Hardly had the flames been extinguished, when in the DP camps, marriages were already celebrated, schools reopened, as if to announce to the entire world: in spite of everything, love exists, faith, too, and also hope.

But not all "adjusted" themselves to the normal conditions of life. Some didn't want to, others couldn't. If their destiny interests you, read this great little book of Cynthia Ozick's: It contains dazzling and staggering pages filled with sadness and truth.

The writing is dense, the dialogues vivid. The author here masters better than ever the art of the short story, by gathering situations and themes, and condensing them to the point at which they burst from within.

Everything in these two related fictions—a short story and a novella—revolves around one woman, Rosa; her niece, Stella; and her infant daughter, Magda, whom she kept hidden in her shawl while they all were inmates of a Nazi death camp. In the short story, **"The Shawl,"** she watches helplessly as a guard finds Magda and flings her to her death. **"Rosa,"** the novella, picks up Rosa's story 30 years later in Miami.

Rosa's impotent but overwhelming anger, her burning memories, her implacable solitude, her hallucinations, her shawl—Ozick speaks of them with so much tact and delicacy that we ask ourselves with wonder and admiration what has she done to understand and penetrate Rosa's dark and devastated soul. Non-survivor novelists who treat the Holocaust ought to learn from Ozick the art of economy and what the French call *pudeur* (modesty). Just a few words speak of Rosa's husband, the son of a Jewish convert. A paragraph recalls that she herself had been violated by the SS. . . .

Fragile and vulnerable, penetrated by anguish and remorse, a page will be turned. But the story will remain the same.

Elie Wiesel, "Ozick Asks Whether There Can Be Life After Auschwitz," *translated by Martha Liptzin Hauptman, in* Chicago Tribune—Books, *September 17, 1989, p. 6.*

FURTHER READING

Gitenstein, R. Barbara. "The Temptation of Apollo and the Loss of Yiddish in Cynthia Ozick's Fiction." *Studies in American Jewish Literature,* No. 3 (1983): 194-201.

Utilizes Ozick's definition of genuine Jewish writing to analyze stories in *The Pagan Rabbi and Other Stories* and *Bloodshed and Three Novellas.*

Greenstein, Michael. "The Muse and the Messiah: Cynthia Ozick's Aesthetics." *Studies in American Jewish Literature* 8, No. 1 (Spring 1989): 50-65.

Asserts that in *The Cannibal Galaxy* and *The Messiah of Stockholm,* Ozick attempts to transcend the limitations she placed on fiction in her critical essays.

Harap, Louis. "The Religious Art of Cynthia Ozick." *Judaism* 33, No. 3 (Summer 1984): 353-63.

Traces the evolution of Ozick's statements on Judaism from her first novel, *Trust,* through her later essays and short stories.

Pifer, Ellen. "Cynthia Ozick: Invention and Orthodoxy." In *Contemporary American Women Writers: Narrative Strategies,* edited by Catherine Rainwater and William J. Scheick, pp. 89-109. Lexington: The University of Kentucky Press, 1985.

Analyzes Ozick's use of postmodern techniques in her stories "Puttermesser: Her Work History, Her Ancestry, Her Afterlife" and "Puttermesser and Xanthippe."

Redmon, Anne. "Vision and Risk: New Fiction by Oates and Ozick." *Michigan Quarterly Review* XXVII, No. 1 (Winter 1988): 201-13.

Identifies the theme of spiritual seeking in Ozick's *The Messiah of Stockholm* and Joyce Carol Oates's novel *You Must Remember This* as a particularly American phenomenon.

Scrafford, Barbara. "Nature's Silent Scream: A Commentary on Cynthia Ozick's 'The Shawl'." *Critique* XXXI, No. 1 (Fall 1989): 11-15.

Analysis of symbols and motifs in this short story.

Marge Piercy

1936-

American novelist, poet, and essayist.

Piercy is a prominent feminist writer whose political commitment informs her works, which focus on individuals struggling to escape restrictive social roles to realize personal potential. Frankly polemical, Piercy's colloquial, free verse poetry passionately excoriates such phenomena as sexism, capitalism, and pollution, using exaggerated imagery and unabashed emotionalism in service of her social commentary. Piercy's novels share these characteristics while concentrating on individuals often deemed marginal by mainstream American society, including working-class Jews, lesbians, urban African-Americans, and immigrants of various nationalities. Although Piercy's depiction of the evils of poverty are often bleakly realistic, her works display a fundamental optimism in the power of the collective will expressed in political action. Susan Mernit remarked: "Marge Piercy is unremitting in showing us how the public world shapes the personal lives of her characters . . . and she infuses ideology with tremendous feeling."

Piercy was born to a Jewish mother and a Welsh father in a working-class neighborhood in Detroit. After attending the University of Michigan as a scholarship student, she moved to Chicago, and received a Masters degree from Northwestern University. Much of Piercy's work of the 1960s and 1970s emerged directly from her involvement in the radical youth organization Students for a Democratic Society. Throughout her career, Piercy has aligned her concern with such social problems as poverty, the destruction of the environment, gentrification of old neighborhoods, and civil and women's rights, to their impact on the private lives of her characters. In her poetry, this is often expressed in an anguished or angry first-person narrative. Piercy's first publication, *Breaking Camp,* is a volume of poetry that balances expressions of outrage at impoverished living conditions in Chicago with personal accounts of joy in love and being alive. *Hard Loving,* her second collection, includes personal and political poems that were praised for their passion and urgency. Dorothy Donnelly commented: "Not highly compatible by nature, poetry and polemics have a hard time integrating, but Marge Piercy's personal intensity combined with her acetylene vocabulary weld the two with more than usual success."

Piercy's politics have evolved over time, as has the political element in her fiction and poetry. In the 1970s, Piercy shifted her emphasis from poverty, racism, and the Vietnam War to the struggle for women's rights. The poems collected in *To Be of Use, Living in the Open,* and *The Moon Is Always Female* reflect her commitment to exposing the damaging effects of patriarchy in contemporary American society, condemning the roles ascribed to women by the male establishment. While Piercy won praise for her attention to details of familiar objects and occurrences, some critics faulted her use of stereotypes to illustrate her propagandistic message.

Piercy's works of the 1980s emphasize the politics of city-planning and the poet's sensual pleasure in such activities as gardening, making love, and cooking. In *The Twelve-Spoked Wheel Flashing,* she captures sense of place within a structure based upon the four seasons. Secure in love, Piercy employs a gentle wit while exploring the vicissitudes of political and domestic life. *Stone, Paper, Knife* contains poems championing nature, women, animals, and the pleasures of gardening, as well as pieces assailing such figures of oppression as the slum landlord, pornographers, and the military. Some critics faulted these poems for excessive, often violent imagery and self-righteous tones. John Kerrigan commented: "There is too much unfocused anger in *Stone, Paper, Knife,* and a great deal of dogma: it's nevertheless enthralling to overhear, or be lectured by, this woman's voice, as it strives to articulate new ways of telling." In her next collection of poetry, *My Mother's Body,* Piercy celebrates the strength of the mother-daughter connection, praising the daily duties and pleasures of womanhood. Sections of *My Mother's Body* and *Available Light* protest the careless proliferation of technology and assert the superiority of living in communion with the earth and seasons. In *Available Light,* Piercy celebrates nature and her Jewish identity. Diane Wakoski remarked: "What Piercy does masterfully and beautifully is present the world of touch, of taste, of texture and even resonance. She is an empress of the vegetable kingdom, sensual, sexual, fecundly Dionysian."

Piercy's early novels, like her first collections of poetry, are explicitly political, often featuring characters victimized by racism, sexism, militarism, and homophobia. Her first novel, *Going Down Fast,* concerns a stable, racially–mixed neighborhood that offers decent, low-income housing but is threatened with demolition by the unified power of city-planners, the nearby university, and the landowners, who want to attract wealthier tenants to their upgraded buildings. In *Dance the Eagle to Sleep,* Piercy imagines an oppressive future society in which a group of youths abandon the city to form a community based on Native American tribal customs. *Small Changes* is a feminist novel in which two women challenge patriarchal dominance in marriage and nuclear family.

Woman on the Edge of Time is Piercy's most highly acclaimed novel. A skillful blend of utopianism and realism, this work is often utilized in women's studies courses. The protagonist, Connie Ramos, is a middle-aged Chicana on welfare whose dire circumstances are relieved by her ability to travel to Mattapoisett, a future society in which racism, sexism, and classism have been obliterated. In the climax of *Woman on the Edge of Time,* Connie takes action against her oppressors in order to ensure the safety of a future that includes Mattapoisett's environmental and spiritual consciousness. Piercy's next novel, *The High Cost of Living,* is set in Detroit and focuses on the types of compromises a lesbian graduate student must make in her search for love, acceptance, financial security, and self-respect. *Vida,* like *Dance the Eagle to Sleep,* is based on Piercy's experiences with Students for a Democratic Society. Davida Asch, the beautiful title character, endures years of loneliness in hiding before she falls in love with another fugitive from the government. Employing a series of flashbacks to the 1960s and early 1970s, Piercy details the radicalization of the "Network" from a loose coalition of anti-war protestors to a highly organized, illegal faction. Jennifer Uglow remarked: "*Vida* may not have the force or coherence of a persuasive argument but it deserves attention, even from those who don't agree, as a powerful novel, written with insight, wit and remorseless energy."

In *Braided Lives,* considered Piercy's most autobiographical novel, the conformist atmosphere of the late 1950s is evoked in intensely poetic language. Essentially a feminist *Künstlerroman, Braided Lives* depicts the protagonist's struggle to become a writer despite the sexist expectations of her parents, professors, and society in general. *Fly Away Home* is perhaps Piercy's most successful attempt to combine political themes with domestic drama. This novel traces the awakening of Daria Walker from the illusions of her marriage. Daria's discovery of her husband's altered character, her decision to aid the tenants' association in its attempt to prove that her husband has been hiring arsonists to burn his own buildings, and her new-found love with a carpenter and power-structure researcher, are turning points that direct Daria back to her working-class roots and her original values. Recalling Piercy's earlier novel, *Woman on the Edge of Time,* Ellen Sweet remarked of *Fly Away Home:* "This may be scaled-down utopia— Piercy's mellowed vision of family and home—but for that

very reason this book should have broad appeal. It may even prove to be more revolutionary than her more obviously radical novels."

Piercy's most recent fiction continues her concern to depict people outside the mainstream of popular fiction. *Gone to Soldiers* concentrates on the ways in which World War II altered women's lives. Along with a variety of male characters, the women in this novel include a pilot, a French Resistance fighter, a Jewish refugee in Detroit, and a war correspondent. *Gone to Soldiers* is considered more accessible than Piercy's previous works and has been commended for its poetic depiction of concentration camps, racial tensions and labor strikes on the home front, and the fear and homesickness experienced by soldiers. *Gone to Soldiers* generally received mixed reviews, with several critics finding Piercy's basic premise and characterization clichéd. *Summer People,* Piercy's most recent attempt to mix politics and personalities, concerns real-estate deals on Cape Cod and the disintegration of a ten-year *ménage à trois.*

(See also *CLC,* Vols. 3, 6, 14, 18, 27; *Contemporary Authors,* Vols. 21-24, rev. ed.; *Contemporary Authors New Revision Series,* Vol. 13, and *Contemporary Authors Autobiography Series,* Vol. 1.)

PRINCIPAL WORKS

POETRY

Breaking Camp   1968
Hard Loving   1969
To Be of Use   1973
Living in the Open   1976
The Twelve-Spoked Wheel Flashing   1978
The Moon Is Always Female   1980
Circles on the Water: Selected Poems of Marge Piercy   1982
Stone, Paper, Knife   1983
My Mother's Body   1985
Available Light   1988

NOVELS

Going Down Fast   1969
Dance the Eagle to Sleep   1971
Small Changes   1973
Woman on the Edge of Time   1976
The High Cost of Living   1978
Vida   1980
Braided Lives   1982
Fly Away Home   1984
Gone to Soldiers   1987
Summer People   1989

Susan Kress

Marge Piercy has been writing novels for almost a decade now. Like Doris Lessing, she is intensely responsive to the political currents of her time, and, like Doris Lessing, her primary concern as a left wing radical is with the "individual conscience in its relation with the collective." Clearly, a writer who is extremely close to contemporary events, and particularly the explosive events of the sixties, is faced with a number of difficult aesthetic choices. How does such a writer achieve distance from her own (acknowledged) strong emotions? Conversely, how does such a writer ensure that rage is controlled but not eradicated? How does such a writer avoid the pitfalls of reporting—or even propaganda? How, in short, does such a writer handle the complexities of fictional form? Close examination of Piercy's five published novels—*Going Down Fast* (1969), *Dance the Eagle to Sleep* (1970), *Small Changes* (1972), *Woman on the Edge of Time* (1976), and *The High Cost of Living* (1978)—reveals that each work represents a different solution to the committed novelist's search for appropriate form. It is the task of this paper to examine the separate formal strategies Piercy adopts, to chart her progress from one novel to another, to reveal the significant patterns that emerge, and, in particular, to understand the logic behind her use of the science fiction genre.

Going Down Fast is a novel which, in reflecting the political and personal convulsions of the sixties, takes its shape from imagery of fragmentation and disintegration. The book's first page sounds the keynote: "The crane bit into a shiny yellow room, turned and with a tidy jerk spat the chewed wall in a dumptruck." A large urban renewal project is under way in Chicago, a project designed to wipe out most of the cheap good housing near the University and to sweep back into the ghetto those who have dared to struggle out to the edges of middle classhood. The local tenants try to organize themselves against the plan to "redevelop," but the massed forces of State, University, planners and developers prove invincible. This area is indeed going down fast, and the implication is that crumbling there, too, in that debris, are some vital but fragile human structures; for in that fringe between University and slum proper—a place of small homes, small shopkeepers, small beginnings toward racial integration—a kind of village neighborhood has bloomed in the heart of the city.

Such breakdown is reflected in the lives of the characters, too. The book offers numerous examples of those who are deliberately or accidentally broken by the system. Rowley, the principal male protagonist, is engaged for the major part of the book in a quest for Black Jack, a singer of considerable power, who has dropped out of sight. Finally, he is discovered in a stinking hotel room, dying and defeated, vomiting his own blood. There are fleeting references to an old woman living in a tenement who refuses to be evicted by city officials, and must be finally removed in a straitjacket. There is a reference to (the real) Louis Sullivan, an architect with a new dream of city who dies in a flophouse worn down by a "Roman dream of empire he couldn't fight." Even Rowley's cat, Yente, in an act of gratuitous cruelty is burned alive. Such examples of irrational violence, of wasted human potential, pervade the book. . . . (pp. 109-10)

None of these characters presents any convincing alternatives, any whole coherent vision for change. Sheldon Lederman, on the other hand, Leon's father and one of the property tycoons involved in the redevelopment scheme, does have a vision of his ideal city. All garish glitter, his "city of light" is a gilded paradise of consumer products. He will sweep away the poor, the ethnic, the misfit in honor of an homogeneous "city of the clean, the fit, the socialized, the acceptable, the good." Against such a nightmare, Black Jack can only propose his own dream of total demolition: "To see this supposed to be great city a hole in the ground." . . .

These characters are cut off from one another, cut off from their roots, cut off from a vision that will counteract the plastic paradise of Sheldon Lederman and carry them into a war against a system they despise. Trapped in history, they are unable to change it. Nor do we get a view of events from outside those characters; no authoritative, omniscient narrator tells this story. Instead, a restricted narrator filters it through the consciousness of a number of characters, sometimes in sequential, sometimes in parallel time. The formal narrative strategy suggests that out of such times, out of such characters, come only partial visions, fragments and approximations.

But Piercy does propose a modest personal, if not political, affirmation at the end of the book. The novel begins in late summer with the breakup of Anna's and Rowley's relationship. Throughout the frozen winter, characters huddle in unheated rooms, smothered in layers of old clothing, seeking each other for warmth. Cold indeed is this city of rubble where the characters try to make connections with each other and with ideas, but rarely succeed. With February, however, come the first thaw and the renewal of the tie between Anna and Rowley. That they are together again is, we must assume, positive, but neither of them is willing to make great claims for a love relationship that failed once and must now struggle along in a society expert in methods of demolition. Nor indeed can they, or the reader, forget the other abortive friendships in the novel (Anna and Leon, Leon and Caroline, Caroline and Rowley, Rowley and Vera) or the disquieting fact that this renewal is achieved in midst of the collapse of their friends' lives—most particularly Leon's who is left to crumble in an institution.

Dance the Eagle to Sleep offers the next stage in revolution, and proposes a very different kind of artistic form. If the characters in *Going Down Fast* have gone down to the bottom, have stripped themselves of illusion, and have analyzed their situation, then those in *Dance the Eagle to Sleep* suggest some ways of acting on that analysis, some ways of rebuilding. The form of *Going Down Fast* is appropriate for showing the perspectives of different characters engaging in reflection and self reflection. In general, the method of the novel is "realistic": the characters' context is carefully specified; there are no outrageous turns of plot or reversals of character. The novel has no chapter headings—only the name of the character whose views are expressed in that chapter—and, significantly, the date. These characters, then, are operating in a particular place (the city of Chicago) at a particular time; indeed, they are trapped in those very particularities, trapped, above all, in the present, the day-to-day, calendar time. In *Dance the Eagle to Sleep,* Piercy seems to have come to the conclusion that if she wants to express a coherent alternative to a capitalist system, she will need to locate the energy for that vision in a different group of characters, and channel that energy through a different formal structure. (pp. 111-12)

The characters are all teenagers, all escaping the horrors of the "Nineteenth Year of Service," a government plan to enforce State service (from army duty to "preschool socialization programs in the ghettoes") on all nineteen year olds not engaged in the study of medicine, engineering, and the sciences. Various representative runaways (including Shawn the rock singer, Billy the brilliant young scientist, Corey the ex-dope-dealing Indian, and Joanna, daughter of an army officer) set up an alternate society based on tribal principles.

It will be obvious by now that Piercy has departed from the "realistic" novel. In a recent issue of the journal, *Frontiers,* devoted to the topic of "Fantasy and Futures," Piercy claims:

> The reason for using a somewhat science fiction format in *Dance the Eagle to Sleep* was to gain some distance from my own very passionate involvement in SDS, and to be able to write about those experiences without aiding and abetting the government.

Elsewhere, she has commented on her notion of the difference between the novel and the tale: the novel deals essentially with character development; the tale is closer to myth, to fairy tale, to ritual, its power deriving not so much from character as from the conflict of large forces. Such a form not only allows artistic detachment, but also, by its very nature, confers universality and timelessness. (pp. 112-13)

The tale is a fascinating formal experiment (and opens the way for *Woman on the Edge of Time*), but does, nevertheless, in important ways, lack conviction. Somehow, the characters do not seem large enough to bear their mythic burden. They are often forced to mouth clichés ("While there are people, we haven't lost. We were right and wrong, but the system is all wrong)," and the imaginative vision itself wears thin toward the end, as Joanna is co-opted back into the system, Corey is killed by a bulldozer that is clearing the ground for a state park and Ginny gives birth to her baby. The symbolism is heavy-handed; dogma weighs down the imaginative structure; and the book comes to a kind of visionary dead end. There is no way for such a band to defeat Empire.

In *Small Changes,* Piercy returns to the novel proper, and writes a book that is more ambitious and more powerful in a number of ways. Finally, Piercy has found a subject that releases her own artistic energy: the lives of women in society. In her previous works, Piercy has certainly been concerned with the roles of women. In *Going down Fast,* Anna drifts from Rowley to Leon and back to Rowley; she is essentially passive—willing to cook, clean, and nurture—a woman without real direction or sense of self; and Piercy grants Rowley most of the important insights. Joanna, in *Dance the Eagle to Sleep,* is a much more self-conscious character. She knows that she does not want to be "somebody else's wife or somebody else's mother. Or somebody else's servant or somebody else's secretary. Or somebody else's sex kitten or somebody else's keeper," but, at the same time she is pulled into the tribe through her intense attraction to Corey. She also perceives that, even in the seemingly "advanced" culture of the tribes, "whatever the rhetoric . . . women mostly ended up running the kitchen," Ginny is a much more revolutionary figure. She progresses from a state of passive self-hatred to one of strength and self-assurance. She is the one who disdains the men of the tribe for being "in love with apocalypse . . . more in love with myths than with any woman;" she is connected to the earth, to human tasks

and aspirations. In *Small Changes,* however, Piercy concentrates predominantly on the lives of women, and charts the changes of the sixties and seventies through the experiences of two women—Miriam and Beth—whose lives converge and diverge.

If Piercy returns to the novel, however, she does so to overturn some of its formal assumptions. This book, unlike those traditional novels about women which *end* with marriage, begins with a wedding. Beth, about to be married, is already rebelling against convention, as, primped and curled and gowned, she is wrapped "like a package" for her husband; and the novel continues its reversal of tradition by documenting her movement away from the convention of marriage. She runs from her husband, sets up house (room) in Boston, joins one then another commune, takes a male lover, a female lover, joins a theatre collective, and finally, pursued by the authorities for the kidnapping of Wanda's children, she and her lover, Wanda Rosario, hide out in Cleveland. Beth's ready exodus from her marriage and her disburdening of the conventional trappings of woman's role in contemporary society seem, perhaps, a shade too easy. For one so young, she seems to have analyzed too fast and acted on that analysis too promptly. Certainly, in terms of the structure of the novel, Piercy means her to offer a contrast with Miriam whose powerful intelligence and vital energy, while promising much, do not save her from following the traditional route of fictional heroines: marriage and children. If Beth is responsible for the novel's theory, for providing a polemical analysis of the plight of women and forcing us to confront the contradictions and inequalities of women's lives, then Miriam is responsible for dramatizing the conflicts of women in transition between old habits and new consciousness.

The book documents a number of changes in women's lives. Beth's odyssey is the grandest, but Dorine, too, moves from the position of house servant in one of the communes to become a woman of strength and self-esteem who becomes immersed in her work as a biologist. She is also primarily responsible for creating an equal relationship with Phil (one of Miriam's former lovers), a very significant accomplishment since he is then able to present the possibility that some men are capable of transcending the old sex roles. Even if people have changed and can change somewhat, however, society does not change much at all. Moreover, most of the small victories are won at enormous personal cost. At the end of *Small Changes,* Miriam is at a turning point. She has realized a number of things about her situation, and perhaps one expects the sequel, Piercy's next book, to portray a Miriam-like character breaking out of her painful dependence on her husband and building an independent future.

The sequel to *Small Changes,* however, is a very different kind of book. It is indeed about the future, but *Woman on the Edge of Time* is a science fiction tale. As we noted, Piercy had tried a "somewhat science fiction format" in *Dance the Eagle to Sleep,* and now she returns to it again for what is her most significant tale. Indeed, it will be worth pausing for a moment, before considering this most important tale, in order to review Piercy's movement toward such a formal strategy. In *Going Down Fast,* Piercy presented a somber vision of disintegration and breakdown—with characters unable to do much more than acknowledge and analyze their plight. Where does a politically committed and responsible novelist go from there? Well, she tries, in *Dance the Eagle to Sleep,* to have her characters, all young people and as yet not fully corrupted by society, form a tribal community based on ideal principles. But it does not, cannot, work because such an ideal society must operate in real time, in a real capitalist context. Nor, artistically, is the particular combination of realism and romance satisfying. Piercy is seemingly still looking for a way to combine political theory with the realistic novel—the novel of ideas and the novel of character. Additionally, the characters in *Dance the Eagle to Sleep* are required to be representative, which tends to undercut the reader's interest in them as particular individuals; and, as participants in a tale, they do not have the kind of imaginative power that will compensate for the overwhelming odds against them—the intractable fact of Empire.

In *Small Changes,* Piercy sharpens and intensifies her focus. She concentrates on the situation of women, and she incorporates her theory in the person of Beth, who is, however dry, still much more compelling and attractive than the characters in *Dance the Eagle to Sleep. Small Changes* offers a powerful critique of society, a critique informed by a passionate yet regulated rage. But Piercy is once again faced with the inflexibility of society itself, and the responsibility for presenting a coherent vision for change. Hence, *Woman on the Edge of Time,* a novel which undertakes an experiment in form that allows Piercy to combine novel and tale—the novel of character and the novel of ideas—with considerable success. This novel represents the culmination of much of the political thinking that has run through the other novels. Here we find caught up, extended, and explored, germs of ideas in the other works, and here, too, we find a coherent, complete, and consistent utopian vision of the future. Finally, Piercy seems to have discovered an integrated form that allows her to solve a number of difficult artistic and political problems. (pp. 113-16)

Connie Camacho Ramos [, the protagonist of *Woman on the Edge of Time,*] is a Chicana, a thirty-seven year old woman from the lower reaches of society, and as such has four counts against her: age, poverty, race, and sex. Unlike the relatively privileged Beth and Miriam from *Small Changes,* this woman has little. Her breakfast of coffee and a scrap of stale bread must be extended with glasses of hot water to stay the pangs of hunger; a highlight of her day is to find in the street a pen that works. When she gets caught in a fight between her niece, Dolly, and Dolly's pimp, she finds herself checked into a psychiatric institution. Disadvantaged before, now she is completely powerless, with no control whatsoever over her own life. What she does have, however, according to the visitor from the future, Luciente, is the gift of receptivity. She is a "catcher," who can "receive" into her present world, Luciente, inhabitant of a future time (2137) and place (Mattapoisett). Through Connie, Luciente is visiting "The Age of Greed and Waste" as part of a time project being carried out in the future.

This is the device that allows Piercy the opportunity to compare the present with the future, as Connie herself visits Mattapoisett and discovers the conditions of life there. But it also allows Piercy to question some assumptions about the nature of that future as well as assumptions implicit in the science fiction genre. When Connie first visits Mattapoisett, she finds a future quite unlike her expectations: " 'No skyscrapers, no spaceports, no traffic jam in the sky' " Mattapoisett is a village world, its roots in the primitive societies of the past; it is an implicit and explicit rejection of present technology (particularly the kind that aims to control and manipulate human beings), and it is further a rejection of those novels about the future that tend to emphasize technological progress at the expense of human values. Connie is also amazed to discover that Luciente is a woman. Judging from her self-assurance, her manner of walking, talking, and taking space, Connie had been convinced she was a man. (Recall Beth from *Small Changes,* " 'We can get outside of roles, finally! We can!' "). The world of the future is a world for men *and* women, a world far removed from present patriarchy, a world where most of the inequalities of the present have been rectified, and most of the repressive institutions and practices have been reformed or abolished. (pp. 116-17)

Piercy has picked an extraordinary protagonist for this tale. Not young. Not beautiful. Not white. Not rich. Not married or about-to-be. Not involved in any relationship with a man. Not brilliant. Not engaged in significant work. She is not even free, but trapped in an institution which monitors her every move. If Piercy does away with all the conventional plot tensions of realistic fiction, how does she maintain interest? At a basic level, she depends on the reader's desire to want to know this world of the future. The ways of Mattapoisett are revealed slowly, a little at a time, over the course of Connie's many visits. But extended exposition is not often guaranteed to compel the novel reader's rapt attention. Hence, plot tension is introduced on two different levels. Brought to the hospital by her niece's pimp, and signed there by her brother Lewis, Connie becomes the victim of a sadistic experiment to alter her brain by means of an implanted electrical device. Nothing could reveal more dramatically the difference between the benign future time and the horrors of the now; "they," in the attempt to get control over Connie's brain, have, as she puts it, "violated her frontiers." She realizes that she is at war, but more important, perhaps, she is made to realize by Luciente, that she is engaged in an even larger war, that the existence of such an ideal future depends on her—and others like her. Only if they fight against the system—and defeat it—will the new order prevail. Indeed, after the dialytrode has been implanted, Connie, while trying to reach Luciente, finds herself in a monstrous, alternate future time confronted by a woman who is a grotesque travesty of "femininity," cosmetically processed for sexual efficiency. And just as we can see Luciente as a possible descendant of Connie, so we can see this alien plastic woman as a possible descendant of Connie's niece, Dolly, who is drugged, smoothed, sleeked and starved—for sexual service. In order to ensure the ascendency of *her* descendants, then, Connie goes to war; tries her best to escape the institution; and when that fails, poisons the doctors' coffee with a substance fortuitously and appropriately stolen from her brother's plant nursery.

Toward the end of *Small Changes,* Phil explains the meaning of "Doing Time":

> "You're a thing in their power. They can beat you, strip you, starve you, take away your letters and your pictures and piss on them and tear them up

in front of you. Tell you what to read, deny you paper and pencil, bust you for staring. They can take your health away real slow or break your back in two minutes. 'Desperate' just has no meaning till you're inside. Then nothing ever is the same again. Not touching a woman, not taking a crap or looking at the sky or buying a paperback or smiling in the mirror. . . . Doing *Time.*"

This passage seems to suggest some of the meanings "Time" has in *Woman on the Edge of Time,* the richness of the concept Piercy has developed in this tale of past, present, and future time. In Connie's experience, exterior time, present time, is State time, system time, and even— male time. She has had her present time taken away from her, and by extension her very life—since life *is* time. She is controlled by institution time, by state time, depending on their time for food, sleep, recreation, medication. And she is at the disposal of their time for experiments and manipulation. Real or present time is her adversary, too, in that she only has so much of it left before the hospital officials, thwarted once in their attempts to implant the dialytrode, implant it again—and for good.

But Connie has her own time in her head, and that is her ally in that it allows her to modulate between past, present, and future. As she perceives it, "these men" wanted to chase "the crouching female animal through the brain with a scalpel," for this individual time, this interior, female time, allows her connections with her past, however painful that is, and her ability to connect with her history differentiates her not only from the characters in *Going Down Fast* (most particularly Rowley who is seeking Black Jack to regain touch with an adopted past), but also with Luciente herself who must, like the other future beings, rely, at least partially, on a "kenner" (a portable computer device) for her memory.

Of course, the primary achievement of Connie's inner time sense involves her ability to cross over into the future. Whether this future is a time outside of Connie's head is questionable. Nobody else in the tale ever corroborates the existence of Luciente; and we know that Mattapoisett is only one of a number of possible futures. Yet Mattapoisett is described in such minute detail. Would a woman like Connie have the means to imagine such a world, and detail so coherently so many practices that, at least initially, shock and dismay her? Piercy's skill is in keeping the matter ambiguous. The reader, too, feels torn between, on the one hand, wanting the future to be "real" and therefore possible, wanting Connie's war in the present to have real consequences in the future, and, on the other hand, wanting Connie, a poor, institutionalized Chicana woman, to be more than a passive "catcher," wanting her to transcend her present with such a vision of the future. If she has no control over her life, she does have control through her vision, for she has vision more powerfully and more clearly than anyone in *Going Down Fast, Dance the Eagle to Sleep,* and *Small Changes.* Unlike the characters in *Going Down Fast,* who cannot imagine a future, who are paralyzed in present, calendar time, Connie is able to touch a future which is truly a vision of light. For she is able, through her female time, to transcend present male time, and to reach a future time that will be a time for women.

Piercy's adoption of the science fiction form has provided

her with the perfect solution to the problem of combining the novel of character and the novel of ideas. In *Woman on the Edge of Time,* Piercy is able to enlist our sympathy for the real, suffering woman, Connie, while she allows Luciente to carry the burden of theory, and assume quite naturally the role of teacher and guide to this new world. She is able to modulate between Connie's anger and Luciente's disengagement. And the notion of a future time utopia enables Piercy to present a compelling and coherent vision of an alternate society of the sort that was impossible in *Dance the Eagle to Sleep.* Additionally, by showing a future that Connie perceives to be radically different from her expectations, Piercy challenges both our normal assumptions about the kind of future we anticipate, as well as the assumptions often found in science fiction novels. Finally, through her brilliant exploration of the concept of time, she is able to draw some illuminating distinctions between the conditions of present patriarchy and future feminism.

There are, of course, some real questions to be raised about this utopian vision. Can any utopia be more than a play world where the complexities of life are simplified out of existence? Is it possible that the reader (so uneducated in the ways of peace and happiness) would find Mattapoisett a nice place to visit but a dull place to live? Is the science fiction form itself, and particularly the time travel motif, an easy way out of present social and political problems? Whether or not she was guided by some such considerations as these, Piercy returns to the "realistic" novel for her latest work. Connie's Mattapoisett is light years away from the world of *The High Cost of Living,* a novel whose bleak vision is reminiscent of *Going Down Fast.* We have come full circle, back to a place where characters make futile attempts to connect with one another, back to the chaotic, painful, absurd present. The main character of *The High Cost of Living* is a lesbian graduate student who forms a friendship with a young girl, Honor, and, reluctantly, with a male homosexual, Bernie. Both Leslie and Bernie fall in love with Honor who seems to deserve neither of them, but instead opts for an affair with Leslie's graduate advisor. Nothing develops from this: a brief connection between Bernie and Leslie is abruptly broken; no real connection between Honor and Leslie ever develops. At the end, Leslie, in spite of his treatment of Honor, still returns to George, her advisor, realizing with some self-disgust that "she needed money and respect and prestige and a toehold in the middle class." Piercy has moved back to the novel of character, but given those characters little to be and less to fight for.

Yet these, perhaps, are the conditions of our times, and it is unfair to Piercy to blame her for reproducing them too faithfully. It is just that *The High Cost of Living* reminds us all too forcefully of how far away we are from Mattapoisett, of what it means to live in the imperfect present. No wonder feminists like Marge Piercy and Joanna Russ opt for science fiction forms; only in some carefully imagined future or on some other planet does it seem possible to create "positive" images of women. As Ellen Morgan says, "the social reality in which the realistic novel is grounded is still sufficiently patriarchal to make a realistic novel about a truly liberated woman very nearly a contradiction in terms." Consequently, those fiction writers who are committed to social and political change must revise old forms or invent new ones. Thus far, Marge Piercy has alternated between the novel and the tale, and found a shape perfectly adapted to her vision in **Woman on the Edge of Time.** (pp. 118-22)

> Susan Kress, "In and Out of Time: The Form of Marge Piercy's Novels," in Future Females: A Critical Anthology, edited by Marleen S. Barr, Bowling Green State University Popular Press, 1981, pp. 109-22.

Jane O'Reilly

Fly Away Home is a romance with a social conscience, a tale of love, betrayal and revenge set against a backdrop of sterile suburbs, confrontational politics, the evils of gentrification and the uses of arson as a slum-clearance tool. As you may gather, Marge Piercy's genre is the didactic page-turner novel, and this is her eighth installment. . . .

[**Fly Away Home**] is packed with the sort of characters we now recognize as Piercy's People. They are definitively American, descended from the crusading woman in Henry James's *Bostonians,* from 19th-century utopians on their farm communes, from our long tradition of vaguely hand-loomed do-gooders who try to translate the notion of social justice into everyday life. In Miss Piercy's relentlessly accurate works, these familiar figures are doggedly earnest even about their jokes, urban even while huddled around a wood-burning stove in a farmhouse. They combine the self-satisfied appeal of the armchair radicals in New Yorker cartoons with a kind of Kafkaesque existential bewilderment. Somewhat randomly educated in the late 20th-century mode (a little Marxism, a little transcendental massage, a little auto mechanics), their inner lives—whether they are planning to rob a bank, get an abortion or cook dinner for 20—run to obsessive list-making.

Probably everyone's inner life runs to list-making, and it is part of Miss Piercy's charm that she never provides elaborate literary flourishes to describe basic human behavior. Her characters may be terrorists or cookbook writers, but they are the salt of the earth. Only Piercy villains, utterly without redemptive qualities, fail to celebrate with their creator the satisfactions of traditional values—family, friendship, the joys of sex, the pleasures of small furry pets, the curative powers of hot homemade soup. For Miss Piercy, a radical social theorist, the feminist celebration of the quotidian is the basis of all humanizing social change.

The heroine of **Fly Away Home** is Daria Porfirio Walker. A cookbook writer, she has mastered the problem of hot homemade soup, but the static comforts of her privileged suburban life are about to literally go up in flames. Forty-three years old, successful ("all but one of her books were still in print"), she and her husband, Ross, "had married so young they had formed each other, she had come to him not fully human, a fish-girl, half jelly and half bones." She has two daughters, and her deepest delight is the 140-year-old house on a hill in Lexington, Mass.

There are problems, though. Ross likes wall-to-wall carpeting. Daria prefers polished wood and Oriental scatter rugs. They don't have much of a sex life anymore. She feels a cringing, desperate desire to please whenever Ross is around. It turns out that Daria has been encapsulated in willful ignorance. She doesn't know how much she makes a year, much less how much Ross makes. She knows he is in business with at least one of her four brothers, but she doesn't know what they do. She doesn't know he is having an affair with a scrawny, rich neurasthenic named Gail Abbott Wisby. . . .

When Ross disappears the weekend of Daria's mother's funeral, she can no longer avoid reality. Then, when an unruly, inner-city crowd of people appear to picket outside her house, she invites them inside "to explain gently and firmly to these people that they had come to the wrong place to complain," being careful to "not take anyone's wraps because she did not want to encourage them to stay long." Such carefully learned politesse becomes irrelevant. "These people" determinedly explain that both Ross and she are slum landlords, arson is epidemic in their buildings and a child has been killed in a fire.

Timorously, Daria begins to ask questions. Ross emerges as a fiend in human form, howling "I want for me, *me!* " and denouncing Daria's books as: "Fat books! That's what they are: fat books!" He actually says: "I'm getting in touch with my feelings," and while this has the echo of authentic male midlife crisis, it does not explain, nor does the author, how Ross has become a grandiose megalomaniac, busy "shaping the future," who also tries to burn up his wife in the house she loves.

Luckily for Daria, the group of protesters has included one of Miss Piercy's heroes, a beau ideal eight years younger, a tender, hulking descendant of New Bedford mill workers and an impoverished librarian. He has also "done power structure research." They make love together powerfully and work together politically and get the goods on Ross, who is convicted of conspiracy to commit arson and manslaughter. Daria, snuggled back into her working-class roots in a double-decker in Allston, is happy with her new rainbow-coalition family. It is an implausible but satisfying story.

> Jane O'Reilly, "Utopians and Firebugs," in The New York Times Book Review, February 5, 1984, p. 7.

John Kerrigan

Already admired in Britain for her novels and polemics, Ms Piercy's reputation can only be enhanced by the publication of **Stone, Paper, Knife.** It is, admittedly, an uneven book: but its recklessness is not uncaring. On the contrary, Ms Piercy's commitment to Life and art (decidedly in that order and with that emphasis) is passionate, unremitting and unashamed; and if her technical command wavers it's because the urgency of her utterance distracts her. There is too much unfocused anger in **Stone, Paper, Knife,** and a great deal of dogma: it's nevertheless enthralling to overhear, or be lectured by, this woman's voice, as it strives to articulate new ways of telling.

Unsurprisingly, perhaps, that telling involves a subversion of the 'straightforward and complete' narratives one 'grew up on'. Thus, in **"A story wet as tears"**, Marge Piercy recalls 'the princess who kissed the frog / so he became a prince' in order to impose on the tale a conclusion unknown to the Opies: 'Though courtship turns frogs into princes, / marriage turns them quietly back again.' In

"Laocoön", she makes the familiar myth of unexpected suffering, where we pity the men attacked, an allegory of men's aggression against women. And, in the first poem of her book, **"Mrs Frankenstein"**, she reformulates a traditional narrative A to Z to communicate the wretched and disjointed story of Heterosexual Love Under the Aegis of Sexism. Having assembled her monster, that is, and married him, and 'rubbed his back' and 'fed' him 'vitamins', the heroine of **"Mrs Frankenstein"** discovers that what she thought was a happy ending was only the start of a catalogue of abuses:

> A is for anguish
> she said, the way I feel
> when you stand on my face. B
> is for beautiful, like this rose.
> No, you don't wipe your ass
> with it usually. C is for
> a very nice part of my body . . .

And so on, through all the permutations of marital misery and resentment, to 'Z', which stands 'not for zoosphere / but, Zanzibar', where the monster apparently fled with a bundle of credit cards 'and his rich / and pliant mistress.'

Ms Piercy is not invariably so tart. **"Being left"**, for instance, deals lyrically with the topos of abandonment, and the result is a feminist variant on 'The Road Not Taken'. For, after chastising her lover for smashing the remains of their affair and gravely wounding her—in the way men do (according to feminist orthodoxy), because they want every story to end with 'blood spurting / to sign finale'—she asks him why he must tie things up and 'raze the ground behind':

> Do you believe if you left
> me alive you would
> be tempted to come back?
> We both know
> back isn't there. The tree
> puts out new leaves or dies.
> What you have abandoned
> is not behind but far ahead
> where we shall never
> now arrive.

A cynic might say of these calculatedly touching lines that the lover knew well enough what the future held for him, and that he chose to abandon it accordingly. Certainly, Ms Piercy makes it clear throughout *Stone, Paper, Knife* that she thinks women and men should move together towards a post-industrial pastoral, where technological development is eschewed for the sake of self-discovery and vegetable-growing. A few poems, like **"Digging in"**, make this austere path forwards almost tempting, but most do not succeed. Readers of Marge Piercy's prose fiction will be surprised by neither the configuration of possibilities which she proposes nor her bias: in what is probably her best novel, *Woman on the Edge of Time,* a heroine, judged crazy by her ruthless and sexist doctors, time-travels or hallucinates into two alternative futures, one technological, oligarchic and sterile, the other ecologically secure and sexually liberated. 'Which,' Ms Piercy seems to ask, 'will be The Road Taken and The Road Not Taken?' The question is Sixties and unfashionable, but hardly insignificant as a gesture towards What Might Be. And whatever one thinks of Marge Piercy's politics, or her verbal finesse, it's a measure of her integrity that a text like **"Being left"**—so immediate, so personal in resonance—should be

continuous in its concerns with her most ambitiously prophetic narrative. (pp. 22-3)

> *John Kerrigan, "The New Narrative," in* London Review of Books, *Vol. 6, No. 3, February 16, 1984, pp. 22-3.*

Ellen Sweet

In place of large visionary utopias, *Fly Away Home* is about a "small" subject all too familiar in recent novels: a conventional woman coming to awareness because of divorce. But Piercy does not disappoint. She manages to turn this hackneyed theme into something new and appealing: a romance with a vision of domestic life that only a feminist could imagine. Although her novel has a strong subplot dealing with social change through political action, at its heart is Piercy's faith in the transforming value of love and intimacy.

Daria Walker, the earthy but cultivated main character, is a Piercy masterpiece. A wife and mother whose marriage raised her out of her working-class background, Daria feels that she is nothing without her husband and her lovely suburban home. But, in fact, she has a talent for cooking that, in her middle age, has gained her a modest fame, book contracts, and her own TV show (shades of Julia Child). All that security is shaken by, first, the death of her mother, followed quickly by her husband's demand for a divorce after 22 years, one daughter's defection to Daddy and his new woman, public accusations that her husband is a crook, and finally the burning of her home.

While trying to untangle the net of deception that her husband has cast around his affair, Daria Walker also is forced to expose the corrupt real estate practices in which he has been involved. Her search for clarity makes [*Fly Away Home*] read a bit like a detective story—the mysterious notes that she steams open, the disguise she assumes to find out where her husband goes and whom he meets, combing through bureaucratic files to uncover his hidden assets, and so on. But the real plot is in Daria's growing awareness of herself and her social context. "Was innocent the opposite of guilty or the opposite of wise?" she wonders. . . .

Piercy presents these transformations in a series of powerful images that reflect her twin skills as poet and novelist: images of ashes and rebirth, death and life, parking lots and gardens, destruction and rehabilitation, fire and earth. As a result, despite the somber subject matter of her novel (the divorce and the business deals are as nasty as they can be), the mood is translucent and affirmative.

The novel's one weakness lies in its characterization of Daria's husband, Ross. Next to her, he seems two-dimensional, a caricature of a man facing a mid-life crisis, a dangerous jerk. What has turned this idealistic young law student with a social conscience into a prejudiced, middle-aged crook? Daria never finds an answer to that question, and since the novel is told entirely through her eyes, neither do we.

Piercy makes up for Ross with Daria's new lover, Tom, a sympathetic, vulnerable, sexy, sharing man who is not a wimp. The life that Daria finally chooses for herself includes Tom, but not exclusively (they share an apartment with a single mother and her young daughter, who also have been burned out of their home). It's a life with creature comforts, but simpler and less conventional than what she had before. This may be scaled-down utopia—Piercy's mellowed vision of family and home—but for that very reason the novel should have broad appeal. It may even prove to be more revolutionary than her more obviously radical novels.

Ellen Sweet, in a review of "Fly Away Home," in Ms., *Vol. XII, No. 9, March, 1984, p. 32.*

John Clute

As *Fly Away Home* opens, Daria Walker is about to celebrate her forty-third birthday. The present her husband Ross gives her is a peignoir. It is too small for her. No reader of commercial romantic fiction could miss the point. She suspects nothing, but the rest of us know that Ross, or more likely his secretary, has muddled up which gift is intended for the wife, and which for the mistress.

This is the first great flaw of *Fly Away Home.* Clearly intended by her creator as an exemplary, Everywoman figure, Daria simply fails to understand the trashy plot Marge Piercy has constructed in order to bare her life to us. . . .

"You pretend you don't catch on to things you don't want to notice", her sister tells her, but by this point her incapacity to understand the world—the story—she inhabits amounts to near-lunacy. For by this point the reader will have noticed not only that Ross is a ruthless male chauvinist, an adulterer, a liberal turned very conservative indeed, a shyster lawyer, and a jogger, but also that he is deeply involved in murder and arson. This is the second great flaw of the novel. While Daria clearly doesn't belong to the world of genre fiction, Ross could easily have stepped out of one of John D. MacDonald's sour exposés of the marriage between business and crime in darkest Florida.

Eventually Ross shows up at the family home to cart away its valuable antiques, while Daria watches bemused. The next day his hired arsonist burns the place down, and she barely escapes with her life. The penny drops at last. The man she has lived with for twenty-two years is a figment. Out of the monster she now recognizes she screws an adequate divorce settlement, and through a protest group trying to save a neighborhood he has been putting to the torch she manages to get him arrested, tried and convicted of arson and other crimes. Such are the consequences, one might be tempted to deduce from Piercy's forthright feminist stance throughout this book, of tangling with a woman who has seen the light.

Though Piercy begs one to caricature her novel in this fashion, it would be unfair to do so. As the protagonist of a novel, Daria is a silly creation, being simply too good, and too dumb, for the world of fiction. But there are moments when her clear, humane decency comes ungarbled through Ms Piercy's elbowing prose, we forget the risible corkscrews of the plot, and feel the presence of a real person deep within the text, crying to get out. For there is reality here: Boston; Daria, and her two difficult, believable daughters; the joys of cooking; the solidarity of neighbours standing together against lawyers and property developers and arson. We are left with a sense of engagement with the decency of human lives, when opened to the eye. That could be the polemical heart of *Fly Away Home.*

John Clute, "Seeing the Light," in The Times Literary Supplement, *No. 4237, June 15, 1984, p. 658.*

Anne Stevenson

Self-explanation is Marge Piercy's line, too, but where Adrienne Rich is dignified and wise, Piercy is impetuous and lusty. *Stone, Paper, Knife* tells us a good deal about the break-up of the poet's marriage, her despair, her loneliness, her cats, her vegetables, her joyous appetite for sex, her fears for love's frailty, her pity for the world's poor, her hatred of American capitalists, her love of justice and her female affinity with the earth. Ultimately she is unquenchable and hopeful. The last line of her book sums it up:

> Hope sleeps in our bones like a bear
> waiting for spring to rise and walk

But is it the bear who will rise and walk or spring? As usual Piercy is not all that fussy about syntax. She is, above all, a great lover, at her best when she is least furious. In **"Being left"**, a gentle poem of understanding she writes:

> What you have abandoned
> is not behind but far ahead
> where we shall never
> now arrive.

This kind of subtle perception, bold though it may be, is greatly preferable to her melodramatic professions of grief:

> Love died like a poisoned
> cat vomiting.
> Sleep has left my bed
> as he has. They curl up
> together downstairs while I
> pore over scenes as if
> reading the palm of a murderer.

The cat in this poem is dead in another, and one wonders if it's the cat or the husband who has most betrayed her. With a new lover, Piercy burns with passion: "What we burn are the books, / the couch, the rug, the bed, the houseplants, / the friends who can't clear out fast enough." Or she swims in luscious pools of flesh: "Wet and sloppy the mutual joy / of stirring our bodies together / warm as breast milk. / . . . A scalpel slits us open like a busted bag of groceries, and out we ooze."

Embarrassing as a lot of this is, you can't help *liking* Marge Piercy, whose poetry seems for the most part to have been poured out and then cut up into lines. Garrulous, comical and bright, she surprises with a number of deliciously delicate poems, in the light of which we forgive her the crude ones.

Anne Stevenson, "Sources of Strength," in The Times Literary Supplement, *No. 4242, July 20, 1984, p. 818.*

Susan Mernit

What should the focus of a feminist novel be? Should it be about ideals and the perils of attaining them, or should it be about things as they are? Should it portray reality, or agitate for change?

Feminists generally agree that in order to change society, we must expose and articulate what is wrong with the society and document the effects of an oppressive system on those under it. Once society can admit the problem, then there are grounds for change. And yet, while the desire to identify a wrong, address it, and expose it is at the heart of much feminist fiction, this impulse is often expressed in intensely personal terms. In accord with the early 1970s axiom, "the personal is the political," many feminist writers address the inequities of contemporary society through focusing on a particular character's life within a relationship, a marriage and a family. The heroine's life and condition is recognized as part of a prevailing social structure, with its own rules and expectations; her acceptance or rejection of them, and the growth that implies, are comments on women in society. Since the individual character is a microcosm of the world which has created her, we are able to see that world through her life.

And yet, for some writers, this is an inadequate way in which to address such social problems as sexism, racism, homophobia and environmental pollution. Can the "personal novel" really reflect these social concerns, or succeed as a catalyst for change? Can it effectively serve the feminist movement? Elinor Langer, writing in the March 4, 1984 issue of *The New York Times Book Review,* would seem to think not. She describes feminist fiction as failing to go beyond the personal to deal with the larger, political issues of American life. Because contemporary novelists focus too much on personal liberation, she asserts, they have failed to create a sufficiently broad context for their feminist beliefs.

While Langer includes Marge Piercy among those writers who have failed to produce appropriately "political" work, Piercy is actually among the few feminist authors writing today whose work is political or even revolutionary in the sense described above. Piercy's controlling idea might be defined as "The political is personal"; all of her novels have been distinctive in showing individuals against a backdrop of social concerns. From her first novel, *Going Down Fast* (1969), through her most recent, *Fly Away Home,* Piercy has consistently sought to show how personal history is shaped by political beliefs and social conditions.

Daria and Ross Walker and their two children, Robin and Tracy, are comfortably ensconced in a large Colonial house in suburban Lexington, Massachusetts. Strange notes and a coldness on her husband's part alert Daria that their comfortable relationship is no longer what it once was. . . . Ross, her handsome husband, has been conducting a mysterious affair and wants a divorce; Robin, her older daughter, will barely speak to her; and worst of all, it seems that Daria's name is down as owner on the deeds to some East Boston rowhouses whose tenants are complaining of being harassed and burnt out. Ross, her husband, has set up some dummy corporations and is caught up in plans to re-shape that part of the city. His liberal concern for the poor has shifted to greed. Now,

having amassed huge real estate holdings, he plans to build an empire and yearns to get Daria out of the way. A ruthless businessman, afraid of his own mortality, Ross wants to make a killing, fast. . . .

On one level, *Fly Away Home* is intensely personal—Daria is another dispossessed, middle-class woman who discovers it is time to wake up and smell the coffee. But the widening distance between Daria and Ross, and her involvement with the members of the East Boston tenants' group, reflect Daria's growing—and reawakening—sense of political responsibility. Why have unscrupulous developers been able to take neighborhoods away from their communities? What is Daria's responsibility, as a building owner, especially after she realizes she has been insulating herself from such problems for years? How can moving away from one's working-class roots become a betrayal of personal and community interests? At what point must someone decide to protest and fight back? Is it better to live in splendid comfort and isolation, or to own less, but share with a community? Ultimately, this rich and entertaining book asks us to consider ourselves as part of a social network beyond the isolated, nuclear family. Are we people like Ross, Daria's husband, who wants to amass as much as he can for himself, or are we like Daria, who wants to create fair, comfortable, conditions for everybody, and who finds other people to help her do it?

Piercy handles these questions by fusing together the personal and the political. Not only do Daria's personal circumstances change, but she and her friends successfully fight some major institutions and gain power for themselves. For Daria, the suburban house, which represents "luxury and adventure" to her, gives way to a communal establishment in Allston where "she was not Mommy and did not always know best." There are few contemporary novelists who so inextricably interweave such large and small concerns. Every personal development of Daria's, from deciding to live in the large house by herself, to researching her husband's holdings for the divorce, to getting involved with Tom, an attractive young carpenter and member of SON [a tenants' rights group], is paralleled by information about Russ' arson-for-hire scheme, the workings of the Boston power establishment and the judicial system. The characters are fairly vivid, but it is the way their lives are made to mirror social issues which makes *Fly Away Home* particularly engrossing. . . .

Marge Piercy is unremitting in showing us how the public world shapes the personal lives of her characters—even to having Daria's husband burn down their house when she refuses to move out—and she infuses ideology with tremendous feeling. Like Meridel LeSueur and other Socialist writers of the 1930s, she attempts to deal directly with what she sees as the pressing issues of American life: class struggle, gentrification, and the emotional impoverishment of the nuclear family. As in her earlier novels, she gives voice to characters who are in some ways considered marginal by virtue of their sexuality, class, or politics—but she never loses sight of how their personal life is linked with their larger environment, and she never ceases to affirm that community struggle is the remedy for many ills.

However, while for the most part *Fly Away Home* does an admirable job of connecting personal experience and social systems, many of Piercy's more marginal characters seem wooden. Their personalities are stiff, their speech unconvincing as they are made to symbolize certain social concerns. Like pieces on a chessboard, they are used to advance the game, but they offer little of the drama and insight that are hallmarks of fiction. Piercy's zeal to tell us how we should live our lives strains her prose; her determination to tell us something specific about our society interferes with the spontaneity of the story. A keen observer, she is capable of dazzling and sensual descriptions; yet, on occasion, her conversations between characters seem trumped-up. As fine as her feeling for language is, here it operates in fits and starts.

Through her portrayals of strong women characters, with committed social values, Piercy demonstrates both that women are essential to every political movement, and that women's lives are political. She sees human beings as interconnected in a social network, having both duties and responsibilities to one another; and it is this conviction, more than anything, that makes her fiction political.

For Marge Piercy, I suspect, the function novels are meant to perform is to challenge and instruct. As a writer with an established audience, she can explore how we do live our lives, and propose how we should, daring to point out wrongs, address them and agitate for change. And yet at the same time, like any good story-teller, she can also afford to delight, spinning an involved family yarn that keeps us absorbed, intently turning the pages. Now that the controversy over what feminist fiction ought to be seems to be heating up, *Fly Away Home* is a reminder that artistic creation is not incompatible with political commitment.

> *Susan Mernit, "Suburban Housewife Makes Good," in* The Women's Review of Books, *Vol. I, No. 11, August, 1984, p. 18.*

Holly Prado

Marge Piercy has published eight novels and nine books of poetry. Obviously, she's no novice. In this new collection of poems, [*My Mother's Body,*] however, there are some lessons she still might learn. As a practitioner of personal poetry, she shou' i remember that such writing must be personally intimate, not symbolically general. It's utterly private detail that urges these kinds of poems to gather meaning and feeling to themselves.

When she writes of her new marriage, Piercy writes with love but falls into the trap of protecting intimacy rather than revealing it. The tone of these poems is the hum of old songs that everybody can sing to a mundane tune: " . . . Each hair of your / head is numbered in my love." With few exceptions, the "wine press of the bed" and the maps that are "all redrawn" and the building of "daily houses brick by brick" don't offer the secret force of love, the powerful jolt that we want when we read fine poetry.

Often, Piercy's other themes have become difficult to write about because of their overexposure in the realm of women's writing: mother-daughter relationships; vehement preference for nature rather than technology; insistence that women have to be angry in order to rebel against traditional roles. . . . In personal poetry, ideas are garnered from the struggle within the poet; they aren't imposed notions but issues that have been wrestled with and fully lived on the page.

This jumpy, uneven book settles into a true voice only when Piercy stops pronouncing on social questions or Marriage—capital *M*—and digs into a tough, thoughtful lyricism that is really hers. Then she's able to move language and image with an exciting mix of wild breath-line and pure rhythmic control. The heightened formality of a poem like **"Tashlich"** collects strong visual elements—starting with the tossing of crumbs and ending with a salty wind that cleanses well-defined envy, greed, betrayal—never letting the writing slip into limp generalizations. In this poem, and in others such as **"What Remains,"** one of the mother poems that really works, or in **"Six Underrated Pleasures,"** Piercy stirs, through her loyalty to her inner view, the reader's trust in her vision. At her best, she offers us the urgent reportage of an unadorned, individual heart. When she pulls this off, we're willing to participate in her poetry because she's been faithful to it herself.

> *Holly Prado, in a review of "My Mother's Body," in* Los Angeles Times Book Review, *May 5, 1985, p. 15.*

Michelene Wandor

Relationships between parents and children go through different phases, and the phases themselves will vary according to the specific parent-child configuration. But in one's middle years, perhaps all of us enter some kind of re-evaluation of these primary relationships, prompted often by the death of a parent. Both [Marge Piercy's *My Mother's Body*] and Hugo Williams' [*Writing Home*] therefore makmoving reading: each explores through the lyric mode the relationship with the parent of the same sex as themselves. For Marge Piercy [in *My Mother's Body*] the fierceness of American-Jewish motherhood, for Hugo Williams the tortured and often unspoken passions between father and son. . . .

Marge Piercy's style is more demanding more expressive through the pull of jagged and often female-biological imagery, than through the ease of a narrative style. Through memory she reaches back into both the material anguish of a daughter who felt her mother wanted her to be different, and also the psychic pain experienced by both mother and daughter, as each has to recognise both their similarity and their difference. As well as the imagistic evocation, she can also come into the clearing of ideas and directness, into a poetic philosophising:

> What is it we turn from, what is it we fear? . . .
> Did I think I would fall into you as into a
>   molten
> furnace and be recast, that I would become
>   you?

But there is also a powerful eroticism in Piercy's work, not just in the poems about sexual relationships, but in the very stuff of the language itself. As I try to think of various ways to describe her style, I keep returning to the word 'fierce' as the most appropriate. It conjures up associations with passionate feeling, with anger, and with a relentless determination not to make things too easy for the reader, as, one feels, the poet herself never allows things to be too easy for her.

> *Michelene Wandor, "Parents and Children,"*

in Books and Bookmen, No. 361, November, 1985, p. 19.

Sandra M. Gilbert

Rough-hewn and "realistic," preferring politics to poetics, Piercy has always presented herself as a raw-boned working-class woman, a woman whose name, as she comically observes in *My Mother's Body,* sounds "like an oilcan, like a bedroom / slipper, like a box of baking soda, / useful, plain." . . . [She] often seems to feel more strongly about what she says than she does about how she says it. Perhaps inevitably, therefore, she lapses at times into clumsiness, into editorializing, even into sloganeering.

"What Remains," the elegiac sequence for the poet's mother which opens this collection, is marred now and then by such lapses. Finding "a bottle-cap flower: the top / from a ginger ale / into which had been glued / crystalline beads from a necklace" among her dead mother's things, Piercy is moved in **"Out of the Rubbish"** to awkward (though socially accurate) meditation:

> A receding vista opens
> of workingclass making do:
> the dress that becomes
> a blouse that becomes
> a doll dress, potholders,
> rags to wash windows.

Similarly, in **"Why Marry at All?,"** one of the poems in the wedding sequence called **"The Chuppah,"** she becomes earnest and flat-footed in her eagerness to communicate key ideas . . . and the opening of her final stanza embarrassingly recalls those Sixties weddings where barefoot girls and boys swore groovy oaths of allegiance to each other on Vermont or California mountaintops:

> This is a public saying to all our friends
> that we want to stay together. We want
> to share our lives.

Again, the obviously heartfelt **"Homage to Lucille, Dr. Lord-Heinstein,"** seems almost parodic in its use of feminist and counterculture jargon. The heroine of this piece is a gynecologist who has "gently, carefully and slowly" opened "our thighs and our vaginas / and show[n] us the os smiling / in the mirror like a full rising moon." . . . I too admire "caring" women, but I care enough about their heroism to wish it could be more imaginatively recorded.

Luckily, despite some of these linguistic lapses, Piercy does—though sometimes, it seems, almost in spite of herself—produce a number of poems in *My Mother's Body* which offer more imaginative and vivid records of female heroism, of the joys of wedded love, and of the pleasures of daily life. As a whole, for instance, the elegiac **"What Remains"** is gravely moving in its expression of grief for the lost mother's hard and wasted life—for "the ugly things / that were" in this women's world "sufficient for every / day and the pretty things for which / no day of hers was ever good enough." And the sequence is poignantly impassioned, too, in its hope for transfiguration of the dead woman's ashes: " . . . just as I knew when you / really died, you know I have brought / you home. Now you want to be roses."

Perhaps less dramatically but just as vividly, the wedding ceremony of **"The Chuppah"** transcends the poet's intermittent proclivity for jargon when, in "Words plain as pancakes. . . . / Simple as potatoes, homely as cottage cheese," she celebrates the ordinary pains and pleasures out of which the extraordinary house of marriage is built. That this new volume ends with a careful but exuberant exploration of **"Six Underrated Pleasures"** ("Folding Sheets," "Picking Pole Beans," "Taking a Hot Bath," "Sleeping with Cats," "Planting Bulbs," and "Canning") suggests that Piercy's sometimes aesthetically problematic political commitment may ultimately arise from an aesthetically energizing talent for attention to the work and play of dailiness, a talent for understanding what is "useful, plain"—and frequently delightful. (pp. 159-61)

Sandra M. Gilbert, in a review of "My Mother's Body," in Poetry, *Vol. CXLVII, No. 3, December, 1985, pp. 159-61.*

Judith Spector

Communication is at the core of . . . Marge Piercy's *Woman on the Edge of Time.* Connie Ramos, a poor Chicana in the ghetto, discovers that she can communicate telepathically with a future utopian, Luciente, who resembles what Connie might have become had hers been a caring, egalitarian society. Piercy provides four perspectives on sexuality as it might exist in differing social contexts: "good" sex under negative social circumstances, a rare exception; "bad" sex (characterized by exploitation, dehumanization, and violence) in the same negative social circumstances (Earth today); "good" sex in a wonderful, egalitarian future society (Earth as it might be); and "horrible" sex in a wretched future society (also Earth as it might be). As in [Joanna] Russ's work, the message is instructive, even didactic at times; polemics is an important part of feminist art. Piercy's basic premise concerning sexuality is political: Women in our culture sell themselves, with or without a choice in the matter, to men who abuse them. As Connie's niece, Dolly, a prostitute, tells her, "Listen, every woman sells it. Jackie O. sells it."

This statement is reinforced by the sexual histories of the characters. Dolly is pregnant by Geraldo, her pimp, and subject to his beatings and coercion; he forces her to have an abortion and to pay for it herself. Dolly and Geraldo commit Connie to Bellevue for her "violence"; in trying to defend the pregnant Dolly against Geraldo, she has broken his nose. Connie, whose lot is little better than her mother's, has tried to escape from her "inheritance," but unsuccessfully: "She had shrieked how much better she was going to live her life, until her father came in and gave her the force of his fists."

But for all her justifiable rage, Connie never attains the good life. Her sexual and sexually related cultural experiences are negative: marriage to a man who beats her, one child who is taken from her after she hits the child in anger, an abortion followed by a beating, a hysterectomy to stop the bleeding, and a one-year term of exploitation as the secretary-mistress to a professor who uses a different Chicana each year. The list goes on, and Connie goes into and out of welfare programs and institutions while remaining a victim of a capitalistic society that uses women as commodities and that ultimately attempts to use her as a subject in psychosurgical brain experimentation. She knows all too well the violence that institutions inflict on the poor. The one good relationship she has had with a man, Claude, a pick-pocket, had come to an end when Claude had died of "experimental" hepatitis in prison.

Connie's pathetically trite conversations with other women in the mental institution in which she is to undergo surgery convey Piercy's bleak analysis of the nature of sexuality in this brutal culture. One woman tells her, "I think we're taught we want sex when we feel unhappy or lacking something. But often what we want is something higher." Connie replies, "For me, sex has more power than that. . . . But I think we often settle for sex when we want love. And we often want love when we need something else, like a good job or a chance to go back to school." Despite her sense of her unfulfilled human potential, Connie has experienced love in her sexual relationship with Claude.

In her contact with the utopian future society of Mattapoisett, she experiences another loving sexual relationship with Bee, a man who reminds her of Claude. Sex in this utopia is without violence. Part of the reason is that by 2137 the citizens of Mattapoisett have eradicated sexual roles. Children are produced in the "brooder" and adopted—and nursed—by three "mothers" of any sex. Connie learns that this society has done away with live childbearing to make the sexes equal and to create an equitable sharing of power, responsibilities, and material possessions. After initial resistance, Connie comes to believe that her own child, who had been taken from her, would be better off in this strange future.

Probably too good to be true, and yet easy enough to believe in for those who want to believe in it, the nonviolent sexuality, love, and sharing in Mattapoisett still represents only one alternative future. Connie accidentally also contacts an antithetical future that is violent, corrupt, patriarchal, and antifeminist. Here she meets Gildina.

> Her body seemed a cartoon of femininity, with a tiny waist, enormous sharp breasts that stuck out like the brassieres Connie herself had worn in the fifties—but the woman was not wearing a brassiere. Her stomach was flat but her hips and buttocks were oversized and audaciously curved. She looked as if she could hardly walk for the extravagence of her breasts and buttocks.

Gildina's behavior and figure are the result of programming and surgery. Connie learns that when Gildina is no longer attractive, she will be dismembered so that the "richies" can use any of her organs that are still functional. For the moment, though, she has the good luck to have a job in "contract sex." Gildina explains, "It means you agree to put out for so long for so much. You know? Like I have a two-year contract. Some girls got only a onenighter or monthly, that's standard."

Gildina's society is based on a rigid class structure that is an exaggerated version of our own, and Gildina occupies the middle stratum. Not very bright, she has access to automatically dispensed "artificial" food, all sorts of drugs—"Risers, soothers, sleepers, wakers, euphors, passion pills, the whole works"—and to "sense-all" pictures. A typical sense-all entertainment is " 'Good Enough to Eat': Toplevel bulger ignores warnings from family and romps in Roughlands. She is captured by mutes. Mass rapes, tor-

ture (inch-by-inch close-up with full Sense-all). Ultimate cannibal scene features close-ups."

That the perspectives on sexuality in such descriptions sound familiar is not at all reassuring to the feminist. But they are an extrapolation of the way things are. In *Woman on the Edge of Time,* Gildina's culture is at war with Mattapoisett. This too is a sex war, between a culture built on sexual enslavement and one that frees people for both love and sex. It is not surprising that in Gildina's culture the sexes are made to seem exaggeratedly opposite, while in Mattapoisett there are only those distinctions that are the result of individual personality differences. Cultures in which the sexes are not at war strive for androgyny, not sexual polarity. (pp. 202-05)

> *Judith Spector, "The Functions of Sexuality in the Science Fiction of Russ, Piercy, and Le Guin," in* Erotic Universe: Sexuality and Fantastic Literature, *edited by Donald Palumbo, Greenwood Press, 1986, pp. 197-207.*

Jonathan Yardley

Marge Piercy, a poet and novelist long associated with the feminist cause, seems to have it in mind to make what publishers like to call a "breakthrough" with this, her ninth published work of fiction. *Gone to Soldiers* is a massive book about World War II that is compared by its publishers to earlier novels by Norman Mailer, James Jones and Herman Wouk, with one ostensibly notable difference: "Never before has a leading woman writer written with such authority about the cataclysmic events and passions of war"—a claim that certainly is open to challenge (nothing in *Gone to Soldiers* rivals the most powerful war scenes in *Gone With the Wind,* for example) but that leaves no doubt we are to approach *Gone to Soldiers* not merely as a "magnificent epic" but also as a woman's view of territory previously occupied largely by men.

If one reads *Gone to Soldiers* solely in that sense, then the novel is not without merit or interest. Though Piercy writes about women's roles in the 1940s from the considerably more advanced point of view of the 1980s, she keeps her rhetoric in check and offers sympathetic but undoctrinaire portraits of several women attempting to transcend the limits traditionally imposed on them. One of them, a dedicated aviator, joins Jacqueline Cochran's Women's Airforce Service Pilots; another fights valiantly for the French resistance; another, a writer of popular romances, signs on as a war correspondent and, in the conflict's final days, reports from the front; another works on the assembly line in Detroit while awaiting her fiancée's return from the Pacific Theater; still another joins the OSS and is assigned to duty in wartime London.

Although from time to time Piercy indulges her own politics and allows these women sentiments echoing Betty Friedan or Gloria Steinem, mostly she is content to let them live their own lives. It is in these passages, in which women confront ordinary reality, that *Gone to Soldiers* is most effective. . . .

But *Gone to Soldiers* is not merely a book about women in wartime; it is also a novel, and as such it is considerably less successful. In writing it—or, perhaps more accurately, assembling it—Piercy seems to have taken on the services of Central Casting. At times *Gone to Soldiers* is an unwitting parody of Second World War fiction, so crammed is it with every stale convention of the genre. As Piercy notes in her concluding acknowledgements, she did a great deal of reading about the war and talked with many people who remember it; but she did not manage to imagine her way out of the clichés that now smother it.

The cast of characters is a variation upon one of those wartime movies in which every foxhole had a proper Bostonian, a hayseed Southerner, a jolly Irishman, a tough Eastern European, a defiant Jew and a noble black; even though most of Piercy's characters happen to be Jewish, they fit the molds created by Mailer, Jones et al., molds that now produce nothing except stereotypes. The result is that *Gone to Soldiers* is merely yet another excursion into all-too-familiar territory, one made no more enjoyable or enlightening by Piercy's leaden prose and lifeless dialogue.

Thus virtually nothing in it is surprising or revealing. When Jeff, brother of Bernice, parachutes into occupied France and falls in love with the brave Resistance fighter Jacqueline, it is a cinch that one of them will die; when Murray, Rosie's fiancée, is taunted by an anti-Semitic sergeant and told that "you're going to die" on Okinawa, it is no less a cinch that one of them will shoot the other; when Lucille and her ex-husband Oscar tease and tantalize each other for nearly 700 pages, it is clear that in the end, one way or another, they will get back together. Even the homosexuality and lesbianism, taboo when *The Naked and the Dead* and *From Here to Eternity* were written, are merely stereotypes, because in 1987 it is a given that any novel of 700 pages that is described as a "magnificent epic" is going to offer homo- as well as heterosexuality.

The problem with *Gone to Soldiers* is not a failure of intentions but a failure of imagination. . . . Piercy has nothing new or arresting to say about a subject that has already been written into the ground, and has been unable to imagine original characters and settings within which to tell her story.

Certainly a case can be made that those big war novels of the late '40s and early '50s failed to give women their due; if we wish to indulge ourselves in the luxury of hindsight, we can criticize them for that. But they possess an energy and immediacy that *Gone to Soldiers,* for all its earnest striving, can only imitate. And as for women and World War II, their story has already been brilliantly told by Diana O'Hehir in *I Wish This War Were Over,* a novel that possesses all the originality *Gone to Soldiers* sadly lacks.

> *Jonathan Yardley, "Marge Piercy's Big War Novel," in* Book World—The Washington Post, *May 3, 1987, p. 3.*

Dorothy Allison

Prejudice consigns women's novels of the war to romance while battlefield accounts are literature. But what Marge Piercy has achieved with her stunning 703-page opus, *Gone to Soldiers,* is unquestionably literature—a novel that moves as easily from battlefield to home front as it does from female to male perspective. . . .

Piercy is as much a poet as a novelist, with a poet's gift for language and capturing the moment in essential details. Though she identifies herself as a political poet, Piercy's work—both poetry and fiction—has been enriched by her emphasis on daily life, love, and human relationships. Her first concern has always been to bring the neglected details of women's experience to the widest possible audience, and her increasingly popular novels turn up as frequently in the hands of housewives and factory workers as they do on the syllabi of women's studies courses.

For 20 years, Piercy has been producing a series of distinctively feminist novels (nine so far); she has also published 10 books of poetry, though as a poet she remains much less well known. Like Margaret Atwood, she has broken through the stubborn categorization of poet and novelist, ignoring the popular bias that assumes "serious" writers choose one specialty and stick to it. The durability of her poetry derives from the strength of her everyday language and descriptions of love and passion rooted in contemporary lives. Her ability to create some of the most believable men and women in modern fiction comes from the same sources. Her characters are marginal, politically committed, and determined to have both love and independence. Many are, like Piercy herself, the children of working-class families: love-hungry Beth in *Small Changes,* wounded Connie in *Woman on the Edge of Time,* underground revolutionary Davida in *Vida,* and Daria Walker, the confused, rejected wife in Piercy's last novel, *Fly Away Home.* Sex roles, love, and class fascinate Piercy, and she is always finding new perspectives from which to examine them.

During the seven years it took her to complete *Gone to Soldiers,* she also wrote the novels *Vida, Braided Lives,* and *Fly Away Home* and the poetry books *The Moon Is Always Female, Circles on the Water, Stone, Paper, Knife,* and *My Mother's Body,* as well as a collection of essays, *Parti-Colored Blocks for a Quilt.* From work to work, the scope of her historical imagination has broadened; she has proved that she, too, possesses the gift she ascribes to her grandmother Hannah: "for making the past walk through the present." *Gone to Soldiers* is solidly grounded in verifiable details of time and place; the reader continually recognizes echoes of survivors' diaries, newspaper accounts, and popular histories. Even for those of us born after the war's end, *Gone to Soldiers* provokes a sense of déjà vu—these are the stories we think we already know, but not the way Piercy tells them.

While Piercy's emphasis is always on women, she doesn't give us that cliché, the women's novel of the home front. *Gone to Soldiers* draws human tragedy so sharply that it reveals not only what women's lives were like in contrast to men's, but also what is missing from most big novels of war—the full impact of loss and turmoil on both men and women. Told from the viewpoint of one character at a time, the novel is structured so that each set of chapters could be read as a separate book. Jacqueline's section, told in 14 chapters, is presented as a series of diary entries until the diary is lost late in 1944; it provides emotional insight into this otherwise reticent partisan. By contrast, Duvey's section—three chapters ending with his death—is a bitter short story that makes him memorable in a way he certainly is not in the chapters told from his sister Ruthie's point of view. Much of the power of *Gone to Soldiers* flows from its overlapping perspectives: Jacqueline writing in her diary about her love for Jeff, Louise meeting Bernice in a transport plane, while half a dozen characters run into the rich and casually bisexual Zach. Surprisingly, none of these many characters ever becomes confused with another. Piercy's soldiers, partisans, Jewish prisoners, women pilots, and factory workers seem to have stepped out of old newsreel images, except that we come to know them far more intimately. (p. 45)

Piercy's women are both recognizable and surprising. Because they are unlike the women portrayed in most World War II fiction, they seem at first too outspoken, too sexually active, too sharp-eyed and thoughtful. But Piercy gradually establishes their reality. Abra, the New England heiress, fielding her sixth proposal of marriage, thinks back on the other men who have wanted to marry her:

> She had disposed of her virginity during her nineteenth summer out on Popham Point where her family had always summered, with a sweet local boy who had settled down by now to lobstering. He had wanted to marry her, and she had understood that to put a nice face upon her apparent acquiescence, she must pretend to be considering marriage . . .

Piercy demonstrates a sure talent for complicated characters who grow and change with time. Her account of the vanity and petty insecurity that mark the relationships between Louise and Abra and the man who has one woman but wants the other reflects the kind of insight gained from painful CR sessions—an understanding of all human beings, male and female, as multifaceted individuals, neither villains nor saints. The husband and lover, Oscar, is less successfully drawn; he is simply too self-centered to hold the reader's attention or to drive the emotions of two such extraordinary women. Piercy is at her best when she explores the internal life of the women: the way Abra slowly pulls herself out of an emotional trap and the equally slow process through which Louise realizes her own desire.

The men of *Gone to Soldiers* are, like the women, just slightly different from what you expect to find in historical novels. There is Oscar, the self-centered professor type, but there is also Jeff Coates, painter and hobo, who wanders from landscape to landscape searching for the home that will inspire his art. For Jeff as for Daniel, a Japanese translator in the army, the war provides a sense of purpose and direction. For others, like the Jewish leftist intellectual Murray, the war imposes a direction they would never have chosen—the brutal confusion that killing to survive can impose. Piercy's male characters are not conventional soldiers; they are neither murderers nor patriots but complex men, hardened by experience yet still trying to understand and choose the shape of their lives. Though Piercy's men have always been sympathetically drawn, these are among her most engaging. None becomes caricature; all, even the unsympathetic ones, are trying to rise above the degradation that war and violence would impose on them.

The consummate soldier of the novel is Jacqueline Lévy-Monot, introduced at the age of 17, living with her parents and twin sisters, Naomi and Rivka—French Jews in Paris in 1939. . . . With only one passport available, Naomi is sent to refuge with American relatives, while the others remain in Nazi-occupied France. When her mother and Rivka disappear into Germany, Jacqueline is suddenly the Jew she never thought herself, and a criminal, alone on the streets of Paris, her only hope to join the underground—to become a soldier of the spirit.

> I practice a discipline as I go around, saying to myself, I know I am not dirty, I am not vile, I am as French as anybody else and as thoroughly imbued with French culture as any of my teachers, so it's not me that this vileness is aimed at and I will simply not accept it.

Much later, struggling to survive at Auschwitz, Rivka uses a similar technique, pared down to essentials: "I will not hate myself because I stink. I will not hate myself because I have no hair. I will not hate myself when they force me to run naked across the yard." (pp. 45, 52)

Naomi has her own heroism. In Detroit, she dreams nightmares through her twin's eyes, nightmares she can tell no one about, for no one would believe that sometimes when she slept, "she slipped into Rivka's body in the noisy filthy cave under the mountain and worked while hunger tore at her and her fingers and toes bled. . . . Naomi was still joined to her twin who lived like a grub inside the cold dark earth, always gutted with hunger, shaking with cold, hollow with exhaustion, till sometimes the death always just under her feet seemed like a soft warm bed." Naomi's telepathic experiences might easily blunt the impact of the novel's realism, but they do not. Her dreams are rendered in lyrical fragments—spare and direct, like Piercy's poetry. There are only enough details to hold the frame in place: the ache of bare feet in icy mud, the claustrophobia of stone walls, the mingling of desire for rest with terror of death. As she did in *Woman on the Edge of Time,* Piercy makes the improbable seem real by her close attention to how such events would feel if they were not strange but matter-of-fact.

At the end of the war, when women pilots are rudely dismissed with none of the benefits of male veterans, the lesbian Bernice Coates decides that since only men are going to pilot planes from now on, she will pass as a man in order to do the one thing that makes her happy. The decision is as reasonable as the calculations Louise made before the war began: "I find people scared that everything will fall apart if women have any independence, any choice. . . . It's the same fear that gripped the nobles when the peasants revolted." Louise knows that with the end of the war will come an attempt to put everyone back in place— particularly the women who had found financial independence on assembly lines, the poor and minority families who had moved to the urban North for factory jobs, and the young men who had found in Europe not only war but a whole new way of looking at the United States. The attempt won't work. None of Piercy's characters tells us this; she uses no political mouthpieces as she sometimes did in her earlier novels. But all her stubborn, hopeful people have changed and will never go back to what they were. The effects of the war are permanent; little and big, they will continue. (p. 52)

> *Dorothy Allison, "Marge Piercy Makes War,"
> in* The Village Voice, *Vol. XXXII, No. 20,
> May 19, 1987, pp. 45, 52.*

Andrea Freud Loewenstein

Like other absorbing pleasures, reading has meant different things to me at different times. Sometimes as I read a novel these days I remember how fiercely my 19-year-old self might have disapproved, or how completely engrossed my 11-year-old self would have been. Marge Piercy's enormous new novel about World War II [*Gone to Soldiers*] pleased and irritated several of these reader selves.

During my first major period of novel-reading, the story was all: I read Dostoyevsky, Jane Austen and Herman Wouk with a certain passionate lack of discrimination. When I was 13 or 14, I was hooked on novels about World War II. These were all more or less alike: long books with a number of simultaneously running stories about various men, each from a different background. (p. 24)

I wonder whether Marge Piercy read these same novels as a child . . . , because *Gone to Soldiers,* while written essentially in the same format as these old books, is exactly what I'd like to have on hand to give to a daughter who was looking for answers and connections about the war. Although Piercy's emphasis is still on the United States, and some sections of her book follow U.S. soldiers on both fronts, others trace the lives of civilians and noncombatant war workers: cryptanalysts and war correspondents in France and Britain, and Resistance workers in France and then Auschwitz. Also, unlike those in the books I grew up on, the majority of Piercy's characters are women, and the majority (and the most interesting) are Jews.

The book's most riveting sections involve a character who is both: Jacqueline, a young Frenchwoman who declares in 1940, "I am as French as anybody else and as thoroughly imbued with French culture . . . so it is not me that this vileness is aimed at." Learning the hard way, Jacqueline goes on to become a hero in the Resistance, bombing trains and killing Nazis as well as rescuing hundreds of Jewish children by leading them over the Pyrenees. She survives torture, the death of her lover and even Auschwitz to emigrate to Israel. If her bravery and independence are so great as to be barely believable at times, I believed anyway, so great was my need for such a character. Creating fiction about concentration camps is tricky, and many have suggested that it shouldn't be done. In following Jacqueline to Auschwitz, Piercy focuses not only on the horror but also on the courage and compassion women in the camps showed toward one another, and those sections are precious. (pp. 24-5)

If you didn't already know about the camps, you wouldn't have learned of their existence by reading *The Naked and the Dead,* or most of the other American and British war books. As a child this omission used to puzzle me; now it strikes me as a way of acquiescing in the silence. Characters in London or Detroit coping with their own war are unlikely to spend time thinking about the death camps in Germany, but I want that omission to be noted, as it is in the empty spaces of Claude Lanzmann's documentary *Shoah.* And Piercy does this: she records the absences as well as documenting the stench and the sounds of genocide. Oscar, a Jewish intelligence officer beloved of two of the other characters, has a sister who disappears from France; Piercy shows us the news reports and reminds us, as well, of what is not reported. Jacqueline has two sisters, who are twins. One, Naomi, is sent to Detroit to stay with American relatives while the other, Rivka, dies in Auschwitz with their mother. While we never hear from Rivka in person, her agony pervades Naomi's sleeping and wak-

ing dreams, and is always in the background of her American life of high school and boyfriends.

While reading *Gone to Soldiers* twenty-five years ago would have fulfilled my need for information, the connections Piercy makes would have deprived me of my 13-year-old patriotic assurances. The camps are not bombed, not attacked, because to "stop the killing in the camps . . . was simply not an Allied priority." And while the Jews are being killed in Europe, Americans on the streets of Detroit persecute both Jews and blacks, making one of the characters, Ruthie, muse,

> You'd think that during a war, people could be satisfied hating the enemy, but no, the enemy is too far away. You want someone to hate right on the next block. . . . Sometimes she wondered if what made Nazis out of Germans wasn't something she felt and saw around her here.
>
> (pp. 25-6)

[In] *Gone to Soldiers,* as in all of Piercy's books, class is an issue for everyone, and if the fighters leave it behind for a while, those who survive must come home to it. And, while the female characters in this book must encounter men in that fierce and unevenly weighted battle of the sexes that is another Piercy constant, this book features a cast of especially strong and independent women, for whom work and autonomy are more important than love.

At 13 I didn't care whether the women characters I encountered were independent or threw themselves under trains for love, as long as their stories were interesting. Being boring is a real risk for an author with a point to make, and it's a fault Piercy's books have not always managed to avoid. But *Gone to Soldiers,* for the most part, is exactly the kind of read I valued most in adolescence: a book that forces itself on you, making you carry it around, sneaking a read on the bus or risking it in the bath. And if you do cheat and skip ahead to find out whether your favorite character survives the war and if so, whom she marries, then you can always go back and read the other sections later.

My younger self objects angrily to any criticism of *Gone to Soldiers,* her favorite book of the moment. But a somewhat older reader, a college freshman who has already declared herself an English major and would not dream of mentioning *Marjorie Morningstar* and *Crime and Punishment* in the same breath, insists that whatever Piercy's virtues in terms of readability and politics, there is a dimension she just does not reach. In-depth portraits of all ten of the main characters whose perspectives we enter and reenter in the course of *Gone to Soldiers* may be too much to ask, but one can suggest complexity of personality without filling it all in. There is a flat completeness about even the most interesting figures here. Each can be summed up by a neat political or socioeconomic tag that is his or her reason for being in the book, and each is remarkably virtuous. . . . Piercy appears to have decided not to waste energy on those who do not provide us with some kind of model for living. With the exception of an otherwise pleasant young man who tries to seduce his 13-year-old niece, the characters whose lives we share harbor no seed of what made the Nazis possible.

Admittedly, my college-freshman self is a romantic. She would have despised the ordered and conscious process that appears to have gone into *Gone to Soldiers,* as well as Piercy's other books. The idea of a writer selecting a good topical issue she believes in, sitting down to make her outline, using a mixing bowl approach to ensure the proper blend of class, sex and religion, going out to do a good year's research in order to get it right, and then shaking it all up to make a novel is repugnant to this critic, who would like to think that inspiration comes into it somewhere, that characters take on a life of their own and do unexpected things, sometimes surprising even the author herself. Piercy rules her characters with an iron hand. She marches them down their ordained paths in language that makes no music and sometimes hurts the ears. "Nothing but fluff," this reading self proclaims, throwing *Gone to Soldiers* onto the large pile of Piercy paperbacks going to the used-book seller. "Good politics alone don't make good fiction."

My final critic, the reader I am today, does not dismiss that pile of paperbacks so easily. Having written one "political" novel that did not sell, I have a new respect for a writer who, year by year, and in the face of increasing caution on the part of mainstream publishers, not only produces books with uncompromising leftist politics but also manages to reach a wide audience. Although I would not take this or any of Piercy's novels with me to a desert island, I'm willing to accept her on her own, unique grounds. (p. 26)

Gone to Soldiers is one of Piercy's best books, but because it is so long and wide-ranging, it also contains samples of some of her worst writing. In the sections about Jacqueline, the Resistance worker and survivor, Piercy's prose takes off as it did in *Woman on the Edge of Time,* a passionate outcry against the oppression of mental patients. Both Jacqueline and Consuelo, the doomed hero of *Woman on the Edge,* are involved in life and death struggles between good and evil forces, and Piercy's storytelling is well suited to such material. Breathless, we race ahead, urging on the forces of good. We don't notice the lack of developed characters; there simply isn't time. In the other successful sections of this book, where Piercy writes of the "ordinary" (actually often courageous and extraordinary) lives of working-class women, she is more like the storyteller in *Small Changes* and *Braided Lives,* a woman telling important secrets to other women around a kitchen table. The voice here is looser and more charming; Piercy relaxes her hold a little and gossips instead of lecturing.

It is only when the lesson overrides the story that the writing becomes boring, and sometimes even embarrassing in its well-intentioned failures. An example is the treatment of Bernice, the lesbian character in *Gone to Soldiers.* Heterosexual sex is a topic Piercy enjoys writing about, just as she likes to write about good food and gardening, and there is plenty of good hetero-sex in this book, all quite hot and convincing. (There is also quite a lot of good food, considering that it's wartime, and somewhat less gardening than usual.) It must have been clear to Piercy that equal representation demanded at least one lesbian in this book, but her sigh as she sets out to invent one is almost audible. Before Bernice manages to come out, far into the book, she has several chapters of sex with a gay man, a sort of compromise solution for Piercy. (The main character in one of her least successful books, *The High Cost of Living,* is also a lesbian whose main relationship is with a gay

man.) When the lesbian scene finally occurs, it takes up one paragraph, concluding with a euphemistic contrast to the sexually explicit straight scenes: "She let Bernice's hand come home." After The Scene, Bernice lives happily ever after (apart from societal persecution, which causes her to cross-dress) in Alaska, "Somehow with Flo. Her Wife."

Piercy has clearly made a decision not to write from the perspective of a black character, probably feeling that to do so without true insight might be even more of a violation. While I don't feel that nonlesbians should not create lesbian characters, Piercy is clearly most effective when writing out of personal, as well as political, conviction. In most of *Gone to Soldiers,* she does just that, and I hope that the book will be a success. The complaints of my second critic aside, it would be good to see it on drugstore counters and in airports, next to *Valley of the Dolls, Part Five* and *Rambo Strikes Again.* (pp. 26-7)

> Andrea Freud Loewenstein, "Iron-Fisted Fiction," in The Nation, *New York, Vol. 245, No. 1, July 4-11, 1987, pp. 24-7.*

Mary Biggs

In an interview I read long ago, Marge Piercy recalled the awful vibrant presence of the Vietnam War at home. She said that she and other activists awoke with the war each morning, retired with the war each night, and lived with it all day; it was never out of their minds. Her earliest books of poems—*Breaking Camp, Hard Loving,* and *To Be of Use*—are tense, urgent, unsparing explorations of the soul of sixties' activism; her novel *Vida,* published four years after the fall of Saigon and focused on a radical activist gone underground, is hot, haunting—a brilliant portrait painted from memory, enriched by perspective.

At its best, Piercy's World War II novel, *Gone to Soldiers,* combines the strengths of those earlier works. Though written as if in the present, it has the wisdom and resonance of hindsight; though it takes place in 1939-46, when Piercy was only 3-10 years old, it has psychological immediacy: we can *feel* the war hovering as it wrenches the characters' lives into unaccustomed shapes. They sleep, eat, work, love and play engulfed by the cloud of it; it is never out of their minds. This is an often nerve-wracking book, and a book so ambitious that it seems petty to find fault with it—as if, in these days of minimalist fiction and inflation of the trivial, Piercy's ambition should be honored regardless of its fruit.

The fruit is rich. The essential problem is its scope and the structure invented to encompass it. Piercy wants everyone: Americans at home, Americans in combat, pre-war French Jews, the French resistance, concentration-camp prisoners, women fliers—and of these, the old and young; male and female; hetero-, homo- and bisexual; sexually faithful and faithless; the working class and the professional intellectuals and the affluent; the gentile and Jewish. Through her attempts to provide a true cross-section, her book becomes almost clinical in outline—like a survey text or one of those "liberal" holiday cards that carefully pictures one child of every color (which is perhaps a bad analogy, as race is the only relevant source of variety left almost, though not quite, unconsidered). . . .

By far the most interesting character is Jacqueline, a French Jew, member of the Resistance and eventually a concentration-camp survivor. She is smart, obstinate, inhumanly demanding, super-humanly tough—a woman who, having seen the corpses of her grotesquely tortured confederates, can still despise her lover for having chosen suicide over extended torture: "I felt that he should choose life at any cost of pain . . . I felt he had deserted me, and I did not forgive . . . I cursed him for choosing death." . . .

Less heroic but almost equally engrossing is Jacqueline's younger sister Naomi, who has been torn from her family—most painfully from her identical twin sister—and sent to the safety of a relative's working-class home in Detroit. Here she grows to adolescence where, along with the "normal" anxieties of that period of life, she suffers the agonies of isolation in a foreign land, separation from family and a growing, almost paranormal, sense that those she loved most dearly are dying. It is a complex, heartbreaking, absolutely authentic portrayal.

But from Jacqueline, Naomi and their people, we are suddenly shifted to the other most-emphasized subgroup, which is delimited by the interlocking love triangles of an insufferable Columbia University professor, Oscar Kahan, and his adoring assistant, Abra, both at work for the OSS; his ex-wife Louise, a writer known best for her slick-magazine romances; and Daniel, a young cryptanalyst of Polish Jewish stock with typical second-generation-American family conflicts. Embraced by their own book, these characters might seem more significant, but here they are tame, their stories often spilling into soap opera as they pop in and out of bed, agonize about their relationships, vent little jealousies and tolerate what are for the most part comparatively small wartime sacrifices. Alongside the marvelously-imagined scenes of combat and bombing, of daily life in the Resistance and the concentration camps, of a grim, dead-tired wartime London, the personal problems of American intellectuals seem frivolous. (Despite Piercy's well-known political history—or, who knows? maybe because of it—her best writing here is about violence real or imminent, and her male characters are believable, objective and compassionately drawn, even when they are unsympathetic.)

Oddly, the sections about the pilot, Bernice, are possibly the weakest in the book, though one might have expected them to be the strongest. A woman who lives to fly and has her chance during the war, only to be cruelly disappointed at war's end, Bernice escapes all prescribed sex roles; eventually, she joins with a woman lover and adopts a male persona in order to continue her career. Symbolically as well as actually, flight represents Bernice's break with bonds of family and gender, yet her story remains earthbound, pro forma, not convincing. She also exemplifies Piercy's proclivity, not limited to this book, for physical stereotyping. Just about every youngish heterosexual woman is slim and notably good-looking; hardly anyone resembles the great majority of real-world women—except for Bernice, the only lesbian and only woman profoundly committed to a "man's" job. *She* is "plain," "big" and distinctly mannish, the stereotypical dyke. I don't want to make too much of this; svelte pretty heterosexuals and large plain lesbians certainly do exist (though the re-

verse is equally true), but the consistency of the descriptions and their conformity to stereotype are irritating.

Gone to Soldiers falls short of the epic stature to which it aspires. Narrowed, deepened, and developed, it would have been much more successful, but it would also have been a different kind of book—one Piercy did not try to write. She chose a canvas of grand dimensions, and although she hasn't covered it with a masterpiece, she *has* produced a work that is vivid and transporting overall and shows greatness in numerous details. Even when she fails her extraordinary expectations of herself, she makes it clear that she is among our finest writers—sensitive, blazingly honest and intelligent, and highly skilled in her craft.

Mary Biggs, "Fiction at the Front," in The Women's Review of Books, Vol. IV, Nos. 10-11, July-August, 1987, p. 23.

Diane Wakoski

What's a critic without a quarrel? So let me begin my praise of Marge Piercy's [***Available Light***] with an argument about why the title of this book is a bad choice. As a long-time appreciator of the art of photography, I can only say that Piercy writes poetry which is related to almost every other sense but the visual. She is neither an abstract writer of perceptions, distortions and shadows, nor even a perceiver of ordinary reality through the eye. What Piercy does masterfully and beautifully is present the world of touch, of taste, of texture and even resonance. She is an empress of the vegetable kingdom, sensual, sexual, fecundly Dionysian. The antithesis of language poets, of *symbolistes* and the avant-garde, she is truly a daughter of Whitman, singing the electric song of material self, glorying in the earthy world; in spite of urban origins, political and polemical banalities, she has found a pure American identity in her body, her geography, landscape, and the knowledge which comes from these things.

Witness ["**Available Light**"] which should draw readers into this book more quickly than an autumn sniff of burning leaves:

> Ripe and runny as perfect Brie, at this age
> appetites mature rampant and allowed.
> I am wet as a salt marsh under the flood tide
> of the full solstice moon and dry as salt itself
> . . .
> I am always finding new
> beings in me like otters swimming in the soup.

Here Piercy declares her natural, cyclical origins, learning the world by animal observation, not cerebrally, and imitating the moon in her rhythms. She knows herself as she knows the land, "The four miles I walk/ every morning."

In fact, if we are starting with quibbles, this reader would edit the book to leave out academic travelogue poems like "**Slides from Our Recent European Trip**" and "**Le Sacre du Printemps**," which seem like pieces of notebook writing by a very accomplished writer. These are quibbles, but I mention them because such poems allow the poet to perceive herself falsely as an eye, not a body, and it is body poetry that she is writing, body poetry such as only Americans at their very best have taught us to write in the last two centuries. This is what the Whitman tradition is all about: recouping the other senses so much outdistanced and undervalued by European aesthetics, where the eye, the abstract eye, ousted every other sense.

Perhaps one of the greatest contributions twentieth-century American women make to poetry is to refuse to let aestheticians and poets forget the body. The earth body, the goddess body, the seasons and cycles, the agrarian root which we must still have even in urban or post-urban culture. Poets like Clayton Eshleman are searching for the mythic cultural root in Paleolithic caves, but every woman knows that she *is* the cave, both primordial and contemporary.

My own prejudice against novelists who write poetry (as if it were something to do in their spare time) has often kept me from Piercy's poetry; but as one of the pioneers of twentieth-century earth poetry, she deserves a different kind of attention from her fellow novelist-poets. Like Judith Minty, William Everson and Robinson Jeffers, she writes about her personal and human identity through her body and its identification with a landscape. Confusingly, perhaps, she insists on her urban Detroit origins; but what she really writes about well is her female body and its connection to her rural garden life. . . . Americans choose their landscape. And these poets are all Dionysian, writing about their dramas through their human bodies, identifying that body with the earth, the land, its scape. Judith Minty writes of Michigan and California as if they are one—they are trees and water, and in both places you find the migrating Monarch butterfly. . . .

The biography of Piercy's poems tells of parents who wanted her to be a boy and her own harsh demands on herself to fulfill early masculine tasks, as she conceived of them. But her poems, her life, perhaps even her beginnings as a novelist (prose=male; poetry=female?) constantly lead her back to her own body and its magnetically earthy center. In a lovely little poem about evolution, **"Baboons in the Perennial Bed,"** couched in her favorite metaphor, gardening, Piercy muses on the hard choice of whether to cut flowers or leave them to look at in the garden. She plays as she constantly does with biblical imagery and allusion—"consider the lilies of the field"—and talks of the flowers flaunting their sexual beauty like the highly-colored hindquarters of baboons; and concludes the poem, "We who are raised to shame/ for the moist orchid between our thighs/ must wish we were as certain of our beauty."

For Piercy, the body is a secret garden, one she did not feel allowed to discover early enough, and thus there is always a powerful tension of surprise and exultation in her poems of the vegetable kingdom. Piercy's politics seem to me to have come out of an early sense that the world put false expectations on her, not only in terms of gender, but also in terms of ethnic reality. This book is full of poems embracing her Jewishness which give the reader a feeling that she has had as hard a time allowing herself to be Jewish as to be a woman. Her ethnicity is divided between the Welsh father and the Jewish mother, just as her sense of landscape has been divided between urban Detroit and pastoral New England. She has wanted to be a man; yet fought militantly to be a woman. Such divisions! Such interesting tensions in the poetry, and perhaps also a focus, not previously achieved in her poems, which is becoming clearer and more precise in *Available Light.*

Diane Wakoski, "Bodily Fluent," in The Women's Review of Books, *Vol. V, Nos. 10-11, July, 1988, p. 7.*

Margaret Randall

[Tess Gallagher, Denise Levertov, Linda Pastan, and Marge Piercy.] Four strong poets. Four poets who speak out of a breadth of female experience and vision. Each has a particular voice and uses it without looking back. Levertov and Piercy especially move through a broad range of concerns, listening to the inner sounding as well as to the larger, more political concerns. Yet perhaps the only particularity these poets share is that energy of naming that emerges from each one's commitment to a retrieval of memory; and, truly, few strong women poets today do not share this. . . .

Of the four books, my favorite is Marge Piercy's *Available Light.* Piercy has been giving us essential poems for as long as she has also been chronicling our discoveries of self and world in her novels. Work, solidarity, issues of sexism and racism, the vital and necessary connections, all are a part of her language. As with Levertov, memory is a physical place, to be risked and conquered. And in her poems Piercy will not leave us until she *has* conquered, often bringing us up short in recognition.

"Hard Time," as in one of Alice Walker's poems, uses the diamond as a metaphor for the exploitation of the Black South African worker. "Do you know/where diamonds come from?" she asks, "Whose suffering is this you wear glinting at your ear/winking from your finger? How many/children's eyes shine in it? . . . /Call it a diamond. Call it the heart of a people." And she ends: "This is not a jewel/I would wear lightly./This is not a jewel/I would wear."

Piercy takes bits and pieces of a system's popular culture, along with the sickness of its social conditioning and the formal conservatism of its fear, and carves metaphors that keep us stumbling upwards in an ever ascendant spiral of discovery. She uses humor. She uses courage. She covers a wide field with the configuration of her line. She takes risks and almost always comes out winning. In her own field, she takes a few shots: "To please a critic you should write little,/a book every ten years. That shows how hard/you work, slow as a glacier advancing,/and critics, who may wish to write/sometimes lying in bed in the morning,/can justify abstention" (from **"The Fecund Complain They Are Not Honored"**).

She writes greatly about our womanness, what it is to *be* woman, and she confronts the ignorant and subversive eye to eye. **"Loving the Crone"** speaks well of woman's aging. In **"Something To Look Forward To"** she addresses menopause, as she once addressed women's work and rape in earlier poems, relentless though humble, without easy sentiment, illuminating all the dark corners. **"Wrong Monday"** is also, in that way, a woman's poem, and here Piercy engages us as well with her taut humor:

First the alarm is mute. Forgot the plunger.
I discover the milk is sour right after
I pour it on cereal. I pad
to the door stepping into what the cat
threw up. I clean the floor and then

my hands smell bad. Washing them
I splash my blouse and have to change.
After driving for an hour I remember
I forgot to pack underwear and the speech
I'm paid to give. The next sign
I see is ROAD CONSTRUCTION
NEXT 144 MILES. At that moment
stalled in traffic, my period starts.

And, as with the other poets reviewed here, Piercy deals in memory. She does so differently from Levertov, more persuasively than either Gallagher or Pastan. In **"How Divine Is Forgiving"** she says: "We forgive those who betrayed us/years later because memory has rotted/through like something left out in the weather/battered clean then littered dirty/in the rain." And towards the end of the same poem: "We forgive mostly not from strength/but through imperfections, for memory/wears transparent as a glass with the pattern/washed off, till we stare past what injured us./We forgive because we too have done/the same to others easy as a mudslide;/or because anger is a fire that must be fed/and we are too tired to rise and haul a log." Piercy is a beautiful gatherer-in, crafting her endings in intelligent flesh.

One reads Piercy's poetry, takes the new collections as entities, and rejoices in the way she chooses and orders, at the way each poem sings in the whole, at how the book is made. Elsewhere she has spoken about how she has refused to include even an obviously fine poem for years, waiting until it fits precisely into a collection. And so her books are also places, where everything happens as it should. With a powerful new volume in hand, there is always the question: Will we find a poem in this book as good as **"A Work of Artifice"** or with the staying power of **"Rape Poem"**? Yes. **"Perfect Weather," "I Saw Her Dancing,"** and **"Maggid"** are such poems, as is **"Burial by Salt,"** about her mother and father. By every poetic measure, *Available Light* is a leap forward for Piercy.

> *Margaret Randall, "Speaking Out of Memory," in* Belles Lettres: A Review of Books by Women, *Vol. 4, No. 1, Fall, 1988, p. 16.*

Stephen Schiff

Like so many of the characters in Ms. Piercy's nine other novels, the romantic threesome of *Summer People,* have invented what some might call an "alternative life style." For 10 years, they've been openly and blissfully bed-hopping in their woodsy Cape Cod retreat (which sounds very like Ms. Piercy's own Wellfleet), and theirs seems an extraordinary rapport; the reader looks forward to acquainting himself with the equally extraordinary people who've managed it. But despite their exotic occupations—Dinah's an avant-garde composer, Willie's a sculptor and Susan's a fabric designer—these three soon prove almost lethally boring. Scandalous sex lives and all.

One sympathizes with Ms. Piercy's plight. She's the sort of radical feminist sage whose fiction and poetry flourished in the 1960's and early 70's, when her *épater le bourgeois* posture, and the ramshackle social architectures she proposed, fit the *Zeitgeist* more snugly. And despite the depredations of the Reagan years, she hasn't changed her mind.

Yet Ms. Piercy seems to have recognized that her time-worn polemic can't enter the 90's blowing the same old steam, so she's not waving banners and fomenting revolt here; she's not even pitting male values against female. The battle lines *Summer People* draws are between the urban and the exurban, between the frozen-souled glamour of 80's New York and the earthy nurturance only Mother Nature can provide. While Dinah and Willie—a Jewish intellectual and an outdoorsy WASP—blossom in the woodlands, Susan, who's fortysomething but full of youthful hot-cha-cha, finds herself drawn to the heady world of Tyrone, a New York financier who carts his entourage of trendies to the Cape with him every summer. . . .

[The more Susan] yearns for him, the less she appreciates Dinah's artsy nobility and Willie's oxlike sincerity. Soon the triad is on the rocks, and Ms. Piercy is asking the age-old question: How ya gonna keep her down on the farm after she's seen SoHo?

Not that the author allows any doubt about her own sympathies. Ms. Piercy describes every leaf scar and peeping tree frog with schoolgirlish awe, mostly by planting us deep inside the mind of her heroine, the fiercely exurban Dinah. Unfortunately, Dinah's meandering mind, profoundly respected though it is among the cognoscenti of the music world, never drifts anywhere very interesting. Its principal occupation, in fact, is the examination and re-examination of what Dinah feels about Susan, what she feels about Willie, what Willie feels about Susan and so on. After a few pages of this stuff, even a colloquy with those tree frogs seems preferable.

Among the distinctions between soap opera and drama, there is this one: soap opera is about who did what to whom, and nothing else; drama is about the same transactions, but it also wants to take in their implications, to bring alive the world in which they take place. In *Summer People*, Ms. Piercy strains for the latter but mainly achieves the former, and the strain shows. The prose feels dogged and woefully earnest; it never stops selling itself. And it's often unintentionally hilarious. One minute Ms. Piercy is waxing neo-biblical: "That first winter and spring of their joining: great fierce winds blew through them." The next minute she's scurrying frantically to rescue her imagery from the snapping jaws of cliché: "Her heart missed a beat. It lurched painfully under her breasts."

And amid all this painful lurching, do we ever begin to understand how a happy, bisexual triangle might work? Afraid not. *Summer People* is full of holes; great fierce winds blow through them.

> *Stephen Schiff, "Red-Hot Pastorale," in* The New York Times Book Review, *June 11, 1989, p. 26.*

Jill Kearney

[*Summer People*] is a novel that yields more in summary than it does in the telling, since the structure of the tale—with its several bisexual characters and interlacing romantic triangles—has the mathematical fascination of a double-helix model. But any such interests are quickly dulled by Piercy's plodding narrative, and what remains is a Harlequin Romance vision of Bohemia, with artists substituted for the dashing doctor or the millionaire.

In the Piercy equation, career constitutes character—and one cares about the characters in direct proportion to the size of the romantic fog enshrouding each one's chosen field. Dinah Nathan has, in Piercy's view, a suitably ennobling job. A composer once married to a famous poet and involved with a sculptor and then a virtuoso musician, Dinah is the implied heroine of this tale. But we don't think much of that millionaire businessman, who lives with his ill-gotten gains across the pond, or of Susan, a mere fabric designer infatuated, to make matters worse, with the millionaire. This Gilligan's Island crew changes partners incestuously over the course of the spring and summer season while telling each other exactly how they feel, and, astonishingly, always knowing: a testament, perhaps, to the fact that Cape Cod is a mecca for psychiatrists. Not one of *Summer People's* characters is hostage to ineffable emotions, and their inner lives are as engrossing as grocery bills. "I love performing, but after a time I lose myself," says the virtuoso flute player to the composer, embarking on yet another detailed dissection of that relationship. "I distract myself from my pain by helping you. You distract yourself from your pain by helping me," says the sculptor to his latest paramour, insightfully. "I think it's beautiful," she responds. "I think being open to each other and helping each other is what being human is all about."

Despite her 14 volumes of published poetry, Piercy's writing seems to be always straining after poetic effects that do not come naturally. Her language lacks a distinctive voice and is mired in cliches: "She had come to Willie ripe but oh so young," she writes, and "her body stirred under his casual glance like a grove of aspens in the wind."

In between such revelations, Piercy numbs the reader with the latest developments in Cape Cod real-estate: quarrels over cesspool design, building permits and beach access rights. These things do obsess Cape dwellers, and though they provide a certain insight into small-town politics and social life, in the absence of a coherent portrait of the social forces at work in the larger town these bites of information have no place to land. Though ostensibly a novel about class conflict and small-town society, *Summer People* does not transcend the domestic dramas of its central characters; there's very little sense of how they integrate into the community, and how, for example, a bisexual triangle would be received by those other winter townspeople who hardly rate a mention—the more conservative Portuguese shop owners and fishermen who share the off-season cape with year-round artists and whose children grow up side-by-side in school. In this sense the novel is guilty of the same oversights and condescensions of which the millionaire stands accused.

But what is most disappointing about *Summer People* is the opportunity Piercy has missed to examine the social structure of the East Coast art world in all its contradictions and hypocrisies. *Summer People* takes the easy road of pitting the "haves," that rich, soulless businessman, against the soulful "have-nots," those artists. How much more interesting it would have been to take on the class structure of the art world itself, the way in which anointed artists—much more than the merely wealthy—rule the Cape Cod social roost; if not in the Hyannis compound of the Kennedys, certainly in the Wellfleet-Provincetown axis where the book occurs. In the real art world, the artist showmen have become the millionaires, buy the most lavish beachfront properties, hire poor artists as their bartenders, and the *nouveau riche* Tyrones hope against hope to be invited in. Sadly, there isn't room in Piercy's imagination for soulless artists and soulful businessmen, or for the sort of contradictions in character that make human beings interesting.

> *Jill Kearney, "Their Love Triangle Was a Double Helix," in* Los Angeles Times Book Review, *July 30, 1989, p. 2.*

Nicci Gerrard

In the sixties and seventies, Marge Piercy was zealous and committed. Her novels might have been bossy and heavy-handed but, fired by dramatic certainty, they managed to express contemporary disaffections and anxieties. *Summer People,* however, is grumpy rather than enraged, and gloomy rather than appalled. Like its main characters, who all flowered in the sixties and are ill at ease in the ageing eighties, the novel flounders in its unfocused pessimism: 390 pages in search of hope or anger.

The plot hardly exists; instead Marge Piercy elaborates upon a claustrophobically middle class situation. At first it is a cosily mobile triangle: Dinah the composer loves Willie the sculptor and his wife, Susan the designer; Willie loves Susan and Dinah; Susan loves Dinah and Willie. They all fuck (Marge Piercy's favourite word) each other, and for ten years the only real complication has been whose bed to use.

Then, when the summer people from New York arrive in Cape Cod and disrupt the artists' *ménage à trois,* it becomes a game of musical chairs, with dum-de-dum melodies and nails sticking out of some of the seats. Susan covertly desires tycoon Tyrone, who takes advantage of her insecure sycophancy but who really wants neighbour Candida of the plunging cleavage; Susan and Willie's easy-going son Jimmy mildly fancies Tyrone's inane daughter Laurie; Dinah falls for frail and brilliant flautist Itzak; Willie just wants everyone to be happy—but few of *Summer People*'s characters manage that. (p. 26)

There is a thread running through the novel, which occasionally tautens and quivers: the artists were swept up by the sixties, and dumped when its energy faded. Their story becomes a struggle against passivity, and their uncontroversial lifestyle is one way of staving off a sour and dulled middle-age. They cannot really make sense of the eighties but neither, it seems, can Marge Piercy, for she spins out and befuddles this central idea. *Summer People* is a novella in shoulder pads, wrongly dressed for its season.

Although a tragic crisis jerks the central characters out of the angst-ridden torpor where they have been churning, and enables them to look to an excruciatingly cheerful future, *Summer People* is not an optimistic novel. Its happy-ever-after ending is a sentimental coda to a lugubrious tale. Love, honesty and doggedness are the trinity of virtues Piercy obviously admires, but all of her cast are opportunistic and fickle. Even the artists, who, in a prolonged fit of cultural snobbery, are "better" than the metropolitan philistines, hurt or deceive each other in the name of love. While she is apparently advocating loyalty and spiritual warmth *à la* west coast of America, Marge Piercy actually gives us a heavily embellished and cunningly overdressed survival of the fittest. It is hard to believe this is her intention. (pp. 26-7)

[*Summer People*] is a sincere and persistent novel but, in the end, tedious. (p. 27)

> *Nicci Gerrard, "Sixties People," in* New Statesman & Society, *Vol. 2, No. 62, August 11, 1989, pp. 26-7.*

Carol Iannone

A major strategy in the current assault on the integrity of art from within the literary world has been the denial of the possibility of transcendence. Any claim that a writer can speak beyond his particular historical circumstances to describe the human experience as lived by all men is considered spurious. What has been seen as the universal truth of literature, we are told, is nothing more than the disguised or unexamined assumptions of the ruling class, sex, and race.

In no way have those making such accusations actually proved them. Do blacks, for example, find unrecognizable the mournful despair of the Trojan people at the death of Hector? Are women incapable of appreciating the restless dissatisfaction that drives Ishmael to join a whaling expedition? Is it beyond the capacity of a person born into the working class to fathom the overreaching ambitions of Macbeth? Of course not—in fact, such suggestions are *truly* "racist," "sexist," and "classist."

Yet the notion that all literature is ideological has enabled its purveyors to clear the way for their own authentically political approaches, entirely relieved of the burden of aesthetic justification. A whole academic/intellectual industry is now thriving on the infusion of politics into literature, much as some people claim whole industries thrive on the manufacture of chemicals that pollute the environment and contaminate the food supply.

Since it seems impossible to make the regnant literary power brokers admit that Shakespeare can be meaningful to anyone other than white males, perhaps the question can be explored profitably from the other end. What is the response nowadays to literature that is *openly* ideological and how powerful a hold does ideologically based literature have on our cultural life? The careers of Alice Walker and Marge Piercy, both of whom are explicitly political writers, and whose latest novels—Miss Walker's third, *The Temple of My Familiar,* and Miss Piercy's tenth, *Summer People*— . . . conveniently lend themselves to an exploration of these questions.

Alice Walker writes as a militant black and an equally militant feminist, while Marge Piercy's novels practically seem to have been produced on commission from some invisible authority on the Left. Unlike such novels as Henry James's *The Bostonians* or Dostoevsky's *The Possessed*, which use politics as a backdrop or a political movement as a subject for fictional exploration, the fiction of Miss Walker and even more that of Miss Piercy is the continuation of politics by other means, often a chance to accom-

plish in art what their favorite movements have failed thus far to achieve in life.

As one critic has written rather grandiloquently of Marge Piercy: "Her real genre is didactic and visionary allegory, . . . she wants her novels 'to be of use' " (the title of one of her books of poetry). In *Small Changes* (1974), for example, this critic continues, Miss Piercy "concentrates upon the creation of a new sexuality and a new psychology, which will permeate and bind a broad, genuine equality." (p. 57)

In looking over the critical reception these two writers have been accorded over the years, we find that the political propagandizing they both do has rarely stood in the way of the accolades they have generally received.

To be sure, some critics apparently see no conflict between the political and the aesthetic dimensions and therefore have no obstacle to overcome in singing the praises of these writers. Thus, according to one reviewer, Marge Piercy, in *Dance the Eagle to Sleep* (1970)—summarized by this reviewer as "the story of some not too distant time in which a small army of youth, drawn together by mutual feelings of alienation and hostility toward an oppressive, demoralized System, declare themselves a nation apart"— gives "fabulous substance to the essential Myth of the Movement."

Yet with a rare exception like John Updike (for whom *Dance the Eagle to Sleep* "fails as a novel of ideas" because "the government becomes one of those almost omnipotent syndicates of evil that Superman did battle with"), even reviewers who recognize that there is a conflict between the aesthetic and the political have tended to insist that Miss Piercy "doesn't allow ideology to overpower the thrust of her narrative," or that her "fierce energy as a novelist redeems the rhetoric."

Indeed, even critics who fully perceive and object to the programmatic quality of Miss Piercy's politics have usually still managed a general endorsement. "The men are monsterized," said a reviewer of *Small Changes.* "Women are made to seem happier without [them]. Children raised in communes are more emotionally secure. Lesbian love is more satisfying than heterosexual love. The end is a propagandist's one rather than a novelist's." Nevertheless, this same reviewer pronounced the novel "engrossing," "absorbing," and "fun." (pp. 57-8)

Although Marge Piercy's new novel, *Summer People,* has received some favorable attention, the bellwether *New York Times Book Review* indicates that patience with her may also be wearing thin [see Stephen Schiff's essay excerpted above].

Summer People tells of a blissfully happy ten-year *ménage à trois* made up of a married couple, Willie (a carpenter and sculptor) and Susan (a fabric designer), and a single woman, Dinah (an avant-garde composer). (The "sexist" implications of two women to one man never seem to occur to Miss Piercy.) The contented trio is broken up by the novel's course of events in which Susan allows herself to be infected/corrupted by Reaganist values like money, status, and glamor. Once Susan has conveniently removed herself by suicide, Dinah and Willie go on to form more traditional arrangements with even more conveniently available others, Dinah with a world-class violinist who not only gives her undying commitment and a baby, but also money, status, and glamor. (Not for nothing did one critic call an earlier Piercy novel "a Harlequin romance in a wolf coat of raised social consciousness.")

The *Times* reviewer "sympathizes with Marge Piercy's plight. She's the sort of radical feminist sage whose fiction and poetry flourished in the 1960's and early 70's, when her *épater le bourgeois* posture, and the ramshackle social architectures she proposed, fit the *Zeitgeist* more snugly." He went on to dismiss the novel for its soap-opera dimension, its willed quality, and its clumsy, theme-conscious prose—all of which have always characterized Marge Piercy's work, though rarely in the past to its detriment in the eyes of reviewers and critics.

Ironically, both of these new novels can actually be seen to be moving, willy nilly, away from "alternative lifestyles" toward more middle-class arrangements. Both authors firmly settle their characters in couples, male and female they settle them, two by two they settle them. . . . One can almost hear Bob Dylan rasping, for a change, *Everybody must go home!*

In their own convoluted ways, and for whatever reasons, Alice Walker and Marge Piercy may also be trying to come home, although most of the critics may be too bored to show up for the homecoming celebration, having already moved on to other preoccupations. If this is so, their careers help reveal the limits of ideology in more ways than one. For as the ideologies they subscribe to are increasingly exposed as empty and false, these writers too may find themselves looking for transcendence, possibly even in (somebody else's) fiction. (p. 59)

> *Carol Iannone, "A Turning of the Critical Tide?" in* Commentary, *Vol. 88, No. 5, November, 1989, pp. 57-9.*

FURTHER READING

Cramer, Carmen. "Anti-Automaton: Marge Piercy's Fight in *Woman on the Edge of Time.*" *Critique* XXVII, No. 4 (Summer 1986): 229-33.

Asserts that Piercy's novel dramatizes a contradiction inherent in the American ideal embodied in the motto *e pluribus unum.*

DuPlessis, Rachel Blau. "The Feminist Apologues of Lessing, Piercy, and Russ." *Frontiers: A Journal of Women's Studies* IV, No. 1 (Spring 1979): 1-8.

Places Piercy's *Woman on the Edge of Time* in context with the "teaching stories" of Joanna Russ and Doris Lessing.

Kessler, Carol Farley. "*Woman on the Edge of Time:* A Novel 'To Be of Use'." *Extrapolation* 28, No. 4 (Winter 1987): 310-18.

Asserts that Piercy's works should be interpreted according to a critical method that acknowledges the power of language to motivate action.

Nowik, Nan. "Mixing Art and Politics: The Writings of Adrienne Rich, Marge Piercy, and Alice Walker." *The Centennial Review* XXX, No. 2 (Spring 1986): 208-18.

Examines the political commitment of these three American writers as expressed in their essays.

Piercy, Marge. "Active in Time and History." In *Paths of Resistance: The Art and Craft of the Political Novel,* edited by William Zinsser, pp. 91-123. Boston: Houghton Mifflin, 1989.

A substantial revision of a previously published essay in which Piercy explores the influence of her urban experiences, especially her childhood in Detroit, on her fiction and her beliefs regarding the function of literature.

———. "Mirror Images." In *Women's Culture: Renaissance of the Seventies,* edited by Gayle Kimball, pp. 187-94. Metuchen, N.J.: The Scarecrow Press, 1981.

Piercy identifies the process and purpose of her writing.

Rose, Hillary. "Laboratory for Dreams." *New Statesman* 114, No. 2954 (6 November 1987): 22-3.

Praises *Woman on the Edge of Time* as one example of how feminist science fiction emphasizes the social context of science and technology.

Sargent, Lyman Tower. "A New Anarchism: Social and Political Ideas in Some Recent Feminist Eutopias." In *Women and Utopia: Critical Interpretations,* edited by Marleen Barr and Nicholas D. Smith, pp. 3-33. Lanham, Md: University Press of America, 1983.

Identifies the fundamental tenets of anarchism in *Woman on the Edge of Time* and other utopian novels.

Sylvia Plath

1932-1963

(Also wrote under the pseudonym Victoria Lucas) American poet, novelist, short story writer, essayist, memoirist, and scriptwriter.

The following entry presents criticism on Plath's novel *The Bell Jar* (1963). For an overview of Plath's complete career, see *CLC*, Vols. 1, 2, 3, 5, 9, 11, 14, 17, 50, 51.

Considered one of the most powerful poets of the post-World War II era, Plath became a cult figure following her suicide in 1963 and the posthumous publication of *Ariel,* which contained her most startling and acclaimed verse. Plath's autobiographical writings poignantly reflect her struggles with despair and mental illness, and her efforts to assert a strong female identity and to balance familial, marital, and career aspirations have established her as a representative voice for feminist concerns. Through bold metaphors and stark, often violent and unsettling imagery, her works evoke mythic qualities in nature and humanity. *Ariel* and Plath's only novel, *The Bell Jar,* which was published just weeks before her suicide, particularly convey her attempts to discover her psychological identity and literary voice.

Born in Boston, Massachusetts, Plath enjoyed an idyllic early childhood near the sea. Her father, a German immigrant, was a professor of entomology who maintained a special interest in the study of bees. His sudden death from diabetes mellitus in 1940 devastated the eight-year-old Plath, and this traumatic experience was significant in establishing her preoccupation with death and her crisis of identity, which later pervaded her writing. Plath began publishing poetry at an early age in such periodicals as *Seventeen* and the *Christian Science Monitor,* and in 1950 she earned a scholarship to Smith College. After spending a month during the summer of her junior year in New York City as a guest editor for *Mademoiselle* magazine, Plath suffered a mental collapse which resulted in a suicide attempt and her subsequent institutionalization. Following her recovery, Plath returned to Smith and graduated *summa cum laude.* While studying at Cambridge University under a Fulbright fellowship, Plath met and soon married Ted Hughes, an English poet. The failure of their marriage during the early 1960s and Plath's ensuing struggles with severe depression eventually led her to commit suicide on February 11, 1963.

The Bell Jar draws heavily upon events from Plath's adolescence, particularly the summer internship in Manhattan and her first suicide attempt. The book was originally published in Great Britain under the pseudonym Victoria Lucas because Plath feared that it might offend those people, especially her mother, on whom the characters are based. Confirming her daughter's suspicions, Mrs. Aurelia Plath was horrified by the story and successfully thwarted publication of *The Bell Jar* in the United States until 1971. The novel details a college student's disappointing adventures during a summer month in New York City as a guest editor for a fashion magazine, her despair upon returning

home, her attempted suicide, and the electroshock treatments and hospitalization she undergoes to "cure" her of depression and lethargy. Esther Greenwood, the narrator of *The Bell Jar,* encounters many of the pressures and problems Plath examined in her verse: her attempts to establish her identity are consistently undermined, she projects an ambivalent attitude toward men, society remains indifferent to her sensitivity, vulnerability, and artistic ambitions, and she is haunted by events from her past, particularly the death of her father. Although initial critical reaction to *The Bell Jar* was mixed, reviewers praised the novel's biting tone and metaphorical language. Laurence Lerner commented: "Sharp, pungent, brittle, [Esther's] images catch at almost indescribable states of mind for an instant, then shift restlessly to catch others. . . . Miss Lucas is tremendously readable, and at the same time has an almost poetic delicacy of perception. This is a brilliant and moving book."

Critics in both Great Britain and the United States have likened *The Bell Jar* to J. D. Salinger's novel of self-discovery and alienation, *The Catcher in the Rye.* Through the quick-witted, sensitive personas of Esther Greenwood and Holden Caulfield, both authors expose superficiality and corruption in adult society. Esther is nineteen when her story takes place, in 1953. A highly intelligent, rebellious, over-achiever from the Boston suburbs, Esther feels she is too tall, too ugly, and too smart to compete for men with the fashionable, flirtatious coeds she encounters at college. Her biggest problem lies in her conflict of interests. As a female in the 1950s, Esther has been taught that being a wife and mother is the only option for her, but she desperately wants to be a poet. Her mother worries about what she perceives to be Esther's impractical interest in literature and encourages her daughter to learn shorthand because, as Esther explains, "an English major who knew shorthand was something else again. Everybody would want her. She would be in demand among all the up-and-coming young men and she would transcribe letter after thrilling letter. The trouble was, I hated the idea of serving men in any way. I wanted to dictate my own thrilling letters."

Esther and eleven other young women win a nationwide writing contest and are awarded summer positions as guest editors for *Ladies' Day* magazine in New York City. Sequestered safely in a women's hotel, they are wined, dined, and shuttled from one photo session to another. Esther's lack of identity is established immediately. She is awed by her sexually attractive roommate Doreen, who represents an adult lifestyle Esther is ambivalent about exploring. Another contest winner, Betsy, is an innocent from Kansas, a virgin with a "Sweetheart-of-Sigma-Chi smile" whom Doreen disdainfully refers to as "Pollyanna Cowgirl." Esther, however, is as much drawn to Betsy's sincerity and warmth as she is to Doreen's brusqueness. She is aware of the capacity for these character traits in herself, but feels that they are just as mutually exclusive as the careers of homemaker and poet. As her adventures in New York continue, Esther experiences confusion between appearance and reality. After attending a gala *Ladies' Day* luncheon, the guest editors become deathly ill, and it is discovered that the elegant food was contaminated. Doreen seems less charming after arranging several disastrous double dates, and her taste in men disgusts Esther, who uses the name "Elly Higginbottom" to conceal her true identity when she is out with Doreen. Esther's last date in New York, Marco, attempts to rape her, and when she fights back and scratches him, he wipes his blood on her cheeks. The only kind man Esther meets while in Manhattan is Constantin, an interpreter for the United Nations, but when she makes sexual overtures, she learns he is a homosexual.

Toward the end of her stay in New York, Esther becomes more impersonalized. Unable to see her own reflection in mirrors, she feels disembodied and anxious. On her last night in the city, Esther climbs to the roof of her hotel and hurls her *Ladies' Day* wardrobe into the wind, symbolically destroying her superficial identity and her unpleasant memories of New York. Betsy loans Esther a skirt and blouse for her train ride home, and Esther takes on Betsy's pristine persona, even though her cheeks are still smeared with Marco's blood. Torn between her desires for chastity and sex, she considers her virginity a colossal burden and longs to be free of it, but in the 1950s, Esther observes dryly, "pureness was the great issue." Her mother had sent her magazine articles with such titles as "In Defense of Chastity," which further complicate Esther's dilemma of wanting to express herself sexually in a repressive society.

Esther is met at the train station by her reproachful mother. Mrs. Greenwood rarely appears in *The Bell Jar,* yet she is one of the novel's most distinct, sharply drawn characters. Vance Bourjaily asserted: "Whatever the abstract roles we decide to assign the characters in *The Bell Jar,* they are never abstractions. It is one of the strengths of the book that each is brought to brief, vivid, and particular life, even the most minor. It's done with snapshot physical description, a quick ear, and a little irony." Mrs. Greenwood has taught shorthand and typing to support her two children after her husband died. Esther believes that "secretly she hated it and hated him for dying and leaving no money because he didn't trust life insurance salesmen." Mrs. Greenwood never allowed her daughter to attend the funeral or to visit her father's grave, and consequently, Esther resents never having been able to mourn. Esther is soon informed that she was not accepted into a prestigious writing class at Harvard, and her already precarious self-esteem plummets. Feeling suffocated in her family's house, and unable to sleep or eat, Esther attempts to write a novel, but fails because, although she has "fifteen years of straight A's," she has no experience in life. Past relationships and events, recalled through flashbacks, provide insight into Esther's eventual breakdown. Buddy Willard, a medical student and former boyfriend, is part of her memories and the principal cause for her hostility toward society's double standards. Buddy dates Esther for several years, insisting they both remain pure for their future wedding night. Buddy worships his mother, a woman who waits on her husband like a servant and represents the kind of relationship and life Esther does not want. Ultimately, Esther discovers that Buddy is not a virgin and is incensed at his hypocrisy.

Living at home, Esther grows increasingly despondent and agrees to see a psychiatrist. Dr. Gordon, a remote, handsome man, makes Esther feel paranoid and foolish, and the framed picture on his desk of his happy, all-American family suggests to her that he will try to reconcile her to a similarly conventional role. A bungled electroshock treatment dissuades her from further visits. Esther decides that suicide is the only answer to her problems, but fails in several different, almost comic, attempts. Finally, hiding in the cellar, she takes fifty sleeping pills and lapses into a coma before being found and revived three days later. Several critics have noted that Esther's failed suicide is an exact description of Plath's own, and that Plath's tone throughout this section, both triumphant and satisfied, adds a poignancy that evokes pity and helplessness. The rest of *The Bell Jar* details Esther's battle to achieve psychological wholeness. She starts competent therapy at an asylum with Dr. Nolan, a woman who wins Esther's admiration and confidence, and undergoes successful shock treatments that erase her fear and depression. Another patient at the hospital, Joan Gilling, is an acquaintance with whom Esther has always competed fiercely. She functions as Esther's *doppelgänger,* something Esther acknowledges when thinking of their past relationship: "Joan was the beaming double of my old best self, specially designed to follow and torment me." As Esther becomes free of her fears and compulsions, Joan becomes more troubled, and ultimately hangs herself. Symbolically, this incident suggests that the distorted side of Esther must die before she can emerge as a whole identity.

As Esther slowly gains confidence and is allowed periodic

leaves from the asylum, she decides she should be sexually active, and with her doctor's blessing, buys a diaphragm. She chooses a Harvard mathematics professor to be her first lover, but experiences hemorrhaging during sexual intercourse and is rushed to the hospital. Remaining composed, Esther simply sends her lover the bill for her emergency surgery. Finally, she seems free of the repressive attitudes that have plagued her life, but *The Bell Jar*'s conclusion is unresolved. Although she is sexually liberated, the conflict of interests remains, and Esther must decide whether to conform to an oppressive society preoccupied with appearances. At the novel's end, in a scene reminiscent of a birth or rebirth, Esther faces the doctors for their approval to leave the asylum.

During the course of the novel, Esther compares her mental state to living in a suffocating bell jar: "wherever I sat . . . I would be sitting under the same glass bell jar, stewing in my own sour air." She later equates the mental hospital patients to college coeds, maintaining that they too live constricted lives. Critics have noted that Esther's final mention of the metaphor parallels Plath's own fears, and foreshadows her imminent suicide: "How did I know that someday—at college, in Europe, somewhere, anywhere—the bell jar, with its stifling distortions, wouldn't descend again?" Esther's battles to find her true, whole self are reflected in the fragmented structure of the novel. The many personalities that Esther feels she must project—courteous daughter, dutiful student, naive virgin, cosmopolitan lover—battle within her, and are intertwined in the story's structure. Esther is witty and intelligent, and it becomes obvious that this separates her from other people, as do her ironic views and melancholy attitude. Detached from others, as well as from herself, Esther lives on the periphery, watching and judging others' lives while obscuring her own. Esther's criticism of society is astute, but she cannot assess herself in the same manner, and numerous critics contend that Esther's struggle to find a place for herself in this larger social situation is Plath's primary focus in *The Bell Jar*. Throughout the novel, there are subtle distinctions made between the "distorted" viewpoint of a madwoman and the actual distortions and irrationalities of the society in which she tries to cope.

Critics praised Plath's style, particularly her poetic skills that enliven the economic intensity of the anecdotes. Plath blends autobiographical elements with caustic social commentary to relate Esther's story, for *The Bell Jar* is as much a satiric portrait of American society in the 1950s as it is a poignant study of the growing disillusionment of a talented young woman. Linda W. Wagner commented: "What *The Bell Jar* ultimately showed was a woman struggling to become whole, not a woman who had reached some sense of stable self." She added: "[The novel must be read as] a testimony to the repressive cultural mold that trapped many mid-century women, forcing them outside what should have been their rightful, productive lives."

(See also *Contemporary Authors*, Vols. 17-20, rev. ed.; *Contemporary Authors Permanent Series*, Vol. 2; *Dictionary of Literary Biography*, Vols. 5, 6; *Concise Dictionary of American Literary Biography: The New Consciousness, 1941-1968;* and *Poetry Criticism*, Vol. 1.)

PRINCIPAL WORKS

POETRY

The Colossus   1960; published as *The Colossus and Other Poems,* 1962
Ariel   1965
Crossing the Water: Transitional Poems   1971
Winter Trees   1971
The Collected Poems   1981

OTHER

Three Women: A Monologue for Three Voices   (radio play)   1962
The Bell Jar   (novel)   1963
Letters Home: Correspondence, 1950-1963   (letters)   1975
Johnny Panic and the Bible of Dreams and Other Prose Writings   (short stories and diary entries)   1977
The Journals of Sylvia Plath   (diary entries)   1982

Laurence Lerner

[*The Bell Jar,* by Victoria Lucas], is the story of Esther Greenwood, who wins a fashion magazine contest and gets, with eleven other girls, a free trip to New York, with free clothes, free meals, free entry to fashion shows, previews, and perhaps a career. Esther feels uncomfortable about it all. New York must have secrets it hasn't yielded to her—in the next taxi, perhaps, in the night club she wasn't asked to. Esther is a nice girl, she appreciates what people are doing for her, but somehow the deputy editor has to ask her if she is really interested in her work. She is gloriously and convincingly young: she sees through everyone, is influenced by everyone.

Slowly, then more quickly, we realize that Esther's ruthless and innocent wit is not just the result of youth and intelligence. It is the sign of a detachment, a lack of involvement, so complete that it leads to neurosis. From satirist she becomes a patient, yet so imperceptibly that after realizing she is sick we don't feel at all tempted to discount her previous shrewdness, or even cease to find her funny, in a rather frightening way. There are criticisms of American society that the neurotic can make as well as anyone, perhaps better, and Miss Lucas makes them triumphantly.

The book has another triumph: its language. The bell jar is Esther's image for her neurosis: 'wherever I sat, on the deck of a ship or at a street café in Paris or Bangkok—I would be sitting under the same glass bell jar, stewing in my own sour air'. Sharp, pungent, brittle, her images catch at almost indescribable states of mind for an instant, then shift restlessly to catch others. The novelist who deals with these elusive states of being usually has to choose between apt and elaborate imagery, or a simplifying and readable clarity. But Miss Lucas is tremendously readable, and at the same time has an almost poetic delicacy of perception. This is a brilliant and moving book.

> *Laurence Lerner, in a review of "The Bell Jar," in* The Listener, *Vol. LXIX, No. 1766, January 31, 1963, p. 215.*

M. L. Rosenthal

Sylvia Plath's *The Bell Jar* was originally published in 1963 under a pseudonym. I very much regret missing it then, for now it is impossible to read without thinking of her personally and of the suicidal poems in *Ariel.* Written in the first person, it is about an American college student who excels in competition, especially academic competition, but who is overwhelmed by her sense of inadequacy and unworthiness. In this novel, Sylvia Plath wanted to clarify the psychological condition, or pathology, of her suicidal compulsion, 'sitting under the . . . glass bell jar, stewing in my own sour air.' She was arranging crucial motifs in her life around this symbol, using flashbacks to give depth to the simple surface account of unexpected breakdown. The motifs occur in the poems of *Ariel,* her other posthumous book, as well—the family's German background (always connoting guilt for Nazism to the girl); her father's death when she was nine; the shock of seeing cadavers, and also of seeing a Caesarian operation, when shown around a hospital by her matter-of-fact boyfriend, a science student; the intertwined fear and fascination toward both death and sex; the longing to be with the dead father, which leads to hatred of her mother for accepting his death and to attempts to destroy herself; the identification of personal and public anguish as functions of one another.

The Bell Jar is an inexpert, uneven novel, but it has magnificent sections whose candour and revealed suffering will haunt anyone's memory. In its capacity as 'Information,' it has a great deal to tell us about the mentality of persons under the desperate internal pressure of the protagonist. The sense of having been judged and found wanting for no externally discernible reason, and the equally terrifying sense of great power gone to waste or turned against oneself—these are the murderous phantoms against which the heroine pitifully contends.

> *M. L. Rosenthal, "Blood and Plunder," in* The Spectator, *Vol. 217, No. 7214, September 30, 1966, p. 418.*

J. D. O'Hara

"Victoria Lucas" first published *The Bell Jar* in England in 1963. But Victoria Lucas was really the American poet Sylvia Plath—or had been; the novel's characters and settings were equally American; and the time of action was the mid-Fifties, not the Sixties. Never much publicized, *The Bell Jar* became something of an unknown favorite, especially among the young. . . .

The novel is a curious combination of stories. It begins in high spirits as a cheerful, shallow, fast-moving, and satirical account of the author's barely fictionalized summer in New York as one of the undergraduate guest editors of *Mademoiselle.* The Barbizon Hotel becomes the Amazon, *Mademoiselle* is simply "a fashion magazine," and Esther Greenwood, a cheerful female Holden Caulfield, tells us about her terrible blind dates, her interest in sex ("When I was nineteen, pureness was the great issue"), and her memories of college and of her Yale boyfriend Buddy Willard. The anecdotes are very well told; after all, Sylvia Plath was a poet (*The Colossus; Ariel*), which means that she knew how to use words economically and unostenta-

tiously. But the narrator's voice is a nineteen-year-old's, pure and simple. When eleven of the twelve guest editors come down simultaneously with ptomaine poisoning, pure and simple Esther comments cheerfully that "there is nothing like puking with somebody to make you into old friends." Remembering the time when Buddy Willard took it upon himself to show her what a naked man looked like, she says:

> He just stood there in front of me and I kept on staring at him. The only thing I could think of was turkey neck and turkey gizzards and I felt very depressed.

But then the New York adventures end, Esther returns to quiet, suburban Massachusetts, and a strange new book begins. The funny incidents are funny in a different way, and suddenly Esther is undergoing psychiatric treatment, and suddenly she's in an asylum.

(The question of where exactly the tone of the novel shifts, where exactly the madness begins, can provoke some very curious discussions, complete with many a sidelong glance. Contestants are likely to take almost any position, some insisting that Esther was never crazy at all, that she was merely the victim of a Communist plot, and others insisting that they knew it from the start, that Esther was crazy to have accepted that first blind date.)

Esther's story of her six months of madness and treatment—the novel ends as she's about to return to Smith College—is bound to be compared, nowadays, to "Hannah Green's" *I Never Promised You a Rose Garden.* Esther's story is better, partly because Sylvia Plath was a better writer, partly because the story is told more swiftly, and partly because the first-person narration fixes us there, in the doctor's office, in the asylum, in the madness, with no reassuring vacations when we can keep company with the sane and listen to their lectures.

Of course the subject matter of the two stories is necessarily similar: Asylums, like happy families, are much alike. The interviews and treatments, the less fortunate and the luckier fellow patients, and the incompetent and the godlike psychiatrist appear in both. In *Rose Garden,* Deborah's mind created a complicated fictional world; fortunately for the reader of *The Bell Jar,* Esther never gets past the opening stages of hers: "My heroine would be myself, only in disguise. She would be called Elaine. Elaine."

Sylvia Plath was herself as two-sided as her novel. She was tall, blonde, beautiful, intelligent, witty, and talented—everyone's dream girl, the American ideal. But we've begun to learn, nowadays, that the safest thing to do in the presence of an Eagle Scout is to turn and run, screaming; and we have also begun to realize that to be a beautiful, intelligent, witty, and talented girl, at least here in mid-century America, is considerably more dangerous than shooting heroin. For such an illness, cures are less common than delays. Born in 1932, Sylvia Plath committed suicide in 1963.

> *J. D. O'Hara, "An American Dream Girl," in* Book World—The Washington Post, *April 11, 1971, p. 3.*

Martha Duffy

[*The Bell Jar*], which is just now scaling the bestseller lists, has actually been around for eight years. It was published in London, without causing much commercial stir, shortly before the author, a young American poet, killed herself. Bringing it out in the U.S.—after years of opposition from the author's mother—was either smart publishing or egregious good luck.

Sylvia Plath is already well known for her last poems, which are brilliant songs of self-destruction, the *ne plus ultra* of confessional verse. *The Bell Jar* is a marvelously unself-conscious, confessional novel dashed off before such documents were in vogue. . . . Like the Lady Lazarus of her poem, she is a virtuoso of death. As she wrote: "You could say I've a call."

She was 30 when she died, an exhausted, mad mother of two, estranged from her poet husband, Ted Hughes. A typically American-looking blonde, she was much admired in English critical circles; half of literary London blamed itself for her death. Yet *The Bell Jar,* like the late poems, makes that tragedy seem a pathetic inevitability.

Not that the novel is either lugubrious or totally morbid. It is by turns funny, harrowing, crude, ardent and artless. Its most notable quality is an astonishing immediacy, like a series of snapshots taken at high noon. The story, scarcely disguised autobiography, covers six months in a young girl's life, beginning when she goes to New York to serve on a fashion magazine's college-editorial board. It ends when she emerges from a mental hospital after a breakdown.

The first part is hilarious. Esther Greenwood, as the heroine is called, is an awkward rube of a girl with "fifteen years of straight A's" behind her but absolutely no experience of life—even as it was known to teen-agers in the '50s. She and her fellow "guest" editors are herded around the city "like a wedding party with nothing but bridesmaids." Upon discovering caviar, Esther consumes a pound or so at a magazine luncheon, paving her plate with chicken slices and smearing on the high-priced spread. But she knows that the whole enterprise is phony, that the girls are smug and dumb and, most important, that she is going against her own grain by participating at all. Before heading back to Massachusetts, she flings all her expensive, uncomfortable new clothes from the roof of her hotel.

At home it is psychic raiment that she lacks. She cannot sleep and will not wash. She longs to write a novel ("That would fix a lot of people"), but cannot write a paragraph. Her mother drives her crazy simply by living in the same house. With the awful logic of the mad, she considers and rejects any amelioration of her condition; she is under a "glass bell jar, stewing in my own sour air." Rescued from a suicide attempt, she starts the long process of mental repair in an asylum.

It is obvious why Sylvia Plath's mother is distressed by the novel. The author remembers every misguided attempt to guide her, every ploy to use her, every complacent piece of advice. Yet her bitterness is so remorseless that it finally becomes poignant, especially since she foresaw the final tragedy. After shock treatments restore Esther's equilibrium, she wonders: "How did I know that someday, at college, in Europe somewhere, anywhere—the bell jar, with its stifling distortions, wouldn't descend again?" (pp. 87-8)

Martha Duffy, "Lady Lazarus," in Time, New York, Vol. 97, No. 25, June 21, 1971, pp. 87-8.

Howard Moss

The story of a poet who tries to end her life written by a poet who did, Sylvia Plath's *The Bell Jar* was first published under a pseudonym in England in 1963, one month before she committed suicide. We have had to wait almost a decade for its publication in the United States, but it was reissued in England in 1966 under its author's real name. A biographical note in the present edition makes it plain that the events in the novel closely parallel Sylvia Plath's twentieth year. For reasons for which we are not wholly to blame, our approach to the novel is impure; *The Bell Jar* is fiction that cannot escape being read in parts as autobiography. It begins in New York with an ominous lightness, grows darker as it moves to Massachusetts, then slips slowly into madness. Esther Greenwood, one of a dozen girls in and on the town for a month as "guest editors" of a teen-age fashion magazine, is the product of a German immigrant family and a New England suburb. With "fifteen years of straight A's" behind her, a depressing attachment to a dreary but handsome medical student, Buddy Willard, still unresolved, and a yearning to be a poet, she is the kind of girl who doesn't know what drink to order or how much to tip a taxi driver but is doing her thesis on the "twin images" in *Finnegans Wake,* a book she has never managed to finish. Her imagination is at war with the small-town tenets of New England and the big-time sham of New York. She finds it impossible to be one of the army of college girls whose education is a forced stop on the short march to marriage. The crises of identity, sexuality, and survival are grim, and often funny. Wit, irony, and intelligence as well as an inexplicable, withdrawn sadness separate Esther from her companions. Being an involuntary truth-seeker, she uses irony as a weapon of judgment, and she is its chief victim. Unable to experience or mime emotions, she feels defective as a person. The gap between her and the world widens: "I couldn't get myself to react. I felt very still and very empty." . . . "The silence depressed me. It wasn't the silence of silence. It was my own silence." . . . "That morning I had tried to hang myself."

Camouflage and illness go together in *The Bell Jar;* moreover, illness is often used to lift or tear down a façade. Doreen, a golden girl of certainty admired by Esther, begins the process by getting drunk. The glimpse of her lying with her head in a pool of her own vomit in a hotel hallway is repellent but crucial. Her illness is followed by a mass ptomaine poisoning at a "fashion" lunch. Buddy gets tuberculosis and goes off to a sanatorium. Esther, visiting him, breaks her leg skiing. When she has her first sexual experience, with a young math professor she has picked up, she hemorrhages. Taken in by a lesbian friend, she winds up in a hospital. Later, she learns that the friend has hanged herself. A plain recital of the events in *The Bell Jar* would be ludicrous if they were not balanced by genuine desperation at one side of the scale and a sure sense of black comedy at the other. Sickness and disclosure are the keys to *The Bell Jar.* On her last night in New York, Esther climbs to the roof of her hotel and throws her city wardrobe over the parapet, piece by piece. By the end of the novel, she has tried to get rid of her very life, which is given back to her by another process of divestment—psychiatry. Pain and gore are endemic to *The Bell Jar,* and they are described objectively, self-mockingly, almost humorously to begin with. Taken in by the tone (the first third of *The Bell Jar* might be a mordant, sick-joke version of *Breakfast at Tiffany's*), the reader is being lured into the lion's den—that sterile cement room in the basement of a mental hospital where the electric-shock-therapy machine waits for its frightened clients.

The casualness with which physical suffering is treated suggests that Esther is cut off from the instinct for sympathy right from the beginning—for herself as well as for others. Though she is enormously aware of the impingements of sensation, her sensations remain impingements. She lives close to the nerve, but the nerve has become detached from the general network. A thin layer of glass separates her from everyone, and the novel's title, itself made of glass, is evolved from her notion of disconnection: the head of each mentally ill person is enclosed in a bell jar, choking on his own foul air.

Torn between conflicting roles—the sweetheart-*Hausfrau*-mother and "the life of the poet," neither very real to her—Esther finds life itself inimical. Afraid of distorting the person she is yet to become, she becomes the ultimate distortion—nothing. As she descends into the pit of depression, the world is a series of wrong reverberations: her mother's face is a perpetual accusation, the wheeling of a baby carriage underneath her window a grinding irritation. She becomes obsessed by the idea of suicide, and one of the great achievements of *The Bell Jar* is that it makes real the subtle distinctions between a distorted viewpoint and the distortions inherent in what it sees. Convention may contribute to Esther's insanity, but she never loses her awareness of the irrationality of convention. Moved to Belsize, a part of the mental hospital reserved for patients about to go back to the world, she makes the connection explicit:

> What was there about us, in Belsize, so different from the girls playing bridge and gossiping and studying in the college to which I would return? Those girls, too, sat under bell jars of a sort.

Terms like "mad" and "sane" grow increasingly inadequate as the action develops. Esther is "psychotic" by definition, but the definition is merely a descriptive tag: by the time we learn how she got to be "psychotic" the word has ceased to be relevant. (As a work of fiction, *The Bell Jar* seems to complement the clinical theories of the Scottish analyst R. D. Laing.) Because it is written from the distraught observer's point of view rather than from the viewpoint of someone observing her, there is continuity to her madness; it is not one state suddenly supplanting another but the most gradual of processes.

Suicide, a grimly compulsive game of fear and guilt, as addictive as alcohol or drugs, is experimental at first—a little blood here, a bit of choking there, just to see what it will be like. It quickly grows into an overwhelming desire for annihilation. By the time Esther climbs into the crawl space of a cellar and swallows a bottle of sleeping pills—by the time we are faced by the real thing—the event, instead

of seeming grotesque, seems like a natural consequence. When she is about to leave the hospital, after a long series of treatments, her psychiatrist tells her to consider her breakdown "a bad dream." Esther, "patched, retreaded, and approved for the road," thinks, "To the person in the bell jar, blank and stopped as a dead baby, the world itself is the bad dream."

That baby is only one of many in *The Bell Jar.* They smile up from the pages of magazines, they sit like little freaks pickled in glass jars on display in the pediatric ward of Buddy's hospital. A "sweet baby cradled in its mother's belly" seems to wait for Esther at the end of the ski run when she has her accident. And in the course of the novel she witnesses a birth. In place of her never-to-be-finished thesis on the "twin images" in *Finnegans Wake,* one might be written on the number and kinds of babies that crop up in *The Bell Jar.* In a gynecologist's office, watching a mother fondling her baby, Esther wonders why she is so separated from this easy happiness, this carrying out of the prescribed biological and social roles. She does not want a baby; she is a baby herself. But she is also a potential writer. She wants to fulfill herself, not to *be* fulfilled. To her, babies are The Trap, and sex is the bait. But she is too intelligent not to realize that babies don't represent life, they *are* life, though not necessarily the kind Esther wants to live; that is, if she wants to live at all. She is caught between the monstrous fetuses on display in Buddy's ward and the monstrous slavery of the seemingly permanent pregnancy of her neighbor Dodo Conway, who constantly wheels a baby carriage under Esther's window, like a demented figure in a Greek chorus. Babies lure Esther toward suicide by luring her toward a life she cannot—literally—bear. There seem to be only two solutions, and both involve the invisible: to pledge faith to the unborn or fealty to the dead. Life, so painfully visible and present, defeats her, and she takes it, finally, into her own hands. With the exception of the psychiatrist's disinterested affection for her, love is either missing or unrecognized in *The Bell Jar.* Its overwhelming emotion is disgust—disgust that has not yet become contempt and is therefore more damaging. (pp. 73-4)

Something girlish in . . . [*The Bell Jar's*] manner betrays the hand of the amateur novelist. Its material, after all, is what has been transcended. It is a frightening book, and if it ends on too optimistic a note as both fiction and post-dated fact, its real terror lies elsewhere. Though we share every shade of feeling that leads to Esther's attempts at suicide, there is not the slightest insight in *The Bell Jar* into suicide itself. That may be why it bears the stamp of authority. Reading it, we are up against the raw experience of nightmare, not the analysis or understanding of it. (p. 75)

> *Howard Moss, "Dying: An Introduction," in* The New Yorker, *Vol. XLVII, No. 21, July 10, 1971, pp. 73-5.*

Elizabeth Hardwick

In Sylvia Plath's work and in her life the elements of pathology are so deeply rooted and so little resisted that one is disinclined to hope for general principles, sure origins, applications, or lessons. Her fate and her themes are hardly separate and both are singularly terrible. Her work is brutal, like the smash of a fist; and sometimes it is also mean in its feeling. Literary comparisons are possible, echoes vibrate occasionally, but to whom can she be compared in spirit, in content, in temperament?

Certain frames for her destructiveness have been suggested by critics. Perhaps being born a woman is part of the exceptional rasp of her nature, a woman whose stack of duties was laid over the ground of genius, ambition, and grave mental instability. Or is it the 1950s, when she was going to college, growing up—is there something of that here? Perhaps; but I feel in her a special lack of national and local roots, feel it particularly in her poetry, and this I would trace to her foreign ancestors on both sides. They were given and she accepted them as a burden not as a gift; but there they were, somehow cutting her off from what they weren't. Her father died when she was eight years old and this was serious, central. Yet this most interesting part of her history is so scorched by resentment and bitterness that it is only the special high burn of the bitterness that allows us to imagine it as a cutoff love.

For all the drama of her biography, there is a peculiar remoteness about Sylvia Plath. A destiny of such violent self-definition does not always bring the real person nearer; it tends, rather, to invite iconography, to freeze our assumptions and responses. She is spoken of as a "legend" or a "myth"—but what does that mean? Sylvia Plath was a luminous talent, self-destroyed at the age of thirty, likely to remain, it seems, one of the most interesting poets in American literature. As an *event* she stands with Hart Crane, Scott Fitzgerald, and Poe rather than with Emily Dickinson, Marianne Moore, or Elizabeth Bishop.

The outlines of her nature are odd, especially in her defiant and extensive capabilities, her sense of mastery, the craft and preparation she almost humbly and certainly industriously acquired as the foundation for an overwhelming ambition. She was born in Winthrop, Massachusetts. Her mother's parents were Austrian; her father was a German, born in Poland. He was a professor of biology, a specialist, among other interests, in bee-raising. (The ambiguous danger and sweetness of the beehive—totemic, emblematic for the daughter.) Her father died and the family moved to Wellesley, Massachusetts, to live with their grandparents. The mother became a teacher and the daughter went to public schools and later to Smith College. Sylvia Plath was a thorough success as a student and apparently was driven to try to master everything life offered—study, cooking, horseback riding, writing, being a mother, housekeeping. There seemed to have been no little patch kept for the slump, the incapacity, the refusal. . . .

Sylvia Plath went on a Fulbright to Cambridge University. She met and later married the distinguished poet Ted Hughes, and after a year or so back in America they returned to live in England. Her first book of poems, *The Colossus,* was published in 1960, the same year her daughter Frieda was born. In 1962, her son Nicholas was born—and then life began to be hard and disturbing, except that she was able to write the poems now being issued under the title *Crossing the Water.* She was separated from her husband, came back to London with two small children, tried to live and work and survive alone in a bare flat during one of the coldest years in over a century. *The Bell Jar* was published under a pseudonym just before she died, in February, 1963. (p. 3)

She has the rarity of being, in her work at least, never a "nice person." She is capable of anything—that we know. [A.] Alvarez reminds us how typical of her nature is the scene in *The Bell Jar* in which she dashes down a ski slope without knowing how to ski; he remembers her reckless ways with horses, and tells of a deliberate smashing of her own car in a suicidal burst before the final one.

It is not recklessness that makes Sylvia Plath so forbidding, but destructiveness toward herself and others. Her mother thought *The Bell Jar* represented "the basest ingratitude" and we can only wonder at her innocence in expecting anything else. For the girl in the novel, a true account of events so far as we know, the ego is disintegrating and the stifling self-enclosure is so extreme that only death—and after that fails, shock treatment—can bring any kind of relief. Persons suffering in this way simply do not have room in their heads for the anguish of others—and later many seem to survive their own torments only by an erasing detachment. But even in recollection—and *The Bell Jar* was written a decade after the happenings—Sylvia Plath does not ask the cost.

There is a taint of paranoia in her novel and also in her poetry. The person who comes through is merciless and threatening, locked in violent images. If she does not, as so many have noticed, seem to feel pity for herself, neither is she moved to self-criticism or even self-analysis. It is a sour world, a drifting, humid air of vengeance. *The Bell Jar* seems to be a realistic account of her suicide attempt during the summer before her senior year at Smith. But the novel is about madness as well, and that separates it from the poems. Death, in the poetry, is an action, a possibility, a gesture, complete in itself, unmotivated, unexamined.

The Bell Jar opens with the line, "It was a queer, sultry summer, the summer they electrocuted the Rosenbergs." The Rosenbergs are in no way a part of the story and their mention is the work of an intelligence, wondering if the sufferings of a solitary self can have general significance. Also with her uncanny recognition of connections of all kinds—sound, sensation—and her poetic ordering of material, the electrocution of the Rosenbergs and the shock treatment at the end of the book have a metaphorical if not a realistic kinship. In the end the Rosenbergs just mean death to Sylvia Plath. "I couldn't help wondering what it would be like, being burned alive, all along your nerves."

After a summer in New York, the girl goes back to Massachusetts and madness begins to close in on her.

> I hadn't slept for twenty-one nights. I thought the most beautiful thing in the world must be shadow, the million moving shapes and cul de sacs of shadow. There was shadow in bureau drawers and closets and suitcases, and shadows under houses and trees and stones, and shadow at the back of people's eyes and smiles, and shadow, miles and miles of it, on the night side of the earth.

Committing suicide is desperation, demand for relief, but I don't see how we can ignore the way in which it is edged with pleasure and triumph in Sylvia Plath's work. In *The Bell Jar* she thinks of slashing her wrists in the tub and imagines the water "gaudy as poppies"—an image like those in her late poems. When she is unable to do the act she still wants to "spill a little blood" for practice. "Then I felt a small, deep thrill, and a bright seam of red welled up at the lip of the slash. The blood gathered darkly, like fruit, and rolled down my ankle into the cup of my black patent leather shoe." These passages, and others much more brilliant in her poems, show a mind in a state of sensual distortion, seeking pain as much as death, contemplating with grisly lucidity the mutilation of the soul and the flesh. (pp. 3-4)

The actual suicide she attempted, and from which she was rescued only by great luck and accident, is very distressing in its details. The girl goes down into a cold, damp, cobwebbed corner of a cellar. There she hides herself behind an old log and takes fifty sleeping pills. The sense of downness, darkness, dankness, of unbearable rot and chill is savored for its ugliness and hurt. "They had to call and call / And pick the worms off me like sticky pearls" (**"Lady Lazarus"**).

In real life there was a police search, newspaper headlines, empty pill bottle discovered; it was dramatic, unforgettable. Sylvia Plath was found, sent to the hospital, had shock treatment, and "the bell jar" in which she had been suffocating was finally lifted. The novel is not equal to the poems, but it is free of gross defects and embarrassments. The ultimate effort was not made, perhaps, but it is limited more in its intentions than in the rendering. The book has an interestingly cold, unfriendly humor. We sympathize with the heroine because of her drudging facing of it all and because of her suffering. The suffering is described more or less empirically, as if it were a natural thing, and the pity flows over you partly because she herself is so hard and glassy about her life.

This autobiographical work is written in a bare, rather collegiate 1950s style, and yet the attitude, the distance and bitter carelessness are colored by a deep mood of affectlessness. The pleasures and sentiments of youth—wanting to be invited to the Yale prom, losing your virginity—are rather unreal in a scenario of disintegration, anger, and a perverse love of the horrible. The seduction of Esther Greenwood, as the heroine is called, is memorably grotesque and somehow bleakly suitable. The act led to a dangerous, lengthy, very unusual hemorrhaging. The blood—an obsession with the author—flows so plentifully that the girl is forced to seek medical help. She rather grimly pursues the young man with demands that he pay the doctor's bill, as if in some measure to get revenge for an action she herself cooperated with in the interest of experience.

The atrocious themes, the self-enclosure, the pain, blood, fury, infatuation with the hideous—all of that is in *The Bell Jar.* But, in a sense, softly, hesitantly. (p. 4)

> *Elizabeth Hardwick, "On Sylvia Plath," in* The New York Review of Books, *Vol. XVII, No. 2, August 12, 1971, pp. 3-4, 6.*

Marjorie G. Perloff

Now that Sylvia Plath has become the darling of those very ladies' magazines that she satirized so mercilessly in *The Bell Jar,* critics have begun to question her claims to literary eminence. Irving Howe, for example, in ["Sylvia Plath: A Partial Disagreement"], a recent reconsideration of Sylvia Plath's poetry, asks, "what illumination—moral, psychological, social—can be provided of . . . the general human condition by a writer so deeply rooted in the extremity of her plight? Suicide is an eternal possibility of our life and therefore always interesting; but what is the relation between a sensibility so deeply captive to the idea of suicide and the claims and possibilities of human existence in general?"

These are by no means easy questions to answer, especially in the case of *The Bell Jar,* which was, after all, originally published under a pseudonym because Sylvia Plath herself regarded it as an "autobiographical apprenticework," a confession which, so she told A. Alvarez, she had to write in order to free herself from the past. The novel's enormous popularity, it would seem, has less to do with any artistic merits it may have than with its inherently titillating subject matter. As the dust jacket of the Harper edition so melodramatically puts it, "this extraordinary work chronicles the crackup of Esther Greenwood: brilliant, beautiful, enormously talented, successful—but slowly going under, and maybe for the last time." (pp. 507-08)

I do not think, in short, that subject matter alone can account for *The Bell Jar's* popular appeal. The novel's most enthusiastic admirers, after all, have been the young, who tend to take health, whether physical or mental, enormously for granted, and whose preoccupations, a decade after *The Bell Jar* was written and two decades after the period with which it deals, are far removed from the fashion world of the *Mademoiselle* College Board, the Barbizon Hotel for Women, the Yale Junior Prom, or even the particular conditions under which shock therapy is likely to benefit the schizophrenic. Yet, although it deals with the now hopelessly anachronistic college world of proms and petting, *The Bell Jar* has become for the young of the early seventies what *Catcher in the Rye* was to their counterparts of the fifties: the archetypal novel that mirrors, in however distorted a form, their own personal experience, their sense of what Irving Howe calls "the general human condition." (p. 508)

In *The Divided Self,* R. D. Laing gives this description of the split between inner self and outer behavior that characterizes the schizoid personality: "The 'inner self' is occupied in phantasy and observation. It observes the processes of perception and action. Experience does not impinge . . . directly on this self, and the individual's acts are the provinces of a false-self system." The condition Laing describes is precisely that of Esther at the beginning of the novel. For example, when Jay Cee, the *Ladies' Day* editor, asks Esther, "What do you have in mind after you graduate?" Esther's inner self observes her own external response with strange detachment: " 'I don't really know,' *I heard myself say.* . . . It sounded true, and I recognized it, the way you recognize some nondescript person that's been hanging around your door for ages and then suddenly comes up and introduces himself as your real father and looks exactly like you, so you know he really is your father, and the person you thought all your life was your father is a sham" (italics mine). In a similarly detached way, Esther listens to the words of Elly Higginbottom, the name she has suddenly and inexplicably adopted in order to cope with the stranger who has picked her up on Times Square. But while Elly prattles on, Esther's real self becomes "a small dot" and finally "a hole in the ground."

If we take the division of Esther's self as the motive or

starting point of the novel's plot, the central action of *The Bell Jar* may be described as the attempt to heal the fracture between inner self and false-self system so that a real and viable identity can come into existence. But because, as Laing reminds us, "everyone in some measure wears a mask," Esther's experience differs from that of so-called "normal" girls in degree rather than in kind. It is simply a stylized or heightened version of the young American girl's quest to forge her own identity, to be herself rather than what others expect her to be.

The dust jacket image of Esther as the brilliant, beautiful, successful girl who is somehow "going under" is, to begin with, wholly misleading. The Esther others see is, from the very first page of the novel, an elaborate contrivance, an empty shell: the fashionable Smith girl with her patent leather bag and matching pumps, the poised guest editor, brainy but no bookworm, equally at home on the dance floor or behind the typewriter. The novel's flashbacks make clear that Esther has always played those roles others have wanted her to play. For her mother, she has been the perfect *good girl*, "trained at a very early age and . . . no trouble whatsoever. [It is fascinating to compare this reference to Esther's infancy with the account given by the mother of "Julie," the chronic schizophrenic studied in the final chapter of *Divided Self*: "Julie was never a demanding baby. She was weaned without difficulty. Her mother had no bother with her from the day she took off nappies completely when she was fifteen months old. She was never 'a trouble'."]. For Mr. Manzi, her physics professor, she is the ideal student, even though she secretly loathes the "hideous, cramped, scorpion-lettered formulas" with which he covers the blackboard. For Buddy Willard, her one serious boyfriend, she is all sweetness and acquiescence. When, for example, Buddy disparages her literary aspirations with the profound remark that a poem is really only "a piece of dust," Esther masks her outrage and replies humbly, "I guess so." Or when, after their first kiss, Buddy says admiringly, "I guess you go out with a lot of boys," Esther, falling in line with his image of her as Popular Girl on Campus, answers, "Well, I guess I do." Even when Buddy has the ridiculous idea that it is time for the virginal Esther to "see a man" and suggests that he disrobe for her inspection, she answers, "Well, all right, I guess so." And the more the false self responds in this contrived and artificial way, the more Esther's inner self nurtures a hatred for Buddy.

The scenes in the present which lead up to Esther's breakdown reveal the same pattern. For Doreen, Esther wears the mask of tough cookie, willing to be picked up by strangers on downtown street corners. For Betsy from the Middle West, she is the fun girl who likes fur shows. For Constantin, the simultaneous interpreter at the UN, she is a no-nonsense type, preparing for a career as war correspondent. Perhaps the final action committed by Esther's external self is the terrible forced smile she bestows on the *Ladies' Day* photographers . . ., a smile that suddenly dissolves in tears. Here the false-self system finally crumbles, and the old Esther must die before she can be reborn as a human being.

Recurrent mirror and light images measure Esther's descent into the stale air beneath the bell jar. In the first chapter, when Esther returns from Lenny's apartment and enters the mirrored elevator of the Amazon Hotel, she notices "a big, smudgy-eyed Chinese woman staring idiotically into my face. It was only me, of course. I was appalled to see how wrinkled and used up I looked." As the self becomes increasingly disembodied, the reflection in the mirror gradually becomes a stranger. Having symbolically killed her false self by throwing her clothes to the winds from the hotel rooftop, Esther rides home on the train to the Boston suburbs and notes that "The face in the mirror looked like a sick Indian." But the "two diagonal lines of dried blood" on her cheeks do not perturb her, for her body no longer seems real. Appearances do not count—Esther no longer washes or changes clothes or puts on make-up—and yet she is constantly afraid of being recognized by others. "In a world full of dangers," writes Laing, "to be a potentially seeable object is to be constantly exposed to danger. . . . The obvious defence against such a danger is to make oneself invisible in one way or another." Thus Esther, hiding behind the bedroom shutters, feels Dodo Conway's "gaze pierce through the white clapboard and pink wallpaper roses and uncover me"; she finds the early morning light so oppressive that she crawls beneath the mattress to escape it, but it seems as if "the mattress was not heavy enough," and, after twenty-one sleepless nights, Esther thinks that "the most beautiful thing in the world must be shadow." Only by returning to the womb in the shape of the basement crawl space at her mother's house and then gulping down a bottle of sleeping pills, does she hope to find the "dark . . . thick as velvet," which is the darkness of death.

Esther's body is recalled to life fairly easily, but the self that emerges from her suicide attempt is hopelessly disembodied. When she looks into the mirror the hospital nurse reluctantly brings her, Esther thinks, "It wasn't a mirror at all, but a picture. You couldn't tell whether the person in the picture was a man or a woman, because their hair was shaved off and sprouted in bristly chicken-feather tufts all over their head. One side of the person's face was purple. . . . The most startling thing about the face was its supernatural conglomeration of bright colors." It is only when she smiles at this funny face, and "the mouth in the mirror cracked into a grin," that Esther is reminded of her identity and sends the mirror crashing to the floor. It will take a long time to pick up the pieces.

But why is Esther's inner self so precarious, so disembodied in the first place? Why must she invent such an elaborate set of masks with which to face the world? To label Esther as "schizophrenic" and leave it at that does not take us very far. For Sylvia Plath's focus in *The Bell Jar* is not on mental illness per se, but on the relationship of Esther's private psychosis to her larger social situation. Indeed, her dilemma seems to have a great deal to do with being a woman in a society whose guidelines for women she can neither accept nor reject. It is beautifully ironic that Sylvia Plath, who never heard of Women's Liberation . . . has written one of the most acute analyses of the feminist problem that we have in contemporary fiction. What makes *The Bell Jar* so moving—and often so marvelously funny—is that the heroine is just as innocent as she is frighteningly perceptive. Far from rejecting the stereotyped world which she inhabits—a world whose madness often seems much more intense than Esther's own—she is determined to conquer it. Fulfillment, the novel implies, must come here or not at all; there is no better world around the corner or across the ocean. Thus Esther's quest for identity centers around her repeated attempts—sometimes funny, but always painful—to find both a female model whom she can emulate and a man whom she need not despise. (pp. 508-12)

Prior to her summer in New York, Esther's world has been safely circumscribed: like a racehorse, she has been "running after good marks and prizes and grants of one sort and another" for as long as she can remember. Now for the first time, she is presented with real alternatives. What does it mean to be a woman, she wonders, and which of the female roles she has studied by observing those around her should she play? Esther is particularly aware of this problem because the person who should be her model—her mother—cannot help her. Characterized in only a few brief flashes, Mrs. Greenwood is a terrifying presence in the novel, and one can hardly be surprised that Sylvia Plath's mother, recognizing herself in the portrait, tried to suppress the book's publication. [In her biographical note on *The Bell Jar,* Lois Ames cites a letter that Aurelia Plath wrote to Harper & Row in 1970: "Practically every character in *The Bell Jar* represents someone—often in caricature—whom Sylvia loved; each person had given freely of time, thought, affection, and, in one case, financial help during those agonizing six months of breakdown in 1953. . . . As this book stands by itself, it represents the basest ingratitude. That was not the basis of Sylvia's personality. . . ." Here Mrs. Plath unintentionally reveals that, precisely like the mother in the novel, she could only regard her daughter's mental illness as an insult to herself. In view of Sylvia Plath's subsequent suicide, it seems strangely irrelevant to talk of her "basest ingratitude."] Here is Esther's first reference to her mother:

> My own mother wasn't much help. My mother had taught shorthand and typing to support us ever since my father died, and secretly she hated it and hated him for dying and leaving no money because he didn't trust life insurance salesmen. She was always on to me to learn shorthand after college, so I'd have a practical skill as well as a college degree. "Even the apostles were tentmakers," she'd say. "They had to live, just the way we do."

The image is one of a hopelessly rigid, strong-willed, loveless person who has survived the battle of life only by reducing it to neat little proverbs and formulas. When her daughter becomes so overtly psychotic that she can neither eat, sleep, nor wash herself, this mother reasons with her sweetly and blandly. When Esther refuses to return to the frightening Dr. Gordon, her first psychiatrist, her mother replies triumphantly, "I *knew* you'd *decide* to be all right again." At the end of the novel, when Esther contemplates her impending return to the world outside the asylum walls, she thinks: "My mother's face floated to mind, a pale reproachful moon, at her last and first visit to the asylum since my twentieth birthday. A daughter in an asylum! I had done that to her. Still, she had obviously decided to forgive me."

Whether or not this portrait of the mother as uncomprehending martyr is unfair to the real-life Aurelia Plath seems to me totally beside the point. What matters is that her daughter *sees* her in this light. Given such a mother image, she must clearly find her models elsewhere. But where? In the course of her quest, Esther is attracted by a bewildering variety of female roles: Dodo Conway, Catholic mother of 6½, whose face is perpetually lit up by a "serene, almost religious smile"; Buddy Willard's mother, professor's wife and leading citizen, whose words of wisdom are regularly quoted by her brainwashed and adoring son; Doreen, the Southern blonde sex kitten who always knows how to get her man; Betsy, innocently happy and uncomplicated Midwestern fashion model; Jody, loyal friend, "practical and a sociology major," who instinctively knows how to spice up scrambled eggs; Philomena Guinea, best-selling novelist, whose endowed scholarship Esther holds at college; and finally, Jay Cee, the successful editor who "knew all the quality writers in the business." Even a Russian girl translator, whom Esther glimpses only briefly at the UN, becomes an object of envy: "I wished with all my heart I could crawl into her and spend the rest of my life barking out one idiom after another . . . ."

But although she envies Dodo's placid contentment, Jay Cee's cleverness, and Betsy's innocence, Esther quickly discovers that each of these women is, despite her particular gift or talent, essentially a flawed human being. Doreen's intrinsic vulgarity and triviality are symbolized by her fluffy cotton candy blonde hair, which is, on close inspection, dark at the roots. Eternally pregnant Dodo is little more than a mindless misshapen animal. Refined and cultured Mrs. Willard lets her husband walk all over her as if she were one of the wool mats she makes as a hobby. Philomena Guinea's novels turn out to be endless soap operas, "crammed . . . with long suspenseful questions" like " 'Would Evelyn discern that Gladys knew Roger in her past?' wondered Hector feverishly." Jay Cee is a walking time clock, devouring manuscripts with mechanical regularity and reserving her emotional commitment for her potted plants. Betsy is "Pollyanna Cowgirl"; the Russian translator is no more than a "little pebble of efficiency among all the other pebbles"; and even Jody, the truly "nice" girl, seems to have a touch of Rosencrantz and Guildenstern in her when she plots with Mrs. Greenwood to distract Esther from her illness by taking her along on a double date.

It seems, in short, all but impossible for a woman to attain what Yeats called Unity of Being. In what I take to be the novel's key passage, Esther, sitting with Constantin "in one of those hushed plush auditoriums in the UN," has a vision of her life branching out like a green fig tree:

> From the tip of every branch, like a fat purple fig, a wonderful future beckoned and winked. One fig was a husband and a happy home and children, and another fig was a famous poet and another fig was a brilliant professor, and another fig was Ee Gee, the amazing editor, and another fig was Europe and Africa and South America, and another fig was Constantin and Socrates and Attila and a pack of other lovers with queer names and offbeat professions, and another fig was an Olympic lady crew champion, and beyond and above these figs were many more figs I couldn't quite make out.
>
> I saw myself sitting in the crotch of this fig tree, starving to death, just because I couldn't make up my mind which of the figs I would choose. I wanted each and every one of them, but choosing one meant losing all the rest, and, as I sat there, unable to decide, the figs began to wrinkle and go black, and, one by one, they plopped to the ground at my feet.

Esther's symbolic tree, appropriately bearing phallic figs, is the objectification of her central malaise, a malaise that is hardly confined to schizophrenics, however starkly and dramatically Sylvia Plath presents Esther's case. I would guess that every woman who reads this passage has felt, at one time or another, that "choosing one meant losing all the rest," that because female roles are no longer clearly defined, women are confronted by such a bewildering variety of seeming possibilities that choice itself becomes all but impossible.

But Sylvia Plath's feminism is never militant; Esther's diagnosis of her situation is totally devoid of self-pity or self-importance. Shortly after describing her vision of the fig tree, she beautifully undercuts her own high seriousness. The occasion is dinner in a Russian restaurant with Constantin: "I don't know what I ate, but I felt immensely better after the first mouthful. It occurred to me that my vision of the fig tree and all the fat figs that withered and fell to earth might well have arisen from the profound void of an empty stomach." So much, Plath sardonically implies, for the profound insights of the weaker sex!

Like her ambivalence to the women she meets, Esther's response to men is hopelessly divided. On the one hand, she is always looking for the perfect lover; on the other, experience repeatedly tells her that men are, however subtly, exploiters and hypocrites. Here, for example, is Esther observing the process of childbirth under the tutelage of her medical student boyfriend, Buddy Willard:

> The woman's stomach stuck up so high I couldn't see her face or the upper part of her body at all. She seemed to have nothing but an enormous spider-fat stomach and two little ugly spindly legs propped in the high stirrups, and all the time the baby was being born she never stopped making this unhuman whooing noise.
>
> Later Buddy told me the woman was on a drug that would make her forget she'd had any pain and that when she swore and groaned she really didn't know what she was doing because she was in a kind of twilight sleep.
>
> I thought it sounded just like the sort of drug a man would invent. Here was a woman in terrible pain, obviously feeling every bit of it or she wouldn't groan like that, and she would go straight home and start another baby, because the drug would make he forget how bad the pain had been, when all the time, in some secret part of her, that long, blind, doorless and windowless corridor of pain was waiting to open up and shut her in again.
>
> The head doctor . . . kept saying to the woman, "Push down, Mrs. Tomolillo, push down, that's a good girl, push down," and finally through the split, shaven place between her legs, lurid with disinfectant, I saw a dark fuzzy thing appear.

It is easy to dismiss Esther's reaction to the delivery as simply "sick"; here is a girl, one can argue, so full of self-loathing and insecurity that she cannot understand the beauty and wonder of a great "natural" event like childbirth. But then, who is it that has always told us of the wonders of childbirth if not men like Doctors Spock, Guttmacher, and the father of natural childbirth, Dr. Grantley Dick Read? Sylvia Plath forces us to forget all the usual clichés about incipient motherhood and to take

a good hard look at the birth process itself; her technique is, as Robert Scholes has argued in his excellent review of *The Bell Jar,* one of *defamiliarization* [See Plath's entry in *CLC,* Vol. 17]. The Russian critic Victor Shklovsky, who coined this term in 1917, held that "art removes objects from the automatism of perception"; its aim is to make "the familiar seem strange by not naming the familiar object." In this scene, for example, Sylvia Plath describes the delivery as if it were happening for the first time in history. From the point of view of the uninitiated observer, childbirth seems to be a frightening ritual in which a "dark fuzzy thing" finally emerges from "the split shaven place" between the woman's legs. In her state of heightened sensitivity, Esther shares the pain of Mrs. Tomolillo, with her "spider-fat stomach," "ugly, spindly legs propped in high stirrups," and "unhuman whooing noise." Only a man, Esther thinks, could conclude that when the woman "swore and groaned she really didn't know what she was doing." And, after witnessing the "sewing up of the woman's cut with a needle and long thread," Esther wonders, not irrationally, "if there were any other ways to have babies."

While Esther wholly identifies with the woman in labor, Buddy, contemplating the birth from his male point of view, is proud of the expert and efficient treatment his colleagues give the patient. As he and Esther leave the delivery room, she notes his "satisfied expression." And no wonder. For beneath the surface of his charming manners and his evident respect for bright articulate girls, Buddy harbors a cynical contempt for women, a contempt that leads him to play off the virginal Esther against the "dirty" waitress he sleeps with. A staunch believer in the double standard, Buddy accepts as axiomatic his mother's wise words that "What a man wants is a mate and what a woman wants is infinite security," or "What a man is is an arrow into the future and what a woman is is the place the arrow shoots off from." It follows that Buddy takes a dim view of woman writers. (pp. 512-17)

Because Esther is, in one sense, an innocent and inexperienced small town girl who drinks out of finger bowls and never knows how much to tip, it takes her some time to realize that "The last thing I wanted was infinite security and to be the place an arrow shoots off from. I wanted change and excitement and to shoot off in all directions myself, like the colored arrows from a Fourth of July rocket." Typing and shorthand—her mother's domain— become the symbols of male oppression: she rejects her mother's practical notion that "an English major who knew shorthand . . . would be in demand among all the up-and-coming young men and she would transcribe letter after thrilling letter." "The trouble was," Esther thinks, "I hated the idea of serving men in any way. I wanted to dictate my own thrilling letters." Naturally, then, Esther cannot love Constantin, the pleasant, polite, but thoroughly conventional UN translator, or Marco, the Latin American woman hater who literally forces her down into the dirt, or Dr. Gordon, the sinister psychiatrist, whose silver-framed family photograph, conspicuously placed on his desk facing the patient, is a tacit reminder that he, at any rate, is a "normal" American male, dwelling in a world of suburban lawns, cute children, and golden retrievers. Esther's final sexual encounter is the most ludicrous of all: having won what she thinks is freedom with the help of birth control, she arranges to have herself seduced by

Irwin, the bespectacled young math professor from Harvard, who takes girls to bed as thoughtlessly and mechanically as Jay Cee reads manuscripts. The outcome of this parody seduction is not passion but severe hemorrhage for Esther, a bloody wound emblematic of the spirit in which Irwin has made love to her—a spirit not of tenderness but of all-out war.

When one considers Irwin's strange unconcern about Esther's hemorrhage, one cannot help wondering who is "saner"—the girl who learns that losing her virginity is not, after all, a great and thrilling adventure, or the man who, ignoring the pain and fear of the girl he has just deflowered, gallantly kisses her hand and bids her goodnight. Whatever the extent of Esther's congenital predisposition to madness, the mad world she inhabits surely intensifies her condition. R. D. Laing's insistence [in his *The Politics of Experience*] that "the experience and behavior that gets labelled schizophrenic is a *special strategy that a person invents in order to live in an unlivable situation,*" may sound extreme but it seems wholly relevant to *The Bell Jar.*

Take, for example, the superbly rendered scene in which Esther, on the verge of total mental collapse, is persuaded to take a volunteer job at the local hospital by her mother's argument that "the cure for thinking too much about yourself was helping somebody who was worse off than you." Esther's job is to take around the patients' flowers, but when she notices, not at all unsensibly, that some are "droopy and brown at the edges," she discards the dead flowers and rearranges the bouquets as attractively as possible. Wheeling her trolley into the maternity ward, she finds that her "helpful smile" is greeted by a furious uproar:

> "Hey, where's my larkspur?" A large, flabby lady from across the ward raked me with an eagle eye.
>
> The sharp-faced blonde bent over the trolley. "Here are my yellow roses," she said, "but they're all mixed up with some lousy iris."

By the time the nurse has arrived on the scene to investigate the cause of the commotion, Esther is overcome by panic and bolts, a reaction that seems at least as sane as the righteous indignation of the women in curlers, "chattering like parrots in a parrot house," who occupy the hospital beds. By society's standards, however, Esther's emphasis on the aesthetics of flower arrangement rather than on its economics (the notion that every woman patient is *entitled* to the flowers bought for her) is dismissed as schizophrenic behavior.

Throughout the novel, Sylvia Plath emphasizes the curious similarity of physical and mental illness as if to say that both are symbolic of a larger condition which is our life today. *The Bell Jar* opens with the following sentence: "It was a queer, sultry summer, the summer they electrocuted the Rosenbergs, and I didn't know what I was doing in New York." This reference to electrocution sets the scene for everything that is to come: before the novel is over, Esther herself will know only too well what it feels like to be "burned alive all along your nerves." The terrible electric shock therapy that Dr. Gordon makes her undergo is a frightening counterpart of the Rosenbergs' punishment; "I wondered," Esther thinks as she goes under, "what terrible thing it was that I had done." Even the bare

room in which the shock treatment is administered resembles the Rosenbergs' prison cell: the windows are barred, and "everything that opened and shut was fitted with a keyhole so it could be locked up."

From the start, when Esther contemplates the terrible fate of the Rosenbergs, sickness is everywhere around her; it begins when Esther finds the drunken Doreen lying on the floor of the hotel corridor: "A jet of brown vomit flew from her mouth and spread in a large puddle at my feet." Here, Sylvia Plath suggests, is the real picture of the desirable debutante, whose smiling photographs grace the pages of the fashion magazines. A similar deception motif occurs in the account of the banquet given by the *Ladies' Day* Food Testing kitchens, at which every girl lucky enough to attend gets ptomaine poisoning from the beautiful avocados stuffed with crabmeat. (pp. 517-19)

In the world of *The Bell Jar,* no one is exempt from illness. Even Buddy Willard, the all-American boy who radiates good health, develops tuberculosis and has to spend a winter in a sanatorium. "TB," he writes Esther, "is like living with a bomb in your lung. . . . You just lie around very quietly hoping it won't go off." There are interesting parallels between Buddy's physical illness and Esther's mental one. Just as Mr. Willard cannot stand the sight of Buddy's sickness "because he thought all sickness was sickness of the will," so Esther's mother is unable to face the truth that her daughter's illness will not disappear by *willing* it to stop. . . . [Both] the TB patient and the mental patient engage in occupational therapy: Buddy makes clay pots while the girls at the asylum play the piano or badminton. "What was there about us, in Belsize," Esther wonders, "so different from the girls playing bridge and gossiping and studying in the college to which I would return? Those girls, too, sat under bell jars of a sort."

Sylvia Plath is no silly sentimentalist; she knows quite well that her heroine *is* different from most college girls, that her bell jar is less fragile, less easy to remove than theirs. But the external or official distinction between madness and sanity, she suggests in her linkage of physical and mental illness, is largely illusory. When, to take the novel's most striking example, Esther breaks her leg skiing, Buddy—and the world at large—regard her broken leg as the most normal of accidents. Yet Esther's account of her mental state as she plummets down the slope suggests that she is never closer to insanity than at this particular moment. A novice skier, she suddenly conceives an overwhelming desire to fly off into "the great, gray eye of the sky." Like the ecstatic speaker of **"Ariel,"** who longs to make the "Suicidal" leap "Into the red / Eye, the cauldron of morning," Esther longs for the annihilation of death. "People and trees receded on either hand like the dark sides of a tunnel as I hurtled on to the still, bright point at the end of it, the pebble at the bottom of the well, the white sweet baby cradled in its mother's belly." Yet this suicidal leap earns Esther no more than a plaster cast, whereas her later, not unrelated suicide attempt precipitates her admission to the dangerous ward of the hospital.

The plot of *The Bell Jar* moves from physical sickness (the ptomaine poisoning) to mental illness and back to the physical, culminating in Esther's hemorrhage. The arrangement of incidents implies that all illness is to be viewed as part of the same spectrum: disease, whether mental or physical, is an index to the human inability to cope with an unlivable situation. For who can master a world where the Testing Kitchens of the leading women's magazine poison all of its guest editors, where a reputable psychiatrist asks a girl, on the verge of suicide, whether there is a WAC station at her college?

But Esther does come back to life. At the end of *The Bell Jar,* her external situation has not appreciably changed—she has found neither a lover nor her future vocation—but now she can view that situation differently. Having passed through death, she learns, with the help of Dr. Nolan, to forge a new identity. It is important to note that Dr. Nolan, the only wholly admirable woman in the novel, is also the only woman whom Esther never longs to imitate or to resemble. The point is that Dr. Nolan serves not as model but as anti-model; she is the instrument whereby Esther learns to be, not some other woman, but herself. The new Esther takes off the mask: she openly rejects Joan's lesbian advances; she can cope with Irwin as well as with Buddy. Best of all, the world of nature, distorted and fragmented in the opening pages of the novel when Esther walks through the "granite canyons" of Manhattan, is no longer inaccessible. Shovelling Buddy's car out of the snow, Esther watches with pleasure as the sun emerges from the clouds: "Pausing in my work to overlook that pristine expanse, I felt the same profound thrill it gives me to see trees and grassland waist-high under flood water—as if the usual order of the world had shifted slightly, and entered a new phase."

As if the usual order of the world had shifted slightly. . . . When Esther pauses on the threshold of the room where the hospital board is waiting to pass final sentence on her, she still sees her future as a series of "question marks," but she has learned something very important. Isolation, Sylvia Plath suggests, the terrible isolation Esther feels when, one by one, her props crumble, is paradoxically the result of negating one's own separateness. The hardest thing in the world to do—and it is especially hard when one is young, female, and highly gifted—is simply to be oneself. Only when Esther recognizes that she will never be a Jody, a Jay Cee, a Doreen, or a Mrs. Guinea, that she will never marry a Buddy Willard, a Constantin, or a Dr. Gordon, that she wants no lesbian affairs with a Joan or a Dee Dee—does the bell jar lift, letting Esther once again breath "the circulating air." As a schizophrenic, Esther is, of course, a special case, but her intensity of purpose, her isolation, her suffering, and finally her ability to survive it all with a sense of humor, make her an authentic, indeed an exemplary heroine of the seventies.

When one compares Esther to Carson McCullers' Frankie Addams, the heroine of *The Member of the Wedding,* written in 1946, the contemporary appeal of *The Bell Jar,* especially for the young, is readily understood. Both Frankie and Esther are sensitive young girls, isolated from friends and family and unable to express their most deep-seated feelings to anyone. But whereas Frankie "gets over" her difficult tomboy stage as well as her brief incarnation as F. Jasmine, the vamp, and emerges at the end of the novel as a happy high school girl, who can share her new interest in Michelangelo and Tennyson with an ideal close friend, Esther can never forget what her mother so ludicrously calls "a bad dream." On the contrary, she remembers everything:

> I remembered the cadavers and Doreen and the

story of the fig tree and Marco's diamond and the sailor on the Common and Doctor Gordon's wall-eyed nurse and the broken thermometers and the Negro with his two kinds of beans and the twenty pounds I gained on insulin and the rock that bulged between sky and sea like a gray skull.

> Maybe forgetfulness, like a kind snow, should numb and cover them.

> But they were part of me. They were my landscape.

Esther's landscape, with its confusing assortment of cadavers and diamonds, thermometers and beans, is, in heightened form, *our* landscape. When Ibsen's Nora slammed the door of her doll's house and embarked on a new life, she nobly refused to take with her any of Torvald's property. The New Woman, I would posit, will not let men off that easily. Esther, having undergone emergency treatment for the hemorrhage induced by Irwin's love-making, calmly sends him the bill. (pp. 519-22)

> *Marjorie G. Perloff, "'A Ritual for Being Born Twice': Sylvia Plath's 'The Bell Jar',"* in Contemporary Literature, *Vol. 13, No. 4, Autumn, 1972, pp. 507-22.*

Mary Allen

In Sylvia Plath's story **"The Fifteen-Dollar Eagle,"** a weathered tattoo artist imaginatively embellishes his customers with colorful images from his own fantasies and from theirs: for one woman, a huge butterfly on the upper legs which appears to flutter every time she moves; for another, the complete scene of Calvary projected on her back. Carmey's wild tales of tattooing are halted when his own Wife appears, a large fleshy woman who hates tattoos. She will oblige none of his artistry on her, remaining "death-lily-white and totally bare—the body of a woman immune as a nun to the eagle's anger, the desire of the rose." Like this resistant woman, and the persona of most of Plath's poetry, Esther Greenwood of *The Bell Jar* spitefully defies the role of *tabula rasa* for the projection of men's images of their dreams and of themselves. Not that this alone is the subject of her scorn, for she is repelled by life generally. But while we may never fully understand her reasons for attempting suicide (there is little self-analysis), her disgust of life is shown expressly in terms of being a woman.

No woman in American literature is quite so thoroughly repulsed by what women are as is Esther Greenwood. She is an unusually ambitious girl, successful in every apparent way with fifteen years of straight A's behind her, who has now won a contest to work for *Ladies' Day* fashion magazine in New York for one month in the summer. (Sylvia Plath won the award to work for *Mademoiselle* in 1953.) But what could be a thrilling experience is a deadening one, like all others in her adult life. The summer concludes with several suicide attempts, all made the more terrible to the reader by the fact of Plath's own suicide in 1963, one month after publication of *The Bell Jar.*

Like Joyce Carol Oates, Sylvia Plath is obsessed with images of blood. Both women see things disintegrating in a world filled with signs of death, where women find no hint of the romantic in their lives and are disgusted by their bodies. But one great difference between the two writers is the intimidation Oates's women feel in relation to outside forces in contrast with the disdain of Esther Greenwood, who projects much more of her own will, self-destructive as it is. If she cannot control what society expects of her, she does dramatically register her disgust for how she is supposed to live and how she is to look, which is perhaps the most overwhelming fact of herself a woman must cope with.

While she is not unattractive, Esther never considers herself a beauty and is overwhelmed by the world of fashion among the clientele of *Ladies' Day*. Like them she buys glossy patent leather shoes from Bloomingdale's, symbolic of the surfacy nature of style. She is at the same time repulsed and envious of girls who are bored by too many love affairs and who spend their days painting their fingernails and keeping up Bermuda tans. The Amazon Hotel, where only girls stay, is presumed by their mothers to keep them safely away from men, announcing an attitude held throughout **The Bell Jar** that men are polluters. Female conversation disgusts Esther, but she is sickeningly drawn to it. She is in awe of the glittery Doreen, who dwells on such trivia as the way she and her friends at college make pocketbook covers of the same material as their clothes so that each outfit matches. Esther confesses that "this kind of detail impressed me. It suggested a whole life of marvelous, elaborate decadence that attracted me like a magnet." Aware of her intrigue with what appalls her, Esther increasingly loathes herself, realizing the great extent to which her image of herself is based on the objects of fashion. A gift for each girl when she arrives in New York is a makeup kit, created exactly for a person of such-and-such a color, the first essential item in establishing her new life. Each girl is photographed carrying a prop to indicate her identity: an ear of corn for one who looks forward to being a farmer's wife, a gold-embroidered sari for another who plans on being a social worker in India. Before Esther leaves New York she mocks a suicide by abandoning her props, the fashionable clothes that have identified her, letting each item float down over the city from the top of her hotel as a way of renouncing the standards of fashion and also of obliterating herself. The climax of Esther's encounter with New York's world of fashion, dramatically proving it to be insidious, comes when a luncheon sponsored by *Ladies' Day* results in the ptomaine poisoning of all the girls who attend.

After her distressing stay in New York, Esther returns to Massachusetts, where she attempts suicide in a way that is particularly gross in terms of its physical distortions. She is found slumped in a crevice in her basement after a dosage of sleeping pills, her face puffed out of shape and badly discolored. The nurse at the hospital has been instructed not to allow her a mirror to see the ugliness, but Esther finds one and takes a look. . . . Esther's attempt to destroy herself is linked specifically with the destruction of her beauty, not merely in the sense that all death is decay, but that by obliterating herself as an object of sexual appeal she can attack the role expected of her as a woman.

The preoccupation with appearance has everything to do with woman as a commodity for man. In her poem **"The Applicant"** Plath poses the prospective bride as an applicant before the buyer bridegroom and his family. She is scrutinized carefully for possible physical imperfections:

"Do you wear / A glass eye . . . / Rubber breasts or a rubber crotch, / Stitches to show something's missing?" Her useful hand becomes a metaphor for the bride's identity as a whole, the bride who is an "it." If "it" does all you tell it, the poet continues sarcastically, "Will you marry it?" At the husband's death, "it" is guaranteed to "dissolve of sorrow," having nothing left of self when the husband is gone.

Esther's loathing of men equals her loathing of women, but she is not obsessed by them and their ways. She is that rare woman who can (once she learns how) truly and devastatingly dismiss men, reducing them to objects for discard. In a brilliant tour de force of the usual male seduction of the virgin, Esther, determined to rid herself of her virginity, which weighs "like a millstone" around her neck, seduces a young professor she picks up on the steps of the Widener Library. Naive but spiteful, she passively requires him to take all the action. He carries her to the bed, where she lazily waits for the event to take place. "I lay, rapt and naked, on Irwin's rough blanket, waiting for the miraculous change to make itself felt. . . . But all I felt was a sharp, startlingly bad pain." If Esther ever had any romantic notions about sexual experience or men, they are permanently dispelled at this cynical stage in her life. In the next few weeks she pesters the bewildered professor to pay off her hospital bill but refuses ever to see him again. Her callousness throughout this brief affair constitutes a thoroughly amoral deflowering of the virgin. The effect of seduction on her is sheerly physical, as she hemorrhages. Otherwise she feels nothing. The same absence of sympathetic emotions is evident in Esther's defiance of Buddy Willard's offer of marriage. The idea of marrying him is so ridiculous her only impulse is to laugh.

But while she is in New York Esther is caught in the old game of trying to be attractive and desirable to men, a need repulsive to her which battles with her impulse to refuse them callously. (Such conflicts between her scorn of conventional attitudes about women and her bondage to them are found throughout the novel.) No idea is more central to the concept of the American girl found here than that of her passion for popularity, which figures above all other considerations, certainly above her value as a good student. In college when Esther is discovered to have a date to the Yale prom she is suddenly thrust into the limelight, something no quantity of good grades is capable of doing. In New York the proof of popularity is established by success with strangers. The first test case is a man in cowboy boots who strolls up to Esther and Doreen, dressed in their best and waiting in the back seat of a taxi. Esther senses that he has come for Doreen, and once this choice is made, putting her at the center of attention, Esther feels herself "melting into the shadows like the negative of a person I'd never seen before in my life." Although there is nothing in this unknown man that she likes or admires, he has the power, by ignoring her, to reduce her self-esteem to nothing. Later in the man's apartment, as he and Doreen grow increasingly intimate, Esther is conscious of herself "shrinking to a small black dot." A further rejection comes from Constantin, the interpreter at the United Nations whom she selects to be her first lover, but who disappointingly makes no attempt to seduce her. From this experience she concludes that she is not only unattractive but intellectually dull: "I thought if only I had a keen, shapely bone structure to my face or could discuss politics shrewdly or was a famous writer Constantin might find me interesting enough to sleep with." Esther looks on at her own adventures with disdain but is unable to free herself of her attitudes, which are expressed with wry honesty and self-loathing.

Esther's revenge on the world for making sexual appeal so important is her rejection and scorn of Buddy Willard, the boy she adores from afar for several years before he finally proposes to her. At first he is a savior, rescuing her from the ordeal of a different blind date each Saturday night and the drab status of bookworm. But getting to know him better she discovers the flaws she always finds in men at close quarters. The ultimate putdown of this ultra-eligible male hero results when, as a gesture of his male pride in a move to both shock and condescend to her, he offers to let her see him in the nude. She has never before seen a man, and he intends this to be one of her great adventures. Esther recalls (with Plath's sarcastic relish of cliché) that her mother and grandmother always said "what a fine, clean boy Buddy Willard was, coming from such a fine, clean family, and how everybody at church thought he was a model person." If he is so clean and fine, she imagines, it must surely be fine to see his clean body. But there is no awe or shock in her response, just the same dulled reaction she has for everything else, which is the perfect putdown: "Then he just stood there in front of me and I kept staring at him. The only thing I could think of was turkey neck and turkey gizzards and I felt very depressed." (pp. 160-65)

Esther sees Buddy as foolish rather than unfortunate for being hospitalized with the tuberculosis he contracts from his work in the hospital. She is relieved to learn that he will be kept out of her way and especially charmed that the good health he was so proud of is gone. Having gained a lot of weight in the sanatorium, Buddy is more ridiculous than ever. At this point he proposes, giving Esther the opportunity to become Mrs. Buddy Willard, which she would have swooned over a few years before. But it now seems hardly worth her trouble even to explain why she could not consider marrying him. He says she is crazy, believing quite sincerely that any girl would be insane to refuse such an offer. She too, to some degree, considers herself a fool for violating the college girl's dream of marrying a handsome medical student, source of wealth and status. But if Buddy and his offer represent a sane choice, she will gladly be considered insane. Horrified at the thought of his mother, who braids fine rugs from her husband's old suits to make kitchen mats that go dull in a few days, Esther knows that what Buddy "secretly wanted when the wedding service ended was for her to flatten out underneath his feet like Mrs. Willard's kitchen mat." She not only despises humiliating service, but she hates "the idea of serving men in any way."

Esther's first big disillusionment with Buddy comes when she finds out that he is not a virgin (she is), an instance revealing her competitiveness and the determination to have as much as men have. She claims bitterly that Buddy is a hypocrite for pretending sexual innocence (which he has never done in any specific way), but the real reason for her anger is that he is one experience ahead of her. She decides she must be seduced in order to catch up. The pursuit of such an experience is entirely sexless, and yet the idea of it as an overwhelming issue remains, not so from any feel-

ing of her own but because of the social import of the event. It is so significant to her at the age of nineteen that "instead of the world being divided up into Catholics and Protestants or Republicans and Democrats or white men and black men or even men and women, I saw the world divided into people who had slept with somebody and people who hadn't."

Purity is a great issue of Esther's time, leaving her at the age of nineteen, arriving in New York as a prize-winning scholar, incredibly naive. Vague information about birth control has filtered to her, but the most emphatic propaganda comes from such tracts as "In Defense of Chastity" from the *Reader's Digest*, admonishing the young girl, "better be safe than sorry." It occurs to Esther that although the article is written by a woman it does not consider the feelings of the girl, an omission reflecting the puritanical notion that sexual pleasure is for men only. Far from representing a hedonistic urge, however, Esther's quest for sexual experience resembles her quest for death, significantly resulting in the blood flow that could have been fatal.

The deflowering of Esther is a bitingly funny scene, reducing the bewildered victim Irwin to the moronic as he fetches towels for his bleeding stranger. After one evening with him she is ready for purity again, vainly craving chastity now that she is convinced of men's worthlessness. Esther is unique among women for being able to ridicule sex, belittle the male, and then turn from men altogether, something Oates's women are incapable of doing. For none of them is there any expectation of pleasure to come from men. But Esther escapes the painful dependency that most women suffer. (pp. 165-67)

Esther sees men very much in types, as predators and as fools. There is little reflection on the death of her father in *The Bell Jar,* which might have changed this view, although she does visit his grave. Plath admittedly uses a persona with an Electra complex in her poetry, but that is not the case here. Mr. Greenwood's death is not shown to have had the profound effect on Esther that Mr. Plath's death had on Sylvia. Even though Esther loathes most women, they are much more individualized and important to her than men are. Many of the women she knows are grotesques, awful images of what she could become if she were to marry and remain in a small town as her mother has done. Very few are admirable. But only women have the possibility of helping her—from the wealthy female novelist, Philomena Guinea, who provides Esther's scholarship, to the female psychiatrist who is responsible for helping her recover from a nervous breakdown.

Esther's mother is a model of the mundane, exhibiting well-meaning but plodding tendencies that are reflected in the lethargy of her daughter. Always faithfully attending to her child, in and out of the hospital, she offers platitudinous encouragement in place of realistic appraisal of her daughter's condition. According to Esther, she never tells her what to do and reasons with her like one intelligent being with another—just the thing to infuriate Esther, to whom reasoning is as meaningless as other formulas. If this mother represents the perpetuation of life, then her child rebels by wishing to end it. After the suicide attempt, Esther must face her mother's sorrowful expression and pathetic questions: "She was sure the doctors thought she had done something wrong because they asked her a lot of questions about my toilet training, and I had been perfectly trained at a very early age and given her no trouble whatsoever." Mrs. Greenwood's belief that a cure "for thinking too much about yourself" is to help somebody "worse off than you" has no relevance to Esther, who for a short time makes a fumbling attempt at charity work in a hospital, with no resultant enlightenment. Like all clichés in *The Bell Jar,* the mother's conventionality is irrelevant and stupid.

But if her own mother cannot help her, Esther seeks a surrogate mother. The worst possible choice she could make would be Mrs. Willard, her potential mother-in-law, whom she hates for her subservience in her home as well as for the way she exemplifies the petty strictures of society. As Esther strolls with a sailor in downtown Boston, boldly letting his arm linger around her waist, she imagines Mrs. Willard to be watching her and instinctively pulls away from the man. The girls Esther meets in New York are, with their shallow sorrows, to which Esther becomes cold-bloodedly indifferent, no more suitable substitutes for mother. When Doreen comes in late after drinking and shakes Esther out of sleep, she feels no compunction at leaving the inebriated girl lying in a pool of vomit in the hall and returning as naturally to bed. "I made a decision about Doreen that night. I decided I would watch her and listen to what she said, but deep down I would have nothing at all to do with her." After the fatal luncheon where the girls are food poisoned, it is during a technicolor movie of boys playing football and girls going to the powder room to say catty things that Esther becomes nauseous, signifying her revulsion against the way the fashion world and the collegiate world exemplify women.

Esther does respect her supervisor at *Ladies' Day,* Jay Cee, a woman the girls immediately label by appearance "ugly as sin." Perhaps it is because she is homely that Esther likes the woman, who, true to the type, appears capable because she cannot be beautiful. Sensitive to something disturbed in her bright young apprentice, Jay Cee calls Esther in to discuss her future. But Esther, in no condition to will her life at the moment, only wishes she had had "a mother like Jay Cee. Then I'd know what to do." The scarcity of female models she can look to is clearly a factor in Esther's limited view of her own life.

When Esther first seeks psychiatric help, the doctor is not the somber and perceptive man she had expected, but rather a handsome and jovial fellow with a photo of his happy family beaming up from the desk. The image is repulsive. What can he say to her? Can he tell her why everything seems so silly because people all die in the end? After shock treatments, which cause a major trauma for Esther, she at last meets a friend, Doctor Nolan, a female psychiatrist who wisely promises her she will not be required to see any more visitors. This woman becomes almost directly a replacement of Esther's mother: in a corner of the hospital room are a dozen long-stemmed roses from Mrs. Greenwood for her daughter's birthday—now stuffed in a trash can. What Esther appreciates in Doctor Nolan is not her training but her natural understanding. Surprisingly affectionate for one in her professional position, she hugs Esther before accompanying her to shock therapy, which she promises will not be traumatic as it was the first time. Esther, the frightened child, pleads with her to be there when the treatments are over. On one occasion she asks Doctor Nolan, " 'What does a woman see in a woman that she can't see in a man?' " The answer is " 'Tenderness.' . . . That shut me up." Characteristics most often attributed to women such as gentleness, and particularly intuition, are the qualities Esther values most. At one point she holds Buddy Willard's scientific mind in awe, but she soon comes to regard him as a fool when she detects his lack of understanding. Only in Constantin does she find the quality she says no American man could have—intuition. She feels that he would not mind a little thing like her being taller than he is. But Esther's real affections are reserved for Doctor Nolan, who proves more worthy than anyone else to be mother and friend.

Sylvia Plath creates antagonism for the mom in *The Bell Jar,* but Mrs. Greenwood is not a clever manipulator. She is only a dowdy and disgusting image of what Esther is determined not to become. Mrs. Greenwood's niceness and her industry to support the family after her husband's death, at a seemingly dull job of teaching shorthand, are repellent to her highly ambitious daughter. Ahead of her time, Esther blasphemes the mystique that a girl must be beautiful, get married, raise children, and do dull work. (pp. 167-70)

Esther's refusal to marry the eligible medical student is a kind of suicidal act in itself. She sees marriage as the plot of men for the subjection of women, especially talented women: "I also remembered Buddy Willard saying in a sinister, knowing way that after I had children I would feel differently, I wouldn't want to write poems any more. So I began to think maybe it was true that when you were married and had children it was like being brainwashed, and afterward you went about numb as a slave in some private, totalitarian state." Even with a man like Constantin, who is not disgusting personally to Esther, she imagines the thought of marriage to him as a process of cooking bacon and eggs for breakfast and then another big meal at night, followed by washing up the dirty plates, to the point of exhaustion. "This seemed a dreary and wasted life for a girl with fifteen years of straight A's, but I knew that's what marriage was like."

Sylvia Plath tells us nothing new in such a formulation of a housewife's existence, which in the last decade has become commonplace. But the bitter, dry tone of *The Bell Jar,* with its ultimate defiance, carries a conviction of its own. It is unlikely that Plath's actual experience of marriage and motherhood is responsible for the view of marriage projected by Esther Greenwood (Plath's best poetry was written after her children were born), but through her we see an *expectation* of what life is like for a housewife in the America where she grows up, a life of mundane stupidity. Plath relates that it was not until she attended Cambridge that a beautiful woman supervisor became her "salvation" for proving, for the first time, that "a woman no longer had to sacrifice all claims to feminity and family to be a scholar!"

Esther has no one to give her such advice and cannot imagine what the course of her life is to be. "I saw the years of my life spaced along a road in the form of telephone poles, threaded together by wires . . . and try as I would, I couldn't see a single pole beyond the nineteenth." This feeling of purposelessness, which can be directly related to her suicidal tendencies, is far more than the discouragement of the moment. What suggestions were there as she grew up of a meaningful life apart from the common route, marriage American style?

If she does nothing, Esther will be stuck at home with her mother, whom she has vowed never to stay with for more than one week. At home she views the worst of possibilities. Probably the most devastating portrait of marriage and motherhood is that of her neighbor Dodo Conway:

> A woman not five feet tall, with a grotesque, protruding stomach, was wheeling an old black baby carriage down the street. Two or three small children of various sizes, all pale, with smudgy faces and bare smudgy knees, wobbled along in the shadow of her skirts.
>
> A serene, almost religious smile lit up the woman's face. Her head tilted happily back, like a sparrow egg perched on a duck egg, she smiled into the sun.
>
> I knew the woman well.

After this sight Esther crawls back into bed, pulls the sheet over her face (we are never far from the image of death), and buries her head under the pillow. Deadened by this sample of womanhood as well as by her mother's obtuse existence, she feels she has "nothing to look forward to." On another occasion, while looking for her father's grave, she contemplates the dreary life she might have by marrying someone like the prison guard who gives her directions to the grave:

> I was thinking that if I'd had the sense to go on living in that old town I might just have met this prison guard in school and married him and had a parcel of kids by now. It would be nice, living by the sea with piles of little kids and pigs and chickens, wearing what my grandmother called wash dresses, and sitting about in some kitchen with bright linoleum and fat arms, drinking pots of coffee.

This heavily sarcastic portrait is followed by her question, " 'How do you get into that prison?' ", meaning, of course, the prison where the guard works, but having unmistakable proximity to the preceding picture of marriage. (pp. 170-72)

Sylvia Plath relates that as a child, when her mother was in the hospital for the delivery of a younger brother, she "hated babies." She felt that the new child would make her a bystander, no longer everyone's favorite. For Esther Greenwood babies are associated with someone like Dodo Conway, whom "everybody loved" and whose swelling family "was the talk of the neighborhood. . . . nobody but Dodo was on the verge of a seventh." She is clearly not envious of this woman in the sense that she wants several children of her own, then or ever, but there is a certain jealous touch in the admission that everyone loves Dodo, which makes sense especially after reading Plath's account of her childhood resentment of the birth of her brother. Esther is an ambitious girl, the golden girl, always winning the prizes that climax in her award of a month at *Ladies' Day*. When she returns to her home in a small town where the neighborhood values are conceived in terms of an advantageous marriage, and the number of children produced is the sign of achievement, she is naturally scornful of the simple animality of the accomplishment. But she may also resent the fact that praise is no longer coming her way. She declares she will write a novel, that will show

them, but momentarily she realizes her lack of experience—no affair, no baby, no closeup view of death. Even the women who are having babies, as repellent as they are to Esther, represent an experience she has not had. If for no other reason than this she envies them, just as she resents Buddy Willard for having sexual experience before she does (although when her own initiation comes it means nothing more to her than an accomplishment).

The most crucial experience having to do with childbirth in *The Bell Jar,* one which emphatically alienates Esther from Buddy Willard, occurs on her visit to his medical school. He is proudly at home there, dressed in white, playing the part of tour guide of the hospital. They are to watch a woman give birth, but what could be an awesome event for Esther is, as usual, a disgusting one. Before directing her to the delivery room Buddy shows her the big glass bottles "full of babies that had died before they were born." One is curled up the size of a frog, another smiling a "piggy smile." Thus, before a baby is associated with life on this occasion, it is associated with death. The scientific atmosphere of the hospital pervades the relationship of Esther and Buddy, making it more sterile than ever. But if he fails with her, he very competently dissects a lung.

The prospective mother is rolled into the delivery room reduced to the status of a thing, a "big white lump" lifted onto an "awful torture table" with its stirrups and strange wires and tubes. With her face covered, all that is visible of the woman is an "enormous spider-fat stomach and two little ugly spindly legs." In giving birth she makes unhuman noises that to Esther can only be signs of pain, despite what she is told of a drug given the woman to kill the pain. The delivery room at this time of birth takes on the quality of a battleground dividing woman from man: he is in control of medication and instruments, apparently performing a violation of the woman, who lies helpless like an ugly animal. (pp. 172-74)

Nothing about a woman in labor is linked to creation. It would be necessary actually to see the baby "come out of you yourself " to make "sure it was yours" figures Esther, to realize the connection, and even that would be momentary. The newborn child, streaked with blood and blue as a plum, is like a foreign object that violates the mother's body, just as men have abused her. On some occasions Plath uses the baby as an image of purity, in one case when Esther emerges from her bath as "pure and sweet as a new baby." But the actual child being born is clearly not an image of anything either pure or sweet.

Not only do children represent a violation of a woman's body, as well as the manifestation of a vulgar life-style such as that of Dodo Conway, but the baby as the embodiment of new life is antithetical to the overriding appeal of death in *The Bell Jar.* Such an appeal is examined by A. Alvarez in his excellent . . . [*The Savage God: A Study of Suicide*], which concludes that while he has learned very little about the motivation for suicide he is convinced that the urge to self-destruction is a long-standing temptation, having all the appeal of other obsessive drives. What the child feels when he childishly blurts out "I wish I were dead" becomes a tantalizingly real possibility later on. Esther regularly reverts to this desire, which becomes a real possibility for her when she is in the community that loves and honors Dodo Conway, mother of seven, making the attempt to destroy life a form of rebellion against the crude breeding of life that Dodo represents. This is not, of course, to suggest that Esther would kill herself merely out of spite, but that she has enough resentment of small-town mores to perform her grossest attempt at suicide in the place which most persuasively suggests such an act to her and where her deed will make the greatest impact.

In reacting against life forces, one of the most important being children, Esther in her suicidal tendencies and in nearly everything else she does is extremely passive. Turn-ing against the life she sees prescribed for women, boring and inactive as it appears, she ironically, in her own way, exemplifies the worst of that passivity. Her movement to-ward death requires that all human ties which might draw her into emotional life be broken, thus allowing her the state of complete inactivity, the state of a thing. (pp. 174-75)

In the midst of New York's activity and opportunity Es-ther enters a numbing depression, as though selection and will are unknown to her, having excelled only in the struc-tured situation of the classroom. "I felt like a racehorse in a world without racetracks or a champion college foot-baller suddenly confronted by Wall Street and a business suit." She is a figure bumped from one hotel to another, incapable of steering herself. In her hotel room she flattens out on the bed trying to think of people who have her phone number and who might call, never considering the possibility of making the calls herself. Rather than attend a fashion show she wants only to stay in bed all day or to lie on the grass in Central Park. Esther considers herself "dealt" to the woman-hater Marco as his blind date, who informs her that it makes no difference if she cannot dance since it takes only one person to dance anyway. All she must do is be on the dance floor with him. Esther has al-ways waited for men to fall in love with her; there is no thought of affection for any of them. Her most decisive ac-tion is the project to unload her virginity, but even in this she merely reclines on the bed and lets it happen.

The situation of the college girl whose self-esteem hinges on a phone call might not merit our attention here if it were not that this stance remains basic in the woman. The passivity that operates in Esther's view of herself as a girl continues in her means of attempting suicide and in the desire for the ultimate passivity in death. Even the fact that she must take some kind of action to accomplish her death is distressing to her, doubly so because of her sense of incapacity. On one occasion she tries bleeding herself with a razor in a warm bath, on the advice of an ancient Roman, but she cannot tolerate the sight of blood. On the calm day of a beach party she tries to drown, diving down several times but popping back into the sunlight from the force of the sea. She asks her timid date Cal how he would try killing himself, and when he tells her he would use a gun she figures "it was just like a man to do it with a gun. A fat chance I had of laying my hands on a gun. And even if I did, I wouldn't have a clue as to what part of me to shoot at." Ineffective as Cal appears to Esther, she grants that as a male he has more nerve, more know-how, and better circumstances than hers for committing a decisive act. Her attempt at hanging is another failure, and she de-spairs at her inability to make a good knot. Her most near-ly successful suicide attempt is carried out with sleeping pills, the easiest and most passive of the methods, offering

a transition through sleep to death, an extension of her earlier retreats into sleep.

In Plath's poetry the urge to die is often given dignity and artistic significance as it is made a kind of awful quest for purity. But there is no grandeur associated with Esther Greenwood's death wish. The tone throughout *The Bell Jar* is grimly humorous, with little pathos developed for the heroine, who is clumsy, unheroic, we could even say shoddy, in her attempts to die. In this coldly realistic and truly ugly version of the suicidal, Plath dispels any roman-tic notions of the subject we might have had. And such a treatment appropriately reflects Esther's spiteful and un-imaginative way of dealing with her own talents: if the world is so heedless of her abilities that the best it can offer her is a job in the fashion industry, she who is one of soci-ety's best female products will commit the ultimate offense by stuffing her body into a crevice and leaving it there to die. We cannot admire her method of attack. But neither can we dismiss her as merely one individually neurotic woman who cannot deal with her problems. The issue of Esther's response to her situation aside, the problem she inherits is a thoroughly dismal view of the expectations for a woman in this country, a view which is not uncommon. The waste of her gifts and her life, even though it is not portrayed tragically, is a crucial loss. It brutally raises the question that must be put to Americans: What is a woman to do with her life if she does not follow the conventional pattern of wife and mother? Is there no other valid exis-tence for her?

Charles Newman says [in "Candor Is the Only Wile"] that *The Bell Jar* gives us "one of the few sympathetic portraits . . . of a girl who refuses to be simply an *event* in anyone's life." It does indeed do this, and it is time such a story was told. Plath presents one of the most unusual and disturbing accounts of a woman ever recorded in American fiction. But no one seems to know where such a story can go or quite what to do with the woman who does not choose to join her life to the lives of others. There is no tradition of women characters dealing with dilemmas that do not revolve around the men or children in their lives. Esther's unconventional pattern can only close off life for her. In her refusal to be like other women she finds no alternative and is trapped in "the bell jar, blank and stopped as a dead baby." The awful irony is that in avoid-ing one blankness, which for her is a hideously empty view of everything female, Esther takes on another, more terri-ble and complete. Her brilliance and accomplishments have no power to lead her to a place in the world. Instead, they drive her out of it. (pp. 176-78)

> *Mary Allen, "Sylvia Plath's Defiance: 'The Bell Jar'," in her* The Necessary Blankness: Women in Major American Fiction of the Sixties," *University of Illinois Press, 1976, pp. 160-78.*

Shelley Orgel

The Bell Jar is composed of small fragments, each one of which might have become a poem. It travels back in time to constitute an autobiography of its heroine, Esther Greenwood, and it shall be interpreted as a disguised auto-biographical account of a period in Sylvia Plath's life. *The Bell Jar* was written as Plath approached the end of the third decade of her life which brought her next major suicide attempt. The writing of the book may be seen as Plath's attempt to return to age twenty in an effort to disrupt the compulsion to repeat the action. She herself described the book as "an autobiographical apprentice work which I had to write to free myself from the past." [In *The Anxiety of Influence*], Harold Bloom has defined the "primordial element" of poetry as "divination, or the desperation of seeking to foretell dangers to the self, whether from nature, the gods, from others, or indeed from the very self." This definition applies to Sylvia Plath's poetry as well as to *The Bell Jar.* Yet the reader is left unconvinced that this self-objectivization will work, and reads her book with an uneasiness only partly the result of her literary skill. Plath takes the reader inside the bell jar, and has him see her surreal world from inside a glass that distorts reality perception, that makes him feel situations without exit. The "outside" is only the glass wall of the entrapped self.

Except for the shock that kills, there is no exit. The heroine-narrator is introduced imagining how the Rosenbergs must have felt being electrocuted, "being burned alive all along your nerves." The book begins with the conflict between excitement and revulsion in contemplating this ultimate, perhaps self-willed, obliteration of the self.

An outline of the plot of *The Bell Jar* will provide some orientation to the aspects of structure and content under consideration. *The Bell Jar* is about Esther Greenwood's descent to a suicide attempt and the beginnings of recovery in her twentieth year. She is a distinguished student at college in the 1950s. After her junior year she wins a prize for creative writing. The award consists of a month in New York with eleven other girls, working as an apprentice at a glossy woman's magazine. Esther is treated to a variety of luncheons, movie previews, fashion shows, and other showcase paraphernalia that should make a small town New England girl happy. However, each externally romantic incident unmasks internal decay. A lunch gobbled up fiercely is poisoned, a street pick-up turns into a sordid seduction of the heroine's friend, while the abandoned Esther falls asleep in the same room, then wakes and makes her way home alone; her glamorous U.N. interpreter date is impotent; another man sadistically tears off her clothes. She returns to her home in New England, and becomes increasingly depressed. Emotionally Esther is out of phase with her mother, and she attempts to run away, to get lost, with a pathetic lack of success. Her repeated, almost comic, attempts at suicide finally culminate in a near-success. Esther crawls into an unused stone cupboard in her house, covers the opening with stones, swallows sleeping pills, and nearly succombs as her mother searches for her everywhere but at home. The last part of the book deals with her hospitalizations, minimal psychotherapy, and electric shock treatment. She has intercourse for the first time and nearly bleeds to death in its aftermath. After this initiation into "womanhood," as she is about to be discharged from a mental hospital, the book ends.

Every major character in *The Bell Jar* is delineated either as a projection of the heroine—either directly or through an "opposite" representation—or represents key figures in her life, each one playing his assigned role in a series of primal fantasies. There are mothers, brothers, the primal-scene parents, idealized or instinctualized fathers, and so on. The created effect is of an outside world that is a projected inner world from which there is no emergence, and no possibility of expansion beyond the borders of a loathed self. The larger dimensions of space as well—the city, a hillside ski run, the ocean, the big hospital—all reinforce her own tiny finiteness. Her constriction is made concrete by her inability to transcend her own boundaries and penetrate into these larger spaces. The world outside comes at her, imprisons her, impales her, and casts her back into herself. Her attempts to conquer the otherness of the "other" by turning it into herself cause her to personify and anthropomorphize the projected inner world with evil ghosts, cadavers, and dead fetuses; the outer world is distorted by her lack of basic trust and sense of alienation.

With shattering effect, this novel conveys the pain of narcissism and dammed up, self-directed aggression in an outer world that allows no resonance, no echoing balance which permits investment and outflow to "collective alternates." Esther Greenwood literally eats and drinks a bad—sadistic or unresponsive—world of objects. A complete range of libido and aggression is traversed in the course of this journey. She becomes, or is invaded by the gobbling mouth and clutching fingers inbibing poison, the black, fetid excretory product, the primal-scene rape of mother, the bleeding, castrated victim of mutilating vaginal penetration, the flying skier (phallus) who collides with someone in her path and breaks her bones, the unsedated victim of electro-shock. [P. Greenacre, in *Emotional Growth*], has commented pertinently on wishes "to restore the lost object not only through one dominant incorporative route, but throughout all of these, which may appear fused or separately." Beginning with the Rosenbergs, each episode confirms her fusion with all objects who are perceived as victims. She fails in one attempt after another to maker herself *willfully* the victim of these objects and their alternative representations, in partnerships that create boundaries through mutual manageable aggression. The word is the state executing the Rosenbergs, and her primitive identification with them creates the art we recognize as Sylvia Plath's. However, in relation to the fragility of the heroine's own boundaries, the quantities and qualities of the world's aggressive energies are greater than her abilities to reproject it. On the first page the electrocutions are contrasted with the heroine's first self-image: "I felt as though I was carrying that cadaver's head around with me on a string, like some black noiseless balloon stinking of vinegar." The balloon is thin, the cadaver-self's skin cannot absorb or discharge traumata; one puncture and the balloon bursts. She attempts to thicken the "skin" of her self in paranoid-like hatred of objects who, in not fighting back appropriately, do not love back either. These include the prosaic mother who loses her and does not know where to look for her; the male psychiatrist (representing the de-idealized father) who is absent and unavailable even when present; the interpreter at the U.N. (the desexualized father) who will penetrate her only with insubstantial words, not physically, who won't seduce her (in part a superego representation); and her boyfriend (equated perhaps with the author's brother) who wants to look and be looked at, but his genitals, which look like a shriveled turkey gizzard and neck, offer no ego or libidinal nourishment (they are the counterpart of the heroine's own balloon head on a string of a neck). Other objects include Esther's father, whose grave has not been visited since his death, so the identifications arising from the mourning process have been unavailable to her; the salesgirl who tells her that no raincoat is water repellent, a reminder that there is no outside barrier to shield her against hostile elements; the other patients in the hospital (her psychopathological self without the redeeming talent) who won't answer her when she attempts a dialogue; the sailor who can't tell her age, who swallows her lies about herself; and the stone cupboard that won't hide her. Her incorporation of each of these elements and her failure to reproject them back into the world creates a loathed, increasingly fragmented, unidealized self.

Perhaps the author said to herself: In writing about them, I can rid myself of them. In one documented instance [the memoir of Nancy Hunter Steiner, Plath's college roommate], it is clear that the character Joan Gilling is given the fears and suicidal compulsions that in fact belonged to Sylvia Plath at the time, just as her heroine becomes free of them. Plath's characterizations of people and things are developed, described with the intensity and imagery of a poet, and then cast off, never to return in their original forms. They are like the New York clothes that Esther throws out of her window on her last night in the city. In the novel, almost every experience with objects is untempered by an admixture of object libido with the narcissism and aggression of both heroine and the "others" she encounters. The exceptions are mother-substitutes who are consciously perceived as such by the heroine; Jay Cee, the editor; Philomena Guinea, the novelist; and Dr. Nolan, the second psychiatrist. However, the weight is on the side of those who penetrate beneath her surface to destroy from within, those who inflict mental or physical trauma. Some objects refuse to hold her with loving firmness, feed her the right amounts of assimilable food, or look into her eyes (in all physical descriptions, her mother has her eyes shut, looks past her to others, or turns her back on her). Others fail to dole out proper balances of rewards and restrictions, or shatter her idealization of them. Still others deprive her of the differentiation of her own identity by not allowing developmental crises; they fail to offer intense love or the possibility of hate, and instead show her indifference, slackness of tension, and lack of challenge. Only the wilder aspects of nature satisfy her, and she turns to them—to the sea, the white ski slope, and her horses for challenging, mutually controlling contact. Esther's cure for fears, disappointments in love, and loneliness is a very hot bath—a coffin which turns into a womb. The stimulating pain of its heat reestablishes boundaries, and the water is a possible recipient of dirt and badness which can then be drained away. She steps out feeling "pure and sweet as a new baby."

Many of the characters are alter-egos, who disappear once they have served their purpose in the psychological structure of the novel. . . . [The] mother is serious, hardworking and complains of having passively endured the father's sexual advances. [Fellow contest winner] Doreen, in contrast, is a flighty, humorous, unindustrious, sexy blonde with big breasts—the golden girl. Doreen aggressively, yet playfully, participates fully in the sexual act which the sleepy heroine only witnesses. Doreen is Esther enjoying fantasies of disguised oedipal triumph, freed of pathological mourning for a dead father. The writer says of Doreen: "Everything she said was like a secret voice speaking straight out of my own bones." Doreen is able to forget everything after sleep; the heroine, sleepless,

never forgets anything. For many days before the heroine's major suicide attempt, she is unable to sleep or eat.

The first chapter closes with: "I liked looking on at other people in crucial situations. If there was a road accident, or a street fight, or a baby pickled in a laboratory jar, I'd stop and look so hard, I never forgot it." The last image is particularly significant. As the person in the bell jar, and as the dead fetus in a permanent womb that she tries to become in her suicide attempt, those eyes do more than just remember. The first two images suggest violent action, and while she may identify with either aggressor or victim, or both, she remains differentiated from what she sees. In the last image, evoking the stillness after the violent encounter, it is clear that she *becomes* the dead infant abandoned in a womb without the nutriment that will make birth into life, and selfhood possible. Her suicidal fate in fusion with victims is predicted throughout the beginning chapter of the novel.

In the course of the novel, many efforts to fight off the final "fusion with the victim object" are described or alluded to. The ultimate failure the author envisions is indicated despite the book's mildly optimistic ending. These defensive attempts at boundary formation are discernible in the form of the novel. The division into brief separated fragments has already been mentioned. Often one can trace the progression of ideas from fragment to fragment with a censoring break between fragments like a break in free association. Later, an example will be given to demonstrate how one can "plot" the broken train of ideas and affects by supplying the missing connections and thus link the fragments as one would in an analytic session.

Another stylistic device that serves and reflects defense while adding immeasurably to the richness of texture and tension of the language, is the use of antithetical, often explicitly bisexual symbolism that creates an affect of conflict and differentiation. . . . I noted earlier that for Sylvia Plath, what attracts also contains elements of danger. The moon, in its capacity to draw the tides, is maternal and fusing, while its bald white face, creating sharp outlines, is differentiating, cold, lifeless, to be avoided. The sea draws her; she wishes to drown in it. Father dwells on the other side and beneath it. The maternal, womb-birth-fusion symbolism of the sea is mixed with the opposite, sadistic, positive oedipal image, in Plath's childhood memory I noted earlier. It will not take her yet—neither father nor mother, neither the murderous nor sweet death. The buoyancy of the sea casts Esther up, and as she emerges, she hears her heart beating: "I am, I am, I am."

A third means of establishing boundaries between self- and object-representations is through the creation of thrown-off alter-egos, opposite twins, both of the same and different sexes. Through them she can live vicariously. With their aid she can project opposing sides of internal conflicts and separate identity fragments. For instance, the heroine's boyfriend, Buddy Willard, can be interpreted as representing a male self through whom she can fantasize having a baby all by herself without heterosexual intercourse. . . . These characters offer the possibility of unpunished gratification of her own drives, but their sharp oppositeness also serves to tell her who she is: at least, she is not they. In one fragment, she goes with Hilda, another alter-ego, to see *The Dybbuk*, and "when the Dybbuk spoke from her [the heroine of the play's] mouth, its voice sounded so cavernous and deep, you couldn't tell whether it was a man or a woman. Well, Hilda's voice sounded just like the voice of that." Dissociated from herself, Hilda is presented in feline images, a phallic-sadistic witch-like girl. Opposite to the heroine, Hilda is happy that the Rosenbergs will be executed. She would murder the primal-scene parents who write in their cells of their sexual longings. But the identity of Esther with Hilda is revealed by the use of one of Plath's favorite symbols for herself. Hilda stares at her reflection in the shop windows, "as if to make sure moment by moment that she continued to exist." Hilda, having her picture taken, holds a "bald, faceless head of a hatmaker's dummy," which is equated with Esther's first image for herself, the detached cadaver head like a balloon. Through this double, one sees the struggle between identification with the aggressor who would kill the Rosenbergs, and identification with the victims, the heroine who imagines *being* the Rosenbergs. Hilda, the girl possessed by the dybbuk, is, after all, described as invaded by an alien identity (the dybbuk) against which her ego is able to struggle.

In the following fragment, the heroine weeps as her picture is taken—possibly the experience is associated with a childhood memory involving her father. Later, looking at a snapshot of herself, she equates it with a newspaper photo of a girl who committed suicide. Still later she weeps for a second time at her father's grave. This resonates with the episode concerning having her picture taken. At the picture-taking, she announces she wants to be a poet. In this identity, she feels the loss of her father who will never see her poems that are written for him in his most idealized, immortal form. She imagines being discovered some day, an anonymous, acclaimed author whose true identity is revealed and who is found to be the clumsy adolescent no one appreciated. By reversal, this is an allusion to the reunion with the family-romance father and mother through writing. The picture-taking is also a mourning for, and an identification with the Rosenbergs (the dead parents) of the previous fragment. Looking in the mirror, "the face that peered back at me seemed to be peering from the grating of a prison cell."

Another double, Joan, a potential suicide, suddenly appears at the end of the novel. The character of Joan Gilling has recently come to life in the form of a memoir by Nancy Hunter Steiner, the model for the character. Mrs. Steiner seems intuitively to have understood Sylvia Plath's oscillation between fusion and differentiation. Steiner writes that she finally had to leave her friend because Sylvia had turned to Nancy to supply a missing piece in herself. Mrs. Steiner realized that she could not offer herself in this capacity without suffering severe emotional consequences, "so I drew back instinctively, allowing some distance to come between us like an invisible barrier."

At the end of the novel, Esther goes to Joan's house, hemorrhaging after her first intercourse. As usual, the author defines Joan unequivocally. "Joan was the beaming double of my old best self, specially designed to follow and torment me. . . . Sometimes I wondered if I made Joan up. . . . She would pop up at every crisis of my life to remind me of what I have been, and what I have been through, and carry on her own separate but similar crisis under my nose." Here is a perfect ironic description of the projected primitive superego precursor. On one level it

represents a defense against homosexual impulses; on another, the narrator indicates that the character will be used to represent her in what is to follow. In a continuation of the same passage, she speaks of how she must resist old women who want to adopt her and turn her into themselves.

Joan takes her bleeding friend to the emergency room of the hospital—none of the doctors she telephoned are available. Then Esther hears that Joan has suddenly killed herself. The suicide is presented almost matter-of-factly, adding to its ominousness. Esther goes to the funeral, "and all during the simple service, I wondered what I thought I was burying." At Joan's funeral, "the coffin loomed in its snow pallor of flowers." The white stands for death here, the death pallor—another instance of the use of antithetical symbolic meanings. Symbolically the whiteness may also be interpreted to represent the blood of the primal scene (the defloration of Esther) and of childbirth killing the victim-mother (represented by Joan). In another passage the "white sweet baby cradles in its mother's belly." In the latter scene, a description of skiing, everything is white with life. Again, what gives life to one self, the active aggressor conquering nature, also brings death to the other self, the passive victim unable to work its way into the outside world.

The character of Joan at the end parallels Doreen at the beginning. But the oppositeness of Doreen is contrasted with the similarities to Joan. Joan's identity is too close to the heroine's to allow Plath to use her for vicarious, instinctual gratification. The similarities to the heroine come through in spite of the author's attempt to deny them. Feelings of dread are evoked in the reader at Plath's failure to successfully project, that is, the author fails to create a Joan-figure who is different enough from her heroine to take on her own life, a figure invested, in a sense, with object-libidinal and differentiating aggressive cathexis.

Joan is obviously a part of the heroine rather than a separate character and is therefore dangerous. In the absence of stable boundaries between them, she must be killed to save Esther from "death" through mutual reincorporation. Steiner has compared her relationship with Sylvia Plath to that between Jesus and Judas. At another time, she notes that Sylvia "referred to me in letters to her mother as her alter-ego and often remarked that we presented a mirror image or represented opposite sides of the same coin." Steiner also describes how Sylvia was visibly shaken when a girl casually remarked that Sylvia had "her" hairdo. (The same hairdo meant a loss of part of the self.) And at another point Steiner describes Sylvia's passionate need to laboriously label two identical bottles of nail polish which were kept on opposite sides of their shared bedroom. These passages give important clues concerning Plath's need to cast off doubles, and her fear of re-fusion. When the projected self appeared to offer the temptation of gratifying her need for incorporation Plath's integrity was threatened. Therefore, the double, Joan, must be presented defensively in unflattering terms. There is a near-paranoid quality given to descriptions of Joan, the repository of those aspects of the author she most criticized in herself.

Like the heroine in the beginning, Joan is forced to witness the primal scene, but when Esther almost bleeds to death afterward, the sexual experience is no longer the casual play of the early episode. At Joan's funeral the heroine comes ominously close to reidentifying with the projected suicidal self. "I wondered what I thought I was burying." Joan's motives for suicide are never explored in the book. We assume that one aspect of Joan's identity represents Esther as female victim. According to Steiner's accounts, Plath courted rape as her first experience in intercourse. The dangerous bleeding was almost consciously sought. . . .[It] represents menstruation, rape, abortion, and childbirth. Joan-Esther is the dying mother giving birth to herself following a sado-masochistic primal scene. Joan-Esther is the child dying in the process of birth. The fusion of the victim's female identities is condensed in Joan's self-destruction by hanging, a method that failed to kill the heroine earlier. It does suggest the strangulation of the unborn fetus in the bell jar.

This manner of killing off of Joan also suggests she may be the victim of the author's death wishes for her brother, who was born when Plath was two and a half. The day her brother was born, Sylvia Plath walked along the beach and for the first time saw "the *separateness* of everything. I felt the wall of my skin. I am I. That stone is a stone. My beautiful fusion with the things of this world was over." On this day, "the awful birthday of otherness, she [the world] became my rival, somebody else." In this "memory" the shoreline represents the separation of conflicting selves and the loss of the mother-child unity. It also represents the barrier between life and death, a barrier which Plath repeatedly sought to obliterate. This early memory is condensed with a later one at the death of her father: "My father died, we moved inland."

The ambivalent pull to return to the sea is multiply determined. It signifies rejoining the family-romance father, re-merging with mother, and replacing brother in the womb. It also means casting off the "other," the tension between observing and observed selves that maintains the defensive counter-cathexis against the regressive loss of a stable sense of identity. To return to the sea and merge with it represents her ego's denial that brother is born and lives, and that father is dead. To go to the border of the sea, yet not to succumb to its lure, is to face the gulf of separateness dividing the living from the dead, the parent from the child, and the poet from the emergent poem. When, in *The Bell Jar,* the ocean casts her up, and her beating heart proclaims "I am, I am, I am," she receives the message with disappointment. She has not gone far enough. Father has sent her back to the living—inland. Mother has sent her alone into the world—brother is born. The pain of the experience leads to a break between fragments.

After the unsuccessful attempt to drown, the next fragment in the novel begins: "the flowers nodded like bright, knowledgeable children." One can interpret the presence of a resistance in this transition which allows resumption of the previous train of ideas and affects when they are disguised by symbolic and allegorical representations. Her wish to distribute only living flowers to new mothers on the maternity ward, to weed out the dead ones (a reaction formation against death wishes toward the baby brother), leads her to mix up mothers and flowers. She gives the wrong flowers (children) to the wrong mothers and is sent away in disgrace from the maternity ward. The birth of

her new self is associated with the loss of mother, the absence of father.

A final means of evading fatal fusion with the idealized victim-object fused with self-representations in *The Bell Jar* is afforded through the search for oedipal and postoedipal identifications and relationships with the father, and through heterosexual activities. The instinctualized relationship to the father is represented by the German language, a language which the academically brilliant heroine cannot grasp. She decides to go to bed with a simultaneous translator at the United Nations with whom she feels a kinship, but they fall asleep chastely, side by side. The death of her father during her latency and her failure to mourn appropriately have prevented the desexualization of id-derivatives from the oedipal phase. For her first lover she chooses a man who is experienced, described as an impersonal, priest-like official, as in the tales of tribal rites.

To understand somewhat more about Plath's relationship to the father and to males, a brief account of the five main male characters in their relationship to the heroine proves illuminating. These include the chaste interpreter, idealized but sexless, and her steady boyfriend, Buddy Willard, who disappoints her when she discovers he has had a previous sexual experience. She projects her oedipal curiosity onto him in the episode where they both strip—perhaps an echo of childhood sexual exploration with her brother. In one of his roles, Buddy represents the primal-scene father, the de-idealized sexual male. He is anti-poetry. She views poetry as the living child (the dead fetus brought to screaming life), as rendering immortality, the return to primary narcissism—"Godly, as a child's shriek. / Spider-like I spin mirrors. / Loyal to my image" (**"Childless Woman"**). This conflicts with Buddy's representation of poetry as the dead thing, symbolized by his dead genitals and sick flesh, which are associated with the cadaver that crumbles into dust and the specimens in jars on the shelf. Buddy, earlier described as a male alter ego, will be discussed further in another context.

A third male is the sadistic, woman-hating Marco, who attempts to rape her at a party in the midst of onlookers, another version of the primal scene. He is made sadistic (like the father in **"Daddy"**) partly to protect against the fusion experience. After the attempted rape, she tosses her clothes "like a loved one's ashes" to the night air. They flutter in the wind, which is inadequate to carry them freely and flowingly. The gesture is self-purification, a casting off of the New York self, the dybbuk, her dress "black as dirt," father's ashes, death itself. The wind which will carry them into the unknown dark heart of New York is her poetic inspiration. The gray scraps, also symbolizing her poems, are (transitional objects) ambiguously poised between life (white) and death (black). But they are only clothes, the outer skin, and, ominously, "the wind made an effort, but failed, and a bat-like shadow sank toward the roof garden of the penthouse opposite."

Dr. Gordon, the fourth important male figure, her first psychiatrist, is narcissistically blind to her. Like the dead father, he is self-satisfied and sufficient like the phallic-exhibitionistic little boy (brother). Finally there is the dead father himself, visited in rain that drenches through to her skin. She takes the place of the mother by wearing a black mourning veil to visit his grave (further antithetical symbolism—the bride wears black, the wedding is a funeral, the sexual flow is tears). The pouring rain under which he lies reminds us of his romance-equivalent, the merman of Arnold's poem. She writes: "I thought it odd that in all the time my father had been buried in this graveyard, none of us had ever visited him. My mother hadn't let us come to his funeral because we were only children then, and he had died in the hospital, so the graveyard and even his death seemed unreal to me." She goes on with ambiguous and ambivalent language: "I had a great yearning lately to pay my father back for all the years of neglect, and start tending his grave. I had always been my father's favorite, and it seemed fitting I should take on a mourning my mother had never bothered with."

The coffin is described as a dirty bathtub. This echoes the earlier bath in which Esther washes off the dirty sensuality of her oedipal Doreen self, returns regressively to mother, and is reborn. Here the image takes on the opposite meaning: not mother's womb, but father's grave. Mother's womb is father's grave, and so the mourned for, idealized father was the victim in the primal scene. Esther breaks down, weeps "into the cold salt rain," and in identification with the dead victim father, she creates her own grave—in mother's house, with pills taken from mother's strong box (another coffin-womb), in which she will die and/or be reborn. It should be emphasized that the libidinal wishes for the oedipal father (unless he is made sadistic, repulsive) and the symbiotic mother create the tendency to surrender to regressive fusion in death; while the aggressive impulses toward the abandoning father and emotionally absent, unresisting mother brings death through internalization of unneutralized defused aggression in the absence of a live object. Both erotic and aggressive wishes to either mother or father on all of the levels discussed here lead inevitably to the compulsion to die. The victory of individuality is choosing the time and form of death. Esther takes fifty pills at one time. The poisoning repeats the food poisoning sequence earlier in the book. In the early episode, however, her identification with her opposite, Doreen, who is also poisoned, maintains a stable projected self-representation that allows rejection of the poison.

The heroine's mother occupies relatively little space in the story. She is first mentioned in the chapter where the heroine meets the Russian United Nations interpreter. Esther sees him as father rediscovered, and sitting next to him, she realizes, "that I was only purely happy until I was nine years old." She then describes her mother's joyless scrimping to give her "advantages," and in the next paragraph, speaking of a Russian girl who accompanies this man, Esther wishes she "could crawl into her and spend the rest of my life barking out one idiom after another"—in an unknowable tongue. Perhaps, she is expressing a regressive wish for re-fusion with the early mother before the distancing discrete cognitive verbal communication began. This is combined with the wish to become the dybbuk, a separate self with her own boundaries within the mother's body. Her mother is introduced into the book in this context and she is equated with those who serve men, who cook and write shorthand. Yet the heroine has an empty stomach, and only a man can feed her assimilable food. However, men all require that she submit sexually, and this act, too, must imply joining together of male and female self in a regressive fusion, or in a continuing defen-

sive sadomasochistic struggle of the sort strongly hinted at in Plath's allusions to her marriage (see **"Daddy"**).

Many of the perceptions of Esther's actual mother in *The Bell Jar* convey the absence of stabilizing constant contact, the failure to provide satisfying libidinal stimulation fused with a differentiating neutralized aggression to promote safe self-object differentiation and secondary identifications against the twin dangers of fusion and object loss. When the mother drives her home from New York, she fails to pursue her curiosity about her daughter's face, cut in an abortive suicide attempt. "My mother climbed behind the wheel and tossed a few letters into my lap, then *turned her back*" (italics mine). "My mother took care never to tell me to do anything. She would only reason with me sweetly, like one intelligent person with another." The enraged child wishes to strangle the mother—either to death or into responsive life. As dawn comes after a sleepless night: "My mother turned from a foggy log into a slumbering middle-aged woman, her mouth slightly open and a snore raveling from her throat. The piggish noise irritated me, and for a while it seemed to me that the only way to stop it would be to take a column of skin and sinew from which it rose and twist it to silence between my hands." When mother leaves for work, Esther crawls under a mattress. It is "like a tombstone. It feels dark and safe under there, but the mattress was not heavy enough. It needed about a ton more weight to make me sleep." It seems obvious enough to interpret the coming suicide attempt as the murder of the mother with the weight of the father upon her turned against the self, and Joan Gilling's suicide lends itself to this interpretation. However, emphasis should also be placed on the stimulus hunger, the absence of pressure against the body, of libidinal nutriment from any animate object that does not disappear and reappear, like a foggy log, silently to take her place beside the daughter.

In the same episode the heroine unsuccessfully tries to split up the hundred letter word on the first page of Joyce's *Finnegan's Wake*. She dimly perceives that the word is somehow associated with the birth of the child and its differentiation from the parents and within its global self-image, but she fails in her attempt at analysis.

The mother's abandonment is also expressed in terms of distortion of self- and object-images. "I watched my mother grow smaller and smaller until she disappeared into the door . . . then I watched her grow larger and larger as she came back. . . . " As mother gets bigger, Esther must be getting tinier. The scene evokes the easy regressibility of her own body image reflecting the inconstancy of the mother's affective distance represented by changes in the mother's spatial distance.

Esther's only satisfying identity is as a poet. Poetry is equated with the ideal abstraction of father, supplying sublimated energy to her ego, and idealizing power to her superego. Winning prizes, the only thing she is good at (except for dying—the final prize—see **"Lady Lazarus"**) is contrasted with her lack of ability and interest in mundane activities associated with her mother and grandmother. In Esther's extended argument with Buddy, she sees poetry as immortal, the part that survives death; he sees it as dust, equivalent to a cadaver. The figure of Esther, who feels her head is like that of a cadaver, conveys the conflict between the two identifications with father (the living soul of the poet, the dead body in the grave) at the very beginning. In this role, Buddy, the son of family-romance parents, is probably partially equated with the author's brother, the intellectual argument originally arising in concrete childhood discussions between brother and sister. For example, one can well imagine the two children discussing "Is father really dead? Will he come back? Is there a soul which survives?" Buddy argues the negative side of all these questions, bringing her back to "the facts of life," as the birth of Sylvia Plath's brother made her aware of otherness. Her brother brought back and represented the degraded sexual father. This endangered her partial identifications with him which nourish her talent, and conjured up the decaying corpse, blotting out the professor, the linguist, and the author of a remembered book. Esther must win the argument to go on living, with her poetic ambitions as her *raison d'être*. In the novel the arguments end inconclusively. Later, in her fantasies, she imagines winning them.

Esther's visit to her father's grave, however, affirms the reality of father (representing poetry) as dust. It is the final, unbearable loss, and completes the chain that ends with the suicide attempt. In it she creates her own coffin in the ashes, and blocks the opening of the hole with *dustcovered* logs. In killing herself in identification with the father as the victim of the ashes, she revives the sea imagery that expresses the union with the primal parent, and she surrenders to the merman of Arnold's poem. The chapter ends: "the silence drew off, bearing the *pebbles* and *shells* and all the *tatty wreckage* of my life." Then, at the rim of vision, it gathered itself, and in *one sweeping tide* rushed me to sleep" (italics mine). She is reborn into a world of women. Her first word spoken by a depersonalized self is: "Mother." The rejection of the symbiotic mother and the search and discovery of the mother who will supply neutralized aggressive dialogue, who will arrange to have her own mother shut out and kept away, supplies the thematic thread of the rest of the book.

Sylvia Plath was one of those individuals described [in *Psychoanalytic Study of the Child*] by Anna Freud in whom

> the survivor's desolation, longing, loneliness are not acknowledged as his own feelings, but displaced onto the dream (poetic) image of the dead, where they are experienced in identification with the dead,. . . . That identification with the lost object, the deserted person, is derived from specific infantile experiences when the dreamer, as a child, felt unloved, rejected, and neglected.

That some such fantasy must have crystallized is strongly suggested by Plath's description of the visit to the father's grave in **The Bell Jar**. . . . [The] heroine feels that "desertion has not been the fault of the lost parent. It had been caused by the surviving parent's intolerable character traits or moral worthlessness." In the climactic scene of the visit to the grave, Esther experiences a double identification with the idealized, dead father whom she wishes to rejoin; and with the unloving mother whom she will destroy by killing herself.

The failure of Esther Greenwood, the fictional representation of Sylvia Plath, to resist the call from the dead for reunion may be interpreted in many ways and is obviously overdetermined. It shows the failure of the ordinarily temporary regressive identification with the lost object of mourning to become resolved, the failure to reestablish self-object differentiation by externalization of aggression onto the surviving parent, and the inability to displace and retain the idealized object in a structured superego, whose formation has its earliest roots in the vicissitudes of the symbiotic relationship with the mother. The need to retain love from the superego (the psychic structure that is the precipitate of former idealized relations) may arise in part from the wished-for unification between self and object, a residue of the original symbiosis. On the other hand, the structuralization of the superego in both its restricting and idealizing aspects as a relatively autonomous agency, using relatively neutralized aggressive energies to maintain counter-cathectic boundaries, protects the ego against being overwhelmed by the wished-for refusion. Its aggressive energies always keep it set apart from the ego, aiding defense against the urge to be reunited with either the primary mother or, in the case of Esther or her creator, the dead father.

The superego sets up unreachable objectives; that they cannot be realized insures the continuance of life as an individual in the face of loss, and prevents the loss of self in the creation of poetry. The unresisting reach toward loss of self is represented most vividly in some of the poems written just before Plath's suicide. One finds this self-abandonment in the form of merging into mirrors, the joining of reflection in water to self, the fusion without conflict with a corpse in **"Edge,"** written in the last week of her life. Everything folds inward—nothing turns outward as "The woman is perfected. / Her dead / Body wears the smile of accomplishment. . . ." The children are "coiled" and "folded"; "Her breasts, empty, are . . . back into her body as petals / Of a rose close"—at night. In **"Words,"** also written during the last week of her life, the external guiding stars are gone. The poet merges with her image in the water. The poem ends: "From the bottom of the pool, fixed stars / Govern a life." A third poem written that week, **"Contusion,"** ends: "The heart shuts, / The sea slides back / The mirrors are sheeted."

To the readers of her poems and novel, Sylvia Plath's suicide may be interpreted as the consequence of her attempt to reach the unreachable, and is viewed by many as a kind of tragic heroism of our times. This interpretation, I suspect, accounts for the growing Sylvia Plath legend in recent years as much as anything else. (pp. 152-67)

> *Shelley Orgel, "Fusion with the Victim: A Study of Sylvia Plath," in* Lives, Events, and Other Players: Directions in Psychobiography, Vol. IV, *edited by Joseph T. Coltrera, Jason Aronson, 1981, pp. 123-72.*

Jeremy Hawthorn

I saw my life branching out before me like the green fig-tree in the story.

From the tip of every branch, like a fat purple fig, a wonderful future beckoned and winked. One fig was a husband and a happy home and children, and another fig was a famous poet and another fig was a brilliant professor, and another fig was Ee Gee, the amazing editor, and another fig was Europe and Africa and South America, and another fig was

Constantin and Socrates and Attila and a pack of other lovers with queer names and off-beat professions, and another fig was an Olympic lady crew champion, and beyond and above these figs were many more figs I couldn't quite make out.

I saw myself sitting in the crotch of this fig-tree, starving to death, just because I couldn't make up my mind which of the figs I would choose. I wanted each and every one of them, but choosing one meant losing all the rest, and, as I sat there, unable to decide, the figs began to wrinkle and go black, and, one by one, they plopped to the ground at my feet.

For Esther Greenwood, heroine of Sylvia Plath's *The Bell Jar,* the choice between mutually exclusive futures clearly poses problems which are related to her later breakdown. Moreover, this choice between these mutually exclusive alternatives is related not just to what she does, but to what she is; the novel indicates from its opening pages that Esther's confusion and despair stem from her having to act a part in various social activities which are little more than charades for her, charades with little or no relationship to her actual feelings and inclinations. It is only in her fantasies that these real feelings and inclinations can be indulged.

Esther, at the start of the novel, is thus in a state comparable to that of Golyadkin at the start of Dostoyevsky's *The Double:* playing a part in society which necessitates the repression and concealment of real feelings, emotions, and desires. It is interesting, therefore, to remember that Sylvia Plath completed an undergraduate dissertation on the theme of the double in two of Dostoyevsky's novels: *The Double* and *The Brothers Karamazov.* There is evidence in this dissertation, written in 1955 (five or so years before the writing of *The Bell Jar*) that Plath used the exercise of writing the study to explore aspects of her own breakdown which had occurred shortly before the writing of the dissertation, and which clearly provides much of the material which is used to create *The Bell Jar.* Plath compares Golyadkin's 'personality structure' to that of a victim of acute schizophrenia, drawing upon information in an article on schizophrenia by Edward W. Lazell included in a contemporary textbook *Modern Abnormal Psychology,* edited by William H. Mikesell (1950). Plath quotes Lazell to the effect that schizophrenia represents a definite type of personality disorganization which limits the patient's ability to adapt himself to reality. The patient's early experiences and conflicts are seen to have caused the repression of instinctive urges and cravings, producing—inevitably—feelings of guilt and insecurity.

Plath accepts this as an adequate explanation of Golyadkin's dissociation, commenting however, that as we meet him 'on the very morning of his schizophrenic outbreak, we cannot be sure of the exact nature of his "early experiences and conflicts.' " Plath's analysis is an interesting one and, bearing in mind the far more limited general knowledge concerning schizophrenia at the time she was writing, a strikingly original one for a young undergraduate. But what is very apparent when we compare this account of breakdown with that given in *The Bell Jar* is that the roots of Esther Greenwood's collapse are not seen to be exclusively situated in her individual past, but are present at large in the world in which she is living. 'Roots' may indeed be an inappropriate metaphor: it is Esther's percep-

tion of the constraints her society places upon her in terms of her present and her future that is intimately related to her breakdown. From the undergraduate dissertation to the novel, then, there is a significant shift of emphasis from the individual's personal history of childhood repression to the pressure exerted upon a mature individual by his or her society. This is not to say that Plath discounts the importance of such early experiences: both in *The Bell Jar* and autobiographical fragments (including references in, and to, poems) Plath stresses the traumatic effect of the death of a father for a young child, and the double-binding nature of other familial relationships. But these experiences are seen in dialectical relation with other, more 'normal' social pressures in the later investigations into breakdown. It is perhaps worth recalling that our earlier consideration of multiple-personality case-histories indicated that both childhood trauma and repression, and adult crisis were needed to precipitate personality dissociation.

What *The Bell Jar* makes particularly clear is that the problems Esther faces in her young adult life are peculiar, for the most part, to the experience of a *woman.* For a man, getting married and being a famous editor—or having children and becoming a famous poet—are not mutually exclusive options. Esther's 'fig-tree' dilemma is not just one which faces anyone trying to decide between different careers; it is specifically the problem of a woman not granted the luxury of a *double* life. Esther is sent an article by her mother on female chastity, cut out from the *Reader's Digest.* This clipping forefronts the whole issue of male double standards for Esther, especially as she has just learned that the seemingly (and avowedly) pure Buddy Willard has had an affair with a waitress:

Now the one thing this article didn't seem to me to consider was how a girl felt.

It might be nice to be pure and then to marry a pure man, but what if he suddenly confessed he wasn't pure after we were married, the way Buddy Willard had? I couldn't stand the idea of a woman having to have a single pure life and a man being able to have a double life, one pure and one not.

Things have not changed so much since the time [Oliver] Goldsmith wrote *She Stoops to Conquer;* women are still expected to be either one thing or another while men have the freedom to be both.

In *The Bell Jar* the younger women are, in general, either virgins or whores, wives or mistresses—compartmentalized in a way roughly comparable to the female divisions outlined by Faulkner in *Absalom, Absalom!,* but without the complication of racial divisions as well. For a sensitive and thinking woman such as Esther the choices are unsatisfactory: the 'whores' like Doreen or the 'virgins' like Betsy and Hilda both offer Esther a chilling vision of a possible future. She wants the security of a close relationship with a man, she wants children, but she demands too the same sexual rights and freedoms men enjoy, along with the same ability to construct a rewarding career in the public world which is not just that of serving men. . . . It is no doubt for this reason that Esther considers Doreen's sexual freedom to be inadequate, for it still involves subservience to a man. Faced with the sordid reality of Doreen's drunken promiscuity, we see Esther hesitating between the two unsatisfactory and mutually exclusive alternatives, and choosing, rather half-heartedly at this stage, to become a 'virgin' rather than a 'whore'.

> I made a decision about Doreen that night. I decided I would watch her and listen to what she said, but deep down I would have nothing at all to do with her. Deep down, I would be loyal to Betsy and her innocent friends. It was Betsy I resembled at heart.

We know, however, that Esther is trying here to persuade herself; she resembles Betsy about as much as she resembles Doreen, and her desperate attempt to find an identity for herself leads her like a shuttlecock from one unsatisfactory alternative to another. It is not accidental that at different times Esther adopts a false name—the ludicrously unsophisticated 'Elly Higginbottom'. Her incipient breakdown is revealed early on in the book when, Lenny (we presume) and Doreen are trying to get her up to let the drunken Doreen in:

> 'Elly, Elly, Elly,' the first voice mumbled, while the other voice went on hissing 'Miss Greenwood, Miss Greenwood, Miss Greenwood, Miss Greenwood', as if I had a split personality or something.
>
> (pp. 117-20)

Elly Higginbottom is Esther's 'Betsy' character (we can recall that Betsy, in the New York group photograph, holds an ear of corn to show that she wants to be a farmer's wife).

> I thought if I ever did get to Chicago, I might change my name to Elly Higginbottom for good. Then nobody would know I had thrown up a scholarship at a big eastern women's college and mucked up a month in New York and refused a perfectly solid medical student for a husband who would one day be a member of the AMA and earn pots of money.
>
> In Chicago, people would take me for what I was.
>
> I would be simple Elly Higginbottom, the orphan. People would love me for my sweet, quiet nature. They wouldn't be after me to read books and write long papers on the twins in James Joyce. And one day I might just marry a virile, but tender, garage mechanic and have a big cowy family, like Dodo Conway.

Esther's descent into breakdown involves a bouncing between these alternatives represented by the different figs on the tree, alternatives which, it needs stressing, are not just mutually exclusive but are also inadequate and unsatisfying in themselves.

Esther's frantic oscillation between being Elly Higginbottom and coolly deciding to lose her virginity is not, then, something that is indicative of an internal imbalance in her basic makeup; it is a response to the contradictory pressures that are placed upon her. It is worth stressing that although Esther is the one who breaks down, *all* the men she comes into contact with have exactly the same double standards with regard to women as oppress her. Eric, the student she talks to after he discovers that his date has eloped with a taxi driver, describes his initiation into sex with a prostitute in 'a notorious whore house':

> (. . .) he had her under a fly-spotted twenty-five watt bulb, and it was nothing like it was cracked up

to be. It was boring as going to the toilet. I said maybe if you loved a woman it wouldn't seem so boring, but Eric said it would be spoiled by thinking this woman too was just an animal like the rest, so if he loved anybody he would never go to bed with her. He'd go to a whore if he had to and keep the woman he loved free of all that dirty business.

Esther considers that Eric might be a good person to go to bed with, as he had already done it and didn't seem dirty-minded or silly when he talked about it, but when he writes to her to say that he thought he might really be able to love her, she realizes that she is the type he would never go to bed with. Esther's rejection of the possibility of a sexual relationship with him, then, *follows* his indication that he himself splits girls into those he loves and those he sleeps with.

In much the same way, the woman-hating Marco divides the female sex into sluts and nuns, and brutally assaults Esther when she says that he will love some one else apart from the cousin who is going to be a nun. Esther's actual soiling here (Marco pushes her in the mud and soils her dress) is paralleled by the symbolic soiling of the mat Mrs Willard (Buddy's mother) makes from strips of wool taken from her husband's old suits. Esther says that she would have hung it on the wall after having spent weeks on it, but Mrs Willard puts it on the floor in place of her kitchen mat, 'and in a few days it was soiled and dull and indistinguishable from any mat you could buy for under a dollar in the Five and Ten.' The symbolic import of this is not lost upon Esther:

> And I knew that in spite of all the roses and kisses and restaurant dinners a man showered on a woman before he married her, what he secretly wanted when the wedding service was ended was for her to flatten out underneath his feet like Mrs Willard's kitchen mat.
>
> Hadn't my own mother told me that as soon as she and my father left Reno on their honeymoon—my father had been married before, so he needed a divorce—my father said to her, 'Whew, that's a relief, now we can stop pretending and be ourselves'?—and from that day on my mother never had a minute's peace.

'Being oneself' is not only easier for a man in Esther's society, it also forces women to be what men want them to be. It is thus appropriate that after her soiling and assault at the hands of Marco Esther returns to her hotel and lets her clothes—the dirty ones stuffed under her bed by Doreen—drift out of the hotel window into the New York night. The action symbolizes Esther's rejection of the identity implied by 'all those uncomfortable, expensive clothes' that she mentions early on in the course of the novel, clothes which define her in a particular way for men, and for herself. (pp. 120-21)

In *The Bell Jar* all the men are hypocrites. I have mentioned Buddy Willard and Eric, and Esther's father. Consider too Irwin, who conceals Esther in his flat while he dissuades another woman from entering, and Doctor Gordon, whose family photograph displays a different personality from that implied by his memories of the wartime WAC station.

It is for this reason that two crucial elements in Esther's recovery are her gaining control over her own reproductive powers through visiting the clinic, and her getting Irwin to pay for her medical treatment.

> 'What I hate is the thought of being under a man's thumb,' I had told Doctor Nolan. 'A man doesn't have a worry in the world, while I've got a baby hanging over my head like a big stick, to keep me in line.'

But while such achievements do constitute the gaining of a certain amount of freedom, Esther is aware that one does not escape from one's past, from the network of social relationships that one has experienced, that easily. Her self is not something that can be defined separately from her contacts with other people, from what they have expected of her, done to her, forced her to be:

> I remembered the cadavers and Doreen and the story of the fig-tree and Marco's diamond and the sailor on the Common and Doctor Gordon's wall-eyed nurse and the broken thermometer and the negro with his two kinds of beans and the twenty pounds I gained on insulin and the rock that bulged between sky and sea like a grey skull.
>
> Maybe forgetfulness, like a kind snow, should numb and cover them.
>
> But they were part of me. They were my landscape.

The Bell Jar is not, however, concerned merely to talk about the split personality forced on to women by men in an abstract and ahistorical way; this theme is given a precise historical and social context in the novel, and it thus meshes in with larger social and political concerns of Plath's, concerns all too clearly expressed in her writing but all too often ignored and distorted. (pp. 122-23)

[We] can see that the novel concerns itself not with a universalized sex-war, but with the complexities of human relationships in a very specific context.

> It was a queer, sultry summer, the summer they electrocuted the Rosenbergs, and I didn't know what I was doing in New York. I'm stupid about executions. The idea of being electrocuted makes me sick, and that's all there was to read about in the papers—goggle-eyed headlines staring up at me on every street corner and at the fusty, peanut-smelling mouth of every subway. It had nothing to do with me, but I couldn't help wondering what it would be like, being burned alive all along your nerves.
>
> I thought it must be the worst thing in the world.

Although Esther Greenwood, rather disingenuously, tells us that 'It had nothing to do with me', we learn a few lines further on that she had heard so much about the Rosenbergs 'I couldn't get them out of my mind.' The novel thus opens with an act of legalized murder that is specifically related to the heroine's depression, and which later on is paralleled by her own treatment through electro-convulsive therapy. Objecting to being given ECT without having previously been warned, she asserts that had she been given such a warning

> I would have gone down the hall between two nurses, past DeeDee and Loubelle and Mrs Savage and Joan, with dignity, like a person coolly resigned to execution.

Through the subtle and economical use of symbol and image, a number of key associations are introduced to the reader in the first few pages of *The Bell Jar.*

> I knew something was wrong with me that summer, because all I could think about was the Rosenbergs and how stupid I'd been to buy all those uncomfortable, expensive clothes, hanging limp as fish in my closet, and how all the little successes I'd totted up so happily at college fizzled to nothing outside the slick marble and plate-glass fronts along Madison Avenue.
>
> I was supposed to be having the time of my life.

The glass shop-front blends in with the image of the bell jar in the novel, and brings with it ideas of the alienating world of commerce and consumerism. It is the Madison Avenue world of New York from which Esther feels cut off, a world in which the people around her come to seem more and more dehumanized. The shop window image is picked up later in the novel when Esther visits Doctor Gordon's private hospital, and Esther tells us that

> (. . .) I felt as if I were sitting in the window of an enormous department store. The figures around me weren't people, but shop dummies, painted to resemble people and propped up in attitudes counterfeiting life.

And of course in that same hospital Esther receives the ECT treatment that calls to mind the execution of the Rosenbergs. Much later on in the novel the same complex of associations reappears, but this time linked to a particular image of mindless 'femininity' in the person of the chillingly brutal Hilda:

> [Hilda] stared at her reflection in the glossed shop windows as if to make sure, moment by moment, that she continued to exist. The silence between us was so profound I thought part of it must be my fault.
>
> So I said, 'Isn't it awful about the Rosenbergs?'
>
> The Rosenbergs were to be electrocuted late that night.
>
> 'Yes!' Hilda said, and at last I felt I had touched a human string in the cat's cradle of her heart. It was only as the two of us waited in the tomblike morning gloom of the conference room that Hilda amplified that Yes of hers.
>
> 'It's awful such people should be alive.'

Such passages build up a family of associations as the novel progresses: the particular mindlessness of Hilda's self-regarding transformation of herself into a sort of beautiful but non-human object (in the group photograph she holds the 'bald, faceless head of a hatmaker's dummy to show she wanted to design hats'); the inhuman world of commerce and its objects cut off from Esther's humanity by the same sort of glass wall which forms her bell jar, and the larger significance of ritual terrorism and brutality involved in the Rosenbergs' execution. We can see here how what appears at first sight to be an essentially private trauma is related 'to the larger things, the bigger things such as Hiroshima and Dachau'. (pp. 125-26)

One important element in *The Bell Jar* is Plath's perception of the dehumanizing effect of commercial medicine;

Joan tells Esther that she could see the dollar signs in her psychiatrist's eyes, and shortly after this a nurse tells Esther that when she has earned enough money to buy a car, she will clear out and take on only private cases. The nurse's behaviour is classically contradictory: her friendly conversation implies that she sees the patients as human beings, but what she actually says implies that she sees them only as means to an end, defines them only in cash terms.

Plath's sense of the threatening nature of human connections doubtless owes much to aspects of her personal biography; she repeatedly talks of the traumatic effect on her of her father's death when she was nine, and in the fragment **"Ocean 1212-W"** (significantly this is a telephone number—a link) she talks of the similar, earlier effect of learning that she had had a brother:

> Hugging my grudge, ugly and prickly, a sad sea urchin, I trudged off on my own, in the opposite direction toward the forbidding prison. As from a star I saw, coldly and soberly, the *separateness* of everything. I felt the wall of my skin: I am I. That stone is a stone. My beautiful fusion with the things of this world was over.

The relationship between an external threat and a sense of purified but nonetheless diminished identity is surely clearly indicated here. In spite of this feeling of dehumanization, connection with the world of separate objects is seen as threatening, for it may once again betray, hurt. Plath's desire to link up personal experience with 'the larger things, the bigger things' is, then, generally successful. The use of images of racial persecution, sexism and commercialism remind us again that it is not just within the family that contradictory double-binds are generated for the individual—and that even within the family such tensions are linked to larger contradictions in the wider society. (p. 133)

> *Jeremy Hawthorn, in his* Multiple Personality and the Disintegration of Literary Character: From Oliver Goldsmith to Sylvia Plath, *St. Martin's Press, 1983, pp. 117-34.*

Linda Huf

[Suicide], or rather attempted suicide, is only of secondary interest in **The Bell Jar,** which is not about thwarted romance at all but about thwarted ambition. Esther Greenwood, as her name implies, is a green, gawky, half-grown girl who has set her heart on becoming a poet. Unfortunately, hers are the times that tried some women's souls: the era of what Betty Friedan has called the "feminine mystique." As an aspiring woman poet Esther confronts the Eisenhower Fifties, when even the maverick Adlai Stevenson maintained that the chief end of woman was service to man. As he told Plath's graduating class in 1955: the Smith College woman would one day be proud to "change diapers" instead of shape policy, make "laundry list[s]" instead of write poetry. A woman, especially an educated woman, had "a unique opportunity" to better the world by influencing men and children. There would be much the Smith graduate could do on behalf of life, liberty, and liberalism in the "humble role of housewife," and Stevenson said he could wish her "no better vocation than that."

More predictably perhaps, the women's magazines, in whose pages Esther dreams of seeing her poems, have their own idea as to what constitutes poetry. "Cooking to Me Is Poetry," proclaimed an article in one of their recent issues, clearly more in the spirit of Betty Crocker than of Betty Friedan. It hardly needs saying that like all artist heroines Esther hates cooking:

> I started adding up all the things I couldn't do. I began with cooking . . . I didn't know shorthand either. I was a terrible dancer.

Lacking traditional feminine interests and abilities, Esther fears herself a monster, a woman *manqué.* Her appearance worries her as well, giving her further reason for seeing herself as a freak. . . . [She stands] five feet ten in her stocking feet, an inch or two taller than Plath herself. Looking down at the boys her age, she feels "gawky and morbid" like "somebody in a side show," and in consequence has taken to slouching—"one [hip] up and one [hip] down." If Esther is as tall as a boy, skinny as a rail, and "barely rippled" in the bust, it is not her boyish body that makes her a monster of her sex but her "mannish" intellect. It is her intelligence that differentiates her from the wonder woman of cold war America—the Keeper of the Kitchenette—and condemns her to the company of the least desirable men. Esther says as much herself when she complains that on skipping downstairs to greet her blind date every Saturday night, she finds "some pale mushroomy fellow with protruding ears or buck teeth or a bad leg." She suspects her friends of intentionally finding her boys whose physical deformities suggest her psychic ones. She grumbles to the reader: "I didn't think I deserved it. After all, I wasn't crippled in any way, I just studied too hard, I didn't know when to stop." Despite Esther's protests to the contrary, Plath means us to understand that her heroine *is* crippled in a way. As a brainy woman she is the natural match for an ungainly man, because both have equal handicaps in the sexual marketplace.

Of course, like all artist heroines Esther is not only smart, she is ambitious and self-driven. Recently she has won a scholarship to an elite woman's college where she has "toted up" a number of honors and prizes, including straight A's. When the story opens, she has won still another prize, first place in a fiction-writing contest—that is, a month in New York as a guest editor on a food/fashion/fiction magazine, *Ladies' Day.* To all appearances, this is her "first big chance" as an artist—her opportunity to meet famous writers and to establish herself as a talent to be reckoned with. She knows that she is supposed to be the envy of every red-blooded American girl who burns to take New York by storm in her black patent-leather pumps and matching pocketbook. But something has gone wrong. There is a crack in the machine of the American Dream.

> I just bumped from my hotel to work and to parties and from parties to my hotel and back to work like a numb trolleybus. I guess I should have been excited the way most of the other girls were, but I couldn't get myself to react. I felt very still and very empty the way the eye of a tornado must feel, moving dully along in the middle of the surrounding hullabaloo.

It is not immediately obvious what is causing Esther, after

fifteen years of collecting prizes and straight A's, to "let . . . up, slow . . . down," and drop "clean out of the race." Some commentators complain that the author gives no cause for her heroine's breakdown at all. We have only to look at *The Bell Jar* as the *Künstlerroman* it clearly is, however, to see why Esther at nineteen is beginning to "balk and balk like a dull cart horse." Like every other creative heroine she is caught in the tug and pull between her aspirations as an artist and her education as a woman.

Esther's aspirations as an artist are obvious enough: she wants to be a writer, specifically a poet. Coming of age in the ultraconservative fifties, however, Esther is getting an education less in becoming an artist than in accepting a restrictive life role. Predictably, it is her mother who serves as the first of her teachers in female accommodation. . . . Mrs. Greenwood wants her daughter to learn shorthand because it will get her a living until she can get her a husband to get her a living; indeed, because it may even get her a husband. (pp. 127-30)

That Esther may get the best possible bargain among marriageable men, Mrs. Greenwood reminds her that she must remain "pure." She mails the scholarship student *Reader's Digest* articles "In Defense of Chastity," which say that although men will "try to persuade a girl to have sex," if she succumbs to their stratagems they will "lose all respect for her" and dump her for somebody else. Men, these articles conclude, "want . . . to be the ones to teach their wives about sex." But, as Esther tells her readers astutely, the one thing these articles did not seem to consider was "how a girl felt."

Indeed.

While male readers frequently find Esther's hostility toward her mother "incomprehensible" and thus a "major flaw" in the book, women usually recognize her resentment. Among those who best understand Esther's feeling of betrayal are women who came of age in the fifties when it seemed (as Adrienne Rich puts it) that mothers had all "gone over to the enemy." While survivors of the fifties invariably acknowledge that Mrs. Greenwood only wants the best for her daughter in this not so best of possible worlds, they also see why Esther, after being alone with her mother for only twenty-four hours, fantasizes strangling her in her sleep.

Esther gets further lessons in growing up female from her boyfriend, Buddy Willard. Buddy, who flatters himself that Esther will one day stop rocking the boat and start rocking a cradle, had once asked her, "Do you know what a poem is, Esther?" and before she had time to answer, had answered himself: "A piece of dust." "And he looked so proud of having thought of this that I just stared at his blond hair and blue eyes and his white teeth . . . and said, 'I guess so.' "

Esther recalls how Buddy would often say to her in "a sinister knowing way" that after she had children she would "feel differently," she "wouldn't want to write poems any more." In fact, Esther worries that Buddy may be right, that after "you were married and had children it was like being brainwashed, and . . . you went about numb as a slave in some private, totalitarian state." That is what happened to Buddy's mother, who, after her marriage, flattened herself out under her husband's feet like a "kitchen mat." It is his mother whom Buddy is always quoting

when he says, "What a man wants is a mate and what a woman wants is infinite security" and "What a man is is an arrow into the future and what a woman is is the place the arrow shoots off from"—all of which, Esther reports, made her "tired." Finally, Esther remembers that when Buddy proposed marriage to her, he phrased the question as if anticipating her annihilation in the union: "How would you like to be Mrs. Buddy Willard?" he had demanded, looking one imagines like Zeus before he swallowed his first wife. When Esther had said she never intended to marry, he had answered ominously, "You're crazy . . . you'll change your mind."

Even the editors of *Ladies' Day* magazine, who are ostensibly giving Esther her "first big chance" as a writer, are in reality only exploiting her femininity on behalf of their magazine. With the exception of Jay Cee, the "plug-ugly" fiction editor, these Madison Avenue madams are interested primarily in procuring her services as a publicist. On her arrival in New York, they taxi her around from fashion show to beauty parlor to gala luncheon to publicity party. Then, having hatted and heeled her, fitted and fêted her, they pose her in front of a camera with eleven other Cinderellas in crinolines and a dozen "anonymous young men with all-American bone structures," who have been "hired or loaned for the occasion." Clearly, Ladies Day Enterprises is less interested in promoting the talent of these young women than in using their talent to promote the feminine mystique on which their Empire is built. It is no wonder that Esther, who is supposed to be having the time of her life, finds her life at this time to be weary, stale, and unprofitable. She is being poisoned not only physically by the ptomaine-contaminated crabmeat prepared in the *Ladies' Day* kitchen, but also spiritually by the culture of couture and coiffure cooked up in the *Ladies' Day* boardroom.

It is hardly surprising then that Esther is confused, a mystique being nothing if not confusing. Thus, when Jay Cee asks her what she intends to do after she graduates from college, Esther is at a loss for a reply for the first time in years. She remembers that only recently she wanted to be "a professor and write books of poems or write books of poems and be an editor of some sort." Until a few weeks ago these plans were on the tip of her tongue. But now they have vanished like a dream in the hard light of morning.

> "I don't really know," I heard myself say. I felt a deep shock, hearing myself say that, because the minute I said it, I knew it was true.

Until recently Esther also wanted a husband and children, but because she has been given to understand that a future of marriage and motherhood precludes any other, she now wonders if it isn't a "dreary and wasted life for a girl with fifteen years of straight A's." (pp. 130-33)

As self spars with self, as woman wars with artist, Esther becomes increasingly schizophrenic. Split down the middle by her conflicting desires and dreams, she takes on a second personality: the promising poet acquires a double or *Doppelgänger*. If among her friends and family she is still Esther Greenwood, the would-be writer and scholarship student who turns out long papers on James Joyce and promises to do herself and them credit, among the men she meets casually in the parks and streets she becomes Elly Higginbottom, a woman of no particular gifts, who dreams only of marrying a garage mechanic or prison guard and having a "big cowy family." She is Elly when she and her friend Doreen pick up a disk jockey on a New York sidewalk and also later when alone she takes up with a sailor on Boston Common. It is interesting that after the first incident, when Esther returns to her hotel room, she is awakened in the middle of the night by two people banging on her door—a drunken Doreen and a sober hotel maid—each calling on one of her identities . . . It is no accident that she plans to write her Senior Honors Thesis on the twin images in James Joyce, just as Sylvia Plath wrote her own thesis on the figure of the double in Fyodor Dostoevsky.

At length, Esther does choose among her several possibilities, just before she leaves New York. As she poses for her official *Ladies' Day* picture, in which she is required to hold a prop suggesting her intended career, the photographer asks her what she wants to be:

> I said I didn't know.
>
> "Oh, sure you know," the photographer said.
>
> "She wants," said Jay Cee wittily, "to be everything."

But Esther, suddenly daring and decisive, chooses a future. Leaving the other figs to rot on the tree, she says emphatically, "I want . . . to be a poet," and bursts into tears. The next evening she takes her entire New York wardrobe to her hotel roof and feeds it—bra, bag, and baggage—to the night wind.

Having decided on becoming a poet, Esther returns to her home in the Boston suburbs, where she learns from her mother that Harvard University has refused her a place in an exclusive summer writing course. Although she feigns indifference in the presence of Mrs. Greenwood (a tireless purveyor of unwelcome wisdom), Esther cannot hide her chagrin from herself. "The air punched out of my stomach." Angry and depressed, she decides to spend the rest of the summer writing a novel that "would fix a lot of people." "My heroine would be myself, only in disguise. She would be called 'Elaine.'" But Esther rolls a blank sheet of corrasable bond into her portable typewriter only to watch it stare her back in the face. Blocked and baffled she succumbs to self-doubt, then to inertia. Rationalizing that she will need more experience if she is to write novels, she gives up the effort with a heavy heart.

That evening Esther yields to her mother's perennial argument that she should learn shorthand—"something practical." But as she sits watching Mrs. Greenwood scribble little curlicues on a blackboard, her mind plays truant. Failing to focus her attention on her lesson, she pleads a headache and goes to bed.

> I didn't know shorthand, so what could I do?
>
> I could be a waitress or a typist.
>
> But I couldn't stand the idea of being either one.

As the summer wears on, Esther spends more and more time in bed, where, unable to sleep, she listens to a pregnant neighbor, Dodo Conway, roll a baby carriage back and forth beneath her window.

Dodo, Esther confesses, interests her in spite of herself. For notwithstanding Dodo's diploma from Barnard College, she spends every day pushing a baby carriage up and down her suburban street as five smudgy children waddle along in the shadow of her skirts. "She seemed to be doing it for my benefit," Esther laments. And in a way Dodo is doing it for Esther's benefit. Albeit unawares, she is portraying for Esther the future Esther fears will be hers if she fails to become a writer. It is no accident that Dodo takes her name from a large clumsy bird, now extinct, whose stunted wings were useless for flying. The thought of ending like Dodo, stunted and grounded, sends the heroine crawling back to bed, where she pulls the sheet over her head. She can no longer "see the point of getting up," she has "nothing to look forward to." Children make her "sick."

Unable to eat or sleep let alone write, Esther agrees to talk with a psychiatrist. Anticipating a kind, ugly, intuitive man who looks up at her and says "Ah!" in an encouraging way, she resolves to tell him everything, including her fear of never writing again and her feeling of "being stuffed farther and farther into a black airless sack with no way out."

As it turns out, however, the doctor is more distressing than the disease. "I hated him," Esther says, "the minute I walked in through the door . . . He was young and good-looking and I could see right away he was conceited." Esther balks at unleashing her demons on a man whose features are too bland and perfect, who smiles too smugly behind his "acre of highly polished desk." But what puts her off most about Doctor Gordon is the photograph that adorns his desk in a silver frame. It pictures the doctor's glamorous wife, his two beautiful children, and what looks like a golden retriever, all bearing witness to his sanity and success. The photograph makes Esther furious:

> I thought, how could this Doctor Gordon help me anyway, with a beautiful wife and beautiful children and a beautiful dog haloing him like angels on a Christmas card?

The picture suggests that Doctor Gordon sees a healthy woman as an ornamental woman, a creative woman as a procreative one. It suggests, in short, that he will try to reconcile Esther to a conventional role. At the end of the hour, just before he dismisses the heroine, Doctor Gordon reveals what he really does have in mind for his recovered patient. The only thing he can remember about the elite school Esther attends is that during the war there was a WAC station nearby, where, he boasts, he was "doctor for the lot." Then sitting back in his chair, he reminisces smugly, tactlessly, irrelevantly to his patient who has not washed her hair or clothes in three weeks: "My, they were a pretty bunch of girls."

Doctor Gordon brings to mind numerous other psychiatrists in recent artist novels by women, men who also ply their lucrative trade in the Freudian Fifties. He recalls Doctor Schrift, Isadora Wing's analyst in [Erica Jong's] *Fear of Flying,* who advises the would-be writer to "Ackzept being a vohman." He reminds one too of Doctor Foxx, the therapist in Lois Gould's *Final Analysis,* who explains to the writing heroine that what she really needs is a man to dominate her. And he conjures up the image of Doctor Popkin, Bettina Balser's psychiatrist in Sue Kaufman's *Diary of a Mad Housewife,* who informs his patient, an aspiring painter, that her "dibs" and "daubs" on canvas are merely "fecal smears," a "graphic expression" of her childish refusal to grow up and accept a woman's destiny. Bettina herself describes the results of his treatment:

> I finally learned to accept the fact that I was a bright but quite ordinary young woman . . . who was equipped with powerful Feminine Drives— which simply means I badly wanted a husband and children and a Happy Home. As I said, it took a lot of doing: in view of earlier aspirations it wasn't the greatest news in the world, and my pride took a bit of a beating, but once I'd gotten it all straight, and bought it, the search for a man was on.

As a result of her therapy, Bettina gives up painting, enrolls in an evening typing course, takes a secretarial job in a hospital swarming with men, and finds a husband. The analysis has been successful but, as it turns out, the patient goes mad.

In a similar way, Esther Greenwood goes increasingly mad under the "care" of Doctor Gordon, Despite a series of electroshock treatments at which he officiates, his bland face offering "a plate full of assurances," she continues to despair. Then one morning, convinced, as her mother later says, that she'll never write again, she crawls into a cobwebbed corner of her cellar, hides herself behind an old log, and gobbles down fifty sleeping pills. Within seconds a tide of darkness sweeps over the "tatty wreckage" of her life, erasing her despair of ever becoming anything but a dodo with her fledglings in tow. But Esther does not die— this time. Bruised and comatose, she is discovered, hospitalized, and "treated" to a smorgasbord of insulin injections, electroshocks, and psychotherapy, none of which gets at the basic problem. The remainder of the book details her struggle to regain wholeness in a world that has divided her against herself. (pp. 133-38)

Esther, who dreams of becoming a poet, is being prepared by precept and example for becoming a mother, a role she has been told is incompatible with writing. Hadn't Buddy Willard insisted that once she had children, she would no longer want to write poetry? It is no wonder then that babies figure ominously in *The Bell Jar.* They wobble along dirty and oppressive in the shadow of Dodo Conway's skirt. They stare back with mock wisdom at Esther from across a gynecologist's waiting room. They insinuate themselves into the features of Eisenhower, whose bald head and blank face remind Esther of nothing so much as a fetus pickled in a bottle.

"Why was I so unmaternal and apart?" Esther asks herself at one point. "Why couldn't I dream of devoting myself to baby after fat puling baby like Dodo Conway?" The answer, of course, is that babies suggest death to Esther—the death of the woman artist. Although babies are occasionally figures of life or rebirth in *The Bell Jar,* as when Esther steps out of a tub feeling "pure and sweet as a new baby," they are more often suggestive of death. For instance, there is the pickled and puckered fetus that smiles a "little piggy smile" at Esther from a jar of formaldehyde in Buddy Willard's medical school. And there is the "white sweet baby cradled in its mother's belly" which awaits Esther at the bottom of a dangerous ski slope. Out of the cradle endlessly rocking, babies grin at Esther—like death's-heads.

Esther's fear of death by motherhood is not an unreasonable one, as Tillie Olsen's book *Silences* confirms in some detail. Down the centuries the care of children, which has fallen almost exclusively on women, has meant the "death" of the woman artist. (pp. 138-39)

Writing as she did in the prefeminist fifties, Sylvia Plath does not think to reproach the other sex with failing to provide one solution to the problem that babies pose for the woman artist. Yet if Plath does not blame men for failing to assume equal responsibility for child care, she does come down hard on them. . . . The author of *The Bell Jar* holds men at least partly responsible for her heroine's predicament. "Men Drive Women Crazy," announced psychologist Phyllis Chesler in a *Psychology Today* article which came out the same year *The Bell Jar* appeared in America. It hardly needs saying that Chesler's thesis (later the thesis of her controversial book, *Women and Madness*) is not universally admired. However, if not everyone agrees that "men drive women crazy" in the world at large, one must concede that they do drive Esther crazy in *The Bell Jar.* Again and again the Eternal Masculine disappoints Esther the woman and denies Esther the artist. At the end of the novel Buddy Willard, having seen two of his former girlfriends go mad, queries Esther nervously: "Do you think there is something in me that drives women crazy?" In assuring him that there is not, Esther lets him off too easily, partly in the hope of exonerating herself of responsibility for Joan Gilling's suicide. The reader, though, is less convinced of Buddy's innocence than Buddy himself, who swallows Esther's assurances in his tea "like a tonic medicine." For Buddy Willard, more than anyone else in *The Bell Jar,* helps to divide Esther against herself.

Buddy is maddening to Esther not only because he dismisses her ambition as a poet but also because he disregards her feelings as a woman. This is most evident in the scene in which he takes her to his hospital to witness a childbirth. As Esther stares in horror at the "torture table" where an Italian woman with a "spider-fat stomach" and "spindly legs propped in high stirrups" screams with pain, Buddy looks on with a "satisfied expression." (pp. 139-40)

As an incarnation of the Eternal Masculine, or uncomprehending male principle, that reappears throughout women's artist novels, Buddy is predictably self-aggrandizing, insensitive, and smug. Characteristically he has won a prize in medical school for "persuading the most relatives of dead people to have their dead ones cut up whether they needed it or not, in the interests of science." For Buddy is happiest, Esther tells us, when he is lecturing, moralizing, and patronizing.

It is no accident that Buddy is portrayed in bird imagery as absurd as that in which the heroine is portrayed is sublime. After taking Esther to witness the childbirth, he escorts her back to his room, where he attempts to complete her sex education by showing her "what a man looks like." Discarding his chino pants and fishnet underwear, he poses before his fiancée with the clear expectation of exciting admiration. Esther, however, mentally sharpening her knife, takes this barnyard bantam and reduces him to giblets. "The only thing I could think of," she tells us, sounding drolly woebegone, "was turkey neck and turkey gizzards and I felt very depressed."

In contrast to Esther, then, who like all artist heroines is a high-flying bird, Buddy is something of a turkey. When Esther informs him that she will probably "be flying back and forth between one mutually exclusive thing and another for the rest of [her] days," he places his hand on hers and says, "Let me fly with you." But like the sailors on Boston Common, who are likened to pigeons, Buddy Willard, whatever else he is, is not a high-flying bird.

Buddy also helps to divide Esther against herself by splitting her sex into the irreconcilable classes of virgin and whore. Believing like many others of his era in separate standards of sexual behavior for men and women, Buddy confesses to having had a summer affair with a "tarty waitress," while he takes it for granted that Esther will remain "pure" for their wedding night. "Pureness," Esther says sarcastically, "was the great issue" when "I was nineteen."

Nor is Buddy the only man in the novel to divide women into strumpets and Snow Whites. Eric, another boy Esther goes out with in college, maintains in his head the same simplistic filing system. "If he loved anybody," the heroine relates what he told her, "he would never go to bed with her. He'd go to a whore if he had to and keep the woman he loved free from all that dirty business." Marco, a sadistic Peruvian with whom Esther has a blind date in New York, also splits her sex into saints and sinners. The woman he loves (a nun!), he says, is chaste; all other women including Esther are "sluts." Conveniently, he uses that epithet to justify himself in assaulting his date, in throwing her in the mud, tearing her dress, and attempting to rape her.

To the extent that the men in the novel demand that Esther be either a madonna or a magdalen, they help to divide her against herself, to drive her schizophrenic or crazy. Accordingly, during the first half of the book, as Esther grows increasingly disoriented, she alternately poses as one or the other—as innocent or jade. Sometimes she imitates Betsy, an ingenue from Kansas with a "bouncing blonde ponytail" and a "Sweetheart-of-Sigma-Chi smile." At other times she copies Doreen, a drugstore blonde whose mouth is set in "a perpetual sneer." As we have come to expect, both foils are blonde in contrast to the artist heroine, who has brown eyes and brown hair.

It is not true, as some critics suggest, that Esther, in alternately copying Betsy and Doreen, is acting out "two aspects of herself": the nice girl and the naughty one. In imitating her foils, Esther is reducing herself to the stereotypes in which the world has long been pleased to cast women. Neither role—vestal or vamp—suits Esther or any woman, really. To cut herself to the procrustean beds of virgin and whore is to deny the human complexity without which she can never become an artist. To try on alternately the roles of ingenue and libertine is to divide herself in two. Ultimately it is to go mad.

Esther's madness in all its suffocating confinement is suggested by the central image of Plath's *Künstlerroman,* the bell jar. Paralyzed by her effort to conform to antithetical roles—writer and woman, naïf and debauchee—Esther sees herself as sitting under a glass jar, stymied, sick, unable to stir. It is as if, she says, she has been "stopped like a dead baby," pickled and preserved like an aborted fetus in a laboratory jar. Arrested as an artist by her socialization as a woman, which demands that she be childlike and decorative, Esther feels as if she has been bottled into paralysis. While the bell jar is clearly a metaphor for the heroine's private madness, it is less obviously a metaphor for the madness of an era, the Feminine Fifties, when all women were glassed into "belle" jars, as it were. (pp. 141-43)

Intriguingly, other women writers have also used the image of the bell jar to suggest the glassing of their sex into juvenescence. In the short story "Under a Glass Bell," Anaïs Nin depicts her heroine Jeanne as living in a changeless, childlike world "under a glass bell," because she is afraid to confront mutability and death. Similarly, in her famous *Diary,* Nin describes herself as feeling trapped "inside a glass bell" when she learns from her father, who abandoned her in childhood, that she is expected to play the dutiful child and solace him in his age. More recently, Silvia Tennenbaum in *Rachel, the Rabbi's Wife* describes her artist heroine's garrulous foil, Golda Garfinkle, as having long ago sealed off her intelligence inside a "bell jar." . . .

Sylvia Plath is only one of a number of women who portray themselves as trapped inside jars, cages, boxes, houses, and madhouses. Traditionally the "weaker vessel," women characteristically see themselves as suffocating inside vessels, particularly inside glass vessels, from which they look out on a world they can neither touch nor affect.

The second half of **The Bell Jar** shows Esther's efforts to free herself from the glass bell of madness. Under the treatment of a woman psychiatrist, Doctor Nolan, Esther plots her escape from the bottle which suffocates her. She sets out to lose her virginity, which she sees as condemning her to a kind of "infantile paralysis." (pp. 143-44)

With the approval of Doctor Nolan, Esther goes to a gynecologist to be fitted with a diaphragm. Telling herself she is "buying [her] freedom"—"freedom from fear . . . from marrying the wrong person"—she climbs onto the examination table. Afterward, with her pestle snugly in her purse, she declares, "I was my own woman. The next step was to find the proper sort of man." He must be both experienced and anonymous, this male who would free her of her burden without incurring any obligation on her part.

The high priest chosen for this ancient ritual is a toad-ugly womanizer named Irwin, a twenty-six-year-old full professor of mathematics at Harvard. With Irwin, Esther sets out to destroy the double standard in sexual relations. She arranges her defloration as coolly as her appointment with her gynecologist, pleased that she feels nothing for the man: "All I felt was a sharp, startlingly bad pain." Afterward, she proclaims the seduction a success: "I smiled into the dark. I felt part of a great tradition." Within minutes, however, she begins to hemorrhage, her blood gushing down her legs, filling her shoes like jugs under a spigot. According to a doctor in the hospital emergency room where she is taken, only one in a million deflowered virgins bleed like this. Later she sends the hospital bill to Irwin. Then, satisfied that her unwitting rescuer from inexperience doesn't know where to find her, she proclaims herself "perfectly free."

Improbably, we are supposed to believe that Esther, in casting off her virginity, has also cast off her madness. In engineering her defloration, she has somehow achieved self-definition and sanity. She has freed herself from the bell jar, and is now directing her own life, defining her own nature. As she puts it herself, she is her "own woman."

It is interesting that the "real life" episode on which Esther's sexual defloration was based was a whole different story. If we are to believe Plath's roommate at that time, the poet's sexual initiation was more a rape by him than a seduction by her. According to Nancy Hunter [in her *A Closer Look at Ariel: A Memory of Sylvia Plath*], Sylvia was sexually assaulted by the real Irwin—who was actually a bespectacled biology professor. Moreover, rather than resolutely cutting the real Irwin out of her life, as Esther does the fictional, by slamming down the phone in his ear, Sylvia "dated" him for some time after his attack. More sobering still, it was not she but her outraged roommate who insisted on sending the rapist the bill for treatment of the hemorrhage. It is clear that Plath considerably altered her actual experience in the interest of her story. Instead of making Esther the passive victim of a rape, she made her the active agent of a seduction in order to show her effecting her recovery by refusing to accept the definition of herself as virgin or whore that the double standard imposed on her.

The best one can say for such a specifically sexual resolution to Esther's larger problem is that it is far from satisfactory. Sexual liberation, after all, is not sex-role liberation. Despite Esther's freedom to couple casually without unwanted consequence, she has in no way settled the conflict between woman and writer which has paralyzed her inside the bell jar. She herself seems to sense as much, for—despite the hopeful note on which she ends her story—she muses uneasily at the last: "How did I know that someday—at college, in Europe, somewhere, anywhere, the bell jar, with its stifling distortions, wouldn't descend again?"

As we now know, of course, the bell jar did descend again—at least on Sylvia Plath, whose last years suggest a kind of epilogue to Esther's story. We learn from Plath's *Letters Home* to her mother that the writer was no more successful than her heroine in reconciling her conditioning as a woman with her aspirations as a poet. After her marriage she put her own work second to her husband's, accepting as a matter of course her supportive role as housekeeper, secretary, bookkeeper, child rearer, and literary agent. While Ted Hughes often had a study in which to work, Sylvia Hughes usually found herself without a room of her own. Moreover, she who had maintained in *The Bell Jar* that babies made her "sick," had the primary responsibility for the daily care of her own. Then in 1963, after having committed herself for seven years to the cult of domesticity, she watched it give way beneath her. The husband to whom she had voluntarily taken a backseat decamped, leaving her with two children and her rage over her seven-year compromise with herself.

In the last weeks of Plath's life, as the bell jar descended for a second and final time, she wrote a number of brilliant if bitter poems indicting among other things domesticity (**"Lesbos"**), patriarchy (**"Daddy"**), and the feminine mystique (**"The Applicant"**). While for the most part critics admired the power of these last poems, they also called

them "bitchy and hard," "brutal" and "mean," "cold-hearted and unkind." "What can we make of a poet so ambitious and vengeful?" they asked. "How can we judge . . . such rage and such deformed passions?" In trying to explain Plath's inordinate bad temper, one of them considered the likelihood that she had been tormented by irreconcilable roles—that as a writer she had been troubled by "the claims of the feminine." However, no sooner had Elizabeth Hardwick considered this possibility than she dismissed it out of hand. After all, Hardwick concluded in [a review in the *New York Review of Books*] that reflected what has long been the majority opinion on the subject, "Every artist is either a man or a woman and the struggle is pretty much the same for both." (pp. 144-47)

> *Linda Huf, " 'The Bell Jar' (1963): The Apprenticeship of Sylvia Plath," in her* A Portrait of the Artist as a Young Woman: The Writer as Heroine in American Literature, *Frederick Ungar Publishing Co., 1983, pp. 125-47.*

Susan Coyle

Sylvia Plath's *The Bell Jar* is replete with metaphor: metaphor of death, of alienation, of losing one's self and, later, regaining that self. From the outset of the novel, where the narrator, Esther Greenwood, is obsessed with thoughts of cadavers, pickled babies, and the execution of the Rosenbergs, to the ending, where Esther consciously and triumphantly goes through a metaphoric rebirth, Plath takes the reader on a remarkable tour of metaphor. Through this use of metaphor, the reader comes to see, feel, and know Esther's world intimately and vividly. Essentially, the novel chronicles Esther's quest for identity, for authenticity, in a world that seems hostile to everything she wants.

Annis Pratt, in *Archetypal Patterns in Women's Fiction,* deals with this idea of "desire for authentic selfhood" in her chapter on the novel of development. Pratt asserts that "a considerable portion of mythology, religion, and literature is devoted to the quest of the youthful self for identity, an adventure often formalized in a ritual initiation into the mysteries of adulthood." In fiction of this type, there is generally "a turning point in the hero's life that is of both personal, psychological import and social significance." In *The Bell Jar,* the young protagonist is in search of herself, but she cannot quite fit herself into the patterns that she sees as available to her. In looking at the future that her society seems to have planned for her, she realizes that if she embraces it, she will be "growing up grotesquely," to use Pratt's terms. This kind of growing fills her with terror. The turning point in the novel, which has all the significance that Pratt indicates, is Esther's madness. After she is institutionalized, she slowly begins to put herself together, to develop a sense of the personally authentic.

Throughout the novel, Esther is known most tellingly through her use of metaphor. Plath's use of imagery changes markedly prior to and after the suicide attempt that leads to the asylum; the images of pre-breakdown are almost unrelievedly negative. The novel contains veritable cadences of death and remarkable images showing the hostility of the world around Esther, but the metaphors of primary interest are the ones that concern self, that reflect her states of mind. In the pre-breakdown part of the novel, Esther's sexual experiences are all somewhat dislocating: she cannot define herself as a sexual being. The patterns that she sees of marriage and motherhood make her loathe more than desire either of these accepted institutions. Esther's negative view of herself as an individual is reflected in her choices of metaphor; these images are frequently very physical, tied to her body. Slowly, she becomes increasingly dissociated from herself, until a sense of the "other" is clearly established, a dark side of herself who acts almost without Esther's volition. Contingently, there is a rebellion of matter: things (clothes in a pile, words on a page) that were previously predictable and inert now acquire an active and malevolent force of their own, a force the diminishing Esther is powerless to control. Language symbols fall apart for the protagonist, and nothing is left to hold on to.

After the turning point of the novel, which certainly does not conform to the traditional idea of an "adventure," unless it is a macabre adventure, these groups of metaphors change radically. Some do not go through any transformation; they die with Esther's madness. Others, such as the body images, change and become more positive, if less physical. In the "recovery" phase of *The Bell Jar,* Esther is known more through her actions and overt assertions, and the metaphors connected with these. The obsessive sense of self has been left behind, and the new self is more concerned with what she will be *doing.* Through her own effort, with Dr. Nolan's help, Esther ultimately forms an authentic self and manages to grow up rather than down.

One of the most interesting clusters of metaphors in the novel is the one that deals with language and language symbols. Since the reader knows that *The Bell Jar* is roughly autobiographical, it is particularly fascinating that Sylvia Plath, in creating Esther's and recounting her own breakdown, would be so sensitive to subtleties of language. . . . [The] reader is aware of Plath the novelist, acutely aware of language: loving the printed word, hating some kinds of language symbols, and ultimately being unable to connect to the kinds of writing she once loved. She establishes Esther's love of the printed word in the story of the Jewish man and the nun, coming together through the fig tree:

> I thought it was a lovely story, especially the part about the fig tree in winter under the snow and then the fig tree in spring with all the green fruit. I felt sorry when I came to the last page. I wanted to crawl in between those black lines of print the way you crawl through a fence, and go to sleep under that beautiful big green fig tree.

She loves the fiction so much that it seems preferable to her reality; she would like to live there, in the created world. She is just as emphatic about the language symbols she does not like, notably, German, physics formulas, and shorthand. When she sees printed German, "the very sight of those dense, black, barbed-wire letters made my mind shut like a clam." She has an equally violent physiological response to physics formulas, and when she enters the classroom, her "mind went dead." On the blackboard there are "hideous, cramped, scorpion-lettered formulas in Mr. Manzi's special red chalk." While she makes it through the physics class, she feels that if she is subjected to any more of these hostile language symbols in chemistry, she will "go mad." Through being a good student and

a good manipulator, she circumvents the chemistry course, but another unpleasant experience confronts her in the form of her mother's touting shorthand. Her mother feels that it is a practical skill that Esther can always fall back on, should her more rarefied academic pursuits fail to support her. Mrs. Greenwood sets up a blackboard and fills it with shorthand, but as her pupil imagines herself as an efficient secretary using shorthand, again her mind goes "blank," and "the white chalk curlicues blurred into senselessness." Esther cannot accept the idea of being subservient, though utilitarian, and the shorthand symbols become the objective correlative of this foreign and unpleasant possibility.

Her most severe dislocation from language comes when she tries to read for her thesis and begins with a Joycean experiment with language: "riverrun, past Eve and Adam's, from swerve of shore to bend of bay, brings us by a commodius vicus of recirculation back to Howth Castle and Environs." In vain she tries to analyze and dissect this passage, and moves through the "alphabet soup of letters" to a word with 100 letters. She tries to pronounce it, and asserts that "it sounded like a heavy wooden object falling downstairs, boomp boomp boomp, step after step." Then, as she fans the pages of the book before her eyes, her perception of the printed word falls apart: "Words, dimly familiar but twisted all awry, like faces in a funhouse mirror, fled past, leaving no impression on the glassy surface of my brain. . . . The letters grew barbs and rams' horns. I watched them separate, each from the other, and jiggle up and down in a silly way. Then they associated themselves in fantastic, untranslatable shapes, like Arabic or Chinese." This is the pivotal point in Esther's life. Running parallel to all the other dislocations she feels, she becomes alienated from language itself, and it is just after this Joycean distress that she can no longer read. In mood, there seems to be a tie to Yeats "The Second Coming," particularly the lines "Things fall apart: the center cannot hold; / Mere anarchy is loosed upon the world, / The blood-dimmed tide is loosed, and everywhere / The ceremony of innocence is drowned." Esther's hopes and prospects, which to an outsider would look bright, seem to be falling entirely apart; the center will not hold. Significantly, the failure of language occurs exactly halfway through the novel. From here there is the full blossoming of the breakdown and the subsequent slow path to recovery. As Esther's inability to connect to the world through language symbols is explored, the metaphor used to describe it anthropomorphizes the symbols, in a sense. Esther can no longer read, and in her perception the letters themselves take on an active and aggressive life: squiggling, fading, growing horns. It is almost as if there is a rebellion of matter, and while Esther tries to decipher and connect, the matter itself will not allow her to.

From this point on, Esther can read only abnormal psychology books (where she finds all her symptoms detailed), and scandal sheets, with stories of suicides, murders, and violent crimes. This narrowed field of perception reinforces her sense of life as a horrendous, hostile, and barely endurable experience. She even sees herself as an exact double of a picture of a dead girl in one of the scandal sheets. She compares her picture to the tabloid photo, and while the dead girl's eyes are closed, she feels certain that if they were opened they would have the same "dead, black, vacant expression" as her own.

Her alienation from language extends to writing and verbal expression too. She tries to write a letter to Doreen, but something within betrays her, and the handwriting which comes out is not identifiably hers at all. It is a large, childish scrawl, unfamiliar to Esther. When Dr. Gordon says " 'suppose you try and tell me what you think is wrong,' " she considers the possible ambiguity of the word "think" in the sentence, and says, "I turned the words over suspiciously, like round, sea-polished pebbles that might suddenly put out a claw and change into something else." While Dr. Gordon's words *are* ambiguous and patronizing, the metaphor gives them an incredible amount of traitorous power. And in the final instance of language failure, she tries to ask Dr. Gordon what the shock treatments will be like, but "no words came out." Her mouth is opened and her thought is formed, but language fails her entirely. The language references and metaphors are dropped during Esther's hospitalization, but there is one final reference after her recovery. When Dr. Quinn tells her, " 'Joan has been found,' " Esther realizes, "Doctor Quinn's use of the passive slowed my blood." It is clear that Esther is back in sync, aware of and sensitive to the subtleties of language.

At the outset of the novel, Esther is an outstanding student, successful and seemingly full of possibility. She sees her life as a metaphoric fig tree, offering multiple possibilities on every branch, yet she is unable to take even one of the figs. . . . Esther is "starving" not simply from indecision but also from an increasing sense of alienation from self and alienation from the world and her potential goals. The husband and children are scathingly undercut by the possibilities that Buddy and Mrs. Willard present. The career potentials are effectively undermined when she becomes unable to read or write. And the lovers become virtually impossible when she fails to gain a sense of herself as a sexual being. She either cannot get to the figs (editor, sex, poet) or the figs no longer represent viable alternatives (marriage, family).

In "The Divided Woman and Generic Doubleness in *The Bell Jar*," Gayle Whittier writes that "Esther Greenwood's primary identity is that of an intellectual woman. According to her society's standards, an 'intellectual woman' is herself a cultural contradiction in terms, a disharmonious combination of biology and intelligence. It is in part from this sense of herself as a living paradox that Esther grows increasingly depressed." Indeed, Esther is struggling to find a synthesis in her life that will allow her to combine her intelligence and ambition with fitting into a socially accepted role. She has been told that she should want marriage and motherhood and is moving toward both of these through Buddy Willard. Yet when she imagines what it might actually be like, she recoils. Her mother and Mrs. Willard are the two role models she has, and she does not want to be like either one. Mrs. Greenwood "never had a minute's peace" in her marriage, and from Mrs. Willard's example she infers that men really want women to be rugs under their feet, ever obliging, ever ready to subordinate themselves." . . . Because of Buddy's suggested life for her, and other models around her, she is also less than ambivalent about motherhood.

While the society's norms have taught her that it is a great good, she sees the novel's actual birth in negative terms and focuses more on the dead fetuses in jars than she does on any live babies. Plath's portrait of Dodo Conway, her chief example of motherhood, is scathing. The very name "Dodo" is insulting. Dodo is forever pregnant, with a "grotesque, protruding stomach," children swarming around her feet, and physically looks like "a sparrow egg perched on a duck egg." After this unflattering description, Esther says that Dodo raises her children on "Rice Krispies, peanut-butter-and-marshmallow sandwiches, vanilla ice cream," and milk. There is an insipid, mindlessly fecund aura around the woman, and one has a sense that she is more like fertile eggs about to hatch than like a person. Esther concludes: "Children make me sick." Through her views on marriage and motherhood, Esther is understandably alienated from these two institutions. To submit to them will leave her, metaphorically, as a rug, and a sick rug at that.

Sexually, Esther cannot find her place in the world. Her sexual metaphors are vivid, sometimes hilarious, and sometimes touched with pathos. When Buddy Willard, the ostensible object of her desire, undresses in front of her in a passionless sort of show-and-tell, she looks at his genitals and thinks of "turkey neck and turkey gizzards." Understandably, she is very depressed. When Buddy suggests that she reciprocate in the undressing display, she refuses and again finds a metaphor to suit the occasion: the suggested disrobing would be tantamount to having her college Posture Picture taken in the nude. Her lack of feeling has much more to do with Buddy than with herself. She *wants* to be a sexual person, but Buddy is unquestionably the wrong person for her. Adding to this confusion, another college boy tells her that having sex (albeit with a whore) is as "boring as going to the toilet." After the negative and thwarting sexual views of the college boys, Esther encounters another sexually warped but even more dangerous man, Marco the misogynist. He is described in a remarkable combination of images: animal, god, and machine. His smile reminds Esther of a snake striking. Like a savage animal, he later tears her dress with his teeth. She concludes, "woman-haters were like gods: invulnerable and chock-full of power." When she punches him in the nose, "it was like hitting the steel plate of a battleship." And this twisted type of man, the animal-machine, adds to Esther's ill-fated and devastating quasi-sexual encounters. So this fig too seems to be downed, falling withered to the ground. While she has a desire to be a sexual woman, the list of lovers seems to evaporate when she is unable to make any kind of meaningful sexual connection.

In terms of sexuality, marriage, and motherhood, Esther is faced with the growing up grotesque archetype. If she takes the routes which her society approves, she will be personally unsatisfied, if not dismal. She is in search of an authenticity but is unable to find it. She wants to both go by the rules and satisfy herself, and it is no wonder that the pressures within her begin to mount and eventually become overwhelming.

The way that Esther perceives her own face is indicative of her intense sense of dislocation and dissociation from self. In the first instance, which foreshadows the later and more dramatic post-breakdown mirror scene, she is in New York, in an elevator that evidently has a reflecting door: "I noticed a big, smudgy-eyed Chinese woman staring idiotically into my face. It was only me, of course. I was appalled to see how wrinkled and used up I looked."

While admittedly the reflection is somewhat distorted, the essential fact remains: she does not recognize herself. (pp. 161-67)

In another instance, she recognizes herself but has a horrible opinion of her face and a sense of detachment. After bursting out crying for the photographer, she looks in her compact mirror: "The face that peered back at me seemed to be peering from the grating of a prison cell after a prolonged beating. It looked bruised and puffy and all the wrong colors. It was a face that needed soap and water and Christian tolerance." Of course she has not been in a prison cell, she has been in New York, supposedly having an enviable time, but in her perception the prison metaphor is more apt. There is also a sense of disconnection in the passage, as if the narrator is somehow separate from "the face." After Marco has marked her face with blood, she says "the face in the mirror looked like a sick Indian." Again, the image is negative and there is a sense of detachment. It is not "I looked like a sick Indian" but "the face" looks like a sick Indian. Later, as she wanders around her mother's house, trying to commit suicide, she contemplates her razor blade scheme: "If I looked in the mirror while I did it, it would be like watching somebody else, in a book or a play. But the person in the mirror was paralyzed and too stupid to do a thing." There is a sense of alienation from self: the person in the mirror is entirely different from the person with the razor. (p. 167)

Esther is having difficulty placing herself in the world, which is reflected in metaphor, and her self-image is also readily discernible through imagery. In the pre-breakdown narration there are virtually no positive self-images and very few positive images of the world around Esther. In New York she sees herself moving through the days that the magazine has planned like a "numb trolley-bus." A trolleybus is a machine, incapable of feeling numb, and Esther, as a human being, could feel numbness, but she feels more like a machine. She seems to combine the worst of both and apply them to herself. When she tries to make a social contact with a man, but finds that he is shorter than she, she feels "gawky and morbid as somebody in a sideshow." In another particularly telling image, she comes back to the Amazon at night and thinks about going to bed, "but that appealed to me about as much as stuffing a dirty, scrawled-over letter into a fresh, clean envelope." She sees herself as dirty and unacceptable.

Many of the metaphors of self are quite physical, describing her body. When Esther is sick with food poisoning, she is "limp as a wet leaf" and the white tiles of the bathroom make a "glittering white torture chamber" which threatens to crush her to pieces. Again and again the same theme occurs: her body is helpless, and the world is assaulting it. She becomes tense and rigid, attempting to withstand the assault, but finally she cannot combat it. Toward the end of her New York stay, she says, "I could feel the tears brimming and sloshing in me like water in a glass that is unsteady and too full." Esther's obvious unsteadiness stems at least partly from being "too full" of disappointment and horror at the world around her. . . . When she loses her absolute control and cries [during her compulsory magazine photograph], she gains something as she feels free of the "terrible animal," but there is more than just control and lack of control here. Esther feels as if her spir-

it, her very self, has been taken, and she is left simply forlorn and bereft. The world is making no sense to her, and she not only cannot place herself within it, she cannot even find herself. She is an abandoned skin, only a residue of what she once was.

During the skiing flashback, Plath uses a metaphor that summarizes Esther's early attitude toward herself and the world. For a few seconds, as she speeds down the hill, Esther is happy. The happiness seems to come from two impulses: self-destruction (she might die on her way down) and rebirth (rushing down the hill is like rushing toward one's birth). Yet, ironically, at this exhilarating moment, she is knocked unconscious. As she slowly comes back to consciousness, her assessment is that "piece by piece, as at the strokes of a dull godmother's wand, the old world sprang back into position." Esther's possibilities for happiness simply do not lie within this world. Self-destruction would deliver her *from* the world, and since the rebirth that excites her is momentary and abstract, it is not very viable. The world as she knows it comes back to her, a gift from a dull godmother.

Aside from her negative view of self and alienation from the world, Esther encounters yet another problem—dissociation from herself. Whenever Esther meets men who might provide sexual adventure, she uses the phony name Elly Higginbottom. Doreen knows this, and early in the novel Doreen and the Amazon night maid are outside Esther's door, one calling "Elly, Elly, Elly" and the other calling "Miss Greenwood, Miss Greenwood, Miss Greenwood." Esther, awakened by these calls, is perplexed at them, thinking that it sounds "as if I had a split personality or something." This early episode foreshadows, on a superficial level, the otherness and doubleness that will occur within Esther. The Esther of *The Bell Jar* has never felt at ease with her body, and so it seems appropriate that the otherness begins with her body. It is as if the foreigner in her blood rises and betrays her. When she is talking on the phone about the writing course that she was not accepted for, she realizes that "my voice sounded strange and hollow in my ears." That in itself is not particularly odd, but only a few lines later the voice is seemingly no longer hers: "The hollow voice" answers the girl on the phone, and Esther listens to it as she would to another person's voice. Just after this, she tries to make another phone call, but again her body is behaving strangely: "My hand advanced a few inches, then retreated and fell limp. I forced it toward the receiver again, but again it stopped short, as if it had collided with a pane of glass." Things are beginning to be out of control; her hand acts as if it had volition.

This revolt in the flesh occurs at the same time as the failure of language: the breakdown has begun in earnest. When she visits her aunt the doctor, the division within her becomes more malevolent: "I tried to speak in a cool, calm way, but the zombie rose up in my throat and choked me off." By the time she goes to Dr. Gordon, she knows that things are definitely amiss and hopes that he can help her "to be myself again." Plath creates a sense of duality and horrific doubleness. Some other has arisen and taken control of her, and whoever she is, she is not herself. Dr. Gordon does not help her; his shock treatments only exacerbate the problem. During the shock treatment, the electricity grabs Esther and she feels like "a split plant" whose "sap" is about to fly out. Afterward, she feels terrible, remembering when a lamp cord shocked her when she was a child. In this childhood memory, she hears her own scream, but "I didn't recognize it, but heard it soar and quaver in the air like a violently disembodied spirit." This description seems especially significant, since the Esther under Dr. Gordon's care is indeed a "violently disembodied spirit" not just in the scream but in all ways. She is separated from herself, and the shock treatment is the culmination of the abuse of the world. The result of the treatment is that she feels "dumb and subdued. Every time I tried to concentrate, my mind glided off, like a skater, into a large empty space, and pirouetted there, absently." Her mind now does what her voice and hand previously did; it does not obey her but acts on its own.

In three of her suicidal forays—razors, strangulation, and drowning—there are contrasting examples of the double within. When she is in the bathroom, contemplating death in the bath, she has a startling realization. . . . What she wants to kill is not herself but the other within her. In a surprising turnabout, Esther exhibits almost a tenderness toward her physical self and does not want to kill it. She is divided, wanting to kill *something* within herself but not wanting to kill *all* of herself.

When she tries to strangle herself (humorously enough, with the silk cord from her mother's bathrobe), she runs into another problem. Her internal dilemmas seem to be solved, and she is determined to really do the deed, but her body sabotages her. Just as she feels herself about to lose consciousness, her hands let go of the cord and she revives. She is annoyed with all the "little tricks" of her body, and resolves "I would simply have to ambush it with whatever sense I had left, or it would trap me in its stupid cage for fifty years." Similarly, when she decides to drown herself, she chooses a method of death with which her body will not cooperate. It keeps popping her back to the surface of the water, and her "heartbeat boomed like a dull motor in my ears. I am I am I am." The painful division is ever-present. When her mind is resolved to do away with the body, the body will not cooperate, and when the body allows for the possibility, her mind hesitates. This feeling of division and alienation from self, the world, and every possibility becomes overwhelming, and Esther devises a plan whereby she can successfully get rid of all the pain. She fails, of course, and ironically enough awakens to a face she does not recognize.

When Esther is in the crawl-space, she crouches "like a troll." Her next awareness is in the hospital, when her head rises, feeling like "the head of a worm." While in the hospital, the staff members look at her as if she were a "zoo animal" and speak to her as if she were "a dull child." There is also the first reference to the bell jar, which Esther is "sitting under . . . stewing in my own sour air." Later, when Joan shows her the scrapbook of clippings about Esther, she notes with a kind of detachment that the picture shows her as a "long, limp blanket roll with a featureless cabbage head" being put into an ambulance. And here the intensely negative metaphors end. The dense, ferocious, and most moving metaphors are reserved for the earlier states of self when Esther is irretrievably alienated and depressed. The later images change and are much less physical, less concerned with her body and more concerned with action and the possibility of a more hospitable world around her.

This is not to say that there is a sense of total resolution in the end of the novel, any unrealistic happy ending. At the end of the book, Esther says that she is "patched, retreaded, and approved for the road." This seems to be accurate, since the reader does not have a sense of her as a brand-new, unblemished tire but of one that has been painstakingly reworked, remade. Madness is still a potential threat; Esther's sexual achievement is not the blissful initiation that the reader would wish for her; everyone does not live happily ever after. But the steps that she does take toward defining herself in the world, the assertions and actions, however tentative, do lead her toward an authentic self that was previously impossible for her.

One of the first signs of recovery is that the bell jar metaphor changes slightly. After Dr. Nolan's shock treatment, "the bell jar hung, suspended, a few feet above my head. I was open to the circulating air." The suffocating barrier has moved, and from a close look at the textual progression, the reader can infer that it moves not only from this supposedly superior form of treatment but from the interaction of Esther and Dr. Nolan and the slow climb out of madness that Esther herself painfully makes. Ostensibly there are two kinds of shock treatments in the novel; certainly Esther's responses to them are different. After Dr. Gordon's treatment, she feels terrible: a "violently disembodied spirit." After Dr. Nolan's, she feels "surprisingly at peace." Her mind will not cooperate with her, as it would not the other time, but this time it seems to be a more positive sort of noncooperation, and Esther is not tense or unhappy about it: "I took up the silver knife and cracked off the cap of my egg. Then I put down the knife and looked at it. I tried to think what I had loved knives for, but my mind slipped from the noose of the thought and swung, like a bird, in the center of empty air." She is attmepting to recollect love (even if love of a knife), and the thought itself is a noose from which she is free. The differing responses suggest that the effect of the second treatment is different and more positive.

Later, Esther refers to the bell jar in retrospect, saying that, "to the person in the bell jar, blank and stopped as a dead baby, the world itself is the bad dream." She exhibits an awareness of the bell jar and an analytical separation from it. Her mother had suggested to her that they forget all about her negative experiences, treating them as if they were a bad dream. Esther makes an important assertion in conjunction with her mother's suggestion: "Maybe forgetfulness, like a kind of snow, should numb and cover them. But they were part of me. They were my landscape." She decides not to hide from the horror that she has felt and been but to accept it as an integral, if dreaded, part of herself. Slowly, these images of self as a multifaceted, good and bad whole, build. In the final reference to the bell jar she admits that she does not know whether it will "descend again," but since she has found her way out from underneath it once, there is a sense of a potential Esther who has more power to combat it, should it descend.

Esther resolves her conflicts about her sexuality and motherhood by accepting how she genuinely feels and acting on those feelings. She realizes that she wants to have sexual relationships but that the chief drawback is "I've got a baby hanging over my head like a big stick, to keep me in line." She accepts her ostensibly unmaternal feelings, stating that "if I had to wait on a baby all day, I would go mad." . . . She also resolves the conflict about marriage, recognizing that if it means marrying someone like Buddy she does not want it at all. She says good-bye to him, and while she does not know who will marry her now that she has her own unorthodox "landscape," one has a sense that she is not particularly worried about it. She has a bright, if tentative, confidence in herself and is no longer belaboring the marriage issue.

Because Esther is integrating herself and losing the sense of otherness within, Joan becomes the objective correlative for this doubleness. At a relatively early point in the asylum, when Joan has town privileges while Esther does not, Esther feels that "Joan was the beaming double of my old best self, specially designed to follow and torment me." Later, when their positions reverse, Esther concludes that Joan's "thoughts and feelings seemed a wry, black image of my own." This double succeeds in killing herself, and Esther goes to her funeral with the puzzling thought that "I wondered what I thought I was burying." She seems to be burying her own dark side, seduced by death in the person of Joan. In another imagistic reprise from early in the novel, Esther, as survivor at the funeral of her dark side, listens to "the old brag of my heart. I am, I am, I am."

While the new Esther shovels snow for Buddy, she looks around her and feels a "profound thrill . . . as if the usual order of the world had shifted slightly, and entered a new phase." This can be contrasted with the earlier idea of a dull godmother forming the world. This time, the world and its possibilities seem bright, and if there has been a godmother, it has been jointly Esther herself and Dr. Nolan working to make the world, or Esther's perception of it, different. In the final scene, Esther goes to her interview with the doctors in a "red wool suit, flamboyant as my plans." The metaphor concerns plans for the future and not just physical self. Esther moves in her red suit into the room where the doctors wait, ready to determine her release. As she describes it, "the eyes and the faces all turned themselves toward me, and guiding myself by them, as by a magical thread, I stepped into the room." This is definitely a birth, or more accurately, a rebirth scene. Esther, dressed in a symbolically bloody color, is the focus of the scene, with the eyes of all the doctors on her. As a baby in the process of birthing would, she "guides" herself by them and is brought back to the world by their authority and help. The "magical thread" is analogous to an umbilical cord, but in this case it seems to be her own volition and self-command that allow her to step into the room, symbolically taking the responsibility and credit for her own rebirth. (pp. 168-73)

> *Susan Coyle, "Images of Madness and Retrieval: An Exploration of Metaphor in 'The Bell Jar',"* in Studies in American Fiction, *Vol. 12, No. 2, Autumn, 1984, pp. 161-74.*

Vance Bourjaily

What happens to the way we read and estimate *The Bell Jar* if we really go along with Sylvia Plath, taking it as the first novel of the young American writer, Victoria Lucas, then living in England, otherwise unknown? Under the Lucas pseudonym it was published, in January 1963, the month before the poet's death, by Heinemann of London—published, locally reviewed, modestly promoted, and briefly sold. With which, as most books do, it disappeared. It was pretty much unheard of, at least in this country, until eight years later, in February 1971, when it was ready to become a major item in a tragic legend, and Harper & Row had the business-wit to bring it out.

I am beginning in this way not to be tough but to be fair. *The Bell Jar* is obviously relevant to the life and death of Sylvia Plath, but the life and death need not be held relevant to *The Bell Jar.* A book is what the author puts between its covers, not what the publisher writes to wrap it in, nor critics and psychologists cull out to analyze, nor elegists to improvise upon. It isn't that I feel like shutting anybody up, out, or away—publisher with books to sell, wan reader wanting fellow-sufferance, ghost seeker, keen case hunter, or grinding biographer in need of grist. The book is here now, one way or another, for all of us, and what shrewd Peter sees in it to talk about may not at all be what young Paul wishes to discuss.

What interests me first is *The Bell Jar,* all by itself—the story, the social report, the view of life, the characters, the organization, the prose, the images and the working out—and what is achieved and with what intrinsic value. Then I'll return (if it's all right with you and Peter and Paul) to the autobiographical problem.

The Bell Jar, by Victoria Lucas, though not so-divided by its author, is nevertheless a novel in three parts. In the first, Esther Greenwood is an academically brilliant, socially insecure, and constantly introspective college junior. She has won, along with eleven others, a fashion magazine contest "by writing essays and stories and poems and fashion blurbs and as prizes they gave us jobs in New York for a month, expenses paid."

In New York, Esther is especially attracted by two of the other winners, both blondes—a decadent, flamboyant platinum number called Doreen, and a sweet, wholesome daisy of a girl named Betsy. Esther can't decide which she'd rather be like. When she attaches herself to Doreen, they are picked up by a disc jockey named Lenny, with eyes for Doreen. Esther invents for herself a drab, protective identity as Elly Higginbottom. When Esther/Elly leaves the pair in Lenny's apartment, to walk back alone to her hotel through the New York night, Doreen and Lenny have been jitterbugging, kissing, and biting, and Doreen is being whirled on the disc jockey's shoulder, belly-down and breasts out. (pp. 134-35)

When Esther attaches herself to Betsy, they do what is expected of them. They behave with girlish propriety—though Esther is covertly gobbling Betsy's caviar—at an elaborate luncheon. This, too, ends in vomit as the whole crew of nice young editors is struck down by ptomaine. Doreen has stayed away.

Recovering, Esther detaches herself, and operates next on her own. She offers her burdensome virginity, one evening, to a United Nations simultaneous interpreter named Constantin. Though they lie down together, he will do no more than squeeze her hand, touch her hair, and go to sleep. Consequently, she fails to catch up in sexual experience with Buddy Willard, the Yale medical student whom it was assumed Esther would marry. Buddy's courtship, told in interspersed flashbacks, has been agreeably gruesome, featuring her attendance at the dissection of cadavers; a tour of the exhibit of pickled, premature babies; a lecture during which sickle-cell anemia victims were wheeled onto the platform; and a bloody childbirth. There was also a ski trip during which Esther broke her leg, an evening when Buddy exhibited himself—and the boy is now tubercular. But Esther's reason for rejecting him, as she does, is Buddy's confessional boasting of a consummated summer affair with a waitress.

At the opening of the book, and recurring as a prelude to Esther's final New York indignity, are passages about the real horror she feels at the impending electrocution of Julius and Ethel Rosenberg. When the indignity occurs, Esther is Doreen's satellite once more. Doreen has arranged a date for her reticent friend.

" 'Honestly,' " Doreen promises, " 'This one'll be different.' " He sure is.

Marco is an immaculate Peruvian who tangos masterfully with Esther, escorts her outdoors, knocks her down in the mud and tries to rape her. When she bloodies his nose, he marks her cheeks with his blood.

The first part, and the New York adventure, end with Esther on the hotel roof, just before dawn, throwing out into the darkness, item by item, the expensive, not-quite-sophisticated wardrobe bought with scholarship money for the trip.

She goes home by train to Route 28, outside of Boston, wearing a silly dirndl skirt and frilled white blouse. Marco's blood is still on Esther's face.

Though the tone of much of this is wry, reminiscently detached, even amusing, it shows us Esther on her way down into melancholia, with little spurts toward recovery after each of which the psychotic despair deepens. There is evidence enough to justify using some harsh, psychiatrist's jargon about her—words like narcissistic and infantile—but if each quality is there, it is so only in such measure as seems normal for a vulnerable, imaginative, mostly appealing young woman, at odds with society. What is not normal is the growing split we are shown into the two selves, Esther and the very-much lesser, unappealing self she has named Elly Higginbottom.

In the second part of *The Bell Jar,* returned to a depressing Boston suburban home with her widowed mother, Esther is neither a Doreen nor a Betsy, but only Elly now. And while poor, dull Elly tells a young sailor, whom she allows to pick her up on the Boston Common, that she comes from Chicago, her real home is underneath a bell jar, an archaic laboratory fixture for displaying specimens. The specimen, on its dark base, is kept airtight, dust-free and out of contact, by a cylindrical glass cover. We can see it well enough, but if we imagine the specimen itself having life inside, the sights and sounds which reach it through the suffocating glass are distorted, muffled, and meaningless.

Our specimen, Elly Higginbottom, doesn't want to be alive. In this second part of the book, she tries, with razor blades, by drowning, and by hanging, to kill herself. At last, using sleeping pills, she so nearly succeeds that the search for and discovery of her drugged body are the subject of tabloid news stories.

During this section she has been seen by a disastrously unprofessional psychiatrist named Gordon with "eyelashes so long and thick they looked almost artificial" and features "so perfect he was almost pretty." When she has finished telling him that she cannot sleep or eat or read, Dr. Gordon asks:

> "Where did you say you went to college?"
>
> Baffled, I told him. I didn't see where college fitted in.
>
> "Ah!" Dr. Gordon leaned back in his chair, staring . . . over my shoulder with a reminiscent smile. . . .
>
> "I remember your college well. I was up there during the war. They had a WAC station, didn't they? Or was it WAVES? . . . Yes, a WAC station. I remember now . . . my, they were a pretty bunch of girls."
>
> Dr. Gordon laughed.

He decides to try electroshock therapy, and bungles it. The sleeping pills are only a few days off, now, for Esther/Elly. She takes fifty of them.

In part three, institutionalized, given increasingly better psychiatric care, and finally successful shock treatments, Elly sees the cover of the bell jar start to rise, and begins to emerge as Esther once again.

In the hospital with her is someone she knew at college named Joan Gilling. Joan has also been a near-fiancée to Buddy Willard, and also a campus achiever. Joan, reading in the papers of Esther/Elly's suicide attempt, a few weeks back, was actually led to emulate it, going off to New York to try to kill herself.

As Esther improves, Joan declines. Near the end of the book, Esther, on parole, finally manages to get rid of her virginity in a painful, rather impersonal way, and is satisfied with herself if not by the instrumental stranger she has chosen, whom she only sees once. Joan's new experience is homosexual, with another inmate. As Esther is ready to face the committee of doctors who will release her to return to college, news comes that Joan has slipped away in the night, to the woods, by the frozen ponds, has hanged herself and is dead.

Death and its agents are epicene in *The Bell Jar.* The sexual outcome is important because movement toward it is the positive movement in the novel. Through emotionally neutral defloration, Esther has become her own woman in a world of inadequate, repressive men. She says, "I hate the feeling of being under a man's thumb." It is in this regard that *The Bell Jar* is a feminist novel, repudiating the double-dealing by means of which society is stacked against talented, independent women.

Negative movement in the book is toward sexlessness—and death, whose woman Joan becomes. There are others, the living dead: Valerie, the snow-maiden whose lobotomy has taken away her anger, and Joan's lesbian partner Dee Dee, rejected by her husband. But it is Joan who is Esther's double in the book. This is a pretty easy point to make, since the author makes it for us. At first, when it is Joan who seems to be recovering faster, Esther is bitterly jealous: "Joan was the beaming double of my own best self, specifically designed to follow and torment me." Later, as Joan relapses, as indicated by the lesbian involvement, "Joan fascinated me. Her thoughts were not my thoughts, nor her feelings my feelings, but we were close enough so that her thoughts and feelings seemed a wry, black image of my own."

Negative and positive again.

"I like you better than Buddy," Joan has said suggestively, and Esther replies: "That's tough, Joan . . . because I don't like you. You make me puke, if you want to know."

Vomit again—but there can be no break this side of the grave between doubles. It is, necessarily, Joan whose help Esther needs when hemorrhaging, after the session with Irwin, the instrumental stranger.

Others have seen *The Bell Jar* as a book full of Esther-doubles, but in my reading only Joan is truly one (and I admire the restraint with which, though it's prepared for early, Joan's effective entrance into the book is delayed). Other characters do not double Esther but double one another, in the positive-negative way I've been discussing. This seems to me true, for example, of Betsy and Doreen—the latter's platinum hair has dark roots. Only Betsy is wholesome, with the emphasis on *whole*.

There are two mother-figures, similarly related: Jay Cee, the magazine editor, whose no-nonsense handling of Esther seems to straighten the heroine out briefly, and the biological mother, Mrs. Greenwood, who nearly drowns in nonsense, and whose well-meaning pushes Esther toward disaster.

There is Buddy Willard's father, trusting, henpecked, and alive. And there is Esther's father, also a professor, a bitter atheist who never gave his wife a moment's peace, and long since dead.

Constantin and Marco are negative-positive, in the sense of harmless and harmful. Irwin the instrument and Dee Dee the lesbian have something of polarity about them. And certainly there are negative and positive psychiatrists—the detestable Dr. Gordon, and Dr. Nolan, who is a warm and capable woman.

It is interesting that polarity and its reversal are characteristic of electricity as well as photography. I am about to quote quite a lot, to show how electricity moves from fearful to benign in Esther Greenwood's life. (pp. 135-39)

Sometime or other, long before the New York trip, Esther decided to move an old floor lamp in her father's former study at home.

> I closed both hands around the lamp and the fuzzy cord, and gripped them tight.
>
> Then something leapt out of the lamp in a blue flash and shook me till my teeth rattled, and I tried to pull my hands off, but they were stuck and I screamed, or a scream was torn from my throat, for I didn't recognize it, but heard it soar and quaver in the air like a violently disembodied spirit.
>
> Then my hands jerked free, and I fell back onto my mother's bed. A small hole, blackened as if with pencil lead, pitted the center of my right palm.

This remembered terror must be part of what is in Esther's mind when, at the opening of the novel, in New York, brooding about the Rosenbergs, she says,

> The idea of being electrocuted makes me sick. . . . I couldn't help wondering what it would be like, being burned alive, all along your nerves.
>
> I thought it must be the worst thing in the world.

This is nearly confirmed at Dr. Gordon's private hospital, when the electrodes are in place on Esther/Elly's temples, and the inept man gives his patient a wire to bite.

> There was a deep silence, like an indrawn breath.
>
> Then something bent down and took hold of me like the end of the world. Whee-ee-ee-ee-ee, it shrilled, through an air crackling with blue light, and with each flash a great jolt drubbed me till I thought my bones would break and the sap fly out of me like a split plant.
>
> I wondered what terrible thing I had done.

Shock treatment itself finally has its own, positive double. Wise Dr. Nolan has promised that, when done right, it only puts people to sleep, that some even like it. Themes come together here:

> I saw the high bed, with its white, drumtight sheet, and the machine behind the bed and the masked person—I couldn't tell whether it was a man or a woman—behind the machine, and the other masked people flanking the bed on both sides. . . .
>
> (Miss Huey, "a tall, cadaverous woman,") set something on my tongue and in panic I bit down, and darkness wiped me out like chalk on a blackboard. . . .
>
> I woke out of a deep, drenched sleep. . . . All the heat and fear had purged itself. I felt surprisingly at peace. The bell jar hung, suspended, a few feet above my head. I was open to the circulating air.
>
> (pp. 140-41)

Whatever the abstract roles we decide to assign the characters in *The Bell Jar,* they are never abstractions. It is one of the strengths of the book that each is brought to brief, vivid, and particular life, even the most minor. It's done with snapshot physical description, a quick ear, and a little irony.

For example, Esther is naïve about tipping:

> A dwarfish, bald man in a bellhop's uniform carried my suitcase up in the elevator and unlocked my room for me. . . . After a while I was aware of this bellhop turning on the hot and cold taps in the washbowl and saying "This is the hot and this is the cold" and switching on the radio and telling me all the names of all the New York stations and I began to get uneasy, so I kept my back to him and said firmly, "Thank you for bringing up my suitcase."
>
> "Thank you thank you thank you. Ha!" he said, in a very nasty, insinuating tone, and before I could wheel around to see what had come over him he was gone, shutting the door behind him with a rude slam.

In the case of an important character, when Joan Gilling

is first mentioned as the girl Buddy Willard has come to see at college, the irony is in unacknowledged jealousy:

> She was a big wheel—president of her class and a physics major and the college hockey champion. She always made me feel squirmy with her starey pebble-colored eyes and her gleaming tombstone teeth and her breathy voice. She was big as a horse, too. I began to think Buddy had pretty poor taste.

If the author is adept at quick-stroke characterization, she is equally so at quick-drawn scenes. I've made occasion to quote some of these, at least partially, and will be quoting others. For now I'll simply do some casual arithmetic, and report that there are seventy-five or eighty distinct scenes in the two hundred pages of *The Bell Jar,* most of them completed in fewer than a thousand words. The effect is movielike, and the movie smartly paced. It is fast, absorbing stuff, except in two stretches. Some of the first-section flashbacks seem uncontrolled and repetitious, and we are not always perfectly oriented in time. Some of the second-section, Elly material is a little tedious, because Elly, obsessed with the how-to of suicide and insensitive to others, is a tedious girl, with whom we lose patience; I do, anyway. But these are partly faults of inexperience in the writer—and there are some vastly experienced novelists around who still have trouble managing time, making dullness interesting and obsession sympathetic; likely we all do.

Much of the prose in *The Bell Jar* is direct, lucid and in no need of ornament. . . . Admittedly, there is careless prose here and there too, as in the lamp-gripping recollection with its tooth-rattling, and its scream torn from the throat, quavering in the air like a disembodied spirit. It isn't like Victoria Lucas to be that Victorian.

Examples like that are rare. Mostly the language and image combination in *The Bell Jar* is of an easy, colloquial voice in which the thing to be visualized can grow as if in a culture. Take this, from the very first page:

> It was like the first time I saw a cadaver. For weeks afterwards, the cadaver's head floated up behind my bacon and eggs at breakfast and behind the face of Buddy Willard . . . and pretty soon I felt as though I were carrying that cadaver's head around with me on a string, like some black, noseless balloon stinking of vinegar.
>
> (pp. 142-43)

The flaws of execution in *The Bell Jar* are not many and not serious. They are outnumbered by examples of felicity by a margin of, say, fifty to one. There is, however, a flaw of intention to consider, though the effects of it are hard to measure. We must leave the text, for now, but not for good, and deal with Victoria Lucas as a mask.

Victoria Lucas was not supposed to be a totally serious writer. She was to write best-sellers. (p. 144)

Victoria Lucas, as I've tried to show, was pretty good. She had her limits. Sometimes she fell below them, more often she exceeded them. In general, she was a necessary fiction through which Sylvia Plath could hold back a really reckless commitment of talent, thought, and feeling at the depths where they are too nearly inexpressible to make for easy reading. I'll need to return to this at the end of my piece, but for now I hope you'll accept it as one of my rea-

sons for not wanting to treat *The Bell Jar* as an autobiographical effort, in which Sylvia Plath demeans herself as Esther Greenwood. The book is something better than a document. It is a work of fiction in which, to sum up, an unhappy, intelligent schizoid, Esther Greenwood, sinks into the lesser of her two selves, becomes Elly Higginbottom—in which Elly must die so that Esther may be reborn.

If I may so describe it, then, *The Bell Jar* is a brave try at a minor work of art, rarely undercut by the inexperience and light intention permitted Victoria Lucas, instead of a nervously clever piece of confession and catharsis. It stands, supported by the poet's reputation but not really in need of it, as a small, rather haunting, American youthbook. (pp. 144-45)

Now, to try to make my view persuasive, let me try to find some of the ways in which Esther, though she shares experiences with Sylvia Plath, is actually a created character.

We can begin, but not get very far, with the only physical trait Esther gives about herself, other than that she was tall, as Sylvia Plath was, too: "This dress was cut so queerly that I couldn't wear any sort of bra under it, but that didn't matter much as I was skinny as a boy and barely rippled." Please turn to any grown-up photograph of Sylvia Plath, including one taken in 1953, *The Bell Jar* year. You will see a buxom enough young woman.

More tellingly, as a college junior, Esther is not a poet. She isn't even much of a writer: "The only thing I was good at was winning scholarships and prizes." Esther is an academic overkiller, with low-key inclinations toward graduate school, or a professorship, or writing poetry, or getting into publishing, or something. There are thousands like her. There are hardly any like Sylvia Plath, who had been dedicated to writing poetry since childhood, who had begun sending out her work in high school, who had, by junior year in college at nineteen, started to accumulate publications.

Listen once more to Esther in New York: "I wasn't steering anything, not even myself. I just bumped from my hotel to work and to parties and from parties to my hotel and back to work like a numb trolleybus. . . . I couldn't get myself to react. I felt very still and very empty." She tags along, camp-follower of women, victim of men, listless, secretive, gluttonous, mostly depressed, and always introverted.

The Sylvia Plath we read about in the biographies could get depressed—horribly, insanely depressed—but she was still no Esther. Even when hellbent, she had energy and discipline. She sparkled, was intense, came on strong to men, women, and situations. She could dominate, entertain, flirt, impress, tease, dissimulate, and win. She was introspective often, at times introverted; we see it in the journals. But we also see in the journals a lively, attractive, passionate, and gifted young woman, probably a genius. Nobody would call Esther Greenwood a genius. I just cannot take her as a portrait of the artist as a young woman. (pp. 145-46)

An author has put ironic distance between self and character when author and reader share an understanding which eludes the character. Okay:

"Hey, Lenny, you owe me something. Remember, Lenny, you owe me something, don't you Lenny?"

I thought it odd Frankie should be reminding Lenny he owed him something in front of us, and we being perfect strangers, but Frankie kept saying the same thing over and over, until Lenny dug into his pocket.

Oh, come on, Esther, don't you see what's going on? Lenny was lounging about under a restaurant awning with some of the guys, when they spotted you and Doreen in the stalled cab. The others watched, laughing about it, while Lenny strolled over and persuaded the two of you to leave your cab and have a drink with him. As the three of you went by the group, Lenny said, "Come on, Frankie." And short, scrunty Frankie came along into the restaurant. Lenny went in first with Doreen. You tried to pretend you didn't see Frankie at your elbow. You sat away from him, close to Doreen. You made awkward conversation. You decided to call yourself Elly Higginbottom. You laughed at and looked down on Frankie when he asked you to dance. You said coldly that you weren't in the mood. Now Lenny and Doreen are giggling together, and Frankie has said he'd better go, stood up, and is asking for a ten-dollar payoff. You don't know what it's for? Sylvia Plath does.

Next example. . . . [About] Doreen, Esther thinks "she really was wonderfully funny."

I've looked at all the dialogue given Doreen on occasions which might produce wit. Here is what I've found:

"The only thing Doreen ever bawled me out about was bothering to get my assignments in by a deadline.

" 'What are you sweating over that for?' "

And: "You know old Jay Cee won't give a damn if that story's in tomorrow or Monday . . . Jay Cee's ugly as sin . . . I bet that old husband of hers turns out all the lights before he gets near her or he'd puke otherwise."

And: "I fitted the lid on my typewriter. . . .

"Doreen grinned. 'Smart girl.' "

And: "In private Doreen called her [Betsy] Pollyanna Cowgirl."

And, in Lenny's apartment, when Lenny is cutting up: " 'What a card. Isn't he a card?' "

And: " 'Stick around, will you? I wouldn't have a chance if he tried anything funny. Did you see that muscle?' "

After the banquet luncheon, given by *Ladies' Day,* when Esther is recovering from food poisoning (Doreen's is the first speech):

"Well, you almost died."

"I guess it was all that caviar."

"Caviar nothing! It was the crabmeat. They did tests on it and it was chockfull of ptomaine."

I had visions of the celestially white kitchens of *Ladies' Day* stretching into infinity. I saw avocado pear after avocado pear being stuffed with crabmeat and mayonnaise and photographed under brilliant lights. I saw the delicate, pink-mottled claw meat poking seductively through its blanket of mayonnaise. . . . Poison.

"Who did tests?"

"Those dodos on *Ladies' Day*. As soon as you all started keeling over like ninepins, somebody called into the office . . . and they did tests on everything left over from the big lunch. Ha!"

Finally, before the blind date with Marco:

"Honestly . . . this one'll be different."

"Tell me about him," I said stonily.

"He's from Peru."

"They're squat," I said. "They're ugly as Aztecs."

"No, no, no, sweetie. I've already met him."

If either of this pair has been given a touch of comic vision or a glint of verbal wit, surely it's Esther, not Doreen.

Shall we believe it's unintentional?

The last example is Constantin, the simultaneous interpreter, who will squeeze no more than a girl's hand. Subtly, Sylvia Plath makes him gay—by association, when he and Esther sit by his colleague, "a stern muscular Russian girl with no makeup . . . in her double-breasted grey suit. To have been more open than this at the outset would, of course, have taken the tension out of the failure of Esther's plan of submission. Constantin's nature never becomes clear to Esther, and the author reveals it to the reader only gradually. In his apartment after dinner, "I asked him if he was engaged or had any special girlfriend, thinking maybe that was what was the matter, but he said no, he made a point of keeping clear of such attachments."

Esther goes into his bedroom, takes off her shoes and lies down.

Then I heard Constantin sigh and come in from the balcony. One by one his shoes clonked on the floor, and he lay down by my side. . . .

I thought he must be the most beautiful man I'd ever seen. . . . I thought if only I had a keen, shapely bone-structure . . . Constantin might find me interesting enough to sleep with.

I woke to the sound of rain. . . .

Constantin . . . was lying in his shirt and trousers and stocking feet just as I had left him when he dropped asleep . . . as I stared down, his eyelids lifted and he looked at me, and his eyes were full of love. I watched dumbly as a shutter of recognition clicked across the blur of tenderness and the wide pupils went glossy and depthless as patent leather.

Constantin sat up, yawning. "What time is it?" . . .

As we sat back to back on our separate sides of the bed fumbling with our shoes . . . I sensed Constantin turn around. "Is your hair always like that?"

"Like what?"

He didn't answer but put his hand at the root of my hair and ran his fingers out slowly to the tip ends like a comb. A little electric shock flared through me and I sat quite still. . . .

"Ah, I know what it is," Constantin said. "You've just washed it."

And he bent down to lace up his tennis shoes.

Now, at the end of all this, I need to speculate, in a way you may feel I have no business doing. I half agree, for I have no proof outside myself that what I'm going to talk about exists, and only intuition to tell me Sylvia Plath contended with it. Yet if I were talking with Peter and Paul, I would insist on this. Shall I fear the coldness of print at my age?

I believe there is a psychic region, corresponding to the unspeakable in general human experience, which is, for writers, the unwritable. In it is that emotional experience which can never be recollected in tranquility, because to recollect it is to become disturbed again. (pp. 147-50)

One of the ways of recognizing the unwritable is that you do keep trying to deal with it, to make something of it, and can, finally if at all, only in one of three ways.

The first, with awe and admiration, I shall set aside, since what comes of it is neither fiction nor poetry, but that direct confession in prose for which the term "agonized" is often used. (p. 150)

The second is more commonly available. It is to fictionalize the unwritable thoroughly enough, by wishing it off on an invented character, so that it's no longer autobiographical. This is what I feel Sylvia Plath was able to do successfully in parts one and three of *The Bell Jar.* In the third, for a final pair of instances, I'm relying on biographical information from which I learned that there was no Joan Gilling failing in the asylum while Esther Greenwood was recovering, and that Irwin the Instrument wasn't one, but another sort of man, met with after the time of maidenhood, and in a less significant way.

It was in part two, about Elly and her attempted suicide, which I've called sometimes tedious, almost antipathetic, that my intuition says the unwritable could not be written in the second way, of making fiction.

This left the third way, which is to reveal the unwritable in a system of symbols, language, allusions, and images so nearly private that only perfect, perfectly dedicated readers, to whom the reading is as serious as writing to the writer, will deserve to make them out.

While Victoria Lucas was working with Esther Greenwood and Elly Higginbottom, Sylvia Plath was writing *Ariel.* (pp. 150-51)

> *Vance Bourjaily, "Victoria Lucas and Elly Higginbottom," in* Ariel Ascending: Writings About Sylvia Plath, *edited by Paul Alexander, Harper & Row, Publishers, 1985, pp. 134-51.*

Linda W. Wagner

One of the most misunderstood of contemporary novels, Sylvia Plath's *The Bell Jar* is in structure and intent a highly conventional *bildungsroman.* Concerned almost entirely with the education and maturation of Esther Greenwood, Plath's novel uses a chronological and necessarily episodic structure to keep Esther at the center of all action. Other characters are fragmentary, subordinate to Esther and her developing consciousness, and are shown only through their effects on her as central character. No incident is included which does not influence her maturation, and the most important formative incidents occur in the city, New York. As Jerome Buckley describes the *bildungsroman* in his 1974 *Season of Youth,* its principal elements are "a growing up and gradual self-discovery," "alienation," "provinciality, the larger society," "the conflict of generations," "ordeal by love" and "the search for a vocation and a working philosophy."

Plath signals the important change of location at the opening of *The Bell Jar:* "It was a queer, sultry summer, the summer they electrocuted the Rosenbergs, and I didn't know what I was doing in New York. . . . New York was bad enough. By nine in the morning the fake, country-wet freshness that somehow seeped in overnight evaporated like the tail end of a sweet dream. Mirage-gray at the bottom of their granite canyons, the hot streets wavered in the sun, the car tops sizzled and glittered, and the dry, cindery dust blew into my eyes and down my throat." Displaced, misled by the morning freshness, Greenwood describes a sterile, inimical setting for her descent into, and exploration of, a hell both personal and communal. Readers have often stressed the analogy between Greenwood and the Rosenbergs—and sometimes lamented the inappropriateness of Plath's comparing her personal *angst* with their actual execution—but in this opening description, the Rosenberg execution is just one of the threatening elements present in the New York context. It is symptomatic of the "foreign" country's hostility, shown in a myriad of ways throughout the novel.

In *The Bell Jar,* as in the traditional *bildungsroman,* the character's escape to a city images the opportunity to find self as well as truths about life. . . . As Buckley points out, however, the city is often ambivalent: "the city, which seems to promise infinite variety and newness, all too often brings a disenchantment more alarming and decisive than any dissatisfaction with the narrowness of provincial life." For Esther Greenwood, quiet Smith student almost delirious with the opportunity to go to New York and work for *Ladies' Day* for a month, the disappointment of her New York experience is cataclysmic. Rather than shape her life, it nearly ends it; and Plath structures the novel to show the process of disenchantment in rapid acceleration.

The novel opens in the midst of Greenwood's month in New York, although she tells the story in flashbacks; and for the first half of the book—ten of its twenty chapters—attention remains there, or on past experiences that are germane to the New York experiences. Greenwood recounts living with the other eleven girls on the *Ladies' Day* board at the Amazon Hotel, doing assignments for the tough fiction editor Jay Cee, going to lunches and dances, buying clothes, dating men very unlike the fellows she had known at college, and sorting through lifestyles like Doreen's which shock, bewilder, and yet fascinate her. Events as predictably mundane as these are hardly the stuff of exciting fiction but Plath has given them an unexpected drama because of the order in which they appear. *The Bell Jar* is plotted to establish two primary themes: that of Greenwood's developing identity, or lack of it; and that of her battle against submission to the authority of both older people and, more pertinently, of men. The second theme is sometimes absorbed by the first but Plath uses enough imagery of sexual conquest that it comes to have an almost equal importance. For a woman of the 1950s, finding an identity other than that of sweetheart, girlfriend, and wife and mother was a major achievement.

Greenwood's search for identity is described through a series of episodes that involve possible role models. Doreen, the Southern woman whose rebelliousness fascinates Esther, knows exactly what she will do with her time in New York. The first scene in the novel is Doreen's finding the macho Lenny Shepherd, disc jockey and playboy par excellance. Attracted by Doreen's "decadence," Esther goes along with the pair until the sexual jitterbug scene ends with Doreen's melon-like breasts flying out of her dress after she has bitten Lenny's ear lobe. Esther has called herself *Elly Higginbottom* in this scene, knowing instinctively that she wants to be protected from the kind of knowledge Doreen has. Plath describes Esther as a photo negative, a small black dot, a hole in the ground; and when she walks the 48 blocks home to the Amazon in panic, she sees no one recognizable in the mirror. (pp. 55-7)

The second "story" of the New York experience is the ptomaine poisoning of all the girls except Doreen after the *Ladies' Day* magazine luncheon. Plath's vignette of Jay Cee is imbedded in this account; the editor's great disappointment in Greenwood (because she has no motivation, no direction) serves to make Esther more depressed. As she comes near death from the poisoning, she also assesses the female role models available to her: her own mother, who urges her to learn shorthand; the older writer Philomena Guinea, who has befriended her but prescriptively; and Jay Cee, by now an admonitory figure. Although Esther feels "purged and holy and ready for a new life" after her ordeal, she cannot rid herself of the feeling of betrayal. No sooner had she realized Jay Cee ("I wished I had a mother like Jay Cee. Then I'd know what to do") than she had disappointed her. . . . Plath's handling of these early episodes makes clear Greenwood's very real confusion about her direction. As Buckley has pointed out, the apparent conflict with parent or location in the *bildungsroman* is secondary to the real conflict, which remains "personal in origin; the problem lies with the hero himself" (or herself).

Esther Greenwood's struggle to know herself, to be self-motivated, to become a writer as she has always dreamed is effectively presented through Plath's comparatively fragmented structure. . . . [Perhaps] we should not be disturbed that the face in [Esther's] mirror is mutable. We must recognize with sympathy, however, that she carries the weight of having to maintain a number of often conflicting identities—the obliging daughter and the ungrateful woman, the successful writer and the immature student, the virginal girlfriend and the worldly lover. In its structure, *The Bell Jar* shows how closely these strands are interwoven.

While Plath is ostensibly writing about Esther's New York experiences and her quest for a female model, she regularly interjects comments about Buddy Willard, the Yale medical student who has proposed to Esther. Early references to him connect him with the haunting childbirth scene and the bottled foetuses and cadavers he has

introduced Esther to. That these images are all connected with women's traditional choices in life—to become mothers—begins to frame the essential conflict between Buddy and Esther. From chapters five through eight Plath describes the romance between the two, but the extensive flashback seems less an intrusion than an explication. Esther is what she is in New York because of the indoctrination she has had at the hands of her socially-approved guide, Buddy Willard. For Buddy, women are helpmeets, submissive to husband's wishes; they have no identity in themself. Esther's desire to become a poet is nonsense (poems are "dust" in his vocabulary); her true role is to be virginal and accepting of his direction—whether the terrain be sex or skiing. More explicit than their conversations are the images Plath chooses to describe Esther during this section, images of frustration and futility.

One central image is that of the fig tree, first introduced after Esther has nearly died from food poisoning and is reading the stories *Ladies' Day* has sent the convalescents. Lush in its green spring, the fig tree nourishes the love of an unaware couple. In contrast, Esther describes her love for Buddy as dying,

> we had met together under our own imaginary fig tree, and what we had seen wasn't a bird coming out of an egg but a baby coming out of a woman, and then something awful happened and we went our separate ways.

When the fig tree metaphor recurs to Esther, she sees it filled with fat purple figs. . . . She sits in the crotch of the tree, however, "starving to death, just because I couldn't make up my mind which of the figs I would choose. I wanted each and every one of them, but choosing one meant losing all the rest." The dilemma of her adolescence—unlike that of most men—was that any choice was also a relinquishing. Greenwood believed firmly that there was no way, in the American culture of the 1950s, that a talented woman could successfully combine a professional career with homemaking. As Mrs. Willard kept insisting, "What a man is is an arrow into the future and what a woman is is the place the arrow shoots off from."

Eventually, in Esther's metaphor, the figs rot and die, a conclusion which aligns the image tonally with the rest of the novel. In her highly visual presentation of Esther's education, Plath consistently shows characters who are poisoned, diseased, injured, bloodied, and even killed. The violence of her characterization seems a fitting parallel for the intensity of her feelings about the dilemmas Greenwood faces as she matures. . . . Greenwood's persona is clearly marked by feelings of uncertainty, based on her all-too-sharp understanding of her "absence of power." When Buddy, who has never skiied himself, "instructs" her in the sport and encourages her in the long run that breaks her leg in two places, she obeys him almost mindlessly. (The fact that she finds a sense of self and power in the run is an unexpected benefit for her.) Buddy's malevolence as he diagnoses the breaks and predicts that she will be in a cast for months is a gleeful insight into his real motives for maintaining their relationship while he is hospitalized for tuberculosis. Esther is his possession, his security, his way of keeping his own self image normal in the midst of his increasing plumpness and his fear of disease.

Buddy's sadistic treatment of Esther prepares the way for the last New York episode, Esther's date with the cruel woman-hater, Marco. Replete with scenes of violence, sexual aggression, mud and possession, this last of the New York stories plunges the reader further into the relentless depravity the city has provided. Marco's brutal rape attempt and his marking Esther with blood from his bleeding nose are physically even more insulting than his calling her *slut*. But even though the men in Esther's life are responsible for these events, Plath shows clearly that Esther's passivity and her lack of questioning are also responsible. Esther's malaise has made her incapable of dealing with aggression either subtle or overt—except privately. Once she has returned to the Amazon, she carries all her expensive clothes to the roof of the hotel and throws them into the sky. Her anger at New York is at least partly misplaced, but Plath has shown that the city and its occupants have exacerbated wounds already given in more provincial and seemingly protective locations. Throwing out her clothes is tantamount to rejecting the traditional image of pretty, smart girl, object for man's acquisition (the use throughout the novel of the *Ladies' Day* photographs of the fashionably dressed coeds also builds to this scene).

Unfortunately, once Plath returns home—dressed in Betsy's skirt and blouse and still carrying Marco's blood streaks on her face—she finds that she has been rejected from the prestigious Harvard writing course. That blow destroys the last shred of self image (Greenwood as writer), and the second half of the novel shows Esther's education not in the process of becoming adult but rather in the process of becoming mad. Again, Plath structures the book so that role model figures are introduced and either discredited or approved. Esther's mother, who appears to think her daughter's insanity is just malingering, is quickly discredited. The irony is that Esther not only must live with the woman; she must also share a bedroom (and by implication, the most intimate parts of her life) with her. Joan Gilling, a Smith student and previous rival for Buddy's affections, presents the option of lesbian life, but her own stability has been irrevocably damaged and she later hangs herself. Doctor Norton, Esther's psychiatrist, is the warm, tolerant and just mentor whose efforts to help Esther understand herself are quickly rewarded. Doctor Norton gives her leave to both hate her mother, and the attitudes she represents, and to be fitted with a diaphragm, so that the previously closed world of sexual experience will be open to her. As Plath has presented both areas of experience throughout the novel, Esther needs to be free from conventional judgments so that she will not absorb so much guilt. (pp. 57-61)

The relentless guilt Esther feels as she looks from her bedroom window and sees the neighbor Dodo Conway wheeling her latest child of six while she is pregnant with the seventh, brings all the scattered images of childbirth and female responsibility to a climax. Unless she accepts this role, Esther will have no life—this is the message her society, even the most supportive elements in it, gives her. But Plath has used one key image during the childbirth scene, that of a "long, blind, doorless and windowless corridor of pain . . . waiting to open up and shut her in again," and that image of relentless suffering recurs throughout the second half of *The Bell Jar*. It is, in fact, the title image, an encasement, unrelieved, where Esther is "stewing in my own sour air." More frightening than the bewildering crotch of the fig tree, the bell jar presents

no choices, no alternatives, except death. Another late image is that of "a black, airless sack with no way out." Choice has been subsumed to guilty depression, and one of the refrains that haunts Esther is *You'll never get anywhere like that, you'll never get anywhere like that.*

And so the second half of the novel becomes a chronicle of Esther's education in suicide and her various suicide attempts. So expertly and completely have the contradictions of her adolescent education been presented in the first ten chapters that Plath needs do very little with background during the second half. Buddy Willard makes only one appearance, wondering sadly who will marry Esther now that she has been "here." Such a scene only confirms the intent of his characterization earlier in the book. Even during the second half of the novel, Esther remains the good student. In her study of suicide, she reads, asks questions, correlates material, chooses according to her own personality, and progresses just as if she were writing a term paper. All factual information is given in the context of *her* needs, however, so the essential charting of Esther's psyche dominates the rest of the book.

Many of the episodes in the latter part of the novel are skeletal. It is as if Plath were loathe to give up any important details but that she also realized that her readers were, in effect, reading two stories. The first half of *The Bell Jar* gives the classic female orientation and education, with obvious indications of the failure of that education appearing near the end of the New York experience. The second half gives an equally classic picture of mental deterioration and its treatment, a picture relatively new to fiction in the late 1950s, important both culturally and personally to Plath. But the exigencies of the fictional form were pressing, and Plath had already crowded many characters and episodes into her structure. The somewhat ambivalent ending may have occurred as much because the book was growing so long as because Plath was uncertain about the outcome of her protagonist. As the text makes clear, the main reason for a fairly open ending is that Esther herself had to remain unsure about the condition of her recovery, about her health in the future: she saw question marks; she hoped the bell jar would not close down again; but she also affirmed that her leaving the asylum was a birth, and that there should be "a ritual for being born twice." The recurrence of the "old brag" of her heart—"I am, I am, I am"—is much more comforting than another time the refrain had occurred, as she contemplated death through drowning.

The Esther Greenwood pictured in the later pages of *The Bell Jar* is a much more confident person. She knows she does not want to be like the lobotomized Valerie, incapable of any emotion. She knows real grief at Joan's funeral, and real anger at Buddy's visit. She understands the enormity of her mother's refusal to accept the truth about her illness, and the corresponding and somewhat compensatory generosity of Doctor Nolan's acceptance of it. Esther is also much more aggressive in her language. For the first time in the years depicted, she speaks directly. " 'I have a bill here, Irwin,' " she says quietly to the man who was her first lover. " 'I hate her,' " she admits to Doctor Nolan about her mother. " 'You had nothing to do with us, Buddy,' " she says scathingly to her former boyfriend. Even early in her breakdown she is quite direct ("I can't sleep. I can't read. . . . ") but the irony in these encounters is that no one she speaks with will attend to what she is saying. Various doctors, her mother, friends persist in translating what she is saying ("I haven't slept for fourteen nights") into meanings that are acceptable to them. (pp. 61-3)

The closing lines of *The Bell Jar* surely draw a birth scene:

> There ought, I thought, to be a ritual for being born twice—patched, retreaded and approved for the road. I was trying to think of an appropriate one when Doctor Nolan appeared from nowhere and touched me on the shoulder.
>
> "All right, Esther."
>
> I rose and followed her to the open door.
>
> Pausing, for a brief breath, on the threshold, I saw the silver-haired doctor who had told me about the rivers and the Pilgrims on my first day, and the pocked, cadaverous face of Miss Huey, and eyes I thought I had recognized over white masks.
>
> The eyes and the faces all turned themselves toward me, and guiding myself by them, as if by a magical thread, I stepped into the room.

In contrast to the doorless blankness of tunnels, sacks, and bell jars, this open door and Esther's ability to breathe are surely positive images.

Inherent in the notion of *bildungsroman* is the sense that such a novel will provide a blueprint for a successful education, however the word *successful* is defined. At times, as in *Jude the Obscure,* education comes too late to save the protagonist, but the issue is more the information to be conveyed than the factual ending of the character's saga. For Jerome Buckley, if the protagonist has the means to give life "some ultimate coherence," then education has been efficacious. *The Bell Jar* gives the reader the sense that Esther has, at least momentarily, gained the ability to achieve that coherence. Because so few *bildungsromane* deal with madness, however, exact comparisons between Plath's novel and those usually considered in such generic discussions are difficult; but because so many women's novels treat the subject of madness, *The Bell Jar* cannot be considered an anomaly. (pp. 64-5)

Among other differences between the conventional *bildungsroman,* which usually deals with a young man's education, and the female novel of experience in adolescence would be the shift in role from father as crucial parent to mother. Much of the process of education is imitative, so that figures which serve as role models will also shift from male to female. A female *bildungsroman* will thus seem to be peopled more heavily with women characters than with men, although cultural patterns would keep men—economically, socially and sexually—prominent. It may be because men must occur in the female novels that they come to play the role of adversary or antagonist, whereas in the male *bildungsroman* women can be simply omitted.

Educational experiences and choices leading to occupations will also differ, but none will be quite so persuasive as the female's need to choose between profession and domesticity. It is the inescapability of that choice that forces many a novel which would well be labeled *bildungsroman* into the category of domestic novel. Underlying what would seem to be the choice of profession is the less obvious issue of sexuality, which again plays a very different role in female adolescence than in male. In the conventional *bildungsroman,* sexual experience is but another step toward maturity. It suggests the eventual leaving one household to establish another. For a man, such a move may mean only that he hangs his hat in a different closet. For a woman, however, the move means a complete change of status, from mistress to servant, person responsible for the housekeeping in ways she would never have been as the young daughter of a house. A parallel degradation occurs in most representations of the sex act. Biological necessity and physical size mean that the female is usually a more passive partner in intercourse. The accoutrements of a sexual relationship are therefore different for women than for men, and the relationship may loom central to the female *bildungsroman,* while it may be almost peripheral to the male. Losing one's virginity unwisely seldom determines the eventual life of the male protagonist; it is the stuff of ostracism, madness, and suicide for a female, however. Plath's concern with Esther's sexual experience is relevant, certainly, for her choices will determine her life. Her aggression in finding Irwin so that she can be sexually experienced is a positive sign, but the characteristic irony—that she be the one in a million to hemorrhage after intercourse—mars the experience and tends to foreshadow the incipient bad luck which may follow cultural role reversal. As Plath knew only too well, society had its ways of punishing women who were too aggressive, too competent, and too masculine.

The apparent connections between Plath's experiences and Esther's are legitimate topics of discussion when *bildungsromane* are involved because the strength of such novels usually depends on the author's emotional involvement in the themes. Buckley points out that a *bildungsroman* is often an early novel, a first or a second, and that much of the life—as well as the ambivalence—of the novel exists because the author is so involved in the process he or she is describing. In Plath's case, *The Bell Jar* was not only her first novel; it was also published under a pseudonym. Limited to British publication in the original 1963 printing, under the authorship of "Victoria Lucas," the novel was an only partially disguised statement of Plath's anger toward a culture, and a family, that had nourished her only conditionally—that would accept her only provided she did "acceptable" things. If one of the goals of writing such a book was self-discovery, then Plath's evident anger may have been as dismaying, for her in the early 1960s, as it was unexpected.

Because it is this tone of wrenching anger that makes *The Bell Jar* seem so different from the novels generally categorized as *bildungsroman.* The wry self-mockery that gives way to the cryptic poignance of Esther's madness has no antecedent in earlier novels of development. It is in tone and mood that Plath succeeded in making the conventional form—which she followed in a number of important respects—her own.

What *The Bell Jar* ultimately showed was a woman struggling to become whole, not a woman who had reached some sense of stable self. And that conclusion, according to Annis Pratt in *Archetypal Patterns in Women's Fiction,* is what any reader might expect from a sensitive woman author. As Pratt observes, even the most conservative women authors create narratives manifesting an acute tension between what any normal human being might desire and what a woman must become. Women's fiction reflects an experience radically different from men's because our drive towards growth as persons is thwarted by our society's prescriptions concerning gender. . . . we are outcasts in the land. . . .

So far as the generic differences are concerned, then, the female hero in a woman's *bildungsroman* will be "destined for disappointment." Pratt concludes, "The vitality and hopefulness characterizing the adolescent hero's attitude toward her future here meet and conflict with the expectations and dictates of the surrounding society. Every element of her desired world—freedom to come and go, allegiance to nature, meaningful work, exercise of the intellect, and use of her own erotic capabilities—inevitably clashes with patriarchal norms."

The Bell Jar must certainly be read as the story of that inevitable clash, a dulled and dulling repetition of lives all too familiar to contemporary readers, and a testimony to the repressive cultural mold that trapped many mid-century women, forcing them outside what should have been their rightful, productive lives. For those of us who lived through the 1950s, *The Bell Jar* moves far beyond being Sylvia Plath's autobiography. (pp. 65-7)

> *Linda W. Wagner, "Plath's 'The Bell Jar' as Female 'Bildungsroman',"* in Women's Studies: An Interdisciplinary Journal, *Vol. 12, Nos. 1-6, 1986, pp. 55-68.*

FURTHER READING

Alexander, Paul, ed. *Ariel Ascending: Writings about Sylvia Plath.* New York: Harper & Row, 1985, 217 p.
> Contains biographical and critical essays on Plath, including pieces by Ted Hughes, Joyce Carol Oates, and Anne Sexton.

Berman, Jeffrey. " 'If Writing Is Not an Outlet, What Is?': Sylvia Plath and *The Bell Jar.*" In his *The Talking Cure: Literary Representations of Psychoanalysis,* pp. 120-53. New York and London: New York University Press, 1985.
> Academic analysis of *The Bell Jar,* paralleling Plath's

psychological problems with those of the novel's protagonist.

Butscher, Edward, ed. *Sylvia Plath: The Woman and the Work.* New York: Dodd, Mead & Company, 1977, 242 p.
> Comprised of biographical and critical essays on Plath, including pieces by Richard Wilbur, Irving Howe, and Gordon Lameyer, a high-school boyfriend of Plath's. Includes bibliography.

Ellmann, Mary. "*The Bell Jar*: An American Girlhood." In *The Art of Sylvia Plath: A Symposium.* Edited by Charles Newman, pp. 221-26. Bloomington: Indiana University Press, 1970.
> Discusses the methods and themes of *The Bell Jar.* Excerpted in *CLC,* Vol. 17.

Lane, Gary, and Stevens, Marcia. *Sylvia Plath: A Bibliography.* Metuchen, N.J. & London: The Scarecrow Press, Inc., 1978, 144 p.
> Detailed, chronological compilation of works by and about Plath.

Scholes, Robert. *"The Bell Jar." The New York Times Book Review* (11 April 1971): 7.
> One of the first American reviews of the novel, it is considered by critics to be an excellent analysis. Excerpted in *CLC,* Vol. 17.

Smith, Stan. "Attitudes Counterfeiting Life: The Irony of Artifice in Sylvia Plath's *The Bell Jar.*" *Critical Quarterly* 17, No. 3 (Autumn 1975): 247-60.
> Examines the structure and psychological case history of the novel. Excerpted in *CLC,* Vol. 17.

Steiner, Nancy Hunter. *A Closer Look at Ariel: A Memory of Sylvia Plath.* New York: Harper's Magazine Press, 1973, 83 p.
> Memoir by Plath's college roommate. Offers substantial insight into the time of which Plath writes in *The Bell Jar.*

Stevenson, Anne. *Bitter Fame: A Life of Sylvia Plath.* Boston: Houghton Mifflin Co., 1989, 413 p.
> Well-regarded, thorough biography. Provides considerable psychological insight into Plath's life and works. Includes index, appendices, photographs.

Wood, David. "Everything You Wanted to Know About Suicide! *The Bell Jar* by Sylvia Plath." *Kyushu American Literature,* No. 25 (July 1984): 7-17.
> Maintains that the focus of *The Bell Jar* is not on suicide, but on an individual's struggle for self-control.

Thomas Pynchon

1937-

(Born Thomas Ruggles Pynchon, Jr.) American novelist and short story writer.

Pynchon is widely regarded as one of the most eminent literary stylists in contemporary American fiction. His novels, often described as labyrinthine or encyclopedic in scope, are characterized by an aura of great mystery and reveal a knowledge of many disciplines in the natural and social sciences. Pynchon's use of sophisticated ideas is balanced by his verbal playfulness with such elements as black humor, outlandish puns, slapstick, running gags, parody, and ridiculous names. Through this blend of serious themes and comic invention and combination of documented fact and imaginative fantasy, Pynchon paradoxically affirms and denies the notion that mundane reality may possess hidden meaning. Living amidst the chaos of modern existence that is mirrored in the fragmented structures of his novels, Pynchon's protagonists typically undertake vague yet elaborate quests to discover their identities and to find meaning and order in their lives. While Pynchon's novels have often been faulted as labored or incomprehensible, all have provoked ongoing scholarly debate and earned widespread popularity among young readers.

Pynchon's literary career began with the publication of several short stories, five of which are included in his 1984 collection, *Slow Learner: Early Stories.* This volume contains an uncharacteristic introduction by Pynchon, who has since the beginning of his career maintained strict anonymity. Although Pynchon's short fiction is regarded as less accomplished than his later novels, many reviewers maintain that his early stories offer insight into his stylistic development. Pynchon's initial novel, *V.,* was compared to works by such authors as Joseph Heller, William Burroughs, Kurt Vonnegut, and John Barth for its experimental format and use of black and absurdist humor. Among other events, the book relates the obsessive quest of Herbert Stencil to discover the identity of a person or thing referred to as "V." in his father's diary. Stencil's quest is complicated by a superabundance of clues that he feels obliged to follow. During his travels, Stencil encounters a group of people known as the "Whole Sick Crew," whose decadence and aimlessness are widely regarded as representative of the moral, social, and cultural decline of Western civilization. Pynchon contrasts the energetic Stencil with the moribund state of the Whole Sick Crew as part of an intensive investigation into the nature of the animate and inanimate. While some critics consider Pynchon to have overelaborated essentially simple themes, others were impressed by the vast historical scale of *V.,* particularly its multiple perspectives on twentieth-century events and the intricate network of referents that serve to expand the implications of Stencil's quest.

Pynchon's second novel, *The Crying of Lot 49,* is regarded as his most accessible work due to its concise development. In this work, Pynchon employs the second law of thermodynamics—a rule of physics that describes entro-py—as a metaphor for the forces that contribute to social decline. *The Crying of Lot 49* centers on Oedipa Maas, who is named the executrix of the will of Pierce Inverarity, a California real-estate mogul and her former lover. In executing Inverarity's will, Oedipa stumbles upon clues suggesting that a centuries-old communications system is secretly competing with the United States Postal Service. Like many of Pynchon's characters, Oedipa is uncertain whether her perception is valid or a result of either her own paranoia or the manipulation of her thoughts by others. Throughout his fiction, Pynchon alludes to paranoia, through which his characters often assign an organizing principle to a world that would otherwise be random and meaningless. Frank Kermode stated: "The shortest of [Pynchon's] novels, *The Crying of Lot 49* most perfectly expresses, as a kind of riddle, the question whether evidence that seems amply to support a theory of universal correspondence, secret networks of significance, covert modes of oppression, is really to be found out there in the world or only in the crazed mind of the person who discerns it." Like many of Pynchon's works, *The Crying of Lot 49* ends before the protagonist's quest is resolved. Critics have offered many interpretations of the novel but have generally praised Pynchon's metaphorical use of the concept of entropy.

Pynchon's third novel, *Gravity's Rainbow,* received a National Book Award and was also nominated for the Pulitzer Prize. While Pynchon's detractors have variously faulted this controversial novel as obscene, nihilistic, or incomprehensible, many designate *Gravity's Rainbow* a masterpiece, contending that Pynchon has fashioned a work of profound implications by connecting a wide variety of human activities and ideas with the mass destruction of World War II. Described as an extended meditation on death, *Gravity's Rainbow* blends factual details and fantastic events, includes scenes of comedy and brutality, develops extensive symbolic implications, and offers several perspectives of historical events. In addition to suggesting that Western society actively promotes a culture of death by perfecting such weapons as the German V-2 rocket, Pynchon links advances in science and technology with historical patterns, political, economic, and social values, and international cartels in their contributions to the war effort. Although considered by some an overrated work, *Gravity's Rainbow* is generally regarded as Pynchon's most significant achievement and an important contribution to contemporary literature.

Nearly seventeen years elapsed between the publication of *Gravity's Rainbow* and Pynchon's next novel, *Vineland.* On one level, the title of this work alludes to America as it was discovered by Leif Ericson prior to Christopher Columbus; on another, Vineland refers to a fictitious county near the coast of northern California, the state's last uncharted wilderness. In the 1980s, Vineland serves as a refuge for middle-aged veterans of the 1960s counterculture who have sought refuge from government repression. The novel focuses primarily upon Prairie Wheeler's search for her long-lost mother, Frenesi Gates, a beautiful former member of a defunct radical group dedicated to exposing the corruption and hypocrisy of the Nixon administration. Prairie eventually learns that Frenesi betrayed the cause and became an informer for Brock Vond, a notorious, fascistic federal prosecutor. During the 1980s, Frenesi disappears after being cut from the payroll of the Federal Witness Protection Program, and a love-obsessed Vond attempts to locate her by leading an assault on the surviving counterculture. Together with characters such as DL Chastain, a "ninjette" and former friend of Frenesi's, and Takeshi Fumimota, an amphetamine addict who serves as a means for Pynchon to parody Japanese espionage films, Prairie attempts to discover her family's past and future. Although the novel contains many subplots and characters, combining elements of soap opera and political thriller, *Vineland* is generally considered less ambitious in scope, thematic complexity, and historical range than Pynchon's previous works. Terrence Rafferty commented: "*Vineland,* for all its wild, abrupt turnings, is the clearest novel Thomas Pynchon has written. . . . This novel is as funny, as smart, as lyrical, and as subversive as any American fiction of the past decade, but the most remarkable thing about it is the purity of its desire to get through to us. These days, Pynchon seems to be writing out of the deepest, most uncontrollable motive for speech: the need to pass along what he has learned before it's lost forever."

(See also *CLC,* Vols. 2, 3, 6, 9, 11, 18, 33; *Contemporary Authors,* Vols. 17-20, rev. ed.; *Contemporary Authors New Revision Series,* Vol. 22; and *Dictionary of Literary Biography,* Vol. 2.)

PRINCIPAL WORKS

V.   (novel)   1963
The Crying of Lot 49   (novel)   1966
Gravity's Rainbow   (novel)   1973
Slow Learner: Early Stories   1984
Vineland   (novel)   1990

Robert D. Newman

Slow Learner collects five of Pynchon's early stories, outlining his writer's apprenticeship. Taken with his entertaining and candid introduction to the collection, they offer an excellent guideline for the aspiring writer, much like a postmodern version of Rilke's *Letters to a Young Poet.* Even though Pynchon wrote **"The Secret Integration"** after the publication of *V.,* all the stories possess the flaws of undergraduate pieces. "My specific piece of wrong procedure back then," he admits, "was, incredibly, to browse through the thesaurus and note words that sounded cool, hip, or likely to produce an effect, usually that of making me look good, without then taking the trouble to go and find out in the dictionary what they meant." Pynchon's showmanship, especially his insistence on calling attention to literary allusions, is unrestrained. Unlike most undergraduate works, however, these stories are brilliantly conceived, although unevenly executed. As is typi-

cal of a thoughtful and probing young man, he forces concepts on structures that will not hold them. Yet the reader is fortunate to be able to witness his process of discovery. In these stories one can observe his sometimes fumbling but consistently penetrating attempts to tunnel into the subterranean underpinnings of our culture. He frequently presents his disturbing findings like a stand-up comic, sometimes betraying his lack of confidence by playing too strongly to his audience. But in his comedy there is always conscience, born of seriousness and fear and wonder.

In Pynchon's first published story, **"The Small Rain"** (1959), the "characters are found dealing with death in pre-adult ways." Like numerous characters in his novels these retreat from feeling: "they evade: they sleep late, they seek euphemisms. When they do mention death they try to make with the jokes. Worst of all, they hook it up with sex." Nathan "Lardass" Levine acquires autobiographical dimensions, having "once dug Lester Young or Gerry Mulligan at Birdland" and being "over six feet and loose jointed." A graduate of the City College of New York, he has enlisted in the army and is stationed at Fort Roach, Louisiana. Levine enjoys the inertia of army life in the middle of nowhere. He passes his time reading pornographic novels like *Swamp Wench* while specializing in mental inanition. Ironically, he is a communications expert, thereby introducing Pynchon's fascination with the relationship between communication and entropy.

Levine is jerked from his self-enclosure when a hurricane strikes southern Louisiana and his unit is ordered into action. Confronted with the decaying corpses that must be dragged from the water, he plunges from a psychological wasteland into a literal one. . . . Furthermore, the students at the college campus where the army takes up residence during the disaster are oblivious to the horror that surrounds them, thereby commenting on Levine's own death-in-life. Lest the reader miss the point, Pynchon self-consciously alludes to T. S. Eliot and Ernest Hemingway to expand this localized situation to universal proportions.

Levine's immersion in this atmosphere of death transforms him. No longer able to derive comfort from evasion, he envisions himself as "Lardass Levine the Wandering Jew, debating on weekday evenings in strange and nameless towns with other Wandering Jews the essential problems of identity." The influence of Jack Kerouac's *On the Road* is certainly here, and Pynchon also points to Helen Waddell's *The Wandering Scholars,* which discusses a group of medieval poets who departed from their cloistered monasteries to experience the broader dimensions of life in the outside world. (pp. 12-15)

Toward the end of the story Levine drives off with a teasing coed who calls herself Little Buttercup. They drive to a cabin in the swamp where she becomes the incarnation of his swamp wench, "a never totally violated Pasiphae" whose lack of touching after the sex act secures her place in the death-in-life labyrinth of avoidance that substitutes for communication. "In the midst of the great death, the little death," Levine says in reference to the seventeenth-century belief that each orgasm diminished one's life by a day. Yet his experience during the disaster also diminishes his interest in returning to Fort Roach at the conclusion of the story. Although he is no Fisher King, we witness in him a temporary rebirth through self-recognition.

While Pynchon self-deprecatingly refers to the narrative voice in **"Low-lands"** (1960) as that of a "smart-assed jerk who didn't know any better," the story is well structured and rich in suggestion. It extends Pynchon's use of Eliot's "The Waste Land," descending into a fantastic underworld to escape from the surface world's stifling rationality. Tony Tanner calls **"Low-lands"** a rewriting of Washington Irving's "Rip Van Winkle." Ironically, however, Pynchon's protagonist enters the dream state through an awakening.

Dennis Flange, a former naval communications officer who is currently a lawyer, stays home from his office to drink muscatel and listen to Vivaldi with the local garbageman, Rocco Squarcione. Much to his wife Cindy's dismay, his former naval buddy, Pig Bodine, appears on the doorstep. Pig becomes Pynchon's archetypal anarchistic slob, and he brings him back for encores in *V.* and *Gravity's Rainbow.* Having lured Flange away on his wedding night seven years ago for a two-week drunken debauch, Pig has been banished by Cindy, who now throws the three men out of the house and tells Flange not to return.

Flange's home life foreshadows the stultifying domesticity that we find on the opening page of *The Crying of Lot 49.* His two-story home is perched on a cliff overlooking the sea; Flange calls it his "womb with a view." It contains concealed passageways and a network of tunnels in the cellar constructed for whiskey-running during Prohibition. However, prohibition in an emotional sense has ascended upstairs, for Flange practices "Molemanship," regressing into fetal positions and inertia. His marriage has attained nothing but bourgeois sterility. (pp. 15-16)

Flange indulges in two forms of escape from the constraints of his home life. His sessions with his analyst, Geronimo Diaz, depart completely from the over-reliance on rationality that defines his life with Cindy. Diaz is the prototype for Dr. Hilarius of *The Crying of Lot 49* and for the scientists of The White Visitation in *Gravity's Rainbow.* He believes he is Paganini and has lost his powers because he sold his soul to the devil. His sessions with Flange consist of imbibing martinis and "reading aloud to himself out of random-number tables or the Ebbinghaus nonsense-syllable lists, ignoring everything that Flange would be trying to tell him."

Flange's other indulgence is his thoughts of the sea with which he withdraws from the monotony of his life, seeking a cushion for his emotional pain. However, his perspective on the sea lacks the important spatial dimension that he acquires when he descends from his house to arrive at sea level in the dump.

Rocco takes Flange and Pig to the dump, which is presided over by a watchman named Bolingbroke (*Henry IV*) who wears a porkpie hat for a crown. In Bolingbroke's shack they swap sea stories over wine in a scene reminiscent of the "Eumaeus" episode of *Ulysses.* Ironically, the story that Flange tells bears no relation to the sea, but recounts a fraternity prank with a stolen female cadaver. His reason for relating this type of story asserts his passivity as a metaphysic:

> But the real reason he knew and could not say was that if you are Dennis Flange and if the sea's tides are the same that not only wash along your veins but also billow through your fantasies then it is all right to listen to but not to tell stories about that sea, because you and the truth of a true lie were thrown sometime way back into a curious contiguity and as long as you are passive you can remain aware of the truth's extent but the minute you become active you are somehow, if not violating a convention outright, at least screwing up the perspective of things, much as anyone observing subatomic particles changes the works, data and odds, by the act of observing. So he had told the other instead, at random. Or apparently so.

Flange invokes Werner Heisenberg's uncertainty principle, which holds that the position of a subatomic particle cannot be precisely determined without disrupting the system, for the paired qualities of position and motion cannot be measured concurrently. For Flange, life and fantasy are precariously balanced, a balance preserved by passivity. To tell a sea story would be to bring the fantasy world to an active level and thus to disrupt the equilibrium of the duality.

The dump is situated fifty feet below street level, a "lowlands," which Flange associates with a Scottish sea chanty:

> A ship I have got in the North Country
> And she goes by the name of the *Golden Vanity,*
> O, I fear she will be taken by a Spanish Gal-la-lee,
> As she sails by the Low-lands low.

In descending from the perspective of his house above the sea to that of the dump at sea level, Flange attains an epiphany through his observation of the borderless expanse of debris. . . . The flat perspective allows him to project his imagination without limitation. The civilizing process, however, is equated to the piling of debris on the dump site, a process that alters the flat perspective and creates the "convexity" that is at the root of Flange's fear. Like the Mondrian angles that preside over the solitude of his sleep, civilized rationality imposes immediate horizons on the free and open perspectives of his fantasy life.

Flange's recognition permits him access to his alter ego, or doppelgänger, as he awakens to a siren voice calling, "Anglo, . . . Anglo with the golden hair. Come out. Come out by the secret path and find me." He leaves the shack, but knocks over a stack of snow tires arranged by Bolingbroke as a booby trap for gypsies. His revival from unconsciousness is accomplished by a beautiful, three-and-a-half-foot "angel" named Nerissa, suggesting both Portia's maid in *The Merchant of Venice* and a mythical sea nymph. She then leads him through a network of underground tunnels emanating from a backless GE refrigerator to her home. The underground complex, he learns, was built in the thirties by a revolutionary group called the Sons of the Red Apocalypse and has been occupied by gypsies since their demise. In her abode Flange encounters her pet rat, Hyacinth, a forerunner of the rat Veronica in *V.* Nerissa reveals that a fortune-teller named Violetta had foretold that Flange would be her husband, and the story concludes with Flange deciding to stay. He looks at Nerissa and sees sea images: "whitecaps danced across her eyes; sea creatures, he knew, would be cruising about in the submarine green of her heart." His transformation into his fantasy world is complete.

The references to Eliot's poem are numerous. Joseph

Slade argues that Flange is the Phoenician sailor who travels in the wasteland. Violetta is Madame Sosostris, and Nerissa the hyacinth girl who offers renewal. The conclusion of the story also suggests the vision of the mermaids at the end of "The Love Song of J. Alfred Prufrock." However, Prufrock's dream life fails to redeem him, while Flange's fantasy offers a positive alternative to the mundane void of his life with Cindy. His vision of Nerissa and the rat as children counterpoints the sterility of his marriage, with the resultant conviction that "a child makes it all right. Let the world shrink to a *boccie* ball." This image, drawn from Marvell's "To His Coy Mistress," indicates a commitment to life rather than a retreat. In this sense Slade's argument that the story is static is fallacious. Instead, Thomas Schaub's contention that it possesses an hourglass shape, so that the ending becomes an inverted mirror of the beginning, appears more accurate. Flange's descent into the underworld of his fantasy life is a return to the imagination's primal wellspring, unencumbered by the sharp angles of rationality that had previously punctured his security.

In his introduction to *Slow Learner,* Pynchon points to the primary weakness in **"Entropy"** (1960): "It is simply wrong to begin with a theme, symbol or other abstract unifying agent, and then to try to force characters and events to conform to it." The abstract unifying agent is stated in the title, and its cultural and metaphysical applications, derived from Pynchon's reading of *The Education of Henry Adams* and Norbert Wiener's *The Human Use of Human Beings,* are suggested by the depressing climate depicted in the epigraph from Henry Miller's *Tropic of Cancer.* References to literature that depicts sexual perversion—de Sade, Faulkner's *Sanctuary,* Djuna Barnes's *Nightwood*—further underscore the theme of decay. While the characters, as Pynchon admits, "come off as synthetic, insufficiently alive," the story is nonetheless important because it is the first full treatment of thematic material that is to form the cornerstone of Pynchon's novels.

Given the combination of engineering and literature in Pynchon's education, the significance of Eliot's "The Waste Land" to his writing is logically succeeded by that of Henry Adams's theories. Adams applies the second law of thermodynamics—that all things tend toward disorder or entropy—to the decay of civilization. Entropy manifests itself in two somewhat paradoxical ways. In one sense order breaks down, resulting in the random dispersement of energy. In the other the distinctions between the elements of a closed system vanish, resulting in a sterile homogeneity. Adams's applications of these physical laws to his observations of culture form definitive metaphors with which Pynchon structures his future work.

The frequent musical references in the story comment upon its fuguelike structure: the events on two floors of a Washington, D.C. apartment building are counterpointed. On the lower floor Meatball Mulligan is giving a raucous lease-breaking party that has entered its second day. Entropic chaos builds as new guests, primarily government workers, coeds, and sailors, arrive. One woman falls asleep in the sink, and, when moved to the shower, she sits on the drain and almost drowns from the rising water. However, this chaos does not occur within a closed system since diversity is constantly added to the apartment party from the street outside. Given two alternatives to dealing with the mess that his party has become—locking himself in the closet until everyone goes away or trying to calm his guests by attending to their individual needs—Meatball chooses the latter. In choosing not to seal himself off from participation in the flux of life and the diversity of the street, he foreshadows the advice that Oedipa Maas receives in *The Crying of Lot 49* to "keep it bouncing," thereby avoiding deterioration into the lifeless sameness that constitutes the entropic system.

In contrast, the apartment on the floor above houses Callisto and Aubade, who live in a "hothouse" environment. Isolating himself from the world, Callisto creates a closed and unchanging system—an entropic state. . . . (pp. 17-24)

Because the temperature outside has registered 37 degrees for three days, Callisto conjures a paranoiac vision of the heat death of the universe. His obsession fills his memoirs, which he dictates to Aubade, Henry Adams style, in the third person. However, Aubade hears noises from the street and the music from the party punctuating Callisto's words: "the architectonic purity of her world was constantly threatened by such hints of anarchy." She is part French and part Annamese and therefore contains the capacity to bring together two worlds. This, plus the musical aspect of her name, casts her in the symbolic role of harmonizer. As the story alternates between Mulligan's party and Callisto's apartment, the reader learns that Callisto is attempting to heal a sick bird by holding it against the heat of his body, thereby resisting mutability. The eventual death of the bird signals the destruction of the self-contained ecological balance in the room, and Aubade smashes the window to allow the outside world to penetrate.

While Meatball restores order to his party by caring for his guests, Callisto's act of love toward the bird fails to prevent disorder. Seeking an equilibrium between inside and out, Aubade permits the street to invade the hothouse uninhibited. Like the protagonists of all of Pynchon's novels, Meatball and Aubade combat personal and cultural entropy by choosing between hothouse and street. They also share with these later characters the fact that their triumphs are often Pyrrhic and always ephemeral.

"Under the Rose" (1961), later reworked as chapter 3 of *V.,* offers an early indication of Pynchon's capacity to piece together historical events within a fictional narrative. The novel's version includes significant alterations. Most importantly, the events are narrated through the perspective of Herbert Stencil, whose obsessive quest for V. causes him to focus on Victoria Wren so that the other characters serve primarily as a backdrop. The novel does not depict, for example, Porpentine's discovery that Goodfellow's Lothario image is a sham when he observes his impotent tryst with Victoria. Nor does it explore Porpentine's compassion, which is also his fatal flaw.

"Under the Rose" is set in Cairo at the time of the Fashoda crisis in 1898, when the British and French were vying for the strategic area in the Upper Nile. The British spies, Porpentine and Goodfellow, attempt to ward off any terrorist acts that might ignite war. Germany, on the other hand, has much to gain from a war between Britain and France. It sends a trio of spies—Lepsius, Bongo-

Shaftsbury, and Moldweorp—to assassinate the English consul-general, Lord Cromer, in an attempt to encourage hostilities.

The British spies have been trained in a tradition where espionage is conducted on a "gentlemanly basis." Despite their opposed allegiances both British and German agents share a code of conduct. They are "comrade Machiavellians, still playing the games of Renaissance Italian politics in a world that has outgrown them." This code centers around an absolutely impersonal approach to the work of espionage and a consequent disdain for the impurities of human feelings. Bongo-Shaftsbury physically converts to a mechanical doll to cleanse himself of his humanity. . . . Pynchon develops here a theme that will dominate his novels: the transformation in world view from the dominance of the human to that of the inanimate, a reworking of Henry Adams's metaphors of Virgin and Dynamo. The reader observes this shift in microcosm when Porpentine meditates on the new generation of spies:

> Time was his fellow professionals became adept through practice. Learned ciphers by breaking them, custom officials by evading them, some opponents by killing them. Now the new ones read books: young lads, full of theory and (he'd decided) a faith in nothing but the perfection of their own internal machinery.

Porpentine dies because he breaks the code of espionage by permitting his feelings to interfere with his work. He and Goodfellow attempt to frustrate the Germans' assassination of Lord Cromer while Cromer attends a performance of Puccini's *Manon Lescaut* at the Cairo opera house. Pynchon's habit of milking his allusions for all they are worth is illustrated by his choice of this particular opera, which comments on the characters and events of the story. The hero, Des Grieux, who had previously rejected the idea of love, is smitten by a beautiful woman and is subsequently victimized by his newfound romanticism. Likewise Porpentine succumbs to human emotions. He responds to Victoria Wren's plea to protect Goodfellow and also expresses personal anger toward a fellow spy. As he leaves the opera house, he violates the code by yelling at Moldweorp to "go away and die." For this he is executed after chasing the Germans across the desert, the setting where Des Grieux also plays his final scene. Before Porpentine is killed, he requests, and is granted, the release of Victoria and Goodfellow. However, the gentlemanly basis for espionage can no longer apply to him: "He'd crossed some threshold without knowing. Mongrel now, no longer pure. . . . Mongrel, he supposed, is only another way of saying human. After the final step you could not, nothing could be, clean."

The story concludes sixteen years later with Goodfellow in Sarajevo, attempting to prevent the assassination of the Archduke Ferdinand, an event that will spark World War I. His age and impotence comment on his ineffectiveness. With the end of the nineteenth century comes the collapse of traditional codes of conduct. The dedicated agent as savior is rendered anachronistic. While Goodfellow clings to the antiquated image of the spy, his latest "conquest" describes him to her friends as "a simple-minded Englishman, not much good in bed but liberal with his money." The modern world is of a different order, and the old rules lack relevance.

"The Secret Integration" (1964) is an initiation tale set in Mingeborough, Massachusetts, in the Berkshire mountains where Pynchon was raised. It involves a group of children who conspire against the hypocritical institutions that their parents engender. Grover Snodd, a boy genius in the Salinger mode, provides the brains behind their plans. He seeks a perfect symmetry of action against the confused patterns offered by the adults. The inner junta of his group consists of Tim Santora, from whose point of view the events are narrated; a practical joker named Étienne Cherdlu (a variant of Etoain Shrdlu from the linotype keyboard); a nine-year-old reformed alcoholic named Hogan Slothrop (Tyrone's brother); and a sixth grader named Kim Dufay, who is aroused by explosives and whose size 28A padded bra permits her to pass for an adult at PTA meetings. Financed by milk money from other malcontented children who enlist in their cause, they conduct Operation Spartacus (the title of which Grover takes from the Stanley Kubrick film). They drop sodium bombs in school toilets and stir up silt in the river to stall machines in the local paper mill. However, many of their acts of sabotage fail because fear of adult authority is so ingrained in the children. In one attack on the school several children are halted by the chalk lines on the playing field which, Grover deduces, remind them of classroom authority.

While Operation Spartacus falters, the story enters a second dimension as Hogan is sent as a joke by the local AA to respond to a call from a black alcoholic, Mr. McAfee. Tim accompanies him, and Grover and Étienne join them later. Hogan's serious response to his assignment moves McAfee, and he exchanges tales with the children. Although he enjoys the spirit of their pranks, his own stories are filled with the isolation caused by his color. His loneliness so affects Tim that he telephones long distance to a girl whose name McAfee has carried in his wallet for years. But, his call for help yields no results. . . . The police then arrive and unceremoniously run McAfee out of town.

Revenge is in order and the children regroup. Their retaliation is an ingenious imposition of color on the bland security of a random group of adults. They don green masks and place green floodlights along a railroad track, suddenly horrifying a trainload of passengers.

One member of the group is a black boy, Carl Barrington, who is later revealed to be a fantasy figure born out of their collective rejection of adult bigotry. A childless couple, the Barringtons, have recently integrated the neighborhood and are subjected to abusive calls from the parents. When the children attempt to help them clean up a load of garbage that has been dumped in their front yard, they discover objects from their own households.

The only integration that can occur in this repressive environment is secretive. With the perverse views of Mingeborough society fully exposed, Carl is no longer safe, even as a fantasy figure, in the children's homes and school. He goes to live in their hideout, the mansion of King Yrjö, which is inhabited by the seven-foot ghost of the king's aide. Only in this detached refuge can he remain intact. Meanwhile, the other children return to their individual homes, to a "hot shower, dry towel, before-bed television, good night kiss, and dreams that could never again be entirely safe." (pp. 24-32)

Robert D. Newman, " 'Slow Learner': Establishing Foundations," in his Understanding Thomas Pynchon, *University of South Carolina Press, 1986, pp. 12-32.*

Brian Stonehill

If self-consciousness can sustain satire, as in William Gaddis, Thomas Pynchon shows us how it can also sharpen the edge of a particular wedge of paradox.

Gravity's Rainbow creates a paradoxical effect: some readers rave about the book, while others cannot read it. Although the Fiction Jury of the Pulitzer Committee unanimously recommended Pynchon's novel for the 1973 Pulitzer Prize, the Committee at large found it "turgid," "obscene," and "unreadable," and voted to withhold its fiction prize that year. Books have already been written on Pynchon, critical studies calling him "the greatest living writer in the English-speaking world"; and even the semi-official gate-keeper, *PMLA,* admitted Pynchon's four-year-old novel into the Academy. Other critics, meanwhile, have called his work "American plastic" and "a failure." *Gravity's Rainbow* is highly controversial; even the fact of its authorship is in dispute.

I would like to suggest that the response to *Gravity's Rainbow* has been paradoxical because the novel is itself paradoxical in *genre.* The entire novel, that is, seeks to produce the specific esthetic effect which I shall call the Power of Paradox: the peculiar suspension of the intellectual and emotional faculties between two equally plausible but mutually exclusive modes of perception or belief. The novel's self-consciousness reinforces its paradoxical effect.

We are already familiar with paradox as an esthetic power—as the "final cause," the "intended effect"—of works of art in other media. In drawing, for example, paradox is sought as the final power in much of the work of M. C. Escher. In the folk art of verbal humor, the power of paradox underlies many jokes, especially puns. Paradox is rarer as the intended effect of literature since it is primarily a local effect, not easily sustained without becoming tedious. (pp. 141-42)

Gravity's Rainbow creates its own paradoxical effect by offering the reader two antithetical perspectives on everything that happens in its pages. Everything in it can be seen either as related *caus*ally, or as related *casu*ally: the novel provides evidence for both conclusions. If events in *Gravity's Rainbow* are related *caus*ally, then a massive conspiracy envelopes Tyrone Slothrop and the other characters. This is confirmed by the novel. If events are related *casu*ally, however, then the apparent links are no more than the characters' (and reader's) paranoid imaginings. This, too, is confirmed by the novel.

Slothrop's amorous successes coincide point for point with the rocket strikes in London: surely cause-and-effect, either precognition or psychokinesis. But both patterns conform to a Poisson distribution: perfect randomness, each point ideally independent of any other. Where does Slothrop see the most pervasive web of conspiracy surrounding him? In a casino—hazard's home. This is the essence of the paradoxical effect of what happens in the novel: the insistence, in every episode, that everything is fixed; inseparable from the insistence, in those same episodes, that everything is random. Does Slothrop escape into the anarchic chaos of "the Zone," asserting his independence of plots and conspiracies? Then the first person he meets there will spontaneously offer him information on "the one rocket out of 6000" that he seeks. Death by bombardment is surely the most random and pointless of fates; but what if voices from the dead say that it all makes sense? Is the world watched over by a spiritual divinity? Or are the conventional restraints on man's bestiality wholly arbitrary? Rhetorically, the novel endorses both Christ and coprophilia. To every question, the action of *Gravity's Rainbow* offers two plausible answers, each a contradiction of the other.

The structure of the novel, although enormously elaborate, may be reduced to two simple opposite movements: the assembly of the Rocket, and the disassembly of Tyrone Slothrop. The more he (and we) learn about the Rocket, the less of Slothrop remains as a character, until there are left only a "few who can still see Slothrop as any sort of integral creature any more." The Rocket, by contrast, first appears in the novel in dispersed fragments, and is only gradually reassembled:

> What it is is a graphite cylinder, about six inches long and two in diameter, all but a few flakes of its Army-green paint charred away. Only piece that survived the burst.

Slothrop, until his own dispersal, collects the fragments of rocket information that ultimately coalesce in the twin rocket sagas of Blicero's Rocket No. 00000 and its repetition, Enzian's No. 00001. The Schwarzkommando's reconstruction of Rocket No. 00001 from scattered debris coincides with the reader's reconstruction of Rocket No. 00000 from scattered details. Just as the reader puts the whole story together, its hero (paradoxically) falls apart. (pp. 142-43)

Pynchon polarizes the characters of *Gravity's Rainbow* into antithetical pairs. Black Enzian, for example, corresponds to white Gottfried: for good or evil, the Rocket launches them both. Bianca Erdmann and Ilse Pokler, fathered respectively by a movie actor and a movie spectator, are "the same child" born on either side of the screen. Suspended like an arch between the paradoxes, Slothrop serves both the Schwarzkommando and "the White Visitation," balanced between "Them" and "the Counterforce." "Everything in the Creation," as Slothrop's Puritan ancestor William put it, "has its equal and opposite counterpart." Containing "opposites together," the Rocket itself is dual in nature, "a good Rocket to take us to the stars, an evil Rocket for the World's suicide, the two perpetually in struggle."

The title of *Gravity's Rainbow* itself proclaims the novel's paradox, in that gravity and rainbows are antithetic phenomena. Gravity pulls mass, while the rainbow has no mass. The rainbow is visible but intangible, gravity tangible but invisible. Only in the title of Pynchon's novel does the rainbow "belong" to gravity; for, like its title, the whole novel yokes contraries, embraces contradictions, propounds paradox. (pp. 144-45)

The self-consciousness of *Gravity's Rainbow* strengthens its paradoxical power. The novel both seems and seems not to be about the reader's "real" world, leaving the reader suspended between two attitudes towards the text itself:

(1) the text is an accurate transcription of reality; and (2) the text is a piece of self-conscious artifice subject to no rules but its own. Like *Ulysses, Gravity's Rainbow* is both minutely mimetic and egregiously ludic; it amalgamates literary realism with surreal fantasy.

On the one hand, the world Pynchon depicts is obviously our own. Our World War Two, with its bombs and its death camps. Our Jack Kennedy, Mickey Rooney, Malcolm X. But on the other, Pynchon's world is obviously made up. The narrator speaks directly to the reader:

> You will want cause and effect. All right. Thanatz
> was washed overboard in the same storm that . . .

Pynchon's omniscient narrator (who does indeed seem to know everything) shows himself making up his story as he goes along. The names he gives people and places are often ludicrously fake: the Russian thief Nocolai Ripov, the German spa Bad Karma. The narrator frequently steps back a frame to suggest that his own narrative voice is but one more deceptive strategy among many:

> (the voice speaking here grows more ironic, closer
> to tears which are not all theatre as the list goes
> on . . .)

The novel characteristically pretends to be a movie: "If there is music for this it's windy strings and reed sections (. . .)." And the narrator takes pleasure in directly challenging the reader:

> (. . .) They are not, after all, to be lovers in para-
> chutes of sunlit voile, lapsing gently, hand in hand,
> down to anything meadowed or calm. Surprised?

In the very paragraphs from which these quotes are taken, however, the narrator proceeds to create illusions of reality that are masterful in their verisimilitude. This same paradoxical process is at work in the novel's opening pages, where, after being "taken in" by wonderfully evocative, detailed description, we learn to our surprise that we have been reading not of events but of a dream.

These two different ways of reading the text—as accurate transcription or as elaborate invention—provoke two antithetical responses. By dramatizing within the novel the relation between *Gravity's Rainbow* and its readers, Pynchon fortifies the central paradox of the causal/casual relation, not only among events in his book, but between his book and real life. If events within the novel are related *caus*ally, and if, as the references to historical figures and actual multinational corporations suggest, the world the novel depicts *is* the world the reader lives in, then the reader's appropriate response to the text is one of paranoia: "nothing less than the onset, the leading edge, of the discovery that *everything is connected,* everything in the Creation (. . .)." One need not be stoned or paranoid to recognize, for example, that the giant German chemical cartel I. G. Farben, which gave the world aspirin and penicillin and the poison for Hitler's gas chambers, was in historical fact preserved from postwar dismantling by the multinational oil companies. Shell Oil did indeed "fight" for both sides during the war. "They," the oil cartels, that is, *have* persisted through outward political upheaval and mass death. Henry Kissinger did work for the family that founded Standard Oil. "They" sponsor much of our public arts and televised entertainment, and own the companies that publish many of our books. It's no joke.

If, however, events in the novel are related merely *casu*ally, and if, as the self-conscious narration, the ludicrously artificial names, and the preposterous plot suggest, the text itself is no more than canard or self-indulgence, then the reader's appropriate response is that of "anti-paranoia, where nothing is connected to anything." To make sense of the novel we are expected to believe not only that a human being named Tyrone Slothrop gets an erection for every German rocket fired at London, but also that he finds a woman to share it with as frequently and in as many places as the rockets fall. The novel's premises are absurd. It's all a big joke. Joke or no joke, the novel offers us the choice: "Is the baby smiling, or is it just gas? Which do you want it to be?"

All three of Pynchon's novels are fictions of "suspended meaning," in Frank Kermode's phrase, as in each case the text withholds its logical conclusions from character and reader alike. In *The Crying of Lot 49,* the heroine never learns the secret of the Trystero conspiracy, since the novel ends just as Oedipa is *about* to hear Lot 49 "cried." The mysterious woman V., whom Stencil pursues in Pynchon's first novel [*V.*], is gradually replaced by prosthetic devices until finally she stops ticking and "comes apart." As V. falls apart before Stencil can learn her secret, so Slothrop falls apart without finding his Rocket. In *V.,* the *object* of the search falls apart; in *Gravity's Rainbow,* the *subject* disintegrates. (The two novels thus juxtapose each other in more ways than the noted recurrence of characters; the phallic V-2 Rocket responds to vaginal V.) And just as disintegrated Slothrop never learns his Rocket's secret, so the reader of *Gravity's Rainbow* never learns the secret of his "own" final rocket, the one about to explode over "our" heads on the novel's last page:

> And it is just here, just at this dark and silent frame,
> that the pointed tip of the Rocket, falling nearly a
> mile per second, absolutely and forever without
> sound, reaches its last unmeasurable gap above the
> roof of this old theatre, the last delta-t.

Will the Rocket bring the flash of inspiration, or the annihilation of death? Pynchon's conclusions are suspended: there is no way to tell.

The prose style of *Gravity's Rainbow* is not single style but an impressive compendium of many styles which contribute considerable power to the paradox within the novel.

> Later, toward dusk, several enormous water bugs,
> a very dark reddish brown, emerge like elves from
> the wainscoting, and go lumbering toward the lar-
> der—pregnant mother bugs too, with baby translu-
> cent outrider bugs flowing along like a convoy es-
> cort. At night, in the very late silences between
> bombers, ack-ack fire and falling rockets, they can
> be heard, loud as mice, munching through Gwen-
> hidwy's paper sacks, leaving streaks and footprints
> of shit the color of themselves behind. They don't
> seem to go in much for soft things, fruits, vegeta-
> bles, and such, it's more the solid lentils and beans
> they're into, stuff they can gnaw at, paper and plas-
> ter barriers, hard interfaces to be pierced, for they
> are agents of unification, you see. Christmas bugs.
> They were deep in the straw of the manger at Beth-
> lehem, they stumbled, climbed, fell glistening red
> among a golden lattice of straw that must have
> seemed to extend miles up and downward—an edi-
> ble tenement-world, now and then gnawed through
> to disrupt some mysterious sheaf of vectors that

would send neighbor bugs tumbling ass-over-antennas down past you as you held on with all legs in that constant tremble of golden stalks. A tranquil world: the temperature and humidity staying nearly steady, the day's cycle damped to only a soft easy sway of light, gold to antique-gold to shadows, and back again. The crying of the infant reached you, perhaps, as bursts of energy from the invisible distance, nearly unsensed, often ignored. Your savior, you see. . . .

The suppleness of this prose is admirable. It creates paradox by embracing within individual sentences a diction that is base, obscene, and suggestive of disorder and decay, and a diction that is lofty, spiritual, and evocative of transcendent harmonies. In the paragraph just cited, the style serves to amplify the paradoxical quality of the thought: impressions both of trivial decay and of holy redemption are rendered with great vividness. Does the mentino of insect excrement heighten the passage's religious values or, on the contrary, is the reference to "your savior" ironic? Again, the reader is suspended between antitheses of great seriousness. The inobtrusive shifts in tense and the recurrent mention of "you" succeed in bringing the reader vividly into the presence of both holiness and filth. Like Nabokov, Pynchon is a practitioner of phrasal tmesis, and a twister of old clichés into new meanings. His "hyperdense metaphors," as Joseph Slade puts it, and the extraordinarily energetic packing of ideas into his sentences make *Gravity's Rainbow* into a virtuoso performance that is beyond the endurance of many readers. While there remains much to be said about Pynchon's style, as about much else in the novel, its significance to this discussion is clear. Pynchon's paradoxically self-conscious style reminds the reader that we are reading a fiction even as we are being taken in by it. As Joseph Slade describes it, "Having begun a sentence of great fragility, Pynchon will cheerfully clamber out upon it to hammer in the last word, and allow the reader to see him do it."

Unlike narrative tragedies or comedies, the genre of paradox requires not a specific sequence of events, but rather the steady elaboration and reiteration of the paradoxical effect. *Gravity's Rainbow* is therefore very loose in form and has, perhaps unfortunately, no necessary beginning, middle, or end. There is always room for more discussions of ideas, scientific principles, historical facts, philosophic controversies, ancient myths, surreal dreams, and drug-induced fantasies that have apparently little or nothing to do with the novel's central action, but which all contain the means to sustain or intensify the paradoxical effect. (pp. 146-50)

Discussions of all scientific paradoxes such as the Heisenberg uncertainty principle *belong* in *Gravity's Rainbow,* although their effectiveness varies with their relevance to what is happening in the plot. The novel's power is intensified, for example, by repeated references to science's inability to reconcile Euclidean and non-Euclidean geometry, classical and Einsteinian physics, and wave and particle theories of light:

> "We seem up against a dilemma built into Nature, much like the Heisenberg situation. There is nearly complete parallelism between analgesia and addiction. The more pain it takes away, the more we desire it. It appears we can't have one property without the other, any more than a particle physicist

can specify position without suffering an uncertainty as to the particle's velocity—"

The narrative techniques of *Gravity's Rainbow,* its structure, characterization, style, and themes are thus all to a certain extent metaphors for the central causal/casual, order-or-chaos paradox. Pynchon has elsewhere been called "an author in search of a metaphor, a fictional scheme to ask and answer the question of what prevails in the physical and in the spiritual universe" [see excerpt by Alan J. Friedman and Manfred Puetz in *CLC,* Vol. 6.] But I would add that the pursuit of metaphor is itself paradoxical. . . . Metaphor, as Pynchon reminds us, is a potentially self-conscious trope: it both asserts an identity and denies it. A is like B but it is really A. Like each of the metaphors of which it is composed, Pynchon's entire novel claims to represent the world as it is, and denies that such representation is possible. *Gravity's Rainbow* is itself both "a thrust at truth and a lie."

Pynchon's novels are thus metaphors for our own reading experience of them. As Edward Mendelson has noted, "To read the encyclopedic *Gravity's Rainbow* is, necessarily, to read *among* the various probable interpretations of the book." In order to find out what happens, that is, we must re-enact Slothrop's effort to read the "holy Text" of the Rocket. Hero and reader are launched on the same quest to distinguish signal from noise, to find a message in the mess. As Frank Kermode observed of the heroine of *The Crying of Lot 49,* "What Oedipa is doing is very like reading a book."

Paranoia is Pynchon's most comprehensive metaphor for both the act of reading and the act of writing, for in this "Puritan reflex of seeking other orders behind the visible," the paradoxical relations between the self and the world are most clearly juxtaposed. Seen from the outside, paranoia is a form of solipsism, in which the victim imagines existence to be an orderly pattern focused upon himself. This is the threat to her sanity that confronts Oedipa Maas in *The Crying of Lot 49: "Shall I project a world?"* It is also the solipsistic madness of Slothrop "finding in every bone and cabbage leaf paraphrases of himself" (*Gravity's Rainbow*).

Seen from the inside, however, paranoia is a form of artistic or exegetical creativity. Every artist is paranoid to the extent that he or she imposes pattern on his experience. And every reader is paranoid to the extent that he or she extracts a "meaning" from a text which, like *Gravity's Rainbow,* both invites and forbids interpretation. As William James observed on behalf of pragmatism, "The actual universe is a thing wide open, but rationalism makes systems, and systems must be closed." The "motive to metaphor," as Northrop Frye calls the esthetic impulse, is thus a paranoid reflex. *Gravity's Rainbow* dramatizes both our need for fictions and the invalidity of our fictions. "The knife cuts through the apple like a knife cutting an apple": the novel is a metaphor for the limitations of metaphor.

Paranoids also see plots wherever they look, just as storytellers do. Even the universe may be made to yield a story, and its title, according to Pynchon, is Entropy. Entropy refers to the inescapable loss of energy in every transaction; it is an irreversible law of nature codified in the Second Law of Thermodynamics which, theoretically extrapolated, predicts an eventual heat-death for the universe.

As Pynchon described it in an early story called, simply, **"Entropy,"** "the entropy of an isolated system always continually increased (. . .) from differentiation to sameness, from ordered individuality to a kind of chaos." Entropy most clearly describes the behavior of heated gases but may also be applied, metaphorically, to the breakdown of biological and political organisms, to the "Energy Crisis," and to the theory of information (as the parlor game of "telephone" neatly illustrates). Because of its irreversibility, entropy is intimately related to time; as Hans Meyerhoff has noted, "Time may be said to move in the direction of an increase in entropy." (pp. 151-53)

Pynchon's novel *enacts* entropy in the eventual falling apart of its hero, Slothrop's decline "from ordered individuality to a kind of chaos." The novel itself knows and acknowledges, in a sense, that it must come to an end, even if that end comes, as it does, in midsentence: "Now everybody—". The incomplete last line shows the novel resisting its own termination, engaging in yet another struggle of opposites between entropy and energy. Entropy seems to have won the day in finally bringing the novel to its end, but the victory is only apparent. For the novel is *not,* as the success of entropy requires, a closed system, but rather it continually absorbs new quantities of energy from both writer and reader, as it is written and each time it is read. The novel demands rereading, with an insistence that denies it is really used up when one has read the last page. In the last line, a rocket is about to explode over "our" heads. The novel's first line describes the sound of a rocket rushing in, *after* the supersonic missile has already exploded: "A screaming comes across the sky." So the novel's conclusion leads us back to its beginning: its ends are joined. The annular structure of *Gravity's Rainbow* refutes the entropic curtailment of its own narrative energy.

Pynchon's metaphors, like those of the Symbolist poets, have no specific referents. They thus invite readings of almost infinite subtlety, an irresistible temptation to some critics. Slothrop's disintegration, for example, can be read as a metaphor for any number of things. I have concentrated on his falling apart as a metaphor for entropy and as a source of paradoxical power. In Joseph Slade's reading, it is a metaphor for the helplessness of innocence before the immensity of power: "He literally fragments, cut to pieces by energy grids, the victim of his innocence, which is no defense against the complexities of the systems that reform after the war." William Plater cleverly reads Slothrop's disintegration as a metaphor for the Heisenberg uncertainty principle: "Slothrop even begins to disperse and spread throughout the Zone as his psychoanalytical observers learn more about the sexual energy he appears to derive from the Rocket." And according to Edward Mendelson, "Slothrop's disintegration (. . .) summarizes the historical fate of literary modernism."

This is not to say, however, that Pynchon's texts mean whatever one wants them to, and that there is no such thing as a wrong reading. David Richter, for example, in an otherwise interesting study, extracts a "thesis" from *V.,* and then blithely admits that "I am unable to understand" why the novel's last two chapters are so ambiguous. Ignoring the possibility that *V.,* like *Gravity's Rainbow,* may be generically paradoxical, Richter wedges the novel into the category of "apologue," and then blames the poor fit on

Pynchon's "failure of completeness." This we may call an erroneous reading.

By opposing each assertion to its own negation, *Gravity's Rainbow* resists the critic's effort to extract a single paraphrasable meaning. As Edward Mendelson has written of Pynchon's novel, "self-conscious narrative can admit serious meanings only through indirection." Good is good and evil is evil, this much is always clear, but the novel never gives either side the upper hand: "Just as there are, in the World, machineries committed to injustice as an enterprise, so too there seem to be provisions active for balancing things out once in a while." The concentration camp Dora is here, and so is a Christmas Eve service in Kent: both are allowed to speak for themselves. The characters live, in a sense, beyond moral distinctions, for even the "good guys" do evil. (pp. 153-55)

Thus, despite its deliberate posturing as allegory, Pynchon's fiction is *not* an ethical statement in disguise. The most unambiguous affirmation in his work, in fact, is the advice of a laid-back musician in *V.* to "Keep cool, but care"; and even this, as David Richter notes, is "mighty slim pickings as affirmations of life go." Keenly aware, as we have seen, of its own ambiguous stance as a fiction, *Gravity's Rainbow* allows itself no such direct moralization. What it offers instead is a sense of *possibility:* that perhaps there is a choice to be made, but perhaps not; that perhaps our lives are our own, but perhaps not; that perhaps fiction may divulge the truth about the human condition, but perhaps not.

To some readers, this sense of certainties suspended is unbearable. Frederick J. Hoffman, for example, complains that one of the "principal faults" of Pynchon's fiction is that "it makes fun of the reasons why it makes fun of everything else." To others, however, including myself, Pynchon's balance of vividly evoked sympathy, humor and passion with an acute recognition of the fiction's own contingency is as enchanting as it is disturbing. If there are some in whom *le goût du paradoxe* is lacking, there are others for whom, as Kierkegaard put it, "Either/Or is the key of heaven." This is not to reduce the evaluation of *Gravity's Rainbow* to a matter of taste, but rather to suggest why, as we noted at the outset, many people cannot read it.

To be certain about any clear message in *Gravity's Rainbow* is thus in some sense to distort the text. And yet, as E. D. Hirsch reminds us, "knowledge of ambiguity is not necessarily ambiguous knowledge." We may reasonably hope to understand, for example, what general rules Pynchon followed in composing *Gravity's Rainbow.* The genre of paradox seems to me a more useful category for interpreting the novel than "encyclopedic narrative," since the latter label implies only that Pynchon threw everything in. The requirements of paradox account for more. The novel is immensely funny, as paradoxes often are, and as no encyclopedia ever is. Puns, as we have noted, are paradoxical, and entire episodes of *Gravity's Rainbow* are contrived for the sake of one. Nor is any encyclopedia self-conscious; but without its self-consciousness *Gravity's Rainbow* would be less paradoxical, and not itself. We have also been able to learn from paradox why the novel is preoccupied with paranoia, with entropy, and with its own relation to the reader's life. Not everything is lost to equivocation, then, for by displaying its own art, *Gravity's Rainbow* obliges us to affirm its value. (pp. 155-56)

> Brian Stonehill, "Paradoxical Pynchon; or, The Real World inside 'Gravity's Rainbow'," in his The Self-Conscious Novel: Artifice in Fiction from Joyce to Pynchon, *University of Pennsylvania Press, 1988, pp. 141-56.*

Christopher Lehmann-Haupt

Vineland in actual history is purportedly the America that Leif Ericsson discovered before Columbus. But in Thomas Pynchon's pyrotechnic new novel [*Vineland*]—his fourth, but his first since *Gravity's Rainbow* was published 17 years ago—Vineland is a very different New World. . . .

On a summer morning in 1984, as Zoyd, wearing "a party dress in a number of colors that would look good on television," prepares to leap through the window of the Cucumber Lounge for the attendant news crews, he discovers in the crowd a "visitor from out of the olden days." It is "Zoyd's longtime pursuer, D.E.A. field agent Hector Zuniga . . . the erratic Federal comet who brought, each visit in to Zoyd's orbit, new forms of bad luck and baleful influence."

Though it turns out that Hector is on the run from an institution that studies and treats "Tubal abuse and other video-related disorders," he warns Zoyd that Frenesi, Zoyd's ex-wife, has gone underground after having been dropped from the Federal Witness Protection Program because of Reagan Administration cutbacks. She is being hunted by a Justice Department strike force led by Brock Vond,

> a federal prosecutor, a Washington, D.C., heavy and . . . the expediter of most of Zoyd's years of long and sooner or later tearful nights down in places like the Lost Nugget.

If these developments seem hard to follow, never mind. The plot of *Vineland* is not the sort you get attached to or wrapped up in. Eventually, Mr. Pynchon's "story" boils down to a contest between Zoyd the hip and Brock the square, with Frenesi as their medium of communication. Mr. Pynchon's fans will recognize this archetypal triangle as an afterimage from *V, The Crying of Lot 49* and even *Gravity's Rainbow.*

Instead of telling a coherent story in *Vineland,* Mr. Pynchon improvises like a jazz musician. At times, his theme is a burlesque of the 1960's; at times it's an elaborate intrigue centering on the Sisterhood of Kunoichi Attentives, a California retreat offering "fantasy marathons for devotees of the Orient"; at times it's the history of the West Coast labor movement. Altogether, it's a little as if Upton Sinclair had been captured by ninja warriors and lived to tell the tale to an R. Crumb high on acid.

At times, the novel is quite funny. Zoyd earns extra money doing lawn and tree work for a landscape contractor named the Marquis de Sod. ("Crabgrass won't be'ave? Haw, haw! No problem! Zhust call—the Marquis de Sod. . . . 'E'll wheep your lawn into shepp!"). A death-obsessed commune of so-called Thanatoids are awakened by "sound chips" playing J. S. Bach's "Wachet Auf," "one of the best tunes ever to come out of Europe."

At other times, it can be annoyingly simplistic, especially when guns are likened to phalluses. . . .

Yet always the reader is fascinated by Mr. Pynchon's amazing fund of knowledge and the ease with which he applies it to everything from popular culture to social history to technology. And now and then, the depth of his paranoid conspiracy theories—or rather those of his characters—is enough to give you shivers. . . .

What does *Vineland* add up to? You don't total Mr. Pynchon's work glibly any more than you "enjoy" it in any conventional sense of the word. For all its batty high jinks, his text here is an intentional subversion of orderliness. You'd deconstruct it by pulling its pin and heaving it.

Still, one senses in it faint signs of optimism. This perception is hard to defend, especially given the parable told near the end by the Head Ninjette of the Kunoichi Sisterhood of an earth so resembling hell that hell's residents finally gave up visiting it. "Why leave home only to find a second-rate version of what they were trying to escape?"

Yet the apocalyptic horror of *V* and *Gravity's Rainbow* is missing from *Vineland.* The ominous underworld of *The Crying of Lot 49* is also lacking. Mr. Pynchon's paranoia seems to have eased. After all, when Brock Vond tries to claim Zoyd Wheeler's daughter as his own, she tells him off: " 'But you can't be my father, Mr. Vond,' she objected. 'My blood is type A. Yours is Preparation H.' "

One may not share Mr. Pynchon's vision that the earth ought to belong to the shaggy and spontaneous. But good things are happening. There are signs that the cold war is ending; that's good. The money has run out on Brock Vond and his system of persecution, that's good too. And in the final paragraph, a "warm and persistent tongue" is licking Zoyd's daughter awake. It's Desmond the dog, "the spit and image of his grandmother Chloe, roughened by the miles, face full of blue-jay feathers, smiling out of his eyes, wagging his tail, thinking he must be home."

Is that good too? Well, like so much of the novel, I can't entirely make sense of it. But unlike so much that happens in Mr. Pynchon's fiction, at least it doesn't forebode the end of the world.

> Christopher Lehmann-Haupt, " 'Vineland,' Pynchon's First Novel in 17 Years," in The New York Times, *December 26, 1989, p. C21.*

James McManus

In the 17 years since *Gravity's Rainbow* was published—the precise literary distance between *Ulysses* and *Finnegans Wake*—the consensus has been growing that its author, Thomas Pynchon, was the most significant novelist writing in English since James Joyce. And if *Gravity's Rainbow,* which took nothing less than 20th Century white western civilization as its subject, was the product of seven years work—what Joyce spent on *Ulysses*—what sort of novel would Pynchon produce after 17 years? We have wondered, extrapolated, passed along rumors and waited.

It turns out that *Vineland,* Pynchon's fourth novel, more closely resembles his second, *The Crying of Lot 49* (1966), than it does his 1973 masterwork. Considerably less ambitious in scale, historical range and thematic complexity, *Vineland* is a correspondingly more manageable book. Like *Lot 49,* it takes place in contemporary California, much of it in the fictional county of Vineland, located up along the coast in redwood country, near Eureka and Arcata. Conspiracies, real and imagined, proliferate, and sexual betrayal is commonplace. . . .

The plot of *Vineland,* such as it is, mainly involves Prairie Wheeler, the 14-year-old daughter of . . . Zoyd, an odd-job specialist suffering from '60s Shock Syndrome. Prairie and Zoyd have gone into hiding from Brock Vond, a federal prosecutor who also heads up PREP (Political Re-Education Program), a clean-cut, zero-tolerance organization.

Frenesi Gates, Prairie's mother and sometime guerrilla documentary filmmaker, has been out of the family picture since Prairie was 2, which was right around the time Frenesi was compromised, "turned" into a double—triple?—agent by Vond. She is even more vulnerable now that her Justice Department job line has been cut from the Reagan-Meese budget. Frenesi is also sexually involved with—who else?—Mr. Vond. Nearly every character, in fact, like the novel itself, is "entangled in other, often impossibly complicated, tales of dispossession and betrayal."

Prairie's antic flight from Brock Vond dovetails with her quest for the facts surrounding her conception. Pynchon establishes dozens of mocking parallels with our culture's fixation on high-tech special effects, whether filmic or military, and such famous bits of hokeyness as the Luke Skywalker-Darth Vader relationship. In one of the novel's lightning segues, Prairie finds herself barreling down Route 101, through an area where parts of *Return of the Jedi* were filmed, in a kind of Stealth Trans-Am painted "with a proprietary lacquer of a crystalline microstructure able to vary its index of refraction so that . . . [it] could easily, except for a few iridescent fringes, have been taken for empty roadway."

The plot is simultaneously preposterous and convincing; but what happens next, what caused which effect, are questions Pynchon tends to subvert, not to answer. His narrative impulses have always been digressionary and poetic, returning again and again to familiar obsessions: TV, narcotics, corporate greed, film, paranoia. "As long as I don't sleep, (an insomniac narc has) decided, I won't shave. . . . That must mean . . . that as soon as I fall asleep, I'll start shaving!" Pynchon then transposes the motif: "At the Steering Committee meeting that night for the newly formed All Damned Heat Off Campus, or ADHOC," there are young men who "cut off pieces of hair from their heads and, too impatient to grow beards, glued it onto their faces."

By this point we have gathered that *Vineland* is both satire and nostalgic meditation on the values of the '60s, as well as a contemptuous send-up of what one female character calls the "Midol America" of the Spielbergian-Reaganite '80s. Pynchon has captured the nuance and vernacular of both periods, allowing their respective idiosyncracies to throw each into sharper relief.

"Brock Vond's genius," he writes,

> was to have seen in the activities of the sixties left

not threats to order but unacknowledged desires for it. While the Tube was proclaiming youth revolution against parents of all kinds and most viewers were accepting this story, Brock saw the deep . . . need only to stay children forever, safe inside some extended national Family.

Pynchon also lets us read how we talk. When her street-tough friend Che suggests punching out a rich, spoiled white kid, Prairie declares, "Che, you're rilly evil?" We also hear Bach's "Wachet Auf " referred to as "one of the best tunes ever to come out of Europe."

Vineland is continually this arch and amusing. What will be missed by inveterate Pynchon readers is the density of weave, the thematic urgency, the structural audacity and grandeur of *Gravity's Rainbow.* There is no part of *Vineland* as evocative as Pirate Prentice's banana breakfast in a London under siege of V-2s, Brigadier Pudding's encounter with Katje Borgesius, let alone the sublime parabolic arc—gravity's rainbow itself—that comprises the structural, ballistic, metaphorical and ferociously erotic lines of force in that novel. What's at stake in *Vineland* is smaller, participates less fully in our hubris and grief. For as unhep and mean-spirited as Nixon, Brock Vond, Ed Meese and Reagan may be, conservative Republicans are small potatoes as villains when compared to Albert Speer, Hitler, Weissman/Blicero and Werner von Braun, with their gravity-defying missiles, the millions they executed, the worlds they intended to conquer.

So the question recurs: Is *Vineland* the sole product of almost two decades of Pynchon's best work? One doubts it. Just as he completed *Lot 49* while working on *Gravity's Rainbow,* Pynchon probably has interrupted work on a much longer novel-in-progress to write *Vineland . . . .*

Is *Vineland* worth reading? Certainly, if only for the Celtic and Laker jokes, and for numerous others as well. No matter how frantic or hilarious it gets, each page retains the ring and brutality of fact—what amounts, in the end, to a blackly comedic assault on what is, in Pynchon's view, Republican America's desire for

> a timeless, defectively imagined future of zero-tolerance drug-free Americans all pulling their weight and all locked into the official economy, inoffensive music, endless family specials on the Tube, church all week long, and, on special days, for extra-good behavior, maybe a cookie.

However persuasive we may find these politics, Pynchon remains our premier connoisseur of uncertainty, wicked tropes, anti-climax, the seductively dangled loose end. No living American writes stronger prose. Scores of passages in *Vineland* flicker with the Tube's own ineluctable accuracy and "coolth," its Paschke-esque palette and nerve.

It is also the case that Thomas Pynchon can do even better than *Vineland,* and that he probably already has.

> *James McManus, "Pynchon's Return," in*
> Chicago Tribune—Books, *January 14, 1990,*
> *p. 3.*

Paul Gray

It is one of the better-known opening lines in American literature: "A screaming comes across the sky." Thus begins *Gravity's Rainbow* (1973), the mammoth and, to many, impenetrable novel that established Thomas Pynchon as the most important and mysterious writer of his generation. . . . Now, at last, comes *Vineland,* Pynchon's first novel in nearly 17 years, and the faithful can again begin the quest for runic meanings, preferably hidden. And right up at the top of the second page of text, something interesting glimmers:

> Desmond was out on the porch, hanging around his dish, which was always empty because of the blue jays who came screaming down out of the redwoods and carried off the food in it piece by piece.

From the sound of a V-2 rocket descending on London in the earlier novel to the cries of birds pilfering dog food in *Vineland:* um, as a Pynchon character might say, there seems to have been a little down*scaling* going on around here. The perception is accurate but also, as things develop, a trifle misleading. True, this time out Pynchon has not tried to top the apocalypse of *Gravity's Rainbow.* He has chosen a subject that may even cause some groaning (Oh, come on, man, grow up) among reviewers and fans: the attempts of some aging hippies to steer clear of the narcs.

Patience at this point is advisable, because it will be rewarded. The year is 1984, although flashbacks soon come thick and fast. The setting is Vineland County, a fictional, fog-shrouded expanse of Northern California where, as one character remarks, "half the interior hasn't even been surveyed."

The spot is a perfect refuge for a remnant of wilting flower children, including Zoyd Wheeler, a part-time keyboard player, handyman and marijuana farmer. Along with his teenage daughter Prairie, Zoyd still mourns the departure and later disappearance of his ex-wife Frenesi, a onetime '60s radical who was seduced into becoming a Government informer by a notoriously malevolent federal prosecutor named Brock Vond. . . .

These details establish the absolutely typical Pynchon plot. An evil, well-organized and immensely powerful enemy sows "the merciless spores of paranoia" among a shaggy, lost group of drifting souls who find the real world threatening under the best of circumstances. The intended victims, not all of whom think too clearly anymore, have other problems as well, including the task of making sense out of what is happening to them while knowing that sense, strictly defined, is a weapon of the other side. Caught between these opposing, mismatched factions is a child, Prairie, who would dearly love to find, and love, her mother.

But the novel is only marginally about dopers and spoilsport law-enforcement types. The showdown looming in Vineland County serves as the melody for a series of dazzling riffs on the 1970s and early '80s. It comes as a surprise to realize that these generations are the lost ones in Pynchon's fiction. *V.* (1963) and *The Crying of Lot 49* (1966) anticipated but arrived just before the triumphant effulgence of television and youth culture in American life; *Gravity's Rainbow* was chiefly set during World War II. So *Vineland* amounts to Pynchon's first words on the way we have been living during the past two decades.

Wretchedly funny excess seems the point of the exercise, not to mention the hallmark of the years portrayed. Pynchon's technique is to turn up the volume on contemporary reality, fiddle with the contrast and horizontal hold, in order to produce scenes that are both distorted and recognizable, and a pretty good indication of where all the current trends may be heading.

The people in *Vineland* have been steeped in TV long enough to become pickled. Some of them are Tubefreeks, whose habits of Tubal abuse alert the vigilant authorities at NEVER (National Endowment for Video Education and Rehabilitation). (p. 69)

The tide of pop culture even swamps the high mountain ridge where sits the Retreat of the Kunoichi Attentives, a commune of women militantly opposed to male militarism. The library there contains hundreds of audiotapes, including *The Chipmunks Sing Marvin Hamlisch.* When a disciple commits a grievous offense against the rules of the order, she faces fearsome punishment, including "the Ordeal of the Thousand Broadway Show Tunes." As a rule, though, piped-in images are perceived as comforting. During her irregular childhood with Zoyd, Prairie sometimes wishes that she could be a member of "some family in a car, with no problems that couldn't be solved in half an hour of wisecracks and commercials." Near the end of the novel, when Prairie gets to meet her mother, nothing will do but that the child sing the theme song from *Gilligan's Island.*

Pynchon's devotion to electronic allusions has been criticized before, and *Vineland* will no doubt increase the number of protests. It is, admittedly, disquieting to find a major author drawing cultural sustenance from *The Brady Bunch* and *I Love Lucy* instead of *The Odyssey* and the Bible. But to condemn Pynchon for this strategy is to confuse the author with his characters. He is a gifted man with anti-élitist sympathies. Like some fairly big names in innovative fiction, including Flaubert, Joyce and Faulkner, Pynchon writes about people who would not be able to read the books in which they appear. As a contemporary bonus, Pynchon's folks would not even be interested in trying. That is part of the sadness and the hilarity of this exhilarating novel. (pp. 69-70)

> *Paul Gray, "The Spores of Paranoia," in* Time, *New York, Vol. 135, No. 3, January 15, 1990, pp. 69-70.*

Rhoda Koenig

Vineland is set, in part, in a town of the same name in California, that sun-drenched compost heap of the American Dream, but its larger setting is everything meant by the country whose northern tip the Vikings knew as Vinland the Good, a place of great natural richness populated by natives they called "wretches," who drove them away. A millennium later, wretches still slink along the roads and through the forests, bending nature and the innocent to their purposes, normalizing dread. Developers pave the land with cheap condominiums. The Thanatoids, people who are dead but won't lie down (who among us does not know a Thanatoid?), not only multiply but hold dances and conventions where the band plays such gloriously depressed favorites as "I Gotta Right to Sing the Blues" and "Don't Get Around Much Anymore." (How did Pynchon ever miss "Moanin' Low"?) . . .

Nature responds with terror of its own in both appearance and act. The sky is "the underside of a beast, countless gray-black udder shapes crawling in front of a squall line, behind it something distantly roaring." A mysterious saurian emerges from the sea to squash a research laboratory with one stamp of its humongous foot. Some Vinelandians try to placate nature, but in ways that are designer-ineffectual and of which nature probably would not approve: A couple forgo bread, because it involves the killing of yeast.

Zoyd Wheeler, a gypsy roofer and pick-up musician, sets off Pynchon's plot, one that is as complicated and improbable as life (well, at least, life in California). *Vineland* begins in 1984 and shuttles backward and forward between that Orwellian, Reaganite year and the sixties. At the fag end of that desperate decade, Zoyd's wife, Frenesi, gave birth to their daughter, Prairie, and took off with Brock Vond, a dark genius of political control. (Though *Frenesi* means "Please love me," the request seems to best apply, sadly, to her daughter, who reproaches Zoyd for never re-marrying and for dating girls her own age, then decides, "You must have always loved my mom, so much that if it couldt'n be her, it wouldt'n be anybody.")

Back in the sixties, Brock realized that the youth revolutions were "not threats to order but unacknowledged desires for it . . . the deep—if he'd allowed himself to feel it, the sometimes touching—need only to stay children forever, safe inside some extended national Family." He sets up a reeducation camp to turn demonstrators into FBI informers, the bait being that they can keep going back to school forever, and becomes obsessed with his prisoner, Frenesi.

Pynchon's plot comprises much besides—endless variations on betrayal, dislocation, disguise, revenge. (While characters and situations are endlessly satirical, the story itself is an intoxicated satire of thrillers and conspiracies.) Zoyd, who must appear continually deranged in order to claim his federal mental-disability check, walks into a loggers' bar carrying a chain saw and wearing a dress. One barhound takes a fancy to him and asks if he is an undercover agent. " 'Nut case,' confided Zoyd. 'Oh. Well . . . that sounds like interesting work too.' " Then, quick as forked lightning, Zoyd is asked to *become* an agent by his persecutor Hector Zuñiga, a Fed, who is then himself revealed to be just a few steps ahead of the men in white coats. Refracted identities occur on a more crudely comic level when Billy Barf and the Vomitones, badly in need of a gig, offer themselves as a replacement band at a Mafia wedding, under the name of Gino Baglione and the Paisans. When Billy-Gino's wig slides off to reveal a turquoise crop, "the bride, to protect her wedding from such possible unlucky omens as blood on the wedding cake," slips out and returns with the *Italian Wedding Fake Book*. . . .
    (p. 66)

Language is for Pynchon not only a stun gun but an assault vehicle. The new novel has its share of sinister acronyms—UHURU here is not Swahili for "freedom" but "Ultra High-speed Urban Reconnaissance Unit"—and dazzlingly silly puns. (The local lawn-care service, The Marquis de Sod, advertises with a jingle that begins, to the tune of the "Marseillaise," "A lawn savant, who'll lop a tree-ee-uh.") The most caressing phrases and actions shiv-

er with menace. Frenesi's father sings "Down Among the Sheltering Palms" to delight his little daughter, but the Vibrating Palm is also the Ninja Death Touch, which a runner-up in California's Dangerous Teen Miss pageant ("Best I could do was Miss Animosity") applies to her victim in the so-called act of love.

There are times when Pynchon's multiple shifts of perspective become exhausting rather than enlightening, times when, drawing back from allusiveness, he becomes overexplicit. But these are minor glitches in a powerful, pitying vision of the reality of America juxtaposed against its promise. In this endlessly inventive novel, Pynchon's unfortunates scrabble away as best they can, with the sketchiest instructions from the great fake book of life. Erased from existence by the press of a computer button, Frenesi hums Pynchon's bleak gospel hymn: "What we cry, what we contend for, in our world of toil and blood, it all lies beneath the notice of the hacker we call God." (pp. 66-7)

Rhoda Koenig, "Worth Its Wait," in New York *Magazine, Vol. 23, No. 4, January 29, 1990, pp. 66-7.*

Terrence Rafferty

Between the final words of *Gravity's Rainbow,* "Now everybody—," calling us to sing together in the last moment before the silent rocket hits, and the first words of *Vineland,* "later than usual one summer morning in 1984, Zoyd Wheeler drifted awake," is a gap of nearly seventeen years. In that time Thomas Pynchon has lain low, vanished into the underground or some self-devised witness protection program, surfacing only occasionally and briefly . . . like a groundhog poking his head out of his hole for a quick look around. This time, Pynchon is taking a good, long look, and that's a hopeful sign: evidence that the pitiless reactionary winter that has been our weather for the last decade and a half might be nearing its end. *Vineland* is about people waking up unusually late, beginning to stir for the first time since the late sixties. One character, trying to fill in some missing history for a teenage girl, says, "It's been what, 15 years, just about your lifetime, full of playin' make-believe, acting on faiths in things that sound crazy now, lying, turning each other in, too much time passed, everybody remembering a different story—" In *Vineland* all the different stories resolve themselves into one, something that everybody, even kids, can understand: a fairy tale about a whole country under an evil spell. And by the end of the book Pynchon, brewing and mixing promiscuously, seems to have broken the spell, revived the sleeping beauties of American life.

The novel begins and ends in the enchanted redwood forest of Vineland County, in Northern California, a mythical community of loggers, aging hippies, marijuana growers, and a group of not quite dead folks known as Thanatoids. But most of the action takes place in the territory of the past, which is truly another country, remote and embargoed, accessible only to the obsessed; everyone else is trapped in the flat present of television . . . In the opening pages of *Vineland* we follow Zoyd Wheeler—an amiable, pot-addled schlemiel who lives with his teen-age daughter, Prairie—as he goes about his business: dressing in women's clothing and hurling himself through the window of the Cucumber Lounge (for the local-news cameras), so he can qualify for a mental-disability check; meeting with a crazed Drug Enforcement Agency man, Hector Zuñiga, who has been trying since the sixties to get him to turn informant ("It was a romance over the years at least as persistent as Sylvester and Tweety's"); finally taking it on the lam when his house is seized by "a Justice Department strike force (with) military backup" under the command of the sinister federal prosecutor Brock Vond. For a while, it's all light weirdness, hippie humor of an unusually high grade, a series of deft, mellow riffs; Pynchon's writing in these passages might make you think of gray, paunchy Jerry Garcia noodling his way through the Grateful Dead songs he has been playing for a couple of decades. Wonderful as this old-guy rock and roll is, we suspect, with some disappointment, that it's *only* rock and roll. But it isn't.

The jokes in the first seventy pages or so of **Vineland** reveal themselves, much later, to be more than jokes: they're the residue of old crimes, shady deals, unavenged betrayals turned weightless and transparent in the thin air of the present. Zoyd, the lovable zany, disappears for practically the rest of the book, and sharp little Prairie takes over as the story's emotional center. She has a livelier sense than Zoyd that something's missing from their lives, something she should know but no one's telling her. She's too cool to admit it, but the ambience of stoned wackiness doesn't satisfy all her needs; and everything that has happened— the state's abruptly swooping down on her and her father and dispossessing them—seems to have to do with her mother, Frenesi, who vanished when Prairie was a baby. The pressure of events, interrupting a generally snoozy, uneventful existence, brings out the Nancy Drew side of her; only slightly more willingly than Oedipa Maas, the girl detective of **The Crying of Lot 49,** Prairie sets off into the secret, unspeakable past, in search of her legacy.

What she finds, with the help of a peculiar couple—DL Chastain, a female Ninja who's an old friend of Frenesi's, and Takeshi Fumimota, a speed freak who runs a "karmic adjustment" service out of a Thanatoid hangout called the Zero Inn—is more strangeness, but of a different kind: not the anomic everyday unreality of her life in Vineland but a more densely textured madness, a dance of obscure compulsions. Everything comes down to the twisted relationship between Frenesi and Brock Vond, the helpless mutual attraction of an arrogantly beautiful sixties radical and a methodical fascist. When, about halfway through the book, Pynchon gets down to the task of telling us, and Prairie, the full, sad story of what happened at the end of the sixties, the writing takes on a darker tone: rapt, horrified, mournful. It's an anatomy of betrayal; a frame-by-frame analysis of the moment when everything turned, when the long troubled sleep, the death in the soul, really began; and a new version of the oldest story in the world— the original sin and the exile from Paradise.

Heavy, we might say. . . . Sure, Pynchon is out to create a mythic history of our muddled and narcoleptic times, but he has the good grace—the grace of American pop culture at its casual, lowdown best—to take his big themes by surprise, cutting in on them in mid-dance, spinning them around the floor a few times, then bopping off somewhere else, with a little thanks-for-a-good-time wave. What makes his vision of America so persuasive is that he shows us a country in which serious things keep happen-

ing to people who are trying, on the whole, not to take things too seriously—whose attempts at "seriousness" are, more often than not, just the manic gravity of children at play. And he finds this play beautiful, recognizes it (as virtually no other big-deal literary novelists do) as an essential part of his own character, and maybe not the very worst part, at that. He's famous for his Byzantine plots, his complex patterns of metaphor, his elaborate paranoia, but his sympathies are always, unambiguously, with the plotted-against: the schlemiels and human yo-yos, the fun-loving goofballs, the dazed innocents who just want to be left alone—Benny Profane in *V.,* Tyrone Slothrop in **Gravity's Rainbow,** Oedipa in **Lot 49,** Zoyd and Prairie here. He seems at times almost ashamed of his ferocious ingenuity, his literary facility, his taste for intricate structures, as if all this were evidence of a hideous and grinning demon inside him, a Brock Vond that never gets sent up the river for his crimes.

The story of Frenesi and Brock, the heart of the novel, is a screwball tragedy, the Road Runner and the Coyote as Romeo and Juliet. They meet, at the book's dead center, in classic thirities-comedy style, trading barbed double entendres, apparently hating each other on sight. Earlier, Pynchon prefigures this fateful moment with a brilliant parody of it, in the first encounter of DL and Takeshi, the novel's good couple. Obeying the rules of romantic comedy, they "meet cute," with a vengeance. DL, hired by a mafioso to assassinate Brock Vond, is disguised as Frenesi, complete with contact lenses that blur her vision so she can't see that the man to whom she is applying the Vibrating Palm (or Ninja Death Touch) in the midst of intercourse isn't the evil prosecutor but hapless Takeshi, who has been mistaken for Vond by the mob's dumb goons. He is confused, but decides, as DL begins to seduce him, to relax and go with the moment—unaware that in a year he'll be due to keel over dead. When they discover the unfortunate error (Takeshi, in a splendid comic-book moment, exclaiming, "My own sleaziness—has done me in!"), they manage to reverse the Death Touch, and then enter into a contract to stick together, with DL commanded to "balance your karmic account by working off the great wrong you have done him." Like everything else that seems random and eccentric in **Vineland,** this pulp-fiction romance has a point: the macabre coupling of DL and Takeshi is an alternate take, salvaged from the cutting-room floor, of the grim union of Frenesi and Brock, a vision preserved of the absurd comedy that this relationship, in a better world (or movie), would have remained.

But in this world, "the spilled, the broken world" that Pynchon is compelled to acknowledge, Frenesi and Brock have no benign karmic forces to call up in time of need, nothing to rely on but their own contradictory characters, the tangled family history mapped on their chromosomes. American history plays itself out in their bed—bad news, especially for Frenesi. On her mother's side, she comes from a strong union family, with roots in Vineland; she was brought up, though, in Hollywood, her father a gaffer, in charge of the lighting on studio pictures, until the blacklist hit. To her mother, Sasha, "the blacklist period . . . thick with betrayal, destructiveness, cowardice, and lying, seemed only a continuation of the picture business as it has always been carried on, only now in political form." Sasha says, "History in this town is no more worthy of respect than the average movie script, and it comes about in the same way—soon as there's one version of a story, suddenly it's anybody's pigeon. Parties you never heard of get to come in and change it. Characters and deeds get shifted around, heartfelt language gets pounded flat when it isn't just removed forever. By now the Hollywood fifties is this way-over-length, multitude-of-hands rewrite—except there's no sound, of course, nobody talks. It's a silent movie." Frenesi finds herself in the picture business . . . in the sixties, as part of a radical documentary-film collective known as 24fps—a true believer in the power of the camera, "in the ability of close-ups to reveal and devastate," and in the merciless truth of strong light. She meets Vond through the lens of "her faithful 16mm Canon Scoopic," zooming in on him as she films in an Oregon courthouse lobby, but it's she, not her subject, who's revealed and devastated: he's got star quality. (So much for light; she falls in love with the Prince of Darkness.) Frenesi is, as Prairie will be later, the victim of something inherited from her mother. Sasha, it seems, has always had a bit of a uniform fetish, a shameful, politically incorrect attraction to men in authority. What was no more than a quirk, a sick joke, in Sasha's character is a catastrophe in her daughter's.

"Brock Vond's genius was to have seen in the activities of the sixties left not threats to order but unacknowledged desires for it," Pynchon tells us. . . . Frenesi's desire for order—in the masterful form of Brock himself—culminates in a monstrous act of treachery. She fingers a shambling, inept campus political guru named Weed Atman (another schlemiel, and a lover of Frenesi's) as a traitor, and slips a gun, supplied by Brock, to another activist leader. (When the prosecutor shows her the gun, she protests, pathetically, "Come on, it's only rock and roll," which couldn't be further from the truth.) Years later, in the split-level home of a surviving member of 24fps, Prairie watches the footage of the climax, the exact moment of Weed's murder somehow missed as the cameraman changes rolls, but the full horror clear enough: Frenesi herself lighted the scene. Just before Weed is shot, the camera picks up "not only the look on his face . . . but the way that what he was slowly understanding spread to his body, a long, stunned cringe, a loss of spirit that could almost be seen on the film . . . some silvery effluent, vacating his image, the real moment of his passing." This raw, unedited piece of film is, of course, the record of the death of the sixties. Or, rather, of the moment when the spirit of a playful, childish time departed the body of ordinary life, passed into the region of vacated images—part of the big-screen silent movie, continuously unreeling, that ultimately replaced experience, glazed our memories, turned us into an extended national family of spectators. It's a terrible and paradoxical image: a quick flaring of consciousness, a last-minute recognition, snuffed out before it can be assimilated or acted on—knowledge arrested at the fruitless, immature stage of simple disillusion.

In the aftermath, Weed enters the ranks of the Thanatoids, the sleepless and the powerless, and ends up wandering through Vineland County with all the other unavenged victims of the country's unconfessed sins; Frenesi, self-appalled, drops out of sight, marries Zoyd, gives birth to Prairie, and then, in a deal engineered by Vond, abandons her family and retreats into the anonymity of the Witness Protection program, to live with what she has done. . . . And Prairie, let into the secret of her heritage

at last, through the ambiguous magic of the movies, is left to ponder the images:

> Her mom, in front of her own eyes, had stood with a 1,000-watt Mickey-Mole spot on the dead body of a man who had loved her, and the man who'd just killed him, and the gun she'd brought him to do it with. Stood there like the Statue of Liberty, bringer of light, as if it were part of some contract to illuminate, instead of conceal, the deed. With all the footage of Frenesi she'd seen, all the other shots that had come by way of her eye and body, this hard frightening light, this white outpouring, had shown the girl most accurately, least mercifully, her mother's real face.

It's a media kid's primal scene: the sight of her mother in bed with a dreadful and absolute figure of authority, screwing and being screwed and, in her transports, without the will to sort out the difference. Like every moment of historical lucidity in *Vineland,* this one comes a little late; Prairie is seeing at fourteen what she should have seen long before. But in this case, Pynchon seems to say, it's not *too* late; Prairie is still young, not yet so done in by life that ugly truths send her running for cover.

In the final section of the novel, a softer illumination takes over: "the light of Vineland, the rainy indifference with which it fell on surfaces, the call to attend to territories of the spirit," the fairy-tale light of resolution, retribution, reconciliation. And the story of America in the sixties and the seventies—worked on, like the movie scripts Sasha describes, by a multitude of anonymous hands until it became perfectly mute—seems to have at last found its voice again. History, poor pigeon, has finally made its way home—for once, carrying a readable message, in heartfelt language. *Vineland,* for all its wild, abrupt turnings, is the clearest novel Thomas Pynchon has written. Drawing both its frame of reference and its extraordinary energy from popular culture, the book has a congenial, unthreatening surface; it doesn't have the encyclopedic grandeur of the earlier novels, the head-spinning structural complexity. For some of his fans, and for the most obsessed of his academic exegetes, the Pynchon of *Vineland* may seem a ghost of his former self. But after all those years away he has come back to haunt us with an urgent purpose—has simplified his means so we won't be able to mistake what he's saying. This novel is as funny, as smart, as lyrical, and as subversive as any American fiction of the past decade, but the most remarkable thing about it is the purity of its desire to get through to us. These days, Pynchon seems to be writing out of the deepest, most uncontrollable motive for speech: the need to pass along what he has learned before it's lost forever.

Not that there's anything didactic about his manner: this history lesson seeps into us as gently as sun in a forest, as insidiously as a song heard over and over on the radio. The setting for the novel's verdant, *Midsummer Night's Dream*-like final act is the annual reunion in Vineland of Frenesi's family, generations together under the trees,

> spinning and catching strands of memory, perilously reconnecting—as all around them the profusion of aunts, uncles, cousins, and cousins' kids and so on, themselves each with a story weirder than the last, creatively improved on over the years, came and went, waving corncobs in the air, dribbling soda on their shirts, swaying or dancing . . . while

the fragrance of barbecue smoke came drifting down from the pits.

With this lovingly detailed vision of untidy, free-form family happiness, Pynchon is actually trying to reëvoke what he calls "the green free America of (our) childhoods": a phrase that popped up earlier, while Zoyd and another sixties survivor are sitting around listening to *The Best of Sam Cooke*. *Vineland* is Pynchon's version of "Wonderful World," a beautiful and wholly convincing imagining of life turning out O.K. for us dumb American kids, even though we don't know much about history (or biology, either). Pynchon, the long-lost relative, has turned up again, only slightly changed, and still (improbably) eager to get that big sing-along going, to whip our flawed, disparate voices into an enveloping chorus. It sounds better than we could have hoped. (pp. 108-12)

> *Terrence Rafferty, "Long Last," in* The New Yorker, *Vol. LXVI, No. 1, February 19, 1990, pp. 108-112.*

John Leonard

Vineland—a multimedia semi-thriller, a *Star Wars* for the counterculture—is easier to read than anything else by Thomas Pynchon except *The Crying of Lot 49*. Like *Crying*, it's a brief for the disinherited and dispossessed, the outlaws and outcasts of an underground America. Also like *Crying*, I suspect it's a breather between biggies. It doesn't feel like something obsessed-about and fine-tuned for the seventeen years since *Gravity's Rainbow*. It feels unbuttoned, as though the author-god had gone to a ball-game; another, darker, magisterial mystification is implied, maybe the rumored Mason-Dixon opus. This doesn't make *Vineland* a Sunday in the Park with George, but at least it can be summarized without my sounding too much like an idiot.

Where is "Vineland"?

In northern California's redwoods, "a Harbor of Refuge" since the middle of the nineteenth century "to Vessels that may have suffered on their way North from the strong headwinds that prevail along this coast." It's also a republic of metaphors, a theme park of sixties obsessions—television, mysticism, revolution, rock and roll, Vietnam, drugs, paranoia and repression. And it refers as well to the Vinland of the old Norse sagas, what the Vikings called America. (I wasted time looking up the Vikings. How far did their dragonships get? Explain that Viking tower in Newport, Rhode Island, and those Minnesota runes. Was Quetzalcoatl actually a Viking? Is Pynchon singing some rock saga about another of his unmapped kingdoms, like Vheissu, the "dream of annihilation" at the heart of *V*?) Anyway, it's symbolic: a Third World.

What happens to whom, and when, in this "Vineland"?

In Orwellian 1984, midway through the Reagan gerontocracy, refugees from the sixties are having a hard time. Zoyd Wheeler, who used to deal dope and play keyboard in a rock band, is a "gypsy roofer" trying to take care of his teenage daughter, Prairie. Prairie's in love with a heavy metal neofascist and misses the mother she hasn't seen since babyhood. This mother, the almost mythical Frenesi, belonged in the sixties to a band of guerrilla movie-makers, the Death to the Pig Nihilist Film Kollective, but she was more or less abducted by the malign federal prosecutor Brock Vond and "turned" into an "independent contractor" for F.B.I. sting operations. When Justice Department budget cuts "disappear" Frenesi from the government computer, Vond is frantic. Expecting her to show up in Vineland, he plots to frame Zoyd, kidnap Prairie and scorch every pot plantation north of "San Narcisco." (Think of Panama.)

In other words, "the State law-enforcement apparatus . . . calling itself 'America' " declares total war on the leftover flower children. It's a made-for-TV rerun. Back in the sixties Vond's feds destroyed a college-campus People's Republic of Rock and Roll and trucked the student revolutionaries off to camps for a Political Re-Education Program (PREP). This is where he turned Frenesi. When Vond invades Vineland, Zoyd and Prairie are assisted in their resistance by the woman warrior DL Chastain; by the Japanese private eye Takeshi; . . . [and by] three generations of Left Coast Wobblies, including Frenesi's mother, Sasha, who may or may not be a member of the Party.

Is any of this funny?

Of course it's funny. Not only does Pynchon know more than we do about almost everything—communications theory, stimulus-response psychology, rocket science, Catatonic Expressionism, entropy, gauchos and stamps—but what he doesn't know, he makes up. In *Vineland,* for instance, ping-ponging between the sixties and the eighties, he makes up TV movies: John Ritter in *The Bryant Gumbel Story*, Pee-wee Herman in *The Robert Musil Story*, Woody Allen in *Young Kissinger*. Not to mention a docudrama about the Boston Celtics with Paul McCartney as Kevin McHale and Sean Penn as Larry Bird. And not even to think about *The Chipmunks Sing Marvin Hamlisch*.

There are, besides, the Bodhi Dharma Pizza Temple, "a classic example of the California pizza concept at its most misguided," and a controlled-environment mall called the Noir Center, with an upscale mineral-water boutique (Bubble Indemnity), a perfume and cosmetics shop (The Mall Tease Flacon) and a New York deli (The Lady 'n' the Lox).

Of all the funny names—Weed Atman, Ditzah and Zipi Pisk, Ortho Bob, Mirage—my favorite is Isaiah Two Four, Prairie's heavy metal boyfriend, named by his parents for the swords-into-plowshares, spears-into-pruning-hooks passage from the Bible. No wonder Isaiah wants to start a chain of Violence Centers, each to include "automatic-weapon firing ranges, paramilitary fantasy adventures . . . and video game rooms for the kids." These centers would presumably compete with the "fantasy marathons" of the Kunoichi Sisterhood that feature "group rates on Kiddie Ninja weekends." I also laughed at a Sisterhood self-criticism session devoted to "scullery duty as a decoding of individual patterns of not-eating." And of the many songs Pynchon's written for his various musicians, the funniest is "Just a floo-zy with-an U-u-zi."

Can we count on the usual entropy, paranoia and Manicheism?

Yes, as well as some terrific rhapsodies on water, cars and

parrots. And the paranoids are right. *They* (narcs, RICOs, yuppies, television anchorfaces, earthrapers, treekillers, random urine-sniffers, sexhating deathloving Wasteland thought police) are out to get *us* (whomever: civil liberties, due process, readers of Pynchon and *The Nation*). *And* they use us against us. (pp. 281-82)

Only this time *we* win. You have to understand entropy not just as the heat-death of a culture but as *equilibrium*. As Pynchon clued us in his first famous short story (**"Entropy"**), with nods to Henry Adams, so he clues us here by quoting another American crazy, Emerson, from William James's *The Varieties of Religious Experience*:

> Secret retributions are always restoring the level, when disturbed, of the divine justice. It is impossible to tilt the beam. All the tyrants and proprietors and monopolists of the world in vain set their shoulders to heave the bar. Settles forever more the ponderous equator to its line, and man and mote, and star and sun, must range to it, or be pulverized by the recoil.

For Pynchon, this is remarkably cheerful. But how are we, a bunch of dopers in the California redwoods, to prevail against the Geeks: Virgins vs. Dynamos? See below.

Will we care any more about these characters than we did about, say, Benny Profane and Tyrone Slothrop?

Probably not, except for DL. Like a Buddhist or a Hume, Pynchon doesn't really believe in a "self." He's more interested in states of being and becoming. Zoyd attitudinizes, Frenesi is a computer dream of patterns, Takeshi is inscrutable, Hector is a clown and Sasha is one of Tolstoy's super-goody, clean old peasants. Even Vond, "like any of the sleek raptors that decorate fascist architecture," adds up to little more than an upwardly mobile social-control freak with a flashy line of psychic yardgoods. But as Vond talks to other men through the holes in women's bodies, so Pynchon talks to his readers through the holes in his cartoon zanies. And what he wants to talk about is "official" reality (a media fabrication) versus "unofficial" alternatives (see below).

Frenesi is Pynchon's excuse to make fun of film. According to her Killective: "A camera is a gun. An image taken is a death performed. Images put together are the substructure of an afterlife and a Judgment. We will be architects of a just Hell for the fascist pig. Death to everything that oinks!" Vond tells her, "Can't you see, the two separate worlds—one always includes a camera somewhere, and the other always includes a gun, one is make-believe, one is real? What if this is some branch point in your life, where you'll have to choose between worlds?" Frenesi brought a gun *and* a camera to the People's Republic of Rock and Roll on the night of its destruction, not to mention fast-film 7242 and a Norwood Binary light meter, for the helicopters and the troops in blackface and "the high-ticket production of their dreams." This is "Reality Time" versus "all that art-of-the-cinema handjob." She'll emerge from hiding and go to Vineland only because Hector promises to star her in *his* movie.

Hector is an excuse to talk about television. Although almost everything happens in *Vineland* in "sullen Tubeflicker," not always "prime time"; and odd birds sit in palm fronds to sing back at the commercials; and Zoyd, dropping acid, hopes Prairie will be there "to help him through

those times when the Klingons are closing"; and Takeshi believes that television "mediates death" . . . ; only Hector is addicted, a Brady Buncher. When his wife kills their TV set with a frozen pot roast, Hector arrests her. He'll escape from a "Tubaldetox" program. Television is the white noise of the garrison state, the elevator Muzak of repression going down.

Zoyd is an excuse to talk about music, which he's given up, from rock in general to heavy metal ("nuke-happy cyberdeath," "Septic Tank and Fascist Toejam") to New Age ("audio treacle," "mindbarf") and even Bach ("the best tunes ever to come out of Europe"). (pp. 282-84)

Whereas Sasha is Pynchon's excuse to talk about one of the alternatives to media reality—the lost history of radical politics in the American West, long before Pacifica or Savio or People's Park; the organizing of loggers, miners and canneries; the strikes against San Joaquin cotton, Ventura sugar beets, Venice lettuce; Tom Mooney, Culbert Olson, Hollywood craft unions and fifties blacklists. This repressed progressive history and its media denial seem at first the subtext of *Vineland.* These people did more for the revolution than sing about it or dope themselves stupid. Nor did they surf.

But this is to reckon without the alternative (and competing) unofficial realities of the Indians and the dolphins and DL Chastain, the kick-ass woman warrior.

In every Pynchon novel, there's a woman we love—Rachel Owlglass in *V,* Oedipa Maas in *Crying,* Katje or Greta in *Gravity's Rainbow*—because in the satiric muddle she seems to point north to a magnetic pole of decencies. DL is the one we care about here. Though trained in a variety of martial arts strategies, from the Vibrating Palm and the *Kasumi* Mist to "the Enraged Sparrow, the Hidden Foot, the Nosepicking of Death and the truly unspeakable *Gojira no Chimpira,*" and equally at home among the Kunoichi Sisters and the YakMaf, she is nevertheless Frenesi's loyal friend *and* Prairie's resourceful protector *and* Takeshi's eventual lover. Like her comrades on a rescue mission into "the Cold War dream" of PREP, we believe in DL's "proprietary whammies"—"the same way in those days it was possible to believe in acid, or the imminence of revolution, or the disciplines, passive and active, of the East." She's also Pynchon's door to the Orient, into which, it seems to me, he disappears.

Now I can sound like an idiot.

I haven't mentioned the Thanatoids, nor their Vineland suburb of Shade Creek. You reach Shade Creek by water and darkness, often with the help of Vato and Blood, those strippers of cars and souls. It's a ghost town, except the ghosts aren't dead yet. They are an "unseen insomniac population," refugees from history, residues of memory, victims of "karmic imbalances—unanswered blows, unredeemed suffering, escapes by the guilty—anything that frustrated their daily expeditions on into the interior of Death, with Shade Creek a psychic jumping-off town." . . . (p. 284)

Think of them as the un-Grateful semi-Dead.

Thanatoids, instead of rock and roll, sing songs like "Who's Sorry Now?"; "I Gotta Right to Sing the Blues"; "Don't Get Around Much Anymore"; "As Time Goes

By." They watch television, although they learned long ago

> to limit themsclves, as they always did in other areas, only to emotions helpful in setting right whatever was keeping them from advancing further into the condition of death. Among these the most common by far was resentment, constrained as Thanatoids were by history and by rules of imbalance and restoration to feel little else beyond their needs for revenge.

Weed Atman, the Timothy Leary-like mathematics professor who rose implausibly to become guru of the People's Republic of Rock and Roll before Frenesi betrayed him, is a Thanatoid. So are many Vietnam veterans, like Ortho Bob. . . . Takeshi, like the Sisterhood of Kunoichi Attentives, sees the moneymaking possibilities of a "Karmology hustle." So, apparently, do Vato and Blood, Charons on the Shade Creek Styx. When Vond comes looking for Frenesi, he'll meet Vato and Blood instead, while the leftover flower children are at a picnic with the leftover Wobblies and a Russian punk rocker who wandered into the redwoods.

According to Takeshi, if none of this other stuff works, "we can always go for the reincarnation option." Takeshi is into the *Bardo Thodol, The Tibetan Book of the Dead,* with souls in transition, denying death, unable to distinguish between "the weirdness of life and the weirdness of death." So, of course, are the Thanatoids. But. . . .

In a way, everybody in *Vineland* is a Thanatoid, a deadhead, full of bad faith; equally guilty, resentful and nostalgic; under(ghost)cover, in motion through varying thicknesses of memory and light toward a reckoning. Zoyd's sixties surfer band, the Corvairs, found "strange affinities" with the subculture of "beer riders of the valleys": both rode a "technowave. . . . Surfers rode God's ocean, beer riders rode the momentum through the years of the auto industry's will." (pp. 284-85)

But there were ghosts before the sixties—the Yorok Indians. Early Russian and Spanish visitors to Vineland felt some "invisible boundary" the Indians

> might have known about but did not share . . . black tips of seamounts emerging from gray sea fringed in brute-innocent white breakings, basalt cliffs like castle ruins, the massed and breathing redwoods, alive forever . . . the call to attend to territories of the spirit.

And there were ghosts even before there were Indians. Past the lights of Vineland, "the river took back its oldest form, became what for the Yuroks it had always been, a river of ghosts" with spirits called *woge,* "creatures who had been living here when the first humans came," who went away, eastward, over the mountains or "nestled all together in giant redwood boats, singing unison chants of dispossession and exile." Trails without warning "would begin to descend into the earth, toward Tsorrek, the worlds of the dead." Eco-freaky hippies tell Vato and Blood that

> this watershed was sacred and magical, and that the *woge* were really the porpoises, who had left their world to the humans, whose hands had the same five-finger bone structure as their flippers . . . and gone beneath the ocean, right off Patrick's

Point in Humboldt, to wait and see how humans did with their world. And if we started fucking up too bad . . . they would come back, teach us how to live the right way, save us.

What's going on? If we put together Shade Creek, flood dreams, technowaves, William James, porpoises and *woge* with Vheissu in *V* and the Trystero underground in *Crying* (clairvoyants, paranoids, outcasts and squatters swinging in "a web of telephone wires, living in the very copper rigging and secular miracle of communication, untroubled by the dumb voltages flickering their miles") and the "Deathkingdoms" and "deathcolonies" Blicero apostrophizes in *Gravity's Rainbow* ("waste regions, Kalaharis, lakes so misty they could not see the other side," original sin, modern analysis), we end up with something that looks a lot like if not a comic-book *Thodol,* then maybe that nonviolent Buddhist "global novel" Maxine Hong Kingston has been going on about recently in the pages of *Mother Jones* and on—gasp!—The Tube. For that matter, Zoyd, Prairie, Takeshi, DL and the Wobblies look a lot like the 108 bandit-heroes of *Water Margin,* the Chinese Robin Hood that Kingston has so much fun with in *Tripmaster Monkey.*

According to *The Tibetan Book of the Dead,* dying takes time. We experience the supreme void as pure light and hope it takes us straightaway to Amitabha, which is for Buddhists what "one big union" was for Wobblies. If the pure light won't take us, we must wrestle with our past, our karma. Only after apparitions both beautiful and monstrous are done with our "conscious principle" will we be reborn—the "reincarnation option"—as something else, somewhere other, on the great wheel. Pynchon calls this place, in the last word of *Vineland,* "home." Wouldn't it be sweet to think so? (pp. 285-86)

John Leonard, "The Styxties," in The Nation, *New York, Vol. 250, No. 8, February 26, 1990, pp. 281-86.*

Brad Leithauser

The further I ventured into Thomas Pynchon's new novel, *Vineland,* the more pressingly I found myself wondering: For whom is this intended? What sort of sensibility would, on turning page 200, say, of this nearly four hundred-page book, find itself cheerfully hoping to be introduced to yet another character who boasts both a funny name and a taste for folksy facetiousness? For this is what, like as not, one will get at any given juncture. (On page 200, incidentally, one reads about Zipi Pisk, Frenesi, Darryl Louise Chastain, and Krishna.) Pynchon introduces by name a cast of well over a hundred, including Scott Oof, Moonpie, Isaiah Two Four, Willis Chunko, Morning, Chef Ti Bruce, 187, Meathook, Cleveland ("Blood") Bonnifoy, Baba Havabananda, Ortho Bob Dulang, Dr. Elasmo, Chickeeta, and Sid Liftoff. Needless to say, the result can be confusing. . . . (p. 7)

Lest all of these details sound disastrously coy and cloying, I hasten to note that *Vineland*—although it tries one's patience at nearly every turn—is far from a disaster. It is manifestly the work of a man of quick intelligence and quirky invention. Many of its episodes flicker with an appealingly far-flung humor. And Pynchon displays throughout *Vineland* what might be called an internal loyalty: he keeps the faith with the generally feckless and almost invariably inarticulate misfits he assembles, tracking their looping thoughts and indecisive actions with a patience that seems grounded in affection. He is true to his creation until the finish; the book's closing pages strike a moving note of sweet inconclusion, of curiosity grading not into enlightenment but into wonder. Nonetheless, such virtues having been tallied, one must note that in view of our expectations the book is a disappointment.

One's sense of letdown derives in part from a condition extrinsic to the book itself: seventeen years have elapsed since Pynchon last released a novel, *Gravity's Rainbow,* and hopes naturally run high, perhaps unreasonably so. But in the end *Vineland* falters in a convincing variety of ways—perhaps chiefly through its failure in any significant degree to extend or improve upon what the author has done before. In its style and diction, in its satirical targets, in the techniques of its plot unfoldings and outreachings toward illumination—in practically everything—*Vineland* marks a return to what was weakest in his patchy novella, *The Crying of Lot 49,* published in 1966. But whereas the earlier book offers the virtue of compression—and, with it, the thrill of watching, at the book's denouement, as the pent-up becomes the pell-mell—*Vineland* is a loosely packed grab bag of a book. And there is no pleasure in *Vineland* to compare with the one great delight of *Lot 49*—its madman-in-a-library's hunger for arcana, as the century-long development of the postal service is pursued with a diligence worthy of a superhuman mailman.

Vineland opens to opening eyes—those of Zoyd Wheeler, a largely unemployed, pot-smoking, fortyish Californian who wakes up one morning in the summer of 1984 to the realization that he must perform "something publicly crazy," preferably before a television camera, if he is to protect his "mental-disability" stipend. He resolves to secure his money, as in years past, by leaping through an enormous plate-glass window. . . . (p. 7)

Although he passes through the window unscathed, Zoyd is, we gradually discern, a wounded man. He has never recovered from the disappearance, many years before, of his wife, Frenesi, who abandoned him for a federal prosecutor named Brock Vond. When the reader meets up with Frenesi, he discovers that she, like Zoyd, is on the public payroll, though not in any humorous, harmless way. A student revolutionary in the Sixties, she has since become an FBI informer and lackey, shuttling from place to place at the behest of her increasingly ruthless and indifferent employers.

Zoyd and Frenesi have a teen-aged daughter, Prairie, who lives with her father and dreams of being reunited with her mother, whom she has not seen since she was a little girl. Her quest is, in fact, one of the book's main themes, for at one point or another most of the principal characters seem to be on the trail of a missing woman. Another theme is the centrality in our culture of television, which is generally referred to as the Tube (capital "T") and which inspires meditations on Tubal abuse and Tubaldetox and Tubeflicker. Whatever the disparities in their outlooks, Pynchon's characters are united in having television serve as their communal well of learning, from which they draw their humor, morality, locutions, analogies. No one reads; everybody watches; and what binds us, soul to soul, is *Wheel of Fortune, The Flintstones, Phil Donahue, Alvin and the Chipmunks, The Mod Squad,* and (a special favorite) *Gilligan's Island.*

At the book's heart—the one theme without which *Vineland* wouldn't be *Vineland*—is political paranoia. The novel asks us to entertain the notion that, beginning with Nixon and culminating with Reagan, our government came to regard its subclass of easy-doping lay-abouts—its Zoyd Wheelers—as meriting not merely contempt but brutal repression and, perhaps, extermination. Deep in the hills of northern California, in the imaginary county of Vineland from which the book draws its title, a military installation has gone up for the evident purpose of sowing domestic terror.

The book's title recalls, of course, the Norse adventure sagas and the North American expeditions they chronicled, but little is made of this connection. A tighter literary link is fixed when Pynchon evokes the white man's discovery of Californian Vineland:

> Someday this would be all part of a Eureka-Crescent City-Vineland megalopolis, but for now the primary sea coast, forest, riverbanks and bay were still not much different from what early visitors in Spanish and Russian ships had seen.

Hovering in the background here, needless to say, is Nick Carraway and his celebrated lament at the close of *The Great Gatsby:*

> And as the moon rose higher the inessential houses began to melt away until gradually I became aware of the old island here that flowered once for Dutch sailors' eyes—a fresh, green breast of the new world.

Pynchon's passage rings a dirgelike note of corroboration. Out there at the New World's newest New World—the coast of California—one catches an echo of hopes mislaid, a continent betrayed.

But to set the two books side by side is unavoidably to highlight one of *Vineland*'s gravest deficiencies: the absence in it of natural beauty. . . . At various points in *Vineland* (beginning with the marvelous photograph on its dust jacket, which depicts a hill of evergreens savagely reduced to clipped and smoking rubble) Pynchon asks us to ponder the rape and poisoning of our environment, but how are we to summon any deep consternation when Nature in these pages engages us so thinly? Pynchon characteristically renders natural detail in a tone of pop flippancy—a "golden pregnant lollapalooza of a moon," a "sun just set into other world transparencies of yellow and ultraviolet, and other neon-sign colors coming on below across the boundless twilit high plain," a "squadron of bluejays stomping around on the roof."

In 1982, not long before he died, John Cheever published a short book, *Oh What a Paradise It Seems,* that likewise treats issues of paranoia and environmental vandalism within a tale of antic folly and reversal. But one of the many lessons offered by that fine, valedictory novel was that contemporary fiction of a comic, even slapstick kind has ample room for the humbling grandeurs and outsize poetry of the natural order. When Cheever informs us that quaint Beasley's Pond, on which the book's New England hero likes to skate, has been poisoned by unscrupulous businessmen, the reader feels heartsick, for Cheever's is a world where "a traverse of potable water" can represent "the bridge that spans the mysterious abyss between our spiritual and our carnal selves." In *Vineland,* one could witness the dynamiting of the entire state of California, redwoods and all, and remain unaffected.

What one longs to meet in *Vineland,* and never does meet, is some moment when Zoyd or one of his buddies would find the stars overhead cutting so deeply into his psyche, or the waves before him breaking with so plaintive a collapse of voices, or the ground underfoot releasing so tangy a mixture of surge and decay that all wisecracks die aborning in the throat. One longs for a sweeping crack of thunder. The rain-whetted smell of toadstools. The shifting flank of a startled deer.

A feeling for the natural world may be welcome in a satirical novel, but it is hardly essential—as is demonstrated by Evelyn Waugh, who in a masterwork like *A Handful of Dust* can hurl the reader into the feverish Amazon jungle without ever evoking much of its infernal beauty. What is essential, however, is freshness; even if the targets that one aims at are in tatters, the darts that one tosses at them must be sharp. When Pynchon takes on laid-back California ("The little portable sign read OPEN KARMOLOGY CLINIC, WALK RIGHT IN, NO APPT. NECESSARY") . . . or militant feminism (" 'It was sleazy, slippery man,' Rochelle continued, 'who invented good and evil, where before women had been content to just be' ") or made-for-television movies ("Pee-wee Herman in *The Robert Musil Story*") all we can give him is a weary smile. This humor has no bite; we've heard it all before.

He's even less successful when he bundles off one of his heroines to Tokyo, where she is sold into white slavery by a bunch of inscrutable technocrats. Lord knows that modern Japan is ripe for satire, and perhaps in time, as the Japanese bury us economically, we may abandon our solicitous but condescending notion that they—unlike the British, the French, the Soviets—are not hardy enough to withstand our chiding. But even if one applauds Pynchon's recognition that to lampoon the Japanese is not necessarily "Japan-bashing," what he actually presents here is not merely bathetic and inane but ("Girl, you have never seen picky till you've been in one of these Jap meat shows") ugly and offensive.

In short, his aim is off. What could be a more rewarding adversary than television, provided you actually had something novel to say about the ways in which it alternately stupefies and imbrutes us? But what Pynchon offers has already been said better in Cheever, in Updike's Rabbit novels, even in Kosinski's *Being There*—and, daily, in the parodies that television unselfconsciously makes of itself. (pp. 7-8)

As satire, *Vineland* is a case not of "too little, too late," but of too much, too late. Given the book's length, there is simply not enough originality to sustain it. Most of it, particularly the sending-up of California, feels a little stale. One is left with a troubling image of an author supplying what he thinks his audience wants, based upon what it embraced in the past. Do his readers like to meet rock bands with unpalatable names like the Paranoids of *The Crying of Lot 49?* This time around he'll give us Billy

Barf and the Vomitones. Have we shown a liking for portentous aphorisms? Okay, then how about "Life is Vegas"? In the end, it's hard to quell a suspicion that Pynchon is—either deliberately or through a sort of unguarded psychological seduction—playing down to his audience.

Although *Vineland* tilts at grand issues, the book is actually at its best in little, unforced moments in which Pynchon puts a spinning zap on his language:

> Why, the man had me scared spitless.

> They arrived at the mouth of an oversize freight elevator, scrambled inside, and began to plunge earpoppingly hellward.

> Dangerous men with coarsened attitudes, especially toward death, were perched around lightly on designer barstools, sipping kiwi mimosas.

Pynchon's style everywhere courts ungainliness. He pursues dissonance over euphony, roughness over smoothness, and, often, confusion over lucidity. For one thing, he adopts into his own expository prose some of the awkward contractions employed by his characters: "to've," "might've," etc. For another, his almost exclusive reliance on the comma, and his penchant for breaking phrases unidiomatically, leads to a prose of jumpy, tumbling disclosures:

> He didn't get to the Cuke quite in time to miss Ralph Wayvone, Jr., in a glossy green suit accented with sequins, who was cracking jokes into the mike to warm this crowd, who in Ralph's opinion needed it, up. . . .

This is writing with a lot of clangor, a lot of racket, in it—as in these thumping repetitions of "out" and "out of ":

> Somewhere down the hill hammers and saws were busy and country music was playing out of somebody's truck radio. Zoyd was out of smokes. On the table in the kitchen, next to the Count Chocula box, which turned out to be empty, he found a note from Prairie.

This sort of discordancy can hardly be attributed to oversight, since it is drawn from the novel's first page and since each succeeding page turns up similar effects. No, Pynchon deliberately hits the ear harshly; reading him is like listening to a song on the radio with the volume cranked up to the point where, now and then, static crackles.

Among contemporary writers Pynchon is, of course, hardly unique in cultivating disharmony. J. D. Salinger and Flannery O'Connor owe many of their most winning effects to an ear attuned to the preposterous ways in which words get mangled around them and to a tongue prepared to go the manglers one better. But both of them reserve such effects until something truly choice happens by. For all the malformations of speech that Pynchon records in *Vineland* (all the phrases like "actin' like a li'l fuckin' army o' occupation") none is so felicitous as when Meeks, in *The Violent Bear It Away,* with a misguided stab at formality, declares, "You figure he might have got aholt to some misinformation." . . . (pp. 8-9)

Why is a surreal, madcap novel like O'Connor's *The Vio-*

lent Bear It Away so much more satisfying than a surreal, madcap novel like *Vineland?* In part because O'Connor's careful clumsinesses are always bumping up against something graceful, or Graceful: human fumbling is set off against divine agency. By contrast, there is little "behind" all the clatter in *Vineland,* nothing transcendently spiritual or beautiful or numinous—or even overarchingly malignant, unless one is prepared to take seriously its (surely satirical?) suggestion that Reagan and his cronies were only a step or two removed from committing Ceauçescu-like pogroms against their own people. *Vineland* lacks the huge, desolating disillusion of, say, Beckett; the abyss that it contemplates is, simply, not very deep.

For some readers, such shortcomings will scarcely matter. *Vineland* by mere virtue of its arrival qualifies as a phenomenon—one that releases, in some quarters, an almost irresistible impulse to announce a masterpiece. How else explain why a highly intelligent critic like Sven Birkerts, reviewing the book for *USA Today,* would liken it to the *Divine Comedy?* Or why Salman Rushdie, in *The New York Times Book Review,* would proclaim it "a major political novel about what America has been doing to itself, to its children, all these many years"? Pynchon inspires cultists, and a cult that has waited nearly two decades for word from its leader will naturally feel uncontainable pressures to declare the wait worthwhile. (Just how powerful this impulse can be was crystallized for me when I discussed *Vineland* with an academic friend. When I complained that most of the book's jokes fall flat, he readily agreed—but added that Pynchon surely had trafficked to such length in leaden humor for some aesthetically sound, if as yet undetermined, reason.)

The cult is fueled, naturally, by Pynchon's celebrated, and greatly refreshing, anonymity. In an era in which the writing of books begins to seem, for many prominent writers, and adjunct to the business of promotion—talk shows, readings, signings, "appearances"—he somehow contrives to make even Salinger look like a party animal. No one appears to know where he lives and how he spends his time; what may be his most recent available photograph dates to his 1953 high school yearbook. The blankness that enfolds him allows each of us to make of him what we will—to convert him into a species of ideal artist or secret friend. In addition, by setting so much of *Vineland* in a Sixties' dope haze, he taps into what for many people remains an era of indestructible nostalgia. How delightful it is as one's joint-passing youth is now revealed to be no mere idyll but—wow! neat!—the stuff of great art.

The common tendency to overrate Pynchon reflects as well his admirable fascination with the ways in which science and technology daily refigure our lives—a subject of curiously little urgency for many American writers, whether traditional or avant-garde. This has been a preoccupation of his from the outset; one of his earliest stories, written when he was little more than twenty, was a meditative piece entitled **"Entropy."** In *Vineland* he muses repeatedly upon the nature of the computer. But if we look outside America to a writer like Stanislaw Lem, we see just the sort of sparks that can fly when a first-rate creative temperament truly immerses itself in scientific issues. In his native Poland in the Fifties—a milieu in which computers were but a distant rumor—he discovered in cybernetics "a new era not just for technological progress but

also for the whole of civilization." Time and again, he has demonstrated a genius for focusing on new or potential technological breathroughs and teasing from them one implication after another, each more striking than its predecessor. After the dizzying meditations on theology and artificial intelligence in a book like *The Cyberiad,* *Vineland* can look embarrassing. . . . (pp. 9-10)

Over the years, Pynchon has clearly established himself as our foremost "experimental" writer—but isn't it equally clear that our country in recent decades has not produced anyone who can compare to Borges, Calvino, García Márquez? Many wonderful things have emerged from those American writers who are regularly grouped, in both age and aims, with Pynchon. Donald Barthelme, for instance, brought to the short story a distinctively oddball humor— his "The King of Jazz" is a gem—but does anyone sincerely wish to hold up one of his collections beside Borges's *Ficciones?* John Barth can be marvelous—particularly in *The Floating Opera* and some of his short stories—but who would set his *oeuvre* beside Calvino's? Where are the recent American novels that one would want to stack up against García Márquez's *One Hundred Years of Solitude?* Or Lem's *Solaris?* Or Kobo Abe's *Woman in the Dunes?* Or Halldor Laxness's *The Atom Station?* Or Juan Rulfo's *Pedro Paramo?* (Ironically, some of the best antirealist American fiction in our time belongs to writers who are generally classified as naturalists. Who would have supposed that Cheever, often dismissed as a chronicler of suburban quandaries, would write some of the best American ghost stories since Henry James?) These are the books against which *Vineland* must be matched; we do no favor to Pynchon when we allow him to flourish in a critical vacuum.

If I concentrate on *Vineland*'s short-comings, and underplay its considerable charms (and how unlikeable can a book be in which one character's haircut was apparently "performed by someone who must have been trying to give up smoking"?), I may do so in an attempt to counterbalance its idolaters. For all its dark moments, the book is closer to farce than tragedy, and to herald it as some sort of weighty masterwork is to place a king's crown on the head of a jester. And although I have no more idea than anybody else about how Pynchon spends his days, I have trouble believing that during the last seventeen years he has devoted himself exclusively to *Vineland:* My guess— and my hope—is that time will reveal this book to have been a lighthearted interlude, one completed while its author was intent on a more substantial, if not necessarily more voluminous, work. Peering hard at that high school yearbook photograph—its pair of earnest probing eyes, its appealing buckteeth—one longs to be able to say, as Prairie says in the last spoken words of the novel, "You can come back. . . . Come on, come in . . . Take me anyplace you want." (p. 10)

> Brad Leithauser, "*Any Place You Want,*" in The New York Review of Books, *Vol. XXXVII, No. 4, March 15, 1990, pp. 7-10.*

Edward Mendelson

To find another novel that is as tedious, as tendentious, and as exhilarating as Thomas Pynchon's *Vineland* you have to search far back through literary history, perhaps as far as *War and Peace*. The tedious part of *Vineland* is its plot, in which radicals and potheads of the 1960s replay in the 1980s their Manichaean struggles against authority. The tendentious part of the book is its historical myth, which explains the repressive 1970s and 1980s as a fulfillment of the secret wishes of the radical 1960s. The exhilarating part is its vision. *Vineland* sees American life of the last two decades in terms of a laconic American Indian legend of a period when no one dies, a legend that the book transforms into a vision of an era when the processes of life and death are suspended, when time stands still. The vision culminates in the moment when that era ends, death resumes, and life triumphs.

To reach the vision, though, you must work your way through the plot. In itself the plot is an unsalvageable tangle of improbabilities, but Pynchon almost rescues it through the intellectual and imaginative energy that he brings to the landscape, the culture, and the language that are the setting of each improbable incident. *Vineland*'s plot is often both programmatic and perfunctory, but its world is richer and more various than the world of almost any American novel in recent memory.

As in most visionary tales, the story begins in a comfortably familiar setting. A few chapters later, when the vision kicks in, this setting, like every ordinary-looking place in Pynchon's universe, proves to be a crossing point on the border between the everyday world and the realm of the mysterious and the miraculous. The book opens on the morning when Zoyd Wheeler is scheduled to perform the annual act of public craziness that assures the continued arrival of his mental-disability checks. It is 1984. Wheeler, the latest of Pynchon's passive and bewildered representatives, is an ex-rock musician around forty who lives a hand-to-mouth existence in the California redwood country with his teenage daughter. Except for his well-planned annual leap through the window of a friend's bar, nothing in his thoughts or actions qualifies him for mental disability payments. The worst that can be said of him is that he seems slow to recognize that the 1960s are really over. But the opening morning of the novel brings him "several rude updates." The loggers' bars have been remodeled and gentrified. . . . And the drug enforcement agent who made his life miserable in the pot-smoking 1960s reappears with news of Wheeler's ex-wife, last seen a dozen years before.

These early chapters are vintage Pynchon, with all the comic extravagance that makes his books so uncomfortable to read while dressed in a stuffed shirt. Here again are the silly names, the dialogue marked by ungrammatical commas to indicate pauses and breathing patterns, the exact ear for elevated and demotic speech. Here also are dozens of interpolated lyrics, some tossed off by otherwise unmusical characters in the course of the action, others crafted by artistic sensibilities who share Pynchon's own indecorous high spirits. (pp. 40-1)

Also present, as always in Pynchon, is a breathtakingly sustained democratic lyricism. No other American writer moves so smoothly and swiftly between the extremes of high and low style, or accommodates so generously the shrill patois of the valley girl and the rotundities of Emerson. (p. 41)

Even at its most lyrical, the style of *Vineland* is less flashy than the style of *Gravity's Rainbow,* a book in which Pynchon created the illusion of switching from English to French to German in the course of a few pages written entirely in English. But *Vineland*'s style is more densely integrated with its emotions and less hesitant to speak in the voices of feeling. What is new in the style and the story of *Vineland* is a deliberately gawky tenderness for the ordinary. Pynchon writes with quiet affection about a modern backwoods America where building supplies are exchanged at swap meets and tow-truck drivers recall lessons from group therapy.

A similar affection informs Pynchon's account of Zoyd Wheeler's love for his daughter, whose name, Prairie, is a discordant 1960s artifact among the shopping malls of the 1980s. . . . The novel treats the relation between father and daughter partly as a détente between the language of two generations, and the complex harmonies of style established here extend back through two more generations before the novel ends.

When Pynchon reprinted his early stories in *Slow Learner* (1984), he wrote an introduction that all but explicitly renounced his first three novels, *V.* (1963), *The Crying of Lot 49* (1966), and *Gravity's Rainbow* (1973), and offered a prospectus for his next one. He recalled that his younger self had "come up with the notion that one's personal life had nothing to do with fiction, when the truth, as everyone knows, is nearly the direct opposite." His early work had ignored what he already knew, that the fiction

> that moved and pleased me then as now was precisely that which had been made luminous, undeniably authentic by having been found and taken up, always at a cost, from deeper and more shared levels of the life we all really live.

The main plot of *Vineland* is built around a diagrammatic story of personal and political obsession that has little to do with lives that anyone has ever lived. But the relations between parents and children in the book, relations often tangential to the main plot, intermittently make *Vineland* "luminous, undeniably authentic," and give it a warmth that the intellectual exoticism of his earlier work excluded.

Zoyd Wheeler and his daughter Prairie turn out to be little more than observers of the main plot, which unfolds as Prairie seeks the secrets of her mother's past. The story centers on the mutual sexual obsession between Frenesi Gates, once a radical filmmaker at Berkeley, later Wheeler's wife and Prairie's mother, and Brock Vond, an antiradical federal prosecutor who got his start in Nixon's Justice Department.

Pynchon performs much fancy footwork to avoid falling into the holes of this plot, but he never bothers to fill the holes because he has little interest in Brock Vond or Frenesi Gates as people. Vond is for Pynchon a local embodiment of impersonal and collective power, deluded by the belief that his acts are the product of his own choice rather than of larger historical energies. Frenesi, more subtly, is an embodiment of the impersonal collective wishes of much of her generation. The actions of both serve mostly to dramatize a single historical and political idea, the idea that the conflict in the 1960s between the radicals and the authorities concealed their shameful longings for each other.

Everything that happens in the story of Frenesi Gates and Brock Vond is designed to confirm Vond's intuition that the rebellions of that era were "not threats to order but unacknowledged desires for it," that the revolution of youth against "parents of all kinds" expressed a "need only to stay children forever, safe inside some extended national Family." Frenesi needs little persuasion from Vond to become first his lover, then his means of spreading distrust and violence among the leaders of a campus rebellion, and finally, under the federal witness-protection program, an agent in sting operations. Through all this, Pynchon is less concerned with her motives or feelings than he is in treating her as an allegory of the willing transformation of the rebellious self-righteous 1960s into the sullen acquisitive decades that followed.

Vineland's account of the past quarter century depends on the imaginative force of its historical myth, not on the analytic power of historical argument. Whether or not a reader believes the myth is probably irrelevant. What matters is whether or not the myth has sufficient resonance to make a reader willing to suspend disbelief for the duration of the novel. Pynchon's mythmaking succeeds, but only after the plot repeatedly brings it close to disaster.

Mythical history, as Pynchon practices it, is not a record of power and domination, it is a record of longings and fulfillments that occur on a vast archetypal scale. Figures like Frenesi Gates and Brock Vond can personify those longings, but they merely act out a struggle much larger than anything they can understand. In *Vineland,* the whole culture of the 1970s and 1980s is the fruit of desires felt in the 1960s for an eternity without change—for a permanent historical love-death like the endless union sought by Tristan and Isolde. Rebellious youth yearned for the conviction that they "were never going to die" (a ubiquitous refrain among the young in this book). Authoritarian age yearned for unchanging certainties that would calm their fears of death. To escape from time and change, the young cried for a parental discipline that would preserve them in eternal youth, and the old were grateful to oblige. The result, in Pynchon's myth, was a brief historical interregnum outside both the sufferings and satisfactions of human time. At the end of *Vineland* this era ends, not with an apocalyptic upheaval, which would mark the end of time, but in a refusal of apocalypse, when human time renews itself, and death and life regain their dominion.

Historical mythmaking is a risky enterprise for a novelist, especially when the myth refuses to point a reassuring and accusatory finger at political groups that the novelist's audience dislikes. Even more risky is the way Pynchon's overtly feminist novel covertly adopts mythical archetypes: the young rebels are portrayed as archetypally feminine, the authority that they yearn for as archetypally masculine. But the historical myth of *Vineland* is cautiously disguised by the tone of the book, a glowingly nostalgic tone that suggests that the spontaneities of the 1960s were unambiguously admirable. The disguise is so effective that the whole myth seems to have eluded many readers who would certainly have censured it if they had noticed it.

The contrast between the achingly nostalgic tone of the story and the harsh judgment of its content is *Vineland*'s most calculatedly unsettling quality. The effect is designed to educate the reader away from the nostalgia that the book itself evokes. *Vineland* adopts the nostalgic wish of its early chapters precisely in order to expose the delusion and fantasy of those wishes later. As Frenesi Gates's story gradually emerges, it becomes clear that *Vineland* is nostalgic only about the events and situations of the 1960s, and that it maintains its nostalgia only as long as it neglects to look at the personalities that figured in those events. The 1960s wedding of Zoyd Wheeler and Frenesi Gates, recalled through Zoyd's memories early in the book, is an image of the peaceable kingdom. Pynchon waits a few chapters before pointing out, almost parenthetically, that the bride married the groom mostly because he knew nothing about her and her past, that she was on the run from multiple acts of sexual and political betrayal and from her direct moral responsibility for the murder of one of her lovers.

Pynchon portrays Frenesi Gates with the same unsettling contrast of tone and substance that he applies to the 1960s ethos that she represents. Virtually everyone in the book spends most of his time passively adoring her or actively seeking her. Her ex-husband Zoyd Wheeler tries to visit her in his dreams. Her ex-lover Brock Vond leads a private army in search of her when her file disappears from a federal computer. Someone else wants to make her the center of a film about the whole adventure of the 1960s. A reader can scarcely avoid getting caught up in the universal mood of admiration, a mood that persists long after it becomes clear that Frenesi's only redeeming virtues are a pair of legs that look arresting in a miniskirt, her "notorious blue eyes," and her ability to affect "the wide invincible gaze practiced by many sixties children, meaning nearly anything at all, useful in a lot of situations, including ignorance." Summarized in a review, this contrast between tone and substance seems stark and obvious. In *Vineland* itself, the process of moral discovery that Pynchon generates from this contrast seems as subtle and nuanced as the patient moral revelations in the late novels of Henry James.

Unlike James, Pynchon brings his most nuanced moral arguments to bear at precisely the points where his narrative seems most garish and unsubtle. The more the melodramatic language of *Vineland* casts Brock Vond as a sadistic villain, the more the logic of the action casts him as a partner in a dance of mutual courtship. Some readers, taking the tone for the substance, have complained that Brock and the other Justice Department heavies in *Vineland* seem disappointingly tame when compared with the real heavies who occupied the department under Nixon and Reagan. But like all literature that tries to make a moral argument, *Vineland* sees little point in placing blame on those who are unlikely ever to read it. It tries to discomfort its readers, first by agreeing with their self-satisfied sense that their unhappiness is the result of others' actions, then by quietly demonstrating that the actions that most afflict them are their own. The 1960s radicals (and the peaceful apolitical potsmokers whom Pynchon treats with sentimental affection) do not even have the satisfaction of defeating Brock Vond, who is defeated by his own side. Ronald Reagan, like a half-conscious deus ex machina, wakes from a dream and, by cutting Vond's budget, interrupts him in mid-villainy.

Vineland's moral argument makes it a far more coherent book than the jumbled catalog of effects suggested by the reviews. But it is not nearly as coherent as Pynchon's earlier novels. One subplot reads as if it scarcely belongs to the rest of the book and probably dates back to a much earlier point of Pynchon's career. Shortly after *Gravity's Rainbow* appeared in 1973, reports circulated that Pynchon planned to complete two novels, referred to in his contract as *The Mason-Dixon Line* and *The Japanese Insurance Adjuster*. *Vineland* is neither of these books, but the Japanese insurance adjuster—his name is Takeshi Fumimota—strayed into it anyway. He seems a bit lost. Some of his episodes, notably one in which he investigates a Japanese electronics plant apparently leveled by the foot of a gigantic reptile, are written in a science-fiction style that resembles parts of *Gravity's Rainbow* and nothing else in *Vineland.* The episodes in which he appears are given over to technological fantasies of the kind that the rest of the book disdains, and are void of moral or emotional intelligence. I won't bother you with details of the Ninjette retreat in California where Takeshi Fumimota recovers from the Ninja Death Touch inflicted on him in a Tokyo brothel by his American partner, a female martial arts specialist named DL Chastain, when she mistakes him for Brock Vond. (pp. 41-2, 44)

Pynchon's vision is sacramental but not otherworldly. Instead of looking away from this world to one somewhere else, he looks for the hidden order and significance of the world he lives in. *Vineland*'s sacramental geography is a vision of a sacred place, the fictional Vineland County in northern California, the place that Zoyd Wheeler comes to recognize as a harbor of refuge, "Vineland the Good." This visionary Vineland occupies the real geography of the California coast from Crescent City to Eureka and the redwood forests nearby. But its name hints that it is an epiphany of that thousand-year-old alternate America founded by Norse sailors, who, unlike the sailors who founded the America we live in, never conquered the land or usurped its indigenous people. (p. 44)

Although *Vineland* satirizes television so obsessively that some reviewers concluded that Pynchon no longer notices anything deeper than "Gilligan's Island," in fact the dust of the library rests on this as on all his books. Often it is in so fine a form as to defy casual notice. Pynchon found the story of the man from Turip in A. L. Kroeber's massive collection *Yurok Myths* (1976), where it appears as a raw unpromising fragment told by an unskilled informant. *Vineland* transforms it partly into the story of Brock Vond's failed pursuit of Frenesi Gates, partly into his historical myth of an era when America sought to live "safe in some time-free zone," exempt from death and excluded from life. The song of triumph that sounds through the prose of the final chapters of the book celebrates the end of that era and prophesies a return to the pains and joys of human time.

Pynchon gives a local habitation to the "time-free zone" by creating a skittishly comic group of persons called Thanatoids, who exist in a state between life and death. They are not as embarrassing as their name makes them sound. Pynchon writes about them with a deadpan Gilbert-and-Sullivan logic that accepts the impossible premise of their existence and proceeds to draw the inevitable consequences. His Thanatoids are not ghosts or ghouls, but ordinary men and women who happen to encounter considerable trouble with banks and credit bureaus be-

cause their heirs have a legal claim on their property. A large population of them lives in a place called Shade Creek, where they watch television and eat fatty foods because they can't think of any reason not to. In the Yurok story, no one died for ten years. Near the end of *Vineland,* the Thanatoids hold their tenth annual reunion. (pp. 45-6)

In these final chapters all the book's generations of the living gather for another reunion, one that joins the families of Frenesi Gates's grandparents. The older members of these two families are Wobblies and Hollywood leftwingers, bearers of a heritage of an alternate and unofficial America. Pynchon treats this alternate tradition as a matriarchal one: the novel traces the ancestry of all its women characters while treating the men as if they sprang directly from the earth. Frenesi's hatred for her newborn daughter, and voluntary separation from her soon afterward, violates that matriarchal line, just as her murderous entanglement with Brock Vond is a sign of what the book's historical myth regards as the betrayal of the true alternate America by the 1960s left.

After so thorough a betrayal no return or recovery can ever be complete. Zoyd Wheeler at last meets Frenesi Gates again—she is remarried with a second child—but her reappearance is a deliberate anticlimax. The book has other futures to pursue than theirs. The final sentence, which focuses on their daughter Prairie, traces a comic variety of matriarchal lineage, this one extending from the grandmother of Prairie's dog down to the dog itself, who has abruptly returned to the scene after his flight from Brock Vond's minions. The sentence looks like a cloyingly sentimental celebration of continuity, home, and love, until you notice that one of its subordinate clauses makes clear that its vision of renewal includes sudden violent death. *Et in arcadia ego,* says the ancient tombstone—death also is in Arcadia. And death makes possible the renewal of life in arcadian Vineland. The fugal interweaving of life and death in these final pages approaches the richness of Shakespearean comedy.

All of Pynchon's books are permeated by one or two central ideas: entropy in *V.,* the manifestation of the sacred in *The Crying of Lot 49,* and the bureaucratization of charisma, as described by Max Weber, in *Gravity's Rainbow.* In *Vineland* the central idea is less abstract than in the earlier books. A fall into an era without life or death, followed by a return to human time, is less a concept than a parable of personal experience. It describes in visionary terms a phase that can occur in anyone's life when all significant relations and events seem bafflingly distant and inaccessible.

What makes this vision luminous (to use Pynchon's word of praise) in *Vineland* is not the tendentious historical myth that attaches to it, but its intensely personal quality. Zoyd Wheeler's years of separation from his wife are his years in a realm without time, when he dreams of an impossible return. But he comes to recognize those same years as the ones in which he learned to value his daughter and their shared harbor in Vineland. This part of the narrative, lightly sketched in the margins of the brightly colored central plot, reads like an allegory of a lived experience of loss and renewal.

For all its silliness and longueurs, *Vineland* is the most troubling and exuberant work of American fiction to appear in many years. It is also the most personal work of an author who relied in the past on an almost anonymous impersonality. Pynchon still refuses to make his personality into a commodity available for packaging and distribution by a publicity machine, and still prefers his readers to attend to his books rather than to himself. Yet *Vineland* says more about its author than anyone could hope to learn from the photograph that is omitted, with honorable reticence, from the dust jacket. (p. 46)

Edward Mendelson, "Levity's Rainbow," in The New Republic, *Vol. 203, Nos. 2 & 3, July 9 & 16, 1990, pp. 40-6.*

FURTHER READING

Black, Joel D. "Probing a Post-Romantic Paleontology: Thomas Pynchon's *Gravity's Rainbow*." *Boundary 2* VIII, No. 2 (Fall-Winter 1980): 229-54.
    Asserts that one narrative strand of *Gravity's Rainbow* "can be traced back to a dissenting scientific strain in Anglo-American and German Romanticism."

Clerc, Charles, ed. *Approaches to 'Gravity's Rainbow'*. Columbus: Ohio State University Press, 1983, 307 p.
    Contains eight essays on diverse aspects of Pynchon's acclaimed novel by such critics as Alan J. Friedman, Joseph W. Slade, and Roger B. Henkle. Clerc's Introduction is excerpted in *CLC*, Vol. 33.

Colvile, Georgiana M. M. *Beyond and Beneath the Mantle: On Thomas Pynchon's 'The Crying of Lot 49'*. Edited by C. C. Barfoot, Hans Bertens, and Theo D'haen. Amsterdam: Rodopi, 1988, 119 p.
    Examination of such topics as language, metaphor, and social and feminist issues in Pynchon's second novel. Includes a brief bibliography.

Cowart, David. *Thomas Pynchon: The Art of Allusion*. Carbondale, Ill.: Southern Illinois University Press, and London: Feffer & Simons, Inc., 1980, 154 p.
    Analyzes Pynchon's use of such forms of media communication as painting, film, music, and literature in his fiction.

Fowler, Douglas. "Story into Chapter: Thomas Pynchon's Transformation of 'Under the Rose'." *The Journal of Narrative Technique* 14, No. 1 (Winter 1984): 33-43.
    Compares Pynchon's original short story with its later revision as the third chapter of his first novel, *V*.

Graves, Lila V. "Love and the Western World of Pynchon's *V*." *South Atlantic Review* 47, No. 1 (January 1982): 62-73.
    Asserts that "the correlation which Pynchon establishes between sexual and cultural decadence owes a substantial debt to Denis De Rougemont's *Love in the Western World*, a work of psychological culture criticism."

Hans, James S. "*Gravity's Rainbow* and the Literature of Renewal." *Essays in Literature* 15, No. 2 (Fall 1988): 267-84.
    Refutes the popular critical notion that Pynchon's portrayal of modern existence as entropic places him in the tradition of the "literature of exhaustion" as practiced by John Barth and other postmodernist authors.

Hite, Molly. " 'Holy-Center-Approaching' in the Novels of Thomas Pynchon." *The Journal of Narrative Technique* 12, No. 2 (Spring 1982): 121-29.
    Examines Pynchon's fiction in accordance with its theme of "holy-center-approaching," which Hite defines as "the epiphanic point in both time and space where the questing hero realizes the full meaning of his life, his search, and his world."

———. *Ideas of Order in the Novels of Thomas Pynchon*. Columbus: Ohio State University Press, 1983, 183 p.
    Study of such elements of order in Pynchon's novels as form, structure, and plot.

Hume, Kathryn. *Pynchon's Mythography: An Approach to 'Gravity's Rainbow'*. Carbondale, Ill.: Southern Illinois University Press, 1987, 262 p.
    In opposition to the popular critical notion that to seek meaning in Pynchon's deconstructive novel is to risk forcing inappropriate assumptions on "an almost unknowable text," Hume suggests that Pynchon has consistently employed a mythology "that conveys, supports, and challenges our cultural values."

Hume, Kathryn, and Knight, Thomas J. "Orpheus and the Orphic Voice in *Gravity's Rainbow*." *Philological Quarterly* 64, No. 3 (Summer 1985): 299-315.
    Asserts that despite the essential ambiguity of Pynchon's novel, several patterns exist, including one that parallels the myth of Orpheus.

Kermode, Frank. "There was another planet." *London Review of Books* 12, No. 3 (February 1990): 3-4.
    A review of *Vineland* and discussion of Pynchon's thematic examination of paranoia, which recurs throughout his work.

Moore, Thomas. *The Style of Connectedness: 'Gravity's Rainbow' and Thomas Pynchon*. Columbia, Mo.: University of Missouri Press, 1987, 311 p.
    In response to the prevailing critical view of Pynchon's novel as a work of nihilism, Moore asserts that "Pynchon's work is more psychologically valid, more culturally responsible, and more compassionate than that of the writers of the Absurd tradition with whom he is often confused."

O'Donnell, Patrick. " 'A Book of Traces': *Gravity's Rainbow*." In his *Passionate Doubts: Designs of Interpretation in Contemporary American Fiction*, pp. 73-94. Iowa City: University of Iowa Press, 1986.
    Examines Pynchon's presentation of what he himself terms "conditions of meaning" and his playful questioning of those assumptions through self-reflexive inquiry.

Olsen, Lance. "Pynchon's New Nature: Indeterminacy and *The Crying of Lot 49*." In his *Ellipse of Uncertainty: An Introduction to Postmodern Fantasy*, pp. 69-83. New York: Greenwood Press, 1987.
    Previously published essay intended as a guide to interpreting Pynchon's novel as a work of postmodern fantasy.

Pyuen, Carolyn S. "The Transmarginal Leap: Meaning and Process in *Gravity's Rainbow*." *Mosaic* XV, No. 2 (June 1982): 33-46.

Asserts that the critical tendency to analyze Pynchon's novel in terms of the standard relationship between reader and text results in an inability to experience direct, personal connections between reader and text.

Redfield, Marc W. "Pynchon's Postmodern Sublime." *PMLA* 104, No. 2 (March 1989): 152-62.
Scholarly essay stressing parallels between Pynchon's postmodern philosophy and the aesthetic category of the sublime, a prevalent vehicle of cultural critique during the eighteenth century.

Schachterle, Lance. "Bandwidth as Metaphor for Consciousness in Pynchon's *Gravity's Rainbow*." *Studies in the Literary Imagination* XXII, No. 1 (Spring 1989): 101-17.
Explores Pynchon's use of bandwidth, a term that refers to the range of electromagnetic frequencies in electronic communications systems such as radios and televisions, as an image of consciousness.

Schaub, Thomas H. *Pynchon: The Voice of Ambiguity.* Urbana, Ill.: University of Illinois Press, 1981, 165 p.
Explores indefinite aspects of Pynchon's fiction.

Seed, David. "Fantasy and Dream in Thomas Pynchon's 'Low-lands.' " *Rocky Mountain Review* 37, Nos. 1-2 (1983): 54-68.
Examination of "gestures of disengagement or subversion" in Pynchon's early short story.

Stark, John O. *Pynchon's Fictions: Thomas Pynchon and the Literature of Information.* Athens, Ohio: Ohio University Press, 1980, 183 p.
Analyzes Pynchon's unusual method of attaining coherency through the use of scientific information and theories in his works.

Swartzlander, Susan. "The Tests of Reality: The Use of History in *Ulysses* and *Gravity's Rainbow*." *Critique* XXIX, No. 2 (Winter 1988): 133-43.
Compares Pynchon's humanism and distrust of history to that of James Joyce.

Tanner, Tony. *Thomas Pynchon.* London: Methuen, 95 p.
Concise biographical and critical analysis. See excerpt in *CLC*, Vol. 33.

Tatham, Campbell. "Tarot and *Gravity's Rainbow*." *Modern Fiction Studies* 32, No. 4 (Winter 1986): 581-90.
Examines Pynchon's use of the tarot as an organizing principle, which Tatham defines as "a *text* whose structure is indeterminate and whose pages (the individual cards) lend themselves to endless rearranging."

Watson, Robert N. "Who Bids for Tristero? The Conversion of Pynchon's Oedipa Maas." *Southern Humanities Review* XVII, No. 1 (Winter 1983): 59-75.
In response to critics who fault Pynchon for ending his novel *The Crying of Lot 49* without identifying the person who claims lot 49 for Tristero, Watson proposes that the book's narrator, Oedipa Maas, may have offered the bid.

Weisenburger, Steven. *A 'Gravity's Rainbow' Companion: Sources and Contexts for Pynchon's Novel.* Athens: The University of Georgia Press, 1988, 345 p.
Detailed guide offering solutions to basic textual and critical questions surrounding Pynchon's controversial novel.

Stephanie Vaughn

19??-

American short story writer.

Vaughn's first short fiction collection, *Sweet Talk* (published in Great Britain as *Able, Baker, Charlie, Dog*), has garnered praise for its evocative mixture of humor and pathos and its insightful portrayal of familial relationships. Most of these stories focus on Gemma, a young woman whose life has been greatly affected by her alcoholic father, a reticent career army officer tormented by his failure to advance in the service. Several pieces are set on a military base near Niagara Falls, one of several posts where the father and his family are stationed. Rapidly shifting the narrative between events in the present and the future to underscore their connection, Vaughn imbues small details of family life with resonance and significance. For example, in "My Mother Breathing Light," Vaughn depicts Gemma's volatile mother's disappointment at her husband's refusal to allow her to sell perfume, then moves the story into the future, where this incident is seen as a lost opportunity to earn money for her expensive cancer treatment.

The stories that concern Gemma's adult life further delineate her peripatetic existence while revealing more legacies from her childhood. Critics commended Vaughn's ability to juxtapose pathetic situations and pithy, humorous observations. In "We're on T.V. in the Universe," for instance, Vaughn describes a car involved in a potentially fatal accident as "throwing its hips" back and forth in a kind of dance. Although some critics noted that the stories without Gemma were less focused and interesting, most found *Sweet Talk* to be an auspicious debut. Michiko Kakutani commented: "Ms. Vaughn emerges as a thoroughly original writer, blessed with a distinctive voice, by turns witty and lyrical, wisecracking and nostalgic."

tinctive childhood are delivered in graceful, honest prose. (pp. 40-1)

A review of "Sweet Talk," in Publishers Weekly, *Vol. 236, No. 23, December 8, 1989, pp. 40-1.*

Publishers Weekly

"Every so often that dead dog dreams me up again." This arresting image opens **"Dog Heaven,"** the final story in [*Sweet Talk*], an accomplished first collection by a young writer whose work has appeared in the *New Yorker*. Vaughn writes mainly in a wry, undistanced first-person voice, creating imaginative language for recognizable young women in varying circumstances and careers. The narrator of **"We're on TV in the Universe"** crashes into a patrol car in winter, looks up at the arriving policeman and sees "the crazed lights on the top of his car slinging snowfish around his head." . . . **"Snow Angel"** tells of a young mother, trapped in the house with her two children during a three-day snowstorm, who manages—just—to keep her sanity and faith with her kids. Most powerful are the stories about Gemma, including **"Kid MacArthur"** and **"Able, Baker, Charlie, Dog"** in which Vaughn's clear-eyed, scalpel-sharp and affectionate observations of a dis-

Michiko Kakutani

When writers talk about having an ear for dialogue, they usually mean a gift for capturing the rhythms of conversation, a gift for hearing how people talk, how they connect or don't connect. As [*Sweet Talk,* an] impressive first collection of stories demonstrates, Stephanie Vaughn clearly possesses such an ear. More than that, she's able to use this gift to map entire lives, to read in her people's pronouncements, circumlocutions and non sequiturs, the secrets of character and personality.

The father in these interconnected stories—most of which chronicle the childhood, youth and adulthood of a woman named Gemma—is an Army officer who tells his children to speak in complete sentences. "Learn to come to a full stop when you complete an idea," he advises. "Use semicolons and periods in your speech." . . .

"He never said, 'You know,'" Gemma recalls,

> never spoke in fragments, never slurred his speech, even years later when he had just put away a fifth of Scotch and was trying to describe the Eskimo custom of chewing up the meat before it was given to the elders, who had no teeth. He spoke with such calculation and precision that his sentences hung over us like high vaulted ceilings, or rolled across the table like ornaments sculptured from stone. It was a huge cathedral of a voice, full of volume and complexity.

On the night he learns that he has been passed over for promotion, he stands with his daughter on a riverbank overlooking the Canadian border—they are living at a missile base near Niagara Falls—and stares at the moonlit ice. "I am looking at that thin beautiful line of Canada," he says. "I think I will go for a walk." As Gemma watches him test the ice, then cross from one ice floe to another, she wonders whether he will slip and fall—it is an image she will remember years later, when she visits a cemetery and looks at the red, white and blue carnations decorating his grave.

Through such scenes, through a combination of lyrical and incongruous details, through the shrewd juxtaposition of time present and time past, Ms. Vaughn admits the reader into one family's private world, revealing the secrets they hide and share with one another, the fictions they invent to glue their lives together. . . .

This sense of now and then, after and before, informs all the best stories in *Sweet Talk,* measuring the dissolution of Gemma's family and her own immersion in the frustrations of adult life. In the space of just five years, she recalls, "my father, always a weekend drinker, began to drink during the week. My grandmother broke her hip in a fall. My mother, a quiet woman, was not helped through her quiet by Valium." Gemma's brother, MacArthur, has gone off to Vietnam and returned, a detached, solitary man, uninterested in finding a job or making any plans; and Gemma, herself, has moved to California, where she leads a vague, aimless existence with a vague, aimless boyfriend. We had "six university degrees between us and no employment," she observes. "We lived on food stamps, job interviews and games."

In its evocative descriptions of small-town life, and its familial configurations (increasingly estranged parents, a son who goes to Vietnam and a daughter who flees to the western edge of the continent), *Sweet Talk* may well remind the reader of Jayne Anne Phillips's *Machine Dreams.* Though not nearly as ambitious as that novel, this volume demonstrates a similar ability to delineate a vanished past, and to make ordinary, unfulfilled lives yield resonance and meaning. At the same time, Ms. Vaughn emerges as a thoroughly original writer, blessed with a distinctive voice, by turns witty and lyrical, wisecracking and nostalgic. She's someone who can conjure up the sadness of "a green, antique island" one moment, the absurd plight of catching lice from a lover, the next.

Actually, Ms. Vaughn's strength as a writer emerges most clearly in the more elegiac, first-person stories devoted to Gemma's childhood and youth. The later tales—some of which abandon Gemma to focus on less clearly defined heroines—tend to veer into self-conscious flippancy. The sense of place, so sure in the Gemma stories, dissolves in the California tales into familiar descriptions of highways and fast-food restaurants; and the prose can turn oddly grandiloquent. For instance: "Tonight for supper they had fish sticks, which had been out of the ocean too long and tasted like small punishments."

Such lapses, however, should not discourage the reader from reading *Sweet Talk.* The Gemma stories are each beautifully observed, emotionally vivid pieces of writing, and together they mark the debut of a wonderful new writer.

> *Michiko Kakutani, "Evoking the Vanquished Past of a Family in Dissolution," in* The New York Times, *January 23, 1990, p. C18.*

Joseph Olshan

This powerful first collection of short stories takes place primarily on highly efficient Army bases and in stucco apartment buildings with phony architectural details. The hard-edged world of *Sweet Talk* is filtered through the gentle lens of Stephanie Vaughn, a gifted writer whose work has previously appeared in *The New Yorker* and *Antaeus* magazines.

Ms. Vaughn's strong suit is an ability to make harrowing situations alternately funny and sad. In **"We're on TV in the Universe,"** a woman is driving, with a caged chicken in the front seat, through a blizzard en route to a birthday party. Suddenly the car hits black ice. "My car did a kind of simple dance step. . . . It threw its hips to the left, it threw its hips to the right, left, right, left, right, then turned and slid, as if it were making a rock-and-roll move toward the arms of a partner."

The image of black ice—a condition that can form suddenly in cold weather, leaving cars without traction—is used more than once as metaphor by Ms. Vaughn, who views relationships as fragile states of motion that can on a whim become derailed. And yet her characters distinguish themselves by having a sense of humor about their own failures.

In **"The Architecture of California,"** Megan realizes that her husband is responsible for her best friend Vera's latest pregnancy. The revelation bubbles up one night when the three are cooking dinner, the author skillfully twining Megan's realization around a debacle of ruined pasta. "You gave me self-rising flour, you didn't give me regular," Vera says to Megan, bursting into tears. "Think of it as an accident," Megan replies. "I couldn't help myself."

We may spend years trying to find friends and lovers who embody the impossible standards set by our parents, Ms. Vaughn suggests. But the disappointment of the adult women in these stories becomes all the more poignant when we compare it to the childhood of Gemma, the narrator of several deeply felt interconnected tales that feature her brother, her mother and her father, Zachary, an Army man.

"Keep your voice low and you can win any point," Zachary advises in **"Able, Baker, Charlie, Dog."** He upholds the power of rhetoric and ethical conduct while torturing the family with emotional distance. Unfortunately, Zachary betrays his own principles by insulting a general. Realizing her father may have sabotaged his career, Gemma watches him flirt with danger by trying to walk across the frozen Niagara River. "The last thing I heard, long after I had lost sight of him far out on the river, was the sound of his laugh splitting the cold air." . . .

In her pithy descriptions, Ms. Vaughn not only brings her characters to life; she invests them with a raison d'être, compelling us to love them. In **"My Mother Breathing Light,"** Gemma's mother goes "up the stairs with a fierce, eager step, the hem of her white robe rippling behind in a satin fury, like water swooshing uphill," a description that evokes the vicissitudes of a woman determined to gloss over the fact that she has terminal cancer.

Ms. Vaughn does not always construct her stories as smoothly as she might, and in a few places she underestimates her emotional building power. In **"Dog Heaven,"** for example, she goes on several paragraphs too long and diminishes the impact. Yet if she occasionally sacrifices form to content, the choice is well worth it; the writing in *Sweet Talk* is pure and elegiac, as though it were piped in directly from the soul.

Joseph Olshan, "Laughter on Thin Ice," in The New York Times Book Review, *February 4, 1990, p. 27.*

Rhoda Koenig

Restless and searching, the women in Stephanie Vaughn's short stories [collected in *Sweet Talk*] are always on the lookout for another man, a new job, a better place to be, and are not about to be held back by any encumbrances. [In **"The Architecture of California"**], Vera, who has slept with six men in six weeks, considers not having another abortion but regards the baby much as one might a dog one receives for Christmas: "I was thinking that maybe I should give it to someone who would like it."

In Gemma's case, the mobility started early. The narrator of most of these stories, she is an Army brat, the daughter of a fact-hound who enjoys tormenting the family with such frustrating exercises as an unwinnable game of twenty questions. "My father revealed the thing he had been thinking of. The thing was 'the rocket's red glare'—the light from exploded gunpowder. Gunpowder, if you analyzed its ingredients, was actually animal, vegetable, *and* mineral—providing you agreed that the carbon component could be derived from animal sources." It is no wonder that such a man drives himself to drink, or that his son, MacArthur, who resents being named after a general who let his men starve in Bataan, stops eating meat. (pp. 61-2)

Gemma's mother is terminally foolish but a comfort in areas that to her logical father are uncharted territory, singing a little made-up song to Gemma on the child's way to the hospital. "I could see her breath misting white in the darkness and it seemed to me she was exhaling light."

Grandma, who completes the brigade, at first seems as tartly stern as her daughter is silly, but it turns out that she has a deep vein of nonsense as well, at least in hindsight. "In the 1950s, she had been a member of something called the Ground Observer Corps. Members of the Corps scanned the skies with binoculars, looking for Russian aircraft." . . .

Vaughn lets herself go a bit more with **"Other Women,"** a story in which Angelina's boyfriend, Harvey, lets his ex-wife sleep on his sofa while she looks for a job, or at least that's his story. A friendly dinner starts going wrong when the ex-wife makes packaged spaghetti accompanied with cottage cheese and canned pineapple and excuses herself with " 'Susu was always a rotten cook, wasn't I, sweetie?' " Susu, Angelina thinks, talks about herself in the third person "as if she's a character even in her own life." Angelina goes on to express her next thought out loud.

Sweet Talk is beguiling all right, though never coy; it's the debut of a writer with a style as engaging as her characters, weighed down in their travels by so much unexpected baggage from the past. (p. 62)

Rhoda Koenig, "Still Magnolias," in New York *Magazine, Vol. 23, No. 6, February 12, 1990, pp. 61-2.*

Lee Lescage

Stephanie Vaughn is a more typical storyteller of these times [than is John L'Heureux]. In *Sweet Talk,* her stories divide into two groups. A seemingly autobiographical series about the life of an Army brat who watches helplessly as her beloved father's career sours early, and a batch of unrelated stories about pathetic women victimized by unattractive men.

The first are familiar, but moderately interesting. The second are familiar and clumsy. Mysteries here get as complex as: "I wonder who my man was sleeping with when he got crabs?" Usually, the answer is, "My best friend."

Ms. Vaughn can write a well-turned sentence: "Aunt Ruda is overweight, fat with the stories of other people's grief." She also can write sentences that chloroform the mind: "Here is the world so green you could taste that greenness on your tongue even from an altitude of ten thousand feet in a jet bomber."

Reading Ms. Vaughn it is easy to find oneself wishing that a bit of Mr. L'Heureux's style or wit would show up. Instead, one gets only a literary wink.

Mr. L'Heureux is a professor at Stanford University. Ms. Vaughn studied at Stanford. One of her female characters needs to consult a doctor on a sensitive matter. "Be sure and ask for Dr. L'Heureux," a friend advises. "Dr. L'Heureux is the one who will be lighthearted and make you feel that the situation is very funny." The introduction of a gynecologist named L'Heureux might pep up Ms. Vaughn's stories, but as elsewhere, she shies away from developing what might have been an interesting moment. Her Dr. L'Heureux is reported on vacation in Hawaii.

Lee Lescage, "God the Meddler," in The Wall Street Journal, *February 13, 1990, p. A18.*

Joshua Henkin

When I was twelve years old, my father was tall and awesome." So says Gemma Jackson in the first sentence of *Sweet Talk,* and from that moment on we are riveted. Insightful, sensitive, at times hilarious, Gemma is the cement that glues together this dazzling first collection of short stories.

Gemma is an army child, and we watch her cope with the vagaries of life on the go. Oklahoma, New York, the Philippines, Italy, Ohio. Mobility, adjustment. Throughout it all, her father, tough but loving, plays teacher. "You have developed a junior-high habit of speaking in fragments," he tells twelve-year-old Gemma at dinner. "Use semicolons and periods in your speech." . . .

Even as a youth, Vaughn's heroine recognizes the misfortune of others. "The newspaper carried stories about people who jumped over the Falls, fourteen miles upriver from our house," she muses. "I thought of their bodies . . . tumbling silently, huddled in upon themselves like fetuses—jilted brides, unemployed factory workers, old people who did not want to go to rest homes, teenagers who got bad grades, young women who fell in love with married men."

In ["Sweet Talk"], an older Gemma asks her adulterous husband for a divorce, as the two of them, "six university degrees between [them] and no employment," travel cross-country in search of a better life. Here, too, Vaughn imbues Gemma with empathy: "It was a shock—feeling the tremble of his flesh, the vulnerability of it, and for the first time since California I tried to imagine what it was like driving with a woman who said she didn't want him, in a van he didn't like but had to buy in order to travel to a possible job on the other side of the continent, which might not be worth reaching." Neither self-absorbed nor self-immolating, Gemma is hurt but remains whole. . . .

Throughout, Vaughn's characters maintain a sense of humor. In **"Other Women,"** one of the few stories not about Gemma, a woman named Angelina finds herself living with her lover Harvey and his siliconized ex-wife Susu, who, it seems, has given them both a case of the crabs. "Every morning for two weeks," Angelina tells us, "Susu has been going into the bathroom with ordinary sleep-flattened hair and emerging an hour later with a rococo tangle of back-combed frizzes and knotted tendrils." "Her hair looks like a place where small animals go to browse in the night," she tells Harvey. "But what am I saying? Her hair *is* a place where small animals go to browse in the night."

There is not a weak story in *Sweet Talk,* and few are less than spectacular. Vaughn's work has already been anthologized in the *O. Henry Prize* and *Pushcart* collections, and more accolades are sure to come. Hers is a wise, touching, extraordinary voice—the sort rarely achieved at the end of a gifted career, let alone at the beginning.

Joshua Henkin, in a review of "The Facets of Gemma," in Mother Jones, *Vol. XV, No. II, February-March, 1990, p. 42.*

Tom Shone

On a scale of literary techniques and their relative difficulty—ranging, say, from pathos to poignancy to parataxis—you might think pointlessness one of the easier effects to achieve. But it can be quite difficult sometimes to halt the clod-hopping intrusion of a Moral, the steady drip-feed of a Big Theme. Stephanie Vaughn's first collection of stories, **Able, Baker, Charlie, Dog,** resists such narrative placebos.

The stories are defiantly slight, depicting a handful of scenes, in no particular order, from the life of our narrator, Gemma: from adolescence in the military bases where her father is stationed, to his alcohol-drenched demise. We see the young Gemma sharing the secret of her mother's cancer, the adult Gemma sharing the misery of crabs with her lover. Admittedly, such subjects sound portentous, but just when you are resigning yourself to sinking beneath some moral lesson, Vaughn sidesteps to tease you with a quirky detail.

Take the ear that crops up in the story **"Kid MacArthur"**. Gemma's little brother, goaded by their father's background, goes to Vietnam and comes back in classic fashion: an emotional zombie. His only attempt at communication is to give Gemma the ear of one of his wounded buddies, which she stows in a brown envelope under the seat of her car. And then just when you thought you were in for another lecture on Vietnam, that ear crops up again. Gemma is trying to sell her car; the sale complete, she walks away, then turns around to warn the new owner of his additional purchase but, in the end, cannot bring herself to do it. The story's point about the barbarism of war is thrown away in favour of the much subtler suggestion of the inscrutability of individual experience. It is not just the Vietnam vet who is unable to express himself. . . .

Vaughn delights in the sort of incongruities that slip through the net of those looking for a 'story', a point. Where we seek profundity, scale, we get absurdity, minutiae, for 'whole worlds will be revealed if the eye looks closely enough at what's under the bark'.

Crabs, lice, cancer, all make their invisible presence felt. Gemma's mother calls the spot on her X-ray a 'development', as if it were something promising, like a housing project'. The metaphor is taken from Gemma's job, building scale architectural models of such projects. Cancer is made into a joke, the big is made small. The crabs from which Gemma and her lover are suffering were given to them by his ex-wife. Recalling their inauspicious meeting, Gemma reflects,

> This the very place where Harvey and I met just nine months ago only months after I hit his parked car, and now here we are raising a family of tiny creatures.

An earth tremor shakes California but manifests itself only in the rattling of Gemma's coffee cup. It provides an apt conjugation of the great and the small which characterises these stories. Of course such a defence of the small things in life, particularly the small things in Californian life, risks straying into *thirtysomething* insignificance, but what saves it is Vaughn's lucid style and, above all, her humour, her willingness to offset worries with wisecracks and world-weariness with whimsy.

Tom Shone, "Consider the Crabs," in The Listener, *Vol. 123, No. 3165, May 17, 1990, p. 22.*

Pamela Zoline

1941-

American short story writer and author of children's books.

Zoline has garnered critical acclaim for her first short fiction collection, which was originally published in Great Britain as *Busy about the Tree of Life* and later in the United States as *The Heat Death of the Universe, and Other Stories*. Although originally printed in science fiction journals and anthologies, the five pieces in this book transcend generic categorization. Structurally unconventional, Zoline's fiction achieves a collage-like effect through such elements as puzzles, lists, excerpts from other texts, and fragmented narration. Compared to Angela Carter for her unrestrained imagination, painterly imagery, and oblique humor, Zoline combines fantasy and realism to explore the psychic trauma experienced by individuals who live under perpetual threat of mass extinction. For example, the frequently anthologized story "The Heat Death of the Universe" focuses on a housewife's attempt to maintain sanity amid her growing obsession with the concepts of time, entropy, chaos, and death. Written in fifty-four numbered paragraphs, this story exhibits the protagonist's, and by extension Zoline's, desire to impose order on a disordered world. Lance Olsen observed: "Zoline's is a jolting new land in the geography of postmodern fiction, where incoherent shards of our culture become momentarily exceptional, where hierarchies are toppled and fantasy becomes fact and every voice becomes a dodecaphonic symphony."

Mark Rose

Pamela Zoline's **"The Heat Death of the Universe"** may represent a borderline case of science fiction in some respects; nevertheless, it adheres closely to the genre's central region of concern. As in [H. G. Wells's] "The Star," the antagonist is nature, the entropic will to chaos that is invading Sarah Boyle's life. The protagonist is the human will to order that Boyle herself embodies. In "The Star" no resolution of the struggle is possible. Here, however, the contention is between directly opposed terms—order and disorder—and in the end the inhuman triumphs over the human, the physical over the spiritual, as Sarah Boyle breaks down in exhaustion and begins hurling glasses, dishes, and eggs about her kitchen. **"The Heat Death of the Universe"** may be regarded as a metaphorical version of the alien-invasion tale. Like someone "taken over" by an inhuman invader—as in *The Invasion of the Body Snatchers*—Sarah Boyle has become the alien, the agent of entropy's spread. The triumph of entropy is not, however, so complete as the narrative alone suggests. Some measure of irresolution, analogous to the irresolution of "The Star," is created by Zoline's formal device of presenting her text in fifty-four conspicuously numbered paragraphs,

many bearing titles such as "Cleaning Up the House" or "Time Pieces and Other Measuring Devices." In this way the text draws attention to itself as an ordering system in which entropy, the story's subject, is contained. Wells's mathematician is able to encompass the destructive forces of nature in his brain; Sarah Boyle is unable to resist entropy, but the text itself implicitly asserts the manner in which nature can be defeated.

Both "The Star" and **"The Heat Death of the Universe"** are concerned with confrontations between the human—represented by science in Wells and by art or the will to order in Zoline—and the nonhuman. (pp. 30-1)

> *Mark Rose, "Paradigm," in his* Alien Encounters: Anatomy of Science Fiction, *Cambridge, Mass.: Harvard University Press, 1981, pp. 24-49.*

Thomas M. Disch

1. The first painting of Pamela's that I saw was of an angel with the most amazing wings. Gorgeous slapdash wings with a fauvist palette and (if memory serves) lots of gold-leaf. That would have been the fall of 1962, the year Pame-

la was at Barnard. To be painting like that already at age 21! It didn't occur to me then how utterly unfashionable her painting was. 1962 must have been the nadir for figurative painting in New York. And *angels?* But a successful angel in its nature transcends fashion. Ask Rilke.

2. The first story of Pamela's that I read was **"The Heat Death of the Universe."** That was in London in spring of '67. It had the same basic out-knocking effect as the angel painting, and then some. At this point Pamela, who had been studying at the Slade School, had produced a small warehouse-full of paintings that confirmed the augery of those gold-leaf wings, paintings at once cerebral and sensuous, quirky and full of the Zeitgeist. And now, here she was, with no visible apprenticeship, producing a short story that out-New-Waved the lot of us, that was the prose equivalent to the wings of that angel.

3. The New Wave. I generally maintain that there never was such a thing. There was a magazine, *New Worlds,* whose editor Mike Moorcock had assembled a small core of SF writers living in and around London, but aside from our propinquity and a general ambition to write science fiction suitable for grown-ups, the nearest thing to a common esthetic would have been Ballard's "mini-novels." These narrative mosaics deliberately fractured the sense of a continuous dramatic scene or even a sustained tone of voice, presenting instead a series of vivid *tableaux vivants* and quick bright bursts of Idea in a raw and indefensible state. These bright ideas characteristically were erotic interpretations of the semes of modern life, i.e., the Consumer Society. Which for Ballard had meant mainly cars, high-rises, and medical technology. (pp. 7-8)

4. The problem with appointing Ballard standard-bearer of the New Wave was that, while his images were trendy and easily (and much) borrowed, his *modus operandi* was inimitable. Except by Pamela, who created, in **"The Heat Death of the Universe,"** the most technically accomplished and humane mosaic fiction produced by the New Wave. A Ballard story for human beings. (p. 8)

6. What I didn't understand about that story, or the others that were to follow, each one so different, each so anomalous in its intention and inspiration, each so neatly balanced between the most rarefied artistry and the most sensational emotional assault-and-battery, what I don't understand is this: What makes Pamela write? That's not quite true. I understand it but was disinclined to believe it: everything Pamela writes has been an act of friendship, the written portion of a much larger dialogue she is carrying on with a particular denizen of the world. Other writers may be motivated by the carrot of a lucrative sale or the *reclam* of appearing in an Important magazine. A few may be genuinely obsessive about their writing and would write if theirs were the only eyes in the world. But Pamela writes for an Other.

7. Pamela lived on Camden High Street when she wrote **"The Heat Death,"** in a duplex flat that was already at that time filled to the rafters with a generous sampling of Everything. Pamela may be particular in her aim as to her audience, but when it comes to her material she is a true Earth Mother. She wants it all, and she wants to *put* it all in her flat, and into her paintings and stories. (Just consider the chutzpah implicit in the title of that first story.) (pp. 8-9)

8. It also seems relevant that Pamela is by nature one of the happiest people in existence. It is a fate ordained by biochemistry: she has abnormally high endorphin levels. This doesn't mean that her fictions or paintings are lacking in tenebrous expanses. Indeed, her encyclopedist tendencies would militate against an all-bright emotional spectrum. She celebrates all gamuts she is party to. But when she is dark, she is hugely and energetically dark. Tragedy might interest her, but she's never been one to kvetch about boredom. That's why, whatever may be going on—a crisis or a moonrise—Pamela is fun to be with and to read.

9. One of Pamela's recurrent "themes"—and something we manage to argue about every time we get together—is the realm of the spiritual/supernatural. She believes in it in a way that I don't, but I'm always happy to *visit* it in her company. She is an excellent guide to the realms of the unseen, the supposed, the otherwise apprehended. (p. 9)

> *Thomas M. Disch, in an introduction to* The Heat Death of the Universe and Other Stories *by Pamela Zoline, McPherson & Company, 1988, pp. 7-9.*

Roz Kaveney

There is little in the work of Pamela Zoline to tie it with links of blood to sf. It is nonetheless historically the case that the greater part of [***Busy about the Tree of Life***] itself the greater part of her output, has been published in sf magazines and anthologies, and that one of her stories, **"The Heat Death of the Universe"**, is, in retrospect at least, one of those moments when shifts in the general direction of the sf genre can be defined.

Zoline is a fabulist whose narrative strategies include the satirical exaggeration of current trends and the suggestion of new ways of looking at how things *are:* ways that involve the ordering both of emotions and scientific principles, but the former as often as not with a refusal of verisimilitude and the latter as a strategy parallelled not by the use of further scientific texts, but the use of tourist guides and cook books. When Zoline outlines the ways in which children might be kidnapped and rehomed as a strategy for deterring nuclear conflict, she does so as a piece of rhetoric, a way of showing the monstrousness of nuclear deterrence, rather than as an adventure story or as a political programme. (p. 26)

"The Heat Death" is a text with many meanings, one of which is an examination of the way in which the scientific concept of entropy might illuminate the expectations which patriarchal society, in its early 1960s incarnation, might hold of an intelligent middle-class woman; another of which is a certain joy in the decision to allow chaos its way.

Zoline is decidedly more radical in her use of technical devices, without being obsessive, than the main body of sf writers. The device which characterises ***Busy about the Tree of Life*** most especially is the use of kaleidoscopic shifts of perspective, both between narrative strands and between narrative, expository, parodic and confessional modes. In "Sheep" we see a variety of wounded pastorals, all of them part dream, part the stories which an implied author tells in her head in a doomed attempt to sleep: stories which involve in Western and spy thriller and confused half-dozing surrealism those sheep which it is traditional to try to count (and cook). And the cooking of those sheep, the elaboration of recipes, is itself a pregnant metaphor: we will all bake together when we bake.

The three more recent stories in this volume are all in large measure meditations on and protests against the possibility of mass nuclear extinction—a threat which has rekindled Zoline as a writer after her early and powerful protest against the tyranny of the mundane.

The protest story, like the utopian story, is an important part of the way in which science fiction adds spice to the fictional mainstream—and learns from that mainstream lessons that it might not glean from its usual contemplation of itself. The stories of Zoline are important to the development of sf without necessarily being more than marginally sf themselves. (pp. 26-7)

Roz Kaveney, "Out of Anger: Feminist SF," in New Statesman, *Vol. 115, No. 2976, April 8, 1988, pp. 26-7.*

Colin Greenland

Pamela Zoline's three themes in the short stories collected [in *Busy about the Tree of Life*] are catastrophe, external and internal; textuality and the need for attentive parsing; and love, which may summon up unexpected strengths and strategies. . . .

["Busy about the Tree of Life"] contemplates a prospect of Armageddon "without a myth sufficiently pluralistic to save us; all the bodies emptied of their urgent contents, the cities deconstructed into dust"; but it does so from the foot of baby Gabriel's family tree, whose branches have all terminated in spectacular disasters, earthquakes and eruptions, the Crystal Palace and the R101. Zoline numbers Gabriel's ancestors and records each conception and extinction with antique pathos or bravura. The implicated ironies of her title are thus comprehensively, if not exhaustively, embodied in the very structure of the piece, every section of which accomplishes its own picturesque destruction.

Thoroughly postmodern, Zoline reticulates her prose with puzzles, lists and ellipses, the obtrusive discourse-shifts of a Robbe-Grillet, the language-knots of a Nabokov. Excerpts from other texts, phrasebooks and dictionaries of dreams have been cut out and pasted in.

All Zoline's stories arise out of compassion for a state or phase of mental exile: the isolation of the infant, the housewife or the insomniac; the estrangement of people beginning to lose their grip. Each is evoked and carefully illuminated. Since travel is one of Zoline's key devices for pluralism, the exile can be geographical too. "The Holland of the Mind" traces the progress of an American couple coming apart in Amsterdam, engaging the metaphor of a precariously reclaimed landscape. . . .

[Because Zoline] is a painter as well as a writer, she is concerned as much with the imagistic values of fiction as with the verbal vagaries of the self-conscious text. "The bald moon casts the sheep and her fellows in stone and soap"; the fluorescent light of a supermarket is "mixed blue and pink and brighter, colder, and cheaper than daylight."

The sense of space and light in these pieces gives a pictorial view, removed but never detached. Perhaps one of her characters interprets it best when she suggests: "Light in some paintings is the equivalent, at least the analogue, of love. God's gaze on the world."

Colin Greenland, "All Kinds of Catastrophe," in The Times Literary Supplement, *No. 4441, May 13-19, 1988, p. 534.*

Gregory Feeley

First published in 1967, "The Heat Death of the Universe" was Zoline's first story, a work that followed the zeitgeist in disdaining narrative conventions but lived to tell the tale. Using the Second Law of Thermodynamics as metaphor for the mortality of a simple individual—its obvious but only similarity to that other things-fall-apart story of the '60s, Thomas Pynchon's "Entropy"—"Heat Death" is a work of conscious but successful virtuosity, bodying forth in its numbered paragraphs a vision of a mechanistic universe ticking toward a dissolution that will encompass Sarah Boyle, reflective housewife and mother, as well as her children, the family turtle and any frame she attempts to impose on her life.

Because it first appeared in *New Worlds,* a British magazine devoted to expanding the frontiers of "speculative fiction," "Heat Death" has exerted virtually all its impact in the science fiction field, where it has been reprinted in numerous anthologies, including the prestigious *The Mirror of Infinity,* in which various critics selected and introduced an especially important work. . . . This comes despite the fact that "Heat Death," like the stories that followed, is not science fiction by any reasonable definition. Nevertheless, Zoline's first several stories were all published in like-minded journals . . . so the author appears to have countenanced her placement in the pigeonhole, from which depths it may have been hard for others to notice her.

Things began to change in 1985, when Zoline published her children's book *Annika and the Wolves,* and was named a PEN New Writer.

To be sure, these five long stories [in *The Heat Death of the Universe, and Other Stories*] all offer varying dissents from consensual reality, evincing the imaginative artist's ambition not to record the world but create one's own. "The Holland of the Mind," the most conventional work, details the slow disintegration of a marriage during an extended stay in Amsterdam. As with the others, its narrative is interspersed with bits of text—travelogue extracts, scraps from phrase books—to create the effect of collage. This technique is of course by now an avant-garde commonplace, and easy to do indifferently, but Zoline uses it with more rigor and success than most.

The two latest and longest stories, "Sheep" and "Busy About the Tree of Life," are more original and daunting than the earlier work, and do well to be prefaced by them. "Sheep," an encyclopedic catalogue of sheep-lore by an insomniac narrator who tries counting them, embraces dream analysis, prophetic dreams and the image of the sheep both in pastoral tradition and tales of the Wild West. Again a collage, the story also includes every lullaby that deals with sheep, plus a few recipes. Despite the organizing principles undergirding it, the story seems fulsome in its commodiousness, and will resist all but the most patient readers. Nevertheless, Zoline's wit and the grace of her style offer considerable pleasures. . . .

"Busy About the Tree of Life" sounds as if it should strike a mythological motif, but the tree is a family tree, that of a young boy who has come to the attention of scientists because all of his forebears for four generations have come to catastrophic ends. Zoline documents this by detailing the brief lives of each forebear, beginning with all 16 great-great grandparents. The rather numbing catalogue of propagation and disaster (both the *Titantic* and the *Hindenberg* are mentioned, along with the great San Francisco earthquake and every opera-house fire of the late 19th century) is balanced by the attractions of Zoline's zest, humor and simple energy, and the story ends movingly.

> Gregory Feeley, "Pamela Zoline: Collage of Wonder," in Book World—The Washington Post, *May 29, 1988, p. 9.*

Caryn James

Nuclear war, obesity, failed marriages, kidnapped children—threats of destruction haunt Ms. Zoline's imagination. [in *The Heat of the Universe, and Other Stories*]. She attacks those fears in fiction that revitalizes the labels "post-modern" and "feminist," by lacing her work with a healthy dose of fantasy that links her to Angela Carter, her nearest literary sibling.

The title story ["**The Heat Death of the Universe**"], originally published in a science fiction magazine in 1967, must have seemed then like the fractured diary of a housewife driven mad by fear of entropy. Sarah Boyle "is a vivacious and witty young wife and mother," we're told, "occasionally given to obsessions concerning Time/Entropy/Chaos and Death." The facts about her are offered only to mock their inadequacy, for in brief numbered paragraphs we run after Sarah's thoughts as they dart about in her mind. Memories of a children's birthday party mingle with ideas about how the universe may be running out of energy, unwinding to its final "heat death," and about the life span of turtles. We find that "sometimes Sarah can hardly remember how many cute, chubby little children she has," and the language challenges the image of the good mother Sarah knows she is expected to be.

Yet—and this is Ms. Zoline's greatest triumph—Sarah is not an abstraction. Her thoughts are illogical but profoundly reasonable, and they come to life through stunning metaphors. "Sometimes, at extremes, her Body seems to her an animal on a leash, taken for walks in the park by her Mind."

Sarah also has what seems to be the author's own appreciation of found art. (Ms. Zoline, who now lives in Colorado, studied at the Slade School of Art in London.) She dishes out Sugar Frosted Flakes to her kids, thinking: "If one can imagine it considered as an abstract object . . . the cereal box might seem a beautiful thing. . . . On it are squandered wealths of richest colors, virgin blues, crimsons, dense ochres, precious pigments once reserved for sacred paintings and as cosmetics for the blind faces of marble gods. Giant size. Net Weight 16 ounces, 250 grams. 'They're tigeriffic!' says Tony the Tiger."

These mental excursions into poetry and art are not merely Sarah's way of preserving her sanity; they reveal how she thinks. The smooth, passive, flowing stream of consciousness does not exist in these stories. Ms. Zoline is more like a juggler of consciousness, reproducing the constant jumble of memory that occupies any intelligent, complex mind. Sarah does not despair of keeping the living room dust-free, but dreams instead of "ordering a household on Dada principles." She knows this is "madness," but the idea remains wildly appealing for her and for the reader. . . .

"Instructions for Exiting This Building in Case of Fire" (1985) has a misleading, metaphorical title that makes sense only after the story has been read. The building is our war-torn nuclear world, and Ms. Zoline offers a chilling solution for avoiding the impending fire. She describes an underground network of spies in the near future, including Dakota ("My mother was a hippy") and her husband, Michael, who travel the country from Key West to the Great Plains. Along the way one of their children is snatched from them, and only at the story's surprising end do we realize how children have become sacrificial victims in a desperate peace-keeping plan. As Ms. Zoline deftly leads us toward her emotionally brutal conclusion, she seems to meander cross-country with the family. We never feel the forced pull of an author's intrusion, so we are doubly shocked when the story turns out to be so tough and unsentimental, fighting one nightmare with another. . . .

As Ms. Zoline proceeds in her playfully unchronological way, the story's predictability becomes a dark joke. It is too pat that Gabriel represents the family of humanity, his forebears' names ranging from Capability Bidwell to Sonia Wang and Guglielmo Lippershey. But when Gabriel's father asks, "When is paranoia not illness, but the appropriate response to the post-modern world?" he frames the unanswerable question all Ms. Zoline's fiction addresses. Gabriel has nightmares because we live "without a myth sufficiently pluralist to save us," and Ms. Zoline offers a striking, original version of such a myth for a post-modern age.

There is only one weak story in the collection, and it is an early one. **"The Holland of the Mind"** (1969) is a studied portrait of a couple who go to Amsterdam and find their marriage drowning alongside the city's canals.

"Sheep" (1981) is much stronger, a sleepwalker's meditation structured by the number of sheep she counts. They jump a fence, trailing behind them fragments of Western culture, from cowboy stories and pastoral myths to the theories of Jung. The dreamy world of **"Sheep,"** dredging truths from the unconscious, is the precise landscape of Pamela Zoline's fiction, a place where "anomie" is a *"fin de* millennial phenomenon" and "the Romantic fallacy has ceased operation." Fortunately for readers, Ms. Zoline does not lament this loss. She posits against it these stories, richer and more astute than the bulkier work of most of her contemporaries.

> Caryn James, "Confessions of a Dadaist Housewife," in The New York Times Book Review, *July 17, 1988, p. 9.*

Steven Moore

The Heat Death of the Universe is Pamela Zoline's first

collection of stories, some dating from the 1960s, most of which appeared in new wave sci-fi magazines. Many science fiction writers begin with an ingenious premise but wrap it in plodding prose; Zoline however matches her ingenious premises with postmodern strategies, a playful sense of humor, and colorful writing to produce a dazzling collection of stories. The longest and most inventive story, **"Sheep,"** is made up of an insomniac's encyclopedic ramblings in quest of sleep. Another story [**"Busy about the Tree of Life"**] features a boy whose geneology consists of the most accident-prone family in literary history, while another offers a different view of [Guy] Davenport's Holland, though in a college style similar to his. Zoline joins Davenport and [Robert] Kelly in the small circle of writers who are making genuine contributions to the short-fiction form.

> *Steven Moore, in a review of "The Heat Death of the Universe, and Other Stories," in* The Review of Contemporary Fiction, *Vol. 8, No. 3, Fall, 1988, P. 159.*

Rebecca Martin

In **"Sheep,"** a novella in Pamela Zoline's debut collection, *The Heat Death of the Universe,* the "Romantic fallacy has ceased operation" for a trio of spies. Engaged in the mysterious activities of the netherworld, they are furiously digging up a pastoral landscape nearby the scattered offices of the Border Control between "two countries ideologically at war . . . there is now no connection between their mood and the constructs of the landscape, the weather, the wind, the light and shadow . . . they are post-modern and altogether sundered from their bucolic and bureaucratic surrounds."

Such is the fate of a good many of Zoline's characters in the two short stories and three novellas that constitute *Heat Death,* though few accept it with the energetic efficiency of the trio. Most flail puny fists at an indifferent universe or look with forcibly calmed desperation on the vast measures of human stupidity and destruction threatening our species and our fragile stories of civilization.

In [**"The Heat Death of the Universe"**], Sarah Boyle is "a vivacious and witty young wife and mother, educated at a fine Eastern college, proud of her growing family which keeps her happy and busy around the house . . . and only occasionally given to obsessions concerning Time/ Entropy/Chaos and Death." . . . Sarah gets through each day cleaning, shopping, changing diapers, or giving birthday parties, and turns housework from a series of chores into a metaphysical battle. She numbers the objects in her living room (819 in all) "in a desperate/heroic attempt to index, record, bluff, invoke, order and placate" while thoughts of "the metastasis of Western Culture," "the end of the world by ice. . . . water. . . . nuclear war" revolve in her mind with the regularity of constellations.

In Zoline's work, hopes of happy endings can never quite surmount the reality principle. Endings in general, those soothing illusions that give coherence and meaning to events, are assigned the same status as the Romantic fallacy: a pathetic projection of human imagination onto alien constructs. Instead, Zoline's stories are self-consciously

fragmented. She pieces shards together seemingly at random, but under her vividly succinct touch a series of pictures, or *tableaux vivants,* emerges.

"Heat Death" comprises numbered fragments that vary between discussions of ontology, entropy, and Sarah, who is seen in a variety of poses: washing, sweeping, serving her children Sugar Frosted Flakes. . . . The fragments are like picture postcards with something askew—a guy in a crowd shot inconspicuously giving the world the finger.

The structural logic in these stories is in the juxtaposition of images—of stereo-typical perfection against the sometimes peculiarly childish, profound, or primordial workings of the human mind. The tension between the "vivacious and witty young wife" and the Sarah who thinks that "all well-fed naked children appear edible" and whose "teeth hum in her head with memory of bloody feastings, prehistory" turns the fragments into an absurd and fascinating portrait of the human condition.

"Sheep," an insomniac's journey into the longest night in human history, reels through the half-meditative, half-dream-like landscapes of the Sleeper's mind with bewildering speed and the grotesque logic of the subconscious. The Sleeper idles for a while in a pastoral escape where the Romantic fallacy is still alive and well: willows sigh and the shepherd and shepherdess, Phoebe and Bion, fuck in lush valleys. Moschus, for lack of a better partner, happily does it with his favorite ewe. The Sleeper sighs, moans, and rolls, as

> *Leftists, down from the hills* [and] *Rightists up from the valley. . . . both laid claim to a recent bombing incident, seventeen people . . . killed in the blowing-up of a fast-chicken restaurant. The uncooked bodies of humans, and the cooked and uncooked bodies of chickens were strewn over the lawn and parking lot.*

Trying to encompass within an "insomniac display of ego, id, and super ego" everything from domestic quirks to global warfare, **"Sheep"** sometimes wobbles beneath the weight of Zoline's encyclopedic tendencies. But in spite of a tremor here and there, Zoline deftly manipulates her subjects. The more weight she piles on, the firmer and truer *Heat Death* stands.

> *Rebecca Martin, "We Fall to Pieces," in* The Village Voice, *Vol. XXXIII, No. 40, October 4, 1988, p. 73.*

Lance Olsen

[*The Heat Death of the Universe, and Other Stories* is an exciting and challenging work] by Pamela Zoline, a painter and writer well known by sci-fi aficionados since the late 1960s for her infrequently published polymathic postmodern pastiches, which, like the house of the protagonist in the title story, add up to "a desperate/heroic attempt to index, record, bluff, invoke, order and placate" "this shrunk and communication-ravaged world." In [**"The Heat Death of the Universe"**], a splendid kind of New Wave cult classic, a housewife descends into a psychological maelstrom on the microcosmic level while the universe descends into maximum disorganization and minimum available energy on the macrocosmic. Elsewhere [in **"The Holland of the Mind"**] descriptions of a failing relationship between a husband and wife visiting Amsterdam alternate with those of the Dutch people's extended struggle to hold back the chaos of the sea. A society of women kidnap children from "friendly" countries and place them in "unfriendly" ones in an attempt to thwart nuclear war because they are convinced that no person would launch an attack against a country in which his or her children live. In the longest piece [**"Sheep"**], more novella than short story, Zoline creates an encyclopedia of (among other things) sheep that apparently sleep with their eyes open and don't dream, and of humans who apparently live with their eyes closed and do nothing but dream. The wackily macabre finale carefully catalogues a colorblind boy's ancestors' grotesque and increasingly horrific deaths.

Contrary to what the cultists might say (Thomas M. Disch wrote the introduction to this collection, J. G. Ballard blurbed it [see excerpt above]), Zoline's heteroglossias have little to do with science fiction and much to do with literary experimentation. They are written with an exquisitely precise painterly eye, a cool irony, and a pop sensibility that feels as comfortable with a box of Sugar Frosted Flakes and fortune cookies as it does with astrophysics and Rembrandt's biography. Angela Carter's love of collage swims in and out of these pieces. So does Pynchon's of science and statistics, Guy Davenport's of magnificent esoterica, and Barthelme's of kooky kitsch. Behind all these swims one of the fathers of postmodernism, Duchamp, who, about the time the representatives of the victorious countries gathered at Versailles and other Parisian suburbs, penciled in a goatee on a reproduction of the *Mona Lisa* and in one stroke generated a radical skepticism that would never again take anything, including its own (non)premises, very seriously. Zoline's is a jolting new land in the geography of postmodern fiction, where incoherent shards of our culture become momentarily exceptional, where hierarchies are toppled and fantasy becomes fact and every voice becomes a dodecaphonic symphony. (p. 22)

Lance Olsen, "Short Stories Everywhere," in The American Book Review, *Vol. 10, No. 6, January-February, 1989, pp. 15, 22.*

☐ Contemporary Literary Criticism

Indexes

Literary Criticism Series
  Cumulative Author Index
Cumulative Nationality Index
Title Index, Volume 62

This Index Includes References to Entries in These Gale Series

Contemporary Literary Criticism

Presents excerpts of criticism on the works of novelists, poets, dramatists, short story writers, scriptwriters, and other creative writers who are now living or who have died since 1960.

Twentieth-Century Literary Criticism

Contains critical excerpts by the most significant commentators on poets, novelists, short story writers, dramatists, and philosophers who died between 1900 and 1960.

Nineteenth-Century Literature Criticism

Offers significant passages from criticism on authors who died between 1800 and 1899.

Literature Criticism from 1400 to 1800

Compiles significant passages from the most noteworthy criticism on authors of the fifteenth through eighteenth centuries.

Classical and Medieval Literature Criticism

Offers excerpts of criticism on the works of world authors from classical antiquity through the fourteenth century.

Short Story Criticism

Compiles excerpts of criticism on short fiction by writers of all eras and nationalities.

Children's Literature Review

Includes excerpts from reviews, criticism, and commentary on works of authors and illustrators who create books for children.

Contemporary Authors Series

Encompasses five related series. *Contemporary Authors* provides biographical and bibliographical information on more than 95,000 writers of fiction, nonfiction, poetry, journalism, drama, motion pictures, and other fields. Each new volume contains sketches on authors not previously covered in the series. *Contemporary Authors New Revision Series* provides completely updated information on active authors covered in previously published volumes of *CA*. Only entries requiring significant change are revised for *CA New Revision Series*. *Contemporary Authors Permanent Series* consists of updated listings for deceased and inactive authors removed from the original volumes 9-36 when these volumes were revised. *Contemporary Authors Autobiography Series* presents specially commissioned autobiographies by leading contemporary writers. *Contemporary Authors Bibliographical Series* contains primary and secondary bibliographies as well as analytical bibliographical essays by authorities on major modern authors.

Dictionary of Literary Biography

Encompasses four related series. *Dictionary of Literary Biography* furnishes illustrated overviews of authors' lives and works and places them in the larger perspective of literary history. *Dictionary of Literary Biography Documentary Series* illuminates the careers of major figures through a selection of literary documents, including letters, notebook and diary entries, interviews, book reviews, and photographs. *Dictionary of Literary Biography Yearbook* summarizes the past year's literary activity with articles on genres, major prizes, conferences, and other timely subjects and includes updated and new entries on individual authors. *Concise Dictionary of American Literary Biography* comprises six volumes of revised and updated sketches on major American authors that were originally presented in *Dictionary of Literary Biography*.

Something about the Author Series

Encompasses three related series. *Something about the Author* contains heavily illustrated biographical sketches on juvenile and young adult authors and illustrators from all eras. *Something about the Author Autobiography Series* presents specially commissioned autobiographies by prominent authors and illustrators of books for children and young adults. *Authors & Artists for Young Adults* provides high school and junior high school students with profiles of their favorite creative artists in the mediums of print, film, television, drama, song lyrics, and cartoons.

Yesterday's Authors of Books for Children

Contains heavily illustrated entries on children's writers who died before 1961. Complete in two volumes.

Literary Criticism Series
Cumulative Author Index

This index lists all author entries in the Gale Literary Criticism Series and includes cross-references to other Gale sources. References in the index are identified as follows:

AAYA: *Authors & Artists for Young Adults,* Volumes 1-3
CAAS: *Contemporary Authors Autobiography Series,* Volumes 1-11
CA: *Contemporary Authors* (original series), Volumes 1-130
CABS: *Contemporary Authors Bibliographical Series,* Volumes 1-3
CANR: *Contemporary Authors New Revision Series,* Volumes 1-29
CAP: *Contemporary Authors Permanent Series,* Volumes 1-2
CA-R: *Contemporary Authors* (revised editions), Volumes 1-44
CDALB: *Concise Dictionary of American Literary Biography,* Volumes 1-6
CLC: *Contemporary Literary Criticism,* Volumes 1-62
CLR: *Children's Literature Review,* Volumes 1-22
CMLC: *Classical and Medieval Literature Criticism,* Volumes 1-5
DC: *Drama Criticism,* Volume 1
DLB: *Dictionary of Literary Biography,* Volumes 1-92
DLB-DS: *Dictionary of Literary Biography Documentary Series,* Volumes 1-7
DLB-Y: *Dictionary of Literary Biography Yearbook,* Volumes 1980-1988
LC: *Literature Criticism from 1400 to 1800,* Volumes 1-14
NCLC: *Nineteenth-Century Literature Criticism,* Volumes 1-28
PC: *Poetry Criticism,* Volume 1
SAAS: *Something about the Author Autobiography Series,* Volumes 1-9
SATA: *Something about the Author,* Volumes 1-59
SSC: *Short Story Criticism,* Volumes 1-6
TCLC: *Twentieth-Century Literary Criticism,* Volumes 1-38
YABC: *Yesterday's Authors of Books for Children,* Volumes 1-2

Author Index

CLC Cumulative Nationality Index

Nationality Index

Nationality Index

CLC-62 Title Index

Title Index

Title Index